Instruments of Science

GARLAND ENCYCLOPEDIAS IN THE HISTORY OF SCIENCE
VOLUME 2
GARLAND REFERENCE LIBRARY OF THE SOCIAL SCIENCES
VOLUME 936

Advisory Committee

Dr. Robert G.W. Anderson
British Museum

Dr. Paolo Brenni
CNR Istituto e Museo di Storia della
Scienza

Dr. Paul Forman
National Museum of American History
Smithsonian Institution

Professor John Law
Keele University

Dr. Ghislaine M. Lawrence
Science Museum, London

Dr. Jeffrey Stine
National Museum of American History
Smithsonian Institution

Dr. Jeffrey L. Sturchio
Merck & Co., Inc.

Professor Peter H. Sydenham
University of South Australia

Professor Gerard L'E. Turner
Imperial College of Science, Technology
and Medicine

Instruments of Science
An Historical Encyclopedia

Editors
Robert Bud
The Science Museum, London

Deborah Jean Warner
The National Museum of American History
Smithsonian Institution

Associate Editor
Stephen Johnston
Museum of the History of Science, Oxford

Managing Editor
Betsy Bahr Peterson
The Science Museum, London

Picture Editor
Simon Chaplin
The Science Museum, London

THE SCIENCE MUSEUM, LONDON
and
THE NATIONAL MUSEUM OF AMERICAN HISTORY, SMITHSONIAN INSTITUTION
in association with
GARLAND PUBLISHING, INC.
A member of the Taylor & Francis Group
New York & London
1998

Library of Congress Cataloging-in-Publication Data

Instruments of Science : an historical encyclopedia / editors, Robert Bud,
   Deborah Jean Warner.
         p.   cm. — (Garland encylopedias in the history of science ;
   vol. 2) (Garland reference library of social science ; v. 936)
      Includes bibliographical references and index.
      ISBN 0-8153-1561-9 (alk. paper)
      1. Scientific apparatus and instruments—History—Encyclopedias.
   I. Bud, Robert. II. Warner, Deborah Jean. III. Series. IV. Series: Garland
   reference library of social science ; v. 936.
   Q184.5.I57   1998
   502.8'4—dc21   97-15296
                                                             CIP

Cover photograph: French equatorium, ca. 1600. Courtesy Board of Trustees of
   the National Museum and Galleries on Merseyside.

Cover design by Karin Badger

Printed on acid-free, 250-year-life paper
Manufactured in the United States of America

Contents

v

Series Introduction

Since World War II, the historical study of science has grown enormously. Once the domain of a few scientists interested in their intellectual genealogy and a scattering of intellectual historians, philosophers of science, and sociologists of knowledge, it is now a mature and independent discipline. However, historians of science have not had a way until now to make the essentials of their subject accessible to high school and college students, scholars in other disciplines, and the general public. The encyclopedias in this series will furnish concise historical information and summarize the latest research in a form accessible to those without scientific or mathematical training.

Each volume in the series will be independent from the others. The focus of a particular volume may be a scientific discipline (such as astronomy), a topic that transcends disciplines (such as laboratories and instruments or science in the United States), or a relationship between a science and another aspect of culture (for example, science and religion). The same entry title may appear in a number of volumes, perhaps with a different author, as individual volume editors and co-editors approach the subject from different contexts.

What is common to each of the volumes is a concern for the historiography of the history of science. By historiography, I mean the recognition that there is never an undisputed explanation of past events. Instead, historians struggle to come to a consensus about the facts and significant issues and argue over the most valid historical explanations. The authors of the entries in this and the other volumes in the series were asked to provide entries that are accurate and balanced, while also being cognizant of how historical interpretations changed over time. Where historiographic debate has occurred, authors were asked to address that debate. They were also given the freedom to express their own positions on these issues.

The extent to which historiographic issues are prominent in the entries varies from entry to entry and from volume to volume, according to the richness of the historical literature and the depth of the debate. Even for a subject with a rich historiographic literature, such as science in the United States, there are topics for which there is little scholarship. The one or two scholars working on a particular topic may still be laboring to uncover the facts and get the chronology correct. For other fields, there may have been too few active scholars for the development of a complex debate on almost any topic.

Each entry also provides a concise, selected bibliography on the topic. Further bibliographic information can be obtained from the volumes in the Garland series Bibliographies on the History of Science and Technology, edited by Robert Multhauf and Ellen Wells.

Marc Rothenberg
Smithsonian Institution

Introduction

Who invented the gyroscope? How has the telescope evolved? For what have bomb calorimeters been used? How has changing gas testing technology been reflected in the cost of instruments? This volume differs significantly from other histories of scientific instruments: its 327 entries address topics ranging from antiquity to the present day and include instruments designed for routine testing as well as those used for cutting-edge research. More than two hundred scientists, instrument pioneers, historians, and sociologists contributed entries, each of which is accompanied by a list of further readings and an illustration.

What Is a Scientific Instrument?
Scientific instruments are central to the practice of science. All too often they have been taken for granted. Nonetheless, while most would agree that telescopes and microscopes are scientific instruments, it has proved as difficult to establish a general definition of the category as it has been to define science itself. One of the first attempts was made by the distinguished British physicist James Clerk Maxwell. Speaking at London's South Kensington Loan Exhibition in 1876, Maxwell defined instruments narrowly as those that were specifically made for scientific experiments. A generation later, the *Oxford English Dictionary* distinguished instruments from tools by their scientific purpose. Today most dictionaries emphasize measurement. In addition to those definitions, lists, catalogues, encyclopedias, and common usage also configure our thinking.

The approach taken in this volume is pragmatic but not unprincipled and has been guided by a sensitivity to the changing historical forms of natural knowledge. There are, therefore, entries relating to the mathematical sciences from antiquity onwards, the natural philosophy of the seventeenth and eighteenth centuries, physics and chemistry and the newly emerging life sciences of the nineteenth and twentieth centuries, and the applied and engineering sciences, which have come to increasing prominence in recent years.

This historicist approach has some important consequences. For example, we have chosen instruments that no longer figure in modern conceptions of science, including early modern drawing instruments and sectors used in mathematics and geometry, the spheres and astrolabes of astronomy, and the cross-staffs and sextants of navigation. At the other end of the spectrum, the recent developments in biology and biotechnology suggested entries that confound traditional conceptions of an instrument, including four organisms that are crucial in biological research—*E. coli*, *neurospora, drosophila,* and the mouse. Reflecting the importance of applied science, we have also explored the uses of instruments in sites of routine testing and monitoring such as the hospital, the petroleum refinery, and the airplane cockpit.

Current Scholarship

The historical significance of instruments has become vastly better understood than was the case even a decade ago. The growing material record preserved in museums has challenged and inspired curators to focus upon its meaning. The practice of science equally has attracted detailed attention from a wide field of historians, philosophers, and sociologists.[1] This volume has benefited from their enormous efforts as well as from the knowledge and experience of practitioners.

Despite such expertise, the complexity and scope of science remain a formidable challenge. While for some instruments we are in a position to locate a detailed understanding within a rich context—intellectual, social, and economic—for others even the establishment of a skeletal chronology has proven difficult. Thus this volume represents current understanding and the questions being raised by scholars today.

Science may be international, but its practice is often affected by local conditions, where both the uses of instruments and their patterns of evolution diverge and where manufacturers, key people, and urgent problems differ. Whereas this volume is international in scope, the emphases of the authors, who work in a dozen countries, naturally reflect their own experience and knowledge. Readers will find themselves challenged to produce accounts reflecting the local conditions most familiar to themselves and to develop further international overviews.

Moreover, in many modern worksites, instruments are often brought together into systems and networks, becoming part of ensembles such as astronomical observatories, mineralogical laboratories, or automobile dashboards. Although our A–Z listing of individual instruments preserves the sense of instruments as distinctive and unique artifacts, we hope that scholars will integrate accounts of individual instruments in ways that this volume could not attempt.

How Significant Is an Instrument?

The instruments discussed in this volume were selected from texts on the history of science, trade catalogues, museum collections, and treatises on modern scientific practice.[2] Although the selection can not be comprehensive, it does encompass most well-known devices, including those that have been important in the creation of new scientific fields and that have been widely used over long periods of time. It also includes many that have been used for practical applications from cell counting to paper-making, as well as some designed for education.

Although all instruments are clearly not of equal importance to the development of scientific practice, allocation of space in this volume could not possibly reflect the scale of such diversity. Cross-references to other entries are indicated by bold type. Lists of further reading suggest the fuller accounts that we could not provide for the history of better-known devices. In other cases, however, this volume's entries bring together for the first time information available in scattered and often obscure sources. Therefore, the space allocated to each of our instruments falls within a relatively narrow range: most entries are approximately one thousand words in length.

The volume is intended to communicate clearly to a wide audience and is itself the product of a diverse community of specialists. In most cases, therefore, modern units, rather than contemporary or archaic measures, are used. Moreover, it has not been possible to standardize to either metric or imperial so both will be found.

The lists of up to five further readings follow each entry. These also serve to provide full references for sources referred to in the text or in picture captions. Many of the photographs come from the collections of the Science & Society Picture Library at the Science Museum or from the collections of the National Museum of American History.

This volume is the result of a collaboration between two major national museums and draws upon the strengths of their object, archival, and picture collections. Their institutional support and accumulated resources have made this volume possible. We are grateful also to the members of the advisory committee who provided valuable guidance throughout the project. Several staff members of the two museums worked hard to ensure the success of this multinational endeavor. We are grateful to Angela Murphy for facilitating the provision of Science Museum photographs, Catherine Cooper for work with copyright clearances, Charlotte Cowling and Tia Snell, who checked bibliographic references, Susan Gordon for her help with computing, and Marjorie Castle, Julia Law, Lorraine Gray, and Margaret Sone, who sustained the network of editors, authors, fax machines, e-mails, and entries with efficiency and good humor. We are also delighted to thank Sarah Angliss, Eunice Petrini, and the production staff at Garland who employed great care, tenacity, and patience to ensure the project would finally finish.

Robert Bud
Deborah Jean Warner
Stephen Johnston

Notes

1. See, for example, such general guides to the history of scientific instruments as J.A. Bennett, *The Divided Circle: A History of Instruments for Astronomy, Navigation and Surveying,* Oxford: Phaidon, 1987; Maurice Daumas, *Scientific Instruments of the Seventeenth and Eighteenth Centuries,* translated by Mary Holbrook, New York: Praeger, 1972; Anthony Turner, *Early Scientific Instruments, Europe 1400–1800,* London: Philip Wilson for Sotheby's, 1987; Gerard L'E. Turner, *Nineteenth-Century Scientific Instruments,* Berkeley: University of California Press; London: Philip Wilson, 1983; Albert Van Helden and Thomas L. Hankins, eds., "Instruments." *Osiris* 9 (1994): 1–250.

2. The search for appropriate entries was carried out over several years. Without being comprehensive, it might be useful to list such general works on current scientific instruments as W.H. Cubberly, *Comprehensive Dictionary of Instrumentation and Control,* Research Triangle, North Carolina: Instrumentation Society of U.S.A., 1988; L. Finkelstein and K.T.V. Grattan, *Concise Encyclopedia of Measurement and Instrumentation,* Oxford: Pergamon, 1994; B.E. Noltingk, *Jones' Instrument Technology,* 4th ed., London: Butterworth, 1985; Peter Payne, *Biological and Biomedical Measurement Systems,* Oxford: Pergamon, 1991; and J.G. Webster, ed., *Encyclopedia of Medical Devices and Instrumentation,* New York: Wiley, 1988.

Contributors

Contributors are listed alphabetically with their affiliations. Titles of articles are listed with their authors. Coauthored articles are indicated by an asterisk preceeding the title.

Agar, Jon
*Centre for History of Science, Technology
    and Medicine*
University of Manchester
Manchester, U.K.
Cosmic Ray Detector
Telescope, Radio

Amsterdamska, Olga
*Department of Science and Technology
    Dynamics*
University of Amsterdam
Amsterdam, The Netherlands
*Van Slyke Gasometric Apparatus

Anderson, Robert G.W.
British Museum
London, U.K.
Balance, Chemical
Distillation
Furnace

Angliss, Sarah
Islington, London, U.K.
Sonometer
Sound Level Meter

Asaro, Frank
Lawrence Berkeley Laboratory
Berkeley, California, U.S.A.
Spectrometer, Gamma Ray

Azzam, Rasheed M.A.
University of New Orleans
New Orleans, Louisiana, U.S.A.
Ellipsometer

Baker, Roger C.
Department of Engineering
University of Cambridge
Cambridge, U.K.
Flowmeter

Band, David
School of Physiology
United Medical and Dental Schools
London, U.K.
Blood Gas Analyzer

Bennett, Jim A.
Museum of the History of Science
Oxford, U.K.
Circumferentor (Surveyor's Compass)
Octant
Plane Table
Quadrant
Sextant
Theodolite

Bennett, Stuart
*Department of Automatic Control
    and Systems Engineering*
Sheffield University
Sheffield, U.K.
Process Controller

Bertolotti, Mario
Department of Energetics
University of Rome La Sapienza
Rome, Italy
Laser and Maser

Betts, Jonathan
National Maritime Museum
and Old Royal Observatory
London, U.K.
Chronometer
Clock, Regulator

Bhattacharya, Asitesh
Bombay, India
Viscometer

Blume, Stuart S.
Department of Science Dynamics
University of Amsterdam
Amsterdam, The Netherlands
*Audiometer

Bohning, James J.
American Chemical Society
Washington, D.C., U.S.A.
pH Meter

Boon, Timothy M.
Science Museum
London, U.K.
Spirometer

Bracegirdle, Brian
Cheltenham, Gloucestershire, U.K.
Microscope, Optical (Modern)
Microtome

Bradbury, Savile
formerly of the Department of Human
Anatomy
Oxford University
Oxford, U.K.
Image Analyzer

Bradley, John K.
Southampton, U.K.
Aircraft Instruments

Brain, Robert
Department of the History of Science
Harvard University
Cambridge, Massachusetts, U.S.A.
Kymograph
Polygraph

Brashear, Ronald S.
The Huntington Library
San Marino, California, U.S.A.
Bolometer
Pyrheliometer

Brenni, Paolo
CNR Istituto e Museo di Storia della Scienza
Florence, Italy
Barograph
Chladni Plates
Meteorograph
Polarimeter and Polariscope
Tuning Fork

Broelmann, Jobst
Deutsches Museum
Munich, Germany
Compass, Gyro-
Log
Traverse Board

Brooks, Randall C.
National Museum of Science and Technology
Ottawa, Canada
Dividing Engine
Micrometer

Brown, C.N.
Science Museum
London, U.K.
Electricity Supply Meter
Wattmeter
Wheatstone Bridge

Bryden, D. J.
formerly of the National Museums
of Scotland
Edinburgh, U.K.
Napier's Rods
Slide Rule

Buchanan, Peta D.
Orpington, Kent, U.K.
Balance, Hydrostatic

Bunney, Anna
Science Museum
London, U.K.
Spectrophotometer, Dobson

Burchard, Ulrich
Mineral Exquisit
Haindlfing bei Freising, Germany
Blowpipe

Burgess, Peter
National Radiological Protection Board
Didcot, Oxfordshire, U.K.
Chamber, Ionization
Dosimeter

Burnett, Charles
Warburg Institute
London, U.K.
Abacus (Western)

Burnett, John
National Museums of Scotland
Edinburgh, U.K.
Galvanometer, String
*Pyrometer
Thermometer

Cahan, David
Department of History
University of Nebraska
Lincoln, Nebraska, U.S.A.
Helmholtz Resonator
Ophthalmoscope

Cambrosio, Alberto
Social Studies of Medicine
McGill University
Montréal, Québec, Canada
*Fluorescence-Activated Cell Sorter

Campbell, W.A.
Department of Chemistry
University of Newcastle
Newcastle on Tyne, U.K.
Nitrogen Determination Apparatus, Kjeldahl
Vapor Density, Boiling Point, and Freezing
    Point Apparatus

Carpine, Christian
formerly of the Musée océanographique de
    Monaco
Current Meter

Carson, John
Department of Science and Technology Studies
Cornell University
Ithaca, New York, U.S.A.
Craniometer

Carter, Debbie Griggs
National Museum of American History
Smithsonian Institution
Washington, D.C., U.S.A.
Magic Lantern

Chapman, Allan
Oxford University
Oxford, U.K.
Nocturnal
Transit Instrument

Charman, W. Neil
Department of Optometry and Vision Sciences
UMIST
Manchester, U.K.
Ocular Refraction Instruments

Clarke, Barry
Department of Civil Engineering
University of Newcastle
Newcastle on Tyne, U.K.
Pressuremeter

Collins, Harry M.
Department of Sociology and Social Policy
University of Southampton
Southampton, U.K.
Gravitational Radiation Detector

Collins, Jeremy P.
Christie's South Kensington Ltd.
London, U.K.
Compass, Aeronautical
*Sextant, Aircraft

Comes, Mercè
Departamento de Arabe
University of Barcelona
Barcelona, Spain
Equatorium

Coulter, Wallace H.
Coulter Corporation
Miami, Florida, U.S.A.
Counter, Coulter

Cox, Ronald C.
Centre for Civil Engineering Heritage
Trinity College
Dublin, Republic of Ireland
Distance-Measurement, Electromagnetic
Distance-Measurement, Optical

Crawforth-Hitchins, Diana F.
Headington, Oxford, U.K.
Balance, General

Crompton, H.
Askham, Penrith, U.K.
Gas Testing Instruments

Dainty, John C.
Blackett Laboratory
Imperial College
London, U.K.
Photon Counter

De Luca, Carlo J.
Boston University
Boston, Massachusetts, U.S.A.
Electromyograph

Dennis, Michael Aaron
Department of Science and Technology Studies
Cornell University
Ithaca, New York, U.S.A.
Gyroscope
Inertial Guidance

den Tonkelaar, Isolde
Zoelmond, The Netherlands
* Ophthalmotonometer

DeVorkin, David
National Air and Space Museum
Smithsonian Institution
Washington, D.C., U.S.A
Photomultiplier

Dörries, Matthias
Deutsches Museum
Munich, Germany
Torsion Balance

Dollimore, David
Department of Chemistry
University of Toledo
Toledo, Ohio, U.S.A.
Thermobalance

Domalski, Eugene S.
Physical and Chemical Properties Division
National Institute of Standards
*   and Technology*
Gaithersburg, Maryland, U.S.A.
Calorimeter, Bomb

Draper, Laurence
Culbokie, Dingwall
Ross-shire, U.K.
Wave Recorder

Dumit, Joseph
Dibner Institute
Cambridge, Massachusetts, U.S.A.
Computer Tomography Scanner
Magnetic Resonance Imaging
PET Scanner

Duncan, Sophie
Science Museum
London, U.K.
Insulation Meter

Ede, Andrew
Edmonton, Alberta, Canada
Microscope, Ultra-
Osmometer

Edmonson, James M.
Dittrick Museum of Medical History
Cleveland, Ohio, U.S.A.
Endoscope

Eggert, Arthur A.
University of Wisconsin Hospital
Madison, Wisconsin, U.S.A.
AutoAnalyzer™

Ehrhardt, George R.
Durham, North Carolina, U.S.A.
Bathythermograph

Eklund, Jon
National Museum of American History
Smithsonian Institution
Washington, D.C., U.S.A.
*Spectrophotometer

Elachi, Charles
Jet Propulsion Laboratory
Space and Earth Science Programs Directorate
Pasadena, California, U.S.A.
Radar, Imaging

Ellis, Darwin V.
Schlumberger-Doll Research
Ridgefield, Connecticut, U.S.A.
Down Hole Sonde

Elzen, Boelie
Centre for Science, Technology and Society
University of Twente
Enschede, The Netherlands
Centrifuge, Ultra-

Ernsting, John
Physiology Group
King's College London
London, U.K.
Centrifuge, Human

Evans, Hughes
The Children's Hospital of Alabama
Birmingham, Alabama, U.S.A.
Sphygmomanometer

Evans, Rand B.
Department of Psychology
East Carolina University
Greenville, North Carolina, U.S.A.
Chronograph
Chronoscope

Evesham, H. Ainsley
Shefford, Bedfordshire, U.K.
Nomogram

Fara, Patricia
Darwin College
University of Cambridge
Cambridge, U.K.
Compass, Variation

Feldman, Theodore S.
Department of History
University of Southern Mississippi
Hattiesburg, Mississippi, U.S.A.
Anemometer
Barometer
Hygrometer
Hypsometer
Rain Gauge

Ferrari, Graziano
Storia Geofisica Ambiente Srl (SGA)
Bologna, Italy
Seismograph
Tromometer

Fisher, Susanna
Upham, Southampton, U.K.
Station Pointer

Fleming, James Rodger
Science and Technology Studies
Colby College
Waterville, Maine, U.S.A.
Nephelescope

Forman, Paul
National Museum of American History
Smithsonian Institution
Washington, D.C., U.S.A.
Clock, Atomic
Lock-in Detection/Amplifier

Gallop, John
National Physical Laboratory
Teddington, Middlesex, U.K.
SQUID

Gaudillière, Jean-Paul
U-158 INSERM
Hôpital Necker-Enfants Malades
Paris, France
Mouse

Genuth, Sara Schechner
Department of History
University of Maryland
College Park, Maryland, U.S.A.
Armillary Sphere

Gökalp, Iskender
LCSR–CNRS
Orléans, France
Laser Diagnostic Instruments

Goldstein, Andrew
IEEE Center for the History of Electrical
    Engineering
Rutgers University
New Brunswick, New Jersey, U.S.A.
Charge-Coupled Device

Good, Gregory A.
Department of History
West Virginia University
Morgantown, West Virginia, U.S.A.
Dip Circle
Magnetometer

Gooday, Graeme J.N.
Division of History and Philosophy of Science
Department of Philosophy
University of Leeds
Leeds, U.K.
Ammeter
Voltmeter

Gossel, Patricia L.
National Museum of American History
Smithsonian Institution
Washington, D.C., U.S.A.
Biolistic Apparatus (Gene Gun)
Counter, Colony

Griffiths, John
Science Museum
London, U.K.
Paper Testing Equipment

Gundlach, Horst U.K.
Institut für Geschichte der neueren
*   Psychologie*
Universität Passau
Passau, Germany
Vocational Aptitude Tests (Psychotechnics)

Hackmann, Willem D.
Museum of the History of Science
Oxford, U.K.
Electrometer
Electroscope
Electrostatic Machine
Galvanometer
Induction Coil
Leyden Jar
Sonar
Thermopile

Hall-Patch, Tony
formerly of the Science Museum
London, U.K.
Rail Track Recording Device

Hankins, M.W.
Department of Biology
Imperial College
London, U.K.
* Electroretinograph

Harden, Victoria A.
National Institutes of Health
Bethesda, Maryland, U.S.A.
Micromanipulator

Hawkes, Peter
Laboratoire d'Optique Electronique
*   du CNRS*
Toulouse, France
* Microscope, Electron

Heckenberg, Norman R.
Physics Department
University of Queensland
Brisbane, Australia
Radiometer, Crookes'

Herléa, Alexandre
Institut Polytechnique de Sévanans
Belfort, France
Indicator

Hessenbruch, Arne
Department of History and Philosophy
*   of Science*
University of Cambridge
Cambridge, U.K.
Geissler Tube

Hirsh, Richard F.
Department of History
Virginia Polytechnic Institute and State
*   University*
Blacksburg, Virginia, U.S.A.
Telescope, X-ray

Holmes, Frederic L.
Department of the History of Medicine
Yale University
New Haven, Connecticut, U.S.A.
Warburg Manometer

Hong, Sungook
Institute for the History and Philosophy
*   of Science and Technology*
Victoria College
University of Toronto
Toronto, Ontario, Canada
Capacitance Bridge
Potentiometer

Howell, Joel D.
Department of Internal Medicine
University of Michigan
Ann Arbor, Michigan, U.S.A.
Electrocardiograph

Hudson, Giles M.
Museum of the History of Science
Oxford, U.K.
Torquetum

Hughes, Jeff
Centre for the History of Science, Technology
*   and Medicine*
University of Manchester
Manchester, U.K.
Chamber, Cloud
Geiger and Geiger-Müller Counters

Hurst, Andrew
Department of Geology and Petroleum
*   Geology*
University of Aberdeen
Aberdeen, U.K.
* Permeameter

Ifland, Peter
Nautica Instrument Co.
Cincinnati, Ohio, U.S.A.
*Sextant, Aircraft

Insley, Jane
Science Museum
London, U.K.
*Odometer
Pedometer
Tide Gauge
Water Sample Bottle

James, Frank A.J.L.
The Royal Institution
London, U.K.
Spectroscope (Early)

Jami, Catherine
REHSEIS, CNRS
Paris, France
Abacus (Eastern)

Johnson, Kevin L.
Science Museum
London, U.K.
Comparator, Length
Transit Circle

Johnston, Sean F.
Department of History
York University
York, U.K.
Colorimeter
Comparator, Lovibond
Photometer
Polarimeter, Chemical
Refractometer

Johnston, Stephen
Museum of the History of Science
Oxford, U.K.
Astrolabe, Mariner's
Drawing Instruments
Pantograph

Kay, Lily E.
Program in Science, Technology and Society
Massachusetts Institute of Technology
Cambridge, Massachusetts, U.S.A.
Neurospora

Keating, Peter
Départment d'Histoire
Université du Québec à Montréal
Montréal, Québec, Canada
*Fluorescence-Activated Cell Sorter

Kidd, Cecil
Department of Biomedical Sciences
Marischal College
University of Aberdeen
Aberdeen, U.K.
Plethysmograph

Kidwell, Peggy Aldrich
National Museum of American History
Smithsonian Institution
Washington, D.C., U.S.A.
Calculating Machine
Planimeter

King, David A.
IGN
Goethe University
Frankfurt am Main, Germany
Astrolabe

Koch, Ellen B.
Bellaire, Texas, U.S.A.
Electroencephalograph
Ultrasound, Diagnostic

Kohler, Robert E.
Department of History and Sociology of Science
University of Pennsylvania
Philadelphia, Pennsylvania, U.S.A.
Drosophila

Kondratas, Ramunas
National Museum of American History
Smithsonian Institution
Washington, D.C., U.S.A.
Polymerase Chain Reaction

Kragh, Helge
Department for the History of Science
Aarhus University
Aarhus, Denmark
Scintillation Counter
Spinthariscope

Krehbiel, David
Krehbiel Engineering, Inc.
Camdenton, Missouri, U.S.A.
Chain, Surveyor's

Kuhn, Hans Jochen
Max-Planck-Institut für Strahlenchemie
Mülheim an der Ruhr, Germany
Actinometer

Lawler, Ronald G.
Brown University
Providence, Rhode Island, U.S.A.
Spectrometer, Nuclear Magnetic Resonance

Lawrence, Ghislaine M.
Science Museum
London, U.K.
Gamma Camera
X-ray Machine

Lederberg, Joshua
Rockefeller University
New York, New York, U.S.A.
Escherichia coli

Lewis, Mitchell
Department of Haematology
Royal Postgraduate Medical School
London, U.K.
Hemoglobinometer

Loebl, Herbert
formerly of Loebl and Company Ltd.
Gateshead on Tyne, U.K.
Microdensitometer

Löhnberg, Anne
Department of Science and Technology
Dynamics
University of Amsterdam
Amsterdam, The Netherlands
* Van Slyke Gasometric Apparatus

Longhurst, Alan
formerly of the Bedford Institute of
Oceanography
Dartmouth, Nova Scotia, Canada
Plankton Recorder

Lovelock, James E.
Launceston, U.K.
Electron Capture Detector

Löwy, Ilana
U-158 INSERM
Hôpital Necker-Enfants Malades
Paris, France
Visceroctome

Lyon, Edwin, III
SRI International
Arlington, Virginia, U.S.A.
Radar

Marks, John E.
Vintage Restorations
Tunbridge Wells, Kent, U.K.
Speedometer

Mauskopf, Seymour H.
Department of History
Duke University
Durham, North Carolina, U.S.A.
Explosives, Instruments to Test the Ballistic
Force of

McMullan, Dennis
Microstructural Physics Group
Cavendish Laboratory
University of Cambridge
Cambridge, U.K.
Microscope, Scanning Optical

McWilliam, Robert C.
Science Museum
London, U.K.
Accelerometer
Concrete Testing Instruments
Fatigue Testing Instruments
Liquid Limit Apparatus
Load Measurement
Skid Resistance Testing Instruments
Strain Gauge (General)

Meidner, Hans
Department of Biological and Molecular
Sciences
University of Stirling
Stirling, U.K.
Porometer
Potometer
Pressure Bomb
Psychrometer, Thermocouple

Merrifield, R.B.
Rockefeller University
New York, New York, U.S.A.
Peptide Synthesizer

Morris, Peter
Science Museum
London, U.K.
Chromatograph
Melting Point Apparatus
* Spectrophotometer

Morrison-Low, A.D.
National Museums of Scotland
Edinburgh, U.K.
Hydrometer

Mörzer Bruyns, Willem F.J.
Nederlands Scheepvaartmuseum
Amsterdam, The Netherlands
Artificial Horizon
Cross-Staff

Moseley, Patrick T.
International Lead Zinc Research
*   Organization*
Research Triangle Park,
North Carolina, U.S.A.
Solid-State Gas Sensors

Mylott, Anne
Department of History and Philosophy of
*   Science*
Indiana University
Bloomington, Indiana, U.S.A.
Auxanometer

Neher, Erwin
Max-Planck-Institut für biophysikalische
*   Chemie*
Göttingen, Germany
Patch Clamp Amplifier

Newbury, Dale E.
National Institute of Standards and
*   Technology*
Gaithersburg, Maryland, U.S.A.
Electron Probe Microanalyzer

Newmark, Ann
Science Museum
London, U.K.
Breathalyzer

Nicolson, Malcolm
Wellcome Unit for the History of Medicine
Glasgow, U.K.
Stethoscope

Nier, Keith A.
Thomas A. Edison Papers
Rutgers, The State University of New Jersey
New Brunswick, New Jersey, U.S.A.
Spectrometer, Mass

Nuttall, Robert H.
Glasgow, Scotland, U.K.
Absorptiometer, Hilger-Spekker

Ory, Thomas R.
Daedalus Enterprises, Inc.
Ann Arbor, Michigan, U.S.A.
Multispectral Scanner

Owens, Larry
Department of History
University of Massachusetts
Amherst, Massachusetts, U.S.A.
Differential Analyzer, Bush

Page, James E.
Harrow, Middlesex, U.K.
Polarograph

Palmer, Rex A.
Department of Crystallography
Birkbeck College
London, U.K.
X-ray Diffraction

Peterson, John I.
National Institutes of Health
Bethesda, Maryland, U.S.A.
Blood Analysis, Optical Devices for

Phillips, Vivian J.
Department of Electrical Engineering
University of Wales
Swansea, U.K.
Oscilloscope
Radio Wave Detector

Phipps, John
Institute of Petroleum
London, U.K.
* Petroleum Testing Equipment

Pinch, Trevor
Department of Science and Technology
*   Studies*
Cornell University
Ithaca, New York, U.S.A.
Solar-Neutrino Detector

Powell, Cedric J.
National Institute of Standards and
Technology
Gaithersburg, Maryland, U.S.A.
Surface Analytical Instruments

Rasmussen, Nicolas
Unit for History and Philosophy of Science
University of Sydney
Sydney, Australia
* Microscope, Electron

Redfern, John P.
Rheometric Scientific Ltd.
Epsom, Surrey, U.K.
Differential Thermal Analyzer
Dilatometer

Redhead, Paul A.
Institute for Microstructural Sciences
National Research Council
Ottawa, Canada
Gauge, Vacuum

Regeer, Barbara
Department of Science Dynamics
University of Amsterdam
Amsterdam, The Netherlands
* Audiometer

Reuben, Bryan
School of Applied Science
South Bank University
London, U.K.
Gauge, Level

Roberts, Lissa
History Department
San Diego State University
San Diego, California, U.S.A.
Calorimeter
Eudiometer

Robinson, Derek A.
Science Museum
London, U.K.
Gas Meter

Rothman, Harry
University of West of England
Bristol, U.K.
Gene Sequencer

Rozwadowski, Helen
Atlanta, Georgia
Depth Sounder

† **Ruddock, K.H.**
Biophysics Section, Blackett Laboratory
Imperial College
London, U.K.
* Electroretinograph

Russell, Iain
National Library of Scotland
Edinburgh, U.K.
Rangefinder

Ryan, W.F.
Warburg Institute
London, U.K.
* Abacus (Western)

Schaffer, Simon
Department of History and Philosophy
of Science
University of Cambridge
Cambridge, U.K.
Atwood's Machine

Seidel, Robert W.
Charles Babbage Institute of Computer
History
University of Minnesota
Minneapolis, Minnesota, U.S.A.
Accelerator

Shapiro, Howard M.
West Newton, Massachusetts, U.S.A.
Flow Cytometer

Sherman, Roger E.
National Museum of American History
Smithsonian Institution
Washington, D.C., U.S.A.
Heliostat

Sherratt, Mike
Stanhope-Seta
Surrey, U.K.
* Petroleum Testing Equipment

Sibum, H. Otto
Max-Plank-Institut für Wissenschafts-
geschichte
Berlin, Germany
Mechanical Equivalent of Heat Apparatus

Skopec, Robert A.
Department of Geology and Petroleum
  Geology
University of Aberdeen
Aberdeen, U.K.
* Permeameter

Slavin, Walter
Bonaire Technologies
Ridgefield, Connecticut, U.S.A.
Spectrofluorimeter
Spectrometer, Atomic Absorption

Small, James S.
Maastricht, The Netherlands
Computer, Electronic Analog

Smith, Denis
Woodford Green, Essex, U.K.
Hardness Testing Instruments
Impact Testing Instruments
Strength of Materials–Testing Instruments

Smithies, Nigel
Fire Research Station
Building Research Establishment
Watford, London, U.K.
Fire Detector

Sokal, Michael M.
Worcester Polytechnic Institute
Worcester, Massachusetts, U.S.A.
Intelligence Test

Sorrenson, Richard J.
Department of History and Philosophy
  of Science
Indiana University
Bloomington, Indiana, U.S.A.
* Pyrometer

Spies, Brian R.
CRC for Australian Mineral Exploration
  Technologies
Macquarie University
New South Wales, Australia
Earth Conductivity Measurements

Staelin, David
Department of Electrical Engineering and
  Computer Science
Massachusetts Institute of Technology
Cambridge, Massachusetts, U.S.A.
Radiometer, Space

Stanley, Peter
School of Engineering
University of Manchester
Manchester, U.K.
Strain Gauge (Electrical Resistance)

Steele, Brett D.
Department of History
University of California at Los Angeles
Los Angeles, California, U.S.A.
Gunnery Instruments

Stock, John T.
Department of Chemistry
University of Connecticut
Storrs, Connecticut, U.S.A.
Absorptiometer, Bunsen
Battery
Gas Analyzer
Gauge, Pressure
Voltameter

Swade, Doron
Science Museum
London, U.K.
Computer, Digital

Sweetnam, George
Manchester, Connecticut, U.S.A.
Diffraction Grating and Ruling Engine

Sydenham, Peter H.
Australian Centre for Test and Evaluation
University of South Australia
South Australia, Australia
Earth Strain Meter
Gauge, Mechanical
Gravity Meter
Infrared Detector
Pendulum

Sykes, Alan H.
Ambleside, Cumbria, U.K.
Calorimeter, Animal

Szabadváry, Ferenc
National Museum for Science and
  Technology
Budapest, Hungary
Burette

Taub, Liba
Whipple Museum of the History of Science
Cambridge, U.K.
Cometarium
Groma
Orrery
Planetarium

Thomas, Roger C.
Department of Physiology
University of Cambridge
Cambridge, U.K.
Ion-Sensitive Microelectrode

Thurtle, Phillip
Department of History
Stanford University
Stanford, California, U.S.A.
Electrophoretic Apparatus
Protein Sequencer

Tsong, Tien T.
Institute of Physics
Academia Sinica
Taipei, Taiwan, Republic of China
Microscope, Field Ion

Tullis, Terry E.
Department of Geological Sciences
Brown University
Providence, Rhode Island, U.S.A.
Friction Measurement Apparatus

Turner, Anthony
Le Mesnil-le-Roi, France
Sector
Sun-dial

Turner, Gerard L'E.
Imperial College of Science, Technology,
*   and Medicine*
London, U.K.
Microscope, Optical (Early)
Telescope (Early)

Turner, Steven C.
National Museum of American History
Smithsonian Institution
Washington, D.C., U.S.A.
Goniometer

Turtle, Alison M.
Department of Psychology
University of Sydney
New South Wales, Australia
Galton Whistle
Tachistoscope

van Helden, Anne C.
Museum Boerhaave
Leiden, The Netherlands
Air Pump

van Leersum, Bert
Zoelmond, The Netherlands
*Ophthalmotonometer

Vaughan, Peter R.
Department of Civil Engineering
Imperial College
London, U.K.
Piezometer

Volkov, Alexeï K.
Department of Mathematics
University of Hong Kong
Hong Kong, China
Counting Rods

Wakeling, T.R.M.
Surbiton, Surrey, U.K.
Penetrometer and Penetration Test

Walters, Alice
Department of History
University of Massachusetts
Lowell, Massachusetts, U.S.A.
Globe

Ward, John
Science Museum
London, U.K.
Camera, Photographic
Camera Lucida
Camera Obscura
Densitometer
Exposure Meter
Stereoscope

Warner, Deborah Jean
National Museum of American History
Smithsonian Institution
Washington, D.C., U.S.A.
Cathetometer
Spherometer

Warwick, Andrew
Centre for the History of Science, Technology
and Medicine
Imperial College
London, U.K.
Interferometer

Watson, Fred G.
Anglo-Australian Observatory
Coonabarabran, New South Wales, Australia
Binocular

Welch, Roy
Department of Geography
University of Georgia
Athens, Georgia, U.S.A.
Camera, Aerial, and Photogrammetry

Wells, David
Department of Geodesy and Geomatics
Engineering
Ocean Mapping Group
University of New Brunswick
Fredericton, New Brunswick, Canada
Global Positioning System

Wess, Jane
Science Museum
London, U.K.
Level

Westwick, Peter
Office for History of Science and Technology
University of California, Berkeley
Berkeley, California, U.S.A.
Chamber, Bubble

Wickramasinghe, H. Kumar
Thomas J. Watson Research Center
International Business Machines
Yorktown Heights, New York, U.S.A.
Microscope, Scanning Acoustic
Microscope, Scanning Probe

Williams, Michael
Department of Computer Science
University of Calgary
Calgary, Alberta, Canada
Harmonic Analyzer
Tide Predictor

Wolfschmidt, Gudrun
Deutsches Museum
Munich, Germany
Comparator, Astronomical
Corona, Instruments for Observing the
Sprectroscope, Astronomical
Telescope (Modern)
Telescope, New Technology

Wolfson, Sidney K., Jr.
Center for Biotechnology and Bioengineering
University of Pittsburgh
Pittsburgh, Pennsylvania, U.S.A.
Glucose Sensor

Worthington, William E., Jr.
National Museum of American History
Smithsonian Institution
Washington, D.C., U.S.A.
Tachometer

Wright, Michael
Science Museum
London, U.K.
Angle, Measurement of
Length, Measurement of
Surface Texture, Measurement of

Wright, Norman E.
Computer Science Department
Brigham Young University
Provo, Utah, U.S.A.
Odometer

Wright, Thomas
Science Museum
London, U.K.
Compass, Magnetic
Dynamometer
Hyperbolic Navigation System

Ziegler, Charles A.
Department of Anthropology
Brandeis University
Waltham, Massachusetts, U.S.A.
Radiosonde

Instruments of Science

Abacus (Eastern)

The abacus, which performs arithmetical calculations, is used today mainly in East and Southeast Asia. It consists of a rectangular wooden frame, the two longer sides of which are joined by several equidistant parallel rods. These rods are divided into two unequal parts by a transverse bar and strung with beads. The abacus currently in use in China (known as *suanpan*) has five beads in the lower part and two in the upper part; the Japanese abacus (known as *soroban*) has four beads in the lower part and one in the upper part. Other variants of the instrument have been used in the past.

The abacus allows a decimal place-value representation of numbers, with powers of ten increasing from right to left, the place of units being chosen for each calculation. A bead in the upper part has the value of five of those in the lower part on the same rod. Digits are represented by sliding beads toward the dividing bar: from zero to four by the same number of beads in the lower part, from five to nine by one bead in the upper part plus the complementary number of unit beads in the lower part. The abacus most commonly used in China has thirteen rows (although some with only eleven rows are also found); the frame's dimensions are approximately 15.5 x 31.5 x 2.5 cm, or 12 x 24 x 2.2 cm. The Japanese abacus has twenty-one rows, its frame being approximately 6.4 x 33 x 1.2 cm in size.

In performing operations, numbers are processed from left to right, the result being gradually overwritten on the initial number. Today the four basic arithmetical operations are performed using the same memorized tables as for written arithmetic, but, traditionally, specific tables were used for each of the four operations: these tables stated, rather than the result of each elementary operation, the way in which the local configuration ought to be altered at each step. They are found in a thirteenth-century text, when they might well have been used for calculations with **counting-rods**, and were still taught at the beginning of this century. For example, the table of division by three reads: "Three one thirty-one, three two sixty-two, encountering three enter a ten." In dividing one (or ten) by three, the quotient three and the remainder one are in two consecutive rows: this reads as thirty-one, and so on.

With an abacus with enough rows one can also perform square- and cube-root extractions or numerical solution of second- and third-degree equations. Very few people master these operations today, the abacus being used mainly for accounting. The most skilled abacus users can perform operations as quickly as accountants using electronic calculators. That, as well as the pedagogical value of abacus calculation, are the two reasons put forward for continuing to teach its use to children.

The instrument's historical origin remains unclear. Its resemblance to the Roman abacus has led some historians to hypothesize a direct derivation, but there is no evidence of transmission. No pictorial representation of the Chinese abacus prior to the fourteenth century is known, and the oldest extant mathematical text describing it and its use dates to the fifteenth century. However, a sixth-century A.D. text describes a calculating device using beads from which the abacus may well have been derived.

The representation and processing of numbers using Chinese counting-rods bear striking similarities to those on the abacus. The latter is usually thought to have gradually replaced the

7 2 3 0 1 8 9
NUMBER REPRESENTED

The figure 7230189 displayed on a Chinese abacus. SM 1863-20. Courtesy of SSPL.

former as the calculating device most commonly used in China between the thirteenth and the sixteenth centuries. Thus, it seems that the two instruments coexisted for some time, used by different social and professional groups: counting-rods were used by specialists in mathematics and other sciences, whereas the abacus was the instrument of popular arithmetic. The falling into disuse of counting-rods is considered to mark the decline of traditional Chinese mathematics. On the other hand, the development of the abacus probably reflects a heightened level of popular numeracy, which could be dissociated from literacy because of the instrument.

The abacus spread from China to Korea and Japan around the fifteenth century. After written calculation was introduced from Europe and adopted by Chinese scholars in the seventeenth century, the abacus remained the standard calculating device in popular culture.

Catherine Jami

Bibliography

Jami, Catherine. "Rencontre entre arithmétiques chinoise et occidentale au XVIIe siècle." In *Histoire de fractions, fractions d'histoire,* edited by Paul Benoit, Karine Chemla, and Jim Ritter, 351–73. Basel: Birkhäuser, 1992.

Lau, Chung Him. *The Principles and Practice of the Chinese Abacus.* Hong Kong: Lau Chung Him, 1958.

Needham, Joseph. *Science and Civilisation in China.* Vol. 3. Cambridge: Cambridge University Press, 1959.

Smith, David Eugene, and Yoshio Mikami. *A*

History of Japanese Mathematics. Chicago: Open Court, 1914.

Vissière, A. "Recherches sur l'origine de l'abaque chinois et sur sa dérivation des anciennes fiches à calcul." *Bulletin de Géographie* 28 (1892): 54–80.

Abacus (Western)

An abacus is an instrument for calculation. In the West it has assumed a number of different forms, of which the principal two are the counting board and the frame abacus. The former involves the laying of counters representing units, or collections of units, on a flat surface ruled in columns to show units, tens, hundreds, and so on (or other collective values); in the latter these counters are replaced by beads that are attached to the instrument and run along grooves or wires. The instrument is probably as old as calculation itself; it aided mental arithmetic, was used side by side with pen-reckoning, and can be said to be the predecessor of the electronic calculators and computers of modern times.

Pebbles (Latin *calculi*) were apparently used for arithmetical calculations in ancient Babylonia, where ruled tables, which could have been used as much for mathematics as for board games, have also been found. Our information becomes more secure for Classical Greece and Rome. The Latin word *abacus* derives from the Greek *abax*, meaning a "flat surface," and the commonest kind of abacus in ancient times seems to have been that using a board made of wood or stone marked with lines on which, or between which, pebble counters could be placed. The best surviving example is a marble board from Salamis whose surface measures 1.49 x 0.75 meters. It is ruled with two sets of parallel lines, one of which is labeled with the decimal steps from 1 to 1,000, the other with Greek money values from one-eighth of an obol to 6,000 drachmas. This board included lines for the half-decimals—5, 50, and 500—as appears to be common in Classical abaci and as is reflected in Roman numerals, which have separate symbols for those values. The frame abacus is also represented among the Romans, in the form of a small metal plate with grooves into which beads were set. An example in the British Museum has a groove for each decimal place, each of which is in turn divided, so that the higher section includes two beads indicating by their position the presence or absence of a "five," whereas the lower section includes four beads, representing units.

This first kind of Classical abacus presumably continued in use into the Middle Ages. Confusion arises because in some Classical and early Medieval documents the word *abacus* refers to a board lightly covered with dust on which geometrical figures and (later) numerals were written. When, from the mid tenth century onwards, the latter began to be Hindu-Arabic numerals (known in the earliest documents as "dust numerals"), we have in this kind of abacus the precursor of pen-reckoning. But from the same mid tenth century we have another kind of abacus, which is a hybrid between the traditional abacus and pen-reckoning. In this instrument—known as the "abacus with *apices*" or the Gerbertian abacus (after Gerbert d'Aurillac, its supposed inventor)—a ruled board and counters are used, but there are separate counters for each digit: that is, nine is represented with a counter with the *apex* (or character) 9 written on it, rather than by nine counters (or a "five" counter and four units). This kind of abacus, on which several treatises *de abaco* were composed between the late tenth and the mid twelfth centuries, was probably used as a teaching tool, and it prepared the way for the use of Hindu-Arabic numerals on parchment. For practical arithmetic, however, it was cumbersome and unworkable. Instead, variations of the traditional board with counters were used.

During the time of England's Henry II (1154–1189), royal accounts were calculated on a black lined cloth spread over a table called a chess-board (hence "exchequer"). The lines marked pennies, shillings, and pounds and higher values; in the spaces in between were placed the counters. Such counting-tables, in which either a reckoning cloth covered the table, or the table itself was marked with lines, were used until the time of the French Revolution. The counters came to be known as *jettons* in English sources and were often minted with very elaborate designs.

Instructions for calculations on a counting-table or board were taught alongside pen-reckoning. H.L. Regius's printed instruction book of 1543 has the significant title *Utriusque arithmeticae epitome,* a summary of both kinds of arithmetic; a woodcut in Gregor Reisch's *Margarita Philosophica* of 1503 aptly contrasts the two methods.

Late medieval abacus and counting board. Gregor Reisch. Margarita Philosophica. *Freiburg im Breisgau: J. Schott, 1535: 267. Courtesy of the Wellcome Institute Library, London.*

The Russian Schety

The earliest commonly used frame abacus in post-medieval Europe may well have been the Russian bead calculator, or *schety* (derived from the verb *schitat'* meaning "to count"), which was first described and illustrated in Russian manuscript books of commercial and chancery arithmetic from the seventeenth cen-tury. The earliest extant specimen is in the Ashmolean Museum in Oxford; it was prob-ably brought to England from Archangel on the White Sea by John Tradescant the Elder in 1618, but was clearly not new when he ac-quired it. This, and the few other seventeenth- or eighteenth-century specimens, as well as those in the manuscript illustrations, are all in the form of a folding case, each half of which holds mounted horizontal wires strung with metal, glass, ivory, bone, or pearl beads. The number of wires varies. The upper rows are strung with nine or ten beads (probably depending on whether Greek-style alphabetical numerals or Western Hindu-Arabic numerals were to be used, although the latter were not officially introduced in Russia until the beginning of the eighteenth century). The bottom short rows could carry variously five, four, three, two, or one bead for calculating fractions (the three- and one-bead rows were probably in use in calculating the rather complicated Muscovite three-field land tax system), and sometimes had a vertical dividing bar in the center. The first full row from the bottom represented units, the next tens, then hundreds, and so on up to very large numbers in some cases. The two center beads in the row were often of a different color from the rest to aid location. Later *schety* tended to be mounted in single frames, and many are of elaborate workmanship. Until quite recently *schety* were in regular use in shops, offices, and schools, and they are still used in some places.

The origin of the *schety* is still a mystery. It was probably first used in the sixteenth century; the Russian historian of the *schety*, I.G. Spasskii, in the only substantial monograph on the subject, suggested that it developed within Russia from bead tallies based on prayer beads, and that monetary reforms in the 1530s in Muscovy had effectively produced a decimal currency system that lent itself to calculation in this way. This is a tenuous hypothesis, and it is not supported by any firm evidence. Whatever the case, however, neither the instrument nor the fairly elaborate written instructions for its use found in a few seventeenth-century manuscripts have an obvious foreign model. The *schety* is unlike the ancient abacus and the Chinese or Japanese bead calculators; its use appears to be restricted to Muscovy proper (it does not seem to have been used in the Ukraine). It was an object of curiosity to Western visitors and was mentioned as such in several travel accounts. Moreover, it coexisted with another, perhaps more widely used, method of calculation with counters (reportedly plum stones) on tables or marked cloths, with horizontal lines for decimal values and spaces for half-decimals, a method similar to West European counting boards from which it probably derives. Captain John Perry, who was employed on a number of engineering and surveying projects by Peter the Great in the years 1698–1712, described the *schety* as a Russian invention, but he had a low opinion of it because although it could be used for very large calculations it could also be the cause of serious error.

Charles Burnett
W.F. Ryan

Bibliography

Barnard, Francis Pierrepont. *The Casting-Counter and the Counting-Board*. Oxford: Oxford University Press, 1917. Castle Cary: Fox, 1981.

Evans, Gillian R. "Difficillima et Ardua: Theory and Practice in Treatises on the Abacus, 950–1150." *Journal of Medieval History* 3 (1977): 21–38.

Pullan, J.M. *The History of the Abacus*. London: Hutchinson, 1969.

Ryan, W.F. "John Tradescant's Russian Abacus." *Oxford Slavonic Papers* 5 (1972): 83–88.

Spasskii, I.G. "Proiskhozhdenie i istoriia russkikh schetov." *Istoriko-matematicheskie issledovaniia* 5 (1965): 269–420.

Absorptiometer, Bunsen

An absorptiometer measures the absorption coefficient of gases. It was first described in 1855 by the German chemist Robert Bunsen, who used it to test the laws put forward by John Dalton and by William Henry concerning the effect of pressure on the solubility of gases. Bunsen defined the absorption coefficient of a gas as that volume of the gas, reduced to a temperature of $0°C$ and a pressure of 0.76 meter of mercury, that is absorbed by a unit volume of liquid at this pressure.

An absorptiometer consists of a graduated glass absorption tube, open at the bottom and attached to a small iron stand and able to travel vertically. A glass cylinder, secured between rubber rings in the foot and in the headpiece, surrounds the tube. When the lid of the headpiece is closed and the top of the absorption tube secured, the entire apparatus can be shaken to expedite the absorption of gas. The cylinder allows the tube, which carries a small **thermometer**, to be water-jacketed. Mercury can be added or removed by means of the funnel with stopcock and the runoff cock.

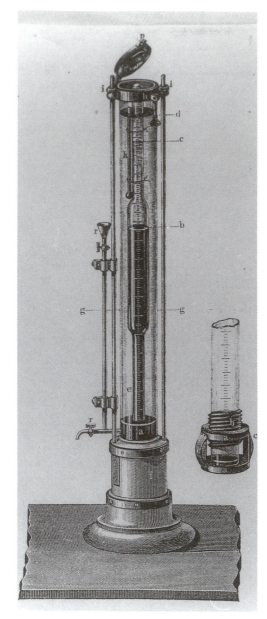

Bunsen's absorptiometer, 1855. Bunsen (1857): 138. Courtesy of John T. Stock.

Water used for absorption measurements must be completely deaerated by prolonged boiling, finishing this in a stemlike-necked bottle as the stem is sealed with a blowpipe flame. When needed, the tip of the stem is broken under mercury, so that the air-free water rises directly into the absorption tube.

In operation, the tube is filled with mercury and stood in a mercury trough. The gas is then introduced and its volume is read with the usual gasometric precautions. A measured volume of air-free water is then admitted. The tube is closed and returned to the cylinder, which contains some mercury, with jacketing water above it. Following a brief opening to equalize internal and external pressures, the tube is closed, the lid is clamped down, and the apparatus is vigorously shaken for one minute. Opening, closing, and shaking are repeated until the volume of the residual gas is constant. The tube is then opened and four readings are noted. These are the upper levels of mercury and of water within the tube, together with the lower mercury level and the upper water level in the cylinder. These readings, along with those of temperature and of barometric pressure, enable the absorption coefficient to be calculated.

Bunsen and his students measured the absorption coefficients of numerous gases in water and in alcohol. They concluded that low-solubility gases generally behave as indicated by the Dalton-Henry laws, but that those of higher solubility do not.

John T. Stock

Bibliography

Bunsen, R. *Gasometry.* Translated by Henry Roscoe, 128–97. London: Walton and Maberly, 1857.
———. "Ueber das Gesetz der Gasabsorption." *Annalen der Chemie und Pharmacie* 93 (1855): 1–50.

Absorptiometer, Hilger-Spekker

The Hilger-Spekker absorptiometer is a photo-electric **colorimeter**. The prototype appeared in 1936, manufactured by Adam Hilger Ltd., of London (the term Spekker being a Hilger trademark). The instrument was originally intended for pathology, pH measurement, and food and water testing, but it soon found use for metallurgical analysis as well. Under the impetus of World War II, and particularly on the basis of E.J. Vaughan's work at the Admiralty Inspection Laboratory in Sheffield, use of the Spekker spread rapidly. It was one of the few British instruments included in Ralph Mueller's extensive compilation on chemical instrumentation (1941). Over the next two decades, this instrument was found in virtually every laboratory in the United Kingdom associated with the ferrous and nonferrous metallurgical industries.

Production of the Spekker was continued during the war, when much of the instrument-

Hilger-Spekker H560 absorptiometer, ca. 1943. Copyright © The Trustees of the National Museums of Scotland, 1997.

manufacturing capacity available in Britain was directed toward the production of military equipment and optical components. Evidently the need to control the quality of steel and other metals was seen as vital for the war effort, while the application of a fluorimeter version of the Spekker for vitamin assay appears to have provided the justification for its wartime introduction and production. By 1945 these two Hilger products had established a dominant market position, and a new version of the absorptiometer was soon introduced. A modernized form of the fluorimeter was available by 1966. Production continued until about 1968, and overall some twelve thousand Spekkers were manufactured.

Method of Operation

At the time of its introduction, the Spekker was seen as taking over the role of the visual colorimeter, primarily of the Duboscq type. Through the use of two of the newly developed barrier-layer photocells, operating in a null mode, Hilger considered that they had gained a significant technical advantage; and though the detailed physical construction and the various control features of the Spekker were significantly varied over the years, the fundamental mode of operation was not.

In all Spekker absorptiometers, a light source with a photocell on each side provided the basic means of operation. In one direction radiation from the lamp passed through the sample, then through a variable aperture (calibrated in optical density) and on to the sample photocell; in the opposite direction the light traversed an iris diaphragm on its way to the compensating photocell. The method of operation was to set up the instrument with the solution to be measured in the sample light beam, and then balance the output EMF of the photocells to zero on a **galvanometer.** The sample was replaced with a reference cell, typically containing water, and the null point again obtained by reducing the light falling on the sample photocell by closing down the calibrated aperture. In this way the light absorption of a colored solution, and thus the concentration of the dissolved light-absorbing substance, could be determined photoelectrically.

The name Spekker has been applied to other Hilger instruments, including a prewar ultraviolet spectrophotometer that combined a quartz spectrograph with a double-beam photometer, and a direct-vision Steeloscope designed for visual survey of a spark source.

Robert H. Nuttall

Bibliography

Haywood, F.W., and A.A.R. Wood. *Metallurgical Analysis by Means of the Spekker Photoelectric Absorptiometer*. London: Hilger, 1944.

Hilger, Adam. "Photoelectric Absorptiometer." *Journal of Scientific Instruments* 13 (1936): 268–69.

———. Hilger material HILG 1/7 and 2/8. London: Science Museum Library Archives.

Mueller, Ralph H. "Instrumental Methods of Chemical Analysis." *Industrial and Engineering Chemistry Analytical Edition* 13 (1941): 667–754.

Vaughan, E.J. *The Use of the Spekker Photoelectric Absorptiometer in Metallurgical Analysis*. London: Institute of Chemistry of Great Britain and Ireland, 1941.

Accelerator

An accelerator uses electromagnetic forces to propel charged ions and subatomic particles to interact with other atoms or with other particles and produce new particles and other phenomena. Many have been developed in the twentieth century. The largest are very costly, and the resources of several nations have been pooled to build them.

The earliest particle accelerators accelerated electrons. In 1895, Wilhelm Conrad Röentgen discovered that cathode-ray tubes produce x-radiation. Shortly thereafter, John Joseph Thomson discovered that the cathode rays were electrons, giving reason to develop such accelerators. In 1924 Gustaf Ising of Stockholm proposed a traveling-wave accelerator to accelerate electrons; this was reduced to practice by Rolf Wideroe in 1928.

The Race for High Voltage

The discovery of the proton by Ernest Rutherford in 1919 led him to call for the development of artificial sources of such particles. European and American physicists then vied to produce up to one million volts potential difference in order to bombard atomic nuclei. At Rutherford's Cavendish Laboratory at Cambridge, John Cockcroft and E.T.S. Walton used a voltage multiplier to apply up to 800,000 volts to tubes to accelerate protons. In 1932, they succeeded in creating a nuclear reaction that transformed lithium atoms into alpha particles.

Robert Van de Graaff's electrostatic generator produced a few million volts in 1933, and the Van de Graaff generator became a workhorse of nuclear physics in the 1930s. Its energies, however, were limited by corona breakdown to less than 10 million electron volts.

Recognizing the shortcomings of these direct-voltage accelerators, Ernest Lawrence forced ions in circular orbits by applying a magnetic field and accelerating them over and over again with the same radio-frequency field. His cyclotron at the University of California at Berkeley overcame the need for high voltages to accelerate particles and became the most successful particle accelerator prior to World War II. Lawrence won a Nobel Prize in physics for this work in 1939.

The discoveries of the neutron by James Chadwick and of deuterium by Harold Urey in 1932, and of artificial radioactivity by Frederic and Irene Joliot-Curie in 1934, made these early accelerators particularly useful in the manufacture of artificial radio-isotopes for medical research and clinical use, and of high-energy beams of neutrons for therapy.

In the late 1930s, Donald Kerst and Robert Serber developed the betatron at the University of Illinois. Instead of magnetic resonance or linear resonance techniques, the betatron used magnetic induction to accelerate electrons.

Cyclotrons were limited by the relativistic increase in mass experienced by particles as they approached the speed of light. Lawrence and his associates hoped to overcome this, either by applying a million volts to the dees of a 184-inch cyclotron or by using the Thomas principle of sector-focusing. These plans were laid aside, however, when World War II began, and cyclotron technology was applied to the electromagnetic separation of uranium-235 isotopes. Accelerators also played an important role in the measurements leading to the design of the first nuclear weapons.

Lawrence and Livingston with the Federal Telegraph magnet used in their first large (twenty-seven inch) cyclotron at Berkeley in 1931. Courtesy of the Lawrence Berkeley National Laboratory.

Post War Accelerators

After the war, Lawrence, Luis Alvarez, Edwin M. McMillan, and William Brobeck brought a new concept—phase stability—to accelerator design. Energies of an order of magnitude larger than designed were achieved with the 184-inch cyclotron after it was modified in 1946. McMillan's electron synchrotron, Brobeck's multi-giga-electron-volt (GeV) Bevatron, and Alvarez's proton linear accelerator, all built at the Radiation Laboratory of the University of California, were emulated in many other institutions. The new Brookhaven National Laboratory in Upton, New York, completed the first large American proton synchrotron, the 2.5 GeV Cosmotron, in the same year.

The Cosmotron and the Bevatron, which came into use two years later, replaced cosmic rays as the primary source of very-high-energy particles like pions, muons, kaons, and "strange" mesons, which began to populate the world of fundamental particles. The Bevatron went a step further when it made the first anti-protons in 1955 and antineutrons in 1956.

In 1952, Milton Stanley Livingston, Ernest O. Courant, and Hartland Snyder at Brookhaven discovered the principle of strong focusing, which made it possible to hold beams of particles into stable, tight bunches as they were accelerated in a proton synchrotron, making possible machines of much greater energies.

The Atomic Energy Commission (AEC) and the Office of Naval Research (ONR) were the primary patrons of accelerator construction after World War II, populating the new national laboratories and many universities with machines that became the primary tools of nuclear and high-energy particle physics. By 1955, the AEC was funding sixty-two accelerators in thirty-two universities in the United States in addition to those in its national laboratories.

The Soviet Union announced that it would build a 10-GeV proton synchrotron in 1955, to which the United States responded with the 12-GeV Zero-Gradient Synchrotron built at Argonne National Laboratory. Unable to compete individually on a national level with the superpowers, European nations formed the European Center for Nuclear Research (CERN) outside Geneva, where they constructed a 25-GeV alternating-gradient synchrotron (AGS) using strong focusing. Brookhaven completed a 32-GeV machine in 1961. Strong-focusing proton synchrotrons were also built in England, Russia, and Japan.

The Radiation Laboratory at Berkeley planned a 200-GeV proton synchrotron in the early 1960s, and a 1000-GeV machine was also planned for later construction at the New York Laboratory. Midwestern physicists won the 200-GeV site selection contest, however, and the 200-GeV machine was completed near Chicago under the leadership of Robert Wilson. Wilson rejected many of the accoutrements of large accelerator laboratories in his design of the Fermi National Accelerator Laboratory, where a two-mile ring buried underground housed the proton accelerator. This machine was modified with superconducting magnets in 1983 to achieve almost a trillion electron volts, and it became known as the Tevatron. CERN built the Super Proton Synchrotron, a 400-GeV machine, in 1976.

In the meantime, the Thomas principle was applied in cyclotrons developed at Berkeley, Oak Ridge, and elsewhere to make sector-focused machines capable of transcending the energies and currents available with conventional cyclotrons, and the linear accelerator was developed for heavy ion acceleration at Yale University and the Radiation Laboratory. In 1973, the Radiation Laboratory's Heavy Ion Linear Accelerator (HILAC), and the Bevatron were combined into the Bevalac. ONR sponsored a series of high-energy electron accelerators at Stanford University, where Wolfgang Panofsky proposed building a half-mile-long electron linear accelerator in 1957. The AEC agreed to fund the Stanford Linear Accelerator Center (SLAC) in 1959.

In the 1960s, colliding-beam machines, such as those suggested by the Midwest University Research Association, made possible the study of very-high-energy interactions by replacing the fixed targets used in conventional machines with beams of particles or antiparticles stochastically cooled and stored in rings until diverted into the path of the main beam. These were pioneered in the ADONE accelerator at Frascati, Italy, and the Cambridge Electron Accelerator in 1967; by the 1980s such devices were in use at CERN, where an Intersecting Storage Ring for protons was built in 1971, and at SLAC, where the Stanford Positron Electron Accelerator (SPEAR) and Positron-Electron Project (PEP) were built in the 1970s. In Europe, other colliders included Germany's DORIS and PETRA and Russia's VEPP, and, in Japan, TRISTAN. CERN's Large Electron Positron Accelerator and Stanford's SLC achieved 100-GeV collisions.

Accelerators also found applications in defense. When the Soviet Union built its first atomic device in 1949, Lawrence and the Radiation Laboratory responded to the need for more raw materials for weapons by constructing a Materials Testing Accelerator at Livermore, California. The prototype machine, a large linear accelerator similar to Alvarez's at Berkeley, was intended to produce enriched nuclear materials. Although the discovery of uranium ores made this machine unnecessary, the discovery of strong-focusing gave rise to speculation about particle-beam weapons of the type later developed for the Strategic Defense Initiative. Accelerators like the half-mile-long Los Alamos Meson Physics Facility were designed with defense and research applications in mind, producing intense beams of particles for studies of neutron effects on materials. Using a Russian accelerating cavity called the radio-frequency quadrupole, Los Alamos fielded a neutral particle beam accelerator in 1989 that operated successfully in space.

The end of the cold war saw a reduced interest in both research and defense accelerators. The Superconducting Supercollider, which was to have been built underground at Waxahachie, Texas, at a cost of $11 billion, was abandoned in 1993. The Strategic Defense Initiative was also cut back, and the development of particle accelerators for its purposes terminated. The hopes of high-energy physicists turned upon further developments at CERN, where European physicists hoped to build a Large Hadron Collider for $3 billion; Fermilab, where the Tevatron produced the last of the quarks predicted by the Standard Model in 1994 and where upgrades to increase beam density were planned; and SLAC, where a B-meson factory was authorized by Congress in 1993.

Robert W. Seidel

Bibliography

Galison, Peter, and Bruce Hevly, eds. *Big Science: The Growth of Large-Scale Research.* Stanford: Stanford University Press, 1992.

Heilbron, John L., and Robert W. Seidel. *Lawrence and His Laboratory.* Vol. 1, *A History of the Lawrence Berkeley Laboratory.* Berkeley: University of

California Press, 1989.

Hermann, Armin N., et al. *History of CERN*. Amsterdam: North-Holland Physics, 1987, 1990.

Livingston, M. Stanley. *Particle Accelerators: A Brief History*. Cambridge: Harvard University Press, 1969.

Accelerometer

The forces on a mass that arise during either acceleration or deceleration can be measured with devices based on the same principles as those used for load measurement. That is, an accelerometer is a form of **dynamometer**. A number of motion measurement devices were developed concurrently in the 1930s as concerns about safety and comfort arose, especially as automobile engines became more powerful.

For many purposes, an indication of the single highest value of acceleration is the only requirement. One simple example is a contact accelerometer in which a break of electrical contact occurs if the load on a cantilevered reed is exceeded. An even simpler, but relatively unreliable, device was the mass-plug accelerometer, whose brittle plug was intended to rupture when a definite value of acceleration had been attained.

Single peak measurements are sufficient in the routine testing of deceleration during braking. Such tests are usually conducted at speeds of 50 km/h or less. Various simple mechanical devices for braking tests were developed around 1930. Some relied on pendulum-type actions, such as the Tapley Meter, the James Decelerometer, and the Churchill Brakemeter, which incorporated magnetic damping. Simpler devices relied on U-tubes or tilting tubes to indicate maximum deceleration. A U-tube is used on the Mintex Brake Efficiency Meter: the liquid columns in both limbs are the same height at uniform speeds. On deceleration different heights are visible, with the smaller bore of one limb ensuring sensitivity and a constriction in the tube joining the limbs providing damping. The Ferodometer contains ball bearings in tubes set at particular angles, which, when a certain deceleration has been reached, let the balls roll up and pivot a colored marker.

More sophisticated mechanical apparatus that record acceleration/time curves were developed by, for example, the Cambridge Instrument Company. Here a mass is supported by springs connected to a member supported on a knife-edge with a recording stylus marking a continuous celluloid film. A very sophisticated example is the Jacklin Accelerometer developed by H.M. Jacklin and G.J. Liddell at Purdue University in 1933. This uses mechanical and optical "levers"; a mirror is attached at the juncture of a double-reed mechanical lever and its motion is further amplified by a light-beam/lens system. The results are recorded photographically.

In the late 1920s high sensitivities began to be achieved by various direct electrical load measurement devices able to be both amplified and recorded with oscillographs. The Telemeter, developed by the U.S. National Bureau of Standards, used a pile of carbon discs, the electrical resistance of which varied with the compressive force acting on the pile. In 1929 the U.K. National Physical Laboratory developed an accelerometer in which the displacement of the armature relative to a fixed, laminated iron core was measured by voltage changes on a secondary winding. Other examples available in the 1930s included the Statham accelerometer (allowing a strain-sensitive filament suspension to serve as a spring), the Brush crystal accelerometer (subjecting piezoelectric Rochelle salt crystals to bending), and the Westinghouse crystal accelerometer (subjecting piezoelectric quartz crystals to compression).

The load cell, which became available in the 1940s, contained an elastic device to which **electrical-resistance strain gauges** were permanently attached. Accelerometers were configured by placing strain gauges on a cantilever beam with a mass attached to its end, and the bending was proportional to the acceleration of the instrument. Load cells are also able to monitor high-frequency dynamic load applications required in vibration testing.

Other electrical devices developed in the early 1960s include the **potentiometer**-based apparatus used to measure vehicle deceleration. This consisted of an oil-damped moving mass, with two wiper arms, supported by leaf springs. Deceleration causes the mass to move and thus slide the wiper arms along the potentiometer wires. When no deceleration is applied, the mass and wiper arms are in a central position. The high lateral rigidity of the springs ensures the device has a low response to transverse acceleration. The output is fed through a resistive bridge unit to a recorder; at frequent intervals during the tests the decelerometer is tilted through 90 degrees, so that it is vertical, subject

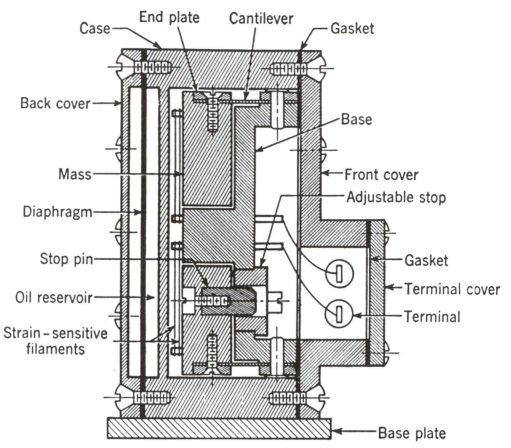

Case — End plate — Cantilever — Gasket
Back cover
Base
Mass
Front cover
Diaphragm
Adjustable stop
Stop pin
Oil reservoir
Gasket
Terminal cover
Terminal
Strain-sensitive filaments
Base plate

Schematic diagram of a Statham accelerometer. Ormondroyd (1950): 320. Courtesy of the Society for Experimental Mechanics.

to an acceleration of 1g, thus calibrating the recording paper.

By the mid 1970s accelerometers had become packaged as one of many types of transducers, devices that convert a physical quantity to a voltage or some other quantity, available from the electronic components industry. Capacitance-sensing transducers, for instance, register the change of position of a test mass. Damping oscillations in the small test masses that provide output signals is achieved by using feedback to prevent the test mass from being displaced relative to the body of the accelerometer, the applied feedback force thus being the accelerometer's output signal. By 1980 such accelerometers were similar in external appearance to other packaged transducers—for example, say, a linear variable displacement transformer (LVDT), with dimensions of 5 cm x 3 cm x 3 cm. They were by then widely used in the automobile and machinery industries.

Robert C. McWilliam

Bibliography

Alexander, A.L. "Vehicle Performance Recording." *Automobile Engineer* 53, (December 1963): 526–31.

Ormondroyd, J., et al. "Motion Measurements." In *Handbook of Experimental Stress Analysis*, edited by M. Hetényi, 301–89. New York: Wiley, 1950.

Road Research Laboratory. *Research on Road Safety*, edited by J.B. Behr. London: Her Majesty's Stationery Office, 1963.

Roads Department, Ministry of Transport. *Technical Advisory Committee on Experimental Work: First Annual Report, Year 1930*. London: His Majesty's Stationery Office, 1931.

Wilson, Ernest E. "Deceleration Distance for High-Speed Vehicles." *Proceedings of the Highway Research Board* 20 (1940): 393–98.

Actinometer

An actinometer measures the intensity of visible or ultraviolet light. It also determines the quantum yields of photochemical reactions. A chemical actinometer, or **dosimeter**, is a chemical system that undergoes a light reaction for which the quantum yield, Φ, is accurately known. Measuring the reaction rate allows calculation of the incident light intensity. Determination of chemical conversion gives the integrated number of photons absorbed by the sample.

Although people had long known that solar radiation causes changes in matter, it was only in the eighteenth century that this phenomenon was used in measuring devices. The use of the first chemical actinometer (oxygen and hydrogen chloride formed in exposed chlorine water, C.L. de Berthollet, 1785) is ascribed to H.B. de Saussure who, in the Swiss mountains in 1790, observed that the rate of the evolved oxygen gas corresponded to the light intensity. Other early **photometers** or tithonometers made use of a dangerous mixture of chlorine and hydrogen. By the mid nineteenth century, researchers were struggling to elucidate the photoreactions of oxalic acid salts of iron and uranium, which are among the most important actinometers today. Dependable actinometers, however, did not appear until 1930, when W.G. Leighton and G.S. Forbes published quantitatively reproducible results on the uranyl oxalate system.

Important theoretical steps in the development of the chemical actinometer include the realization by Theodor von Grotthuß (1817) and John W. Draper (1843) that only radiation that is absorbed can cause a chemical reaction (Grotthuß-Draper absorption law); the Stark-Einstein law, which states that light is absorbed in quanta as discrete photons; and the Bunsen-Roscoe law of reciprocity, which states that the product of light intensity and exposure time determines photochemical conversion.

Chemical Actinometry

To determine the quantum yield of a photochemical reaction (Φ), a sample (S) and a standard chemical actinometer (CA) are irradiated with monochromatic light under equal conditions, usually in a merry-go-round device or through a beam splitter dividing the incoming beam with a known ratio. The chemical change in CA then allows one to calculate the number of photons absorbed by either sample, which, together with the chemical change in S, allows one to calculate Φ. (The quantum yield of a photochemical reaction is defined as Φ = the number of events—for example, molecules formed or destroyed, divided by the number of absorbed photons.)

An ideal CA works independently of wavelength, medium, concentration, and temperature, responds linearly and sensitively (high absorption coefficient, ε and high Φ), yields stable product(s) with low ε, is stable in the dark and against heat or oxygen, is nontoxic, easy, and cheap to prepare and purify, and allows simple, accurate, and straightforward analysis and evaluation. Most systems in use today do not meet all of these demands.

Today the most widely accepted standard CA is the Hatchard-Parker system, aqueous potassium tris(oxalato)ferrate(III), $K_3[Fe(C_2O_4)_3]\cdot3H_2O$, which undergoes photoreduction of the iron(III) at 250–500 nm with $\Phi = 1.25\ldots0.9$. Analysis is by measuring the absorbance at 510 nm of the intensely colored 1,10-phenanthroline complex of iron(II).

Electronic Actinometry

Chemical actinometry is often prone to experimental errors resulting from improper handling of the chemicals, variations of the light flux, insufficient absorbance of samples, and elaborate methods of analysis. To minimize these difficulties, the photochemistry research group at Geneva University designed an electronic system in 1974 (W. Amrein, J. Gloor, and K. Schaffner). This included a chemical quantum counter, photocells, and a digitizer/integrator unit, and owed much to the progress in electronics and fluorescence spectrometers. The idea was taken up at the Max-Planck-Institut für Strahlenchemie and perfected and implemented into a small series of instruments (W. Küpper, 1976) when Schaffner moved to Mülheim as director of the institute. Today some ten to fifteen of them may be in use in photochemical laboratories in Europe, Japan, and the United States.

Integrating electronic actinometers of the MPI Mülheim Model type measure and integrate the amount of light absorbed by the sample during irradiation, largely independent of the absorbance. The incident monochromatic light is split into a sample beam and a reference beam. At the rear of the sample compartment the beams hit quantum counter cells (Rhodamine B in 1,2-ethanediol) coupled with photodiodes that produce voltages that are then electrically matched.

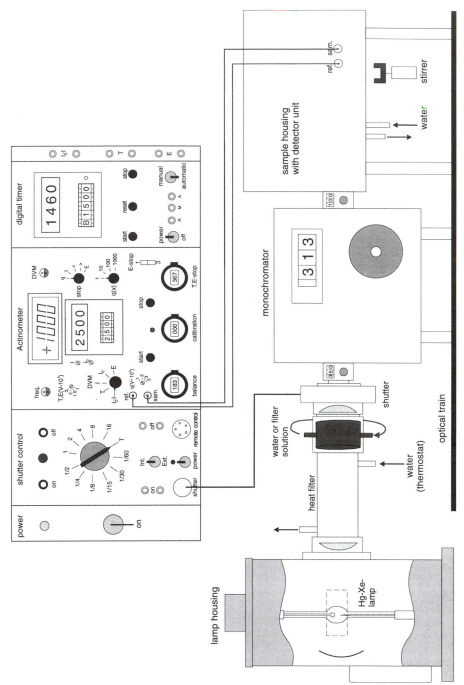

Schematic diagram of an MPI Mülheim Integrating Electronic Actinometer. Courtesy of Hans Jochen Kuhn.

During irradiation of an absorbing sample, the difference of the light intensities before and behind the sample is continuously computed by comparison with the reference beam and converted into a frequency that is integrated, counted, and displayed. The instrument allows continuous reading of the absorbed photon flux and the application of a preset amount of quanta to the sample. It takes into account any variations of the light source and of the absorbance of the sample. The complete optical and electronic setup is calibrated by chemical or physical methods determining the photons-per-count relationship for the wavelengths applied. Continuous monitoring of the absorbance or computerized operation are optional.

Hans Jochen Kuhn

Bibliography

Amrein, W., J. Gloor, and K. Schaffner. "An Electronically Integrating Actinometer for Quantum Yield Determinations of Photochemical Reactions." *Chimia* 28 (1974): 185–88.

Eder, Josef Maria. *Ausführliches Handbuch der Photographie.* Halle (Saale): Wilhelm Knapp, 1892–1903.

Kuhn, H.J., S.E. Braslavsky, and R. Schmidt. "Chemical Actinometry." *Pure & Applied Chemistry* 61 (1989): 187–210.

Sheppard, S.E. *Photochemistry.* London, 1914.

Wightman, E.P. *Photographic Science & Engineering* 3 (1959): 64–87.

Aerial Camera and Photogrammetry

See CAMERA, AERIAL, AND PHOTOGRAMMETRY

Aeronautical Compass

See COMPASS, AERONAUTICAL

Air Pump

Although compressors of various sorts had been known since antiquity, the invention of the air (or vacuum) pump is commonly attributed to Otto von Guericke, an alderman in Magdeburg, and dated around 1647. Guericke's pump was not the first instrument to create a macroscopic void—credit for that rests with the Torricellian tube (see **barometer**)—but it did make it much easier to do experiments in a vacuum. The English scientist Robert Boyle exploited this possibility in the 1660s, thus transforming the air pump from merely a means to create a vacuum into an established research tool, and eventually the emblem of the new experimental science.

The air pump was one of the high tech instruments of its time, expensive to make and difficult to use. The main problem was leakage, and its reduction required, among other things, the production of perfectly straight cylinders with a smooth inner surface. There were probably no more than fifteen air pumps in existence before 1670. Most of these were built and maintained by Guericke, Boyle's assistant Robert Hooke, or Christiaan Huygens in Paris.

Commercial production of air pumps began in Paris in the 1670s. The Musschenbroek workshop in Leiden began making pumps in 1675, and within a few years it had become the leading supplier in continental Europe. Customers could choose from a variety of models (up to five variants in 1711), ranging in price from 175 to more than 500 Dutch guilders (half a university professor's annual salary). The workshop met serious competition only in the early eighteenth century, when Jacob Leupold in Leipzig and Francis Hauksbee the elder in London started their activities.

Typical customers for these instruments were societies, rich individuals, and, somewhat later, universities. Most of these pumps were used to copy or demonstrate the experiments of Boyle and Guericke. Notable exceptions were Hauksbee (see **electrostatic machine**) and Huygens, but the number of scientists doing new research with air pumps never was very large.

The 1670s saw several efforts to make pumps easier to use. Denis Papin invented a double-barrel air pump that required less force and pumped twice as fast as the single barrel design; and the Leiden physics professor Wolferd Senguerd introduced a pump that could both evacuate and compress. A commercially successful variant of Papin's model was introduced by Hauksbee in the early eighteenth century. A table-top version of this pump remained on the market for almost two centuries.

The prime concern since the mid eighteenth century has been pumps capable of reaching ever lower pressures. Three important obstacles hindered the production of a better vacuum: the dead space at the bottom of the cylinder, the valves, and the vapor pressure of the lubricant. Around 1750 the English engineer John Smeaton designed a two-stage

A double-barrelled table-top pump by George Adams, late eighteenth century. SM 1927–1310. Courtesy of SSPL.

air pump, in which the dead space of the first stage was evacuated by the second. Thus the air that was left in the cylinder after compression was not at atmospheric pressure, and was therefore no longer a limiting factor. An entirely different solution was given in 1855 by the glassblower and mechanic J.H.W. Geissler, who needed vacuum tubes in order to study the effect of electric discharges in gases (see **Geissler tube**). Geissler's solution was to use a mercury piston. The flexible mercury would fill the holes and corners of the cylinder, leaving no room for dead space. Based on the Torricellian tube, the idea was to use the void above the mercury to evacuate a larger vessel. Every now and then this idea had popped up,

but Geissler's design was the first that was actually applied. In fact it became the starting point of several new developments. A notable example was Wolfgang Gaede's rotary mercury pump of 1905, which combined low pressure with large capacity.

The problem with valves was mostly a matter of convenience. The early eighteenth century knew two patterns: hand-operated stopcocks, and valves made of bladder that were opened and closed by the current of air. These latter were the more convenient, but they always needed a minimum difference of pressure to open up. In effect this set a limit to the vacuum that could be reached. Various improved valves were proposed and rejected, but eventually most makers settled on mechanically steered valves, which were introduced by the Amsterdam instrument maker John Cuthbertson in 1787.

The earliest air pumps were usually lubricated with a mixture of water and oil. For that reason alone, the lowest attainable pressure could not be lower than 10^3 Pa (0.01 Bar). During the eighteenth century the deliberate admixture of water was dropped, but still the oil would contain water. It was only at the end of the nineteenth century that the search for mineral oils with low vapor pressures began. A more drastic option was to do away with lubrication altogether. In 1865, the Parisian instrument-maker L.J. Deleuil designed a piston that did not need lubrication. And, of course, Geissler's mercury pump did not need to be lubricated either. Therefore the limiting factor with this pump was the vapor pressure of mercury (10^{-1} Pa). Geissler's design did not get that far, but subsequent improvements did a lot better. Pressures even below the vapor pressure of mercury were reached by the end of the century.

All the pumps discussed so far were displacement pumps. In the early twentieth century, the German physicist Wolfgang Gaede invented two pumps in which the individual molecules were, in a manner of speaking, hit toward the outlet of the pump. In Gaede's mercury vapor diffusion pump, these molecules diffused into a current of mercury atoms. When struck by one of the mercury atoms, the molecules would gain a velocity toward the outlet, where they would be pumped off by a traditional vacuum pump. This same hitting of individual molecules was applied in the so-called molecular pump. This time it was a fast moving wall in the vessel that did the hitting. A more recent class of pumps does not remove the gas from the vacuum chamber. The molecules are removed from the gaseous phase by physical or chemical binding, but they remain inside the vessel. These pumps need a more traditional pump to evacuate to a sufficiently low pressure to start with, but with a suitable combination pressures below 10^{-9} Pa can be reached.

Although air pumps have been standard pieces of physics equipment since the late seventeenth century, they were often used for demonstration rather than research. Geissler's work initiated the first application of vacuum pumps in industry, if one is prepared to call the production of Geissler tubes industrial. The first major use of vacuum technology in industry occurred about 1900 in the manufacture of electric light bulbs.

Anne C. van Helden

Bibliography

Shapin, Steven, and Simon Schaffer. *Leviathan and the Air-pump: Hobbes, Boyle and the Experimental Life*. Princeton: Princeton University Press, 1985.

Turner, Gerard L'E. *Nineteenth-Century Scientific Instruments*. Berkeley: University of California Press/London: Philip Wilson, 1983.

van Helden, Anne C. "The Age of the Air-pump." *Tractrix, Yearbook for the History of Science, Medicine, Technology & Mathematics* 3 (1991): 149–72.

Westcott, G.F. *Handbook of the Collections Illustrating Pumping Machinery*. Part I and II. London: Science Museum, 1932, 1933.

A

Aircraft Instruments

Aircraft instruments monitor the flight performance of an aircraft and its engines and equipment. Their arrangement on the instrument panel has been determined by the operational and ergonomic experience of pilots, and by safety regulations and standards arising from accident investigations. The instrument panel is also an identity, as characteristic of a particular airplane as its silhouette. It has evolved from the few mechanical instruments of the single-engine World War I fighter, through the complex analog instrument panels of civilian and military airplanes, to the microprocessor-based visual display screens and head-up displays of current aircraft.

The basic flight performance measurements common to all aircraft are airspeed (airspeed indicator or machmeter), altitude (altimeter and rate of climb meter), attitude (**artificial horizon,** turn and bank indicator, and trim indicators), and direction (**gyro and magnetic compass**).

Airspeed is measured by the differential pressure from the pitot-static head, and altitude by changing barometric pressure. Both are aneroid instruments. Attitude and direction are measured with gyroscopic instruments, with longer turn monitoring by some form of gravity level and magnetic compass

Instrument panel in the cockpit of a De Havilland Comet 1A jet airliner, 1952. SM 1994-222. Courtesy of SSPL.

respectively. Other instruments, such as those measuring temperature, pressure, and position, provide information on engine and fuel management, fire monitoring, electrical and hydraulic power supplies, automatic flight control, control surfaces and undercarriage, navigation, environmental conditioning, and so forth, and all are backed up by alarm systems to alert the pilot to any malfunction. Although similar instruments can be found in other forms of transport, those designed for aircraft must meet the severe acceleration and environmental conditions of high-speed and high-altitude flight.

The number of flight instruments has increased as the speed, altitude, and range of aircraft has increased, and this number doubled when a second pilot was added. The number of engine instruments increased directly with the number of engines, further increased with more demanding engine performance, and again when jet engines replaced piston engines. The instruments have been grouped in different locations to meet changing aircrew responsibilities, such as engine, electrical, and hydraulic power instruments for the flight engineer, navigation instruments for the navigator, and communication equipment for the wireless operator. Later, these instruments were relocated back to the pilot as equipment became more automatic and reliable and the crew members responsible for monitoring them were no longer needed. The number of alarms increased as the potential number of victims per accident and the publicity given to accidents increased. Any abnormal condition is now annunciated to the pilot, and nothing is left to the pilot's alertness.

Aircraft instrumentation started with self-contained, self-powered instruments actuated directly by hydrostatic, centrifugal, gyroscopic, magnetic, or thermal expansion forces. This changed to electromechanical devices as aircraft became larger and measurements had to be transmitted longer distances to the flight panel. Accuracy was improved by servo transmission, and interpretation was improved by integrating the display of associated measurements. More recently, instruments have become an image on a computer screen. Accuracy, readability, reliability, low weight, and low power consumption have been the overriding design criteria throughout this development.

Engine speed indicators received early attention, as sustained flight depended on the maximum revolutions from low-powered and unreliable engines. Airspeed indicators were next in importance, indicating the narrow margin of safety between stalling at low speed and structural damage at higher speeds. As airplanes struggled higher, the altimeter was added, initially more as an instrument of achievement than to assist its return to earth; as flight distances increased, the compass was added to assist navigation.

The overwhelming problem facing early aircraft instrument designers was the engine vibration transmitted through the airframe, which vibrated instrument pointers into an unreadable blur and made the compass card rotate continuously. The engine speed indicator needed little modification, as it was designed for motor vehicles with some vibration, but the altimeter and airspeed indicator proved more difficult. Successful balloon or mountaineering altimeters proved useless, except as handheld instruments, and better balanced mechanisms had to be designed. The liquid U-tube manometer was successfully used for pitot-static air speed indication for some years until a successful dial instrument was designed. For the compass, reversing the pivot and cup arrangement to put the pivot on the card proved the simple solution.

World War I brought the need to navigate through clouds. Early attempts proved hopeless, especially in rotary engine scout planes, which easily developed a spin once the pilot lost sight of the visible horizon and from which there was no known recovery procedure at that time. The only instrument to assist the pilot was the compass, but any slight bank caused the compass to respond to the vertical component of the earth's magnetic field and indicate a false heading, which added to the confusion when the pilot tried to correct it. Instrument designers knew that the solution was a gyroscopic instrument, but no small, reliable gyroscope mechanism was available, nor became available until after the war. A temporary solution was achieved with the static turn indicator, which indicated bank by measuring the hydrostatic pressure between the wingtips.

By 1920, the mechanical design of the basic aircraft instruments had been established. This early development was European, and American instruments were mainly copies of successful European ones. Later, however, American makers quickly took a leading role. The high development and flight testing costs of aircraft instruments and the relatively small market meant that only a few instrument-makers specialized in the trade, and that number fell further as instrument systems became electronic.

John K. Bradley

Bibliography

Bradley, John K. "The History and Development of Aircraft Instruments—1909 to 1919." Ph.D. dissertation. Imperial College London, 1994.

Chorley, R.A. "Seventy Years of Flight Instruments and Displays." *Aeronautical Journal* 70 (1976): 313–42.

Coombs, L.F.E. *The Aircraft Cockpit: From*

A

Stick and String to Fly by Wire. Wellingborough, U.K.: Stevens, 1990.

Pallett, E.H.J. *Aircraft Instruments: Principles and Applications.* London: Pitman, 1972.

Stewart, C.J. "Modern Developments in Aircraft Instruments." *Journal of the Royal Aeronautical Society* 32 (1928): 425–81.

Aircraft Sextant

See SEXTANT, AIRCRAFT

Ammeter

An ammeter measures alternating (ac) or direct (dc) electric current. Its name is a contraction of "ampere-meter," the ampere being the standard unit of current. A great variety of forms are commercially available, ranging from the stout devices that handle thousands of amperes in industrial power plants to delicate laboratory microammeters that can read as low as 10^{-6} ampere; a **galvanometer** is required for currents smaller than that. Numerical readings are generated by the current's effect on an electromagnetic or electrothermal mechanism.

Whatever their operational principle and construction, all ammeters are built to have as low a resistance as possible. When placed in series with a circuit, this feature ensures that the instrument does not significantly reduce the current it is being used to measure. This contrasts with the high-resistance **voltmeter**, which is always connected in parallel with a device when measuring the potential difference across it. In their early development, the ammeter and voltmeter were otherwise closely related devices.

Prehistory

Before 1878 the predominant electrical industry in the United States and Europe was telegraphy, which required instruments only to detect tiny fluctuating signal currents. However, the advent of electric lighting and power transmission around 1878 brought new devices. Commercial concerns for economy, safety, and control demanded fast and accurate means for measuring large currents and voltages. The "fishbone" galvanometer, produced in 1880 by the Parisian electrical engineer Marcel Deprez, was popular as a robust, portable, and "deadbeat" device that could measure large currents next to vibrating electrical machinery—a feat of

which delicate laboratory apparatuses were certainly not capable.

Deprez's device belongs to the "moving iron" type of electromagnetic instrument: a current passing through the coil magnetizes the set of sixteen "fishbone" iron needles; under the influence of the horseshoe magnet this magnetized iron then rotates, causing the coil and the attached pointer to deflect according to the size of the current. As with other contemporary industrial instruments of the moving iron sort, it could not be directly calibrated in units of current. This was due to the inconstancy of the iron magnet's restoring force, and the nonstandardizable relation between current and angular dial readings. To translate the angle reading into a current value, engineers had to refer to empirical calibration plots, redrawn frequently as the qualities of the magnet varied.

Prototypes

In early 1881 two London-based academics and practicing engineers, William Ayrton and John Perry, collaboratively produced a "portable absolute galvanometer for strong currents." This was based on Deprez's device but reconfigured with an ellipsoid moving soft-iron piece to give dial readings directly proportional to the current; if not creating an original principle (J.T. Sprague, British patent [1873] no. 1558), Ayrton and Perry were unique in realizing it consistently enough for commercial practice. Although the instrument's "constant" of proportionality had to be recalculated daily because of the variations in the magnet's strength, an engineer could easily use it to work out a current simply by multiplying up the dial reading. This handy device quickly proved popular among lighting engineers. It sold widely under the new name of the Am-meter, the name that Ayrton and Perry gave it in the summer of 1881, the "ampere" having just been ratified as the international unit of current. A high-resistance version was concurrently christened the Voltmeter.

Facing heavy competition in 1882 from the Siemens's electrodynamometer, Ayrton and Perry sought to overcome their instruments' dependence on multiplication constants, working on a model that would instead be "direct-reading." In late 1883 they produced ammeters that could at last be engraved with a permanent, trustworthy scale marked in divisions of an ampere. They achieved this with a screw adjustment that enabled the instrument's user to com-

Ayrton and Perry's direct-reading spring ammeter by Latimer Clark, Muirhead and Co., patented in 1883. NMAH 315,363. Courtesy of NMAH.

pensate for deviations in the magnet's strength and other imperfections produced in their hand manufacture (W.E. Ayrton and J. Perry, British patent [1883] no. 2156). The same patent also presented a proportional magnifying helical spring upon which they based a new solenoidal moving-iron ammeter. In this instrument, the current-carrying coils "sucked" an iron core downwards, thereby extending the spring attached to it and rotating the spring to produce a deflection. Capable of yielding accuracies up to 1 percent in their skilled hands, these spring ammeters and voltmeters became Ayrton and Perry's most popular models from 1884.

Modern Instruments

Ayrton and Perry's instrument dominated the early market and set challenging standards of robustness and precision to rivals who increasingly adopted their taxonomy of "ammeter" and "voltmeter." These were superseded in 1888, however, by moving-coil meters manufactured by a British emigré, Edward Weston, in New Jersey. In these instruments he dispensed with the troublesome hysteresis-prone piece of soft iron that often caused inaccuracy among Ayrton and Perry's devices. Weston developed instead a way of winding and mounting the current-carrying coil in the field of a permanent magnet (U.S.

patent 392,386 of November 6, 1888) so that it alone could generate a deflection.

Unable to meet the challenging task of measuring the increasingly ubiquitous alternating current, the Weston Electrical Co. meters were nonetheless soon recognized as the most accurate available to electricians for direct current work—and also the most expensive. The use of Weston's ammeter by elite specialists was complemented by a proliferation of rival manufacturers' cheaper and often ingenious alternatives for use in both ac and dc power industry. Prominent among these were William Siemens's dynamometer ammeter, and the ampere-balance developed by William Thomson for the purpose of precision standardization. During the twentieth century, Weston's moving coil ammeter and Ayrton and Perry's moving iron ammeter have remained popular among engineers and scientists alike, especially since it was found that the consistency of instruments could be improved by artificially "aging" their magnets.

Although some electrical measurement devices in the 1920s used thermionic valves, it is only since the 1960s that traditional devices with pointers deflecting over continuous scales have been displaced by electronic technologies. The use of analog to digital converters has enabled the construction of instruments that give readings in discrete numbers, up to eight digits in advanced models. The advantages of this display technology are that it eliminates parallax errors and allows much faster and more precise measurements to be made even by unskilled observers. Multimeters are especially convenient devices for the digitized ac and dc measurement of current, voltage, and resistance.

Concepts of Usage

Ammeters and voltmeters were originally invented for use in the electrical industry, and operated analogously to the mechanical engineer's pressure gauge. By contrast, typical Victorian electrical instruments such as the tangent galvanometer were not usually directly calibrated. These required painstaking determinations of mass, length or time followed by calculation with a standard formula to produce a reading. Physicists thus at first regarded the ammeter and voltmeter not as instruments for scientific measurement but as unrigorous and rather unreliable "indicators" that did not strictly belong in the laboratory.

Around the turn of the century, however, the rapid growth of experimental science led a new generation of scientists increasingly to use high-quality Weston-type instruments to expedite electrical measurement. The discovery of electrons in 1897 moreover supported the view that electrical phenomena could genuinely be measured without reduction to mass, length, and time. The adoption of the ammeter and voltmeter in laboratory science thus symbolized this new concept and practice of electrical measurement.

Graeme J.N. Gooday

Bibliography

Ayrton, W.E., and J. Perry. "Direct-Reading Instruments." *Proceedings of the Physical Society of London* 6 (1884): 59–67.

Edgcombe, K. *Industrial Electrical Measuring Instruments.* London: n.p., 1908.

Gooday, Graeme. "The Morals of Energy Metering: Constructing and Deconstructing the Precision of the Victorian Electrical Engineer's Ammeter and Voltmeter." In *The Values of Precision,* edited by M. Norton Wise, 239–82. Princeton: Princeton University Press, 1995.

Mazda, F.F. *Electronic Instruments and Measurement Techniques.* Cambridge: Cambridge University Press, 1987.

Stock, John T., and Denys Vaughan. *The Development of Instruments to Measure Electric Currents.* London: Science Museum, 1983.

Analog Computer

See COMPUTER, ELECTRONIC ANALOG

Anemometer

Compared with temperature, atmospheric pressure, and humidity—concepts that proved elusive to early modern natural philosophers—the speed of the wind seems a simple quantity. Its measurement by the anemometer (Greek, *anemos,* "wind" + *metron,* "measure"), nevertheless, presented great difficulties and required a surprising expenditure of mechanical ingenuity. Two categories embrace the nearly numberless variations of the anemometer's design: in the pressure anemometer the wind's dynamic pressure, acting on some obstacle, deflects an indicator; in the rotation anemometer the velocity of a windmill is supposed to be nearly proportional to the speed of the wind.

Although Leonardo da Vinci has often been credited with the invention of the anemometer, the instrument had been described by Leon Battista Alberti around 1450, the time of Leonardo's birth. The idea for this elementary pressure anemometer, in which a little board swung along a graduated arc, may have come from watching a sign swinging in the wind. The board was faced into the wind by a vane. Robert Hooke made a swinging-plate anemometer around 1660, for his program to develop a "history of the weather."

In 1625, Santorio Santorre described a normal-plate (or vertical-plate) anemometer, in which the plate is held normal to the wind. During the seventeenth and eighteenth centuries, a variety of linkages and sources of resistance (which gravity supplies in the swingingplate version) were developed for the normal-plate anemometer: weights, columns of liquid, fusees, chain balances, pulleys. A vertical-plate anemometer designed by Follett Osler in 1837, in which the plate presses against a spring, was one of the first such instruments durable and cheap enough for continuous use at meteorological stations. An Osler anemometer remained in continuous operation at Royal Greenwich Observatory from 1841 well into the twentieth century, and hand instruments of the vertical-plate type were in use during World War I.

The first pressure-tube anemometer suitable for meteorological use was built by the physician James Lind of Edinburgh in 1775, although Pierre Daniel Huet and Stephen Hales had constructed versions earlier in the century. The pressure-tube anemometer has a U-shaped tube, open at both ends and filled with water. As the wind blows into one side of the U through a brass elbow, the water along the other side rises against a graduated scale. Lind's instrument was not very sensitive, since a breeze of about sixteen knots is required to displace his water-column one-tenth inch. In 1858, W. Snow Harris replaced the graduated side of the U with a narrow tube, one-quarter the diameter of the original, bent into a rectangular shape. This arrangement magnified the motion of the water in the side exposed to the wind by a factor of sixteen.

An important modification of the pressuretube anemometer was developed by amateur British meteorologist William Henry Dines

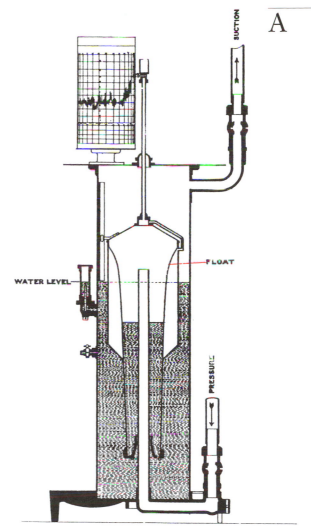

Float and recording drum of the Dines pressure tube anemograph, 1890s. William Henry Dines. Collected Scientific Papers. *London: Royal Meteorological Society, 1931: 11. Courtesy of the Royal Meteorological Society.*

around 1890. Dines's instrument derived from studies done earlier in the century in the United States, which measured the suction generated in chimneys by the passage of the wind across their open ends. In the Dines anemometer the pipe leading from the head of the tube (where the wind enters) is annular, and through the outer cylinder a dozen small holes are drilled into the annular space. The wind blowing past these holes creates a suction that varies as the square of the wind speed. The inner pipe leads up into the hollow space under a float riding on water in a sealed chamber, so that the pressure from the wind tends to raise the float; the suction is led from the outer pipe into the space above the float. The hollow space within the float is so shaped that the change in the float's displacement varies with the square of the distance it has risen from equilibrium. In this way the instrument's scale is rendered linear. The Dines anemometer had no moving parts requiring oiling or other attention, and the exposed part could be mounted high on a pole, while the pipes led to the recording apparatus placed in a convenient location. On the other hand, the large number of variations recorded—as many as twenty in a minute—make it difficult to draw any conclusions about the general condition of the free atmosphere. The Dines anemometer remains in current use.

Robert Hooke probably invented the first rotation or windmill anemometer around 1672. He recorded the number of rotations of the mill by punches placed on toothed wheels geared so as to rotate one revolution for every one hundred, one thousand, and so on turns, and he estimated the wind's speed from the number of punchmarks made in a given interval of time. Several windmill anemometer-designs, with both vertical and horizontal axes, appeared in the eighteenth and early nineteenth centuries.

The rotating cup anemometer was invented by the Irish astronomer Thomas Robinson in 1846. This works consistently over a long period of years, develops considerable motive power, moves slowly relative to the wind, and, thanks to the momentum of the cups, is not overly sensitive to gustiness or alterations in wind velocity. Moreover, it needs no vanes to face it into the wind, and it is easily duplicated. Numerous versions of the cup anemometer appeared over the course of the century. Since its invention coincided with early applications of electromagnetism, the instrument was arranged so that an electrical circuit was closed at a given number of revolutions, and a mark made on paper via an electromagnet.

All anemometers are difficult to calibrate. Robinson, mounting his instruments on a carriage, found that the cups rotated at one-third the wind speed. Later studies showed this simple relation to be unreliable; in fact, the so-called "anemometer constant," or the ratio of rate of cup rotation to wind speed, varies with the dimensions of the cups and the cross-arms holding them, as well as with the velocity and gustiness of the wind. The exact ratio must be determined experimentally for each type of instrument. Because of the inertia of the cups and arms, the cup anemometer will record a high value for wind speed when the wind is gusty.

Different anemometers render disparate values for wind velocity. Aside from the difficulties already mentioned, plate and pressure-tube anemometers measure wind pressure (rather than velocity), which varies with the obstacle presented by the instrument, the density of the air, even the mass of rain carried by the wind. Finally, there is the problem of exposure. Any flat surface exposed to the wind produces a local eddy, and a few degrees difference in the instrument's orientation may have a considerable effect on its record. The layer of atmosphere near the surface of the ground, where instruments are necessarily installed, is unsatisfactory for the measurement of the wind's velocity, because of obstacles and the friction of the air with the ground itself. Even when an anemometer is housed in a tower of open ironwork on an open space of level ground, distant geographical features will affect its reading.

Theodore S. Feldman

Bibliography

Middleton, W.E. Knowles. *Invention of the Meteorological Instruments.* Baltimore: Johns Hopkins University Press, 1969.

Shaw, William Napier. *Manual of Meteorology.* Vol. 1. Cambridge: Cambridge University Press, 1926.

Turner, Anthony J. *Early Scientific Instruments: Europe 1400–1800.* London: Philip Wilson for Sotheby's, 1987.

Angle, Measurement of

Angles are measured either by using some instrument with a graduated scale, by means of linear measurement and trigonometry, or by comparison with standards verified in one of these ways.

The trigonometrical method is much used in metrology. A right-angled triangle is set up, usually with its hypotenuse precisely defined by the use of a sine bar, and another side is adjusted to length using slip gauges or a similar means of accurate measurement. In other applications, trigonometry provides a convenient and precise way of setting out or measuring small angles.

The majority of instruments for measuring angles contain graduated scales. There may be

Watts autocollimator with polygon being used to check a dividing table, 1930s. Hume (1980): 171, Figure 59. Courtesy of Rank Taylor Hobson Ltd.

verniers, and microscopes with or without eye-piece micrometers, to facilitate reading or to obtain subdivision of the scale, but the scale itself is the main concern; whether it occupies a full circle or only an arc, it almost invariably derives ultimately from original division of the circle, which is usually regarded as a mechanical speciality in its own right.

Until about 1850, the greatest accuracy on scales of large radius was obtained by highly skilled operators working *ab initio* on each scale, using simple tools. A celebrated exponent of this art, John Bird, published a full account of his method in 1767.

Original division is an exacting and tedious, and hence expensive, operation, and ways were sought of achieving the same result by machine. The first really effective **dividing engine** was Jesse Ramsden's second attempt, of 1774, of which his own account was published in 1777.

Ramsden's engine comprised a circular table rotating in a fixed frame, its edge cut into 2,160 teeth, engaged by a worm, connected to the frame, that was rotated by set amounts to move the table round step by step. At each step a scribing cutter jointed to the framework was used to cut a graduation. The performance of this and similar early engines could not equal the best original division on large scales but provided a satisfactory and much quicker alternative for the graduation of smaller instruments such as **sextants**. Graduations were typically accurate to within ten seconds. William Simms's engine of 1843 became in 1850 the first to be used to divide a large important instrument, Airy's **transit circle** for the Royal Observatory, Greenwich. The precision of more modern instruments is enhanced to within a second by a correction cam, its profile adjusted to correspond to calibrated errors in the division of the teeth; a follower bearing on the cam gives a compensating movement to the worm, and hence an adjustment to the angular position of the table. The arrangement was first employed by Bryan Donkin, in a linear dividing engine, in 1826.

However accurately a circular scale may be divided, even a small error of concentricity in mounting it for use can lead to serious errors of reading. For a scale 100 mm in diameter, eccentric by only 0.001 mm, the maximum error in reading is about 8 seconds of arc. Where the scale is a full circle, this error may be nearly eliminated by averaging the readings of two indices placed opposite one another. By combining the readings of a greater number of equally spaced indices one can reduce error due to irregularities in the scale itself.

The bubble level, invented by Robert Hooke, only later became an instrument of precision. Levels can in many instances be used in combination with other apparatuses for the measurement of angles. Sensitive bubble levels are readily available to measure a few seconds of arc per division, allowing estimation to less than one second. Modern electronic levels, in which a **pendulum** forms part of an induction transducer, can be even more sensitive. The clinometer combines a level with a circular scale for the measurement of a line or surface inclined to the horizon.

The autocollimator detects small differences in angle. Here, light from a bright object in the focal plane of a converging lens is collimated into a parallel beam; this is reflected back to the instrument by a mirror to form an image in the focal plane, where it is observed though a simple or compound microscope. Angular deviation of the mirror is indicated by the lateral movement of the image, which is independent of the distance of the mirror from the instrument. The microscope may be fitted with an eyepiece micrometer allowing the operator to obtain repeatable readings to a quarter of a second of arc. The autocollimator may also be fitted with a photoelectric microscope, which provides greater sensitivity and consistency than is attained with visual observation.

In metrology and the checking of machinery and other apparatus, the autocollimator is a valuable tool for examining errors of alignment, straightness, and flatness.

Angle gauges with accurately lapped flat faces, to be used in combination by *wringing* together, just as is done with slip gauges in linear measurement, were developed by George A. Tomlinson in 1941. The practical use of such blocks is often awkward; moreover their angular values have to be verified by reference to other means of measurement, and when used in combination their errors are compounded. For these reasons their use has been limited.

Polygons with facets of optical quality were subsequently developed by Cecil O. Taylerson, and have proved valuable in the calibration and setting of divided scales. They are made of glass or steel lapped to a mirror finish, or with separate reflecting facets. The facets are used as target mirrors for one or more autocollimators. Polygons need not be regular, although they usually are, but the angles are checked and calibrated to $1/2$ second using self-proving methods. The polygon gives accurate and repeatable results when used with an autocollimator because there is no need for it to be centered.

The "Ultradex" indexing table, developed in 1953, comprises two components with identical serrations on the faces of annular rings; when forced into contact, any irregularity in the serrations is taken up by elastic deformation and a very high precision of angular setting is obtained. With a more recent form having 1,440 serrations, settings at the $1/4$-degree intervals are claimed to be repeatable to 0.02 second and accurate to 0.1 second. The addition of a micrometer tangent screw allows intermediate values to be obtained with similar accuracy.

Michael Wright

Bibliography

Brooks, John. "The Circular Dividing Engine: Development in England, 1739–1843." *Annals of Science* 49 (1992): 101–35.

Evans, J.C., and C.O. Taylerson. *Measurement of Angle in Engineering.* London: Her Majesty's Stationery Office, 1986.

Hume, Kenneth J. *A History of Engineering Metrology.* London: Mechanical Engineering, 1980.

Moore, Wayne R. *Foundations of Mechanical Accuracy.* Bridgeport, Conn.: Moore Special Tool, 1970.

Rolt, Frederick Henry. "The Development of Engineering Metrology." *The Sir Alfred Herbert Paper, 1952.* London: Institution of Production Engineers, 1952.

Animal Calorimeter

See CALORIMETER, ANIMAL

Armillary Sphere

The armillary sphere was produced both as an instrument of observation and a tool for demonstrating astronomical principles. Both forms were composed of rings (known in Latin as *armillae*), from which the instrument got its name. These rings represented the great circles of the celestial sphere. In the observational armillary, the rings were kept to a minimum so as not to block out the sky, and one or two carried movable sights. These rings were calibrated to measure degrees of latitude and longitude with respect to the ecliptic, or declination and right ascension with respect to the equator. In the demonstrational armillary, the polar circles and tropics of Cancer and Capricorn were delineated in addition to the colures, equator, and ecliptic. A central ball marked the position of the earth or, sometimes, the sun.

Observational Armillary Spheres

The earliest armillary spheres were strictly for observation, and these were derived from the *astrolabon* described by Ptolemy in the *Almagest*. Ptolemy's instrument was adjustable for the observer's geographical latitude; it enabled astronomers to determine the positions of stars and planets directly in ecliptic coordinates—the format required by Ptolemy's planetary theory—without having to go to the mathematical trouble of converting altazimuth observations into the ecliptic form. This type of

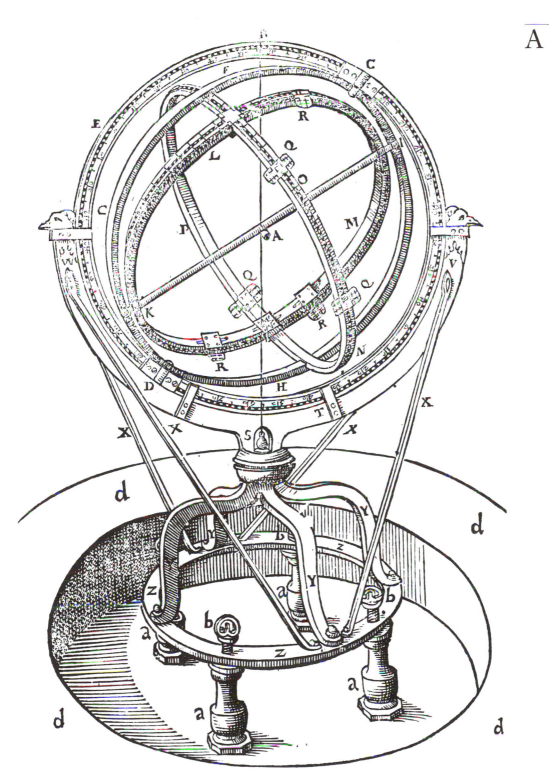

Tycho Brahe's zodiacal observational armillary sphere. Tycho Brahe. Astronomiae Instauratae Mechanica.
Wandesburgi, 1598. Courtesy of SSPL.

armillary sphere was known as zodiacal. Later forms of the instrument gave positions directly in equatorial coordinates, and were known as equatorial armillaries. Both types were used in medieval Islamic observatories.

Knowledge of the observing instrument was probably transmitted from the East to the West in the late twelfth century, when Gerard of Cremona translated the *Almagest* from Arabic into Latin. A description of the armillary sphere was also included in the *Libros del Saber,* compiled in the mid thirteenth century at the request of Alfonso the Wise of Castile. During the fifteenth and sixteenth centuries, Bernard Walther, Nicolas Copernicus, and Tycho Brahe employed zodiacal armillaries. Observing planets between 1488 and 1504, Walther was able to achieve an accuracy within 10 minutes of arc with his instrument.

Tycho Brahe was not satisfied with the zodiacal armillary, complaining that its lack of symmetry and great weight imposed uneven stress on the instrument causing it to warp. He preferred the equatorial form and built three. The first two were fairly traditional in design, but were noteworthy for being made of steel, brass, and wood held together by screws ("for an astronomer ought to be a citizen of the world," Tycho wrote, putting a positive spin on the political reality that astronomers often needed to relocate their "fixed" apparatus to lands that would better support their work). These armillaries were 1.5 meters in diameter and divided into minute intervals. His third equatorial armillary was more radical in design. It consisted of a large declination circle (2.72 meters in diameter and reinforced by cross-braces) that revolved around a polar axis set within a semicircular arc fixed in the equatorial plane. This armillary could be read to 15 seconds of arc, although in practice Tycho's accuracy was within 40 seconds. Tycho's observatory was the last to employ large observational armillary spheres.

The observational armillary developed independently in China, where it was also a key piece of observatory equipment.

Demonstrational Armillary Spheres
With interlocking rings to represent the celestial sphere, the armillary sphere could also serve as a model of the universe, and scaled-down versions of the large observational instrument were used to teach elementary astronomical principles, solve basic astronomical problems, and make rough calculations in much the same way that globes were used. For this reason, the pedagogical functions of armillaries were often reviewed in manuals concerning the use of the globes.

Armillaries intended as teaching tools were sometimes mounted on handles, but often they were set like globes into cradles so that the rotating sphere could be adjusted to represent the heavens as seen from any latitude. To illustrate the geocentric system, a small terrestrial globe was fixed to an ecliptic-polar axis in the center of the outer sphere, while a series of nested, movable rings (or skeletal spheres) portrayed the paths of the moon, sun, and planets. Some fancy armillaries used gearwork to shift inner and outer celestial spheres in order to demonstrate precession of the equinoxes or trepidation. Others replaced the planetary rings with eccentric disks in order to illustrate the Ptolemaic theory of deferents and epicycles. Star pointers were sometimes soldered to the instrument's outermost sphere, which represented the firmament.

Although planetary rings may have been added to the armillary as early as the fourth century, no record of the demonstrational instrument has been found in the Islamic world. The didactic Ptolemaic instrument appeared in Christian Europe perhaps as early as the late tenth century (for Gerbert of Aurillac seems to have owned one). It was used for teaching the doctrine of the sphere up through the nineteenth century.

In the seventeenth century, Copernican armillary spheres became paired with Ptolemaic ones as teaching tools. In these heliocentric instruments, a small globe representing the sun was fixed to the central axis of the armillary sphere and planetary rings revolved around it. New rings were later added to accommodate the discovery of Uranus (1781), Neptune (1846), and the larger asteroids, Vesta, Juno, Ceres, and Pallas (1801–1807). In some Copernican armillaries, a planetarium replaced the planetary rings.

Most demonstrational armillaries were made of brass or other metals, but wood, pasteboard, and paper were also used, particularly by some central-European craftsmen of the fifteenth and sixteenth centuries, and many French makers of the late eighteenth and early nineteenth centuries.

Long recognized as a standard piece of equipment for astronomers, teachers, and scholars, the armillary sphere became an emblem of astronomy in particular, and learning in general. In manuscripts, cathedral sculpture, books, and paintings, astronomers (and their muses) were often portrayed holding an armillary sphere, and scholars were depicted in their studies with an armillary near at hand. Even today, the image of the armillary serves as a marker of erudition and breeding, appearing on university brochures and posters advertising lectures and programs of study.

Sara Schechner Genuth

Bibliography

Brahe, Tycho. *Tycho Brahe's Description of His Instruments and Scientific Work* as given in *Astronomiae Instauratae Mechanica (Wandesburgi 1598)*. Translated and edited by Hans Ræder, Elis Strömgren, and Bengt Strömgren. Copenhagen: Ejnar Munksgaard, 1946.

Needham, Joseph. *Science and Civilisation in China*. Vol. 3. Cambridge: Cambridge University Press, 1959.

Nolte, Friedrich. *Die Armillarsphäre*. Erlangen: M. Mencke, 1922.

Poulle, Emmanuel. *Les sources astronomiques (textes, tables, instruments)*. Typologie des sources du Moyen Âge Occidental, no. 39. Turnhout, Belgium: Brepols, 1981.

Price, Derek J. "A Collection of Armillary Spheres and Other Antique Scientific Instruments." *Annals of Science* 10 (1954): 172–87.

Artificial Horizon

An artificial horizon replaces the apparent horizon when it is obscured, such as by fog, intervening land, or darkness, and is used with an instrument to measure the altitude of a celestial body above the horizon. Early instruments for measuring altitudes, the nautical **quadrant** and the **mariner's astrolabe**, were based on vertical reference. These instruments were suspended so that they would hang truly vertically, and had to remain motionless during the observation.

Two basic types of artificial horizons should be distinguished. The first type is fitted to the instrument with which the altitude is measured, or placed nearby, on the level of the observer's eye. It was developed in several variations, of which the bubble level and the gyroscopic type became predominant, and used on both ships and aircraft. The second type consists of a reflecting surface, in which the image of the celestial body can be seen. The surface could be made of glass, or could consist of oil, water, mercury, or even treacle. As oil, water, and treacle absorb much light, mercury, protected by glass from disturbance by the wind, was used predominantly in the nineteenth century. The angle between the heavenly body and its reflection was measured. This type was not very practical on a ship or aircraft in motion, and was used mainly for land surveying.

History and Development

An artificial horizon was mentioned in Pedro de Medina's *Arte de Navegar* (Valladolid, 1545), an authoritative navigation manual that was written in Spanish and translated into French, Italian, Dutch, and English. Medina described a contraption with a horizontal bar that had to be fixed to the observer's ship, to substitute for the obscured horizon, when observing with a **cross-staff**. Robert Hooke reputedly used a mercury trough as an artificial horizon at Oxford, but George Adams is credited with the invention of the mercury tray with glass cover in the mid eighteenth century.

In 1728, the Englishman John Elton patented a back-staff fitted with two bubble levels. The invention of the **octant** and the **sextant** in 1731 and 1757 respectively stimulated the invention of new and more sophisticated types of artificial horizons. John Hadley, the inventor of the octant, fitted his instrument with a bubble level in 1733. Around 1740, John Serson invented a gyroscopic speculum artificial horizon that, apparently, was no success.

In 1834 Lieutenant A.B. Becher RN designed an artificial horizon consisting of a small **pendulum**, to be fitted to a sextant, and whose motion was damped in oil. The English Captain Christopher George, in 1868, patented a horizon consisting of a mercury reservoir from which a glass-topped chamber could be filled. P.J. Kaiser developed an artificial horizon for the Dutch navy around 1880. This consisted of a reservoir made of leather and filled with mercury, and a hollow tray on top, covered with a lid made of mica. When the reservoir was squeezed, the mercury would flow onto the tray. A French admiral, G.E. Fleuriais, in 1890 invented a gyroscopic artificial horizon. The **gyroscope** was spun by a special mechanism, and after being attached to the sextant would spin for several minutes.

Fleurais artificial horizon, attached to a sextant, 1890s. Courtesy of SSPL.

With the development of aircraft, at the beginning of the twentieth century, the bubble level was further perfected. In the United Kingdom the bubble-sextant, or bubble-octant as it was named by airmen (see **sextant, aircraft**), was developed and manufactured by the London firms of Heath & Co. and H. Hughes & Son, mainly for use in aircraft. They remained in use until about 1960, when astronomical navigation started to become obsolete. In Germany, around 1935, the Hamburg firm of C. Plath developed and manufactured a sextant with a built-in gyroscopic horizon, which had to be activated by an **air pump**. It was used in U-boats during World War II when these, for safety, could surface only during darkness.

Willem F.J. Mörzer Bruyns

Bibliography

Cotter, C.H. *A History of the Navigator's Sextant*. Glasgow: Brown, 1983.
An Inventory of the Navigation and Astronomical Collections, Vol. 1, *Artificial Horizons*. London: National Maritime Museum, 1970.
Mörzer Bruyns, W.F.J. "Historische Kunstkimmen." *NTT De Zee* 1 (1972): 214–18.
Williams, J.E.D. *From Sails to Satellites: The Origin and Development of Navigational Science*. Oxford: Oxford University Press, 1992.

Astrolabe

The astrolabe was the favorite instrument of medieval and Renaissance astronomers. It is essentially a model of the universe that one can hold in one's hand and it has many uses in astronomy, time-keeping, astrology, and surveying. The astrolabe inspired the development of the astrolabic clocks found in various European cathedrals, although there is little evidence of Muslims or Christian monks having actually used astrolabes to regulate their prayer times.

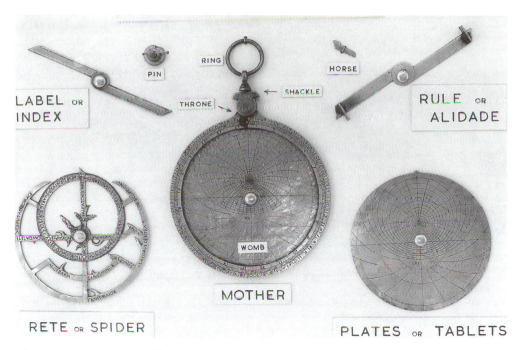

The parts of a standard astrolabe. Courtesy of SSPL.

A charming medieval Arabic anecdote relates that while riding a donkey, Ptolemy dropped a celestial sphere and the beast trod on it: the result was an astrolabe. Only the donkey is fictional. The astrolabe, whose principle was known to Ptolemy, is a two-dimensional model of the celestial sphere, achieved by a mathematical projection known as stereographic. The plane of the projection is the celestial equator.

The astrolabe consists of two main parts. The movable rete—the celestial part—shows various bright stars and the ecliptic; each fixed plate—the terrestrial part—shows the projections of the horizon and meridian for a specific terrestrial latitude, as well as circles of altitude above the horizon. The stereographic projection ensures that the circles on the celestial sphere are projected as circles, and that angles between these circles are preserved. The back of the astrolabe bears an altitude scale and is fitted with an alidade, a sighting device used to measure altitudes on the scale.

To use the astrolabe, one first measures the altitude of the sun or a given star with the alidade, and then sets the appropriate marker on the rete on top of the appropriate altitude circle on the plate for the latitude in question. The ensemble shows the instantaneous con-figuration of the heavens with respect to the local horizon. And since one complete rotation of the rete corresponds to twenty-four hours, any rotation can be converted into an interval of time. Thus, by moving the sun back to the eastern horizon, one can measure the time elapsed since sunrise. Or by moving the sun to the meridian below the horizon, one can measure the time remaining until midnight. One can also see the configuration of the ecliptic with respect to the local horizon and meridian—the points of intersection, known as the ascendant and descendant, and upper and lower midheaven, respectively, are of prime importance in mathematical astrology. Some astrolabe plates have markings for the astrological houses; these enable the user to read off the positions of the twelve houses at any time, and thus lay the foundation for casting a horoscope. Astrolabes also have more mundane uses in surveying.

The theory of stereographic projection was apparently known to Hipparchus (ca. 150 B.C.), and the application to the needs of spherical astronomy was described in Ptolemy's *Planisphaerium* (ca. A.D. 125). The "astrolabe" described in Ptolemy's *Almagest* is a three-dimensional **armillary sphere**. The "planispheric astrolabe" with which we are concerned here was apparently described in a lost treatise by Theon of Alexandria (ca. 300), and the earliest instruments of which we have any record were made in Alexandria and Harran (now southeast Turkey) in the seventh and eighth centuries. What is believed to be the earliest surviving astrolabe (now preserved in a museum in Baghdad) has star positions that correspond to about the year 800. This astrolabe has three plates, whose six sides together with the base of the front of the instrument (known as the mater) serve the latitudes of the seven geographical climates of classical antiquity, and the back bears no markings beyond an altitude scale. The design of the rete is close to that of the sole surviving astrolabe with Greek inscriptions (now in Brescia) from the year 1062.

The astrolabes made in Baghdad and Iran in the ninth and tenth centuries, and associated texts on the construction and use of the instrument, attest to the scientific achievements of the early Muslim astronomers. Innovations included azimuth circles on the plates, trigonometric grids on the back, and occasionally a luni-solar gear mechanism for showing the phases of the moon. An ingenious set of markings on the back can be used with the alidade to find the time of day as a function of solar latitude for any time of the year and any terrestrial latitude. These horary markings appear on virtually all European astrolabes, even though the underlying formula, which is necessarily approximate, did not work well for the latitudes of northern Europe. Between the tenth and thirteenth century numerous astrolabes of great beauty were constructed by Muslim craftsmen.

The spherical astrolabe was also developed in Iraq and Iran at this time; the only complete surviving example comes from fourteenth-century Egypt or Syria. The linear astrolabe, with which all of the standard problems of spherical astronomy could be solved for a single latitude (this is the closest thing to a medieval slide-rule), was developed in twelfth-century Iran. A universal astrolabe that would work for all latitudes with a single plate was devised in Andalusia in the eleventh century. The most sophisticated astrolabe ever made was conceived and constructed by Ibn al-Sarraj of Aleppo in the early fourteenth century; its various components can be used for any terrestrial latitude, in five different ways. Many very beautiful and highly accurate astrolabes were produced in the seventeenth century, particularly in Iran. The majority of surviving Islamic astrolabes, which number about one thousand, are late Indo-Persian in provenance. Fake instruments are still being made in India and the Maghrib for tourists.

The earliest European astrolabe (now in a museum in Paris) dates from tenth-century Catalonia. It was copied from an early Andalusian astrolabe, and the Arabic inscriptions of the original were transliterated in Latin characters or translated into Latin. A few European astrolabes date from the twelfth and thirteenth centuries and a few more from the fourteenth century; most of these are unsigned and undated. By the fourteenth century, several regional schools of astrolabe production had come into being in Northern Italy, France, and England.

In the fifteenth century, we can for the first time associate European astrolabes with specific individuals. Some twenty pieces survive from the workshop of Jean Fusoris in Paris, and about a dozen from the Vienna workshop of Peuerbach and Regiomontanus. In the early sixteenth century Georg Hartmann in Nuremberg produced hundreds of astrolabes after the model of the Regimontanus pieces; close to thirty astrolabes signed by him survive, many with batch-letters engraved on their component parts. The main European workshop in the late sixteenth century was in Louvain, and equally competent pieces were produced in Elizabethan England. Astronomers in Flanders in the seventeenth century reinvented most of the unusual forms of astrolabes that Muslim astronomers had devised in the ninth and tenth centuries.

David A. King

Bibliography

Gunther, Robert W.T. *The Astrolabes of the World.* Oxford: Oxford University Press, 1932. London: Holland, 1976.

King, David A. "Astronomical Instruments between East and West." In *Kommunikation zwischen Orient und Okzident,* edited by H. Kühnel, 143–98. Vienna: Austrian Academy of Sciences, 1994.

———. *Islamic Astronomical Instruments.* London: Variorum, 1987.

North, John D. "The Astrolabe." *Scientific American* 230 (January 1974): 96–106.

The Planispheric Astrolabe. London: National Maritime Museum, 1979.

Astrolabe, Mariner's

A mariner's astrolabe measures the height of the sun or a star above the horizon, and is used together with astronomical tables to find the latitude of the observer. It was developed for and first used by Portuguese navigators as they explored progressively further down the west coast of Africa in the late fifteenth century.

The mariner's astrolabe is a simplified version of the planispheric **astrolabe**. In its initial form it consisted of a circular disc suspended vertically from a hinged ring, with an alidade moving over a scale of degrees on the limb. Subsequent developments were intended to adapt it to the often difficult observing condi-

tions on board an unsteady ship at sea. For instance, if a breeze were blowing it was difficult to keep the instrument hanging vertically while taking observations. To reduce the effect of the wind, an open, wheel-type body was introduced in the early sixteenth century to replace the complete disc. Observation at sea was also eased by fixing the sights on the alidade closer together than those on a planispheric astrolabe. Stability was further improved by making the instrument as heavy as practicable: the body was made of cast metal, and during the sixteenth century an integral ballast weight was added to Portuguese and Spanish instruments.

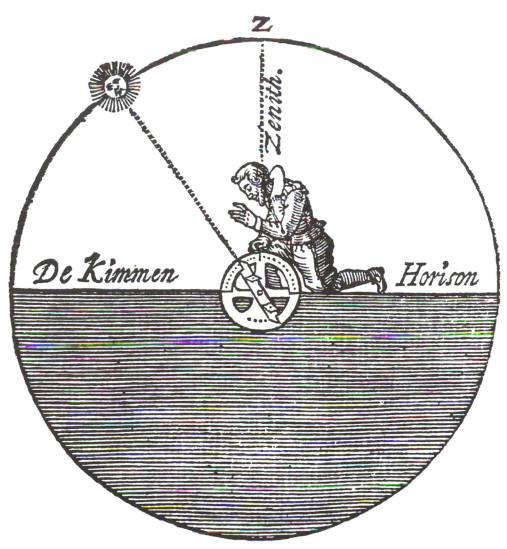

Mariner's astrolabe in use. Adriaan Metius. De genuino usu utriusque globi tractatus. *Amstelodami: Fronecker, 1624. Courtesy of the Museum of the History of Science, Oxford.*

The mariner's astrolabe was used in two different ways depending on whether the sun or a star was being observed. Solar observations were made at noon when the sun crossed the local meridian. The instrument was suspended and its alidade adjusted so that the sun's rays came through small holes on both of the alidade's sights. The alidade then indicated the sun's altitude against the instrument's degree scale. Using tables of the sun's declination for each day of the year, the observed altitude could be used to calculate latitude. Stars were observed directly by holding the sighting alidade up to the eye and reading their altitude against the degree scale. Larger pinholes were provided for stellar observations but they became less common during the sixteenth century as the **cross-staff** was increasingly adopted for taking the height of stars at sea.

The Spanish state sought to ensure the quality of mariner's astrolabes and other instruments for astronomical navigation by stipulating that they be submitted for expert approval before use. Official regulations enacted in the early sixteenth century required all such instruments to be submitted for examination by the Pilot Major at the Casa de Contratación in Seville. Some surviving instruments bear stamped markings to show that they had been duly approved.

Spanish and Portuguese navigators continued to use the mariner's astrolabe into the eighteenth century, with few changes in the form of their instruments after the sixteenth century. The instrument did however undergo further development in northern Europe, especially by the Dutch. The Dutch East India Company issued its navigators with astrolabes in which the ballast weight was moved to the crown of the instrument, directly underneath the suspension ring. Another Dutch innovation was the introduction of a semicircular form of the mariner's astrolabe, in which only the two upper quadrants of the instrument were retained. Used in exactly the same way as the full circular version, it could provide a larger diameter (and hence improved accuracy) without a corresponding increase in weight. But despite these changes, the mariner's astrolabe was displaced by other instruments, with the cross-staff and back-staff becoming standard devices for northern European navigators prior to the introduction of Hadley's **octant** in the eighteenth century. The Dutch East India Company had stopped issuing the mariner's astrolabe by 1675.

Like other instruments used as working tools, very few mariner's astrolabes were preserved in private and museum collections, and only ten were known to researchers in 1957. Since then the picture has been changed by the rapid growth of underwater archaeology and exploration of wreck sites. By 1988 more than sixty mariner's astrolabes had been reported and documented.

Stephen Johnston

Bibliography
Stimson, Alan. *The Mariner's Astrolabe. A Survey of Known, Surviving Sea Astrolabes.* Utrecht: HES, 1988.
Waters, David. "The Sea- or Mariner's Astrolabe." *Agrupamento de Estudos de Cartografia Antiga*, 15 Seção de Coimbra. Coimbra: Junta de Investigaçõs do Ultramar, 1966.

Astronomical Comparator
See COMPARATOR, ASTRONOMICAL

Astronomical Spectroscope
See SPECTROSCOPE, ASTRONOMICAL

Atomic Absorption Spectrometer
See SPECTROMETER, ATOMIC ABSORPTION

Atomic Clock
See CLOCK, ATOMIC

Atwood's Machine
A device designed in the 1770s by the Cambridge mathematician George Atwood to demonstrate the motion of bodies under constant forces. Built by the London maker George Adams the younger, it consisted of a 2-meter wooden column supporting a platform carrying conical pivots for two pairs of brass wheel bearings to minimize friction. A long silk cord ran over a brass pulley riding on these bearings, and attached at either end of the cord were equal stacks of wooden or brass cylindrical weights. Additional weights, small perforated discs or thin bars, could be placed on either stack. Fitted to the wooden column was a thirty-minute weight-driven pendulum clock, and set between the platform and the stand behind the cord was

George Atwood's machine with (right) an enlarged illustration of the clock, pulley, wheel bearings, scale and ring for removing weights. Atwood (1784): Figures 78–83. Courtesy of the Whipple Library, Cambridge.

a divided rule with two small movable stops, the lower to terminate the weights' fall, the other an open ring designed to instantaneously remove projecting bar weights from the cylinder as it moved down through the ring.

Atwood first used this machine in lectures at Trinity College Cambridge from 1776, and published a detailed description in 1784. Whereas in "books of mechanics no account is found of methods by which the principles of motion may be subjected to decisive and satisfactory trials," this machine would allow such trials, because the cord's weight, the effect of air resistance, and the friction at the pulley would all be negligible. Different accelerations could be produced by changing the number of weights and the motion started with a control rod. "The proper method is to attend to the beats of the **pendulum** until an exact idea of their succession is obtained, then the extremity of the rod being withdrawn from the bottom [of the stack] directly downward at the instant of any beat, the descent will commence at the same instant." A dozen trials demonstrated the relations between elapsed time, space fallen, initial speed, final speed attained, and accelerating force. The final speed could be measured by removing a supplementary weight from the falling stack as it passed through the open ring, so as to make the weights in the two stacks equal. The further distance moved by the stack in known time under no net force would allow the calculation of the speed attained at the moment when the ring was reached. In an important adaptation of this experiment, removing weights from the falling stack would render it less heavy than the rising stack and the machine could be used to demonstrate the behavior of falling bodies under a retarding force.

"To form an adequate idea of the laws that are observed in the communication of motion, the bodies impelled should be conceived to exist in free space and void of gravity," the situation Atwood's Machine allegedly produced. Cambridge mathematicians often assumed that they could prove that motions depended entirely on external forces, and that they could refute the doctrine of living force. Atwood advertised his machine as a superior substitute for the early-eighteenth-century experiments in which the force of falling bodies was estimated by the size of the impression they made on some resisting substance whose resistance was hard to measure exactly. While Atwood's Machine was often used to test Newtonian mechanics,

late-eighteenth-century Cambridge mathematicians equally often assumed the truth of this doctrine and used the machine simply to clarify the concepts on which it depended.

The distribution of the machine helped disseminate these views on Newtonian mechanics. In the 1780s, the Portuguese entrepreneur Jean Magellan had already helped acquire machines from Adams for several European academic and noble clients, including the Pavia natural philosophy professor Alessandro Volta. "The result has always corresponded to the theory with a precision which one could not wish to be greater," Volta exclaimed. William and Samuel Jones took over the machine's production in 1795, and four years later Harvard University ordered a machine from them. By the first decades of the nineteenth century, makers such as John Newman in London, and Nicolas Pixii and Nicolas Fortin in Paris, were supplying these machines worldwide. American makers, such as Alva Mason at Philadelphia and William Welch at New York, produced versions from the 1840s. Designs often varied considerably from Atwood's original, with improved clocks, a bell to signal the impact of the falling weights, and an automatic lever attached to the clock gearing for releasing the weights and starting the clock simultaneously. In an important, and distinctly cheaper, nineteenth-century modification, the moving weight was held in place electromagnetically, released by breaking electrical contact, and its subsequent motion measured by observing the trace left by a plate vibrating against a smoked cylinder attached to the pulley or by successively cutting a paper strip pasted to the vertical rod. As these devices became ever more common in physics classrooms, the machine came more usually to be interpreted as a means for measuring the acceleration due to gravity assuming the truth of Newton's second law, as a means of illustrating that law's meaning rather than a stiff test of its empirical adequacy.

Simon Schaffer

Bibliography

Atwood, George. *A Treatise on the Rectilinear Motion and Rotation of Bodies: With a Description of the Original Experiments Relevant to the Subject.* Cambridge, England, 1784.

Greenslade, Thomas B. "Atwood's Machine." *Physics Teacher* 23 (1985): 24–28.

Magellan, Jean Hyacinthe de. *Description d'une nouvelle machine de dynamique inventee par Mr. G. Atwood.* London, 1780.

Schaffer, Simon. "Machine Philosophy: Demonstration Devices in Georgian Mechanics." *Osiris* 10 (1994): 157–82.

Wheatland, David P. *The Apparatus of Science at Harvard 1765–1800.* Cambridge: Harvard University Press, 1968.

Audiometer

Audiometers are used to assess hearing acuity, and to determine the existence, type, and severity of hearing problems. They are also used to obtain data on normal hearing (psychophysics) and to investigate various aspects of sound. The pure tone audiometer, which generates tones of different frequencies and levels, has replaced the use of tuning forks for testing hearing loss. The speech audiometer is used instead of conversational voice tests.

Electric or Induction Coil Audiometer

In this instrument, two primary coils of different sizes were fixed on either side of a wooden bar that was divided into two hundred parts. A large induction coil, connected to a telephone, moved along the bar. By periodically interrupting the primary circuit, an alternating current was induced in the secondary circuit, producing sounds in the telephone receiver. The intensity depended on the position of the secondary coil on the bar.

Arthur Hartmann in Germany constructed an electric hearing-testing device in 1878; he was followed by Endre Högyes (1879) in Hungary, and by David Hughes (1879) in Great Britain. The English physician Benjamin Richardson coined the term audiometer in 1879 to describe Hughes's device. Although Richardson performed various experiments with Hughes's instrument and advocated its clinical use, neither Hughes nor Richardson did apply it clinically. The early instruments were bulky and difficult to keep in running order. Moreover, since the frequency and the intensity range were limited, they had little diagnostic value. Nevertheless, Thomas Hawksley produced Hughes's audiometer commercially until 1912.

The first clinically useful audiometer was developed in 1919 by Lee Dean and Cordia Bunch at Iowa State University. It contained an electric generator, which had been developed in 1914 by A. Stefanini in Italy and which produced an alternating current across a wide range of frequencies. It was called "pitch range audiometer" because it produced all tones between 30 and 10,000 Hz "pure enough for all practical purposes." The intensity could be varied from below the threshold of audibility up to

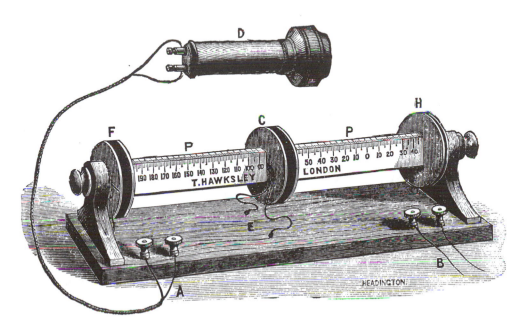

Commercial model of the Hughes sonometer by Thomas Hawksley. William B. Dalby. Diseases and Injuries of the Ear. *London: J. and A. Churchill, 1885: 65. Courtesy of the Wellcome Institute Library, London.*

that of discomfort. This audiometer was never produced commercially.

Electric Valve or Vacuum Tube Audiometer

With the advent of the electric valve tube, oscillating currents of almost any frequency could be generated. The vacuum tube audiometer was the first instrument capable of making precise measurements throughout the human auditory range, and it was the first commercially feasible audiometer. The first audiometers of this generation were the Otaudion in Germany (1919) and the 1-A audiometer of the Western Electric Co. in the United States (1922). The 1-A (which, at $1,500, was very expensive) was soon followed by a portable model 2-A, which found its way into general use by otologists. An audiometer that could measure bone conduction as well as air conduction was developed in 1924 by Knudsen and Jones and produced by Sonotone Corp. It included a masking noise source (probably the first recognition of the need to mask a good ear while testing the poorer one).

Speech Audiometers

In 1904, William Sohier Bryant presented a phonograph audiometer based on the Edison phonograph design. A speech signal was emitted through stethoscope tubes, with the intensity controlled by a valve. The technique of recorded speech testing via the phonograph reached its apogee in 1927, in the Western Electric 4A audiometer. Entire classes of school children could be tested because twenty to forty earphones could be used to listen to the recording. This approach to testing big groups was replaced by pure-tone screening tests in the late 1940s. Speech audiometry acquired new importance during World War II in the military aural rehabilitation centers.

Modern Audiometers

The pure-tone audiometer provides a range or a discrete set of frequencies (125–8,000 Hz) by means of an oscillator, presented as sound via a transducer (headphones, loudspeakers, bone conductor). For each frequency the intensity is changed with an attenuator (usually in steps of 1 or 5 dB) by the tester, and the patient signals when the tone becomes audible. The intensity at which tones are just audible is plotted against the frequency in a pure tone audiogram. The audiometer is calibrated in terms of hearing loss relative to the hearing threshold for the average normal ear at each frequency.

In the Békésy automatic pure-tone audiometer developed in 1947 by George von Békésy, the oscillator is driven by a motor in order to increase the frequency automatically while the subject manipulates the intensity continuously so that the tone remains just audible. The subject presses or releases the button, increasing the intensity when the signal is not heard and decreasing the intensity while the signal is heard, resulting in a curve zigzagging around the hearing threshold.

A speech audiometer, which reproduces standard speech material at known intensity, measures a patient's ability to hear in daily life. It provides inputs from a microphone, from a tape recorder or a CD-player, and from a masking-noise generator. The output of the amplifier is directed through an attenuator to headphones or loudspeakers. The speech audiometer produces a speech audiogram that shows a plot of the word score (percentage of correctly identified words) against intensity. The 50 percent level (intensity at which 50 percent of the words are heard) is called the speech reception threshold (SRT).

The screening audiometer is a very simple and often portable pure tone audiometer that has a limited number of frequencies and intensities. It is used by general practitioners, consultation bureaus, company medical officers, armed forces, and schools to screen for hearing impairment. Békésy audiometers are often used in industrial testing, as they are time-efficient. Diagnostic and clinical audiometers can in addition perform bone conduction tests, to discriminate between conductive and sensorineural hearing loss, and speech audiometric tests. They provide a wider frequency and intensity range than the screening audiometer. They also provide masking facilities: white noise, speech noise, or narrow-band noise. A modern clinical audiometer, as used in a hospital or audiological center, may cost about $5,000–6,000.

Stuart S. Blume
Barbara Regeer

Bibliography

Glorig, Aram, and Marion Downs. "Introduction to Audiometry." In *Audiometry: Principles and Practices,* edited by Aram Glorig, 1–14. Baltimore: Williams and Wilkins, 1965.

Katz, Jack, ed. *Handbook of Clinical Audiology.* 3rd ed. Baltimore: Williams and Wilkins, 1985.

Mester, A.F., and S.D.G. Stephens. "Development of the Audiometer and Audiometry." *Audiology* 23 (1984): 206–14.

Stephens, S.D.G. "David Edward Hughes and His Audiometer." *Journal of Laryngology and Otology* 93 (1991): 1–6.

AutoAnalyzer™

The AutoAnalyzer™ was used in clinical laboratories to measure the amount of a chemical or chemicals in blood, urine, or other body fluids. It resulted from the work of Leonard Skeggs, who in the 1950s studied the properties of fluid streams segmented by air bubbles. The instrument automatically mixed equal amounts from successive specimens with appropriate amounts of reagents and then measured the resulting color changes of each mixture.

Before the invention of the AutoAnalyzer™, patient specimens were processed manually. Each specimen was placed in a test tube, reagents were added in a fixed time sequence, and the reactions were allowed to proceed for a fixed length of time. The results were determined by visual observation or by a photometric detector. This procedure lacked good precision and accuracy.

The AutoAnalyzer™ has six basic components: turntable, pump, manifold, bath, photometer, and chart recorder. Standards for calibration, controls to test the calibration, and specimens are loaded onto the turntable. At regular intervals the turntable indexes one position, and a sampling probe enters the next specimen to remove material for analysis. Between specimens, the probe aspirates wash solution to minimize carryover between specimens. The probe is raised by gears and levers, to prevent damage when the turntable rotates to the next position.

The specimen leaves the turntable and enters clear tubing of fixed wall thickness and known inner diameter. A peristaltic pump forces the specimen along the tubing in the longitudinal direction. Other pieces of tubing of the same wall thickness but of various inner diameters also pass through the pump. These tubes are connected to bottles of reagents. The result is that the reagents and specimens are pumped forward at the same rate, but the relative proportions of reagents to specimen are determined by the ratios of the inner diameters squared of the various tubes.

The contents of the various tubes are mixed at the manifold. Air bubbles are added to the specimen stream to reduce the longitudinal diffusion of the specimen resulting from the drag of the tubing walls. The liquids in the various tubes are then combined at Y-junctions and mixed in small glass coils. Because some analytes in blood can be measured only if other natural chemicals of the blood are removed, chemicals with small molecules are separated from those with large molecules using dialyzer blocks. The specimen stream passes on one side of a semipermeable membrane, and a pickup stream passes on the other side. An amount of the smaller molecules proportional to their concentration in the specimen passes through the membrane and is absorbed by the pickup solution. This solution was then mixed with the reagents to perform the analysis.

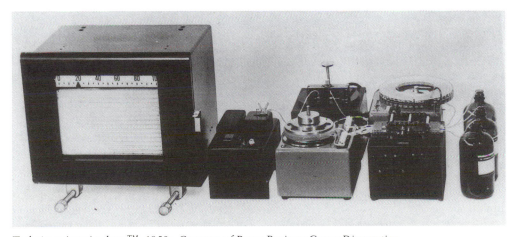

Technicon AutoAnalyzer™, 1950s. Courtesy of Bayer Business Group Diagnostics.

The reagent mixture then enters a large glass coil immersed in a water bath that keeps the reaction mixture at a constant temperature. The length of the coil determines the amount of time for the reaction to proceed to a known percentage of completion. The stream then enters a **photometer**, which measures the light at a wavelength where the amount of product formed or reagent consumed could be related to the concentration of the desired chemical species in the specimen. Later ion-specific electrodes were also used as reaction detectors for some species.

The analog electrical signal from the detector is amplified, if necessary, and displayed on a chart recorder. Because the specimens are aspirated sequentially into the same tube with only brief separation between them, the output on the recorder is a series of peaks and troughs, where the peak heights are related to the amount of unknown present. Excessive carryover between specimens can be detected as inadequate troughs between sample peaks.

The Technicon Corp. of Tarrytown, New York, was formed to manufacture and distribute the AutoAnalyzer™. The analyzer eliminated pipetting and timing errors, and thus provided more reproducible results than did manual methods. Mechanization also enhanced productivity and lowered costs.

The original AutoAnalyzer™ used relatively large amounts of specimen and reagents. It was susceptible to the presence of clots, and the tubing deteriorated. Each AutoAnalyzer™ required significant benchtop space, and numerous instruments were required to cover a laboratory's menu. Producing calibration curves was sometimes error-prone and time-consuming.

Subsequent models eliminated most of these operational problems by combining more and more tests together using the same sampler probe, and progressively reduced the size of all system components. The SMA (Sequential Multiple Analyzer) series and the SMAC (Sequential Multiple Analyzer with Computer) series moved the state of the art from one test per specimen per minute to more than twenty tests per specimen every twenty-four seconds. The SMAC did its own calibration and internal diagnostics and transmitted results directly to a laboratory computer.

Arthur A. Eggert

Bibliography

Eggert, Arthur A. *Electronics and Instrumentation for the Clinical Laboratory.* New York: Wiley, 1983.

Programmed Instruction for the Basic Auto-Analyzer™. Tarrytown, N.Y.: Technicon Instruments Corporation, 1969.

Skeggs, Leonard T. "An Automated Method of Colorimetric Analysis." *American Journal of Clinical Pathology* 28 (1957): 311–22.

———, and Harry Hochstrasser. "Multiple Automatic Sequential Analysis." *Clinical Chemistry* 10 (1964): 918–36.

Auxanometer

An auxanometer measures the rate of growth of a plant by amplifying the minuscule changes in the size of the plant. The modern meaning of the term and the extensive use of the apparatus began with Julius Sachs in Germany in the 1860s. Over time physiologists and their instrument-makers have devised ways to track ever smaller elongations in ever shorter time periods.

The Englishman Stephan Hales (*Vegetable Staticks,* 1727) described a method of measuring plant growth by making marks on young shoots and leaves, and measuring their displacement on the mature structure. In 1843 the German August Grisebach coined the term "auxanometer" for the small toothed wheel he used to mark plants for such observations. Later a horizontally mounted **microscope** was used to measure growth in length and thickness, and to confirm the accuracy of auxanometers; it was also used for classroom demonstrations. The German Wilhelm Pfeffer recommended this method when the organism was too small to tie to an auxanometer, or to keep the latter's tension from affecting growth. Beginning in the 1870s, calipers, **spherometers**, and *Fühlhebel* were employed to gauge growth in thickness. In the twentieth century, time lapse films have also been used.

In 1818, Pierre Picot suggested to Auguste-Pyramus de Candolle applying a device to a plant in such a way that the elongation of a branch would be magnified to make the slightest change observable by the naked eye. Sachs described three instruments of this sort. In 1868 he used a pointer on a thread that ran from the plant, over a pulley, to a weight. As the plant grew the weight moved downward and a needle attached to the weight moved along a ruler.

The pointer on an arc added the lever principle. A thread ran from the plant, over a pulley, to a weight. Shortly before the weight, the

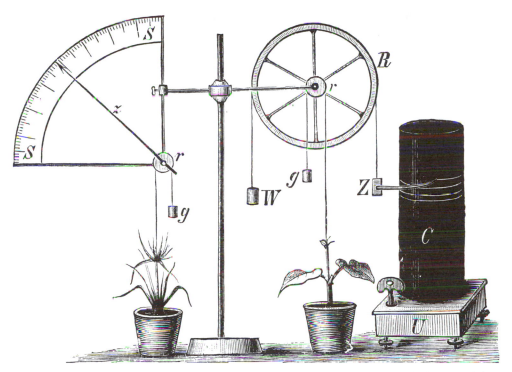

Lever-auxanometer and self-registering auxanometer. Eduard Strasburger et al. Lehrbuch der Botanik für Hochschulen. *Jena: G. Fischer, 1898: Figure 190. Courtesy of SSPL.*

thread was fixed to one point on the edge of a wheel. A long pointer was attached at one end to the wheel and the other end moved in front of a graduated arc. As the plant grew, the weight was able to pull the thread downward, turning the wheel and hence the pointer. The long pointer translated small extensions in the plant into easily perceptible revolutions along the arc. Sach's student Johannes Reinke (1876) borrowed measurement techniques from physics to improve the precision of this instrument. As in other branches of physiology, precision was a constant theme in accounts of new apparatuses. Botanists stressed their care in construction, elimination of sources of error, and the recording of ever smaller growth increments.

Sachs's self-registering auxanometer (1871) was inspired by the **kymograph**. A simplified pointer on an arc left a trail on a rotating cylinder of lamp-blacked paper. The trace was nearly a horizontal line; each time the cylinder went around, the plant had grown somewhat and thus the line was a little further down the paper. The distance between lines gave the amount of growth per cycle of the cylinder. Sachs's apparatus rotated once an hour for a total of 22 hours per sheet of paper; it was able

to measure growth rates on the order of 2 mm per hour. Later he multiplied the precision by placing a **spherometer** between the plant and the thread.

Jagadis Chandra Bose in India constructed an auxanograph (or crescograph) in 1919. In this instrument, the plant growth was first magnified by a lever whose movement was magnified by another lever, producing a ten-thousand-fold magnification. In the same year, the English physicist H.R. Arnulph Mallock used an **interferometer** to measure growth in thickness. Fritz Laibach, professor of botany at Frankfurt a. M., wanted to introduce interferometers into plant physiology, but Martin Möbius (1937) doubted whether "with these overrefined methods a noteworthy new result has been achieved." He considered the interferometer far too costly and its use far too complicated, requiring long study before the botanist could work with it.

Elaborating on a demonstration device of the American William T. Bovie, Victor Jacob Koningsberger of Utrecht devised a way to measure plant growth that could be used in total darkness or with a clinostat. The growing plant, by means of a very delicate contact arrangement, closed a weak electric current. This indirectly lifted the contact a fixed distance (the weak current passed through a relay that activated an electromagnet whose armature turned a rachet wheel attached to a micrometer screw, which in turn lifted the contact). The plant then had to grow this distance (on the order of 10μ) before it closed the circuit anew. Another part of the mechanism drew lines corresponding to how many seconds it took the plant to grow the fixed distance (in contrast to previous devices, which recorded how far the plant grew in a fixed time).

Anne Mylott

Bibliography

Koningsberger, Victor Jacob. "Tropismus und Wachstum." Doctoral dissertation. University of Utrecht, 1922.

Metner, Helmut. *Pflanzenphysiologische Versuche.* Stuttgart: Gustav Fischer Verlag, 1982.

Möbius, Martin A.J. *Geschichte der Botanik von den ersten Anfängen bis zur Gegenwart.* Jena: Fischer, 1937.

Pfeffer, Wilhelm. *Pflanzenphysiologie: Ein Handbuch der Lehre vom Stoffwechsel und Kraftwechsel in der Pflanze.* Vol. 2. Leipzig: Englemann, 1897–1904.

Sachs, Julius. "Ueber den Einfluss der Lufttemperatur und des Tageslichtes auf die stündlichen und täglichen Aenderungen des Längenwachsthums (Streckung) der Internodien." *Arbeiten des Botanischen Instituts Würzburg* 2 (1872): 100. Reprinted in Sachs, Julius. *Gesammelte Abhandlungen über Pflanzen-Physiologie.* Vol. 2, pp. 677–772. Leipzig: Engelmann, 1892.

B

Balance, Chemical

Representations of balances are known from Egyptian papyri, in which hearts of the dead are weighed against truth. The mode of suspension of the beam is not clear, but pans are hung from the beam ends and weights may be moved along the beam to attain their balance. An example of such an illustration is found on a British Museum copy of the *Book of the Dead* dating from ca. 1320–1290 B.C. Roman balance beams and steelyards survive in some numbers, and there can be no doubt that weighing was a common procedure in the ancient world (see **balance, general**).

The earliest balances developed for a chemical purpose are probably those used in assaying processes, for which small globules of gold need to be weighed. A manuscript of Thomas Norton's *Ordinall of Alchimy* of the late fifteenth century contains an illumination of a laboratory in which distillation processes are occurring. On a sturdy table stands a balance in what appears to be a glazed case.

The development of assay, pharmaceutical, and coin balances appears to have remained independent of improvements to increase the sensitivity of chemical balances: the former continued to be conservative in design. For example they retained the solid, rodlike beam and swan-neck ends long after the latter had abandoned them for more rigid beams and more precise suspension systems.

It could be argued that chemical balances developed from **hydrostatic balances** of the early eighteenth century. These were used to determine the specific gravity of liquids by determining the weight of a metal mass immersed in water and then in the liquid to be determined. These balances were described by John Harris in his *Lexicon Technicum* of 1710 and at least two examples survive, one in the Royal Museum of Scotland having been used by Andrew Plummer, the professor of chemistry at Edinburgh University, in his work on the spa water of Moffat in the south of Scotland.

The earliest surviving balance used for a published series of chemical experiments is said to be that used by Plummer's successor at Edinburgh, Joseph Black, who described work on the alkaline nature of magnesia alba (basic magnesium carbonate) in his doctoral thesis of 1754. This was an important experiment because it led to the discovery of fixed air (carbon dioxide), the first gas to be chemically identified. The balance is crudely made with a simple suspension of the beam on a knife edge. The beam has swan-neck ends from which the pans are hung directly by cords. Tests have shown that the balance is sensitive enough to have provided the results recorded by Black, even though Lyon Playfair referred to it in 1876 as "a grocer sort of balance . . . no better than a grocer's scales."

Though chemists demanded higher levels of sensitivity, balance makers tended to be conservative. Even though Antoine Laurent Lavoisier's balances were constructed to the highest level of craftsmanship by Nicolas Fortin and Pierre Bernard Megnie, they show few innovations. Significant improvements were to be introduced by work directed through the Royal Society and commissioned by the British government, which needed accurate measurements of the specific gravity of water-alcohol mixtures in order to exact taxes in a scientific manner. A brilliant instrument-maker, Jesse Ramsden, was given the task, and he realized that the inaccuracies of existing balances were caused by the flexing of beams when they were loaded. This

Short-beam analytical balance by Sartorius, 1876. SM 1876-380. Courtesy of SSPL.

he tackled by creating a much more rigid beam from two hollow brass cones joined at their bases. They carried a central steel knife that turned on an agate plane. Pan hangers used a suspension known as "slide and knives." These two features reduced the variation in the exact point of suspension present in earlier balances. Ramsden's balance provided the accuracy required, but the long, massive beam swung very slowly and each measurement took a very great time to take.

The problem of the need for lightness and rigidity in balance beams was successfully tack-led by a London manufacturer, Thomas Charles Robinson, who has been described as the first manufacturer of precision balances. Around 1820 he supplied the chemist William Hyde Wollaston with a short beam balance, the beam being of a perforated triangular design. Adjustments could be made to each end of the beam and there was a short vertical pointer that moved over a scale to determine the null point. This beam design was soon widely adopted, and analytical chemists could order similar instruments from precision makers: Andrew Ure from F.W. Breithaupt in Kassel, Germany, and J.F.

Jacob Berzelius from C.E. Littman of Stockholm, for example. The Berlin maker Ludwig Oertling settled in London in the early 1850s and for the rest of the century—and beyond—his firm was the leading manufacturer in Britain. In Germany, Paul Bunge of Hamburg built short-beam analytical balances from 1866 that had highly engineered knives and planes. Florenz Sartorius, who founded his firm in Göttingen in 1870, was the first to use aluminum in beam construction.

Many refinements were introduced at a time when the chemical community was rapidly expanding, thus offering a flourishing market to manufacturers. For instance, the rider system, a small wire weight that could be suspended from a beam with graduations, offered additional accuracy, and was introduced in 1851. Semiautomatic systems for adding or subtracting weights without the need to open the balance case were introduced from about 1880, notably by A. Rueprecht of Vienna. Christian A. Becker patented a fine chain to add weights to the beam in 1915 and termed it the *Chainomatic*.

A major advance in balance construction was the introduction of so-called substitution weighing. One side of the beam is constantly loaded. The object to be weighed is placed in a single pan, and the weights, which begin by being fully loaded on the pan, are removed one by one until equilibrium is reached. The balance always carries a constant load, no matter what the mass of the object is. Balances using this principle were popularized by the Swiss firm of E. Mettler, the production models dating from 1947. Weighing was much speedier than before because knob-operated dials controlled a system of cams that enabled various combinations of weights to be raised and lowered. The total weight removed left a discrepancy within one gram of the weight of the object. The remaining weight needed to restore the exact balance point was estimated on a scale projected onto a screen by an optical system. Such balances were generically named "single pan balances."

For weighing very small masses, various microbalances have been developed. These often used beams made of quartz rods. A quartz fiber runs through the central position. When displacement occurs, the fiber is twisted to restore equilibrium and this provides a measure of the mass. The beam can, alternatively, be restored electromagnetically, the current change

being measured. The principle on which such electro balances were based was first described in 1956.

Chemical balances have, by and large, become simpler and quicker to operate over the years. Less skill and less understanding of the technique are required, while considerable gains in accuracy have been made.

Robert G.W. Anderson

Bibliography

Child, Ernest. *The Tools of the Chemist.* New York: Reinhold, 1940.

Jenemann, Hans R. *Die Waage des Chemikers.* Frankfurt am Main: Dechema, 1979.

————. "Zur Geschichte der Waage in der Wissenschaft." In *Beitrage zur Geschichte der Laboratoriumstechnik und deren Randgebiete,* edited by E.H.W. Giebeler and K.A. Rosenbauer, 97–119. Darmstadt: G-I-T Verlag Ernst Giebeler, 1982.

Stock, John T. *Development of the Chemical Balance.* London: Her Majesty's Stationery Office, 1969.

Balance, General

Until analytical investigations started around 1750, scientists needed balances to make up chemical mixtures reasonably consistently (see **balance, chemical**), but, as their ingredients were not consistently pure or reliable, there was little point in having precise quantities of each ingredient. Any competent scale-maker could supply an equal-arm balance that would indicate with a sensitivity of one in one thousand, or 1 grain with a load of 500 grains in each pan. The coin-scales made between 1632 and 1750 will turn with that load (although greatly more than they were designed to take) and still indicate 1 or 1.5 grains, in spite of extensive use and considerable deterioration. Equal-arm balances with box-end beams up to 10 in. in length would weigh up to 2 lb. avoirdupois, or 14,000 grains.

Joseph Black, the first British scientist to regularly define quantities by weight, initially used ratios to express his investigations, such as "3 or 4 times its quantity." By 1756 he was using apothecaries' weights regularly: "27 grains of magnesia" or "weighed, as nearly as I could guess, one third of a grain." The implication is that although Black could state that "a sediment amounted to half a grain" he could

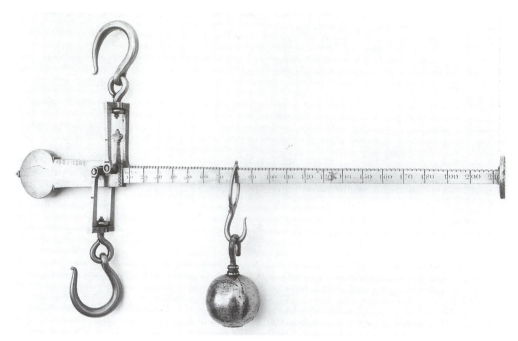

A classic British turn-over steelyard with a maximum capacity of 200 Troy ounces, eighteenth century. SM 1927-1205. Courtesy of SSPL.

not weigh a third of a grain accurately on his Scottish-made swan-neck-end scales, with their sensitivity of about one in fourteen thousand.

The weighing process was simplified when makers suspended the beam from a pillar and used a cord-lift to raise the beam and pans. The box-ends protected the knives from dust, and wear was minimized by having the scales checked annually and the knives replaced when necessary. The fear that the beams would bend (as shown by the construction of cone-beams) was reduced by not placing too great a load in the pans and by using beams of oval cross-section. The knowledge that metals expand when heated was of no significance in relation to beams until experiments using balances became much more precise after 1834 and the manufacture of the new Imperial Standards.

Steelyards were used for experiments on air pressure, magnetic attraction, or leverage, commonly indicating pressure or force to the nearest 1 oz. troy. The steelyards made by instrument-makers between about 1690 and 1780 were often made of brass with a circular cross-section. Scale-makers, at that time, made their steelyards from wrought iron of rectangular and diamond-shaped cross-section, with a sensitivity of about one in twelve hundred and commonly marking them in 4-oz. avoirdupois

units. The Romans used knife-edges in their steelyards by about A.D. 300 (as exemplified by steelyards found in Triers), but they were not perfectly in equilibrium, because the knives' centers were in a straight line on turnover steelyards, producing a "fast" (unstable) steelyard when one way up to weigh smaller loads, and even faster when used the other way up to weigh greater loads. This problem was not resolved in Britain until some time after 1758, when the knives were arranged to produce a straight line at the tip of the knives being used, whichever way the steelyard was used.

People began using compact spring-balances about 1750. The early spring balances with helical springs could weigh up to 60 lb. with a sensitivity of one in one hundred twenty, at a tenth of the cost of a steelyard of that capacity. Pendulum balances, first patented in Britain in 1772, were also compact, provided instant "read-out," and were sensitive to 1 grain with a load of 300 grains; but the knife-edge fulcrum had to operate over a range of angles, 30° from the vertical on each side of the knife. The wear would have been considerable on both the fulcrum and on the pivot of the load pan. Lambert's pendulum scales, documented in 1758, were particularly used for determining the salt content of liquids.

Around 1750, scale-makers began producing larger equal-arm beams with box-ends. Samuel Read made 36-in. beams that will indicate 50 grains when loaded with 14 lb. in each pan, even today when in a dilapidated condition; these had, at the least, a sensitivity of one in five thousand.

In the early nineteenth century, as chemicals became purer and scientists more exacting, instrument-makers tried to make balances more accurate. They added agate bearings to reduce the wear of steel knives and arrestment mechanisms to relieve the fulcrum, and later to relieve all three pivots; increasingly, scientists would pay for a glass case to protect against drafts and corrosive fumes. (Glass cases were quite common in laboratories by 1750, but the makers did not supply them automatically, and it was only well after 1850 that customers realized their efficacy.) Beams were made so that the arm length could be finely adjusted. Materials that would not deteriorate were introduced: platinum, glass, mother-of-pearl, paktong, nickel-plating. Mechanisms for placing minute weights without opening the glass case were investigated. Specialized attachments were supplied for specific experiments.

By 1850, because of the work of T.C. Robinson during the 1820s and 1830s (advertising that he worked to a sensitivity of one in one hundred thousand) and of L. Oertling, good-quality balances were within the means of students. And, although assay balances, inspector's beams, and bullion balances of good sensitivity have continued to be made by scale-makers until the present day, scientists began looking to precision instrument-makers rather than to scale-makers for most of their needs.

Instrument-makers also made scales for trade, for the military, and for weighing coins. Makers may have supplied every size from 3 in. to 6 ft. long, but, because of the lack of surviving examples, it cannot be ascertained whether they made all sizes themselves or purchased scales from specialist scale-makers. Scale-makers were working in all major British towns by the early 1700s; many in London had prosperous establishments.

Diana F. Crawforth-Hitchins

Bibliography

Equilibrium. Journal of the International Society of Antique Scale Collectors.

Morton, Alan Q., and Jane A. Wess. *Public and Private Science: The King George III Collection.* Oxford: Oxford University Press in association with the Science Museum, 1993.

Balance, Hydrostatic

Hydrostatic balances demonstrate the principle of Archimedes that a body immersed in a liquid is buoyed up by a force equal to the weight of the liquid displaced. They are also used to weigh objects in air and then in water, and thus determine their specific gravity. Archimedes, who knew that gold is substantially heavier than other common metals, is said to have used the hydrostatic principle to determine if the King's crown was actually made of gold.

As Europe became an increasingly industrialized economy in the seventeenth and eighteenth centuries, the public was urged to check the standard of all coins, and many handheld coin scales were produced. Designs in which a pillar was fixed to the scale box gave the best results. In these scales one pan had short strings enabling a pair of pincers to be hung beneath it to hold the coin first in air and then in water. The principles of hydrostatic weighing could be learned from lectures and illustrated manuals, and demonstration apparatus as were made by leading instrument manufacturers.

Interest in the composition of all substances, including gases, increased in the latter part of the eighteenth century. **Balances** suitable for hydrostatic weighing with greatly increased sensitivity, made by manufacturers such as Jesse Ramsden, were supplied to learned societies and their patrons. These improved standards were also used by governments demanding more accurate weights and measures and a more reliable taxation system for alcoholic liquids. The balances were substantially built, with beams of 24 in. or more in length. The central knife rested on a "crystal" plane with the pointer at the end of the beam and provision for weighing large globes of gases suspended under the case.

In the early 1820s, Thomas Charles Robinson produced hydrostatic balances that were precise and inexpensive. With a delicate, openwork 5 in. beam and three pans it was accurate to one-hundredth of a grain (0.0006 g). The provision of a third pan on short strings made the balance dual-purpose. The strings were soon replaced by fine platinum chains that were in turn replaced by pans with fixed bows and a

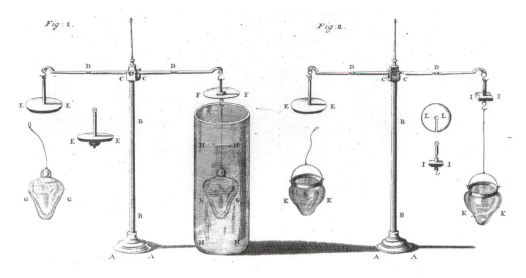

Hauksbee's hydrostatic balance. John Harris. (1710). Courtesy of SSPL.

hook under the top of the bow. A more specialized design had one-half of the beam evenly divided to take large calibrated riders shaped like horseshoes and a thermometer in a plummet of known mass to allow for corrections to be made for the temperature of the water.

Work on the periodic table in the latter part of the nineteenth century demanded ever more accurate figures for atomic masses of elements and the vapor densities of gases. Lord Rayleigh (John William Strutt), an English physicist, determined the density of pure nitrogen by suspending flasks of gas under the case of a long beam balance. The steady increase in the quality of balance construction during the nineteenth century provided greater accuracy and sensitivity, and a technique used to improve quality control became a diagnostic tool.

P.D. Buchanan

Bibliography

Brande, W.T. "Description of the Balance Represented in Plate V fig 1." *Quarterly Journal of Science Literature and the Arts* 11 (1821): 280–81; 12 (1822): 40–41.

Brauer, E.A. *The Construction of the Balance According to Underlying Scientific Principles and According to Its Special Purpose.* Translated by H.C. Walters. 3rd rev. ed. Edinburgh: Incorporated Society of Inspectors of Weights and Measures, 1909.

Griffin, J.J. *Chemical Handicraft.* London: J.J. Griffen, 1866.

Harris, John. "Hydrostaticall Balance." In *Lexicon Technicum; or, An Universal Dictionary of Arts and Science,* Vol. 2, *Art.* London, 1710.

Shuckburgh, George Evelyn. "An Account of Some Endeavours to Ascertain a Standard of Weight and Measure." *Philosophical Transactions of the Royal Society* 38 (1798): 133–82.

Barograph

A barograph automatically records the variations of atmospheric pressure, and thus obviates the tedious routine of periodically reading and transcribing **barometers**' indications. Furthermore, the barographic chart (diagram) provides a clear and immediate graphical presentation of pressure over time. Different designs have been proposed since the end of the seventeenth century, but it was only during the nineteenth century that these instruments became necessary for the needs of modern meteorology. Several of them were incorporated into complex **meteorographs**.

The first barograph was probably a modification of Robert Hooke's wheel barometer, and was developed by Hooke himself while he was improving Christopher Wren's meteorograph. In this instrument, a float in a siphon barometer was mechanically connected to a pen that inscribed the variation of pressure on a lined chart. This chart was fixed on a disk, a drum, or a table, which was moved by clockwork. Other instru-

Richard type aneroid barograph, English, early twentieth century. Courtesy of the Fondazione Scienza e Tecnica, Florence.

ments of this sort were developed in the eighteenth century. The clockmaker Alexander Cumming made a splendid siphon barograph for George III in 1765; Antoine Assier-Perricat and Pierre Changeux devised similar instruments in France; and in Florence, Felice Fontana made a barograph in which the floater activated a strip of recording paper instead of the writing pen. Recording siphon barometers were quite popular until the 1850s, followed by about half a century during which other kinds of barographs were preferred. At the beginning of the twentieth century, a few improved and effective siphon barographs were again proposed.

The balance barometer was conceived by Samuel Morland in the late seventeenth century but, apart from a 1726 description by Jacob Leupold, it was not used in a barograph until its reinvention by Angelo Secchi in 1857. The tube in these instruments was suspended by a balance beam, and the changing height and weight of the mercury column produced a movement of the beam that was connected to a writing system. In a few models, such as the one by André Crova, the tube was fixed and the cistern was suspended.

Among the many other balance barographs invented in the nineteenth century, some of the most interesting were those proposed by Heinrich Wild, Rudolf Fuess, Alfred King, Filippo Cecchi, and Paul Schreiber. Their conditions of stability depended on their construction (equal or unequal arms of the beam). Although they were often quite precise, they were also heavy, complicated, and expensive. Adolph Sprung introduced a rolling weight barograph in the late 1870s. In this type of instrument, a rider with a writing pen traveled along a steelyard beam (supporting the tube) so that it always oscillated slightly around the equilibrium position. During the same period, Daniel Draper invented a successful barograph, whose tube was fixed and whose cistern, which was bearing a pen, was supported by a couple of springs.

Some barographs produced a point-wise recording of the pressure, which avoided the constant friction of the pen on paper. The barographs of George W. Hough and of Friedrich C. Müller eliminated friction through complicated electrical servomechanisms. After 1850 most barographs used different techniques for automatically correcting the pressure readings to the atmospheric temperature. Other barographs with less common solutions were proposed. Some included a floating tube or a rotating tube of a particular shape, and Fuess even described an unusual magnetic barograph.

Photographic techniques were applied to barographs surprisingly quickly. Since 1839 it had been proposed to use a beam of light to illuminate the mercury column, whose shadow would then be recorded on a movable band of photographic paper. The culmination of this design was the Kew Barograph, which never gained popularity outside the British observatories.

The introduction of efficient aneroid barometers composed of one or more metallic vacuum chambers made it possible to develop a new class of cheap, portable, and simple barographs. Although the Breguet firm had presented the first aneroid barograph in 1867, this instrument achieved popularity around 1880 through the design and technical improvements introduced by the French maker Jules Richard and his brother (trading as Richard Frères). In this design, an aneroid chamber is mechanically connected to a light aluminum arm bearing a pen. This pen traces the pressure variations onto a clockwork-driven drum covered by a chart with curved hour lines. At the end of the century, barographs (and other meteorological recording instruments) of the Richard type were sold by many European and American instrument-makers, and they are still in use today with only minor modifications. These instruments, often enclosed in an elegant glass cabinet, also became popular as home scientific furniture. Light aneroid barographs were often part of sounding-balloons and kite meteorographs. Microbarographs, statoscopes, and variographs were particular types of modified aneroid instruments that were used mainly to record minor and fast variations of pressure.

Paolo Brenni

Bibliography

Middleton, W.E. Knowles. *Catalog of Meteorological Instruments in the Museum of History and Technology.* Smithsonian Studies in History and Technology 2. Washington, D.C.: Smithsonian Institution Press, 1969.
————. *The History of the Barometer.* Baltimore: Johns Hopkins University Press, 1964.
Multhauf, Robert P. "The Introduction of Self-Registering Meteorological Instruments." *Contributions from the Museum of History and Technology.* United States National Museum Bulletin 228, paper 23. Washington, D.C.: Smithsonian Institution Press, 1961.
Richard Frères. *Notice sur les instruments enregistreurs construits par Richard Frères, comprenant le rapport de M. le Colonel Sebert à la Société d'encouragement pour l'industrie nationale et l'exposé des perfectionnemente et applications nouvelles.* Paris, 1889.

Barometer

A barometer (Greek *baros,* "weight" + *metron,* "measure") measures atmospheric pressure (which was confused with the atmosphere's weight when the word was coined). Most commonly it is a glass tube, some 860 mm long and closed at one end. Filled with mercury, it is inverted so that it stands vertically with its open end immersed in a reservoir of the same liquid. The pressure of the atmosphere balances a column of mercury in the tube, above which a near vacuum subsists, and whose height provides a measure of that pressure. The aneroid barometer (Greek *a,* "without" + *neros,* "wet, damp") substitutes for the fluid column an evacuated box, upon whose elastic lid the atmosphere presses.

The barometer's prehistory lies in the practical hydrostatics of the early seventeenth century. Welldiggers and mining engineers found that their pumps and siphons would not raise water more than about 30 ft., and this led natural philosophers to reflect on the pumps' operation. Galileo Galilei supposed that the "force of the vacuum" inside the pump could hold up a column of water just so high, while Isaac Beeckman, Giovanni Baliani, and others held that the weight of the external air balanced the internal column. The discussion continued until, around 1641, Gasparo Berti attached a lead tube some "forty palms" long to the wall of his house in Rome, its top closed by a glass flask and its bottom standing in a cask of water. When filled by means of a set of stopcocks, the tube held a column of water suspended about 18 cubits above the level of the water in the cask.

Vincenzio Viviani and perhaps Galileo himself had imagined that different liquids would stand at varying heights in these experiments, and it was Viviani who in 1644, at the suggestion of Evangelista Torricelli, carried out the famous experiment with mercury in a glass tube. The external air, Torricelli argued, balanced the mercury column, whose height was proportionally smaller than that of Berti's water column by the ratio of the specific weights of mercury to water.

This experiment, the issue of researches by a number of natural philosophers, was not yet a barometer. Although at one point Torricelli described his experiment as "an instrument which might show the changes of the air," the debate over the vacuum and the hydrostatic balancing of air and mercury dominated his and his successors' discussion for two decades. The device, variously called "Torricellian tube" or simply "tube," "quicksilver experiment," "Torricellian experiment," or "experiment with a vacuum," remained a demonstration experiment, not a measuring instrument. Pascal, when he had provided the tube with a paper scale so that the mercury traveled "up or down according as the weather is more or less overcast," called it the 'continuous experiment,' because one may observe, if he wishes, continuously." His remarks represent a stage in the gradual transition from demonstration experiment to measuring instrument, which Robert Boyle finally named the "barometer" in 1663.

The decade or so following 1660 was one of extraordinary fertility of invention, especially in England, and produced numerous variations on the barometer, many from Robert Hooke's hands. These included the siphon barometer, in which the mercury reservoir is eliminated by curving the barometer tube upwards at the bottom; Hooke's wheel barometer, which magnifies the instrument's motions by passing a string from a float atop the mercury in the short end of the siphon over a pulley, the axle of which carries a long pointer; double and triple barometers, in which columns of different liquids above the mercury column magnify the mercury's motions; and the diagonal barometer, where the last few inches of the tube are inclined, with the same effect. Hooke executed his designs in the context of concurrent microscopical investigations and a continuing preoccupation with hydrostatics; his language makes clear that he intended his barometers as atmospheric microscopes, so to speak, that would magnify tiny and otherwise imperceptible variations of the air.

This fecundity of invention did nothing for the barometer's accuracy; Hooke and his contemporaries never expressed a concern for precision. The barometer's gross inaccuracy, however, frustrated cartographers and surveyors, who found the instrument convenient for measuring heights, knowledge of which required

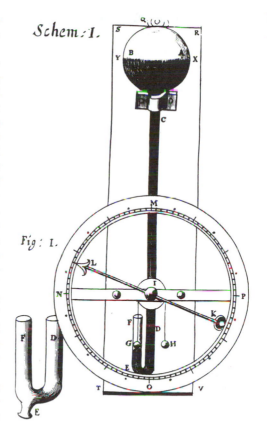

Hooke's wheel barometer, 1665. Robert Hooke. Micrographia. *London, 1665: Plate 1, Figure 1. Courtesy of SSPL.*

reduction of survey measurements to sea-level values. The proliferation of military and national surveys after the Seven Years' War, along with the fashion for Alpine mountaineering, sharpened demand for accurate barometers. Jean-André Deluc, a Genevan mountaineer and natural philosopher, designed a portable one around 1770, accurate to 0.01 in. Deluc's innovations included boiling the mercury to remove dissolved air, methods for leveling the barometer and for reading the mercury meniscus, and corrections for temperature-expansion of mercury, glass, and the ambient air. Deluc also introduced methods of systematic, repeated observation and correction for observational error that contemporaries regarded as revolutionary.

Deluc's methods spread rapidly, especially in England, where Jesse Ramsden constructed barometers accurate to 0.001 in. Ramsden and other British craftsmen, highly capitalized and using proto-industrial methods of manufacture, held a considerable lead over the French, whose craft-based organization of instrument manufacture remained nearly medieval. But the French government's attentive cultivation of the scientific instrument trade, the dissolution of the guilds during the Revolution, and explosion of demand for instruments for military purposes and for metrification, helped a few French instrument-makers to modernize toward the end of the Old Regime and in the Revolutionary and Napoleonic period. One result was Nicholas Fortin's barometer. Fortin closed his cistern at the bottom with a leather bag, which a screw could press upwards, until the mercury in the cistern touched the tip of an ivory pointer that was the zero of the instrument's scale. A glass window offered a view of the operation. The barometer, read to 0.002 in. or 0.1 mm, became standard in the nineteenth century.

The barometers of Deluc, Ramsden, Fortin, and their contemporaries were essentially modern instruments. Further developments in the nineteenth century included marine barometers, high-precision "primary" barometers, and the aneroid barometer. Hooke had invented a marine barometer whose constricted tube prevented the shipboard tossing of the mercury and consequent shattering of the glass tube. This device was forgotten and subsequently reinvented by Edward Nairne around 1770. British imperial expansion and the efforts of the Kew Committee of the British Association for the Advancement of Science fostered the development of the marine barometer to its modern form between about 1845 and 1860, and the so-called Kew barometer became standard on ships. Around the same time, Admiral Fitzroy developed a "gun" barometer, whose tube was packed in vulcanized rubber to protect it from the vibrations of naval gunfire.

The multiplication after the mid nineteenth century of nationally supported networks of weather observers generated demand for highly sophisticated precision "primary" barometers, against which observers' instruments could be calibrated. These barometers used elaborate methods of cleaning and filling the tube; obtaining the vacuum above the mercury (the Sprengel pump was first used in the 1880s); and reading the mercury level, using optical aids including **microscopes, telescopes, micrometers, cathetometers,** and image projection. Primary barometers were also employed in precision measurement in physics and physical chemistry.

Gottfried Wilhelm Leibniz had suggested the idea for what, when it was eventually constructed, would be called the aneroid barometer.

He proposed in 1698 "a little closed bellows that would be compressed and dilate by itself, as the weight of the air increases or diminishes." The pressure of the air would be counterbalanced by a steel spring within. The first successful aneroid barometer, designed in 1844 by Lucien Vidie, was a brass box with a corrugated diaphragm supported by some thirty-three helical springs. The aneroid became popular with mountaineers and travelers, and as a "weather-glass" and marine barometer. In the twentieth century, metallurgical advances and the requirements of aviation produced aneroids reliable and accurate enough to replace mercury barometers at many meteorological stations.

Theodore S. Feldman

Bibliography

Bennett, J.A. *Le Citoyen Lenoir: Scientific Instrument Making in Revolutionary France.* Cambridge: Whipple Museum of the History of Science, 1989.

Feldman, Theodore. "Late Enlightenment Meteorology." In *The Quantifying Spirit in the 18th Century,* edited by Tore Frängsmyr, J.L. Heilbron, and Robin E. Rider, 143–78. Berkeley: University of California Press, 1990.

Middleton, W.E. Knowles. *The History of the Barometer.* Baltimore: Johns Hopkins University Press, 1964.

Turner, Anthony J. *From Pleasure and Profit to Science and Security: Etienne Lenoir and the Transformation of Precision Instrument-Making in France, 1760–1830.* Cambridge: Whipple Museum of the History of Science, 1989.

Turner, Gerard L'E. *Nineteenth-Century Scientific Instruments.* Berkeley: University of California Press/London: Philip Wilson, 1983.

Bathythermograph

A bathythermograph (commonly called a BT) simultaneously measures ocean temperature and pressure, and plots them with a stylus on inexpensive smoked glass slides that can be easily removed from the instrument and read against a calibration chart. The instrument is lowered from the back of a stationary or moving vessel, and measurements are continuously taken upon the BT's ascent. Its development in the late 1930s allowed for the first time a synoptic view of the world's oceans.

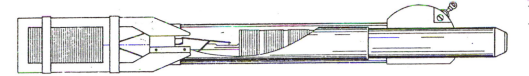

B

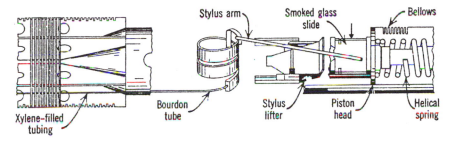

Temperature element   Pressure element

Stylus arm — Smoked glass slide — Bellows

Xylene-filled tubing   Bourdon tube   Stylus lifter   Piston head   Helical spring

Schematic diagram showing the overall form (top) and components (bottom) of a bathythermograph. Weyl (1970): 171, Figure 11.13. Copyright © 1970 John Wiley & Sons Inc. Reprinted by permission.

Before the invention of the bathythermograph, oceanographers could measure subsurface temperatures only at discrete points, by lowering Nansen bottles equipped with reversing thermometers into the ocean from a stationary surface vessel, and recovering them once the measurements had been taken (see **water sample bottle**). While the individual measurements were quite precise, the observation points were far apart vertically and even more so horizontally. This proved to be a particularly acute problem for the Massachusetts Institute of Technology meteorologist Carl-Gustav Rossby, who was attempting to extend his work on atmospheric vorticity into oceanography, particularly by studying the eddies of the Gulf Stream. By the time a string of Nansen bottles had been lowered and recovered, the eddies had moved on, and it was impossible to gain a complete picture of their structure. In the summer of 1934, Rossby designed and built an oceanograph to rapidly and continuously measure ocean temperature to a depth of several hundred feet. When this proved to be unwieldy, Rossby gave the task of redesigning the instrument to Athelstan Frederick Spilhaus, a young South African meteorology student with a background in mechanical and aeronautical engineering.

After a brief return to South Africa, Spilhaus returned to work with Rossby in 1936. By the summer of 1937 he had designed and tested his first bathythermograph. The pressure element, which proved so satisfactory that it remained nearly unchanged from the initial design, consisted of a hermetically sealed sylphon (a concertina-like metal bellows) containing a guide and compression spring to give the requisite pressure range. Attached to the outside was a bimetal strip with a fine stylus, which inscribed a trace on a small, oil-coated, smoked glass slide that was rigidly mounted inside the rectangular housing. Since the motion of the bellows would be at right angles to the expansion of the bimetal from temperature change, the needle would trace on the slide a curve measuring temperature versus pressure, the latter of which would reveal the depth of the reading. The accuracy of the reading could be measured for a stationary vessel by comparing the path of the needle on the descent against the path drawn on ascent—the two should be nearly coincidental.

Early tests aboard the Woods Hole Oceanographic Institute's research vessel *Atlantis* showed that measurements were generally accurate to a depth of 150 meters. However, the temperature element was overly sensitive to the vibrations created by exposure to moving sea water. Spilhaus solved this problem by substituting a bourdon tube thermometer for the bimetal model. In this newer model, the **thermometer** bulb could be exposed to the rushing sea water, while the spiral containing the mercury or other expansible liquid could be shielded within the instrument housing. The thermometer was now physically unconnected to the pressure element, so the slide holder was attached to the bellows of the pressure element, with the stylus being attached to the end of the bourdon spiral. For mobile vessels, a Nansen bottle clamp with tripping mechanism was attached so that the stylus could be removed from the slide at the point of furthest descent. So completely was vibration eliminated by the bourdon type bathythermograph that it could be used by a vessel moving at speeds up to 11 knots. Spilhaus received a patent for the BT in 1937 and subsequently turned it over to the Submarine Signal Company of Boston, which produced the early models for scientific research.

After the outbreak of hostilities in Europe, Spilhaus and Woods Hole director Columbus O'Donnell Iselin became concerned about the number of ships sunk by German submarines. They speculated that it was because the Germans had learned to hide in the thermocline, the region of rapid temperature changes that separates the surface waters from the deep ocean, where the sound waves produced by **sonar** are greatly diffracted, effectively creating a shadow zone. The BT could be used, they believed, to map the thermocline, allowing adjustments to sonar readings that would help locate enemy submarines. Spilhaus brought this to the attention of the British naval attaché in Washington, and in short time the British requested two hundred BTs. These were produced at Woods Hole, where Iselin had already begun an American naval oceanographic research program. It was here that William Maurice Ewing of Lehigh University and his graduate student Allyn Vine began to make improvements in the BT, streamlining its design and increasing its response to temperature change so that it could be lowered and raised from a fast-moving warship. After the United States entered the war, all American destroyers were equipped with BTs. Soon the Woods Hole scientists were at work designing and producing a modified BT for use in Allied submarines operating in the Pacific theater. By the end of hostilities, some sixty thousand slides had been collected from the North Atlantic alone.

After the war, bathythermographs came into wide scientific use and were produced in many countries, notably the United States, Great Britain, Japan, and Argentina. The modern BT is remarkably little changed from the general design of Spilhaus's patent. Xylene is now used instead of mercury or other liquids in the

bourdon tube thermometer, in order to produce a faster response to temperature changes. Several models of BT were constructed for use at varying ocean depths. It is primarily used, however, only for readings down to about 300 meters, or more usually down to the bottom of the thermocline. The usefulness at great depths is hindered by the great lengths of wire necessary when used from a rapidly moving vessel. For measuring depths down to about 460 meters, electronic expendable bathythermographs (XBTs) were developed in the 1960s. The bomb-shaped XBT uses a thermistor (heat-sensitive bead) attached to a coil of thin copper wire that is attached to an electronic monitoring device on the vessel (or even on an aircraft). The depth is calculated from the constant fall velocity and the length of time following release.

George R. Ehrhardt

Bibliography

Baxter, James Phinney, III. *Scientists against Time.* Boston: Little, Brown, 1952.

Revelle, Roger. "The Oceanographic and How It Grew." In *Oceanography: The Past,* edited by M. Sears and D. Merriman, 10–24. New York: Springer-Verlag, 1980.

Schlee, Susan. *The Edge of an Unfamiliar World: A History of Oceanography.* New York: E.P. Dutton, 1973.

Spilhaus, Athelstan. "A Bathythermograph." *Journal of Marine Research* 1 (1937–1938): 95–100.

———. "A Detailed Study of the Surface Layers of the Ocean in the Neighborhood of the Gulf Stream with the Aid of Rapid Measuring Hydrographic Instruments." *Journal of Marine Research* 3 (1940): 51–75.

Weyl, Peter K. *Oceanography: An Introduction to the Marine Environment.* New York: Wiley, 1970.

Battery

A battery is an assembly of cells in which electricity is produced by electrochemical action. A primary battery functions as soon as assembled; a secondary (or storage) battery requires electrical charging before use. By 1990, the value of the world battery market probably exceeded twenty-three billion dollars.

The first battery was the "pile" described by Alessandro Volta in 1800. This was a stack

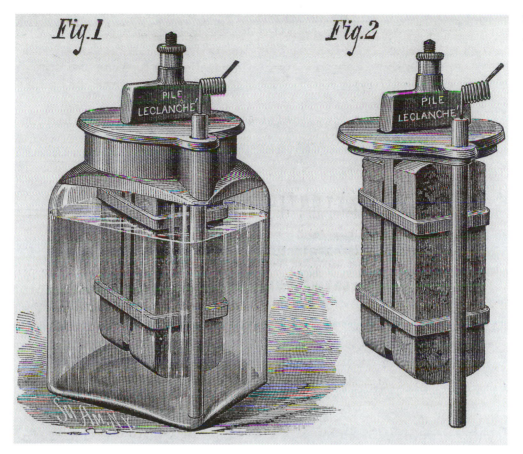

Leclanché cell, immersed in (left) and removed from the ammonium chloride solution. "The New Leclanché Battery." Scientific American 42, no. 13 (1880): 198. Courtesy of NMAH.

of alternating zinc and copper or silver discs separated by pieces of brine-wetted cloth. Subsequent versions consisted of cells containing dilute sulphuric acid as the electrolyte, a copper plate positive electrode, and an amalgamated (mercury-coated) zinc electrode.

The output of these cells decayed rapidly. Early workers attributed this defect to hydrogen evolution at the copper electrode, which partially isolated it from the electrolyte, and they realized that hydrogen is not evolved if the electrolyte is a powerful oxidizing agent such as concentrated nitric acid. Since, however, nitric acid destroys both zinc and copper, William Robert Grove (1839) replaced the copper with platinum, which is not attacked by nitric acid. In Grove's divided-cell battery, a porous septum separates the nitric acid from the dilute sulphuric acid in which the zinc electrode was immersed. In 1840, John Thomas Cooper showed that carbon could replace the expensive platinum as the positive electrode.

Around this time, Robert Wilhelm Bunsen constructed high-current versions of the carbon-zinc battery especially to power electric arc lights, which required a heavy current. Because of the concentrated nitric acid, the cells had to be partially taken apart before the battery could be stored.

Robert Warington had shown in 1842 that a potassium dichromate-sulphuric acid solution could replace nitric acid in a Grove-type cell. Bunsen examined this idea and developed a battery of single-solution cells that could be stored, then restored to use immediately. An overhead winch lifted all electrodes clear of the cells when storage was necessary.

Several attempts were made to develop batteries that did not deteriorate when left fully assembled. One of the most successful used the cell developed by Georges Leclanché in 1868. Here, a porous pot contains the carbon electrode, packed in a mix of manganese dioxide and powdered carbon. The pot and the zinc negative electrode are immersed in ammonium chloride solution. The modern "dry battery" is a modification of Leclanché's "wet" version. A carbon rod is surrounded by a manganese dioxide mix. A thin paper or gel separator lies between the mix and the zinc chloride/ammonium chloride paste on the inside of the zinc cylinder. Although more expensive, the "alkaline battery," the paste of which contains potassium hydroxide with added zinc oxide, is often chosen for heavy-duty applications.

Long life, very small size, and steady output are required from batteries in electric watches, hearing aids, and the like. Typical is the 1.35-volt zinc-potassium hydroxide-mercuric oxide cells. With silver oxide in place of mercuric oxide, a voltage of 1.6 can be obtained. These voltages can be approximately doubled by replacing zinc by lithium, which, however, reacts with water. An example, successfully used in cardiac pacemakers, is the lithium-iodine cell, the contents of which are entirely solid.

Storage Batteries

Indications that electricity might be stored in a cell system were noted in the early 1800s. The first practical storage battery was invented by Gaston Planté in 1860. The plates in each cell were rolled-up sheets of lead, separated by cloth and immersed in sulphuric acid. Storage capacity was improved by "formation," the electrochemical activation of the lead surfaces. Two major improvements appeared in 1881. By coating the plates with lead dioxide paste, formation was made easier and storage capacity was improved. Poor adherence of the paste led to the introduction of gridlike plates, so that pasting materials could be forced into and retained in the openings. At that time, the electricity needed for charging could be provided by a dynamo, so the general use of storage batteries was favored. By 1900, portable batteries were common; since then, construction and performance have steadily improved. Modern automobile batteries are compact and often completely sealed. Battery manufacture is presently estimated to consume about 40 percent of world lead production.

Nickel-iron and nickel-cadmium storage batteries appeared in 1901. Their popularity declined around 1930, but recovered with the rise of portable electrical appliances.

Battery-driven cars began to appear in the 1890s but, having to rely on lead batteries, were limited in range and performance. Since the 1980s there has been renewed interest in the development of high-performance, low-weight batteries. The sodium-sulfur battery appears to be the most promising, but it must be heated to 300° to 400°C before it can operate.

Fuel Cells

Grove noted in 1839 that hydrogen can be oxidized in a fuel cell to produce electricity rather than heat. Fuel cells became important in the mid 1950s, when Francis Thomas Bacon developed a practical hydrogen-oxygen battery. Fuel cells found use in space-vehicle programs. Much research is now focused on the development of fuel cells, and multimegawatt stationary versions have been demonstrated. Fuels such as methanol and diesel oil have been used, usually by decomposition to yield hydrogen. Air is commonly used instead of oxygen.

John T. Stock

Bibliography

Pickett, A.P. "Fuel Cells." In *Encyclopedia of Physical Science and Technology,* edited by R.A. Meyers, 731–44. London: Academic, 1992.

Stock, J.T. "Bunsen's Batteries and the Electric Arc." *Journal of Chemical Education* 72 (1995): 99–102.

Vinal, G.W. *Storage Batteries.* London: Chapman and Hall, 1955.

Vincent, C.A., and F. Bonino. *Modern Batteries.* London: Arnold, 1984.

Binocular

It is only since the third quarter of the nineteenth century that the adjective "binocular" (that is, two-eyed) has been used on its own as a noun. Though originally it was used for any binocular instrument (including **microscopes**), it was most commonly a contraction of "binocular field glass" or "binocular theater glass," and its definition as a dual **telescope** for use with both eyes soon became its exclusive meaning. The term was eventually corrupted to the plural form commonly used today.

The story of binoculars goes back to the invention of the telescope itself. Hans Lipperhey, while seeking a patent for his new distance glass from the Assembly of the States General of the Netherlands in October 1608, was instructed to build a version for both eyes. This he apparently succeeded in doing and, though his patent was not granted, he can be credited with the invention of the binocular. Only a few opticians attempted to construct similar instruments over the succeeding two centuries. Chérubin d'Orléans made a large Galilean binocular in the 1670s that is preserved in the Museum of the History of Science in Florence. Probably the first binocular with today's simple hinge adjustment for eyepiece separation was made by the Venetian optician Selva in the 1750s.

The first commercially successful binocular was produced in 1823. It was an opera glass, consisting of a pair of small Galilean telescopes whose bodies were joined by metal bridges; it was made by Johann Friedrich Voigtländer in Vienna. Within a few years, center-wheel focusing had been added to produce the familiar Galilean binocular. These instruments were made for both theater and field use in very large numbers. They had limited field of view and a magnification of typically three times (and seldom more than five); they changed little as the nineteenth century progressed.

Binoculars consisting of two side-by-side terrestrial telescopes began to appear in the last quarter of the century. These "binocular telescopes" were long and ungainly compared with the Galilean type, but had a larger field of view and higher magnification. They were also more expensive. In 1888, for example, John Browning's prices for binocular telescopes started at £5, compared with £1 5s for their Galilean field glasses.

Prismatic binoculars had their origins in the early 1850s, when an Italian artillery officer, Ignazio Porro, devised two forms of a prism system that could be placed between the objective and eyepiece of a Keplerian (inverting) telescope to turn the image upright. He constructed monocular telescopes using both forms, but it was left to a Frenchman, A.A. Boulanger, to patent the first prismatic binocular in 1859. A rare example of Boulanger's instrument survives in the Science Museum, London. It was not a commercial success, and was gradually forgotten.

The idea of a binocular using image-erecting prisms was independently arrived at by Ernst Abbe of the University of Jena in the 1870s. His collaboration with the instrument-maker Carl Zeiss and the glass-maker Friedrich Otto Schott eventually yielded the technological advances necessary to manufacture it. In 1894, he was awarded a German imperial patent for a binocular that used Porro-type

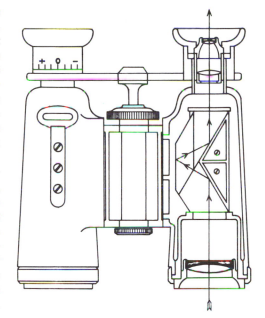

Hensoldt binocular using roof prisms to render the image upright, ca. 1905. Courtesy of SSPL.

prisms to increase the separation of the objectives, thereby enhancing the stereoscopic effect. The instrument was introduced by the Zeiss company during the same year, in 4x, 6x, and 8x versions, and was an immediate success.

Competing manufacturers also introduced prismatic binoculars, and the need to avoid patent infringement spawned a rich variety of turn-of-the-century designs. Schütz adopted the less-common second form of Porro prism, while Hensoldt used roof prisms. Abbe's patent expired in 1908 and, by the outbreak of World War I, the majority of new binoculars were of the now-familiar Zeiss "stereo-prism" pattern. Zeiss continued to innovate with 7x50 night glasses (1910), wide-angle Erfle eyepieces (patented 1917), and lightweight binoculars (1933). In Britain, Barr & Stroud, together with Ross, introduced cemented-prism night glasses around 1929, while the robust American-style body was introduced by Bausch & Lomb in 1934.

Another world war saw the increasing use of antireflection coatings, developed primarily by Zeiss in the late 1930s. During the postwar years, binocular development continued more slowly, but once again Zeiss took the lead in the 1950s. The West German factory produced a series of innovative models, including the 1964 slim-line 8x30 "Dialyt," whose Schmidt roof-prisms are found in almost half the binoculars manufactured throughout the world today. Shortly afterwards, a number of well-known British names disappeared as Japanese imports became more common.

The picture today is of a buoyant worldwide industry producing a remarkable variety of binoculars. At technology's leading edge are specialist instruments with such capabilities as image-stabilization and night vision.

Fred G. Watson

Bibliography

Seeger, Hans T. *Feldstecher: Ferngläser im Wandel der Zeit*. Borken: Bresser Optik, 1989.

Watson, Fred. *Binoculars, Opera Glasses and Field Glasses*. Princes Risborough: Shire, 1995.

Biolistic Apparatus (Gene Gun)

A Biolistic apparatus uses high-velocity microprojectiles to deliver deoxyribonucleic acid (DNA) or other substances into cells and tissues. Its inventors derived the name "Biolistic" from biological ballistics. The instrument is also known as the "gene gun" or the "particle gun," and the technique is called the "biolistic process," "particle bombardment," or "microprojectile bombardment."

The advent of genetic engineering in the 1970s generated a search for methods to introduce foreign DNA into a variety of organisms. Plants, with their rigid cell walls, posed special problems for many of the available methods of DNA delivery. Most systems used protoplasts (plant cells stripped of their cell walls). However, most plants did not regenerate well from single cells. John C. Sanford, a Cornell University plant geneticist, thought a good way to deliver foreign DNA into plants in situ would be to use genetically transformed pollen, provided he could find a way to put foreign DNA into a pollen grain. From 1980 to 1983 he tried several existing methods (irradiation, direct DNA uptake, electroporation, infectious vectors like *Agrobacterium*, microinjection, and holes made with microlasers), all to no avail. Either the wall of the pollen grain blocked effective delivery, or the cell cytoplasm leaked out through the holes.

Prototypes

The concept of using small particles (1–4 microns in diameter) both to create a hole in the cell wall and actively carry DNA into a cell emerged in 1983 in discussions Sanford had with Edward D. Wolf, director of the National Nanofabrication Facility at Cornell. They had Nelson K. Allen, a skilled machinist in the School of Electrical Engineering, make a series of prototype instruments. Allen modified an ordinary air pistol to see if it would shoot tungsten particles into onion epidermal cells. Visible cytoplasmic streaming in these cells made it apparent that some of the bombarded cells remained alive after the blast, and the particles could be seen moving along with the cell's cytoplasm. The inventors created two more sophisticated prototypes driven by gunpowder charges, further demonstrating the viability of the concept using the onion epidermis model.

Initial research on the apparatus was funded by a Cornell Biotechnology Program grant designed to encourage innovative collaborations. The grant supported postdoctoral fellow Theodore M. Klein, who worked in Sanford's laboratory for two years to refine the method. Klein successfully bound RNA and DNA to tungsten particles and showed that the molecules retained their biological activity and were expressed when delivered into a variety of target cells.

The fully functional prototype used a gunpowder charge to force a high-density polyethylene plunger (macroprojectile) down a barrel at the speed of 250 meters per second. A layer of DNA-coated particles of tungsten or gold (microprojectiles) covered the front face of the plunger. When the plunger hit a special stopping assembly, the accelerated microprojectiles passed through a small aperture into a partially evacuated chamber and hit the target cells. The partial vacuum helped preserve particle speed. Gas and gunpowder debris from the blast were vented into a surge tank. The method and apparatus are covered by United States patents no. 4,945,050 (July 31, 1990) and no. 5,036,006 (July 30, 1991).

Gunpowder Particle Gun

In October 1986 Sanford and Wolf formed a company in Ithaca, New York, called Biolistics, Inc., to market their invention. Cornell University transferred the technology to the company as part of a licensing agreement for the patents. Biolistics, Inc., leased the apparatus for research purposes—initially a ten-year lease cost $50,000 for industry and $30,000 for universities, although prices soon dropped. By 1989 Biolistics, Inc., had placed about thirty instru-

Biolistic Particle Delivery System prototype III, built by John Sanford, Edward D. Wolf, and Nelson K. Allen, 1985. Courtesy of NMAH.

ments internationally, each built to order by the Rumsey-Loomis Co. of Ithaca, New York. E.I. du Pont de Nemours and Co. of Wilmington, Delaware, purchased all rights to the technology in 1989, retaining Sanford and Wolf as consultants. Biolistics, Inc., dissolved the following year. DuPont distributed the gunpowder apparatus as the DuPont Biolistic™ PDS-1000 Particle Delivery System.

Helium Particle Gun

An improved biolistic apparatus, which replaced the gunpowder acceleration mechanism with a high-pressure helium gas shock, was devised by Sanford in collaboration with Stephen A. Johnston at Duke University in 1990. They also developed a handheld model of the helium apparatus for medical applications. The Rumsey-Loomis Co. made prototypes of both. DuPont gave an exclusive license on the helium biolistic technology to Bio-Rad Laboratories of Hercules, California, in 1991. Bio-Rad currently (as of 1995) manufactures and sells or leases the helium version of the particle gun as the Biolistic™ PDS-1000/He. The helium system provides higher velocities and better particle distribution, and it is less damaging to target tissue.

Electric Particle Gun

Dennis E. McCabe and his colleagues at Agracetus, Inc., in Middleton, Wisconsin, devised an electric version of the particle gun in 1987. Agracetus, a subsidiary of W.R. Grace and Co., develops transgenic products for the biopharmaceutical and fiber industries. The Accell™ Gene Delivery system uses high-voltage electricity to vaporize a drop of water suspended between two electrodes, creating a shock wave that accelerates DNA-coated gold particles on a carrier sheet toward a retainer screen. The screen stops the carrier sheet, but allows the DNA-coated particles to pass through the screen and penetrate the target tissue on the other side. Agracetus designed a handheld version of the Accell™ gene gun especially for use with mammalian tissues and live mammals. Research on the use of Accell™ gene guns as inoculators for direct delivery of vaccines and other therapeutics started in 1992. The Accell™ system and the handheld electric gene gun are covered by United States patents no. 5,120,657 and no. 5,149,655 (September 22, 1992).

Agracetus established a collaboration with Bio-Rad Laboratories in 1994 to manufacture and distribute Accell™ technology to the research community. Agracetus controls production of clinical-grade devices.

Conclusion

In less than ten years, DNA particle guns have become one of the standard laboratory options for gene transfer. The physical nature of the technique gives it unusual versatility. Particle guns reduce the need for sophisticated regeneration systems required of other DNA transformation technologies. They have been used successfully to genetically transform plant, insect, and animal tissues, both in culture and *in situ*, as well as pollen, algae, fungi, bacteria, and cellular organelles. Their use for the genetic transformation of major crop plants such as maize, rice, wheat, sugarcane, soybean, cotton, papaya, and tobacco has given the biolistic process significant economic importance. Promising research on genetic immunization using handheld versions of the gene gun suggests it may also have important medical applications.

Patricia L. Gossel

Bibliography

Christou, Paul, Dennis E. McCabe, and William F. Swain. "Stable Transformation of Soybean Callus by DNA-Coated Gold Particles." *Plant Physiology* 87 (1988): 671–74.

Sanford, John C. "The Biolistic Process." *Trends in Biotechnology* 6 (December 1988): 299–302.

———, et al. "Delivery of Substances into Cells and Tissues Using a Particle Bombardment Process." *Particulate Science and Technology* 5 (1987): 27–37.

———, et.al. "An Improved, Helium-Driven Biolistic Device." *Technique—A Journal of Methods in Cell and Molecular Biology* 3 (February 1991): 3–16.

Yang, Ning-Sun, and Paul Christou, eds. *Particle Bombardment Technology for Gene Transfer.* Oxford: Oxford University Press, 1994.

Blood Analysis, Optical Devices for

Many of the optical devices used for blood analysis—notably **colorimeters, spectrophotometers,** fluorimeters, turbidimeters, nephelometers, and flame **photometers**—are similar to chemical laboratory instruments. There are, however, three kinds of optical instrumentation methods developed for blood analysis that measure blood components directly without the use of sampling and laboratory methodology. They are oximetry, optical sensors for monitoring pH, PCO_2, and PO_2, and noninvasive spectrophotometry.

The determination of the oxygen saturation of blood by oximetry is one of the most important clinical measurements to assess respiratory competence in critical care, emergency treatment, and especially anesthesiology, because it can be done quickly and continuously. A measurement of the "blood gas" concentrations—pH, PCO_2, and PO_2—provides more detailed information on the behavior of the respiratory system.

Oximetry

Oximetry, the oldest and most frequently used technique, assesses the ratio of oxygenated hemoglobin to total hemoglobin in the blood. In 1933 the British physiologist G.A. Millikan reported what may be the first description of a clinical colorimeter intended specifically for oximetry. It distinguished between oxy- and deoxy-hemoglobin by a combination of two color filters and the spectral selectivity of a mercury arc lamp, acting differentially on copper/copper-oxide photocells connected to a galvanometer. Previous methods had required optical techniques of visual comparison. The physiologists Kurt Kramer and Karl Matthes in Germany also developed photoelectric instruments in the early 1930s to measure the optical density of blood for oximetry. Subsequent development has progressed along two paths: transcutaneous sensors placed against the skin to measure changes in the neighboring tissue, and devices for a direct measurement by means of intravenous catheters.

The first transcutaneous instrumentation for clinical use was G.A. Millikan's ear oximeter of 1942, which used a lamp and photocell to measure the transmission of light through the earlobe. In this and other early devices, the transmission of red light (related to variation in hemoglobin oxygenation) was compared with transmission in the green (which was less sensitive to variation in oxygen saturation). Later investigators preferred measurements in the near-infrared, because the photocells had good sensitivity in that region, and because blood is too optically dense in the green to transmit light effectively. For this method to work, it was necessary to heat or otherwise treat the location of the sensor to increase blood flow, to make it more nearly representative of arterial blood. It was also necessary to remove the blood from the tissue temporarily (for example, by squeezing the ear) to allow a measurement to correct for the light scattering and attenuation in the tissue.

Efforts to circumvent these difficulties led to instruments in which the pulsing component of light attenuation represents the arterial blood volume, and the steady component represents the correction to be subtracted for tissue scattering and venous blood absorption. This work began in 1975 when the Japanese biomedical engineers Susumu Nakajima and co-workers developed an ear oximeter that measured the light transmitted through the tissue at the peak and low point of the blood flow pulsation. In 1980, the Japanese biomedical engineers I. Yoshiya et al. described a fingertip oximeter with a fiber-optic connection between finger and instrument. Pulse oximeters are now widely used, especially in fingertip form, and many commercial instruments are available.

Catheter sensors provide accurate measurements in a precise location, such as in the pulmonary artery. The first ones were miniature optical cells at the end of a catheter, but in 1962 the physiologists Michael Polanyi and Robert Hehir showed the advantage of using a reflectance measurement at the end of an optical fiber in an optically dense medium such as blood. Fiber-optic instruments can be used for the combined measurement of percent saturation and dye-indicator dilution curves. The latter allows an observation of the rate of dilution of injected dye, which measures perfusion. Fiber-optic catheter sensors have been made commercially available for oximetry.

Optical Sensors for pH, PO_2, and PCO_2

While oximetry measures the fraction of hemoglobin that is oxygenated, a more accurate assessment of the status of blood respiration requires the determination of total oxygen concentration, carbon dioxide concentration, and pH. Electrode measurement of blood samples has long been an accepted method, but optical measurement offers the advantage of immediate and continuous measurement by either an arterial catheter or sensors in the extracorporeal blood flow line of an oxygenation machine.

In the 1970s, the German physiologists Dietrich Lübbers and Norbert Opitz originated the concept of optical measurement of these components by their diffusion from blood through a membrane into a dye-containing solution for their spectrophotometric or fluorimetric mea-

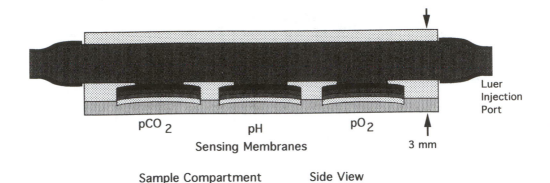

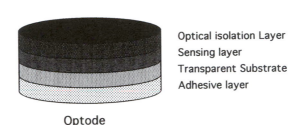

Schematic diagram of an optode cell for in vitro blood gas measurement. Courtesy of Marc J. P. Leiner/ Elsevier Science.

surement. Concurrently, the chemist John Peterson and biomedical engineer Seth Goldstein in the United States developed the idea of fiber-optic sensors for physiological measurements, based on dye-indicators fixed at the tip of an optical fiber. These approaches have had extended development.

The extracorporeal sensors, based on principles originally developed for fiber-optic sensors, take the form of disc optodes (fiber-optic chemical sensors) in flow-through cells, as exemplified by the recent work of the Austrian chemist Mark Leiner. The pH sensor consists of an adhesive layer, a transparent support, a sensing layer with an immobilized fluorescent indicator dye, and an opaque optical isolation layer having a membrane permeable to the blood component to be analyzed. The PCO_2 sensor is similar in construction, but its outer membrane is black silicone, permeable only to gaseous CO_2, and the dye layer contains sodium bicarbonate solution. The PO_2 sensor also has a black silicone outer layer that is permeable to oxygen, but here the indicator dye is adsorbed onto silica particles in a silicone matrix. This senses oxygen by its quenching of the fluorescence of the indicator.

In all three types of optode, the component to be measured diffuses through the outer mem-brane, and its concentration in the sensor equili-brates with its blood concentration. The dye fluorescence, indicating concentration, is measured by the attached optical system. The instrument consists of a disposable flow-through cell with temperature control, a tungsten light source, wavelength selection filters, photodiode detectors, and fiber optics to connect the individual optodes to the light source and measuring system. The light intensity is monitored by a digital signal-processing system with appropriate calibration.

Fiber-optic sensors, which were originally developed for measurement of pH, PCO_2, and PO_2 in blood vessels, are small, and they don't need a reference electrode. Recently much commercial development has gone into making fiber-optic catheters that combine the three measurements. Both catheter and extracorporeal optical sensors are currently being tested for commercial production.

The original fiber-optic sensors consisted of a flexible plastic optical fiber with a hollow-fiber membrane at its end that was ion-permeable for pH measurement, or gas-permeable for PCO_2 and PO_2 measurement. The pH sensing dye was an optical absorbance indicator, phenol red, fixed to a support of polyacrylamide microspheres containing smaller polystyrene microspheres for light scattering. Other versions used a mirror surface or a continuous fiber bent in a U shape to provide a return of the light transmitted through the indicator for measurement of the optical absorption.

A dye indicator has two forms, acidic and basic, and the equilibrium ratio of these forms varies with pH. Since the two forms have different optical absorption or fluorescence spectra, the ratio can be measured optically and translated to pH. A single indicator can cover only a narrow pH range, but recent work by John Peterson in the United States and the physicist Francesco Baldini in Italy suggests the possibility of multiple indicators for a broader range.

The original PO_2 sensor was based on quenching of dye fluorescence by oxygen. The effect occurs commonly with dyes, but certain aromatic and metal-organic compounds show it strongly. The fiber-optic instrumentation consists of a light source, either tungsten or diode, wavelength-selection filters, intensity-sensing detectors, and a digital signal-processing system. In addition, a variety of optical arrangements have been used to insert the light into a fiber and collect it from the fiber.

Quenching of fluorescence by oxygen can also be measured by determining the fluorescence lifetime, its mean rate of decay. With most dyes the lifetime is in the nanosecond range, and elegant instrumentation is required to measure it. Some metal-organic compounds of platinum and palladium have lifetimes in the microsecond range, and these can be measured easily by simple instrumentation, as described by the Brazilian biomedical engineer Pedro Gewehr and British medical physicist David Delpy.

Noninvasive Spectrophotometry

The success of pulse oximetry as a direct optical method has heightened interest in the possibility of other noninvasive blood measurements, especially for glucose. Invasive probes for physiological sensing of blood components have had many difficulties in application, primarily because of a lack of materials biocompatibility. Noninvasive measurement in the near-infrared is based on the relative transparency of blood and tissue in that spectral region, but the difficulty of weak optical absorption of the blood component in a relatively high and variable background has not been yet overcome. Encouraging results have been obtained on blood samples by the academic chemist Mark Arnold and co-workers, and some workers have experimented on a fingertip device. Another promising idea, pursued for several years, is measurement of a blood component by its optical density, through the resolution of photon travel time through tissue on a picosecond scale. This has been applied to the measurement of blood components by Britton Chance and other physiologists.

John I. Peterson

Bibliography

Leiner, Marc J.P. "Optical Sensors for In-Vitro Blood Gas Analysis." *Sensors and Actuators B-Chemical* 29 (1995): 169–73.

Lübbers, Dietrich W. "Blood Gas Analysis with Fluorescent Dyes as an Example of Their Usefulness as Quantitative Chemical Sensors." In *Chemical Sensors, Proceedings of the International Meeting on Chemical Sensors, Fukuoka, Japan, September 19–22, 1983,* edited by T. Seiyama et al., 609–19. New York: Elsevier, 1983.

Millikan, G.A. "The Oximeter, an Instrument for Measuring Continuously the Oxygen Saturation of Arterial Blood in Man." *Review of Scientific Instruments* 13 (1942): 434–45.

Peterson, John I., et al. "Fiber Optic pH Probe for Physiological Use." *Analytical Chemistry* 52 (1980): 864–69.

Wolfbeis, Otto S., ed. *Fiber Optic Chemical Sensors and Biosensors.* Boca Raton, Fla.: CRC, 1991.

Blood Gas Analyzer

A blood gas analyzer measures the partial pressures of oxygen (PO_2) and carbon dioxide (PCO_2) in blood, and the pH of the sample. The typical instrument is self-flushing and -calibrating, and normally operates at body temperature. Some generate their own standard gases from CO_2 and room air, correcting the values for barometric pressure with an internal aneroid. The gas results are presented as either mm Hg or Kp_a, and the pH values are usually referred to the NBS pH scale. Some analyzers incorporate a polymeric ion-selective potassium electrode, and some measure the hemoglobin as well as the PO_2.

Starting from a few specialist centers using laboratory-built equipment in the 1960s, the industry expanded rapidly; in 1993 approximately 150 million measurements were made in the United States. This revolution has been brought about by a continuous development of instruments in which rapid measurements can be made by unskilled operators, rather than by any major advances in the sensor technology. The actual electrodes that make the measurements in any modern machine would be instantly recognizable to their original inventors.

Blood gas analyzers use a minimum of three electrochemical sensors. The pH and PCO_2 electrodes are modifications of the glass pH electrode, while the oxygen electrode is a polarographic cell. The first two are potentiometric; their output is a voltage that is determined by the quantity being measured. An external voltage is applied to the oxygen electrode, and the current passed is the output.

In the 1880s, the German chemist Walter H. Nernst brought together the concepts developed by Svante Arrhenius, Jacobus van't Hoff, and J. Willard Gibbs, and formalized them in an equation that relates the changes in voltage of the pH and PCO_2 electrodes to the quantity being measured. Nernst also contributed the idea of the equi-transferent bridge, and he introduced the concentrated potassium chloride that is still widely used as the reference contact with the blood or calibrating buffer solutions. His assistant Heinrich Danneel was the first to show that the current passed by a negatively charged platinum electrode is dependent upon dissolved oxygen—in effect the first oxygen electrode.

The biologist Max Cremer discovered that a thin glass membrane separating two solutions of different acidity would generate a voltage. In 1925 the biochemist Phylis T. Kerridge made the first glass electrode for blood pH, and many ingenious electrode designs followed. Losses or gains of gas from the sample had to be prevented. Blood pH is affected by temperature, and so accurate temperature control was required. A small sample volume was an advantage. The narrow range of blood pH necessitated a highly reproducible reference against which to measure the voltage of the sensing electrode and highly precise standard buffers to define the pH scale.

In 1958 the Danish clinical chemists Ole Siggaard-Andersen and Poul Astrup demonstrated the Radiometer micro pH electrode, which could be used at the bedside and which gave a reproducibility of 0.002 pH. Many still consider this electrode to be the gold standard for blood pH work. In this electrode, the glass sensing element was blown as a capillary tube into which the analyte was sucked. The reference contact was between the blood in the tip of a specially shaped plastic capillary and saturated KCl. Most modern analyzers have reverted to a more conventional electrode shape to facilitate replacement and servicing but have retained a concentrated KCl solution as the reference junction.

In 1952 the property of CO_2 to diffuse through membranes and affect the pH of a solution at a distance was used by Richard Stow, a medical physicist working at Ohio State University, to adapt a glass pH electrode so that it would respond to changes in PCO_2. A film of solution was trapped against the surface of the glass behind a plastic membrane through which the CO_2 diffused from the sample until it reached equilibrium. The anesthesiologist John W. Severinghaus made the important modification of adding sodium bicarbonate to the electrolyte film. The excess bicarbonate was effectively constant, and the hydrogen ion concentration of the film was forced to approximate to a linear function of the PCO_2. This is essentially the electrode used today, with only minor alterations to the geometry to fit into the particular analyzer.

By the 1950s the measurement of dissolved oxygen by polarography was well developed, but blood poisoned the cathode at which the reduction was occurring. In 1954 Leland Clark, working at Fells Institute in Ohio, used an oxygen-permeable plastic membrane to keep the blood away from the active cathode. By choosing a plastic of suitable oxygen permeability and reducing the cathode diameter, the membrane became the dominant limiting factor in the diffusion process and the current passed became a function of the partial pressure of oxygen in the blood driving it through the membrane. The current from such an electrode may fall by less than 2 percent when calibrated with an equilibrated solution, as compared with the reading in the gas phase.

The electrical resistance of the pH electrode is typically >100 MΩ and the signal from the PO_2 electrode <1 nano amp. High quality insulation and specialized electronic circuits are therefore required. This has been greatly simplified by the advances in low-leakage-current, high-input-impedance solid state devices and by digital processing of the signals.

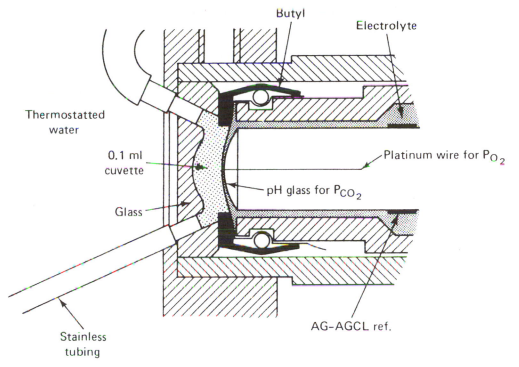

Butyl

Electrolyte

Thermostatted water

0.1 ml cuvette

Platinum wire for P_{O_2}

pH glass for P_{CO_2}

Glass

AG-AGCL ref.

Stainless tubing

Cuvette design for mounting either PCO_2 or PO_2 electrodes. Leslie Cromwell et al. Biomedical Instrumentation and Measurements. *New Jersey: Prentice-Hall, 1973: 59, Figure 4.21. Courtesy of John Severinghaus.*

In order to recognize the importance of the grouping of the measurements of pH, PCO_2 and PO_2, it is necessary to consider that blood may become abnormally acid as the result of two quite separate causes.

1. Hypo-ventilation (under-breathing) results in the concentration of CO_2 in the alveolar gas, which is in equilibrium with the arterial blood, rising until the quantity exhaled by the reduced breathing again matches the rate at which it is being produced by the tissues. The P_aCO_2 therefore rises, as does the concentration of dissolved CO_2 in the plasma. A fraction of the dissolved CO_2 is hydrated to form carbonic acid, and so hydrogen ions are formed and the pH falls. The majority of the hydrogen ions are buffered by other buffers in the blood. Bicarbonate ions are formed from the retained CO_2 and the bicarbonate concentration rises at the same time as the pH falls. This pattern of disturbance is called respiratory acidosis.

2. Fixed acids may appear in the blood and drive the pH down. Lactic acid is pro-

duced normally in strenuous exercise, but there are many pathological causes for what is termed metabolic acidosis. The CO_2/bicarbonate system buffers these acids and as the pH falls the bicarbonate concentration falls as CO_2 is driven off through the lungs. In a normal individual the fall in pH is reduced by hyperventilation which lowers the P_aCO_2, providing some respiratory compensation at the expense of a further fall in bicarbonate.

Clinically all the possible combinations of acidosis and alkalosis are encountered. The modern analyzer incorporates this collective wisdom in calculating derived parameters that help the clinician to recognize the underlying problem.

In a normal individual, if the P_aCO_2 is low, the P_aO_2 will be high and vice versa. However in many clinical situations this is not so. For example, the distribution of blood and gas flow in the lungs may not be matched. Since at the normal P_aO_2 the blood is nearly saturated with oxygen, any blood that escapes through the lungs without being properly oxygenated lowers the PO_2 of the final mixture in a way that cannot be compensated for by hyperventilation. A combination of a low P_aCO_2 with a low P_aO_2 can result.

The measurements provided by the blood gas analyzer, together with the derived parameters, form a pattern that can change very rapidly. The speed and ease with which the results can be obtained is one of the major advances of the last forty years.

David Band

Bibliography

Cremer, M. "Ueber die Ursache der electromotorischen Eigenschaften Der Gewebe, zugleigh ein Beitrag zur Lehre von den polyphasischen Electrolytketten." *Zeitschrift für Biologie* 47 (1906): 562.

Danneel, H.L. "Ueber den durch diffundierende Gase hervorgerufenen Reststrom." *Zeitschrift für Electrochemie* 4 (1897–1898): 227–42.

Kerridge, P.T. "The Use of the Glass Electrode in Biochemistry." *Biochemical Journal* 19 (1925): 611–17.

Nernst, W.H. "Die electromotorische Wirksamkeit der Ionen." *Zeitschrift für physikalische Chemie* 4 (1889): 129–81.

Severinghaus, J.W., and P.B Astrup. *History of Blood Gas Analysis*. Boston: Little, Brown, 1987.

Blowpipe

A blowpipe is a curved tube with a small orifice at one end through which the operator can blow a stream of air. By directing the air through the flame of a candle or burner onto a test sample the size of a pepper seed, intense temperatures can be attained that would normally be expected only in a smelting furnace. The reactions in the oxidizing or reducing zone of the flame can easily be observed with charcoal, clay, glass, or platinum serving as support. The samples are subjected to various tests with the blowpipe and examined with the addition of fluxes or reagents. The metal components of salts can generally be positively identified by the coloration of the flame, the resulting oxide coating or a fused glass bead. Much experience and talent is needed for efficient work with the blowpipe. Rubber bellows can be attached to the blowpipe to bring about a more steady and continuous stream of air.

The origin of the blowpipe is lost in antiquity, but it was probably an invention of the Egyptians. Depictions of goldsmiths using metal blowpipes appear on tomb wall paintings at Sakkara dating to ca. 2400 B.C. The use of the blowpipe for chemical investigations was pioneered in the seventeenth and eighteenth centuries by German scientists such as Georg Ernst Stahl, Johann Andreas Cramer, and Andreas Sigismund Marggraf. Swedish mineralogists and metallurgists used blowpipes for quick qualitative tests of minerals, ores, and smelter products, and chemists such as Torbern Bergman, Axel Frederik Cronstedt, and Johann Gottlieb Gahn developed analytical methods and tools for the blowpipe. Through the efforts of the chemist Jöns Jakob Berzelius, who between 1805 and 1828 discovered three new elements, the blowpipe became the "stethoscope of the chemist." These methods were further refined at the Mining Academy of Freiberg in Saxony, where Eduard Harkort in 1826 introduced implements for quantitative blowpipe analysis of silver by cupellation. Karl Friedrich Plattner expanded Harkort's ideas, and his *Manual of Qualitative and Quantitative Analysis with the Blowpipe* is the culmination of all the knowledge in this field.

Blowpipes were usually made of brass or silver. The length normally varied from 20 to 24 cm and could be adjusted so the sample could be easily seen. Most mouthpieces were either silverplated or made out of ivory, horn, or wood. A metalworker's blowpipe is a tapering conical tube, the narrower end bent at a right angle; here, however, saliva collects and blocks the jet hole. Cronstedt's blowpipe has a hollow ball attached below the middle of the tube to collect the saliva. In Gahn's very popular design, a cylindrical moisture chamber was attached at the lower end of the blowpipe, and small platinum tips with different hole sizes could be attached according to requirements. Julius Hirschwald designed a holder for a cobalt glass filter used to observe flame coloration. Joseph Black's blowpipe, which was used mainly in England, had a straight tube that widened at the bottom without a moisture chamber, and the tip was screwed into the side. Smithon Tennant's blowpipe was similar, but had a bent and fully rotatable tip just above the lower end of the tube. William Hyde Wollaston's blowpipe consisted of three conical parts that could be stored one inside the other, reducing the size to that of a small pen-

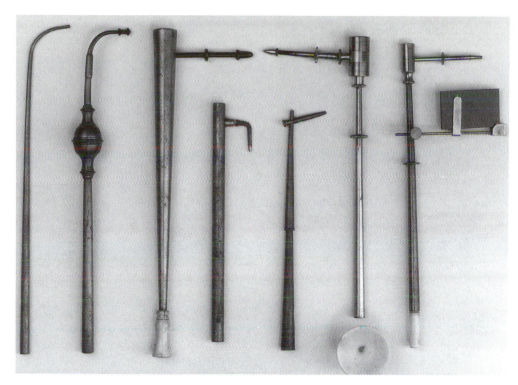

Simple, Cronstedt, Black, Tennant, Wollaston, Gahn, and Hirschwald blowpipes. Courtesy of Ulrich Burchard.

cil. Friedrich Wilhelm Voight's blowpipe (also known as Peppy's blowpipe) had a flat disk functioning as a moisture chamber, and a tip movable about the central axis.

Early mineralogical pocket laboratories contained the bare essentials of blowpipe analysis, including bottles of the three main fluxes: borax, phosphorous salt, and soda. The Plattner or Freiberg apparatus manufactured by Lingke in Freiberg was a self-sufficient traveling laboratory, including tools and implements for sample preparation, fuels, chemicals, and a collapsible analytical balance. Letcher in Truro, Cornwall, made relatively simple and inexpensive blowpipe kits that were widely distributed. Some models had a drawer with crushed mineral samples for reference. These Letcher kits may be obtained in specialty shops even today.

The displacement of the blowpipe began around 1860, with the introduction of the Bunsen burner and of spectral analysis. Nevertheless, blowpipes have played an important role in science since about 1760 and were instrumental in the discovery of more than fifteen elements.

Ulrich Burchard

Bibliography

Berzelius, Jöns Jakob. *The Use of the Blowpipe in Chemical Analysis and in the Examination of Minerals.* Translated by J.G. Children. London: Baldwin, 1821.

Burchard, Ulrich. "The History and Apparatus of Blowpipe Analysis." *Mineralogical Record* 25 (1994): 251–77.

Jensen, W.B. "Development of Blowpipe Analysis." In *The History and Preservation of Chemical Instrumentation,* edited by J.T. Stock and R. Orna, 123–48. Dordrecht: Reidel, 1986.

Plattner, Karl Friedrich. *Probierkunst mit dem Löthrohr.* 4th ed. Leipzig: Van Nostrand, 1865.

Bolometer

The bolometer measures the total amount of radiant heat incident upon it. Its main use in scientific research has been for the measurement of infrared radiation. Its name derives from the Greek *bole* (ray), and *metron* (measure). The bolometer works on the principle that the resistance of its metallic detector varies proportionately with the amount of heat applied to it. The

Langley bolometers, 1880s. SM 1890-39, 1880-40. Courtesy of SSPL.

variation of the detector's resistance is measured by placing it in one of the arms of a balanced electrical circuit known as a **Wheatstone bridge**. When the detector is heated, thus changing its resistance, the resulting current in the bridge can be measured.

The bolometer's detecting element could theoretically be chosen from a variety of metals, but platinum was initially favored because of its strength when fashioned into thin strips for use in measuring discrete sources of thermal radiation. The detectors are often used in pairs, each one being on a different arm of the Wheatstone bridge. One is exposed to the radiation and the other is shielded from it. The shielded element serves to reduce the effects of ambient thermal radiation. Because of the small currents encountered when the bridge goes out of balance, **galvanometers** were commonly used for measurement.

Prior to the invention of the bolometer, the standard instrument for the measurement of radiant heat was the **thermopile**. By the late nineteenth century, however, researchers were straining to measure fainter and more discrete sources of heat and the thermopiles of that time were not adequate for the task. Thomas Alva Edison attempted to remedy the situation in 1878 with his tasimeter, but his instrument was erratic, had a slow response time, and had a nonlinear response. Samuel Pierpont Langley, director of the Allegheny Observatory near Pittsburgh, Pennsylvania, and a leading solar physicist, was acutely disappointed by Edison's failure. Langley had corresponded with Edison

in 1877 regarding the need for a new instrument, especially for measuring the radiant heat from the invisible infrared solar spectrum. With no useful instrument forthcoming, Langley set about in late 1879 to construct one on his own. Working from a suggestion of Edison's (which he had at first dismissed as impractical), within a year Langley had constructed the prototype bolometer.

Langley tried various metals for the detecting element before settling on platinum, although he would constantly experiment with new materials as they became available to him, particularly selenium and carbon filament. Langley's initial platinum detectors were 1 mm wide and 10 mm long. With these detectors and a Thomson galvanometer, Langley's bolometer proved to be about fifteen times more sensitive than the current thermopiles. Langley was impressed with the sensitivity of the bolometer and tested it on his expedition to Mount Whitney, California, in 1881. His discovery of the extension of the solar spectrum deep into the infrared on this expedition demonstrated to other scientists the power of the bolometer.

Shortly after Langley built a satisfactory version of the bolometer, he arranged for William Grunow, a New York City instrument-maker, to produce bolometers commercially. By the end of 1886, Grunow had made a total of eight bolometers for researchers and instrument-makers such as Aleksandr G. Stoletov at Moscow, Hermann von Helmholtz at Berlin, Eugène-Adrien Ducretet at Paris, and André P.P.

Crova at Montpelier. Within a few years the bolometer proved to be a useful instrument, particularly in the growing field of black body radiation research.

Langley, with Grunow's assistance, continued to make improvements in the bolometer and its auxiliary apparatus, especially the galvanometer. Grunow and Langley were able to make detector strips as narrow as 0.05 mm and developed more efficient blackening techniques. After moving to the Smithsonian Astrophysical Observatory in Washington, D.C., Langley's assistant, Charles Greeley Abbot, made a number of additional improvements to the bolometer casing. He also experimented with placing the detecting elements in a vacuum to improve the instrument's performance. By 1898, the bolometer had been well sealed and made more portable. The number of electrical connections and lead wires was reduced and the instrument was made more manageable for the new user. Langley was able to claim that he had made his bolometer four hundred times as sensitive as his earliest models.

Although the bolometer proved to be a successful instrument, it did not become the preeminent detector in radiant energy research. Improvements to the **radiometer** by Ernest Fox Nichols and to the thermopile by Heinrich Rubens gave physicists a choice of useful instruments. The bolometer's disadvantages were a "drift" in the readings caused by unequal warming of the strips, and interference from local air currents arising from the heat produced by the electric current. Advantages included its quick response time, which made it the superior device for working with rapidly changing sources.

Platinum, in the form of thin foil, remained the element of choice in bolometers up through the 1940s. In that decade, researchers worked on improving the response of the bolometer by using a variety of detecting elements. While some experimented with evaporated films of nickel or gold, better success was achieved at Bell Laboratories with thermistor (*therm*ally sensitive re*sistor*) elements made from combinations of nickel, manganese, and cobalt oxide alloys. The thermistor bolometer has been widely used for military and space systems.

Another major improvement in bolometers resulted in the ability to cool the detectors to very low temperatures. Cooling allows bolometers to use superconducting elements, to reduce the thermal capacity of the elements resulting in faster response times, and reduce the effects of background radiation in conjunction with shielding. Superconducting columbium nitride and low-temperature carbon-composition resistor bolometers were tested, but perhaps the most successful was Frank J. Low's low-temperature germanium bolometer. Developed in 1961 using a single crystal of gallium-doped germanium, the Low bolometer has become a very important detector for astronomical infrared research.

Currently, metal-film and thermistor bolometers are still in general use, but in research on the far infrared or on faint astronomical sources, cooled semiconductor bolometers are required. Additionally, researchers are continuing to test new detecting materials in efforts to improve the sensitivity of bolometers.

Ronald S. Brashear

Bibliography

Coblentz, William Weber. "Instruments and Methods Used in Radiometry." In *Investigations of Infra-red Spectra,* 152–76. Washington, D.C.: Carnegie Institution of Washington, 1906.

Hudson, Richard D., Jr., and Jacqueline Wordsworth Hudson, eds. *Infrared Detectors.* Stroudsburg, Pa.: Dowden, Hutchinson and Ross, 1975.

Langley, Samuel P. "The Bolometer and Radiant Energy." *Proceedings of the American Academy of Arts and Sciences* 16 (1881): 342–59.

———, and C.G. Abbot. *Annals of the Astrophysical Observatory of the Smithsonian Institution.* Vol. 1. Washington, D.C.: Government Printing Office, 1900.

Smith, Robert Allan, F.E. Jones, and R.P. Chasmar. *The Detection and Measurement of Infra-red Radiation.* Oxford: Clarendon, 1957.

Bomb Calorimeter

See CALORIMETER, BOMB

Breathalyzer

A Breathalyzer measures the alcohol content of exhaled breath, and thus indicates the level of a person's intoxication. The name Breathalyzer was given to the instrument designed by Robert F. Borkenstein, an American chemist, in 1954. It was the first to allow fairly precise

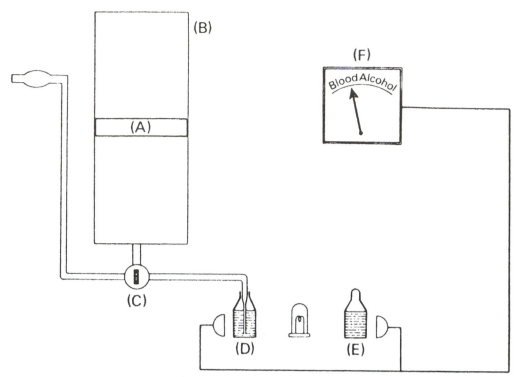

The principle of the Breathalyzer. Breath is blown into a reservoir (B), from which a measured volume is passed through a heated solution of potassium dichromate and sulphuric acid (D). Presence of alcohol causes formation of green chromium sulphate, detected against the control solution (E). Denney (1979): 86, Figure 9. Courtesy of Robert Hale Ltd./R. C. Denney.

analysis and became widely used in the United States, Canada, and Australia. Breathalyzer later became the generic name for "blow-in-the-bag" breath analysis instruments. Among the general public, this has come to be extended to include all breath analysis instruments.

Rolla Neil Harger, an American chemist, and others showed that the amount of alcohol in a sample of exhaled breath is proportional to the amount in a blood sample. Harger's Drunkometer, described in 1931 and introduced in 1938, was the first practical roadside instrument to measure breath alcohol in the United States. It used a purple solution of potassium permanganate in sulfuric acid, which oxidizes alcohol, the solution fading to a pale straw color. The Breathalyzer employed a similar oxidation reaction using potassium dichromate solution. A standard amount of breath, collected in a metal cylinder, was heated to 45–50°C, and passed through an ampoule containing the solution with a silver salt catalyst. The decrease in the orange/yellow color of the dichromate was measured colorimetrically to give the alcohol content. The Breathalyzer gave

consistently low readings, which varied more than expected with results from analysis of subjects' blood alcohol. However, its use became widespread, and it had a profound effect on the control of drink-related road accidents. Later models, such as the Breathalyzer 1000, developed in the 1970s, overcame these problems and were designed with digital printouts for convenience. The main disadvantage with these instruments is the corrosive nature of the acidic solutions on which they depend.

The "blow-in-the-bag" breathalyzers of the 1960s and 1970s, such as the Alcolyser or Alcotest, used sealed glass ampoules containing yellow dichromate crystals saturated with sulfuric acid. The subject blows through the opened ampoule into a bag. Alcohol in the breath changes the crystals green (to chromium sulphate), the extent of the green stain depending on breath alcohol level.

Disposable instruments used by police at the roadside were introduced in the early 1960s. One such was the Kitagawa detector tube, made in Japan. Here the breath blown into a balloon is transferred to a detection tube using a pump, and alcohol is measured by comparing the color change of the reagent with a reference chart. It was not very accurate, as the rubber balloon was slightly permeable to alcohol and color matching was subject to human error.

Since the 1970s, a number of reliable and rapid techniques have been introduced to replace the wet chemistry methods described above. Gas chromatography was used in such instruments as the Alco-Analyzer and the Gas Chromatographic Intoximeter. Their chief disadvantage is that a supply of an inert carrier gas is necessary for operation. Samples were either analyzed directly or field samples were collected and analyzed subsequently.

Alcohol molecules show a characteristic absorption of infrared energy, a property that was used in the CMI Intoxilyzer. The much greater accuracy of infrared and gas chromatography instruments allowed them to be used for evidential testing in court cases in the United States. The Lion Intoximeter 3000, another infrared device, was introduced in the United Kingdom in 1983 and rapidly became the standard equipment in police stations, displacing blood and urine testing for law enforcement purposes.

In the late 1970s devices that employed electrochemical fuel cell detectors were developed both as battery-powered portable roadside instruments and as larger evidential testers with printout facilities. The Lion Alcolmeter instruments are the most common of this type. These measure the electric current generated at a platinum electrode when alcohol is oxidized at its surface. The development of passive detectors working on the same principle is a further refinement. Lion Laboratories in Wales collaborated with the Insurance Institute of Highway Safety in Washington, D.C., to produce a passive device that incorporates a fuel cell detector in a flashlight. When shone in a subject's face, a pump draws in exhaled breath for analysis. This enables a police officer to screen drivers without causing inconvenience or embarrassment to sober individuals. Introduced in the 1980s, it also bypassed the possible refusal of drivers in the United States to give a breath test by invoking the Fourth Amendment, claiming that to comply would be self-incrimination.

Ann Newmark

Bibliography

Borkenstein, Robert F. "A New Method for Analysis of Alcohol in the Breath: The Breathalyzer." United States patent no. 2,824,789, 1958.

Denney, Ronald C. *Drinking and Driving*. London: Hale, 1979.

Jain, Naresh C., and Robert H. Cravey. "A Review of Breath Alcohol Methods." *Journal of Chromatographic Science* 12 (1974): 214–18.

Jones, A.W. "Physiological Aspects of Breath-Alcohol Measurement." *Alcohol, Drugs and Driving* 6 (1990): 2–25.

Bubble Chamber

See CHAMBER, BUBBLE

Burette

A burette is a glass tube with stopcock that delivers small, measured quantities of a liquid. It is used in volumetric analysis (titrimetry), in which a reagent solution of known concentration (titrant) is added to the sample solution until the material to be determined (determinand, titrand) is transformed. The end point of the reaction is indicated by a visually observable change (for example, if a base is titrated with an acid, by the color change of an indicator), or by an abrupt change in potential of an indicator electrode. With knowledge of the chemical reaction involved, the amount of the determinand can be calculated from the volume of titrant added to reach the end point. The titrant is usually added from a burette to the sample solution measured out with a pipette (a small tube, often graduated), but the opposite arrangement may also be used.

Volumetric analysis became a quantitative analytical technique only after the introduction of the pipette and burette. Both tools were invented and introduced into practice by the French chemist and pharmacist Francois Antoine Henri Descroizilles, who described them in a 1795 paper concerning a new method for checking with indigo solution the appropriate concentration of hypochlorite solution used in textile bleaching. Descroizilles's burette was a graduated cylinder from which it was difficult to discharge minute portions of solution. Descroizilles called the tool "bertholli-mètre" after a contemporary, Claude Louis Berthollet, who developed the method of textile bleaching with chlorine. In an 1806 paper on an acid-base determination method, Descroizilles described an "alcalimètre," which permitted fine dosing of liquids.

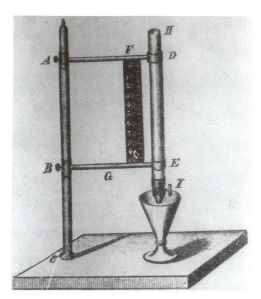

Cock burette, 1850s. Friedrich Mohr. Lehrbuch der chemisch-analytischen Titrirmethode. *Braunschweig: F. Vieweg, 1855: Figure 8. Courtesy of Ferenc Szabadváry.*

The names "burette" and "pipette" originated with Joseph Louis Gay-Lussac, in a paper published in 1824. When the burette was tilted, the solution was discharged through a thin tube dropwise. Gay-Lussac's burette was the only such tool mentioned in Karl Heinrich Schwarz's *Praktische Anleitung zu Massanalysen* (1853), the first book on volumetric analysis. The French word *burette* originally means a small can with a thin outlet tube, while the word *pipette* means a wine tester.

In 1846 Étienne Ossian Henry described his new glass burette with a copper tap. In his *Lehrbuch der chemisch-analytischen Titriermethode* (1855), the German pharmacist Friedrich Mohr introduced a "clip-burette" and an all-glass "cock-burette." All-glass cock-burettes of this sort became common as glass-blowing techniques improved in the latter decades of the nineteenth century. They are still in use today, although their sizes have been reduced in accordance with the requirements of microanalysis.

Ferenc Szabadváry

Bibliography

Szabadváry, Ferenc. *History of Analytical Chemistry,* 195–247. Oxford and London: Pergamon, 1966.

Bush Differential Analyzer

See Differential Analyzer, Bush

C

Calculating Machine

A calculating machine, broadly speaking, is a machine that adds, subtracts, multiplies or divides. Numbers are represented digitally, rather than by continuous quantities as in a **slide rule**. The term has also been used more narrowly to describe those machines that have a moveable carriage or other mechanism that makes it possible to multiply other than by strict repeated addition. In this usage, machines designed only for addition (and possibly subtraction) are called adding machines.

People have used objects to help them keep track of computations from antiquity. A fascination with computations and mechanisms led the German natural philosopher Wilhelm Schickard to envision a mechanism that would carry a one in summing two numbers. Schickard described his machine in a 1623 letter to Johannes Kepler, but it remained unknown until Kepler's correspondence was published early in the twentieth century. On Schickard's machine, one was to enter numbers by pulling out toothed shafts; the carry mechanism involved a gear with a single tooth. The French mathematician Blaise Pascal invented a somewhat more successful adding machine in 1642; several examples survive. In these machines, one enters a number by rotating wheels with pins protruding from them. A weight linked to the pins falls to bring about the carry.

In the late seventeenth century, the mathematician and natural philosopher Gottfried Leibniz introduced another way of representing numbers on a computing device, the stepped drum. This was a cylindrical gear with nine teeth of varying length along its side. Setting a digit on such a machine engages the corresponding number of teeth on the appropriate gear. Rotating the cylinder then adds this digit to the total already calculated. Although Leibniz's stepped drum calculating machine had little immediate influence, stepped drums would reappear on important later machines. A few calculating machines were made in the eighteenth century, but they remained mechanical marvels. One was the adding machine built in 1725 on the principles of Pascal by Jean Lepine, watchmaker to the king of France. Later in the century, the German sun-dial- and clock-maker Philip Matthäus Hahn made a small number of stepped drum calculating machines.

Practical devices date from 1820, when the insurance executive Charles Xavier Thomas of Colmar presented an arithmometer to the French Société d'Encouragement pour l'Industrie Nationale. In this machine, a digit was entered by pulling a lever which, in turn, engaged the appropriate number of gears on a stepped drum. Pulling a ribbon or, in production models of the machine, rotating a crank, entered the digit into the machine. Thomas arithmometers sold slowly at first, but he steadily made improvements. By 1878, about fifteen hundred machines had sold. Later stepped drum machines included the Burkhardt, Layton, Madas, Muldivo, Peerless, Saxonia, Tate, Tim, and Unitas. A handheld stepped drum machine, developed by the Swiss entrepreneur Curt Hertstark, sold well after World War II.

During the 1870s, Witgold Odhner, a Swede living in Russia, and Frank S. Baldwin of St. Louis and later Philadelphia both introduced pinwheel calculating machines. The wheels on these machines had retractable pins. Setting a digit by a lever or key caused that number of pins to protrude from the edge of the wheel. Pinwheel calculating machines proved compact

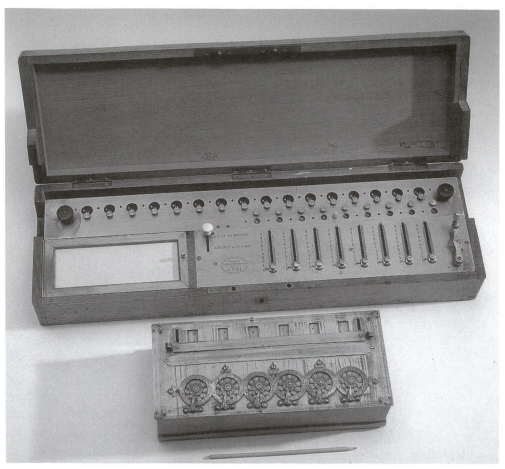

Two calculating machines: (rear) arithmometer, by Thomas de Colmar, late nineteenth century; (front) replica of Blaise Pascal's adding machine. SM 1926-192, 1967-69. Courtesy of SSPL.

and relatively durable. Models included the Odhner from Russia and then Sweden, Brunsviga from Germany, and such later examples as the Britannic, Lusid, Dactyle, Marchant, and Muldivo.

On early adding and calculating machines, numbers were generally set by rotating a wheel with a stylus or moving a lever. D.D. Parmalee obtained an American patent for a key-driven adding machine in 1850; and the Swiss clockmaker Victor Schilt exhibited a key-driven machine with ten keys at the Great Exhibition in London in 1851. Such devices did not become practical products, however, until Dorr E. Felt of Chicago patented a key-driven adding machine in 1887. Felt's Comptometer had eight or more columns of keys, with one column for each digit of a number. This "full-keyboard" was widely adopted in many twentieth-century machines. William S. Burroughs, for instance,

introduced a full-keyboard adding machine on which numbers were set on keys and then entered by rotating a crank. Burroughs adding machines printed the results of computations; it was, in the language of the day, a "listing" adding machine. This feature greatly interested banks and other customers wishing to have a written record of transactions. Reliable Burroughs machines were sold by the American Arithmometer Co. of St. Louis, Missouri, from 1895; this firm later moved to Detroit, Michigan, and became the Burroughs Adding Machine Co.

None of the machines mentioned thus far could multiply two numbers together directly— on early calculating machines one set up the multiplicand, added it as many times as the first digit of the multiplier, shifted the carriage, and again added repeatedly. A machine allowing for direct multiplication was developed by Léon

Bollée in France between 1888 and 1892, but never manufactured as a successful product. In 1895, O. Steiger patented a machine that did make it possible to multiply directly. This hefty instrument, manufactured by Hans W. Egli of Zurich under the name Millionaire, was used particularly by actuaries and astronomers, who multiplied extensively. A second machine of this type, designed especially for bookkeepers, was invented by Hubert Hopkins in 1903, and sold as the Burroughs Moon-Hopkins.

The introduction of these full-keyboard adding machines did not preclude development of devices with nine or ten keys like that of Schilt. James L. Dalton of Poplar Bluff, Missouri, and then Cincinnati, Ohio, began manufacturing Dalton adding machines at the turn of the century. In 1927, the Dalton Adding Machine Co. merged with Remington Typewriter and Rand Kardex Bureau to form Remington Rand. Ten-key adding machines remained among the new company's products for decades. Other ten-key adding machines included the British Summit, the German Rheinmetall, and one form of the American Victor. In the 1950s, companies such as the Italian firm of Olivetti began to manufacture ten-key machines that could multiply and divide directly. The use of keys on a calculator keyboard continued through the 1970s, even as calculating machines were replaced by handheld and desktop electronic calculators.

The development of several other digital computing devices is linked to that of calculating machines. From the 1820s, the Englishman Charles Babbage experimented with a difference engine, a machine intended to compute successive values of a function from its power series expansion. Babbage never completed his engine, although difference engines were built by the Swedes Georg and Edvard Scheutz and the American George Grant. In the late 1870s, James and John Ritty of Dayton, Ohio, patented a machine for keeping track of the cash received in a business—that is to say, a cash register. Their patents were the basis of the National Cash Register Co., founded in 1884. NCR, Remington Rand, and Underwood Sunstrand would also manufacture machines that, like the Moon-Hopkins, combined typewriters and one or more adding units to form bookkeeping machines. Finally, in 1890, Hermann Hollerith began supplying the U.S. Census Bureau with machines for tallying census data, punched on cards. Improved tabulat-

ing equipment, as sold by the descendant of Hollerith's firm, International Business Machines, would prove of considerable use in dynamical astronomy in the 1930s and 1940s.

In the 1920s, an analog device known as the **differential analyzer**, introduced by Vannevar Bush of the Massachusetts Institute of Technology, proved more rapid in solving complex mathematical equations than calculating machines. Differential analyzers, in turn, gave way to electromechanical and electronic **computers** at mid century. Calculating machine manufacture continued throughout the 1950s and 1960s, with some competition late in this period from transistorized desktop electronic calculators. The introduction of microchips and inexpensive desktop and electronic calculators in the 1970s signaled the end of the calculating machine era.

Peggy Aldrich Kidwell

Bibliography

Cortada, James. *Before the Computer: IBM, NCR, Burroughs, and Remington Rand and the Industry They Created, 1865–1956.* Princeton: Princeton University Press, 1993.

Kidwell, Peggy A., and Paul E. Ceruzzi. *Landmarks in Digital Computing: A Smithsonian Pictorial History.* Washington, D.C.: Smithsonian Institution Press, 1994.

Martin, Ernst. *Die Rechenmaschinen und ihre Entwicklungsgeschichte.* Pappenheim: J. Meyer, 1925. English translation, *The Calculating Machines: Their History and Development,* edited by Peggy A. Kidwell and Michael R. Williams, MIT Press, 1992.

Turck, J.A.V. *Origin of Modern Calculating Machines: A Chronicle of the Evolution of the Principles That Form the Generic Make-up of the Modern Calculating Machine.* Chicago: Western Society of Engineers, 1921.

Williams, Michael R. *A History of Computing Technology.* Englewood Cliffs, N.J.: Prentice-Hall, 1985.

Calorimeter

The word "calorimeter" was coined in 1789 by Antoine Laurent Lavoisier, to refer to the heat-measuring instrument that he and Pierre Simon Laplace had developed. It denoted his belief that

Sectioned diagram of Lavoisier's calorimeter. Lavoisier (1780): Plate 1. Courtesy of SSPL.

heat was a material substance (caloric), and was deployed as part of a campaign to discourage reliance on alternative sorts of heat measurement. The name now refers to instruments that measure heat by thermoelectric effects, by time-dependent temperature difference, and by local temperature difference, as well as those instruments, like that of Lavoisier and Laplace, that measure heat in terms of phase transition. The calorimeter's history thus stands as tribute to an instrument's ability to transcend the theory that it was originally intended to embody and the historically complex issue of relating words to things.

Lavoisier used the name to differentiate the calorimeter from **thermometers**, which measure temperature—the portion of caloric absorbed by a thermometer, Lavoisier argued—but which could not detect the entire quantity of caloric in a given system. To measure the entire quantity of heat released in a given operation, including that which resulted in a body's change of physical state without a rise in temperature, Lavoisier and Laplace designed an instrument that measured heat in terms of melted ice. Johan Carl Wilcke had previously experimented with melting snow as a means of measuring heat, but Lavoisier and Laplace improved on his idea by

encasing their instrument with an insulating compartment and lid filled with crushed ice, which shut the instrument's interior off from external interference. A second chamber, also filled with crushed ice, sat within the outer envelope, surrounding a central basket that housed any substances or animal upon which Lavoisier and Laplace wanted to experiment. At its bottom were a screen, sieve, cone, and tube through which the ice that was melted by experiments conducted in the inner space flowed for collection and final measurement. The machine was approximately 30 cm high and 45 cm in diameter. The cost of the first two calorimeters Lavoisier commissioned was 600 livres.

While the ice calorimeter did measure the release of heat in a way that differed from that of thermometers, Lavoisier and Laplace admitted when they introduced it in their *Memoir on Heat* (1783) that interpretive flexibility was a built-in characteristic of their instrument. What mattered first and foremost, they argued, was its technical superiority to other methods. Particularly, they had in mind the "method of mixture," developed by Joseph Black in the 1750s to 1760s and championed by Adair Crawford in his *Experiments and Observations on Animal Heat* (first edition, 1779). This approach involved taking equal weights or volumes of chemically nonreactive substances, measuring their initial temperatures, and then mixing them. Once uniform temperature was achieved, it was measured again and the reading was translated into a statement of the involved substances' specific heats. Lavoisier and Laplace criticized this approach because it was carried out in an open space, which allowed a sizable quantity of heat to escape measured detection. Further, a state of uniform temperature was extremely difficult to ascertain, and the method was generally useless for investigating combustion and respiration phenomena.

In 1788, Crawford published an account of an experimental apparatus he designed, partially in response to Lavoisier's and Laplace's criticisms. Because he was convinced that animals absorb more heat while breathing at lower temperatures, he thought it imperative to maintain the same temperature inside his instrument as in the surrounding environment. Thus, while it too was composed of three nested compartments, the outer insulating layer of his apparatus contained fine down rather than ice, while the next, inner section contained water. Crawford measured the release of heat from his instrument's innermost chamber by examining whether and to what degree the water rose in temperature. Ironically, while Crawford did not accept the existence of caloric, the instrument he designed to counter Lavoisier's views subsequently became known as a water calorimeter.

While Crawford's criticisms of Lavoisier and Laplace's work stemmed from his support of Priestley's phlogiston theory and his belief that heat did not chemically combine with other substances, the ice calorimeter was criticized for a number of other reasons as well. The calorimeter was extremely delicate, and operable within only a small range of ambient temperatures. As Lavoisier admitted, it was relatively expensive and complicated to work with. Moreover, its readings were known to vary, and so could not be taken as exact. Nonetheless, Lavoisier and Laplace published tables containing data of an incredibly exact nature. Opponents such as Richard Kirwan and William Nicholson criticized Lavoisier, not only for his questionable show of accuracy, but more fundamentally for trying to use empirical precision as an argument for the truth of his theoretical belief in caloric and its role in the "new" chemistry.

Josiah Wedgwood was concerned that some water remained trapped in the crushed ice as it melted in the inner compartment, thereby keeping the calorimeter from providing an accurate reading. This critique was widely repeated and led some to prefer water calorimeters and others to modify the ice calorimeter itself. The most successful redesign was by Robert Bunsen, first described by him in 1870.

At the center of Bunsen's calorimeter was a small glass tube filled with water at 0°C. in which between 0.3 and 4.0 grams of a hot substance could be placed. The tube was fused inside a larger glass vessel that was filled with air-free water frozen over mercury. This vessel was then surrounded by an external jacket containing an ice-water mixture in which a capillary tube was placed. When heat was released or absorbed in the innermost tube, the surrounding ice melted or froze, giving rise to a change in volume that was marked by the movement of mercury up or down the capillary tube. It was this calibrated motion that provided a measure of heat. Because of the instrument's structure, heat could not escape by convection from the enveloping ice water to the surroundings. Nonetheless, Bunsen's ice calorimeter was a temperamental instrument whose use required taking a number of precautions.

Because of operational difficulties, calorimeters were not widely used in the first half of the twentieth century. Today, however, a number of reliable and easy-to-operate calorimeters are available, and calorimetry has become a widespread practice. Some of these modern calorimeters rely on traditional mercury thermometers, while others employ electron beams and thermocouples. What these instruments all share is their use in the analysis of heat fluxes and specific capacities, and their vast distance from debates about the existence of caloric.

Lissa Roberts

Bibliography

Bunsen, Robert. "Calorimetric Researches. I. The Ice Calorimeter." Translated by F. Jones. *Philosophical Magazine* 41 (1871): 161–82. First published as "Calorimetrische Untersuchungen. I. Das Eiscalorimeter." *Annalen der Physik und Chemie* 141 (1870): 1–31.

Lavoisier, Antoine Laurent, and Pierre Simon Laplace. "Mémoire sur la chaleur." *Mémoires de l'Academie des Sciences* 1780 (1783), 355–408. Translated by

Henry Guerlac as *Memoir on Heat*. New York: Neale Watson, 1982.

Lodwig, T.H. and William A. Smeaton. "The Ice Calorimeter of Lavoisier and Laplace and Some of Its Critics." *Annals of Science* 31 (1974): 1–18.

Roberts, Lissa. "A Word and the World: The Significance of Naming the Calorimeter." *Isis* 82 (1991): 198–222.

Calorimeter, Animal

Antoine Lavoisier used his ice **calorimeter** to show that animal metabolism is a slow combustion that can be measured as accurately as the combustion of carbon. Since then, a number of techniques have been developed to measure the "sensible" heat loss of man and animals (by radiation, convection, conduction) and the evaporative heat that together make up the total heat loss.

Direct calorimetry is complex and expensive, and thus is not used as often as other methods, but it has been the source of much exact and now classic work on energy metabolism. Using both direct and indirect methods, Max Rubner, professor of hygiene at Berlin, determined the physiological fuel values of carbohydrates, fat, and protein in the diet; showed the importance of surface area as a determinant of metabolic rate; and described the role of chemical and physical factors in body temperature homeostasis. Wilbur Atwater, a professor of chemistry at Wesleyan University in Middletown, Connecticut, from 1873 and, briefly, Chief of the Office of Experiment Stations of the U.S. Department of Agriculture, and his school established that human metabolism is precisely measurable and obeys physical laws, thus leaving no room for "vital forces." They also validated the use of indirect calorimetry. Atwater's pupils (Henry Armsby, Francis Benedict, Graham Lusk, Raymond Swift), Americans with interests in nutrition, established the principles of energy metabolism in animal nutrition. Theodor Benzinger used his gradient layer calorimeter to demonstrate the role of central and peripheral receptors in human temperature regulation.

Four types of apparatus are recognized: heat sink, gradient layer, convection, and differential.

Heat Sink Methods (Adiabatic Calorimeters)

The sensible heat is absorbed by a current of water while the animal chamber is kept at a constant temperature with no heat loss through the surrounding walls. Despite later advances in instrumentation, the calorimeter completed in 1899 by Atwater and his colleague Edward Rosa, professor of physics at Wesleyan University, still stands as the classic example of this type of apparatus. It was a double-walled metal box, the inner wall of copper, the outer of zinc, large enough to allow a man complete freedom of movement and to perform measured work on a bicycle ergometer. The chamber was surrounded by three wooden walls enclosing air spaces. The inner and the outer space contained circulating air at a constant temperature so that there was no exchange of heat across the insulating middle layer of static air. Inside the chamber a water-cooled heat exchanger with metal fins absorbed heat emanating from the subject. The temperature of the water, its rate of flow, and the position of the exchanger could all be adjusted to ensure that a constant room temperature was maintained. Fresh air for ventilation was cooled to remove moisture, then rewarmed before entering the chamber; on leaving it was cooled again and the amount of condensate measured for the calculation of evaporative heat loss. A sample of air was passed through CO_2 absorbers to estimate heat production indirectly. Later a closed circuit system was used to remove CO_2 and water and to admit oxygen. The temperatures of the copper and zinc walls were closely monitored by means of an array of 304 thermocouples that could measure differences of 0.007° C. Calibration tests with burning alcohol showed that an accuracy of 0.2 percent could be achieved. The heat sink principle has been developed in a portable form by Paul Webb, a contemporary American physician, with his human suit calorimeter. Underlying an insulated outer garment is a network of water tubing that carries away body heat. The evaporative heat loss from the skin cannot be measured, which therefore restricts its use to nonsweating conditions.

Gradient Layer Methods

Heat loss through the internal wall is proportional to the temperature gradient across it when precautions are taken to ensure that its outer surface is kept at a constant temperature. This principle was used by Jacques Arsène d'Arsonval, a French physiologist who worked briefly in Claude Bernard's laboratory, and by Max Rubner, who measured changes of pressure or volume of the air in the gap between the inner and outer walls of the chamber as a response to

The large animal gradient layer calorimeter at the Hannah Research Institute, Ayr. Courtesy of John A. McLean.

the heat evolved by the enclosed animal. These changes could be transformed into the sensible heat loss after calibration with burning alcohol. Later workers constructed a more uniformly insulated wall and the temperature gradient across it was measured with thermocouples. The technique was brought to a high level of perfection by Theodor Benzinger and Charlotte Kitzinger, physiologists at the Institute of Naval Medicine, who used several thousand thermocouples to obtain a true mean value for the gradient across the whole of the chamber, which could accommodate an adult man. The inner wall was constructed from uniform sheets of a poorly conducting material, an epoxy resin, around which were entwined continuous strips of alternating copper and constantan in such a way that thermocouples were situated alternately on the inner and outer surfaces. The couples were joined in series and produced a single, additive EMF representing the mean temperature gradient across the walls of the entire chamber. The temperature of the outer surface of the gradient layer was held constant by water circulating through pipes brazed onto the outer surface. Later models had an air conditioned space between the

gradient layer and the external wall. The gradient therefore depended upon the temperature of the inner surface exposed to the heat emanating from the subject. Evaporative heat loss was measured by two smaller gradient layers, one at the inlet for saturated air rewarmed to the chamber temperature and one at the outlet for the air, which was cooled to the dew point (the temperature of the air entering the chamber) so that the extra water contributed by the subject condensed and gave up its latent heat. A small number of gradient layer calorimeters have been built around the world and they have also been manufactured commercially in a number of sizes. The suit calorimeter has also been adapted to the gradient layer principle by the use of a network of resistance thermometers on both sides of the inner layer instead of the water cooling.

Convection Methods

The sensible heat of the animal is used only to raise the temperature of the surrounding air, there being no other avenue of heat loss. This method was used by Rubner and others in the nineteenth century, but satisfactory results were not achieved until the advent of very sensitive instruments for measuring air flow, temperature, and humidity. Since all the animal heat has to be transferred to the circulating air, it is essential that the chamber walls be kept at a constant temperature. In one modern installation the chamber air is recirculated on both sides of the inner wall and a radiation screen of polished metal ensures that the walls do not absorb heat from this source.

Differential Methods

The heat loss from the animal chamber is matched by the measured heat production from another source, usually electrical, in an identical chamber. This principle had been used by early workers on the subject including Rubner in his second type of direct calorimeter. An interesting example is that of the Danes Christian Bohr, a physiologist, and Karl Hasselbalch, a biochemist, who constructed a very small calorimeter to hold an incubating hen's egg. Both chambers were of copper connected together by a constantan bridge. The compensation chamber contained an electrical resistance heater that could be adjusted to balance the heat produced by the egg as indicated by the thermocouple connecting the two chambers.

The classic example of this type of calorimeter was described by Adriaan Noyons, professor of physiology at Louvain, Belgium. Two copper cylinders, placed horizontally in an enclosure that provided identical conditions for both, held either the animal or a heating element. The latter could be controlled by a variable resistance and indicating meters to balance the temperature recorded in the animal chamber. In later models the humidity in the compensation chamber could be controlled through a wetted muslin wick, and the evaporative heat lost estimated from the volume and humidity of the ventilating air stream. This type of calorimeter has not been widely used, hardly at all for man and large animals. It is capable of responding very rapidly, for example, to changes in posture.

Alan H. Sykes

Bibliography

Lefevre, Jules. *Chaleur animale et bioenergetique*. Paris: Masson, 1911.

McLean, J.A., and G. Tobin. *Animal and Human Calorimetry*. Cambridge: Cambridge University Press, 1987.

Webb, Paul. *Human Calorimeters*. New York: Praeger, 1985.

Calorimeter, Bomb

A bomb calorimeter measures the heat produced by the reaction of a substance with oxygen or another oxidant. The apparatus has two main parts, the bomb and the **calorimeter** proper. The bomb is a closed metal cylinder with a thick wall, in which the reaction takes place at a pressure of 3.0 MPa (30 atm.). The substance to be reacted is placed in a small cup or crucible inside the bomb, and the bomb is immersed in a cylindrical calorimeter vessel that contains from 2 to 3 liters of water. The calorimeter is separated from a larger water bath or jacket by an air space of about 1 cm. The reaction is initiated by passing an electrical current through a fuse wire in contact with or in proximity to the substance. The energy from the reaction produces a temperature rise in the calorimeter that is measured by a temperature sensor. The mercury **thermometers** of the 1800s were superseded in the 1900s by thermistors, platinum resistance thermometers, or quartz thermometers.

The first bomb calorimeter was made by T. Andrews, an Irish physical chemist, who reported the results of his oxygen combustion measurements in 1848. Oxygen at atmospheric pressure was reacted with liquids and solids in a thin-walled copper cylinder having a volume of 4 dm³. In 1885, M.P.E. Berthelot and P. Vieille, French calorimetrists, described a bomb calorimeter applicable to the combustion of liquids and solids of low volatility. They used oxygen under a pressure of 2.5 MPa and obtained nearly instantaneous and complete combustion for many substances. Berthelot's bomb was lined with platinum to prevent corrosion from acidic vapors and solutions (see figure).

American calorimetrist H.C. Dickinson provided a detailed description of procedures and calculations for measurements in a bomb calorimeter in 1915. He concluded that benzoic acid is the most suitable standard substance for the calibration of bomb calorimeters, and to this day it is used worldwide. Uncertainties as small as 0.01–0.03 percent in the energy of combustion have been common since the 1930s.

Dickinson used a combustion bomb made by K. Kroeker, a German bomb manufacturer. His calorimeter, like that used by Andrews and Berthelot, was a variation of the isoperibol design. That is, the temperature of the calorimeter at the beginning of the reaction is below the temperature of the jacket, and the energy from the reaction brings the final temperature of the

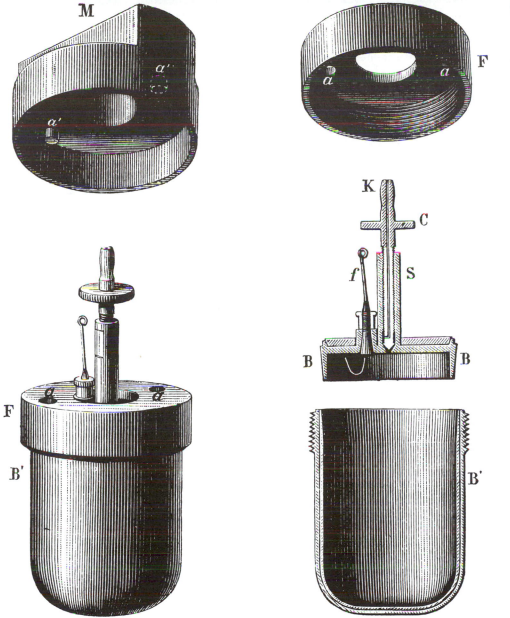

Schematic diagram of a Berthelot bomb. Berthelot and Vieille (1885): 546. Courtesy of Eugene S. Domalski.

calorimeter vessel very close to that of the isothermal jacket. A correction for the stirring energy and heat exchange from the surrounding jacket is accounted for in the calculation of the reaction energy.

E.W. Washburn, an American physical chemist, recommended that every bomb calorimetric experiment be corrected to the internal energy of combustion of the isothermal reaction at 298.15K and 1 atm. for each reactant and product to eliminate unstandardized variables. In 1956, S. Sunner, a Swedish calorimetrist, G. Waddington, and W.N. Hubbard, both American calorimetrists, described the development of the rotating bomb calorimeter for reactions that produce an aqueous solution. The energetics of the final thermodynamic state of this product must correspond to that for a homogeneous solution. Without rotation, the solution is inhomogeneous and its final thermodynamic state is uncertain. Fluorine bomb calorimetry emerged in the late 1950s and early 1960s and is useful in studying compounds not amenable to oxygen bomb calorimetry, such as inorganic fluorides. The reaction of chemical elements with fluorine to form fluorides is particularly advantageous because the enthalpy of reaction and enthalpy of formation are equivalent.

A major driving force behind the development of bomb calorimetry has been the need to determine the calorific content of solid and liquid fuels. Since the early 1980s, similar calorific data have been required for waste materials so that they may be disposed of in an environmentally acceptable manner. In the early 1990s, in the United States, a commercial bomb calorimeter costs between $13,000 and $30,000, excluding accessories.

Eugene S. Domalski

Bibliography

Andrews, T. "On the Heat Disengaged During the Combination of Bodies with Oxygen and Chlorine." *Philosophical Magazine* 32 (1848): 321–39, 426–34.

Berthelot, M.P.E., and P. Vieille. "Nouvelle methode pour mesurer la chaleur de combustion du carbon et des composes organique." *Annales de chimie et de physique* 6 (1885): 546–56. See also Berthelot, M.P.E., *Traité pratique de calorimetrie chimique*. Chapter 8, "Chaleurs de combustion." Paris: Gauthier-Villars, 1905.

Dickinson, H.C. "Combustion Calorimetry and the Heats of Combustion of Cane Sugar, Benzoic Acid, and Naphthalene." *Bulletin of the National Bureau of Standards* 11 (1915): 189–257.

Waddington, G., S. Sunner, and W.N. Hubbard. "Combustion in a Bomb of Organic Sulfur Compounds." In *Experimental Thermochemistry*, edited by F.D. Rossini, chapter 7. New York: Interscience, 1956.

Washburn, E.W. "Standard States for Bomb Calorimetry." *Journal of Research of the National Bureau of Standards* 10 (1933): 525–58.

Camera, Aerial, and Photogrammetry

An aerial camera records photographs from airplanes, satellites, and balloons, and these photographs are often used to produce highly accurate measurements and maps by photogrammetric techniques. These techniques have developed in response to requirements for improved methods of military reconnaissance and topographic mapping.

The French sports balloonist Felix Tournachon ("Nadar") used cameras for aerial observation in 1856. Another Frenchman, Aimé Laussedat, used a glass-plate camera in a tethered balloon in 1858 and made maps from the photographs.

The period from 1860 until the beginning of World War I saw the development of photogrammetric principles by scientists and inventors in Austria (Eduard Dolezal), Germany (Carl Pulfrich), Great Britain (Henry Fourcade), Canada (Edouard G. Deville), and the United States (Cornele B. Adams). Among the first aerial camera designs were those of J. Fairman (1887) of the United States and Theodor Scheimpflug (1906) of Austria. The first recorded photographs taken from an airplane were made in 1909 and are credited to Wilbur Wright of the United States and to M. Meurisse of France.

The use of airplanes for reconnaissance purposes and the gathering of intelligence in World War I led to improved cameras, including the automatic film camera of Oscar Meester (Germany), which was used to obtain strip mosaics of much of France, Belgium, and Russia, and the efficient single-lens aerial camera produced by Zeiss in 1917. James Bagley of the United States developed a three-lens mapping camera that was used by the U.S. Army in World War I, as was the handheld or turret-mounted K-1 Folmer Schwing film camera.

Postwar developments were rapid and widespread. In the United States, aerial cameras for civilian use were produced by Aero Service Corp., Mark Hurd, Abrams Aerial Survey Corp., and Park Aerial Surveys, Inc. On the military front, names such as Fairchild, Folmer-Graflex, Bausch and Lomb, and Chicago Aerial Surveys were prominent. In Europe, George Poivilliers (France), Ermenegildo Santoni (Italy), Heinrich Wild (Switzerland), and Carl Zeiss (Germany) were associated with aerial camera design and manufacture.

The forerunner of modern mapping cameras appeared in the mid to late 1930s. These frame cameras featured a single wide-angle lens of good resolution and correctable distortion (such as the Metrogon, with a focal length of 15 cm) with a between-the-lens shutter mecha-

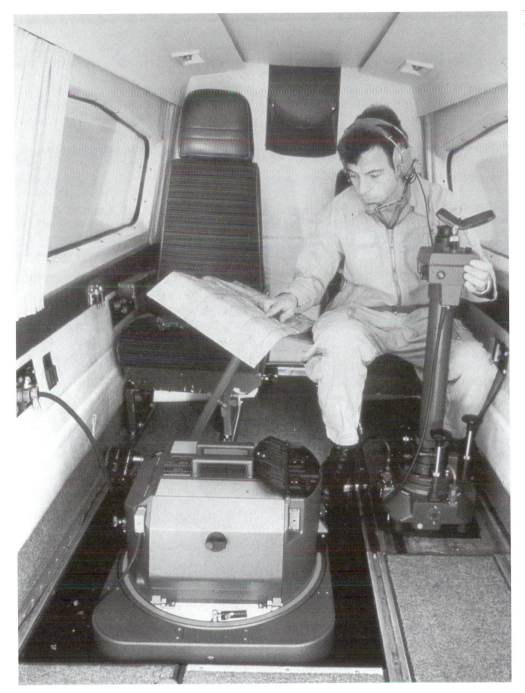

Aerial camera in use, 1995. Courtesy of Leica U.K. Ltd.

nism. Photographs of 18 x 18 cm or 23 x 23 cm format were recorded on roll film contained in a magazine attached to the camera body. These cameras were designed to acquire photographs with overlap in the along-track direction, to allow stereoviewing or mapping the terrain in three dimensions. During World War II, aerial cameras were used to acquire mapping photographs of most of the earth's land surface.

World War II also saw the development of improved reconnaissance cameras. These included frame cameras with lenses having focal lengths up to and beyond 120 cm. The longer focal lengths provided greater magnification and hence improved resolution of military features recorded from aircraft operating at altitudes in excess of 10,000 meters. In order to obtain the fastest possible shutter speeds and thereby minimize image motion to ensure acceptable ground resolution, some of these cameras were equipped with focal plane shutters, rather than the between-the-lens shutter mechanisms used in mapping cameras.

The continuous strip camera was also refined in support of wartime military operations and used for low-altitude, high-speed reconnaissance. A continuous photograph of the terrain was obtained by passing the film over a stationary slit in the focal plane of the lens at a speed synchronized with the velocity of the ground image across the focal plane.

During the Cold War, the military intelligence communities on both sides of the Iron Curtain placed emphasis on developing cameras capable of recording high-resolution photographs of restricted territories from fast-moving, high-altitude aircraft and, after 1960, from earth-orbiting satellites. The primary requirements for such cameras were a long focal-length lens (generally greater than 60 cm), a fast shutter mechanism, a large aperture to admit sufficient light to expose fine-grained, high-resolution films, and a mechanism for image-motion compensation. Efforts in the 1950s by companies such as Fairchild, Itek, Perkin-Elmer, and Vectron in the United States and Williamson Manufacturing Company Ltd. in the U.K. resulted in panoramic cameras that combined high resolution with wide swath width. Because of their narrow angular field of view and sophisticated lens design, panoramic cameras produced resolutions well in excess of 100 lpr/mm. A disadvantage of panoramic photographs was the geometric distortion that occurred outward from the center of the photograph in the cross-track direction. Panoramic cameras were used in military intelligence reconnaissance programs to obtain up-to-date and accurate assessments of the Soviet Union's intercontinental ballistic missile (ICBM) system between 1960 and 1972; in the *Apollo* program, panoramic cameras produced high-resolution photographs of the lunar surface.

Camera design for civilian mapping purposes focused on improving lens quality, reducing radial lens distortion, and increasing resolution, the latter primarily through the efforts of film manufacturers to produce fast, fine-grain black-and-white, color, and color infrared emulsions with resolving powers in excess of 50 lpr/

mm for low-contrast targets. Two European companies emerged as the dominant manufacturers of aerial mapping cameras for the civilian community, Wild-Heerbrugg of Switzerland (later acquired by Leica) and Carl Zeiss of Oberkochen, West Germany. These cameras had excellent "distortion free" lenses with reduced illumination fall-off, as well as improved camera mounts, film metering devices, film flattening prior to exposure, intervalometers (for overlap control), between-the-lens rotary shutter mechanisms, and devices for recording auxiliary information in the margins of the photos. By the mid to late 1980s, many survey cameras also had devices for image motion compensation and automatic exposure control, and survey aircraft were being equipped with **Global Positioning System** (GPS) equipment that enabled the aircraft crew to fly precise flight lines and automatically trip the camera shutter at predefined coordinate locations. With aerial photographs obtained by modern survey cameras and computer-based softcopy photogrammetric techniques, measurements accurate to better than one part in twenty thousand of the flying height can be obtained. Thus, many surveying and mapping tasks previously undertaken by the field surveyor are now handled by photogrammetrists using high-resolution aerial photographs.

Roy Welch

Bibliography

American Society of Photogrammetry. *Manual of Photogrammetry.* 4th ed. Falls Church, Va.: American Society of Photogrammetry, 1980.

Babington-Smith, Constance. *Air Spy. Evidence in Camera: The Story of Photographic Intelligence in World War II.* London: Chatto and Windus, 1957.

Goddard, George W. *Overview: A Life-long Adventure in Aerial Photography.* Garden City, N.Y.: Doubleday, 1969.

McDonald, R.A. "CORONA: Success for Space Reconnaissance, A Look into the Cold War, and a Revolution for Intelligence." *Photogrammetric Engineering and Remote Sensing* 61 (1995): 689–720.

Odle, J.E. "Aspects of Airborne Camera Development from 1945 to 1966." *Photogrammetric Record* 5 (1967): 351–65.

Camera, Gamma
See GAMMA CAMERA

Camera, Photographic

The photographic camera was derived from the portable **camera obscura** used by artists in the eighteenth and early nineteenth centuries. It normally consists of a light-tight box with a lens at one end and a light sensitive film or plate at the other. W.H.F. Talbot's early cameras (ca. 1835–1839) were reputedly built by a carpenter and fitted with a microscope lens. Commercial camera production followed the public announcement of the daguerreotype process in 1839, when L.J.M. Daguerre authorized Alphonse Giroux of Paris to make and sell these instruments. Giroux's camera consisted of a single achromatic lens in a wooden box that slid into another to allow focusing. It took daguerreotype images on a plate of 8 x 6 in., the original whole-plate size from which later plate sizes were derived. Instrument-makers were soon making cameras of this sort. However, some used Wollaston-type achromatic meniscus lenses for landscapes, or doublet lenses of the type pioneered by Joseph Petzval for portrait photography.

Rigid sliding-box cameras remained popular throughout the nineteenth century and into the twentieth, but portable cameras with hinged sides that collapsed inward and bellows cameras that collapsed longitudinally were also known. The first popular bellows cameras were produced to an American design patented by J.J., W., and W.H. Lewis in 1851. One of the most influential bellows designs in Britain was that introduced in 1857 by a Scottish photographer, C.G.H. Kinnear.

Because of the long exposure times required, early cameras were usually mounted on a tripod or stand. No shutters were required, and the ground glass focusing screen made viewfinders or **rangefinders** unnecessary. Typically, sensitive silver salts in a suitable carrying medium were coated onto individual plates that were loaded into the camera in a simple plate-holder prior to each exposure. More sensitive commercially manufactured dry plates were introduced in the 1870s, and roll film soon after. As the film became faster, handheld cameras with shutters and viewfinders began to be mass produced. The introduction of new optical glasses by Abbe and Schott in 1888 allowed for the production of lenses corrected for astigmatism and having a reasonably flat field. The first anastigmatic lenses appeared in the 1890s.

The trend toward smaller cameras led to a fashion for disguised or concealed (detective) cameras. Many were novelties of limited practical use, but experience in manufacturing these models led to improved production techniques and useful experience in handling new materials. The most influential detective camera was the original Kodak of 1888, the first of many popular roll film cameras that was to bring millions of amateurs to photography. The Kodak was supplied loaded with film adequate for one hundred exposures, and when all were exposed the customer returned the camera to the factory for development and printing.

Motion picture photography began, in large part, with the efforts of scientists to study animal and human motion. In 1878, using batteries of plate cameras fitted with electromagnetic shutters, Eadweard Muybridge produced animated sequences of animal motion. In 1882 Etienne-Jules Marey recorded bird flight with a gun camera that derived from one designed by the astronomer Pierre-Jules-Cesar Janssen and that incorporated a clockwork motor that rotated a circular plate by means of a maltese cross mechanism. Marey later developed a plate camera with a rotating disk shutter. His film camera (1888–1890) was the first instrument to employ all the essential elements of the motion picture camera.

The increasing refinement of sensitized materials and the widespread availability of 35mm film after 1896 accelerated the trend toward smaller cameras. The 35mm Leica designed by Oskar Barnack in 1913, and introduced to the market in 1925, was the first successful precision-manufactured miniature camera with high-quality lenses, and it has influenced camera design up to the present day.

Subsequent innovations include interchangeable lenses, the pentaprism reflex, and the 35mm single lens reflex (SLR), which can make fine focus adjustments of a moving object up to the moment of exposure. Commercial SLRs began to be mass marketed around 1900, but they were heavy and bulky. The first true 35mm SLR camera was the Ihagee Kine Exakta of 1936. With through-the-lens metering, automatic focusing, and other electronic features, modern cameras now take over many of the functions previously left to the judgment of the photographer.

The twin lens reflex camera is essentially two identical box cameras, one mounted above the other, linked by a common focusing mechanism. The upper box acts as a viewfinder. These

Leica I (model A) 35mm camera, by Ernst Leitz, introduced in 1925. Courtesy of SSPL.

were introduced around the same time as the SLR and were initially more popular, but they too were bulky and soon fell from favor. The introduction of the compact, precision-constructed Rolleiflex camera in 1928 led to a revival of interest, and twin lens reflex cameras remained popular with press photographers until the 1960s.

The camera has become one of the most useful recording instruments of modern science. Camera bodies have been attached to optical instruments such as **microscopes, telescopes,** and **polariscopes** since the earliest days of photography. **Aerial cameras** survey the earth from both aircraft and spacecraft.

Specialized cameras are used to record phenomena that are too fast or too slow to be appreciated by the human eye. Talbot took a high-speed photograph in 1851 using a conventional camera illuminated by a 1/100,000th of a second spark from a battery of **Leyden jars.** Similar techniques were used by Ernst Mach and P. Salcher (1885) and C.V. Boys (1892) to photograph bullets in flight. In 1903, Lucien G. Bull designed a rotating-drum spark camera that took fifty-four stereoscopic images at rates of up to two thousand a second; this was used to analyze the wing-beats of insects. Modern high-speed cameras are much faster. The camera built to record the beginnings of the fire ball of

the first British atomic explosion (1952) was a rotating mirror camera taking eighty images at a rate of half a million a second.

John Ward

Bibliography
Coe, Brian. *Cameras.* London: Marshall Cavendish, 1978.

The Focal Encyclopedia of Photography. Rev. ed. London: Focal, 1965.

Gernsheim, Helmut, and Alison Gernsheim. *The History of Photography from the Camera Obscura to the Beginning of the Modern Era.* London: Thames and Hudson, 1969.

Hicks, Roger. *A History of the 35mm Still Camera.* London: Focal, 1984.

Thomas, D.B. *The Science Museum Photography Collection.* London: Her Majesty's Stationery Office, 1969.

Camera Lucida

The camera lucida was devised by William Hyde Wollaston as "An Instrument whereby any person may draw in Perspective, or may Copy or Reduce any Print or Drawing." Wollaston filed an application for a British patent in 1806, and in June of the following year he published articles describing his invention. Within months, instrument-makers such as Dollond and Newman were selling camera lucidas, with appropriate instructions for their use.

Wollaston introduced the term "camera lucida" (literally, room of light) in 1807, perhaps wishing to distinguish his instrument from the **camera obscura**, an artist's aid known for centuries. He may also have been referring in some way to the unrelated "light room" invented by Robert Hooke in 1668. Hooke's term was translated into the Latin as camera lucida in the eighteenth century, and appeared as such in most later dictionaries and works of reference.

Wollaston's camera lucida usually consisted of a four-sided reflecting prism mounted on the end of a supporting arm. When sited above a horizontal sheet of paper, it is possible to see a reflected image of the scene in front. By looking over the edge of the prism, an artist can trace the image onto the paper below. In practice, it is a difficult instrument to master. William Henry Fox Talbot recorded: "For when the eye was removed from the prism—in which all looked beautiful—I found that the faithless pencil had only left traces on the paper melancholy to behold."

Talbot's fruitless attempts to produce satisfactory drawings with the device led him to resume experiments with the camera obscura, and subsequently to the invention of his negative-positive photographic process. Talbot's friend John Herschel, however, was more successful. Indeed, it has been suggested that Herschel did not proceed with his own photographic experiments partly because he was content to record the world around him with pencil sketches produced with the aid of the camera lucida.

The camera lucida was used by many English gentleman travelers during their trips abroad. It was also received enthusiastically in Europe and there were several suggestions for improved instruments. A modified form was described by Professor Ludicke after seeing a German translation of Wollaston's description in 1812. However, the most notable attempt to improve the camera lucida was made by the Italian physicist Giovanni Battista Amici, professor of mathematics at the University of Modena. Amici purchased a camera lucida in Paris in 1815 and published a paper describing his improvements in 1819. The paper, originally published in Italian but translated into French in 1823, was illustrated with diagrams produced by

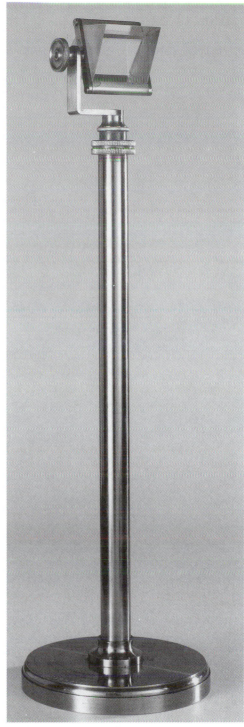

Wollaston camera lucida by Ladd, London, ca. 1872. SM 1876-16. Courtesy of SSPL.

the French instrument-maker N.M.P. Lerebours. Despite Amici's reputation, his modified instrument was not a commercial success, even in

France where the camera lucida was manufactured and sold in large numbers.

As an artist's aid, the camera lucida remained popular until the end of the nineteenth century, when the boom in amateur photography and widespread social change contributed to the decline of sketching as a leisurely pastime. Camera lucidas continued to be manufactured in small numbers well into the present century, primarily as aids for draftsmen producing perspective drawings. Several novelties based on the principle of the camera lucida have also been marketed as children's toys.

John Ward

Bibliography

Gernsheim, Helmut, and Alison Gernsheim. *The History of Photography from the Camera Obscura to the Beginning of the Modern Era.* London: Thames and Hudson, 1969.

Hammond, John, and Jill Austin. *The Camera Lucida in Art and Science.* Bristol: Adam Hilger, 1987.

Schaaf, Larry J. *Tracings of Light: Sir John Herschel and the Camera Lucida: Drawings from the Graham Nash Collection.* San Francisco: Friends of Photography, 1989.

Wollaston, W.H. "Description of the Camera Lucida." *Philosophical Magazine* 27 (1807): 343–47.

———. "An Instrument Whereby Any Person May Draw in Perspective, or May Copy or Reduce Any Print or Drawing." British patent no. 2993.

Camera Obscura

A camera obscura (literally, a dark chamber) is an optical device that forms an image of an external scene on a wall or screen within a darkened room or box. The photographic camera derives directly from the portable camera obscura used by gentlemen artists in the eighteenth and early nineteenth centuries as an aid to sketching.

Chinese texts from as early as the fifth century B.C. record the creation of an inverted image with a pinhole on a screen. The effect was also known to Aristotle, who further noticed that the smaller the hole the sharper the image. The instrument itself was described by the tenth-century Arabic scholar Alhazan. By the sixteenth century it is likely that the camera obscura was widely known and unremarkable to European philosophers, and its invention has been attributed to such diverse personalities as Roger Bacon, Leo Battista Alberti, Leonardo da Vinci and, most consistently, Giovanni Battista della Porta. Porta gave a very detailed description of the instrument in 1558 and was possibly the first to suggest its use as an aid to drawing.

Improvements to the camera obscura were soon forthcoming, such as a converging lens in the small hole, and a diaphragm to sharpen the image. It was also noted that the inverted image could be corrected by means of a mirror placed at an angle of 45° to reflect the view onto a table. Concave mirrors were suggested for the same purpose but the results were unsatisfactory. In his *Ars Magna* (1646), Athanasius Kircher described a portable camera obscura that could be carried like a sedan chair by two men using horizontal bars. One of Kircher's pupils, Gaspar Schott, described a small portable box camera obscura in *Magia Universalis* (1657), and Robert Boyle in 1669 wrote of a similar instrument he had constructed. The first reference to a portable reflex camera obscura was by Johann Christoph Sturm in 1676. In 1685 Johann Zahn illustrated several types of small reflex box cameras that have been described by one authority as prototypes of nineteenth century box and reflex cameras. Almost no further development of the camera took place until the mid nineteenth century.

In the seventeenth century, astronomers such as Johann Hevelius and Johann Kepler used room-sized camera obscuras to study the sun, and philosopher magicians and charlatans used them to produce optical illusions and "magical" effects. Artists used portable instruments as a guide to form and perspective. The camera obscura became immensely popular in the eighteenth century and descriptions of it are to be found in most encyclopedias and works on optics, painting, and popular entertainment. Portable models formed an essential part of the luggage of every traveler with artistic pretensions.

Thomas Wedgwood made the first photographic experiments with a camera obscura in 1799. Wedgwood was unsuccessful, but it is no accident that Nicephore Niepce, Louis Jacques Mande Daguerre, and William Henry Fox Talbot were all familiar with the camera obscura before beginning their investigations leading to the first practicable photographic processes. Their first camera pictures were made with in-

Portable "Artist" camera obscura, by Jones, ca. 1790. The screen is missing, revealing the angled mirror below. SM 1918-270. Courtesy of SSPL.

struments almost indistinguishable from the standard camera obscura of the period.

During both world wars, the Royal Air Force used room camera obscuras for observation during bombing practice. A few room camera obscuras survive as tourist attractions, perhaps the most notable being on Castle Hill in Edinburgh and in Douglas, Isle of Man. However, the camera obscura survives today primarily as the ubiquitous photographic camera found in multifarious forms all over the world.

John Ward

Bibliography

"Camera Obscura." In *The Cyclopaedia; or, Universal Dictionary of Arts, Sciences, and Literature,* edited by Abraham Rees, Vol. 6. London: Longman, 1819.

Gernsheim, Helmut, and Alison Gernsheim. *The History of Photography from the Camera Obscura to the Beginning of the Modern Era.* London: Thames and Hudson, 1969.

Hammond, John H. *The Camera Obscura: A Chronicle.* Bristol: Hilger, 1981.

Capacitance Bridge

The principle of the capacitance bridge followed from that of the **Wheatstone bridge**, which was used to derive an unknown value of resistance from the known values of resistances. The demand for exact measurement of the capacitance of condensers emerged in the 1860s when condensers began to be widely used in long-distance submarine telegraphy. The first capacitance bridge was devised by C.V. De Sauty of the Eastern Telegraph Company. Here a condenser of unknown capacitance (X) and a condenser of known capacitance (C) are put in the two adjacent branches of a Wheatstone bridge; two resistances (R and S) of known values, in the other two branches, are connected in such a way that R is adjacent to X and S is adjacent to C. A dc **battery** was connected between a point on the middle of the two condensers and one on the middle of the two resistances, and a **galvanometer** circuit was made in diagonal to the battery circuit. When there is no current on the galvanometer, the relation between these two capacitances and resistances is XR = CS, that is, X = CS/R. From the known values of C, S, and R, the value X can thus be derived.

In 1873, William Thomson added a variable resistance to the De Sauty bridge. He also introduced an ingenious way of connecting and breaking several branches of the bridge circuit, which rendered efficient charging and discharging of the condensers possible. J. Gott in 1881 improved Thomson's bridge by connecting one branch of the circuit to the earth (ground). However, De Sauty's, Thomson's, and Gott's bridges had a defect, in that the methods yielded a stable result only when the two capacitances were nearly the same.

James Clerk Maxwell suggested a different kind of capacitance bridge in his *Treatise on Electricity and Magnetism* (1873). Here a condenser of unknown capacitance is put in a branch of the Wheatstone bridge and the other

Capacitance bridge type A-168-A, by Muirhead and Co. Ltd., 1958. SM 1989-960. Courtesy of SSPL.

branches are resistances. A commutator rapidly charges and discharges the condenser. When there is no current on the galvanometer, the capacitance of the condenser can be expressed in terms of the known resistances. Maxwell had used a tuning fork as the commutator, but more stable commutators of revolving type were later devised by R.T. Glazebrook, J.J. Thomson, and J.A. Fleming. In his lectures at Cambridge University in 1878–1879, Maxwell also suggested a capacitance bridge consisting of four condensers in each branch. The method was first practiced by W. Nernst in 1897.

In 1891, Max Wien suggested methods to use alternating current (ac). A telephone or an ac galvanometer was substituted for the ballistic galvanometer that had been used with dc batteries. When an ac source with a telephone was used, however, it was very difficult to obtain a balance. This was because each capacitance branch has its own resistance and reactance components that cause losses. Wien also suggested the series resistance method to overcome this weakness, in which a resistance in series with the known capacitance compensates for the loss in

the unknown condenser. Wien's method was later modified by F.W. Grover (1907), K.W. Wagner, and H. Schering (1920) and became one of the standard capacitance bridge methods that is still being widely used.

Sungook Hong

Bibliography

Campbell, Albert. "Capacity, Electrical, and Its Measurement." In *A Dictionary of Applied Physics,* edited by Richard Glazebrook, Vol. 2, 103–44. London: Macmillan, 1922.

Fleming, J.A. "Prof. Clerk Maxwell Lectures on Electricity taken during the Session 1878–1879." Cambridge University Library, *MS Add* 8083.

Hague, Bernard. *Alternating Current Bridge Methods.* London: Pitman, 1930.

Cathetometer

A cathetometer measures the difference of level between two points. It originated in France in the early years of the nineteenth century, as

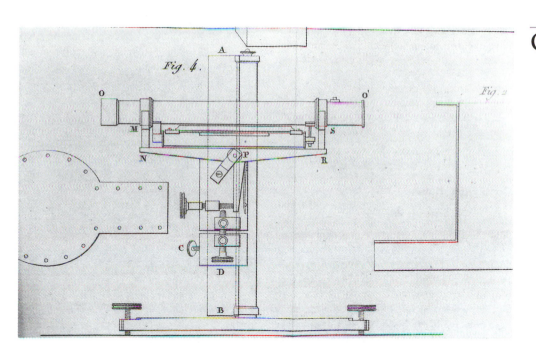

Dulong and Petit's cathetometer. Pierre Louis Dulong and Alexis Thérèse Petit. "Recherches sur la mesure des températures et sur les lois de la communication de la chaleur." Annales de chimie et de physique 7 (1817): Figure 4. *Courtesy of NMAH.*

physics was being transformed from a qualitative science into a rigorous discipline based in large part on precision measurements. As the search for precision intensified, extremely sophisticated cathetometers were developed for several national laboratories, from Washington to St. Petersburg, and educational models were developed for lecture demonstrations or laboratory exercises. In the twentieth century, as the precision enterprise was muscled aside by a growing interest in atomic and nuclear physics, cathetometers were moved from working laboratories into museum collections.

François Arago credited Joseph Louis Gay-Lussac with having invented the cathetometer, in order to determine capillary action under various conditions. Most accounts, however, point to Pierre Louis Dulong and Alexis Thérèse Petit, who used an instrument of this sort in their efforts to determine the absolute dilation of mercury at various temperatures between 0 and 300°C. This investigation brought the two young physicists the 3,000 franc prize offered by the Institute de France; it was widely acclaimed as a model of experimental method, and described in numerous nineteenth-century physics texts. Cathetometers could also be used, as Felix Savart did in the 1830s, to measure the elasticity of wires and the distance between the

nodes as that wire was caused to vibrate. Perhaps the most important advocates of cathetometers, however, were those meteorologists wedded to the ideology of precision, who used cathetometers to measure the height of the mercury column in their **barometers.**

The term "cathetometer" came into use in the mid 1840s; previously these instruments had been described as simply a sort of **micrometer.** In 1857, as the cathetometer was becoming a standard piece of laboratory apparatus, James David Forbes, a professor of natural philosophy in Edinburgh, claimed that it was not a French invention. Rather, it had actually been invented in 1698 by the English botanist Stephen Gray. Forbes was technically correct, but it is unlikely that Gray had influenced the French physicists. Forbes was also correct in regarding the cathetometer as a French instrument. Henri Prudence Gambey, the most prominent precision instrument-maker in post-Napoleonic France, had made Dulong's and Petit's first cathetometer, and he and his successors controlled the cathetometer market until the 1870s when, following the unification of Germany, German makers began to dominate the precision instrument market. By the turn of the century, the leading manufacturer of precision instruments in general, and cathetometers in particular, was the Société

Genevoise pour la Construction d'Instruments de Physique, located in Geneva, Switzerland.

Deborah Jean Warner

Bibliography
Warner, Deborah Jean. "Cathetometers and Precision Measurement: The History of an Upright Ruler." *Rittenhouse* 7 (1993): 65–75.

Centrifuge, Human

A human centrifuge exposes human subjects to increased accelerative forces under controlled conditions for periods extending from several seconds up to many hours. They are used to simulate as closely as is possible in a ground-based machine the accelerative forces to which humans can be exposed during flight in aircraft and in space vehicles. Human centrifuges are used principally to investigate the physiological effects of exposure to increased accelerative forces, to develop and assess methods of enhancing human tolerance of these effects, and to instruct aircrew in the use of protective maneuvers and equipment.

Centrifugation of human subjects was first performed early in the nineteenth century as a treatment for nervous disorders. The best documented of these early machines is that which was in use at La Charité in Berlin between 1814 and 1818. This centrifuge had a diameter of 13 feet and was rotated by a rope and pulley system. The patient was placed along the long axis of the arm where rotating exposed him to either headward or footward acceleration. Numerous similar machines were used to treat mental illness, gas engines replacing manual power toward the end of the century. Later, captive flying machines in which members of the public sat in "boats" suspended by radial wires from a central vertical mast that was then rotated became popular at fun fairs. Indeed, the first recorded instance of acceleration-induced loss of consciousness (GLOC) occurred in England in 1903 when A.P. Thurston was exposed to an accelerative force of 6.87 times gravity during trials of the Captive Flying Machine. This machine, built by Hiram Maxim, a British inventor and aviation buff, later operated at the Crystal Palace park in South London for some forty years.

The first modern human centrifuges were constructed in 1935 by Harry G. Armstrong and J.W. Heim at Wright Field in the United States, and by H. and B. von Diringshofen in

The human centrifuge installed in 1955 at the Royal Air Force Institute of Aviation Medicine, Farnborough. Courtesy of the Royal Air Force School of Aviation Medicine.

Berlin. The lengths of the arms of these first two machines were 2.6 and 4.2 meters, respectively, and they could produce centrifugal accelerations up to 20 g.

World War II saw the construction of human centrifuges in several countries including Canada (Toronto, 1941), the United States (Mayo Clinic, 1942; Wright Field, 1943; University of Southern California, 1944; and Pensacola, 1945), Japan (Tachikawa, 1942), and Australia (Sydney, 1942). A further group of human centrifuges were built in France (1956), Sweden (1954), the United Kingdom (1954), and the United States (1950–1962). These machines typically had an arm length of 2.6 to 3.9 meters, were capable of a maximum acceleration of 15 to 20 g, and had a rate of onset of acceleration of 0.5 to 2 g sec^{-1}. They were used extensively for aeromedical research and development.

A human centrifuge consists essentially of a structure comprising an arm that is rotated in the horizontal plane about a fixed vertical axis by a powered drive mechanism, generally an electric motor. The gondola that contains the human subject is mounted at the end of the arm. The subject is usually supported in a seat or on a couch that is mounted in an orientation that results in the accelerative force being applied along the desired axis of the body: (g_z longitudinal, g_x transverse, and g_y lateral). The gondola is usually mounted in bearings so that it is free to rotate around its longitudinal (fore and aft) axis—that is, in roll—so that it aligns with the vector sum of the radial acceleration produced by the rotation of the arm and earth's gravitational field. Some machines incorporate active control of the alignment of the gondola, which requires a gimbal suspension and drive motors. Active control in the pitch axis reduces the disorientation that is normally experienced during changes in the angular velocity of the arm of the centrifuge.

The advent of fighter aircraft capable of sustaining 7 to 9 g with onset rates of 10 to 15 g sec^{-1} in the mid 1970s and the subsequent incidence of GLOC resulting in fatal aircraft accidents led to a resurgence in acceleration research and the need for human centrifuges with a higher performance. The 1980s saw the acceptance of the need for the training of fighter aircrew in g-protective maneuvers and equipment in human centrifuges.

Several countries have installed or are planning to install new centrifuges or to update their existing centrifuges so that the g high-onset rates of modern fighter aircraft can be reproduced either for research or for training aircrew. The performance of these machines is typically a maximum 15 to 20 g, with maximum onset rates between 3.5 and 6.0 g sec^{-1} for training and up to 10 to 12 g sec^{-1} for research. The centrifuges employed for research are extensively equipped with physiological and human performance monitoring and recording equipment.

John Ernsting

Bibliography

AGARD, *High G Physiological Protection Training AGARDograph no: 322.* Advisory Group for Aerospace Research and Development. Neuilly sur Seine, France, 1990.

Howard, Peter. "Introduction to Accelerations." In *A Textbook of Aviation Physiology,* edited by J.A. Gillies, 517–50. Oxford: Pergamon, 1965.

White, William Joseph. *A History of the Centrifuge in Aerospace Medicine.* Santa Monica, Calif.: Biotechnology Branch, Douglas Aircraft, 1964.

Centrifuge, Ultra-

As a scientific instrument, the ultracentrifuge is currently used primarily in biochemical research to sediment substances from a solution. A rotor with containers holding the solution is spun at high speeds, causing the solute to move toward the periphery of the container under the influence of the generated gravitational fields. Historically, however, ultracentrifuges were developed for analytical purposes to determine the size of colloidal particles.

In the early years of the twentieth century, the noted Swedish chemist Theodor Svedberg was interested in determining the particle sizes of colloids in solution. One of the methods he used exploited the phenomenon that these particles gradually separate from the solvent under the influence of gravity. The speed with which this occurred gave information on the size of the particles. In an attempt to achieve greater accuracy, he modified gravity, one of the constants of his method. To do so he used high-speed centrifuges, and was eventually able to subject the colloid particles to forces up to 5,000 g (five thousand times the force of gravity). In analogy with the more common methods of ultrafiltration and the ultramicroscope, he called his apparatus an ultracentrifuge.

Svedberg used the new apparatus to determine the sizes of inorganic and organic colloids. He expected that protein particles, like inorganic colloids, would be characterized by a wide distribution of particle sizes. However, when he analyzed hemoglobin, it seemed as if all particles had the same size. This might imply that this protein would be a well-defined molecule, a conclusion that ran counter to the ideas of most of his contemporaries. To be sure, however, further analyses would be needed, using fields of the order of 100,000 g.

This twentyfold improvement was not easy to achieve, but after investing huge sums of money and conquering a variety of problems, he succeeded in developing a suitable instrument. The rotor was driven by oil-turbines that facilitated lubrication of the bearings. The rotor spun in a hydrogen atmosphere that conducted away the heat generated in the bearings but did not overheat the rotor. The substance to be analyzed was put in a so-called sedimentation cell, and the sedimentation of the particles under influence of the gravitational forces could be registered by illuminating the process with a special light source and taking photographs at regular intervals. Some hours of calculation were needed to deduce the particle sizes from these photographs.

On the basis of experiments with this new ultracentrifuge, Svedberg concluded that hemoglobin is indeed a monodisperse protein. After this surprising result, research at his

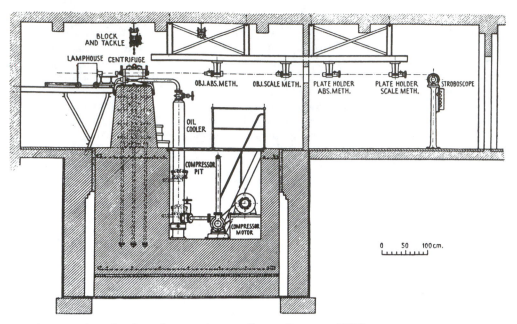

Side elevation of an oil turbine ultracentrifuge installation. Courtesy of SSPL.

laboratory became almost exclusively focused on proteins.

In 1926 Svedberg was awarded the Nobel Prize in chemistry. This increased his reputation even further, and enabled him to attract funds for further research. A large portion were used to further develop ultracentrifuges, especially to increase the forces that could be generated. Almost every part of the apparatus was optimized, such as the shape of the turbines and turbine chambers, oil inlets, bearings, the type of oil used, the balancing of the rotor, and rotor size.

In 1937 Svedberg concluded that, after more than a decade of development, further improvement was no longer possible. He kept using his latest ultracentrifuge, which could generate 400,000 g, until his retirement in 1949, after which the protein research was continued by his former colleagues. It was not until the mid 1970s, half a century after the first apparatus was developed, that the oil-turbine ultracentrifuge was taken out of use.

Another Line of Development
The American optical physicist Jesse Wakefield Beams developed rapidly rotating mirrors that were mounted on small, conically shaped spinning tops (of the order of 1–2 cm in diameter) driven by compressed air. After 1930 he started to make these tops hollow, thus creating small

centrifuges. Because of their high speeds, Beams called them ultracentrifuges. He identified a wide variety of applications for the apparatus, including Svedberg's method of determining molecular weights.

Edward Greydon Pickels, one of Beams's students, developed the apparatus further. This appeared quite problematic because the high speeds heated the rotor, thus causing convection currents in the sedimenting solution. By 1935 Pickels had designed an instrument in which the rotor proper spun in vacuum. A small wire, which passed through a vacuum-tight gland, connected the rotor to the driving air-turbine. This appeared to solve all convection problems, making possible forces up to 1 million g.

This ultracentrifuge attracted the attention of scientists at the Rockefeller Institute for Medical Research in New York, and they hired Pickels to develop the apparatus further for them. He developed two different concepts. His analytical ultracentrifuge could be used to determine particle sizes, analogous to Svedberg's method. His preparative ultracentrifuge was used to separate a substance from a solvent and was used primarily for concentrating viruses.

Distribution
Beams designed his apparatus to be as simple as possible, and through the work of his instrument-makers, his ultracentrifuges

achieved a limited distribution in the scientific world. Around 1937 his vacuum ultracentrifuge was marketed by an American company, which, however, became a commercial failure.

Svedberg was also prepared to sell ultracentrifuges made by his instrument-makers, but the apparatus was extremely expensive, on the order of $20,000. It was marketed by a Stockholm company in the early 1940s, but it too became a commercial failure.

In 1946 Pickels was approached by a California salesman interested in marketing an ultracentrifuge based on Pickels's design. Together they formed Spinco (Specialized Instruments Corp.). Because Pickels considered his design too complicated, he developed a more easily operable, "fool-proof" version. Sales, however, remained low, and Spinco almost went bankrupt.

Pickels subsequently concentrated on developing the preparative ultracentrifuge for the market. The success of this product gave Spinco sufficient financial power to continue production of the analytical ultracentrifuge as well, although in small numbers. Over the years, that number gradually rose.

The scientists who used ultracentrifuges for biochemical research formed a community, with organizing symposia and conferences at regular intervals. The expansion of this community, with more scientists articulating their own approaches and interests, stimulated further development of the apparatus. A variety of designs were developed, and the ultracentrifuge became a common instrument in many types of biochemical research.

Boelie Elzen

Bibliography

Beams, Jesse Wakefield. "High Speed Centrifuging." *Reviews of Modern Physics* 10 (1938): 245–63.

Elzen, Boelie. "The Failure of a Successful Artifact—The Svedberg Ultracentrifuge." In *Center on the Periphery: Historical Aspects of 20th-Century Swedish Physics*, edited by Svante Lindqvist, 347–77. Canton, Mass.: Science History, 1993.

———. "Scientists and Rotors—The Development of Biochemical Ultracentrifuges." Ph.D. dissertation. University of Twente, Enschede, 1988.

Pickels, Edward Greydon. "High-speed Centrifugation." In *Colloid Chemistry*, edited by J. Alexander, Vol. 5, 411–34. New York: Chemical Catalog, 1944.

Svedberg, Theodor, and Kai O. Pedersen. *The Ultracentrifuge*. Oxford: Clarendon, 1940. New York: Johnson Reprint, 1959.

Chain, Surveyor's

The surveyor's chain, used primarily for making land measurements, was developed by Aaron Rathborne, who mentioned "the making and use of the Decimal Chayne, used only by myself" in his book *The Surveyor* (London, 1616). Rathborne's chain had ten links to the pole (16.5 feet), and each link was marked with ten increments. It soon replaced the traditional wooden poles and rope or cord that surveyors had used to measure horizontal distances.

A more successful version was introduced in 1620 by Edmund Gunter, an English mathematician and astronomer. Gunter's chain lessened the possibility of measuring errors because, unlike Rathborne's, it could be used with either end forward. Despite its clumsiness, it remained the surveyor's standard measuring device until the development of the steel tape in the mid 1800s.

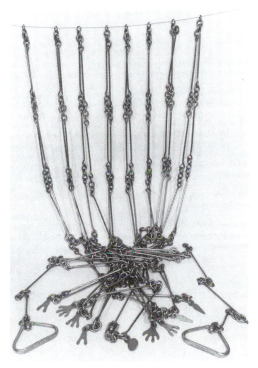

Gunter's chain, 100 links (66 feet), by Baker, mid-nineteenth century. SM 1872-78. Courtesy of SSPL.

Gunter's original chain was 66 feet (four poles) long, and composed of one hundred links, each 7.92 in. in length. A 33-foot (two-pole) version was easier to handle and more commonly used. Each wire link was connected to the others by two rings that were generally oval, sawed, and well-closed. The ends of the wire forming the hook were filed and bent close to the link to prevent kinking. Brass tally markers of various design identified every tenth link. The accuracy of the chain was enhanced by the length adjustment at the handles, which compensated for the lengthening of the chain through use. Chains with brazed links were required for the U.S. public land surveys after 1881.

Chains are known to have been manufactured in England, France, Germany, Sweden, and the United States. There were many variations, and the following descriptions should help in their identification:

Engineer's chain	50 or 100 feet long; 50 or 100 12-in. links
Spanish vara chain	10 or 20 varas long; 50 or 100 links
French meter chain	10 or 20 meters long; 50 or 100 links
Pennsylvania chain	33 or 66 feet long; 40 or 80 links

In 1843, a prominent maker of link chains, J. Chesterman of Sheffield, England, patented a cloth tape reinforced with fine wire. The first American patent for a steel tape was issued to Eddy and Company of Brooklyn in 1867. Chains were quickly replaced by the 100-foot steel tape, and by the turn of the century were rarely used. However, the term "chaining" continues to be used interchangeably with "taping."

David Krehbiel

Bibliography

Rathborne, Aaron. *The Surveyor in Foure Bookes.* Preface, Book 3. London, 1616.

Chamber, Bubble

A bubble chamber records the tracks of elementary particles in a superheated liquid. The chamber holds a liquid under pressure above its boiling point, then suddenly releases the pressure through expansion. A charged particle passing through the chamber further heats the liquid and leaves a line of vapor bubbles in its wake. A photograph of this track of bubbles provides a permanent record of the particle's path.

Donald Glaser, a physicist at the University of Michigan, devised the bubble chamber in 1952 to detect cosmic rays. Most detectors at the time relied, like the bubble chamber, on thermodynamic instabilities. The **cloud chamber** supersaturated a gas by suddenly expanding the chamber volume, and recorded the droplets formed by the passage of ions. The expansion cloud chamber suffered from a slow cycle time; the diffusion cloud chamber solved this problem by providing a continuously sensitive detector. But cloud chambers in general suffered from the paucity of interactions offered by a diffuse gas. Film emulsions used a solid and yielded more interactions, but also constantly recorded tracks and hence complicated the resolution of occurrence times. Glaser's bubble chamber provided a liquid alternative, with sufficient density for numerous interactions and a fast cycle time.

Glaser initially used a glass bulb, 0.75 in. diameter by 1.25 in., filled with liquid diethyl ether. A high-speed camera filmed the first tracks on October 18, 1952. Glaser's results, announced at the meeting of the American Physical Society on May 2, 1953, attracted the attention of **accelerator** physicists. One implication in particular intrigued them: the possibility of a bubble chamber filled with liquid hydrogen. Liquid hydrogen, with its simple nucleus, already served as a target for interaction experiments in accelerators. A hydrogen bubble chamber would combine target and detector in one device.

Glaser collaborated with a group at the University of Chicago in designing a hydrogen bubble chamber for use in the pion beam of the Chicago accelerator. Glaser also used one of his chambers on the Brookhaven Cosmotron. But the first and greatest success with the hydrogen bubble chamber came to the University of California at Berkeley and the group under Luis Alvarez. In late 1953, John Wood of Alvarez's group produced the first tracks in a hydrogen chamber. As important, Wood's chamber, 1.5 in. in diameter, demonstrated that the accidental boiling induced by imperfections at the chamber walls did not impair performance. This discovery made possible the use of "dirty" chambers with metal walls, rather than the smooth and clean glass walls recommended by Glaser. No longer constrained by all-glass vessels, the Berkeley group soon scaled up to chambers of 2.5-in., 4-in., and 10-in. diameters. In

The seventy-two-inch liquid hydrogen bubble chamber at the Lawrence Berkeley Laboratory, 1959. Courtesy of the Lawrence Berkeley National Laboratory.

1955, Alvarez audaciously proposed a 72- x 20- x 15-in. hydrogen bubble chamber, in order to accommodate the greater interaction lengths of hyperons and other strange particles.

The 72-in. chamber, completed in 1959, presented technical problems beyond those originally faced by Glaser. The highly volatile liquid hydrogen required safety precautions and cryogenic expertise; the metal walls had to bear enormous stresses at low temperatures; an intricate optical system illuminated and photographed the interior of the chamber through the single window; the vast numbers of events led to computerized data reduction and analysis. The coordination of the physicists, engineers, and technicians performing these diverse tasks produced an organizational structure more familiar to the corporation than the laboratory.

The Berkeley bubble chamber marked the growing importance accorded the detector in accelerator experiments. It also signaled a decisive shift from the table-top device of Glaser, designed for cosmic-ray physics, to the big science of high-energy physics. The relative cost of the two instruments represents the magnitude of this transition: Glaser built his first bubble chamber for $2,000; the big Berkeley detector came in at $2,100,000.

Bubble chambers also employed heavy liquids, such as propane, xenon, and halogen compounds, as an alternative to hydrogen as a medium. The higher densities of heavy liquids provided more interactions and greater stopping power, and proved particularly effective for the detection of photons, through electron pair production, and neutrinos. The heavy liquid chambers also cost less than hydrogen chambers.

Bubble chambers advanced the field of particle physics. Data from the smaller Berkeley detectors confirmed the Lee-Yang theory of parity violation, for the case of L hyperons; produced a new particle, the X°; and provided evidence of the strange resonances Y*(1385), K*(890), and Y*(1405). These discoveries, along with others produced by bubble chambers at Argonne, Brookhaven, and CERN, supported the SU(3) particle classification. When turned to the study of neutrino interactions, bubble chambers detected weak neutral currents and helped confirm the electroweak theory.

In 1960, Glaser joined the bubble-chamber group at Berkeley. The same year he received the Nobel Prize in physics for his discovery of the instrument. Alvarez won the Nobel Prize in 1968 for the results obtained with the hydrogen bubble chamber. Both Glaser and Alvarez eventually drifted away from experimental nuclear physics, citing disillusionment with the routinization, specialization, and automation that had come to characterize laboratory work, trends that the bubble chamber had helped to bring about.

Peter Westwick

Bibliography

Alvarez, Luis W. *Alvarez: Adventures of a Physicist*. New York: Basic, 1987.

Galison, Peter. "Bubble Chambers and the Experimental Workplace." In *Observation, Experiment, and Hypothesis in Modern Physical Science,* edited by Peter Achinstein and Owen Hannaway, 309–73. Cambridge: MIT Press, 1985.

Glaser, Donald A. "Elementary Particles and Bubble Chambers." In *Les Prix Nobel en 1960,* edited by M.G. Liljestrand, 72–94. Stockholm: Norstedt, 1961.

Heilbron, J.L., Robert W. Seidel, and Bruce R. Wheaton. *Lawrence and His Laboratory: Nuclear Science at Berkeley, 1931–1961*. Berkeley: Lawrence Berkeley Laboratory and Office for History of Science and Technology, University of California, 1981.

Shutt, R.P., ed. *Bubble and Spark Chambers: Principles and Use*. New York: Academic, 1967.

Chamber, Cloud

Invented in the late nineteenth century as a means of producing clouds in the laboratory for the study of meteorological and optical phenomena, the cloud chamber (*see* nepheloscope) has come to be better known in the twentieth as an instrument for making visible and photographing the tracks of ionizing radiations. It played such a central part in the elicitation, detection, and characterization of subatomic particles in physics that Ernest Rutherford described it as "the most original and wonderful instrument in scientific history."

Its origins lie in the attempts of Charles Thomson Rees Wilson to reproduce in the laboratory some of the effects he had seen produced by the sun shining through clouds surrounding the hilltop at Ben Nevis Observatory in 1894. Working in the Cavendish Laboratory at the University of Cambridge, Wilson drew on work by Jean Paul Coulier and John Aitken to construct an apparatus for producing condensation in a closed vessel by the sudden expansion of saturated air. A series of modifications led to the construction of about three serviceable expansion chambers that successfully reproduced natural phenomena.

In 1910, Wilson constructed a new, cylindrical, flat-topped expansion chamber 7.5 cm in diameter in order to explore whether fast-moving ionizing particles could be made "visible" by photographing the droplets of water condensing along their trajectories. He obtained and published the first such photographs in 1911; thereafter the cloud chamber and photography were inextricably linked, as the cloud chamber came to provide compelling visual evidence of the trajectories of individual atoms and electrons and of the encounters and collisions of one atom with another—evidence, moreover, that could be taken away from the chamber itself and analyzed at leisure.

As the potentialities of the method for the study of ionizing radiation became clear, a larger version of the chamber (16.5 cm in diameter and 3.4 cm high) was constructed to allow improved photographs to be taken. This instrument is now housed in the Cavendish Laboratory Museum. In 1913 the Cambridge Scientific Instrument Co. began manufacturing a "Wilson Expansion Apparatus," priced at £20.0.0. About ten instruments were made in 1913, and they were soon in use in several European and North American laboratories. The company also marketed a series of fifteen lantern slides illustrating Wilson's own photographs of particle tracks (price £1-10-0).

The 1910 Wilson apparatus allowed only single expansions to be obtained in a relatively slow and time-consuming operation, and obtaining photographs was somewhat tedious. In 1921, Takeo Shimizu, a student of Rutherford's at the Cavendish Laboratory, designed a cloud chamber with a reciprocating mechanism and variable expansion ratio, capable of fifty to two hundred expansions per minute (T. Shimizu, British patent no. 177,353). Operated by hand or electric motor, the relatively small chamber (5.5 cm in diameter and 1 cm high) was illuminated by a pointolite lamp, allowing photographs to be taken of large numbers of expansions in rapid succession. Stereoscopic photographs could be obtained with motion picture film and a system of mirrors similar to that used in **rangefinders**. A commutator allowed the electrostatic field to be cut off during cloud formation, and rotating lead segments allowed the entry of radiation to be synchronized with the operation of the chamber.

The Cambridge Scientific Instrument Binocular Co. manufactured and marketed this instrument as the "Wilson-Shimizu Ray-Track Apparatus." Stereoscopic cameras were supplied as optional accessories. In 1926, the company introduced a simplified version of the Shimizu instrument, designed for use by schools, colleges, and technical institutes. This employed a fixed expansion ratio and was hand operated, illumination of the chamber being from a metal-filament incandescent lamp. It was mainly for demonstration purposes and was not suitable for photography. Both these devices were widely distributed, over fifty instruments being made between 1922 and 1927. Two of the demonstration models were among the most popular exhibits in the science section of the Festival of Britain Exhibition in 1951.

During the 1920s and 1930s, cloud chambers were among the most important research tools in radioactivity and nuclear physics. For these purposes, custom-built chambers were often used, and experimentalists usually specialized in the use of such instruments. At the Cavendish Laboratory, for example, Patrick Maynard Stuart Blackett, a virtuoso in cloud chamber technique, designed and constructed an apparatus in which the camera shutter was linked to the expansion mechanism, so that photographs of atomic tracks were taken automatically just as the expansion was completed. With this device, capable of producing a pho-

Wilson cloud chamber made by the Cambridge Scientific Instrument Co., 1913. SM 1981-2175. Courtesy of SSPL.

tograph every 13 seconds, Blackett and others obtained a great deal of data concerning atomic and nuclear processes.

From the late 1920s, cloud chambers also began to find use in studies of the penetrating radiations from earth's atmosphere (cosmic rays). They were sent aloft in balloons, sited on high mountains, and taken down deep mines in order to obtain information about the constitution of cosmic radiation at different altitudes. In the early 1930s, an automated cloud chamber was devised by placing two or more **Geiger-Müller counters** above and below the chamber, such that the passage of a particle through the counters triggered the expansion and the camera shutter. Used in conjunction with a strong magnetic field, this arrangement yielded valuable information about subatomic particles, particularly through the creation of "showers" of particles by secondary processes occurring inside the chamber.

During the 1930s, the cloud chamber, surrounded by an increasingly complex ensemble of photographic, electronic, and magnetic apparatus, was central to the discovery of the

C

positron, the mesotron, and other high-energy subatomic particles. It became so deeply constitutive of the practice of nuclear and particle physics that it was, according to Rutherford, "the final court of appeal by which the validity of our explanations can be judged." Chambers gradually became larger, so that by the early 1940s they typically measured between 25 x 25 x 7 and 80 x 60 x 30 cm. High-pressure chambers increased the number of observable interactions, though at the expense of increased time between expansions.

With the development of large particle accelerators in the early 1950s, cloud chambers were unable to keep pace with the rate at which particles could be produced, and were gradually replaced by **bubble chambers**. They remain in use, however, for some applications involving low-energy particles or highly charged heavy fragments that do not have a measurable range in a bubble chamber.

Jeff Hughes

Bibliography

Barron, S.L. C.T.R. *Wilson and the Cloud Chamber.* London: Cambridge Scientific Instrument Co., 1952.

Cattermole, M.J.G., and A.F. Wolfe. *Horace Darwin's Shop. A History of the Cambridge Scientific Instrument Company, 1878–1968.* Bristol: Hilger, 1987.

Galison, Peter, and Alexi Assmus. "Artificial Clouds, Real Particles." In *The Uses of Experiment: Studies in the Natural Sciences,* edited by David Gooding, Trevor Pinch, and Simon Schaffer, 225–74. Cambridge: Cambridge University Press, 1989.

Gentner, Wolfgang, H. Maier-Leibnitz, and W. Bothe. *An Atlas of Typical Expansion Chamber Photographs.* New York: Interscience, 1954.

Henderson, Cyril. *Cloud and Bubble Chambers.* London: Methuen, 1970.

Chamber, Ionization

An ionization chamber generates an electrical current when it is placed in an ionizing radiation field. Its output is intended to be linearly or nearly linearly dependent on the intensity of a radiation field of defined radiation type, particle or photon energy, and direction of incidence. It is also reasonably independent of the particle or photon energy and direction of incidence of those particles or photons over a defined energy range and for a particular quantity of measurement such as, for example, exposure, air kerma, or tissue dose rate.

Its operation is simple in principle. For the measurement of exposure, or its modern analog for x and γ radiation, air kerma, it contains a defined volume of air surrounded by air equivalent materials, that is, materials that have an atomic number close to that of air and thus interact with both the x and γ radiation and the resulting secondary electrons in a manner similar to that of air. The radiation generates positive ions and electrons, which almost immediately attach themselves to oxygen atoms, forming negative ions. These charges are separated by an electric field and the charges of one or other sign are collected, amplified, and displayed in some convenient manner. The currents involved are very small, typically in the range 10^{-15} Å to 10^{-9} Å, and special care must be taken to ensure a very high level of insulation resistance between the collector and other parts of the circuit. The device is essentially simple, and satisfactory examples can be obtained with polystyrene coffee cups rendered conductive with graphite and provided with conventional coaxial connectors.

The history of the ionization chamber is closely tied to the development of radiation dosimetry. Early measurements used **electroscopes**, but in 1908 Paul Villard proposed the use of an ionization chamber connected to an electrometer. The ionization chamber became the principle method of precision measurement and radiation standards, being modified to allow the measurement of radiations of greater or lesser penetrating power. Variations include the free air chamber with unimpeded entrance and exit windows, which is used to measure low energy, and hence relatively nonpenetrating radiations.

Early development concentrated on radium activity and x-ray exposure rates, both of which were important for medical treatment. Some radiologists measured their exposure to radiation with very small ionization chambers worn as finger rings. The use of ionization chambers in medicine is still important.

A typical modern instrument comprises a range of detectors designed for different x, γ energies, and intensities, connected to a preamplifier that converts the dc current to a digital signal that is then further processed by the display unit. Medical measurements are of much higher accuracy than radiation protection measurements, as they normally deal with much more closely defined conditions. Early instruments used precision **ammeters** with mirror scales to display the indication. Digital presentation was introduced around 1977.

Ionization chamber instruments for radiation protection became increasingly important with the development of nuclear weapons, nuclear power, and the increasing industrial and research uses of radiation. Normal applications involve a high-volume chamber of several hundred cm^3, necessary to generate a sufficient current at the low dose rates that are acceptable, connected to an electrometer. Most instruments, up to around 1965, used an electrometer valve as the input amplifier. This was succeeded for a short period by the vibrating reed electrometer, which used a vibrating capacitor as an input element that generated an ac potential depending on the current flowing. This ac signal is much easier to amplify than a dc signal. By about 1975, however, the majority of instruments used a MOSFET transistor as the input element.

Early instruments used a moving coil ammeter to display the amplified current, typically marked from 0 to 5 in increments of 0.1, combined with a range switch giving multipliers of x 1, x 10, x 100, and so on, to cover the desired dose rate or dose range. Modern instruments increasingly use a liquid crystal display often giving both a digital display with a relatively high reading precision and an analog display to indicate trends. Radiation protection measurements are relatively inaccurate, in comparison with medical measurement of radiation, and apparently very high uncertainties of ±25 percent are normally quite acceptable. Radiation fields can also vary rapidly with time and space and, hence, the high reading precision of a digital display is often both unnecessary and in fact disadvantageous, when compared with the ease with which the human eye and brain can deduce an average from a varying analog display. The form of a typical modern instrument has changed little from that of the immediate postwar equipment, but the display has been improved and the batteries reduced from the up to five units, all of which were different and some of which gave up to 30 volts, down to two conventional cells. The battery life is also much higher.

Peter Burgess

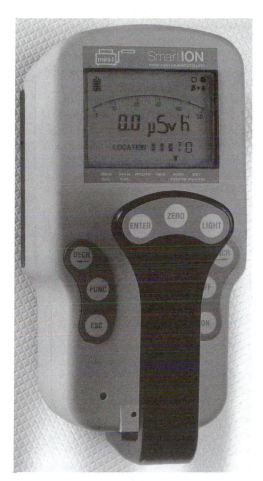

A Smart ION ionizing radiation meter, by Mini Instruments, 1995. Courtesy of Mini Instruments Ltd.

Bibliography

Attix, F.H., W.C. Roesch, and E. Tochlin, eds. *Radiation Dosimetry.* 2nd ed. New York: Academic, 1966.

Charge-Coupled Device

A charge-coupled device (CCD) is an electronic component that stores and manipulates information by controlling the flow of electric charges within itself. It uses semiconductor phenomena to store electric charges and conduct them in discrete bunches. Ordinary electric wire can conduct charge, but CCDs can do more than wire because, by using an external signal to control conduction, they can speed up, slow down, or even halt for a limited period the movement of electric charge. Because the discrete packages of charge conducted by the CCD can represent analog signals or digital information-tion, CCDs have a wide variety of applications in signal processing and computer memories. More important, CCDs are able, because of their chemical composition, to generate their own electrical signals when exposed to light. The combination of photosensitivity and precise control over electrical signals makes CCDs excellent for imaging devices such as cameras and optical scanners.

A CCD passes electrical signals down its length as a bucket brigade conveys water. Throughout the body of the CCD is a regularly spaced series of regions, called potential wells, where electrons naturally collect. The potential wells are separated from one another by insulating barriers. Since the electrons tend to stay in the potential wells, shunning the insulating barriers, they can be made to move down the body of the CCD by simply changing the location of the potential wells. This is done by applying a voltage from an external control signal to very specific areas of the CCD through a series of electrodes that sit atop the device. When an electrode has sufficient voltage, it creates a potential well beneath itself within the CCD. When the voltage on an electrode drops, it returns the region of the CCD underneath to its insulating state. Rippling a voltage change down a row of electrodes causes a wave of insulating barriers to turn temporarily into potential wells, while the potential wells that adjoin them on one side are converted back into insulating barriers. This action squeezes the electrons out of the old potential wells into the new ones while the two are briefly coupled together. By applying voltage in a particular pattern down the row of electrodes atop the CCD, the electrons are marched down the length of the device.

The CCD was invented in 1969 by Bell Labs scientists Willard S. Boyle and George E. Smith. The pair, urged by Bell Labs to create a semiconductor integrated circuit for the storage and manipulation of digital bits that was analogous to magnetic bubble technology, sought to create a device that eschewed the traditional circuit concepts that had evolved during the era of discrete components. Influenced also by the program to develop a silicon diode array camera tube for AT&T's PICTUREPHONE, Boyle and Smith used MOS (metal-oxide semiconductor) technology to fabricate a chip with a 0.1-mm x 0.1-mm array of aluminum electrodes insulated from doped silicon by a thin layer of silicon dioxide. Their prototype was successful. Many colleagues quickly contributed significant improvements, and Boyle and Smith announced

their new device in the spring of 1970. Their suggestion that CCDs might be applied to serial shift registers (to function as computer memory) and imaging devices, reflected the role of magnetic bubbles and silicon diode arrays in inspiring the invention. Other suggested applications included delay lines, logic arrays, and display functions.

The CCD caused an immediate sensation among electron-device engineers. Excited by the potential for high-density memories, simple signal-processing circuits, and rugged solid-state imaging devices, technologists undertook large-scale research and development during the 1970s to adapt CCDs to a wide range of functions. It is in imaging where they achieved their greatest success.

When light is focused on a CCD, the energy from the photons liberates electrons from the semiconductor (usually silicon, but sometimes gallium arsenide) that makes up the device. These fall quickly into nearby potential wells within the CCD and can then be conducted out in an orderly fashion, generating an electrical signal that carries the original optical information. Photons of all visible wavelengths will produce electrons, so CCDs are sensitive to all colors. Imagers made of CCD chips are rugged and reliable. They offer high sensitivity and demand little power. It is easy to pinpoint where on the CCD a particular photon struck, and the device's linear response—the number of electrons produced is proportional to the number of photons falling on the imager—makes measurements of light intensity straightforward. These features, along with the prospect for accelerated development resulting from the high interest in CCDs for other, nonimaging purposes, convinced the American astronomical community—NASA and the Jet Propulsion Laboratory in particular—to throw their support behind developing CCDs as astronomical detectors. Within a decade, CCDs became an important astronomical tool, functioning in space-bound and ground-based observatories. Other significant imaging applications include facsimile machines, photocopiers, video cameras, and machine vision, as well as industrial robots, mail sorters, and bar-code readers.

CCDs have made a less pronounced impact in nonimaging applications. The development of other technologies and persistent production difficulties with CCDs (such as achieving a defect-free semiconductor substrate that could

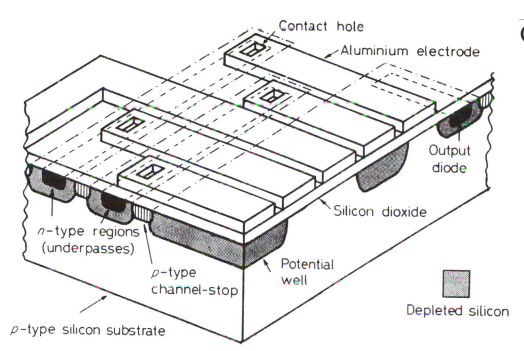

Contact hole
Aluminium electrode
Output diode
Silicon dioxide
n-type regions (underpasses)
p-type channel-stop
Potential well
p-type silicon substrate
Depleted silicon

Section of an aluminium gate CCD. Howes and Morgan (1979): 82, Figure 2.1. Copyright © 1979 John Wiley & Sons Inc. Reprinted by permission.

transfer a very high percentage of charge from well to well) combined in the beginning to limit the number of successful CCD applications. CCD memory chips, handicapped by their inherently serial nature, proved less attractive than RAM chips made by VLSI (Very Large Scale Integration) techniques, which improved dramatically in the 1970s. During that same period, analog signal processing using CCDs suffered from a preference among engineers to convert analog signals and process them digitally. Recent developments, however, including falling prices, point to an important role in the future for CCDs in low-power, high-complexity analog signal processing. Promising avenues include using CCDs for delay lines by briefly storing a signal within the device; for encrypting signals by varying the speed at which portions of them are conducted through a CCD; for analog-to-digital conversion; and for multiplexing and demultiplexing.

Andrew Goldstein

Bibliography

Amelio, Gilbert F. "Charge-Coupled Devices." *Scientific American* 230 (February 1974): 22–31.

Boyle, Willard S., and George Elwood Smith. "The Inception of Charge-Coupled Devices." *IEEE Transactions on Electron Devices* ED-23 (July 1976): 661–63.

Howes, M.J. and D.V. Morgan, eds. *Charge-coupled Devices and Systems.* Chichester, U.K.: Wiley, 1979.

Smith, Robert W., and Joseph N. Tatarewicz. "Replacing a Technology: The Large Space Telescope and CCDs." *Proceedings of the IEEE* 73 (July 1985): 1221–35.

Chemical Polarimeter

See POLARIMETER, CHEMICAL

Chladni Plates

Chladni plates borrow the name of the German scientist and amateur musician Ernst Florens Friedrich Chladni who, in 1787, published his discovery concerning a simple but effective system for visualizing two-dimensional mechanical oscillations. Although a considerable amount of work had been done on the vibrations of strings, organ pipes, rods, and membranes, almost nothing was known about vibrating solid plates. For his researches, Chladni clamped a glass or metallic plate to a wooden pillar, covered the plate with a thin layer of sand, and ran

Chladni plates, Italian, ca. 1850. Courtesy of the Fondazione Scienza e Tecnica, Florence.

a violin bow along its edge. As the plate vibrated, the sand accumulated along the nodal lines where no oscillatory motion occurred. Chladni noticed that the sand patterns depend on the vibration mode of the plates: simple figures generally correspond to low-frequency tones, higher tones generate more complicated figures. The theoretical description of Chladni figures is not yet fully understood. In 1931 it was demonstrated that the sand does not rest exactly along the nodal lines, but rather on curves that approach the nodal lines for oscillations of large amplitude.

Chladni's research had been stimulated by the electric figures discovered in 1777 by Georg Christoph Lichtenberg. By spreading an electroscopic powder (generally a mixture of yellow sulphur and orange lead oxide) on an electrically charged surface, Lichtenberg was able to produce beautiful arborescent patterns, which reproduced the distribution of charges.

Chladni experimented with circular, square, and rectangular plates, and later with more complicated shapes (elliptical, hexagonal, and triangular), eventually describing more than 240 different sand figures. He traveled extensively in Europe, demonstrating his experiments and performing on the musical instruments that he had invented (euphonium and clavicylinder, both

modifications of the glass harmonica) to the leading scientists of his time. Chladni was also able to measure the velocity of sound in gases other than air. His investigations were continued by such physicists as Félix Savart, Michael Faraday, and Lord Rayleigh (John William Strutt).

During the nineteenth century, Chladni plates became a popular demonstration device. They were widely used in acoustics courses, and they were available from Rudolph Koenig and many other instrument-makers. In many instances they were used with the forked tube covered by a membrane, invented by William Hopkins in 1835, to demonstrate the interference that occurs by combining the vibrations of two different sectors of a plate. In recent years, Chladni figures have been used to study the vibration modes of musical instruments such as violins and guitars.

Paolo Brenni

Bibliography

Brenni, Paolo. *Gli Strumenti del Gabinetto di Fisica dell'Istituto Tecnico Toscano, I. Acustica.* Firenze: Provincia di Firenze, 1986.

Chladni, Ernst Florens Friedrich. *Entdeckungen über die Theorie des Klanges.* Leipzig: Weidmanns Erben und Reich, 1787.

Tyndall, John. *Sound: A Course of Eight Lectures Delivered at the Royal Institution of Great Britain*, 140–50. 2nd ed. London: Longmans, 1869.

Ullmann, Dieter. "Chladni und die Entwicklung der experimentellen Akustik um 1800." *Archive for the History of Exact Sciences* 31 (1984): 35–52.

Chromatograph

A chromatograph separates the chemical components of a mixture. Most chromatographs incorporate a reservoir for the mobile phase in which the mixture is added to a liquid or gas, a "column" (which is now often a coil) for the subsequent stationary phase, and instrumentation to detect each component as it leaves the column. The separation is a result of the differing affinity of each compound for the stationary phase relative to the mobile phase; the compounds with the greatest affinity for the stationary phase are the last to exit the column. Nearly all commercial chromatographic systems now use dedicated computers and the chromatograph can be "hyphenated" to other analytical instruments, notably **mass spectrometers** and Fourier-Transform infrared **spectrophotometers**.

Chromatography is divided into liquid and gas chromatography, and further subdivided into liquid-solid, liquid-liquid, gas-solid, and gas-liquid. Liquid-solid and gas-solid chromatographs use columns of active materials in powdered form, and the solid interacts directly with the mixture in the mobile phase. Liquid-liquid and gas-liquid chromatographs use columns of inactive powders coated with an active liquid or layer. They depend on partition chromatography because the mixture is distributed between the mobile phase and the immiscible liquid on the inert solid.

Other variants of chromatography include thin-layer chromatography (TLC), paper chromatography; (HPLC) initially said to stand for high-pressure liquid chromatography, but now taken to mean high-performance liquid chromatography), ion-exchange chromatography (IEC), and gel-permeation (or gel-filtration) chromatography (GPC).

Development

The Italian-born botanochemist Mikhail S. Tsvett (or Tswett) used liquid-solid column chromatography to separate plant pigments in 1903, and he described his method in two detailed papers three years later. He displayed the colored bands produced in the column by a solution of plant pigments in petroleum ether at a meeting of the German Botanical Society in June 1907. He called the colored bands a chromatogram (from the Greek for "color" and "letter"; chromatography means "color" and "writing"). This new technique was slow to take off, but was independently revived in the 1930s to purify carotenoids by Edgar Lederer and László Zechmeister. The technique is still used today. In cases where there are several bands, or when the bands cannot be detected by the eye, a turntable with a large number of containers can be used to collect the different fractions.

Liquid-liquid column chromatography arose out of Archer J.P. Martin's need to separate mixtures of acetylated amino acids in the course of his work on the structure of wool. Counter-current distribution using two immiscible liquids had proved unsatisfactory, and Martin (with Richard L.M. Synge) in 1940 developed the idea of passing a chloroform/alcohol mixture over silica gel. Their key paper, published in 1941, predicted that this technique could be used with gases as well as liquids.

Gas-absorption chromatography had been developed in the late 1940s by Erika Cremer at Innsbruck and Courtney Phillips at Oxford, and pioneering (but almost wholly unrecognized) work on gas-liquid chromatography was carried out in 1943 by G. Damköhler and H. Theile. However it was the announcement of Martin's and Tony James's work on gas-liquid chromatography in 1951 that led to the explosive development of this technique. By the mid 1960s, commercial gas chromatographs dominated chromatography. This situation began to change with the introduction of HPLC. Although Martin and Synge had predicted the development of high-speed liquid-liquid chromatography with the use of very fine powders and high pressures in 1941, the instrumentation of HPLC systems owes much to gas chromatography. The first separations using high-pressure liquid chromatography were carried out by P.B. Hamilton in 1960, followed by C. Karr in 1963. The first commercial HPLC chromatograph was marketed by Isco of Nebraska in 1961; the firm later gave licenses to Waters Associates and Varian Associates.

Paper chromatography was used to analyze dyes by F.F. Runge in the 1850s and was soon

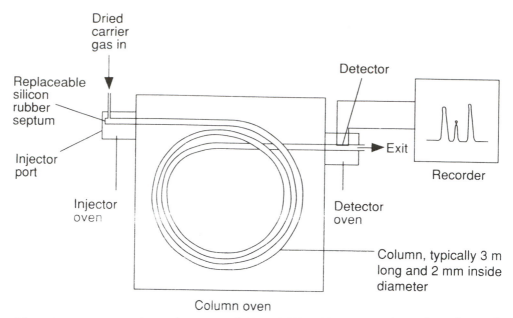

Dried carrier gas in

Replaceable silicon rubber septum

Injector port

Injector oven

Detector

Exit

Recorder

Injector oven

Detector oven

Column, typically 3 m long and 2 mm inside diameter

Column oven

Schematic representation of a gas chromatograph. Faust (1992): 132, Figure 17. Copyright © The Royal Society of Chemistry. Courtesy of the Royal Society of Chemistry.

developed as "capillary analysis" by F. Goppelsröder. Martin introduced modern paper chromatography with R. Consden and A.H. Gordon, along with the ninhydrin spray as an indicator for amino acids, in 1944. Paper chromatography uses specially made filter paper and airtight development tanks containing the solvents.

The history of thin-layer chromatography stretches back to the work of M.W. Beyerinck and H.P. Wijsman at the end of the nineteenth century. In 1938, N.A. Izmailov and M.S. Schraiber at the University of Kharkov used a circular form of TLC as a rapid method of analyzing materia medica. Between 1945 and 1954, J.G. Kirchner at the U.S. Department of Agriculture developed TLC in order to analyze fruit juices. Rather than filter paper, TLC uses small plastic strips (formerly glass plates) that are coated with active solids similar to the ones used in liquid-solid chromatography.

Ion-exchange chromatography arose from the need to separate rare earth ions for the Manhattan Project in World War II, although Harold Urey at Columbia University in New York had used a 130-foot column to separate lithium-6 from lithium-7 in 1938. Ion-exchange chromatography operates on the basis of the ion-exchange resins (such as Permutit, a commercial water softner).

Gel permeation chromatography began in 1959 with the discovery by J. Porath and P.

Flodin in Uppsala that cross-linked dextrin gel could be used to separate large molecules according to their size. It was soon improved by J.C. Moore, who introduced polystyrene gels that were marketed as Styragel.

Applications
Chromatography has become one of the most significant tools in twentieth-century chemistry and has found wide application in many industries. Gas chromatography and HPLC are by far the most important forms of chromatography used today, and the only ones commonly used in tandem with other scientific instruments.

Gas chromatography (GC) is useful for the analysis of volatile hydrocarbons, and the petroleum industry has been closely associated with the development of GC since the early 1950s. Denis Desty of BP Research was one of the leading pioneers of the technique. GC is used for the analysis of fuels, lubricants, crude oils, chemical feedstocks, additives, and gases. The separation of volatile components in a gasoline mixture typically uses a tightly coiled column 100 meters long but only a quarter of a millimeter thick. The inside wall of the coil is coated with fused silica, which carries out the separation. The temperature of the column is slowly built up to 170°C. The carrier gas is helium and the exit gases are fed into a flame ionization detector, which detects components by

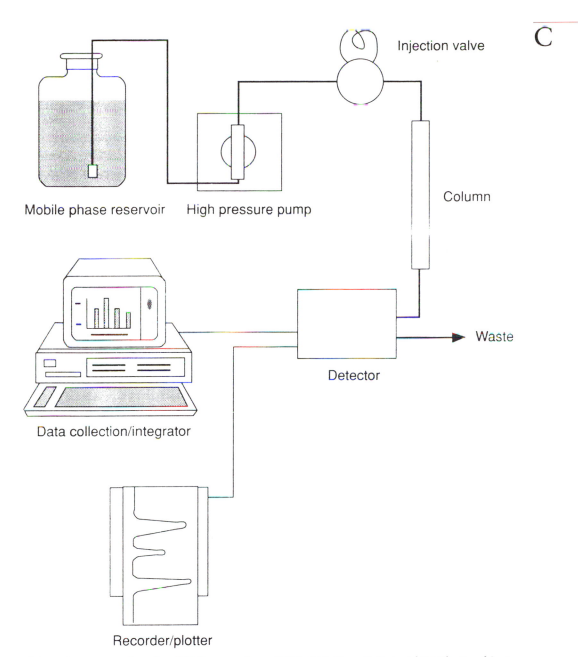

Injection valve

Column

Mobile phase reservoir   High pressure pump

Waste

Data collection/integrator

Detector

Recorder/plotter

Schematic representation of an HPLC system. Faust (1992): 124, Figure 9. Copyright © The Royal Society of Chemistry. Courtesy of the Royal Society of Chemistry.

the increase in the conductivity of a hydrogen-air flame when foreign compounds are introduced.

HPLC has become an essential and ubiquitous analytical tool in the pharmaceutical industry, contributing in a significant way to the rapid advances in drug therapies over the past two decades. A typical HPLC system has four basic parts: a solvent delivery device, a solvent reservoir, a pump unit, and a gradient mixer capable of delivering the carrier solvent in a precise and constant manner. An automated sampling system injects liquid samples repeatedly onto the column, which is a highly packed slurry of very fine particles. The separated components are eluted from the column into a detector, which typically employs ultraviolet absorbance, fluorescence, refractive index, mass spectroscopy, or electrochemical methods. The range of solvent delivery systems manufactured are capable of delivering solvent volumes from microliters to liters per minute, thus permitting the entire range of separations from trace analysis to production line. The development of diode array and other multidimensional detectors have been the most significant advances in recent years. These innovations allow vast quantities of information to be gained from each individual separation.

Peter Morris

Bibliography

Braithwaite, A., and F.J. Smith. *Chromatographic Methods*. 4th ed. London: Chapman and Hall, 1985.

Ettre, L.S., and A. Zlatkis, eds. *75 Years of Chromatography: A Historical Dialogue*. Oxford: Elsevier Scientific, 1979.

Faust, C.B. *Modern Chemical Techniques*. London: Royal Society of Chemistry, Education Division, 1992.

Laitinen, Herbert A., and Galen W. Ewing, eds. *A History of Analytical Chemistry*. Chapter 5, "Analytical Separations." Washington, D.C.: Division of Analytical Chemistry of the American Chemical Society, 1977.

Opheild, Mike. "Separated for Thirty Years." *Laboratory Practice* 37 (1988): 19–23.

Chronograph

Chronographs provide a written record of time intervals. They were used in astronomical observatories to determine the times of star transits, in psychological laboratories to measure human reaction time, and in physiological laboratories to measure the rate of neural transmission. They were also used to calibrate other timing devices, and to record events.

The drum chronograph is basically a cylinder, driven by hand or some mechanical or electrical device and covered with paper on which the desired information is recorded.

Chronographs with External Time Calibration

The earliest drum chronographs were devised for astronomers, and used the electrical pulse of the observatory clock for their calibrated timeline. John Locke of Cincinnati, Ohio, developed an instrument of this sort as part of the astronomical clock he built for the U.S. Naval Observatory in 1849. It was equipped with several pens, one of which was controlled by the clock. Since the pens moved upwards a fraction of an inch on each revolution of the drum, much information could be recorded on a single sheet of paper. The drum was turned with an accurate clockwork mechanism.

A similar drum chronograph, devised by American clock-maker George Bond, was installed at the Harvard Observatory and demonstrated in England in 1851. Bond's chronograph was adopted at the Greenwich Observatory in 1854, and later by the U.S. Coast Survey in its measurement of longitude.

C. Krill's drum chronograph was widely used in astronomical observatories in Europe, for longitude determinations.

Drum Chronographs with Internal Time Sources

The Dutch physiologist F.C. Donders devised his Noemotachograph around 1868. It was a simple chronograph used to measure human reaction times. The horizontally mounted drum was turned by hand; as it was turned it moved upward, allowing the recording track to spiral across the drum. Mounted on the drum mechanism was a 250-vibration-per-second tuning fork that marked its vibrations on the paper with a small spring. Because of these markings, the speed of the drum did not have to be absolutely constant.

Swiss clock-maker Matthäus Hipp developed a similar chronograph but with a very accurate clockwork mechanism that also supplied pulses for the time line. It was a two-channel drum device in which one pen produced the timing line and the other recorded the interval. The pens were controlled by individual electromagnets.

By the late nineteenth century there were a wide variety of quite accurate drum chronographs on the market. The German psychologist Wilhelm Wundt designed an instrument for the Leipzig psychological laboratory that became the standard chronograph for most psychological laboratories. It was equipped with an electrical tuning fork time calibration channel, and was advertised as being accurate to 1/10,000th of a second.

Continuous Paper Chronographs

These are similar to drum chronographs but have a continuous flow of paper guided by rollers. The paper feed device is sufficiently accurate to produce a relatively constant feeding

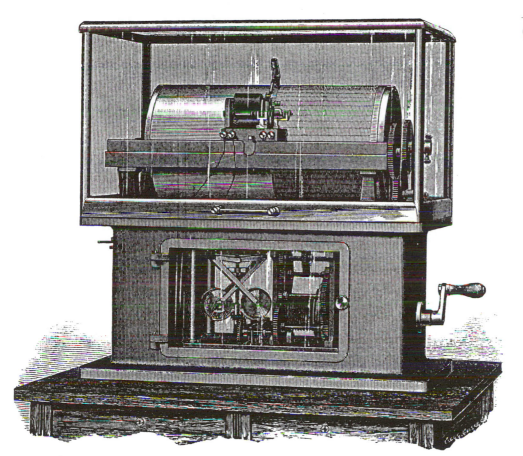

American astronomical chronograph, ca. 1890. George Chambers. A Handbook of Descriptive and Practical Astronomy. *Volume 2, Fourth Edition, Oxford: Clarendon Press. 1890: facing page 215. Courtesy of SSPL.*

rate. Often there is a time-line channel, but often the rate of paper feed is matched to pre-printed, calibrated paper on which the timing of events is calculated.

Pendulum Chronographs

Another major class of chronographs used a swinging pendulum. These were similar to the pendulum **chronoscopes**, but here the pendulum was outfitted with a high-voltage spark contact that swung in close proximity to a metal plate on the base of the device. Between the two was a sheet or strip of paper. The release of the pendulum coincided with the beginning of the timed interval, and a spark jumped from the contact to the metal plate through the paper at the end of the interval, thus marking the paper. By knowing the period of the pendulum, the time difference could be calculated. The Bergström Chronoscope was available commercially with this additional function as a spark chronograph.

There were also several pendulum chronographs created specifically for that purpose. Hathaway's Pendulum Chronograph and Seashore's Spark Chronograph, both based somewhat on Bergström's design, were manufactured as late as 1940.

Rand B. Evans

Bibliography

Bond, G.P., and R.F. Bond. "Description of an Apparatus for Making Astronomical Observations by Means of Electro-magnetism." *Report of the British Association for the Advancement of Science* (1851), Transactions of the Sections, pp. 21–22.

Donders, F.C. "Twee Werktuigen, tot Bepaling van den Tijd, voor Psychische Processen Benoodigd" ("Two Instruments for Determining the Time Required for Mental Processes"). In *Attention and Perfor-*

mance II, edited and translated by W.G. Koster, 432–35. Amsterdam: North Holland, 1969.

Favarger, A. *L'Électricité et ses applications à la chronométrie*, 515–19. 3rd ed. Paris: Girardot, 1924.

Locke, John. *Report of Profesor John Locke, of Cincinnati, Ohio, on the Invention and Construction of His Electro-Chronograph for the National Observatory in Pursuance of the Act of Congress, Approved March 3, 1849*. Cincinnati, Ohio: Wright, Ferris, 1850.

Stoelting, C.H., Co. *Apparatus, Tests and Supplies for Psychology, Psychometry, Psychotechnology, Psychiatry, Neurology, Anthropology, Phonetics, Physiology and Pharmacology*, 74–75. 4th ed. Chicago: C.H. Stoelting, 1940.

Chronometer

A chronometer is a portable watch or clock capable of high-precision timekeeping. The English definition has always stipulated that a chronometer must have a spring detent escapement, but the Swiss apply the term to any highly accurate portable timekeeper. Under this definition, quartz watches capable of specified standards of performance may also be considered chronometers.

Origins and Function

Portable timekeepers have existed since the invention of the mainspring in the late fifteenth century. Watches were made in south Germany in the early sixteenth century, but these were exceedingly poor timekeepers, at best accurate to about ±15 minutes a day. The primary incentive for the invention of a better portable timekeeper was navigation at sea.

From the mid seventeenth century, with increasing numbers of lives and shipments of cargo being lost every year, ways were sought to navigate the oceans safely and chart their coastlines. To establish any position on the earth one needs to identify that position's latitude north or south of the equator and the longitude east or west of the home meridian. Because the earth spins on its axis, time is a function of longitude. If, at an unknown position, "home time" were recorded accurately on a portable clock, a comparison with the local time would indicate how far around the globe from home that position was.

Thus arose the need for an accurate portable clock that could cope with the motion of the ship and wide temperature variations. Many European scientists sought solutions, and clock designs were attempted, *inter alia*, by Robert Hooke in Britain, Christiaan Huygens in Holland, and Gottfried Leibniz in Germany.

Several European nations promised large monetary prizes for a solution to the problem; the British government offered £20,000 in 1714, awards to be administered by its Board of Longitude. If a timekeeper were to be considered for the full prize, it would have to perform better than ± 3 seconds per day.

In spite of a great flurry of interest, it was to be more than half a century before the prize was won (in 1773), by the self-taught English clock-maker John Harrison. He had begun in 1730 by designing and building a truly remarkable sea clock (now known as "H1"), with two balances incorporating temperature compensation, an automatic maintaining power to keep the machine working while being wound, and a movement (the whole mechanism) that needed no lubrication. Though very encouraging, this clock did not capture the prize money. Nor did Harrison's two further attempts, "H2" and "H3," the latter (1740) incorporating his inventions of the bimetallic strip and the caged roller bearing. Harrison's winning design ("H4," completed in 1759) was on the scale of a large watch. Although very complicated and expensive (a copy made by Larcum Kendall cost the board £500), H4 was in fact the forerunner of all precision watches. It demonstrated that portable precision timekeepers needed a relatively light, high-frequency oscillator with high stored energy. It provided a fully developed system of maintaining power, and it employed a bimetallic compensator, which would be the basis for almost all later compensation balances.

In France, Pierre LeRoy had been following Harrison's work (he is said to have visited him in 1738), and in 1770 LeRoy published a memoir stating three requirements for a practical chronometer: a compensation balance, a detached escapement, and an isochronous balance spring. However, his actual designs were not practical and had little influence on the developed chronometer. In England, Thomas Mudge attempted, in the 1770s, to improve on Harrison's work by introducing further complications, and although one of his machines performed very well on trial at the Royal Ob-

Harrison's No. 1 Chronometer, 1735. Courtesy of SSPL. 0340. On display at the National Maritime Museum, Greenwich.

servatory at Greenwich, the design was not practicable.

The term "chronometer" had been coined by both William Derham and Jeremy Thacker in 1714 but, while it was used occasionally later in the century to describe precision timers, Harrison referred to his instruments as timekeepers or sea clocks. The term chronometer was first properly applied by John Arnold and Alexander Dalrymple in 1780 to describe Arnold's pocket chronometer No. 36, which had performed so magnificently at Greenwich when on trial the year before.

It was John Arnold who, virtually single-handed, simplified Harrison's model. Arnold introduced his own design for a compensation balance which, when heated, automatically compensated for the weakening spring and expanding balance by decreasing the moment of inertia of the balance using rims made of bimetals. LeRoy had independently invented such a balance, and both were undoubtedly inspired by Harrison's work. Arnold also invented the helical balance spring with terminal curves, making the balance's swings effectively isochronous, and a version of a detached escapement that allowed the balance to receive impulse with as little interference from the clockwork as possible. Arnold then produced practicable and relatively inexpensive versions for marine and pocket chronometers, the marines costing between 60 and 80 guineas.

Following Arnold's work, Thomas Earnshaw standardized the design and production of marine chronometers and was almost certainly the first to have rough marine chronometer movements made for him in Lancashire—a practice employed for many years before by watchmakers and that became standard practice for chronometer-makers. Earnshaw introduced his simple spring detent escapement, and enclosed the movement in a brass bowl, suspended in gimbals in the familiar cube-shaped mahogany box. By 1800, thanks to Earnshaw's refinements, the chronometer in England was developed virtually to its modern form, and provided the basis for those manufactured all over the world in the following century and a half.

Popularity

During the last quarter of the eighteenth century, the Royal Observatory began more regularly to put chronometers on trial for the Board of Longitude. In the early voyages of exploration, beginning with those of James Cook in the 1770s, chronometers were increasingly used to establish the longitudes of coastlines and of positions inland. However, the Royal Navy was skeptical and it was the merchant service that first introduced chronometers on a regular basis, though these usually still had to be bought privately by captains.

Once Harrison and Arnold had demonstrated the scale on which a portable chronometer should be made, the wider implications for their use were realized. Pocket chronometers became popular as personal precision timekeepers, not only for navy captains but also for astronomers and others interested in science. Until the introduction of the electric telegraph, chronometers were used to fix longitude differences between observatories by transporting large batches of them between the two places. Chronometers used by astronomers were usually rated to sidereal (star) time; their dials normally had twenty-four numerals rather than twelve, and they used Arabic rather than Roman figures on the dial. A particular version of this type of chronometer, produced from the latter end of the nineteenth century and designed for surveying, was used in conjunction with a tape chronograph and enabled the longitudes of landmarks to be established quickly and accurately.

Improvements

By the mid nineteenth century, chronometers were big business, and such London firms as Dent, Frodsham, Mercer, and Kullberg were exporting chronometers all over the world. As demand and production increased, prices fell— a typical two-day marine chronometer made during the second half of the nineteenth century cost about £20. Technical improvements concentrated on the compensation balance, chiefly to correct for middle temperature error caused by the elasticity of the steel balance spring changing with temperature in a nonlinear progression. With the invention by French metallurgist Charles-Edouard Guillaume of Invar (1898) and Elinvar (1918) (alloys almost unaffected by temperature changes), production chronometers were capable of timekeeping to better than 0.5 second per day in varying conditions.

Most chronometers were so well made that by 1900 there was a glut of serviceable instruments, many still doing sterling service after one hundred years of use. The two great world wars induced a new demand, however. The Americans produced a fine new design in the 1940s, the Hamilton model 21, based on the Swiss original by Ulysse Nardin of around 1900.

In theory, once Marconi's wireless telegraphy had appeared early in the twentieth century, the marine chronometer's days were numbered. But in practice there was no substitute for having home time indicated on board, and Western navies continued to issue them to warships until the 1970s. Now, cheap and reliable quartz clocks have replaced them and indeed almost all other forms of mechanical chronometer.

Jonathan Betts

Bibliography

"Chronometer." In *The Cyclopaedia; or, Universal Dictionary of Arts, Sciences, and Literature,* edited by Abraham Rees, Vol. 8. London: Longman, 1819.

Gould, Rupert T. *The Marine Chronometer: Its History and Development.* Reprint. Woodbridge, Suffolk: Antique Collectors' Club, 1989.

Howse, Derek. *Greenwich Time and the Discovery of the Longitude.* Oxford: Oxford University Press, 1980.

Mercer, Tony. *Chronometer Makers of the World.* Colchester, U.K.: N.A.G., 1991.

Whitney, Marvin. *The Ship's Chronometer.* Cincinnati, Ohio: A.W.I., 1985.

Chronoscope

Chronoscopes are a family of instruments that measure, automatically, brief elapsed time intervals. The term is often used interchangeably with **chronograph**, although chronographs leave a written record of the timed interval, while with chronoscopes the interval is read directly from a dial or calculated from the mechanism (**pendulum** swings, **galvanometer** displacement, and so forth). Chronoscopes were originally created to measure the velocity of projectiles fired from guns. This was accomplished by breaking a circuit (a thin wire) as the shell was fired from the muzzle; the circuit was remade when the shell struck its target. Later the device was used in physics to measure short periods of time and particularly to demonstrate the rate of fall of objects from various heights. The primary use of chronoscopes after the 1880s, however, was in experimental psychology, where it was used to measure the time it takes for an individual to respond to a stimulus. Its use in the "reaction-time experiment" was crucial in the development of psychology as an experimental discipline.

Electro-mechanically Linked Clockwork Chronoscopes

Charles Wheatstone devised a chronoscope in 1840 utilizing an accurate clockwork system in which the interval between the opening and closing of an electromagnet was measured. Activated, the electromagnet engaged an indicator hand with the moving clockwork mechanism. Deactivated, it disengaged and stopped the hand. The elapsed time was read on a calibrated dial. The Swiss horologist Matthäus Hipp modified Wheatstone's design. Marketed in the 1840s as the Hipp Chronoscope, it was accurate to 1/1,000th of a second and was the preferred research instrument for measuring short durations until the 1920s.

Pendulum Chronoscopes

Pendulum chronoscopes come in two forms, direct reading and indirect reading.

Direct Reading Pendulum Chronoscopes

In 1895 F.W. Fitz, a physiologist at Harvard University, devised a chronoscope using a pendulum swing to measure an elapsed time. At the beginning of the interval to be measured, the solid metal pendulum was released to swing through its arc. A loosely attached pointer swung with the pendulum. At the end of the interval an electromagnet disengaged the pointer from the

Hipp chronoscope, ca. 1889. SM 1889-38. Courtesy of SSPL.

pendulum and held it fast to an indicator scale. Elapsed time was read off of the calibrated scale. J.A. Bergström's modification of the design in 1900 allowed measurements of 1/100th of a second. It became the standard for that type of chronometer through the 1920s.

Indirect Reading Pendulum Chronoscopes

In 1890, the psychologist E.C. Sanford of Clark University introduced a chronoscope with two pendulums, using the principle of the vernier. Charles Wheatstone had developed a similar device as early as 1840, but it appears never to have gone beyond the prototype stage. Sanford's Vernier Chronoscope became popular in student instructional laboratories for measuring human reaction times from its commercial introduction in 1898 well into the 1930s. Mounted on a frame were two pendulums with weighted bobs. The pendulums were set at different lengths. At the start of the timed interval, the longer pendulum was released. At the end of the timed interval, the shorter pendulum was released. Because the lengths of the pendulums are known, counting the number of swings it takes for the shorter pendulum to catch up with the longer allows calculation by formula of the elapsed time. Accuracy of this device was approximately 1/100th of a second.

Electrical Chronoscopes
These chronoscopes use purely electrical devices for measuring elapsed time.

Pouillet's Chronoscope
This instrument, devised in the 1830s by the French physicist Claude Pouillet, is sometimes called the ballistic galvanometer. When a current is sent through a galvanometer coil, the coil is deflected proportionately to the amount of electrical current. Assuming the amount of the current remains constant, the deflection produced by a brief pulse of current will be proportional to the duration of the pulse. Properly calibrated, the galvanometer functions as a chronoscope for very brief time intervals. A modification of Pouillet's chronoscope by Paul Klopsteg of Northwestern University, was available as late as 1939.

Ewald's Chronoscope
In 1889, the German physiologist J.R. Ewald devised an electric chronoscope using a small electromagnet whose armature rocked back and forth in synchrony to an alternating current produced by an electrical tuning fork. The armature played between the teeth of a one-hundred-tooth cog wheel that was set to move in one direction. A pointer, directly attached to the wheel, moved one increment for every alternation of the armature, each representing 1/100th of a second.

Synchronous Electric Chronoscopes
Synchronous electric motors revolutionized the manufacture of chronoscopes in the 1920s.

Dunlap's Chronoscope
In 1917 Knight Dunlap, a psychologist at Johns Hopkins University, produced a chronoscope using a form of synchronous electric motor. Ten electromagnets were arranged around the periphery of a circle within which the armature of the chronoscope turned. The motor was powered by a calibrated alternating current and ran at a constant speed. The indicator dial was engaged and disengaged to the armature by an electric clutch activated by the making or breaking of an electric circuit. Accurate to 1/1,200th of a second, it quickly replaced the Hipp chronoscope.

Standard Stopclock
By the late 1920s a miniature synchronous motor was made available by the Warren Telechron Co. of Ashland, Massachusetts. The telechron motor, coupled to an electrically controlled clutch to start and stop the timer hands, was marketed by the Standard Clock Co. of Springfield, Massachusetts, in the mid 1930s as the Standard Stopclock. Its accuracy of 1/100th of a second and its ease of use made it the "standard" laboratory stopclock until the development of electronic elapsed time counters in the 1950s.

Rand B. Evans

Bibliography
Dallenbach, K.M. "Two New A.C. Chronoscopes." *American Journal of Psychology* 48 (1936): 145–51.
Fitz, G.W. "A Location Reaction Apparatus." *Psychological Review* 2 (1895): 37–42.
Stoelting, C.H., Co. *Apparatus, Tests and Supplies for Psychology, Psychometry, Psychotechnology, Psychiatry, Neurology, Anthropology, Phonetics, Physiology, and Pharmacology.* Chicago: C.H. Stoelting, 1939.
Titchener, E.B. *Experimental Psychology: A Manual of Laboratory Practice.* Vol. 2, Part 2. New York: Macmillan, 1905.
Wheatstone, Charles. "Le chronoscope electromagnétique." *Comtes rendus de l'Académie des Sciences* 20 (1845): 1554–61. Reprinted in *The Scientific Papers of Sir Charles Wheatstone,* 143–51. London: Physical Society of London, 1879.

Circumferentor (Surveyor's Compass)
The traditional and proper meaning of the term "circumferentor" is a surveyor's **compass**—that is, a magnetic compass fitted with sights so as to take bearings with reference to the magnetic meridian. There are, however, types of survey-

Tintype of an unidentified surveyor and chainman with circumferentor (center), ca. 1870. Courtesy of NMAH.

ing compasses that have never been called circumferentors: prismatic compasses, for example, or compasses housed in square wooden boxes with sliding or folding lids and folding sights or pivoted sighting tubes. More significantly, in recent decades there has been a wide-

spread use of the term "circumferentor" to denote an instrument for taking bearings with a pivoted alidade that, in the time of its manufacture and use, would have been called a theodolite. This leads to confusion when reading primary sources.

The essential characteristics of a circumferentor are a glazed circular compass box in brass or wood, a degree scale, a pivoted magnetic needle, and two sights fixed to the box, often on extended arms. A **theodolite** may be aligned with the meridian using a magnetic compass, but bearings are indicated by an index that moves over a stationary degree scale. In a circumferentor the index is fixed, since it is a magnetic needle, and the scale moves with the sights. Many of the instruments incorrectly referred to today as circumferentors have both facilities. Typical of these is the "common theodolite" described by George Adams, in which the index or alidade, moving over the outer fixed scale, also carries a compass box with a needle and divided scale. Nonetheless, this was not referred to as a circumferentor in its day, and was quite a different instrument.

The very earliest circumferentors were modeled on the mariner's compass, in which the needle was invisible beneath a compass card. The card, with its graduations, was attached to the needle, which in turn was mounted on a vertical pin. Such cards could be engraved in the traditional manner with east to the right of north (holding north upright): since the card remained fixed, turning the sights to the east gave an eastward reading. It was simpler, however, to balance the needle above the card, which was then attached to the base of the box and, unlike the needle, moved with the sights. This arrangement was quickly adopted and became general from the late seventeenth century. One consequence, however, was that a traditionally designed card would then give a westward reading beneath the needle as the sights were turned to the east. As a result, circumferentor cards usually have east and west transposed from the familiar arrangement.

The circumferentor was popular through the eighteenth and into the nineteenth century, but it became increasingly associated with particular settings for surveying practice, and in these settings its design became refined and specialized. One feature, which became popular in Ireland and the United States, was a vernier mechanism used to adjust the instrument for the ever changing magnetic variation. While the theodolite could reproduce the artificial features of a settled landscape—buildings, boundaries, roads, and so on—the circumferentor's fundamental reference to a natural feature, the magnetic meridian, made it particularly suited to an undeveloped topography, and so it became used in colonial survey. The preferred instrument of surveyors in Ireland and in America became the circumferentor, and it was soon the most commonly made surveying instrument by manufacturers in both countries. In America it became the starting point for a whole family of instruments represented by "the American transit," in which a telescopic sight is carried by A-frame supports above a central compass. Although a vertical circle would be added for taking altitudes and even a horizontal scale of the type found on a theodolite placed outside the compass box, a prominent magnetic compass remained characteristic of surveying instruments made in America.

The second situation to which the circumferentor was well suited was the still more featureless environment of an underground mine. The "miner's dial" is usually some form of circumferentor, often with the addition of a clinometer or some other feature for taking inclinations or altitudes. A good many instruments for mine survey have been designed to try to cope with this uncompromising environment, and they represent a second line of development from the basic circumferentor. The problem associated with all surveying compasses, magnetic variation, presented a difficulty above ground, but there at least the sun was available for finding the true meridian and thus measuring variation; underground the problem was much more intractable.

Jim A. Bennett

Bibliography

Bennett, J.A. *The Divided Circle: A History of Instruments for Astronomy, Navigation and Surveying*. Oxford: Phaidon, 1987.

Clock, Atomic

Atomic clocks are not what a general public misled by journalists generally understands by this term: they are not radioactive isotopes (such as "radiocarbon") whose relative abundance in particular material objects serves to measure—but never very precisely—the time elapsed since the formation of that object. Atomic clocks, properly speaking, are extremely precise (and extremely accurate) electronic instruments—more exactly stated, quantum-electronic instruments—that use as their

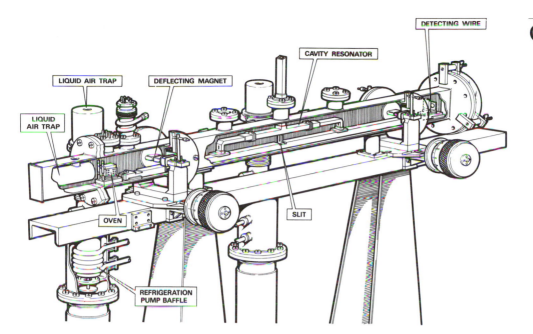

LIQUID AIR TRAP

DEFLECTING MAGNET

CAVITY RESONATOR

DETECTING WIRE

LIQUID
AIR TRAP

OVEN

SLIT

REFRIGERATION
PUMP BAFFLE

Schematic diagram of the cesium beam chamber at the British National Physical Laboratory, 1955. Courtesy of SSPL.

"pendulum" an atom or molecule experiencing a transition between two well-defined energy states. On this physical basis the instrument generates a constant-period electromagnetic oscillation, and may further supply an elapsed time by counting up the number of those constant-period oscillations occurring since a specified instant.

In most types of atomic clock, indeed in all possessing high long-term stability, the "clock" transition is between two hyperfine energy levels—that is, between two orientations of the spinning atomic nucleus with respect to the surrounding cloud of electrons and the frequency of the "clock" transition is in the microwave range, 5–50 gigahertz. By convention, atomic frequency standards (such is the term generally used in lieu of "atomic clocks" in the technical literature) are typed on two axes into four categories: active/passive, laboratory/commercial. Active standards are masers and lasers. They are "active" in that the electromagnetic oscillation appearing as the output of the instrument is the very radiation generated in the atomic transition serving as its "pendulum." The ammonia maser was the first of the active standards (Charles Townes, 1954; Nobel Prize 1964). Hydrogen masers (Norman Ramsey, 1960; Nobel Prize 1989) stand before all other standards in stability. More recently rubidium and cesium masers, and several types of stabilized

lasers, have also appeared as experimental devices.

Passive standards use an electronic feedback mechanism in order to adjust the frequency of an electronic oscillator to that of the "clock" transition. The output oscillation of passive standards thus derives from the electronic oscillator, and only indirectly from the atomic transition. The first type of passive clock to be proposed (1945), and still by far the most important type in use, is the cesium atomic beam frequency standard. This instrument inverts the research apparatus introduced by I.I. Rabi in the late 1930s in order to measure magnetic moments of atomic nuclei: the hyperfine transition of the Cs^{133} atom ceases being that which is measured, becoming that which measures. Indeed, in 1964 the General Conference on Weights and Measures redefined the second as 9,192,631,770 of these oscillations. Other "passive" standards include those based on an optically pumped rubidium gas cell (Robert Dicke, 1955), the most compact (some are smaller, even much smaller, than a fist) and the least expensive of the atomic frequency standards; "passivated" versions of the maser frequency standards (in order to render them more compact); and, recently, frequency standards based upon hyperfine transitions in cooled ions stored for long times in electromagnetic traps (Hans Dehmelt; Nobel Prize, 1989).

Consideration of size and cost brings us to the second dimension of our matrix: laboratory versus commercial standards.

The notion of natural, invariable, and universal physical standards that inspired the late-eighteenth-century originators of the metric system remained the cynosure of physicists qua metrologists in the following two centuries. Of all the metric standards, it was, however, the one taken over from millennia-long tradition—the unit of time as a fraction of the period of rotation of the earth—that was amenable to the most precise determination. (Indeed, to the present day, time/frequency is, far and away, the most precisely determinable physical quantity.) The instability of the earth's rotation—about one part in 10^8—came gradually into evidence over the first four decades of the twentieth century, first through the advance of mechanical clocks, and then, more clearly still, through the development of quartz-crystal oscillators. Already a half century earlier, James Clerk Maxwell had proposed (1873), in the wake of Kirchhoff's and Bunsen's (1859) spectroscopic revelations, that "in the present state of science the most universal standard" of time would be the period of vibration of some species of atom (and the standard of length, the wavelength of the light emitted by that atom in so vibrating).

Although steps toward the realization of an atomic standard of length were taken before the end of the nineteenth century by A.A. Michelson, the proposal of an atomic standard of time had to remain wholly theoretical in the absence of any means for counting those atomic vibrations. It would be seven decades before the development of radio electronics, and more particularly of microwave **radar**, created such means. The locking of the frequency of an electronic oscillator to a molecular transition was achieved in several laboratories, academic and industrial, immediately following World War II (using the absorption line arising from the inversion transition in ammonia), but it was only national standards laboratories that were well equipped to count those atomic vibrations with the help of their calibrated crystal oscillators and frequency standards based on chains of electronic frequency multipliers.

First to achieve this was the U.S. National Bureau of Standards (now National Institute of Standards and Technology), creating great éclat with the announcement of its ammonia absorption clock in January 1949. Subsequent work there on a cesium beam device bogged down and was overtaken by that at the British National Physical Laboratory (1955), whose work, continued in the following years, provided the basis for the redefinition of the second in 1964. The National Bureau of Standards pulled ahead in the 1960s, but was rivaled by Canada's National Research Council and, later, Germany's Physikalisch-Technische Bundesanstalt. These, followed by many other national standards laboratories, pushed the development of atomic clocks—first and foremost cesium beam clocks, and, secondarily, hydrogen masers—in the direction of the greatest attainable accuracy and stability. Often this was the direction of increasing length (transit time), for the Heisenberg uncertainty principle sets the limiting accuracy of a frequency standard proportional to the length of time during which a "pendulum" atom is, on average, kept under observation. These laboratory standards have attained accuracies better than one part in 10^{13}. Devices based upon cooled ions stored in electromagnetic traps hold out the prospect of accuracies a few orders of magnitude greater still.

Commercial standards, by contrast, are, as the adjective implies, made seriatim, packaged compactly, and marketed. Cost counts, although to the military, the principal customer, not so much as size and weight. As has been true since the seventeenth century, the principal incentive to devising more stable and accurate clocks is the wish to be able, thereby, to determine not time, but position. And after position comes encryption, as well as the above-board timing needs of communication systems, power networks, and so on.

The first commercial atomic clock was the Atomichron® (1956), a cesium beam device conceived and promoted by Jerrold Zacharias at M.I.T. and developed at the National Co. in suburban Boston. It stood $2^1/_2$ meters high, weighed 250 kg, and cost $50,000. Since 1964 Hewlett Packard's model 5060, one tenth as tall and as heavy but only half the price, has dominated the commercial market, with an accuracy approaching one part in 10^{12} and an extraordinary reliability. In recent years the market for atomic clocks has been reduced through the ready availability of time signals from the atomic clocks carried in **Global Positioning System** satellites. The commonest use of atomic clocks as scientific instruments, narrowly construed, is in very-long-baseline radio astronomy (**interferometry**), in which the ex post facto re-construction of the phase difference between the signals received at the widely separated antennae depends upon those signals having been recorded along with time markers from extremely stable and accurately calibrated frequency standards.

Paul Forman

Bibliography

Barnes, James A., and John J. Bollinger. "Clocks, Atomic and Molecular." In *Encyclopedia of Physics,* edited by Rita G. Lerner and George Trigg, 154–55. New York: VCH, 1990.

Forman, Paul. "Atomichron®: The Atomic Clock from Concept to Commercial Product." *Proceedings of the IEEE* 73 (1985): 1181–1204.

For greater detail and bibliographic references on many aspects of atomic timekeeping, see the following special issues on time and frequency of the *Proceedings of the IEEE*: 79 (July 1991); 74 (1986); 60 (May 1972).

Clock, Regulator

A regulator is a fixed and highly accurate **pendulum** clock. A regulator dial has a central minute hand, with the hours and the seconds as subsidiary dials within the center.

In the early seventeenth century, when ordinary clocks were capable of keeping time only to within about 15 minutes a day, the Swiss-born clock-maker Jost Burgi introduced a new clock escapement, specifically to improve timekeeping capability, known as the cross beat. It was, however, only with the invention of the practical pendulum clock by Christiaan Huygens in 1657 that clocks could keep time to within a few seconds per day. The pendulum clock was rapidly developed, especially in England, and by the end of the century almost all the technical improvements for the modern mechanical clock were in place.

Huygens had introduced clocks with long pendulums to England in the early 1660s and was the first to observe their greater stability as timekeepers. Joseph Knibb in London supplied the astronomer James Gregory with two precision longcase clocks, the direct forerunners of the regulator, for the University of St. Andrews, Scotland, in 1673. Other English makers made longcase clocks with long pendu-

lums—some without striking work, some with unusual dialing, and a few with equation of time indication to enable them to be set accurately with a **sun-dial**. These clocks might be capable of a performance within a few seconds a week, but only if the temperature were relatively constant.

Much of the impetus for the improvement in clockwork came from the desire to determine longitude at sea (see **chronometer**). The Royal Observatory at Greenwich, founded in 1675 for this purpose, acquired two year-going clocks from Thomas Tompion in London in 1676. These clocks had 13-foot pendulums and a dead beat escapement which, unlike all previous ones, did not cause the wheels to reverse at each swing of the pendulum. John Flamsteed, the first Astronomer Royal, used these clocks to measure star positions and to determine that the earth spins on its axis at a uniform rate. In the 1720s, George Graham made several precision clocks with his dead beat escapement and regulator dial for Edmund Halley, the second Astronomer Royal.

Temperature Compensation

When clocks get warmer they generally go slower. Heat causes a pendulum to expand and thus beat time more slowly, a concept that was understood from the early eighteenth century.

George Graham, partner and successor to Tompion, realized that as long as the effective length of the pendulum remains the same, the clock will keep time, and in 1715 he invented the mercurial compensated pendulum. This was basically a glass jar containing a short column of mercury, attached to a steel rod. With a rise in temperature, as the rod expands downwards, the mercury expands upwards, and the center of mass remains the same distance from the suspension point. John Harrison's gridiron pendulum of 1725 has a series of brass and steel rods and works on the same principle. As the steel expands downwards, the brass expands upwards, and the bob stays where it is. Clocks with a compensation pendulum could maintain correct time to within about a second a week. Harrison's compensation pendulum was more stable and convenient than Graham's, and it became the standard for most eighteenth-century regulators. The only competitor was the design by John Ellicott based on the same idea but using levers to raise the pendulum bob; these enjoyed a certain amount of use from the

C

Regulator no. 1906 by E.J. Dent & Co., London, ca. 1870. Courtesy of the National Maritime Museum.

1750s, but probably owing more to Ellicott's influence and business acumen than to their performance.

Regulator

During the eighteenth century, traveling versions of regulator clocks were carried on several expeditions to determine the difference in gravitational pull at various places in the world, and thus derive the shape of the earth.

In December 1760, Nevil Maskelyne ordered an astronomical clock, costing £33.12.-, for use in observing the 1761 transit of Venus, and his order specifically used the term "regulator." This clock was made by John Shelton, foreman to George Graham. Based on Graham's original instrument, and provided with a regulator dial, dead beat escapement, compensation pendulum and maintaining power, it became the standard for all ordinary regulators to be made during the following century and a half. French regulators, by such makers as Ferdinand Berthoud, Robert Robin, and Antide Janvier, usually had conventional dials with concentric hour and minute hands, and were generally more complex and lavish.

About 1745 John Harrison produced a regulator for which he claimed the astonishing potential of a second in one hundred days. This had his grasshopper escapement and gridiron pendulum with cycloidal cheeks, and ran without lubrication. Justin Vulliamy and his son

Benjamin made a small number of regulators based on Harrison's design. Around 1800 there was a vogue for regulators with constant force escapements, mostly using Alexander Cumming's or Thomas Mudge's gravity escapements, or Thomas Reid's or William Hardy's spring pallet escapements. Although very few survive, these regulators were apparently made in some numbers.

Until the mid nineteenth century, the primary function of a regulator was to keep accurate time. With the invention of telegraphy and electric clocks, "master" regulators were used additionally to distribute time to a series of "slave" clocks. The first official electric regulator, by Charles Shepherd, was fitted at the Royal Observatory in 1852.

Related Instruments

The "domestic regulator" introduced in the nineteenth century had a conventional dial and an hour-striking movement, but a dead beat escapement and (usually) a wood-rod pendulum. This might also be termed a "regulator clock," as the term "clock" referred to a timekeeper that strikes a bell.

From the early nineteenth century, watch- and clock-makers began providing their shops with a regulator, usually with a glass door for viewing the pendulum, for regulating their own clocks and watches and for the benefit of their clientele. Wealthy amateur astronomers also began to acquire such instruments for their observatories.

Improvements

In 1831, T.R. Robinson at Armagh Observatory noticed that a regulator supplied by Thomas Earnshaw in 1794 was performing so well that he could distinguish errors caused by changes in barometric pressure, and Robieson introduced a small barometric compensator to the pendulum. In the 1860s, the firm of William Bond and Sons of Boston made a series of complex detached escapement regulators that were also capable of detecting errors caused by barometric changes. In 1870 E.J. Dent made his celebrated regulator (No. 1,906) for the Royal Observatory with detent escapement and, in conjunction with a zinc and steel temperature-compensated pendulum, a full mercury-tube barometric compensator.

At the end of the century, the German Sigmund Riefler made regulators accurate to a few seconds in a year. These had a mechanical movement with an electrically rewound remontoir, all enclosed in a constant-pressure vessel. Meanwhile, in France, the Leroy Company was working on a similar idea, but with the pendulum impulsed by a form of spring pallet escapement. William Hamilton Shortt's free pendulum clock, with a master pendulum in a partially evacuated cylinder, was capable of about ±1 second in a year. The master pendulum was impulsed by a gravity arm that was released electrically by a secondary slave pendulum outside the cylinder. The Shortt system was superseded only when quartz technology was sufficiently well developed in the 1940s, providing a time standard more stable than one second in ten years.

Jonathan Betts

Bibliography

"Clock." In *The Cyclopaedia; or, Universal Dictionary of Arts, Sciences, and Literature,* edited by Abraham Rees, Vol. 1, London: Longmans, 1819.

Howse, Derek. *Greenwich Time: And the Discovery of the Longitude.* Oxford: Oxford University Press, 1980.

Roberts, Derek, Antiques. *An Exhibition of Precision Pendulum Clocks.* Tunbridge Wells: Otter, 1986.

Cloud Chamber

See CHAMBER, CLOUD

Colony Counter

See COUNTER, COLONY

Colorimeter

A colorimeter is used to match or measure colors. The term "colorimetry" was employed by chemists in the 1860s to refer to the measurement of the concentration of a liquid sample by its color, and instruments designed for this purpose are sometimes referred to as color comparators. By the first decade of the twentieth century, the word "colorimeter" was being used to describe the instruments that quantify and describe color itself. Both classes of instrument generally employ the technique of matching. Colorimeters, unlike their simpler counterpart, the visual **photometer**, rely on a number of psychophysical characteristics. Three perceptual attributes are particularly important: hue (or tint), color saturation (or purity), and brightness.

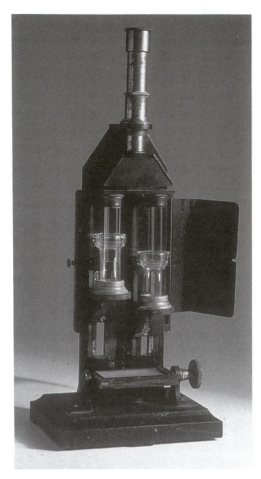

Duboscq colorimeter, by Cogit, early twentieth century. SM 1976-420. Courtesy of SSPL.

The **Lovibond comparator** and other commercial colorimeters found wide use in the grading and testing of products such as beer, flour, and oils. With the advent of standardized methods, deviations in quality or the presence of impurities could be quantified. Such methods frequently employ an indicator chemical that tints the sample. The reference material used in the color matching is typically a set of solutions of known concentration, or a manufactured item such as a dyed fabric swatch or painted card. For routine chemical tests such as pH determination, water purity, and blood analysis, permanent glass filters were manufactured concurrently with the instruments themselves.

Comparators and colorimeters for quantitative analysis were refined in the early twentieth century. The field of view was carefully specified to ensure a side-by-side comparison of colors, and schemes were devised for precisely adjusting the reference color to obtain a match. With the Duboscq colorimeter, the light passing through two vials of liquid was combined at an eyepiece. A rack and pinion varied the depth of a glass plunger immersed in the sample liquid and located in its light path, thereby changing the sample's effective thickness. Despite such elaborations, colorimetric analysis or "indicator testing" remained of limited application until World War II, with most analytical chemistry involving "wet" gravimetric or volumetric methods.

Colorimetry in its psychophysical sense was increasingly researched from the turn of the twentieth century. The competition between various gas and electric light sources motivated photometric comparison, which was hindered by their dissimilar color characteristics. Such research became more organized in the interwar period at the U.S. National Bureau of Standards, the National Physical Laboratory in London, and commercial laboratories such as the General Electric Nela Research Laboratory in Cleveland and the Munsell Color Co. in Baltimore.

F.E. Ives developed the first "trichromatic" colorimeter in 1908. This consisted of an optical arrangement to combine the light passing through blue, green, and red filters at the observer's eye. Adjusting the width of diaphragms placed over the filters allowed the relative intensities to be changed, and a wide range of colors to be synthesized by the addition of three primary colors. An alternate additive scheme for "mixing" colors was the spinning disk covered with sectors of differently colored paper. This idea, popularized by James Clerk Maxwell and later William Abney in the late nineteenth century, was revived in disk colorimeters of the 1930s for use with standardized color patches such as those of the Munsell system. Other instruments subtracted spectral components from a single "white" light. The Eastman subtractive colorimeter (1920), for example, employed graded wedges of selectively absorbing materials, for which the thickness and optical density vary from end to end, or as a function of angle. The wedges, placed in the single reference beam, successively removed controllable amounts of the spectral complements of blue, green, and red light.

Such instruments were refined in the interwar period, but were hampered by a lack of standardization in light sources and filter characteristics. Among the issues studied were the selection of a standard source of light, the importance and variability of the color vision of the human eye, and the optimal choice of color filters.

The exclusively vision-based colorimeter was challenged from the 1920s, when photoelectric measurement of light intensity became practicable. With the advent of photoelectric cells sensitive to light across the entire visual spectrum, commercial colorimeters were introduced. The first wave of photoelectric instruments used vacuum phototubes, which were relatively delicate, demanded high-voltage power supplies, and employed either sensitive galvanometers or amplifiers to observe the weak signal. Later instruments frequently used one or more flat-plate photocells constructed using selenium, silicon, or other material. Photoelectric colorimeters generally measure three components of the light transmitted through or reflected from a colored sample. These three components are defined by the spectral responses of the photocells alone or as modified by the spectral transmittance of three sets of color filters.

The replacement of visual by physical methods permitted color evaluation to be automated. This, together with the increase in the production of dyes and mass-produced goods, led to a rapid expansion of industrial colorimetry. An additional incentive to the use of colorimeters was the 1931 Commission Internationale de l'Eclairage (CIE) agreement on a standard system of color description. This quantified language of color was reflected in instruments calibrated for the new CIE units, the system of color specification that remains the most widespread today. Colorimeters proliferated after 1932, but commercial and industrial implementations through the 1930s led to some dissatisfaction with the reliability of colorimeters by the end of the decade. Tristimulus colorimeters found little application to quality-control problems. The employment of only three color attributes proved inadequate to fully characterize certain materials, particularly those having glossy, heterogeneous, or fluorescent surfaces. The color comparator and, for more thorough evaluation, the more accurate but complex **spectrophotometer** have found the most widespread application.

Sean F. Johnston

Bibliography

Abney, William de Wiveleslie. *Colour Measurement and Mixture*. London: SPCK, 1891.

Campbell, Norman R. "Photoelectric Colour Matching." *Journal of Scientific Instruments* 2 (1925): 177–87.

Committee on Colorimetry of the Optical Society of America. *The Science of Color.* New York: Thomas Y. Crowell, 1953.

Johnston, Sean F. "A Notion or a Measure: The Quantification of Light to 1939." Ph.D. dissertation. University of Leeds, 1994.

Luckiesh, Matthew. *Colour and Its Applications.* London: Constable, 1915.

Cometarium

Cometariums are models showing the orbital motion of a comet around the sun. The earliest date from the eighteenth century, when various models of astronomical motion became increasingly common. Most of these **planetariums** did not attempt to demonstrate the elliptical (Keplerian) motion of the planets, which is difficult to do on a small-scale model. Because planetary orbits almost resemble circles, this was not a major drawback to the usefulness of planetariums. However, any reasonable model of a comet must indicate its elliptical orbit.

John Theophilus Desaguliers was credited with the invention of what was called the cometarium by James Ferguson. Desaguliers described his device, which demonstrated the first two laws of Johannes Kepler, showing that planetary orbits are elliptical and that an imaginary line from the planet to the sun would sweep out equal areas in equal increments of time. Taking advantage of the public interest in the predicted return of Halley's

Cometarium, by W. and S. Jones, early nineteenth century. SM 1909-202. Courtesy of SSPL.

comet in 1758, the London instrument-maker Benjamin Martin advertised an "improved" version. Martin called his instrument a "cometarium," and marketed it along with his book *The Theory of Comets Illustrated* (1757). The instrument-maker William Jones brought out a new design in the early years of the nineteenth century. William Pearson, who wrote extensively on planetary models, was probably involved in the design of a cometarium with elliptical gear-wheels made by the London instrument-maker Robert Fidler (ca. 1810–1822).

Liba Taub

Bibliography

Desaguliers, J.T. *A Course of Experimental Philosophy,* Vol. 1, 451–66. London, 1734.

Ferguson, James. *Astronomy Explained upon Sir Isaac Newton's Principles,* 254–56. London, 1756.

King, Henry C., and John R. Millburn. *Geared to the Stars: The Evolution of Planetariums, Orreries, and Astronomical Clocks.* Toronto: University of Toronto Press, 1978.

Macdonald, Angus, and A.D. Morrison-Low. *A Heavenly Library: Treasures from the Royal Observatory's Crawford Collection.* Edinburgh: Royal Observatory, 1994.

Millburn, John R., and Henry C. King. *Wheelwright of the Heavens: The Life and Work of James Ferguson, FRS,* 64, 299. London: Vade-Mecum, 1988.

Comparator, Astronomical

An astronomical comparator is used to compare the spectra or star images on different astronomical plates.

Spectrum Comparator

Ernst Abbe's comparator (1874) was used in the 1890s to measure wavelengths and the line shifts of spectra. Abbe's comparator was precise but slow—the measurement of one spectrum might take up to several days, while photographs could be taken in about an hour. A more precise and more efficient comparator was designed by Johannes Hartmann in 1906 and produced by Carl Zeiss of Jena. With this instrument one did not need to know the wavelength absolutely. Rather, the measurement was taken relatively, for instance to the solar spectrum. This reduced the time of analysis to one-third. Since the 1920s, comparators have been replaced by photoelectric microphotometers, in which the spectrum is scanned onto photographic paper for further measurements.

Stereo and Blink Comparators

Carl Pulfrich of the Carl Zeiss Optical Workshop developed the stereo comparator in 1899, basing his instrument on the stereoscopic distance-measuring device of 1893. Pulfrich presented his idea in May 1900 to Max Wolf, a Heidelberg astronomer who had been working with stereo photography since 1892, and he demonstrated a prototype showing a three-dimensional image of the moons of Saturn at the meeting of the international Astronomische Gesellschaft in Heidelberg in September 1901. This instrument, later used by Wolf, has belonged to the Deutsches Museum in Munich since 1933.

As early as 1901, Wolf had suggested that the new device could be used to measure the relative proper motion of fixed stars and for other astronomical applications. Following Wolf's advice, Pulfrich soon discovered a new asteroid on one of Wolf's photographic plates. But the main use of stereo comparators was to search for variable stars, which are hard to find with the naked eye. During the first test of the stereo comparator in 1901, ten new variables in the Orion nebula were found.

The stereo comparator could not be used by people who have defective vision in one eye—as had Pulfrich himself! Thus, in 1904, he developed the blink comparator, and this was soon widely used for astronomical applications. In a blink comparator one views two negative photographic plates of the same star field taken at different times. Since brighter stars blacken the photographic plate more deeply than faint stars, variable stars can be identified as black dots with different sizes on photographic plates exposed at different times. A variable star appears to "blink" because the light path is switched rapidly between the two photographic plates. The blink comparator soon led to the discovery of hundreds of variable stars.

With objects that move rapidly relative to the stars, one has to look not for a blinking but for a jumping object. A spectacular success was Clyde W. Tombaugh's discovery of the planet Pluto in 1930; he used a Zeiss blink comparator and photographic plates taken with a 13-in. refractor at the Lowell Observatory.

Stereo comparator, by Carl Zeiss, early 1920s. Courtesy of the Deutsches Museum.

An improved model of the blink comparator was developed by Walther Bauersfeld of the Zeiss Works in 1932, following an idea of Paul Guthnick, director of the Observatory Berlin-Babelsberg. Even today the blink comparator is used from time to time, such as for checking the older photographic plates if a supernova is discovered.

Gudrun Wolfschmidt

Bibliography

Hartmann, Johannes. "Ein neues Verfahren zur Messung der Linienverschiebung in Spektrogrammen." *Publikationen des Astrophysikalischen Observatoriums zu Potsdam* 18, no. 53 (1906): 1–47.

Pulfrich, Carl. "Ueber neuere Anwendungen der Stereoskopie und über einen hierfür bestimmten Stereo-Komparator." *Zeitschrift für Instrumentenkunde* 22 (1902): 65–81, 133–41, 178–92, 229–46.

Schneller, Hans. "Der neue Blinkkomparator von Zeiss." *Zeitschrift für Instrumentenkunde* 52 (1932): 480–84.

Wolf, Max, and Carl Pulfrich. "Briefwechsel über den Stereokomparator 1901–1920." Deutsches Museum, Archive/ Sondersammlungen/Dokumentationen HS 3287–98, 1901–1920.

Wolfschmidt, Gudrun. "Die Weiterentwick-

lung von Abbes Geräten bei Zeiss Jena und ihre Bedeutung für die Astronomie in der ersten Hälfte des 20. Jahrhunderts." In *Carl Zeiss und Ernst Abbe— Leben, Wirken und Bedeutung,* edited by R. Stolz and J. Wittig, 331–62. Jena: Universitätsverlag, 1993.

Comparator, Length

Standards for cubit measures from ancient Egypt bear testimony to the importance of accurate length measure to the earliest civilizations. Most early length standards were end measures, which were checked against a bed measure or gauge, with any difference being apparent. The need for more precise measures was recognized by the eighteenth century, being driven by emerging disciplines such as surveying. The result was scientifically constructed line standards, their length being the distance between two precisely ruled lines. The consequent improvement in length standards required a commensurate means to verify the improved accuracy. The outcome was a whole new family of measuring instruments to verify the new line-measure standards. This class of apparatus must be distinguished from those used in engineering metrology, often grouped under the heading of comparators. These include measuring instruments such as optimeters and dial gauges.

The role of the length comparator in verifying length measures and standards has three distinct applications. Each relates to a different level of precision that has a recognized path of traceability, from the primary standard to local tertiary standards. At the top of the pyramid is the comparison made between the primary material standard and the current natural length standard, the wavelength of light. Lower in precision is the comparison made between primary length standards and secondary reference standards. These secondary standards are copies of the primary one, and are themselves compared with local standards. The local working standards are in turn used to verify length measures used in commerce.

The bed measure, or gauge, by its very nature cannot be used to a high order of accuracy. By the nineteenth century the improved precision of line measures resulted in most end measures being relegated to use as local standards. Later instruments allowed direct comparison between line standards and end measures. A good example is that constructed by Troughton and Simms for the British Standards Department. Comparisons are made on the apparatus with two pairs of moveable plates that slide against a line reference scale. The final measurement is read from a vernier scale with a **microscope**. Flexure of the standards is avoided by the use of two sets of supporting rollers.

In tandem with the construction of precision line standards, scientific instruments were developed capable of evaluating them. The features and general design of these line comparators had become well established by the start of the twentieth century. These can be explained by reference to the "Geneva" Comparator produced in 1902 by the Swiss company Société Genevoise. This comparator consists of a pair of **micrometer** microscopes fixed rigidly over each end of a double-walled water bath. The standards to be measured lie on two adjustable girders in the inner tank of the water bath. The tank itself rests on a wheeled carriage that allows each standard to be moved under the measuring microscopes. The comparator stands on a concrete pillar isolated from the rest of the building and is insulated to improve thermal stability. In operation, each of the line standards is alternately compared under the micrometer microscopes

Commercial length comparator for both end and bed measures, made by Troughton and Simms, 1869. SM 1933-388. Courtesy of SSPL.

and then reversed and exchanged to avoid any optical distortions. These measurements are then reduced by simple calculations to give a length value at a fixed temperature. Comparison made over a range of temperatures will give the coefficient of expansion. Such differences are important, as the International Prototype Meter is defined at 0°C, while the Imperial Yard is specified at 62°F.

The use of the wavelength of light as a natural length standard was suggested in the early nineteenth century. By 1864, the French physicist Armand Fizeau had used an **interferometer** to measure the coefficient of expansion of the platinum alloy later used in meter standards. Subsequent work undertaken at the Bureau International des Poids et Mesures in Paris resulted in successful comparisons with meter line standards. Subsequent line comparators incorporated optical interferometers into their design, as can be seen in the "Tutton" wave comparator. In this instrument a light interferometer is coupled to one of the micrometer microscopes on an otherwise conventional line comparator. Measurement of the interference fringes gives a very precise value of the displacement of the micrometer microscope. By the 1930s, improvements pioneered at the National Physical Laboratory near London allowed end standards to be measured using wavelength comparators. Today the international standard of length, the meter, is defined as the distance traveled by Laser light in a vacuum during $1/299,792,458$ of a second.

Kevin L. Johnson

Bibliography

Barrel, H.A. "A Short History of Measurement Standards at the National Physical Laboratory." *Contemporary Physics* 9 (1968): 205–26.

Hume, Kenneth J. *A History of Engineering Metrology.* London: Mechanical Engineering, 1980.

Johnson, W.H. "Comparators." In *A Dictionary of Applied Physics,* edited by Richard Glazebrook, Vol. 3, 233–57. London: Macmillan, 1923.

Rolt, F.H. *Gauges and Fine Measurement.* London: Macmillan, 1929.

Comparator, Lovibond

Joseph Lovibond was a London brewer who began in the 1870s to seek a way to grade the color of beer. Although he spent several years investigating schemes of color matching, he had little time for theorizing. Rather, he confined himself to empirical experiment, which "enabled the author to devote much of his time and energy to actual work, which would otherwise have been employed in profitless controversy." The outcome of his studies was a practicable color classification system and reliable comparison instrument, the Tintometer, which was put on the market in 1887.

The Tintometer employed previously established principles of color measurement, namely the comparison of the sample with a calibrated reference consisting of a combination of three primary colors. Lovibond's development of a suitable reference is what distinguished his instrument from competitors and promoted its commercial success. Schemes of color "mapping" had been proposed by others, but Lovibond was particularly successful in generating a system of color description based on a quantitative numerical index.

The original Tintometer consisted of two viewing tubes about 25 cm long, converging at an eyepiece. The transparent sample was placed in one tube, and filters from graded sets were combined in the other to match it when viewing "white" light illuminating a white surface (or the sample itself, if opaque). The matching color was thus obtained by subtracting components from nominally balanced light. In a period when artificial lighting was poorly controllable, nonstandardized, and distinctly yellow in hue, Lovibond recommended using diffused north daylight on a misty or overcast day as the ideal "white" light source to be used with the comparator. The colored glass filters, produced in magenta, yellow, and cyan hues, were scaled from nearly colorless to highly saturated. The units of this empirical color scale were arbitrary except that three colored filters of the same value yielded a grey or neutral tone, and filter values of the same color could be combined additively. This ability to combine filters arithmetically allowed several million colors to be generated.

The Tintometer found use in industries as diverse as oil production, water quality measurement, and agricultural grading. The instrument was used in two distinct ways: either to label an unknown color in terms of its equivalent filters (for example, a colored wool being described as 3 Red, 6.6 Yellow, and 6 Blue) or as a means of quantitative analysis. Lovibond showed that his method could correlate the color of flour to its market price, and accurately infer the concentration of carbon in steel. As important as the instrument itself were the colorimetric methods developed by its inventor and users. To determine the concentration of lead in water, for example, an indicator solution consisting of a drop of acetic acid and two of sulphuretted hydrogen solution would be added to a half pint of water and used to fill a 4-in.-long Tintometer cell; the colored solution would be matched to filter series 52, and the number of "degrees" divided by forty to give the grains of lead per gallon of water. Later versions of the instrument employed disks of filters calibrated for particular analyses such as the measurement of the pH of water. By World War I, the Tintometer was the basis of formal standards in the petroleum industry, leather trades, and boards of health, and it was the recipient of awards by several scientific societies.

The Tintometer was increasingly criticized from the 1920s (when color research was particularly active at British and American standards laboratories) for three reasons: the combination of more than two or three filters could introduce errors owing to reflections; the "steps" of the color scale were not precisely uniform; and, matching relied on the characteristics of the uncontrolled "white" light source as well as the sample and reference filters. Later variants such as the Lovibond Schofield Tintometer (1939) employed only two colors and a means of adjusting light intensity through the filters to make it compatible with the newer Commission Internationale de L'Eclairage (CIE)

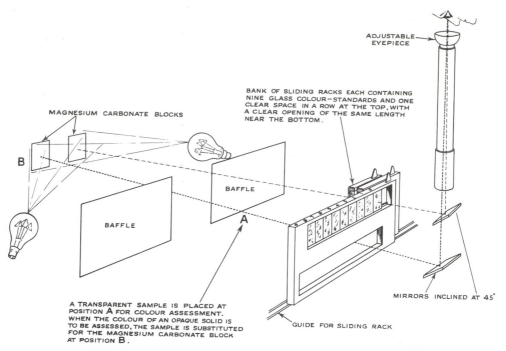

ADJUSTABLE
EYEPIECE

BANK OF SLIDING RACKS EACH CONTAINING
NINE GLASS COLOUR—STANDARDS AND ONE
CLEAR SPACE IN A ROW AT THE TOP, WITH
A CLEAR OPENING OF THE SAME LENGTH
NEAR THE BOTTOM.

MAGNESIUM CARBONATE BLOCKS

B

BAFFLE

BAFFLE

A

A TRANSPARENT SAMPLE IS PLACED AT
POSITION A FOR COLOUR ASSESSMENT.
WHEN THE COLOUR OF AN OPAQUE SOLID IS
TO BE ASSESSED, THE SAMPLE IS SUBSTITUTED
FOR THE MAGNESIUM CARBONATE BLOCK
AT POSITION B.

MIRRORS INCLINED AT 45°

GUIDE FOR SLIDING RACK

Schematic diagram of the tintometer colorimeter. Courtesy of SSPL.

system of color measurement introduced in 1931. With such adaptations, the Tintometer and its color system remain in active use a century after its introduction.

Sean F. Johnston

Bibliography

Gibson, Kasson S., and F.K. Harris. "A Spectrophotometric Analysis of the Lovibond Color System." *Journal of the Optical Society of America* 12 (1926): 481–86.

Hunt, Robert W.G. *Measuring Colour.* Chichester: Ellis Horwood, 1987.

Johnston, Sean F. "A Notion or a Measure: The Quantification of Light to 1939." Ph.D. dissertation. University of Leeds, 1994.

Lovibond, Joseph W. *Light and Colour Theories and Their Relation to Light and Colour Standardization.* London: E. and F.N. Spon, 1915.

———. *Measurement of Light and Colour Sensations.* London: George Gill and Sons, 1897.

Compass, Aeronautical

Like **compasses** used on land or at sea, an aeronautical compass provides a fixed line of reference from which angles can be measured as bearings. It indicates directions, primarily north and south, and minimizes errors due to magnetic dip, precession, turning errors, and easterly and westerly speed effect.

The development of aeronautical compasses followed the use of balloons in the late nineteenth century, and the invention of airships and aircraft soon thereafter. In 1909 Samuel Cody flew a cross-country exercise, navigating with a liquid filled marine compass.

First Attempts

The first satisfactory compass for aircraft use was developed during World War I, and was eventually known as the P4 or P6 Aperiodic Aero Compass. Around 1915 the P250 pattern was constructed with the compass bowl resting on a horseshoe pad in the base of an outer case. Henry Hughes & Son Ltd. began producing the P259 in 1915. This model was difficult to manufacture on account of problems with card suspension.

The P2 (1923) had a grid wire method of course indication. Damping was obtained by the use of four layer magnets, and the totally enclosed instrument was suspended by sorborubber packs. Alan Cobham used this type on his flights to the Cape and Australia. The P3

Type 5/17 "Quick Period" aircraft compass, ca. 1919. SM 1919-531. Courtesy of SSPL.

(1926) had a vertical card with glass window for dashboard use. With the P7 (1938), the magnet system could be viewed from beneath, via a mirror.

These compasses were made so that bearings could be taken with a suitable sighting arrangement similar to that used on marine compasses. Some were fitted with electrical illumination. By 1942 the N series was introduced as a course-checking compass. This was a dashboard instrument, and could be fitted to pilots' or navigation panels. It is still in use as the E series, and forms the basic direction-checking facility on many military and private aircraft.

Further Development

The Distant Reading Compass with gyro-stabilization was devised in the late 1920s, and service tests were carried out before World War II. This uses a pivoted sensitive magnetic system monitoring a horizontal axis gyro, which in turn stabilizes an azimuth scale. Magnetic heading is obtained at a master unit and is transmitted to repeater units at crew positions.

The German firm of Karl Bamberg produced the first remote indicating compass for aircraft use. Another German compass of this period was the Askania Selenium DR compass, a complicated instrument using selenium cells.

In the U.K., Henry Hughes & Son Ltd. produced the Holmes telecompass in 1929. The master unit consisted of an ordinary liquid-fitted compass, the bowl being kept in alignment with the magnetic element by means of a follow-up motor. The liquid was made conductive and the two electrodes were fitted to the bowl and card. These electrodes were used as a **Wheatstone bridge**. When the bridge was unbalanced the current fed to the follow-up motor.

The first American remote indicating compass, the Pioneer Magnesyn, appeared in 1940. The sensitive element is a magnet supported by a float in a liquid-filled bowl. This magnet induces a current in a torroidal wound coil, the strength of the current depending on the aircraft's heading. The electrical effect thus gives a remote indication. Another American example was the Pioneer Gyro Fluxgate Compass, which used a gyro-stabilized fluxgate instead of a magnetic system. This system was unusual in that the fluxgate element with gyro was placed in the wing of an aircraft, the remote indicator being on the pilot's panel.

The German Patin Compass was yet another wartime development. A liquid-damped magnetic element was housed in a gimbal system and positioned away from adverse magnetic effects. Repeaters were linked to an ordinary gyro or to the automatic pilot.

After World War II, distant-reading compasses gave way to those with the Power Selsyn transmission system used to lock the gyro unit in alignment with the earth's magnetic field. The G4 series of compasses contained all the advantages of the older instruments, but was more adaptable to aircraft of varying types. The G4B system, for example, was composed of a gyro unit, master indicator, flux-valve detector unit, amplifier, and control unit. This popular compass was highly accurate and easy to use, and probably the ultimate aviator's compass system before the introduction of computerized technology.

Jeremy P. Collins

Bibliography

Davidson, Martin. *The Gyroscope and Its Applications.* London: Hutchinsons Scientific and Technical, 1946.
McMinnies, W.G. *Practical Flying: A Complete Course of Flying Instruction.* London: Temple, 1918.
Molloy, E. *Air Navigation.* London: George Newnes, 1942.
Weems, P.V.H., and Charles A. Zweng. *Instrument Flying.* Annapolis, Md.: n.p., 1957.

Compass, Gyro-

A gyrocompass serves as a substitute for a magnetic **compass**, using rotating wheels instead of magnetic needles. Its development is characterized by the interaction of several inventors and scientists and the blend of mechanical skill and mathematical analysis. The gyro gained popularity with demonstration models like the "machine to demonstrate the laws of rotation of the Earth" developed by the German Johann v. Bohnenberger (1817), the rotascope of the American Walter Johnson (1831), and the **gyroscope** of the Frenchman Léon Foucault (1852). Foucault's gyroscope was mechanically precise, enabling him to claim that a spinning gyro that was free to move on a horizontal level had a tendency to align its axis to the axis of the rotating earth and to adjust parallel to the meridian, and thus could serve as a north-seeking compass.

The gyroscope had great influence on scientists, as in the gyrostatic models of elasticity by William Thomson, and on inventors, as in the stabilization or guidance of vehicles. The use of iron and steel in ships severely disturbed their traditional course indicator, the magnetic compass. Thomson's proposals for a "gyrostatic model of the magnetic compass" in 1884 are to be found in a patent by the Dutchman Marinus van den Bos, of the same year, "to improve the Mariner's Compass," replacing the compass needle and card with an electrically driven wheel. Werner Siemens bought this patent to utilize the potential of the new instrument commercially, but gave up after testing a prototype in 1889 without success. Likewise, attempts to electrify Foucault's gyroscope, conducted by the French navy, were not continued.

As the mechanical difficulties were obvious to experts, private inventors took up the challenge. The German Hermann Anschütz-Kaempfe, whose plan to reach the North Pole in a submarine had focused on developing a suitable direction indicator, presented his gyro instrument for patent in 1904. By then, the Siemens Company had commissioned the physicist Oscar Martienssen to conduct a feasibility study and a mathematical analysis. He concluded that a gyrocompass was unsuitable for use in a ship, as it would be disturbed by the

A Brown gyrocompass, with four-inch gyro wheel, early twentieth century. SM 1948-345. Courtesy of SSPL.

ship's movement. This in fact turned out to be the major problem in gyrocompass design.

Anschütz-Kaempfe, then joined by his cousin Max Schuler, a graduate engineer, succeeded in demonstrating and selling a prototype to the German navy in 1908; from 1910, this instrument was also built under license by Elliott Bros. in England.

In the Anschütz gyrocompass, the spinning axis of the gyro was driven by ac at twenty thousand revolutions per minute; since the casing floated in mercury, it was free to move about the horizontal and vertical axes. The gyro was suspended in such a manner that the forces of precession brought its axis into line with the north-south axis of the earth. The following oscillations about this direction, resulting from gyroscopic inertia, were dampened by special devices.

The pendulous suspension was liable to errors caused by accelerations of the vehicle, known as ballistic deflection. Schuler found that a pendulous device with a period of 84 minutes—equal to a pendulum of the earth's radius—automatically corrects for the disturbing influence of ship accelerations. This essential effect, later called Schuler tuning, is fundamental to gyro-navigation systems.

The American inventor Elmer Sperry visited Germany and Anschütz in 1909, and later England and the inventor Sidney Brown. In 1911 the Sperry Gyroscope Co. presented their first gyrocompass, also suspended pendulously but using a wire suspension like that of Foucault.

During sea trials by the German navy and tests conducted by James Henderson for the British navy, both types of gyrocompass showed rolling or quadrantal errors, deviations caused if the ship, rolling in a seaway, took courses between the cardinal points. Both designs were altered with additional gyros. By 1912, the Anschütz Tri-Gyro-Compass had suppressed these errors of the single gyrocompass; Sperry introduced a single auxiliary gyro two years later.

In 1916 the English professor John Perry, together with Sidney Brown, patented a gyrocompass with a nearly frictionless vertical axis on a pulsating cushion of oil; this also had a liquid level control using interconnected boxes and applying a controlling couple to the single gyro. This turned out to be unaffected by the motion of the ship in a seaway. A similar device, called a mercury ballistic, was used to improve the existing Sperry compass.

Because of the similarities in the design of these instruments, a great deal of energy was mobilized in priority claims and patent infringements. In 1914 the Anschütz Co. started patent litigation against Sperry; Albert Einstein, a physicist and former patent expert, was to assess the case, which Sperry lost. In 1927 the British Admiralty set up a committee to investigate the relation between the Sperry compass and the Brown compass with reference to the level control. The committee found that Brown and Henderson had the original conception.

World War I provided the testing ground for the gyrocompass, and revealed a number of defects in the instrument. Anschütz-Kaempfe sought to mount the gyro system in a frictionless spherical case surrounding the gyros that enabled it to float without contact to the case. Einstein provided the solution for centering the floating sphere with a magnet coil.

The advantage of the gyrocompass is that it can be connected via transmitters to distant repeaters and course recorders, and it can also be used together with automatic pilots, which were gradually introduced into merchant navies during the 1920s.

Jobst Broelmann

Bibliography

Fanning, A.E. *Steady as She Goes. A History of the Compass Department of the Admiralty.* London: Her Majesty's Stationery Office, 1986.

Hughes, T.P. *Elmer Sperry: Inventor and Engineer.* Baltimore: Johns Hopkins University Press, 1971.

Lohmeier, D., and B. Schell, eds. *Einstein, Anschütz und der Kieler Kreiselkompaß.* Heide: Westholstein, 1992.

Rawlings, A.L. *The Theory of Gyroscopic Compass and Its Deviations.* London: Macmillan, 1929.

Compass, Magnetic

A magnetic compass indicates the direction of the magnetic pole. Its main element is a pivoted magnetic needle (or set of needles) attached to a graduated compass card. The pivot is fixed in a bowl that is in turn mounted in gimbals, to isolate the compass from the motions of the ship. A lubber line is marked on the rim of the bowl that is aligned parallel to the vessel's fore and aft line. The angular difference between the lubber line and north as indicated by the card is the course or heading of the ship. Some compasses are provided with an azimuth mirror, allowing bearings of objects to be read off the card. Providing the variation and deviation are known, the true course or bearing can found.

Although the directional properties of the lodestone had long been known, the earliest realistic European and Chinese references to a compass date to A.D. 1187 and A.D. 1111 respectively. These compasses appear to have been simple magnetized needles made to float in a bowl of water by means of a pierced reed, an arrangement workable only in calm weather. Until the mid 1700s, compass needles were made from soft iron and magnetized by stroking them with lodestone.

The first known reference to a dry pivoted compass is dated 1269, to a compass card 1380, and to gimbals 1537. The earliest surviving compasses are those excavated from the *Mary Rose*, a British ship that sank in 1545. The most complete example from this wreck is a bowl with pivot mounted in gimbals; unfortunately, both needle and card perished with their long immersion. By 1550 it was standard practice to graduate the compass card into thirty-two equiangular points, and with the adoption of the azimuth compass in the eighteenth century to divide the card into degrees as well.

Knowledge of magnetic variation (the discrepancy in direction between magnetic and true north at any point on the earth's surface) began to appear around the middle 1400s, and to counter its effects the north point of the card was frequently offset from the axis of the needle so that the north indicated by the card was approximately true north. This practice declined as voyages became longer and the variable nature of variation became known. Although the first variation chart is said to have been made in the mid 1500s, the first recognizable world variation chart was published by Edmund Halley in 1701.

Although the compass gradually became more complex, it was not until 1837 that dissatisfaction with the performance of compasses supplied to the Royal Navy led to the founding of the Admiralty Compass Committee. From this time the magnetic compass was systematically developed and its performance analyzed, particularly by Captain F. Evans R.N. and the Scottish lawyer/mathematician Archibald Smith.

The introduction of increasing amounts of iron into ships during the nineteenth century led to further errors, called deviation, affecting compasses. In his surveying voyage to Australia in 1801, M. Flinders compensated for this effect by placing a vertical soft iron bar immediately aft of the compass. In 1824 the French mathematician and physicist S.D. Poisson published a rigorous analysis of the deviation problem, which provided the basic mathematics, to be later developed by Archibald Smith. In 1835 the Admiralty measured the deviation of all points of the compass on the iron paddle steamer *Garry Owen*. The results were analyzed by the Astronomer Royal, G.B. Airy, who advocated a system of compass correction by means of compensating magnets. This system consisted of a variety of "hard" (permanent) magnets to compensate for the permanent magnetism of the ship, and "soft" iron masses to compensate for transient magnetism induced by virtue of heading and position. Airy's ideas were later amended in light of Smith's and Evan's collaborative work.

Toward the end of the nineteenth century, dry card compasses were gradually replaced by liquid-filled compasses (particularly in naval applications) in which the card was semibuoyant and the effect of the liquid (usually a form of

William Thomson's ten-inch compass and binnacle with correctors for quadrantal semicircular and keeling errors, 1870s. SM 1879-33. Courtesy of SSPL.

alcohol) was to reduce the card's sensitivity to error induced by ship motion, vibration, and gunfire. Associated with these efforts is the work of E.S. Ritchie, W.R. Hammersley, and William Thomson.

The marine magnetic compass has changed relatively little since the beginning of the twentieth century. The problem of adapting the magnetic compass for submarines was overcome by mounting the compass outside the hull and reading the card by means of a periscope. The basic marine magnetic compass was also developed for use in land vehicles, including tanks.

During World War II, a series of sun compasses were developed and used by Allied forces operating in North Africa. These were sun-dials worked in reverse. Knowing the local solar time (gained from a knowledge of the vehicle's longitude, Greenwich Mean Time, and the equation of time), the compass plate was oriented so that the shadow cast by the gnomon lined up with the local solar time inscribed on the compass's disk. North was indicated by what amounted to the direction indicated by the time 1200.

With the widespread introduction of ever smaller and more robust **gyrocompasses** following the war, the marine magnetic compass has tended to be viewed as a standby emergency instrument, except for the smallest of craft. Their biggest users are merchant ships, on which they are required to be fitted by law.

Thomas Wright

Bibliography

Bagnold, R.A. "Navigating Ashore." *Journal of the Institute of Navigation* 6 (1953): 185–93.

Fanning, A.E. *Steady as She Goes: A History of the Compass Department of the Admiralty.* London: Her Majesty's Stationery Office, 1986.

Hine, A. *Magnetic Compasses and Magnetometers.* London: Hilger, 1968.

May, W.E. *A History of Marine Navigation.* Henley on Thames, U.K.: Foulis, 1973.

Compass, Surveyor's

See CIRCUMFERENTOR (SURVEYOR'S COMPASS)

Compass, Variation

Magnetic variation (or declination) is the angle between a magnetic meridian and a geographical meridian. In other words, it is the angle between the orientation of a compass needle and a line pointing toward geographic north. The variation alters irregularly, depending both on location and on time, and European navigators had recognized the problems this posed by at least the fifteenth century. People using compasses for practical purposes developed modifications helping them to make corrections for variation, whereas natural philosophers and scientists interested in terrestrial magnetism designed instruments to measure variation precisely.

The early chronology is contested, but during the fifteenth century, German craftworkers were marking their compass **sun-dial** with an offset line to allow for variation. In the sixteenth century, Portuguese navigators, notably Pedro Nuñez and João de Castro, described and used an instrument for calculating variation by comparing the shadows cast by the sun at two different times of day onto a dial oriented magnetically. In England William Borough discussed this double altitude method in 1581.

Seamen deployed various techniques of compensating their compasses for variation, such as permanently rotating the card relative to the needle, or using a rectifier with two concentric dials enabling the variation to be read directly. By the end of the seventeenth century, the most important navigational instrument for measuring variation was the azimuth compass. This was a round, wood-cased steering compass suspended in a wooden box and fitted on top with a circular sighting mechanism—either one or two vertical sights and a string—for observing the bearing of the sun or a star of known position. The circumference of the compass card was divided into degrees, so that the angular location of the string's shadow, and hence the variation, could be recorded. Like all marine compasses of this period, these instruments were inaccurate and poorly made. They were also difficult to use, especially at night or in stormy weather.

In the middle of the eighteenth century, Gowin Knight and John Smeaton introduced numerous modifications intended to make azimuth compasses more precise and reliable. These included a high-quality narrow steel needle balanced on a fine suspension point, sturdy nonmagnetic brass casing, a light card with radial adjustable weights, and an outer brass ring accurate to half a degree. Such compasses cost about £5. By the end of the century, more complex models had been invented, most importantly by Kenneth McCulloch, who replaced the string with a double lens system, and by Ralph Walker. Selling at 10 to 15 guineas, these compasses had elaborate sighting devices and were said to be more stable and easier to use when at sea. However, users unaware of the effects of nearby iron continually complained that readings were inconsistent, and many navigators queried the value of using such precise instruments.

During the nineteenth century, with the advent of iron ships and collaborative international projects of terrestrial mensuration, the British Navy paid far more attention to instructing its officers in using, maintaining, and correcting compasses, and in routinely measuring

Philos. Trans. N.° 495 TAB. III. *p. 51*.

C

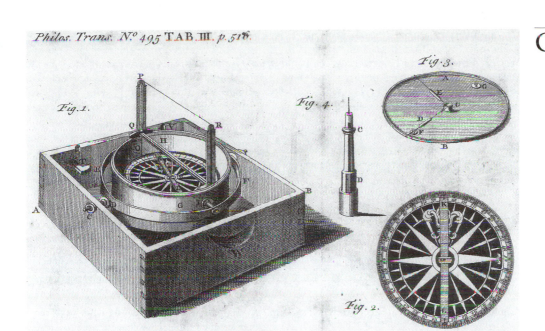

Gowin Knight and John Smeaton's azimuth compass, 1750. Knight (1750): facing page 115. Courtesy of SSPL.

variation. Many new designs were tested, and in the 1840s the Admiralty Standard Compass became the principal compass for the next fifty years, also being adopted by many foreign governments. The final version had four needles, interchangeable cards for different conditions, and an azimuth circle with two verniers giving readings accurate to 1 minute of arc. In the last quarter of the century, William Thomson introduced an azimuth mirror that reflected the image of a distant object onto a magnified portion of the compass card. Similar instruments are used today for rapid readings.

While navigators at sea needed robust and portable compasses that would measure any value of variation reasonably accurately, natural philosophers on land required instruments yielding extremely accurate readings over a small range. Borough and William Gilbert illustrated similar double-altitude semicircular instruments and during the seventeenth century, Henry Gellibrand and Edmund Gunter both systematically investigated the changes in magnetic variation.

Unlike navigators, natural philosophers stressed the importance of keeping a compass's environment free of iron. In conjunction with instrument-makers, they successively modified variation compasses to obtain more precise readings. In the 1720s, the watch-maker George Graham measured the variation with thin needles balanced on steel points by crystal caps, able to rotate 20 degrees either side of a zero line he established by stretching strings across his house. By the middle of the eighteenth century, George Adams was selling a variation compass (probably designed by Knight) with an integral microscope and a vernier scale for accurately recording the position of a slender steel needle about 30 cm long. Such compasses were used to record local changes in variation with time, and to measure the variation in different parts of the world. In the 1770s, Henry Cavendish described further refinements to make the instrument more convenient and accurate to use, incorporating a telescope for aligning it with a geographical meridian. He also discussed ways of assessing and reducing instrument error. In France in the 1780s, Jean Jacques Cassini measured the variation by suspending, rather than balancing, an asymmetrical needle about 30 cm long.

During the nineteenth century, scientists around the world built iron-free magnetic observatories with permanently built-in delicate instruments, and later developed photographic techniques for recording their readings. Surveyors and explorers used smaller, more portable, variation compasses, typically about 20 cm long, with a flat, square-ended needle that was protected by a glass and brass case and was able to swing 15 degrees either side of zero.

From around the 1820s, scientists increasingly used the unifilar **magnetometers** first introduced by Christian Hansteen, which could measure intensity as well as variation. These relied on heavier and shorter cylindrical needles, pointed at each end and suspended by a long silk thread. Intensity was found by counting the oscillation rate, while, for variation, the instrument was accurately aligned with the geographic meridian before observing the rest position of the magnet.

Patricia Fara

Bibliography

Cavendish, Henry. "An Account of the Meteorological Instruments Used at the Royal Society's House." *Philosophical Transactions of the Royal Society of London* 66 (1776): 375–401.

Chapman, Sydney, and Julius Bartels. *Geomagnetism,* Vol. 2, 898–937. Oxford: Clarendon, 1940.

Hewson, J.B. *A History of the Practice of Navigation,* 47–72, 120–54. Glasgow: Brown, Son and Ferguson, 1983.

Knight, Gowin. "A Description of a Mariner's Compass Contrived by Gowin Knight, MB FRS." *Philosophical Transactions of the Royal Society of London* 46 (1750): 505–17.

McConnell, Anita. "Nineteenth-Century Geomagnetic Instruments and Their Makers." In *Nineteenth Century Scientific Instruments and Their Makers,* edited by P.R. de Clercq, 29–52. Amsterdam: Rodopi, 1985. Atlantic Highlands, N.J.: Humanities Press, 1985.

Computer, Digital

A digital computer uses discretely variable physical entities for its essential operation. **Electronic analog computers** use continuously variable quantities.

Automatic digital computation can be traced to Charles Babbage's Difference Engine, conceived in 1821. The purpose of the Difference Engine was to eliminate human errors in the production of printed mathematical tables, navigational tables in particular. The Difference Engine was designed to tabulate polynomial functions using the method of finite differences. This method allowed successive tabular values to be generated by repeated addition, which is comparatively easy to mechanize, and eliminated the need for the multiplications and divisions ordinarily required to evaluate each term in a polynomial expression. Except for a few partial assemblies, Babbage failed to complete any of his engines in physical form. Georg and Edvard Scheutz, a Swedish father and son team, built three difference engines. A prototype was completed in 1843. The first production machine (1853) was purchased by the Dudley Observatory, Albany, New York, for astronomical work; the second (1859) was made for the General Register Office, London, and used in the preparation of the English Life Table of 1864. Martin Wiberg's compact difference engine (ca. 1860) was used to prepare volumes of tables published in Swedish, German, French, and English. A motor-driven difference engine by George Grant was exhibited in Philadelphia in 1876.

Babbage's Difference Engine is a **calculating machine** in the sense that its use is confined to a fixed set of operations determined by its wheelwork. It earns its place as the starting point of the digital computer because it was automatic—that is, it was the first machine to sucessfully incorporate mathematical rule in mechanism. Unlike its manual predecessors, it did not rely on the informed intervention of the operator to provide useful results. However, it was not a general-purpose machine. Babbage's Analytical Engine, conceived by 1834, represents the first design for an automatic general-purpose calculating machine. This could be programmed with punched cards to perform the four basic arithmetic functions in any sequence. It was capable of iteration and conditional branching, and its internal architecture featured the functional separation between the Store, where information and results were held, and the Mill, which processed information fetched from the Store. The separation of the Store and Mill is a fundamental feature of the modern electronic digital computer described by John von Neumann in 1945. Babbage saw the Engine as a universal calculating machine capable of evaluating almost any algebraic expression.

Although Babbage developed his designs to an advanced stage, only a small experimental model was built during his lifetime, and the Analytical Engine had little direct influence on subsequent design. Another isolated design was Percy Ludgate's 1909 plan for a mechanical digital general-purpose program-controlled calculator.

A number of transitional machines mark the passage from mechanical to electronic machines. In Germany Konrad Zuse built a series of general-purpose automatic digital machines using sliding mechanical plates and electromechanical relay components as switching elements. The mechanical prototype Z1 (1938) used, as did his later machines, binary rather than the decimal number system. The Z2 had a mechanical memory and an electromechanical arithmetic unit. The Z3 (1941) was entirely electromechanical and ranks as the first successful general-purpose program-controlled calculator. The stimulus for Zuse's work was the need to reduce the drudgery and time taken to solve simultaneous linear equations for aircraft design. In the United States, Howard Aiken's giant electrically driven mechanical calculator, the Harvard Mark I, was completed in 1943, jointly funded by IBM and the U.S. Navy. The Mark I was used for mathematical calculation and for the production of printed mathematical tables. The stimulus for Aiken was to reduce the volume of numerical computation required for the solution of differential equations.

The earliest electronic machines used thermionic valves or vacuum tubes as their active elements. Vacuum tubes offered the prospect of high switching speeds and wear-free operation. John Atanasoff, professor of physics at Iowa State University, and his assistant Clifford Berry built an experimental electronic computing device in 1939. Wartime conditions stimulated the development of electronic computing devices. In Germany, Helmut Schreyer, a colleague of Zuse's, developed experimental vacuum tube circuits. At Bletchley Park in the U.K., Thomas H. Flowers, a post office engineer, built the first Colossus, not for arithmetic calculation but for high-speed trial-and-error testing of cipher keys for decoding intercepted enemy radio messages. The electronic signals represented alphabetic and numerical characters rather than simple number values, and the machine represents an early example of a computing device used as a symbol manipulator rather than a straightforward number cruncher. The first fully functional electronic calculator was the ENIAC (Electronic Numerical Integrator and Computer) built in 1945 at the Moore School of Electrical Engineering at the University of Pennsylvania, by John Mauchly and Presper Eckert. ENIAC was developed for the rapid production of ballistics firing tables. It failed to see wartime service but was used shortly after for complex calculations associated with the design of the H-bomb. John von Neumann, who was associated with the ENIAC project, described a general-purpose stored-program digital computer, the EDVAC, in a seminal paper written in 1945. The principles formulated by von Neumann dominated computer design for the next forty years.

C

ENIAC computer at the University of Pennsylvania, late 1940s, with J. Presper Eckert and John W. Mauchly in the foreground. Courtesy of University of Pennsylvania Archives.

Postwar developments moved the computer from the engineer's laboratory into the office. In Manchester, England, a team that included Frederick Williams and Tom Kilburn ran the first electronic stored program in 1948 on the SSEM (Small Scale Experimental Machine). Subsequent collaboration between the Manchester group and the Ferranti Company produced several commercial computers including Pegasus (1956), Mercury (1957), and Atlas (1962). These saw both commercial and scientific use.

In the Mathematical Laboratory at Cambridge, England, a team led by Maurice Wilkes built the EDSAC (Electronic Delay Storage Automatic Calculator), which first ran in 1949. Unlike most of the earlier experimental machines, EDSAC was specifically designed to provide computing services for academic research. EDSAC 1 computed planetary orbits, the wave functions of chemical molecules, and the calculations to determine the structure of the protein myoglobin. EDSAC 2 played a central role in radio astronomy work at the Cavendish Laboratory. Subsequent collaboration with the J. Lyons & Company (a major catering company) led to a series of commercial computers called LEO (Lyons Electronic Office). LEO I, which first ran test programs in 1951, was the first computer designed specifically for business use.

At the National Physical Laboratory in England, Alan Turing, a mathematician and former Bletchley Park code-breaker, designed the ACE (Automatic Computing Engine) in 1946. An experimental version ran in 1950, and a fully engineered version (Deuce) was produced by the English Electric Company in 1955. In the United States, Eckert and Mauchly delivered the first UNIVAC (Universal Automatic Computer) to the Census Bureau in 1951. IBM delivered the first IBM 701 computer to Los Alamos in 1953. Of the nineteen 701s produced, eight went to aircraft companies, seven to government agencies and large corporations, and three to universities. IBM went on to dominate the computer mainframe market and its products successfully straddled scientific and commercial use.

The invention of the transistor in 1947 by William Shockley, John Bardeen, and Walter Brattan at Bell Laboratories, New Jersey, led to a new generation of more compact and comparatively power-efficient computers in the early 1960s. Jack Kilby at Texas Instruments established in 1958 that different electronic components could be manufactured on the same block of semiconductor material, and in 1959, Robert Noyce, at rival Fairchild Semiconductors, devised a way of interconnecting and integrating such components. The invention of the integrated circuit (IC) is jointly credited to Noyce and Kilby, though not without controversy. The integrated circuit, or microchip, laid the foundation for the microelectronics revolution, and successive generations of faster and larger machines were manufactured in large production runs by major manufacturers.

M.E. (Ted) Hoff at Intel Corp. conceived of putting most of the essential logical elements of a computer on a single microchip, and the microprocessor was announced in 1971. This led to the electronic pocket-calculator boom in the early 1970s, and to the personal computer boom that followed the first production desktop computers in 1977, notably the Apple II and the Commodore Pet. The history of computer hardware since then is largely the history of microelectronics that offered increasing miniaturization and corresponding increases in component density. With the rapid growth of the microelectronics and computer industries, the contributions of individuals become lost in the anonymity of corporate research-and-development teams.

Doron Swade

Bibliography

Aspray, William, ed. *Computing before Computers.* Ames: Iowa State University Press, 1990.

Augarten, Stan. *Bit by Bit: An Illustrated History of Computers.* London: Allen and Unwin, 1985.

Lavington, Simon. *Early British Computers: The Story of Vintage Computers and the People That Built Them.* Manchester: Manchester University Press, 1980.

Lindgren, Michael. *Glory and Failure: The Difference Engines of Johann Müller, Charles Babbage and Georg and Edvard Scheutz.* Translated by Craig G. McKay. 2nd ed. Cambridge: M.I.T. Press, 1990.

Williams, Michael. *A History of Computing Technology.* Englewood Cliffs, N.J.: Prentice-Hall, 1985.

Computer, Electronic Analog

A general-purpose direct-current electronic analog computer is a computational device in which problem variables are represented by continuously varying electrical voltages. It is typically used either as a mathematical tool to automate the solution of differential equations, or as a device for modeling and simulating the dynamics of physical and abstract systems (be they mechanical, chemical, pneumatic, economic, or biological). A standard commercial system has four basic computing components: dc operational amplifiers, **potentiometers**, multipliers, and function generators. The key component is the operational amplifier, which can be configured to perform the mathematical operations of addition, integration and differentiation, inversion, and scaling. To set up (or program) the computer system, individual computing devices are interconnected by cables via a central patch-bay. When the computation is started all components operate in unison and computation is almost instantaneous.

The chief advantages that electronic analog computers offered over their digital rivals were high computing speed and an interactive man-machine user context. Their parallel computer architecture and electronic components permitted real and faster than real-time computing. Problems were relatively easy to set up and modify, parameter values could be changed by turning a knob, and the results could be immediately observed on a cathode ray tube or plotter. The "hands-on" analog computing environment enabled users to gain insight into, and get a feel for, the problems being studied. Electronic analog computers were thus particularly useful for exploratory studies.

Prior to 1945, the foremost and most versatile analog aids to computation in science and engineering were the mechanical **differential analyzers** and the electrical network analyzers developed in the United States and elsewhere during the 1920s and 1930s. Yet, though functionally similar, electronic analog computers did not originate from attempts to apply electronics to either of these established computing technologies. The origins of post–World War II electronic analog computers lie instead in more than two decades of research and development in vacuum-tube-based amplifiers for communications, and in wartime work on electronic devices, servomechanisms, **radar**, and special-purpose control applications.

The adoption and adaption of electronic amplifiers for computing purposes began with the Automatic Control Analyzer, a special-purpose electronic analog simulator developed by George A. Philbrick at the Foxboro Instrument Company in the United States in 1938–1939. This was designed to simulate and thus simplify the study of control loops, and to help engineers solve problems in the design of industrial process controllers.

In 1940, and entirely independently of Philbrick's work, C.A. Lovell and D.B. Parkinson initiated a development program at Bell Laboratories to replace the mechanical analog computing components of antiaircraft gun controllers by electronic devices. This involved the design, development, and application of dc operational amplifiers and laid much of the technological foundations for the postwar development of electronic analog computers. Nevertheless, the first concrete steps to codify operational amplifiers into a generalized computing system for mathematical analysis and simulation were taken within a National Defense Research Council project at Columbia University in New York. The chief goals of the project were the evaluation of new designs for airborne bomb navigation devices and gunfire controllers. In order to develop a means of doing so in the laboratory rather than in the field, the researchers adopted and modified computing amplifiers developed at Bell Laboratories. In 1947 J.R. Ragazzini, R.H. Randall, and F.A. Russell, published details of their wartime work at Columbia University, and introduced the term "operational amplifier."

After the war, electronic analog computers were developed in response to the increasing complexity of technical systems, and the impracticality and inadequacy of existing analytical and empirical design methods. Notable computational demands were associated with the development of guided missiles and aircraft. Projects funded by governments and the military played a crucial role not only in laying the technical foundations for electronic analog computers but also in their commercialization and further development. In the United States, the Office of Naval Research funded Projects Cyclone and Typhoon. Established in 1946, Project Cyclone was carried out by the Reeves Instrument Company of New York. It led to the introduction in 1947 of the first commercial general-purpose dc electronic analog computer system, the REAC (Reeves Electronic Analog Computer). Project Typhoon, established in 1947 at the Radio Corporation of America in Princeton, led to significant technical improvements in the overall performance of dc operational amplifiers.

By the mid 1950s, a dozen American firms were manufacturing general-purpose dc elec-

Electronic analog computer installation by Electronic Associates Inc., ca. 1962. Courtesy of the National Archive for the History of Computing, Manchester.

tronic analog computer systems on a commercial basis. In addition, many private firms, universities, and research laboratories developed "in-house" systems that were never commercialized. Commercial analog computer systems ranged in size from desk-top to room-size, and in cost from a thousand dollars to several hundreds of thousands of dollars. One of the most influential and successful American manufacturers of general-purpose electronic analog and hybrid computer systems is Electronic Associates, Inc. (EAI). In the 1950s EAI's most successful analog computer system was the PACE 231-R (Precision Analog Computer Equipment). Among the other major American manufacturers of general-purpose electronic analog computers in the 1950s were the Goodyear Aircraft Company with its GEDA (Goodyear Electronic Differential Analyzer) range of equipment, Beckman Instruments, Inc. with its EASE (Electronic Analog Simulation Equipment) product range, the Boeing Aircraft Company, the Reeves Instrument Company, George A. Philbrick Researches, Inc., the GPS Instruments Company, and Applied Dynamics, Inc.

During the 1960s manufacturers turned their attention increasingly toward the development of hybrid computer systems, which combined analog and digital technologies, and the replacement of vacuum-tube amplifiers by transistors. The Ci 5000, introduced in 1964 by Comcor, Inc., was the first fully transistorized

general-purpose analog computer specifically designed to be interfaced to and controlled by a general-purpose **digital computer**. By the late 1960s, several firms were manufacturing all-transistor hybrid computer systems.

In Britain, hardware development and commercialization ran a few years behind that in the United States. In the mid to late 1950s, the leading British manufacturers of general-purpose electronic analog computers were Elliott Brothers (London) Ltd., E.M.I. Electronics Ltd., English Electric Company Ltd., Fairey Aviation Company Ltd., Saunders-Roe Ltd., Short Brothers and Harland Ltd., and Solartron Ltd. The first commercial computer system was introduced by Short Brothers and Harland Ltd. in 1953. The most successful of the British electronic analog computer firms was Solartron Ltd. In the early 1960s, Solartron's chief analog/hybrid computer product ranges were the 247 Series of analog computers, and the HS7 Series of hybrid computers.

By the late 1950s analog computers were in widespread use in chemical, mechanical, and electrical engineering applications. Nevertheless, their principal application domain was aeronautical engineering and aerospace. Indeed, by 1960, every major aircraft and aerospace company, military aircraft and missile development, and test facility in the United States and Britain had a general-purpose electronic analog computer. In the United States in the 1960s and 1970s, electronic analog and hybrid computers were used by NASA and its contractors during America's manned space programs, including Apollo. In Britain, they were used in the development of the *Concorde,* in nuclear engineering, and in the electrical power and electronics industries. Electronic analog computer development and use was also widespread in France, Germany, Japan, and the former Soviet Union.

Though military patronage, economic considerations, and high computing speeds were significant factors in the success of postwar electronic analog computers, they do not explain the appeal of these computer systems as a tool of engineering design. Much of this appeal lay in the fact that electronic analog computers resonated with and were shaped by an engineering pedagogy that emphasized empiricism, trial-and-error, and parameter-variation design methods. This tradition stressed the value of visualization and tacit forms of technological knowledge over analytical methods and theory expressed as mathematical formulae. By redefining scale-model building techniques and enabling dynamic systems to be simulated in real time, electronic analog computers enhanced traditional engineering design practices. They helped engineers bridge the gap between the limits of theory and existing empirical methods and the complex real-world systems that they were constructing.

James S. Small

Bibliography

Bekey, G.A., and Karplus, W.J. *Hybrid Computation*. New York: Wiley, 1968.

Holst, P.A. "George A. Philbrick and Polyphemus—The First Electronic Training Simulator." *Annals of the History of Computing* 4 (1982): 143–56.

Korn, G.A., and T.M. Korn. *Electronic Analogue Computers*. New York: McGraw-Hill, 1952.

Ragazzini, J.R., R.H. Randall, and F.A. Russell. "Analysis of Problems in Dynamics by Electronic Circuits." *Proceedings of the IRE* 35 (1947): 444–52.

Small, J.S. "General-Purpose Electronic Analog Computing: 1945–1965." *Annals of the History of Computing* 15 (1993): 8–18.

Computer Tomography Scanner

Since the discovery of x-rays in 1896, physicians have desired a way to produce better images of objects in the body. Traditional radiography had two fundamental problems. First, it reduced a three-dimensional body to a two-dimensional image, necessarily overlapping structures such as organs and bones. Second, although x-rays are attenuated (stopped) in direct proportion to the amount and density of the material they pass through, they do not satisfactorily distinguish small differences in tissue density, such as between muscle and fat.

In the first two decades of the twentieth century, many researchers attempted to correct these problems using what German physicist Gustav Grossman called tomography (*tomo* in Greek means "cut" or "slice"). Scientists Alessandro Vallebona of Italy and Bernard George Ziedes des Plantes of the Netherlands moved the x-ray source and the film in opposite directions such that one cross-sectional plane in the body (one "slice" in a loaf of bread) remained in focus and the rest of the body appeared blurred. The technique yielded images that were helpful in resolving some objects, but were still of very low contrast; moreover, it involved large doses of radiation.

Computerized tomography approached the question of imaging a cross-sectional slice as a problem of image reconstruction from projections. Treating the slice as a two-dimensional matrix of densities (attenuation coefficients), multiple images from different angles around the slice are taken and a computer is used to calculate the attenuation at each point in the matrix.

This process involves a number of steps. In the fan-beam approach to scanning, for example, the x-ray source is collimated (filtered) so that it irradiates in a fan only in the plane of interest. These x-rays penetrate the body and are attenuated in proportion to the total density of objects in their path. Those that pass through the body are detected by a scintillation crystal (such as sodium chloride), which in turn emits a photon of light. These photons then enter a photomultiplier tube where highly charged electrical plates translate the amount of photons into an electrical signal, which is then counted by a computer. This signal constitutes the radiographic image of the slice from that projection (angle). In such earlier configurations, the x-ray source and the bank of detectors are then rotated and another projected image is acquired. Contemporary configurations use a ring of detectors that remain stationary while the x-ray source rotates, simplifying the engineering requirements.

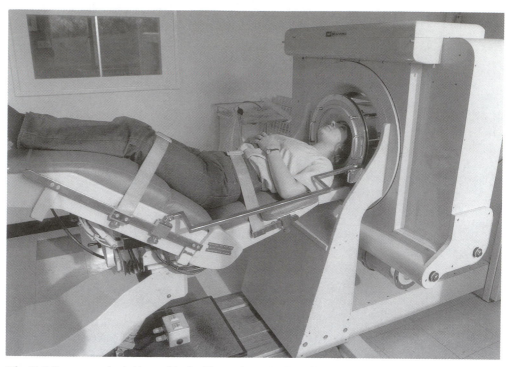

The EMI Scanner at the Atkinson Morley Hospital, 1970s. SM 1980-811. Courtesy of SSPL.

When enough projections have been acquired to form a statistically valid image, the computer mathematically reconstructs the slice from the counts, using an algorithm (for example, algebraic, iterative, filtered, or fourier transform). The result is a matrix of approximate densities throughout the slice. This matrix can be displayed as a table of numbers or, with ranges of these numbers converted to colors or levels of gray, as the familiar CT images.

One of the greatest values of the CT scanner is the ability to separate a narrow range of densities into a wide range of colors, allowing muscle and fat, for instance, to be clearly visualized. These images can be displayed on a computer screen, transferred to radiographic film, or stored on magnetic tape.

History

The first suggestions for computerized tomography in medicine were made in 1956 by engineer Roy Q. Edwards and physician David E. Kuhl, who, while working with emission tomography (see **PET Scanner**), developed a method of transmission tomographic imaging that used a back-projection algorithm. The process was advanced by William H. Oldendorf, an American neurosurgeon seeking better ways to

image the brain, in 1967. Oldendorf's method consisted of sequentially blurring all but one point in the brain, and then plotting each point.

The concept of reconstructing images from projections was first published by the mathematician J.H. Radon in 1917. In 1956, the physicist Alexander MacLeaod Cormack, working in a radiotherapy unit in South Africa, solved the problem of calculating the matrix of densities in a body and, with his undergraduate assistant David Hennage, built and tested a prototype CT scanner.

The first practical computerized tomographic scanner was envisioned by the electrical engineer Godfrey N. Hounsfield, starting in 1967, working at Electrical and Musical Industries (EMI). Hounsfield applied pattern recognition ideas to the computerized reconstruction of an image from projections and realized that this could be useful in medicine. With the help of EMI, he succeeded in building a prototype that took nine hours to acquire enough data to reconstruct one slice. He then worked in secret with neuroradiologist James Ambrose to produce a clinical diagnostic device. The first EMI scanner, which produced images only of slices of the head, was installed at Atkinson Moreley Hospital in Wimbledon, England, in 1971, and announced to the public in 1972. Three EMI units were installed in North America the next year. For their work on CT, Hounsfield and Cormack shared the 1979 Nobel Prize in physiology and medicine.

In 1973, physician and physicist Robert S. Ledley at Georgetown University built the first whole-body "ACTA" scanner. This was marketed by Pfizer. By 1976, twenty companies were involved in making CT scanners and almost six hundred scanners had been installed worldwide.

In the early 1990s in the United States and the U.K., especially, the tremendous cost of these scanners (about $100,000 for installation and $100,000 per year maintenance) raised grave concerns over inequality of access to high-tech health care and the wisdom of high-cost medicine in general. The CT scanner's cost contributed to the revamping of a Medical Device act within the FDA.

By the mid 1980s, CT had been established as a necessary diagnostic imaging modality. Though **magnetic resonance imaging** (MRI) has better resolution overall, CT is more common and less expensive. It can also can provide better images of bone, and even of metal, which MRI cannot.

Joseph Dumit

Bibliography

Kaplan, Bonnie. "Computers in Medicine." Ph.D. dissertation. University of Chicago, 1983.

Seeram, Euclid. *Computed Tomography Technology.* Philadelphia: Saunders, 1982.

Stocking, Barbara, and Stuart L. Morrison. *The Image and the Reality: A Case-study of Medical Technology.* Oxford: Oxford University Press for the Nuffield Provincial Hospitals Trust, 1978.

Susskind, Charles. "The Invention of Computed Tomography." *History of Technology* 6 (1981): 40–80.

Webb, Steve. *From the Watching of Shadows: The Origins of Radiological Tomography.* Bristol: Hilger, 1990.

Concrete Testing Instruments

Concrete differs from most other structural materials in that its quality is highly dependent on the workmanship on site. Even if a suitable ready-mixed concrete is brought to site from a well controlled central mixing plant, its handling on site may affect its subsequent properties. These properties change with time and can be greatly affected, especially while the concrete is curing, by temperature and humidity.

Much of the equipment used for testing concrete and its ingredients is similar to that used, for example, in process control, strength of materials testing, and load measurement. The vibrating wire **strain gauge** is particularly suitable for casting or embedding into concrete to measure strain from creep, shrinkage, and stress distribution.

Concrete is composed mainly of cement, water, and aggregates. Cement is the principal active ingredient and its reactivity is brought into effect by mixing with water. "Ordinary Portland Cement" patented by Joseph Aspdin in 1824 is now the most widely used cement. It did not, however, become well known until samples were displayed at the Great Exhibition in London in 1851. John Grant was the first engineer to test Portland Cement on a scientific basis, and his results led to the selection of cement for London sewers in 1859.

Lime had been used to make concrete long before the introduction of cement, and equipment used before 1859, such as Vicat's needle, to test lime was later used to test cement. The subsequent use of concrete in large structures required the development of tests to establish the strength of hardened concrete. Later tests were evolved to monitor the characteristics of concrete when it was being placed and when "fresh."

Cement Testing

There are three basic cement tests: Vicat's needle, Grant's test of tensile strength, and Le Chatelier's test for soundness. Setting-time was first reckoned using the needle apparatus devised by L.J. Vicat in 1818 for dealing with hydraulic lime. A needle with a flat point of 0.1 in. diameter, loaded with a weight usually of 3 pounds, is placed against a cement sample every ten minutes, where it is allowed to remain for 1 minute. When the needle left no appreciable mark the sample was considered hard. This test remains in use throughout the world.

Grant's test, designed to establish the tensile strength of cement, was performed on a small briquette of neat cement, made in a brass or gun-metal mold, left 24 hours to harden in air, and then placed in water. The cement was tested seven days later by breaking the briquette with a small lever testing-machine. Various configurations of the machine had evolved by the

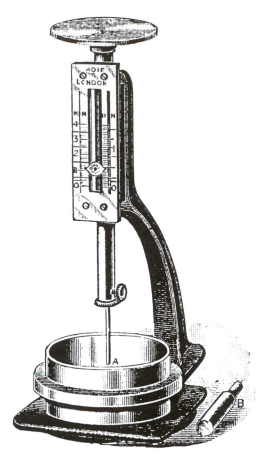

Vicat needle, 1923. Baird & Tatlock Ltd. Standard Catalogue of Scientific Apparatus: *Vol. 1,* Chemistry. *London, 1923: 654. Courtesy of SSPL.*

turn of the century, all purporting to apply the load at a regular rate and without shock. Designs included water to fill a cistern, a rolling weight, a worm screw acting on a spring balance, and a receiver for lead shot dispensed by a shot-dropper. An almost identical test has only recently been phased out of industrial use (ASTM C 190 was discontinued in 1991).

Cement is said to be unsound if, during the hydration of hardened cement paste, excessive expansion causes cracking and reduction in strength. In the simple test for soundness developed by H. Le Chatelier in the 1870s, cement paste is placed in a split brass cylinder fitted with two indicator stems (termed a Le Chatelier mold) and cured under water at 20°C for 24 hours. The separation of the stems is then measured. The mold is then immersed in water that is brought to a boil in 30 minutes and held there for an hour, and after cooling the separation of the stems is again measured. The change repre-

sents the expansion of cement. The test remains in use throughout the world.

Compressive Strength Tests

Most concrete structures are designed under the assumption that concrete resists compressive stresses but not tensile stresses; thus, for purposes of structural design the compressive strength is the criterion of quality. The earlier papers on cement and concrete, such as White's 1851 introduction to Portland cement, mention compressive strength, but with tests only on mortar blocks. By the 1880s concrete specimens were taken, cured, and tested by engineers as a check on quality on critical larger works. However it was not until the 1920s that industrywide standard tests began to appear (for example, ASTM C 31 in 1920).

Tests for Fresh Concrete

The increased use of steel reinforcement in concrete has required that fresh concrete be readily worked into place. The term "workability" has been coined to describe the ease with which a concrete mix can be handled from the mixer to its final compacted shape. None of the tests used for workability measure individual rheological characteristics, such as consistency, mobility or compactability.

There are four common methods of measuring workability. The simple slump test, developed by Cloyd M. Chapman in the United States in 1913, is useful only for quality control. The compacting factor test was developed, initially as a laboratory test, by the British Road Research Laboratory in 1947. The Vebe test dates from 1940 and is named after the initials of its inventor, V. Bährner. It is more expensive than the others, and requires electric power. The Vebe apparatus is usually found only in precast works and ready-mix concrete plants. The Kelly Ball was devised by the American J.W. Kelly in 1955 as a simple substitute for the slump test.

In 1918 Duff Abrams at the Lewis Institute, Chicago, formulated his "law" that: "for the same materials and conditions of test, the strength of fully compacted concrete at a given age depends only on the ratio of water to cement used in the mix." The need to determine the cement content of freshly mixed concrete as quickly as possible has resulted in a number of techniques being developed. One of the most interesting is the Rapid Analysis Machine (RAM), first reported in 1974 by the British Cement and Concrete Association. The current model is an integrated unit with an operating cycle of 15 minutes to determine the cement content of an 8-kg sample of fresh concrete.

Robert C. McWilliam

Bibliography

Dhir, Ravindra K., and Neil Jackson. "Concrete." In *Civil Engineering Materials,* edited by Neil Jackson, 107–209. 3rd ed. London: Macmillan. 1983.

———, John G.L. Munday, and Nyok Yong Ho. "Analysis of Fresh Concrete: Determination of Cement Content by the Rapid Analysis Machine." *Magazine of Concrete Research* 34 (June 1982): 59–73.

Grant, John. "Portland Cement: Its Nature, Tests and Uses." *Minutes of Proceedings of the Institution of Civil Engineers* 62 (1880): 98–179.

Hadley, Earl J. *The Magic Powder: History of the Universal Atlas Cement Company and the Cement Industry.* New York: Putnam, 1945.

Troxell, George Earl, and Harmer Elmer Davis. *Composition and Properties of Concrete.* New York: McGraw-Hill, 1956.

Corona, Instruments for Observing the

Coronagraph

A coronagraph produces an artificial solar eclipse, thus enabling astronomers to photograph the corona, the hot and outermost layer of the sun. Before its invention in 1930 by the French astrophysicist Bernard Lyot, the corona could be observed only during a total solar eclipse, and all efforts to photograph it had failed. Lyot's original coronograph was a refracting **telescope** of 8 cm aperture, diaphragmed to 3 cm, equipped with an occulting disk and a tilted flat mirror that reflected most of the sunlight off to one side. This disk was later replaced by a highly reflecting metal cone at the focus.

His second instrument, in use in 1931, had a second diaphragm in front of the camera lens. Lyot erected these instruments on the Pic du Midi in the Pyrenees, and succeeded in photographing the corona and the coronal spectrum.

The next two coronagraphs were built at Arosa in the Swiss Alps and at the High Altitude Observatory at Climax, Colorado. Coronagraphs twice the size of Lyot's were later built at Sacramento Peak Observatory in New Mexico and at Climax, Colorado. The Russian Academy of Sciences has two very large coronagraphs in the Caucasus Mountains and in Siberia; these have an aperture of 54 cm, and a focal length of 8 meters.

In order to observe the corona, it is absolutely essential to prevent stray light. Thus, the objective lens must be free from scratches, streaks, and bubbles, it must have an excellent polishing, and it must be cleaned very often during the period of observation. Also, coronagraphs work best in observatories located at high altitudes with a very clear sky. To reduce stray atmospheric light still further, Gordon A. Newkirk, Jr., introduced coronagraphs in stratospheric balloons. Space missions proved even more successful, and famous photographs were provided by the coronagraph on Skylab in 1974.

Hα Filter

The corona is not usually observed in white light. Thus, the development of monochromatic filters was important for this work. In 1933, Lyot described a polarization interference monochromator (red Hα filter, 6563 Å) for observing prominences and corona. This consists of an alternating combination of birefringent calcite or quartz crystals and polarization filters (quarter-wave plates). These crystals have two indices of refraction that split the light in two opposite polarized beams, producing a phase difference that depends on the thickness of the crystal. Through

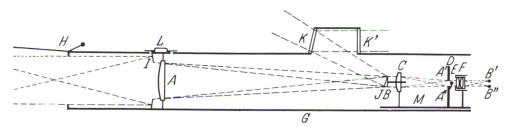

Path of rays in Lyot's coronagraph, used at the Pic du Midi, 1931. Lyot (1932): 77. Courtesy of the Deutsches Museum.

interference, the desired radiation is amplified and other radiation blanked out. The minima of interference vary with the thickness of the crystal. The more pairs of quartz plates and polarization filters one takes, the higher the efficiency of the monochromator.

Since double refraction depends on temperature, the filter must be kept at a constant temperature. In 1937, Yngve Öhman produced a filter of the band-width 50 Å using four quartz plates. In the 1950s, the firm Optique et Précision de Levallois produced filters with a transmission band of 0.75 Å. Today, corona filters have a bandwidth of 1.0 to 0.1 Å, while for observing solar prominences, filters with a bandwidth of 1 Å to 100 Å are fine. The Hα filter works because the narrow band in the red region of the spectrum in which hydrogen emits energy is isolated.

Using a Hα filter, Lyot was able to take the first motion pictures of the movements of solar prominences in 1939. This work was developed by the Zürich astronomer Max Waldmeier working at Arosa, and by Donald H. Menzel and other Harvard astronomers working at Climax. Today these filters are combined with heliographs that automatically photograph the active sun. The universal birefringent filter (UBF) of Sacramento Peak, an extremely narrow interference filter whose transmission band can be varied quickly, allows observations in different wavelengths. The resultant filtergrams reveal phenomena and dynamics at different heights and give the opportunity to reconstruct the three-dimensional structure of the solar atmosphere.

Spectroscopic Observations of the Coronal Emission Lines

The bright green coronal emission line (5303 Å) was discovered in 1869 and attributed to the otherwise unknown element "coronium," but its interpretation remained a mystery until 1939, when Walter Grotrian and Bengt Edlén explained that it originated from highly ionized iron atoms (Fe XIV). That solution suggested, in contrast to the ideas of that time, a very high temperature in the corona. Lyot observed other emission lines with his first coronagraph in 1930.

The spectrographs for coronal work are of moderate dispersion because the lines are faint and broad. For example, the 12.5-cm coronagraph at Climax has a Littrow spectrograph of 210 cm focal length and of 7.5 cm aperture with a grating of 600 lines/mm. The curved slit can be set to any position angle and covers an arc of 120° on each exposure.

With a corona **spectroscope**, like the one made by Carl Zeiss of Jena in 1943 and used in the solar observatory of the Fraunhofer Institute at Wendelstein in the Bavarian Alps, it was possible to observe the intensity variations of the coronal lines, which vary markedly during the sunspot period. As a comparison light source a tungsten lamp was used. In contrast, the observations at Climax and Sacramento Peak were done photographically. Since the 1950s photoelectric coronal **photometers** have been developed. But even today, a detailed study of the coronal structure, the brightness, and the spectrum of the outer corona can be made only during an eclipse.

Corona Observation with X-ray Optics

The first photograph of the sun in soft x-rays was taken in 1960, using a pinhole camera in a rocket. This made it possible to observe the hot emission regions of the corona just above the solar disk. A Fresnel zone plate produces much sharper images of the corona: by an appropriate combination of filters, the hard x-rays are absorbed and only soft x-rays (10–100 Å) can pass through.

A photograph by Leon Golub (1989) taken during a rocket flight with the NIXT (normal incidence x-ray telescope) shows extremely fine details of the hot solar corona. The active regions can be studied with a spatial resolution of 500 km. The image is taken at a wavelength of 63.5 Å, a line of highly excited iron formed at temperatures between two and three million kelvin. With x-ray optics, information about density and temperature of hot emission regions in the corona is available.

Gudrun Wolfschmidt

Bibliography

Evans, J.W. "The Coronagraph." In *The Solar System*, edited by Gerard P. Kuiper, Vol. 1, 635–44. Chicago: University of Chicago Press, 1953.

Hufbauer, Karl. "Artificial Eclipses: Bernard Lyot and the Coronagraph." *Historical Studies in the Physical and Biological Sciences* 24 (1994): 337–94.

Lyot, Bernard. "Étude de la couronne solaire en dehors des éclipses." *Zeitschrift für Astrophysik* 5 (1932): 73–95.

———. "Le filtre monochromatique polarisant et ses applications en physique solaire." *Annales d'astrophysique* 7 (1944): 31–49.

McMath, Robert R., and O.C. Mohler. "Solar Instruments." In *Encyclopedia of Physics,* edited by S. Flügge, Vol. 54, 1–41. Berlin: Springer, 1962.

Cosmic Ray Detector

The cosmic ray detector has not been one stable type of instrument, but rather an assemblage of such instruments as **electrometers**, balloons (see **radiosonde**), **Geiger counters**, and **cloud chambers** that have been used to record the passage of penetrating radiation from above the earth's atmosphere.

The instruments used have been shaped by debates over the origins and nature of the radiation. The controversial claim that a component of penetrating radiation came from above (literally *Höhenstrahlung*) was made and tested through measurements made at different heights above the ground. Ballooning provided a relatively inexpensive method of lifting instruments. The device taken by balloon-borne investigators was the Wulf electrometer, developed by Theodor Wulf and manufactured by the firm of Gunther and Tegetmeyer as a rugged field instrument combining portability and accuracy. The gold leaves of a conventional electrometer were replaced by two shock-resistant conducting fibers. The Wulf electrometer coevolved with balloon technology in the years following 1910 as investigators such as Victor Hess and Werner Kolhörster, claiming an extraterrestrial origin of the radiation, responded to criticisms leveled at the design of the instruments. The minimization of temperature and pressure effects on electrometers (also called "ionization chambers") accompanied innovation in balloon design, for example the Swiss Auguste Piccard's airtight cabins, and, later, Robert Millikan's and Erich Regener's self-recording instruments aboard sounding balloons.

Millikan was a late convert to the idea of an extraterrestrial origin of the penetrating radiation, but he quickly cemented this interpretation through coining and publicizing the term "cosmic ray" in 1925. He interpreted cosmic rays as extremely high energy photons, a "birth cry of atoms" produced as light elements coalesced in space, which formed part of his wider synthetic program of science and religion. This commitment led him into conflict over two developments in cosmic ray research and instrumentation in the 1920s and 1930s: the large-scale geographical survey, and the introduction of particle counters from nuclear physics.

If a component of cosmic rays was charged and corpuscular, then intensity would vary with geomagnetic latitude. The Carnegie Corporation paid for both Millikan and his rival Arthur Compton to study the geographical variation of cosmic ray intensity. These surveys and expeditions relied on the collaboration of scientists across the world. For Compton's 1932 survey, each group of investigators was supplied with identical portable recording electrometers, along with calibration instructions. Millikan attacked the method and data of Compton and his co-workers when they declared a confirmation of the latitude effect.

The interpretation of cosmic rays as high-energy photons was further challenged by physicists adapting the new instruments of nuclear physics. In the coincidence counter, the near simultaneous discharge of a pair of Geiger counters recorded the passage and direction of a charged particle. Walter Bothe and Kolhörster, following Dimitry Skobeltzyn's 1927 attribution of tracks in cloud-chamber photographs to high-energy cosmic ray particles, used a coincidence counter made of two Geiger counters surrounded by 5 cm of iron and 6 cm of lead to directly demonstrate the corpuscular character and high energy of cosmic rays in 1929. Geiger-counter techniques were further adapted for use in cosmic ray research by Bruno Rossi in Italy.

Guiseppe Occhialini brought experience of Rossi's coincidence counter techniques to the Cavendish laboratory at Cambridge University in 1931. Patrick Blackett and Occhialini incorporated another new device into their Cavendish cosmic ray detector: the cloud chamber. The discharge of Geiger counters triggered the expansion of the cloud chamber and operated a camera, recording photographically the tracks of cosmic ray particles, deflected according to charge and energy by a magnetic field.

Coincidence counters and cloud chambers provided a smaller scale alternative to particle **accelerators** for the investigation of the particles of high-energy physics. The positron was discovered in the course of cosmic ray studies by Carl Anderson in 1932, and V-particles in Manchester in the 1940s. New particles were found to be created in intense events called showers, a phenomenon studied using networks of cosmic ray detectors. Programs of cosmic ray

Carl D. Anderson (right) and H. Victor Neher with telemetering device used for cosmic ray research, 1953. The ionization chamber is the black sphere above the radio equipment. Courtesy of the Archives, California Institute of Technology.

research grew in many countries including Britain, Italy, Japan, Germany, the United States, and the Soviet Union. During the postwar years, other instruments developed for use in accelerators, such as counters made of photomultipliers amplifying the Cerenkov radiation of high-energy particles, have been adapted for cosmic ray research. Another postwar development has been the transport of cosmic ray detectors above the earth's atmosphere on probes and satellites such as HEAO-3 and Ariel 6.

Jon Agar

Bibliography

De Maria, M., M.G. Ianniello, and A. Russo. "The Discovery of Cosmic Rays: Rivalries and Controversies between Europe and the United States." *Historical Studies in the Physical Sciences* 22 (1991): 165–92.

De Maria, M., and A. Russo. "Cosmic Ray Romancing: The Discovery of the Latitude Effect and the Compton-Millikan Controversy." *Historical Studies in the Physical Sciences* 19 (1989): 211–66.

Galison, Peter. *How Experiments End*. Chicago and London: University of Chicago Press, 1987.

Sekido, Yataro, and Harry Elliot, eds. *Early History of Cosmic Ray Studies: Personal Reminiscences with Old Photographs*. Dordrecht: D. Reidel, 1985.

Ziegler, Charles A. "Technology and the Process of Scientific Discovery: The Case of Cosmic Rays." *Technology and Culture* 30 (1989): 939–63.

Coulter Counter

See COUNTER, COULTER

Counter, Colony

A colony counter magnifies and illuminates colonies of bacteria as an aid to manual counting. The most common version is the Quebec Colony Counter, a metal box with a slanted top and a circular, clear-glass counting grid on its surface to hold the bacterial culture or Petri dish. It is lit from below by a 40-watt electric bulb and uses a series of mirrors to indirectly illuminate the colonies, which are counted through a 1.5X magnifying glass suspended on an adjustable focusing arm.

Accessory electronic devices have been developed to mark and tabulate the colonies simultaneously. Fully automated colony counters use a television scanner coupled to a magnifying lens and an electronic counter.

History

Public health laboratories began counting bacteria in the 1880s as part of the examination of food, milk, and water supplies for the presence of disease-causing bacteria. The technique of counting colonies developed in the laboratory of Robert Koch at Berlin. Under the **microscope**, living bacteria were indistinguishable from dead bacteria, so they estimated the number of viable bacteria by counting their "colo-

nies," the visible accumulation of bacteria that occurs when a single bacterium grows and divides on a solid gelatin or agar surface. The number of colonies grown from a standardized sample provided a quantitative measure of the level of bacterial contamination. Colony counting is widely used in the dairy industry to monitor cleanliness.

Counting colonies was tedious and fraught with error. Tiny, "pinpoint" colonies could be overlooked easily and confused with debris or bubbles in the substrate. Variations in the time the culture was incubated or the conditions of viewing the colonies contributed additional error. Colony counters evolved with attempts to reduce counting error.

Early Colony Counters

The earliest colony counting aids magnified but provided no illumination. In 1886, Erwin von Esmarch, a colleague of Koch, devised a hand-held, adjustable test-tube clamp for counting a "roll-tube" culture. The bacterial colonies were grown on a thin sheet of agar "rolled" onto the interior surface of a test tube and were counted through a magnifying lens placed over a sliding aperture in the clamp. In the United States, Bausch and Lomb Optical Company sold these devices in 1900 for $4.00. Many laboratories devised makeshift counting stands that held a magnifying lens over a Petri dish holder. Mirrors mounted below the dish transmitted light through the transparent substrate to highlight the opaque colonies.

Ruled patterns were available by 1900 to ease counting. These divided the area of a circular Petri dish into equal sections of 1 cm^2. The patterns of Gustav Wolffheugel, another associate of Koch, H.W. Jeffers of the New York State Veterinary College at Cornell University, and A.H. Stewart of Philadelphia became commercially available. Wolffheugel's pattern remains the standard ruling provided with today's manual colony counters.

After small reliable electric lights became available, bacteriologists developed illuminated boxes with overhead magnifiers to hold the counting grids. One of the first, developed by A.H. Stewart in 1906, used a 16-candlepower electric light placed below and to one side of the box. It cast oblique light onto the Petri dish, which he placed on a dark blue background to provide contrast. This arrangement avoided reflecting light directly into the observer's eyes and drowning out the colonies. Later refine-

Earliest commercial version of the Spencer Quebec colony counter, 1943. Courtesy of NMAH.

ments, like T.C. Buck's 1928 version, altered the location of the light or added mirrors to reflect light both from above and below the Petri dish.

Quebec Colony Counter

In the 1930s, efforts to improve the accuracy of colony counts focused on the need to standardize illumination. Archie Hunt Robertson of the New York State Food Laboratory, a referee for the Committee on Standard Methods of Milk Analysis of the American Public Health Association, constructed several of the commonly used colony counters and distributed them to laboratories for comparative trials. The dark field colony counter designed in 1937 by Mac H. McCrady and his colleagues at the Laboratories of the Quebec Ministry of Health in Montreal received the most favorable reports. Robertson and McCrady enlisted the Spencer

Lens Company of Buffalo, New York, by then the instrument division of American Optical Company, to make an affordable version. Spencer's Oscar W. Richards patented the improved Dark Field Quebec Colony Counter in 1943. It sold for $30. Still the standard colony counter, it uses an annular reflector above a 40-watt bulb and a series of mirrors to provide uniform oblique lighting that highlights the bacterial colonies against a dark field. American Optical continues to make the Quebec Colony Counter today; in Europe it is made by Reichert Instruments.

Electronic marking and tallying accessories, like that designed in 1935 by Philip L. Varney of St. Louis, Missouri, are now common. The operator touches each colony with a metal electrode that completes a circuit and trips a magnetic counter. Today Manostat Company in New

York City makes a portable, battery-operated electronic counter that looks like a felt-tipped pen with a digital liquid-crystal display.

Automated Colony Counters

The Allen B. DuMont Laboratories of Clifton, New Jersey, was commissioned in 1953 by the U.S. Army Chemical Corps to develop a fully automated colony counter. The "flying-spot, optical-electronic transducer instrument" scanned Petri dishes with a cathode-ray tube and optical system similar to that used in television, but slowed the scanning rate to obtain better resolution. Whenever light from the scanning spot was occluded by an opaque colony, a pulse was produced by a phototube. These instruments were commercially available by the 1970s, but their expense limited their use to the food and dairy industry. In 1973, J.E. Gilchrist and his colleagues at the Food and Drug Administration in Cincinnati, Ohio, devised an automated inoculation system that deposited a set volume of the sample on a rotating agar plate in the form of an Archimedes spiral.

The 1980s saw new approaches to the assay of microbial (bacteria, yeast, and mold) populations that took advantage of the biochemical and biophysical properties of microbial metabolism. Among the new strategies are instruments that use bioluminescence to measure ATP (adenosine tri-phosphate) content, microcalorimetry to measure the heat produced by growing microbes, changes in the flow of electric currents as microbes convert substrates into smaller molecules, or radiometry to measure the metabolites of isotopically labeled substrates. These costly computerized instruments are used almost exclusively to monitor processes in the food and pharmaceutical industries and in large medical diagnostic laboratories. None of them have displaced the Quebec Colony Counter of 1943.

Patricia L. Gossel

Bibliography

Archambault, Jacques, J. Curot, and Mac H. McCrady. "The Need of Uniformity of Conditions for Counting Plates." *American Journal of Public Health* 27 (1937): 809–12.

Dziezak, Judie D. "Rapid Methods of Microbiological Analysis of Food." *Food Technology* (July 1987): 56–73.

Esmarch, E. "Ueber eine Modification des Koch'schen Plattenverfahrens zur Isolirung und zum quantitativen Nachweis von Mikroorganismen." *Zeitschrift für Hygiene* 1 (1886): 293–301.

Mansberg, H.P. "Automatic Particle and Bacterial Colony Counter." *Science* 126 (1957): 823–27.

Richards, Oscar W., and Paul C. Heijin. "An Improved Darkfield Quebec Colony Counter." *Journal of Milk Technology* 8 (1945): 253–56.

Counter, Coulter

A Coulter counter counts the individual cells in a sample, and provides cell size distribution. The number of cells counted per sample is approximately one hundred times greater than the usual **microscope** count, and so the statistical error is reduced by a factor of approximately ten. It uses a nonoptical scanning system providing a counting rate in excess of six thousand individual cells per second with a counting interval of 15 seconds. A suspension of blood cells is passed through a small orifice simultaneously with an electric current. The individual blood cells passing through the orifice introduce an impedance change in the orifice determined by the size of the cell.

The patented Coulter principle of volumetric impedance, discovered by Wallace Coulter in 1948, calls upon the principle of displacement as a measure of volume. Blood cells are suspended in a conductive fluid into which electrodes are placed. As a blood cell passes through an aperture between the electrodes, it displaces its own volume of electrolyte, and there is a measurable change in the electrical resistance of the system. This change becomes a precise measure of cell volume and permits three-dimensional evaluation.

Working in a Chicago basement on electronic component projects and experiments, Coulter conducted his initial experiment with rubber bands, cellophane, and a sewing needle. His discovery provided medical and industrial researchers with a fast, accurate method of counting cells and small particles, and of obtaining a great deal of additional information about cell size and size variations.

Within a few years after its introduction, the Coulter principle was cited as the foremost reference method for cell and small particle counting and sizing and was universally recognized as a landmark contribution to the particle measurement field. The Coulter counter was the first automated system that provided a true measurement of cell volume and cell distribution and the basis for the first viable **flow cytometer**.

Instruments

Coulter assembled a simple model to demonstrate his principle to staff of the Office of Naval Research, in a quest for a grant to build a working prototype for testing there and at the National Institutes of Health. With the grant, Wallace Coulter and his brother Joseph R. Coulter, Jr., assembled two prototypes with parts purchased from various sources and modified to suit Wallace's specifications.

Model A, introduced in 1953, was the first commercial venture in diagnostic medicine for the Coulter brothers. It revolutionized the study of biological cells and other small particles, opening the gateway to a new world of discovery in science. After receiving many inquiries from industrial laboratories, the Coulters developed an industrial version of the Model A suitable for measuring a wide range of particles, including clay powders, chocolate powders, phosphors on color-television picture tubes, solid fuel, rocket loadings, missile nose cone materials, and others. The modified Model B Industrial Particle Analyzer was developed during the period 1958–1960.

In 1958 Wallace and Joe Coulter launched Coulter Electronics, Inc. In 1995 this corporation had over five thousand employees working in manufacturing facilities and sales, service, and education operations in twenty countries around the world.

Many other companies have developed instruments using Wallace Coulter's principle, and at least 95 percent of the automated blood counts in the world today are done on Coulter instruments, or their clones.

Wallace H. Coulter

Bibliography

Breitmeyer, M.O., and M.K. Sambandam. "Holography of Red Cells Moving Toward an Orifice: Verification of a Model." *Journal of the Association of Advanced Medicine* 6 (1972): 365.

Coulter, W.H. "High Speed Automatic Blood Cell Counter and Cell Size Analyzer." In *Proceedings of the National Electronics Conference, Hotel Sherman, Chicago, Illinois. October 1–2, 1956,* edited by George W. Swenson, Jr., et al. Chicago: National Electronics Conference, 1957.

Jones, A.R. "Determination of Hematocrit: Macroscopic Examination of Centrifuged Blood." In *A Syllabus of Labora-*

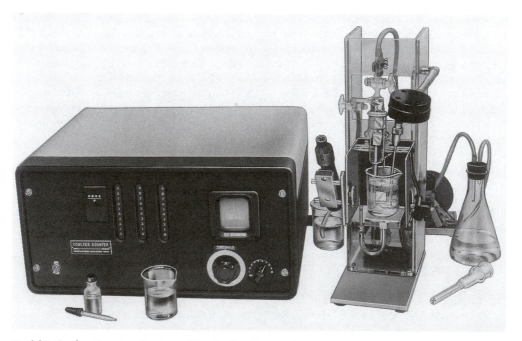

Model A Coulter Counter. Courtesy of the Coulter Corporation.

tory Examinations in Clinical Diagnosis; Critical Evaluation of Laboratory Procedures in the Study of the Patient, edited by Thomas Hale Ham. Cambridge: Harvard University Press, 1950.

Price-Jones, C. Blood Pictures: An Introduction to Clinical Hematology. 2nd ed. London: J.S. Wright, 1920.

Waterman, C.S., et al. "Improved Measurement of Erythrocyte Volume Distribution by Aperture-Counter Signal Analysis." Clinical Chemistry 21 (1975): 1201–11.

Counting Rods

Counting rods were used in ancient and medieval China, medieval Korea, and Japan to perform arithmetical and algebraic calculations. In China, the instrument had different names: ce, suan, chou, chousuan, chouce, suanchou, suanzi; the latter was its most common name beginning from the Song dynasty (960–1279).

The most ancient specimens of counting rods were excavated recently from Chinese tombs dating from the second to first centuries B.C.; some of them are made of bamboo and some of bone. The first detailed description of the instrument is found in the Qian Han Shu (History of the Early Han Dynasty) by Ban Gu (32–92). The rods were round bamboo sticks of six Chinese inches (cun) long and 1/10 cun in diameter (one cun of that time is approximately 2.3 cm). A standard set contained 271 rods. Later sources mention colored round counting rods: white and black (or red and black) to represent, respectively, positive and negative numbers. According to other sources, the signs of numbers were also represented with different cross-sections of the counting rods (triangular for positive numbers and square for negative ones).

The arithmetical operations performed with counting rods are partly described in one of the most ancient extant mathematical manuals, Jiu zhang suan shu (known as Nine Chapters on the Mathematical Art, compiled around the first century A.D.), and there is evidence of their use in a recently unearthed mathematical treatise, Suan shu shu (Book on Calculations, dating from the early second century B.C.). The operations performed with the instrument were four basic operations (addition, subtraction, multiplication, and division) for integers, decimal and common fractions, extraction of square and cube roots, solution of simultaneous equations with a generally valid algorithm. There is evidence that at that time a general procedure of numerical solution of equations of second degree was elaborated; the method of numerical solution of equations of higher degrees (up to the tenth degree), and a method of representation and solution of simultaneous nonlinear equations were developed in China later, during the eleventh to fourteenth centuries.

The calculations with counting rods were performed on a flat surface with decimal positions, most probably on a table covered with a special cloth. It is not known if the decimal position was marked on its surface as square (or rectangular) cells or whether they had imaginary boundaries. Some authors believe that operations were performed on a special counting board (with drawn cells), yet the existence of such an instrument is not attested in ancient and medieval Chinese sources. In Japan a sheet of paper was used.

The method of representation of numbers was as follows. One of the positions on the counting surface was fixed as that of units, then the first to the left was that of tens, the next one was that of hundreds, and so forth. The positions to the right of that of the units were used for 10^{-1}, 10^{-2}, and so on, respectively. A digit n from one to five is represented with n counting rods and a digit n from six to nine as $(n-5)$ counting rods of the same orientation and one perpendicular rod symbolizing five units; for zero the position is left empty. The orientation of rods in a given decimal position (horizontal or vertical) depended on the power of 10 corresponding to the position: vertical for 10^{2n} and horizontal for 10^{2n+1}. Common fractions were represented as pairs of integers.

Chinese mathematicians Jia Xian (fl. 1050), Liu Yi (not earlier than the mid twelfth century), Qin Jiushao (1202–1261), Li Zhi (1192–1279, often transliterated as Li Ye), Yang Hui (fl. 1257), and Zhu Shijie (fl. 1299) provided an algorithm for the numerical solution of algebraic equations of higher degree with counting rods. Presented in modern algebraic notation, this algorithm is similar to the so-called Ruffini-Horner method—that is, to a calculational scheme that includes consecutive divisions of polynomials $a_0x^n + \ldots + a_{n-1}x + a_n$ by $x - x_0$ for an approximate value of the root x_0. The polynomials are represented with counting rods as columns of their

Chinese counting rods, illustrating the figures 1971 (top) and 1976. An hui Sheng bo Wu Shan. "He fei xi jiao sui mo." Kao Gu 2 (1976): Figure facing page 140. Courtesy of the Syndics of Cambridge University Library.

coefficients—that is, one row was fixed as the position of units, the rows above (or below it, according to conventions adopted by the authors) were used to set the coefficients of x, x^2, x^3 . . . represented with counting rods. Zhu Shijie introduced the rules of operations with the polynomials, such as their addition, subtraction, and multiplication, as well as the special case of division just mentioned. He also provided a technique of representation of polynomials of several (up to four) unknowns: beginning from a given position on the counting surface (set as that of units) the successive positions in four directions were used to display the coefficients of successive power of the four unknowns, and the position at the intersection of the i-st row and j-st column was used to represent the coefficient of the $u^i v^j$ for unknowns u and v.

In China, beginning in the second half of the fourteenth century, counting rods were progressively replaced by the **abacus** and soon disappeared. In Korea and Japan, counting rods and related mathematical procedures were in use until the nineteenth century.

Alexeï K. Volkov

Bibliography

Hoe, John. *Les systèmes d'équations polynômes dans le Siyuan Yujian (1303)*. Paris: Collège de France (*Mémoires de l'Institut des Hautes Études Chinoises 6*), 1977.

Horiuchi, Annick. *Les mathématiques japonaises à l'époque d'Edo*. Paris: Vrin, 1994.

Jami, Catherine. "History of Mathematics in Mei Wending's (1633–1721) Work." *Historia Scientiarum* 4, no. 2 (1994): 159–74.

Martzloff, Jean-Claude. *Histoire des mathématiques chinoises*. Paris: Masson, 1987.

Needham, Joseph. *Science and Civilisation in China*, Vol. 3. Cambridge: Cambridge University Press, 1959.

Craniometer

A craniometer measures features of the human skull. Craniometers can range from simple devices that determine basic head diameters to more complicated instruments able to provide angular as well as linear measurements from any two points on a skull. Physical anthropologists have used craniometers, in conjunction with statistical methods of aggregating data, primarily to create racial and other group-based quantitative norms.

Interest in defining physical characteristics that would distinguish humans from each other and from other animals can be traced to Aristotle. Artists and anatomists in the sixteenth and seventeenth centuries proposed particular sets of diameters or angles they deemed useful in defining the shape of a face or head. In the eighteenth century, naturalists such as Carl Linnaeus (1735), George Louis Leclerc de Buffon (1749), and Johann Friedrich Blumenbach (1775) directly addressed questions of human classification and racial or species difference. Because the head was considered the most distinctive feature of the body, facial or skull characteristics were important features in all classificatory schemes, although few attempts were made to produce quantitative cranial measures. Samuel T. von Sömmerring (1784) used a length of cord to measure the skulls of Europeans and Moors; Charles White (1799) used calipers to measure various skeletal parts; and Charles Bell (1809) suspended "White" and "Negro" crania on an iron rod and compared the angles formed.

The first craniometric instruments originated in the 1820s and 1830s with phrenologists, who were interested in relating the precise shape of the skull to a person's mental character. The phrenological calipers, designed to measure general head size, had two curved arms connected at one end by a central pivot, and a ruled scale that marked the distance between the two pointed ends. The first instrument termed a craniometer was designed around 1824 by the Edinburgh phrenologists Robert Ellis and William Gray to measure the distance from the top of the spinal marrow, where each phrenological organ was assumed to originate, to the point where the organ reached the surface of the brain. The Ellis and Gray craniometer had a semicircular frame that encircled the head, and whose ends were centered on each ear via thin rods. A graduated rod indicated the distance from the top of the head to the center of the circle, which was assumed to lie at the top of the spinal marrow.

The craniometer soon became popular within the developing field of anthropology. Adrien Antelme's cephalometer (1838) added a ruled circular disk going around the head between the eyes and ears and attached to the semicircular frame carrying the measuring rod. The cephalometer defined the plane of measurement, determined the position of each point measured in terms of the two circular coordinates, and allowed for the ready calculation of such features as the facial angle.

In the United States, Samuel Morton and John Turnpenny developed a facial **goniometer** also designed to allow the "exact determination of facial angle in 2 to 3 minutes" in the 1830s. This instrument had an adjustable three-sided frame with sliding ear rods and two hinged verticals. The skull was placed so that the jaw touched the cross piece of the frame, and the vertical bar, equipped with a hole for the nasal ridge, rested on the forehead, paralleling the angle of the face.

Although further improvements were made in the craniometer and facial goniometer in the 1840s and 1850s, the major period of instrumental innovation occurred from 1860 to 1900, when physical anthropology flourished around the Société d'Anthropologie de Paris. Paul Broca wrote over forty papers on craniometric instruments, introducing such tools as the cranioscope, craniophore, millimetric roulette, micrometric compass, pachymeter, and craniostat. Among his major contributions, most often produced in conjunction with the surgical-instrument-maker Mathieu, were the stereograph (1865), which provided a two-dimensional projection of a section of a skull; an improved facial goniometer (1864); the spreading calipers (1865); the sliding calipers (1865); the occipital goniometer (1872), which measured angles at the back of the skull; and the median facial goniometer (1874). Emile Duhousset developed a sliding calipers (1875) that facilitated internal measurements; Gustave LeBon and the surgical-instrument-maker Molteni created the coordinate sliding calipers (1878); and Paul Topinard, who worked with the instrument-maker Collin, created a modified median facial goniometer (1881) that was easier to use with living subjects.

In Britain, George Busk introduced a craniometer (1861) that made possible quick mea-

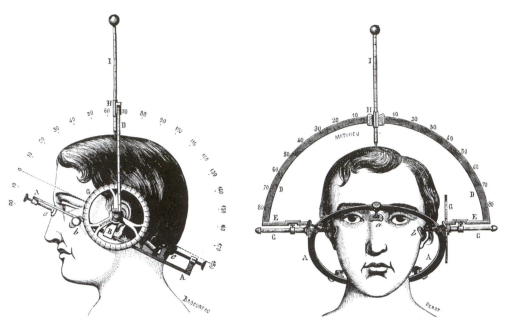

Adrien Antelme's cephalometer. Alphonse Bertillon, ed. Dictionnaire des Sciences Anthropologiques. *Paris, 1883: 251. Courtesy of SSPL.*

surement of skull length and width; William H. Flower invented a calipers (1879) with the point-to-point measuring capability of the spreading calipers and the greater accuracy of the sliding calipers; and George M. Atkinson introduced a goniometer (1881) that measured the angle between the visual plane and the line connecting any two points on the front of a face. In the German-speaking world, Moriz Benedikt developed a craniophore (1888) that measured angles in several directions and planes; Aurel Von Török combined several instruments into a universal craniometer (1890); and Rudolf Martin improved the basic designs of the sliding calipers, spreading calipers, and craniophore (1889).

Much of the impetus to create new or improved craniometric instruments can be traced to physical anthropologists' increasing belief that quantitative norms based on numerous individual measurements must serve as the means to distinguish races and groups. As Broca remarked in 1862: "The goal . . . is to substitute for evaluations that . . . depend on the sagacity of the observer and on the exactness of the glance . . . mechanical and uniform procedures, which permit . . . the grouping of observations in series, submitting them to calculations, obtaining mean measurements, and thus avoiding as much as possible the misleading influence of individual variations." In addition, as crania studies prolif-

erated because of the growing institutionalization of anthropology, together with the expanding European colonization of Africa and Asia and a number of European archaeological finds, it proved increasingly difficult to constitute simple quantitative differences between the various human races and subgroups. Still committed to constructing group differences, and often to placing those groups in a hierarchy based on their presumed level of intellect, physical anthropologists used their new instruments to produce ever more elaborate sets of measurements, in the process often disagreeing about the "proper" diameters and angles to measure and which points defined them.

By 1900, two distinct styles of physical anthropology had emerged. Broca's influence loomed large in Britain, France, and the United States, and there simple, inexpensive, and easily transported instruments were preferred. In the German-speaking world, physical anthropology was conducted primarily as a laboratory science, and elaborate, expensive, and precise instruments predominated. These investigative styles and craniometric instruments persisted well into the twentieth century.

John Carson

Bibliography

Broca, Paul. "Instructions craniologiques et craniométriques." *Mémoires de la*

Société d'Anthropologie de Paris 2, no. 2 (1875–1882): 1–204.

Hoyme, Lucile E. "Physical Anthropology and Its Instruments: An Historical Study." *Southwestern Journal of Anthropology* 9 (1953): 408–30.

Martin, Rudolf. *Lehrbuch der Anthropologie.* 3 vols. Jena: G. Fischer, 1928.

Spencer, Frank, ed. *Ecce Homo: An Annotated Bibliographic History of Physical Anthropology.* New York: Greenwood, 1986.

Topinard, Paul. *Eléments d'anthropologie générale.* Paris: Delahaye et Lecorsnier, 1885.

Crookes Radiometer

See RADIOMETER, CROOKES

Cross-Staff

The cross-staff was used to measure the altitude of a celestial body above the horizon at sea. With the altitude, and with the knowledge of the declination of the observed body, a seaman could find his latitude. The cross-staff is also known as the Jacob's staff and as the fore-staff. Thomas Hood suggested that the name Jacob's staff was based on Genesis 32:10, where it is said that Jacob held a staff while crossing the River Jordan. Another explanation refers to Genesis 28:12, where it is said that Jacob dreamed of a ladder between heaven and earth. After the introduction of the back-staff, the cross-staff was sometimes referred to as the fore-staff.

A cross-staff consists of a four-sided staff and one or more vanes, all made of wood. The average staff, made of ebony or lignum vitae, is about 800 mm long, and the sides, on which the graduations are cut, about 16 mm wide. The vane, usually made of pearwood, is shorter than the staff, flat, and about 40 mm wide. In the middle it has a hole just large enough for the staff to pass through, so that the observer can slide the vane along the staff.

In use, the flat eye-end of the staff was placed near the observer's eye and the other directed at a point approximately halfway between the horizon and the celestial body. The vertically placed vane was then slid along the staff, until its upper edge "touched" the celestial body and, at the same instant, the lower edge "touched" the horizon. The vane was then clamped to the staff and the altitude read from the scale.

The cross-staff was introduced at sea by the Portuguese around 1515. At that time it had only one 0°–90° scale, which was used to measure the altitude of the pole star only. The cross-staff should be distinguished from the older astronomer's staff or radius astronomicus, and the surveyor's staff or radius geometricus. However, the adaption for use at sea was probably inspired by the kamal, an instrument for the measurement of altitudes at sea used by Arabs and seen by Vasco da Gama in 1498. With the diffusion of navigational knowledge from the Mediterranean, the cross-staff became available in Northern Europe. In 1571, in England, William Bourne first described in print how the sun's altitude could be measured with a cross-staff. He also discussed ocular parallax, the instrumental error of the cross-staff, as well as the use of a colored glass at the end of the vane to protect the eye from bright sunlight.

In 1580, the Flemish scholar Michiel Coignet described three scales, each representing a section of the 0°–90° graduation; this meant larger degrees and thus easier reading. The Dutch pilot Lucas Janszoon Waghenaer published a scale for zenith distance, the complement of altitude, in 1584. With this scale the calculation of latitude from the sun's altitude was made easier. In 1595, the English seafarer John Davis provided a method to eliminate ocular parallax. He also described how to observe with the back to the sun. In this way two problems were avoided: the need to look into bright sunlight and the "blinking" of the eye between the ends of the vane. The Dutch developed a variant of Davis's backward observation which, in England, became known as the "Dutch fashion." In 1633, the Dutchman Jacob Aertszoon Colom wrote that staffs were made with combined scales for both altitude and zenith distance on three sides, and by the 1650s staffs were graduated in this manner on all four sides. Around this time, the Dutch introduced two improvements for the backward observation. They were a brass aperture disk, named by the English "Dutch shoe," and a bone vane fitted to the smallest or horizon vane. These innovations meant that, by the second half of the seventeenth century, the cross-staff was the most accurate instrument for the measurement of altitudes at sea. This remained so until, in 1731, Hadley's quadrant (**octant**) was invented. By 1750, the octant was generally accepted, and

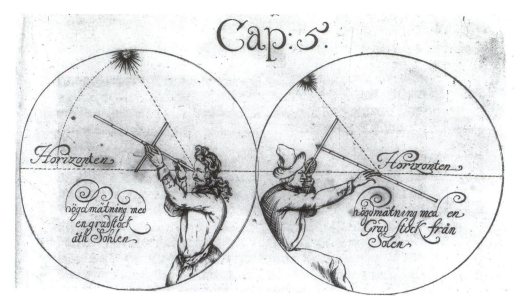

Illustration showing the operation of a cross-staff, Amsterdam, 1690s. Courtesy of the Nederlands Scheepvaartmuseum.

the use of the cross-staff diminished. The last reference to it in the first edition of a navigational manual was in 1768. Surviving examples indicate that production continued until the early nineteenth century. However, from written evidence it is clear that, by then, they were not being used by officers in the service of large organizations such as the East India Company and the Admiralty.

Originally cross-staffs were made by the seamen who used them. Names of professional makers are known from the end of the sixteenth century onward. Often these makers were not involved in the production of other scientific instruments. Of the ninety-five known cross-staffs (as of 1994), sixty-five were made in the Netherlands. Another eleven probably originate from that country. Others were made in England, Scandinavia, Germany, France, Spain, and North America. The Amsterdam firm of Van Keulen (1680–1885) made the majority of the surviving staffs. Other eighteenth-century Dutch makers responsible for surviving staffs are Johannes Loots, Joachim Hasebroek, and Lambertus Dankbaar, all from Amsterdam. Even so, from archival evidence it is clear that only a fraction of manufactured cross-staffs have survived. For example, the Van Keulens sold 1,148 to the Dutch East India Company between 1731 and 1748. This figure does not include sales to other branches of shipping, nor the production of other makers. Production fig-

ures of Dutch makers, the number of surviving Dutch staffs, and the Dutch influence on the development of the cross-staff, lead to the conclusion that, in the seventeenth and eighteenth centuries, the Dutch were predominant in the production and diffusion of the navigational cross-staff.

Willem F.J. Mörzer Bruyns

Bibliography

Mörzer Bruyns, Willem F.J. *The Cross-Staff: History and Development of a Navigational Instrument.* Zutphen: De Walburg Pers, 1994.

Current Meter

A current meter measures the direction and speed of water currents. Although mariners had long recognized the existence of steady and persistent currents, it was not until the eighteenth century that oceanographers began to study currents and to appreciate their significance for physical and biological phenomena. The subsequent development of instruments to permit precise and reliable measurements took place over an extended period.

Many different instruments have been used to measure direction and speed, the two essential parameters, yet technological constraints have led to common design responses. Direction can be measured only with a magnetized needle or bar. Speed is usually determined with a propeller or rotor.

Unlike floats and passive drifters, which indicate an average current direction, current meters must remain immobile during use. They have frequently been operated from stationary ships and their indications observed from on board. A current meter of this sort was devised in 1845 by the French oceanographer Georges Aimé and used in 1847 by the Danish admiral Carl Irminger. Aimé's apparatus used a fixed vane and a compass needle to register a single observation of direction. While in the water, the vane oriented the apparatus in the direction of the current, and the angle between the vane and magnetic north was recorded by locking the compass needle in place. By contrast, the instrument conceived by Thorsten Arwidsson in 1880 could not indicate direction but was capable of recording speed on a dial. Its axis was vertical and the instrument was operated by being inverted, using two lines to set it going and to stop it.

Most later current meters were unable to register speed and direction in real time. Sometimes they gave the two parameters in incomplete form: direction at the moment of recovery and mean speed during immersion (Ernst Mayer, 1877; John E. Pillsbury, 1885); sometimes they were reduced to a very simple mechanism (Stepan Makaroff, 1882). Fridtjof Nansen created a genuine recorder in 1901 based on the displacement of a pendulum. When placed on the sea bed, this indicated the speed and direction of the current for several minutes. It was taken up in more elaborate form by Yves Delage in 1918.

The propeller-type current meter of V. Walfrid Ekman (1903) was reliable and easy to control for up to 60 minutes of operation. The machine was positioned on the bottom, and the rotation of the propeller triggered the release of small steel balls whose number was proportional to the speed of the current. Since the balls were collected in compartments on a plate oriented by a compass needle, the apparatus also indicated the current's direction. A good approximation was thereby obtained for work that did not require too great a precision. Ekman's simple and robust current meter was used by numerous oceanographers until after World War II.

But new techniques were also sought. In 1909 Jacob P. Jacobsen introduced a simple bubble level device to permit the continuous measurement of both speed and direction from

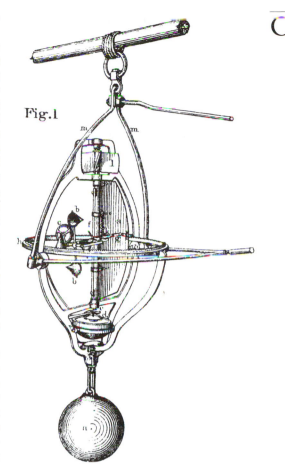

Fig.1

Diagram of Pillsbury's first current meter, 1885. Courtesy of SSPL.

on board an immobile ship. Although this technique was imprecise in practice, its inventor used it for many years.

The first true recording apparatus, created in 1910 by Otto Pettersson, used film to make a periodic record of speed and direction. The axis of the rotor was vertical and its relation with the watertight interior was made by a magnetic coupling. This photographic system was further developed and alternative recording media were introduced. In 1927, Pierre Idrac's recorder photographed the data on a 35-mm film that unrolled over seven days thanks to a clockwork movement. In the apparatus of the Japanese Kohei Ono, conceived in 1950 for tidal currents, the measures were transcribed in colored points on a roll of paper. Fjelstad's machine transcribed the data in the form of figures stamped on a roll of tin.

The methods applied today make use of perfected rotors, electric or magnetic transducers, and magnetic tape recorders. When current meters are attached to buoys, their position is often determined by satellite; the data can be transmitted by radio in real time or at regular intervals and later processed by computers.

The measurement of currents in rivers is easier than in the ocean, because the river bank is always close and the direction of the current is obvious. In many cases direct measurement is possible, simply holding the apparatus by hand. Perhaps for this reason, but also because electrical insulation was better in fresh water, the Swiss Jacob Amsler-Laffon conducted the first trials of his current meter in the Rhine, near Schaffhouse, from 1876. He devised what was without doubt one of the first methods of telemetry, using an electrical contact on the propeller of the instrument to ring a bell on land.

The explorer Sven Hedin used a current meter developed by Thorsten Arwidsson, conceived during the 1880s especially for shallow depths in fresh water. The rotor was made of four hemispherical cups contained within a frame that protected the rotor and assisted the action of the current. Needles indicated tens and hundreds of revolutions on dials, and recording was begun and stopped by pulling on a line.

Some instruments designed for ocean measurements were later also used for fresh water, and this trend continues with measuring and recording instruments today. Ekman's current meter was applied universally and was used for studies in large lakes and rivers. One of the most frequently used pieces of apparatus was that devised by the American William G. Price and constructed on the same principle as Amsler-Laffon's, though the rotor cups on its vertical axis were conical. The instrument was provided with optional ballast and a rudder to orient it in the water, and it was suspended from a cable that allowed it to operate at considerable depths. An electrical conductor transmitted the signal to a receiver and the frequency of its audible pips was proportional to the rotor's speed of rotation and thus to the current.

A quite different principle was used solely for fresh water measurements (its use would have been difficult at sea); it was based on the eighteenth-century invention of Henri Pitot. A right-angled tube is immersed in running water and the level of water in the tube's vertical section rises as a function of water pressure and hence speed of current. Improved versions of this simple device provide precise and measurable results. A related device is Carl E. Bentzel's apparatus in which the two vertical branches of a U tube are immersed and entirely filled with water that is moved by the measured current. Several devices have been conceived to display the speed of the current on a graduated scale. Thrupp's method can also be mentioned, in which the speed of a surface current is determined by the angle of the wake created by the immersion of a thin rod in the water stream.

Christian Carpine

Bibliography

Aimé, G. "Courants de la Méditerranée." In *Recherches de physique générale sur la Méditerranée*, 181–91. Paris: Imprimerie royale, 1845.

Boyer, M.C. "Streamflow Measurement." In *Handbook of Applied Hydrology*, edited by V.T. Chow, 15-1–15-41. New York: McGraw Hill, 1964.

Ekman, V.W. "On a New Current-Meter Invented by Professor Fridtjof Nansen." *Nyt magazin for naturvidenskaberne* 39 (1901): 63–187.

Frazier, Arthur H. *Water Current Meters in the Smithsonian Collections of the National Museum of History and Technology*, Smithsonian Studies in History and Technology 28. Washington, D.C.: Smithsonian Institution Press, 1974.

Idrac, P. "Sur un appareil enregistreur pour l'étude océanographique des courants de profondeur." *Comptes rendus de l'Académie des Sciences* 184 (1927): 1472–73.

Pillsbury, J.E. "Methods and Results, Gulf Stream Explorations: Observations of Currents." *Report of the United States Coast and Geodetic Survey* (1885). Appendix 14, 495–501.

D

Densitometer

A densitometer determines the density of the silver deposit in a photographic image, usually by measuring the intensity of a beam of light before and after it passes through a small part of the image. The ratio between these values is called the opacity of the parts measured, while the inverse ratio is the transparency. Density values may be plotted against the logarithm of the exposures that produced them to obtain the characteristic curve of the material, or they may be used for simple exposure determination.

There are two ways of measuring the transmission density of a negative. Specular density is derived from the intensity of a beam of light at a distance from the area to be measured. Diffuse density involves measurement of the total amount of light passing through the selected part of the negative. The selected dense part is measured when in contact with a sheet of light-scattering opal glass. Specular density methods are more important in projection printing, diffuse density methods in contact printing. The measurement of densities is complicated by the Callier effect, the selective scattering of light in an optical system and when it strikes the dense area.

The procedure for measuring reflection densities from a photographic print is similar to those of transmission densitometry. Normally, the incident light is directed to the surface of the print at an angle of 45° and measured at an angle of 90° in order to avoid specular reflection.

In the last quarter of the nineteenth century, two industrial chemists working in Lancashire, England, Ferdinand Hurter and Vero C. Driffield, showed that the density of a photographic image is proportional to the mass of silver developed per unit area. They also showed that the response of any photographic emulsion to light can be expressed only by a curve or series of curves relating densities developed under known conditions to the logarithms of the exposure times. These H&D curves were long used as the basis of a speed rating for photographic films and plates. Photographic emulsion manufacturers continue to produce such curves routinely.

Hurter's and Driffield's first densitometers (ca. 1886) were simple adaptations of the Bunsen grease-spot **photometer**, and they were used to compare a known light source with one transmitted through a developed photographic plate. Hurter and Driffield later devised a bench photometer based on a type then used to measure the illuminating power of coal gas. In 1891 Hurter and Driffield devised a sector wheel apparatus that incorporated a wheel cut by angular apertures that was sited and turned between a photographic plate and a light source. The plate was subjected to a series of exposures of known ratio, developed, and the density of the silver image calculated.

The accuracy of Hurter's and Driffield's early instruments, and thus the validity of their conclusions, were challenged by a distinguished photographic scientist, William de Wiveleslie Abney, partly on account of what later came to be known as the Callier effect. It is now accepted that Abney's criticisms did not invalidate Hurter's and Driffield's work.

Commercial densitometers fall into three main types: variable-intensity densitometers, constant-intensity densitometers, and photoelectric densitometers.

Variable-intensity instruments use an optical wedge to equalize the illumination of two

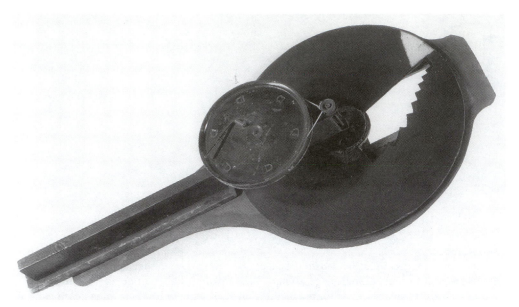

Hurter's and Driffield's revolving-disk densitometer, 1891. Courtesy of The Royal Photographic Society Collection, Bath, England.

areas, as described in 1910 by Emanuel Goldberg, professor of graphic arts in Leipzig. As the wedge increases in thickness arithmetically, the optical density of the screen that is proportional to the thickness also increases arithmetically. Optical wedge densitometers were marketed over a very long period. The Sanger-Shepherd density meter, first advertised in 1911 at a cost of ten shillings and six pence, consisted of a small box pierced by two holes below each of which was an inclined mirror. The density to be measured was placed over one hole, and the calibrated wedge was placed over the other. On looking through an eyepiece at the end of the box, the viewer saw a circle made up of half the image of the first hole and half the second. The wedge was adjusted until the illumination was judged to be equal, and the density was read from the position of the wedge. Variations were marketed by several manufacturers. As late as 1948, Ilford advertised a simple densitometer that depended on matching two beams of light from low-voltage bulbs, one beneath the negative under test, the other beneath an annular wedge.

Variable-intensity densitometers were unsatisfactory at high and low densities, either because the eye was dazzled or because there was insufficient light to make a judgment. Instruments with a balanced photometric field of constant intensity avoided these problems. Here one area receives constant illumination, but the light that falls on the second area passes through the unknown density and then through the wedge. When the system is balanced, the sum of the known and unknown densities must be constant and the light transmitted constant and equal to the illuminated area. A reflection instrument of this type was designed for motion-picture work by J.G. Capstaff and R.A. Purdy around 1927. A modified version of the Capstaff-Purdy instrument was developed by Kodak for a wider market. A 1950 review of the Model 2 claimed that it "should meet all requirements of the color photographer, the motion picture laboratory and the many industrial and scientific applications of photography that call for sensitometric control."

Densitometers that rely on photoelectric cells are more accurate and less tiring to use than visual instruments. The British Photographic Research Association automatic recording densitometer based on a design by F.C. Toy in the 1920s and manufactured by W. Watson and Sons, allowed an operator to take about one thousand measurements a day, a task quite impracticable using visual instruments. Recording instruments can be traced back as far as Goldburg, early in the twentieth century, who coupled his optical wedge to a writing mechanism mounted over graph paper. Photoelectric recording densitometers are widely used in industrial laboratories.

Direct-reading photoelectric densitometers have also been widely available since World War II. Some simply equate two light intensities using a photoelectric cell. The E.E.L. Densitometer, marketed in England in the 1950s, passed current generated in the photocell directly to a microammeter calibrated in optical densities. The manufacturers claimed that it would remain accurate throughout its working life. This instrument was designed to read in specular densities for transmission work but could also be simply adapted for reflection densities. A rather different design was the Baldwin vacuum cell densitometer, which incorporated a photoemissive vacuum cell with a vacuum tube amplifier.

John Ward

Bibliography

Ferguson, W.B., ed. *The Photographic Researches of Ferdinand Hurter and Vero C. Driffield.* London: Royal Photographic Society, 1920.
The Focal Encyclopedia of Photography. Rev. ed. London: Focal, 1965.
Lobel, L., and M. Dubois. *Basic Sensitometry.* 2nd ed. London: Focal, 1967.
Thomas, D.B. *The Science Museum Photography Collection.* London: Her Majesty's Stationery Office, 1969.

Depth Sounder

A depth finder measures depth of water, customarily in fathoms (1 fathom equals 6 feet). Traditional sounders consisted of hempen line attached to a lead, deployed from the bow of a boat. A sailor cast the lead and line over the side, let it run through his hands, and counted markings on the line until he felt it hit bottom. Depth sounders were navigational tools used by mariners everywhere. In the nineteenth century, particularly in the United States and Britain, hydrographers began to deploy them in conjunction with surveying techniques for precise charting.

Exploration, charting, and especially submarine telegraphy demanded sounders that could measure deep water accurately and recover bottom sediments. In the 1840s, American naval hydrographers began using a 32-pound shot attached to twine. Even when hundreds of fathoms of this thin line were wet, the heavy shot preserved the same weight ratio of lead to line as in shallow water. Theoretically, this allowed hydrographers to observe when the line stopped running out, but the moment of impact was not always so clear. Also, the practice of cutting the line forfeited a sample.

A better method of identifying the moment a sounder struck bottom emerged in the late 1850s and 1860s, when hydrographers adapted a technique suggested early in the century by polar explorer John Ross. As each hundred fathoms of line ran out, the time was recorded and intervals computed. Intervals increased steadily with depth, but shortened noticeably after the sounder struck bottom, which allowed depth to be extrapolated. During the same decades, steam-powered vessels and deck engines were adopted for deep-sea sounding.

In 1852, John M. Brooke of the U.S. Navy introduced a sounder with a detachable weight, and a sampling tube that could be recovered. In this device, a rod was fitted into a hollow cast shot that rested in a cord harness. When the device hit bottom, the sounding line slackened, releasing an arm that held the harness and shot. During the next two decades, numerous other sounders were designed, built, and tested by American and British hydrographers on virtually every deep-sounding vessel at sea. Bonnici's claw, for instance, invented in 1856 by a blacksmith on HMS *Spitfire,* was similar to Brooke's instrument, but with a simpler and more reliable detaching mechanism.

Three types of depth sounder emerged in this period, and all were greeted enthusiastically by the naturalists and microscopists who pioneered marine zoology. Skead's sounder, developed in 1857 by Francis Skead, master of HMS *Tartarus,* used a small cup for collecting sediments. The early cup leads relied on tallow to pick up a few grains of the bottom, but, as submarine telegraph companies demanded bigger samples, valves were added to trap more sediment. Still larger samples were recovered by a grab sounder developed in 1860 by the engineers and naturalist of HMS *Bulldog.* The Bulldog sounder was fitted with India rubber springs that snapped two cups together when the sounding line slackened. The third type was the corer devised by the blacksmith and two sailors on HMS *Hydra* in 1868. This had a spring that threw off the sinker after the sampling tube had been driven into the bottom.

The substitution of steel piano wire for hemp in the 1870s marked a dramatic shift. In

D

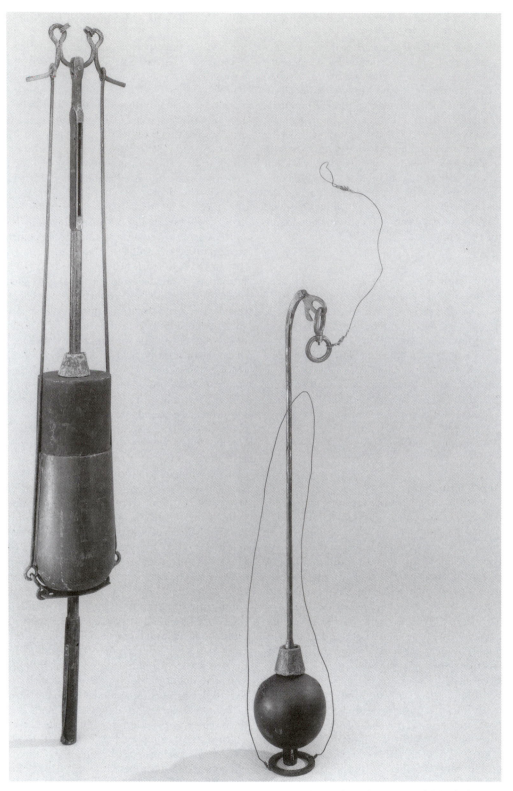

Two deep-sea sounders: (left) modified version of Brooke's sounder used on the voyage of H.M.S. Cyclops, 1857; (right) Brooke's sounder, 1856. SM 1876-833, 1876-832. Courtesy of SSPL.

1872, the physicist William Thomson designed a wire sounding machine not only to meet cable company needs, but equally for safer navigation. Thomson integrated into a self-contained machine all the rigging and equipment for paying out, measuring, and reeling in wire. The small version of this machine, equipped with 300 fathoms of wire, sold for £20, while the deep sea version cost £127/10. Two American hydrographers, George Belknap and Charles D. Sigsbee, improved Thomson's machine by modifying the brake and accumulator. Thomson's and Sigsbee's sounding machines were adopted for cable surveys until displaced by a machine invented by Francis Lucas in 1887. The Lucas sounder used an easily regulated, spring-loaded paying-out wheel and became standard equipment on hydrographic vessels and cable ships. Before World War I, lineless sounders never replaced lines and leads. Efforts had been made to develop waywiser sounders, similar to ships' logs, as well as devices that measured pressure as a function of depth, but neither of these survived. Echo-sounding and sidescan sonar replaced traditional sounders for measuring depth beginning in the 1920s, but old sounders retained the task of collecting bottom samples.

Helen Rozwadowski

Bibliography

McConnell, Anita. *No Sea Too Deep: The History of Oceanographic Instruments.* Bristol: Adam Hilger, 1982.

Maury, Matthew Fontaine. *The Physical Geography of the Sea.* New York: Harper and Brothers, 1855.

Sigsbee, Charles D. *Deep Sea Sounding and Dredging: A Description and Discussion of the Methods and Appliances Used on Board the Coast and Geodetic Survey Steamer "Blake."* Washington, D.C.: Government Printing Office, 1880.

Differential Analyzer, Bush

Midway through World War II, M.I.T.'s Rockefeller Differential Analyzer (RDA) was put to work calculating firing tables and profiles of radar antennae. Built by Vannevar Bush with support from the Rockefeller Foundation, this electronic analog computer weighed almost a hundred tons and comprised some two thousand vacuum tubes, over a dozen disk integrators, several thousand relays, 150 motors, and automated input units and printers. The largest computer in the United States in operation at the end of the war, the Rockefeller Analyzer was supposed to mark the start "of a new era in mechanized calculus." Its development had been inspired by the success of a series of earlier, almost entirely mechanical, analyzers built at the end of the 1920s and widely imitated inside and outside the United States: at General Electric, Aberdeen Proving Ground, and the universities of Pennsylvania, California, and Texas, and in England (at Manchester and Cambridge), Ireland, Germany, Norway, and Russia.

The provenance of the analyzers was two-fold: more generally, in an engineering culture that flourished after the turn of the century and that stressed shopwork, hands-on skills, and practical mathematics; and more particularly, in the severe mathematical difficulties confronted by electrical engineers concerned with the development of vacuum tubes, telephone lines, and, especially, long-distance power transmission lines. Relevant to the origin of the analyzers were equations like that derived for long lines by John Carson of Bell Telephone:

$$I = A(t)E\sin\theta + Ep\cos(pt+\theta)\int_0^t \cos p\delta A \bullet (\delta)d\delta$$

$$+ Ep\sin(pt+\theta)\int_0^t \sin p\delta \bullet A(\delta)d\delta,$$

where I was the entering current, and $(E)\sin(pt+\theta)$ the voltage suddenly applied to the sending end of an initially unenergized transmission line. Solution by hand required first the calculation of the products under the integral signs with the help of tables of functions, their plotting, the determination of the areas under the curves (and thus the integrals) with the use of an Amsler planimeter and finally the necessary multiplication and addition of curves to give, in graphic form, I versus t.

With the help of Herbert Stewart, F.D. Gage, Harold Hazen, and Samuel Caldwell, Bush had developed by 1931 a machine that computed continuous solutions to differential equations by almost entirely mechanical means. The Differential Analyzer, as it was named, consisted of a long tablelike framework crisscrossed by interconnectable shafts.

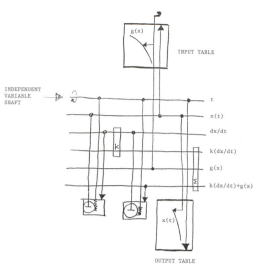

$$d^2x/dt^2 + k(dx/dt) + g(x) = 0$$

Diagram illustrating how subunits of the 1931 analyzer would have been connected in order to solve the falling body equation. Courtesy of Larry Owens.

Along one side were arrayed a series of drawing boards and along the other, six disk integrators. The device traced functions on some boards, while other boards allowed the input of other functions by hand. The heart of the analyzer and the means by which it performed the operation of integration was the disk integrator (known earlier by Thompson), a variable friction-gear consisting of a disk resting on a wheel at a variable distance from the wheel's center. The geometry of the integrator forced its constituent shafts to turn in accordance with the relationship:

$$y = \int_a^b f(x)dx$$

In essence, the analyzer was a device cleverly contrived to convert the rotations of shafts one into another in a variety of ways. By associating mathematical variables with shaft rotations and by employing an assortment of gearings, the operator could cause the machine to add, subtract, multiply, divide, and integrate. All in all, the analyzer constituted an elegant kinetic model of the differential equation it was set up to solve. The diagram above illustrates the manner in which the subunits of the 1931 analyzer would have been connected in order to solve the falling body equation

(with k and Σ representing multiplying and adding gears):

$$\frac{d^2x}{dt^2} + k\frac{dx}{dt} + g(x) = 0$$

or

$$\frac{dx}{dt} = -\int \left[k\frac{dx}{dt} + g(x) \right] dt$$

By 1935, the analyzer was helping physicists around the world see through the mathematical thickets of quantum mechanics and cosmic rays. Success plus the frustration of time-consuming problem setup encouraged the group at M.I.T. to embark on the seven-year development of the larger, more precise Rockefeller Differential Analyzer able to switch rapidly from one problem to another in the manner of an automatic telephone exchange. The project got underway in 1935 with a preliminary study grant of $10,000 from the foundation, followed the next year by a full development grant of $85,000. More precise integrators were developed with little difficulty, as were the servomechanisms and electronic amplifiers needed to create the electrical connections between elements. Other problems proved more difficult, the most frustrating of which involved automatic control. Earlier analyzers had been dedicated machines, assembled anew each time an equation was to be solved. The RDA, intended to compute multiple problems simultaneously, needed to reassign computing elements quickly, efficiently, and automatically, even as one problem finished and another began. The matter introduced extraordinary difficulties into the design of the machine that were not completely solved even by the end of the war. The matter of multitasking is still difficult, of course, and it isn't surprising that Bush and his team should have found it unsettling in the 1940s.

The RDA never lived up to its promise or potential. In the different institutional climate at M.I.T. after the war, Bush's analyzers seemed antiquated and irrelevant—slow, imprecise, rooted in an older, shop-oriented engineering tradition, and unappealing to the physicists and others who found the new electronic **digital computer** a machine more suited to new demands. The analyzer was granted a stay of execution when it was adopted by Stark Draper and put to work during the Korean

War doing yeoman work in the design of computing gunsights. But by 1954 it had reached the end of its life. In a two-week feeding frenzy, the massive machine was picked entirely apart, pieces showing up at the Boston Museum of Science, the Franklin Institute in Philadelphia, at Purdue and the University of Connecticut, in the equipment stores of M.I.T.'s physical plant, in the Railroad Club, Rocket Society, and even as components of other, newer computers.

Larry Owens

Bibliography

Bush, Vannevar. "The Differential Analyzer." *Journal of the Franklin Institute* 212 (1931): 447–88.

———, and Samuel H. Caldwell. "A New Type of Differential Analyzer." *Journal of the Franklin Institute* 240 (1945): 255–326.

Owens, Larry. "Vannevar Bush." In *Dictionary of Scientific Biography,* edited by Frederic L. Holmes, Vol. 17, 134–38. New York: Scribner, 1990.

———. "Vannevar Bush and the Differential Analyzer: The Text and Context of an Early Computer." *Technology and Culture* 27 (1986): 63–95.

Differential Thermal Analyzer

A differential thermal analyzer (DTA) measures the difference in temperature between the sample to be studied and an inert reference material as a function of temperature as both are subjected to the same temperature regime in a controlled environment heated or cooled at a controlled rate. Temperature difference (ΔT) is plotted against time or temperature. DTA measures the energy changes occurring on heating (or cooling) and enables enthalpies of reactions and phase changes to be obtained.

In the 1830s F. Rudberg used an iron crucible suspended by four platinum wires in a large iron vessel fitted with a lid and a thermometer whose bulb was in the sample. Molten material was placed in the crucible while the outer vessel was filled with snow, as was the lid. Thus a controlled cooling curve could be obtained, and with it Rudberg studied lead, tin, zinc, and some alloys. DTA, which is much more sensitive in its ability to measure temperature effects in materials, was made possible by H. L. Le Châtelier's pioneering work on the reliability and reproducibility of thermocouples. In the 1890s, William Roberts-Austen and his assistant, A. Stansfield, perfected equipment for studying the effects of small admixtures of certain elements on the properties of iron, copper, and lead. They devised a method for measuring the temperature difference between the sample and the reference material (platinum) placed side-by-side in an identical thermal environment. The first published DTA curve was of iron cooling. Subsequent improvements in electric **furnaces** that permitted accurate temperature control led to the widespread use of DTA.

Although Roberts-Austen had used an automatic photographic system for recording the differential emfs using a vertical line of light falling on a photographic plate moved vertically by a clockwork motor, manual plotting was

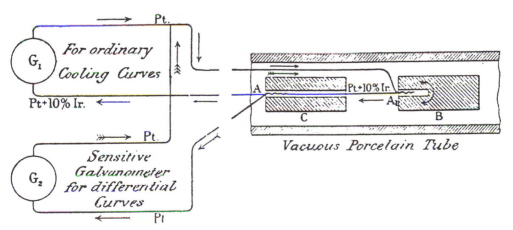

Differential thermocouple arrangement used by Roberts-Austen in 1899, using platinum as the reference material. Roberts-Austen (1899): 38.

widely used until the introduction of potentiometric recorders.

Until the 1950s most DTA instruments were individually built by the research worker. The first commercial instrument, introduced by the Eberbach Corp. in 1948, was a portable device used for mineral prospecting in the field. Other commercial instruments quickly followed from various countries. Nowadays the market is dominated by some seven or eight well-known manufacturers with equipment prices around $20,000 to $30,000.

While early DTA instruments operated in air with no control of the atmosphere around the DTA cell, it was the work of Robert Stone, and the introduction of his commercial apparatus in 1962 with close atmosphere control in the DTA cell, that underlined the significant part the atmosphere can play. Now atmosphere control is considered essential for all DTA experiments.

The earliest paper describing a DTA instrument working subambient is probably that of T.I. Taylor and H.P. Klug in 1936, who used DTA from -75°C to 160°C to study molecular rotation in copper sulfate pentahydrate. The two wells of the DTA cell were cooled in solid carbon dioxide. However, no curves below 10°C were shown. The first published DTA subambient curve is due to A.T. Jensen and C.A. Beevers. In their instrument, the copper foil nib attached to the base of the DTA cell was lowered by an electric motor into liquid air to give a linear temperature/time curve. High-temperature DTA has been carried out up to >2400°C using tungsten heating elements introduced in the late 1950s.

There are other significant landmarks in the history of DTA instruments: (1) Miniaturization. Using the drilled-out beads of the thermocouple-measuring system as the crucibles, C. Mazieres studied samples as small as 1μg. In 1968 E.M. Bollin described a DTA instrument carried on a Mars mission used to study samples scraped by robot from the planet's surface. The instrument was based on a 1-in. gold cube. (2) In 1955 F. Paulik et al. described the development of a complex thermoanalytical instrument (called the derivatograph) measuring and recording simultaneously the weight change (TG), its derivative (DTG), and the rate of enthalpy change (DTA) against the temperature. Commercial simultaneous TG-DTA (or DSC) instruments are widely available, as they give fuller information than the separate techniques.

(3) In 1964 a power-compensated differential scanning **calorimeter** (DSC) was introduced. This was based on a theory developed by M.J. O'Neill, in which separate heaters were positioned in contact with the sample and reference crucibles so that the heat generated was electrically compensated. A heat flux DSC was introduced in 1968. This was based on S.L. Boersma's work published in 1955 and quickly followed by all the major manufacturers. Now DSC is the predominant technique—apart from high-temperature work above 1700°C. (4) Finally, the use of computers has greatly facilitated the use of DTA and DSC. Now the techniques are very widely used for research and development and for quality control in many industries.

The early use of DTA was mainly in the study of minerals and in their identification, providing an alternative to x-ray crystallography. These early studies also underlined the importance of careful experimental procedure. The range of applications expanded in the early years to include metals and alloys, inorganic compounds, cements, and ceramics. As commercial instrumentation became more sensitive, sample sizes smaller, and base lines more precise, the range of applications grew so that today the biggest field for DSC (and DTA) is undoubtedly polymer chemistry along with other fields such as pharmaceuticals, oils, fats, and foods. With the powerful software programs now available, the information obtainable is considerable, including the evaluation of enthalpies, the extent of crystallization, purity, kinetics, heat capacity, glass transition temperature, and the like.

John P. Redfern

Bibliography

Mackenzie, Robert C. "Origin and Development of Differential Thermal Analysis." *Thermochimica Acta* 73 (1984): 307–67.

Paulik, F., J. Paulik, and L. Erdey. Hungarian patent no. 145,332, 1955.

Redfern, John P. "Low Temperature Studies." In *Differential Thermal Analysis,* edited by Robert C. Mackenzie, Vol. 2, 119–45. London: Academic, 1972.

Roberts-Austen, William. "Fifth Report to the Alloys Research Committee: Steel." *Proceedings of the Institution of Mechanical Engineers* 35 (1899): 35–107.

Smothers, W.J. and Y. Chiang. *Differential*

Thermal Analysis: Theory and Practice.
New York: Chemical, 1958.

Diffraction, X-ray
See X-ray Diffraction

Diffraction Grating and Ruling Engine

The modern diffraction grating is a reflecting surface crossed by thousands of parallel lines per inch that break light up into one or more spectra through the phenomenon of interference. The machines used, historically, to produce diffraction gratings are called ruling engines. The larger apparatus in which a grating is placed to record spectra is called a spectrograph (see **spectrophotometer; spectroscope (early); spectroscope, astronomical.**)

Uses

Diffraction gratings and prisms are the two principal devices that disperse light into component colors or wavelengths. From the time of Isaac Newton's analysis of light in the seventeenth century until roughly the twentieth century, prisms predominated as research tools. However, diffraction gratings are today preferred for precise determinations of wavelength. Also, reflection gratings eliminate the light absorption that takes place when light passes through a prism.

Gratings and prisms, used in spectrographs, today make possible highly sensitive chemical analyses in the laboratory, based on the distinctive light emissions of specific atoms and molecules. Astronomical spectrographs attached to **telescopes** furnish the raw data from which astronomers determine the elemental composition, temperature, and other properties of luminous celestial objects. Until the quantum-mechanical model of atoms emerged in the 1920s, laboratory spectra also represented a challenge to physicists, who attempted for more than a half-century to explain the spectra of the elements based on some mechanical picture of the atom.

Origins

Italian physicist F.M. Grimaldi observed in the seventeenth century that the edges of shadows are not completely sharp, but possess fringes or diffraction bands. The American David Rittenhouse was the first to place multiple edges next to each other, in 1785, and observe that the ensemble spreads light from a small opening into multiple colored lines if placed between the opening and the eye. His device was a transmission grating, 0.5 in. square, composed of fifty hairs stretched between two parallel fine screws.

The principal founder of diffraction spectroscopy was Joseph von Fraunhofer, a Munich optician who also worked on achromatic lenses. He mapped the solar spectrum, showing the positions of 350 lines, assigned the now-familiar letter designations to the most notable ones, and measured the wavelengths of specific lines. Fraunhofer used fine wires rather than hairs to create a larger grating in the 1820s. He also developed gratings of the modern type: lines ruled on a substrate such as glass. He ruled fine parallel lines in a layer of grease on a glass plate, and also in a layer of gold foil; he used a diamond point to rule lines directly on glass; and he scribed lines on a glass surface covered with black resin, creating in that case a reflection grating. Thomas Young in England had used similar gratings as early as 1802, but Fraunhofer developed a body of practical and theoretical knowledge along with his instruments.

To automate the line-ruling process, Fraunhofer created the first ruling engine, which produced gratings with a density of thousands of lines per inch. He discussed the possible effect of periodic ruling errors on the resulting spectra (this became a *bête noire* around 1900), and the effects of groove shape. He did not, however, publish details of his ruling engine.

Spectroscopy received new impetus in 1859 from the realization by Gustav Kirchhoff and Robert Bunsen that dark absorption lines in the solar spectrum correspond to bright emission lines from specific chemical elements in the laboratory. In the 1860s, using a transmission grating made by the Pomeranian instrument-maker Friedrich Nobert, Anders Ångström of Sweden made a drawing of the solar spectrum that showed some one thousand dark lines. The unit most commonly used for wavelength today, 10^{-10} meters, is named after Ångström.

American Manufacture

An American lawyer and amateur astronomer, Lewis M. Rutherfurd, developed his own ruling engine in the 1860s and 1870s, and spectra from his reflection gratings were acclaimed as brighter and better-defined than any diffraction spectra then produced. Rutherfurd's largest gratings

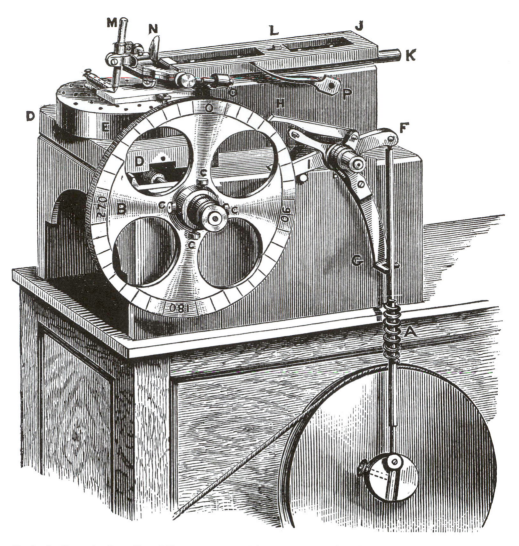

Rutherfurd's engine for ruling diffraction gratings. The American Cyclopedia, *Vol. 15. New York: D. Appleton, 1881: 243. Courtesy of NMAH.*

were about two inches wide. William A. Rogers, an astronomer at Harvard, attempted to improve on Rutherfurd's achievement, but was in turn quickly surpassed by Henry A. Rowland, the first professor of physics at Johns Hopkins University.

Rowland Gratings

Working with a mechanic, Rowland created a ruling engine that produced gratings that were larger and more finely ruled than Rutherfurd's, creating spectra accordingly brighter and sharper. These gratings, ruled on speculum metal, measured up to 6 in. wide. According to Rowland, who was an engineer by training, the critical component of the ruling engine was a highly uniform screw that controlled the spacing be-

tween the grooves. Rowland also conceived of ruling on a concave surface, which brought spectra into focus without the need for collimating and focusing lenses, with their attendant light-absorption, as required by conventional gratings.

Concave and plane gratings produced under Rowland, and later under other physicists trained at Johns Hopkins, set the standard for fifty years or more. These gratings took a few days and nights of nonstop ruling. They were sold at cost, or below, and shipped all over the world, demand constantly exceeding supply. A 1911 catalogue from the firm that acted as distributor for Johns Hopkins shows that grating prices ranged from $20 to $400, depending on size and quality. Spectroscopy was still a major branch of physics, and many fundamental observations of the elements were achieved with these instruments. Rowland himself produced a photographic map of the solar spectrum, recording twenty thousand absorption lines with unprecedented accuracy. Nonsolar astronomy, however, got little benefit from gratings until technical advances in the 1930s made plane-grating spectra still brighter.

The first significant rival to Johns Hopkins in the United States was Albert A. Michelson at the University of Chicago, but the Chicago ruling operation produced many fewer gratings. In 1916, George Ellery Hale hired the head of the Johns Hopkins ruling operation, John Anderson, to produce gratings at the Mount Wilson Observatory. Hopkins, the University of Chicago, and Mount Wilson remained the only sources of large gratings into the 1940s, although a number of shops made smaller gratings. Engine owners could be secretive, which limited spread of the craft.

Modern Improvements

By the 1940s, the favored material for gratings was highly reflective aluminum on glass, which wore out the diamond ruling tip more slowly than did speculum. Control of groove shape, or "blazing," concentrated more light into desired spectra. By the late 1940s, work on ruling engines began at the Massachusetts Institute of Technology and at a commercial firm, Bausch & Lomb. Both organizations received engines formerly used at Chicago. Other institutions and companies soon entered production as well. At M.I.T., George Harrison, the postwar master of the art, developed interferometric control of ruling, an idea of Michelson's, to ensure accurate groove placement. The misplacement of grooves at regular intervals caused "ghosts," or unintended spectral lines, which were a curiosity to Fraunhofer but a plague to later makers. Along with increasing brightness and definition, fine mechanical control has gradually brought the virtual elimination of these ghosts. By the 1960s, grating widths reached 10 in. or more.

In the late 1940s, gratings were reproduced chemically by pouring a resin onto machine-made gratings. When the resin was removed, it formed a usable grating itself, not necessarily better than the original, but cheaper to make. In the late 1960s, laser interference fringes recorded on a photosensitive material provided yet another nonmechanical means of grating production. Once a source of puzzlement in

physics, spectroscopy is now a routine tool in chemistry and astronomy.

George Sweetnam

Bibliography

Fraunhofer, Joseph. *Prismatic and Diffraction Spectra,* edited and translated by J.S. Ames. New York: American Book, 1900. Reprint. *The Wave Theory, Light and Spectra.* New York: Arno, 1981.

Harrison, George R. "The Production of Diffraction Gratings. I. Development of the Ruling Art." *Journal of the Optical Society of America* 39 (1949): 413–26.

Sweetnam, George. "Precision Implemented: Henry Rowland, the Concave Diffraction Grating, and the Analysis of Light." In *The Values of Precision,* edited by M. Norton Wise, 283–31. Princeton: Princeton University Press, 1995.

Warner, Deborah Jean. "Lewis M. Rutherfurd: Pioneer Astronomical Photographer and Spectroscopist." *Technology and Culture* 12 (1971): 190–216.

———. "Rowland's Gratings: Contemporary Technology." *Vistas in Astronomy* 29 (1986): 125–30.

Digital Computer

See COMPUTER, DIGITAL

Dilatometer

A dilatometer measures changes in length as a specimen is subjected to a controlled temperature program, thus determining the coefficient of expansion of the material. Similarly, a thermomechanical analyzer measures dimensional changes, such as expansion, penetration, tension, and flexure. Dilatometry (or thermo-dilatometry) is one of a whole family of thermal analysis techniques (see **thermobalance** and **differential thermal analyzer**).

The development of thermal analysis began with the development of reliable thermocouples, due principally to Henri Le Châtelier, a French metallurgist and chemist in 1886, and the electric **furnace,** by G. Charpy in 1895. Josiah Wedgwood, an English potter, used the shrinkage of china clay samples to describe a temperature scale in 1782. He placed a clay piece of standard size in the furnace, took it out after firing, allowed it to cool, and measured its shrinkage in a V-notch arrangement calibrated

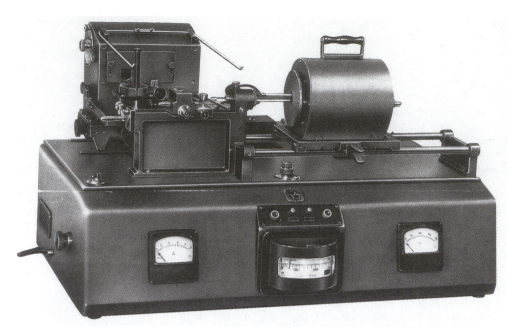

Early commercial Automatic Recording Dilatometer, by Netzsch Geratebau, 1954. Courtesy of Netzsch Geratebau.

in "degrees Wedgwood." He did not allow for the nonlinearity of shrinkage, and so came up with the surprising results that the melting point of iron was >10,000°C. These experiments were, in effect, the reverse of dilatometry in that shrinkage is used to define temperature rather than temperature to measure shrinkage.

In a simple modern dilatometer, the specimen is mounted in the center of a constant temperature zone in the controlled furnace. The specimen's expansion is measured by means of a push rod, whose movement is monitored by a precision **micrometer**, a dial gauge, an **interferometer**, a **telescope**, x-ray diffraction patterns, a thermoresistor bridge using a light beam and mirror arrangement, or, nowadays most commonly, a linear variable differential transducer. Alternatively a **laser** beam may be used. The signal is then recorded on an X-Y recorder or by a computer so that a *dl/t* (that is, change in length plotted against temperature) curve is obtained. For accurate work, corrections have to be applied for the expansion of the rod or an alternative arrangement involving a differential system and a second rod parallel with the first, of the same material as the rod in contact with the sample. When penetration is required to measure the softening point, a weight is added mechanically or electrically to the top of the rod. Various geometries for the rod tip may be used. Changes

in tension are measured by holding the material in two clamps, one anchored and the other positioned on the bottom of the rod, which is counterweighted so that the sample is under a known tension. This method is used for textile and polymer fibers and films.

D. J. Evans and C. J. Winstanley described a simple, inexpensive dilatometer that operates down to liquid nitrogen temperatures. Descriptions of other early instruments are given by W. D. Kingery in 1952, Wesley W. Wendlandt in 1964, and Paul D. Garn in 1965.

In 1950 Netzsch Geratebau, a manufacturer of machinery for the ceramic industry, began developing a range of testing and analytical instruments to overcome problems encountered with the raw materials. Netzsch was based in Selb, Bavaria, Germany, the home of Rosenthal China. They introduced their first commercial recording dilatometer in 1954. This had an automatic temperature control for a fixed heating rate of 5°/minute. Recording of both temperature and changes in length was made photo-optically. The changes in length had the possibility of magnification steps of 125, 250, 500, and 1000 referred to a theoretical sample length of 100 mm, which was then related to the actual length by a lever system. One of the early Netzsch instruments sold in the U.K. in 1959, was recently reported to be still in use in a department of the

British General Electric Company. Another early model was supplied to what was then British Steel. Other companies manufacturing thermobalances and differential thermal analyzers quickly followed suit, introducing the more versatile thermomechanical analyzers.

In 1954 F. Paulik et al. in Hungary described an instrument for carrying out the work of a thermobalance and a differential thermal analyzer simultaneously; they called it a derivatograph. They subsequently incorporated a simple dilatometric device into their equipment so that they could obtain a simultaneous record of weight changes, rate of weight change, energy changes, changes in length, and rate of change of length all against temperature.

The latest developments are the expected ones of extending the temperature range both to lower and to higher temperatures. There has also been the computerization of the equipment for data acquisition, processing, and control. Most recent was the introduction of the dynamic thermal mechanical analyzer (or dynamic mechanical analyzer), in which the specimen is subjected to an oscillating load that enables the viscoelastic properties of materials to be determined over the temperature range of interest. This provides data essential for design engineers.

John Redfern

Bibliography

Garn, Paul D. *Thermoanalytical Methods of Investigation.* London: Academic, 1965.

Mackenzie, Robert C. "De Calore: Prelude to Thermal Analysis." *Thermochimica Acta* 73 (1984): 251–306.

———. "Origin and Development of Differential Thermal Analysis." *Thermochimica Acta* 73 (1984): 307–67.

Paulik, F., J. Paulik, and L. Erdey. Hungarian patent no. 145,332, 1955.

Redfern, John P. "Complementary Methods." In *Differential Thermal Analysis,* edited by R.C. Mackenzie, Vol. 1, 138–41. London: Academic, 1970.

Dip Circle

A dip circle measures the angle made with the horizon by a magnetic needle, freely suspended near the earth. It is also known as a dipping circle, dipping needle, or inclinometer.

In 1544, Georg Hartmann noticed that the north-seeking end of a magnetized needle dips toward the earth in the Northern Hemisphere.

While Hartmann sought to eliminate dip by means of a counterbalanced compass needle, Robert Norman, an English hydrographer and instrument-maker, called for extensive measurements of dip and conducted the first known systematic experimental investigation of this geomagnetic phenomenon. Other sixteenth-century navigators and instrument-makers may have also noted the dip of compass needles. In *The Newe Attractiue* (London, 1581), Norman described a device with a 6-in. magnetized steel needle with a horizontal axle fixed at its center of gravity, and mounted within a vertical graduated circle. The sharpened ends of the axle rested in hollowed glass receptacles and rotated in the magnetic meridian—that is, that plane defined by the zenith and by magnetic north. It is notable that while Hartmann's measured dip of 9° was much too small for his Bavarian location, Norman's value of 72° was much too large for London. The difficulty of measuring dip was often commented on during the next few centuries.

The next published description of a dip circle appeared in William Gilbert's *De Magnete* (1600). Gilbert's dip circle was mechanically crude, with an axle of steel wire inserted into holes drilled in a brass frame. Although Gilbert suggested that the dip might be used to indicate latitude, friction at the pivot was a serious obstacle to accurate measurement. Instrument-makers for the next three hundred years tried many means to minimize this friction. They lined the pivot points and cups with gold alloys, bell metal, or jewels. A system in the nineteenth and early twentieth centuries attached knife edges to the needle and rested them on agate plates.

The dip circle presented other problems. The center of gravity of the needle rarely coincided with the axis of the needle's rotation. Moreover, it was difficult to ensure that the axis was at the center of the graduated circle. The first problem was addressed in the mid eighteenth century by Tobias Mayer, who purposefully separated the center of gravity from the axis of rotation. Solutions to the second problem included various design niceties and an observational protocol that included reading both ends of the needle, reversing the needle, reading both ends again, and averaging the readings. A last problem, the influence of air currents on the needle, was alleviated by enclosing the needle and circle in a box of glass and wood or brass.

D

Dip circle, by Nairne and Blunt, ca. 1775. SM 1900-129. Courtesy of SSPL.

More extensive use of dip circles in research began in the eighteenth century. Johan Carl Wilcke published a map of lines of equal dip in 1768. Jean-Charles Borda, E.P. de Rossel, and Alexander von Humboldt introduced the method of oscillating the dip needle in the magnetic meridian to measure total magnetic intensity. James Clark Ross used a dip circle in 1831 to locate the northern magnetic pole.

By the eighteenth century dip circles were widely used. Edward Nairne of London sold a brass instrument to Harvard College in 1765 for £18/3, including its lined mahogany box. Étienne Lenoir of Paris produced instruments for Charles Coulomb and Jean-Baptiste Biot. Henri-Prudence Gambey produced a widely used dip needle beginning in the 1820s.

With the spread of geomagnetic surveys from the 1830s on, a period of rapid innovation in instrument design was quickly superseded by decades of commercial availability of a relatively few standard designs. Some new makers of magnetic instruments included Moritz Meyerstein of Göttingen, Friedrich Wilhelm Breithaupt of Kassel, and Thomas Grubb of Ireland. Robert Were Fox designed a robust dip circle suitable for expeditionary use on land and sea; it cost £26/2 in 1844 from the instrument shop of Mr. George of Falmouth. Another design by Henry Barrow was comparably priced at £25, but it was not as versatile. A third design, the Kew Pattern Dip Circle, was made in the shop of John Dover.

A final flurry of innovative design occurred at the Department of Terrestrial Magnetism of the Carnegie Institution of Washington. Their so-called Universal Magnetometer of 1911 included a dip needle. The name came from its incorporation of a unifilar **magnetometer** in the box of the dip circle, thus making for a lightweight, versatile, field instrument.

Dip circles had also long been used in mining and prospecting, although the historical details on this story are obscure. Prospectors' dipping needles were produced into the twentieth century by firms including W. and L.E. Gurley, Keuffel and Esser, and Eugene Dietzgen. Adolf Schmidt, as head of the Prussian geomagnetic observatory, developed a "vertical balance" in about 1915 for studying the variation of dip and the vertical component of the magnetic field. Schmidt's instrument was useful in mineral prospecting, as was the "Hotchkiss Superdip," patented by W.O. Hotchkiss in 1929.

Although these instruments represent pinnacles of dip circle design, new methods of determining magnetic inclination were already being developed. The most important of these was the null-method earth inductor, a device using a rotating coil and a **galvanometer** to locate the direction of the earth's magnetic field. Models were in use in observatories and in field research by World War I. Earth inductors were just the first indication of electrical and electronic systems that in the decades ahead made the dip circle essentially obsolete. Indeed, dip is not generally measured directly any more, but is more commonly calculated from measurements of the horizontal and either the vertical or the total intensity.

Gregory A. Good

Bibliography

Crichton Mitchell, A. "Chapters in the History of Terrestrial Magnetism. Chapter III: The Discovery of the Magnetic Inclination." *Terrestrial Magnetism and Atmospheric Electricity* 44 (1939): 77–80.

Forbes, A.J. "General Instrumentation." In *Geomagnetism*, edited by J.A. Jacobs, Vol. 1, 51–142. London: Academic, 1987.

McConnell, Anita. *Geomagnetic Instruments before 1900: An Illustrated Account of Their Construction and Use.* London: Harriet Wynter, 1980.

Multhauf, Robert P., and Gregory A. Good. *A Brief History of Geomagnetism and a Catalog of the Collections of the National Museum of American History,* Smithsonian Studies in History and Technology 48. Washington, D.C.: Smithsonian Institution Press, 1987.

Parkinson, W.D. "Geomagnetic Instruments." In *Sciences of the Earth: An Encyclopedia of Events, People, and Phenomena,* edited by Gregory A. Good. New York: Garland, 1997.

Distance-Measurement, Electromagnetic

Electromagnetic distance-measurement (EDM) instruments transmit an unmodulated pulsed or continuously modulated electromagnetic wave, the signal being reflected (passive systems) or retransmitted (active systems) from the remote end of the measured line back to the instrument. The slope distance is obtained from measurements of the time taken for the pulse to travel the double distance (the pulse echo technique) or by measuring the difference in phase angle between transmitted and reflected signals and counting the complete number of cycles of the measuring wavelength (the phase difference technique). EDM instruments may be classified according to the nature of the wave employed. Accuracy depends on the characteristics of the signal and the precision of the measuring techniques employed.

Phase-Measurement Techniques

Here the return signal travels through an internal light path, the length of which can be varied by one full unit of the measuring wavelength. Phase difference is measured directly in terms of length, by recording the displacement of moving prisms required to null a null-indicator. In the analog method, a reference signal having the same characteristics as the transmitted signal is delayed until a zero phase lag with the return signal is obtained. In the digital method, the transmitted signal is compared with the return signal. Here the original sinusoidal signals are converted into square waves. A gate is opened when the reference signal begins a new cycle, and closed when the return signal does the same. While the gate is open, pulses from a high-frequency oscillator are accumulated in a counter. Most modern instruments use this method.

These optical-mechanical methods resulted from efforts by Armand Fizeau (toothed wheel, 1849), Leon Foucault (rotating mirror, 1862), Albert Michelson (rotating prism, 1926), and others to determine the velocity of light. Using mechanical methods of modulating the light to give an approximately square wave form and estimating by eye the phase difference of transmitted and received signals, these experiments suggested a method of determining distance by the timing of electromagnetic waves.

In the electro-optical alternative, an optical shutter (Kerr cell, 1929) provides a much faster rate of interruption of light. This was used by Erik Bergstrand in Sweden in his determination of the velocity of light (1943), and later in his prototype electro-optical distance-measuring instrument, the Geodimeter. The first commercial version, manufactured by AGA of Sweden, appeared in 1953. Geodetic surveyors were attracted by the possibility of applying the principles to the accurate measurement of the sides of large triangulation networks and baselines for the control of national mapping. Early instruments were heavy and bulky and required considerable external power supplies.

A. Bjerhammar applied super-heterodyning techniques to electro-optical distance meters in order to obtain accurate phase measurements at lower frequencies. The AGA Geodimeter 6A, with coaxial optics and an electromechanical resolver, was introduced in 1967. This instrument, although still heavy, could be carried as a backpack. The Kerr cell was superseded by an electronic shutter, the KDP-crystal.

Parallel developments in radio ranging led to the development by T.L. Wadley in South Africa in 1954 of a microwave distance meter. The first of these, the Tellurometer MRA1, was introduced commercially in 1957.

Research on gallium arsenide light-emitting diodes in the 1960s led to their incorporation in short-range electro-optical EDM instruments. Such instruments are currently widely used in surveying and civil engineering construction and for industrial metrology.

Microwave Instruments

A frequency-modulated carrier wave is transmitted from the "master" instrument to a similar instrument at the remote end of the line. The "remote" instrument amplifies the signal and returns it to the "master," where the phase difference between the transmitted and returned signals is measured and displayed. The effective modulated measuring wavelength is typically 10 m, and phase resolution to 0.1 percent results in a basic precision of about 10 mm.

The MRA101 Tellurometer (1970) employed a klystron or cavity resonator to generate frequency-modulated microwave emissions. Solid-state Gunn diodes replaced klystrons. The first lightweight microwave distance meter (Tellurometer CA1000) became available in 1972. A recent microwave instrument, the Tellumat CMW20, has a range of 25 km, built-in aerial, and a beam width of only 3°. Similar instruments were developed by Wild in Switzerland and by Cubic in the United States.

Electro-Optical Instruments

A transmitted amplitude-modulated beam is reflected by a passive retroprism reflector at the remote end of the line. The variations in intensity of the returning signal are detected and transformed into variations of current. Silicon avalanche diodes are normally used in short-range EDM, and photomultipliers in long-range EDM.

In 1968, Wild of Switzerland introduced the Wild/Sercel DI-10 Distomat, the first of many short-range electro-optical distance meters using light-emitting diodes. The Tellurometer MA100 followed in 1969, and the Zeiss SM11 in 1970. The most important feature of the gallium arsenide diode is that the radiation can be directly modulated in intensity, thus eliminating the need for modulating devices, such as the Kerr cell.

Landmark EDM instruments representing an advance on previous instruments include the Kern DM500 (1974), the AGA Geodimeter 12 (1975), the Sokkisha SDM-1C (1976), and the Topcon GTS-1 (1980). Precision of short-range electro-optical instruments is typically 10mm.

Electro-optical distance meters may be mounted on optical **theodolites** or combined with electronic theodolites to form electronic tacheometers, or so-called "total stations."

Tellurometer MRA1, ca. 1960. SM 1967-34. Courtesy of SSPL.

Pulsed Distance Meters

A short intense signal (frequently a pulsed laser) travels to a reflective target and back, the so-called double flight time being determined to about 0.1 ns, equivalent to an accuracy of about 15 mm. Pulsed distance meters were pioneered by Eumig for industrial purposes, the first surveying instrument using the method being the Geo-Fennel FEN 2000 (1983), followed by the long-range Wild Distomat DI 3000 using prism reflectors (1985) and the reflectorless Wild DIOR3002S with a range of about 350 meters. Other instruments include the IBEO Pulsar 100 and the handheld Leica DISTO.

Precision Distance Meters

The first high-precision EDM instrument, the Mekometer, was built by K.D. Froome and R.M. Bradsell in 1961 at the National Physical Laboratory in the U.K. and introduced commercially in 1973 as the Kern Mekometer ME 3000. In the Mekometer, the carrier signal is produced by a Xenon flash tube (later replaced in the ME 5000 by a HeNe laser) and modulated with a KDP crystal. A modulation wavelength of 0.6 meter is derived from a quartz cavity resonator connected to the atmosphere through soft bellows. Phase comparison is achieved optomechanically. The Geomensor CR204 (United States) operates on a similar principle. Other instruments include the long-range laser Geodolite 3G and the Georan 1 and Terrameter LDM2, which use two different color light sources in order to filter out the effects of atmospheric refraction.

Ronald C. Cox

Bibliography

Burnside, C.D. *Electromagnetic Distance Measurement*. 3rd ed. Oxford: BSP Professional, 1991.

Deumlich, Fritz. *Surveying Instruments*. Translated by Wolfgang Faig. Berlin: Walter de Gruyter, 1982.

Rueger, J.M. *Electronic Distance Measurement: An Introduction*. 3rd rev. ed. Berlin: Springer, 1990.

Distance-Measurement, Optical

Optical distance measurement is the technique of determining horizontal and vertical distances between two or more points by optical methods based on the solution of a plane triangle formed through the point of observation and the remote point. The various solutions are known collectively as *tacheometry* (from the Greek *tacheos,* "quick," and *metron,* "measure").

Background

One of the effects of the first industrial revolution was to increase the value of land and create a need for more accurate and rapid land-measuring techniques. The construction of transportation systems required by industry, such as canals, railways, and roads, made great demands on surveyors and engineers. Measuring distances directly with graduated ropes and chains was slow and tedious and alternative optical methods began to be considered. By the end of the nineteenth century, surveying telescopes could be provided with a diaphragm incorporating intersecting lines defining the line of sight and a number of horizontal parallel lines, so-called stadia lines or hairs. Continuous development of optical distance measuring instrumentation over nearly two hundred years, principally in Great Britain, Germany, Switzerland, France, and Italy, progressed in line with improvements in optical and mechanical systems design.

Stadia Tacheometry

The slant distance from a sighting instrument to a graduated rod, held either vertically or normal to the line of sight at a remote point, is proportional to the length of intercept(s) on the rod subtending a constant angle formed by a pair of parallel wires or lines (the stadia) in the diaphragm of the instrument. Slant distance may be reduced to the horizontal by multiplication by the cosine of the angle of inclination. G.F. Brander used this technique in Augsburg in 1764, and William Green described it in 1778. Both men used instruments incorporating a refracting **telescope** fitted with a **micrometer** in the focus of the eyepiece, with lines having either a fixed or variable separation; but neither recognized that an additional instrument constant was required to correct the measured distances. In 1805, Georg Reichenbach in Munich developed a formula that included this term.

In 1823, the Italian Ignazio Porro placed between the object glass and eyepiece a third (or anallatic) lens whose focus coincided with that of the object glass, thus eliminating the troublesome additive constant. In the early twentieth century, Heinrich Wild produced a virtually anallatic internal-focusing surveying telescope, in which the additive constant became negligible.

Stadia methods became standard practice for detail surveys, but the reduction of slant distances was tedious, necessitating the use of tables. Henry Homan Jeffcott (1912) varied the stadia interval in his direct-reading instrument, one stadia line being fixed, the other two being moved by cams fitted to the horizontal axis of the telescope, providing a form of autoreduction. These ideas were later embodied in designs introduced in 1955 and 1963 by the firm of Kern.

Tangential tacheometry required two pointings of the telescope to determine the staff intercept. These methods required much computation, and the accuracy obtained was often low.

Reduction Tacheometers

In order to reduce the amount of computation required with stadia methods, instruments known as tacheometers were developed with varying forms of autoreduction device, for example, tangent and contact tacheometers by J. L. Sanguet (1860) and C.A. Eckhold (1868). Shift or projection tacheometers were introduced around 1870. Such instruments consisted of a basic sighting instrument (**theodolite**) modified to accept a form of mechanical reduction device by means of which the horizontal distance and vertical difference in height were determined di-

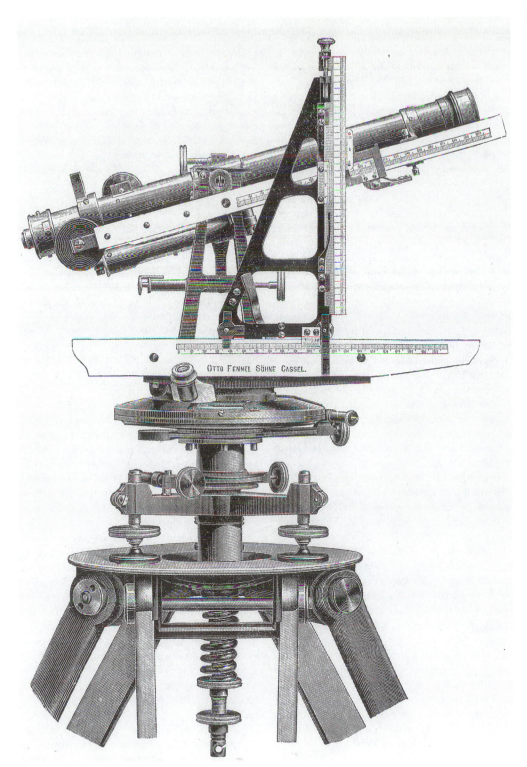

Wagner-Fennel shift tacheometer, 1901. Otto Fennel Söhne, Export-Catalog I: Gruben-Theodolite. *Cassel, 1900: 35. Courtesy of SSPL.*

rectly without further computation. The instruments were, however, heavy and cumbersome.

The concept of optically projecting a reduction diagram into the field of view of the main telescope is usually attributed to the Italian engineers G. Roncagli and E. Urbani in 1890. Ernst von Hammer of Stuttgart developed a diagram with a distance curve and two branch height curves, and Adolf Fennel manufactured the first diagram tacheometer in 1900. All diagram tacheometers use a zero circle, as well as distance and height curves that are related to the stadia reduction equations. The differences that developed between instruments were in the actual appearance of the curves in the field of view and in the methods of moving the curves or measuring lines to correspond to the reduction equations. Later examples are the Wild RDS and Zeiss RTa4 instruments.

Optical Wedges

Around 1890 the concept of using an optical measuring wedge with a vertical rod was developed in the United States and Europe. A glass wedge, placed either in or in front of the telescope causes a light ray to be deflected by a known amount, usually arranged so that there is one unit deflection on the rod for every one hundred units of distance from the wedge. Andrew Barr and and William Stroud in England in 1888 designed the first single-observer **rangefinder**, in which two separate images of a distant object, reflected from wedges or prisms located at opposite ends of a short fixed base, are brought into coincidence. The relative movement of the two images is the basis for the measurement of the distance.

In 1924, Rondolphe Bosshardt designed a double-image tacheometer that employed a pair of contra-rotating wedges mounted in front of the telescope objective lens. The wedges rotated with change in vertical angle, slant distance being related to the relative displacement of two sections of a staff mounted horizontally. The residual interval was measured with a plane-parallel plate micrometer. Slant distance was reduced to horizontal by the rotation of the wedges. Zeiss marketed the idea in 1929; Kern used the concept in their DK-RT instrument of 1947, and Wild in their RDH tacheometer of 1950.

Subtense Tacheometry

Accurate determinations of horizontal distance may be made by repeated measurements of the horizontal angle subtended at a precise theodolite by a horizontal subtense bar of fixed length located at the remote point and oriented normally to the line of sight from the theodolite. Such methods were used to measure distances in control surveys to accuracies similar to those obtained with steel taping.

Optical distance-measuring techniques began to be replaced in the 1960s by electromagnetic distance measurement (see **distance-measurement, electromagnetic**).

Ronald C. Cox

Bibliography

Cox, Ronald C. "The Development of Survey Instrumentation 1780–1980." *Survey Review* 28 (January 1986): 247–55.

Deumlich, Fritz. *Surveying Instruments.* Translated by Wolfgang Faig. Berlin: Walter de Gruyter, 1982.

Hodges, D.J., and J.B. Greenwood. *Optical Distance Measurement.* London: Butterworths, 1971.

Distillation

As late as the nineteenth century, some chemists were still conducting their experiments with ordinary domestic utensils such as wine glasses. Distillation is one process, however, that requires either specialized apparatus or a complex combination of nonspecific items. In distillation, a mixture of liquids is heated to boiling, at which point it is possible to concentrate or completely separate off one of the components by condensing the vapor.

Archaeologists have claimed that distillation was carried out in the distant past, supporting their views by proposing that unusually shaped vessels were used as stills. It has been suggested that ceramic bowls with a double rim from Tepe Gawra on the Tigris, of ca. 3,500 B.C. were used to distill off alcohol, which would then drip through plants to leach out pharmaceutical products. Hemispherical vessels with spouts from Taxila in the Indus Valley, dating from 90 B.C. to A.D. 25, have been identified as being retort heads. Both these proposals are highly conjectural.

A form of distillation vessel called an alembic may have been developed in Hellenistic Alexandria by the second century A.D. An alembic is a dome-shaped hemispherical vessel with an internal gutter at its rim. The liquid being separated off is boiled in a vessel below the alembic and the vapor condenses inside the dome.

Eighteenth-century practical chemistry laboratory, with apparatus for distillation. Universal Magazine
December 1747: Plate 23, facing page 331. Courtesy of NMAH.

Liquid droplets run into the gutter and into a tube attached to the side. Such vessels are illustrated in two late copies of a Greek manuscript showing Alexandrian apparatus. The process of distillation was transmitted to the Arab world, and the earliest physical evidence for the alembic may date from the eighth to the tenth century A.D. Alembics of a design indistinguishable from that of a millennium earlier were being used in Iran by alchemists as recently as the 1970s and probably still continue in use in various countries.

Distillation in China appears to have developed independently. The Chinese still is fundamentally different from that used in the West, in that it uses a concave condensation surface as opposed to the convex surfaces of the alembic and later retort. The early history of the still in China is no less uncertain than that in the Near East and Europe, as virtually no secure evidence from archaeological sources survives. In the West, there is material evidence of distillation from the fourteenth and fifteenth centuries. In a number of medieval sites, mainly castles and monasteries, alembics and associated vessels such as cucurbits (gourd-shaped vessels in which liquids were boiled) and aludels (for sublimation, especially for purification of sal ammoniac) have been appearing in recent years. The retort, a globular vessel with a curved spout, developed later than the alembic, though it did not replace it. It was widely used, in glass, ceramic, and metal forms. The English ceramicist Josiah Wedgwood made retorts for his scientist friends at the end of the eighteenth century.

The distillation vessels described so far are inefficient, partly because of the escape of vapor. Water-cooled condensation columns were developed at the end of the eighteenth century to reduce this effect, seemingly by three independent discoverers: Christian Ehrenfeld Weigel of Göttingen (published 1771), P.J. Poisonnier, for the French Ministre de la Marine (published 1779), and the Swede Johann Gadolin (published 1791). This form of condenser is usually called the counter-current or Liebig condenser, though Justus von Liebig was not born until 1803. It consists of concentric tubes, the distillate flowing along the inner tube while cooling water flows in the opposite direction in the outer one. Liebig popularized the apparatus through books such as the *Handwörterbuch der Chemie* (1842), and the rise of organic chemistry, in which low-boiling-point solvents are frequently used, guaranteed its utility and, indeed, its ubiquity. The basic design continues in use today for simple laboratory processes.

Throughout the nineteenth century improvements were made to the effectiveness of stills, largely by French chemists. Most of the new models were produced for industrial purposes, but a number of general principles were developed that could be incorporated on a laboratory scale. Most important was the technique of vacuum distillation, proposed by Philippe Lebonin in 1796 and later described by Henry Tritton in 1818 and by John Barry in 1821. This allowed liquids to boil at lower temperatures, reducing the likelihood of molecular decomposition. Such benefits could also be obtained by steam distillation, in which compounds that are sparingly soluble in water may be distilled by heating with water or by blowing steam through the mixture.

If a distillation column is arranged vertically rather than at a downward angle, a mixture of liquids can be separated if they boil off at different temperatures. This was first effected by Charles Mansfield, who separated off fractions of coal tar in the mid 1800s. Columns were developed in hundreds of different shapes and forms. Hugues Champennois introduced the principle of bubble-cap plates in 1854; here, the column is split up into a series of stages, liquid and vapor being in equilibrium at each stage. In 1880, Walter Hempel suggested that packing the columns with glass beads would increase the efficiency. Since then, a wide variety of packing units have been developed in different shapes and materials. The ease with which components forming a distillation arrangement can be substituted was greatly increased from the 1950s, when standard ground glass joints began to be generally introduced.

Since the mid twentieth century, laboratory distillation apparatus has become increasingly automated. Heating could be controlled by contact **thermometers**, the rate of evaporation determined by differential manometers and reduced pressures maintained. Measurements of various data were recorded automatically. All the components required for distillation were built into a single complete unit.

Robert G. W. Anderson

Bibliography

Forbes, R.J. *A Short History of the Art of Distillation*. Leiden: Brill, 1970.

Krell, Erich. *Handbook of Laboratory Distillation*. 2nd ed. Oxford: Elsevier, 1982.

———. "Zur Geschichte der Labordestillation." In *Historia Scientiae naturalis: Beiträge zur Geschichte der Laboratoriumstechnik und deren Randgebiete*, edited by E.H.W. Giebeler and K.A. Rosenbauer, 51–78. Darmstadt: G-I-T Verlag, 1982.

Moorhouse, Stephen. "Medieval Distilling-Apparatus of Glass and Pottery." *Medieval Archaeology* 16 (1972): 79–121.

Sifalakis, George. *A Century of Distillation*. Den Haage: Privately published, 1967.

Dividing Engine

Dividing engines are employed to delineate the linear and circular scales of measuring instruments used in astronomy, navigation, and other sciences. The first mechanical dividing device was conceived in 1674 by Robert Hooke to divide scales of large astronomical **quadrants**. Like every subsequent engine until recently, Hooke's engine used the revolution of a precision screw to advance the scribe from one line to the next. The first actual circular dividing engine was built by the clockmaker Henry Hindley around 1738. Jesse Ramsden laid down the principles of successful construction and technique in 1777. Modern dividing engines employ computer-controlled optical encoders. Scales may be photographically reproduced or encoders mounted on the measuring instruments, making engines unnecessary.

Although dividing engines evolved from horological gear-cutting machines, their development was prompted by the fabulous prizes offered by European governments in the early eighteenth century for methods to determine longitude at sea. These awards stimulated construction of marine **chronometers** by John Harrison (1736, 1759) and Pierre LeRoy and Ferdinand Berthoud (1763). Following these highly publicized efforts, instrument makers realized that the new navigational techniques required **octants** or **sextants** with precisely graduated scales, and that these could be made in a reasonable time only with mechanical means. The large circles of primary astronomical instruments, however, continued to be divided by hand until the mid nine-

Ramsden's 45-inch dividing engine completed in 1774. Jesse Ramsden, Description of an Engine for Dividing Mathematical Instruments. *London: J. Nourse, 1777: Plate 1. Courtesy of SSPL.*

teenth century, when smaller diameter circles could match or surpass them in accuracy.

Circular dividing engines are relatively easy to construct because, as the circle closes on itself, any division may be compared with any other. Linear dividing engines, however, must be compared with a standard that itself is subject to errors. To construct either type, a scale must be originally divided as a guide to the placement of teeth for the precision worm-wheel or rack that drives the engraving tool carriage. Hindley's circular engine, not following that principle, would not have been very successful.

Dividing engines were built in the 1750s by Daniel Ekström of Stockholm and Georg Brander of Augsburg. Brander was particularly adept at engraving glass grid **micrometers**, a precursor of **diffraction gratings**. The Duc de Chaulnes built several engines in the 1760s, and his description (1768) demonstrates a good understanding of the technical requirements and a desirable method of approach. Most notably, he used micrometer **microscopes** as the points of a compass to successively bisect and compare angles. Modern measurements of Chaulnes's 1761 engine, however, and the apparent lack of divided instruments from his hand, suggest limited success. Lack of skilled workmen and quality tools probably undermined his endeavor.

Ramsden completed his first circular engine in 1766, and a linear engine in 1768. The latter had disappeared by 1790 when Sir George Shuckburgh tried to substantiate the claimed 1/4,000-in. accuracy. A second circular engine (1774–1775), 45 in. in diameter, earned Ramsden a £6,000 prize from the Board of Longitude and contracts to divide octant and sextant scales for competitors. Ramsden's success was attributable to his unmatched mechanical skill and the specialized lathe with which he made the worm screw that was then used to delineate the teeth on the wheel's limb. John Troughton made a similar machine in 1778. His brother Edward completed a 30-in.-diameter engine in 1783 using the same principles as Chaulnes.

Some thirty linear and circular dividing engines had been made by 1800. The best of these circular engines were said to perform to 1 arcsecond, but the fact that stellar parallax was not measured until 1838 reflects scale inaccuracies in excess of this—errors overcome only by use of statistical methods, analysis of scale errors, and attention by observers to such details as differential expansion of scales from body heat.

In the first half of the nineteenth century, some thirty dividing engines were made by such noted instrument makers as James Watt, J.-F. Richer, Nicholas Fortin, F.-A. Jecker, Henry Cavendish, Henry Kater, James Allan, William J. Young, Henri Gamby, Bryan Donkin, Andrew Ross, and George Merz. William Simms automated the driving and engraving mechanism in 1843. With each attempt to perfect the engine, new understanding of the problems was gained, such as the metallurgical characteristics of the scale material, the importance of axial centering of the workpiece, the role of the instrument-maker's body heat, and methods to correct screw errors.

Many of these early engines survive, with the major collections being held in the Science Museum, Conservatoire des Arts et Métiers, National Museum of American History, and Deutsches Museum. The earliest extant engine is that of Chaulnes, now in the Museo de Storia Scienza (Florence).

Louis Perreaux began making dividing engines for sale to other instrument makers around 1850, and his participation in the Paris Exposition of 1856 resulted in orders from various countries. The Société Genevoise d'Instrument de Physique completed their first linear dividing engine in 1863, and soon thereafter their first circular engine with a scale delineated by Marc Thury in a manner similar to that used by Edward Troughton. The firm soon became the largest manufacturers of quality dividing machines, and they remain so to this day.

For the specialized linear dividing engines used to produce gratings for diffraction spectroscopy, see **diffraction grating**.

Randall C. Brooks

Bibliography

Bennett, James A. *The Divided Circle: A History of Instruments for Astronomy, Navigation and Surveying.* Oxford: Phaidon Christie's, 1987.

Brooks, John. "The Circular Dividing Engine: Development in England, 1739–1843." *Annals of Science* 49 (1992): 101–35.

Brooks, Randall C. "The Precision Screw in Scientific Instruments of the 17th–19th Centuries." Ph.D. dissertation. Leicester University, 1989.

Chapman, Allan. *Dividing the Circle: The Development of Critical Angular Measurement in Astronomy 1500–1850.* New York: Horwood, 1990.

Evans, Chris. *Precision Engineering: An Evolutionary View.* Bedford: Cranfield, 1987.

Dobson Spectrophotometer

See SPECTROPHOTOMETER, DOBSON

Dosimeter

A dosimeter assesses the exposure to ionizing radiation for the purposes of medical treatment, radiation protection, or industrial exposure control. There are several types, depending on

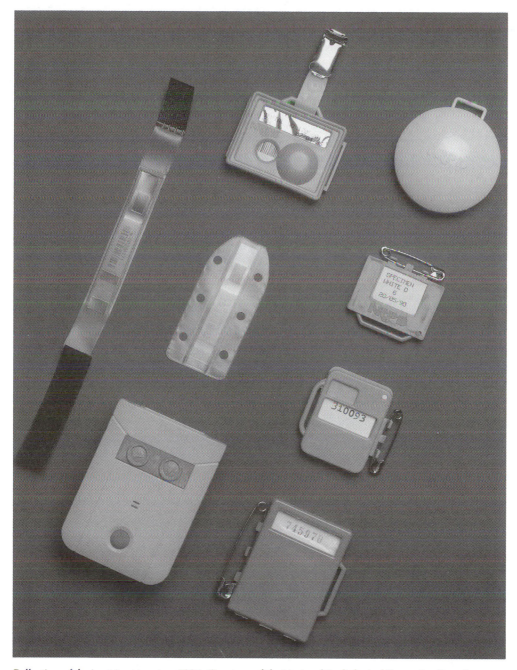

Collection of dosimetric apparatus, 1994. Courtesy of the National Radiological Protection Board.

the target object, the radiations used, and the dose to be measured.

Ionization Chamber

For clinical dosimetry and treatment planning, an ionization chamber connected to an **electrometer** has been the method of choice since 1925, because of its convenience, versatility, sensitivity and reproducibility. Ionization chambers are used in conjunction with phantoms, essentially plastic water-filled tanks, to predict the dose at the center of a tumor within the human body. The phantom scatters and absorbs radiation in a way similar to that of the patient's body.

There is increasing interest in the impact of radiological examination on patients, where x-ray images are produced, and considerable pressure to optimize doses for any particular investigation. Ion chambers fixed to x-ray equipment thus allow the measurement of the total energy of radiation used in a particular examination.

Film Dosimetry

The discovery of radioactivity in 1895 was a result of the sensitivity of photographic film to ionizing radiation, and film has long been used to control an individual's exposure to radiation. Increasingly versatile dosimeters have been developed from 1950 onwards, culminating in the U.K. in the AERE/RPS film badge introduced in 1963. This uses a series of plastic filters and metal filters of different materials (aluminum, tin and lead, cadmium). By measuring the optical density under each element and combining these densities using an algorithm, an acceptable measurement of dose at the position of the dosimeter can be made over a range of doses from approximately 0.2 mSv (equivalent to 1 percent of the current annual recommended maximum) up to 10 Sv, which would be fatal in the case of a whole body exposure to penetrating γ radiation.

Thermo Luminescence Dosimetry (TLD)

This technique, which also dates back to 1895, uses the property of certain materials that generate light when heated if they have been exposed to ionizing radiation. Ionizing radiation generates free electrons, a proportion of which are trapped in the crystal lattice in a relatively stable energetic state. Heating the crystal allows these electrons to escape from these traps and return to the ground state by emitting light. This light is normally picked up by a photomultiplier, converted to an electron current, amplified, and processed to yield a value of the radiation exposure. For radiation protection purposes, lithium fluoride is the most common material. Its mean atomic number is close to that of tissue, and hence the doses deposited in lithium fluoride are often numerically close to doses that would be deposited in tissue under the same circumstances. This makes the assessment of tissue dose a much simpler process when compared with the process required for film.

Body dosimeters often include two volumes of lithium fluoride. One, under a relatively thick plastic cap, removes relatively nonpenetrating radiations such as beta rays so that doses

to relatively deep body organs can be controlled. The other, a thin layer of material under a thin plastic cover, allows the measurement of skin dose. Extremity dosimeters often take the form of finger stools, which have a thin layer of thermoluminescent material under a thin cover. These have the advantage that the dose to the hands can be assessed when radioactive materials are manipulated, as the hands are often much closer to the material than the body and hence subject to a much greater exposure.

Radio Photo-Luminescence Glass

Many materials operate in a way analogous to that of TLD. In this case electrons are ejected from their traps using UV light, and return to their ground state by emitting visible light that, again, can be detected with a photomultiplier tube. A filter interposed between the dosimeter and the photomultiplier eliminates scattered UV light. Silver activated phosphate glass is a suitable material, but it has a much higher atomic number than does tissue and hence an energy correction filter is required if a sufficiently wide range of x- and γ radiation (for example, 50 keV to 3 MeV) is to be measured.

Other Optical Methods

Dyed polymethyl methacrylate can be used for high-dose dosimetry, such as that encountered in the radiation sterilization of scalpel blades. Red perspex, a particular dyed plastic, has been in use in various forms since 1951 for this purpose. Radiation exposure produces an increasing blackening of the material.

Neutron Dosimeters

Neutron dosimetry produces special problems, mainly because of the wide energy range of neutrons encountered, from thermal at 0.025 eV up to in excess of 20 MeV. Current methods include counting tracks of energetic protons produced by neutron/hydrogen collisions in photographic film, and methods using plastics such as poly allyl diglycol carbonate, which can be etched in sodium hydroxide solution in a high electric field. Neutron dose equivalent is proportional to the density of damage pits produced in the exposed plastic.

Radon Dosimeters

Approximately 70 percent of the average population radiation exposure is caused by radon and its radioactive decay progeny. Radon doses are very unpredictable and show large variations within, for example, a row of houses. Dosimetry is performed using the same plastic used for neutron dosimetry, but in this case a simpler etching process using sodium hydroxide only is required because of the high density of energy deposition produced by the alpha particles involved in radon decay.

Peter Burgess

Bibliography

Attix, Frank H., William C. Roesch, and Eugene Tochlin, eds. *Radiation Dosimetry*. 2nd ed. New York: Academic, 1966.

Down Hole Sonde

A down hole sonde is used to explore properties of the earth's crust without taking physical samples. This procedure, known as geophysical well logging, was developed for the petroleum industry as an alternative to the expensive and time-consuming operation of coring and the subsequent analysis of the extracted rock's physical properties, such as porosity, permeability, and the presence of hydrocarbons. Well logging consists, in part, of lowering the down hole sonde into a well by an armored cable. As the sonde is withdrawn from the well, continuous measurements are made by sensors in or on the down hole sonde of physical properties of the rock formations that are intersected by the well bore. The cable provides power for the sonde, a means for communicating the measurements to the surface equipment, and tensile strength for its withdrawal.

Superficially, all logging sondes resemble one another, because of the borehole environment in which they operate. They are generally sealed, pressure-resistant, cylindrical devices, often resembling long pieces of pipe, with outside diameter on the order of 10 cm. This permits their operation in the majority of boreholes drilled by the petroleum industry. Specialized sondes with diameters of less than 5 cm are for use in small-diameter boreholes or in producing wells where access to the region of interest is through a small-diameter pipe known as production tubing. Some sondes are designed to be operated in a centralized position in the borehole, achieved by the use of bow-springs attached to the exterior, or by more sophisticated hydraulically actuated "arms." Some measurements require that part of the sonde, called a pad, be held in contact with the formation. The length of commercially operated sondes, typically on the order of several meters, depends on the size of the sensor arrays and the complexity of associated electronics. It is possible to fasten a number of sondes together for a common descent into the well, forming tool strings as long as 30 meters.

The first down hole sonde, designed by Conrad and Marcel Schlumberger and used by Henri Doll to measure the resistivity of the subsurface formations in the Pechelbronn oil field in France in 1927, consisted of 3-meter-long Bakelite tubes fastened together. The sensors, three copper electrodes, were attached to the outer surface. Three spark plug wires, one connected to each of the electrodes, suspended the sonde weighted by lead shot, and provided the means of measuring the formation resistivity, through the conductive drilling fluid in the bore hole, with readings taken at 1-meter intervals. Currently more than fifty types of modern down hole sondes exist, and they are generally operated by commercial service companies. These sondes are considerably more elaborate and are instrumented not only to measure the resistivity of the down hole formations, but also for measuring mechanical and nuclear properties.

Down hole sondes for determining the electrical properties of formations are of many varieties, ranging from multielectrode devices descended directly from the original 1927 sonde, to induction sondes whose sensors are coils, excited at low frequencies (tens of kHz), inside a nonconductive sonde, that can measure formation conductivity even when the well bore contains resistive fluids that limit the use of electrode devices. High-frequency (MHz) devices with antennas mounted on articulated pads to provide close contact with the formation, regardless of the borehole diameter fluctuations, measure the dielectric properties. Sondes with sensors such as **magnetometers** or **gyroscopes** for orientation information coupled with articulated pads containing multiple electrodes that push against the surface of the borehole can provide the three-dimensional orientation (dip and strike) of subsurface rock layers, or even an electrical image of the borehole wall that strongly resembles a photograph of the extracted whole core from the well. Sondes that combine induction coils and specially shaped magnets (earlier sondes used the earth's magnetic field) are used to exploit nuclear magnetic resonance of the proton to measure the hydrogen content of the formation.

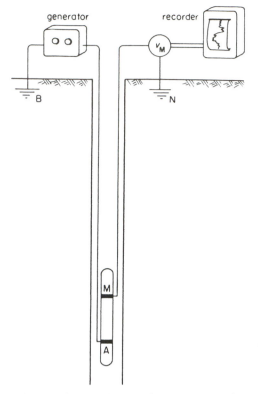

Schematic diagram showing the arrangement of electrodes in a normal logging circuit, showing source (A) and sink (B) electrodes. The difference in potential is measured between M and N. Edwin S. Robinson, Basic Exploration Geophysics. *New York: Wiley, 1988: 517, Figure 14-14. Copyright © 1988 John Wiley & Sons Inc. Reprinted by permission.*

Sondes for measuring the acoustic/mechanical properties of formations employ arrays of transmitters and receivers, typically magnetostrictive or ceramic materials with piezoelectric properties, to measure the compressional and shear wave velocity. These velocities vary principally with the porosity of the rock and typically are much less than the velocity in the sonde material. This results in innovative sonde designs with elaborate means to delay or attenuate the so-called direct arrival so that acoustic energy from the formation is measured. A sonde equipped with a rotating transducer can produce, as it is withdrawn from the well, an acoustic image of the borehole wall.

Sondes that exploit nuclear measurements range from passive devices containing only a gamma-ray detector for measuring the natural formation radioactivity to sondes that contain either radioactive gamma ray or neutron sour-

ces. Some have miniaturized **accelerators** that can produce bursts of high-energy neutrons, to probe the nuclear properties of the formations. Unlike conventional electrical sondes, these sondes make possible measurements of formation properties even in wells that are cased with a sheath of cement and steel pipe.

Sondes used to measure the density and photoelectric absorption properties of the formation contain a source of gamma rays (usually ^{137}Cs) and several scintillation detectors. Neutron scattering is used for the determination of subsurface formation porosity since porous rock filled with either water or hydrocarbons moderates neutrons more or less strongly, depending on the hydrogen content. Commercial neutron porosity sondes generally consist of a source of neutrons (a mixture of Am-Be or Pu-Be) and several gaseous detectors.

Specific measurements of the formation geochemistry can be made from the spectroscopy of neutron-induced gamma rays in the manner of neutron activation analysis. This technique relies on the prompt emission of one or more characteristic gamma rays, which accompanies the capture of thermal neutrons by most of the formation nuclei. The sonde uses a pulsed source of neutrons, and gamma ray detectors. Spectroscopic detection of the gamma rays allows the identification of the nuclei and a quantification of their abundances. The overall rate of decay of the gamma ray spectra measures the thermal neutron absorption cross-section, a quantity used in the petroleum industry as a method of distinguishing the relative fraction of brine and hydrocarbon in the pore space. Another more direct method relies on a measurement of gamma rays from the inelastic excitation of C and O nuclei, which can frequently be performed by the same sonde.

Darwin V. Ellis

Bibliography

Allaud, Louis, and Maurice Martin. *Schlumberger, The History of a Technique.* New York: Wiley, 1977.

Ellis, Darwin V. *Well Logging for Earth Scientists.* New York: Elsevier, 1987.

Hearst, Joseph R., and Philip H. Nelson. *Well Logging for Physical Properties.* New York: McGraw-Hill, 1985.

Tittman, Jay. *Geophysical Well Logging.* Orlando: Academic, 1986.

Drawing Instruments

The earliest drawing instruments were developed in antiquity from craft tools used by artisans to mark out lines and measure dimensions. Pre-Roman civilizations used large-size dividers and rulers in setting out buildings, and such instruments were still in use by medieval craftsmen. Smaller drawing instruments such as dividers, rules, and set squares survive from the Roman period. Drawing instruments became much more important in the fifteenth century, as technical design became increasingly separated from manual construction. Scale drawing on paper was introduced in architecture, engineering, and cartography, and the new design practitioners appealed to mathematics as the basis of their work. From the sixteenth century, drawing instruments were included in the repertoire of the mathematical instrument maker, and made with the same materials and to the same standards as instruments for surveying, navigation, and astronomy. Those instruments produced for learned and wealthy clients were often finely decorated, housed in elaborate cases, and intended for presentation and display.

Drawing offices became large and complex departments of railway and engineering companies in the nineteenth century, and of aerospace companies in the twentieth. The tolerances and detailing required in these fields demanded the highest precision in drawing. In the last quarter of the twentieth century, some traditional drawing practices have been displaced by computer-aided design and plotters providing direct output from screen-based drawings. Laser printers now offer the possibility of creating drawings without the use of pens at all.

Most individual drawing instruments have retained a recognizable and familiar form throughout their history, despite the introduction of detailed improvements and new materials. The oldest drawing instrument is the stylus. Here a blunt point scribes a line that can be filled in freehand with ink if required. The direct application of ink for straight line drawing is accomplished with a ruling pen. As with styli, examples of ruling pens survive from ancient Rome, and similar types were still in use during the Renaissance. Early forms used either a single piece of metal folded over on itself as the blade, or two separate blades whose separation could be controlled by a ring sliding on the pen's shaft. A development of the latter type, in which the separation of the two steel blades was controlled by a screw, became standard in the eighteenth century; one of the blades was often hinged to permit easier access for cleaning. The nineteenth century saw a proliferation of variations, such as the road or rail pen with two sets of blades for drawing pairs of parallel lines.

Although charcoal has been used for drawing since antiquity, graphite pencils were introduced only in the sixteenth century. Experiments in the eighteenth century adding clay to graphite led to the development of pencils of differing degrees of hardness. These new pencils were cheaper to produce than the traditional form and their properties could be tailored to the requirements of their users. Specialist makers supplied these pencils to a greatly expanded nineteenth-century market.

From antiquity onward, two-legged compasses with plain points have been used to scribe circles. In the sixteenth century they were provided with ink, crayon, or pencil points that could be interchangeably attached to one of the compass's legs. During the eighteenth century there were attempts to provide all the permutations of possible drawing and tracing points in a single instrument. Turn-up compasses had double-ended fittings on each leg that could be turned around to match either an ink, pencil, or plain point against another plain point. Napier compasses with folding legs were a nineteenth-century variant. Pillar compasses had hollow legs in which the reversible attachments were housed.

Specialized compasses abound from the sixteenth century onwards. Greater precision in the separation of the legs was achieved in wing compasses and screw compasses: the former have an arc over which one of the legs can be moved and secured; the latter use a horizontal screw through both legs. Beam compasses, designed for circles of large radius, consist of a bar supplied with points for the fixed center and for drawing. The separation of the points and thus the radius of the circle is set by adjusting the position of the points on the bar. Bow compasses, spring bows, and pump compasses are used to draw small circles.

Compasses with two plain points came to be known as dividers and were used principally for transferring dimensions. They were made not only in many of the same forms as compasses, but also in particular, specialized versions. Single-handed dividers for use with sea charts date from the sixteenth and seventeenth centuries. Proportional dividers, used to transfer dimensions in enlarged or reduced ratio,

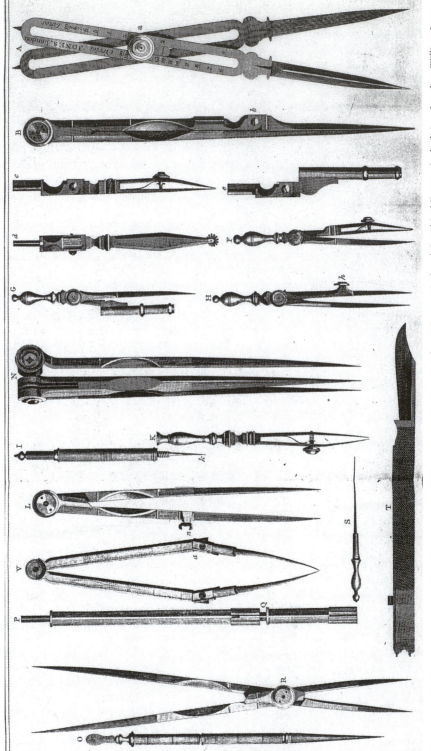

Compasses, dividers, and proportional dividers, by George Adams, ca. 1800. George Adams. Geometrical and Graphical Essays, 2nd edition. London: William Jones, 1797: Plate 1. Courtesy Museum of the History of Science, Oxford.

consist of two hinged legs with four points, one at either end of each leg. The position of the joint determines the ratio between the separation of the two sets of points. Fixed proportion instruments were found in the Roman ruins at Pompeii and the same basic design was popular in Renaissance and early modern Europe. In the late sixteenth century, Jost Burgi devised a version with slotted legs in which the position of the joint was adjustable. Its legs were engraved with scales to enable the transfer of variable proportions for geometrical figures as well as straight lines. Similar instruments continued to be made into the twentieth century.

Dividers were frequently used with scale rulers. Besides providing a straight edge for use with a ruling pen, these rulers carried scales divided with varying degrees of sophistication. Diagonal scales, which were common in the eighteenth century, offered the finest subdivisions of measuring units. Scales of equal parts, with varying numbers of divisions per unit, were suitable for cartographers and were featured on sixteenth-century instruments. Trigonometrical and logarithmic scales were added in the seventeenth century, and such arrangements as Gunter's scale and the plain scale remained popular into the nineteenth century.

Simple rulers for drawing parallel lines survive from the sixteenth century. They were made of two linked rules, with a third sometimes added to provide a wider separation. A later alternative to the simple links between the rules was a scissor linkage that better maintained a given spacing. A late-eighteenth-century innovation was the rolling parallel ruler, in which a rod with milled wheels at either end was incorporated into a rectangular rule. This offered unlimited movement, and its larger versions became standard equipment in nineteenth-century drawing offices. Pocket-sized versions in ivory were frequently engraved with a variety of scales to produce a compendious instrument.

Protractors appeared as distinct instruments in the late sixteenth century, for use with sea charts. Semicircular forms with rectangular bases were advertised as especially suitable for surveying in seventeenth-century English texts, but plain semicircular protractors in various materials became the standard portable style. For more accurate work, larger circular or semicircular protractors appeared in the second half of the eighteenth century. These were typically provided with a vernier scale and a magnifying glass to ease scale reading, along with a pricking point at the end of their rotating arms.

Pens, compasses, dividers, rules, parallel rulers, scales, and protractors, as well as squares and sectors, were included in the sets of drawing instruments produced from the sixteenth century onwards. The most lavish instruments were of finely engraved silver, occasionally with the added use of gold. Brass was used for less prestigious instruments, while steel remained the favored material for points and blades. During the nineteenth century new materials such as aluminum and electrum were tried, and cheaper instruments were introduced for the expanding student market that followed the growth of technical education.

The larger sets of drawing instruments sometimes included curve-drawing devices. Elliptic and semielliptic trammels were in use from the sixteenth century and provided the simplest means of tracing ellipses. Since trammels cannot draw small figures, several late-eighteenth- and early-nineteenth-century makers such as Gourdin, Farey, and Clement devised ellipsographs to overcome this problem. Trammels and ellipsographs have now largely been replaced by plastic templates with standard curvatures. Templates had been used in the nineteenth century, especially in the form of railway curves, which provided engineers with standard curvatures for their drawings. Other curve-drawing instruments such as conchoidographs and parabolagraphs are much more specialized and have only ever been made as prototypes or in very small numbers.

Stephen Johnston

Bibliography

Dickinson, H.W. "A Brief History of Draughtsmen's Instruments." *Transactions of the Newcomen Society* 27 (1949–1951): 73–84.

Hambly, Maya. *Drawing Instruments, 1580–1980*. London: Sotheby's Publications, 1988.

Petroski, Henry. *The Pencil*. New York: Knopf, 1990.

Scott-Scott, Michael. *Drawing Instruments 1850–1950*. Princes Risborough: Shire Publications, 1986.

Drosophila

Drosophila melanogaster, the common fruit fly, is a premier example of a "standard" experi-

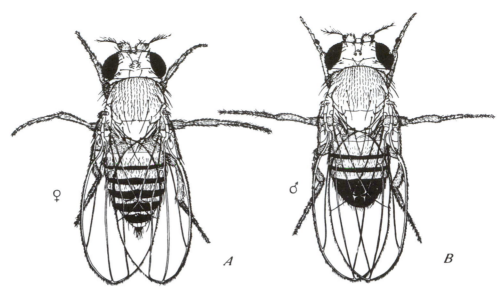

The wild type female (left) and male of Drosophila melanogaster. *Thomas Hunt Morgan, Calvin B. Bridges, and Alfred H. Sturtevant,* The Genetics of Drosophila. *The Hague: Nijhoff, 1925: Figure 1. Reprinted by permission of Kluwer Academic Publishers.*

mental organism. Other familiar examples are the white rat and **mouse**, *Neurospora* (a bread mold), the bacterium *Escherichia coli*, and *Zea mays*, or Indian corn. It may seem odd to think of living creatures as physical instruments, but in fact they are partly human artifacts, rebuilt by inbreeding and genetic manipulation so that all individuals are, for the purposes of experiment, the same. The advantage of standard organisms is that experiments done in different places give comparable results.

D. *melanogaster* is one of more than a thousand species of the genus *Drosophila* that live by eating yeasts. It is a cosmopolitan species, which has dispersed around the world in a commensal relationship (the word means "feeding at the same table") with humankind, another cosmopolitan animal much given to fermentation and a prodigious producer of vegetable waste. *D. melanogaster* is, in short, a weed, part of our portmanteau biota long before it joined in the business of doing experiments. A native of Southeast Asia, it spread around the world in the company of agricultural peoples, appearing in Boston and New York in the 1870s. There, a few decades later, it established a new niche in biological laboratories.

Drosophila was first used in laboratory work around 1900, most notably by William Castle at Harvard University and Thomas Hunt Morgan at Columbia University. Contrary to legend it was not initially used for genetic ex-

periments, but rather for a variety of odd jobs— student projects, classroom demonstrations of insect behavior, and in Morgan's laboratory, an untried line of work on experimental evolution. This situation was dramatically transformed by the appearance in 1910 of the famous white-eyed mutant, which, because it was sex-linked, suggested that the units of heredity were physically located on particular chromosomes. As more mutants appeared it further became clear that these factors, or "genes," were arranged in a fixed order that could be mapped by measuring the frequency with which they remained linked together in genetic crosses. The first map was constructed in 1912 by Morgan's young student Alfred Sturtevant, and in the same year Sturtevant and his fellow student Calvin Bridges began a systematic project of mapping the three known chromosomes of Drosophila (a fourth soon turned up). From this student project evolved the vast enterprise of modern cytogenetics.

It was this systematic mapping that transformed *Drosophila* from a wild creature into a laboratory instrument. Standardization was essential for mapping genetics. Unlike other modes of Mendelian genetics, mapping was a quantitative practice and depended on precision and reproducibility for its credibility. Wild drosophilas are genetically extremely variable. Their chromosomes contain modifying genes that affect the results of mapping experiments, and this variability undermined the credibility of mapping, a controversial mode in the early years. Morgan's group solved the problem of variability by defining standard conditions of fly culture and constructing a standard fly, breeding out all the hidden modifying genes that caused actual results to diverge from those predicted by Mendelian theory. Over the course of a decade and at the cost of immense labor, Bridges, Sturtevant, Hermann J. Muller, and others created a family of standard mutant flies, whose chromosomes conformed to their new theory of genes and gene maps. This "standard" fly was the instrument and embodiment of the new cytogenetics.

Invention, of course, is only half the story of how instruments become standard; they must also be adopted by everyone as "standard." A characteristic feature of the drosophilists' practice was an elaborate system of exchange of mutant stocks. It was the drosophilists' custom to share stocks and know-how freely, on the presumption that everyone would benefit from free access to the best tools. An elaborate set of customs and moral rules grew up around the exchange of stocks. Recipients of stocks, for example, were expected to disclose fully what they intended to do with them, and to reciprocate with their own stocks and know-how. Drosophilists also discouraged workers from reserving particular tools or problems as their own private property, and they gave credit for achievements not to those who had an idea first but to those who did the experiments and got the results. Production came first: that was the golden rule of the fly people. These customs of exchange —no trade secrets, no monopolies, no poaching, no ambushes—were highly effective in making *D. melanogaster* and genetic mapping the standard everywhere, driving competing organisms and modes of practice from the field.

Drosophila has proved to be an extraordinarily versatile laboratory instrument. Initially it was used principally for genetic mapping and for studying the physical mechanism of transmission (segregation, recombination, crossing over). This narrow focus was criticized by biologists who felt that Morgan's school had abandoned the more fundamental biological problems of development and evolution. The Morgan group tried between 1910 and 1930 to use the standard fly for such work but failed. In the 1930s, however, new methods were invented that did extend *Drosophila*'s range. Theodosius Dobzhansky showed how wild species of *Drosophila*, especially *D. pseudoobscura*, could be studied in the field to illuminate the dynamics of local populations and their role in the formation of subspecies and species. This work became a major growth field after World War II. Others discovered developmental mutants that enabled them to begin to unravel the process of morphogenesis. This slow and exacting work was overshadowed in the 1950s and 1960s by the more spectacular developments in bacterial molecular genetics, but in the 1970s *Drosophila* again became a popular and widely used tool among developmental biologists, an experimental cornucopia once more.

Robert E. Kohler

Bibliography

Allen, Garland E. *Thomas Hunt Morgan: The Man and His Science.* Princeton: Princeton University Press, 1978.

Carlson, Elof Axel. *Genes, Radiation, and Society: The Life and Work of H.J. Muller.* Ithaca, N.Y.: Cornell University Press, 1981.

Kohler, Robert E. *Lords of the Fly: Drosophila Genetics and the Experimental Life.* Chicago: University of Chicago Press, 1994.

Dynamometer

A dynamometer measures both force and mechanical power. The word, which derives from the Greek, first appeared in Edmund Regnier's article "Description et usage du Dynamomètre . . ." (1798).

During the nineteenth century, dynamometers were at the forefront of the development of engineering instrumentation. Absorption dynamometers measured the power produced by primary power sources such as steam engines, while transmission dynamometers measured power transmitted between machines. In the former, losses due to friction were designed to be a maximum; in the latter they were minimized.

Absorption Dynamometers

The fundamental invention of the absorption dynamometer appears to be the work of the leading French engineer G.F.C.M. de Prony (1822), who envisaged encasing the output shaft of an engine in a wooden collar that could be progressively tightened by means of a lever

D

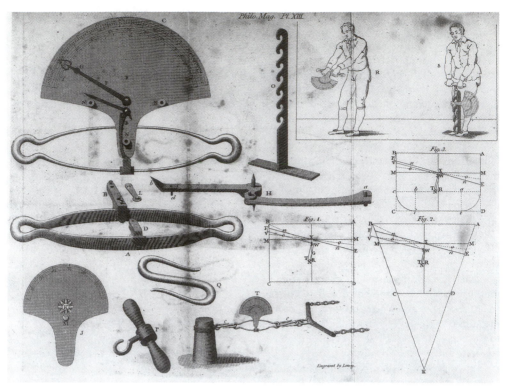

Regnier's dynamometer, 1798. Edmund Regnier, "Description and Use of the Dynamometer; or, Instrument for Ascertaining the Relative Strength of Men and Animals." Philosophical Magazine 1 (1798): Plate XIII. Courtesy of NMAH.

fitted with a sliding mass of known weight. For a constant shaft speed, the opposing torque developed by this brake was simply the product of the weight and its distance from the center of the shaft. Although simple in concept, Prony's friction brake tended to be cumbersome and erratic. Nevertheless, a substantial number of these instruments were developed throughout the nineteenth century.

In 1877, an English engineer and the founder of ship hydrodynamics, William Froude, invented the water brake to measure the power absorbed by a ship's propeller. This had two symmetrical casings, one fixed to the ship's shaft and the other free to move, the propeller having been removed. The casings formed an elliptical annular space around the shaft that was penetrated by a series of radial vanes. By filling this space with water and turning the shaft, the vanes created a series of internal vortices that acted as the principal dissipative mechanism. The torque needed to restrain the free casing, which became coupled to the fixed casing through the vortices, was measured by a weighted lever fixed to the free casing.

Electromagnetic absorption dynamometers began to appear toward the end of the nineteenth century. These used either the production of eddy currents as the frictional mechanism, or else were simply dynamos whose output was easily measured.

Transmission Dynamometers

The basic transmission dynamometer was simply a spring balance indicating force on a graduated scale. These were used extensively for experimental investigations throughout the eighteenth and nineteenth centuries and, although simple in concept, they required considerable ingenuity to apply. The seminal transmission dynamometer is undoubtedly that of the French engineer and soldier A.J. Morin, who, in 1841, published the results of his experiments on the forces and work expended by horse-driven carriages. The spring unit consisted of two flat bar springs fixed at each end to each other. The center of one was attached to the pulling shaft, and the center of the other to the carriage; the midpoint separation of the two springs indicated the traction force. An innovative feature of Morin's dynamometer was the use of a stylus that recorded the traction force on a paper cylinder geared to the carriage wheels; for longer runs an integrator was incorporated into the recorder that allowed the work done to be read off.

William Froude built an ingenious single-linear-spring recording dynamometer in 1870 to measure and record the drag force experienced by a scale model of the ship HMS *Greyhound*. The results were extrapolated to the full size by means of Froude's famous scaling law, and the resulting prediction compared with that measured on a towing trial of the actual ship. For this second trial Froude used a recording dynamometer with a piston working in a hydraulic cylinder. The piston's movement, under the action of the towing force, increased the pressure of the oil, and this resulted in the deflection of a smaller spring-backed piston.

In 1876 G.A. Hirn invented a transmission dynamometer that measured the angular torsional deformation of a shaft. Various improvements to this method ensued. The best known is probably the Thring-Hopkinson torsion meter (1906). This employed a sleeve surrounding the shaft, with one end fastened to it and the other free. The relative twist and displacement between the shaft and sleeve was measured by

reflecting a beam of light off a mirror that deflected and twisted with the shaft's deformation.

Small spring-loaded pulleys were used, in the period before electrification, to measure the tension of the belts that distributed power from source to machines.

Modern Developments

With the massive growth in electronics and new materials since the 1950s, mechanical dynamometers have been supplanted by a range of force, torque, and strain sensors whose output is an electrical current proportional to the force measured. The term "transmission dynamometer" has died out, and "dynamometer" is usually taken to mean an absorption dynamometer. The adapted Prony brake is still used for small powers, with larger powers being handled by hydraulic and electric brakes.

Thomas Wright

Bibliography

Jervis-Smith, F.J. *Dynamometers*. London: Constable, 1915.

Regnier, E. "Description et usage du dynamomètre, pour connâitre et comparer la force relative des hommes. . . ." *Journal de l'École Polytechnique* 2 (1798): 160–78.

E

E. coli
See ESCHERICHIA COLI

Earth Conductivity Measurements

Earth conductivity measurements are primarily used as a geophysical technique to infer information about the structure and geology of the earth from its electrical properties. By measuring the conductivity of the earth, early prospectors sought to detect hidden ore deposits and follow underground extensions of known ore bodies. Later, as measurement techniques became more quantitative and the depth of investigation was increased, the measurements were also used for groundwater detection and mapping rock strata for engineering applications and also for studies of the tectonics and crustal structure of the earth.

The earliest recognition that earth materials are conductors of electricity dates back to 1729, when the Englishmen Stephen Gray and Granville Wheler tabulated the electrical conductivity of rocks and minerals. William Watson independently discovered that the earth is an electrical conductor in 1746 and also noted the presence of naturally varying telluric currents in long grounded wires.

In 1830, Robert Fox mapped natural electric currents associated with sulphide ore deposits in Cornwall, England. Fox used copper plates as electrodes and a 0.75-in. compass needle enclosed by twenty-five turns of wire as a galvanometer. By the late 1800s, this self-potential method had become an established geophysical exploration tool.

Techniques for mapping the natural potential field near ore deposits evolved into earth investigations using artificial current sources. Leo Daft and Alfred Williams used an ac source and telephone receiver connected to search electrodes to detect variations in earth conductivity in 1902. In 1912, the Frenchman Conrad Schlumberger improved this technique by using a dc current source and nonpolarizing potential electrodes connected to a sensitive **galvanometer**. Equipotential lines were mapped by tracing the locations of zero potential difference between one location and the next. Departures of these maps from the theoretical response of a homogeneous earth indicated regions of anomalous conductivity.

The first attempts to make quantitative measurements met with limited success. Fred Brown in 1902 and Peust in 1905 used a **Wheatstone bridge** circuit to measure the resistance of the ground between two metal electrodes. But these measurements were extremely sensitive to the contact resistance at the electrodes and suffered from electrode polarization.

The development by Frank Wenner at the U.S. National Bureau of Standards in 1915 of a practical four-terminal-bridge design paved the way for measurements of earth resistivity that were unaffected by contact resistance. Wenner's array consisted of two outer current injection electrodes and two inner potential electrodes, all equally spaced but at different depths. An alternating current at about 300 Hz eliminated electrode polarization. The current was measured with an **ammeter**, and the potential difference between the inner electrodes was measured with a sensitive galvanometer in a **potentiometer** circuit affixed with a variable inductance to cancel out phase shifts associated with inductive effects. A simple expression was used to convert the current and potential values to "effective resistivity," which is the resistivity of a uniform medium that matches the observed

Schlumberger's dc resistivity apparatus, ca. 1927. Courtesy of Schlumberger-Doll Research.

data. The four-electrode measurement gives an average of the earth resistivity in the vicinity of the array, extending down to around one-half of the outer electrode spacing.

The Schlumberger brothers developed an alternative array in 1921, in which the potential difference is measured between two closely spaced electrodes located midway between the outer current electrodes, with the data converted to "apparent resistivity." Schlumberger's early system operated with nonpolarizing electrodes at dc, with the current reversed periodically to eliminate drift. The Schlumberger array became popular for deep soundings that required large electrode separations.

Instruments

Use of the four-electrode array triggered the development of a number of earth-resistivity measuring devices. The instruments had to be rugged for field use and contend with various sources of noise and biases: natural potentials caused by variations in electrolyte concentration in the soil, electrode polarization, telluric fluctuations, and inductive coupling between wires. In the United States, O.H. Gish and W.J. Rooney designed an instrument based on the

Wenner configuration in 1924. Here current was reversed sixteen times per second to eliminate natural and electrode polarization potentials, and a double commutator rectified the current flow in the potentiometer so that the signal always read the same polarity, while noise appeared as random fluctuations. Later improvements included offsetting segments of the potentiometer commutator with respect to the current commutator to allow the current to reach its equilibrium value after reversal, and the addition of an auxiliary capacitor circuit to steady the galvanometer fluctuations.

Schlumberger steadily improved his dc apparatus for field reliability and greater sensitivity. The initial system used nonpolarizing electrodes and a potentiometer circuit with periodic reversal of injected current to reduce the effects of stray currents and leaks from the current into the potential-measuring circuit. Simpler copper electrodes were introduced in 1925, and an auxiliary **battery** and rheostat were used to compensate for polarization potentials. A small adjustable transformer canceled the voltage spike associated with inductive effects when interrupting the current. This equipment was capable of large electrode separations and, since it operated near dc, the depth of investigation was not limited by inductive skin effects. In 1929, a resistivity sounding was carried out with an outer electrode spacing of 200 km.

In parallel to the development of quantitative resistivity devices primarily designed for geophysical prospecting, compact instruments called Megger (short for megohmer) Earth testers were developed to test the grounds of power stations and transmission lines. The Megger differed from the Gish-Rooney instruments primarily in that a direct-reading ohmmeter read the ratio of voltage to current so that resistance was measured directly, and a hand-powered magneto was used to generate the test current at a repetition rate of about fifty times per second. The original Megger had four electrodes corresponding to the Wenner configuration, but later models incorporated a third potential electrode for other configurations. The Megger gave systematically lower resistivities than the Gish-Rooney equipment, because some of the current flows through the measuring coils; it was suitable only for shallow measurements at high signal levels.

Electrode resistivity devices operating near dc that are in use today are similar in concept to their counterparts developed in the 1920s and have an important niche in engineering and groundwater studies in the intermediate depth range of several meters to several hundred meters.

Techniques of estimating earth conductivity based on electromagnetic induction evolved from electromagnetic prospecting methods in the early 1930s. Both frequency-domain and time-domain instrumentation is in use today, in ground and airborne modes. Modern induction techniques include shallow-probing (of around 1 meter) "terrain conductivity" meters suitable for rapid reconnaissance surveying in geotechnical and environmental applications, and high-power systems suitable for conductivity mapping down to depths of many kilometers.

Brian R. Spies

Bibliography

Ambronn, R. *Elements of Geophysics as Applied to Explorations for Minerals, Oil and Gas*. New York: McGraw-Hill, 1928.

Edge, A.B. Broughton, and T.H. Laby, eds. *The Principles & Practice of Geophysical Prospecting*. Cambridge: Cambridge University Press, 1931.

Gish, O.H., and W.J. Rooney, "Measurement of Resistivity of Large Masses of Undisturbed Earth." *Terrestial Magnetism* 30 (1925): 161–88.

Heiland, C.A. *Geophysical Exploration*. New York: Prentice-Hall, 1940.

Van Nostrand, R.G., and K.L. Cook. *Interpretation of Resistivity Data*. Geological Society Professional Paper No. 499. Washington, D.C.: Government Printing Office, 1966.

Earth Strain Meter

An earth strain meter measures the strains in the earth's crust arising from the phenomenon of solid tides. Solid tides have the same cause as the more familiar tides observed in the sea. While the earth rotates in its orbit around the sun, its distance from the other astronomical bodies in the solar system varies. As distance varies, so does gravitational attraction, and the earth's shape deforms because of these changing forces. As with ocean tides, the moon has the dominant effect in solid tides.

Understanding the tidal effects caused by motions of the astronomical bodies would make possible their elimination from observations and thus reveal the anomalies caused by geological structure and gravity waves intercepted by the earth. However, the magnitude of the strains created by solid tides is extremely small and difficult to measure, and the effects recur in cycles ranging from years to one-third of a day. Observations are usually made deep underground to minimize the daily cycle of thermal expansion caused by the heat of the sun. But the observed strains also depend on local topography and how instruments are installed.

Jean Baptiste Joseph Fourier predicted solid earth tides in the mid nineteenth century, but the first observations were not made until the twentieth century. It is still not possible to confirm some aspects of his findings because of local effects. H. Benioff made the first measurements around 1930 using a 20 meter long steel tube of 2-in. diameter. One end of the tube was clamped to a concrete pedestal on the floor of a chamber. A sensor monitored the other, free end of the tube and recorded the movements resulting from solid tides. This instrument had however been built as a seismometer and could not measure signals of very long period. Moreover, the steel tube was subject to unwanted thermal expansion effects, and quartz (fused silica) was soon used in other instruments.

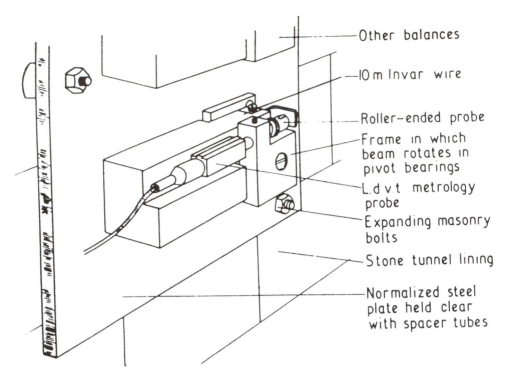

Labels on diagram:
- Other balances
- 10 m Invar wire
- Roller–ended probe
- Frame in which beam rotates in pivot bearings
- L.d v t metrology probe
- Expanding masonry bolts
- Stone tunnel lining
- Normalized steel plate held clear with spacer tubes

Prototype catenary strain meter, by Peter Sydenham, 1969. Courtesy of Peter Sydenham.

It was also difficult to accurately measure the minute displacements taking place over the long length of the tubes or arms required in the apparatus. Although optical interferometry could in principle provide the necessary precision, it proved tedious and troublesome in experimental practice. Not until the mid 1960s did laser sources provide the properties needed for solid tide measurements by interferometry. Laser **interferometers** were built in the United States, U.K., and Australia to detect displacements of around 10–9 meters in a 10-meter apparatus. However, the apparatus was complex because the interferometer had to be operated in vacuum to obtain signal stability.

A simpler approach was adopted in 1969 by Peter H. Sydenham, who designed an inexpensive solid tide meter using a 100-mm-long gravity balance connected to solid rock by a 10m-long Invar wire hanging in a catenary shape. Minute rotation of the balance resulting from rock tides altering the mounting length was sensed by an electronic displacement sensor. Three units were built and installed in the Queensbury Triangle railway tunnel in Bradford, U.K. Using a laser instrument from the University of Cambridge, Sydenham and his colleagues produced the first comparable simultaneous records of solid tides by two different instrument types.

The development of earth strain meters has continued through the use of fused-quartz instruments, in which 1-meter "canes" of fused quartz are hooked together to form a 10-meter chain. A 1-meter long quartz rod instrument that could be used in short bore holes was investigated in the 1970s by Peter Sydenham, but this smaller device was not sufficiently sensitive and stable.

Peter H. Sydenham

Bibliography

Benioff, H. "A Linear Strain Seismograph." *Bulletin of the Seismological Society of America* 25 (1935): 283–309.

Blair, D., and P.H. Sydenham. "A Tidal Strain Model for Hillgrove Gorge, Eastern Australia." *Geophysical Journal of the Royal Astronomical Society* 46 (1976): 141–53.

King, G.C.P., R.G. Bilham, V.B. Gerard, and P.H. Sydenham. "New Strain Meters for Geophysics." *Nature* 223 (1969): 818–19.

Sydenham, Peter H. *Measuring Instruments:*

Tools of Knowledge and Control. London: Peter Peregrinus for the Science Museum, 1979.

———. "Where Is Experimental Research on Earth Strain Headed?" *Nature* 252 (1974): 278–80.

Electricity Supply Meter

The introduction of incandescent electric lighting in the 1880s created a market for electricity from central power stations and a need to measure the electrical energy customers used. The unit of measurement, the kilowatt-hour, known in Britain as the Board of Trade unit, was established at an early stage. Measuring kilowatt-hours was not easy; many early meters actually measured ampere-hours but were calibrated in kilowatt-hours on the assumption that the supply voltage was constant. True kilowatt-hour meters became the norm later.

Thomas Edison designed the first successful supply meter in 1882, as part of the system for supplying customers using his incandescent lamp. It used an electrolytic process—to "read" the meter the electrodes were removed and weighed—but remained in use for some years. Direct-reading electrolytic meters were developed later, and some remained in use until the 1930s.

Other meters were designed to use many different electrical effects, with varying degrees of success. Mechanical integrating meters with an intermittent action, which sampled the power con-

Edison's electrolytic electricity supply meter, used between 1882 and 1885. SM 1926-743. Courtesy of SSPL.

sumption at fixed intervals, were popular in France for a while. In the clock meter introduced commercially by Hermann Aron in Berlin in 1884, electromagnetic forces between a fixed coil and a pendulum made a clock run slower or faster than normal. Most versions used two clock mechanisms and differential gearing to show electricity consumption directly. They were still highly regarded in the 1950s.

Most supply meters used a form of electric motor operating against a brake. The number of revolutions measured the electricity consumption. Sebastian de Ferranti produced mercury motor meters from about 1883. Electromagnetic forces caused mercury in a small chamber to rotate, carrying with it a small fan attached to the counter. Viscous forces provided the retardation. In Britain the first meter to use an ordinary motor with a commutator was supplied by the firm of Chamberlain and Hookham in about 1888. It had a braking mechanism that became standard, a metal disk rotating between the poles of a permanent magnet. Eddy currents induced in the disk provided the retarding force. Another commutator motor meter with eddy current brake was patented by Elihu Thomson in the United States in 1890; it was used for many years. The sliding contacts of a commutator were potentially troublesome, and for alternating-current meters they could be avoided by using an induction motor. Galileo Ferraris in Italy and Nikolai Tesla in the United States described induction motors independently in 1888. The Westinghouse Electric Co. marketed the first induction motor meter, designed by O.B. Shallenberger, in 1889.

For direct-current supplies, a mercury motor meter of a type first made in Britain by Chamberlain and Hookham in 1892 became standard. The current passed radially through a disk armature, the mercury serving as a sliding contact, and eddy current braking was used. Most supplies were, and nowadays practically all are, alternating current, and the form of meter used almost universally is an induction motor meter in which the armature is a rotating disk that also serves as the disk for the eddy current brake. Chamberlain and Hookham supplied the first meter of this type in 1895. Subsequently many companies made these meters, but modernization of the industry has reduced the number.

Meters for industrial supplies pose additional problems. Induction motor meters are used to measure energy consumption, as for domestic supplies. For three-phase circuits two meter movements are combined in a single instrument. Transformers or resistances are used to adapt meters to the higher voltages and currents supplied. The size of supply cables needed depends on the maximum demand for power, and it is usual to provide a maximum demand indicator that records the maximum consumption in (typically) any half-hour period. With inductive loads, larger currents flow than are indicated by the energy consumption, making larger supply cables necessary, and another type of meter may be provided to allow for this.

By about 1980 electronic supply meters were becoming available. They are used increasingly for industrial supplies, to cope with the greater sophistication of the energy market in the 1990s. For domestic supplies the induction motor supply meter remains supreme for the time being. It has proved a remarkably enduring instrument, manufactured in enormous numbers at low cost and retaining its accuracy with no maintenance over a long working life.

C.N. Brown

Bibliography

Brown, C.N. "Charging for Electricity in the Early Years of Electricity Supply." *Proceedings of the Institution of Electrical Engineers* 132, Part A (1985): 513–24.

Ferns, J.L. *Meter Engineering*. London: Pitman, 1932.

Forbes, George. "Electric Meters for Central Stations." *Journal of the Society of Arts* 37 (1888–1889), 148–59.

Solomon, Henry G. *Electricity Meters*. London: Charles Griffin, 1906.

Stumpner, W. "Zur Geschichte des Elektricitätszählers." *Elektrotechnische Zeitschrift* 47 (1926): 601–5, 646–50. Reprinted in *Geschichtliche Einzeldarstellungen aus der Elektrotechnik* 1 (1926): 78–98.

Electrocardiograph

The electrocardiograph, also known as the cardiograph, records the electrical currents associated with the heartbeat. In the United States, the instrument is abbreviated as both "ECG" and "EKG," the latter abbreviation reflecting a German spelling of the name. The graphic tracing that the instrument produces is called an electrocardiogram.

Frank Wilson's electrocardiography apparatus. Courtesy of NMAH.

The tracing represents the signal recorded at specific places on the body. The different combinations of places from which one might record are known as leads. The most important waves that are seen in the electrocardiograph tracing are the P wave, which reflects depolarization of the upper cardiac chambers, the atria; the QRS complex, which reflects depolarization of the lower chamber, the ventricles; and the T wave, which reflects repolarization of the ventricles. These waves have a different appearance in the different leads.

Origins

Most nineteenth-century attempts to record the electrical action of the heart used recordings taken directly from the heart's surface, an approach that obviously limited the clinical utility of this technique for use on human beings. In May 1887, Augustus Waller demonstrated at St. Mary's Hospital in London that he could use an instrument known as a capillary **electrometer** to produce a graphic record from the human heart from outside of the body. The instrument, however, had several serious technical difficulties, which made its use extremely difficult.

The electrocardiograph's invention, therefore, is usually attributed to a Dutch physician and physiologist, Willem Einthoven, who witnessed Waller's demonstration and spent several years working with the capillary electrometer. Despite the problems inherent in the tool, Einthoven was able to derive reasonable tracings. From these he named the waves of the electrocardiogram, using names that are still in use at the end of the twentieth century. He selected letters from the middle of the alphabet, PQRST, leaving room for other waves to be named later.

Seeking to overcome the limitations of the capillary electrometer, Einthoven eventually turned to a different type of instrument to record the subtle electrical signals produced by the heart. The heart of his new instrument was a **string galvanometer,** a device similar to one developed in 1897 to measure telegraphic signals coming across a transatlantic cable, but the extent to which Einthoven based his description on the telegraphic device is a matter of dispute. Einthoven described an electrocardiograph machine based on the string galvanometer in a preliminary paper in 1901. For this work he received the 1924 Nobel Prize in medicine and physiology.

Following an unhappy relationship with a German manufacturing company, Einthoven turned to the Cambridge Scientific Instrument Co. (CSI), which delivered its first electrocardiogram machine in 1908. The CSI played a key role not only in marketing the instrument, but also in making it more durable and more accurate, and in helping it become not only a device for experimentation but also a trusted clinical tool.

Clinical Application

To detect abnormal cardiac rhythms, the machine was used in a manner analogous to that of the **polygraph,** an earlier instrument that had been used to record arterial and venous pulses graphically. This work covers the period to the mid 1920s, and was led by Thomas Lewis, a London physician. Use of the machine primarily to diagnose arrhythmias reinforced British physicians' role as superb diagnosticians who needed instrumental tools to train their senses, but who did not wish such machines to become part of their daily routine.

The next phase of clinical investigation was focused on use of the machine as a tool for measuring the form of the waves produced by the heart's electrical action, a use for which the unaided senses could not substitute. These applications, which were primarily done in the United States, led to clinical use of the machine for the diagnosis of coronary artery disease, often manifest as myocardial infarction or "heart attack."

During the first decades of the twentieth century, the number of leads was expanded. Einthoven had used three leads—leads I, II, and III—formed by different pairings of a person's limbs. Three more leads—aVR, aVL, and aVF—were created by changing the ways in which the signals from the limbs are connected. These original six leads measure signals within the frontal plane of the body. Six additional leads—V1 through V6—measure signals orthogonal to the plane of the body, by placing an electrode upon a person's chest. The electrocardiogram is thus able to measure electrical activity in two planes. The key figure for this period of work, from the 1920s through the 1940s, was Frank Wilson, a physician working at the University of Michigan, in Ann Arbor.

Instruments and Applications

The initial versions of the electrocardiograph machine were cumbersome and difficult to use. Key developments included smaller machines that could be taken to the bedside or even carried out into the community. At first, people had to immerse their limbs into buckets of saline to have an ECG recorded; later, electrodes were devised that could be simply attached to the limbs. The tracings were made at first by recording the motion of the string galvanometer on a photographic plate, which needed to be developed before the tracing could be seen. Use of the electrocardiogram was made much easier by the development of direct-writing machines in the 1950s, as well as by the later invention of machines that could simultaneously record three or more leads.

Much of late-twentieth-century medical care uses devices that are fundamentally based on applications of the electrocardiogram. Cardiac monitors are used in coronary care units, obstetric delivery suites, and operating rooms. Portable electrocardiograms with built-in computers can accurately read rate, rhythm, and cardiac axis. Artificial pacemakers implanted in the heart can read the heart's rhythm and adjust their own output. Continuous recording of the electrocardiograph for periods of twenty-four hours, or more, aids in the diagnosis of both abnormal rhythms and of cardiac ischemia. However, in the late twentieth century, there is increasing concern that too much routine use of the electrocardiogram may cost a great deal and not lead to any significant improvement in patients' health or longevity.

Joel D. Howell

Bibliography

Burch, George E., and Nicholas P. DePasquale. *A History of Electrocardiography* [1964]. Reprint, with a new introduction by Joel D. Howell. San Francisco: Norman, 1990.

Burnett, John. "The Origins of the Electrocardiograph as a Clinical Instrument." *Medical History* Supplement No. 5 (1985): 53–76.

Frank, Robert G. "The Telltale Heart: Physiological Instruments, Graphic Methods, and Clinical Hopes: 1854–1914." In *The Investigative Enterprise: Experimental Physiology in Nineteenth-Century Medicine,* edited by William Coleman and Frederic L. Holmes, 211–

90. Berkeley: University of California Press, 1988.

Howell, Joel D. "Early Perceptions of the Electrocardiogram: From Arrhythmia to Infarction." *Bulletin of the History of Medicine* 58 (1984): 83–98.

Katz, Louis N., and Herman K. Hellerstein. "Electrocardiography." In *Circulation of the Blood: Men and Ideas,* edited by Alfred P. Fishman and Dickinson W. Richards, 265–351. New York: Oxford University Press, 1964.

Electroencephalograph

An electroencephalograph (EEG) measures the weak electrical activity in the brain by amplifying and recording electrical waves detected by electrodes attached to the scalp. Diagnosis is based on analysis of the strength, wave frequency, and duration of the electrical pulses.

The EEG evolved from research among physiologists in the 1800s on the electrical properties of animals. In 1875, Richard Caton of Liverpool, England, published reports on his detection of electrical activity in animal brains. Fifteen years later, a Polish physiologist, Adolf Beck, detected regular electrical patterns in the cerebral cortexes of dogs and rabbits.

The successful introduction of Einthoven's **electrocardiograph** (EKG) in 1902 for disease diagnosis inspired further research on the brain. Investigators working on electrical activity of the brain quickly adopted the highly sensitive Einthoven string galvanometer. In 1914 Napo-

leon Cyblusky and S. Jelenska-Macieszyna at the University of Crakow published their tracings taken with an Einthoven galvanometer from a dog during an epileptic seizure. The development of the triode amplifier for small voltages in radio signaling during World War I made it even easier to record the very small electrical changes in the brain.

Hans Berger, a German psychiatrist at the University of Jena, detected electrical activity through the intact skull in the early 1900s, thus making the technique applicable to humans. Many other investigators in England, France, Italy, Rumania, Russia, and the United States in the 1920s and 1930s studied the electrophysiology of the central nervous system, and many had seen, if not recorded, the characteristic patterns of electrical pulses in the brain. Berger's observations of the decrease of electrical activity during sensory stimulation were made in 1924 and published in 1929. Berger's work was little known, however, until Edgar Douglas Adrian (an unimpeachable authority in British neurophysiology) and his colleague at the University of Cambridge, B.H.C. Matthews, demonstrated Berger's findings at meetings of the Physiological Society in Cambridge in 1934, and the International Congress of Psychology in 1937.

Clinical Applications

The human brain had long been inscrutable and Berger's EEG with surface electrodes was easy, inexpensive, safe, and noninvasive. The greatest concentration of EEG research on humans dur-

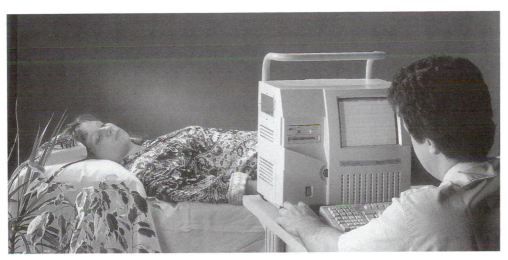

Medelec DG Discovery portable digital EEG system in use, 1995. Courtesy of Medelec Ltd./Vickers Medical.

ing the late 1930s and early 1940s was accomplished in North America, by researchers already skilled in working on laboratory animals: W.G. Lennox, and Erna and F.A. Gibbs at the Harvard Medical School, H.H. Jasper and Donald Lindsley at the Emma Pendleton Bradley Home associated with Brown University, and Wilder Penfield at McGill University. Their work was supported largely by the Rockefeller and the Josiah Macy, Jr., foundations, both of which held as their mission the support of interdisciplinary research into psychiatry, deviancy, and social ills. Research on the EEG seemed to offer the promise of social reform based on scientific knowledge; if brain disorders such as epilepsy were inherited traits, then screening for these disorders would allow individuals to make wise choices about marriage partners and procreation, thus eventually lowering the incidence of the disorders. After a decade of clinical application, the EEG was so well accepted that the U.S. Army and Navy used it to screen inductees for epilepsy and other disorders associated with abnormal electrical patterns.

By 1950 the medical community had amassed enough information about the EEG to realize that EEG tracings were not as definitive as they had at first believed. Clinicians continued to use the EEG throughout the 1950s and 1960s to differentiate different types of epilepsy, to monitor the effect of treatments on psychiatric patients, and to study electrical activity in sleep, but they also approached the EEG with greater caution, using it as an adjunct to other diagnostic techniques, rather than as a definitive diagnosis by itself.

The EEG found a new function in the increasingly technical world of the hospital. As artificial respiration and cardiac resuscitation made it possible to keep people "alive" indefinitely after the brain had ceased to function (and the cost of keeping such patients alive continued to escalate), the EEG increasingly provided a definition of death. The flat or isoelectric EEG as an indication of death, first proposed in 1963 by R.S. Schwab and colleagues, was further legitimated in 1968 when the Harvard Medical School Ad Hoc Committee to Examine the Definition of Brain Death pushed for its adoption. The flat EEG as an indicator of death has been hotly debated since then, but its use continues to rise in parallel with the increasing need for an objective, legal definition of death (as in decisions about when organ transplants may be done).

The EEG has changed little since its first human applications in the 1920s, but its function has reversed completely, from providing a characteristic tracing of life to demonstrating its absence.

Ellen B. Koch

Bibliography

Cobb, W.A., ed. *Handbook of Electroencephalography and Clinical Neurophysiology: Appraisal and Perspective of the Functional Exploration of the Nervous System.* Vol. 1. Amsterdam: Elsevier, 1971.

Hill, Denis, and Geoffrey Parr. *Electroencephalography: A Symposium on Its Various Aspects.* New York: Macmillan, 1963.

O'Leary, James L., and Sidney Goldring. *Science and Epilepsy: Neuroscience Gains in Epilepsy Research.* New York: Raven, 1976.

Russell, Louise B. *Technology in Hospitals: Medical Advances and Their Diffusion.* Washington, D.C.: Brookings Institute, 1979.

Report of the Ad Hoc Committee of the Harvard Medical School to Examine the Definition of Brain Death. "A Definition of Irreversible Coma." *Journal of the American Medical Association* 205 (1968): 85–90.

Electromagnetic Distance-Measurement
See DISTANCE-MEASUREMENT, ELECTROMAGNETIC

Electrometer
Throughout the eighteenth century electrometry was dogged by two major problems: it was necessary to determine what was actually being measured, and units of measurements had to be formulated; all the factors influencing the operation of the measuring instruments had to be elucidated. In fact, it was not possible with confidence to compare readings between instruments, calibrate instruments, or replicate measurements without first resolving these issues.

A standard or absolute electrometer must be capable of measuring in fundamental units and be constructed in such a way that its results are at all times reproducible. The vague eighteenth-century electrical concepts based on actual experiments began to be defined more clearly in the

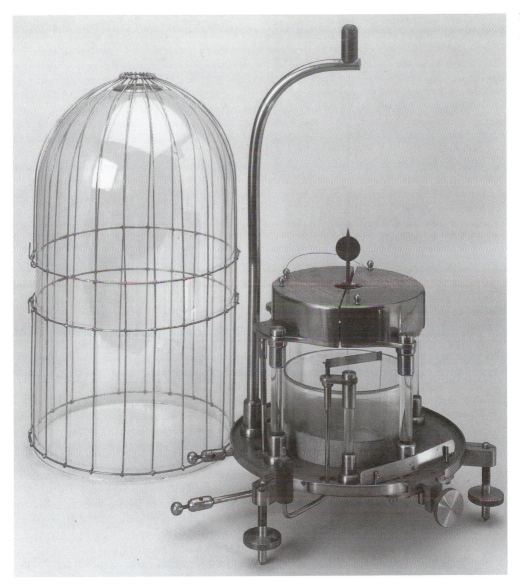

William Thomson's quadrant electrometer, by Elliott Bros., 1857. SM 1926-284. Courtesy of SSPL.

nineteenth century, so that in the mid 1830s the difference between "tension" (potential) and "intensity" (strength of an electric field) was understood, clearing up this particular ambiguity. Ohm's law of 1826 gave for the first time a clear formulation of that other vague concept, "resistance" but it took Charles Wheatstone's energetic pursuit of Ohm's work in the 1840s before its full significance was appreciated.

Mathematicians started the process of the mathematization (or mathematical idealization) of electrical phenomena in the 1780s, using the data gathered by the experimentalists. Key to this process was the determination of the in-verse-square law of electrostatic force. That such a law existed had been suspected for at least forty years because of the analogy with gravitational force, and had been anticipated by Joseph Priestley (1767) and elegantly demonstrated by Henry Cavendish by means of his "globe and hemispheres" experiment (1771), what William Thomson was to call the "null method." But Cavendish never published this experiment.

The first clear demonstration was achieved by Charles Augustin de Coulomb by means of his **torsion balance** (1785). He determined that the torsion angle as indicated by the torsion-micrometer had to be increased four times to halve the distance between the fixed ball and the repelled lever-arm at any constant charge, and from this deduced the inverse-square law. Modern replication experiments have shown the extraordinary difficulty of manipulating this instrument. That Coulomb was a very exacting experimenter is not in doubt, but he also knew what result he was looking for. At about the same time the Scotsman T.R. Robinson achieved the same result with his steelyard repulsion electrometer. This instrument measured the force of electrostatic repulsion in terms of the weight in grains, and he determined the inverse-square law by noting the different amount of repulsion at constant charge but with the arms at different angles. Coulomb's torsion balance was modified by J.F.G. Dellmann (1842) and Rudolph Herrmann Arndt Kohlrausch (1847). The suspension was of different materials. Coulomb used both silver and a single silk fiber, while Kohlrausch used a glass torsion fiber. William Snow Harris (1831) developed a "bifilar" suspension. Thomson used a similar suspension in some of his electrometers.

Coulomb was one of the first of the new breed of mathematical physicists who made their appearance in the late eighteenth century. His empirical investigation and mathematical formulation of electrostatic force was followed in 1822 by M.D. Poisson's mathematical description of the distribution of charge on the surface of conductors, which was extended by G. Green in 1823. This formed the basis for the evolution toward standard or absolute instrumental measurements that came to fruition in the 1860s through the work of Johann Karl Friedrich Gauss, Wilhelm Eduard Weber, James Clerk Maxwell, and Thomson.

The first phase of electrometer development came to an end with Alessandro Volta's series of straw electrometers (see **electroscope**). These were essentially indicators and not meters. During the second half of the nineteenth century a great deal of attention began to be paid to the mechanical design and construction as well as the electrical action of these instruments. Every electrometer (like any other indicating instrument) consists of two systems: one fixed and the other moving in such a way that this movement bears some simple relationship to the quantity being measured. Absolute and direct reading instruments could be developed only after all the factors (mechanical and electrical) were understood.

Thomson, in particular, was very interested both in the theory and the practicalities of electrometer construction. He was central to the development of the electrometer into a true measuring instrument. His electrometers, including his absolute (long-range) pattern of 1855/1870, were developed from two of the techniques used in the eighteenth century: Coulomb's frictionless fiber (torsion) suspension and Volta's attracted disk balance electrometer (1787). Thomson's extraordinary versatility as an instrument designer is attested to by his range of electrometers: a divided ring electrometer with a useful range of from less than 100 to about 500 volts (1857/1860), a portable electrometer with a range from about 0.5 to about 5,000 volts (1867), the very popular quadrant electrometer in which a large aluminum needle moved between four brass quadrants supported on glass pillars (1867), sensitive to about 0.01 volt, and the electrostatic balance, which was a form of attracted disk or long-range electrometer. In the improved version the range was from 0 to 100,000 volts. Thomson also designed a series of commercial electrostatic **voltmeters** during the 1880s for use in the rapidly expanding lighting and electric power industry. The simplest version was a modification of the quadrant electrometer designed in such a way as to give direct reading on a scale graduated in volts. A more accurate instrument was the multicellular electrostatic voltmeter (1888), designed for measuring both direct and alternating currents. The quadrant electrometer became especially popular, and versions were designed by George M. Minchin (1880), Friedrich Dolezalek (1897), Arthur Holly Compton (1919), and Frederick Alexander Lindemann (1924), among others.

Other types of electrometers were also developed, sometimes for specific purposes. A case in point is the capillary electrometer, in which current potential was indicated by the minute movements of mercury observed with a microscope and recorded photographically. It was invented by Gabriel Lippmann in 1872, but an improved, portable version is named after the German physicists Friedrich Wilhelm Ostwald and C. Robert Luther. The first **electrocardiograph** was made with a capillary electrometer by Augustus D. Waller in 1887, and this electrometer was extensively used by Willem Einthoven, among others.

In the generation after Thomson, electrical measuring instruments reached the peak of their development, and the way forward was to eliminate as much as possible the mechanical component, first by applying the electronic properties of the thermionic valve (the first valve meter was marketed in 1922), and then, in the 1960s by transistors. More recently, the analogous pointer readout has been replaced by digital number displays.

Willem D. Hackmann

Bibliography

Green, George, and John T. Lloyd. *Kelvin's Instruments and the Kelvin Museum.* Glasgow: University of Glasgow, 1970.

Hackmann, Willem D. "Eighteenth-Century Electrostatic Measuring Devices." *Annali dell'Istituto e Museo di Storia della Scienza di Firenze* 3 (1978): 3–58.

Smith, Crosbie, and M. Norton Wise. *Energy and Empire. A Biographical Study of Lord Kelvin.* Cambridge: Cambridge University Press, 1989.

Tunbridge, Paul. *Lord Kelvin: His Influence on Electrical Measurements and Units.* London: Peter Peregrinus for the Institution of Electrical Engineers, 1992.

Electromyograph

An electromyograph measures the signal that originates in muscle and nerve tissues when they are excited either by a signal from within the body or by an external electrical excitation. The related term "electromyography" was first used by Etienne-Jules Marey in his book *Physiologie du mouvement: Les vols des oiseaux* (1890).

Electromyographs have evolved into two categories: those that measure the individual pulses from a small group of muscle fibers (approximately less than twenty), and those that measure the electrical activity from large groups of fibers throughout the muscle. The shape of the individual pulses provides information concerning myopathies and neuropathies; the amplitude of the signal indicates the force produced by a contracting muscle; and the characteristics of the frequency spectrum of the signal provide indices of accumulating fatigue during muscle contractions. Clinical versions also measure the velocity of signal propagation along nerves.

Description

Current forms of the device consist of electrodes to detect the signals (ranging from 0 to 10,000 microvolts [rms] in amplitude), amplifiers and filters to condition the signal, and some means of displaying or storing the signal.

There are three types of electrodes: needle, surface, and wire. The needle electrode contains a small, relatively inert metallic detection surface (typically, a platinum-iridium compound or tungsten) lodged into and exposed at the tip of a needle that is inserted into the muscle and kept in place for the duration of the measurement. This electrode is preferred by neurologists for diagnostics of neuropathies and myopathies. The surface electrode consists of electrically conductive surfaces (typically silver, silver chloride or high-carbon stainless steel) having a variable area and shape to suit the size of the muscle over which it is placed on the skin. For the past decade, the trend has been to house the front stage of the amplification chain with the detection surfaces, rendering what has become known as the "active electrode." This arrangement considerably improves the fidelity of the recorded electromyographic signal. This electrode is preferred for measurements related to the movement, force, and fatigue of contracting muscles. The wire electrode consists of electrically insulated wires 25 to 100 µm in diameter exposed at the tip. The wires are lodged into the muscle by a needle that is removed. This electrode finds applications in studies of movement where muscle selectivity is of concern.

Signal Amplification

A differential amplification arrangement is used to magnify the relatively low-amplitude electromyographic signal in the presence of much greater ambient electrical signals, such as those from power lines. The input from two detection surfaces is subtracted and amplified. The differential amplifiers require balanced input impedances in excess of 10^{12} ohms in parallel with 5 pF. To maximize the signal-to-noise ratio, the signals are filtered at 20 to 500 Hz for surface electrodes, at 10 to 10,000 Hz for needle electrodes, and 20 to 2,000 Hz for wire electrodes. Complete technical aspects have been described by John V. Basmajian and Carlo J. De Luca in their book *Muscles Alive*.

History

The earliest reference to electricity generated in muscles comes from Francesco Redi, who in 1671 described an experiment he conducted in 1666: "It appeared to me as if the painful action of the electric ray was located in these two sickle-shaped bodies, or muscles, more than in any other part." The concept of "animal electricity" was raised to scientific consciousness by

E

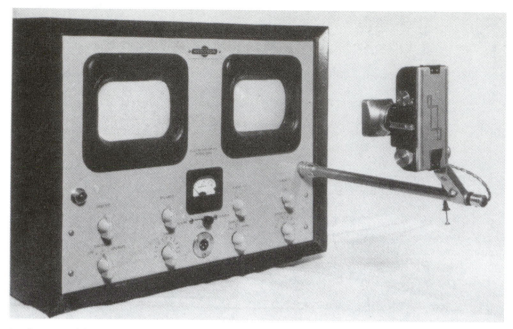

Meditron Model 200 electromyograph, 1948. Randall L. Braddom, "1991 Presidential Address. AAEM: The First Five Years." Muscle and Nerve 15 *(January 1992): 118–123, Figure 3. Copyright © 1992 John Wiley & Sons Inc. Reprinted by permission.*

Luigi Galvani, who reported his work on frog muscles in his influential book *De viribus electricitatis* (1791). But it remained for Carlo Matteucci (1844) to prove that electric currents originated in muscle tissue. Emil Du Bois-Reymond constructed a sensitive **galvanometer** to which he connected electrodes made of blotting paper immersed in a jar of saline solution; he reported electrical activity in a contracting human muscle in *Untersuchungen über thierische Elektricität* (1849).

H. Piper described the use of metal surface electrodes in *Elektrophysiologie menschlicher Muskeln* (1912). The display medium was improved considerably by the invention of the cathode ray tube by Braum in 1922. H.S. Gasser and J. Erlanger used an oscilloscope consisting of amplifiers and a cathode ray tube to "see" the individual impulses from nerve tissue, and won a Nobel Prize for this work in 1944. These technical developments, along with the introduction of needle electrodes by Edgar Douglas Adrian and Detlev Bronk (1929), set the stage for the modern electromyograph.

Up to the early 1940s, electromyographs were considered research equipment, and only a few clinicians had seen one, let alone used one. In 1948, the Meditron Co. marketed the first self-contained clinical electromyograph.

By the late 1950s, most physical medicine specialists and a growing number of neurologists considered it required equipment. In the early sixties, John Basmajian popularized the wire electrode through numerous kinesiological studies.

Advances in electronics over the past three decades have produced versatility, miniaturization, and ease of use. Improvements in surface electrodes have made it possible to use the electromyograph as a biofeedback device to inform the patient and the clinician of the intensity of a muscle contraction, thus making it an important tool for modern rehabilitation techniques. Its use for measuring muscle fatigue is beginning to have an impact in ergonomics.

Carlo J. De Luca

Bibliography

Adrian, Douglas Edgar, and Detlev W. Bronk. "The Discharge of Impulses in Motor Nerve Fibers. Part II. The Frequency of Discharge in Reflex and Voluntary Contractions." *Journal of Physiology* 67 (1929): 19–151.

Basmajian, John V., and Carlo J. De Luca. *Muscles Alive: Their Functions Revealed by Electromyography.* 5th ed. Baltimore: Williams & Wilkins, 1985.

Gasser, H.S., and J. Erlanger. "A Study of the Action Currents of Nerve with a Cathode-Ray Oscillograph." *American Journal of Physiology* 62 (1922): 496–524.

Matteuci, Carlo. *Traité des phenomènes electrophysiologiques des animaux.* Paris: Fortin Masson, 1844.

Redi, Francesco. *Esperienze intorno a diverse cose naturali, e particolarmente a quell, che ci son portate dall'Indie . . . scritte in una lettera al . . . Atanasio Chircher.* Florence, 1671.

Electron Capture Detector

The electron capture detector (ECD) is an exquisitely sensitive chemical analytical device that can detect a few fg (10^{-15} gram) of a halogen compound such as sulphur hexafluoride. What makes the ECD notable is that this sensitivity is limited to a small range of substances, many of which are environmentally significant, and among which are some that are toxic, carcinogenic, and ozone depleting.

The ECD was invented in 1957 by James Lovelock, who was investigating the damage suffered by living cells when frozen. Lovelock knew that the response to freezing varied with the fatty acid composition of cell membrane lipids, but he lacked the means to analyze these lipids. Archer Martin and Tony James, Lovelock's colleagues at the National Institute for Medical Research in London, were willing to make the analysis with their gas **chromatograph** if Love-lock would provide a larger sample or invent a more sensitive detector.

Lovelock had previously invented an ionization **anemometer** that could detect air movements as slow as 5 mm per second, but its practical use was disturbed by traces of smoke or vapor. He wondered if this drawback might become the basis of a sensitive detector for gases and vapors. Ionization detectors that had been tried for gas chromatography were simple ion chambers in which a radioactive source set free ions from the gas. They were known to be less sensitive than Martin's gas density balance, but experience with the anemometer suggested that they might be made sensitive. Lovelock built one of these detectors using a 2-ml ion chamber enclosing a seventy-four million Becquerel ^{90}Sr source of ionizing radiation. When connected to a 120-volt battery, the ion current in nitrogen was about 5 nA, easily measured by a thermionic valve **electrometer**. He connected this detector to the outflow from one of James's gas chromatograph columns and tested its response to different volatile compounds. It was, as expected, insensitive.

When the polarizing potential was reduced to 10 volts, the instrument became wonderfully sensitive, but only to a few compounds—notably halocarbons like chloroform, nitro compounds like nitromethane, and a few oddities like cyclooctatetrene and diacetyl. The presence of vapor caused the ion current to decrease as if by electron capture. With different carrier gases and different potentials, Lovelock was able to detect almost all organic vapors, includ-

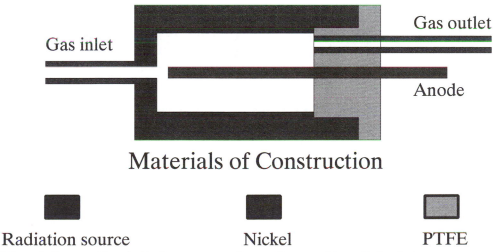

Schematic diagram of Lovelock's electron capture detector. Courtesy of James E. Lovelock.

ing fatty acid esters. The "argon" detector was widely used for several years before the flame ionization detector replaced it.

Lovelock went on to confirm that the low-potential detector worked by electron capture. The reaction between gas phase free electrons and solute vapors is second order, and complicated by subsequent reactions involving the dissociation of the negative ions. Positive ions are always present and serve to scavenge by recombination the negative molecular ions. The electron current decreases in proportion to vapor concentration but nonlinearly. The modern ECD is a 1-ml nickel "test tube" in which vapors react with a dilute suspension of free electrons in nitrogen. The electron abundance is sampled by brief pulses of potential. The frequency of the pulses, the signal, varies with vapor concentration. The ECD is usually part of a gas chromatograph.

Lovelock described the ECD during a lecture in Oxford in April 1958 and, with Sandford R. Lipsky of Yale University, published his first paper on the subject in 1960. The early ECD was difficult to use. Nevertheless, J.O. Watts and A.K. Klein of the U.S. Food and Drug Administration conscripted it to analyze pesticide residues in foodstuffs. Their work and that of E.S. Goodwin and colleagues in the U.K. revealed halogenated pesticides everywhere they looked. It gave Rachel Carson the data for her influential book *Silent Spring,* said to have started the Green movement. The ECD is the nose that smelled the onset of environmental corruption. It discovered the global distribution of the CFCs, the pesticides, and the PCBs, and it is still used to monitor their abundance. New uses of the ECD include the detection of perfluorocarbons used as tracers to measure air and water mass movements.

James E. Lovelock

Bibliography

Lovelock, James E. "Affinity of Organic Compounds for Free Electrons with Thermal Energy: Its Possible Significance in Biology." *Nature* 189 (1961): 729–32.
———. "The Electron Capture Detector Theory and Practice." *Journal of Chromatography* 99 (1974): 3–12.
———. "Ionization Methods for the Analysis of Gases and Vapors." *Analytical Chemistry* 33 (1961): 162–78.
———, and Sandford R. Lipsky. "Electron Affinity Spectroscopy. A New Method for the Identification of Functional Groups in Chemical Compounds Separated by Gas Chromatography." *Journal of the American Chemical Society* 82 (1960): 431–33.
———, and A.J. Watson. "Electron Capture Detector Theory and Practice. II." *Journal of Chromatography* 158 (1978): 123–38.

Electron Microscope
See MICROSCOPE, ELECTRON

Electron Probe Microanalyzer

This is a vacuum electron/x-ray optical instrument for measuring the elemental composition of a microscopic volume of solid matter, with lateral and depth dimensions on the order of micrometers. It is used to characterize chemical microstructure in a wide range of physical, biological, and technological fields.

Physical Principles

A focused beam (1 nm to 1 μm in diameter) of energetic electrons strikes a solid specimen. Inelastic scattering limits the penetration range of the beam electrons to a depth of 0.1 to 10 μm, while elastic scattering causes lateral spreading to about the same extent as the range. Within this excited volume, which has a mass of 0.1 to 10 pg, a beam electron can cause ejection of a bound inner shell electron from an atom. De-excitation through intershell electron transitions causes emission of an x-ray photon, which has a sharply defined energy that is characteristic of the original atom. The complex shell structures of heavier atoms yield extensive families of characteristic x-rays. These characteristic x-rays are observed as peaks above a continuous background formed by electron *Bremsstrahlung* caused by deceleration in the coulombic field of the atoms. The x-ray spectrum is measured with the wavelength dispersive **spectrometer,** which separates the different x-ray energies (wavelengths) through the phenomenon of diffraction from a crystal (for example, LiF), and the energy dispersive spectrometer, which directly measures the photon energy through photoelectric capture to deposit charge in a semiconductor crystal. Wavelength dispersive spectrometry provides the highest spectral resolution (peak width less than 10 eV), but has only narrow spectral coverage requiring mechanical scanning with several diffraction crys-

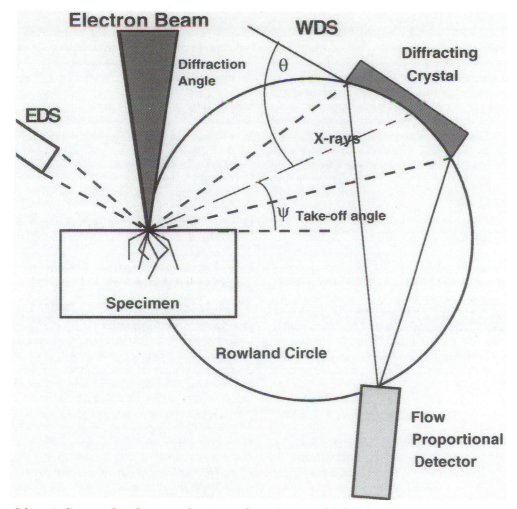

Schematic diagram of an electron probe microanalyzer. Courtesy of Dale E. Newbury.

tals to examine the entire x-ray spectrum. Energy dispersive spectrometry suffers from poor spectral resolution, but simultaneously views the entire x-ray spectrum from 100 to 50,000 eV.

Qualitative analysis is based upon the application of the atomic number systematics originally observed by H.G.J. Moseley in 1913: wavelength (or energy) of the x-ray peak(s) identifies the elements present in the excited volume. Practical limitations on the performance of x-ray spectrometers make beryllium the lowest atomic number element that can be measured. Quantitative analysis relies on the comparison of the peak intensity measured from the specimen with the peak intensity measured under the same beam conditions for the same element from a standard of known composition. Very simple standards can be used, such as a pure element (such as iron), a binary

compound for those elements not in solid form in a vacuum at room temperature (such as gallium arsenide), or a microscopically homogeneous mixture of elements such as a glass or certain mineral crystals (such as quartz).

True elemental concentrations are derived from these intensity ratios through the application of multiplicative correction factors based upon physical descriptions of the interaction of electrons (backscattering and stopping power) and the generation and propagation of x-rays through matter (absorption and secondary fluorescence of x-rays of lower energy). All correction factors are themselves compositionally dependent, requiring a calculation that involves an initial estimate of composition followed by iterative procedures. The accuracy achieved with this "matrix correction procedure" for polished specimens is described by a distribution of errors such that 95 percent of test analyses lie within ± 5 percent relative of the true concentration. The fractional limit of detection is somewhat element- and matrix-dependent and is generally approximately one thousand parts per million for energy dispersive spectrometry and one hundred parts per million for wavelength dispersive spectrometry, although in the most favorable situations ten parts per million can be detected. For an excited mass of one pg, the limit of detection in terms of absolute mass sensitivity is 10 ag to 1 fg. Complete qualitative and quantitative analysis typically requires 10 to 1,000 seconds per beam location, depending on the number of elements to be determined and the limit of trace detection required.

History
The development of the electron probe microanalyzer has its roots in experiments in electron optics in Germany in the 1930s (E. Ruska, M. Knoll, and others) and in the United States in the 1940s (V. Zworykin and J. Hillier). The first successful electron probe microanalyzer was developed by Raymond Castaing of France in 1951. Castaing also identified the significant physical processes that affected quantitative analysis and proposed the systematic approach to establishing correction factors. Castaing's instrument had a fixed probe, and it used an optical microscope to locate the specimen target. P. Duncumb and V.E. Cosslett of the U. K. introduced scanning capability in 1956 that made possible direct visualization of compositionally heterogeneous microstructures through x-ray compositional mapping. The parallel development (1948–1960) in the U. K. of the scanning **electron microscope** by C.W. Oatley, D. McMullan, K.C.A. Smith, and others produced high-resolution electron imaging of topography, composition, magnetic and electrical fields, and crystal structure to complement x-ray microanalysis.

A modern electron probe microanalyzer costs $250,000 to $1,000,000. It consists of a high-performance scanning electron microscope, a mechanical stage for precisely positioning a specimen 10 cm (or even larger) in dimensions, one or more wavelength dispersive x-ray spectrometers with multiple crystals (*see* **spectrophotometer**), a fixed-focus light **optical microscope** for accurate positioning of the specimen relative to the focusing ellipsoid of the wavelength dispersive spectrometers, an energy dispersive spectrometer, and a computer automation system for unattended operation with control of all aspects of

the system. The electron probe microanalyzer provides the powerful combination of comprehensive visualization of the microstructure and accurate measurement of the elemental composition.

Dale E. Newbury

Bibliography
Castaing, R. "Application des sondes électroniques á une méthode d'analyse ponctuelle chimique crystallographique." Thesis. University of Paris, 1951.
Goldstein, J.I., et al. *Scanning Electron Microscopy and X-ray Microanalysis.* New York: Plenum, 1992.
Heinrich, Kurt F.J. *Electron Beam X-ray Microanalysis.* New York: Van Nostrand Reinhold, 1981.
———, and D.E. Newbury, eds. *Electron Probe Quantitation.* New York: Plenum, 1991.

Electrophoretic Apparatus
Electrophoresis is an important method used to characterize and prepare molecules of biological and chemical interest. When an electric field is applied to a solution, molecules are separated on the basis of their electrical charge. Alexander Reuss, a Russian physicist, performed the first recorded electrophoretic experiment in 1807. He placed two pieces of glass tubing filled with water in a slab of wet clay, carefully layered sand at the bottom of each tube, and connected the tubes to a voltaic pile (*see* **battery**). Water at the end of the tube connected to the positive pole became milky, as clay particles migrated through the sand. In 1879 Hermann Helmholtz generalized experimental observations into an equation on electrophoresis.

Although the electrophoretic separation of proteins was imprecise and erratic, it was fairly nondisruptive. Consequently, researchers used electrophoresis to understand proteins and other large molecules of biological interest. In 1900, W.B. Hardy quantitatively determined the mobility of separated proteins, and in 1908 Karl Landsteiner separated protein from blood sera.

In the 1920s, The Svedburgh, the inventor of the **ultracentrifuge**, encouraged his student, Arne Tiselius, to improve electrophoretic techniques. Over the next few decades, Tiselius transformed the electrophoresis apparatus into a powerful analytical instrument. He used a U-shaped tube as the electrophoresis chamber. The tube was in three parts: the upper channels connected to electrodes, the middle channels through which the solutions

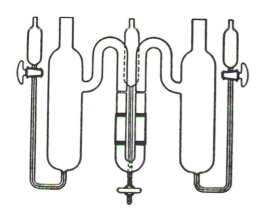

Tiselius's electrophoresis cell, 1939. Stern (1939): 154, Figure 5. Courtesy of the New York Academy of Sciences.

migrated, and a bridge connected the two migratory chambers. Tiselius is credited with three major improvements in electrophoresis. He created a cooling system. The application of an electric current to the buffer caused the electrophoretic apparatus to heat up, creating convection currents in the sample chamber. These currents blurred the boundaries of the migrating zones of molecules. Tiselius reduced the convection currents by immersing the electrophoretic chamber in a bath of near-freezing water, cooling the chamber to 4°C. Secondly, he adapted a Schlieren optical system to visualize the refraction boundaries of colorless solutions. The differences in densities between layers of substances cast a shadow through properly adjusted lenses. These could be photographed as dark bands on a light background. The Schlieren optical system took up most of the 20-foot length of the Tiselius apparatus. Finally, Tiselius used a plunger lowered by a clockwork mechanism that produced a counterflow that held the fastest migrating boundary stationary while the slower boundaries appeared to have a net negative velocity. This allowed for the separation of substances that would normally migrate to the end of the tube. Tiselius used this apparatus to describe the moving boundaries corresponding to α, β, and γ-globulin in blood serum, and received the Nobel Prize in chemistry for his work in 1948.

Despite its expense ($6,000 to build and $5,000 a year to maintain and operate), there were fourteen Tiselius stations in existence in the United States by the end of 1939. In 1945 the first commercial Tiselius apparatus was sold by Klett Manufacturing at a price of $4,000.

Visualization of colorless substances improved with the adaptation of stains and the development of radio nucleotide labeling. Separated proteins, for instance, could be easily seen by staining with amide black or by measuring the radioactivity of labeled samples in a **scintillation counter** or by exposing the radioactive electrophoresis products to film. The elaborate and bulky Schlieren optical system was hence abandoned.

Zone electrophoresis eventually passed the Tiselius apparatus in popularity. Here molecules migrate through a solid matrix infused with buffer. This sharpened the migration boundaries of the substances by further reducing the effects of convection currents. Compared to the Tiselius apparatus, in which only the fastest and slowest migrating components could be separated, zonal electrophoresis separated each component into distinct bands. Finding a suitable support proved a problem, though. Some of the substances tried included agar, potato starch, cellulose, glass, sponge rubber, and polyurethane foam. With the use of paper in the late 1940s, zonal electrophoresis received general interest. It allowed for separation of large amounts of solute, making preparative electrophoresis attractive. The low adsorption of polyacrylamide gel, first used by S. Raymond and L. Weintraub in 1959, further increased resolution. In 1961, S. Hjérten used agarose, created by eliminating the charged sulfur-containing component from agar, as a support.

In capillary electrophoresis, researchers even further reduced convection currents through the use of small-diameter electrophoretic chambers. Small tubes dissipate heat more efficiently, providing a more uniform temperature throughout the electrophoretic chamber. In 1967, Hjéten used a tube with a 3-mm inside diameter for gel-free zonal electrophoresis. J.W. Jorgenson and K.D. Lukacs showed high separation efficiency in capillaries less than 100µm in diameter in 1981. The use of sensitive detection techniques allows researchers to visualize the small amount of sample used in capillary electrophoresis.

Today zonal electrophoresis apparatus is found in almost all laboratories interested in studying proteins and nucleic acids. Models are designed for a wide variety of applications. For example, researchers use agarose supports to separate whole chromosomes or polyacrylamide to separate nucleic acids a few nucleotides in length. Electrophoretic apparatus is now very inexpensive—the cheapest can be purchased for under $200. The smallest zone electrophoresis chamber is under 6 in. in length and requires much less sample for analytical runs. Once large enough to demand special centers with teams of workers, now electrophoretic apparatus fits unobtrusively on a researcher's bench top.

Phillip Thurtle

Bibliography

Kay, Lily. "Laboratory Technology and Biological Knowledge: The Tiselius Electrophoresis Apparatus, 1930–1945." *History and Philosophy of the Life Sciences* 10 (1988): 51–72.

Morris, C.J.O.R., and P. Morris. "Experimental Methods of Electrophoresis." In their *Separation Methods in Biochemistry,* 664–770. New York: Interscience, 1963.

Shafer-Nielson, C. "Steady-state Gel Electrophoresis Systems." In *Gel Electrophoresis of Proteins,* edited by Michael J. Dunn. Bristol: Wright, 1986.

Stern, Curt. "Method for Studying Electrophoresis." *Annals of the New York Academy of Sciences* 39 (1939): 147–86.

Vesterberg, Olof. "A Short History of Electrophoretic Methods." *Electrophoresis* 14 (1993): 1243–49.

Electroretinograph

An electroretinograph records the gross electrical potential generated by the retina of the eye in response to light stimulation. The study of electrical activity in the retina began with Du Bois-Reymond's 1849 discovery of the "negative variation" elicited from the optic nerve by light stimulation of the eye. This work prompted the Swedish physiologist Frithiof Holmgren (1865) to place electrodes on the skin close to the eyes, which revealed electrical activity in response to light, observed as deflections of a **galvanometer**. These occurred both at the onset and extinction of the light stimulus, and Holmgren's account of his observations, published in Swedish, provides the first description of the electroretinogram response. In the introduction to his paper, he commented: "It would be of great importance to devise a method by means of which it were possible to find an objective expression of the effect of light upon the retina. The following contains an attempt to solve this problem." J. Dewar and J.G. McKendrick, the two Scottish scientists who published an account of an electroretinogram in 1873, were acquainted with Holmgren's work.

Progress in the understanding of the electroretinogram reflected technical advances in electrophysiology. The first significant development was the application of the **string galvanometer** by the British physiologist F. Gotch in 1903. This was sufficiently fast to resolve temporal components of the ERG, and led Gotch to identify in the frog all the currently recognized component features of the response. Numerous studies followed, including Einthoven's application of the string galvanometer, with which he established that the general form of the electroretinogram is common to all vertebrate eyes. Subsequent analysis of the electroretinogram has rested on the application of microelectrode techniques, first introduced by H.K. Hartline (1938) and R. Granit and G. Svaetichin (1939), which facilitated identification of the neural generators of its different compo-

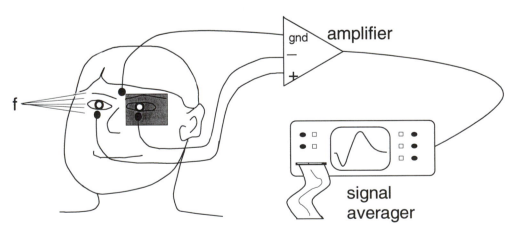

Recording the electroretinogram in response to a light flash (f). The response is recorded differentially with a ground reference electrode, typically locatxed on the forehead. The amplified output is averaged over a number of flash responses. Courtesy of M.W. Hankins and K.H. Ruddock.

nents. Since the early nineteenth century, descriptions of the electroretinogram have been included in textbooks of physiology.

Electroretinography in Humans

Dewar and McKendrick recorded light-evoked electrical potential changes in the human eye in 1877, but such measurements remained an academic curiosity until 1924, when R.H. Kahn and A. Lowenstein began to record electroretinograms with a view to clinical application. Significant advances were also made by Hartline and Sachs, but progress was constrained by the limited temporal resolution of the capillary galvanometer. The development of vacuum-tube amplifiers; their introduction into electrical recording systems resolved this problem and allowed S. Cooper, R.S. Creed, and R. Granit (1933) to record electroretinograms generated in the central and peripheral regions of their own eyes. Clinical applications were undertaken, and in 1945 G. Karpe published outline procedures for clinical electroretinography. His recording system in the Ophthalmological Clinic of the Karolinska Institute, Sweden, consisted of an oscillograph with a directly coupled vacuum-tube amplifier; records of electroretinograms from both normal and pathological eyes were stored photographically. Electrode connections to the patient's eyes were formed by two silver-silver chloride electrodes with saline-impregnated cotton wicks, the reference electrode being applied to the forehead and the recording electrode to the anesthetized cornea.

Developments in the design of recording electrodes and of signal averaging devices have established electroretinography as a valuable clinical diagnostic technique. Contact lens electrodes yield highly reproducible responses, but require anesthesia of the cornea and sclera. The latter can be avoided by the use of gold foil electrodes that are hooked over the lower eyelid. Signal averaging to improve signal-to-noise ratios was originally achieved by superimposition of photographic traces, but is now performed digitally by commercially available instruments such as those developed in the 1970s by Medelec. Modern electroretinographs contain integrated instruments, which not only generate the light stimuli, but also filter, amplify, average and store the signal, and provide hardcopy output of the resulting electroretinogram.

M.W. Hankins
K. H. Ruddock

Bibliography

Cooper, S., R.S. Creed, and R. Granit. "A Note on the Retinal Action Potential of the Human Eye." *Journal of Physiology* 79 (1933): 185–90.

Dewar, J., and J.G. McKendrick. "On the Physiological Action of Light." *Transactions of the Royal Society of Edinburgh* 27 (1873): 141–66.

Du Bois-Reymond, Emil. *Untersuchungen uber thierische Elektricitat*. Berlin: Reimer, 1849.

Holmgren, F. "Method att objectivera effecten av ljusintryck pa retina." *Upsala lakareforenings forhandlingar* 1 (1865): 177–91.

Kahn, R.H., and A. Lowenstein. "Das Electroretinogram." *Graefe's Archives of Ophthalmology* 114 (1924): 304–31.

Karpe, G. "The Basis of Clinical Electroretinography." *Acta Ophthalmologica* 24 (1945): 1–118.

Electroscope

The earliest electrical indicator was William Gilbert's "versorium," in essence a horizontally pivoted magnetic needle, described in his *De magnete* (1600). Forty years later Francis Hauksbee the elder suggested an indicator consisting of a few threads enclosed in a glass bottle. In the 1730s electrical activity was indicated by means of a single thread suspended from a stick. Granville Wheler showed that two repelling electrified threads diverge equally in opposite directions—a view that fit with contemporary ideas about symmetry in nature. Jean Théophile Desaguliers used this technique in 1741 to display the symmetrical distribution of charge on differently shaped conductors. Both of these conclusions, which implied that indicators could be used to measure the degree of electricity, were confirmed by J.H. von Waitz's 1745 observation that the divergence of the two threads of an indicator is inversely related to the mass of the weight suspended from their ends.

In 1747 Jean Antoine Nollet wrote to Benjamin Franklin suggesting that the divergence of such threads could be used as a measure of electricity. He called his device an "electrometer," but noted that it would be better to call it an "electroscope," as it did not accurately correlate degree of divergence with magnitude of electricity. The term "electrometer" was also coined by Daniel Gralath in early 1747 for the modified balance with which he tried to "weigh" the electric force. John Ellicot had reported a similar instrument the previous year. The floating repulsion electrometer by P. Le Chevalier d'Arcy and Jean Baptiste Le Roy measured the force of electrostatic repulsion in units of weight.

The many eighteenth-century variations in electroscope design can be grouped in four main classes: those operating on electrostatic repulsion and attraction; those measuring the force of the spark discharge; those measuring spark length; and those measuring the heating effect of the spark discharge. The first discharging-electrometer was devised by the apothecary Timothy Lane in 1766 for use in electrical treatment, but was later also much used to compare the output of **electrostatic machines**. The first instrument using the heating effect of the discharge was Ebenezer Kinnersley's "electrical air thermometer" of 1761.

John Canton's electroscope of 1753 had two small balls made from the pith of elder, each one suspended by a fine linen thread and enclosed in a narrow wooden box. In later models, produced by Kinnersley, William Henley, and Edward Nairne, the instrument was enclosed in a glass vessel and thus protected from drafts. In Tiberius Cavallo's influential "portable electrometer" of 1779, the pith balls were suspended from fine silver wires that made electrical contact with a large brass cap to which the charge to be measured was communicated. Cavallo also glued two tin-foil strips to the inside of the glass vessel, which conveyed excess charge from the diverging wires to earth, thereby preventing this charge from accumulating on the glass and affecting the reading.

Cavallo's electrometer was improved by H.B. de Saussure, Alesandro Volta, and Abraham Bennet. Bennet's gold leaf electroscope of 1786 incorporated Cavallo's "earthing strips" and a process of "doubling" the charge that was based on Volta's parallel plate condenser. Weak charges were increased by alternately charging and grounding two varnished brass disks placed on the flat cap of the electroscope. The doubler is the precursor of the mechanical induction machine, the best known example of which is the Wimshurst machine of the early 1880s.

By replacing Cavallo's silver wire with light straws, Volta produced an instrument that gave readings almost directly proportional to the intensity being measured. Using a graded series of straw electrometers, Volta was

Gold leaf electroscope, Ayrton's improved form, ca. 1890. SM 1975-284. Courtesy of SSPL.

able to investigate contact potential, and this led to the discovery of his electrochemical pile of 1800 and to a host of unforeseen electrical phenomena.

William Henley's "quadrant electrometer" of 1770 consisted of a semicircular scale divided in degrees and secured to a wooden or brass stem. The divergence was indicated by a light wooden rod terminating in a small pith or cork ball, and pivoted at the center of the scale. This must not be confused with William Thomson's much more sophisticated instrument of the 1860s (see **electrometer**).

The early electroscopes were used primarily to study atmospheric electricity and the output of the increasingly sophisticated electrostatic machines. By the last quarter of the eighteenth century, research had switched from large-scale phenomena to the study of extremely small electric charges, made possible by the new generation of instruments based on Volta's electrophorus (1775) and parallel plate condenser (1780).

The behavior of Volta's pile was initially explained in terms of electrostatics, and the earliest current-measuring instruments were based on the gold leaf electroscope. Bischoff's "galvanometer" of 1801 consisted of a single gold leaf and a brass sphere actuated by a micrometer screw. A more sensitive instrument was T.G.B. Behrens's dry pile gold leaf electroscope, which indicated both the polarity and the intensity of the current, as the single gold leaf was deflected to the pole of the pile of the opposite charge. This type was further developed, especially in Germany, by J.G.F. von Bohnenberger (ca. 1814), G.T. Fechner (ca. 1829), and Wilhelm Gottlieb Hankel, who added a microscopic eyepiece and used it in 1850 in his piezoelectric and thermoelectric studies of crystals. In 1827 James Cumming replaced the dry pile with a horseshoe magnet; when a current passed through the strip of gold leaf held loosely at both ends in forceps, it was either attracted to or repelled from the poles of the magnet, depending on the direction of the current. This was the precursor of Willem Einthoven's **string galvanometer**.

The gold leaf electroscope was also used in the early work on radioactivity. Radiation intensity was measured by observing the collapse of the divergence of the charged electroscope as charge leakage accelerated because of the ionization of the air. With his "tilted" electroscope of 1903, C.T.R. Wilson could achieve two hundred eyepiece divisions per volt over a limited range.

Willem D. Hackmann

Bibliography

Hackmann, Willem D. "Eighteenth-Century Electrostatic Measuring Devices." *Annali dell'Istituto e Museo di Storia della Scienza di Firenze* 3 (1978): 3–58.

————. "Leopoldo Nobili and the Beginnings of Galvanometry." In *Leopoldo Nobili e la cultura scientifica del suo tempo,* edited by G. Tarozzi, 203–34. Bologna: Nuova alfa editoriale, 1985.

Heilbron, John L. *Electricity in the Seventeenth and Eighteenth Centuries; A Study of Early Modern Physics.* Berkeley: University of California Press, 1979.

Electrostatic Machine

An electrostatic machine produces an electrostatic charge. Modern electrical research began with William Gilbert, author of *De magnete* (1600), who tried to distinguish between the attractive properties of the magnet and those of a rubbed "electric" such as amber, glass, or sulphur. Some sixty years later, Otto von Guericke of Magdeburg devised what scholars later realized was the first electrostatic machine, more commonly known as an electrical machine. It consisted of a sulphur ball "about the size of a child's head," which was both rotated and rubbed by hand. Although Guericke observed many of the properties of electrostatics, he did not recognize them as such, as his intention was to demonstrate his cosmological theories. According to him, there existed in nature a number of forces, including the attractive force, which he equated with gravitation. His device was a model of the earth—an electric terrella to counter Gilbert's magnetic terrella—and the friction of the hand was the air that rubs against the revolving earth creating an attractive force, gravitation.

According to many sources, Isaac Newton improved the electrical machine by replacing the sulphur globe with one of glass, but that is incorrect. Newton did, however, demonstrate that glass is a good "electric" with strong attractive properties when rubbed.

The next stage in the development of the frictional electrostatic machine was achieved in 1706 by Francis Hauksbee the elder, the unofficial "curator of experiments" at the Royal Society. Some thirty years earlier, the French astronomer Jean Picard had observed that when he moved **barometers** in his observatory in Paris, a mysterious glow would sometimes appear above the level of the oscillating column of mercury. Hauksbee showed that the glow was caused by the friction of the mercury on the glass barometer tube, which produced electricity, and that the same phenomenon could be produced by rotating a glass globe with a woollen cloth or the open hand.

Hauksbee's machine did not immediately become popular. Instead it continued to be used for repeating his experiments with the electric glow (hence it was referred to in Germany by Christian Wolff as the *Lichtmaschine*), while conventional electrical experiments were made by rubbed glass or resinous rods (or tubes).

The development of the electrostatic machine followed a number of key discoveries con-

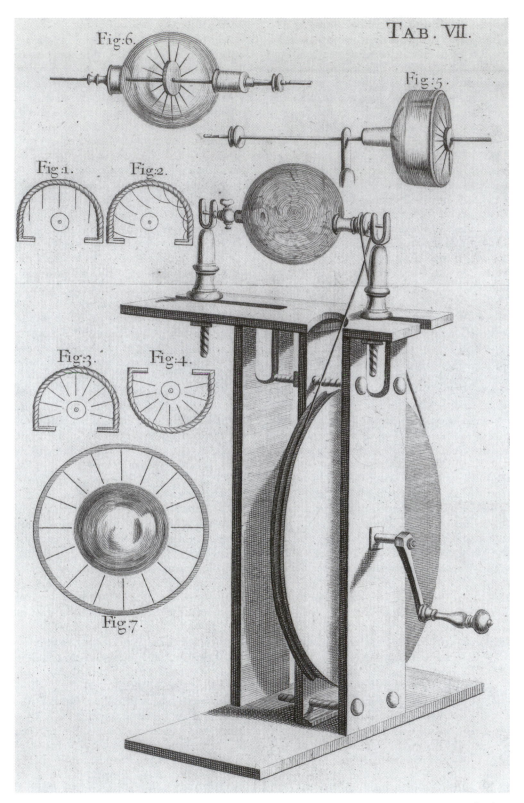

Francis Hauksbee's electrical machine. Francis Hauksbee. Physico-Mechanical Experiments. *Second Edition. London, 1719: Plate VII. Courtesy of SSPL.*

cerning the behavior of electric charge that made it possible to distinguish between electrics and nonelectrics, insulators and conductors. At least two men in Leipzig were using Hauksbee's globe machine for electrical experiments in the 1730s: Georg Matthias Bose, then an assistant lecturer in mathematics and physics at Leipzig and later at Wittenberg and Christian A. Hausen, professor of mathematics at Leipzig. Bose's machine was made from the spherical body of an alembic. The charge from the globe, still rubbed by hand, was accumulated on a person insulated either by being suspended from silk cords (cords dyed blue were thought to be the best insulators), or by standing on a thick cake of pitch or sealing wax. In 1743 Bose replaced the person by a tin-plate telescope tube suspended in the same way. He may have been the first person to insert a bundle of threads in the end of the tube nearest to the glass to facilitate the transfer of charge from globe to tube. He also used multiglobe machines to increase the charge. The illustration of an electrical machine in the frontispiece of Hausen's *Novi profectur in historia electricitatis,* published posthumously in 1743, caught the imagination of the scientific community.

It was, however, Johann Heinrich Winckler, professor of classics at Leipzig, who developed the primitive generators of Bose and Hausen and made the electrostatic machine universally popular. Working in association with a local turner, Johann Friedrich Giessing, they adapted the electrical machine to be driven by a foot treadle rather than cranked by hand, and introduced a cushion of leather or linen stuffed with a soft material to rub the rotating glass globe. Their conductor was made of a long metal tube supported on an adjustable stand by means of blue silk threads. In 1744 Winckler developed an improved arrangement for exciting electricity in a vacuum, and the following year he described a multiglobe machine in the *Philosophical Transactions.* At about the same time either Winckler or the Scottish monk Andreas Gordon replaced the globe by a glass cylinder.

A Winckler electrical machine was presented to the Royal Society of London in 1745. Five years later, the court painter Benjamin Wilson described a "compact" cylinder machine in which all the features were combined on a single table. He introduced the "collecting comb" consisting of a comblike arrangement of metal wires that could be set nearer or further from the rotating cylinder to act as a collector of electricity, replacing the threads or chains previously used.

During the second half of the eighteenth century the electrical machine established its basic form, but there were numerous variations. The glass was rubbed by a leather cushion whose pressure could be adjusted, and the charge was collected by an insulated metal tube called the "prime conductor." The only radical innovation was the plate electrical machine developed in the 1750s, in which the globe or cylinder was replaced by one or more thick glass disks. This allowed for a more compact arrangement. While no single inventor can be named, contenders include Martin Planta, Sigaud de la Fond, Johann Ingenhousz, and Jesse Ramsden. Ramsden and Peter Dollond both began trading in plate machines in the 1760s. The English form was the more compact: four cushions adjustable by screws rubbed against the glass supported between two wooden uprights; the prime conductor was a brass tube supported on a glass pillar or a **Leyden jar,** and with its arms terminating in either single or multiple-point collectors. The Continental type, often erroneously associated with Ramsden, is much larger. The high point was the plate machine made in 1783 by the English instrument-maker John Cuthbertson, at that time resident in Amsterdam, for Martinus van Marum. Its huge, twin glass plates produced discharges two feet (61 cm) long—that is, about 500,000 volts. This machine can still be seen at the Teyler's Museum in Haarlem, and a modern duplicate at the Utrecht University Museum. Interest switched from electrostatics to current electricity with the invention of the voltaic pile by Alessandro Volta in 1800 (*see* **battery**).

The early development of the electrostatic machine was predominantly empirical. Its insulated prime conductor and collecting points were based on discoveries made with very crude equipment, although experiments were performed within a conceptual framework. Further advances in design during the second half of the eighteenth century were much more influenced by theoretical considerations, in particular Franklin's single-fluid theory of electrical action.

Willem D. Hackmann

Bibliography

Hackmann, Willem D. *Catalogue of the Pneumatic, Magnetic, Electrostatic, and Electromagnetic Instruments in the Museo di Storia della Scienza.* Florence: Giunti, 1995.

———. *Electricity from Glass: The Development of the Frictional Electrical Machine 1600–1850.* Alphen aan den Rijn: Sijthoff and Noordhoff, 1978.

———. "The Relationship between Concept and Instrument Design in Eighteenth-Century Experimental Science." *Annals of Science* 36 (1979): 205–24.

Ellipsometer

An ellipsometer measures the transversal elliptical vibration of the electric vector of a beam of monochromatic light. This elliptical polarization is produced when linearly polarized light is reflected at oblique incidence from a mirror-like surface, which may be coated with a thin film. From the incident and reflected polarizations, the ratio of amplitude reflectances (expressed as the tangent of an angle ψ) and the differential reflection phase shift (angle Δ) of the components of the electric vector that oscillate parallel and perpendicular to the plane of incidence are determined. The equations of light reflection, which were first derived by Augustin Fresnel (1815) and Paul Drude (1889), are then used to derive from ψ and Δ the optical properties of the reflecting medium or the thickness and refractive index of the film coating.

Since ellipsometry involves analysis of the polarization of reflected light, its history may be traced to E. Louis Malus (1809) and David Brewster (1815), who discovered the polarization of light by reflection. J. Jamin (1851) and John William Strutt, Lord Rayleigh (1892) investigated experimentally the residual elliptical polarization caused by reflection from presumably clean liquid and solid surfaces at and near the Brewster angle. However, the theory and practice of ellipsometry was founded largely by Paul Drude (1889). In the 1920s and 1930s, Leif Tronstad and A.B. Winterbottom at the Norges Tekniske Hogskole in Trondheim used a visual "ellipsometer" (then called polarization spectrometer) to study film formation on metal surfaces in liquid and gaseous environments. The word ellipsometer was coined by Alexandre Rothen in 1945. Advances in photoelectric detection, electronics, and **digital computers** led to a renaissance and increased use of ellipsometry in the second half of this century; this was brought to an early focus at the first international conference on ellipsometry at the U.S. National Bureau of Standards in 1964.

Analysis of elliptical polarization, which dates back to H. de Senarmont (1840), involves the use of wave retardation plates and crystal or sheet polarizers. In a typical null measurement, the retardation plate and polarizer are adjusted to extinguish the transmitted light. (The retardation plate is also called a compensator because it transforms the incoming elliptical polarization into linear polarization, which

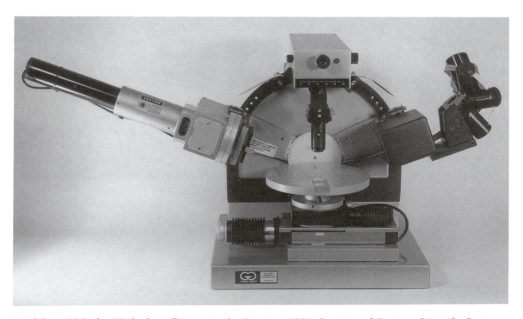

Model L115S Stokes Waferskan ellipsometer, by Gaertner, 1994. Courtesy of Gaertner Scientific Corp.

is then crossed with the polarizer.) Azimuth angles and phase retardation have to be known to high precision (0.01°) to determine the parameters of the polarization ellipse accurately. Fast and automatic self-nulling ellipsometers with no moving parts are realized by using the electro-optic (Pockels) effect to produce phase retardation, or by using the Faraday effect to replace mechanical rotation with optical rotation. Such instruments are important in applications that require real-time monitoring of surface reactions.

Modern ellipsometers use Fourier analysis of a periodic photodetected signal, generated by a rotating polarizer or an electro-optic or photoelastic modulator, to determine ψ and Δ. Spectroscopic ellipsometry over the visible and near-visible spectrum is now possible using commercial instruments built in the United States, France, and Japan. Ellipsometry has also been extended to soft x-rays, infrared and far-infrared radiation, microwaves, and even elastic waves in solids.

The newest instruments, which do not use any moving parts or modulators, are based on developing multiple (≥ 4) signals by several detectors simultaneously using division of wavefront (Edward Collett, U.S. patent [1979] no. 4,158,506) and division of amplitude (Rasheed Azzam, U.S. patents [1987 and 1994] nos. 4,681,450 and 5,337,146). One such design uses only four partially reflective silicon detectors to measure all four polarization Stokes parameters of light. A commercial instrument based on this principle is available from Gaertner of Chicago.

Rasheed M.A. Azzam

Bibliography

Azzam, Rasheed M.A., ed. *Selected Papers on Ellipsometry*. Bellingham, Wash.: SPIE Optical Engineering, 1991.

———, and N.M. Bashara. *Ellipsometry and Polarized Light*. Amsterdam: North-Holland, 1977.

Passaglia, E., R.R. Stromberg, and J. Kruger, eds. *Ellipsometry in the Measurement of Surfaces and Thin Films*. Washington, D.C.: Government Printing Office, 1964.

Proceedings of the First International Conference on Spectroscopic Ellipsometry. Amsterdam: Elsevier, 1993.

Proceedings of the Second, Third, and Fourth International Conferences on Ellipsometry. Amsterdam: North-Holland, 1969, 1976, and 1980.

Endoscope

An endoscope is used to examine the interior of a canal, hollow organ (viscus), or body cavity. It consists of a tube or shaft, light source, and optical system. Observation may take place through a natural body orifice, surgical stoma, fistula, or surgical incision. Intended for diagnosis, endoscopes have acquired therapeutic importance in recent decades.

Although specula to peer into body orifices existed in Roman times, endoscopes date from Philipp Bozzini's "light conductor" of 1805. Bozzini, a Frankfurt physician, devised this instrument for several diagnostic procedures, including examination of the mouth, nose, ears, vagina, uterus, male and female urethra, female urinary bladder, and rectum. In clinical trials by the faculty of the Josephakademie in Vienna, candle and concave mirror provided inadequate illumination, while the viewing tube without a lens provided inadequate images. Caustically worded critiques soon spelled the demise of Bozzini's instrument.

Subsequent endoscopy development centered in urology, but illumination problems and restricted field of view affected the instruments of French physicians Pierre Salomon Segalas (1826) and Antonin Jean Desormeaux (1853). Desormeaux, who introduced the term "endoscope," employed a spirit lamp (later fueled by gasogene, a mixture of alcohol and turpentine) to furnish brighter light, and his instrument was produced commercially by Charrière and Luer in Paris. Widespread clinical acceptance came only when Max Nitze, a Dresden urologist, introduced the cystoscope for viewing the urinary bladder interior in 1879. Nitze, in collaboration with Vienna instrument-maker Josef Leiter, installed a light at the distal end of the instrument that improved illumination but radiated only minimal heat. (The first light featured a platinum wire lamp, followed by an incandescent lamp in 1886.) The Nitze-Leiter cystoscope achieved a wider field of view by a lens/prism combination. These changes, which appeared on subsequent instruments, ushered in the era of electroendoscopy.

Endoscopy of the alimentary tract originated in 1868 with the rigid open-tube gastroscope of Adolf Kussmaul, but the procedure languished until 1911, when Hans Elsner added a light and lens to the instrument. Even then, gastroscopy was harrowing for patients and remained uncommon until the advent of the semiflexible Wolf-Schindler gastroscope in

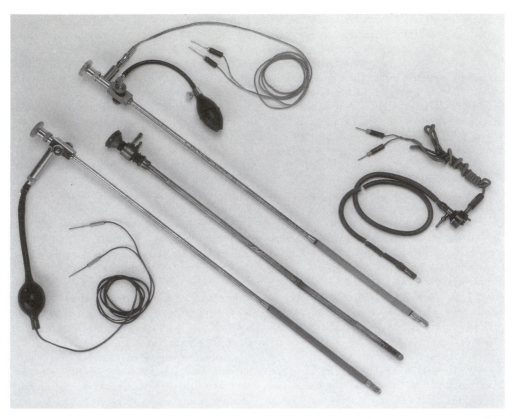

Early twentieth-century gastroscopes: (from left) semi-rigid gastroscope, by the Genito-Urinary Manufacturing Co., ca. 1950; gastroscope by J. Leitner, ca. 1900; Taylor gastroscope, ca. 1940; Kuttner's gastrodiaphanoscope, ca. 1920. SM 1979-707/1, A600263, 1983-881/1088, A647516. Courtesy of SSPL.

1932. Rudolf Schindler, a Munich gastroenterologist, worked with Georg Wolf of Berlin to fashion a "flexible" instrument that bent 34° (achieved by placing a series of short-focal-length lenses in a spiral of bronze, sheathed in rubber). Schindler departed Germany in 1934, and subsequent development of semiflexible instrumentation took place in America. Gastroscope modifications included controlled tip deflection (1941), biopsy forceps (1948), and endoscopic photography (1948).

Bronchoscopy began in 1898 when Gustav Killian of Freiberg adapted a rigid esophagoscope for viewing the trachea and bronchi through a tracheostomy opening. The procedure developed slowly until American laryngologist Chevalier Jackson devised an instrument to be inserted through the mouth in 1907. Instruments designed by Jackson, and produced by Pilling of Philadelphia, propelled bronchoscopy from retrieving foreign objects to diagnosing esophageal and respiratory disease. Bronchoscopes changed little until recently, ex-

cept for illumination by Fourestiere's quartz light rod (1952).

Laparoscopy is the visual examination of the abdomen, specifically the interior of the peritoneal cavity, by means of an endoscope. Dresden surgeon Georg Kelling first performed the procedure in 1901 by inserting an instrument through an abdominal wall incision. In 1910, Hans Christian Jacobaeus of Stockholm, utilizing a cystoscope, established the clinical viability of the procedure and named it "laparoscopy." After 1930 John C. Ruddock and Edward B. Benedict of the United States refined instruments ("peritoneoscopes") for diagnosing liver diseases, ascites, neoplasms of the stomach and colon, and gynecological diseases. Therapeutic laparoscopy in general surgery dates from 1987, when Philippe Mouret, Francois Dubois, and J. Perissat in France introduced laparoscopic cholecystectomy (gallbladder surgery). Laparoscopy is used extensively for appendectomy, gynecological surgery, and a broad spectrum of abdominal surgical procedures. Since 1990, disposable laparoscopic instrumentation has proliferated (now over 70 percent).

Fiberoptic endoscopy dawned in February 1957 when Basil Hirschowitz, in Ann Arbor, Michigan, passed a gastroscope down his throat and, a few days later, down that of a patient. Hirschowitz and colleagues C. Wilbur Peters, Larry Curtis, and Marvin Pollard, inspired by work on fiberoptics by Hopkins and Kapany, had produced coated optical glass fibers and fashioned a prototype endoscope with a bundle of these fibers. Persuaded of the instrument's potential, American Cystoscopic Manufacturers, Inc., (ACMI) introduced the ACMI 4990 Hirschowitz fiberoptic gastroduodenoscope in October 1960. This instrument diminished patient discomfort by enhancing instrument flexibility and by reducing instrument bulk. Notable endoscope refinements of the late 1960s and early 1970s included repositioning of lenses for wider field of vision, addition of channels for biopsy forceps, suction, air, or water, and four-way controlled tip deflection. Endoscopists, citing these improvements, contended that instruments had reached a final developmental plateau. Indeed, fiberoptic technology spread rapidly from gastroscopy to colonoscopy, bronchoscopy, and other endoscopic domains.

Fiberoptics also enhanced the therapeutic potential of endoscopy. For example, the fiberoptic colonoscope, introduced by Olympus and Machida in 1965, was modified by William I. Wolf and Hiromi Shinya in 1971 to perform polypectomies using a wire loop snare. Therapeutic gastrointestinal endoscopy that followed included cannulation of the pancreatic duct (1972), removal of biliary stone (1975), and placement of feeding tubes by gastrostomy (1979).

Video endoscopy began in 1982 when Welch-Allyn, Inc., placed a **charge-coupled device** at the distal end of a gastroscope; the image captured by the CCD was processed by a computer and viewed on a television screen. Clinical trials by Michael Sivak in Cleveland, Ohio, confirmed the instrument's viability, while refinements by Circon/ACMI, Storz, Olympus, Fujinon, and others spawned another revolution in endoscopy. The diameter of controlled-tip, flexible instrument shafts, for example, can be reduced to a mere 2.8 mm, rendering video endoscopes less cumbersome than fiberoptic models. Arthroscopy, laparoscopy, and other endoscopic surgery burgeoned with the advent of video, and continue to displace conventional, invasive surgery.

Coupling the computer and endoscope has transformed the management and manipulation of endoscopic images. Video endoscopy now offers unique advantages for documentation, review of findings, objective comparison of repeated examinations, and teaching. In the future, computers will likely enhance endoscopy still further by facilitating three-dimensional imaging, robotics, and computer simulation of procedures.

James M. Edmonson

Bibliography

Edmonson, James M. "History of the Instruments for Gastrointestinal Endoscopy." *Gastrointestinal Endoscopy* 37 (1991): 27–56.

Hirschowitz, Basil I. "The Development and Application of Fiberoptic Endoscopy." *Cancer* 61 (1988): 1935–41.

Reuter, Hans Joachim, and Matthias A. Reuter. *Philipp Bozzini and Endoscopy in the 19th Century.* Stuttgart: Max Nitze Museum, 1988.

Sivak, Michael, Jr. "Video Endoscopy, the Electronic Endoscopy Unit, and Integrated Imaging." *Bailliere's Clinical Gastroenterology* 5 (March 1991): 1–18.

Stellato, Thomas. "The History of Laparoscopic Surgery." In *Operative Laparoscopy and Thoracoscopy,* edited by Bruce V. MacFayden and Jeffrey L. Ponsky, 3–12. Philadelphia: Lippincott-Raven, 1996.

Equatorium

The word "equatorium" comes from the Latin verb *equare*. One of the verb's medieval meanings is "to calculate the equation of a planet"— that is, to calculate the correction that must be applied to the angular coordinates in order to determine the true longitude of a planet. An equatorium, then, was a computing instrument used to determine the longitude of any one of the planets for any given time, which spared astronomers the tedium of numerical computation, mainly when great accuracy was not required.

Equatoria can be divided into three different groups: geometrical, mathematical, and mechanical. Geometrical equatoria faithfully reproduce the geometrical construction of the planetary models. Mathematical equatoria show the calculation process of the planetary positions, giving the components of the astronomical tables. Mechanical equatoria include

French equatorium, ca. 1600. Courtesy Board of Trustees of the National Museums and Galleries on Merseyside.

gear wheels or other mechanical elements, giving the planets a speed that matches their real motion, in order to show it graphically.

The earliest treatises on this instrument were written in Arabic in Muslim Spain by Ibn al-Samḥ, al-Zarqālluh, and Abū-l-Ṣalt (eleventh and twelfth centuries). However, al-Jazīn (Baghdad, tenth century) may have described a kind of astrolabe-equatorium in his recently found *al-zīj al-ṣafāʾiḥ*. Most of the surviving treatises, how-ever, except that of al-Kāshī's (Samarkand, fifteenth century), were written in Latin Europe between the thirteenth and seventeenth centuries.

Almost all equatoria are based on the Ptolemaic epicyclic theory and assume that planets move in the ecliptic plane. Since the angle between the ecliptic and the plane of the planet's orbit is in all cases small, very little precision is lost in longitude calculations if this angle is made zero, while there is a great gain in simplicity.

According to Ptolemaic theory, the planets move with uniform angular velocity in a small circle (epicycle), the center of which revolves in turn around a larger circle (deferent), eccentric in relation to the center of the universe. Their angular speed is not uniform with regard to the center of the universe, or to its own center, but to a third point called the "equant" placed between the center of the deferent and the center of the universe. These three points are situated on an apse-line whose direction in space is different for each planet and depends on the position of the planet's apogee. The true longitude of a planet, then, can be regarded as a function of two independent variables, the mean longitude (the motion of the epicycle's center in the deferent) and the anomaly (the motion of the planet in the epicycle). There are slight differences between the models of the different planets: the models for Venus, Mars, Jupiter, and Saturn follow the above mentioned rules; the model for the sun is even simpler, as it has no need of an epicycle, nor an equant point, and the theories of Mercury and the moon are more complicated because the center of their deferents is not fixed, but moves along a small circle.

The construction and use of an equatorium requires the consideration of two elements: the parameters of each planet (the eccentricity, the radius of the deferent and the epicycle, and the position of the apogee) and their angular coordinates (the motions of the apogee, of the center of the epicycle on the deferent, and of the planet itself on the epicycle).

The use of an equatorium requires access to mean motion tables for the planets and knowledge of their apogees. Once the movement of the planet in its epicycle and the position of the center of the epicycle in the deferent are known, the only thing that remains is to place the epicycle in the correct position and mark in it the position of the planet. Then with the aid of the alidade it is possible to read the true longitude of a planet directly in the paraecliptic.

We do not know if the Arabic equatoria were known in Latin Europe, although they are mentioned in the Hebrew treatises on these instruments. Be that as it may, several characteristics of the earliest European equatoria suggest the possibility that the Latin authors, like the Hebrew authors, knew of the work of their Arabic predecessors and, taking it as a basis, did their best to improve on it.

Arabic, Hebrew, and the first Latin descriptions of equatoria suggested the use of brass. However, most Latin equatorists used paper or cardboard for their instruments. Of 136 Latin equatoria described by Poulle, in only nine is the use of brass suggested.

The first Latin treatise on the equatorium was the work of Campanus of Novara, who conceived his instrument as a pedagogical aid to his book on the theory of the planets. Equatoria were introduced in university teaching at the end of the twelfth century, but with the advent of printing they became more widely known. Most books on the subject contained the instrument on mobile paper disks. One of the most beautiful and prestigious was the *Astronomicum Caesareum* (1540) of Petrus Apianus.

Henry Bates of Malines, Jean of Linieres, Geoffrey Chaucer, Jean Fusoris, and Guillaume Gilliszoon were among the writers who described geometric equatoria.

The development of mathematical and manual or automatic mechanical instruments began in the fifteenth century. Among the former, the *Organa* by Sebastian Münster, Johann Schöner, and Johann Werner and the *Albion* by Richard of Wallingford were the most important. The most impressive and complex mechanical equatorium was the Astrarium of Giovanni de Dondi, although some others, such as the planetary clock attributed to Oronce Fine and the one made by Baldewein, also deserve mention.

Mercè Comes

Bibliography

Benjamin, Francis S., and Gerald J. Toomer, eds., trans., and authors of commentary. *Campanus of Novara and Medieval Planetary Theory. Theorica planetarum.* Madison: University of Wisconsin Press, 1971.

Comes, Mercè. *Equatorios andalusies: Ibn al-Samḥ, al-Zarqālluh y Abū-l-Ṣalt.* Barcelona: Universidad de Barcelona, 1990–1991.

Kennedy, Edward S. *The Planetary Equatorium of Jamshīd Ghiyāth al-Dīn al-Kāshī.* Princeton: Princeton University Press, 1960.

North, John D., trans., author of introduction, and commentary. *Richard of Wallingford.* Oxford: Clarendon, 1976.

Poulle, Emmanuel. *Les instruments de la théorie des planètes selon Ptolémée: équatoires et horlogerie planétaire du XIIIᵉ au XVIᵉ siècle.* Paris: H. Champion, 1980.

E

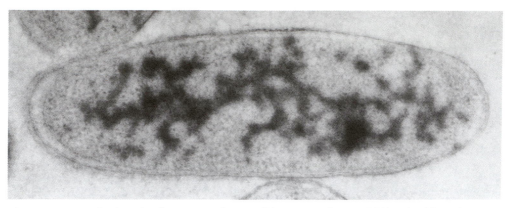

Electron micrograph of an ultrathin section of an E. coli *bacterium, showing DNA stained by an immunological procedure. Carl Robinow and Eduard Kellenberger, "The Bacterial Nucleoid Revisited." Microbiological Reviews 58 (1994): 211-232, Figure 14(c). Courtesy of the American Society of Microbiology.*

Escherichia coli

E. (Escherichia) coli is a small bacterium universally found in the intestinal tract of birds and mammals, including humans. Most strains are part of the normal microflora of healthy individuals, and they probably play some beneficial role in crowding out other, pathogenic bacteria and in providing some traces of rare vitamins.

It may be curious to regard *E. coli* as an instrument. August Krogh had noted, in 1929, "For a large number of problems there will be some animal of choice, or a few such animals, on which it can be most conveniently studied." We do generalize from "animals" to organisms more broadly, from bacteria to yeast, maize, fruit flies, and mice, not to mention human cells for direct experimentation, and human individuals and populations for observation. Except for the difficulties in laboratory culture of many species, it may also be true that every organism is superbly suited to the study of some particular problem. For the difficult to culture, that is already the challenge.

E. coli has become the species of choice for a wide range of biological problems. In 1994, according to the database of the Institute for Scientific Information (ISI), 2,703 published articles included *E. coli* in their titles. This compares to 1,244 for **Drosophila**, 9,156 for the **mouse**, 1,575 for guinea pigs, but only 115 for *Shigella* and 619 for *Salmonella*. The latter two are related bacteria whose importance in disease far outweighs that of *E. coli*. The numbers for mice and guinea pigs reflect the widespread use of these animals for routine tests of toxicity of new drugs and other chemicals. All these numbers are underestimates by a factor of two or so,

as the species name is not always given in the title. For mechanical or electrical instruments, it would be even more problematical how to estimate their importance by counting the literature. But for comparison, 1,733 articles had "mass-spec . . ." in their titles (*see spectrometer, mass*).

The name *Escherichia* honors Theodor Escherich, a German pediatrician who discovered and characterized "Bacterium coli" in 1885 as a common saprophyte in the human colon. It was renamed in 1919 in a revision of bacteriological nomenclature after the term "Bacterium" had become overloaded with too many diverse forms. *E. coli* thus dates to the very origins of modern bacteriology, most of which was preoccupied with dangerous pathogens like the "bacilli" for tuberculosis, pneumonia, cholera, and diphtheria. From the beginning, *E. coli* was used as a representative, harmless bacterium that could be safely and easily cultivated even on synthetic media. With its rapid growth, almost three doublings an hour, it forms readily visible colonies from single cells overnight on agar media. In liquid media, the cloudy growth is readily dispersed, so that single-cell colonies or clones are readily cultivated by simple plating procedures. It is also helpful that several chromogenic media have been devised (Eosin-Methylene Blue; X-gal; tetrazolium) that give vivid reports of various metabolic functions, reflected in colony pigmentation. During the first half of the twentieth century, *E. coli* was probably the single most studied bacterial species for basic physiological and metabolic investigation, but it was rarely mentioned in general biology texts.

The turning point of *E. coli*'s popularity came in the mid 1940s with a series of investigations on bacteriophages grown on *E. coli,* and the demonstration of a form of sexual genetic recombination in the same species. *E. coli* was chosen for these studies because of its favorable husbandry. Soon, the very accumulation of knowledge, mostly concentrated on a single strain, "K-12," made it more likely that it would be a prototype for still further studies. This strain was found to harbor a lysogenic bacteriophage, lambda, which has seeded a scientific industry of its own, and it is the seat of a number of plasmids—intracellular DNA particles transmitted by conjugation. The latter in turn provided the basis for gene-splicing, genetic engineering, and modern biotechnology.

Strain K-12 was isolated in 1922 from human feces and kept for many years as a stock strain in the bacteriology department at Stanford University. In the 1940s, Charles E. Clifton used it for studies of nitrogen metabolism, and his colleague Edward L. Tatum borrowed it initially as a source of the enzyme tryptophanase in his work on the biosynthesis of tryptophane from indole and serine. During many years of cultivation in the laboratory, the strain has lost many of its "Smooth" surface antigens, which is just as well, as it provides further assurance of its harmlessness to people. K-12 entered the domain of genetics with Tatum's pioneering studies on the production of nutritionally deficient mutants in 1944. That work attracted my own attention and led to a collaboration and discovery of sexual recombination in 1946. Since then, K-12 has been used by thousands of other investigators for innumerable genetic studies, and its genome has by now been almost completely mapped and much of its DNA sequenced. In retrospect, we know how lucky was the choice of strain K-12. With the methods used in 1946, only one *E. coli* strain in twenty, chosen at random, would have been successfully crossed.

Some of the most important of the scientific applications have been in the field of gene regulation, and the elaboration of the concept of the "operon," with work centered at the Pasteur Institute in Paris. The Nobel prizes earned by Francois Jacob and Jacques Monod are but two of the dozen that by my account are affiliated with *E. coli*. The operon is a cluster of DNA structures that are repressed or activated to regulate the activities of several genes downstream on the same DNA strand. Monod is attributed with the aphorism that "what is true for *E. coli* will be true for the elephant," and by

implication the human. He had in mind particularly the theory of tissue differentiation in embryological development. This has proven to be somewhat overoptimistic, and it points to one of the limitations of *E. coli* (or other bacteria) as a model for general biology. The chromosome structure of *E. coli,* generally a simple circle, is far less convoluted than that of eukaryotic cells, which are complexed with histones and subject to several orders of folding to generate the compact visible chromosomes. This is in keeping with the modest genome size of bacteria, measured in millions of nucleotide units, compared with three billion for the human. Nor do bacteria show the complex patterns of differentiation characteristic of higher eukaryotes. A simple, unicellular eukaryote, yeast, has come a long way to filling in this instrumental gap, as is reflected in its 2,435 articles in the ISI database.

For many years, another serious limitation of *E. coli* was the difficulty of introducing extraneous DNA into its cells; this has now been overcome with tricks like electroporation (high-voltage zaps) and exposure to calcium phosphate gels.

What more could be asked of this instrument? I have four suggestions:

1. To isolate or select for still more rapid growth, perhaps at higher temperatures. However, *E. coli* may already be close to the theoretical limits set by the pace of biosynthetic machinery.
2. To excise extraneous segments of DNA and reduce its genome size by half or more, partly in the service of more rapid growth.
3. To enhance the efficiency of spontaneous uptake of DNA, to emulate, for example, *Acinetobacter.*
4. To introduce the capacity for durable spores, to assist in the long-term preservation of cultures—which now entails liquid nitrogen temperatures.

But it is doubtful if these advantages would be worth giving up any of the existing panoply, and especially the enormous backlog of knowledge represented in a literature that must now encompass perhaps fifty thousand publications. It may not be too fanciful to expect that these enhancements could be achieved with the continued reengineering of strain K-12 itself.

Joshua Lederberg

Bibliography

Krogh, A. "The Progress of Physiology." *American Journal of Physiology* 90 (1929): 243–51.

Lederberg, J. "Edward Lawrie Tatum." *Biographical Memoirs of the National Academy of Sciences* 59 (1990): 357–86.

———. "Genetic Recombination in Bacteria: A Discovery Account." *Annual Review of Genetics* 21 (1987): 23–46.

Miller, Jeffrey. *A Short Course in Bacterial Genetics: A Laboratory Manual and Handbook for* Escherichia coli *and Related Bacteria.* Cold Spring Harbor, N.Y.: Cold Spring Harbor Laboratory, 1992.

Neidhardt, Frederick C., ed. Escherichia coli *and* Salmonella typhimurium: *Cellular and Molecular Biology.* Washington, D.C.: American Society for Microbiology, 1987.

Sussman, M. "Theodor Escherich (1857–1911): A Biographical Note." In *The Virulence of* Escherichia coli, edited by M. Sussman, 1–4. London: Academic, 1985.

Eudiometer

By any normative account, the eudiometer would be classified as a failed instrument. From a technical viewpoint, its structure and calibration were never standardized. In terms of application, its various uses tied the eudiometer to long-abandoned beliefs such as phlogiston chemistry and aerial medicine. To the historian of science, however, the eudiometer opens a fascinating and enlightening tale of the relations among instrumentation, theory development, and social context.

Based on Joseph Priestley's "nitrous air test," which he first described in his *Experiments and Observations on Different Kinds of Air* (1774), natural philosophers such as Felice Fontana and Marcilio Landriani designed a variety of instruments in which a test air might be combined with nitrous air (now known as nitric oxide) over water or mercury, and the consequent diminution of its volume measured. Landriani coined the term "eudiometer" to indicate that the level of diminution was taken as a measure of the test air's "goodness." Priestley had intended his nitrous air test to serve as an objective alternative to testing the salubrity of air by smelling it or timing how long a mouse survived in it, but none of the instrumental designs promoted for standardizing the test were accepted as providing stable and reliable readings. Technical reasons reported at the time include the expense and chemically active nature of mercury, the propensity of water to imbibe airs that sat over it for extended periods of time, and the apparent inability to standardize the nitrous air used in different places and at different times.

The eudiometer inhabited a web of contention that encompassed far more than narrowly defined technical issues, however. When Priestley and his associates spoke of an air's "goodness," they sought to link the study of atmospheric virtue and health with phlogiston chemistry. Arguing that good air supported both combustion and respiration, and that it was sensibly diminished when mixed with nitrous air, they placed airs on a sort of sliding scale of phlogistication, associating the wholesomeness of air with its ability to absorb the greatest quantity of exhaled phlogiston possible. Armed with this theoretical perspective, eudiometers were recruited for a variety of enlightenment projects intended to monitor and improve the atmosphere in which the public lived and worked. They were used to determine the relative healthfulness of various locales, ranging from factories and graveyards to marshlands, potential urban sites, and farmlands. The success of these projects, and therefore practical acceptance of the eudiometer, rested on establishing a link between the data eudiometers generated and contemporary beliefs about environmental causes of ill health, and simultaneously on the backing of royal patrons to pursue such projects. With the decline of enlightened despotism in Italy and growing conservatism in Great Britain by the end of the eighteenth century, support for eudiometric monitoring of public health was abandoned.

Beginning in 1777, Allesandro Volta introduced a modification in eudiometric procedures by combining and firing his test gases with an electric spark. This reconfiguration of the eudiometer's instrumental space provided a path that linked this "sparking eudiometer" to another, equally complex, social and theoretical trajectory. Taken up by Lavoisier in service of his expectation that combining inflammable and vital airs (hydrogen and oxygen) would yield an acid, it became the preliminary site for his claim that their combination actually yielded water. Once convinced that water was a compound substance, Lavoisier and his associates employed their claim as potent evidence for the truth of the "new" chemistry. Ironically, then,

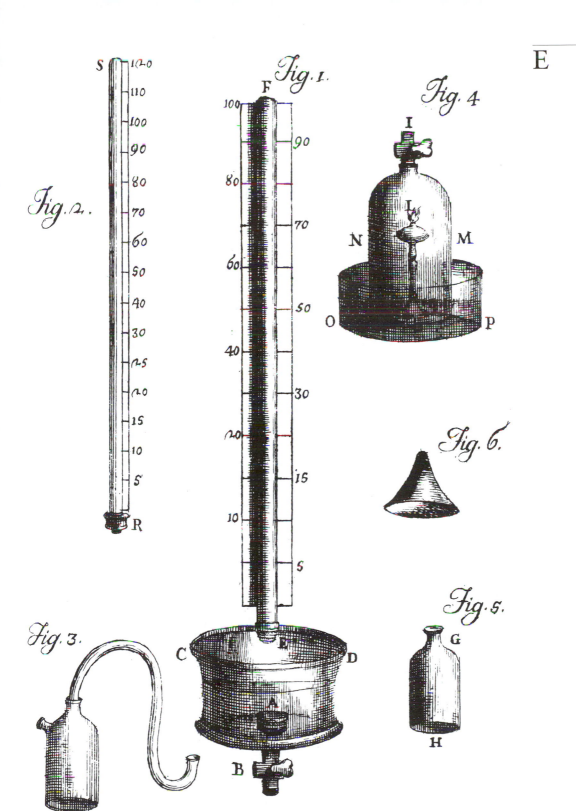

Landriani's apparatus for testing "the goodness of the air." Marsilio Landriani, Ricerche fisiche intorno alla salubrita dell'aria. *Milan, 1775: Plate 2. Courtesy of the Wellcome Institute Library, London.*

while the eudiometer owed its initial conception to the claimed existence of phlogiston, its deployment in a different experimental and theoretical setting enmeshed it in a system that would eclipse the work of Priestley and other phlogistonists.

Eudiometers were still employed both experimentally and didactically in the early nineteenth century, but their connection to the initial settings of phlogiston chemistry, environmental medicine, and ancien régime reform projects faded. Nitrous air eudiometers ceased to be an active research site, while further modifications of Volta's "sparking eudiometer" and instruments that relied on various chemical reactions retreated back within chemical laboratories, where they were used to measure the oxygen content of gaseous mixtures. Divorced from chemical controversy and ambitious reform programs, they retired to a life of humble and uncontentious laboratory service, finally dying out from benign neglect.

Lissa Roberts

Bibliography

Fontana, Felice. "Account of the Airs Extracted from Different Kinds of Waters." *Philosophical Transactions of the Royal Society of London* 69 (1779): 432–53.

Golinski, Jan. *Science as Public Culture: Chemistry and Enlightenment in Britain, 1760–1820.* Cambridge: Cambridge University Press, 1992.

Landriani, Marsilio. "Lettre." *Observation sur la Physique* 6 (1775): 315–16.

Magellan, Jean-Hyacinthe. *Description of a Glass Apparatus for Making Mineral Waters.* London: W. Parker, 1777.

Priestley, Joseph. *Experiments and Observations on Different Kinds of Air.* London: J. Johnson, 1777.

Schaffer, Simon. "Measuring Virtue: Eudiometry, Enlightenment and Pneumatic Medicine." In *The Medical Enlightenment of the Eighteenth Century,* edited by Andrew Cunningham and Roger French, 281–318. Cambridge: Cambridge University Press, 1990.

Explosives, Instruments to Test the Ballistic Force of

Exterior Ballistics

The standard means of testing military powder throughout the eighteenth century was the mortar-eprouvette. This was a small mortar that used a fixed amount of powder to project a cannon ball of standard size and weight in an open field. The mortar-eprouvette received constant criticism for imperfections and irregularities in its results; most seriously, it came to be recognized that denser, larger-grained powders exerted less apparent ballistic force in the mortar even though the reverse was true in actual cannon. Yet it continued in use into the second half of the nineteenth century.

But a more sensitive instrument, with which it was feasible to deduce actual projectile velocities, had long been available. This was the ballistic pendulum invented by the military engineer and mathematician Benjamin Robins, first described in his *New Principles of Gunnery* (1742).

In order to determine muzzle velocities from the ballistic pendulum data, it was necessary to know something about how the ballistic velocity fell off with distance from the pendulum. The principal factor was air resistance; Robins was the first student of ballistics to develop both theoretical and experimental data on this. His work was the point of departure for over a century of investigation. The relationship of air resistance to projectile velocity proved to be very complicated.

Robins conducted his experiments with a comparatively small apparatus. A century later, massive ballistic pendulums could take firings from large cannon. The American ordnance officer Alfred Mordecai used a ballistic pendulum weighing 9,358 pounds (empty) and 24- and 32-pounder test guns in the extensive ballistic tests he carried out at the Washington Arsenal in 1843 and 1844.

Electroballistic **chronographs** permitted the measurement of the velocity of a projectile while it was in flight. They also had the advantages of greatly reduced bulk and superior portability. Finally, they could measure velocities of projectiles shot by guns in positions other than the horizontal. This family of ballistic instruments depended on developments in electromagnetism. Charles Wheatstone introduced the idea around 1840, and it was taken up by ballistic inventors all over Europe almost immediately. They all operated on the same principle: the rupturing of a sequence of target electrical circuits by a fired projectile; the consequent deactivation of electromagnets contained in each circuit caused a succession of marks to be made on a recording apparatus. The intervals between the marks were convertible into the time intervals between target ruptures and hence, velocity data, since the distances between targets were predetermined.

Most electroballistic chronographs permitted the velocity between only two targets to be determined at a time. However, Schultz's chronograph (1864) enabled velocities between several consecutive targets to be measured. Improved ballistic chronographs (for example, using the fundamental frequency of a quartz crystal in place of the tuning fork as the timing device) continued in use until the middle of the twentieth century.

Interior Ballistics

All explosions or detonations involve rapid volumetric expansion of explosive gases; it is the pressure generated by the sudden thermal and volumetric change that propels the projectile down the gun barrel. Attempts to measure the volumetric changes of gunpowder explosion began in the late seventeenth century; early determinations were in the range of 220 to 240 times the volume of the powder sample itself, at normal temperature. Taking account of the elevated temperature of actual explosion, Benjamin Robins concluded that volumetric expansion was about one thousand times the volume of the powder; hence, the maximum pressure of fired powder was 1,000 atm. or " 6 Tun Weight" per square inch.

Robins assumed instant explosion of gunpowder when a gun was fired, and he asserted that there is a linear relationship between gunpowder "density" (volumetric proportion of firing chamber filled by powder) and pressure. These assumptions, as well as Robins's maximum pressure determination, were challenged by the American expatriate Benjamin Thompson (Count Rumford) and others. In experiments conducted in Munich in 1793, Rumford attempted to measure the pressure of gunpowder explosions. He was able to plot a curve correlating powder quantity to explosive pressure that disputed Robins's linear correlation. And he determined pressures that were vastly greater than Robins's maximum of 1,000 atm.: experimentally over 10,000 atm., by extrapolation from his curve for maximum pressure over 29,000 atm., and factoring thermal expansion, 128,000 atm. Although Rumford's values proved to be much too high, they were lauded as the first attempt to directly measure the pressure of fired gunpowder.

The next advance on Rumford's measurement of interior pressure was made in the late 1850s by an American ordnance officer, T.J.

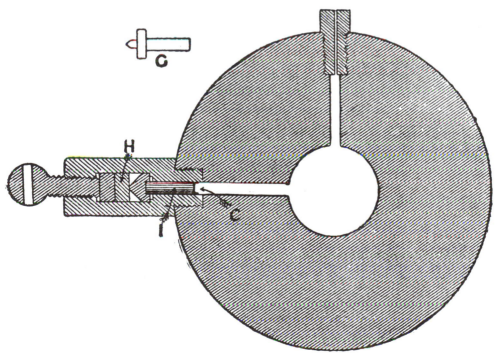

Major Rodman's pressure gauge to calculate pressure at various points along the bore of a gun. Noble (1906): 488. Courtesy of SSPL.

Rodman. Rodman was particularly concerned with controlling the pressure generated by gunpowder explosion in the bore of the gun, both to minimize the dangers of guns bursting from too high an initial pressure in the breech (which had become a major problem in large breech-loading guns) and to improve the ballistic effectiveness of the powder charge. Rodman took a systemic approach to these challenges, by developing an instrument for determining the gunbore pressure, and by experimentally determining the shape for powder—the "perforated cake cartridge"—that would most nearly equalize the pressure down the gun bore and thus ensure maximum muzzle velocity.

His own name for his pressure-measuring instrument, the "indenting apparatus" (subsequently referred to as the Rodman pressure or cutter-gauge), aptly describes the modus operandi of the instrument. Placed either in the cartridge at the base of the bore or screwed into the bore wall, the instrument consisted of a piston with a knife edge in contact with a disk of soft metal such as copper. The explosion pressure acted on the piston and forced the knife edge into the metal disk, the penetration of the knife correlative with the degree of pressure.

Rodman's pressure gauge was rapidly adopted. In England, Andrew Noble produced the crusher gauge, primarily by getting rid of the knife edge and substituting a cylinder of copper for Rodman's disk, the compression of which against an anvil is correlative with the pressure. The modern descendant of these pressure gauges is the pressure transducer, the most popular of which, the piezoelectric transducer, uses a quartz plate, the compression of which produces an electric charge as a signal. However, for large guns, the copper crusher gauge was still cited as being in use in 1979.

Seymour H. Mauskopf

Bibliography

Fisher, E.B. "Research Test Techniques Applied to Gun Interior Ballistics." In *Interior Ballistics of Guns,* edited by Herman Krier and Martin Sommerfield, Vol. 66, 281–306. [New York]: American Institute of Aeronautics and Astronautics, 1979.
Noble, Andrew. *Artillery and Explosives.* London: John Murray, 1906.
Robins, Benjamin. *New Principles of Gunnery.* London: J. Nourse, 1742. Reprint. Richmond, Surrey: Richmond, 1972.
Steele, Brett D. "Muskets and Pendulums: Benjamin Robins, Leonhard Euler, and the Ballistics Revolution." *Technology and Culture* 35 (1994): 348–82.
Thompson, Benjamin Count Rumford. "Experiments to Determine the Force of Fired Gunpowder." In *Collected Works of Count Rumford,* edited by Sanborn C. Brown, Vol. 4, 395–471. Cambridge: Harvard University Press, 1970.

Exposure Meter

An exposure meter (commonly, but imprecisely, termed a light meter) measures light intensity for photographic purposes. The measure obtained may be applied to a table or calculator or shown directly as an exposure setting for a camera.

Exposure time has always been an important factor in the production of photographs. Early photographic processes required long exposure times, and the individually prepared sensitive materials responded inconsistently. A photographer would commonly calculate exposures by trial and error using experience to produce acceptable results. This changed in the 1880s with the widespread introduction of mass-produced dry plates that had a consistent and predictable response and that allowed exposure times of fractions of a second. The first scientific investigation into the characteristics of photosensitive materials were carried out by Ferdinand Hurter and Vero Charles Driffield during this period. They established a method whereby each batch of dry plates could be given a speed number that could form the basis of a reliable calculation of exposure. An exposure meter or calculator now became a much more useful aid, and most exposure meters date from the 1880s or later.

All exposure meters can be classified into one of four types: **actinometers**, visual or extinction meters, comparison **photometers**, and photoelectric meters. Actinometers (sometimes called tintmeters) employ a small piece of sensitive paper and measure the time taken for it to darken to standard tint. Typically, the meters incorporated a roll or disk of sensitive paper. A fresh piece of this paper was placed next to the standard tint and exposed to light falling on the subject of the photograph. When the two tints matched, the time taken was then used to calculate the length of exposure by reference to tables. In a variation of the idea, the sensitive paper was exposed for a fixed time under an optical wedge with windows of gradually increasing density.

The principle of the actinometer was suggested by W.H.F. Talbot as early as 1840, as a means of calculating the time needed to print-out a negative. Several instruments known as print meters were devised for this purpose in subsequent years, notably for printing-out processes such as carbon tissue and platinotype, in which the formation of the image could not be directly inspected. The introduction of the fast dry emulsions, which established the need for exposure meters, also promoted a boom in amateur photography, and many inexpensive, practical actinometers were introduced in the 1880s and 1890s. Some of the most popular instruments were based on a patent of January 27, 1890, by Alfred Watkins of Hereford, England. Watkins's patent described a tubular form of combined tintmeter and calculator, the first of several Watkins actinometers successfully marketed for over thirty years. Watkins's most successful instrument was a watch form meter based on a patent of 1902. Introduced as the Bee meter, variations of the model were sold in enormous numbers up until 1939.

Although actinometers were very popular around the turn of the century, they were gradually displaced from favor after World War I. They were slow in action compared with other methods, not suitable for use with panchromatic materials, and could not be used in artificial light.

The visual or extinction meter was designed to assist the eye to make a direct measure of light intensity. It normally consisted of a tube or disk containing an optical wedge, a variable-density filter linked to a numbered scale through which the photographer viewed the subject. The wedge was adjusted until an appropriate part of the subject just became invisible. This gave a reading of the brightness at that part which could then be used to calculate an exposure.

The first extinction meter to be widely used was patented in 1887 by J. Decoudin. This was a disk-shaped meter that measured the brightness of a selected area on the ground glass focusing screen of a camera. An early tubular meter was the Tylers Pickard exposure meter of 1889, which, like other meters of this type, was held to the eye like a telescope. Simple, inexpensive visual meters of both disk and tubular type were widely sold in the 1920s and 1930s. These visual meters worked well at very low light levels. They were produced well into the 1950s,

but disappeared when their limitations for color photography became apparent and the price of more accurate photoelectric meters was dramatically reduced.

A major source of error when using visual meters was due to accommodation adjustments and variations in the eye of the user. Such errors could be eliminated if the light measured could be compared with a standard source. The well-tried laboratory photometer was adapted for photographic purposes by Harold Dennis Taylor of England, who patented a portable instrument in 1885. Taylor's photometer used a candle in a tubular housing as the standard light source. It was described in a contemporary handbook as an "elaborate instrument" but "very perfect in action." Comparison instruments using luminous material as the standard light source were offered to photographers from the 1880s to about 1930 but were never popular. Photometers using electric light sources were designed for the photographic market in the 1920s and 1930s, and enjoyed a little more success. Improved versions were introduced after World War II. Although some of the later models of the spot photometer, such as the S.E.1. introduced in England in 1947, were particularly accurate, they always sold in small numbers. As was the case with other forms of exposure meters, comparison photometers were displaced from the photographic market in the 1950s by the widespread availability of inexpensive, reliable photoelectric meters.

The photoelectric exposure meter was made possible by the discovery in the 1870s that the element selenium has an electrical conductivity that varies according to the quantity of light falling on it. Although exposure devices making use of this property were described in the 1880s, the first photoelectric exposure meter to be widely sold was the American Rhamistine Electrophot, marketed in 1931. This contained a selenium cell connected to a 3-volt battery and meter. A year later, Weston of Newark, New Jersey, produced the Universal 617 meter, the first commercial photoelectric meter to use the output of a selenium cell alone. During the next few years, a plethora of photoelectric meters were marketed in America and Europe. Designs were produced for both photographic and cinematographic work. Two main types of meter evolved. The reflected-light meter was pointed at the subject to be photographed, recording the light reflected from it. The incident-light meter was pointed at the light source and recorded the light falling on the subject. The latter type derived from P.C. Smethurst's British

Avo-Smethurst High-Light exposure meter, by the Automatic Coil Winder and Electrical Equipment Co. Ltd., 1937. SM 197. Courtesy of SSPL.

sulphide cells, in which light falling on the cell causes a change in resistance, began to replace selenium cells in the late 1950s. Although requiring a battery, they were much smaller and more sensitive than the earlier selenium cells. The concept of the camera's incorporating a photoelectric exposure meter was also developed in this period, and the fully automatic camera is now commonplace.

The separate exposure meter is now used largely by professional photographers and cinematographers in special situations. Models adapted from photoelectric exposure meters and scaled in lux units are employed by interior designers, shopfitters, conservators, and museum and gallery curators to measure light levels in areas containing paintings, historic artifacts, or sensitive fabrics.

John Ward

patent of 1936, which suggested covering the photo cell with a diffusing medium. This was marketed in 1937 as the Avo-Smethurst High-Light Meter.

In 1938 Eastman Kodak marketed the first camera incorporating a photoelectric cell for exposure control. In the years following World War II, new production techniques lowered the price of photoelectric meters to the point where they displaced all other types of exposure meter from the market. Cadmium

Bibliography

Coe, Brian. *Cameras: From Daguerreotypes to Instant Pictures.* London: Marshall Cavendish, 1978.

Hurter, Ferdinand, and Vero C. Driffield. *The Photographic Researches of Ferdinand Hurter and Vero C. Driffield.* Edited by W.B. Ferguson. London: Royal Photographic Society, 1920.

Stroebel, Leslie, and Richard Zakia, eds. *The Focal Encyclopedia of Photography.* Rev. ed. London: Focal, 1965.

Thomas, D.B. *The Science Museum Photography Collection.* London: Her Majesty's Stationery Office, 1969.

F

Fatigue Testing Instruments

Fatigue is defined as the damage to a structural member caused by repeated application of stresses that are insufficient to induce failure by a single application. The phenomenon was described in 1843 by W.J. Macquorn Rankine, afterwards professor of engineering at the University of Glasgow, and named "fatigue" by J. Braithwaite in 1854. In 1917 Bernard P. Haigh identified the related phenomenon, now known as corrosion fatigue, in which metals suffer reductions in load resistance if they are subjected to alternating stress and to the action of corrosives.

In 1850 the Institution of Mechanical Engineers, then based in Birmingham, England, held a series of discussions on the deterioration of wrought-iron railway axles. Archibald Slate described a fatigue testing machine in which he had subjected a bar, 1 in. square, to a constant load of 5 tons and an additional load of 2.5 tons that was reversed up to ninety times per minute, for a period equivalent to ninety years' life in railway service. Slate did not find any harmful effect on the iron and continued to believe that the phenomenon occurred only if the elastic limit of the material was exceeded. Nevertheless, axles designed to these limits kept breaking.

The first comprehensive investigations of fatigue were made by a German railway official, August Wöhler, between 1860 and 1870. He made repeated stress tests in bending, torsion, and axial load on prepared specimens. Although his machines were slow, his conclusions regarding material fatigue limits was a percentage of ultimate tensile strength remain unchallenged.

Wöhler's name survives in his rotating cantilever test-piece. Here the test-piece is gripped at one end in a chuck and loaded at the other by a dead weight acting through a ball race. (Wöhler's 1858 machine had used a spring and a ring-bearing with two such cantilevers aligned on either side of a pulley wheel.) The shape of the Wöhler test-piece is now defined in international technical standards such that changes in cross-section are gradual and well-radiused to avoid points of high stress concentration. The cantilevered test-piece is rotated so that each portion is alternately stressed in tension and compression.

In 1890 Jerome Sondericker introduced a rotating beam test-piece supported at both ends and loaded vertically at two points equidistant from the center. This gave a uniform bending moment over the middle of the test-piece and avoided the shear stresses found in the cantilever method. The specimen is reduced in the center to avoid fracture in the areas of stress concentration, and the supports are pivoted about horizontal axes perpendicular to that of the specimen.

Since wire has a uniform cross-section, a rotating beam test is most likely to fracture at the grips. This difficulty was overcome in a machine patented by Haigh and Thomas S. Robertson in 1932. Here the test-piece is flexed as a strut so that the maximum bending moment occurs in the mid span. The machine operated at around fifteen million revolutions per day. The R.R. Moore reversed-bending fatigue machine, made for the Southwark Division of the Baldwin Locomotive Works in the United States, subjected cylindrical specimens to pure bending moments free from transverse shear forces at speeds of 12,000 rpm.

In the 1850 Birmingham discussions, John Ramsbottom noted that since the railway axles always failed at the inner edge of the wheel seats, the whole design should be considered. As

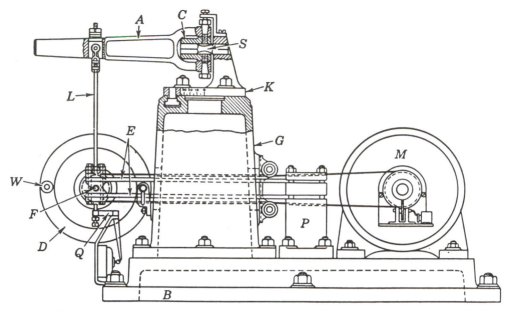

Combined Torsion-Bending-Fatigue machine developed at the British National Physical Laboratory.
Handbook of Experimental Stress Analysis, *edited by Miklos Hetényi. New York: Wiley, 1950: 57, Figure 2-27. Courtesy of the Society for Experimental Mechanics.*

was later confirmed, the shape and configuration of components could be more important in assessing likelihood of failures than the fatigue limit of a carefully prepared sample.

Several direct stress machines based on constant deflection or constant amplitude were developed in the early twentieth century. The simpler models were restricted to prepared samples in which simple stresses were induced by bending, axial, or torsion loads. Simple bending examples include the 1934 fixed-cantilever constant amplitude fatigue machine by G.N. Krouse, the Avery Co. reverse bending machine, and the 1940 inertia flexure machine designed by the Sonntag Scientific Corp.

Axial loads, both tension and compression, can be applied by attaching different fixtures to the Sonntag machine. Other axial load machines include the 1925 Jasper Co.'s constant deformation spring-type machine; Haigh's 1926 machine in which the specimen was moved back and forth between two electromagnets; the Avery Co.'s 1954 Pulsator, which operated by the oscillation of a coil spring excited by a motor-driven out-of-balance rotating mass; and the 1960 hydraulically operated machine, made by the Losenhausen firm, which had a dynamic load range of 50 tons imposed by an oil pump setting up pulsations at frequencies up to six hundred cycles per minute.

Torsional fatigue has been investigated with a number of ingenious machines, such as the 1934 constant deflection torsion fatigue machine by H.F. Moore and the Vibrotor of 1954, in which the test-piece is carried in a stator in which torsional oscillations are produced by turning a toothed rotor within it.

In 1934, Britain's National Physical Laboratory developed a mechanical simulator, especially to test the torsion-bending fatigue found in crankshafts. The test-piece can be swiveled in relation to the lever through which the alternating load is applied. When the lever is out of line with the test-piece it applies a combination of bending and torsion, the latter increasing in proportion to the sine of the angle between lever and test-piece.

Biaxial tensile repeated stresses, as found in tubular specimens subjected to fluctuating internal pressure and axial stress, were also mimicked mechanically, but in the 1930s the fastest rate possible for such a configuration was two hundred cycles per minute. This limitation was passed in the 1940s by reliable electromagnetic resonant frequency vibrators. In the Amsler Co.'s 1959 Vibrophone, the load is applied at the natural frequency of the specimen plus loading train, and the load amplitude is a function of the driving current in the electromagnet. Changes in frequency are achieved by changes in the mass of the loading train.

Resonant machines operated at higher frequencies than contemporary mechanically driven machines. In the 1970s the former had load capacities up to 450 kN, the latter up to 1,000 kN.

Since the 1960s, servo-controlled machines have provided a more flexible way of mimicking dynamic loads. Here the signal from the load- (or displacement- or strain-) measuring device is compared with a command input signal representing the controlled variable, using a differential amplifier. The output from the differential amplifier then drives the servo-valve that controls the machine's actuator. There is thus a control loop that enables the machine response to follow the command. Selected service load histories and random loading as well as block program and constant amplitude testing can be undertaken with such a machine.

Since the 1930s, special testing rigs have been used for box-girders, aircraft-engine mounts, and locomotive driving axles. Since the 1950s, complete air-frames have been tested to destruction in a test-rig that simulates cabin-pressure changes and wing flexing during flight. Since the 1980s, reliable high-speed actuators and digital servo-hydraulic controllers have permitted simulation of the loads imposed on vehicles on test tracks, or on industrial equipment, from recordings of actual conditions in remote sites. Such systems were promoted as "digitally integrated testing laboratories."

Wheel-tapping, the most popular nondestructive test for a manufactured component in service, also originated in the 1850 Birmingham discussions on railways. The sharp impact of the hammer sets up a vibration, and any change in vibration due to a hidden fatigue-induced crack may be detected by a difference in the sound.

Robert C. McWilliam

Bibliography

Gough, Herbert J., and H.V. Pollard. "The Strength of Metals under Combined Alternating Stresses." *Proceedings of the Institution of Mechanical Engineers* 131 (1935): 3–103.

Lazan, B.J. "Some Mechanical Properties of Plastics and Metals under Sustained Vibrations." *Transactions of the American Society of Mechanical Engineers* 65 (1943): 87–104.

Moore, H.F., and J.B. Kommers. *The Fatigue of Metals.* New York: McGraw-Hill, 1927.

Peterson, R.E. "Fatigue Tests of Large Specimens." *Proceedings of the American Society for Testing and Materials* 29, part 2 (1929): 371–79.

Timoshenko, Stephen P. *History of the Strength of Materials.* New York: McGraw-Hill, 1953. Reprint. New York: Dover, 1982.

Field Ion Microscope

See MICROSCOPE, FIELD ION

Fire Detector

A fire detector automatically senses the presence of fire by responding to heat, smoke, or infrared or ultraviolet radiation. It is normally referred to by the type of sensing element it contains, and it is usually linked to other devices to form a fire alarm or automatic extinguishing system. New types and applications of fire detectors have often resulted from the application of new technologies from other areas of science or industry. This has led to a large number of patents, but poor historical documentation of developments.

The early fire alarm systems used electrical transmission techniques to summon the fire brigade but relied on human detection of the fire. Alarms of this sort were installed in Berlin in 1849 and in Boston in 1852. Automatic detection using heat sensors was developed approximately twenty years later.

Heat Detectors

Early sensors responded solely to heat, and were commonly referred to as thermostats. More than thirty different makes appeared on the market between 1873 and 1900. Some used the differential expansion of metals in the form of a bimetallic strip to close electrical contacts; others used the expansion of a range of fluids, including air and ether, to expand bellows. A modification of the mercury in glass thermometers was also used as a heat-sensitive switch.

Thermostats would be set to trigger at preset temperatures of between 55 and 70°C. It was realized that, in temperate climates, this could represent a substantial rise in temperature. However, since lowering the trigger tempera-

Fox-Peterson fire detector, ca. 1901. Harold G. Holt. (1913): 162, Figure 93. Courtesy of SSPL.

ture could result in false alarms, detectors were developed with a two-stage approach. The Fox-Peterson Detector (1901) had two separate sets of contacts designed to give a caution warning followed by an alarm if the upper temperature limit was exceeded.

A heat detector that can respond to rate-of-rise of temperature is potentially more sensitive than fixed-temperature devices, and, by 1913, eight different systems of this sort had been approved by the Fire Offices' Committee in the U.K. Some sensed conditions at a point, while others used small-bore tubing that could be ceiling mounted and monitor average temperatures over a substantial area. The fluid in the tubing was normally air, which, when it underwent thermal expansion, would exert a force within bellows attached to one end of the tubing. A small pilot hole in the wall of the tube near the bellows would leak air in a controlled manner. Hence low rates of temperature rise would cause no increase in pressure, but higher rates of rise would close an electrical contact.

The May-Oatway system, unusual because of its size and simplicity, used a copper wire sensor, the ends of which were connected to a short compensating steel channel fixed to the ceiling. A rapid rise in temperature would cause the copper to expand, and either lower a silvered cone onto electrical contacts or tilt a mercury switch. A gradual rise in temperature would cause both the copper wire and the steel channel to slowly expand in unison and hence the copper would not sag to the same extent. However, the coefficient of expansion of copper is approximately 1.5 times that of steel, and so the detector would switch before excessively high temperatures were reached.

Smoke Detectors

These were developed for use on ships and aircraft where large volumes of smoke would be generated before there was any significant increase in temperature. They were in use in buildings in the 1950s but were not officially approved in the U.K. until the early 1960s. There are two types of smoke detectors. The photoelectric detector senses the obscuration or scattering of a beam of light. The **ionization chamber** senses changes in the conductivity of air bombarded by alpha particles.

With the early photoelectric detectors, a beam of light was projected across a space, and the receiver measured the change in intensity resulting from the partial obscuration of the light source by smoke. Such a system was also incorporated into point-type devices; here the transmitter and receiver with a small beam path were mounted in one unit. Other point-type devices sensed the scattering of light as smoke entered a chamber containing a light source and sensor mounted in such a way that the sensor does not normally receive any light. Smoke particles entering the chamber reflected light onto the sensor to trigger the detector.

Early photoelectric detectors used tungsten filament bulbs with a life expectancy of approximately 5,000 hours and relatively inefficient sensors. Photoelectric detectors in the 1980s used pulsed infrared light-emitting diodes and fast, low-current photodiode sensors. Current consumption of point-type sensors is typically short-duration 100 µA peaks at intervals of 5 seconds or more.

The ionization chamber smoke detector developed in the 1960s consisted of one or two ionization chambers and associated current-sensing and switching circuits. Air within the chambers was bombarded with alpha particles from a small radioactive source. A dc voltage of approximately 200 volts applied across the chambers caused the ions to migrate and produce a small flow of current. Smoke particles entering one of the chambers collide with ions and reduce the migration rate, thus causing a small but detectable reduction in current. Early devices used a cold cathode trigger tube to provide the output signal.

The advent of the field effect transistor and its ability to amplify currents of nano-amps, together with low-cost electronic amplifiers, made it possible to use a smaller ionization chamber running at much lower voltages and to produce a commercially viable ionization chamber smoke sensor. Linking this technology with high-efficiency piezoelectric sounders and long-life batteries produced the domestic single-point smoke alarm of today.

Nigel Smithies

Bibliography

Crosby, Everett U., and Henry A. Fiske. *Hand-book of Fire Protection for Improved Risks.* Boston: Standard, 1904.

Holt, Harold G. *Fire Protection in Buildings.* London: Crosby Lockwood, 1913.

Tryton, George H., and Gordon P. McKinnon, eds. *Fire Protection Handbook.* 13th ed. Boston: National Fire Protection Association International, 1969.

Underwood, G.W. *Electrical Fire Alarm Systems.* London: Lomax, Erskin, 1946.

Flow Cytometer

Cytometry refers to the measurement of physical or chemical characteristics of cells or other biological particles. In a flow cytometer, measurements of such characteristics as electrical impedance, light scattering behavior, and the fluorescence of cell-bound labeled antibodies and other dyes are made while the cells pass through the measuring apparatus in a fluid stream. On the basis of measured parameter values, subpopulations of cells in mixed populations can be identified, counted, and separated for further study.

Prehistory

Between the 1930s and the 1950s, the basis for much of modern cytometry was established by Torbjörn Caspersson and his colleagues in Stockholm. They combined microscopy and spectroscopy, using precise measurement of the ultraviolet and visible absorption of individual unstained cells to quantify changes in nucleic acid (DNA and RNA) and protein content during normal and abnormal cell growth.

In 1934, Andrew Moldavan proposed counting cells by using a photoelectric sensor to detect changes in optical extinction as a cell suspension flowed through a capillary tube; his phraseology, however, suggested that the device had not yet been reduced to practice.

It was known by the 1920s that light scattering, observed in a dark-field **microscope**, could be used to visualize viruses and other objects below the resolution limit of transmitted-light **microscopes.** In the 1920s and 1930s, instruments incorporating such **ultramicroscopes** were built for analysis of flowing colloidal suspensions and for detection, counting, and sizing of particles in aerosols.

Prototypes

In 1947, Frank Gucker and colleagues reported the use of one such instrument to detect bacterial spores in aerosols. The Gucker particle counter injected the air sample into a rapidly flowing stream of filtered air, which confined the particles of interest to the central portion of the stream, in which they were subjected to dark-field illumination. The light source was an automobile headlight; a **photomultiplier** tube was used as a detector. In 1953, P.J. Crosland-Taylor described a similar device for counting cells in saline solution; commercial development of such instruments for clinical hematology laboratories was subsequently pursued by several organizations.

Also in 1953, Wallace Coulter received a patent for a device for counting cells based on measurement of the small changes in electrical impedance produced when cells, which are relatively poor conductors, pass through a small orifice connecting two saline-filled chambers. **Coulter counters** came into wide use in the early 1960s. Since the measured impedance change is proportional to cell volume, a Coulter orifice can be used for volume measurement, as well as cell counting. In 1965, Mack Fulwyler described sorting of cells of different volumes; the saline stream containing cells was broken into droplets by applied acoustic energy at a point downstream from the Coulter orifice, and electronic circuitry was used to charge droplets containing selected cells. The droplet stream then passed through an electrostatic field, resulting in charged droplets being deflected into collecting vessels. This sorting mechanism was adapted from one designed by Richard Sweet for use in ink jet printing.

While measurements of cell volume alone, or of any other single parameter, are of limited use in identifying different types of cells, it is possible to improve discrimination of cell types by making multiple measurements of each cell. In 1965, Louis Kamentsky and his colleagues, working at the International Business Machines Corp. and aided and inspired by Caspersson's group, described an optical flow cytometer that could measure four parameters per cell. The apparatus incorporated a dedi-

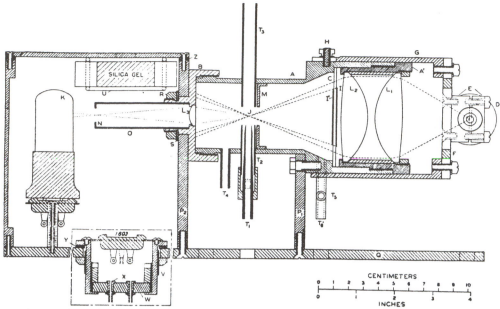

Frank T. Gucker's photoelectronic particle counter. A dilute stream of smoke is subjected to dark-field illumination (J) from a source (D). Flashes caused by individual particles are detected by the photomultiplier tube (K). Gucker et al. (1947): 2423, Figure 1. Courtesy of the American Chemical Society.

cated minicomputer for data analysis; at that time, this would have been inconceivable had it been developed elsewhere. By 1969, Kamentsky et al., Marvin Van Dilla and his coworkers, and Wolfgang Göhde and his had, independently, made fluorescence measurements in flow cytometers; later that year, Leonard Herzenberg and colleagues sorted cells based on fluorescence, also using Sweet's electrostatic droplet deflection principle.

Modern Flow Cytometers

In Gucker's apparatus, each particle spent approximately 3 ms in the illuminating beam. Because the observation period in later optical instruments is much shorter (1–10 µs), more intense light sources, such as short arc lamps and lasers, are needed. Typical instruments employ 488 nm (blue-green) illumination from low-power, air-cooled argon ion lasers, and measure light scattering at small and large angles from the beam and fluorescence in three or four (green, yellow, red, and orange) spectral regions. More elaborate systems add one or more additional illuminating beams, usually in the ultraviolet or red regions.

Multiparameter data acquisition and analysis are done with personal computers. While sorting by droplet deflection is still common, fluid switching sorting mechanisms are becoming popular because they are simpler to operate and because they do not generate potentially biohazardous aerosols. In the early 1990s a typical fluorescence flow cytometer costs approximately $75,000; more elaborate instruments cost over $300,000. By 1994, approximately seven thousand fluorescence flow cytometers were in use worldwide. More instruments, employing impedance or light scattering measurements, are used primarily for cell counting; the simplest of these are available for less than $10,000 (see **flourescence-activated cell sorter**).

Fluorescence flow cytometers are currently used to count and characterize cells from blood and the immune system (for example, the helper T-lymphocytes affected by HIV infection), and to determine cell DNA content and proliferative activity, which, in clinical settings, help assess prognosis and determine treatment for patients with cancer. Other uses include cross-matching organs for transplantation, isolating human chromosomes for genomic analysis, separation of X- and Y-chromosome bearing sperm for animal breeding, and analysis of microorganisms in clinical and environmental samples. Instruments have been built with sensitivity sufficient to detect single molecules of proteins, nucleic acids, and organic dyes; applications in microbiology, molecular biology, and analysis of cellular signal transduction are likely to assume increased importance in the future.

Howard M. Shapiro

Bibliography

Fulwyler, Mack J. "Electronic Separation of Biological Cells by Volume." *Science* 150 (1965): 910–11.

Gucker, Frank T., Jr., Chester T. O'Konski, Hugh B. Pickard, and James N. Pitts, Jr. "A Photoelectronic Counter for Colloidal Particles." *Journal of the American Chemical Society* 69 (1947): 2422–31.

Kamentsky, Louis A., Myron R. Melamed, and Herbert Derman. "Spectrophotometer: New Instrument for Ultrarapid Cell Analysis." *Science* 150 (1965): 630–31.

Melamed, Myron R., Tore Lindmo, and Mortimer L. Mendelsohn, eds. *Flow Cytometry and Sorting.* 2nd ed. New York: Wiley-Liss, 1990.

Shapiro, Howard M. *Practical Flow Cytometry.* 3rd ed. New York: Wiley-Liss, 1995.

Flowmeter

A flowmeter measures the volumetric or mass flow of a liquid, gas, granular solid, or mixture of these in a pipe, usually in commercial applications. In some designs the meter measures momentum, and the actual volume or mass flow has to be deduced from the density of the fluid. The term is sometimes extended to equipment for open-channel flow measurement and to probes that measure the local details of flow and are more commonly used in research. Flowmeters are used in almost every industry for a huge range of fluids (gases, food, drink, fuel, water, slurries, sewage, and chemicals), and only a selection of the one hundred or more types that make use of many physical principles will be considered.

The first crude form of flowmeter for open channels may have been a weir used by the Egyptians about 3,000 years ago. Herschel (1899) points out that Hero of Alexandria, who lived sometime after 150 B.C., concluded: "Observe always that it does not suffice to determine the section of flow, to know the quantity of water furnished by the spring. . . . It is necessary to find the velocity of the current, because the more rapid the flow, the more water the spring will furnish, and the slower it is, the

less it will produce." Frontinus (A.D. 40–103) claimed that there were dishonest water consumers in Rome. The problem was caused by flow rationing rather than measuring. Each consumer paid for the lease of a certain continuously running discharge, so that the dishonest fitted larger pipes at their discharge to increase the flow. Leonardo da Vinci illustrated flow over a weir and proposed the **anemometer** for measuring wind. Edme Mariotte suggested a float to measure liquid velocity in an open channel. Flumes and weirs are now used in rivers and open channels to measure the flow rate.

The name of Daniel Bernoulli is linked to the equation that governs the momentum flowmeters of which the venturi is one. Credit for the instrument, one of the earliest true flowmeters, should really go to Clemens Herschel, a nineteenth-century graduate of Harvard University, who named it after Giovanni Battista Venturi and patented the device. Walter Kent saw the possibilities of the device and obtained an agreement in 1894 for world rights excluding North America, and thus linked the first of a line of notable flow measurement engineers with his company (now ABB Kent-Taylor). They include J.E. Grant, J.L. Hodgson, H.E. Dall, and R.S. Medlock, from whose historical writing this piece has greatly benefited. In the venturi, flow is smoothly constricted and accelerated through a throat and into a diffuser, where pressure recovery is so good that the venturi is used where little pressure loss in the pipe can be accepted. The pressure difference for deducing the flow is between inlet and throat. Measurement uncertainty in modern instruments is typically 0.5–1.5 percent.

The most common momentum flowmeter is the orifice plate, developed from the end of the nineteenth century up to the middle of the twentieth. Flow through the orifice (of diameter less than the pipe), in a thin plate across the pipe, creates a pressure drop in the flow, which is used to deduce the flow rate. Typical measurement uncertainty is 0.5–1.5 percent.

The variable-area meter consists of a float buoyed up in a conical tube by the upwards flow. As the flow increases the float rises higher in the tube, and the flow is deduced from this height. Measurement uncertainty is typically 1.5–3 percent. G.F. Deacon produced a design that resembled a variable-area meter in 1873. A device of this kind was devised by J. Alfred Ewing in about 1876.

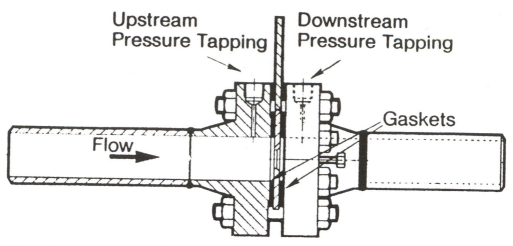

Schematic diagram of a typical industrial orifice plate assembly. Courtesy of Hartmann & Braun (UK) Ltd.

In 1790 Reinhard Woltman described the application of a spoke-vane meter for river flow, the design of which he ascribed to Schober, but which in various forms still bears his name. This was the forerunner of the turbine meter, in which a propeller in the flow rotates and the speed of rotation allows the volumetric flow rate to be deduced. Measurement uncertainty is typically 0.1–0.5 percent.

The positive displacement flowmeter is another volumetric flowmeter. Its rotors are so constructed that fluid is divided into compartments that are carried through the meter, and the flow rate can be deduced from the number of revolutions of the rotors. Measurement uncertainty is typically 0.1–0.5 percent for liquids. The nutating-disk flowmeter for liquids was developed in 1850. The rotary piston meter appeared in the late nineteenth century. Samuel Clegg (1815) should have credit for the wet **gas meter**, and William Richards (1843) for the diaphragm-type dry gas meter.

In the vortex flowmeter a bluff body across the pipe sheds vortices at a frequency proportional to the flow rate of the fluid. Measurement uncertainty is typically 0.5–1.5 percent. Some of Leonardo da Vinci's drawings suggest that he was aware of the phenomenon, but it was Roshko in 1954 who investigated the possibility of using the phenomenon for flow measurement. In 1959 W.G. Bird took out a patent for a flow measurement device, but the invention of the first successful commercial meter has been credited to the work of Alan Rodely in the 1960s.

Michael Faraday was aware of the fact that the flow of water through a magnetic field gen-erated a voltage across the flow. It was E.J. Williams in 1930 who succeeded in measuring the voltage generated across a pipe in which copper sulphate flowed through a magnetic field, and although his work sprang only from scientific interest, it provided the basis for today's most common designs of electromagnetic flowmeter. In these a liquid flows through a tube that has an internal insulating liner and across the tube is a magnetic field. Electrodes on each side of the tube sense the voltage that is generated and is approximately proportional to the flow rate. Measurement uncertainty is typically 0.2–1.0 percent.

There are two main types of ultrasonic flowmeter. The Doppler meter depends on reflection of the ultrasound off moving particles in the flow, and from the resulting Doppler shift in the frequency the velocity can be deduced. The transit time meter depends on the time taken for pulses of ultrasound to cross the pipe at an oblique angle to the flow. The first is not very accurate, while the second can give measurement uncertainty of about 0.5–2 percent. Devices of this type were reported in the 1950s. Various improvements relating to electronics and head design followed.

The third family of flowmeters measures mass flow rate. In the thermal flowmeter a fluid is heated and the temperature change in the flowing fluid provides a measure of the mass flow rate for a particular fluid. In some devices, a heated probe is kept at constant temperature and the heat flow is measured. Measurement uncertainty is typically 0.5–2.0 percent. C.C. Thomas appears to have been the first to report on this type of instrument in 1911, and the Calendar electric air-flow meter was in existence by 1920.

In the Coriolis flowmeter a tube is vibrated so that, for part of its length, it experiences a rotational motion. This, combined with the flow of the fluid along the rotating tube, results in a Coriolis acceleration that in turn creates a force proportional to the mass flow rate. Measurement uncertainty is typically 0.1–1.0 percent. An early device of this type was introduced by Y.T. Li and S.Y. Lee in 1953, but it was not until the late 1970s that a device based on such principles was commercially successful.

The precision of local velocity measurements will depend on the calibration of the probe and the expertise of the experimenter. The Pitot tube, for which Bernoulli's equation provides the basis, is sometimes used without calibration and may then be expected to give a measurement uncertainty of order 1 percent if correctly designed and used. It was described by Henri Pitot in 1732, and Henry D'arcy developed it almost to its present design. This device measures the velocity of the fluid at a point by bringing the fluid to rest in the entrance of the Pitot tube and by relating the consequent pressure rise to the velocity. A device consisting of a bar across the pipe with several upstream-facing holes and a smaller number of downstream-facing holes, and known as an averaging Pitot tube, is sometimes used as a bulk flowmeter. Its measurement uncertainty is typically 1–3 percent.

Many of the technologies described above are used in probes. An important alternative to the Pitot tube for research is the hot wire anemometer. Very fine wires are heated and the heat loss from the wire is used to obtain a measure of the flow of the gas at a point. L.V. King in 1914 gave the relationship between heat transfer rate and velocity. Hot film probes are used for liquid flows.

The laser Doppler anemometer was proposed by Y. Yeh and H.Z. Cummins in 1964 (see **laser diagnostic instruments**). By crossing two coherent beams of laser light, a fringe pattern can be set up. Spacing of the fringes can be deduced from light frequency and optical geometry and, as particles in the fluid pass through, the frequency of reflected light off the bright fringes gives a measure of the particle velocity and hence indirectly of the fluid carrying the particles. Alternative systems use other methods to achieve the same result.

All the flowmeters described are suitable for both liquid and gas where the term "fluid" has been used. Uncertainties are those achievable after calibration on a standard rig.

Roger C. Baker

Bibliography

Baker, R.C. *An Introductory Guide to Flow Measurement*. London: Mechanical Engineering, 1989.

Herschel, Clemens, ed. *The Two Books on the Water Supply of the City of Rome of Sextus Julius Frontinus*. Boston, 1899; reprint Boston: New England Water Works, Association, 1973.

Herschy, R.W. *Streamflow Measurement*. 2nd ed. London: Chapman and Hall, 1995.

Medlock, R.S. "The Historical Development of Flow Metering." *Measurement & Control* 19 (June 1986): 11–22.

Miller, R.W. *Flow Measurement Engineering Handbook*. New York: McGraw Hill, 1989.

Ower, E., and R.C. Pankhurst. *The Measurement of Air Flow*. Oxford: Pergamon, 1966.

Spink, L.K. *Principles and Practice of Flow Meter Engineering*. 9th ed. Foxboro, Mass.: Foxboro, 1967.

Fluorescence-Activated Cell Sorter

A fluorescence-activated cell sorter is a type of **flow cytometer** used to count and classify thousands of cells per second into distinct populations. The cell identification occurs when cells tagged with a fluorescent antibody pass through a vibrating flow chamber that breaks the cell stream into droplets. Laser illumination of the cells contained in the droplets allows for discrimination between them on the basis of light scatter and fluorescence. Cells of interest can be individually collected for further inspection by having the droplets containing the cells pass through an electric field. From its inception in the late 1960s, the apparatus has undergone several changes. For instance, while the early models detected only one fluorescent reagent, today's models can simultaneously detect up to five different dyes and thus perform multiparametric measurements. The performance of computers connected to the device, especially in the domain of data analysis, has also been enhanced by the

Bernard Shoor (left) and Leonard A. Herzenberg (right) with one of the early commercial flow cytometers, Becton-Dickinson's FACS II. Courtesy of Edward W. Souza/Stanford University News and Publications Service.

adoption of increasingly sophisticated software. The acronym FACS is the trademark of an apparatus marketed by Becton-Dickinson. Similar cell-sorting equipment is marketed by other companies under different trademarks.

Prototypes

The FACS apparatus was developed by a multidisciplinary research team at Stanford University, led first by Elliott Levinthal, then by Leonard Herzenberg. The impetus to build this apparatus stemmed from two sources: the automation of clinical-diagnostic practices such as the Pap test for the diagnosis of cervical cancer, and the automation of biological equipment for unmanned space flights. Their instrument brought together previous work that had sought to automate standard methods of biological analysis.

The team was able to draw on two devices that had been developed by 1965. The first was the result of a collaborative effort of a group that was led by Louis A. Kamentsky of the IBM Watson Laboratory at Columbia University and that included Mike Melamed and Leo Kass of the Sloan-Kettering Cancer Center. Two systems of cell separation were developed: the first, demonstrated in December of 1963, used an electrostatic field to deflect droplets containing cells of interest. This however was abandoned,

as it was believed that the target cells were too large and would block the nozzle. Moreover, IBM had a new typewriter technology incorporating a fluidic switching device etched on a molybdenum plate. Thus, by 1963, a fluidic switch that drew targeted cells out of the flow was developed and patented.

The second prototype emerged within the context of a technology transfer at the Los Alamos National Laboratory when, in 1960, Marvin Van Dilla, a physicist, began working with a pathologist, Clarence C. Lushbaugh, in an attempt to combine the pulse height analyzers Van Dilla had been using in gamma ray spectroscopy with a **Coulter counter** used to enumerate red blood cells. By 1965, Van Dilla's student Mack J. Fulwyler was able to separate cells on the basis of cell volume by adding a vibrating nozzle invented by a Stanford engineer, Richard G. Sweet.

In 1966, the demand for biological equipment for unmanned space flights led the Stanford University Instrumentation Research Laboratory, in concert with the Department of Genetics of the Stanford University Medical School, to apply for and receive a substantial NASA grant to develop instrumentation for use in outer space. Funding was subsequently provided by the National Institutes of Health. Starting with the

Kamentsky prototype and the Sweet-Fulwyler nozzle, the Levinthal-Herzenberg team developed an instrument in which the fluorescent readings were taken as the cells came out of the nozzle and were suspended in midair. It was named the fluorescence-activated cell sorter and received a patent in 1974.

Modern Usage

The success of the apparatus was linked to the development in 1975 of monoclonal antibodies used as labeled reagents in the machine. Whereas the term "FACS" was once sufficient to describe the activity of cell sorting, the FACS at present is but one of a number of devices in the much larger field of flow cytometry. In addition to an extensive variety of research uses, a number of clinical applications have been developed, the most prominent involving cell counts in AIDS, cancer diagnosis, and the monitoring of organ transplants.

Peter Keating
Alberto Cambrosio

Bibliography

Herzenberg, Leonard A., Richard G. Sweet, and Leonore A. Herzenberg. "Fluorescence-Activated Cell Sorting." *Scientific American* 234 (March 1976): 108–17.

Keating, Peter, and Alberto Cambrosio. "'Ours Is an Engineering Approach': Flow Cytometry and the Constitution of Human T-Cell Subsets." *Journal of the History of Biology* 27 (1994): 449–79.

Longobardi Givan, Alice. *Flow Cytometry: First Principles*. New York: Wiley, 1992.

Shapiro, Howard M. *Practical Flow Cytometry*. 3rd ed. New York: Alan Liss, 1994.

Friction Measurement Apparatus

Friction is a resistance to sliding between two bodies that results from pressing the bodies together. Apparatus designed to measure friction must be able to apply and measure the shear and normal forces between the two moving bodies. Because of the wide range of normal forces and stresses that are of interest in various applications, a wide variety of devices have been designed. Most of these instruments use the known force resulting from gravity, or they apply a force through an elastically deformed element and measure the distortion of that element.

A simple and classic way to measure friction is to use gravity to apply both the normal and shear forces by placing a block on an inclined plane and increasing the angle θ of the incline. If the weight of the block is W, then the normal force is W cos θ, and the shear force is W sin θ.

For more careful measurements, various configurations of the bodies have been used. Commonly one of the bodies is a small cylinder or pin with a hemispherical tip, and the other is a large flat surface. Much of this work was done and the apparatus developed in the Department of Physical Chemistry at the University of Cambridge beginning in the 1930s. The flat surface can be moved in a linear fashion as was done there by F.P. Bowden and L. Leben in 1939, or it can rotate relative to the pin similar to the motion of a phonograph record under its needle, as was done in the same lab by J.R. Whitehead in 1950. A rotating pin-on-disk apparatus has the advantage that indefinitely large amounts of relative displacement can be attained.

Measurements of frictional resistance can also be made by sliding along the interface between two large bodies. This is generally done by earth scientists studying the friction of rocks in order to understand the sliding resistance on faults associated with earthquakes. The first measurements of friction of rocks under significant normal stress were made by John C. Jaeger in the 1950s in the Research School of Earth Sciences at the Australian National University (ANU). He placed a cylindrical sample containing an oblique cut or fracture in a pressure vessel and measured the resistance to sliding along the cut when one end of the cylinder was pushed toward the other end. This type of friction measurement has become known as triaxial geometry, because the stresses along all three principal axes are nonzero. It was used because shear faults form in an oblique orientation at about 30° to the specimen axis when an intact cylinder of rock is compressed at elevated confining pressure. The triaxial apparatus for measuring friction is an adaptation of the apparatus for measuring the deformation of rocks at elevated pressure. This was first developed by the geophysicist David T. Griggs in the 1930s working in the high-pressure laboratory of the physicist Percy W. Bridgman at Harvard and later in his own lab at UCLA. Many other workers have followed this general design in performing friction measurements on rocks. A group of students at MIT working with William

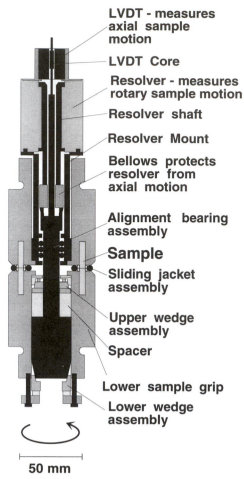

Rotary shear sample assembly for measuring friction, developed at Brown University, 1980s. The assembly is mounted inside a gas-medium pressure vessel and coupled to a rotatable piston. Courtesy of Terry E. Tullis.

F. Brace in the Earth Sciences Department did much work in refining friction measurements both there and later in their own laboratories.

Other geometries of friction apparatus have also been used to measure rock friction. Several of these use only two nonzero principal stresses. Here the magnitudes of the normal forces cannot be as high as those involved in earthquakes, because the rocks will crush if too much stress is applied in the absence of high all-around pressure. Nevertheless, there are technological simplifications when the experiments do not have to be done inside a pressure vessel. The two main geometries used are termed double direct shear and biaxial geometry. The double direct shear involves pushing a middle rectangular block between two others while applying normal force across the two boundaries between the three blocks. This was introduced by Earl R. Hoskins, an American who worked with John C. Jaeger in the 1960s at ANU, and who applied the normal stress with flatjacks (essentially flat steel envelopes filled with pressurized oil) inside a rigid framework and applied the force to slide the middle block with a hydraulic ram. Subsequent use of this geometry has involved hydraulic rams to provide both the normal forces and the relative motion. In biaxial geometry, a rectangular block with a diagonal cut normal to the largest face has forces applied to the other two pairs of faces with either flatjacks or hydraulic rams. When the forces are applied with flatjacks, the forces involved are determined by measuring the pressure in the flatjacks. When hydraulic rams are used, the forces are known either by measuring the pressure in the rams or by using load cells in series with the rams.

If indefinitely large displacements are desired, a rotary shear configuration can be used in which a cylinder is split perpendicular to its axis and one part rotated about the axis relative to the other part. If one or both cylinder halves are made hollow with walls of moderate thickness, the variation in velocity from the inside to the outside is less serious. An apparatus using this geometry inside a pressure vessel was developed by Terry E. Tullis in the Geological Sciences Department at Brown University in the 1980s, and it has the advantage of combining large displacement with the ambient pressure needed to prevent crushing of the rock. As with other apparatus using high pressure, some contribution to the measured frictional resistance arises from the sliding or deformation of the jacket assembly used to isolate the pressurizing fluid from the pore space of the rock.

Friction-measuring devices range greatly in size and cost, from something as simple as sliding a block down an inclined plane to the high-pressure apparatus that can be 2 or 3 meters in size and cost as much as a few hundred thousand dollars.

Terry E. Tullis

Bibliography
Bowden, F.P., and D. Tabor. *The Friction and Lubrication of Solids*. Parts I and II. Oxford: Clarendon, 1950–1964.
Griggs, David, and John Handin. "Rock Deformation." *Geological Society of*

America, Memoir 79 (1960).

Jaeger, J.C., and N.G.W. Cook. *Fundamentals of Rock Mechanics*. London: Methuen, 1969.

Tullis, T.E., and J.D. Weeks. "Constitutive Behavior and Stability of Frictional Sliding of Granite." *Pure and Applied Geophysics* 124 (1986): 383–414.

Furnace

The need for a source of heat is fundamental to operations in the chemistry laboratory. Furnaces are, of course, used in all kinds of contexts and need not be specific for such operations to be carried out. In the earlier period of laboratory work they were built in to the fabric of the building especially for the purpose of experiment, but their form was not developed in a specialized manner. Later, perhaps in the seventeenth century, chemical furnaces as such were designed.

Very little has been written about the internal arrangements of chemical laboratories before the eighteenth century. None has survived in its original form, and there are few enough that have survived in any form at all. Archaeological work has not shed much light on medieval laboratories, though a little of the equipment used in them has been found (see **distillation**).

An engraving of the laboratory built in 1682 in the University of Altdorf, Germany, shows furnaces of the built-in variety. These were very inflexible. The heat output could be changed only slowly and the vessels had to be moved to where the heating level was appropriate. Portable furnaces are shown in illustrations in texts from the seventeenth century onwards. They are made of iron with various furnace linings, but they too were difficult to use. The German alchemist Johann Joachim Becher described a variety of arrangements of such furnaces in his *Tripus Hermeticus Fatidicus*, posthumously published in 1689. These were made of parts that could be added or removed from the furnace body, which meant that the furnace could be adapted for specific uses such as fusion, cupellation, calcination, reverberation, cementation, digestion, distillation, and sublimation.

A major improvement, made by the Scottish chemist Joseph Black in the 1750s, was described by one of his students, August Christian Reuss, in 1782. A panel of holes with plugs in the side of the portable iron furnace could be opened or closed to regulate the airflow and thus the temperature. This form was valued by Joseph Priestley in 1791 (when his laboratory was destroyed by a mob) at £3/13/6 and was being sold by the firm of Griffin in 1866 for £4/10/0 and £6/6/0 (large oval form). It was still being advertised in trade catalogues at the beginning of the twentieth century. All the furnaces so far described used solid fuel. With the development of an efficient oil-burning system by Ami Argand in 1780, which introduced air on both sides of a cylindrical wick, oil lamps (or "lamp furnaces") were introduced to laboratories. A particularly effective variety with two concentric wicks was being advertised in 1804.

For very high temperatures, burning lenses or mirrors could be used to concentrate the heat from the sun. A vast double lens was constructed for Graf von Tschirnhausen and was used by the Académie Royale des Sciences from 1702 to 1709. In 1772, it was used by Lavoisier and colleagues to show that diamond would burn in air.

Coal gas supplies to towns were available from about 1820, and gas was used for both lighting and heating laboratories. Michael Faraday described in 1827 a burner that consisted of a tube with an open funnel below and a gas jet inside it so that the coal gas was mixed with air when it burned, creating a hotter flame. The more famous "Bunsen burner" was produced by Robert Bunsen and Henry Roscoe in 1857 and was manufactured by the Heidelberg University laboratory technician Peter Desaga. This was developed into the model that allows air to mix with the gas by introducing air in through a hole in a collar at the base of the gas tube by the manufacturer John Joseph Griffin. The temperature of the flame can be controlled by allowing in more or less air. The design revolutionized laboratory heating sources and it remains in very widespread use at the end of the twentieth century. That is not to say that the design was the only one developed. The Warrington firm of Fletcher, Russell and Co. (in the north of England) developed a range of gas laboratory furnaces, **blowpipes**, water heaters, and ovens from 1860, and these came into widespread use in laboratories throughout the world.

Electrical heating devices were introduced when electrical supplies became readily available. They were particularly appropriate where gentle or constant heat was needed and were frequently found in the form of drying or ster-

Reconstruction of Joseph Black's portable chemical furnace. SM 1977-529. Courtesy of SSPL.

ilizing ovens or as evaporating baths. Initially, constant temperatures were not easy to maintain, as the heating wires did not have sufficient resistance to oxidation and the thermostats were unreliable. A bimetallic thermo-regulator, designed by T.B. Freas in 1908 at the University of Chicago, solved the latter problem, the former being dealt with by enclosing the heating element within a double wall. In 1924 a specialist firm to provide ovens and water baths was started in Newark, New Jersey, by V. Weber, the Electric Heat Control Apparatus Co. Later, electrical heating mantles and tapes were developed, and these remain common in late-twentieth-century laboratories.

Robert G.W. Anderson

Bibliography
Anderson, R.G.W. "Joseph Black and His Chemical Furnace." In *Making Instruments Count,* edited by R.G.W. Anderson, J.A. Bennett, and W.F. Ryan, 118–26. Aldershot: Variorum, 1993.
Child, Ernest. *The Tools of the Chemist.* New York: Reinhold, 1940.
Kohn, Moritz. "Remarks on the History of Laboratory Burners." *Journal of Chemical Education* 17 (1950): 514–16.

F

G

Galton Whistle

This small whistle was designed in England by Francis Galton to produce tones of very high frequency and was used to detect the highest pitch audible to humans and animals. Galton's interests in such detection related to his broad evolutionary and reformist interests; subsequently psychologists used it to test theories of pitch perception. It was also used medically to determine amount of deafness, as well as in the physical examination of schoolchildren.

Galton, a man of independent means and tremendous creative energy, described his whistle in 1876. The lower end of a brass tube was closed with a piston that could be turned by a screw to various depths to make possible the production of varying notes: the shorter the bore the higher the note. The screw was attached to a cap covering the body of the whistle, one turn of which turned the plug $1/25$ in. The plug and whistle were calibrated on the outside so that the precise note produced could be determined by reading from these and referring to a table. To preserve a viable proportion between diameter and depth, Galton found it necessary to make instruments with very narrow bores (internal diameter of $1/16$ in.), but he still had problems obtaining high notes that were both powerful and pure. He experimented with gases lighter than air to increase the shrillness and came to favor hydrogen, using an India rubber ball and tubing. William Wollaston before him had described the upper limits of pitch perception as varying considerably in human adults under different conditions and had used small pipes to demonstrate individual differences; Galton found this ability to decline with age. Galton also experimented on a variety of animal species, carrying a whistle at the end of a hollow walking stick fitted with an India rubber tube squeezed at the handle during his peregrinations around the London Zoological Gardens and Europe. The whistle was made by at least two London instrument manufacturers, Hawksley and Tisley, then by Stoelting of Leipzig, and a later version (Edelmann's) by Spindler and Hoyer of Göttingen.

In the second half of his life, Galton became absorbed with the techniques of collection and analysis of anthropometric data as well as with their potential for application for the public welfare. The philosophy behind this was eugenics, or "race improvement," a program for speeding up the process of natural selection of human beings. At his instigation the Biology Section of the British Association for the Advancement of Science in 1875 established an Anthropometric Committee that conducted extensive surveys of thousands of persons throughout Britain. Galton urged it to include mental as well as physical characteristics, and in 1882 he published a plan for an "Anthropometric Laboratory" to apply simple physiological and psychical tests, including measures of keenness and discrimination of the senses. In 1884 he set up such a laboratory at the International Health Exhibition at South Kensington, most of the instruments being of his design. The use of the measurements was described as individual (a check on rate of personal development) and statistical (to determine the performance of the British population overall and the direction of any change). In 1885 he moved his equipment to the Science Galleries in the South Kensington Museum where it remained until 1894, by which time it had amassed records on more than nine thousand visitors. Galton justified his focus on simple psychological processes by claiming that

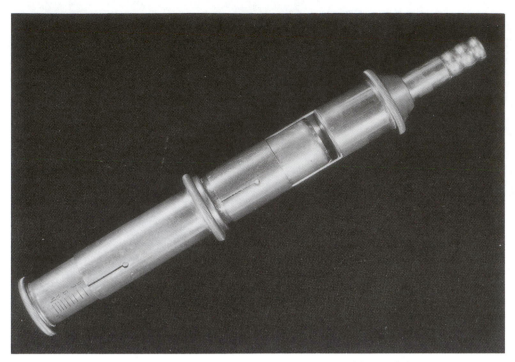

Galton whistle, by Stoelting, Leipzig, late nineteenth century. Courtesy of the Psychology Museum, University of Sydney.

the intellectually able have greater sensory acuity than the less able.

Anthropometric techniques were transported to the United States by James McKeen Cattell, who in 1890 coined the term "mental test" to describe the administration of a single item such as the blowing of the whistle; the notion of the generalizability of results thus obtained to more complex capacities was however abandoned when empirically disconfirmed a decade later. Gradually, intelligence tests of twentieth century design, composed of multiple items purported to tap complex abilities directly, came to be included in anthropometric surveys when measures of ability were wanted.

Psychologists however continued to use the whistle in their laboratories. Here the subject would be seated about a meter from the experimenter and required to indicate when a tone could be discerned. The experimenter began by setting the whistle to produce a fairly low tone, gradually shortening its length until the point was reached when the subject could no longer hear a tone. The experimenter would then proceed in the opposite direction, lengthening the whistle until the subject just perceived a sound. Various modifications appeared, but none overcame the whistle's chief inadequacy, which is that it did not emit a tone of constant pitch: its notes varied considerably according to the pressure of the wind blowing it. Use of a series of **tuning forks** and, more recently, the threshold **audiometer**, has proved more satisfactory.

Alison M. Turtle

Bibliography

Galton, Francis. "Hydrogen Whistles." *Nature* 27 (1882–1883): 491–92.

———. *Inquiries into Human Faculty and Its Development*. New York: Macmillan, 1883.

Myers, C.S. *A Text-book of Experimental Psychology with Laboratory Exercises*. 2nd ed. Cambridge: Cambridge University Press, 1911.

Turtle, Alison M. "Anthropometry in Britain and Australia: Technology, Ideology and Imperial Connection." *Storia della Psicologia e delle Scienze del Comportamento* 2 (1990): 118–43.

Wollaston, William Hyde. "On Sounds Inaudible by Certain Ears." *Philosophical Transactions of the Royal Society of London*. Part 1(1820): 306–14.

Galvanometer

There are many parallels between electrometry in the last quarter of the eighteenth century and galvanometry in the first quarter of the nineteenth. In both instances a variety of electrical phenomena were used as measuring techniques. The terms "galvanoscope" and "galvanometer" were first applied in the early 1800s to very sensitive gold-leaf electroscopes modified to measure the recently discovered "galvanic" or electric current (named after the Italian physiologist L. Galvani). Shortly after the discovery by H.C. Oersted in 1820 that the compass needle is deflected by a wire carrying a current, J.S.C. Schweigger, professor of chemistry at Halle University, showed how this could be turned into a sensitive device for detecting small currents. He tried out various coil arrangements and called his device a *Verdoppelungs-Apparat* (doubling-apparatus). It was later known as a "multiplier," a term probably coined by Thomas Johann Seebeck, the discoverer of thermo-electricity.

Johann Christian Poggendorff designed a coil (the precursor of the astatic) galvanometer in 1821, which he called a "condenser," analogous to Alesandro Volta's electrostatic condenser for magnifying electrostatic phenomena. Poggendorff appreciated the measuring capabilities of his instrument and demonstrated the correlation between number of turns of the coil and gauge of wire with increased sensitivity, but he could not establish a simple law relating needle deflection to the strength of the current.

The most sophisticated of these early coil galvanometers was designed in Britain by James Cumming, who described his "galvanometer" (for measuring) and "galvanoscope" (a sensitive detector) in April and May of 1821. Cumming did not use the direct method of the deflection of the magnetic needle. Instead of a coil, he used a single wire that could be moved closer to or further away from the magnetic needle until a standard deflection was obtained. The relative strength of the current was given by the position of the single wire on a scale. He concluded that the tangent of the deflection of the needle varied inversely as the distance of the sliding wire from the magnetic needle. Here Cumming combined the law of deflection of a galvanometer needle in a transverse horizontal field and the law of the magnetic force for a long, straight wire. The latter had already been determined experimentally in France by Jean Baptiste Biot and Félix Savart, by timing the oscillations of a suspended magnet. Cumming, too, used his sensitive instruments to investigate Seebeck's discovery of thermo-electricity, and he may have discovered this effect independently.

Cumming used a complicated system of permanent magnets to reduce the effect of the earth's magnetic field on his galvanometer. This idea was developed by William Thomson in the third quarter of the nineteenth century. However, it was André Marie Ampère who associated the name "galvanometer" with this electromagnetic indicator, and who developed the astatic principle as a way of neutralizing the earth's magnetic field. In Ampère's *aiguille aimanteé astatique* of 1820, the magnetic needle was mounted so that it turned and inclined parallel to the earth's magnetic field and dip. His second method, described the following year, is the one that has become known as the astatic system (although Ampère did not use this term in this context). Two parallel magnetic needles of almost equal strength but with their poles in opposite directions were attached to a brass wire bent at the top and suspended on a steel point in such a way that the upper needle was just above the current-carrying wire. The needles aligned themselves to the earth's magnetic field but were barely influenced by it. This arrangement formed part of Ampère's series of experiments on the properties of current in wires (which became much favored as classroom demonstrations). Previous investigators of the astatic effect of magnetic needles were Antonio Maria Vassalli-Eandi, professor of physics at Turin, and Jean Louis Trémery, a French mining engineer.

The Italian physicist Leopoldo Nobili developed the astatic principle into the ubiquitous astatic galvanometer. His instrument incorporated the multiturn coil of Schweigger et al., the thread suspension developed by Charles Auguste Coulomb for his electrostatic **torsion balance**, and Ampère's astatic needles. One other precursor was Amadeo Avogadro, professor of mathematical physics at Turin, whose *voltimetro multiplicatore* of 1821–1822 had all the elements apart from the astatic needle.

It was said that Nobili was the savior of the frog, as the most sensitive indicator of electric current before his astatic galvanometer was freshly prepared frogs' legs. Between 1825 and 1830 Nobili made a series of astatic galvanometers, and his portable model was reproduced by many instrument-makers all over Europe. Charles Wheatstone used such a version made by Watkins and Hill of London (ca. 1845) for his experiments on the velocity of electricity.

G

Astatic galvanometer used by Wheatstone, 1840s. SM 1884-87. Courtesy of SSPL.

Most makers followed the pattern of Nobili's astatic galvanometer established by the French maker Heinrich Daniel Ruhmkorff.

Until about 1837 the deflection of the magnetic needle was taken to be simply proportional to the magnetic effect in the galvanometer coil. Moreover, apart from debate over the nature of electricity, there was much debate about what was actually being measured: quantity of current, or its intensity. Faraday concluded in 1833 that the deflection of the needle was proportional to the quantity of the current and not its intensity (potential), but his conclusion was open to criticism as his galvanometer was not a direct-reading instrument. Difficulties were compounded by the absence of a standard voltaic cell. An important step forward was the demonstration by Cumming and by Ludwig Friedrich Kaemtz that

the magnetic effect of the current on the needle is proportional to the number of turns of the coil. Kaemtz also gave the correct mathematical formula when the needle is acted upon by two uniform magnetic fields at right angles to each other.

Electromagnetic measuring techniques were of three types: (a) timing the oscillations of the magnetic needle under the influence of the magnetic field (Biot and Savart, 1811); (b) null-point method using a torsion galvanometer (William Ritchie, 1830); and (c) direct readings with the tangent and sine galvanometers invented by Servais Mathias Pouillet in 1837. William Eduard Weber's moving-coil galvanometer or electrodynometer of 1845 was the first instrument capable of measuring current in absolute terms without involving the horizontal component of the earth's magnetic field. It now became possible to define the absolute electromagnetic unit of current and the electromagnetic force of the standard voltaic cell.

Galvanometer development increased dramatically from the 1840s. Their principles were now better understood, and there was great commercial pressure from the rapidly expanding electrical industry, in particular telegraphy. In Thomson's sensitive mirror galvanometer (1863), the magnetic needle was replaced by a small magnet attached to the back of a small suspended mirror and the deflection was magnified by a spot of reflected light. This instrument was further improved by Friedrich Paschen and Arthur Charles Downing.

Other important classes of galvanometers also underwent a great deal of development. The earliest moving-coil galvanometer with a permanent magnet was probably devised by William Sturgeon in 1824. The first commercial instrument of this type was Thomson's syphon recorder of 1867, developed for transatlantic telegraphy. This rather specialized instrument was developed by, among others, Marcel Deprez and Jacques Arsène D'Arsonval, who placed the coil in the annular gap of the permanent magnet. It evolved into a robust, portable, direct-reading instrument in the hands of Cromwell Fleetwood Varley and Edward Weston. In 1903, Robert Paul introduced his "unipivot" meter, in which the coil was supported in such a manner that the meter would operate without accurate leveling. William Edward Ayrton and J. Perry introduced the first direct-reading **ammeters** and **voltmeters** in 1881. Thomson's ampère gauge, in which the moving iron was controlled by gravity, was patented in 1888. All of these were superseded by more efficient designs with lower power consumption.

The differential galvanometer developed by Hermann von Helmholtz consisted of two coils and could be used to compare two currents. Cumming suggested a (vibrating) string galvanometer (in which the string was a gold strip) in 1827. The instrument was refined by Willem Einthoven for **electrocardiography** and further improved by William DuBois Duddell, who used a thin strip of phosphor bronze (1897). His "oscillograph" (used with photographic recording) was the precursor of the electronic **oscilloscope**.

Galvanometers operating on the heating effect of a current (using either a wire or a thermocouple) were used to measure both direct and alternating currents, but they were not particularly robust and their power consumption was high. The first person to "weigh" a current may well have been A.C. Becquerel in 1837, but Volta had already used such a technique to measure electrostatic charge. Thomson designed a range of current balances for 0.01 to 2,500 ampères. The instrument consisted of two movable coils, one attached to each end of a beam balance, and suspended between two pairs of fixed coils. The current flowed in such a way that the movable coil at one end was attracted and the other end repelled. The balance was restored by a weight sliding on a steelyard. The weight displacement was proportional to the square root of the current, and could be read directly in ampères. This remained very much a laboratory instrument.

In recent years the term "galvanometer" has come to denote sensitive laboratory instruments, while "ammeter" is more generally used for less sensitive portable instruments measuring electric currents greater than 1 μA.

Willem D. Hackmann

Bibliography

Chipman, R.A. "The Earliest Electromagnetic Instruments." *Contributions from the Museum of History and Technology.* United States National Museum Bulletin 240, paper 38. Washington, D.C.: Smithsonian Institution Press, 1966.

Gooday, Graeme J.N. "The Morals of Energy Metering: Constructing and Deconstructing the Precision of the Victorian Electrical Engineer's Ammeter and Voltmeter." In *The Values of Precision,* edited by M. Norton Wise, 239–82. Princeton, N.J.: Princeton University Press, 1995.

Hackmann, Willem D. "Leopoldo Nobili and the Beginnings of Galvanometry." In *Leopoldo Nobili e la cultura scientifica del suo tempo*, edited by Gino Tarozzi, 203–34. Bologna: Nuova alfa editoriale, 1985.

Vaughan, Denys, and John T. Stock. *The Development of Instruments to Measure Electric Current.* London: Science Museum, 1983.

G

Galvanometer, String

A string galvanometer was a highly sensitive form of galvanometer in which the coil was reduced to its minimum, a single wire. In its most sensitive form, as part of the **electrocardiograph**, the wire was a filament of quartz coated with metal. The vibration of the string was illuminated by a point light source, and the shadow was recorded on a photographic film.

The idea of using the movement of a single filament hung between the poles of a magnet was suggested by James Cumming in 1827. This kind of instrument was realized by Clément Ader in 1897, but in a form that showed, rather than measured, the variation of the current passing through the filament. Of more importance to the string galvanometer was a paper written by André Eugène Blondel in 1892 on the design of the oscillograph, which explained that the instrument should be as fully damped as possible, have minimum self-induction, negligible hysteresis and eddy currents, and that its period should be less than one-twentieth of the frequency of the alternating current. These were the properties that were required of the string galvanometer.

The Prototype ECG

The string galvanometer was devised by Willem Einthoven, professor of physiology at Leiden. His first instrument evolved in 1900–1903: it filled two rooms, the electromagnet had to be water cooled, and five people were needed to operate it. It proved to be extremely sensitive, but it was not immediately practical. Over the next decade Einthoven continued to improve it, but the most important step he took was to write to the Cambridge Scientific Instrument Co.(CSI) at the end of 1903, to ask whether they would manufacture the instrument. He also carried out important work in demonstrating the medical value of the ECG. Einthoven won the Nobel Prize for Medicine in 1924.

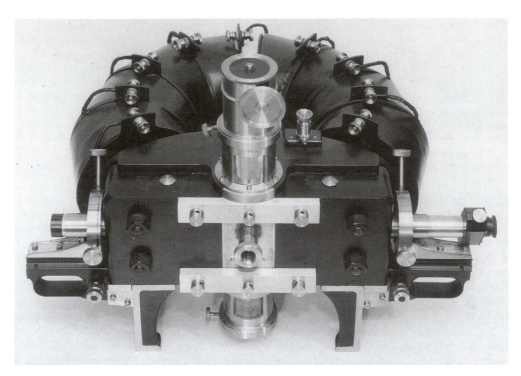

String galvanometer designed by H.B. Williams and built by Charles F. Hindle, for use with an electrocardiograph. The first of these instruments was delivered to Dr. Alfred E. Cohn in May 1915 and is now in the NMAH collections. NMAH M-6773-6776. Courtesy of NMAH.

Practical Instruments

CSI built the first practicable string galvanometer in 1905 and their first complete electrocardiograph three years later. Fifty-seven string galvanometers had been sold by 1912, and 140 by 1914, mostly for cardiology, though a few were bought by wireless telegraphy companies. Einthoven declined to patent his invention, so CSI soon had competitors: Max Edelmann of Munich, Boulitte of Paris, and Kunsch und Jaeger of Rixdorf. The first ECG in America (1909) was an Edelmann machine, though they were soon being made there by Charles Hindle. American physicians were more committed to the use of instrumentation, and the market developed rapidly, though cardiological research with the ECG was carried out equally on both sides of the Atlantic.

Later Developments

In 1920 the electrocardiograph was still five feet long and weighed over 600 pounds. Its size was reduced in the following decade, but its design was completely changed after the production of the first instrument based on the vacuum tube (1929). The electrocardiograph no longer required either the sensitivity of the string galvanometer or a complex moving camera.

John Burnett

Bibliography

Barron, S.L. *The Development of the Electrocardiograph with Some Biographical Notes on Professor W. Einthoven.* London: Cambridge Instrument, 1952.

Burch, George E., and Nicholas P. DePasquale. *A History of Electrocardiography.* Chicago: Year Book Medical, 1964.

Burnett, John. "The Origins of the Electrocardiograph as a Clinical Instrument." In *The Emergence of Modern Cardiology,* edited by W.F. Bynum, C. Lawrence, and V. Nutton, 53–76. London: Wellcome Institute for the History of Medicine, 1985.

Einthoven, Willem. "Un Nouveau Galvanomètre." *Archives Néerlandaises des sciences exactes et naturelles.* Série 2 (1901): 625–33.

Gamma Camera

Gamma cameras are the instruments around which medical radioisotopic imaging is based.

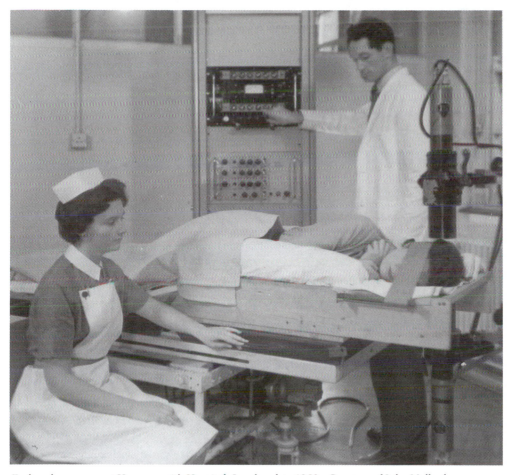

Early color scanner at Hammersmith Hospital, London, late 1950s. Courtesy of John Mallard.

Essentially detection systems for gamma radiation, they are used to image either function or structure in the body after the patient has received, usually by intravenous injection, a gamma-ray emitting radionuclide attached to a metabolically active substance. Before the development of the gamma camera by H.O. Anger in 1959, early studies of a similar type were carried out moving a **Geiger-Müller tube**, which accepted gamma-rays only through an aperture in a thick sheet of lead (a collimator) at centimeter intervals by hand over organs such as the thyroid gland. Counts were recorded every half minute with a stop watch and plotted on graph paper. Constructing isocount contours produced a crude image from the quantitative data. The radioisotope used for thyroid scans was Iodine-131, which was taken up by the gland. Cold spots (areas of relative inactivity) could indicate tumors, while hot spots suggested thyrotoxic nodules.

In the late 1950s rectilinear scanners were connected to mechanical printers. The patient was moved in a rectilinear raster on a floating top couch, and a sodium iodide **scintillation counter** was used. Multihole collimators added to these systems improved spatial resolution, and brain tumors were localized initially using Iodine-131-labeled albumen, then Technetium-99m.

The addition of many **photomultiplier tubes** in a system using a very large scintillation crystal (50 cm in diameter and 1 cm thick in a modern gamma camera) and a collimator with many parallel holes (several thousand in modern instruments) created the gamma camera. It was no longer necessary to move either the patient or the scanner to achieve an image. Detections are made simultaneously from all over the field of interest. Gamma-ray emissions, representing the distribution of the radionuclide in the body part under examination, pass through the collimator to interact with the thallium-activated sodium iodide crystal. Each interaction causes a tiny flash of light that is detected by the array of photomultiplier tubes on the back of the crystal. Resultant electronic signals are processed to give position coordinates and gamma-ray energy. Over several minutes, an image can be built up. Display mode can be analog or digital, and all modern systems are fully digitized.

Radionuclide imaging using gamma cameras has found greatest application in bone scans, using labeled phosphate analogs taken up by bone. Increased uptake may indicate secondary cancer deposits or other abnormality. Abnormal structure or function may also be revealed in organs such as the liver, kidneys, heart, or lungs. In this last instance a radioactive gas (Krypton-81m) can image the air passages. Detection of radio-labeled monoclonal antibodies against, for example, tumor antigens, is a developing field.

From the outset, radionuclide imaging was distinguished from conventional x-ray imaging by its ability to perform dynamic studies of body metabolism. Attachment of image processing computers to gamma cameras has considerably enlarged their potential in this respect. For example data collection in heart studies can be triggered by particular waves of the patient's **electrocardiograph** and thus linked accurately to their cardiac cycle. Image processing computers are essential for SPECT (single photon emission computed tomography). Gamma camera scanners for SPECT were developed in the mid 1970s. For SPECT, the camera is moved around the patient on a ring gantry, and the computer processing is similar in principle to that used in x-ray computed axial tomography. SPECT is particularly useful for brain function imaging, when labeled brain bloodflow agents are used to distinguish certain brain disorders and dementias (see **PET scanner**).

Development of radiopharmaceuticals for use with gamma camera imaging has proceeded apace. Over 80 percent of examinations now use Te^{99} as the radioactive label, which, for various reasons including its short half life (six hours), is suitable for most procedures.

Ghislaine M. Lawrence

Bibliography

Brecher, R., and E. Brecher. *The Rays: A History of Radiology in the United States and Canada.* Baltimore: Williams and Wilkins, 1969.

Glasser, Otto. *Wilhelm Conrad Röntgen und die Geschichte der Röntgenstrahlen.* Berlin: Springer, 1931.

Mould, Richard F. *A History of X-rays and Radium with a Chapter on Radiation Units: 1895–1937.* Sutton: IPC Building and Contract Journals, 1980.

Pallardy, Guy, Marie-Jose Pallardy, and Auguste Wackenheim. *Histoire illustrée de la radiologie.* Paris: Roger Dacosta, 1989.

Pasveer, Bernike. "Knowledge of Shadows: The Introduction of X-Rays into Medicine." *Sociology of Health and Illness* 11 (1989): 360–81.

Gamma Ray Spectrometer

See SPECTROMETER, GAMMA RAY

Gas Analyzer

The discovery of oxygen in 1774 activated the study of gaseous reactions. Information could be obtained by exploding mixtures of a combustible gas with oxygen. With hydrogen as the combustible, Henry Cavendish established the composition of water. John Dalton used methane and ethylene to establish the law of multiple proportions.

Technical gas analysis began in the 1850s, when Robert Bunsen used solid absorbents to examine blast **furnace** gases. In the 1870s, Walther Hempel designed a liquid-absorbent pipette, and Clemens Winkler systematized qualitative gas analysis. These led to the development of compact, portable gas analyzers.

Flue-gas Monitors

Too little air in a furnace gives rise to incomplete combustion ("smoking chimney"); too much air wastes fuel. One way to control coal-fired furnaces was to measure the carbon dioxide in the flue gases. The earliest apparatus, developed in Germany and patented by M. Arndt in 1893, relied on the density of carbon dioxide being greater than that of air. In 1898, Arndt patented an absorption type monitor. In this, a known volume of gas was mixed with a potassium hydroxide solution that absorbed carbon dioxide; the decrease in volume indicated the amount of carbon dioxide in the sample. Fully mechanized instruments, which recorded the prevailing percentage of carbon dioxide on a clock-driven drum, appeared around 1900 and were soon common.

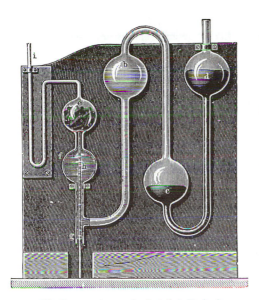

Hempel hydrogen pipette, by Baird & Tatlock, early twentieth century. Baird & Tatlock Ltd. Standard Catalogue of Scientific Apparatus: *Vol. 1* Chemistry. *London, 1923: 712. Courtesy of SSPL.*

Some analyzers, the earliest the work of M. Chopin in 1918, responded to changes in electrolytic conductivity caused by bubbling flue gas through an alkaline hydroxide solution. Absorptive removal of carbon dioxide, then catalytic oxidation to produce more of this gas, was also used by Eric Rideal and Hugh Taylor in 1919 to determine carbon monoxide in furnace gases.

Modern monitoring relies on the paramagnetic determination of oxygen, a method that is virtually specific for this gas. The principle was introduced by Erwin Lehrer and Edgar Ebbinghaus of Ludwigshafen in 1950. In one form of device, a nitrogen-filled dumbbell responds to the percentage of oxygen. In another form, the flue gas flows through a magnetic field containing a heater. The oxygen attracted by this field becomes less paramagnetic when heated, and is displaced by the more strongly attracted cold gas. The "magnetic wind" thus produced passes over a temperature-sensitive element that is the actual sensor.

Thermal Conductivity Devices

These appear to have been introduced by Leon Samzee around 1880. They have been used for gases such as carbon dioxide, sulphur dioxide, or chlorine, which are less thermally conducting than air. The high thermal conductivity of hydrogen is the basis of a patent, granted in 1904 to the Vereinighte Maschinen Fabrik company of Nürnberg, to determine the hydrogen in watergas (essentially a mixture of hydrogen and carbon monoxide). Thermal methodology is still used to determine hydrogen in gas mixtures.

With a katharometer, a term introduced by the British scientist Gilbert Shakespear in 1918, gas flows at a constant rate over a heated metal filament. The temperature of the filament, and hence its electrical resistance, decreases as the thermal conductivity of the gas increases, and vice versa. Measurements are made with respect to the constant resistance of a second filament, over which a reference gas flows. Sometimes two analytical and two reference filaments are used.

A catalytic analyzer can determine combustibles such as hydrogen, carbon monoxide, or various hydrocarbons in a gas stream. The platinum filament has a coating that catalyzes the oxidation of the combustible, thus causing the temperature of the filament to rise.

Infrared Analyzers

Gases that exhibit characteristic infrared spectra can be analyzed with a spectrometer (see **spectrophotometer**). Dispersion spectrometers, which scan a desired spectral range by a quite complex optical arrangement, are used primarily in laboratories. The relatively simple and robust nondispersive instruments are much used in industry. These may respond only to a specific component of the gas mixture, but when the general composition of a process stream is known, the monitoring of one component may provide ample control.

A nondispersive spectrometer uses the entire spectral range of the infrared source. However, some degree of dispersion can be obtained by filtering out unwanted portions of the spectrum. The radiation is split into two beams that are continuously chopped, so that illumination rapidly alternates between the two cells. The reference cell has a path length equal to that of the cell through which the sample gas flows. The transmitted beams alternate in reaching the detector. This detector, developed in Germany during World War II by Karl Friedrich Luft, is filled with the pure component to be measured. A flexible diaphragm, which forms a capacitor with an adjacent fixed plate, divides the detector into two compartments. Unless the sample gas is free from carbon monoxide, the compartment beneath the sample cell will receive less radiation than the other compartment. Unequal heating of the detector gas causes the diaphragm to deflect. This changes the capacitance, and hence the response of the associated electronics. The differential output from a pair of solid-state temperature sensors may replace that of the Luft detector.

Narrow-range optical or gas filters can be inserted when needed. For example, in the determination of a low concentration of another gas in carbon dioxide, the response of the latter can be masked by using filters that contain carbon dioxide.

Optical analyzers based on ultraviolet or visible-range spectroscopy, or on chemiluminescence (chemically produced emission of light) are less common than infrared instruments. Some analyzers are based on coulometric or other electrochemical techniques.

The increasing interest in air quality has directed attention to low-concentration determinations of a wide range of possible pollutants. Ozone or nitric oxide in the parts-per-billion range can be determined by chemiluminescence techniques. Much use is made of gas chromatographic methods, especially for the simultaneous monitoring of several pollutants.

John T. Stock

Bibliography

Colthup, N.B., L.H. Daly, and S.E. Wilberly. *Chemical, Biological and Industrial Applications of Infrared Spectroscopy.* 2nd ed. New York: Academic, 1975.

Miller, B. "Methods Available for the Measurement of Toxic Substances in the Workplace Atmosphere: An Overview." *Analytical Proceedings* 27 (1990): 267–68.

Stock, John T. "Flue Gas Monitoring: An Early Application of Mechanized Analysis." *Trends in Analytical Chemistry* 2, (1983): 14–17.

Verdin, A. *Gas Analysis Instrumentation.* New York: Wiley, 1973.

Gas Meter

Gas meters measure and record the quantity of gas supplied in a system and are capable of measuring the rate of flow at any time. In inferential meters, the quantity of gas flowing may be calculated from any of the following measurements: rotational speed of a turbine, pressure loss across an orifice, difference between static and kinetic pressures, change of temperature in a heated wire, height of a rotating float in a tapered tube, ultrasonic time of flight with and against the gas flow. In positive displacement meters, a volume of gas is measured by displacement through one of the following: bellows or diaphragms, compartments submerged in a liquid, spaces between impellers or vanes.

In the U.K., gas made by the carbonization of coal became available for lighting in the early nineteenth century. Charges were based upon the number of lights installed and the length of time for which the supply was provided. Frequent abuse of this system and the desire to use gas during working hours led to the development of gas meters, so that charges could be based on the volume supplied. In the United States, such a system of charging was not mentioned until 1885.

The first wet displacement meter, devised by Samuel Clegg in 1815, used a hollow drum divided into four compartments, rotating on a shaft in a cylindrical tank, part filled with water. Incoming gas lifted each compartment, in turn, out of the water and the displaced water flowing back into the compartment pushed the gas to the outlet. Clegg, in an improved version (1817), and John Malam, in an alternative design awarded the Society of Arts gold Isis medal in 1819, established the principles of an efficient wet meter that with modifications continued in practical use into the second half of the twentieth century.

Metered supplies achieved the ascendancy in the 1840s, following the development of the dry diaphragm meter by Miles Berry (1833) and improvments by Nathan Defries (1838), Thomas Peckston (1841), and Alexander Wright (1844). The diaphragms in the dry meter are alternately inflated and deflated by the pressure of the gas, the movements of the diaphragms operating slide valves controlling the passage of the gas in and out of the measuring compartments. These features are evident in the demonstration meter illustrated. The diaphragm meter became the preferred type for new domestic installations in the late nineteenth century, and it still dominates the domestic scene.

Development has concentrated on producing smaller, more compact meters, capable of passing increasing volumes of gas with minimal pressure losses. Meter cases have progressed through tin plate to unit construction pressed steel, or die-cast aluminum for higher pressure operations. Internally phenolic valves, acetal resin bearings, and synthetic diaphragms have been introduced. Digital indexes have made for easier and more reliable reading, and various methods of remote reading have been explored.

A demonstration version of George Glover's dry gas meter, ca. 1885, with glass sides to show the diaphragm, valves, linkages, and metering indexes gearing. SM 1887-113. Courtesy of SSPL.

Regulations

The Sale of Gas Act of 1859 provided the first legal standard for the measurement of gas in the

U.K. This prohibited the sale or use of all meters that could by any means be made to vary more than 2 percent in favor of the supplier, or 3 percent in favor of the consumer. The act also required that gas meters be tested and stamped by a government inspector. Similar regulations were introduced in Massachusetts in 1861.

In the nineteenth century gas quality was determined in terms of illuminating power. As use of gas for heating and cooking increased, gas quality was determined by its heat content. The Gas Act of 1948 required that gas sold to domestic customers be measured in positive displacement meters.

Metering Outside the Domestic Sector

Until the U.K. converted to natural gas, over the period 1967–1977, the diaphragm meter had been able to cope with most loads. Larger industrial loads were measured by the rotary displacement meter, while intermediate-level industrial loads were also measured by the BM meter, a wet displacement meter patented in Vienna in 1929.

The great increase in commercial and industrial customers with relatively high uniform loads, resulting from the availability of natural gas transmitted nationwide by a high-pressure grid, resulted in the widespread installation of rotary displacement and turbine meters. Correction techniques, never considered economical for domestic metering, became a necessary adjunct.

Rotary displacement meters fall into two main types. The Roots-type, introduced in the 1920s, measures gas by trapping fixed volumes between two intermeshing impellers and the casing of the meter. Although this meter actually measures gas by displacement of volumes, it has been classed as an inferential meter because its accuracy is not maintained when passing small volumes. The vane and gate or rotary vane meters have an annular measuring chamber formed between the casing and a central, stationary cylinder. Vanes rotate around the chamber, trapping fixed volumes of gas between them and passing the gas from inlet to outlet. A rotor geared to the vanes forms a gate that allows the vanes to return to the inlet but prevents gas from by-passing the measuring chamber.

All the remaining meter types described in this section are inferential meters. Turbine meters fall into two main categories. In the axial flow meter designed by Hans Gehre in 1936, the gas flow impinges on the blades of a turbine, and is streamlined by the contour of the casing. The speed of the turbine is proportional to the velocity of the passing gas. Since the area of the bore of the meter is known, the volume passing can be computed from the speed of the turbine, which drives an index counter calibrated to read volumes of gas directly. In the second category, the turbine is an **anemometer** mounted vertically. In the rotary meter patented by Thomas Thorp in 1902, the gas passes through a series of circular ports of known area and is directed on to the vanes of a vertical anemometer.

Three types of meter indicate gas flow by measuring differential pressures. The simple and inexpensive orifice meter, first experimented with by Thomas Weymouth in 1904, is the most commonly used. Being capable of operation at high pressures, it is frequently used for measuring the flow of gas through transmission networks. It has a noncorrodible, thin metal plate mounted with its precisely bored orifice concentric with the pipe bore, together with a system for measuring the pressure drop across the plate. The venturi meter works on the same principle, but is used on low-pressure systems, having the advantage of creating a lower pressure loss because a considerable amount of static pressure is regained as the gas stream slows down after passing through the throat. The pitot tube meter, advocated in 1891, is generally used as a portable device for spot checks on mains networks. It measures the kinetic head, being the difference between the impact pressure on a tube pointing precisely into the path of the flowing gas and the static pressure on the side of the tube.

Other Inferential Meters

In the hot wire anemometer, gas flows over an electric heater situated between two resistance **thermometers**. These control the heater so that a set temperature rise results in the flowing gas. The energy required to do this is measured electrically by a watt-hour meter.

The rotameter, commonly used in laboratories and on gas appliance test rigs, consists of a float in a transparent, tapered vertical tube. Gas flows up through the annular gap around the float and creates a pressure difference. Suspended on the upward flow of gas, the float rotates by virtue of the small slots in its outer edge. The height of the float in the tube is proportional to the rate of flow of the gas, and the calibrated instrument has its tube graduated accordingly.

Commercial sonic meters, available by 1977, measured natural gas flows in high pressure pipelines. These had no parts permanently inside the pipe, and they could be transferred from one location to another. The same principles are at the heart of a domestic, ultrasonic gas meter approved and introduced in 1994. Ultrasonic impulses are transmitted both with and against the flow in a measuring tube containing two transducers. From the difference in transit times the velocity of the gas flow is calculated and the volume of gas consumption accurately displayed. The instrument will operate for ten years on its original battery and is intelligent in recognizing both internal faults and external interference.

Derek A. Robinson

Bibliography

Bonner, Joseph A., and Lee, Winston, F.Z. "The History of the Gas Turbine Meter." Paper presented at the 1992 American Gas Association Distribution/Transmission Conference, Kansas City, Mo., May 3–6, 1992.

Jasper, George, ed. *Gas Service Technology.* London: Benn in association with the British Gas Corp., 1979–1980.

Smyth, Ormond Kenneth. "Meters—The Gas Man's Secret Weapon." *Gas Engineering & Management* 24 (1984): 363–71.

Tweddle, Robert. "Metering—Past, Present and Future Considerations." *Gas Engineering and Management* 17 (1977): 307–15.

Gas Testing Instruments

The use of hydrocarbon gases for wickless illumination was considered in the late eighteenth century. It became a major industry in the Victorian period, and gas testing began with the Metropolitan [London] Gas Act of 1860. Lighting power was controlled by means of a **photometer**, which compared the brightness of a sample of gas burning in a standard burner with a standard illuminant: a candle of sperm wax of a definite diameter and burning at a fixed rate; or a Vernon-Harcourt lamp, which burned butane under fixed conditions; or, in the early twentieth century, a standard electric lamp. The Bunsen, Rumford, and Joly photometers were developed for gas testing. The most accurate optical photometer—the Lummer-Brodhun, which used an arrangement of prisms to direct a central disk image of one of the sources sur-

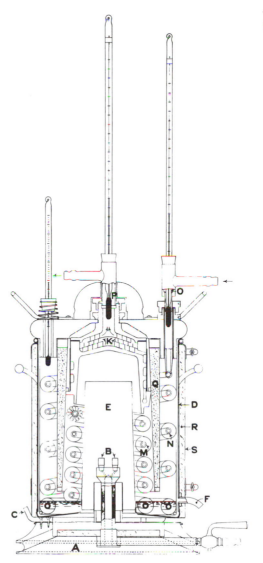

Cross section of a Boys gas calorimeter. SM 1932-533. Courtesy of SSPL.

rounded by a ring of light from the other into an eyepiece—was eventually replaced with flicker photometers, which were better able to match sources of different colors.

Following the late-nineteenth-century invention of the incandescent gas mantle, in which the light was generated by the mantle rather than by the gas itself, and the competing electric filament lamp, gas began to be sold for heating purposes, and **calorimeters** were used to rate its heating value. In a water flow calorimeter, a continuous supply of gas is burned at a constant rate, and the heat of combustion is absorbed by a steady flow of water. By noting the inlet and outlet water temperatures and measuring the quantity of water flowing while a fixed amount of gas is burned, the calorific value may be calculated.

The first successful water flow calorimeter was introduced by Junkers in 1893 and produced in Germany. A modification was developed by the American Gas Institute and the National Bureau of Standards, and widely used in the United States. Another modification of Junkers' instrument, designed by C.V. Boys, became the preferred instrument in Britain. Yet another variation, known as the Simmance-Abady calorimeter, was used in Canada and the United States. These basic instruments could make spot checks only, but recording versions such as the Fairbrother based on the Boys calorimeter were soon on the market to satisfy the needs of larger users.

While many of the recording calorimeters were merely modifications of older designs, the Sigma calorimeter was an inferential device in which a small flow of gas supplied at virtually atmospheric pressure was burned inside a bimetallic chimney. The differential expansion occurring with a change of calorific value actuated a recorder pen. Another group of instruments used air water to absorb the heat of combustion. One of these was designed in 1920 by Carl Thomas in the United States. A modification, the Cutler Hammer, achieved some importance in the 1980s.

With the worldwide replacement of manufactured gas by natural gas, the demand for calorimeters fell dramatically. While each gas works had needed its own instrument, one instrument now sufficed for a whole gas field. Moreover, because of the change in combustion properties, most water flow calorimeters required significant redevelopment. The Thomas and Cutler-Hammer instruments were preferred under the new conditions and eventually replaced most of the other models on the market.

The one new instrument was the Honeywell calorimeter, an inferential device that burned natural gas in a variable stream of air. A monitor in the flue varied the air supply until the effluent gases contained no excess oxygen. The air supply volume was then taken as a measure of the calorific value.

In 1955 a Fairweather calorimeter and auxiliary equipment cost approximately £2,500, or more than twice the annual income of an average worker in Britain. The Thomas group of instruments cost approximately £40,000 in 1985. Thus, over the period of use of these mechanical calorimeters, the equipment cost remained constant in labor terms.

Mechanical calorimeters were eventually replaced by gas analysis. The idea that the calorific value of a gas could be calculated as the weighted sum of the calorific value of its component parts had been recognized by M. Berthelot. Traditional methods of gas analysis depended on wet chemistry, which was far too inaccurate for calorific valuation. The development of gas chromatography opened an entirely new route to measurement.

A modern calorimeter such as the Daniels "Danalyser" consists of three parts. A valve samples the line gas at frequent intervals, interposing a reference sample at fixed intervals. A **chromatograph** analyzes the gas samples. And a computer compares the samples with the standard and calculates the calorific value. The printout may include other data derived from the analysis, such as the gas density, the air for combustion, or the Wobbe index, which is a measure of the interchangeability of a gas with others. A typical chromatograph is more reliable than the mechanical equipment it replaced. Costing less than £20,000 and requiring minimal housing, it is substantially less expensive.

H. Crompton

Bibliography

Coe, A. *The Science and Practice of Gas Supply, Including the Economics of Gas Supply.* Vol. 2. Halifax: Gas College, 1934.

Hyde, C.G., and M.W. Jones. *Gas Calorimetry: The Determination of the Calorific Value of Gaseous Fuels.* London: Benn, 1932.

Ministry of Fuel and Power, Great Britain. *Gas Act, 1948: Gas Examiners General Directions.* London: His Majesty's Stationery Office, 1948.

Starling, S.G., and A.J. Woodall. *Physics.* 3rd ed. London: Longmans, 1964.

Gauge, Level

A level gauge measures the level of a liquid or solid. Common examples include a pole set in a container, or a series of marks on the side of the container. For opaque containers, dipsticks or sight glasses may be appropriate. A dense liquid in a U tube at the side of a tank reduces the distance of travel in the sight glass and makes for more convenient reading. Plumb lines indicate marine depths, and poles are used in ski resorts to indicate snow depth.

Some methods depend on the movement of a float on a liquid surface, often attached to cords and pulleys, **potentiometers** and rheostats, torque tubes, and other devices. Water clocks (clepsydra) with floats were developed in Babylonia, Egypt, and China. A recent technique, involving a system of reed switches inside a stainless steel tube with a toroidal magnet floating on the liquid surface outside, provides a sterilizable system for use in fermenters.

There are two main pressure methods. In the hydrostatic method, one measures the pressure due to the height of a liquid, or the pressure difference between the surface and bottom levels of a liquid. In the bubbler method, one measures the pressure required to drive bubbles out of a tube reaching to the bottom of the liquid. The advent of automatic washing machines has led to the development of plastic diaphragm-operated pressure switches that move to the next section of the machine program when the water level reaches an appropriate level.

Transit times for reflection of sonic, ultrasonic, infrared, or microwave beams from phase interfaces give both depths and distances. **Sonar** was used in both world wars, and **radar** in World War II. It has been possible since the 1960s to measure the nanosecond transit times for infrared beams with sufficient accuracy for them to be used in photography and level measurement.

Since the weight of a container depends on the level of material in it, load cells can be used to measure levels. Levels can also be measured by the resistance or capacitance between electrodes standing in a tank and partially covered by the liquid, and by the blocking of radiation from a radioactive source. Methods of flow measurement are now so accurate that levels may be measured by subtracting flows out of a tank from those into it.

Phase contrast systems similar to those used for automatic focusing cameras can be employed, especially for solids. When an image is in focus on a raster-fronted photovoltaic cell, its output goes through a minimum. A single image can be brought into focus and the range determined. Alternatively, two images from separated viewfinders can be superimposed on the photovoltaic cell, and the angle between the viewfinders determined. Variants of the latter method have long been used for navigation (shooting the sun), and for estimating the height of trees, mountains or buildings.

Methods under development are based on interferometry. Coherent beams of sinusoidally intensity-modulated light are reflected from the phase boundary, and the phase difference of the modulating signal between the emitted and returning light is measured.

Ullage Rods

When a cask is partly filled, it is said to be on ullage. The depth of liquid is described as the wet ullage, and the space above it as the dry ullage. The determination of the contents of a vessel with a dipstick is simple in principle but often complicated in practice. Casks are curved in two dimensions, and their contents may have to be measured when they are upright or lying on their sides.

A treatise on gauging was mentioned in 1347, and more than sixty manuscripts and printed texts are known between 1450 and 1650. There were also gauging secrets, songs, and traditions. Gaugers were employed by villages, by producers and shippers, and especially by tax-gatherers for customs, excise, and revenue. While the tax-man was primarily interested in alcoholic drinks, gaugers also measured volumes of such commodities as malt, green starch, dry starch, and soap.

The crucial measurements required for gauging a cask were the bung diameter (diameter at the widest point), the head diameter (the diameter at the end), and the length. These could be measured externally with calipers or internally with rods plus plumb lines. Ullage rods were used to measure internal bung diameters, liquid depths, and the length of the diagonal from the bung hole to the point at which the staves joined the head of the cask. The diagonal rod had a cubic scale and was used to estimate the total volume of a cask of given shape. Other rods, or scales on the same rod, had squared scales and were applied vertically, the final calculation involving the square of the diameter.

The "square rod" and "cubic rod" probably originated in south Germany and Austria, respectively. The early rods, and some later ones, were calibrated by pouring known amounts of liquid into a cask of more or less standard shape. The geometry of the system was worked out in 1615–1616 by Johannes Kepler, whose experience with ellipses in astronomy enabled him to work out the volumes

Excise officers checking liquor barrels with ullage rods in the Port of London, eighteenth century. Courtesy of SSPL.

of the truncated conic sections (frustums) making up a cask.

In 1643, when England began levying a duty on beer, there were several different sizes of gallons and different standard casks for beer (36 gallons), brandy (60), claret (45), port (57), sherry (54), madeira (46), and so on. The Imperial gallon (277.274 cubic inches; 4.546 liters; 1.201 Queen Anne wine gallons) was introduced in 1825 in the U.K., but the United States has retained the Queen Anne wine gallon for all purposes, so that "a fifth" of bourbon contains 742 ml compared with the present European standard wine bottle of 750 ml and spirits bottle of 700 ml.

Multiscale slide rules, which simplified the calculations, were introduced by Thomas Everard in 1683 and improved by J. Vero, C. Leadbetter, and others. These often had a scale of inches, a squared scale, a cubic scale, a logarithmic scale (like a modern slide rule), and a scale on which the gradations lessen and then increase, reflecting the volumes required to fill a barrel to a particular depth.

Fuel Gauges

The development of internal combustion engines led to gauges to measure the gasoline level els in closed tanks in moving vehicles. These are now probably the most widely used of all level gauges.

Dipsticks to measure fuel continued in use into the 1930s, often as a reliable backup to a pressure or electrical method. Since gasoline evaporates rapidly from a dipstick, special coatings were applied to give a well-defined line (as in the Boyce Universal Petrol gauge of 1926).

Opening the gas tank was messy, inconvenient, and carried a fire hazard, and the dipstick might introduce dirt into the tank, which could subsequently block the carburetor. The 1904 MMC had a glass sight tube set in the side of the gasoline tank. The Cossor gauge (1904), mounted on the dashboard, was a sight gauge that read gasoline density as well as level when a tap was turned. The 1922 Morris Oxford Tourer had a dipstick, but the 1923 Bullnose Morris had a gas tank in the scuttle behind the dashboard at the same level, as well as a dashboard-mounted sight glass.

In 1904, G.P.B. Smith invented a method in which a float on the end of a swinging arm operated a pointer spindle on the outside of a tank, and G.W. Gregory proposed a device in which an Archimedean screw was rotated by a float, thus turning a needle. These ideas were improved in the Simms Magnetic gauge, invented in the United States by Morris Martin in 1912. One variant consisted of a vertical tube with a spiral slot. Inside the tube was a float carrying a magnet that coupled with another magnet turning the needle on a dial outside the tank. As the gasoline level rose or fell, and the float moved up or down, the floating magnet rotated and turned the magnet and needle.

The second type of Simms gauge consisted of a float that raised and lowered an arm attached to gears, which transmitted the motion of the float to a magnet coupled, again, to an external magnet and needle. Simms gauges were fitted to the more expensive cars in the early 1920s and soon passed into general use. The tube-based gauge is particularly useful in tanks containing many baffles, and it is still used in small boats and the tank-mounted gauges on trucks. The device was airtight, dust-tight, fireproof, and did not require electricity, but it had the drawback of not being mounted on the dashboard.

Most of the early remote-reading gauges depended on hydrostatic pressure. A vertical tube in the tank reached to about 1 cm from the bottom, and a small-bore tube from it was led to a pressure-reading device on the dashboard. The device could be a manometer (with a partial vacuum on one side to compensate for differences of height between the tank and the dashboard) or an aneroid/Bourdon type of **pressure gauge**, similar to those in **barometers**. It was unreliable, especially if the tank dried out and air leaked in or out of the tube. A similar system with a closed tube was used to measure the temperature in the automobile radiator. A variant was a bubbler-type gauge, developed by Smiths Industries. The driver operated a knob that pumped air through a vertical tube in the tank, and a pressure device measured the pressure required to force bubbles out of the bottom of the tube.

Electrical methods were introduced in the late 1920s. The sensor was a copper or tinned iron float on an arm attached to a circular rheostat, or else moving a contact up and down a vertical rheostat. Movement of the float varied the rheostat resistance. The level gauge consisted of an electrical circuit containing an **ammeter** and the **rheostat**, the latter being in the grounded side to avoid sparking. The current depended on the rheostat resistance. An early example with a vertical rheostat was the 1932 Alvis.

The problem was to avoid rapid fluctuation of readings as the automobile was driven. The gasoline tank contained baffles. In the 1930s, the ammeter was a moving-iron **galvanometer**, which responded only slowly to changes in current, and this was damped further by its bearings and by damping springs.

In 1961 the bimetal resistance instrument was developed. A bimetallic strip linked to a pointer is heated by resistance wire, the current being determined by the variable float-controlled resistance in the fuel tank. This required an independent voltage stabilizer but was less expensive and less unstable than the moving iron instrument. It is still in standard use.

In the 1970s, damped air-cored moving coil galvanometers were introduced. They were more stable than moving iron galvanometers and more accurate than the bimetal system. They too are in current production.

The float/rheostat sensor has remained largely unchanged since 1950 except that the metal float has been replaced by gasoline-resistant plastics such as nylon. This certainly appeared in the 1964 Alvis but probably originated earlier. Prices of fuel gauges in 1994 were about $70.

Bryan Reuben

Bibliography

Bolton, W. *Instrumentation and Process Measurements*. Rickmansworth: Longman, 1991.

Day, John. *The Bosch Book of the Motor Car*. London: Collins, 1975.

Everard, Thomas. *Stereometrie Made Easie*. London: Playford, 1864.

Judge, A.W., ed. *Modern Motor Cars*. London: Coxton, 1924.

Yeo, William. *The Method of Ullaging and Inching All Sorts of Casks and Other Utensils Used by Common Brewers, Victuallers, Distillers &c*. London, 1749.

Gauge, Mechanical

Mechanical gauges are used to rapidly determine dimensions of many kinds of manufactured components. They have been widely used since the Industrial Revolution to ensure precise control in the mass production of interchangeable parts. Many varieties and sizes have been

Micrometer, believed to have been made and used by James Watt, ca. 1772. SM 1876-1370. Courtesy of SSPL.

created to match the wide range of applications in which they are used.

The most mechanically simple gauges are those that provide a shape against which a part can be checked. These have a long tradition in craft practice and depend on the skill of the worker in judging fineness of fit. More sophisticated is the go/no-go gauge, which identifies objects whose relevant dimension falls within a specified range of tolerance. The gauge has two parts, each an appropriately shaped gap, shaft, or cylinder (depending on the form of the objects to be tested). One part is set to the maximum limit and the other to the minimum, so that an acceptable object will enter or pass the first but not the second. Both parts of the gauge can be incorporated into a single tool.

The British engineer Joseph Whitworth described the go/no-go gauge in a paper of 1876, but earlier, less sophisticated, examples are known. For example, cannon ball production used gauges to ensure the ball would fit the barrel yet not be so tight as to foul on firing.

The go/no-go gauge determines whether a dimension falls within a specified interval. Linear gauges indicate how far the actual dimension departs from an ideal value. The earliest known form is the sliding caliper gauge, in which a slide moves on an L-shaped frame to form a variable distance between the gauge's jaws. The caliper is placed around the object to be measured and the slide moved in to make firm contact. The gauge's scale can then be used to read a measurement of size. Alternatively, the slide may be locked in place by hand or with a holding screw to enable comparisons to be made between two parts. Although workshop use of such measuring devices was not common until the nineteenth century, there is evidence that this form of device existed in China as early as A.D. 9.

While a sliding caliper provides a direct measurement, the human eye cannot read its scale to a high level of precision. In the seventeenth century, Pierre Vernier invented a mechanical method of effectively amplifying the scale. He introduced a second short scale whose intervals differed slightly from those of the main measuring scale. This second scale moves along the main scale and the fine determination is made by noting the coincidence of lines on the main scale and the short, vernier scale. The principle has since been used on numerous instruments. Vernier calipers are still in use today as the least expensive way to measure down to 20 micrometers or 1/1,000th of an inch. However, modern caliper gauges often do not use the vernier principle but, instead, use a friction-driven roller to rotate an easily read pointer or electronic digital readout indicator.

The most familiar tool for engineering measurement is the **micrometer**, which measures objects in the variable gap between its two jaws. The separation of the jaws is controlled by a fine precision screw thread. If the pitch of the thread is chosen conveniently, each rotation of the screw will change the gap by a convenient amount, such as 25/1,000 of an inch. The screw carries a graduated thimble that is read against a fixed datum line to yield subdivision into the finest increments. The principle of the micrometer was introduced in astronomical instruments in seventeenth-century England, and James Watt made a screw micrometer for his own use in 1772. But commercial manufacture for engineering use was only begun by the American firm of Brown and Sharpe in 1867. Modern electronic versions digitize the rotation of the screw to provide a numerically indicated measurement.

The typical industrial micrometer is a handheld device, but larger sizes are also made. However, problems are encountered when the caliper reach exceeds half a meter: the frame deforms unless made prohibitively heavy, and measurements are also influenced by temperature variations that expand the metal and thus alter the reference length. These problems were overcome in the 1960s by making the frame from resin-reinforced carbon fiber, which is less subject to deformation and has a smaller temperature dependency.

The expansion in the use of gauges and measurements in late-nineteenth-century engineering highlighted the problem of how gauges themselves were to be calibrated. Rather than have very many reference gauge blocks each of a useful size, the Swedish engineer Carl Edward Johansson developed a more compact system of block and slip gauges. Introduced in 1908, Johansson's blocks quickly became fundamental to practical engineering metrology. The set consists of 102 highly precise and smoothly machined blocks of stable metal each having a different size. By simply wringing blocks together their faces adhere. Therefore if a particular length is required for calibration purposes, it can be built up by combining several blocks. Typical blocks range in thickness from 50/1,000ths of an inch to several inches. Metric sequences also exist.

Gauges of all types remain essential instruments in manufacturing. Some forms incorporate optical techniques to magnify scale readings, while electronic techniques are increasingly employed. Although the line between gauges and measuring sensors is now often difficult to draw, there has been a trend, especially since the 1960s, to replace gauges by displacement sensors that supply electronic signals to computers.

Peter H. Sydenham

Bibliography

Burstall, Aubrey F. *A History of Mechanical Engineering.* London: Faber and Faber, 1963.

Gordon, Robert B. "Gaging, Measurement and the Control of Artificer's Work in Manufacturing." *Polhem* 6 (1988): 159–72.

Needham, Joseph. *Science and Civilisation in China.* Vol. 4, part 1, section 26. Cambridge: Cambridge University Press, 1962.

Rolt, Frederic Henry. *Gauges and Fine Measurements,* edited by Richard Glazebrook. London: Macmillan, 1929.

Uselding, Paul. "Measuring Techniques and Manufacturing Practice." In *Yankee Enterprise: The Rise of the American System of Manufactures,* edited by Otto Mayr and Robert C. Post, 103–26. Washington, D.C.: Smithsonian Institution, 1981.

Gauge, Pressure

Standard pressure, used to compare pressure-sensitive quantities such as the volume of a gas, has been defined as equivalent to that of 760 mm of mercury, an average barometric pressure. Industrial pressure gauges often read in pounds per square inch (psi). High pressures, such as in compressed-gas cylinders, may be expressed in atmospheres (1 atm. = 14.7 psi). Low pressures are expressed in the Torr (1 Torr = 1 mm of mercury; it is named for Evangelista Torricelli, a pioneer of barometry). The millibar (mb) is sometimes encountered (1 mb = 0.750 Torr), as is the pascal (Pa) (1 Torr = 133.3 Pa) and the kilopascal (KPa).

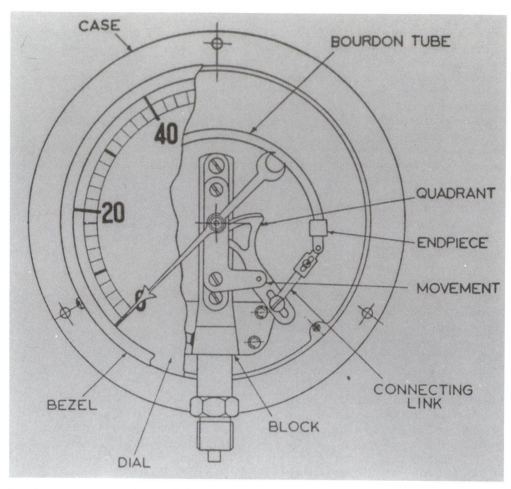

Bourdon pressure gauge, 1956. Budenberg (1956): Figure 1. Courtesy of the Institute of Measurement and Control.

The **barometer**, introduced in the early seventeenth century, is actually a gauge of atmospheric pressure. Another form of pressure gauge is the manometer; this is a liquid-filled, U-shaped tube, one limb of which is open to the atmosphere. In 1777, William Roy used a form of this ancient device to measure the thermal expansion of air. A closed-end U-tube containing mercury was used by the firm of Boulton and Watt in 1808 to indicate the nominally 5 psi steam pressure in a boiler made for a London brewery.

The use of steam for industry and especially locomotives fostered the need for direct-reading pressure gauges. By 1850, two main types had evolved. In the diaphragm gauge, typified by that of Ernst Schäffer in Germany, the upward flexing of a diaphragm under pressure causes a pointer to rotate. Replacing the diaphragm with a stack of interconnected cap-sules or a cylindrical bellows allows even greater flexing.

The use of a curved, flattened tube as a pressure-sensitive element began almost simultaneously in France and Germany. However, it was the French instrument-maker Eugène Bourdon who realized the full potentialities of this design. His patent of 1849 shows more than seventy drawings concerning his invention. Bourdon gave an account of the origin of his gauge to the Institution of Civil Engineers in 1851. In bending tubing into a helix, a partial flattening had occurred. To rectify the error, Bourdon had closed the helix at one end and forced water into the other. The resultant partial uncoiling of the helix suggested that this effect might be used to measure pressure.

Although various modifications and improvements of the Bourdon gauge have appeared, the flattened-tube principle remains unchanged. Tubes may be of varying stiffness, so that Bourdon gauges are available for pressure measurements in the approximate range from 10 to 80,000 psi.

The piezoelectric effect, which is the development of a voltage when certain crystals or ceramics are compressed, can also be used to directly measure moderate to high pressures. An indirect method involves the coupling of a **strain gauge** to a diaphragm or other element that flexes under pressure. In essence, a strain gauge is a fine wire, the electrical resistance of which increases on being stretched.

John T. Stock

Bibliography

Budenberg, C.F. "The Bourdon Pressure Gauge." *Transactions of the Society of Instrument Technology* 8 (1956): 75–88.

Hunt, L.B. "The History of Pressure Responsive Elements." *Journal of Scientific Instruments* 21 (1944): 37–42.

Lambert, L.B. "A History of Pressure Measurement." *Transactions of the Society of Instrument Technology* 15 (1963): 169–80.

Gauge, Vacuum

A vacuum gauge, or manometer, measures gas pressures less than atmospheric (1.013×10^5 Pa, or 760 Torr). The range of sub-atmospheric pressures that need to be measured in practice is so vast (760 Torr to 10^{-13} Torr or less) that several different types of vacuum gauges are required. Different units are widely used for the measurement of subatmospheric pressure; the S.I. unit is the Pascal (N/meter^2) = 7.5×10^{-3} Torr (mm Hg) = 10^{-2} mbar. Vacuum gauges are essential in all vacuum systems used for research and production to monitor the degree of vacuum achieved.

Mechanical Manometers

Mechanical gauges measure true pressure, independent of the nature of the gas. Other gauges measure some other physical property of a gas that can be related to pressure by calibration; here the signal is in all cases dependent on the nature of the gas being measured.

The first measurement of pressure in the vacuum range was made with a liquid manometer by Robert Boyle, who inserted a mercury manometer into an evacuated bell jar in the late 1650s. In 1874, H.G. McLeod used a mercury

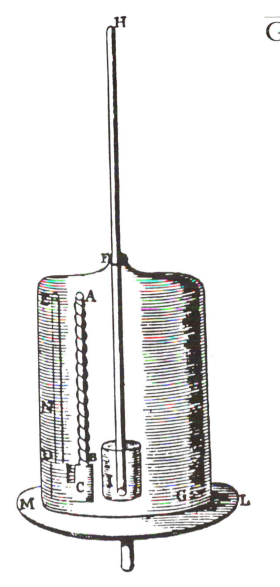

Boyle's "Mercurial gauge." *Robert Boyle.* New Experiments Physico-Mechanicall, Touching the Spring of the Air and Its Effects. *London, 1660. Courtesy of P.A. Redhead.*

column to compress a gas to a higher pressure, which could be readily measured, and then used Boyle's law to calculate the original low pressure. Although modern versions of the McLeod gauge can cover the range range 10^{-2} to 10^{-7} Torr, they are used only to calibrate other vacuum gauges, largely because they are difficult to use and they need a cold-trap (liquid nitrogen).

Other mechanical manometers use the deflection of a metal diaphragm or tube linked to a needle that registers pressure on a calibrated dial. One of the most widely used of this type of gauge was the Wallace and Tiernan absolute pressure indicator, capable of covering the range from 760 to 0.2 Torr.

In the capacitance manometer, the displacement of the diaphragm is measured by the change in capacitance between the diaphragm and a fixed electrode. The diaphragm is usually restored to its undeflected position by an electrical force. Here the volume on one side of the diaphragm must be evacuated to a pressure lower than the lowest pressure to be measured. This type of gauge was first developed by A.R. Olsen and L.L. Hirst in 1929, and various commercial versions are now in widespread use in the range from atmospheric pressure to 10^{-5} Torr.

Viscosity Gauges

The first vacuum gauge dependent on the viscosity of the gas was developed by W. Sutherland in 1887. A disk suspended on a quartz fiber was caused to oscillate in the vacuum, and the decrease of oscillation amplitude measured to yield an estimate of pressure. Irving Langmuir in 1913 developed a rotating disk gauge in which a disk was suspended on a quartz fiber and closely spaced to a disk rotating at a high speed. The deflection of the suspended disk was measured by reflecting a beam of light from a mirror attached to the fiber. This gauge was capable of measuring pressures as low as 10^{-7} Torr and was the only gauge available to measure pressures this low until the advent of the ionization gauge.

Viscosity gauges were resurrected in the 1950s by Jesse W. Beams, who showed that a magnetically levitated steel ball, spun up to about a million revolutions per second and allowed to coast in vacuum, could be used as a vacuum gauge by measuring the decrement in rotational frequency. This device was developed further, with sophisticated electronics, to yield a direct pressure reading, by J.K. Fremery. The spinning rotor gauge is now commercially available and is used as a secondary standard for calibrating other types of vacuum gauges in the range from 10^{-2} to 10^{-7} Torr.

Thermal Conductivity Gauges (Pirani and Thermocouple)

These gauges are based on the fact that the thermal conductivity of a gas is a function of pressure. The change in temperature of a heated filament, as the result of heat loss through the gas, yields an indication of pressure. In 1906,

Marcello Pirani invented the first thermal conductivity gauge in which the temperature of a heated filament is sensed by measuring its resistance. Other forms of thermal conductivity gauges using a thermocouple or thermistor to measure filament temperature were developed later. The instruments are simple and rugged; the pressure indication depends on the nature of the gas, and the calibration curves are in general nonlinear. They are commercially available in a great variety of models, and are the preferred type of gauge in most applications for the pressure range from atmospheric to 10^{-4} Torr.

Knudson or Radiometer Gauges

In 1910, Martin Knudsen demonstrated that the radiometric force could be exploited as the basis of a vacuum gauge. This force is proportional to pressure and independent of the molecular weight of the gas. The Knudsen gauge was developed further by other experimenters to cover the range 10 to 10^{-8} Torr, and was used in laboratories for about three decades. Commercial versions were available until the 1950s.

Ionization Gauges, Hot-Cathode

Electrons emitted from a hot-cathode are accelerated to about 100 volts and collide with gas molecules to produce a current of positive ions, which can be used as a measure of pressure. Otto von Baeyer proposed this method of measuring pressure, and O.E. Buckley developed a practical vacuum gauge in 1916. The triode vacuum gauge based on Buckley's design was capable of measuring from 10^{-3} to 10^{-8} Torr, and was widely used until 1955, replacing all other instruments in this pressure range. The sensitivity was constant, but was dependent on the nature of the gas.

By the 1940s it was known that the triode gauge, with its large, cylindrical electrode to collect ions, could not measure below about 10^{-8} Torr. Wayne B. Nottingham suggested in 1947 that this limitation was caused by soft x-rays (resulting from the impact of electrons on the grid) producing a current of photo-electrons that is indistinguishable in the measuring circuit from the positive-ion current. In 1950, R.T. Bayard and Daniel Alpert developed a gauge that reduced the area of the collector electrode exposed to soft x-rays by using a fine wire on the axis of the grid as the ion-collector. The Bayard-Alpert gauge, with suitable modifications and the use of modulation methods, is now capable of measuring pressures down to about 10^{-12} Torr, and has completely replaced the triode ionization gauge. It is the gauge most widely used in the high vacuum (10^{-3} to 10^{-8} Torr) and ultrahigh vacuum ranges (less than 10^{-8} Torr).

Several other hot-cathode vacuum gauges have been developed for use in the ultrahigh vacuum range. The commercially available Extractor gauge, developed in 1966, can measure to about 10^{-12} Torr, and a modified form of the Extractor gauge has measured down to 10^{-16} Torr in the laboratory.

Ionization Gauges, Cold-Cathode

A self-sustained discharge can be maintained in a cold-cathode gauge having mutually perpendicular magnetic and electric fields, and the current in the discharge is a function of pressure (usually nonlinear). Although the cold-cathode discharge in a magnetic field was first demonstrated by C.E.S. Phillips in 1898, its use as a vacuum gauge was first implemented in 1937 by F.M. Penning. The Penning or Phillips gauge was rugged and simple, and had a range of 10^{-3} to 10^{-6} Torr, but it had a nonlinear current-vs.-pressure characteristic. It was widely used until the 1960s.

In the late 1950s, as the need for vacuum gauges for the ultrahigh vacuum range developed, Paul A. Redhead developed the Inverted-Magnetron and Magnetron cold-cathode gauges. The magnetron gauge has the geometry of a cylindrical magnetron; in the inverted-magnetron, the positions of the anode and cathode are interchanged. The discharge in both these gauges is well trapped to prevent the escape of electrons, and this extends the lowest pressure at which the discharge is maintained to 10^{-12} Torr or below. Unlike hot-cathode gauges, there is no x-ray limit to the lowest pressure measurable with cold-cathode gauges. The inverted-magnetron gauge is commercially available in several forms.

Partial Pressure Gauges

In many applications it is necessary to identify the various gases present in the vacuum system. This is done with a suitably modified **mass spectrometer**, which is known as a partial pressure gauge, or residual gas analyses (RGA). Several different types of mass spectrometers have been used as RGAs, including the omegatron, time-of-flight, and magnetic sector instruments, but none received wide acceptance. The quadrupole mass spectrometer, invented by W. Paul in 1953

and modified to perform residual gas analysis by about 1960, is now commercially available in a great variety of types and is virtually the only type of RGA now in wide use. The quadrupole RGA with an electron multiplier to amplify the signal can measure the partial pressures of the various gases in a vacuum system to as low as 10^{-16} Torr. Quadrupole RGAs have been used to perform residual gas analysis at total pressures as low as 10^{-13} Torr.

Paul A. Redhead

Bibliography

Berman, A. *Total Pressure Measurements in Vacuum Technology.* New York: Academic, 1985.

Leck, J.M. *Total and Partial Pressure Measurement in Vacuum Systems.* Glasgow: Blackie, 1989.

Redhead, P.A. "History of Ultrahigh Vacuum Pressure Measurements." *Journal of Vacuum Science and Technology A* 12 (1994): 904–14.

———. "The Measurement of Vacuum Pressures," *Journal of Vacuum Science and Technology A2* (1984): 132–38.

Geiger and Geiger-Müller Counters

Geiger and Geiger-Müller counters detect ionizing radiation. In conjunction with suitable ancillary apparatus, they allow individual charged particles to be registered and counted. Used mainly as a research tool in radioactivity and nuclear physics before World War II, they came to be much more widely distributed in the second half of the twentieth century with the growth of the nuclear industry. Many forms are available for a wide range of scientific, medical, and industrial uses.

The instruments evolved from efforts in the early 1900s to use electrical methods for the detection and quantification of radiation. The prototype was devised at the University of Manchester in 1908 by Hans Geiger and Ernest Rutherford, in an attempt to find an independent means of verifying results obtained by the scintillation method of counting alpha particles. A thin coaxial wire at high negative potential (about 1,300 volts) was arranged inside a brass cylinder, 15–25 cm in length and 1.7 cm in internal diameter, containing carbon dioxide at low pressure. A charged particle entering the chamber through a window at one end caused sufficient ionization by collision with other

G

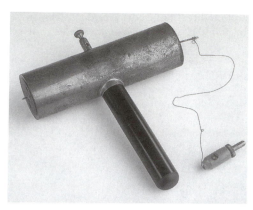

Geiger counter, built by Hans Geiger for James Chadwick, 1932. SM 1982-1707. Courtesy of SSPL.

particles to produce a voltage step on the central wire. This could be registered as a ballistic throw on the needle of a sensitive **electrometer**. This arrangement allowed five to ten particles per minute to be counted.

In 1910 Rutherford and Geiger developed a modified electrical counter consisting of a metal rod and spherical electrode supported by a stopper inside a metallic hemisphere containing helium at low pressure. In this arrangement, the magnified ionization current caused by the passage of a charged particle produced a kick in a Laby string electrometer; a series of such kicks could be counted directly or recorded on a moving strip of photographic film, producing a permanent record of the passage of charged particles through the chamber that could be taken away from the instrument and analyzed at leisure. Up to one thousand alpha particles per minute could be recorded in this way.

Three years later, after a series of trials involving variation of the dimensions and form of the electrode and the nature and pressure of the gas in the tube, Geiger, now working at the Physikalisch-Technische Reichsanstalt in Berlin, produced another modification of the 1908 prototype. This *Spitzenzähler* ("point counter"), 2 cm in diameter and 4 cm long, with a sharply pointed steel needle as anode and with the chamber at atmospheric pressure, could count both alpha and beta particles, together with other types of radiation.

The *Spitzenzähler* found immediate use in problems connected with radioactivity and was soon used in several laboratories, some of them supplied with tubes by Geiger himself. Many of these early instruments were plagued by "natural disturbances" and other "spurious" phenomena (later interpreted as being due to penetrating radiation from the earth's atmosphere—"cosmic rays"), and were so capricious that their successful use demanded a high degree of skill or luck.

Owing to their unpredictability, the devices' mode of operation became the subject of much research in the 1920s. In 1928, Geiger and his student Walther Maria Max Müller found conditions under which the electrical counter could be made to register particles consistently and reliably. Differing from earlier instruments chiefly in the use of a finer central wire and in its electrical characteristics, the device was considerably more sensitive than its predecessors, and normally had to be shielded from background radiation by lead plates. Labeled the *Elektronenzählrohr* by its inventors, the instrument became better known in the English-speaking world as the Geiger-Müller counter (often abbreviated to G-M or, more confusingly, just Geiger counter). Like its predecessors, the G-M counter required an **electrometer** or other apparatus to register the passage of a charged particle. In conjunction with electronic amplification methods made possible by vacuum tubes from the expanding radio industry and the development of increasingly sophisticated circuitry, however, the passage of particles could be registered as clicks in a loudspeaker, giving a direct audible indication of the presence of radiation, or by an electromechanical counting device.

Like the earlier devices, the G-M counter was a laboratory instrument, which was both a research tool and an object of scientific investigation in its own right. At first, the small number of laboratories using the device constructed their own instruments or obtained them directly from Geiger, adding the ancillary registration equipment themselves. Commercial manufacture of G-M counters seems to have begun in the United States around 1930, when firms such as Herbach & Rademan, Eck and Krebs, the Victoreen Instrument Co., and a few others began to market proprietary instruments aimed at the fast-expanding fields of nuclear, particle, and (especially) medical physics.

The G-M counter was rapidly adopted in the emergent field of nuclear physics, where it soon replaced the obsolescent scintillation method of particle counting. The device also found use in the study of cosmic rays, often in conjunction with a **cloud chamber**. With suitable electronic circuitry, two or more counters could be used together to record the near-simultaneous passage of a particle through both—the "coincidence" counting method.

As the instrument became more widely adopted in physics laboratories and elsewhere, further experimental work was devoted to finding the optimum conditions for the detection of different kinds of radiation. The metal cylinder and central electrode were often sealed inside a glass tube, increasing the durability and versatility of the instrument. During the 1930s, the recovery time of the device—the time for it to return to its original state after registering a particle—was significantly reduced by adding a quenching agent (often ethyl alcohol or, later, a halogen) to the gas (usually argon) in the sealed tube. Parallel improvements in electronic counting circuitry in the 1930s meant that by the end of the decade G-M counters were capable of counting up to ten thousand particles per minute.

Work in the development of nuclear weapons and nuclear energy during and after World War II brought a large and pressing demand for robust, reliable, and ever-more specialized radioactivity detection and measurement equipment. This led to an explosion in the number, types, and designs of Geiger and Geiger-Müller counters available. This trend continued in the post-war period, which also witnessed a rapid increase in the number of manufacturers (including government establishments and commercial concerns) and suppliers in the boom field of nucleonics. Instruments were now designed and marketed for the increasingly specialized uses demanded by the nuclear industry and other users of radioactive materials, varying considerably in size and characteristics according to the type of radiation to be measured. Prices of proprietary instruments typically ranged from a few dollars for the simpler individual tubes to some hundreds of dollars for self-contained, battery-operated counters.

Widely available off the shelf from the 1950s (though since supplanted for many uses by solid-state devices). G-M counters resemble many other instruments in their historical trajectory from recalcitrant laboratory device to robust, portable, and relatively unproblematic measuring instrument. They are also among the few types of instruments to have enjoyed a significant cultural presence beyond the laboratory, appearances in the press, literature, and film having made the clicking Geiger counter emblematic of the optimism and anxiety of the nuclear age.

Jeff Hughes

Bibliography

Korff, Serge A. *Electron and Nuclear Counters: Theory and Use*. New York: Van Nostrand, 1946.

Nucleonics (1947–1969), passim.

Rheingans, Friedrich G. *Hans Geiger und die elektrischen Zählmethoden 1908–1928*. Berlin: D.A.V.I.D., 1988.

Trenn, Thaddeus J. "The Geiger-Müller Counter of 1928." *Annals of Science* 43 (1986): 111–35.

Geissler Tube

A Geissler tube is a partially evacuated glass tube with two or more electrodes fitted through its walls. It is named after Heinrich Geissler, a glass blower of Bonn, who began to supply the local professor of mathematics and physics, Julius Plücker, with the tubes in the 1850s. Tubes of this nature were popular in the second half of the nineteenth century and were often named after the most prominent researchers using them: Plücker tubes, Hittorf tubes, and Crookes tubes. The term "cathode-ray tube" also became common after 1880. Most tubes were no more than 3–4 cm in diameter, but the tubes used for public displays could be as big as 15 cm. These early vacuum tubes led to the light bulb, the x-ray tube (see **x-ray machine**), and the **oscilloscope**, all depending upon the passing of electricity through an evacuated glass tube. The term "Geissler tube" was frequently used for early x-ray tubes.

Production

Geissler tubes were made by glass blowing, and special techniques were required to fit the electrodes into the glass wall. A simple technique was to put a fine platinum wire through a hole in the glass wall that was subsequently melted down onto the platinum and then blown out uniform. However, the inequality of the expansion coefficients of the glass and the platinum often led to cracks, and so it was general practice to introduce an intermediate material.

As glass blowing was a common laboratory skill, many of the simpler tubes were blown locally. But since the tubes produced spectacular color effects, they were also produced as commodities for consumption beyond the laboratory. New tubes were constantly devised for these purposes. They became increasingly expensive because they depended upon specialized glass blowing skills and ancillary technologies,

A variety of commercial Geissler tubes, 1924. John J. Griffin & Sons Ltd. Scientific Handicraft: An Illustrated and Descriptive Catalogue of Scientific Apparatus. *London, 1914: 948, Figure 3-7950/2. Courtesy of Fisher Scientific U.K. Ltd.*

especially electricity supply and vacuum techniques. Dependable and controllable effects required relatively strong and regular currents of high tension. The development of electrical motors and accumulators was important in this respect. A fast and effective technique of evacuation was also important, and the introduction of the electrical light bulb revolutionized vacuum techniques in the 1880s. The illustration shows some tubes advertised by Geissler's successors, probably from the 1890s. These tubes would have been beyond the capabilities of most glass blowers.

Use

Geissler tubes fascinated audiences, especially in the 1860s and 1870s. By placing uranium glass inside the tube, striking and beautiful effects were obtained. By employing different residual gases, all colors of the rainbow could be produced. The light could also be concentrated in parts of the tube and even made to follow the curves imparted to the glassware.

The use of Geissler tubes in scientific discourse was very diverse, certainly spanning the disciplines of physics and chemistry. The most general issue that the electrical discharge within the tube could illuminate was the relationship between electricity, matter, and (sometimes) the ether. Within that larger theoretical framework,

three fields of scientific inquiry must be emphasized: stratification, spectroscopy, and the nature of cathode rays.

Spaces of lightness and darkness could be produced within the tube, normally called stratification. The relationship between the shape and size of tube, degree of vacuum, electrical tension, and so on, was investigated by Auguste De la Rive, John Peter Gassiot, Plücker, and William Spottiswoode.

The spectroscopic composition of the light emanating from a Geissler tube discharge (or from its point of impact) prompted detailed research. The change of pressure, temperature, and electrical conditions of the discharge would alter the character of the spectra, sometimes quite dramatically, leading to intensity differences, broadening, or the reversion of lines. Some of the better-known investigators included William Crookes, Eugen Goldstein, Friedrich Paschen, William Ramsay, and Arthur Schuster.

At the higher vacuums achieved in the 1880s, the discharge turned into a "ray" with a linear path. This ray was called a "cathode ray," and its nature was a third large field of inquiry involving the use of electrical and magnetic fields. It was particularly difficult to achieve the stable vacuums required for the production of cathode rays, and so it was also difficult to achieve stable experimental results. It is not surprsing that cathode rays were believed to be electromagnetic in nature in Germany, and material in Britain. Joseph John Thomson's "discovery of the electron" in 1897 settled the matter, at a time when relatively much higher vacuums could be produced. On the German side, Wilhelm Hittorf, Goldstein, Hermann Helmholtz, and Heinrich Hertz were involved; on the British, Crookes, George Stokes, and Thomson.

Arne Hessenbruch

Bibliography

Harvey, E. Newton. *A History of Luminescence from the Earliest Times until 1900*. Philadelphia: American Philosophical Society, 1957.

Lehmann, O. *Die elektrischen Lichterscheinungen oder Entladungen in freier Luft und in Vacuumrohren zum Theil auf Grund eigener Experimentaluntersuchungen*. Halle a. S.: Wilhelm Kapp, 1898.

Waran, H.P. *Elements of Glass-Blowing*. London: G. Bell, 1923.

Gene Gun

See BIOLISTIC APPARATUS (GENE GUN)

Gene Sequencer

A gene sequencer, often termed a DNA sequencer, is used to automate the sequencing of bases in DNA, one of the most important tools of modern biology. It is especially important to scientists working on the regulation and functioning of genes, medical genetics, and the Human Genome Project, which has the goal of mapping and sequencing the three billion base pairs of the human genome and its estimated 50–100,000 genes.

After the discovery of the structure of DNA by James Watson and Francis Crick in 1953, it was realized that the hereditary properties of living organisms could be coded by the sequence of the four nucleotide bases, adenine (A), thymine (T), cytosine (C), guanine (G). From this followed the perception of genes, the units of heredity, as ordered sequences of nucleotides found in particular positions on specific chromosomes, and by the end of the 1960s molecular biologists had established the basic characteristics of the genetic code. The physical composition of genes could then, in theory, be established by sequencing. In practice, however, this proved a technically difficult task, and by 1968 the longest determined DNA sequence was only twelve base pairs.

DNA sequencing can be regarded as a conceptual extension of work done in the 1950s on sequencing proteins, and in the 1960s on sequencing RNA. In the mid 1970s, effective sequencing techniques were discovered more or less simultaneously by Frederick Sanger and colleagues at the University of Cambridge and by Allan Maxam and Walter Gilbert at Harvard University. Gilbert, Maxam, and Sanger shared one-half of the 1980 Nobel Prize for chemistry for their "contributions concerning the determination of base sequences in nucleic acids." In 1958 Sanger had received the Nobel Prize in chemistry for his research on protein sequencing.

The two methods use different approaches. Sanger's method was enzymic, using DNA polymerase and inhibitors that terminate newly synthesized fragments of DNA at specific bases. Maxam's and Gilbert's approach used a series of chemical reactions able to cleave DNA at a particular base. Both methods provided nested sets of radioactive labeled fragments that could be fractionated using polyacrilamide gel electrophoresis in four lanes, one for each base. The radioactive marker produces a band on a film at the position of each fragment end in the gel, and the sequence is read by determining the order of fragment size in each lane. Both techniques led to the development of a wide range of molecular genetic studies and complemented the other great advance of the same period, artificially recombinant DNA—for which Paul Berg received the other half of the 1980 Nobel Prize for chemistry.

Gene Sequencers

Despite their elegance and efficacy, the Sanger and the Maxam and Gilbert techniques were time consuming and labor intensive. For example, autoradiograph band patterns are complex and need skilled interpretation and data transcription. Throughout the early 1980s, therefore, attempts were made to automate various steps in the sequencing process and develop the DNA sequencer.

The earliest successful attempt was at Leroy Hood's laboratory at the California Institute of Technology, where in the early 1980s Lloyd Smith developed an approach that used fluorescent dyes and lasers. The aim was to allow the acquisition, storage, and analysis of sequence information directly by computer during gel electrophoresis. This work paved the way for a pro-

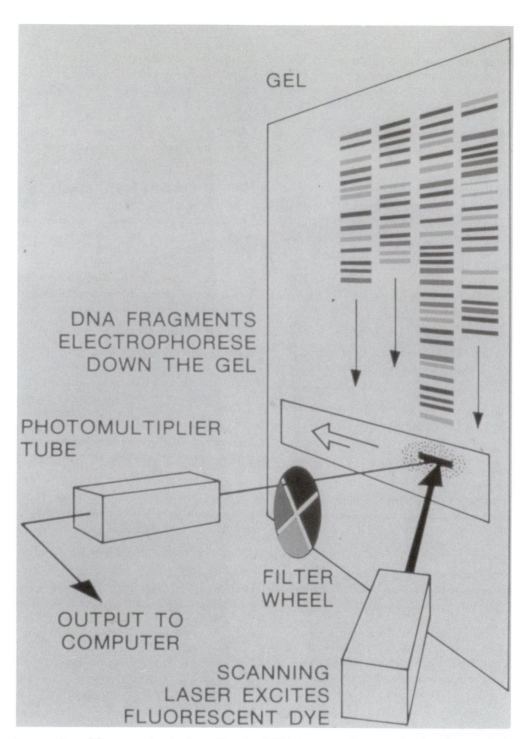

GEL

DNA FRAGMENTS
ELECTROPHORESE
DOWN THE GEL

PHOTOMULTIPLIER
TUBE

FILTER
WHEEL

OUTPUT TO
COMPUTER

SCANNING
LASER EXCITES
FLUORESCENT DYE

Laser reading of fluorescent dyes in electrophoresis of DNA fragments. Courtesy of Perkin Elmer/Applied Biosystems.

ductive collaboration between the Caltech group and Applied Biosystems, Inc., also located in California. The Caltech team announced a prototype sequencer in June 1986, and by the beginning of 1987 Applied Biosystems was marketing a commercial version, the ABS 370A.

The ABS 370A automated the gel electrophoresis, raw data acquisition, and base reading steps of DNA sequencing. The system consisted of an electrophoresis module and electrophoresis detector unit linked to a PC computer that ran special software for data display, interpretation, and storage. To use this system, it was first necessary to carry out a series of laborious sample preparation procedures to produce a set of DNA fragments labeled by fluorescent dyes. The DNA fragments were then loaded onto a single lane of a gel and electrophoresed down the gel over a period of several hours, separating according to size. The detector unit scanned the gel with an argon laser, whose beam caused the dyes to fluoresce. The emitted light was passed sequentially through four filters, each of which passed light corresponding to the maximum emission wavelength of one of the four dyes, each dye matching a specific base. The filtered light was passed through a photomultiplier tube able to produce a digitized signal, which was sent to the computer. The software on the computer was then able to convert this data into a base sequence reading. The instrument could process about three hundred bases per lane per run; since it was able to run sixteen lanes simultaneously, the ABI 370A could, in theory, determine about forty eight hundred bases in a twelve-hour run. It had an accuracy of 99 percent.

Similar developments occurred elsewhere. Both DuPont and EG & G Biomolecular marketed sequencers in the United States. In Europe, Wilhelm Ansorge's group at the European Molecular Biology Laboratory (EMBL) at Heidelberg developed the Automatic Laser Fluorescent (AFL) system; this was later commercialized by Pharmacia. In Japan, the Science and Technology Agency since 1981 supported a sequencer development group led by Akiyosi Wada; Hitachi Instruments developed and marketed a sequencer.

While the EG & G Acugen machine continued the practice of radioactive labeling of the DNA fragments, the other instruments used variants of fluorochrome labeling and laser activated fluorescence detection systems to identify separated products of sequencing reactions in real time as they migrated through the gel. Two basic approaches to fluorochrome labeling have been used in commercial DNA sequencers. One uses four fluorescent labels with single lane separation, as in the Applied Biosystems 370A and in the Genesis 2000 sequencer developed by DuPont. The other uses a single fluorescent label with four lane separation; this was pioneered by workers at EMBL and researchers at Hitachi Instruments of Japan.

Future Developments

Since DNA sequencers are costly—the original IBS sequencers cost about $90,000—small to medium-scale projects still use the less expensive, traditional hand-sequencing methods, usually the Sanger. The consensus is, however, that manual methods will be replaced by automated methods for megabase projects. Such projects are associated with organizational structures more akin to industrial production lines than academic laboratories; a pioneering and successful example of that approach was the Généthon Laboratory opened in 1990 at Évry near Paris.

The DNA sequencer automated only parts of the overall sequencing process, those dealing with running gels and reading sequences. The process of cloning and preparing DNA for sequencing remains laborious, and developments are occurring in laboratory robotics and automation for speeding up these front end stages. In the sequencers themselves, incremental improvements are expected in the short term. This is not to say that revolutionary breakthroughs may not occur, for alternative, but still speculative, approaches are under investigation to achieve the economy, speed, and accuracy of sequencing needed to complete the Human Genome Project.

Harry Rothman

Bibliography

Connell, C., et al. "Automated DNA Sequence Analysis." *Biotechniques* 5 (1987): 42–348.

Hideki, Tetsuo Nishikawa, Yoshiko Katayama, and Tomoaki Yamaguchi. "Optimization of Parameters in a DNA Sequenator Using Fluorescence Detection." *Biotechnology* 6, (1988): 816–21.

Prober, James M., et al. "A System for Rapid DNA Sequencing with Fluorescent Chain-terminating Dideoxynucleotides." *Science* 238 (1987): 336–41.

Smith, Lloyd M., et al. "Fluorescence Detection in Automated DNA Sequence Analysis." *Nature* 321 (1986): 674–79.

Voss, Hartmund, et al. "Direct Genomic Fluorescent On-line Sequencing and Analysis Using In-vitro Amplification of DNA." *Nucleic Acids Research* 17 (1989): 2517–27.

G

Global Positioning System

The Global Positioning System (GPS) is a constellation of twenty-four satellites and several monitor and uplink stations on earth that determine and predict positions for the GPS satellites and uplink data to them. Users with a microprocessor-controlled radio receiver can accurately determine their position and velocity, and recover precise time.

The need for a continuous worldwide accurate position and velocity measurement system was identified in 1968 by the United States Joint Chiefs of Staff. The Navigation Satellite Program and the Four Service Navigation Satellite Executive Steering group were established to determine the technical feasibility, usefulness, and viability of a satellite-based navigation system. From 1969 to 1974, with cooperation from government laboratories, research organizations, and industry, this group developed the basic concept, system configuration, frequencies, codes, performance, cost, and planned applications for what became the GPS. The GPS initial design included contributions from the operational Transit system and two developmental concept studies: the Navy Timation system and the Air Force System 621B. Cicada, a system similar to Transit, and GLONASS, a system similar to the GPS, were developed concurrently in the Soviet Union. All these systems use satellites as space-borne navigation radio beacons that transmit line-of-sight signals to users, containing accurate orbital descriptions. Transit, developed between 1958 and 1964 at the Johns Hopkins University Applied Physics Laboratory (and still operating in 1995), made a number of lasting contributions to satellite-based positioning, and to GPS in particular.

Satellites with stable and predictable orbits were designed, carrying precise clocks and reliably transmitting radio signals for many years. The predictability of satellite orbits was greatly improved by refining models for the nonuniformities in the earth's gravity field (based on unexpected orbital motions of Transit and other satellites). Methods to account for the effect of the earth's atmosphere on radio signals from satellites were developed. Precise satellite locations are provided to users by storing them in satellite memory and reading them out as modulations of the navigation radio tone. However, users must independently determine their altitude and the trajectory of their vehicle during the 10–15 minute tracking period required for each Transit fix, of which there are only a few dozen per day.

The Naval Research Laboratory established the Timation program in 1964 to explore ways of providing continuous three-dimensional positioning (as well as velocity and time), based on pseudo-ranging (or passive ranging, or one-way ranging), a concept developed at NRL in 1960. The transmission of a navigation signal is controlled by a clock in the satellite, while signal reception is controlled by a different clock in the user's receiver. The mis-synchronization of these clocks is treated as a fourth unknown quantity to be determined (in addition to latitude, longitude, and altitude). To do this, GPS receivers must track at least four satellites, and all satellite clocks are assumed to be precisely synchronized. The Timation program designed satellite constellations that could provide continuous worldwide coverage by at least four satellites and developed space-borne precise atomic clocks. The GPS adopted the pseudo-ranging concept, a constellation related to the Timation designs, and atomic clocks in the satellites.

The U.S. Air Force System 621B program also investigated the use of satellite-based systems for determining position, velocity, and time, including satellite constellations providing coverage by at least four satellites. The most important 621B contribution to GPS was the development and navigational use of pseudo-random noise (PRN), a repeated sequence of binary bits (ones and zeroes) with noiselike properties. PRN modulations on a radio tone permit range (or pseudo-range) measurements that are precise, secure, and resistant to jamming. PRN codes are easy to generate but hard to determine if the code is not known, and they are, in effect, readings of the satellite clock. GPS uses two families of PRN codes: coarse-acquisition (C/A) PRN codes, and a precision (P) code. User's receivers must generate the PRN codes of the satellites being tracked. The basic GPS pseudo-range measurement is the time shift required to align the code generated within the receiver with the corresponding code on the signal arriving from the satellite. These measurements, together with accurate knowledge of the satellite positions (transmitted by the satellites in a data message to users), allows GPS receivers to determine their position, velocity, and time.

The GPS program was approved in the early 1970s, and a GPS Joint Program Office established, responsible for the design and deployment

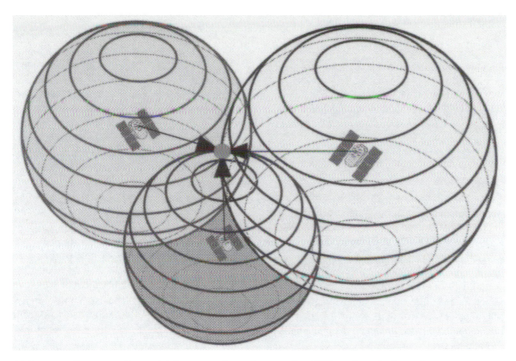

GPS position location using multiple ranges. Assuming a perfect GPS receiver clock, each range measurement can be portrayed as the surface of the sphere. These intersect to produce two possible position fixes, one of which is located far out in space. Courtesy of University of New Brunswick, Department of Geodesy and Geomantics Engineering.

of military GPS receivers, the ground station infrastructure, and several blocks of GPS satellites. Ten Block I development satellites were launched between 1978 and 1985. Twenty-four Block II and IIA operational satellites were launched between 1989 and 1994. The GPS was officially declared fully operational in April 1995. Up to fifty-eight additional GPS satellites will be available to maintain twenty-four satellites in orbit well into the twenty-first century.

GPS signals are available free of charge to all users, both military and civilian. For security reasons, the satellite clock and orbital information available to civilian users has been deliberately degraded since 1991 (a process called "selective availability"). Since 1994 the P-code has been encrypted, so that civilian receivers can track only the C/A-code (a process called "anti-spoofing").

GPS three-dimensional accuracy (16 meters for military users, 150 meters for civilians, 95 percent of the time) is far surpassed by its differential accuracy (tracking the same satellite signals simultaneously at two or more locations). Many networks of public and private civilian reference GPS stations have emerged, transmitting differential GPS (DGPS) corrections to users, and of-

fering 10-meter to submeter accuracies. Receivers have been developed that track all satellites in view (up to twelve), use the GPS radio tones as well as PRN codes for positioning, and make much more accurate PRN code measurements than originally possible. DGPS navigation accuracies of a few centimeters are feasible. Static baselines have been determined to an accuracy of a few millimeters, or a few parts per billion of long baseline lengths.

Civilian use of GPS has had a major impact on transportation and "smart" vehicles, on precision farming, on marine and air navigation and "electronic charts," on natural resource management and utility mapping, and on earth science (directly measuring continental drift, for example). In 1995 there were over one million GPS receivers in use, with sixty thousand per month being produced for the automobile market alone, prices dropping to a few hundred dollars, and a monthly magazine, *GPS World,* dedicated to emerging applications of the system.

David Wells

Bibliography
Langley, Richard. Moderator, Canadian Space Geodesy Forum (CANSPACE).

Uniform Resource Locator (URL) :http://
degaulle.hil.unb.ca/Geodesy/
CANSPACE.html

Parkinson, Bradford W., et al. "A History of
Satellite Navigation." *Navigation* 42
(1995): 109–64.

Wells, D.E., et al. *Guide to GPS Positioning.*
Fredericton, New Brunswick: Canadian
GPS, 1986, 1987.

Globe

Throughout their history globes have served
dual roles, as scientific and didactic instruments
and as symbolic and prestige ornaments. Western globe-makers have produced three types of
globes: terrestrial globes detailing the geographical and other characteristics of the earth;
celestial globes depicting the appearance of the
geocentric vault of the heavens; and globes displaying the physical features of other celestial
bodies, such as the moon or Mars. At minimum, terrestrial and celestial globes constructed
with some attention to accuracy provide (respectively) the coordinates of terrestrial locations (latitude and longitude), or locate the
fixed stars (usually at a fixed point in time, or
epoch) with respect to a traditional astronomical reference system that includes the celestial
equator, ecliptic, and poles. With these basic
features, globes can be used as analog computers to facilitate solution of a range of geographical and astronomical problems.

Globes consist of three main parts: a
sphere, which can be made of metal, wood,
papier maché, or other materials; a map, either
produced directly onto the sphere, or separately
as a set of gores that are then fitted on the
sphere; and the apparatus (if any) in which the
globe is mounted. Globe-makers varied each
according to the demands of learning, patrons,
or intended markets. Globes produced in Europe and America have ranged in size from
mass-produced "pocket globes" of around 3 in.
in diameter, to single, manuscript instruments
of several feet in diameter, although printed
globes have rarely exceeded 30 in. in diameter.
The maps of antique globes are of greatest interest to the historian, as their engravers often
took great care to accurately reflect the extent
of contemporary geographical and astronomical knowledge, as well as to create an aestheti-
cally pleasing product. The apparatus furnished
with a globe might be a simple stand for display,
or it might include various devices intended to

facilitate or extend the range of calculations
possible on globes.

Although the scientific principles of depicting both the celestial sphere and terrestrial geography on globes were known to the ancients, and
although literary evidence indicates that globes
were produced in the ancient world, little is
known about the objects themselves. The only
known surviving ancient globe is the Farnese
Atlas, a decorative celestial globe of about 25 in.
in diameter that shows the outline of constellations against a coordinate system; this piece appears to postdate the codification of ancient astronomy and geography by the Alexandrian
scholar Claudius Ptolemy around A.D. 150.

Ptolemy's approach to astronomy and geography dominated these sciences in the medieval world; so, for example, the relative rarity
of medieval terrestrial globes reflects Ptolemy's
preference for depicting the earth on flat maps.
Ptolemy's influence also extended to Arabic
astronomy, and thus to Islamic celestial globes.
However, these devices varied in two important
respects from Ptolemy's model, in that they located the stars at a fixed epoch, thereby ignor-
ing the change in their positions resulting from
precession, and they depicted the figures of the
constellations facing outward, toward the user,
rather than inward, toward the center of the
globe. The first innovation was subsequently
adopted by European makers.

Celestial globes continued to outnumber
terrestrial in Europe until the fifteenth-century
publication of Ptolemy's *Geography,* and the
voyages of discovery stimulated renewed interest in the art of depicting the geography of the
earth on the sphere. As a consequence, from the
fifteenth through eighteenth centuries, celestial
and terrestrial globes were made and sold as
sets.

The introduction of printing revolutionized the production and marketing of globes.
Printing shifted the production of globes from
the private studies of astronomers, and the
workshops of those engaged in the creation of
luxury goods for the elite, to an industry situated at the intersection between the book, map,
and scientific-instrument trades.

Production of printed globes demanded
considerable capital investment, mostly to cover
the cost associated with large copper-plate en-
gravings; consequently, globe-makers were always eager to market their goods to as large an
audience as possible. In the sixteenth and seventeenth centuries, globes were often constructed

Two terrestrial globes by John Senex, 1740s. SM 1915-395, 1917-53. Courtesy of SSPL.

to serve as cartographic and navigational aids; for example, Gerard Mercator included rhumb lines, or loxodromes, on the terrestrial globe he produced in 1541. Even into the eighteenth century, globe-makers continued to insist that their products were indispensable to the practicing navigator. However, navigators apparently concluded otherwise, judging globes as more expensive, inconvenient, and fragile than maps and charts. Consequently, over the course of the seventeenth century, globes gradually lost their place on board ships.

With the decline in their navigational use, globes became primarily instructional tools and "showpieces" of wealth and prestige. The roles were often not compatible. As luxury furniture, seventeenth- and eighteenth-century globes were priced beyond the reach of all but the wealthiest; in 1740, London globe-maker John Senex advertised his 28-in. globes "fit to adorn the Libraries of the Curious" for 25 guineas. Senex's 9-in. globes cost only £3, and his 3-in. "pocket globes" a mere 10 shillings, but neither would have been considered by teachers large enough for the student to carry out precise calculations. Concern over the cost of large globes inspired several eighteenth-century English schoolmasters to design and market inexpensive substitutes for both celestial and terrestrial globes. The effort to produce globes, or their equivalents, inexpensive enough for students accelerated in the nineteenth century, with the invention of folding or collapsible globes, the development of new types of planispheres, and, most important, the replacement of copperplate engraving with lithography, which significantly lowered production costs.

The nineteenth century witnessed the greatest revolution in the globe industry since the introduction of printing. In addition to new production methods, the European globe industry also responded to the demands of nationalism, producing globes in a variety of languages, including Russian, Danish, Armenian, and Hungarian, while across the Atlantic the American globe industry took root and flourished. The nineteenth century also marked the decline of the celestial globe, which became less popular as a knowledge of positional astronomy became less useful and necessary; at the same time, new types of thematic terrestrial globes became available, reflecting new research in geology, meteorology, oceanography, and other geophysical subjects.

Alice Walters

Bibliography

Dekker, Elly, and Peter van der Krogt. *Globes from the Western World*. London: Zwemmer, 1993.

Der Globusfreund: Wissenschaftliche Zeitschrift für Globen- und Instrumentenkunde. Vienna, 1951–.

Krogt, P.C.J. van der. *Globi Neerlandici: The Production of Globes in the Low Countries*. Utrecht: HES, 1993.

Stevenson, Edward Luther. *Terrestrial and Celestial Globes: Their History and Construction*. New Haven: Yale University Press, 1921.

Glucose Sensor

When a physician first tasted a patient's urine for purposes of diagnosing "sugar diabetes," the initial glucose sensor was identified: the human tongue. The Brahmin text Suruta described diabetes mellitus with remarkable accuracy in the A.D. fifth century. The sweet taste of diabetic urine was mentioned as least as early

as the eleventh century, but not proven due to sugar until the eighteenth century. Full understanding of etiology and treatment methods did not occur until the discovery of insulin by Frederick G. Banting and Charles H. Best in 1921. With the ability to diagnose and treat diabetes mellitus, came the need of precise methods for measuring body glucose levels, including blood and urine. In 1962 Leland Clark proposed a family of sensors, including glucose, derived from his amperometric oxygen sensor.

Glucose sensors are now used in environmental monitoring, food science, fermentation, clinical laboratory and other chemical analytic applications, and within the body of experimental animals and patients. In the latter two cases the term "biosensor" may be applied, and that is the context for the remaining discussion. The requirement for different applications determines the form and design of the sensor as well as materials that may be used.

Continuous information about blood glucose would be invaluable for regulating therapeutic regimes for brittle (Type I) diabetics and for treating patients in acidotic coma or having hypoglycemic reaction from insulin overdoses. A completely implanted sensor would find its greatest expression as part of a closed loop artificial pancreas device, providing feedback for control of the insulin infusion pump. Many of the technical components for an artificial pancreas are available and in use, but the transducer or sensor is still wanting.

All glucose sensors generate an electrical signal that can be read directly, recorded, or used in feedback control of an insulin pump system. They then are capable of being hardwired or completely implantable, using techniques such as telemetry. Some utilize measurements of chemical or electrochemical reactions, others employ physical measures such as temperature or optical phenomena, and some are small enough to fit into a hypodermic needle. The following examples are not to be considered inclusive or necessarily the best in their class.

Electrochemical Sensor

There are two main categories. The first uses an electrode (anode) usually of noble metal or metal black to directly oxidize glucose to a product such as gluconic acid and then capture the electrons transferred in this process. Rate of reaction, as indicated by current flow, is a function of glucose concentration. Examples are the

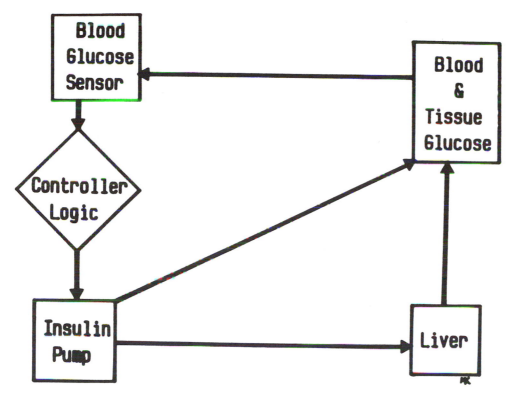

Schematic diagram showing control loop for an artificial pancreas device to regulate blood glucose. Courtesy of University of Pittsburgh, School of Medicine.

early efforts of Kuo W. Chang et al. in the 1970s and, more recently, John F. Patzer II et al. Electrodes may be polarized to a set voltage and current measured or scanned over a voltage domain in a process called cyclic voltammetry. In both, the specificity depends on reactions occurring at the selected voltage where current is sampled. In the cyclic method the scan may include an electrode reactivation voltage phase or "pulse."

The second and largest category is composed of sensors in which an enzyme such as glucose oxidase provides the selectivity, and the measurement depends upon directly capturing the electron of the enzyme catalytic reaction, oxidation of a product of the reaction (H_2O_2 in the case of glucose oxidase), or measuring the oxygen consumed. This is the type proposed by Clark. Glucose oxidase electrodes have been constructed and tested in vitro and in vivo in animals and humans by many investigators. Some have worked well for short periods of time, some have been coupled to insulin pumping systems and actually controlled carbohydrate metabolism for short periods. Electrodes that directly oxidize glucose will suffer interfer-

ence from any substance that is capable of oxidation at the potential chosen, thus specificity is a problem. The enzyme electrode has the problem of enzyme lability and thus a short functional life.

Optical Glucose Sensors
Optical isomerism is a property of sugars such as glucose that have an asymmetric carbon atom in the chain. The concentration of the isomer can be determined from the degree of rotation of plane polarized light. Wayne F. March has proposed a microminiature **polarimeter** focused on the anterior chamber of the eye and mounted on an eyeglass frame. This system would be noninvasive, but its problems include the small degree of rotation to be expected from the physiologic glucose variation and possible interference of other metabolites exhibiting optical isomerism. Fluorescence methods using optical fibers have been used with several glucose sensing strategies. Dietrich W. Lubbers et al. have applied the principle of fluorescence quenching by O_2 in a system containing glucose oxidase. Jerome S. Schultz et al. have used a fiber optic system in which binding of fluores-

cein labeled dextran to ConA is altered by competition with glucose for binding sites. This reversible reaction takes place in a dialysis hollow fiber that is implanted in an appropriate glucose monitoring site. Chemiluminescence in a peroxidase-luminol-H_2O_2 system has been applied to glucose measurement by Yoshihito Iarriyama. This was tested on the lab bench but not actually miniaturized to fiber optic size.

Calorimetry

Klaus Mosbach has used thermistors to measure heat generated by the glucose oxidase or hexokinase reaction. His work was in an in vitro flow through apparatus but could be applied to an implantable version.

Summary

Though there is not yet a long-lived, reliable, stable, and easily calibrated device suitable for implantation or even extended bedside applications, work continues because of the great demand for better metabolic control of diabetes mellitus. The recently completed diabetes control and complications trial (DCCT) has convincingly shown what many believed: that close control of plasma glucose leads to significant reduction in the complications that are the source of most diabetic morbidity and mortality. Close control requires close monitoring, and hence a renewed impetus for a reliable sensor. The best way to approach near perfect control is with an implantable closed-loop insulin pumping system (artificial endocrine pancreas). Further impetus comes from the economic and human cost of this disease. In 1992, direct inpatient cost for diabetes care, including its complications, is estimated to have been $39 billion for the United States alone. Outpatient care was an additional $6.2 billion. To this $45 billion for direct costs can be added another indirect $46.6 billion (lost productivity and premature death), for a total cost of $91.8 billion in 1992.

Sidney K. Wolfson, Jr.

Bibliography

Chang, K.W., et al. "Validation and Bioengineering Aspects of an Implantable Glucose Sensor." *Transactions of the American Society for Artificial Internal Organs* 19 (1973): 352–60.

Clark, L.C., Jr., and C. Lyons. "Electrode Systems for Continuous Monitoring in Cardiovascular Surgery." *Annals of the New York Academy of Sciences* 102 (1962): 29–45.

Fischer, U. "Fundamentals of Glucose Sensors." *Diabetic Medicine* 8 (1991): 309–21.

Patzer, J.F., II, et al. "A Microchip Glucose Sensor." *ASAIO Journal* 41 (1995): M409–M413.

Wolfson, S.K. "Glucose Sensors, Blood and Tissue, Implantable." In *Encyclopedia of Medical Devices and Instrumentation,* edited by J.G. Webster, 1410–28. New York: Wiley, 1987.

Goniometer

In its most basic sense, a goniometer measures angles. Although specialized goniometers have been used in several fields (such as surveying, physics, and craniometry), the most common and historically significant goniometers were those used by mineralogists to measure the face angles of crystals.

The first goniometers were handheld instruments. Like the protractor on which they were based, these contact goniometers used two movable arms to directly measure angles. If the crystal were large and the faces smooth, it was easy to measure angles to within 1° or 2°. Under optimal conditions, the accuracy of this type of direct measurement might extend to 0.5°.

The first systematic use of a contact goniometer was by Jean-Baptiste Romé de l'Isle, whose *Cristallographie* (1783) is considered the first scientific treatise on the subject. Using an instrument invented for the purpose and constructed by his assistant Carangeot, he made systematic measurements that established the invariability of the angles of certain simple forms of crystals.

Romé tried to establish crystallography as the basis of mineral identification. This approach to the study of minerals was influenced by his views on the nature of scientific inquiry. Romé supported the *nomenclateurs* (as their opponents called them), who agreed with Linnaeus in viewing classification to be one of the chief ends of the natural sciences. The *systémateurs* were more interested in building general systems on the basis of hypotheses that were not necessarily based on empirical research.

Romé's empirical approach stood in contrast to the work of René-Just Haüy, who attempted to classify crystals according to a mathematical system that presumed the existence of basic "primitive forms" from which all crystals were derived. A mathematical idealist, Haüy insisted on the principle of the "simplicity of nature," and stubbornly rejected any measurements that disagreed with the predictions of his theory. It is noteworthy that, even after more precise instruments were available, Haüy continued to use the less accurate contact goniometer.

In 1809, in an apparent attempt to refute Haüy's speculations, the English chemist William Hyde Wollaston invented the reflecting goniometer. Using the principle of the optical lever, Wollaston's simple and inexpensive instrument ingeniously solved the problems inherent in earlier goniometers. It consisted of a brass circle, graduated on its edge and mounted on one end of a horizontal axis. The crystal to be measured was mounted on the other end of the axis. The observer adjusted the crystal until a distant image was reflected off one of the facets into the observer's eye, rotated the crystal until the next surface reflected the same image (the eye being kept stationary), and then read the angle between the two crystal faces from the graduated circle. Wollaston's original instrument could measure the angle between two crystal faces to an accuracy of 5 minutes, and could measure crystals with faces as small as $1/_{50\text{th}}$ of an inch.

Wollaston never actually named Haüy in the article announcing his invention, but he characterized his work as "a result deduced from the supposed position . . . of the surfaces, and from other seducing circumstances of apparent harmony by simple ratios." He also noted an error of over 30 minutes in Haüy's measurement of the calcium carbonate crystal, and predicted that his new instrument "will probably afford corrections to many former observations."

The reflecting goniometer is credited with separating mineralogy from chemistry as a discrete area of study. In his 1830 review of scientific progress, John Herschel characterized Wollaston's "elegant invention" as the prototype of a scientific instrument: "What an important influence may be exercised over the progress of a single branch of science by the invention of a ready and convenient mode of executing a definite measurement, and the construction and common introduction of an instrument adapted for it cannot be better exemplified than by the instance of the reflecting goniometer. This simple, cheap, and portable little instrument has

Wollaston's reflecting goniometer, by Cary, ca. 1820. SM 1927-116. Courtesy of SSPL.

changed the face of mineralogy, and given it all the characters of one of the exact sciences."

Although instruments nearly identical to Wollaston's original design continued to be used in classrooms throughout the nineteenth century, more precise versions were also introduced. The two most successful types were those developed by the French physicist Jacques Babinet in 1839, and by Eilherd Mitscherlich, professor of chemistry at the University of Berlin, in 1843. Babinet's reflecting goniometer had a horizontal graduated circle and was equipped with two **telescopes**, one serving as a collimator for the light source and the other for viewing the image. As Babinet was noted for his work with **diffraction gratings**, it is not surprising that his goniometer proved to be particularly well suited to spectroscopic investigations. In their 1890 *Catalogue*, the Société Genevoise described their Babinet goniometer as an instrument that "may be used without modification as a spectrometer" (*see* **spectrophotometer**).

Mineralogists found the Babinet goniometer advantageous when measuring large crystals or those attached to a large piece of rock. Physicists saw it as one of the most valuable instruments in the laboratory. In the goniometer form it could be used to measure the angles of crystals, find the index of refraction of solids or liquids, and study dispersion. In the spectrometer form, it could be used to measure wavelengths. Edward C. Pickering, who developed the first college physics laboratories in the United States, recommended that each laboratory acquire "one large and very accurate" Babinet goniometer and "others of smaller size for work requiring less precision."

Mitscherlich's basic design had a vertical graduated circle and two telescopes. The measurement was made when the illuminated reflection of the cross hairs in the first telescope were made to coincide with those in the viewing telescope on successive crystal faces. Over the years, instrument-makers produced a wide variety of Mitscherlich-type goniometers of increasing complexity. Although offering extreme precision, these elaborate instruments required patience and skill to operate properly.

Although the optical goniometer was largely replaced by other types of measurement in the early twentieth century, it continues to have limited applications in mineral identification.

Steven C. Turner

Bibliography

Turner, Steven C. "The Reflecting Goniometer." *Rittenhouse* 27 (1993): 84–90.

Usselman, Melvyn C. "The Reflective Goniometer and Its Impact on Chemical Theory." In *The History and Preservation of Chemical Instrumentation,* edited by John Stock and Mary Virginia Orna, 33–40. Boston: Reidel, 1986.

Wollaston, William Hyde. "Description of a Reflective Goniometer." *Philosophical Transactions of the Royal Society of London* 99 (1809): 253–58.

Gravitational Radiation Detector

According to most interpretations of the general theory of relativity, moving masses should generate gravitational radiation just as moving electrical charges produce electromagnetic radiation. The energy associated with a moving mass is, however, vanishingly small, and there are no plans to try to detect gravitational waves that are generated on Earth. Supernovae, or other exciting cosmic scenarios, should, however, generate a flux of radiation detectable by a sufficiently sensitive gravitational "antenna."

There are broadly three generations of antennae. The first device was built by Joseph Weber at the University of Maryland in the late 1960s. A "Weber Bar" is a cylinder of aluminum alloy, perhaps a couple of meters in length and a meter in diameter. The bar is suspended in a metal vacuum chamber on a thin wire, the suspension being supported by a sandwich of lead and rubber sheets. It is hoped that the bar is thus insulated from electrical, magnetic, thermal, acoustic, and seismic forces. The bar is connected to strain gauges or other transducers that detect vibrations putatively caused by the passage of pulses of gravitational radiation.

The transducers will show effects due to thermal excitation of the bar and to any other forces that have not been completely excluded. Therefore the signal of putative gravity "waves" has to be extracted from noise. A method of major importance is to look for coincident excitations between bars separated by thousands of miles. The heyday of this first generation of room-temperature detectors lasted until around 1975. During the early 1970s various coincident signals were apparently seen. Calculations suggested, however, that the first generation of Weber Bars was too insensitive to detect the weak flux of radiation that cosmologists found credible. By 1975, encouraged by the forcefully presented data analyses of Richard Garwin, all detector builders other than Weber had stated that there were no coincidences to be found.

The second generation of gravitational antennae were based on the same principles as the Weber Bar but used advanced techniques to increase sensitivity. Single crystals of sapphire could be used, or the bars could be cooled with liquid-helium. In the mid 1990s there are three liquid-helium-cooled bars "on air," one in Louisiana, one in Italy, and one in Australia. A similar device built by William Fairbank at Stanford University is no longer in use. The Louisiana group suggest that they are able to detect a disturbance at the end of their 3-meter bar equivalent to substantially less than the diameter of an atomic nucleus. No one has claimed to find gravitational waves with these bars, though they seem to be many orders of magnitude more sensitive than the room-temperature antennae.

In the mid 1990s a third generation of detectors is being constructed. The emphasis is now on laser-**interferometers** with a baseline of

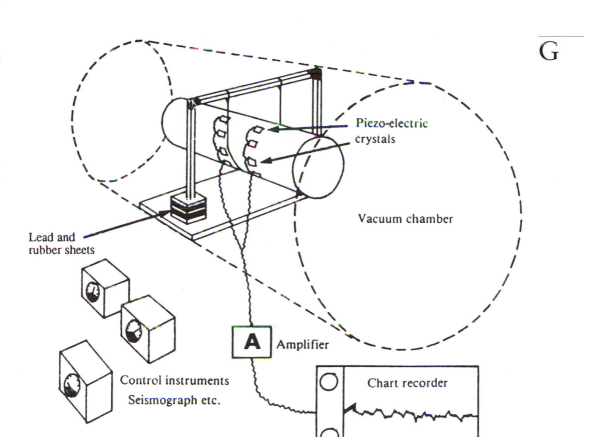

Piezo-electric
crystals

Vacuum chamber

Lead and
rubber sheets

A Amplifier

Control instruments
Seismograph etc.

Chart recorder

Weber-type gravity wave antenna. Harry Collins and Trevor Pinch. The Golem: What Everyone Should Know about Science. *Collins and Pinch. (1993): 93. Courtesy of Harry Collins/Cambridge University Press.*

kilometers (Laser-Interferometer Gravitational Observatories or LIGOs). This new "big science" of gravitational astronomy (costing hundreds of millions of dollars) is intended to detect pulses at least 10^9 smaller in magnitude than those detectable by the early Weber Bars. What is more, laser interferometers are better able to resolve pulse shapes, whereas bars respond best to signals around their resonant frequency. Broad bandwidth interferometers may be able to extract more information from the flux of gravitational radiation but will be correspondingly more difficult to isolate. They are not expected to be producing signals for a decade or more. It has been argued that a proportion of the sums being spent on LIGO would be better used developing more sophisticated resonant bars, but cooperation in looking for coincident signals between the two types of detectors is the most likely outcome of the debate.

As in many stories, historical divisions are never as neat as they first appear. One of the very

first detectors was a small laser-interferometer built by Robert Forward (a student of Weber's) at Hughes Aircraft Research Laboratories in California, and Joseph Weber has continued to press his early claims to have detected gravitational radiation. Weber claims that differences between his devices and those of others account for their failure to see coincidences. For example, he says that a crucial difference between his devices and the liquid-helium-cooled detectors is the means of recognizing vibrations—centrally mounted **strain-gauges** and end-mounted **accelerometers**, respectively. Further, in 1982, a paper by Ferrari, Pizzella, Lee, and Weber claimed that detectors in Rome and Maryland had seen coincidences with a statistical significance of 3.6 standard deviations above chance. Weber and Pizzella also believe they have seen signals corresponding to the 1987 supernova; theirs were the only antennae operating at the time, to the embarrassment of low-temperature groups. In 1984, supported by the Italian theorist Guiliano

Preparata, Weber claimed that previous calculations of the sensitivity of bar-type detectors were wrong and that a correct calculation, treating the bar as a coherent ensemble of pairs of atoms, gave a much greater cross-section, which was consistent with his coincidence findings. Very few other scientists accept the validity of the 1982 results, the 1987 gravitational sighting of the supernova, or the recalculation of the bar cross-section, but Weber remains undaunted.

The Louisiana State University (LSU) group, who were one of the first to build a low-temperature detector, have designed a resonant device in the shape of a faceted sphere 3 meters in diameter that is intended to be both sensitive, free of directional bias, yet able to resolve the direction of origin of a pulse. The sphere, which has an accelerometer on each of its ten faces, is equivalent to five bars joined at their centers. They believe that if it is built it will be more sensitive than a LIGO, albeit in a narrow bandwidth. The new design is know as a Truncated Icosohedral Gravitational Antenna—TIGA (LSU's mascot is a tiger!).

For all but a few physicists, the Weber story shows how things can go wrong when a scientist cleaves too strongly to a preferred interpretation of events. On the other hand, nearly all acknowledge that Weber is an ingenious and determined scientist whose pioneering of an "impossible" experiment set in motion what might one day be an important branch of astronomy.

Harry M. Collins

Bibliography

Blair, David G., ed. *The Detection of Gravitational Waves.* Cambridge: Cambridge University Press, 1991.

Collins, Harry M., and Trevor J. Pinch. *The Golem: What Everyone Should Know about Science.* Cambridge: Cambridge University Press, 1993.

Saulson, Peter R. *Fundamentals of Interferometric Gravitational Wave Detectors.* Singapore: World Scientific, 1994.

Gravity Meter

A gravity meter measures g, the acceleration due to gravity that arises from the force of attraction between a host heavenly body (usually the earth) and a nearby mass. Measurement can be made in an absolute sense or be relative to a measurement at a nearby defined location.

Absolute measurements provide the baseline measurements for the gravity map of the world. They usually involve laboratory-style instruments set up at a fixed location and observed to the best possible limits of precision. Within the grid established by absolute determinations, relative gravity instruments are used. They have greater sensitivity and more portability but are less stable over time. The most sensitive and stable relative instrument is the earth tidal meter used to measure the earth's solid tides.

Until recently, the **pendulum** provided the principal means for absolute determinations of gravity. The pendulum method has now been replaced by a falling ball apparatus timed by laser interferometry. A known mass is first tossed upward in an evacuated chamber and then its fall is measured. Tossing the mass upwards overcomes the difficulty of releasing the ball without an initial force component.

Relative instruments require portability and ease of use to gain access to virtually any global location. They are used for geophysical investigation of the nature of the earth and also for exploration of natural resources, notably oil. By mapping fine changes in the value of g, any anomalies in a region's gravity map are revealed. Coupled with other knowledge these anomalies can suggest such geological features as salt domes, in which oil is often to be found.

Gravity meters for relative measurements come in many forms and sizes to cope with use from aircraft and helicopters, in submarines, down boreholes, and in trucks across rough terrain. Pendulum-based systems have been used, but the largest group of relative instruments are spring-mass units.

Gravitational attraction creates a small force between the mass of the earth and a small test mass. If the test mass is suspended on a spring, gravity variation can be observed as a displacement in the spring. To obtain worthwhile results, the spring must deform sufficiently in response to the minute variations to be detected, yet be stable with time and with temperature change. Torsion balances have been used since the nineteenth century as spring-mass gravity meters.

The use of an elastic fiber as a torsional balance can be traced back to the explanation of material elasticity by Robert Hooke in the seventeenth century. Notable eighteenth- and nineteenth-century users of the torsion balance in their own historic devices were Simon Ohm,

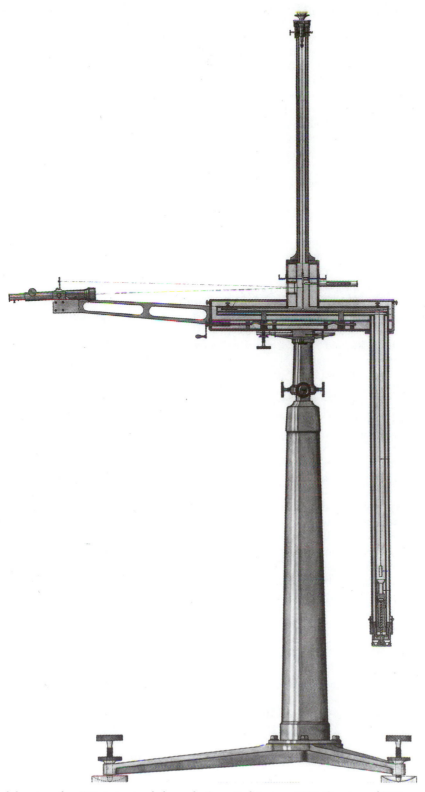

Sectional drawing of an Eötvös torsion balance, by Suss, Budapest ca. 1888. Courtesy of SSPL.

Charles Augustin Coulomb, Hans Christian Oersted, and William Thomson. However, the first use of the torsion balance to detect minute changes in gravitational attraction was made in 1888 by the Hungarian physicist Baron Roland von Eötvös. In Eötvös's balance, a hanging torsion wire supports an arm carrying equal small gold masses at each end. One of these gold masses is additionally suspended from the end of the arm by a thread 0.6 meter long. When set up in six different directions, the rotations of the arm can be used to calculate g. The balance can detect 10^{-13} gram force changes but is tedious to use. Some forms combine two arms to speed up observation. Several forms of the Eötvös-type balance were used from 1900 to 1930: well-known examples include Suss and proprietary models from the instrument-makers Askania and Oertling. Everett Lee der Golyer is credited with pioneering their use in oil exploration.

However, Eötvös balances gave way to a simpler, more easily used arrangement using only one test mass. Richard Threlfall and James Arthur Pollock devised a single mass instrument in Australia in 1898. Building on Charles Vernon Boys's work on quartz fibers, they used a horizontal quartz thread as a torsional spring. Gravitational attraction on the attached mass causes a minute rotation of the quartz thread and the angle of rotation is read against a precise **goniometer** scale.

Although contemporary with the Eötvös method, this simpler arrangement only gradually came to prominence as mechanical means to magnify the displacement and hence improve sensitivity were devised. Electrical sensing was added in the 1970s and improved metal spring materials have also been adopted. The simple quartz spring form, read by an optical reading magnifier and notoriously delicate, has now been superseded by the electrically observed torsional type using a robust metal spring. Manufacture of spring-mass gravity meters is internationally distributed, with key makers including LaCoste and Romberg in the United States, Scintrex in Canada, and Askania in Germany.

Peter H. Sydenham

Bibliography

Hugill, Andrew. "An Electronically Read Gravity Meter." Ph.D. dissertation, Flinders University of South Australia, 1984.

Hunter, James de Graaf. "Gravity Survey." In *A Dictionary of Applied Physics*, edited by Richard Glazebrook, Vol. 3, 398–415. London: Macmillan, 1923.

Lenzen, Victor F., and Robert P. Multhauf. "Development of Gravity Pendulums in the 19th Century." *Contributions from the Museum of History and Technology*, United States National Museum Bulletin 240, paper 44. Washington, D.C.: Smithsonian Institution Press, 1965.

Sydenham, Peter H. "Early Geophysical Practice—The BMR Instrument Collection." *BMR Journal of Australian Geology & Geophysics* 3 (1978): 241–48.

Threlfall, R., and J.A. Pollock. "On the Quartz Thread Gravity Balance." *Philosophical Transactions of the Royal Society of London A* 193 (1899): 215–58.

Groma

The groma was the principal Roman surveying instrument. Knowledge of the groma comes from written references (some of which are ambiguous, not least of all because of variants of terminology) and archaeological evidence (which is often difficult to interpret).

What is generally regarded as the only known example of a groma was excavated at Pompeii in 1912, but only the metal parts survive. This instrument (now in the Archaeology Museum, Naples; reconstruction in the Science Museum, London) was made in what was apparently the workshop of a surveyor possibly named Verus. The groma was composed of an X shape mounted on a pivoting bracket, which was in turn fitted to a straight stick. By aligning pairs of plumb-bobs that were suspended from the cross-arms, the groma was used to survey straight lines and right angles. The advantage of the pivoting bracket, which permitted the arms of the groma to be off-center in relation to the supporting staff, was to allow sighting to be unhindered by the supporting staff, which might otherwise create a visual obstruction. The presence of the pivoting bracket is often understood to be the defining characteristic of the groma; earlier cross shapes that might have been used in surveying are regarded as being precursors to the groma itself. However, the actual intended use of some purported "surveyor's" crosses has been debated. For example, an archaeological find from Eichstatt, Germany, has been variously described as a groma, as a predecessor to the groma, and as a grain measure.

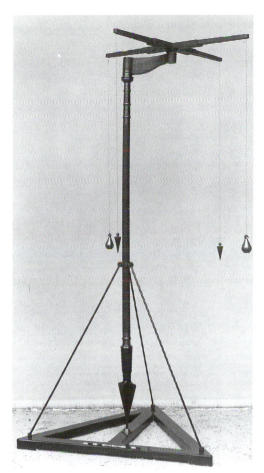

Reconstruction of Roman groma, first century A.D., *based on pieces excavated at Pompei. SM 1923-395. Courtesy of SSPL.*

Prior to the excavation at Pompeii, the groma was known from written references and from a representation of what may have been a groma on a tombstone found at ancient Eporedia (modern Ivrea in northern Italy), now in the Museo Civico. The tombstone was erected by a first century B.C. surveyor, Lucius Aebutius Faustus, for himself and his family and depicted various symbols of office.

The groma allowed straight lines and rectangles to be surveyed and had both civilian and military uses, including the determination of the kardo (north-south line) and decumanus (east-west line) essential to the orientation of a temple or to the division of a military camp. The groma may have been used in conjunction with other instruments (such as **sun-dials,** used to establish direction). It is significant that other surveying instruments were excavated from Verus's

workshop, including a folding ruler, bronze compasses, the endpieces of a measuring rod, and a portable sun-dial.

Liba Taub

Bibliography

Della Corte, Matteo. "Groma." *Monumenti Antichi* 28 (1922): 5–100.

Dilke, O.A W. *The Roman Land Surveyors: An Introduction to the Agrimensores.* Newton Abbot: David and Charles, 1971.

———. "Roman Large-Scale Mapping in the Early Empire." In *The History of Cartography,* edited by J.B. Harley and David Woodward, Vol. 1, 212–33. Chicago: University of Chicago Press, 1987.

Kelsey, Francis W. "Groma." *Classical Philology* 21 (1926): 259–62.

Turner, A.J. *Mathematical Instruments in Antiquity and the Middle Ages: An Introduction,* 299. London: Vade-Mecum, 1994.

Gunnery Instruments

Europeans began using instruments to control and analyze projectile motion in the late fifteenth century, an activity that significantly influenced both science and warfare by the late eighteenth century. While Western artillery hardware had Asian rivals, especially in the Ottoman Empire, the new mathematical theories and instruments gave Western gunners a tactical advantage during the Renaissance. This success helped transform mathematics into a strategic commodity. Along with navigation and *trace italienne* fortification design, gunnery linked the rise of Western science with the rise of Western military power.

Early modern artillery had four basic degrees of freedom: the elevation angle of the gun barrel, the traverse angle of the gun carriage, the incline angle of the gun carriage's axle, and the muzzle velocity of the projectile fired. Niccolò Tartaglia described the gunner's **quadrant** for measuring the barrel's elevation angle in his *Nova scientia* (1537). This instrument consisted of a right-angle frame with a plumb line and an angular scale. The gunner placed the quadrant inside the gun barrel and measured the elevation angle by observing where the plumb line intersected the scale. While Tartaglia presented the quadrant as his invention, its use was documented as early as 1471 by Martin Mercz, a

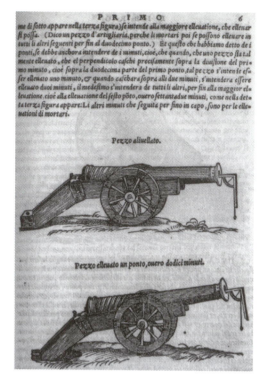

me di sotto appare nella terza figura)se intende alla maggiore elleuatione, che ellenar
si possa. (Dico un pezzo d'artigliaria, perche li mortari poi se possono elleuare in
tutti li altri seguenti per fin al duodecimo ponto.) Et questo che habbiamo detto de i
ponti, se debbe anchora intendere de i minuti, cioe, che quando, che uno pezzo sta tal
mente elleuato, che el perpendicolo caschi precisamente sopra la diuisione del pri
mo minuto, cioe sopra la duodecima parte del primo ponto, tal pezzo s'intende esser elleuato uno minuto, & quando caschara sopra alli due minuti, s'intendera essere
elleuato duoi minuti, il medesimo s'intendera de tutti li altri, per fin alla maggior elleuatione, cioe alla elleuatione del sesto pōto, ouero settantadue minuti, come nella det-
ta terza figura appare: Li altri minuti che seguita per fino in capo, sono per le elle-
uationi di mortari.

Pezzo aliuellato.

Pezzo elleuato un ponto, ouero dodici minuti.

The use of the gunner's quadrant explained. Niccolò Tartaglia. La nova scienta. *Venice, 1558: 6. Courtesy of the Museum of the History of Science, Oxford.*

German master gunner. By the 1520s, the artillery schools of Burgos and Venice were providing instruction in the use of the gunner's quadrant. Because of the difficulty in holding the plumb line still in field combat, most gunners restricted its use to heavy cannons and mortars in siege warfare. Lord Mountjoy verified this trend when he personally sited an artillery battery with his quadrant at the Siege of Kinsale in 1600.

To provide a gun with its proper traverse angle, a gun crew lifted the tail stock to pivot the gun carriage until the layer sited the target along the upper edges of the breech and muzzle. He ensured that this line of sight coincided with the gun bore's axis by placing a simple dispart sight on the muzzle. When elevated above 0°, however, the muzzle often obstructed the target. To site a gun regardless of the elevation angle, gunners employed calibrated breech sights. During the Thirty Years' War, this involved a vertical scale with small holes through which the gun layer sited the target. Jean-Baptiste de Gribeauval, the eighteenth-century reformer of French artillery, developed the tangent sight,

consisting of a horizontal bar that moved vertically on two linear scales. When properly used, breech sights enabled gun layers to control the elevation angle without a quadrant. Jean-Louis Lombard's analytical gunnery tables for the Gribeauval artillery pieces (1787) specified barrel elevations in terms of a standardized tangent sight's scale.

Gunners have routinely employed clinometers to control the vertical incline of a gun carriage's axle since the seventeenth century. For accurate shooting, this slope must be zero—a difficult requirement for heavy artillery on uneven or soft ground. Otherwise, the shot will move laterally away from the sited target toward the axle's lower side. The gunner's clinometer consisted of a **pendulum** that pivoted along an angular scale. When placed on the breech, perpendicular to the bore, the pendulum's position displayed the axle's incline angle.

Master gunners faced a complex question when provided with a solid stone or iron shot of unknown weight: how much gunpowder should be used when a particular ratio of charge-to-shot weight is specified? Galileo Galilei invented his military compass to provide a rapid means of solving this cubic-proportionality problem in 1606. This compass, or **sector**, also solved proportionality problems in general, especially those found in fortification design, surveying, and infantry command, as well as compound-interest and monetary-exchange calculations.

Benjamin Robins invented the ballistic pendulum, the first instrument that successfully measured the instantaneous velocity of projectiles. He described it in *New Principles of Gunnery* (1742), a book that revolutionized ballistics. By shooting musket balls into the lower face of this rigid-body pendulum, and observing its back swing, Robins calculated these bullets' velocities just before impact by applying the conservation of momentum. After obtaining such velocities at different ranges, Robins calculated the projectile's air-resistance function with respect to velocity by applying Newton's second law of motion. This is how he discovered the sound barrier. The ballistic pendulum became the principal gunnery research tool during the second half of the eighteenth-century. It provided the data such eighteenth century mathematicians as Robins, Leonhard Euler, Johann Heinrich Lambert, Jean-Charles Borda, Papacino d'Antoni, Charles Hutton, Georg Friedrich von Tempelhoff, and Lombard required to analyze complex interior and exterior ballistics problems with rational mechanics. The ballistic pendulum remained the most accurate instrument for measuring projectile velocities until the development of the ballistic **chronograph** in the 1860s (see also **chronoscope**).

Robins also invented the whirling arm to investigate the aerodynamic drag of low-speed projectiles. It involved a thin beam that pivoted on a horizontal plane; a falling weight set it in motion. By observing the whirling arm's angular velocity with and without objects attached to the outer end, Robins deduced the air resistance they generated. This instrument was modified in the 1760s by Borda and James Smeaton for hydraulic and windmill experiments, respectively. Such nineteenth-century aeronautical pioneers as George Cayley, Horatio Phillips, Hiram Maxim, and Samuel P. Langley also employed the whirling arm. Although it was displaced by the wind-tunnel for most aerodynamics research in the twentieth century, the aerospace industry continues to use it in rain-impact investigations.

Brett D. Steele

Bibliography

The Compleat Gunner [1672]. East Ardsley, 1971.

Dolleczek, Anton. *Geschichte der Österreichischen Artillerie* [1887]. Gratz, 1973.

Galilei, Galileo. *Operations of the Geometric and Military Compass* [1606]. Translated by Stillman Drake. Washington, D.C.: Smithsonian Institution Press, 1978.

Lombard, Jean-Louis. *Tables du tir des canons et des obusiers.* Auxonne, 1787.

Steele, Brett. "Muskets and Pendulums: Benjamin Robins, Leonhard Euler, and the Ballistics Revolution." *Technology and Culture* 35 (1994): 348–382.

Gyrocompass

See Compass, Gyro-

Gyroscope

Invented by Jean Bernard Léon Foucault in 1852 as an independent method for demonstrating the earth's rotation, the gyroscope has become one of the most useful scientific instruments. In the century and a half since its invention, the gyroscope's history has become inseparable from the history of the growing military and commercial needs of the world's great powers. At the height of the Cold War, American and Soviet gyroscopes were fundamental components of the inertial guidance systems for submarines, missiles, and aircraft, systems that guaranteed the retaliatory Armageddon that lay at the core of the doctrine of Mutual Assured Destruction. In a sense, gyroscopes helped keep the long, cold peace.

Although best known for his pendulum and its demonstration of the earth's rotation, Foucault believed that the gyroscope offered a better and clearer proof of this phenomenon. Composed of a rigid disk (the rotor) through whose center an equally rigid axle was passed and mounted in a gimballed frame that allowed freedom of movement in all directions, Foucault's rotor was then spun up to a high speed of rotation using a separate tooth gearing mechanism. A fixed optical sighting instrument focused on the rotor. As the gyroscope maintained its angular orientation in space, a displacement developed between the fixed observing platform and the unmoving gyroscope rotor, a displacement caused by the rotation of the earth and the concomitant movement of the observing apparatus. Hence, the name "gyroscope," which means, literally, "to view the turning." Foucault's demonstration employed a gyroscope with three degrees of freedom; that is, there was complete freedom of movement about the spinning, horizontal, and vertical axes. Although unable to build a rotor that could operate over long periods of time at a constant speed, Foucault argued that a gyroscope with only two degrees of freedom—that is, one in which only two gimbals moved with complete freedom—would be affected by gravity and align itself with the earth's axis of rotation. Hence, a gyroscope with two degrees of freedom would function as an indicator of true north, a **gyrocompass**.

If Foucault was the first to build and name the gyroscope, he was not the first to recognize that a spinning mass maintains a constant direction. In the early 1740s, Captain John Serson, an English mariner, invented a "whirling speculum," essentially a mirrored top, which provided an artificial horizon to assist in making sextant observations when the actual horizon was invisible. An example of Serson's device survives in the collections of the Science Museum of London; unfortunately, Serson perished aboard the ill-fated H.M.S. *Victory* in 1750 and his device never achieved great popularity among navigators. Serson was the first of many who would at-

Foucault gyroscopic apparatus, ca. 1880. SM 1883-10. Courtesy of SSPL.

tempt to harness the gyroscope to aid in the problem of navigation; it remains unclear to what extent, if any, that Foucault drew upon this tradition of practical use in his own invention.

During the remainder of the nineteenth century, the gyroscope inhabited at least two not entirely distinct worlds: one academic, another commercial. As a central problem in natural philosophy, a growing number of individuals, including James Maxwell and William Thomson worked to perfect the gyroscope as a pedagogical apparatus. In turn, the mathematics of gyroscopic motion became increasingly sophisticated. We need not focus upon that math, simply the basic observation that a gyroscope will move at right angles to the direction of a force acting upon it. This basic principle made the gyroscope the center of a series of important inventions throughout the next century. Equally important, American and French scientists perfected an electric gyroscope that eliminated the problem of maintaining constant spin; William Thomson also described and built a gyrocompass. Although Thomson was unable to sell his instrument to the British Navy, his attempt set the stage for the wedding of the gyroscope and the state during the twentieth century.

Foucault and the nineteenth-century students of the gyroscope worked out the device's rules, but it would require resources unavailable to individuals to harness the gyroscope's powers of stability and direction. What the sociologist Donald MacKenzie has called "gyro culture" emerged during the years before World War I in Germany, Britain, and the United States. Gyro culture had several important characteristics, including the role of individual inventors, private firms, and interested military bureaucracies. The latter had important technical problems to solve, especially as the larger new battleships, like H.M.S. *Dreadnought,* came into existence during the pre–World War I Anglo-German arms race. The widespread use of metal hulls made traditional magnetic compass navigation inadequate. In Germany, Herman Anschütz-Kaempfe, and in the United States, Elmer Sperry, developed working gyrocompasses that they sold to their respective nations' navies. In Britain, Arthur Pollen developed a gyroscopically stabilized platform for the control of the Dreadnought-class guns. In the wake of the Allied victory, the Sperry Gyroscope Co. dominated the market for gyroscopic-based apparatus for both military and civilian needs.

During the interwar period, Sperry extended its market by entering into the development of aircraft instruments, a domain in which the gyroscope excelled. By its very nature, the gyroscope provided a stable reference frame in the new, three-dimensional domain. Sperry and other firms worked with the government in the development of standard aeronautical devices, especially equipment that would allow pilots to navigate under conditions of poor visibility. In addition, Sperry continued the development of fire-control equipment for naval vessels, becoming the U.S. Navy's main supplier, while the Vickers Co. performed a similar service for the Royal Navy.

With World War II, gyro culture underwent a fundamental change. Before the war, firms carried out research and development and then sold this work to interested parties, especially the armed services; during and after World War II, the military paid for research and development as well as finished equipment. Gyroscopes became central to the postwar military strategies of the superpowers as they sought to develop means of navigation with which the enemy could not interfere. In this new social, political, and technical context, a new breed of researcher appeared—one capable of spanning the boundaries separating the civilian and the military, the academic and the industrial. In turn, new types of gyroscopes emerged, such as the laser ring gyroscope and various computer simulations of gyroscopic motion that may ultimately replace Foucault's powerful instrument and its descendants.

Michael Aaron Dennis

Bibliography

Foucault, Léon. *Recueil des travaux scientifiques de Léon Foucault.* Paris: Gauthier-Villar, 1878.

Hughes, Thomas Parke. *Elmer Sperry, Inventor and Engineer.* Baltimore: Johns Hopkins University Press, 1971.

MacKenzie, Donald A. *Inventing Accuracy: A Historical Sociology of Nuclear Missile Guidance.* Cambridge: M.I.T. Press, 1990.

Moskowitz, Saul. "The Development of the Artifical Horizon for Celestial Navigation." *Navigation* 20 (1973): 1–16.

Sumida, Jon Tetsuro. *In Defence of Naval Supremacy: Finance, Technology, and British Naval Policy 1889–1914.* Boston: Unwin Hyman, 1989.

G

H

Hardness Testing Instruments

In an engineering context, the hardness of a metal is generally defined as its resistance to surface abrasion or penetration, but precise terminology and a standard testing technique proved difficult to achieve. To determine the hardness of a metal it is necessary to deform the surface under controlled conditions and then measure the deformation produced. Traditionally, a craftsman would scratch the surface with a file for an approximate assessment of hardness. Scratch tests of this sort were best suitable for brittle materials.

The indentation technique, developed at the end of the nineteenth century for ductile materials, was the first scientific apparatus for this work. In this procedure a standard hard object is forced into the surface of the test piece by a given load, and the resulting deformation measured. The indentation was produced, in some of the early tests, by a falling weight, but a gradually applied load was eventually found to be preferable. One of the pioneer hardness testing instruments in Britain was developed in 1897 by W.C. Unwin, professor of civil engineering at the Central Technical College at South Kensington (now Imperial College).

The body of Unwin's Hardness Tester was a cast iron guide block about 4 in. wide and 8 in. high. The indenting tool was a short, square bar of tool steel, one corner of which acted as a knife-edge, and equipped with a vernier scale for measuring the depth of indentation. The test piece was a bar, 0.375 in. square and about 2.5 in. long. The instrument was placed in a conventional testing machine where the load was applied. The design made it possible to take into account the compression of the instrument itself.

J.A. Brinell in Sweden introduced his self-contained, bench-top hardness tester in 1900. In this popular instrument, the indentation is made by a small hardened-steel ball pressed into the specimen with a load of 500 kg for softer metals, or 3,000 kg for the harder ones. Various machines for making the Brinell test were devised with the load applied directly by means of a lever, by screw gearing, or by hydraulic pressure. The Brinell hardness number is determined by dividing the load in kilograms by the curved surface area of the indentation in square millimeters. The curved area of indentation is usually computed from the diameter across the top, measured with the aid of a **microscope**.

The Vickers Hardness Testing Machine was designed in the 1930s to speed up routine industrial testing. In this floor-standing device, the indenter was a pyramid of diamond. The machine frame carries the specimen stage and a beam of 20:1 ratio. The load is applied through a thrust rod, and the tube carries the diamond indenter at its lower end. The plunger, in contact with the cam, controls the application and release of the test load. When the starting handle is depressed, the sequence starts and is driven by the weight. The width of the indentation is read through a microscope, which can measure to 0.001 mm. With a large throughput of tests, it was usual to make all the load tests first, then, by means of a jig, replace the specimens on the stage and then take the microscope readings. The whole process is automatic and a competent operator could carry out up to two hundred tests in a hour.

The Rockwell Hardness Tester is a static machine that was widely used in the United States. This instrument uses either a small steel ball or a diamond indenter. The load is applied

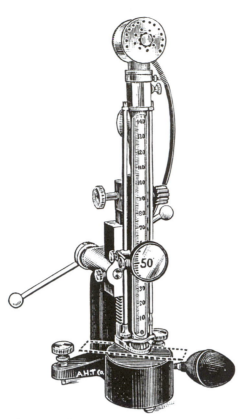

Shore Model C Scleroscope, ca. 1912. Arthur H. Thomas Company. Laboratory Apparatus and Reagents. *Philadelphia, 1921: 339, Figure 6124. Courtesy of SSPL.*

by means of a hand screw, and the hardness number read off directly from a dial gauge with two scales, one for the ball and the other for the diamond indenter. The instrument is rapid, permitting up to 250 tests per hour. Graphs were provided to relate the Rockwell ball readings to the Brinell hardness numbers.

The Shore Scleroscope Hardness Tester provides a dynamic test by means of a falling weight. The instrument comprises a vertical glass tube about 10 in. high and 0.5 in. in diameter. A small diamond-pointed weight of about 40 grains falls inside the tube and strikes the surface of the material to be tested. The tube is graduated with 140 divisions, and the height of rebound is taken as the measure of hardness of the material. The result depends on the permanent deformation produced at the point of impact, the rebound being reduced on account of the work of deforming the test piece. It was usual to take a series of readings for one specimen and take the mean as the measure of hardness. In this case it was neces-

sary to move the specimen for each test so that the localized work-hardening effect did not affect the reading.

Denis Smith

Bibliography

Popplewell, William Charles. *Experimental Engineering,* Vol. 2. Manchester: Scientific, 1901.

Unwin, W.C. *The Testing of the Materials of Construction.* 2nd ed. London: Longmans, 1899.

Walker, E.G. *The Life and Work of William Cawthorne Unwin.* London: Unwin Memorial Committee, 1938.

Harmonic Analyzer

Harmonic analysis is the process of taking a complex wave form, such as a recording of the heights of tides or other natural phenomena (see **tide predictor**), and breaking it down into a sum of much simpler periodic functions, such as cosines. In modern terminology it is often described as finding the Fourier Transform of the original data. The process is of great practical interest because if one can approximate a complex wave by a sum of elementary functions, then it is possible to perform both theoretical investigations and practical calculations on the phenomena—jobs that are impossible when all one has are the original data points.

The first mechanical harmonic analyzer was proposed by William Thomson in 1876. It was a modification of his integrating machine, but it was not a practical device and little use was made of this type of instrumentation; the main method of finding the coefficients of the cosines was still by laborious calculation. Because of the practical nature of the problem and the difficulty of doing the job by hand, several attempts were made to modify various integrating machines to aid harmonic analysis.

The first practical device was marketed by the firm of G. Coradi in Zurich in 1894, and it remained as part of their product line, in several different versions, for many years. The Coradi machine consists of one to five delicate ground glass balls mounted in a frame. Gently touching each ball were mechanisms that would communicate the motion of the full machine across the paper and the motion of its line tracer along the length of the machine to the glass balls. The motion of these balls would, in turn, be re-

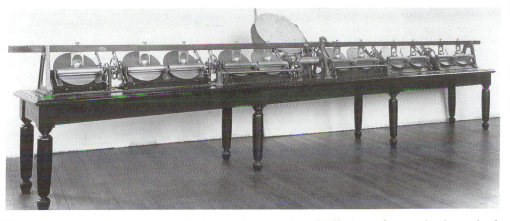

Kelvin harmonic analyzer, 1879, used by the British Meteorological Office to analyze graphical records of daily changes to atmospheric pressure and temperature. SM 1946-343. Courtesy of SSPL.

corded on the small dials arranged around the equator of each ball. Great care had to be taken to set the machine up correctly: the user had to ensure that it was arranged parallel to the x axis of the graph to be traced, and that all the appropriate dials and adjustments were properly set before beginning to trace the data line. Once a complex curve had been traced, a series of readings would be taken that could then be used to find the coefficients of the sines and cosines, the sum of which would approximate the traced curve. Machines with a greater number of mechanisms would produce the coefficients for a greater number of sines and cosines and, thus, a more accurate approximation to the input curve.

A completely different principle was used by two Americans, A.A. Michelson and S.W. Stratton, who were attempting to correct the inaccuracies of Thomson's tide predictor. Michelson and Stratton realized that their new concept could not only be used to evaluate the cosine series, but was also capable of determining the coefficients to be used in the series by feeding the original data into the machine. Rather than relying on rolling motions communicated to delicate recording devices, the Michelson-Stratton Analyzer consisted of a series of springs that would be stretched or compressed as the device traced out a curve. These springs, acting in unison upon the position of a cylinder, would eventually result in the cylinder's reaching an equilibrium position. After stability had been achieved, the coefficients of the required cosines could be determined by measuring the displacement of each spring. The Michelson-Stratton Analyzer was a large instrument consisting of eighty individual sets of springs and levers, each of which had to be manipulated to produce the eventual result. It was also remarkably accurate (even considering the problems of getting that many springs to each behave according to theory) and could be used to great effect.

None of these devices were ever in common use. The expense of their manufacture, the delicacy of their nature, and the complexity of the problems they were attempting to solve limited their use to only those with demanding problems and healthy budgets. People who had the occasional need for such a device would normally resort to careful measurement of the graphs and then long and tedious calculations to find the coefficients of the cosines. It was only after the advent of the modern digital computer, and the so-called Fast Fourier Transform algorithms, that the routine use of harmonic analysis has been seen.

Michael Williams

Bibliography

Henrici, O. "Calculating Machines." In *Encyclopedia Britannica*, Vol. 4, 972–981. 11th ed. Cambridge: Cambridge University Press, 1910.

Michelson, A.A., and S.W. Stratton. "On a New Harmonic Analyzer." *Philosophical Magazine* 45 (1898): 85–91.

Heliostat

A heliostat reflects a beam of sunlight in a fixed direction, using a movable mirror driven by clockwork to counteract the apparent movement of the sun. The resulting stationary beam is used either when an intense light is needed, or when the properties of solar radiation are to be studied.

All heliostats are based on the principle that a ray reflected from a plane mirror lies in the plane defined by the incident ray and the perpendicular to the mirror, and it is reflected at an angle equal to the angle of incidence. Thus, if the reflected beam is to remain motionless, the perpendicular to the mirror must continually bisect the angle between the sun's position and the desired direction of the beam. For certain beam directions a simple arrangement suffices to satisfy this "heliostat condition." For example, a mirror, properly positioned on a shaft rotating parallel to the earth's axis once in twenty-four hours, will reflect a stationary beam toward either celestial pole. To send the beam in another direction, a second, stationary, mirror must be added. A more complex mechanism, however, can send a beam in any desired direction using only one mirror. Heliostats of this kind are generally delicate, costly, and complicated to set up. But the single reflection results in less loss of light than in the two-mirror instruments.

The first to consider the problem of designing a heliostat was Giovanni Borelli of Italy, in the mid seventeenth century. Perhaps stimulated by the experiments of the Florentine Accademia del Cimento on the speed of light, he analyzed the motions required for various configurations of a single-mirror device. Borelli's ideas remained unpublished and had no influence.

The concept of the heliostat, and the first one actually built, came to the attention of the scientific world in 1742, in an influential textbook by the Dutch physicist Willem Jacob 'sGravesande, who also coined the name "heliostat" (from the Greek words for "sun" and "stand"). 'sGravesande's motivation was to facilitate the experimental demonstrations for his lectures on optics. His heliostat had one stand supporting a mirror free to turn in all directions, and a second stand carrying a clock with an arm that moved to follow the sun. When the mirror and clock arm were properly positioned and connected by a sliding joint, the reflected sunbeam was stationary. 'sGravesande's heliostat became widely known through descriptions and illustrations, but it is unlikely that many were actually made.

Intense development of heliostats began around 1800, and lasted until handy, powerful sources of electric light became readily available in the 1880s. These were used in microscopy, photography, spectroscopy, testing the consequences of the undulatory theory of light, and in many other fields of experimental and instructional endeavor that required a strong and steady light. The extensive discussion in the literature suggests that heliostats held considerable interest for nineteenth-century physicists. Only the most important designs can be mentioned here.

The French physicist Jacques A.C. Charles, celebrated for his experimental lectures in the late eighteenth century, was the first to improve 'sGravesande's machine. His chief contribution was mounting the mirror support and the clock on a common base, somewhat rationalizing the setting-up process. The physicist Étienne Malus introduced a slightly different design in 1809.

A cheaper, more convenient alternative was the two-mirror design, in which the first mirror, mounted directly on a clock-driven polar axis, reflects the beam along this axis. This idea, first conceived in the seventeenth century, was repeatedly revived and reinvented in the nineteenth. Its popularity increased after the invention in the 1850s of highly reflective silvered-glass mirrors, which made the loss of light in the second reflection of little consequence.

Another simple type of heliostat also has a mirror mounted directly on the polar axis of the clockwork, but in this case the plane of the mirror contains this axis. If it makes one rotation in 48 hours, the reflected beam remains stationary. This scheme, first conceived in the seventeenth century, was revived by the German E.F. August in 1839 but never became popular. Yet its special property of reflecting a nonrotating (as well as nonmoving) image of celestial bodies led to its transformation into the coelostat, an instrument for astronomical photography.

The Paris instrument-maker Henri Gambey introduced his single-mirror heliostat in 1823. Although more compact and easier to set up than the earlier designs, Gambey's instrument was still complicated and delicate. In 1824, the Italian Pietro Prandi introduced his design, similar in principle to that of 'sGravesande, but better arranged and far simpler to set up. The most successful model, however, was that introduced by J.T. Silbermann of France in 1843. It was compact, simple, and relatively inexpensive and became popular in both Europe and America.

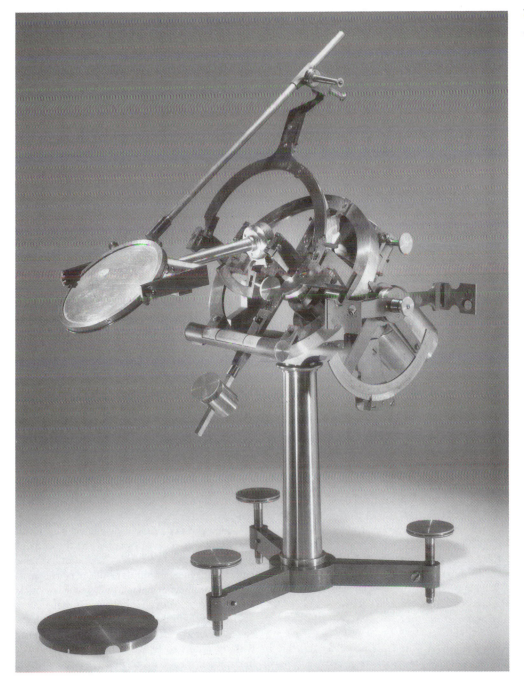

Gambey's heliostat, designed in 1823. The driving clock is not visible. The polar axis points to the upper left; the instrument is set for a latitude of about 45° N, about noon, reflecting its beam to the north. NMAH 315,645. Courtesy NMAH.

In 1862, the French physicist Leon Foucault refined the original 'sGravesande design, making the construction solid and mechanically sound, the mirror large, and the setting-up procedure easy. Shortly before his death in 1868, Foucault developed it into the siderostat for astronomical use by moving the driving clock to the upper end of the polar axis and making the construction even larger and sturdier.

The expense of heliostats tended to keep them out of the hands of individuals such as amateur photographers and microscopists, who nevertheless needed steady solar illumination. In 1869, the Irishman George Johnstone Stoney introduced a heliostat specifically designed to be low in cost. It was similar to Gambey's in its linkwork, but it had a larger mirror. It had some popularity in Germany and the English-speaking world. In 1879, Rudolf Fuess of Berlin introduced the last important heliostat design. Its mechanism resembled Stoney's, but it was constructed more expensively.

Heliostats remained popular long after electric light became convenient to use. Research and teaching laboratories, built in great numbers in the late nineteenth century, were often provided with heliostat shelves outside the windows. As late as 1931, a Chicago firm was offering two kinds of heliostats, describing them as "practically indispensable" aids for the study of solar radiation. That characterization remains true today.

Other mirror instruments with similar names or functions may be confused with heliostats. The heliograph is a signaling device for military use that reflects a beam of sunlight to a distant observer, with provision for interrupting the beam to send a message by Morse code. The heliotrope of Carl F. Gauss is a similar device for surveying, whose reflected beam serves as a beacon for triangulation over long distances.

Roger E. Sherman

Bibliography

Middleton, W.E. Knowles. "Giovanni Alphonso Borelli and the Invention of the Heliostat." *Archive for History of Exact Sciences* 10 (1973): 329–41.

Mills, Allan A. "Portable Heliostats (Solar Illuminators)." *Annals of Science* 43 (1986): 369–406.

Radau, Rudolph. "Sur la Theorie des Heliostats." *Bulletin Astronomique* 1 (1884): 153–60.

Repsold, Joh. A. *Zur Geschichte der Astronomischen Messwerkzeuge von 1830 bis um 1900*, Vol. 2: 8, 116, 119, 127. Leipzig: Emmanuel Reinicke, 1914.

Helmholtz Resonator

The original Helmholtz resonator was created to conduct a subjective, largely qualitative analysis of sounds, above all to hear upper partial tones. Modern resonators (in rather changed form) are used for spatial acoustics, both for aural frequency analysis and to absorb or eliminate certain sounds.

The first half of the nineteenth century witnessed the transformation of acoustics from a subject that, prior to 1800, had been of interest almost exclusively to musicians and mathematicians, into one that became a branch of the new discipline of physics. Above all, the pioneering experimental work of Ernst Chladni on sounding plates, vibrating strings, and rods, and the publication of his *Die Akustik* (1802), proved decisive for the emergence of acoustics (*see* **Chladni plates**). Moreover, the development of new acoustical instrumentation, such as the siren (developed during the 1830s and 1840s) for generating sound, became essential. In turn, Chladni's work stimulated the Weber brothers, Ernst Heinrich and Wilhelm, to their own pioneering study of sound waves (*Die Wellenlehre*, 1825), while the siren led in the 1840s to (opposing) attempts by August Seebeck and Georg Simon Ohm to develop a definition of tone as a function of periodic impulses.

The Ohm-Seebeck dispute was resolved in the late 1850s when the German scientist Hermann von Helmholtz developed a new, more complex definition of tone. Helmholtz entered into the dispute as part of his larger quest to reform physiological acoustics. In the mid 1850s, he invented his resonator in an attempt to isolate and analyze certain sounds (especially upper partials) from background noise. In this way he could, inter alia, test his resonance theory of hearing and analyze vowel sounds in human speech.

Helmholtz's original resonator was a hollow glass sphere with openings at the ends of two short necks. In effect, as he and others saw, any bottle, vase, or similar hollow object with a cavity and made of glass, brass, or some other material constitutes a Helmholtz resonator. One opening of Helmholtz's resonator had a sharp edge, while the other, funnel-shaped opening was designed to fit into the ear. To prevent harming the ear and to make for a good fit, Helmholtz coated the funnel-shaped opening with sealing wax before inserting it into the ear. (And he plugged the other ear with sealing wax to dampen external noise.) Resonator and ear together formed, as he wrote, "an elastic system" that allowed the sphere's prime tone to be set in oscillation and to be heard directly by the ear. Helmholtz claimed that his instrument was so effective that even individuals with untrained ears could readily recognize such tones.

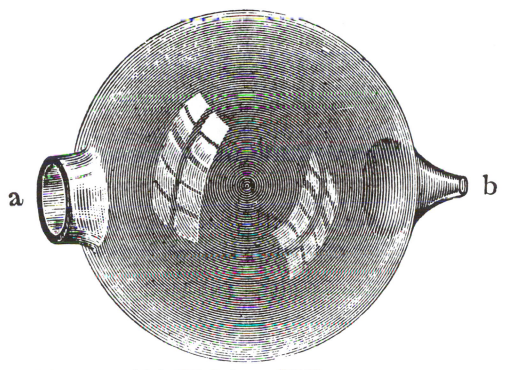

a   b

Helmholtz's resonator. Helmholtz (1877): 43. Courtesy of NMAH.

To conduct his physiological experiments, he constructed a tuned series of such resonators which, in combination, proved particularly effective at picking up even faint tones. After making his first set of rather primitive resonators himself, Helmholtz turned to Rudolf Koenig, an instrument-maker in Paris, to have an entire series of tuned glass resonators constructed. Helmholtz's resonator was, mathematically speaking, a device for analyzing sounds into their sinusoidal components. The air within such a resonator displays simple harmonic motion, with the air inside the neck acting like a mass and that inside the sphere like a spring. The natural frequency ω_0 of any such Helmholtz resonator (assuming no correction for the opening, a straight neck, and no damping) is thus

$$\omega_0 = \frac{c}{2\pi}\sqrt{\frac{S}{lV_0}}, \text{ where}$$

c is the velocity of sound, S is the area of the neck, l is the length of the neck, and V is the volume of air inside the sphere. Helmholtz's resonator and his accompanying analysis greatly advanced the understanding of musical tones, presented by Helmholtz in his pathbreaking musicological masterpiece *On the Sensations of Tone as a Physiological Basis for the Theory of Music* (1863). That work, though not without its critics, revolutionized and greatly stimulated research in acoustics during the second half of the nineteenth century and beyond, just as the Helmholtz resonator (in its various forms) became an essential piece of equipment used in physics teaching laboratories.

Helmholtz resonators have come to form a part of modern sound technology, where they constitute the nucleus of one of several types of sound absorbers. In particular, a large number of such resonators can be connected in parallel to constitute a perforated-plate absorber. When attached to the interior walls of ducts wherein sound is propagated, such resonators attenuate sound. Another, similar form of the modern Helmholtz resonator is a wooden plate with holes extended a certain distance in front of a wall. The plate and the air volume between it and the wall act together as a Helmholtz resonator for reducing echo time (for low frequencies). Moreover, modern Helmholtz resonators sometimes become part of the very architecture of a room itself, as in the concert hall of the Berlin Philarmonie, where such resonators (in the form of hollow pyramids) hang from the hall's ceiling. They thus at once serve both a visually and an optically aesthetic function. Finally, Helmholtz resonators are now also sometimes used in microphones to eliminate an undesired frequency from an acoustical system. For frequencies of less than 300 Hz, they thus become microphone tuners, and they too are often used in concert halls, among other places.

David Cahan

Bibliography

Fletcher, Neville H., and Thomas D. Rossing. *The Physics of Musical Instruments,* 13, 153–55. New York: Springer-Verlag, 1991.

Helmholtz, Hermann von. "On the Physiological Causes of Harmony in Music." In *Science and Culture: Popular and Philosophical Essays,* edited by David Cahan, 46–75. Chicago: University of Chicago Press, 1995.

———. *On the Sensations of Tone as a Physiological Basis for the Theory of Music.* Translated by Alexander J. Ellis, 7, 43–45, 51, 111–12, 372–74. 2nd English ed. London: Longmans, 1885. Reprint. New York: Dover, 1954.

Meyer, Erwin, and Dieter Guicking. *Schwingungslehre,* 233–35. Braunschweig: F. Vieweg, 1974.

Vogel, Stephan. "Sensation of Tone, Perception of Sound, and Empiricism: Helmholtz's Physiological Acoustics." In *Hermann von Helmholtz and the Foundations of Nineteenth-Century Science,* edited by David Cahan, 259–87. Berkeley: University of California Press, 1994.

Hemoglobinometer

Hemoglobin was the name given in 1864 to the red pigment of blood by the German chemist Felix Hoppe-Seyler, who had discovered its absorption spectrum. The importance of this substance had been appreciated since the seventeenth century: Robert Boyle, in his *Memoirs for the Natural History of Human Blood* (1683) considered that blood serves a respiratory function, and he also pointed out the importance of the iron content of blood.

The development of methods to estimate the amount of hemoglobin in blood dates from in 1877, when Louis Malassez compared the color of blood with that of a carmine-picric acid solution—blood itself being too unstable to serve as a standard. In 1878, William Gowers described *An Apparatus for the Clinical Estimation of Haemoglobin.* His standard was glycerine jelly tinted with carmine-picric acid to the color of diluted normal blood; hemoglobin in a patient's blood was then estimated by the extent to which a sample of 20 mm^3 (20 µl) was diluted to give the same color. Georges Hayem simplified the procedure by providing a set of colored disks representing a range of hemoglobin values. In 1900, Theodore Tallquist of Finland compared the color of a drop of blood on blotting paper with a graded set of red to pink colors. This crude method is still being used in some parts of the world.

A major development came from the 1901 observation by the English physiologist John Scott Haldane that the blood pigment could be made more stable by exposing it to coal-gas, which converted hemoglobin to carboxyhemoglobin (HbCO), and that the "coloring power" of blood was proportional to its oxygen capacity. In 1894 G. Hüffner had shown that 1 g of hemoglobin had an oxygen-binding capacity of 1.34 ml. Haldane found that the average normal oxygen capacity of blood (in men) was 18.5 percent. He defined as a standard a 1-percent solution of normal blood (as HbCO), so that 100 percent hemoglobin was 138 g/l, using Gower's instrument. He also noted that in women hemoglobin was, on average, 11 percent lower and in children 13 percent lower than in men.

The Haldane-Gowers hemoglobinometer became widely used in the British empire. Meanwhile, Hermann Sahli of Bern was attempting to overcome the problem of instability by converting hemoglobin to a brown colored derivative, acid hematin, to be read against a brown glass standard. The Sahli hemoglobinometer, described in 1902, became popular in Europe and the United States.

Further developments occurred on two fronts, instruments and standards. In 1906, Johann Plesch of Budapest, working in Berlin, described a selenium cell-galvanometer for measuring hemoglobin based on the principle that the color of the solution was inversely proportional to its concentration. In due course, increasingly sophisticated **colorimeters, comparators, photometers,** and **spectrophotometers** were developed to measure color intensity and light absorbance. These instruments were intended for various analytic measurements, but some were developed with ap-

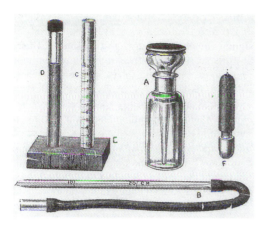

Gower's hemoglobinometer, 1923. Baird & Tatlock Ltd. Standard Catalogue of Scientific Apparatus: *Vol. 3* Biological Sciences. *London, 1923: 284. Courtesy of SSPL.*

propriate filters to function specifically as hemoglobinometers.

The need was also recognized for a simple, portable instrument that could be used outside a laboratory. One such instrument was the grey-wedge photometer, invented by Earl J. King in 1937 and further developed by the British Medical Research Council. In this instrument the density of a dilute sample of blood transmitted through a green absorbing filter is matched against the light transmitted by a rotating grey wedge.

As measuring methods improved, the need for a reliable standard became apparent. The Sahli method was unsatisfactory, as the specifications of the "standard" appeared to vary with the maker, with 100 percent ranging between 130 and 170 g/l. In Britain, standardization of the Haldane method led, in 1942, to a British standard (BS 1079) with the primary color standard, representing "100% Hemoglobin," being maintained at the National Physical Laboratory. However, in 1947, Earl King and his colleagues found, by iron analysis and gasometric determinations, that the original Haldane measurements had been incorrect; they revised the BSI standard of 100 percent Haldane to 148 g/l—thus requiring a recalculation of normal English values, which then fell into line with the normal values that had been established in Continental Europe and the United States.

But there were still alarming discrepancies in measurements between laboratories. To try to ensure a universal standard, in 1963 the (then) European Society for Haematology set up a working group that was to become the International Council for Standardization in Haematology. In 1965, this expert group established specifications for a standard of hemiglobincyanide; its concentration was determined by spectrophotometric measurement on the basis of the molar mass of hemoglobin, as determined in 1961 by G. Braunitzer et al. and by its molar area absorbance. This preparation, which has a stability of at least eight to ten years, was adopted by the World Health Organization as an international standard, and it is now used worldwide to calibrate modern hemoglobinometers.

Mitchell Lewis

Bibliography

Gowers, W.R. "An Apparatus for the Clinical Estimation of Haemoglobin." *Transactions of the Clinical Society of London* 12 (1879): 64–67.

Haldane, John. "The Colorimetric Determination of Haemoglobin." *Journal of Physiology* 26 (1901): 497–504.

King, E.J., et al. "Determination of Haemoglobin: II. The Haldane Haemoglobin Standard." *Lancet* 2 (1947): 789–92.

———, et al. "Determination of Haemoglobin: VI. Test of the M.R.C. Grey-wedge Photometer." *Lancet* 2 (1948): 971–74.

Plesch, Johann. "Über objektive Hämoglobinometrie." *Biochemische Zeitschrift* 1 (1906): 32–38.

Sahli, Hermann. "Über ein einfaches und exactes Verfahren der klinischen Hämometrie." *Verhandlungen der Deutsche Gesellschaft für innere Medizin* 20 (1902): 230–44.

Hilger-Spekker Absorptiometer

See ABSORPTIOMETER, HILGER-SPEKKER

Human Centrifuge

See CENTRIFUGE, HUMAN

Hydrometer

A hydrometer measures the specific gravity of a liquid, and hence its strength. Hydrometers were mentioned by Hypatia around A.D. 400 and by the poet Rhemnius three centuries earlier. German salt workers were using hydrometers to test the strength of brines by the latter Middle Ages. Robert Boyle, who introduced hydrometers into scientific discourse in England in 1675, probably learned about hydrometers from his landlord in Oxford, John Cross, who was the leading apothecary in that town. In the eighteenth century, hydrometers were used primarily for mineral water analysis and to measure the strength of alcoholic beverages for commercial and tax purposes.

The oldest extant hydrometers are made of turned ivory weighted with lead shot and may date from the seventeenth century. Copper hydrometers, graduated for alcoholic proof, were introduced around 1725 by John Clarke, a "turner and engine worker" in London. Clarke's early instruments were provided with weights that screwed on below the bulb, for use with liquids of different densities. He later added other weights to compensate for temperature variation. Clarke's hydrometer was adopted by the English Excise Department in 1762, and it was made the legal definition of proof for levying duty by an act of Parliament in 1787. This 1787 act also sought further verification of proof, and led Charles Blagden, secretary of the Royal Society, and George Gilpin to undertake a long series of very precise measurements to determine the specific gravity of various mixtures of alcohol and water at different temperatures.

In 1802 the Board of Excise held a competition to find a better instrument than Clarke's hydrometer for revenue purposes, and nineteen instruments were submitted for consideration. The winning design was that of Bartholomew Sikes, a peripatetic London employee of the excise commissioners. Sikes's hydrometer was enshrined in legislation in 1816 and remained the legal standard until 1907. Sikes's hydrometers were supplied to the excise by his son-in-law, Robert Brettell Bate, and later by Dring & Fage, while two of Bate's former workmen, Edward Ladd and Thomas Streatfield, won the contract with the Inland Revenue.

Clarke was just one of many British inventors who brought forth new hydrometers. Matthew Quin, for instance, designed an instrument that won a Silver Medal of the Society of Arts in 1781. The instrument patented in 1790 by John Dicas of Liverpool was adopted by the U.S. government for estimating the strength of imported liquors, and remained the American standard for some sixty years.

The story was similar elsewhere in Europe. Antoine Lavoisier introduced a hydrometer designed for tax purposes in 1768, but that designed by the more obscure Cartier proved more successful. Antoine Baumé, a pharmacist in Paris, introduced several hydrometers designed for chemical and pharmaceutical use, and his scales for liquids lighter and heavier than water remained in use for many years. Johann Georg Tralles, a physicist in Berlin, undertook another study of the relation between alcoholic strength and specific gravity in 1805 and later introduced a hydrometric scale that would gain popularity in German-speaking countries. Joseph Louis Gay-Lussac undertook yet another study of the relation between alcoholic strength and specific gravity in 1822, and on the basis of it he introduced a hydrometer with a centessimal scale.

The importance of the hydrometer in brewing was more demand-led than fiscally imposed. It was important for brewers to keep the quality of their product constant for their thirsty customers; and, indeed, by 1760 five London breweries were each producing over fifty thousand barrels each year and consequently spending more than £30,000 on malt and hops, thus it was important to ensure that production was uninterrupted by mistakes. This led to the development of the saccharometer, a hydrometer that measured the specific gravity of wort, or sugar solution. The saccharometer designed by John Richardson of York was made by the Troughtons of London in the 1790s. R.B. Bate's saccharometer, patented in 1822, was adopted in Ireland, while Allan's saccharometer, improved by Thomas Thomson of Glasgow University, continued to be used in Scotland for much of the nineteenth century.

Other hydrometers were designed for other purposes: the lactometer for measuring the richness of milk; the oleometer for measuring the specific gravity of oils; the urinometer to detect diabetes; the acetometer to measure the strength of vinegar; and many others as well. These instruments were essentially alike—most were made of noncorrosive glass, with lead shot as ballast—but they carried different hydrometric scales.

Another method of determining specific gravity, discovered in the mid seventeenth century by members of the Accademia del Cimento in Italy, involved glass beads of different buoyancies that could be dropped successively into a liquid until one was found that was just dense enough to sink. Reinvented in the 1750s by Alexander Wilson of Glasgow, these hydrostatic "bubbles" proved popular, especially in Scotland. Manufactured principally by immigrant Italian glassblowers, they were used in the dairy

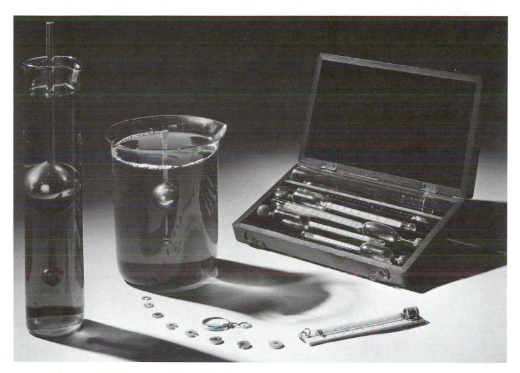

Nineteenth-century hydrometers: (from left) oleometer by Dring & Fage, ca. 1870; portable Sike's hydrometer by Dring & Fage, ca. 1873; set of four glass hydrometers in case, ca. 1830. SM 1954-384, 1954-377, 1954-390. Courtesy of SSPL.

and bleaching industries, but more generally in brewing and distilling.

A.D. Morrison-Low

Bibliography

Burnett, John. "William Prout and the Urinometer: Some Interpretations." In *Making Instruments Count*, edited by R.G.W. Anderson, J.A. Bennett, and W.F. Ryan, 242–54. Aldershot and Brookfield, Hampshire: Variorum, 1993.

"Hydrometer." In *Encyclopedia Britannica*, Vol. 4, 161–65. 11th ed. Cambridge: Cambridge University Press, 1910.

McConnell, Anita. *R.B. Bate of the Poultry, 1782–1847: The Life and Times of a Scientific Instrument-Maker*. London: Scientific Instrument Society, 1993.

Matthias, Peter. *The Brewing Industry in England 1700–1830*. Cambridge: Cambridge University Press, 1959.

Tate, Francis G.H., and George H. Gabb. *Alcoholometry: An Account of the British Method of Alcoholic Strength Determination*. London: His Majesty's Stationery Office, 1930.

Hydrostatic Balance

See BALANCE, HYDROSTATIC

Hygrometer

A hygrometer measures humidity (Greek *hygros*, "wet," + *metron*, "measure"). In the mid fifteenth century, Leon Battista Alberti and Nicholas of Cusa mentioned hygrometers in which a **balance** reads the weight gain of a sponge or wool as they absorb moisture, and Leonardo da Vinci described a sponge hygrometer. In the early seventeenth century, Santorio Santorre used alum or tartar in balance hygrometers; he also described cord and wood hygrometers, in which the hygroscopic substances alter their dimensions as they absorb water vapor. The twisting with humidity of the awn or "beard" of wild oats and other seeds had long been known "to children and Juglers"; according to Robert Hooke, "some of those last-named persons" displayed the beard as "the Legg of an Arabian Spider, or the Legg of an inchanted Egyptian Fly," attaching it on occasion to an index or cross. Hooke's well-known oat-beard hygrometer, constructed around the middle of the seventeenth century, included these among its forebears, as well as more serious versions by Emmanuel Maignan, Cardinal Giovanni de Medici, and Evangelista Torricelli.

Like the **thermometer** and **barometer**, the hygrometer developed a wealth of variation in the late seventeenth and early eighteenth centuries. The new designs, however, employing twisting cords, expanding boards, and other hygroscopic substances, along with various linkages to the index, contributed little to the measurement of humidity. As Johann Heinrich Lambert observed in 1769, hygrometers remained in much the same condition as at the moment of their invention: "It seems indeed that effort has been directed towards ornamentation and variation rather than to closer study, aimed at understanding their language and rendering it intelligible."

Lambert himself, along with Jean-André Deluc and Horace Bénédict de Saussure, addressed this problem beginning around 1770. Lambert and Deluc opened their investigations with careful statements of the fundamental principles of instrumentation. Preeminent among these were comparability among instrument scales, established by setting fixed points, and a known and linear correspondence between the instruments' indications and quantities being measured. Lambert, collaborating with the instrument-maker Georg Friedrich Brander of Augsburg, achieved some success in marking on his gut hygrometer fixed points of absolute dryness and absolute humidity (that is, saturation) and attempted to determine actual quantities of moisture in the air corresponding to its readings. Lambert's experiments were crude, though, and gut is unsuitable as a hygroscopic substance. Deluc's choice of whalebone for his hygrometer, combined with a systematic approach to calibration, weighed in his favor, but his choice of immersion in water to fix the point of saturation was unwise. De Saussure, departing from the traditional reliance on nonhuman substances to mirror nature's changes, chose for his hygrometer a human hair—the delicacy and sensitivity of which remains unsurpassed among natural hygroscopic substances. He subjected the instrument to systematic and exhaustive experiments designed to ensure precision and eliminate sources of error—an approach that, like Deluc's, was characteristic of the late eighteenth century. His work bore theoretical fruit, leading him to abandon the currently favored "solution" theory of evaporation, according to which evaporating water dissolves into the air, in favor of the existence of water vapor as an independent "elastic fluid" (that is, a gas). He arrived at a statement of the independence of the pressures of water vapor and the air in which it is mixed—that is, Dalton's law of partial pressures for the special case of air and water vapor. De Saussure's hygrometer remained in use into the twentieth century; it was especially valuable at near-freezing temperatures, where other designs failed.

Besides instruments depending on an alteration of weight or spatial dimension of some hygroscopic substance, there are two other principal types of hygrometer: the condensation hygrometer and the psychrometer. Ferdinand II, Grand Duke of Tuscany and patron of the Accademia del Cimento, invented the first condensation hygrometer in 1655. A glass vase, pointed at the bottom, was filled with ice. The rate at which drops of condensed water fell from its outer surface into a vessel below provided a measure of the humidity. Later variations included weighing the condensed water instead of counting drops. In 1750 Charles Le Roy, professor of medicine at Montpellier, suggested using as the measure of humidity what we call the dew point: the highest temperature at which water will condense out of the air onto a surface. Beginning early in the nineteenth century, John Frederic Daniell, Henri-Victor Regnault, and others developed dew-point hygrometers, in which a thermometer registers the temperature of a surface cooled by evaporating ether, until water condenses upon it.

The psychrometer (Greek *psychr-*, "cold"; so named by Ernst Ferdinand August in 1825) exploits the cooling that accompanies the evaporation of water. This phenomenon, well-known and long used for refrigeration in tropical countries, was noticed by European natural philosophers as early as 1681 and correctly ascribed to evaporation by William Cullen, René Antoine Ferchauld de Réaumur, and Michael Cristoph Hanow around 1755. According to his biographer, John Playfair, James Hutton conceived the idea of using evaporative cooling to measure humidity; "the degree of cold *ceteris paribus* will be proportional to the dryness of the air." In 1795 John Leslie devised a differential thermometer, in which the difference in temperature between wet and dry thermometer bulbs measures the rate of evaporation. The problem was to relate this temperature difference to humidity—or, properly speaking, to the vapor pressure of water in the ambient air. James Ivory arrived, in 1822, at a formula based on theoretical considerations that is substantially correct: $e = e' - b(t - t')/1200$,

Assmann psychrometer, by Casella, 1950s. C.F. Casella & Co. Ltd. Meteorological and Scientific Instruments Catalogue 684A. London, 1952: 105. Courtesy of Casella Ltd.

where e is the vapor pressure in the atmosphere, e' the saturation pressure at the temperature of the wet bulb, b the barometric pressure in inches of mercury, and t and t' the temperatures of dry and wet bulbs, respectively. Several others, including August and Henri-Victor Regnault, elaborated on the theory of the psychrometer. Meteorologists, however, considered the instrument untrustworthy until the development of Richard Assmann's ventilated psychrometer (1892), in which a fan draws the air at a known rate past thermometers that are shielded from disturbing radiation. Americans preferred Arago's whirled psychrometer, set up in a thermometer shelter. The sling psychrometer, whose two thermometers, held in a sling, are whirled by the observer, remained popular among travelers and explorers. Despite the theoretical understanding of the psychrometer, each of these instruments requires special tables worked out for known rates of ventilation.

Theodore S. Feldman

Bibliography

Archinard, Margareta. "L'apport Génevois à l'hygrométrie." *Gesnerus* 34 (1977): 362–82.

De Saussure, Horace Bénédict. *Essais sur l'hygométrie.* Neuchâtel, 1783.

Feldman, Theodore S. "The History of Meteorology, 1750–1800: A Case Study of the Quantification of Experimental Physics." Ph.D. dissertation. University of California, Berkeley, 1983.

Middleton, W.E. Knowles. *Invention of the Meteorological Instruments.* Baltimore: Johns Hopkins University Press, 1969.

Hyperbolic Navigation System

A hyperbolic navigation system allows a craft to locate its position on a series of intersecting hyperbolic lines radiating out from the base lines of a number of synchronized radio transmitting stations.

All points on a hyperbola have the same difference in distance with respect to two foci. Thus in the figure below, given A and B as the foci, points D1, D2, and D3 lie on the same hyperbola, as the distances AD1 - BD1 = AD2 - BD2 = AD3 - BD3 = k1. By changing the parameter k1 to k2, another hyperbola is generated. The perpendicular bisector of the base line AB will form an axis of symmetry so that similar hyperbolae to those on the right will be generated for similar values of k, on the left. From a navigational perspective, if the value of k can be measured, a craft will be able to place itself on a defined hyperbola with respect to the foci A and B. If a similar exercise is carried out with respect to another set of foci, say A and C, then a position can be fixed by the intersection of the two hyperbolae.

Theoretically it makes no difference how the distance differences are measured, but in practice hyperbolic navigation systems use radio transmissions as their measuring medium. In principle, three radio transmitters transmit synchronized signals. A receiver onboard the craft will measure either time differences if the signals are pulsed, or phase difference if continuous wave. Since radio waves propagate through the earth's atmosphere in different ways depending upon frequency, the accuracy and range of a particular system is in general a function of the frequency employed.

Position fixing is accomplished either by using specially prepared charts with the hyperbolae marked upon them, or by incorporating information processing to yield a direct readout of position.

History

The history of hyperbolic navigational systems began in World War I, when the British, French, and Germans developed sound-ranging systems to locate the position of enemy gunfire. These systems used a series of spaced listening stations, each equipped with a sensitive microphone that could discriminate between the sound of the gun's report and the louder shell shock wave. The signal from the microphone was sent back by land line to a central head-

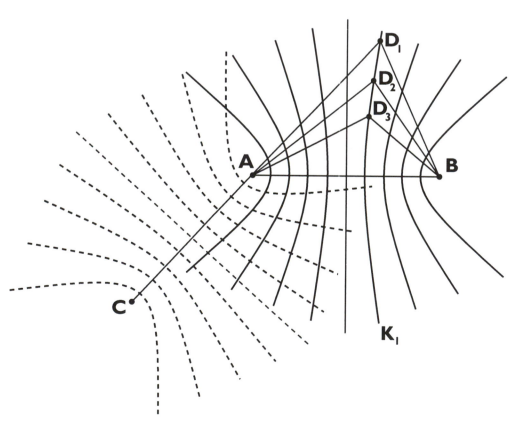

Hyperbolic navigation system, with transmitting stations at A, B, and C. Courtesy of SSPL.

quarters that recorded each signal on a timed film base. The time differences between the various listening posts provided the hyperbolae that crossed to locate the artillery position. Since sound was used as the signal medium, the accuracy could be affected by meteorological conditions, although accuracies of 100 to 150 yards over distances of several miles were reported.

Between the world wars, a series of patents were published for various types of hyperbolic systems using radio transmissions, but it was not until the navigational needs of Allied bombers over Germany became important that the first fully operational hyperbolic system called Gee (for the first letter of Grid, which in turn represented the pattern formed by the families of intersecting hyperbolae), came into being. The key technical advance was the ability to generate and transmit steep-fronted, short-duration radio pulses, a result of the intensive research undertaken into the development of **radar;** much of the development of Gee is associated with R.J. Dippy, a British government scientist working at the Bawdsey Research Station. Gee consisted of a chain of three stations with base lines of fifty to eighty miles transmitting a pulse of length 6 μs with a carrier frequency of 20–90 MHz. The system became operational in July 1941 with a range of about 350 miles, enough to cover large parts of Germany. The onboard equipment consisted of a cathode ray tube that displayed the arrival of the pulses, allowing the time difference to be read off. Although Gee was proposed as an international navigation aid after the war, it was overtaken by competing systems, notably LORAN.

In 1940, Alfred Loomis, chairman of the Microwave Committee of the American National Defense Research Committee, suggested that a LOng RANge hyperbolic system be constructed, with ranges of three hundred to five hundred miles, to cover ships and aircraft crossing the Atlantic. This system would use pulsed transmissions with stations separated on base lines of several hundred miles with a carrier frequency of 2 MHz, which extended the range but reduced the accuracy. In order to overcome any problems of ambiguity as to which was the leading signal, a constant time difference between pulses transmitted by the stations was built into the system. LORAN was developed at the Radiation Laboratory of M.I.T. and is particularly associated with the work of J.A. Pierce; the full system entered service in 1943.

The hyperbolic system that later became the Decca Navigator was invented and developed by the Americans W.J. O'Brian and H.F. Schwarz under the aegis of the British Admiralty and the Decca Gramophone Co. Development took place under the name of QM, between 1940 and 1944. QM used continuous wave (CW) transmissions and measured the phase difference. Given a suitable operating frequency, the measurement of phase difference produces a very accurate system when compared with an equivalent pulsed system. To overcome the problem of the transmitted CW signals of identical frequency mixing and creating a single wave, O'Brian and Schwarz arranged for the signals transmitted to be harmonics of a base frequency. The base frequency was transmitted by a master station and the harmonics by one or more slaves. The onboard receiver translated the two different signals into a common frequency and measured the phase difference, which was read off on a dial. Accuracies of up to 20 yards were reported during the D-Day landings.

With phase measurement it is impossible to tell whether the phase difference measured is 20° or 20° + 360° or 20° + 720°. To remove this ambiguity, the transmissions were periodically altered according to a set scheme that allowed lane identification to take place.

Further Developments

After the war, Gee was not adapted to civilian use to any significant degree. QM was taken over by the Decca Co. and renamed the Decca Navigator, the first commercial chain coming into operation in 1946.

The original LORAN, or LORAN A as it became known following an abortive attempt to develop a high-accuracy LORAN B, was finally withdrawn from use in 1980. LORAN C had been under development by the U.S. Coast Guard since 1956 and was based on a similar system originally developed for the U.S. Air Force. The first LORAN C chain of three stations was erected in 1957, and by 1990 there were some twenty-three chains consisting of sixty-nine stations excluding a compatible system based in the USSR. A short-range tactical version known as LORAN D was also developed, but its use was not pursued.

LORAN C uses ground-wave transmissions with pulses that both limit interference from sky waves and provide a means of cycle identification. The improved accuracy of LO-

RAN C is achieved by using carrier phase comparison and domain filters and correlation techniques when conditions are poor. All LORAN C transmitters operate at 100 kHz, providing a coverage of over 1,000 nautical miles. The emergence of the microprocessor in the 1970s brought improved performance and information display, including the ability to provide position in terms of geographical coordinates. Since 1974 LORAN C has been the national radio navigation system for use in U.S. coastal waters. The system continues to be developed for land vehicles and for handheld portability.

The Decca Navigator has continued in constant use for the purposes of coastal navigation, covering seven important coastal areas throughout the world, in particular Northern Europe. Master frequencies range from 14.0 to 14.4 kHz, giving coverage of from 240 nautical miles by night to about 500 nautical miles by day, the difference being due to the contamination of the ground wave by sky waves. High accuracy and specialized portable variants have also been developed.

By 1955 it had become technically feasible to use low-frequency radio waves to construct a worldwide navigation system with an accuracy of 2 to 4 nautical miles anywhere on the earth's surface, using only a small number of transmitting stations. Development of the system was undertaken by the U.S. Navy in association with J.A. Pierce, who had worked on LORAN. It was given the name Omega, and the first stations began operation in 1966. The system consists of eight permanent stations transmitting in the 10–14 kHz range using continuous waves and phase comparison to determine the hyperbolic position line. Differential Omega uses a fixed station to monitor Omega transmissions and send corrections to users fitted with special receivers who are navigating in the vicinity. This technique can improve accuracy to about 0.5 nautical mile within a radius of about 50 nautical miles of the fixed station.

Thomas Wright

Bibliography

Colin, R.I. "Pioneer Award to W.J. O'Brien and H.F. Schwarz." *IEEE Transactions on Aerospace and Electronic Systems* (1969): 1014–20.

Frank, R.L. "History of Loran C." *Navigation* 29 (1982): 1–6.

Pierce, J.A. "Memoirs of John Alvin Pierce: Invention of Omega." *Navigation* 36 (1989): 147–55.

Powell, C. "Hyperbolic Origins." *Journal of Navigation* 34 (1981): 424–36.

Hypsometer

The hypsometer (Greek *hypsos,* "height" + *metron,* "measure") is now used to calibrate **thermometers,** but in the nineteenth century it served to measure height through a determination of the boiling point of water. The Paris academicians Pierre Charles Le Monnier and Jean-Antoine Nollet had noted the dependence of the boiling point of water on atmospheric pressure in the 1740s, and in the 1760s the Genevan meteorologist and Alpinist Jean-André Deluc undertook extensive studies of the phenomenon. For his investigation Deluc designed what might be called a hypsometer: a thermometer provided with a **micrometer** to measure fractions of a degree in an interval below 100°C, a copper and tin boiler in which the thermometer was held an inch above the bottom of a water bath and a stove. Deluc took this apparatus on several journeys to peaks in the vicinity of Geneva. His object, however, was not thermometric but barometric hypsometry— that is, the measurement of height with the **barometer**—and while his tables relating the boiling point to air pressure might have been used for the former purpose, he intended them for the calibration of a correcting thermometer that he supplied with his mountain barometer.

Francis Hyde Wollaston constructed the first true thermometric hypsometer in 1817. Wollaston's "thermometrical barometer," as he called it, consisted of a sensitive thermometer with a cavity just above the bulb to hold the mercury until the heat reached near boiling point. Beyond the cavity a scale of an inch per degree Fahrenheit could be read by a vernier to thousandths of a degree. Wollaston exposed his thermometer only to the steam in the boiler, whose temperature held steadier than that of boiling water. He claimed that this instrument could detect differences in boiling point arising from the height of a common table! Ganot's well-known textbook modestly claimed 10 feet.

The French physicist Henri-Victor Regnault added several improvements to this instrument, which he called a "hypsometric thermometer." He reduced the size of the instrument, secured its zero, and worked out very precise tables for the vapor pressure of water at temperatures near 100°C. (Wollaston had assumed a linear relation between boiling point and height.) Later versions placed the thermometer inside a double-walled telescoping chamber, which shielded it from cooling by air currents and made possible its nearly total immersion in steam. Advocates of the instrument, which was only about 15 in. long, touted its accuracy and its portability as superior to that of the 32-in. barometer "for the traveller in difficult country."

The hypsometer was perfected at the end of the nineteenth century by the Norwegian meteorologist Henrik Mohn. Mohn regarded his instrument, which read through a telescopic sight to thousandths of a degree, accurate enough for the calibration of barometers and the determination of gravitational constants at meteorological stations. But the uncertainty over the instrument's name ("thermo-barometer" and "thermometrical barometer," "mountain thermometer," "hypsometric thermometer," "hypsometric apparatus"—note that "barometer" in this context includes the notion of measurement of heights) reflects a kind of oscillation of purposes: what was being measured, height, boiling point, atmospheric pressure, or the earth's gravity? The instrument may never have become popular enough among explorers and travelers to settle the issue in favor of height, and in the twentieth century it has reverted to a device for the calibration of boiling points on thermometers.

Theodore S. Feldman

Bibliography

Mohn, Henrik. *Das Hypsometer als Luft-druckmesser und seine Anwendung zur Bestimmung der Schwerekorrektion.* Christiania: J. Dybwad, 1899.

Negretti and Zambra. *A Treatise on Meteorological Instruments: Explanatory of Their Scientific Principles, Method of Construction, and Practical Utility.* London: Negretti and Zambra, 1864.

Regnault, Henri-Victor. "Note sur la température de l'ébullition de l'eau à différentes hauteurs." *Annales de Chimie et de Physique* 14 (1845): 196–206.

Wollaston, Francis Hyde. "Description of a Thermometrical Barometer for Measuring Altitudes." *Philosophical Transactions of the Royal Society of London* (1817): 183–96.

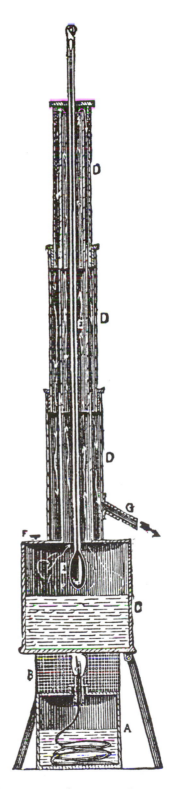

Mountain thermometer or hypsometrical apparatus, by Negretti & Zambra, 1864. Negretti & Zambra. (1864): 95, Figure 73. Courtesy of SSPL.

I

Image Analyzer

A standard **microscope** gives an image that observers interpret in morphological terms. Color, shape, and relationships can be appreciated subjectively but little quantitative data can be obtained. The exception is linear dimensions, which have been measured since Leeuwenhoek's time. Other parameters such as number, area, perimeter, and shape could, until recently, be only estimated or described subjectively.

Image analysis quantifies and subsequently classifies such parameters in identifiable parts of an image. Almost inevitably, image analysis must be preceded by image processing—that is, manipulations performed on an image in order to improve its quality and suitability for measurement. These may involve increasing the contrast, enhancing the boundaries of objects of interest, and separating touching objects. Image analysis thus involves image capture, now usually in digital form; image processing; definition of the regions of interest and their separation from the background, known as "segmentation"; and measurement, analysis, and classification of the relevant parameters.

Since the mid nineteenth century, attempts have been made using grids superimposed on the image to measure parameters such as area fraction and, with hemocytometer slides, to count the number of objects in a microscopical sample. All such techniques are laborious if statistically significant sizes of samples are to be measured, and the results are subject to inaccuracies. Much effort has been expended in the last forty years in an effort to automate the analysis of microscopical images. Such methods may be manual with limited instrumental aid, semiautomatic, or fully automatic. All, with the exception of manual-interactive techniques,

require scanning, either in the plane of the source, in the object plane, or in the image plane.

The first generation of image analyzers derive from the "flying spot" microscope introduced by J.Z. Young and F. Roberts in 1951. This used a TV raster on a cathode ray tube placed over the eyepiece of a microscope used in reverse, so that the objective produced a very small spot of light that scanned the specimen on the stage. The transmitted light (determined by the density of the specimen) was measured by a **photomultiplier** whose output modulated the raster on a second cathode ray tube. Three years later, Cooke-Yarborough and Whyard introduced a stage-scan system with a photomultiplier mounted over the microscope eyepiece, for the automatic counting of red blood cells. In 1963 the first image analyzers using the now universal scan with a television camera in the image plane were produced by Metals Research Ltd. These prototypes of the Quantitative Television Microscope (QTM) type A had no computer memory, were analog, and could not distinguish separate objects in the field of view. The results were displayed on a moving coil meter that represented the proportion of the field seen as either black or white or, alternatively, the number of changes from black to white in any field. The QTM B was introduced two years later and sold until 1970. This had a small amount of memory (using an analog delay line) that allowed the comparison of events on successive scan lines, and thus the measurement of individual objects. Some instruments presented the output on a meter, but later models showed the results as direct digital readout. By 1968 Zeiss had introduced a

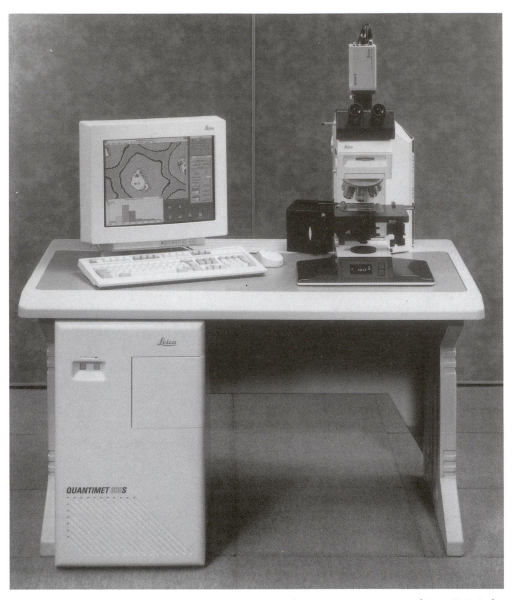

Quantimet QTM 600 image processing and analysis system, by Leica, 1994. Courtesy of Leica U.K. Ltd.

similar instrument, the Micro-Videomat, while Leitz followed with the Classimat.

In 1969 the second generation of image analyzers began with the introduction of the digital PMC marketed by Bausch & Lomb. This had a small amount of memory that could not store a complete black and white image but only the coordinates where a line scan changed from black to white or vice versa. In the same year the Quantimet 720 was placed on the market by Metals Research Ltd. (later taken over by Cambridge Instruments). Here the crystal-controlled scan was broken up into separate

picture points, or pixels, a practice followed in all subsequent image analyzers. The analog output of the QTM 720 scan was digitized into six bits, giving sixty-four separate recognizable grey levels. The scan rate of ten frames/second gave what was then a remarkable spatial resolution but at the expense of a flickering display image. Computer memory was insufficient to allow image storage when the large number of pixels forming an image was considered. Most of the image analysis functions in these early instruments were carried out in dedicated, hard-wired modules.

The principal development in the 1970s was an increase in memory so that a system could store measurements on separate objects in a field and keep and treat them as separate. This made it possible to take different measurements on the same object, leading to shape recognition and classification. In 1974 Leitz brought out their Texture Analysis System (T.A.S.), which introduced the techniques of erosion and dilatation. Joyce-Loebl's Magiscan I, introduced in 1977, may be regarded as the first of the third generation of image analyzers in which hard-wired modules for image classification were replaced with **computers** running specific software. By 1980 software-based image analyzers were standard. The Kontron IBAS had an image array-processor working in conjunction with a large image memory, with a separate microprocessor controlling the system operations. Similar changes were introduced by Cambridge Instruments in their Quantimet series and by Joyce-Loebl in the Magiscan II of 1981.

The fourth generation of image analyzers first appeared in the late 1980s. These were provided with ever-increasing amounts of memory and hard disk storage so that images could be digitized at an eight-bit level in full color. Data handling was much improved with graphic overlays, and there was much easier operator sequence control. The Kontron KICS introduced in 1988 and Kontron IMCO 1000 in the following year allowed for user-defined image memory so that the images could be captured, stored, and analyzed at sizes and resolutions of from 64 x 64 to 4096 x 4096 pixels.

The availability of small desk-top computers containing large amounts of memory prompted various workers (such as Jarvis, 1988; Russ, 1990) to use them with software written "in house" as small stand-alone image-analysis systems. Current trends (in the mid 1990s) are toward physically smaller commercial instruments (such as the QTM 500, 570, and 600) with large image memories and storage facilities and fast processors, run with their system operating under the familiar "Windows" environment. As of 1997 there were several commercial image-analysis programs that ran on standard personal computers. The image, provided from a **camera** or other source via a frame-grabber board, is stored on the computer's hard disk. All the subsequent image manipulations, measurements, and statistical analyses of the results are carried out by the software. It seems probable that this will prove a popular way for image analysis to be carried out in future.

Savile Bradbury

Bibliography
Beadle, C. "The Quantimet Image Analysing Computer and Its Applications." *Advances in Optical and Electron Microscopy* 4 (1971): 361–83.
Jarvis, L.R. "Microcomputer Video Image Analysis." *Journal of the Royal Microscopical Society* 150 (1988): 83–97.
Moss, V.A. "Image Processing and Image Analysis." *Proceedings of the Royal Microscopical Society* 23, pt. 2 (1988): 83–88.
Russ, John C. *Computer-Assisted Microscopy: The Measurement and Analysis of Images.* New York: Plenum, 1990.
Young, J.Z., and F. Roberts. "A Flying Spot Microscope." *Nature* 167 (1951): 231.

Imaging Radar
See RADAR, IMAGING

Impact Testing Instruments
The advent of railway construction in the early nineteenth century produced new types of loading, and structural designers had to take into account the effects of vibration and shock. The reciprocating pistons of the steam locomotive could not be completely balanced by rotating weights fitted to the driving wheels, and this unbalanced force delivered a vertical, cyclical, "hammer blow" load to the rails. The first generation of cast-iron rail frequently failed as increasingly heavier locomotives pounded the tracks. Designers felt that the normal tensile tests did not predict the behavior of metals under impact loading. The first investigations of resistance to this type of loading were made by simple drop-weight tests, in which a span of the metal was subjected to the blow of a known weight falling through a given height. This technique was gradually refined and standardized, but did not lead to the design of specific testing equipment.

By the end of the nineteenth century impact tests were made on a standard 3-foot span of sample rail, and the weight and height of fall was adjusted according to the size of rail section. For railway tires and axles, the specification required that they should sustain a certain

Izod impact testing apparatus. Frederick V. Warnock. Strength of Materials. *London: Pitman, 1941: 329, Figure 136. Courtesy of Pitman Publishing.*

number of blows from a given weight falling through a particular height without failure.

In the early twentieth century, machines were designed to deliver impact loads to small, specially prepared specimens of metals. Of the various forms of dynamic load test, one has come into universal use. That is the notched-bar impact test, in which the specimen is tested as a beam under the action of a pendulum hammer. Although opinion differed as to the significance and value of the notched-bar test, it soon became clear that the test was more sensitive as the notch was made sharper. More-over, the result did not depend greatly on the

type of machine used, and it was not greatly influenced by the striking velocity. Some felt that the term "impact testing" was misleading, as the result did not indicate the material's resistance to shock or impact so much as differences of condition of the material that were not demonstrated by other tests. In fact, the real value of the test was considered to lie in revealing the effectiveness of the heat treatment of the metal.

In the Charpy Impact Tester, a pendulum carries a vertical knife, and the notched specimen is supported horizontally from each end. To conduct the test, the pendulum is raised by means of a worm gear, and then allowed to fall and fracture the test piece. In its upward movement the pendulum carries a pointer over a semicircular scale that is graduated in degrees. The energy absorbed in breaking the specimen is read from a table that indicates the angle through which the pointer is carried by the moving pendulum.

The Izod Machine is similar in principle, but larger and floor-standing. It has a pendulum about 4 feet long that can swing through an angle of about 120°. A small vice, fixed to the base of the machine, grips the specimen in a vertical position, as a cantilever, with the notch facing the hammer. The knife-edge on the hammer strikes the specimen and fractures it. The hammer will have swung through 60° before striking the specimen, and through less than 60° from its lowest position. The difference between these angles is recorded on the scale and is a measure of the energy absorbed in striking the specimen. As it is usual to make at least three tests on a specimen, the Izod test piece is often provided with notches on three faces. Graphs facilitate comparisons between results obtained on the Charpy and Izod testing machines.

Denis Smith

Bibliography

Carrington, Herbert. *Experimental Mechanics of Materials*. London: Pitman, 1930.

Popplewell, William Charles. *Experimental Engineering*. Vol. 2. Manchester: Scientific, 1901.

Unwin, William Cawthorne. *The Testing of Materials of Construction*. 2nd ed. London: Longmans, 1899.

Indicator

Indicators measure and record the pressure exerted by steam or gas in an engine, and through it other mechanical magnitudes such as power, work, speed, and acceleration. They consist of three basic elements: a pressure pickup, an amplification system, and a recording device. Indicators were exclusively mechanical during the major part of the nineteenth century. Later ones incorporated optical, electrical, and electronic elements.

The quality of an indicator is defined by its sensitivity to the slightest changes of pressure, and this quality becomes difficult to maintain as the speed of evolution increases. Thus the inertia of the instrument, of the elements submitted to pressure, must be as low as possible. The history of indicators is that of the improvement of their performance, which can be described in terms of the evolution of their self-frequency. The Watt-Southern indicator had 6 Hz, the indicator with mechanical amplification up to 150 Hz, the micro-indicator up to 400 Hz, the manograph up to 25,000 Hz, and the piezo-electric indicators up to 50,000 Hz before World War II, and up to 150,000 Hz in the 1970s.

Use

Indicators can be used on all engines through which a gas or steam under pressure produces or conveys mechanical energy: thermal engines (steam engines, internal combustion piston engines, jet engines), pneumatic machines, canons and guns, and so forth. They allow us to follow and to record the evolution of pressure during one or several working cycles, which is essential for all studies concerning power, efficiency, mechanical strength, and thermodynamic calculations. Indicator diagrams relate pressure to time or to volume. The surfaces of these diagrams are proportional to the indicated work done by the working fluid (but different from the work measured on the crankshaft by means of dynamometric brakes). The British engineer R.H. Thurston, at the end of the nineteenth century, described the indicator as the engineer's **stethoscope.**

Indicators also played a major role in the establishment and rise of thermal engine theory. Thus Emile Clapayron, inspired by the indicator diagrams of the steam engines, traced in 1834 the Carnot cycle in a pressure-volume coordinate system.

History and Types of Indicators

The development of the indicator was linked to the use of the new steam engine (using steam expansion) patented by James Watt in 1782. Around 1790, Watt built an instrument with a cylinder enclosing a piston that moved in equilibrium between steam pressure and a spring. The piston was linked to a pointer, soon to be replaced by a pen and flat chart. The movements of the pointer or pen were proportional to the volume generated by the piston movement. This improved "work measurer" or "ergometer" was developed by John Southern, Watt's collaborator. His instrument was kept hidden in Boulton's & Watt's workshop, and first mentioned in an English publication in 1822.

I

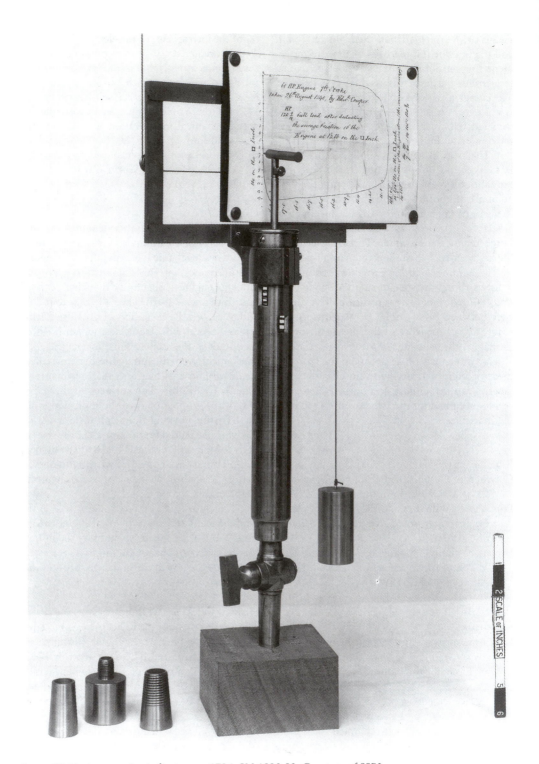

James Watt's steam engine indicator, ca. 1796. SM 1890-83. Courtesy of SSPL.

Around 1830 John McNaught replaced the flat chart with a rotating drum. Arthur Morin and Paul Garnier of France introduced indicators that could record successive closed diagrams as well as indicators able to measure the work developed during a period of time.

Mechanical Amplification Indicators. In 1862, the American C.B. Richard invented the first mechanical indicator designed to reduce the inertia of the moving parts as well as spring vibrations. Instruments of this sort were equipped with low-flexibility springs that allowed only a short stroke of the piston, and a mechanical linkage that amplified the movement and thus increased the scale of the record. Other inventors tried to increase the self-frequency of the spring, but could not go beyond 300 Hz.

Stroboscopic Indicators. Around 1870, the German engineer G.A. Hirn and the Frenchman Marcel Deprez created a method for raising a "stroboscopic diagram" that made it possible to reduce if not to eliminate the inertia of moving parts. It supposed that at each turn of the crankshaft only one point of the diagram was registered, all the diagrams being a succession of points obtained after a high number of cycles. Two types of indicators were built to exploit this method: those for which pressure is chosen in advance and the piston position is revealed, and those for which the piston position is fixed and the pressure is revealed. Deprez built the first type in 1875; Alphonse de Dion and George Bouton built the second in 1904. Stroboscopic indicators were abandoned in the 1930s.

High-Frequency Mechanical Indicators and Micro-Indicators. These use an encased stem as a spring that permits the self-frequency to be increased to 1,200 Hz and are characterized by very small diagrams. The microindicator is based on a strong reduction of the instrument dimensions and the elimination of the amplification device. The first microindicator was probably built by O. Mader in 1912. These indicators were abandoned in the 1930s.

Optical Indicators or Manographs. The manograph is characterized by an optical amplification system. Here the pressure element is connected with one or two small mirrors on which a light beam is focused, and a screen or photographic plate replaces the drum of the mechanical indicator. Deprez created the first manograph in 1877; this was a two-mirror instrument. The first commercially successful manograph, built by the British professor John Perry in 1890, had one mirror and a self-fre-

quency of 500 Hz. Manographs were constantly improved until World War II. The most efficient one was built by the French professor Max Serruys in 1932; it had a self-frequency of 25,000 Hz.

Electric and Electronic Indicators. The first electric indicators were created in the United States in the late 1920s, and they rapidly eliminated all competitors. They incorporated a pressure pickup (transducer) that delivered, after amplification with an electronic device, an electrical signal to a galvanometer or a cathode tube registering system. The use of transistors after 1950, and microprocessors after 1980, greatly increased the efficiency of the amplifier.

Pressure transducers, which use deformations of an elastic diaphragm, are of several forms. One is the magnetic transducer, in which an iron core fixed on the diaphragm under pressure moves inside a coil creating an electrical current. Another is the capacity variation transducer, which uses a condenser capacity with movable plates to control the electric current. The stroboscopic method was often used with indicators of this sort.

The other major type of pressure transducer uses modifications of the intrinsic properties of the item submitted to pressure. The major categories here are electric resistance variation transducers, which use the electric variation of small carbon disks submitted to a pressure, and quartz-pressure transducers, which are based on the piezo-electric properties of quartz (namely the creation of electric charges when a crystal is compressed under specific conditions). Discovered by Jacques and Pierre Curie in 1880, this phenomenon was applied to indicators in the middle of the 1930s by the German professors Kamm, Rickert, and Kieln. Modern quartz-pressure transducers are the most efficient and the most common.

Alexandre Herléa

Bibliography

De Juhasz, Kalman John. *The Engine Indicator: It's Design, Theory and Special Applications.* New York Instruments, 1934.

Herléa, Alexandre. "Les indicateurs de pression: Leur évolution en France au 19e siècle." In *Studies in the History of Scientific Instruments: Papers Presented at the 7th Symposium of the Scientific In-*

struments Commission of the Union Internationale d'Histoire et de Philosophie des Sciences, edited by Christine Blondel, et al., 193–234. London: Rogers Turner, 1989.

Labarthe, André. *Nouvelles méthodes de mesure mécanique.* Paris: Ministère de l'Air, 1936.

Roberts, Howard Creighton. *Mechanical Measurements by Electrical Methods.* Pittsburg, Pa.: Instruments, 1946.

Zelbstein, Uri. *La piezo-electricité appliquée à l'etude des moteurs.* Paris: Ministère de l'Air, 1947.

Induction Coil

An induction coil produces high-voltage sparks. It usually consists of two sets of windings that are either wound close to, or on top of, one another. Current from a **battery** is passed through the primary winding, which has a small number of turns, and is rapidly interrupted either by a mechanical or an electrical device. This sudden make-and-break in the current of the primary coil induces an emf (voltage) in the secondary coil, which has a much larger number of turns. The amount of emf is related to the ratio of the number of turns in the two coils, and this can be many tens of thousands of volts, depending on how well the coil has been constructed. The interrupter has its origin in early-nineteenth-century medical electricity, when physicians began to use voltaic batteries. They were so used to the intermittent shocks produced by the previous generation of **electrostatic machines** that they devised mechanically operated interrupters to "break up" the continuous current of the battery.

Much of the early pioneering work was done independently by Nicholas Joseph Callan, a priest who taught physics at Maynooth College near Dublin, and by Charles Grafton Page, a physician and designer of electrical instruments of Salem, Massachusetts. At this time the basic principles were determined almost entirely by means of trial and error.

The induction coil and the related terminology (inductance, self-inductance, and inductive current) originated from research with flat spiral coils of copper ribbons insulated with silk that was conducted by Joseph Henry, a young instructor at the Albany Academy in Albany, New York. Page continued this work, inventing the first autotransformer in which different portions in the same coil acted as primary and secondary circuits.

Callan was influenced by the electromagnetic researches of his friend William Sturgeon, the shoemaker turned scientific lecturer and inventor of electrical instruments, and also by Henry and Faraday, in that order. His earliest induction coils (1836) were derived from his electromagnets (1834). His device was still an autotransformer similar to Page's 1835 configuration, except that now the wires of the two coils were of different thicknesses. His repeater energizing the coils was a rocking wire whose ends dipped alternately into cups of mercury, operated by a clockwork motor. The electric shocks were taken from the beginning of the first and the end of the second coil, but by 1837 he kept the two coils separate and took the shock only from the secondary coil. This was the configuration of the genuine induction coil.

During the second phase of development, the prototypes became marketable products. Sturgeon made an autotransfomer on the Callan plan, but instead of using long coils, he made them by winding on the wooden bobbin first the thick copper wire (primary), connected to and followed by many more strands of the thin wire (secondary coil). He compared the behavior of a soft iron solid core with a soft iron multicore and observed that coils with the latter produced more intense sparks. George Henry Bachhoffner, the founder of the Polytechnic Institution in London, had made the same observation with one of Sturgeon's coils two weeks earlier.

Sturgeon also devised several interrupters. In the 1840s a popular medical coil pattern had both a manual and an electromagnetic interrupter, so that either strong or weak shocks could be administered (depending on the speed of the interruptions). A particularly popular type was based on Barlow's wheel, in which the stars of the wheel rotated by hand would dip into a mercury trough during rotation. A key factor was the development of the electromagnetic interrupter begun by Page in 1837, but this too had several antecedents, including Callan's rocking repeater. Page's most successful design was a precursor of the automatic hammer break, or vibrator, similar to the device that has become so common with the electric bell. A similar device was described by James William McGauley in 1837 and developed further by the physician Golding Bird, the London instrument-maker William Neeves (1838), Ernst Neeff (1839), and others.

Medical induction coil, by the Medical Supply Association, 1920–1950. SM 1966-1955. Courtesy of SSPL.

By the early 1840s the medical coil had come of age and had assumed its characteristic appearance: primary and secondary coils wound on a bobbin, a central multicore of soft iron, and an electromagnetic interrupter. This device was widely retailed, and the impetus from the market led to minor improvements.

The third phase of development began in the early 1850s, when this instrument was increasingly used as a serious research tool in physics. Improvements were now related to the criteria of this research: whether the coil was required as a high-energy source for x-rays (1895) or radio waves (Hertz in 1888; Marconi and Popov in 1895). This phase started effectively with Heinrich Daniel Ruhmkorff, who improved all aspects of the induction coil: better insulation, an enormously increased secondary coil, the addition of a current reverser to change the direction of the primary circuit, and most important of all, the addition of a large condenser (or capacitor) in the base that was connected across the breaker contacts in order to quench the fierce sparks and prevent the platinum contacts from fusing. This improvement had been suggested by Armand Fizeau in 1853. The device became generally, and unfairly, known as the Ruhmkorff coil, especially after Ruhmkorff was awarded a large sum by Napoleon III at the Paris Exposition of 1864. This caused resentment in the American scientific community, which felt that the award took no account of the improvements made by Edward S. Ritchie to which Ruhmkorff's attention had been drawn in 1858. It is however undeniable that, although Ritchie had improved the coil's windings, it was Ruhmkorff who developed the characteristic form of the coil to which his name became associated.

Other makers made similar improvements. A. Apps in London made a very large induction coil for William Spottiswoode in 1877 that produced 42-in. sparks. The need for powerful discharges and continuous use led to improvements in interrupter design, such as the electrolytic interrupter and the centrifugal mercury interrupter. These large items were worked separately from the coil. Smaller, simpler portable induction coils continued to be manufactured for medical treatment and diagnosis.

By the 1920s, the induction coil's role as a generator of radio waves was taken over by high-powered electron valves (or tubes) in special circuits. In this final phase, the instrument also developed into the closed magnetic circuit transformer made from soft iron stamping, patented in 1885–1886 by Karl Zipernowsky, Max Deri, and Otto Titus Blathy of Budapest, as a consequence of its use in the transmission of electricity in lighting systems (arc and incandescent lamps).

Willem D. Hackmann

Bibliography

Brenni, Paolo. "19th Century French Instrument Makers: IV. Heinrich Daniel Ruhmkorff (1803–1877)." *Bulletin of the Scientific Instrument Society* 41 (June 1994): 4–8.

Colwell, Hector Alfred. *An Essay on the History of Electrotherapy and Diagnosis.* London: Heinemann, 1922.

Hackmann, Willem D. "The Induction Coil in Medicine and Physics 1835–1877." In *Studies in the History of Scientific Instruments: Papers Presented at the 7th Symposium of the Scientific Instruments Commission of the Union Internationale d'Histoire et de Philosophie des Sciences. Paris 15–19 September 1987*, edited by Christine Blondel, et al., 235–50. London: Rogers Turner, 1989.

Rowbottom, Margaret, and Charles Susskind. *Electricity and Medicine: History of Their Interaction.* London: Macmillan, 1984.

Shiers, G. "The Induction Coil." *Scientific American* 224 (May 1971): 80–87.

Warner, Deborah Jean. "Compasses and Coils: The Instrument Business of Edward S. Ritchie." *Rittenhouse* 9 (1994): 1–24.

Inertial Guidance

Developed in the United States and the Soviet Union during the Cold War, inertial guidance was both a new form of navigation as well as the upshot of a new way of organizing the production of knowledge, especially in the United States. An inertial guidance system allows any moving vehicle to determine its own position without reference to any external data. The only input required is the exact starting position and time. With that, the guidance system measures the craft's acceleration and derives from that the vehicle's velocity and distance traveled. Practitioners often refer to inertial guidance as "astronomy in a closet," since they are attempting to perform a basic navigational task, one that often uses the heavens as a guide, as if they were observing the stars from a sealed room. Because their self-contained character made them invulnerable to enemy countermeasures, inertial guidance systems were originally developed for military applications in aircraft, guided missiles, and submarines. A civilian market for these technologies developed only in the early 1970s.

A classical inertial system measures acceleration through sophisticated instruments called **accelerometers**, which are mounted on a

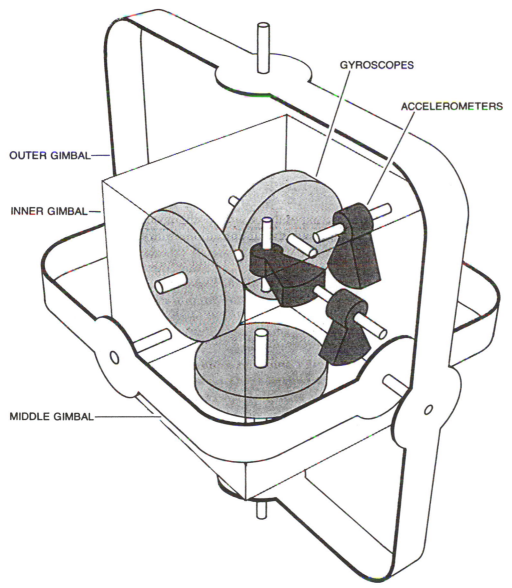

GYROSCOPES

ACCELEROMETERS

OUTER GIMBAL

INNER GIMBAL

MIDDLE GIMBAL

Schematic diagram of an inertial guidance system, showing three pairs of gyroscopes and accelerometers. Kosta Tsipis. "The Accuracy of Strategic Missiles." Scientific American 233 (July 1975): 18. Copyright © 1975 Scientific American, Inc. All rights reserved.

gyroscopically stabilized platform. Accelerometer output is integrated twice. The first integration yields the velocity, the second, the distance traveled. As the vehicle moves, the **gyroscopes** maintain the platform's stability through a complex set of servomechanisms. A fundamental problem in inertial guidance emerges once we set the system in motion: how do we separate the acceleration of the vehicle from the acceleration of gravity? Imagine a plumb line in an airplane. When the plane is at rest, or moving at a constant velocity, the line will indicate the "true" vertical direction; however, when the aircraft accelerates, the line fails as an indicator. Solving this problem demands a platform whose orientation will remain constant throughout the duration of the voyage; deviations from this orientation generate errors that accumulate during the course of the trip. The development of gyroscopes and accelerometers to meet these demanding needs is at one with the history of inertial guidance. More recently, nonmechanical gyroscopes, such as the laser-ring gyroscope, and the use of powerful digital computers have eliminated certain problems related to the design and manufacture of such precision instrumentation.

Herman Anschütz-Kaempfe tried to develop a semi-self-contained guidance system for a submarine voyage to the North Pole in 1902. He wanted to use a gyroscope to compensate for the problems introduced by the submarine's steel hull, which made a magnetic **compass** untrustworthy. However, it proved difficult to design a gyroscope that would maintain its orientation over time, especially under the conditions of acceleration. Anschütz-Kaempfe ultimately abandoned this effort to build a guidance device and developed a **gyrocompass** for the German Navy. In the United States, the Sperry Gyroscope Co. expressed an interest in developing a self-contained guidance system during the late 1930s, but corporate researchers believed it impossible to separate the vehicle's acceleration from that of gravity.

During World War II, German rocket designers at Peenemünde developed a quasi-inertial set of instruments consisting of two gyroscopes that kept the V-2 stabilized and corrected the flight path, while an accelerometer measured the missile's velocity and shut down the rocket motor. After engine cutoff, the weapon continued upon its ballistic trajectory. The V-2 control system was adequate for hitting its target, metropolitan London, but we cannot call it an inertial guidance system because the missile followed a well-known trajectory. The V-2 devices could not guide an aircraft over a long, complicated flight path.

With the Allied victory and the division of German technical talent between the Soviet Union and the United States, the development of inertial guidance began in earnest. Two very different institutions played a role in making inertial guidance a technical reality in the United States: Charles Stark Draper's Instrumentation Laboratory at M.I.T., and the Autonetics Division of North American Aviation. Both institutions were able to exist and prosper because the military was interested in producing a self-contained navigational system for use against the Soviet Union. Only the postwar American and Soviet nation states possessed the huge financial resources necessary to develop this radically new technology.

Draper is generally acknowledged as the inventor of inertial guidance in the United States. His Instrumentation Laboratory was responsible for such fundamental innovations as the Single Degree-of-Freedom Floated Integrating Gyroscope, which has served as part of nearly every major American nuclear missile guidance system from the Minuteman to the MX and Trident II. Technical innovations alone, however, did not guarantee the acceptance and development of this technology. Originally, inertial guidance was seen as one of many technologies that might work to guide American aircraft and cruise missiles to their targets in the Soviet Union. Radio-based systems were easier to design and use, plus the success of **radar** and microwave-based landing systems had been one of the most impressive wartime technical accomplishments. The ultimate use of inertial guidance systems rested upon the complex interaction of technical and political factors.

The development of inertial systems for aircraft flights was the original problem that occupied Draper and his students after the war. Guiding aircraft over long distances, especially over enemy territory, demanded gyroscopes with a drift rate (the rate at which the gyro moved from its original orientation) several orders of magnitude smaller than anything in existence at war's end. The floated gyro, which used a viscous fluid to aid in reducing the friction in a gyro's bearings, was one of Draper's main inventions in the race to reduce gyro drift rates, as was the use of new materials such as beryllium. Equally important was the move from aircraft to ballistic missiles as the main technologies for the delivery of thermonuclear weapons. With their shorter flight times, the missiles needed sophisticated gyros, but they would have to work for only a few minutes, rather than the hours of aircraft flight time. Draper and his students turned their attention toward the development of new, more sensitive accelerometers. Technology alone did not make inertial guidance the backbone of the American deterrent. Draper also created a set of informed consumers for inertial systems through the Weapons Systems Program in M.I.T.'s Department of Aeronautical Engineering. It was not simply coincidence that Draper students were engaged in the top management of nearly every American missile project.

Inertial guidance represented more than a highly sophisticated and technical self-contained navigation system. It represented the wedding of science and the modern nation state in a fundamentally new way. No longer did the military allow firms to develop technologies independently and then sell these same devices to the armed services. Instead, the military was intimately involved in the design and development of inertial guidance from the earliest moments in Draper's laboratory. Today, commercial aircraft use inertial systems for long-range navigation, but that is changing as the **Global Positioning System**, a network of earth-orbiting satellites, begins to function as the preferred means for determining location. Only in the most secure missions, those related to the use of nuclear munitions, will inertial systems remain in place. Inertial guidance, a product of the postwar state's need to wage global war, may yet never function in the circumstances for which it was designed.

Michael Aaron Dennis

Bibliography

Draper, C.S. "The Evolution of Aerospace Guidance Technology at the Massachusetts Institute of Technology, 1935–1951: A Memoir." In *Essays on the History of Rocketry and Astronautics: Proceedings of the Third through the Sixth History Symposia of the International Academy of Astronautics,* edited by R. Cargill Hall, 219–52. Washington, D.C.: NASA, Scientific and Technical Information Office, 1977.

———, W. Wrigley, and J. Hovorka. *Inertial Guidance.* New York: Pergamon, 1960.

Hughes, Thomas Parke. *Elmer Sperry: Inventor and Engineer.* Baltimore: Johns Hopkins University Press, 1971.

MacKenzie, Donald A. *Inventing Accuracy: An Historical Sociology of Nuclear Missile Guidance.* Cambridge, Mass.: M.I.T. Press, 1990.

Wrigley, Walter. "History of Inertial Navigation." *Navigation* 24 (1977): 1–6.

Infrared Detector

An infrared detector senses the invisible rays in the electromagnetic spectrum that humans observe as heat. Although infrared radiation has

Boys' infrared radio micrometer, by Cambridge Scientific Instruments, 1912. Baird & Tatlock Ltd. Price List of Apparatus for Experiments in Practical Physics. *London, 1912: 553. Courtesy of SSPL.*

characteristics similar to those of visible rays, its longer wavelength requires the use of different materials and detectors. Several types of instruments have been used as infrared detectors.

The first major experiments were conducted by William Herschel in 1800, although Isaac Newton had earlier used glass **thermometers** to investigate how heat was transferred in a vacuum. In his observations of the sun's rays, Herschel realized that black filters did not completely block all radiation. He set up an experiment to disperse solar rays with a prism, using thermometers to detect radiation at angles beyond that of red light. Herschel's thermometers could discriminate only about 0.25°F, and he used two at each measuring position, one being shielded to act as a reference. Improvements in measuring techniques were reported in 1804 by John Leslie, who used a thermometer in which the differential heating of two hollow spheres caused a column of liquid to move around a calibrated connecting tube.

The first really sensitive infrared detector, however, was the **thermopile**, credited to the Italian Leopoldo Nobili. It was improved upon by Macedonio Melloni around 1830 to be able to detect as small a variation as 0.0005°C. Subsequent developments in the nineteenth century led to the creation of the **bolometer**.

In 1887 Charles V. Boys, noted for work with fine quartz-fiber suspensions, devised a radio-micrometer after a design by Jacques Arsène d'Arsonval. His unit was said to respond to "a quantity of heat no greater than that which would be radiated onto a halfpenny by a candle flame 1,530 feet away from it." In other words, Boys' apparatus could detect 0.000002°C. Boys set up an apparatus to measure the heat of the moon, as did Hugh Callendar in 1900 using a similar apparatus with a current balance. An 1889 experiment by Boys used a 16-in. concentrating mirror to detect a candle 3 miles away. The minute detector he used also had a response time far superior to that of the former thermopile units.

As in many other scientific and technological fields, electronic devices have played an increasingly prominent role in infrared detectors in the second half of the twentieth century. Solid-state electronic detectors have found a key application in aircraft detection, as the basis for modern heat-seeking missiles that can "see" plumes of rocket and jet engines many kilometers ahead.

Peter H. Sydenham

Bibliography

Allen H.S., and R.S. Maxwell. *A Text Book of Heat.* London: Macmillan, 1944.

Griffiths, Edgar A. "Radiant Heat and Its Spectrum Distribution, Instruments for the Measurement of." In *A Dictionary of Applied Physics,* edited by Richard Glazebrook, Vol. 3, 699–708. London: Macmillan, 1923.

Jones, R.V. "Some Turning Points in Infra-Red History." *Radio & Electronic Engineer* 41 (1972): 117–26.

———. *Most Secret War.* London: Hamilton, 1978.

Sydenham, Peter H. *Measuring Instruments: Tools of Knowledge and Control.* London: Peregrinus for the Science Museum, 1979.

Insulation Meter

Since the introduction of electric lighting and the subsequent need for power transmission, the ability to determine insulation resistances has become important—originally to ensure safety, but later out of a desire to prevent damage to equipment from leakage currents.

In the mid nineteenth century, the most common method for measuring insulation resistances used a moving-coil **galvanometer** and **battery**. This was problematic in that the current measurement was made up of two inseparable components, the leakage current and the surface current. Moreover, this technique was not easily accomplished outside a laboratory, and there was a growing need to measure insulation for testing electrical installations, determining good from defective wires during manufacture, predicting the deterioration of insulation, and so forth.

Several portable, robust, direct-measurement instruments for measuring insulation resistance were developed in the 1880s, and most were based on the ohmmeter invented in 1881 by William Ayrton, professor of physics and electrical engineering at Finsbury Technical College, London, and his colleague John Perry. The ohmmeter was capable of directly measuring the resistance of any part of a circuit through which current was passing, but it could not be used for very high resistances.

The ohmmeter has two coils of wire mounted at right angles to each other, with a soft iron needle pivoting between the two coils. One coil is connected in series with the resistance to be determined and carries the same

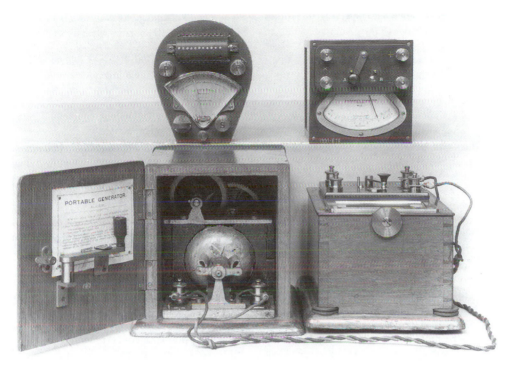

Clockwise from top left: an early Ohmmeter for testing insulation, by Ayrton & Perry, 1881; Evershed Ohmmeter No. 2, by Evershed & Goolden 1889; Ohmmeter and generator for testing insulation, by Evershed & Vignoles, 1890s. SM 1909-26, 1926-1067, 1926-1068, 1931-670. Courtesy of SSPL.

current, while the other is connected across the supply voltage, and hence carries a current proportional to the voltage. The needle aligns with the resultant field, which is proportional to the ratio of the applied voltage and the current. Ohm's law states that the resistance is equal to the ratio of voltage to current, and thus the deflection of the needle is a measure of resistance. By suitable graduation of the scale, the resistance can be read directly from the instrument. The ohmmeter readings are independent of voltage, as any change in the voltage has a corresponding effect on the current.

By exchanging the positions of the coil and the magnet, the problems with stray magnetic fields were eliminated. The two coils, fixed at an angle to one another, were pivoted between the poles of a large fixed magnet. The resultant field of the coils aligns itself with the field of the magnet. Carpentier, a French scientific instrument-maker, was one of the first to use such a system.

The first insulation meter, patented by two English electrical engineers, W.T. Goolden and S. Evershed, in 1889, combined an ohmmeter with a hand-cranked generator to provide the voltage required. It was adapted in 1890 by the introduction of an astatic moving system to minimize the effect of the external magnetic field, and in 1894 by the substitution of a soft iron tube for the magnetic needle. The Megger, introduced by the English firm of Evershed and Vignoles Ltd. in 1905, was the most widely known instrument. It used the moving coil arrangement, and the meter and generator were combined in the same unit so that the same group of four magnets were used to excite the generator and operate the meter.

Although ohmmeters are independent of the applied voltage, steady voltage is essential for cable testing. A constant voltage was achieved by either driving the generator with a small motor or, in the case of a hand-cranked generator, making use of a clutch between driving handle and generator. When the handle is turned at a speed greater than the critical speed, typically 100 rpm, the clutch slips, maintaining the voltage, typically 1,000 volts, to within one part in one thousand. To compensate for stray fields, an additional coil was put in series with the voltage coil and wound in the opposite direction. The coil rotates outside the magnetic field of the instrument, and since it is equally affected, but in the reverse direction by any stray fields, it provides the required compensation.

Insulation meters were also used as ground testers. The resistance of the ground depends on its water content and other factors. The Megger Earth Tester, comprising the generator and an ohmmeter designed to measure low resistances, was popular for this type of work.

The Bridge Megger was soon introduced. This could be used either as a **Wheatstone Bridge**, to measure resistances over a wide range of values (the generator replacing the battery and the ohmmeter replacing the galvanometer), or as a Megger to measure insulation resistance.

The Metrohm, made by the London firm of Everett Edgcumbe, used the same principle as Evershed's Megger but had separate magnets for the meter and generator, and the coils were arranged differently. The Omega by G.W. Harris was also based on the ohmmeter principle, and a number of ranges could be obtained by using switches to introduce a suitable series of resistances and to interchange the functions of the two coils. It was possible to measure from 0.01 ohm to 100 megohms. The Ohmer, invented by Oswald Cox (an English electrical engineer) in 1902, employs the principle of electrostatics and stands apart from the instruments already mentioned. Here the indications were independent of the voltage of the generator, so the speed at which the handle was turned was unimportant. Also, it was unaffected by external magnetic fields. Neither the Omega nor the Ohmer seem to have been widely used.

Ohmmeters operating on similar principles are still in use today. Models with a hand-cranked generator are still made, but most work from dry cells. Transistorized electronic circuits produce the high voltages needed for high insulation testing. As the voltage can be controlled very precisely, there is no need for a special movement of the Megger type, and in many cases an ordinary meter is used instead. Though still available, these electromagnetic instruments are being superseded by electronic instruments using digital processing and display.

Sophie Duncan

Bibliography

Drysdale, C.V., and A.C. Jolley. *Electrical Measuring Instruments,* Vol. 2. London: E. Benn, 1924.
Evershed and Vignoles Ltd., and Evershed, S. Patent no. 11,415. May 1905.
Goolden, W.T., and S. Evershed. Patent no. 2,694. February 1889.
Melsom, S.W. "Resistance Measurement of Insulation." In *A Dictionary of Applied Physics,* edited by Richard Glazebrook, Vol. 2, 683–92. London: Macmillan, 1923.

Intelligence Test

Most early scientific attempts to evaluate "faculties" of individuals—such as Johann Caspar Lavater's late-eighteenth-century distillation of the folk wisdom of physiognomy and the influential science of phrenology—emphasized aspects of character and personality, rather than the all-too-vague concept of intelligence. As phrenology's authority waned half a century later, physical anthropologists such as Samuel George Morton adapted its craniometric techniques and instruments to characterize the human races. In the late nineteenth century, the English polymath Frances Galton sought to extend anthropometric concerns to mental traits, and looked to the laboratory-based "new psychology" then emerging in Germany. But as psychologists emphasized what they defined as the elements of mental life—that is, sensations and perceptions—rather than what they termed the "higher mental processes," the anthropometrists' new procedures simply measured their subjects' reaction times and abilities to bisect lines.

The first self-identified series of "mental tests," developed in the 1890s by James McKeen Cattell of Columbia University, extended Galton's program to measure, among other traits, short-term memory and the keenness of the senses under varying conditions. Like Galton's, Cattell's interests centered on gathering data on how individuals differed from one another—that is, on the variations that made natural selection possible. He thus lacked an overarching functional view of how these traits helped people live their lives. His tests produced results that had no meaning for anyone, and by 1901 most psychologists had abandoned them.

But even as Cattell's tests failed, Americans sought psychological expertise more than ever before, for the following reasons: to help educators "Americanize" the millions of children of the new immigrants from southern and eastern Europe, and to help them deal with the large number of "feeble-minded" boys and girls revealed by compulsory education laws; to help corporations select workers for new industries; and (for eugenicists) to determine who should be allowed to enter the country. Psychologists at state schools for the feeble-minded most steadily attacked this problem, and in 1908 New Jersey's Henry H. Goddard discovered the tests that had been developed in France in 1905 by Alfred Binet and Theodore Simon to help their country's educators deal with similar problems. These tests called for school children to perform various "age appropriate" tasks, such as counting coins at age four, explaining similarities at age eight, repeating five digits backward at age twelve and, for the "superior," explaining proverbs. The level at which children performed determined what the testers called their mental age; mental age divided by a student's chronological age yielded the intelligence quotient, or IQ.

By 1909, Goddard had revised these tests for use in America, and schools like his soon found them extremely useful in designing programs for the children in their care. Other Americans developed analogous individual tests, which large urban school systems began using to help deal with the influx of immigrant children. In 1916, Lewis M. Terman and his collaborators at Stanford University issued the long-standard first edition of the "Stanford Revision and Extension of the Binet-Simon Intelligence Scale." Like almost all of their predecessors, the Stanford psychologists explicitly denied the value of defining intelligence apart from its relation to the functional skills their tests measured.

When the United States entered World War I in 1917, psychologists mobilized themselves to aid the war effort and to "put psychology on the map." Their most general program, led by Robert M. Yerkes of the University of Minnesota, produced two intelligence tests. The Army Alpha examination, designed for men literate in English, asked its subjects to solve arithmetical problems, identify synonyms and antonyms, determine if disarranged sentences were true or false, and complete analogies and number series. The nonverbal Army Beta examination, designed for illiterate men and for those literate only in other languages, asked its subjects to follow mazes, count cubes in complicated structures, decipher digit-symbol codes, and complete pictures and symbol series. Unlike most earlier psychological tests, the army tests called for subjects to be tested in large groups, to write their own responses on test blanks that psychologists later scored, and to select the "right" answer from among multiple choices.

These procedures revolutionized psychological testing and, while observers still disagree whether the army found them useful, the tests clearly "put psychology on the map." The 1920s saw a boom in group psychological testing. Colleges used these as admissions tests, schools used them to section classes on the basis of tested "ability," and the College Entrance Examination Board sought to replace its essay examinations with a more "objective" and easily scored Scholastic Aptitude Test. Eugenicists and others also cited the results of army tests—which showed that native-born Americans scored higher than immigrants, and that immigrants from northern and western Europe scored higher than those from southern and eastern Europe—to argue successfully for immigration restriction. By the end of the decade, however, environmentally based criticisms by cultural anthropologists, led by Columbia University's Franz Boas, statisticians, and other psychologists, led testers to downplay and even retract some of their earlier claims for the value of their work.

Through the 1930s, however, schools still used intelligence tests extensively, and testing gained notoriety with radio programs like "Dr. IQ" and personality tests like Hermann Rorschach's "inkblots." To respond to the growing influence of cultural anthropologists' environmental perspective—which helped shape Gunnar Myrdahl's highly influential study *The Negro in America* (1944)—Raymond B. Cattell at University College, London, and later at Clark University, developed successive versions of what he called "culture-fair" tests that relied on nonverbal or "performance" procedures. Other testers developed complex and often contradictory definitions of intelligence and paid greater attention to issues of statistical validity and standardization. In 1939, for example, David Wechsler, of New York's Bellevue Psychiatric Hospital, combined verbal and nonverbal procedures in his adult-oriented Bellevue Intelligence Scale (from 1955, the Wechsler Adult Intelligence Scale, or WAIS), and based its norms on a carefully defined sample of scores obtained from thirty-five hundred subjects. Publishers offered automated scoring of standardized test-blanks by the mid 1930s, and in 1938, Oscar K. Buros began serving both testers and their clients with his first *Mental Measurements Yearbook* (11th ed., 1992). As the post–World War II baby boom forced schools to deal with an even more diverse population, intelligence testing

Test 6

Picture Completion Test, Group Examination Beta, U.S. Army Psychological Testing Program, 1918. Courtesy of NMAH.

boomed, and in 1949 the Psychological Corp. published the Wechsler Intelligence Scale for Children (or WISC).

The call for equal opportunity in the 1960s led radical educators to attack all tests as necessarily reflecting class or race biases, and their allies found racism and a desire for social control at the root of all testing. As competition for college admission became stiffer, attacks on the cultural and gender biases of the SAT became common. Defenders claimed that, by demonstrating previously hidden abilities in individuals of all races, tests served to create opportunity; they also revealed real differences in the mental functioning of individuals of different racial backgrounds that educators had to deal with. The criticisms gained support with the (recently challenged) charge that the British psychologist Cyril Burt based his claims for inherited differences in intelligence on data he created. But educators still argue that individual tests serve important clinical functions in, for example, the diagnosis of learning disabilities. And the call for educational accountability in the 1990s has led to the introduction of computer-administered tests to assess what students know and how they learn it.

Michael M. Sokal

Bibliography

Fancher, Raymond E. *The Intelligence Men: Makers of the IQ Controversy.* New York: Norton, 1985.

Gould, Stephen Jay. *The Mismeasure of Man.* New York: Norton, 1981.

Hearnshaw, Leslie S. *Cyril Burt, Psychologist.* Ithaca, N.Y.: Cornell University Press, 1979.

Kamin, Leon J. *The Science and Politics of I.Q.* Potomac, Md.: Erlbaum, 1974.

Sokal, Michael M. "Essay Review: Approaches to the History of Psychological Testing." *History of Education Quarterly* 24 (1984): 419–30.

———, ed. *Psychological Testing and American Society, 1890–1930.* New Brunswick, N.J.: Rutgers University Press, 1987.

Interferometer

An interferometer exploits the wave properties of light in the following way: when a beam of light from a point source is divided into two beams that are subsequently recombined, the resultant beam will display visible interference fringes. Any alteration in the optical path traversed by one of the split beams before recombination will cause the interference pattern (known as the interferogram) to shift visibly. Because the light waves generating the interferogram are very short, a minute change in either the length or refractive index of the optical path will produce a measurable effect.

Interferometers are often categorized according to the method they employ to split the initial beam. The technique of allowing the beam to fall on two separate apertures—the method employed by Thomas Young, who first described the interference of light in 1802—is known as aperture or wave-front division. The technique of allowing the beam to fall on a partially reflecting surface (so that part of the beam is transmitted and part reflected) is known as amplitude division. A third technique, known as polarization division, uses a polarizing filter or prism to split polarized light into two polarized beams.

Early Instruments and Applications

One of the earliest practical instruments to employ optical interference was built by the Frenchman Jules Jamin, in 1856, and was designed to measure refractive index. This used two glass plates to achieve amplitude division. One beam was passed through the test substance, while the other traversed a standard path, and the fringe shift gave an indirect measure of the refractive index of the test substance. Jamin's instrument was developed and improved throughout the second half of the nineteenth century. In 1862, Hippolyte Fizeau introduced a collimator to produce a truly parallel light beam from a point source. He also showed how the interferometer could be used to test the accuracy of lenses and prisms. In 1891, Ernst Mach and Ludwig Zehnder adapted Jamin's interferometer for the measurement of airflow in wind tunnels. In 1896, Lord Rayleigh (John William Strutt) designed an improved aperture-splitting instrument to measure the refractive index of gases. Variant forms of most of these instruments are still in regular use today.

The most important contributor to the development of the interferometer in the late nineteenth century was the American physicist Albert Michelson. At the time, it was widely believed that light was a wave motion in a universal medium or ether. In an effort to measure the earth's motion through this ether, Michelson designed a new form of interferometer that has since borne his name. Michelson used a partially silvered mirror to amplitude-split a beam of light, the two beams traveling at right angles to one another before being recombined to form an interferogram. Michelson hoped that the "ether wind" due to the earth's orbital motion would produce a differential shift in the interference fringes as the interferometer was slowly rotated. His failure to detect this effect led to important developments in electromagnetic theory, which, in turn, prepared the way for Albert Einstein's special theory of relativity.

Michelson interferometer, from University of Illinois, 1920s. NMAH 334,757. Courtesy of NMAH.

The Michelson interferometer was an extremely sensitive instrument with many important applications beyond the original experiment. Michelson showed, for example, how the form of the interferogram could provide information about the spectral properties of the light source. He also demonstrated the importance of the interferometer to metrology by showing how the length of the standard meter could be measured with extreme accuracy in terms of light waves. Modified forms of Michelson's interferometer have an enormous range of other applications. In 1916, for example, F. Twyman and A. Green built a Michelson interferometer (adding a Fizeau-type collimator and viewing eyepiece) that is especially suitable for testing lenses and prisms. When it is suitably adjusted, the interference fringes in the Twyman-Green interferometer provide a "contour map" of the optical surface.

Another widely used instrument is the multiple-beam interferometer, the most common being based upon a design built originally by Charles Fabry and Alfred Perot in 1897. The Fabry-Perot interferometer consists of two partly silvered parallel glass plates illuminated by a collimated beam from a point source. The beam undergoes repeated amplitude division as it is partially reflected back and forth between the plates, and this generates an interferogram of exceptional contrast and clarity. This versatile instrument can measure distances several hundred times smaller than one wavelength of light and has applications in all of the areas mentioned above.

Stellar Interferometry

In 1920, Michelson measured the diameter of stars using an interferometric technique suggested originally by Fizeau. In an aperture-dividing interferometer, the form of the interferogram depends on the separation of the apertures and the finite size of the source; the further apart the apertures, the smaller the source must be to generate visible fringes. In Michelson's stellar interferometer, two mirrors (3–4 meters apart) provide two images of the star, which are optically combined and viewed through a large telescope. By separating the mirrors until the interference pattern disappeared, Michelson was able to estimate the angular diameter of the star. The measurement of stellar diameters was continued after World War II, using the intensity interferometer developed by Robert Hanbury Brown and Richard Twiss.

Modern Developments

The use of interference between beams of electromagnetic radiation is by no means limited to the visible band of the spectrum. Since World War II, lower frequency radiation from infrared to radio waves has also been exploited. Indeed, interference phenomena have been especially well studied in radio astronomy, where the long wavelength of the radiation makes it difficult to produce a detailed picture of the source. It is, therefore, convenient to use **radio telescopes** in pairs, or larger arrays, to gain spectral information by interferometric techniques. A detailed picture of the source can then be built up using mathematical analysis.

The appearance of a number of new devices has also led to new applications and to the improvement of interferometers. The laser now provides a powerful point source of monochromatic light that simplifies the design and operation of many instruments. Optical fibers have made it possible to guide infrared and other radiation for interferometric purposes, and to coil a long optical path into a small physical space. The optical sensitivity of such fibers to changes in the local physical environment also renders the interferometer an extremely effective sensor device. Finally, automatic recording techniques and the electronic **computer** have now made mathematical analysis of the interferogram a practical possibility for a wide range of applications.

Andrew Warwick

Bibliography

Candler, C. *Modern Interferometers*. London: Hilger and Watts, 1951.
Haubold, B., H.J. Haubold, and L. Pyenson. "Michelson's First Ether-Drift Experiment

in Berlin and Potsdam." In *The Michelson Era in American Science 1870–1930,* edited by S. Goldberg and R.H. Stuewer, 42–54. New York: American Institute of Physics, 1988.
Steel, W.H. *Interferometry.* 2nd ed. Cambridge: Cambridge University Press, 1983.

Ionization Chamber

See CHAMBER, IONIZATION

Ion-Sensitive Microelectrode

An ion-sensitive microelectrode measures the free ion concentration in living cells and tissues. It consists of a glass probe with a sharp, sensitive tip about one micron in diameter, filled behind the tip with an aqueous electrolyte solution. The tip contains an ion-sensitive material that generates a voltage that varies with the free concentration or activity of an ion in an aqueous solution with which it is in contact. To measure this voltage, and hence the ion concentration, a second, ion-insensitive or reference microelectrode must also be in contact with the solution. Ion-sensitive microelectrodes have been used in many studies of sodium, pH, and other intracellular ion regulation in nerve, muscle, and other animal cells, and also of extracellular ions in tissues such as the brain. They are not commercially available, but are usually made by the experimenter who plans to use them.

Precursors

pH-sensitive glass, the first reliable ion sensor used for laboratory electrodes, was first used for

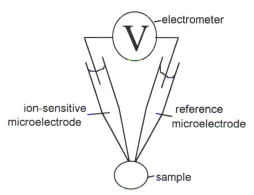

Schematic diagram showing the arrangement of ion-sensitive and control microelectrodes. Courtesy of Roger C. Thomas.

measurements in very large animal cells by Peter Caldwell in England in the 1950s. Sodium- and potassium-sensitive glasses were described in 1957 and soon used to make what were described as microelectrodes by Joseph Hinke. This tip design, shown in the illustration was still too large for any but the largest cells. It was later miniaturized to some extent, but when smaller than about 10 µm the sensor tip had too high an electrical resistance to be practical.

Microelectrodes with Glass Sensor

The inherent high electrical resistivity of ion-sensitive glass requires that considerably more than a square micron be exposed to the sample to be measured, or the microelectrode resistance will make it too unstable. A usable resistance (from 10^9 to 10^{11} ohms) is achieved in the design that was perfected in 1970 by recessing a length of sensitive glass behind the open tip of the insulating glass outer sheath. Only the very tip of the outer sheath needs to cross the cell membrane. This design is difficult to construct, and the response time is inherently slow.

Microelectrodes with Liquid Sensor

The development of organic liquid ion sensors for laboratory electrodes in the late 1960s was followed by attempts to incorporate them into the tips of glass microelectrodes for intracellular use. Glass is normally water-absorbing, so organic fluids tend to be displaced from the tip of untreated microelectrodes. In 1971, John Walker in Salt Lake City devised the first successful method of making microelectrode tips water-repellent, and made the first reliable potassium and chloride-sensitive microelectrodes with sub-micron tips. He treated the micropipettes with a silane solution in chloronapthalene, and then baked them at 250°C for an hour. Many variations on this basic procedure have been published. Finally the micropipette is filled with an aqueous backfill solution and a length of sensor sucked up into the tip.

Liquid ion sensors are now available for many ions of biological interest. Microelectrodes are much easier to make with liquid than solid sensors, and since the liquid-sensor is at the tip they are also inherently faster-responding. Both types of microelectrode are easy to calibrate, and the electrical signal they generate is simple to record and analyze.

New fluorescent indicator dyes for calcium and pH are in many ways less damaging and faster responding than microelectrodes, although the apparatus required is much more elaborate and calibration may be difficult. As they are much easier to use on small cells, fluorescent dye techniques are already more widely used than microelectrodes.

Roger C. Thomas

Bibliography

Ammann, D. *Ion-selective Microelectrodes: Principles, Design and Application.* Berlin: Springer, 1986.

Hinke, J.A.M. "Glass Micro-Electrodes for Measuring Intracellular Activities of Sodium and Potassium." *Nature* 184 (1959): 1257–58.

Thomas, R.C. *Ion-sensitive Intracellular Microelectrodes: How to Make and Use Them.* London: Academic, 1978.

Walker, J.L. "Ion Specific Liquid Ion Exchanger Microelectrodes." *Analytical Chemistry* 43 (1971): 89–92A.

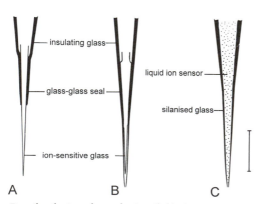

insulating glass

liquid ion sensor

glass-glass seal

silanised glass

ion-sensitive glass

A　　　　B　　　　C

Details of microelectrode tips: (left) glass sensor electrode; (center) glass sensor electrode with recessed tip; (right) silanized glass microelectrode with liquid sensor. The scale bar on the right represents 50 µm. Courtesy of Roger C. Thomas.

K

Kymograph

Carl Ludwig, a nineteenth-century German physiologist, devised the kymograph in order to study the connections between respiration and the systolic and diastolic rhythms of the heart, and he was to see his instrument become an essential tool of the biomedical sciences. Wilhelm Wundt, a medical student in Berlin at the time of its appearance, remarked how even "old school" physiologists proclaimed that the kymograph was destined to "accompany the physiologist in all of his future pathways" for its ability to capture the interrelationships of physiological functions. Because of its invasiveness, the kymograph was never used directly in studies of human physiology. Ludwig's work, however, led other physiologists, notably Helmholtz, Vierordt, and Marey, to build similar devices—such as the myograph, sphygmograph, and the cardiograph—to record the movements of other physiological functions. The word derives from the Greek, meaning wave-writer.

Prehistory

Traditional Galenic physicians determined qualitative characteristics of the pulse in the wrist or feet, especially those concerned with arterial expansion or rate. In the seventeenth and eighteenth centuries, many physicians sought to make visible and measurable the vast range of qualitative perceptions available to clinicians. Stephen Hales, for instance, fastened a long glass tube in the lateral wall of a vessel and determined the blood pressure by measuring the height of the vertical column of blood in the tube. Hales's tube was fitted at its lower extremity with a short copper tube, bent at a right angle and directed toward the heart.

In the 1820s, by measuring the difference in the time of the pulse in the external maxil-

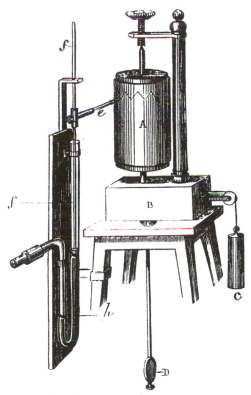

Carl Ludwig's kymograph. Étienne Jules Marey. Du Mouvement dans les Fonctions de la Vie. *Paris: Balliere, 1868: 132. Courtesy of SSPL.*

lary artery and in the dorsalis pedis artery, Ernst Heinrich Weber demonstrated that the pulse waves radiate from the root of the aorta into all the arteries toward the periphery. Comparing these measures with the velocities of undulating water in rubber tubes, Weber concluded that the pulse-wave cannot be regarded as a short wave traveling along the arteries, but one so long that a single pulse-wave cannot find room in the entire distance from the beginning of the aorta to the artery of the big toe. In 1828, Jean-Leonard-Marie Poiseuille, an engineer turned physician, extended these investigations to the problem of the interaction between respiration and venous and arterial circulation. He used a U-shaped manometer, which he inserted laterally by means of a rigid connecting piece into the wall of the vessel. With this instrument, which he called a hemodynamometer, Poiseuille measured the force imparted to the blood in both the carotid and peripheral arteries.

Modern Instruments

Ludwig's original instrument consisted of a tube and cannula connecting the manometer to the artery; the manometer and stylus; and the clockwork and recording cylinder. For the cannula, Ludwig used a brass tube with a side opening that could be closed tightly with a stopper. The tube was filled with a solution of sodium bicarbonate and inserted into the animal artery at right angles to its axis. The cannula was fitted to the manometer with an india-rubber binding. For the manometer Ludwig bent a glass tube of uniform diameter into a U shape and filled it with mercury. To this he added a float made of a tiny ivory cylinder, to which was affixed a small three-sided rod made of hard wood. To the rod he attached a quillholder and a goose quill. The quill recorded upon a sheet of smooth vellum that was stretched upon a brass cylinder that revolved at uniform speed. The cylinder moved by means of a clock, was driven by a weight, and regulated by a rotating spindle. For the self-registering component of his apparatus, Ludwig claimed to have "followed the principles of graphic representation laid out by the English mechanician Watt" in his indicator diagram, which charted the variations in pressure in the cylinder of a steam engine. Ludwig may have adapted the chronometric element of his apparatus from one of many similar devices often attached to dynamometers during the 1840s.

After constructing his first kymographs, Ludwig turned to the instrument-maker Baltzar, who made small modifications to the writing system. For two decades the firm of Baltzar and Schmidt in Leipzig produced Ludwig-Baltzar kymographs. In 1864 Ludwig's student Adolf Fick devised a kymograph based on Bourdon's principle of hollow-spring manometers, long used in aneroid **barometers** and steam engine **indicators**. The spring kymograph was nearly free from the "proper motion" seen to be an occasional defect in Ludwig's design, and consequently made possible measures of the fine variations of arterial pressure in the course of each pulse interval.

In 1883 the Harvard Physiological Apparatus Co. began to mass produce kymographs and other physiological instruments at one-tenth the cost of instruments produced individually. The new, affordable kymographs made possible distribution on an unprecedented scale, and kymographs became an indispensable fixture in all modern physiology laboratories and medical teaching institutions.

Robert Brain

Bibliography

De Chadevarian, Soraya. "Graphical Method and Discipline: Self-Recording Instruments and Nineteeth-Century Physiology." *Studies in the History and Philosophy of Science* 24 (1993): 267–91.

Ludwig, Carl. "Beiträge für Kenntnis des Einflusses der Respirationsbewegungen auf den Blutlauf im Aortensysteme." *Archiv fuer Anatomie, Physiologie und wissenschaftliche Medizin* [1847], 242–302. Reprinted in *Classics in Arterial Hypertension,* edited and translated by Arthur Ruskin, 61–73. Springfield, Ill.: Charles C. Thomas, 1956.

Reiser, Stanley Joel. *Medicine and the Reign of Technology.* Cambridge: Cambridge University Press, 1978.

Schroer, Heinz. *Carl Ludwig: Begründer der messenden Experimentalphysiologie 1816–1895.* Stuttgart: Wissenschaftliche Verlagsgesellschaft, 1967.

L

Laser and Maser

Lasers and masers use stimulated emission to produce coherent radiation in the visible-infrared or microwave range. Laser is the acronym for light amplification by stimulated emission of radiation, while maser is the same for microwave radiation. Early lasers were termed optical masers.

A traditional laser or maser consists of an active medium in an inverted state (more excited than low-energy levels) put into a resonant cavity. Masers use molecular rotovibrational levels or Zeeman split levels of paramagnetic solids. Lasers generally use electronic levels. Once an inverted population has been created, some of the excited states may decay, spontaneously emitting a photon that by stimulated emission starts a cascade of photons. The resonant cavity provides the feedback to generate coherent emission. The device works when the gain due to stimulated emission overcomes the losses (absorption at walls, or mirrors in the case of lasers, scattering, and so on).

Albert Einstein introduced the concept of stimulated emission through an elegant demonstration of Planck's distribution law (1916). Due to stimulated emission an excited state decays emitting a photon with the same frequency and traveling direction as the stimulating photon. Stimulated emission was used in theoretical calculations of dispersion by Hendrick Anthony Kramers (1924) and by Kramers and Werner Heisenberg (1925). Rudolf Walther Ladenburg and his collaborators measured its effect in a series of experiments on electrical discharges in neon, performed between 1926 and 1930. J.H. van Vleck and Richard C. Tolman also considered the role of stimulated emission (1924). In 1940, V.A. Fabrikant in the Soviet Union suggested using it to obtain amplification of radiation. In 1950, Willis E. Lamb and R.C. Retherford treated the subject in connection with their research on the fine structure of hydrogen. In his experiments on adiabatic fast passage in 1946, Felix Bloch obtained a transient inverted population of spins. E.M. Purcel and R.V. Pound introduced the concept of negative temperature to describe systems of inverted population in 1951, obtaining an inverted spin population by a sudden reverse of a static magnetic field, and measuring for a short time a negative absorption. Nobody, however, paid attention to the possibility of making practical devices using this effect, probably because only transient population inversions were obtained.

Works on optical pumping by J. Brossel and A. Kastler in 1949 are also important because they introduced this technique as a means to change the level populations.

During World War II, the development of **radar** strongly enhanced microwaves, introduced the new field of microwave spectroscopy, and produced a strong demand for high-frequency sources; many scientists acquired competence in the microwave field. Surplus radar equipment become common in American universities after the war. The invention of the maser may be seen as a natural consequence of these circumstances.

History

Joseph Weber described a microwave amplifier based on stimulated emission at the Electron Tube Conference held in Canada in 1952. Although he observed that amplification could be obtained if the number of oscillators in the upper states could be made greater than the number in the lower state, none of his methods has ever worked.

The first operating device based on stimulated emission was assembled by Charles Townes and his students, J.P. Gordon and H.J. Zeiger, by using the inversion transition in ammonia. The work started in 1951. The first mention of the operation of an oscillator appeared in a report dated April 30, 1954.

In the Soviet Union, Alexander Mikhailovich Prokhorov and Nikolai Gennadievick Basov considered increasing the sensitivity of microwave **spectroscopes** by artificially varying the level populations. In October 1954 they published a theoretical study of molecular beams in microwave spectroscopy and discussed the application to a molecular generator, as they named it. They had already pointed out the possibility of producing microwaves by using stimulated emission at an All Union conference on radio spectroscopy in May 1952.

The ammonia maser emitted a narrow line at a rigorously fixed frequency. It was an ideal frequency standard but had few chances for other applications in, for example, communications. Basov and Prokhorov suggested the use of three levels in a gas system in 1954, but their proposal did not allow one to build a tunable system and was never developed. Several people considered using paramagnetic solid crystals in 1955. Townes, J. Combrisson, and A. Honig studied a two-level system, and M.W.P. Strandberg and others suggested the use of solid-state materials. A. Javan worked on a three-level maser (publishing his result in 1957). Most important was Nicolaas Bloembergen's proposal to use a three-level system in paramagnetic solid materials (1956). H.E.D. Scovil at Bell Laboratories worked out a similar proposal.

The first operating three-level maser was assembled in 1957 at Bell Laboratories by Scovil, G. Feher, and H. Seidel by using Gd^{3+} paramagnetic ions in a host lattice of lanthanum ethyl sulphate. In 1958, Alan L. McWhorter and James W. Meyer at M.I.T. Lincoln Lab used Cr^{3+} in $K_3Co(CN)_6$ for the first amplifier. Contemporarily, C. Kikuchi and co-workers at the University of Michigan showed that ruby was a good material for these masers, but they had to operate at very low temperatures. A ruby maser at 60K was reported by C.R. Ditchfield and P.A. Forrester in 1958, and independently by Theodore H. Maiman in 1959. Operation at 195K was reported by Maiman in 1960. It was a ruby

maser that allowed A. Penzias and R.W. Wilson in 1965 to discover the 3K black-body radiation remnant from the Big Bang.

In 1965 maser action was found to occur in nature in several molecules in regions near new stars or where stars are at the end of their life cycle.

Lasers came as an extension of the maser principle to the infrared-visible range. In 1951, Fabrikant and his students filed a patent in the Soviet Union for the amplification of electromagnetic radiation (UV, visible, infrared, and radio waves) in an inverted medium. As the patent was published only in 1959, it did not exert any influence on the independent discovery of lasers.

Robert H. Dicke introduced the concept of superradiance in 1954, suggested the use of the Fabry-Perot **interferometer** as the resonant cavity in 1956, and obtained a patent in 1958. Schawlow and Townes made a complete proposal for a laser, discussed the Fabry-Perot cavity, and made some suggestions of possible media in 1958; they received a patent in March 1960, having filed their application in August 1958. In 1957 Gordon Gould had a public notary authenticate a notebook with proposals for making a laser, using a Fabry-Perot cavity and a number of potential systems. He filed a patent application on April 6, 1959, and used this notebook to contest the Shawlow and Townes patent. Gould eventually received a patent just as the Shawlow and Townes patent expired.

The work by Shawlow and Townes inspired others to try different materials and design philosophies. The first operating laser was made by T.H. Maiman and announced in the *New York Times* on July 7, 1960. This used ruby in a three-level scheme pumped optically by pulsed flash lamps. A few months later, Sorokin and Stevenson obtained a four-level laser at low threshold by using $U^{3+}:CaF_2$ emitting at 2.5 µm, and in 1961 in $Sm^{2+}:CaF_2$ at 708.3 nm.

J. H. Sanders and A. Javan both proposed inversion of population in gaseous systems by electric discharge in 1959. Javan, W. R. Bennett, Jr. and D. R. Herriott obtained emission on several lines near 1.15 µm in a mixture of helium and neon pumped by a radiofrequency electrical discharge in December 1960. After A.J. Fox and T. Li studied numerically modes in Fabry-Perot cavities in 1960, and G.D. Boyd and H. Kogelik in 1962 considered cavities made with spherical mirrors by using a confocal configu-

T.C. Wang and J.P. Gordon listening to beats between the first two ammonia beam masers, Columbia University, January 1955. Courtesy of NMAH.

ration, A.D. White and J.D. Rigden in 1962 obtained emission in He-Ne at 632.8 nm. By changing the reflectivity of external mirrors, A.L. Bloom, W.E. Bell, and R.C. Rempel had laser action at 3.39 µm in 1963.

The introduction of spherical mirrors cavities, and the demonstration of the relative ease with which lasers could be made, produced a proliferation of lasers and applications of them in military and civil fields. Examples are ruby laser radars and **rangefinders**, mechanical working with high-power ruby and CO_2 lasers, and medical applications.

In a private communication to John Bardeen in 1954, John von Neumann mentioned the possibility of making an injection semiconductor maser. On April 22, 1957, Y. Watanabe and J. Nishizawa in Japan filed a patent describing recombination radiation at about 4 µm in Te. P. Aigrain in France discussed the extension of maser action to optical frequencies by using semiconductors in 1958. Other proposals were made by H. Kroemer and H.J. Zeiger in 1959. In the Soviet Union, Basov's group began dis-

cussing semiconductors in 1957. The possibility of obtaining stimulated emission in semiconductors by transitions between conduction and valence bands was discussed in a complete and exhaustive manner in 1961 by M.G.A. Bernard and G. Duraffourg by using the concept of Fermi quasilevel giving a fundamental relation to be fulfilled to have laser effect. This relation was also derived independently by the Basov group in 1962.

In January 1962, D.N. Nasledov et al. at the A.F. Ioffe Physicotechnical Institute in Leningrad reported that the linewidth of radiation emitted by a GaAs diode at 77K showed a narrowing at high current densities, suggesting that this could indicate stimulated emission. When William P. Dumke at IBM showed that only direct gap semiconductors such as GaAs should be considered for making lasers, all discussions on Si and Ge were ruled out and a competition started among several American groups using GaAs. Robert N. Hall at General Electric in Schenectady announced the first GaAs laser diode on September 24, 1962. Similar lasers were announced by Marshall I. Nathan et al. at IBM Yorktown Heights on October 4, by T.M. Quist et al. at M.I.T. Lincoln Labs on October 23, and by Hol-nyak et al. at General Electric at Syracuse on October 17.

All these lasers were made with a pn-junction in GaAs at 77K, pumped with microsecond pulses of high density current between 8,500 and 100,000 A/cm². Holonyak and Bevacqua used a GaAsP pn-junction obtaining emission in the visible at 6,000–7,000 Å, while GaAs emitted near 8,400 Å. After these results, the Basov group made a laser diode at FIAN. The use of heterojunctions was suggested by Kroemer in 1963, and by Zh. I. Alferov and R.F. Kazarinov at Ioffe. In 1969 these structures were built by I. Hayashi and Panish at Bell Labs, and by H. Kressel and D.F. Nelson at RCA. These made possible continuous wave and room-temperature operation and opened the way for extensive applications of lasers for optical fiber communication and many opto-electronic devices. Laser action was discovered in recent years also in interstellar dust near forming stars.

Mario Bertolotti

Bibliography

Bertolotti, M. *Masers and Lasers: An Historical Approach*. Bristol: Adam Hilger, 1983.

Bromberg, Joan Lisa. *The Laser in America*. Cambridge: M.I.T. Press, 1991.

Schawlow, A.L., and C.H. Townes. "Infrared and Optical Masers." *Physical Review* 112 (1958): 1940–49.

Laser Diagnostic Instruments

Laser diagnostic instruments can measure various thermodynamic and chemical parameters in reacting and nonreacting fluids. Since the 1980s they have replaced most of the earlier measurement techniques based on material probes and opened new areas of investigation previously considered impossible.

Laser diagnostics use such well-known physical phenomena as emission spectroscopy, which has been used at least since Joseph Swan's observations of emissions from flames in 1857; the Doppler effect, which was discovered in 1842; the elastic scattering of light, which Lord Rayleigh used in 1871 to explain the blue color of the sky; and the scattering effect that Chandrasekhara Raman discovered in 1928 and for which he was awarded the Nobel Prize.

But it was the unique properties of lasers as light sources, namely their power, coherence, and spectral purity that permitted older techniques to be used more efficiently and new ones to be discovered and applied.

The other important components of a laser diagnostic system are those that provide light emission and collection. Lenses focus the laser beam onto the measurement volume or the light collector. Various optical elements such as beam separators, polarizers, mirrors, interferential filters, and, more recently, optical fibers are put together to use the laser light emission and collect the scattered light. At the end of the light collection chain is the photodetector, which senses the electromagnetic radiation. **Photomultipliers**, which can detect single photons of light, are the primary means of signal detection for almost all of the major laser diagnostics. After the conversion of radiation energy into electricity, the signal is processed, analogically or numerically, according to the information sought. Finally, the data corresponding to the parameter measured are stored in computers for post-processing.

During the first phases of the development of laser diagnostics (late 1960s and 1970s), these optical elements were put together at each utilization site by taking into account the specific utilization purpose. The advent of optical fibers and advanced optical systems, and the complete integration, standardization, and packaging of the emission and collection systems meant that nearly no knowledge in optics was needed to use laser diagnostics. Progressively this component of laser diagnostics was black-boxed.

Various physical phenomena can be monitored with laser diagnostics. The Raman scattering of light from molecules indicates temperature. Species concentrations can be measured with Laser-Induced Fluorescence (LIF), which is species specific and capable of detecting minor species, such as flame radicals at trace levels. Laser Doppler anemometry is capable of simultaneously measuring the three components of the velocity vector; phase-Doppler velocimetry provides size and velocity information on the dispersed phase in two-phase flows; and particle-image velocimetry (PIV) gives access to the whole velocity field rather than the velocity at a single point in the flow.

Laser Doppler anemometry (LDA), or velocimetry, was the first, and is still the most developed, laser diagnostic technique. It has a

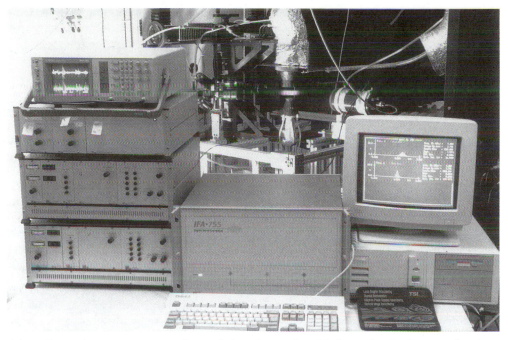

A laser diagnostic system to measure flow turbulence in a methane/air flame, showing burner and optics (rear) and LDA processor (front center). Courtesy of Iskender Gökalp/Centre National de la Recherche Scientifique.

wide spectrum of applications in flow velocity measurements. In its impact on various fields of engineering sciences, this instrument can be taken as the exemplar of laser diagnostics.

The hot-wire anemometer, introduced in the 1930s, was the only instrument able to determine the flow velocity in turbulent flows, until LDA became available in the early 1970s. Y. Yeh and H.Z. Cummins (1964) proposed the idea of using Doppler-shifted laser light scattered from small particles introduced in the flow to determine the flow velocity. This was obtained by mixing the scattered light with the transmitted light. The mixing (or beating) provides the beat or the Doppler shift frequency, which is directly proportional to the velocity of the particle, which should be small enough to exactly follow the instantaneous streamlines. Early LDA instruments used a reference beam technique in which the reference beam, using heterodyne terminology, becomes the local oscillator. Today, the so called dual-scatter or dual-beam technique has become the most widespread arrangement.

Like the other laser diagnostics, LDA is nonintrusive, and no calibration is required. The desired component of the velocity is measured directly, in any complex geometrical configuration, and independent of flow tempera-

ture, pressure, or composition. LDA provides very-high-frequency response and dynamic range and excellent spatial resolution. Its applications vary from very low velocities, as in biological flows, to measurements in hostile media, as in chemically reacting turbulent flows, and to complex flow situations, as in internal combustion engines.

Combined with the other laser diagnostics listed above, LDA has become one of the main scientific instruments in many domains in which the fluid flows matter. It has contributed to the development of new research areas and the establishment of a new instrument culture, namely in engineering sciences, by more tightly bridging laboratory research and design, as it can be used with equal confidence both in research and design sites.

Iskender Gökalp

Bibliography

Durst, Franz, A. Melling, and J.H. Whitelaw. *Principles and Practice of Laser-Doppler Anemometry.* 2nd ed. London: Academic, 1981.

Eckbreth, Alan C. *Laser Diagnostics for Combustion Temperature and Species.* Cambridge: Abacus, 1988.

Gökalp, I. "Turbulent Reactions: Impact of

New Instrumentation on a Borderland Scientific Domain." *Science, Technology & Human Values* 15 (1990): 284–304.

———, L. Bagla, and S.E. Cozzens. "Introduction of Laser Techniques in Turbulence and Combustion Domains: A Case Study on the Impact of Instrumentation on Science." In *Invisible Connections: Instruments, Institutions and Science,* edited by Robert Bud, and Susan E. Cozzens, 180–98. Bellingham, Wash.: SPIE Optical Engineering Press, 1992.

Length, Measurement of

Units of length are arbitrary; the problem of measurement is to relate any actual length to an agreed standard. Early standards were bars intended to be of an exact length overall—that is, "end standards." A bar of this sort, made in the sixteenth century, remained the English legal standard yard until 1824, when it was replaced by a line standard, a longer bar having lines engraved at a separation that defines the unit of length. The *Mètre des Archives* of 1792 is an end standard, while the *International Prototype Metre* of 1875, which replaced it, is a line standard. In principle, comparisons with an end standard may be made either by contact or optically, while precise reference to a line standard can be made only by using **microscopes.**

Since 1960, standards of length have been defined in terms of the wavelength of light: the meter is 1,650,763.73 wavelengths of the orange radiation in a vacuum of the krypton-86 isotope, and the yard is now defined as 0.9144 meter. Secondary, tangible, standards are verified by interferometry (see **interferometer**).

The most common way of measuring length has always been to use a divided scale. Today, the divisions on the cheaper articles are stamped, printed, or etched with no great pretensions to precision; formerly they were incised by hand using a dividing knife. Since the late eighteenth century, better scales have been made with a linear **dividing engine,** by means of which the graduations are ruled individually at intervals regulated by the machine.

It is not practicable to make or use graduations very much finer than half-millimeters or fiftieths of an inch. Even so, under favorable conditions and with experience, a dimension may be estimated more closely. The scale may be read using a simple magnifying lens or a compound microscope with a graticule in the focal plane of the eyepiece. The diagonal scale, known to Tycho Brahe, also affords a way of measuring with greater precision.

A scale may be built into an instrument to measure the displacement of one part relative to another. In most cases, however, the scale is separate from the article that it is used to measure, and a pair of calipers or compasses is used to transfer the measurement to or from the scale. The uncertainty of the measurement and the inconvenience of making it are thereby increased.

Calipers with a lever magnification, such as the watch-maker's douzième gauge, were introduced in the eighteenth century. So too were slide calipers with a vernier scale. These may be read to 1/1,000th of an inch or 1/50th of a millimeter. More recently there have been instruments in which a dial with a pointer, geared to a pinion engaged with a fine rack, is substituted for the vernier. In 1973 electronic slide calipers were introduced with a digital display reading to 0.0001 in. or 0.001 mm. They act by counting moiré interference fringes between fixed and moving scales etched on glass.

The principle of the screw **micrometer,** in which the axial movement of a screw is subdivided by measuring the arc through which it is turned, was known in the seventeenth century. It was applied to linear measurement late in the eighteenth century by James Watt, and later by John Barton, Henry Maudslay, and others. It was gradually introduced as a method of adjustment in machine tools, but became a widely used method of measurement only after the introduction of Jean Laurant Palmer's handheld gauge in 1846. The modern micrometer gauge, developed from this instrument, readily measures to 1/1,000th of an inch or 1/50th of a millimeter, or to an order better than that by the application of a vernier to the circular scale.

The micrometer principle has also found an important use in **comparators,** in which the length of a component is checked against a standard of similar length. In his most delicate measuring machine, Joseph Whitworth compounded the micrometer with worm gearing, claiming sensitivity to 1/1,000,000th of an inch, but recent work suggests that this claim was probably not well founded. Other principles have been applied to the comparator, such as the dial indicator in which the movement of a plunger is magnified through gearing and displayed by a hand on a scale (first used in the factory production of watches in the late nine-

The tolerance in the length of each block in a set of the highest grade is less than 0.0001 mm, and the thickness of the wringing film between blocks, when manipulated with care, is less than a tenth of that. The lengths of the blocks are verified by instruments such as the Eden-Rolt comparator or by interferometry.

Especially in manufacture, linear dimensions are often controlled by the use of either fixed or adjustable gauges. The dimensions of gauges, and often of manufactured components themselves, may be verified with a measuring machine. There are many designs, single-purpose or versatile, but all have a very accurately calibrated scale for each movement; the gauging points on the article to be measured are sighted optically or sensed by a delicate electromechanical or pneumatic contact system.

Michael Wright

Bibliography

Glazebrook, Richard, ed. *A Dictionary of Applied Physics,* Vol. 3. London: Macmillan, 1923.

Hume, Kenneth J. *A History of Engineering Metrology.* London: Mechanical Engineering, 1980.

Moore, Wayne R. *Foundations of Mechanical Accuracy.* Bridgeport, Conn.: Moore Special Tool, 1970.

Rolt, Frederick Henry. "The Development of Engineering Metrology." *Proceedings of the Institution of Production Engineers* 32 (1952): 130–32.

———. *Gauges and Fine Measurements.* London: Macmillan, 1929.

Eden-Rolt slip gauge comparator, 1918, accurate to one-millionth of an inch. SM 1928–1171. Courtesy of SSPL.

teenth century), and by magnification by levers and by optical means. An important example of the latter is the Eden-Rolt comparator, devised in 1918 by Edgar Mark Eden and Frederick Henry Rolt of the National Physical Laboratory, by which a difference of 1/1,000,000th of an inch really can be detected.

The slip gauges invented by Carl Edvard Johansson in 1896 provide a highly accurate and portable standard of length for engineers. These are blocks of hardened steel or other similarly hard, stable material capable of accepting a fine finish, the end faces of which are lapped optically flat and parallel and to closely determined separations. The flatness allows the graduated blocks to be *wrung* into close contact so that they adhere, so that any required length within the capacity of the set can be made up.

Length Comparator

See COMPARATOR, LENGTH

Level

A level determines the level line—that is, a line at the surface of the earth that cuts the direction of gravity everywhere at right angles. It can also be used to find the difference in altitude between two points.

The plumb-bob level for use in carpentry and masonry can be traced back to ancient Egypt, remaining essentially the same until the nineteenth century. Roman land surveyors used plumb-bob levels for routine work and more sophisticated instruments for laying out water supply and aqueducts. In Vitruvius we find a

Abney level and clinometer, ca. 1880. SM 1887-62. Courtesy of SSPL.

description of the "chorobates," a large water-filled channel cut lengthwise in a plank of wood. The surface of the water gave the level. Hero of Alexandria, (fl. A.D. 62), described a water-filled horizontal tube that had two vertical glass sections at each end. Movable sighting slits could be made to coincide with the surface of the water in each of the vertical sections.

The large-scale water supply projects of the late seventeenth century caused a revival of the level. Jean Picard, working at Versailles and Marly, described a plumb bob level in 1684, as did Christiaan Huygens and Olaf Rømer at about the same time. Philippe de La Hire designed an improved water level. The most important development in these instruments was the incorporation of telescopic sights.

In 1661 Melchisedech Thevenot invented a level in which a bubble of air is trapped in a vial of spirit. The problems with sealing were eventually overcome and by 1725 bubble levels suitable for surveying were being produced by Jonathan Sisson and Thomas Heath, both of London. Heath went on to devise a "double" level, consisting of two **telescopes** at 180°, to en-

able forward and back sights to be taken without resetting. Sisson responded in 1734 with the Y or "wye" level, in which the telescope was held in Y-shaped bearings and could be rotated on its axis or reversed. The bubble was slung below. Sisson's design remained the standard for a century. One modification was the drainage level, which had a small vertical arc of adjustment.

The next generation of levels began with those of Jesse Ramsden and Edward Troughton, dating from the end of the eighteenth century and the second decade of the nineteenth century respectively. Troughton's level had the bubble partially imbedded in the telescope with no separate adjustment for either. Although it satisfied the demands of the railway age for a level that could be used more easily than the Y, it was obvious before 1850 that William Gravatt's level, the principal rival, would be the favorite.

Gravatt's level, developed in the 1830s, used a large aperture object glass with a short focal length, which because of better centering of lenses could be mounted without separate adjustment. The tube was shorter and the observer could read the staff directly. It also had a cross bubble, and an inclined mirror to enable the bubble to be read simultaneously with taking a sight. The Gravatt level became known as the "Dumpy" level for obvious reasons.

By the mid nineteenth century the bubble had replaced the plumb bob on the handheld instruments used for masonry and carpentry. Smaller handheld surveying instruments were also developed: Colonel Burel's reflecting level in 1829, William Barrie's hand level in 1856, and William de Wiveleslie Abney's level in 1870. The last consisted of a semicircular protractor, bubble, and sighting tube.

Many modifications were suggested for the level in the late nineteenth and early twentieth centuries. The most notable were the precision level manufactured by J. Kern & Company in Switzerland, and the Zeiss-Wild level, designed in 1910, which incorporated a method of viewing the bubble using prisms. Tacheometric stadia began to be placed in the eyepieces of the best "precision" levels at around that time. However the Dumpy level did not supersede the Y level until the 1950s, when a modification of the Dumpy level, the tilting level, was introduced. The tilting level had a small vertical arc of adjustment so that the refinements of the Y were incorporated into the sturdy Dumpy. More fundamental changes came with the self-adjusting or automatic design introduced by Zeiss in the mid 1960s. The optical system that was suspended inside the **telescope** tube allowed only level rays to pass through. The latest development, popular since the mid 1980s, is the electronic level. This uses electronic-image digital processing in which a bar-coded rod is viewed by the telescope, the image is compared with an image held in the memory of the machine, and the result is displayed and stored.

Jane Wess

Bibliography

Bennett, J.A., and O. Brown. *The Compleat Surveyor.* Cambridge, U.K.: Whipple Museum of the History of Science, 1982.

Dilke, O.A.W. *The Roman Land Surveyors: An Introduction to the Agrimensores.* Newton Abbott: David and Charles, 1971.

Simms, Frederic W. *Treatise on the Principal Mathematical Instruments Employed in Surveying, Levelling and Astronomy.* 6th ed. London: Troughton and Simms, 1844.

Stanley, William Ford Robinson. *Surveying and Levelling Instruments, Theoretically and Practically Described, for Construction, Qualities, Selection, Preservation, Adjustments and Uses; With Other Apparatus and Appliances Used by Civil Engineers and Surveyors in the Field.* London: Spon, 1890.

Leyden Jar

A Leyden jar stores electric charge. It consists of a glass jar, coated inside and out with unconnected metal (originally lead or tin) foils, and a central conducting rod connected to the inner foil and held in place by an unconducting lid. The jar is charged from an **electrostatic machine**: equal positive and negative charges are stored on the corresponding foils creating a potential between them. The jar is discharged with a loud crack and a flash when the two foils are connected together. This device was central to the development of electrical theory in the second half of the eighteenth century.

There are three contenders for the honor of having invented the Leyden jar: Ewald Jürgen Kleist in Germany (October 1745) and Peter Musschenbroek and Andreas Cunaeus in Holland (January 1746). The earliest and most detailed account of this invention occurs in Daniel Gralath's "Geschichte der Electri-cität" published by the Natural Philosophy Society of Dantzig in 1747. The most influential was Joseph Priestley's *History and Present State of Electricity* (1767), but he altered his account in the third edition (1775) after reading Gralath.

While Kleist clearly observed this phenomenon on October 11, 1745, his description was not adequate for others to replicate his experiment. Musschenbroek, however, wrote a detailed description of experiments conducted in Leyden, causing Jean Antoine Nollet to name the device "bouteille de Leyden." In Germany it is still sometimes referred to as the "von Kleistische flache."

Musschenbroek never claimed the invention as his own, and in a letter describing the astonishing effects produced by an electrified bottle containing water, written to Réne Antoine Ferchault de Réaumur in January 1746, he indicated that the experiment was performed by several people in his Leyden laboratory. Most French historians of electricity have opted for Musschenbroek as being the

Leyden jar, coated with lead foil and filled with iron filings, late eighteenth century. SM 1927-1273. Courtesy of SSPL.

by means of a wire dipped into it and connected to the prime conductor of the frictional electrical machine. Glass was used for the vessel as it was a good barrier, which prevented electricity "poured" into the water from being conducted away in the atmosphere. In the course of this experiment Cunaeus received a powerful electric shock when he unhooked the electrified jar from the prime conductor of the electrical machine. According to contemporary practice, however, the glass jar would have been insulated, as it was commonly believed that electricity was not only excited by but also passed through glass. Thus, while the amateur Cunaeus might have performed this experiment, Musschenbroek was a professional, and he knew too much about electrical theory to attempt it.

Whatever the truth of the matter, the discovery was very important, for it not only made it possible to study more powerful electrical phenomena, it also helped with the formulation of new concepts such as that of the electric circuit, intensity or level of electrification (or charge), capacity or area of coated surface electrified, and quantity of charge. These concepts were implicit in the hydrostatic model of the fluid theory, but the Leyden jar made them explicit. Even its shape suggested that such a relationship between charge, area of coated surface, and intensity (or electrical pressure) ought to exist, for it could readily be compared to the behavior of liquids flowing from vessels of different sizes. The analysis of its behavior, in particular that of the dielectric medium (in this case glass) led to the discovery of the "plate of air condenser" by Benjamin Wilson (1746), Franz Ulrich Theodosius Aepinus (1756), and Alesandro Volta, who developed the parallel plate condenser further (1778). This device was crucial for the discovery of "adhesive" or "contact" electricity in the 1790s. This in turn led to the invention of the voltaic pile (1799–1800), the first source of continuous low-voltage electricity, and a new era in the study of electricity. Attempts to explain this extraordinary device in terms of the behavior of the Leyden jar failed, and it was soon realized that other concepts such as current intensity and electrical resistance were necessary.

The water in the original jar was soon replaced by metal—for example, lead shot (by Benjamin Franklin), crumpled gold foil, "Dutch metal" (an alloy of copper and zinc), lead or tin foil, or brass iron filings, poured into the jar or

Dutch inventor of the instrument, while most Germans have favored Cuneaus, as did Priestley in the third edition of his *History*.

According to the standard account, Musschenbroek and his colleagues were trying to increase the power and longevity of electricity generated by electrifying water in a glass bottle made to stick to a shellac coating painted onto the glass's surface. Any kind of glass was used, and early jars were often made from narrow-necked medicine bottles. Tiberius Cavallo in the 1770s invented the "medical Leyden jar," which retained its charge longer by improving the insulation of the central conducting (or discharging) rod. A flat version of the Leyden jar consisting of a plate of glass sandwiched between metal foil was also soon developed by Franklin and others, but the jar shape remained the favorite. Furthermore, it did not take long for jars to be assembled in **batteries** to augment charge.

The Leyden jar also had a key role in the early development of wireless telegraphy (radio). Oliver Lodge demonstrated in 1890 by means of his "syntonic" Leyden jar experiments the importance of tuning both to improve the signal and prevent interference. The Marconi Wireless Telegraphy Co. developed the multi-disk variable condenser in the early 1900s to tune the radio receiver circuit. The inspiration of this device may well have been William Thomson's "multicellular" electrostatic **voltmeter** (1888), in which he used a series of fixed and movable condensers stacked on top of one another. In the course of its evolution, the Leyden jar moved from a storer of charge in the eighteenth century to a tuner of electronic circuits in the early twentieth.

Willem D. Hackmann

Bibliography

Hackmann, Willem D. *Electricity from Glass. The History of the Frictional Electrical Machine.* Alphen aan den Rijn: Sijthoff and Noordhoff, 1978.
———. "The Relationship between Concept and Instrument Design in Eighteenth-Century Experimental Science." *Annals of Science* 36 (1979): 205–24.
Heilbron, John L. *Electricity in the Seventeenth and Eighteenth Centuries; A Study of Early Modern Physics.* Berkeley: University of California Press, 1979.

Liquid Limit Apparatus

The Liquid Limit is defined as the water content, expressed as a percentage by weight of the oven-dry soil, at which the soil passes from the liquid state to the plastic state. In other words, when the soil will just begin to flow when jarred slightly. Soils at the Liquid Limit have a very small but definite shear resistance, which may be overcome by the application of little force, and their cohesion is practically zero. The Liquid Limit was identified by A. Atterberg in 1905 as a specific attribute that could be used in forecasting a soil's performance in, for example, an embankment having to withstand the loads imposed by a road and its traffic.

The Liquid Limit used to be determined with general-purpose equipment. A soil sample was placed in a small porcelain evaporating dish, shaped into a smooth layer about 1 cm thick at the center, and divided into two portions by means of a grooving tool of standard dimensions. The dish was held firmly in one hand and tapped lightly ten times against the heel of the other hand. If the lower edges of the two portions did not flow together the water content was below the Liquid Limit. If they flowed together before ten blows were struck, the water content was above the Liquid Limit. The test was repeated with more or less water as required, until the two edges met exactly after ten blows.

In 1932 Arthur Casagrande described a mechanical device that achieved consistent results when calibrated against the hand method. The soil is mixed with water, placed in the brass cup, shaped into a smooth layer, and grooved. The cup is then attached to the carriage of the machine and dropped through a distance of 1 cm a sufficient number of times to close the groove. This process is repeated for several water contents. The object of the procedure is to obtain a sample of such consistency that the number of drops or shocks to the cup required to close the groove will be both below and above twenty-five. A "flow curve" is plotted on semilog graph paper using the water contents as abscissae on the arithmetic scale and the number of shocks as ordinates on the logarithmic scale. The water content corresponding to the intersection of the flow curve with the twenty-five shock ordinate is the Liquid Limit of the soil. The test continues to be used by the principal geotech-nical research centers in most countries. The apparatus has not changed in appearance since 1932, although most hand-operated models now incorporate a revolution counter. Motorized versions, also fitted with an integral blow counter, have been produced.

In 1989 the Casagrande apparatus was recognized as worthy of international review as part of the Strategic Programme for Innovation Transfer (SPRINT), administered by the Euro-

Instruments for liquid limit testing: Cone penetrometer (right) and Casagrande apparatus, both ca. 1967. Courtesy of SSPL.

pean Commission, to identify the similarities and differences in geotechnical testing standards. It was found that use of the Casagrande chart was consistent across European and U.S. (the American Society for Testing and Materials [ASTM], in this instance) systems, and there was a broad degree of harmonization. However, when the slight differences in test procedures were examined in detail they were seen to be liable to affect test results.

In 1958 Arthur Casagrande wrote : "The Liquid Limit tests as defined by Atterberg and as performed mechanically with the (Casagrande) Liquid Limit device is in reality a dynamic shear test. This is a serious disadvantage because it does not provide a uniform basis of comparison for fine-grained soils which differ in their reactions when subjected to a shaking test. A simple direct shear test or an indirect shear test, e.g., a static penetration test, would eliminate many of the difficulties one faces in the use of the Liquid Limit device. Unfortunately, so far none of these tests has been simplified to an extent that it could compete in simplicity and cost with the present form of the Liquid Limit test."

These comments renewed interest in the search for alternative methods. The principal alternatives are based on penetration tests of laboratory-prepared soil samples (compare in situ **penetrometers** and **penetration test**). In Sweden "the fall-cone test" has been in use since 1922 to find a "fineness number" whose numerical value corresponds to the Casagrande Liquid Limit in the 40 percent region; at higher Liquid Limit values the "fineness number" tends to be lower than the Casagrande Liquid Limit. In 1949 A.M. Vasilev, working in Moscow, introduced the "Russian Cone method." Although its results do not correspond exactly to Casagrande values, the Russian Cone was reported to have been used satisfactorily in New Zealand in 1958. At the same time H.L. Uppal and H.R. Aggarwal, working in New Delhi, developed the heavier "Indian Cone Method," and various tests in the United States and Scandinavia in the 1960s found consistent relations between the Indian and the original Casagrande results. The latter was also true of the Georgia Institute of Technology Cone method, which is similar to the Russian apparatus but requires the cone to be restrained to fall slowly for 10 seconds, whereas the Russian method allows the cone to fall freely.

By 1966 the Laboratoire Central des Ponts et Chaussées (LCPC) in Paris had developed the Cone Penetrometer apparatus. The method is similar to the other cone tests—in other words, a static test depending on the soil shear strength. It is based on the relationship between water content and the penetration of a cone into the soil sample under controlled conditions. A linear graph of percentage moisture content and the penetration is plotted and the best straight line is drawn through the plotted points. The moisture content corresponding to the cone's penetrating 20 mm in 5 seconds is taken as the Liquid Limit of the soil. Since the 1970s the LCPC method has begun to replace the Casagrande test in some countries, notably Ireland and the United Kingdom.

Robert C. McWilliam

Bibliography

Allen, Harold. "Classification of Soils and Control Procedures Used in Construction of Embankments." *Public Roads* 22 (February 1942): 263–82.

Casagrande, Arthur. "Notes on the Design of the Liquid Limit Device." *Géotechnique* 8 (June 1958): 84–91.

———. "Research on the Atterburg Limits of Soils." *Public Roads* 13 (October 1932): 121–30, 136.

Sherwood, P.T., and M.D. Ryley. *An Examination of Cone-Penetrometer Methods for Determining the Liquid Limit of Soils*. Crowthorne, Berkshire, U.K.: Road Research Laboratory, 1968.

SPRINT RA bis, Comprehensive Report. Lyngby, Denmark: Danish Geotechnical Institute, 1993.

Van Alboom, G. "Report from Task Group 1: Soil Identification Tests. Atterberg Limits: Liquid Limit." In *Quality Assurance in Geotechnical Engineering. Phase 2, Recommended Practice in Geotechnical Laboratory Testing,* edited by Per Bjerregaard Hansen, Appendix B (1993–02–26), 40–55.

Load Measurement

The accurate measurement of load is required in the development and testing of new materials and devices, and in the control of the quality of materials for use in design and construction. Laboratory testing machines combine a means for applying load to a specimen with a means for measuring the applied load. In some machines these features are superimposed on each other, in others they are entirely separate. Testing machines also feature various accessories, such as devices for gripping or holding test pieces, power units, controllers, recorders, speed indicators, and recoil or shock absorbers. Self-contained load-measuring instruments are built into test rigs and prototype devices, and, latterly, industrial equipment that is being monitored.

The simplest method of measuring load is the direct application of weights of known magnitude as an applied load. The earliest strength-of-materials tests known, by Galileo, used dead weights to establish the strength of copper rods. Dead weight is still used for nondestructive testing of complex structures.

Prior to 1729, Peter van Musschenbroek of the University of Leyden used a crude steelyard, with no means to keep the steelyard level, to test wooden and metal specimens. Many developments in testing were made at the École des Ponts et Chaussées after 1760. One, introduced by Jean Baptiste Rondelet, was the use of knife edges and a screw for keeping the steelyard level. This was known as "strain compensation."

Joseph Bramah's hydraulic press, patented in 1795, provided another means of applying static load. One of its earlier applications at Brunton's chain works in Musselburgh, Scotland, in 1813, seems to have used a counterweighted manometer to indicate load. By 1829 riveted joints were being tested at Merthyr Tydfil, South Wales, by a hydraulic machine able to apply 130 tons' load with dead weights acting through levers with knife edge fulcra for measuring the load. Lever systems were also used to measure load with the other type of powered loading machines that had been introduced at the same time: namely, the screw-gear machines, such as the cable-proving machine designed by Samuel Brown.

Increasingly larger, more accurate, and more refined powered loading machines appeared throughout the nineteenth century. Lever systems evolved to include multiple-lever and movable poise as well as pendulum weighing devices. Hydraulic machines were developed in which the pressure in the loading ram could be measured by a Bourdon tube gauge. An early form of this was in use in Dunn of Manchester's 1866 machine for the Portsmouth Dockyard.

A hydraulic machine developed by Desgoffe and Ollivier in Paris in 1868 had one end of the test piece secured to the end of a hydraulic ram and the other end to the short arm of a lever with knife edges. The long arm of a second lever in the system bore on a rubber diaphragm secured to an auxiliary weighing cylinder. A manometer measured the pressure in the auxiliary cylinder, and hence the load in the test piece, giving a continuous reading without the need to balance a lever.

This idea was further developed by M.H. Thomasset of Paris in his 1872 machine. It was in turn perfected by A.H. Emery during the development of the 500-ton machine built for Watertown Arsenal by the Ames Manufacturing Co. and known as the "United States Testing Machine." The Watertown machine had a closed flexible hydraulic capsule that could transmit the actual load to the gauges without the losses found in hydraulic cylinders and pistons. Lessons learned during the operation of the Watertown machine included the difficulty of maintaining the diaphragm that bridged the gap between the ring and the measuring column without auxiliary support. The resulting "Emery capsules," which are still being made, incorporate a bridge ring between the ring and the column. Hydraulic capsules installed in a testing rig are a form of **dynamometer**—a self-contained load-measuring instrument.

Many self-contained measuring instruments rely on Hooke's Law—that is, on the elastic deflection of a spring, a beam, a frame, or a ring. They may be applied directly in the line of the loading axis or used in conjunction with multiple levers for larger loads. They range in sophistication from the pendulum dynamom-

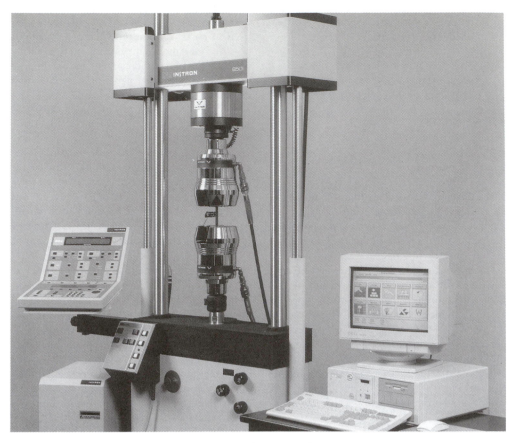

Instron 8501 load testing system, 1994. Courtesy of Instron Ltd.

eter introduced by M. Amsler of Schaffhausen in 1904 to the direct reading of spring balances with closely wound helical springs. Concurrent with these developments was the standardization of testing being pioneered by, for example, David Kirkaldy.

The evolution of the standard proving ring and the load-proving frame was expedited by the mass production of dial gauges. Dial gauges were introduced in 1890 by D.C. Ames and initially regarded as a novel, and less accurate, form of **micrometer**. Improved manufacturing techniques have ensured that a dial gauge rigidly mounted in a proving ring and accurately aligned on the loading axis has repeatability within 0.2 percent of indicated load and accuracy of calibration load of ±0.02 percent at each load applied.

In the 1930s the largest precision testing machines, up to 2,000 tons, still included weighing based on levers with moving poise. However the 1930s also saw the beginnings of developments that led to direct electrical load-measuring devices. These "load cells" contain an elastic device to which electrical-resistance strain gauges have been permanently attached [see **strain gauge (electrical)** and **strain gauge (general)**]. One of the earliest applications was in the Instron tester developed at M.I.T. in the 1940s. Load cells have the additional advantage of being able to monitor high-frequency dynamic load applications required in fatigue testing. Load cells have become increasingly sophisticated as strain gauges have developed.

Robert C. McWilliam

Bibliography

Davis, Harmer E., George Earl Troxwell, and George F.W. Hauck. *The Testing of Engineering Materials.* 4th ed. New York: McGraw-Hill, 1982.

Gibbons, Chester H. "Load-Weighing and Load-Indicating Systems." *ASTM Bulletin* 100 (October 1939): 7–13.

Hindman, H., and G.S. Burr. "The Instron Tensile Tester." *Transactions of the*

American Society of Mechanical Engineers 71 (1949): 789–96.

Kennedy, Alexander Blackie William. "The Use and Equipment of Engineering Laboratories." *Minutes of Proceedings of the Institution of Civil Engineers* 88 (1887): 1–80.

Smith, Denis. "David Kirkaldy (1820–1897) and Engineering Materials Testing." *Transactions of the Newcomen Society (London)* 52 (1982): 49–65.

Lock-in Detection/Amplifier

"Lock-in" detection refers to a signal-processing technique—employing a lock-in amplifier—whereby an otherwise indiscernible object of observation, or response of an experimental system, is made to stand out from the enveloping noise by "looking" alternately, at some fixed frequency, at the signal source, and at the same source in the absence of the signal. If this alternation is at a low audio frequency, it is then possible to "subtract out" the noise by means of a multiplier/rectifier "locked" by a synchronous reference voltage to the desired signal. Moreover, the combination of synchronous reference signal and multiplier, followed by a low-pass filter, functions as a narrow band-pass system, yielding the sought-for signal, free of a great part of the systemic noise.

The first detection instrument based upon synchronism between signal and reference voltage was, apparently, that devised by C.R. Cosens for, and manufactured by, the Cambridge Instrument Co. Ltd., in 1932–1934. This was a balance detector for alternating current bridges, which was sensitive only to the ac frequency applied to the impedances to be balanced. During the later 1930s, some geophysical and astrophysical experimenters incorporated the principle of lock-in detection into apparatus to observe weak signals against an irremediably noisy background—for example, observation of the sun's corona in daylight, and measurement of light scattered by the upper atmosphere from a searchlight beam. The refinement of the lock-in amplifier as a frequency- and phase-sensitive detector was taken on especially by Walter C. Michels and his students at Bryn Mawr College for women.

World War II was a watershed in that, afterwards, as never before, accepted standards of physical experimentation required systematic consideration of the limitations imposed by noise. This new sophistication among physicists about the process and conditions of measurement resulted principally from wrestling with the problem of how best to discern in the noisy output of a **radar** receiver the faint reflection of a "real" target. Among all the war work with this common goal, the single piece that most strongly affected the physicists' postwar approach to noise reduction in experimental design was the microwave radiometer designed by Robert H. Dicke at the M.I.T. Radiation Laboratory. This "tele-pyrometer" used lock-in detection to measure the difference between the noise temperature of the source toward which the horn antenna pointed and the noise temperature (300K) of the antenna itself, and, further, in order to achieve this measurement, to diminish the effect upon the instrument's output both of the much higher white noise temperature of the receiver, and of the slow random variations ("1/f noise") in the operating parameters of the instrument.

The principle of operation of the instrument was as follows: A synchronous motor rotated a disk, appropriately shaped and partially inserted into the waveguide between antenna and receiver, such that during one-half of the disk's 30-Hz cycle the receiver "saw" the signal source, and during the other half "saw" the disk, which thus served as a 300K signalless noise source. To function as a radiometer—that is, a microwave noise meter—the receiver had to have a wide frequency acceptance, and the noise power received across this spectrum was the signal sought. In order, however, to retain this signal while greatly reducing instrumental noise in subsequent stages of the detection process, the output of the wideband receiver is followed by an amplifier accepting only a narrow band around the 30-Hz alternation frequency. The output of this bandpass amplifier is fed into a "mixer," where it is multiplied by a synchronous 30-Hz reference signal from a generator driven by the same synchronous motor rotating the "300K noise" disk. The result is that all signal components coming through the detection system synchronous with the reference signal produce dc outputs, while nonsynchronous (that is, instrumental noise) components appear at harmonics of 30 Hz. Putting the output thus obtained through a lowpass filter, one gets a dc measure of the desired quantity, the difference between source noise temperature and antenna noise temperature, and, moreover, a measure that is immune to drifts in the instrument's op-

RADIATION LABORATORY
MASSACHUSETTS INSTITUTE OF TECHNOLOGY
CAMBRIDGE   MASSACHUSETTS

REPORT
787

R. H. Dicke
July 16, 1945

THE MEASUREMENT OF THERMAL RADIATION AT MICROWAVE FREQUENCIES

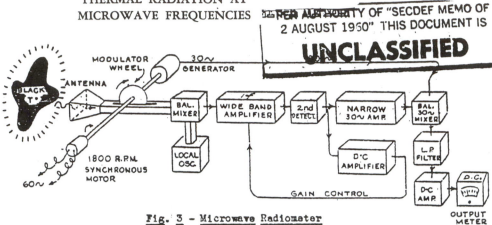

Fig. 3 - Microwave Radiometer

In Fig. 4 there is plotted the average power against frequency for the output of the second detector of Fig. 3.

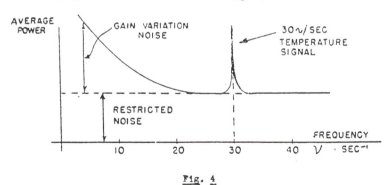

Fig. 4

It is to be noted that the signal, appearing as it does at 30~/sec., avoids the "gain variation noise".

Montage from Robert H. Dicke's report on the microwave radiometer, 1945. Courtesy of Paul Forman/NMAH.

erating parameters occurring on a time scale greater than 1/30 second.

With Dicke's microwave radiometer as exemplar, lock-in detection was quickly and widely adopted in physical experimentation, perhaps first in **nuclear magnetic resonance**, but soon followed by microwave spectroscopy. Dicke published the principle of operation of his radiometer but never details of the circuits, and so he found himself often responding to requests for diagrams. When, in the early 1960s, Dicke and several colleagues established Prince-

ton Applied Research Corp. but not having much commercial success with their initial repertoire of instruments—power supplies and so forth—Dicke proposed to his partners the lock-in amplifier—that is, a single unit incorporating, together with the conveniences of input filters and preamplifiers, a multiplier of input signal and of synchronous reference signal, and a lowpass filter to reject non-dc outputs due to noise. In response to their skepticism, Dicke pointed to the great number of circuit diagrams he had mailed out, and he estimated at least one hundred potential customers; they sold more than one hundred lock-in amplifiers in the first year they were offered. In ever more sophisticated forms, the lock-in amplifier has remained the best known and most distinctive product of this successful firm.

Notwithstanding the many other techniques for "signal recovery" developed in the last several decades, lock-in detection continues to be the most widely applied in scientific research. A survey in the early 1980s (Meade)—still apparently the only book devoted to the subject—listed some eighty fields of application, from "absorption spectroscopy" and "ac bridges" to "Young's modulus" and "Zeeman effect."

Paul Forman

Bibliography

Dicke, Robert H. Interview by Joan L. Bromberg, and Paul Forman, May 2, 1983. Transcript on deposit at the Niels Bohr Library, American Institute of Physics, College Park, Maryland.

———. "The Measurement of Thermal Radiation at Microwave Frequencies." *Review of Scientific Instruments* 17 (1946): 268–75.

Forman, Paul. "'Swords into Ploughshares': Breaking New Ground with Radar Hardware and Technique in Physical Research after World War II." *Reviews of Modern Physics* 67 (1995): 397–455.

Meade, Michael L. *Lock-In Amplifiers: Principles and Applications.* London: Peter Peregrinus on behalf of the Institution of Electrical Engineers, 1983.

Log

A log measures the speed of a ship relative to the surrounding water, and is used to determine the position of a ship at various points during its voyage. Navigation based on the distance run on various courses was known as "dead reckoning."

A simple method of speed estimation, the chip log, used a floating object or piece of wood—hence the word "log"—that a sailor threw overboard and observed moving from one mark to another along the side of the ship. This kind of logging by eye was probably used in the period of Columbus and the voyages of discovery. Despite the shortness of time of the observation and the difficulty of knowing when the object was abreast of the two marks, this log

was still found on Dutch ships at the end of the eighteenth century and was even recommended in navigation manuals of the twentieth century. With the "Dutchman's log" the resulting speed of length and time measurement was determined by conversion tables engraved in personal objects like tobacco boxes.

The Englishman William Bourne described a log in 1574. In an improved form it was attached to a line and floated behind the ship, thereby increasing the time of observation. This log was constructed of wood, weighted with lead to make it float upright, and attached to the line by means of a small bridle that kept it in a position of maximum resistance. The line was usually 150 fathoms long (1 fathom equals 6 feet). To enable the navigator to determine how much line had payed out, the line was knotted at regular intervals, which provides the origin of the expression of ships' speeds in "knots."

The growth of seaborne trade in the seventeenth and eighteenth centuries increased the need for a more accurate measurement of a ship's speed, and several inventors developed self-recording logs. These were based on the principle that a spiral or screw in moving its own length in the direction of its axis through a resisting medium, revolves about its axis. If the revolutions of the screw were communicated to wheels and clockwork inboard the ship and registered, the number of times it moved its own length through the water would be known. Several attempts were made, but they all suffered from friction in the wheelwork at the inboard end, which falsified the readings.

The first successful self-recording log was that developed by Edward Massey and patented in 1802. The Massey log was similar to its predecessors, but varied in several important details. It consisted of a more sensitive and reliable form of rotator, and it recorded the distance traveled on a series of dials in a box near the rotator, which could be read when the log and its line were retrieved from the sea. Massey's nephew, Thomas Walker, developed the "Harpoon" log, which placed the dials in the outer casing of the rotator; this was patented in 1861. More convenient forms of rotating logs were introduced about 1879, which placed the dials for easier reading at the other end of the line on the ship, mostly attached to the taffrail, therefore their name, taffrail logs.

Bottom logs are not towed astern, but protrude from the ship's bottom. The Chernikeeff log, developed in 1915 by Basil Chernikeeff, a

Heures.	Nœuds.	Braſſes.	Routes. Rumbs.
2	3	2	Cap au Nort $\frac{1}{4}$ du Nordeſt.
4	2	4	Cap au Nort-nordeſt.
6	4	2	Cap au Nordeſt.
8	5	3	Cap au Nordeſt.
10	2	3 $\frac{1}{2}$	Cap au Nort $\frac{1}{4}$ du Nordeſt.
12	3	5	Cap au Nort-nordeſt.
2	2	3	Cap au Nordeſt $\frac{1}{4}$ de l'Eſt.
4	2	4	Cap au Nordeſt.
6	6	1	Cap au Nort.
8	6	3	Cap au Nordeſt $\frac{1}{4}$ du Nordeſt.
10	6	2	Cap au Nort $\frac{1}{4}$ du Nordeſt.
12	3	4	Cap au Nort-nordeſt.

Log, log line, and log board. Samuel Champlain. Les Voyages de la Nouvelle France Occidentale. *Paris, 1632: 49–51. Courtesy of SSPL.*

captain of the Russian Navy, relies on a small impeller in a retractable tube that can be raised and lowered so that in its running position it protrudes 15 to 18 in. below the bottom of the ship. The rotation of the impeller is transmitted electrically to a distance recorder. Interest in impeller logs has revived in recent years as a result of the technical advances in the design of impellers, bearings, and electronic instrumentation and the upsurgence in small pleasure boats.

They are, however, susceptible to wear and fouling in the ocean environment.

Other type of bottom logs use different principles. The pitotmeter log is based on an invention by Henry Pitot in 1730 and the measurement of dynamic water pressure. This device consists of a tube with an opening on its forward side, receiving the dynamic pressure, which is compared with the local static pressure in a surrounding tube.

The electromagnetic log, or EM log, uses the potential difference generated in water by its movement relative to a magnetic field, which is produced by an electromagnet. This principle was first, but unsuccessfully, applied for water-flow measurement by Michael Faraday in 1831 (see **flow meter**); it was patented in the form of a ship's speed sensor in 1917. By Faraday's Law this voltage is directly proportional to the water-flow velocity relative to the magnetic field. The EM log consists essentially of a rodmeter, a strut of streamlined cross-section, with a sensing device near its tip. As the conducting sea water cuts the magnetic field, it develops a signal voltage proportional to the speed of the water. An indicator transmitter indicates the speed on a dial in the navigation room.

Jobst Broelmann

Bibliography

Admiralty Manual of Navigation, Vol. 1. London: HMSO. 1938.

Griswold, L.W. "Underwater Logs." *Navigation* 15 (1968):127–35.

Hewson, J.B. *A History of the Practice of Navigation.* Glasgow: Brown, Son and Ferguson, 1963.

Hutchinson, W. *A Treatise on Practical Seamanship* [1777]. Reprint. London: Scolar, 1979.

Waters, D.W. *The Art of Navigation in England in Elizabethan and Early Stuart Times.* London: Trustees of the National Maritime Museum, 1958.

Lovibond Comparator

See COMPARATOR, LOVIBOND

M

Magic Lantern

Magic lanterns, which project individual images from glass slides onto a wall or screen, were precursors to modern slide, overhead, and motion-picture projectors. Over a period of three hundred years they were used for scientific and artistic education, as well as general entertainment. The basic elements are a metal or wood body, an illuminant, a condensing lens, and a focusing lens.

The first published account of the illumination and projection of images appeared in the first edition of Athanasius Kircher's *Ars Magna Lucis et Umbrae* (1646). Christiaan Huygens, who was possibly inspired by Kircher's work, projected images illuminated by artificial light rather than sunlight in 1659; he termed his modifications a "lanterne magique." In the second edition of *Ars Magna Lucis et Umbrae* (1671), Kircher published illustrations of glass lantern slides, and of the apparatus used by Thomas Walgensten, who had traveled through Europe giving magic lantern demonstrations in 1664–1670.

Despite these and other developments, lantern projection remained a novelty until Étienne Gaspar Robertson premiered the "Phantasmagoria" in Paris in 1799. Influenced by this gothic horror show with demons, spirits, and thunderstorms, lantern projection quickly grew in popularity, only limited by the cumbersome apparatus. The public attended presentations in museums and entertainment theaters. Students at universities were exposed to science through magic lantern projection. In England and the United States, the lantern designed to project scientific equipment became known as the "German Lantern," reflecting the success of German educators in improving the magic lantern.

Magic lanterns were widely used during the second half of the nineteenth century, especially after developments in illumination and construction made them safer, more portable, and less expensive. The first common illuminant was limelight, a cylinder of lime brightly lit when exposed to a mixture of oxygen and hydrogen gas (introduced by Thomas Drummond in 1826 and used to light stages in entertainment halls). Gasbags were heavy and dangerous because of their combustible contents and the use of weights to slowly push the gas out. Explosions at lantern exhibitions were a common hazard. Cylinders of oxygen and hydrogen were available by 1878, and within ten years they had replaced the gasbag. The Sciopticon, patented in 1869 by Lorenzo J. Marcy, a Philadelphia optician, was fueled by kerosene and was still considered the first real advance in illumination twenty years later. Laverne & Co. of Paris manufactured a lantern with three to five wicks that could show opaque or transparent objects.

The optical system of lanterns also underwent considerable development. There were lanterns with two or three sets of lenses and only one illuminant, suitable for classes and other large groups (such as the Triunial lantern that Rev. St. Vincent Beechey showed at the London International Exhibition of 1851); lanterns with two lenses that projected concentric circles (such as John Benjamin Dancer's of 1878); lanterns that could dissolve from one view to another (such as the Stereopticon patented by Albert G. Buzby in 1872–1874); and lanterns that could project images of horizontal as well as vertical images and objects (developed by Jules Duboscq in Paris and Henry Morton in Hoboken, New Jersey). In 1893, J.B. Colt and Co. of New York introduced the Cri-

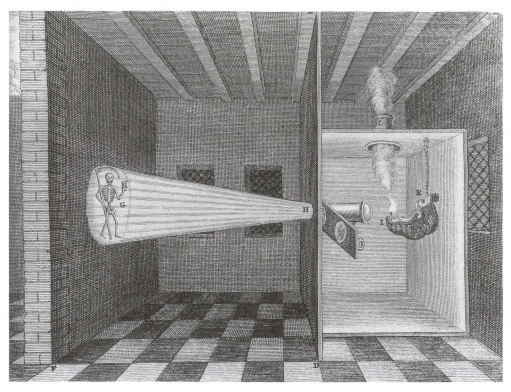

Magic lantern, seventeenth century. Athanasius Kircher. Ars Magna Lucis et Umbrae. *Second edition, Rome, 1671: 768. Courtesy of SSPL.*

terion lantern, illuminated by the carbon arc lamp and provided with exposed bellows and lenses. This configuration, with only the illumination housed, allowed the parts to be easily adjusted or removed and a platform or apparatus added for scientific experiments. The Ernst Plank Co., established in 1866 in Nuremburg, was a major producer of toy, as well as professional magic lanterns.

The early lantern slides were hand painted on glass. Hand-cranked mechanisms produced elaborate special effects, such as planets revolving around the sun, the sun rising or setting over a landscape, or ghosts appearing and fading from view. The Langenheim brothers of Philadelphia introduced photographic lantern slides in 1850. Lewis Wright in England designed a lantern that could project microscopic slides.

Solar **microscopes**, related to magic lanterns and also invented in the seventeenth century, used sunlight to project an enlarged image of a microscopic object. Colleges and universities in Europe and the United States were the major purchasers of solar microscopes until their popularity declined in the mid nineteenth century.

Debbie Griggs Carter

Bibliography

Carter, Debbie Griggs. "Projection Apparatus for Science in Late Nineteenth Century America." *Rittenhouse* 7 (1992): 9–15.

Chadwick, W.J. *The Magic Lantern Manual.* London: [N.p.], 1878.

Warner, Deborah J. "Projection Apparatus for Science in Antebellum America." *Rittenhouse* 6 (1992): 87–94.

Wright, Lewis. *Optical Projection: A Treatise on the Use of the Lantern in Exhibition and Scientific Demonstration.* London: [N.p.], 1891.

Magnetic Resonance Imaging

Magnetic resonance imaging (MRI, or MR, or nuclear magnetic resonance imaging) is a technique for noninvasively producing images of cross-sections of human anatomy at very high resolution (~1 mm). In an MR scanner, a patient is placed in a magnetic coil and radio-frequency waves are used to excite protons (hydrogen nuclei) that in turn give off energy that can be detected and used to produce a detailed map of tissue characteristics. Unlike **computer tomogra-**

John Mallard with his prototype MRI device, Aberdeen, 1970s. Courtesy of John Mallard.

phy scanners, which image tissue density, MR can discriminate specific biochemical properties of tissues, including water content, blood flow, organ contraction and relaxation, and pathologies such as cancer metastases. Also, where CT has difficulty imaging tissue surrounded by bone, MR ignores bone altogether and can image such tissue clearly. The disadvantages of MR include its extreme expense and its strong magnetic field, which prevents patients with pacemakers and other embedded ferromagnetic objects from being studied.

Principles

MR depends on three sets of scientific principles: nuclear magnetic resonance, gradient field separation, and computerized reconstruction. An MR scanner incorporates a magnet large enough to produce **nuclear magnetic resonance** effects. Giant permanent magnets (~125 tons), resistive (electro)magnets, and superconducting magnets have all been used, though superconducting magnets are the most common in the 1990s. These magnets are larger than a human and arranged on top of and below a hollow tube where the person lies.

Gradient field separation allows a specific area of the person to be studied. Gradient coils alter part of the magnetic field inside the MR scanner, isolating a particular slice so that the radio-frequency pulses activate only those nuclei within the slice. In advanced scanners, gradient coils may be arranged so as to isolate more than one slice at a time, to decrease the scanning time required. A radio-frequency transceiver produces the pulses and a radio-frequency receiver captures the resonant pulses. Three parameters (proton density, T1, and T2) can be selectively emphasized by different pulse programs produced by the transceiver. These programs are controlled by the MR operator.

Transforming the pulse information into a map of proton density or tissue contrast requires computer reconstruction. This is typically accomplished using a two-dimensional Fourier transform, as with CT. The resultant image reflects the parameters chosen; different T1/T2 weights emphasize different kinds of pathologies, such as metastases. Reading an MR image thus requires experience and knowledge of the different kinds of appearances of tissue under varied imaging conditions.

MR imaging can also be performed using contrast agents, paramagnetic and supermagnetic chemicals that function like tracers, allowing physiologic processes to be imaged (see **PET scanner**).

History

The principle of using nuclear magnetic resonance to measure different tissue properties was independently developed by two physics groups, one led by F. Bloch at Stanford, and the other by E. Purcell at Harvard. These two men won the Nobel Prize for physics in 1952 for this work. The idea of using NMR to identify and type cancerous tissue was developed by physician and biophysicist R. Damadian in 1970 and published in 1971. The application of NMR to imaging was invented in 1973 by the chemist P. Lauterbur, who realized that magnetic gradients could be used to isolate and study just one section of an object. Lauterbur's term "zeugmatography" was never taken up, however. Instead, **nuclear magnetic resonance** imaging was used up through the early 1980s, when "nuclear" was dropped because of its negative connotation of radioactivity.

By 1974, two groups in England, one at the University of Aberdeen (including J. Mallard, J. Hutchinson, and C. Gold), and one at Nottingham (including E. Andrew, P. Mansfield, and W. Hinshaw) were building bigger MR scanners. Hutchinson et al. published the first MR image of an animal, a dead mouse, and Hinshaw et al. improved image formation and greatly reduced scanning time. By 1976, commercial firms, especially EMI (which was producing the first CT scanners by then) were beginning to investigate MR. Damadian et al. published the first image of a live animal, a mouse abdomen in 1976.

Competition was intense between the groups. Hinshaw et al. published surpassingly good images of a human wrist in 1977, and Damadian et al. built the first MR scanner for humans. By 1981, commercial interests had taken over MR development. Damadian formed his own company, FONAR, and installed four prototype "QED80" scanners in the United States, Japan, Mexico, and Italy. EMI's "Neptune" scanner was installed in Hammersmith Hospital with the assistance of the British DHSS. Phillips had a whole-body prototype, and the Aberdeen group had an alliance with the Japanese firm Asahi and had formed their own British company, M&D Technology. General Electric, Technicare, and Picker were also active. By 1982, twenty firms had invested in MR imaging and fifteen MR scanners had been installed. In 1983, L. Kaufman and L. Crooks at the University of California at San Francisco produced the first multislice MR. That same year, V. Runge et al. suggested the use of paramagnetic contrast agents for MR, greatly expanding the repertoire of uses of the device.

In the United States, FDA medical device approval retarded MR growth until 1984, when it began to approve MR scanners for clinical use in hospitals and the Health Care Finance Administration began allowing Medicare and Medicaid to cover MR procedures. Installation of MR in hospitals required significant capital and structural investment. In addition to liquid helium to cool the superconducting magnets, magnetic shielding had to be developed, and, often, separate buildings had to be built to isolate the side effects of the large magnets. The cost of purchasing and installing a scanner (~$3 million) and the consequent cost per scan (~$1,200–$3,000) focused attention onto the relative value of diagnostic imaging (including CT and PET), as well as onto issues of democratic access to such expensive technology.

Joseph Dumit

Bibliography

Andrew, E.R. "A Historical Review of NMR and Its Clinical Applications." *British Medical Bulletin* 40 (1984): 115–19.

Blume, S. *Insight and Industry: On the Dynamics of Technological Change in Medicine.* Cambridge: M.I.T Press, 1992.

Damadian, R. "Tumor Detection by Nuclear Magnetic Resonance," *Science* 117 (1971): 1151–53.

Eisenberg, R.L. *Radiology: An Illustrated History.* St. Louis, Mo.: Mosby Year Book, 1992.

Lauterbur, P.C. "Image Formation by Induced Local Interactions: Examples Employing Nuclear Magnetic Resonance." *Nature* 242 (1973): 190–91.

Magnetometer

Magnetometers measure the intensity of the earth's magnetic forces, and sometimes magnetic declination as well. They developed from the magnetic **compass**, emerged in the late eighteenth century from a complex of innovative instrumental designs related to experiments using thread-suspensions, and were first used extensively in the nineteenth century.

By 1723 the London clock-maker George Graham had measured the intensity of the earth's magnetism by observing the oscillations of a **dip circle**. Frederick Mallet used an oscillating magnetic compass needle of the typical pivoted design to measure the horizontal intensity in 1769.

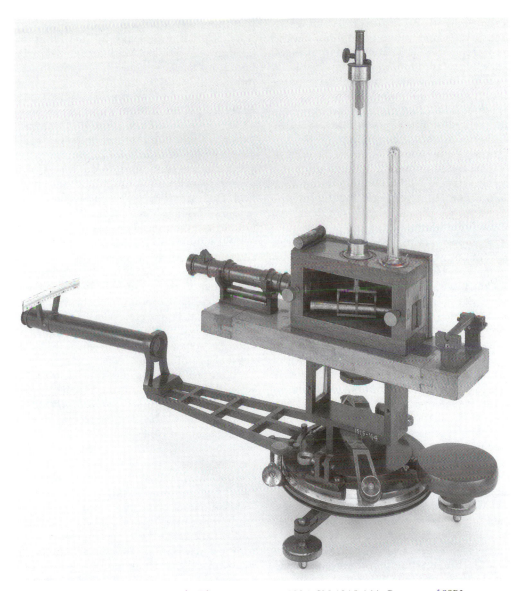

Kew pattern unifilar magnetometer by Thomas Jones, ca. 1836. SM 1915-144. Courtesy of SSPL.

The friction of pivoted needles, however, hindered intensity measurement. The fiber-suspension was much more suitable. Charles Coulomb constructed a magnetic compass in 1776 in which the needle was suspended on a fiber; his instrument might have been made by Étienne Lenoir in Paris.

As scientists such as Coulomb and Alexander von Humboldt became interested in terrestrial magnetism, more attention was devoted to this new breed of magnetic instrument. The Norwegian Christopher Hansteen in the years following 1810 was especially active in improving the design of an instrument for measuring magnetic intensity. He called it a magnetometer (perhaps the first use of this word). He also standardized the technique, taking the time required for three hundred oscillations of a suspended needle as the measurement of the earth's magnetic intensity at a given location.

Hansteen ordered his magnetic needle from London instrument-maker George Dollond, and soon Dollond was marketing variants of Hansteen's instrument. Another prominent instrument-maker who included magnetometers in his repertoire was Henri-Prudence Gambey in Paris. He combined the intensity function of the suspended needle design with reading **microscopes** in some cases and with a transit **telescope** in others, to allow precise measurement of declination and its changes. These were called by various names: variation transits, declinometers, and declination compasses. They all had several functions.

A dramatic change in magnetometer design and procedure was effected in the 1830s by Carl-Friedrich Gauss and Wilhelm Weber. Until then, all measurements of geomagnetic intensity depended on oscillations of a magnetic needle, either in a **dip circle** (for total intensity) or in a Hansteenian magnetometer (for horizontal intensity). The intensity at, say, Paris, was known only relative to the value at some other place, in terms of the comparative number of oscillations performed by the same needle in both places. Humboldt had assumed a value of 1.0 at a place in Peru on the magnetic equator, where he thought the total intensity was maximum. As one traveled toward the earth's poles, the intensity decreased, as shown by the increased period of a needle's oscillations.

Gauss and Weber proposed a system of "absolute" measurement, in which they were able to determine the value of the magnetic intensity in units of mass, distance, and time. This involved oscillations as before, plus a second step. The needle used in oscillations was then used to deflect a compass needle. By combining equations derived from these two measurements, Gauss and Weber obtained their "absolute" result.

Gauss and Weber also introduced a new kind of magnetometer, the bifilar or two-fiber magnetometer. The magnetic needle (actually a heavy bar) was held approximately perpendicularly to the normal direction of a magnetic compass by twisting the two fibers. As the horizontal intensity varied, this was indicated directly by a change in position of the bar. The bifilar magnetometer was sometimes called a variometer.

Another instrument was designed by Humphrey Lloyd in the early 1840s to indicate changes in the vertical intensity of the earth's magnetism. Basically a balanced dip needle, it was called Lloyd's balance, balance magnetometer, or a vertical force magnetometer. Descendants of this instrument and of the bifilar magnetometer were incorporated in the late 1840s into the first photographically self-registering magnetographs, which became the staples of geomagnetic observatories until about World War II. The best of these instruments and of

portable magnetometers were designed by Adolf Schmidt in Germany, by the staff of the Carnegie Institution of Washington, and by D. Lacour in Denmark in the early twentieth century.

The period of classical instrumentation ended around World War II with the application of electronics to instrumentation. The first breakthrough was the saturable-core or fluxgate magnetometer. The core of these magnetometers has a high magnetic permeability, which allows them to detect small variations in the geomagnetic field. These were first used for detection of submarines and for airborne magnetic surveys. The proton precession magnetometer was developed in the 1950s. Here a current flowing through a coil wrapped around a container of a material rich in protons, such as water, sets the protons precessing. With the current interrupted, the precession is proportional to the ambient geomagnetic field. Proton precession magnetometers have been used to map the magnetic striping of the ocean floor as well as the magnetic field high above the earth's surface.

One last magnetometer that has been developed since the 1960s is the **SQUID** (Superconducting QUantum Interference Device). Because it must be used at the temperature of liquid helium, it is best suited for laboratory work, not in the field.

Very little historical investigation has focused on any period of magnetometer development. The extensive literature and relatively good collections of old instruments would certainly repay many historians' efforts. Questions of the relations of instrument-makers with researchers, of the development of the instrument-making trade, and of the roles of scientists in instrument development are possible topics.

Gregory A. Good

Bibliography

Forbes, A.J. "General Instrumentation." In *Geomagnetism,* edited by J.A. Jacobs, Vol. 1, 51–142. London: Academic, 1987.

McConnell, Anita. *Geomagnetic Instruments before 1900, an Account of Their Construction and Use.* London: Harriet Wynter, 1980.

Multhauf, Robert P., and Gregory A. Good. *A Brief History of Geomagnetism and A Catalog of the Collections of the National Museum of American History.*

Smithsonian Studies in History and Technology 48. Washington, D.C. Smithsonian Institution Press, 1987.

Parkinson, W.D. "Geomagnetic Instruments." In *Sciences of the Earth: An Encyclopedia of Events, People, and Phenomena,* edited by Gregory A. Good. New York: Garland, 1997.

Smith, Julian. "Precursors to Peregrinus: The Early History of Magnetism and the Mariner's Compass in Europe." *Journal of Medieval History* 18 (1992): 21–74.

Mariner's Astrolabe

See ASTROLABE, MARINER'S

Mass Spectrometer

See SPECTROMETER, MASS

Mechanical Equivalent of Heat Apparatus

The determination of the mechanical equivalent of heat should demonstrate the existence and the value of a constant relationship between heat and mechanical work, the most important quantitative link needed to construct the concept of energy in general and of energy conservation in particular. Historians of science have described the experimental determination of this work equivalent as a major episode, lasting from the 1830s until the concept of conservation of energy was developed in the 1850s. But experiments to determine and redetermine this conversion factor occurred throughout the nineteenth century.

The most prominent example is James Joule's paddlewheel experiment, conducted during the years 1843–1849 and repeated in an extended version in 1875–1877. After having measured the heating effect of electric currents (the so-called indirect method), Joule decided to determine the mechanical value of heat by measuring the heat developed through the friction of water (the so-called direct method). His apparatus consisted of a copper vessel filled with water and a brass paddlewheel that stirred the liquid when driven by falling weights. Joule found that when a weight of about 57 pounds descends through a space of 105 feet, the temperature of the water in this copper vessel is raised half a degree Fahrenheit. He then calculated the ratio of the work done and the temperature difference to be 722.69, and he called

this result the mechanical equivalent of heat, later named Joule's equivalent, J.

The only surviving part of Joule's original experimental setup is the paddlewheel device, now displayed in the Science Museum, London. One replica, examined by Joule himself, was sent in 1958 to the National Physics Laboratory in New Dehli, India. The Manchester Museum of Science and Industry has a few relics and a replica of the paddlewheel. The physics department of the Carl von Ossietzky University, Oldenburg, Germany, has a replica of the complete experimental setup.

By reworking Joule's experiment, a deeper understanding of the process has been gained. For example, a replica based on the design of the paddlewheel shown in Joule's 1850 publication did not provide sufficient resistance to counterbalance the mechanical force of the falling weights. Only a second replica, based on the device in the Science Museum, allowed a mechanical performance like that described in the publication. But the size of the working handle, which is proportional to the size of the other parts of this device, is insufficient to work with. Joule could have used this particular setup as a demonstration device only. Furthermore, in order to perform the experiment, even when using a longer handle, the mechanical work must have been done by a second, physically well-trained person who was able to wind up the weights in the short time available without increasing the room temperature through sweating.

Thermometry is also important in this experiment. Although Joule's **thermometers** were destroyed, we were able to get a quite good understanding of the quality of his instrument. From the Manchester instrument-maker Benjamin Dancer, Joule had obtained a traveling **microscope**. This low-power microscope moved on an axis horizontally by rotating a screw. The distance of travel could be determined from a graduated disk at one end of the screw. Joule placed a glass tube underneath the microscope, introduced a 1-in. column of mercury into the narrow bore of the tube, and marked the distance between the two endpoints of the drop. By moving the drop so that one of its ends is at one of the previous points, a second measure could be taken. In each position the probably varying length of the column could be ascertained to 1/4,000th of an inch. If the bore is of constant diameter, successive distances will also be constant. The bore of Joule's thermometer was conical and gradually diminishing in diam-

Replica of Joule's paddlewheel apparatus, made by the Research Group on Higher Education and History of Science, Carl von Ossietsky University, Germany. Courtesy of the Whipple Museum of the History of Science, Cambridge.

eter. The mean cross-sections near the two ends of the tube differ by about 20 percent. This process of checking the bore helped in selecting the best quality of glass tubes and it enabled Joule to "calibrate the thermometer by the graduation itself." In dividing the scale, Joule decided to make allowance for the variations in the tube's capacity. The process described above enabled him to identify the varying length of the mercury column. Afterwards, these different distances were each graduated into fifty divisions. This method gave Joule an arbitrary scale, but a most sensitive thermometer.

Complex skills were also needed to perform the experiment with sufficient accuracy. In order to prevent disturbing temperature fluctuations, the experiment could not be performed in public, nor could Joule invite his (heat-radiating) colleagues to witness the performance in the brewer's cellar. In the brewing culture, Joule acquired the thermometrical skills necessary for his heat measurements, as well as other material and human resources.

Apart from Joule's own attempts, a fundamental redetermination of the mechanical equivalent of heat was performed by Henry A. Rowland at the new physics laboratory at Johns Hopkins University in Baltimore during the years 1876–1879. Rowland's apparatus is now in the National Museum of American History in Washington, D.C. Rowland applied advanced engineering technologies to improve previous measurements and to give a value of the mechanical equivalent of heat in absolute units. His research on air thermometers became the premise for solving the conflict about a proper value for the mechanical equivalent of heat.

Since the 1860s, the measurement of the mechanical equivalent of heat has appeared in many physics courses. In 1876 J. Puluj announced a tabletop apparatus that was later distributed through the German firm of E. Leybold's Nachfolger. In 1884, the Cambridge Scientific Instrument Co. (CSI) successively sold apparatus devised by C.V. Boys and G.F.C. Searle, a demonstrator of experimental physics at the Cavendish Laboratory at the University of Cambridge. The latter device is similar to Puluj's (now held in the Cavendish Laboratory archive) and was distributed through the CSI in 1902. In 1904 CSI offered an advanced apparatus designed by Professor H.L. Callendar, announcing that for the expense of £12/10/0 the lecturer could "obtain a value of 'J' correct to $1/2$ per cent. in about 10 minutes, in the presence of a class of students." Equipment designed on the basis of Joule's paddlewheel device was suggested by C. Christiansen at the University of Copenhagen and manufactured in Erlangen, Germany. Around 1900, the scientific instrument firm Max Kohl from Chemnitz even offered a complete replica of Joule's paddlewheel experiment. Apparatus employing the indirect method—that is, the determination of heat produced by means of an electric current—were equally popular but still required an agreement about the exact relation between mechanical and electrical units.

H. Otto Sibum

Bibliography

Joule, James Prescott. "On the Mechanical Equivalent of Heat." *Philosophical Transactions of the Royal Society of London, 140* (1850) 61–82; "New Determination of the Mechanical Equivalent of Heat." *Philosophical Transactions of the Royal Society of London,* 169 (1879): 365–83. Reprinted in *The Scientific Papers of James Prescott Joule,* 298–328, 632–57. 2 vols. London: Taylor and Francis, 1884.

Puluj, J. "Ueber einen Schulapparat zur Bestimmung des mechanischen Wärmeaequivalents." *Annalen der Physik und Chemie* 17 (1876): 437–46; and "Beitrag zur Bestimmung des mechanischen Wärmea-

equivalents." *Annalen der Physik und Chemie* 17 (1876): 649–56.

Rowland, Henry A. "On the Mechanical Equivalent of Heat, with Subsidary Researches on the Variation of the Mercurial from the Air Thermometer, and on the Variation of the Specific Heat of Water." *Proceedings of the American Academy of Arts and Sciences* 15 (1880): 75–200.

Schuster, Arthur. "On the Scale-Value of the Late Dr. Joule's Thermometers." *Philosophical Magazine* 39 (1895): 477–501.

Sibum, Heinz Otto. "Reworking the Mechanical Value of Heat: Instruments of Precision and Gestures of Accuracy in Early Victorian England." *Studies in History and Philosophy of Science* 26 (1995): 73–106.

Mechanical Gauge

See GAUGE, MECHANICAL

Melting Point Apparatus

A melting point apparatus measures the melting points of solid compounds, especially crystalline organic compounds. Before the introduction of spectroscopic and similar methods of characterizing organic compounds, melting points were the only definite way to physically characterize solid organic compounds. Consequently, liquid compounds (for example, ketones) would be converted into crystalline derivatives (such as dinitrophenylhydrazones) with well-defined and known melting points. The identity of a compound could be confirmed by the lack of any depression of the melting point when mixed with a known sample of the compound. Melting points are also sensitive indicators of the purity of organic compounds, as impure compounds have a depressed melting point. Two temperatures are noted: the point at which the first drop of liquid is formed, and the point at which the solid mass becomes a clear liquid.

The use of melting points to characterize organic compounds and their purity was introduced by Michael Chevreul during his study of fatty acids in the 1810s. The thin capillary tube closed at one end, still used today, was employed by Robert Bunsen in the 1830s. Samuel P. Mulliken at the Massachusetts Institute of Technology published extensive tables of melting points in his *Methods for the Identification of Pure Organic Compounds* (1899–1904).

Frederick A. Mason's melting point apparatus, by Gallenkamp, 1929. A. Gallenkamp & Co. Ltd. Catalogue of Chemical and Industrial Laboratory Apparatus. *London: 1929: 620. Courtesy of Fisher Scientific UK Ltd.*

The most common melting point apparatus was a small heated beaker half filled with concentrated sulfuric acid (glycerin and mineral oil were also used) in which was suspended a **thermometer** and a capillary tube held together by a thin rubber band. The observation of the melting point could be improved by using a magnifying glass. Somewhat safer apparatus, which enclosed the sulfuric acid, was introduced by such chemists as Richard Anschütz and E.A. Schluze (1877), Carl Franz Roth (1886), and Frederick William Streatfeild. Several improvements were made to the melting point tube, especially the b-shaped tube introduced by Johannes Thiele (by 1907). However, these changes were not widely used.

The most radical change to the melting point apparatus was the electrically heated metal block introduced in the 1920s. F.A. Mason patented a version in 1924 that was marketed by Gallenkamp. The now familiar apparatus with a metal heating block and a magnifying glass incorporated into one piece of equipment appeared in the early 1960s and, finally, displaced the sulfuric acid bath. For more sophisticated work, the heated **microscope** stage has been used since World War II. An entirely new approach was developed by Laureate Instruments in 1989–1991. Here a powdered sample of the compounds is put on a simple hot plate; a complete melting point curve is obtained within 3 minutes and stored on computer.

Peter Morris

Bibliography

Price, T. Slater, and Douglas F. Twiss. *A Course in Practical Chemistry.* 3rd ed. London: Longman, Green, 1922.

Meteorograph

A meteorograph is a composite self-registering meteorological instrument. It was developed to automatize the periodic and tedious task of reading and transcribing the indications from different devices. Furthermore, its charts enable one to immediately compare diagrams of different meteorological parameters. A meteorograph that records only atmospheric pressure and temperature is called a barothermograph.

The first true meteorograph was probably the "weather clock" proposed by Christopher Wren around 1650, later modified by Wren himself, and largely improved by Robert Hooke. Several meteorological recording instruments were proposed during the eighteenth century, but few attempts were made to combine them into a meteorograph. In the nineteenth century, as the systematic and generalized recording of weather parameters became necessary for science and navigation, many meteorological observatories were founded, and an increasing number of systematic weather reports were published. Many earlier ideas were developed, and several scientists, inventors, and instrument-makers conceived and realized complex meteorographs.

At London's Great Exhibition of 1851, George Dollond presented a purely mechanical meteorograph that could register eight different weather parameters, even including atmospheric electricity. Around 1843 Charles Wheatstone had suggested the use of electricity in meteorological instruments. After about 1850, electromechanical equipment (sometimes borrowed from telegraphic technology) was often employed in order to overcome friction, and also to make possible the installation of external sensors such as windmills and wind vanes far away from the recording instruments.

At the Paris Exposition of 1867, several meteorographs were shown by Matthäus Hipp and by Hasler & Escher of Switzerland, by Jules Salleron of France, and others. Axel G. Theorell of Sweden, who exhibited an electromechanical meteorograph, later improved this instrument by adding a remarkable printing mechanism that recorded the results in figures. But the most impressive meteorograph presented in Paris was the one developed by the Italian Jesuit Angelo Secchi. This huge apparatus (1.5 meters long x 0.6 meter deep x 2.7 meters high) included a balance **barometer**, a metallic **thermometer**, an electric wind vane and cup-**anemometer**, an electric psychrometer, and a special pluviometer

for recording the time and the amount of rainfall. The parameters were recorded by twelve pens on two clockwork-driven boards. Secchi's instrument was extremely expensive (18,000 French francs) and only a few were made.

Other meteorographs were introduced by Paul Schreiber, Peter Stevenson, and George W. Hough. But these large and complex instruments were expensive, and they were generally installed only in important observatories.

The era of the large meteorograph came to a sudden end in the early 1880s when the French instrument-maker Jules Richard and his brother introduced a series of simple, portable, and very efficient recording meteorological instruments. These instruments, made and marketed by Richard Frères, employed a compact and lightweight system of levers which, activated by sensors (aneroid barometer, Bourdon-tube thermometer, **hygrometer**, and so forth), inscribed a graph on a small revolving drum with a clockwork mechanism. Made with interchangeable parts, they were much less expensive (only a few hundreds francs) than the previous meteorographs, and thousands were sold. Many other important instrument-makers copied Richard Frères instruments, and sometimes improved them.

From the late nineteenth century, very light and simple meteorographs (often made of aluminum) were carried by kites, by captive and sounding balloons, and later by aircraft. After World War I, these instruments were gradually replaced by **radiosondes**, which transmitted meteorological information via electromagnetic signals. But the Richard-type recording apparatus is still widely used today, not only in meteorology but also for recording indoor humidity, pressure, or temperature wherever those parameters must be regularly kept under control.

Paolo Brenni

Bibliography

Brenni, Paolo. "Il meteorografo di Padre Angelo Secchi." *Nuncius* 1 (1993): 197–247.

Middleton, W.E. Knowles. *Invention of the Meteorological Instruments,* 245–63. Baltimore: Johns Hopkins Press, 1969.

Multhauf, Robert P. "The Introduction of Self-Registering Meteorological Instruments." *Contributions from the Museum of History and Technology.* United States National Museum Bulletin 228, paper 23. Washington, D.C.: Smithsonian Institution Press, 1961.

Secchi's large meteorograph, originally presented at the Paris Exposition, 1867. It could automatically record seven different weather parameters. Courtesy of the Osservatorio Astronomico e Copernicano di Roma.

Radau, Rodolph. "Die Meteorographische Apparate, Mitteilungen über auf der Pariser Austellung Befindlichen Physikalischen, Mathematischen and Astronomischen Instrumente una Apparate." *Carl's Repertorium für physikalische Technik* 3 (1867): 281–362.

Microdensitometer

A microdensitometer measures the optical density of micro-images on photographic plates, film, and other transparencies and, where required, the distances between images or any parts of them. The conventional applications of these instruments were in astronomical and metallurgical emission spectroscopy. Since the variations in image density between measuring points are usually very rapid, the optical density of an exceedingly small area of the plate must be measured.

The first microdensitometer was described by the German J. Hartmann in 1899. This was a double-beam system, employing two **microscopes** with a common eyepiece and a Lummer-Brodhun cube. One microscope was for measuring the image, and the other for the comparison beam. The plate was covered with a diaphragm with a very small aperture, and a neutral wedge was moved until photometric balance was obtained. A precision stage enabled any part of the plate to be brought into the center of the field of the microscope in the measuring beam.

In 1915, the Frenchmen C. Fabry and H. Buisson described another type of double-beam microdensitometer, again employing a neutral wedge. Since no microscopes were used, it was not possible to examine areas of the plate as small as could be viewed in the Hartmann instrument.

Even the early instruments used neutral wedges made from glass dyed with fine carbon particles. The wedge performed the conversion from transmission to density values, which are more convenient for handling because they are linear. E. Goldberg, head of the first department of scientific photography in the world, at the Technical University, Dresden, produced neutral, or grey wedges, by casting dyed gelatine in metal molds in 1910.

The early instruments were visual. Later instruments used photodetectors—that is, photoemissive or photovoltaic cells, and in some instances **thermopiles**. The image of the source filament was focused on the plate. A micro-

scope close to the plate formed a magnified image on a diaphragm with a small, variable opening. Magnifications of up to 50x were usually sufficient to obtain the required resolution. In its simplest form, the photodetector was placed behind the diaphragm. The measurements were again calibrated by a neutral wedge.

A more sophisticated double-beam system was described by the Englishman G.M.B. Dobson and others in 1923. In this design, the photodetector was illuminated alternately by light transmitted through the plate and the neutral wedge.

The instruments so far described required the balancing of the wedge and the recording and plotting of the optical densities at every point of a spectrum line by hand, a laborious procedure. The first recording microdensitometer was described by the German P.P. Koch in 1912. Although the recording media available at the time were not very convenient, this development marked a considerable step forward. Many types of microdensitometers were then developed, both in laboratories and commercially, using the increasingly more sensitive photodetectors and recording devices that had become available.

Peter B.M. Walker, working at the Biophysics Research Unit of the Medical Research Council, King's College, London, described a much faster and more convenient recording microdensitometer in 1951, originally developed for measuring the absorption of stained and living biological cells. While using a conventional double-beam system with a neutral wedge, this instrument incorporated a number of novel features. The wedge, which was coupled to the recording pen, was driven into photometric balance by means of a very fast servo system. The table carrying the photographic plate or film was rigidly coupled by a fixed but variable-ratio arm, thus eliminating previous problems in obtaining a precise gearing between sample and recording. To ensure the accurate recording of maxima even at high recording speeds, a second servo system permitted optimum plate advance, so that for minimum rate of rise of optical density the advance was maximum, and for maximum rate, minimum. The response of the system was extremely fast—that is, 0.5 second for full-scale deflection of the recording pen—yet the reproducibility of pen deflections and positions was better than 0.5 percent. The use of a photomultiplier provided high sensitivity, making possible the measurement of optical densities to 6D. Magnifica-

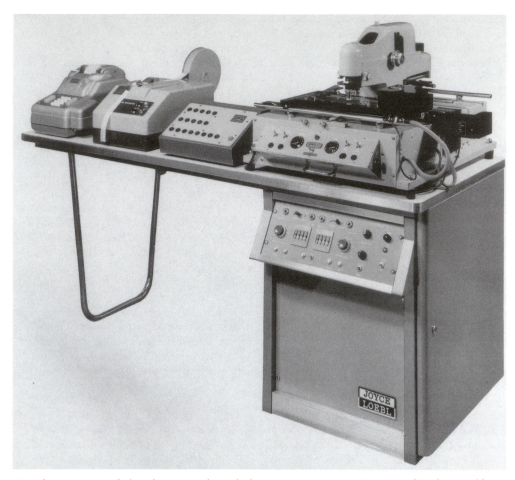

Microdensitometer with digital printer and punched-tape output, ca. 1955. Courtesy of Herbert Loebl.

tions of the image projected onto the diaphragm plane from 4x to 80x were provided. The effective diaphragm was variable from 6 x 1 mm down to 50 x 1 µm.

The instrument was manufactured and marketed from 1955 by the Joyce Loebl Co. of Gateshead, England. Continuous developments of the instrument included punched-tape output and, eventually, integral microcomputers for manipulating the readings, including the integration of the areas under Gaussian and other types of curves, with baseline correction, measurements between maxima, and so on. The step resolution was variable from 0.5 to 12.5 µm in the X axis and 5 µ in the Y axis. The slewing rate was 400 to 1,500 steps/second, depending on step size selected. Facilities for microreflectance measurements were added later.

More than two thousand instruments were produced. At the same time, Joyce Loebl developed the production of neutral wedges of great linear accuracy from grey glass, with density ranges of 0.5D to approximately 6D.

The instrument was well received by spectroscopists and early molecular biologists for the evaluation of x-ray diffraction patterns and Debye Scherrer diagrams. The availability of a convenient and fast-recording microdensitometer for ever-improving photographic plates and film, and, indeed, for other types of transparencies, encouraged the development of novel scientific methods in many fields, including ultrahigh temperature measurement by line broadening (in fusion research), lunar mapping, quantitative radiography in the structural analysis of wood, weight determination of organic molecules from photographs of **ultracentrifuge** separations, mineral content and metacarpal density of bone (by an x-ray method), interference microscopy, quantitative microautoradiography, shockwave phenomena, absorption spectroscopy, emulsion research, lens testing, and cytology.

There are applications in which the tracing of lines of equal density yields information not obtainable by any other means. An instrument for this purpose was described in 1950 by the Australian H.W. Babcock, who called it a Contouring Microphotometer, although such instruments are now more generally called Isophotometers, or more correctly, Isodensitometers. An attachment to the Walker-Joyce Loebl Recording Microdensitometer for this purpose was developed by Technical Operations, Inc., of Burlington, Massachusetts, in the 1960s. Apart from astronomy, particularly heliography, a number of specialized applications attracted attention in the scientific and general press. These included the location of a Surveyor space probe lost in moon dust after conventional methods available to astronomers had failed, the overturning of a verdict of murder, and the attempt to devise methods of designing concert halls by a photographic analog of acoustic principles.

Herbert Loebl

Bibliography

Dobson, G.M.B. "A Flicker Type of Photo-Electric Photometer Giving High Precision," *Proceedings of the Royal Society of London* Series A 104 (1923): 248–51.

Fabry, C., and H. Buisson. "Description et emploi d'un nouveau microphotometre," *Journal de physique* 8 (1919): 37–46.

Hartmann, J. "Apparat und Methode zu photographischen Messung von Flächenhelligkeiten," *Zeitschrift für Instrumentenkunde* 19 (1899): 97–103.

Koch, P.P. "Über die Messung der Schwärzung photographischer Platten in sehr schmalen Bereichen," *Annalen der Physik* 38 (1912): 507–22.

Walker, Peter M.B. "A High Speed Recording Microdensitometer Suitable for Cytological Research," *Experimental Cell Research* 8 (1955): 567–71.

Micromanipulator

A mechanical device for holding and maneuvering extremely small tools used within the field of a **microscope**. Micromanipulators use wedges, gears, hydraulic drives and other means to translate the movements of the operator's hands into the tiny movements necessary for operating such instruments as micropipettes, microneedles, microelectrodes, and micromagnets. Movement along the three spatial coordinates may be supplemented by revolving and tilting to increase flexibility of operation.

Features of micromanipulators vary according to the type of work to be accomplished. Instruments capable of three simple rack-and-pinion motions, for example, are suitable for operations requiring low magnification of up to 200 diameters. Instruments for use at higher magnification require greater sensitivity. They usually offer coarse initial positioning and separate fine controls. Manually controlled micromanipulators of great precision permit positioning in 5-μm increments. Some motorized models offer positioning in 1-μm increments. Most micromanipulators are solidly built to minimize vibration, and many utilize remote controls to further eliminate transmission of vibrations in the user's hand to the microtools.

More than two dozen commercial companies make micromanipulators. Some of the best known are the Leitz lever-activated instrument, the Zeiss sliding micromanipulator, the pneumatic De Frönbrune instrument, and the thermal expansion B-D-H, made by the American Optical Co. Prices vary from less than $1,000 to more than $12,000 according to an instrument's sensitivity to movement and precision of control.

Micromanipulators developed as accessory instruments to the compound microscope, which underwent rapid and significant improvement between 1830 and 1880. Mid-nineteenth-century microscopists were primarily interested in biological and medical research, hence the tools they developed to exploit their instruments were designed to prepare biological specimens and to facilitate dissection and manipulation. These included **microtomes** for cutting thin sections of biological materials, microtools for performing operations in the microscopic field, and, as an obvious necessity, micromanipulators for maneuvering the microtools. In 1859, Henry D. Schmidt, a histologist trained at the University of Pennsylvania, developed the first micromanipulator. Schmidt used his instrument to guide a microinjector, which he had also developed, to resolve the question of the termination of the bile ducts of the liver and their origins in the intercellular capillaries. His micromanipulator used clamps to hold the specimen and the dissecting tools; screws attached to the clamps provided maneuverability.

Schmidt's instrument and other early micromanipulators were operated in the space between the specimen and the microscope objective. This

M

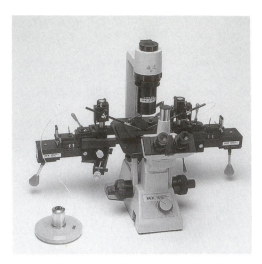

Micromanipulator used for in vitro fertilization, by Research Instruments, 1995. SM 1995–732. Courtesy of SSPL.

ipulators are used to mount individual crystals for research. Artists, archaeologists, museum curators, and forensic experts use micromanipulation to examine textile fibers, pigments, and paints for purposes important to each discipline. Entomologists use the instruments for work as varied as neurological research on insects and artificial insemination of queen honeybees for controlled breeding and inheritance experiments.

Victoria A. Harden

Bibliography

Barber, Marshall A. "A New Method of Isolating Micro-organisms." *Journal of the Kansas Medical Society* 4 (1904): 489–94.

Bracegirdle, Brian. *A History of Microtechnique: The Evolution of the Microtome and the Development of Tissue Preparation.* London: Heinemann Educational, 1978.

El-Badry, Hamed M. *Micromanipulators and Micromanipulation.* New York: Academic, 1963.

Schmidt, H.D. "On the Minute Structure of the Hepatic Lobules." *American Journal of the Medical Sciences* 37 (1859): 13–40.

Serafin, Donald. "Microsurgery: Past, Present, and Future." *Plastic and Reconstructive Surgery* 66 (1980): 781–85.

limited their use to microscopes with low-power objectives. In 1904, Marshall Barber at the University of Kansas introduced a micropipette and a micromanipulation method that permitted isolation of a single microscopic organism in a drop hanging from the undersurface of a cover slip. Because the microtools were manipulated below the cover slip, this device permitted the investigator to use microscopes with high-power, oil-immersed objectives.

By the 1920s, improvements in micromanipulators made microsurgery possible. In 1921, the Swedish physician Carl Olof Nylèn operated on the tiny structures of the middle ear using magnification and a micromanipulator. Reattachment of severed limbs followed, but limitations in knowledge about immunology inhibited the application of microsurgical techniques to tissue and organ transplantation until the 1970s. In the 1980s, micromanipulation techniques became essential to assisted fertility strategies such as in vitro fertilization and implantation of fertilized embryos. They have also become important in manipulation of cell nuclei and chromosomes in recombinant DNA research and gene therapy.

Although best known in biological research, micromanipulators have become indispensable in other fields as well. Preparation of microgram and nanogram samples for chemical analysis is accomplished by micromanipulative methods. A micromanipulator-guided micropipette makes possible the identification of airborne particulate matter. In **x-ray** diffraction studies, microman-

Micrometer

Micrometers can measure small objects, separations, or subdivisions of linear and angular scales, and have been widely used by machinists as well as by astronomers and microscopists. Filar micrometers incorporate one or two screw-driven fiducials, which are commonly stringers from spiders' webs or drawn silver. Machinists' tools such as bench micrometers and **comparators** are simpler, with the latter reaching a high level of precision by around 1860. Heliometers, placed in front of a **telescope**, consist of two halves of a lens or mirror moved relative to each other by screws. Ocular micrometers, placed in an eyepiece, often have fine lines scratched on transparent material. Beginning in the 1970s, micrometer dials and verniers have been replaced by magnetic or optical encoders connected to **computers**.

The first micrometer was devised by Lucas Brunn and made by Christof Treschler, Sr. (ca. 1609). This innovative device, which relied on the number and fraction of turns of a screw, was destroyed in Dresden around 1945. Other craftsmen followed Treschler's lead, and, from the late 1620s, made micrometers for practical purposes.

Although the English astronomer William Gascoigne inserted a micrometer into the path of a telescope (1638–1639), micrometers were not regularly or widely applied to scientific studies until Adrien Azout drew attention to their usefulness to the Académie Royale des Sciences (1665). Innovations were soon made by Johannes Hevelius, Richard Townley (who had acquired and made a modified version of Gascoigne's micrometer), and Robert Hooke. John Flamsteed used Townley's device to measure solar and planetary diameters, and Abbé Picard, working at the Observatoire de Paris, used micrometers to measure diameters of the Sun and sunspots. Calibration of micrometers was by geometric means using a card with lines of known separation and observed at a measured distance (200 to 300 meters). Calibration errors of a few seconds of arc, due to the closeness of the card, were not recognized.

Ole Rømer made the first micrometer designed on mechanically sound principles (1672). It provided for screw backlash adjustment, allowed the fiducial hairs to be moved to different segments of the screw to average screw pitch errors, and had carefully machined, dove-tailed ways for the moving stage. The filar micrometer was successively improved by such eighteenth-century English makers as John Rowley, George Graham, John Bird, and Jesse Ramsden, and reached its nearly final form at the hands of Edward Troughton by 1810. George Merz, Johann Repsold, Thomas Grubb, and Warner & Swasey increased the complexity and size of micrometers, but the only real advances were the impersonal micrometer of Repsold (1893) and use of micrometers with **chronographs**.

Hevelius and Hooke applied micrometer screws to read astronomical **quadrant** scales in the 1660s. Abraham Sharp, working for Flamsteed at the Royal Observatory, more successfully applied screws to scale measurement, though not without discovering the problems. The scale micrometers designed by Louville (ca. 1714) influenced subsequent instrument-makers and astronomers' observational methods. Graham and Bird further perfected scale micrometers, and their quadrants were used for important astronomical discoveries (such as aberration and nutation). Success was partly

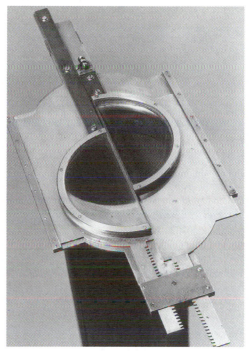

Object glass micrometer (heliometer) by John Dollond, used with James Short's thirty-six-inch telescope to observe the transit of Venus in 1769. SM 1900-136. Courtesy of SSPL.

due to the strategy employed: primary scale divisions (5°, 2¹/2°, or 1°) were divided with great care, with micrometers subdividing these small arcs. Ramsden's compact filar micrometers were successfully applied to surveying apparatus, and he was also responsible for fitting nautical **sextants** with drum micrometers (ca. 1783). Edward Troughton mounted several magnifying micrometers over scales of astronomical and surveying instruments from 1791 to average scale-division errors and to correct errors caused by eccentric circles or decentered axes of circular instruments. The Duc de Chaulnes had previously adopted this strategy using microscope micrometers to delineate the wheel of his 1768 dividing engine.

Heliometers were conceived by Servington Savery (1743) and Pierre Bouguer (1748) to measure solar diameters. Designs by James Short and John Dollond, popular in the 1750s, employed a bisected lens with each half mounted to slide along the cut by the rotation of a precision screw. Friedrich Bessel used a 6¹/4 in. Fraunhofer heliometer to measure the stellar parallax of the star system 61 Cygni (1838). This was the first direct confirmation of the Copernican view of the solar system—a critical observation that had eluded astronomers for three hundred years.

The most noteworthy ocular micrometers are by Georg Brander (ca. 1760) and Fraunhofer. James Watt made the first recognizable workshop "C-shaped" micrometer (see illustration for **gauge, mechanical**), as well as tachymeters with fiducial lines drawn on glass (1769). Related are Alfred Nobert's test plates made to calibrate filar micrometers mounted on **microscopes**; the finest, his "twenty band" plate, was made around 1873. Combining micrometer and microscope was first tried by Stephen Gray (1698) to measure the height of mercury in a **barometer** (see **cathetometer**). Benjamin Martin incorporated a micrometer in his drum microscopes from 1738. Most microscope micrometers were of the filar type and of similar design to astronomical micrometers but of lower precision.

Randall C. Brooks

Bibliography

Brooks, Randall C. "The Development of the Micrometer in the Seventeenth, Eighteenth, and Nineteenth Centuries." *Journal for the History of Astronomy* 22 (1991): 127–73.

Kiely, Edmond R. *Surveying Instruments, Their History and Classroom Use.* New York: Bureau of Publications, Teachers College, Columbia University, 1947.

McKeon, Robert M. "Les débuts de l'astronomie de précision." *Physis* 13 (1971): 225–88; 14 (1972): 221–42.

Microscope, Electron

An electron microscope produces a magnified image through a specimen's interaction with a beam of high energy electrons, usually 50–200 kilovolts. There are two principal forms of this instrument. In a transmission electron microscope (TEM), an electron beam at least as large as the imaged area passes through the specimen and forms an image on a fluorescent screen or photographic film. In a scanning electron microscope (SEM), an electron beam that is small compared with the imaged area passes over the specimen in a regular pattern, and a picture of the specimen surface is reconstructed on a video tube. Image contrast is formed in many ways. In the TEM, electrons are deflected by atoms inside the specimen, without absorption, creating a shadow pattern of greater and lesser electron transmission. In the SEM, interaction of the beam with the specimen surface produces varying intensities of backscattered and secondarily released electrons for each position in the scan, and these are registered by a detector placed appropriately near the specimen. Signals from x-rays, fluorescence, and other phenomena can also be utilized. All electron microscopes depend on the capacity of magnetic and electric fields to alter the path of electron beams according to the laws of optics; all include an electron gun, an evacuated column accommodating the linear beam path, magnetic lenses along the column's length, as well as pumps to maintain high vacuum and electronic components maintaining constant beam voltage and lens current. They are capable of much greater resolving power than a light microscope because of the shorter wavelength of electrons.

Early History

The electron microscope can be regarded as a natural outgrowth of cathode-ray technology, particularly the cathode-ray oscillograph (see **oscilloscope**). The theory and technique of this device, improved electronic tubes and vacuum technology, and the matter-wave theory of Louis de Broglie (implying that optical theory was applicable to electrons), all generated favorable conditions for the electron microscope's development around 1930. In 1928, Hans Busch showed that a circular coil affects electrons as a glass lens affects light; shortly thereafter, electrical engineers Max Knoll and Ernst Ruska began building a TEM in Berlin. By the mid 1930s numerous independent microscope projects had sprung up throughout North America and Europe. In 1937 Siemens engaged Ruska to build a commercial transmission microscope, which first reached market in late 1939. The Radio Corp. of America (RCA) similarly engaged Toronto physicist James Hillier to develop a commercial TEM, the first of which was delivered at the end of 1940. Though Siemens continued research and limited production into 1944, the impact of World War II on Europe effectively put RCA in the lead until the late 1950s with its popular postwar "Universal" microscope, or EMU, pictured on page 383. Despite wartime efforts to develop the SEM at labs associated with both RCA and Siemens, it was not until 1965 that one became commercially available, through the work of Charles Oatley,

Dr. James Hillier operating the EMU electron microscope, 1940s. Courtesy of the David Sarnoff Research Centre.

Dennis McMullan, and Ken Smith, at the University of Cambridge. Today's leading microscope producers include Hitachi, Philips, and Zeiss.

Life Science Applications

Although biomedical applications were anticipated in the 1930s, difficulties presented by biological specimens stymied early electron microscopists. The electron beam demands a vacuum, so specimens cannot be alive and require drying in some minimally destructive way. Since electrons interact strongly with matter, the beam penetrates only very thin specimens. Moreover, the beam heats specimens, and so can alter volatile biological materials. Contrast is another obstacle, since the different substances in living things vary little in opacity to electrons. Specimen preparation techniques to overcome these problems (ways to dry, slice thinly, preserve chemically, and enhance contrast) developed gradually.

Methods for biological electron microscopy were initially explored in Germany, America, and Belgium, but because of the war, the foundation for later developments was laid principally in the United States. RCA sponsored methodological research beginning in 1940, working with prominent biologists from institutions near RCA's New Jersey labs. In addition to the circle introduced by RCA to the instrument, there were also biologists at a handful of American universities with some access to an electron microscope during the war. Since sufficiently thin sections of tissues could not be cut, the earliest successful applications involved dispersed specimens such as viruses, bacteria, and shredded muscle fibers. Contrast was enhanced by staining with reactive metal solutions or evaporating thin metal films onto specimens.

In the later 1940s, ultramicrotome (that is, sectioning-apparatus) design developed rapidly, and with the introduction of plastic embedding material in 1949, study of cell and tissue structure with the TEM became feasible. Specimens are chemically fixed (typically, in osmium tetroxide), soaked with a solvent such as ethanol to replace water (that is, dehydrated), infiltrated with plastic resin, hardened, and finally sectioned for TEM imaging. The development of these techniques for cell biology in the 1950s is associated with contributions of Keith Porter and George Palade at New York's Rockefeller Institute, and of Fritiof Sjöstrand at Stockholm's Karolinska Institute. Since the later 1960s, methods involving rapid freezing have supplemented traditional chemical fixation. For the SEM, wet biological specimens are fixed and dehydrated as usual, dried under pressure above the solvent's critical point (thus eliminating surface tension forces), then metal coated to make surface features electron-dense and conductive. Alternatively, replicas of wet specimens may be used. Technique for biological specimen preparation remains an active research area.

Physical Science Applications

Many of the problems bedeviling biological microscopy are less serious for the specimens of interest to physicists, chemists, and metallurgists. It is often easy to prepare these in the form of films, thin enough to be traversed with negligible energy loss by electrons of 100–200 kilovolts. Conductive specimens can frequently be imaged by SEM without preparation. The effect of vacuum is usually slight, and contrast is generated naturally. During the war, the TEM found employment in rubber and plastic manufacture, and in metallurgy associated with ordnance and uranium-diffusion separators, among other projects.

With crystalline specimens, of great interest in metallurgical research, direct information can be obtained about crystal lattice defects and about the all-important interfaces in semiconductors. A major landmark was the observation by James Menter in 1956 of the lattice spacing in platinum phthalocyanine. The theoretical work of Peter Hirsch, Archie Howie, Michael Whelan, and Hatsujiro Hashimoto on the propagation of electron waves through crystals contributed vitally to interpreting these images. For crystalline materials, it is important that the TEM generate not only an image (individual atoms in the lattice can today be visualized), but also a diffraction pattern. Thus, detailed crystallographic information is rendered immediately accessible by arranging that the electrons fall on the specimen in a convergent rather than parallel beam. Many ingenious ways of exploiting diffraction data have been devised.

With amorphous specimens, the contrast mechanisms are similar to those associated with biological specimens, and the same problems can arise. Polymers, for example, may be damaged by the electron beam itself, and they remain one of the more difficult kinds of specimen to observe. As with biological specimens, it is sometimes more convenient to study a replica than the original: for instance, in 1966 Hermann Träuble and Uwe Essmann observed the magnetic field distribution in superconducting lead by evaporating iron onto the surface of the lead and studying the resulting pattern in the microscope. Differences between field patterns at different temperatures were thus recorded.

The newest instruments are capable of near-atomic resolution. They continue to provide information of fundamental interest in solid-state physics and great practical value in areas such as catalysts, semiconductors, and integrated circuit design.

Nicolas Rasmussen
Peter Hawkes

Bibliography

Hawkes, Peter, ed. "Beginnings of Electron Microscopy." *Advances in Electronics and Electron Physics* 16 (1985): Supplement.

Newberry, Sterling P. *EMSA and Its People: The First Fifty Years,* edited by Mary Schumacher. Milwaukee, Wisc.: Electron Microscopy Society of America, 1992.

Rasmussen, Nicolas. "Making a Machine Instrumental." *Studies in the History and Philosophy of Science* 27 (1996): 311–49.

———. *Picture Control: The Electron Microscope and the Transformation of Biology in America, 1940–1960.* Stanford: Stanford University Press, 1997.

Reisner, John. "An Early History of the Electron Microscope in the United States." *Advances in Electronics and Electron Physics* 73 (1989): 134–233.

Microscope, Field Ion

The field ion microscope (FIM), an outgrowth of the field emission microscope, is the first microscope to achieve atomic resolution. It was invented by Erwin W. Müller in 1951 at the Fritz-Haber Institute, and later developed by him and co-workers at Pennsylvania State University. In 1956–1957, Müller obtained an atomic image of the surface of a tungsten tip, thus becoming the first person to see atoms. In the next twenty years, research was focused on understanding how field ion images were formed, field ion emission phenomena, and high field effects at metal surfaces. Major contributors to these subjects include Müller himself, R. Gomer, M. Southon, T.T. Tsong, and others. Applications of the FIM to problems in metallurgy were also actively pursued by M. Drechsler, D. Brandon, S. Brenner, B. Ralph, S. Nakamura, O. Nishikawa, D. Seidman, H. Nordin, their co-workers, and others during this early period.

In the FIM, the sample must be a sharp tip with an apex radius of less than 0.15 μm. It is usually prepared by electrochemical polishing of a piece of thin wire. The tip is cooled down below 80K by being kept in thermal contact with a helium refrigerator or cryogenic cold finger. The FIM chamber is filled with an inert gas, helium or neon, to a pressure in the range of 10^{-4} to 10^{-5} Torr. With a positive voltage of several to more than 10 kilovolts applied to the tip, a field of a few tens of volts per nanometer can be established above the tip surface. The emitter surface is first smoothed by field evaporation, which is desorption of substrate atoms at low temperature by a high electric field. In a field of a few tens of volts per nanometer, each apex site of the emitter atoms in the more protruding sites is field adsorbed with an image gas atom. Additional image gas atoms, which are attracted to the emitter surface by a polarization force, will hop around the surface until they are field ionized when they pass through the ionization zones right above the protruding surface atoms. Once ionized, they are accelerated to the screen about 10 cm away to form a field ion image of the surface atoms.

Field ionization of helium and neon requires a field of about 45 volts/nm and 38 volts/nm, respectively. The evaporation fields of different materials depend on the cohesive or binding energies of surface atoms, the work functions of the surfaces, and the ionization energies of the atoms of these materials. They range from about 57 volts/nm for tungsten to 35 volts/nm for iron, nickel, cobalt, and gold, and 5 to 1 volts/nm for alkali metals. If the FIM is to yield a good atomic image of a material, its evaporation field has to be greater than or nearly equal to the image field of the image gas used. In addition, to obtain a good FIM image, the field ion emitter surface must be atomically smooth. This cannot be achieved by field evaporation for semiconductor surfaces because of their large field penetration depth. These requirements limit the material applicability of the FIM to about twenty metals and their alloys.

Ideally, a microscope can show not only the structure of an object, but also its elemental distribution. This chemical analysis aspect of the FIM is done by opening a probe-hole at the screen and having a time-of-flight **mass spectrometer** connected behind the probe-hole. By mounting the tip to a gimbal system, surface atoms can be selected from the field ion image using the probe-hole, and then having them mass analyzed one by one by field evaporating them off the surface. As field evaporation proceeds from the step of a surface layer, the composition of each surface layer can be analyzed also by a proper aiming of the probe-hole. Although there

M

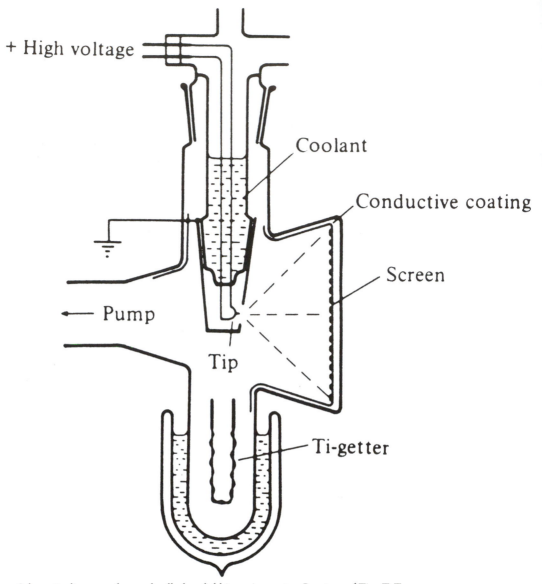

+ High voltage

Coolant

Conductive coating

Screen

Pump

Tip

Ti-getter

Schematic diagram of an early all-glass field ion microscope. Courtesy of Tien T. Tsong.

are several types of microscopes having atomic resolution, the atom-probe FIM is the only instrument capable of atom by atom and atomic layer by atomic layer chemical analysis of materials. Pulsed field evaporation required for a time-of-flight mass analysis can be done by using nanosecond high-voltage pulses as originally done by Müller, or by using ps laser pulses as later introduced by Tsong and G. Kellogg. Laser pulses have the advantage of being able to field evaporate semiconductor surfaces and achieve good mass resolution easily but the disadvantage of greater difficulty in finely controlling the field evaporation.

Magnetic-sector atom-probes were developed by Müller, D.F. Barofsky, and T. Sakurai, but they still lack the single atom detection sensitivity required of an atom-probe. The time-of-flight atom-probe FIM was further developed into an imaging atom-probe by J. Panitz, and three-dimensional atom-probes by A. Cerezo, G.D.W. Smith, D. Blavett, and their co-workers. Using the latter instruments, the three-dimensional elemental distribution of an alloy sample can be mapped out with a spatial resolutions of about 1 nm or better, thus it is most powerful in the atomic scale analysis of materials.

One of the most impressive applications of the FIM is the study of surface diffusion of single atoms and small atomic clusters and atomic interactions at metal surfaces, other atomic processes in the dynamical behavior of metal surfaces, and high field effects on surface atoms such as field evaporation and field gradient induced surface diffusion. Principal contributors to this area of research are G. Ehrlich, D. Bassett, Tsong, W. Graham, Kellogg, and their co-workers. In these studies, the diffusion paths of single atoms and atomic clusters can be mapped out and their diffusion mechanism and energetics studied in unsurpassed detail. The oscillatory and weak interaction between adsorbed atoms on metal surfaces can be observed and measured. The FIM has also been used to study surface and field promoted chemical reactions. Field ionization and evaporation have also been developed into ion sources for use in mass spectroscopy as well as in scanning ion microscopy. The FIM and the atom-probe FIM, while very limited in material applicability, are without doubt powerful and invaluable instruments for atomic-scale studies in surface and materials sciences.

The field emission and field ion microscopes, developed out of the desire of scientists to see and analyze individual atoms, are finding applications in point electron and ion sources, the scanning ion microscope, and vaccum microelectronics. As high-tech material structures continue to be reduced in size, atomic revolution microscopes such as the FIM will surely become increasingly important tools in their development.

Tien T. Tsong

Bibliography

Müller, Erwin W., and Tien T. Tsong. *Field Ion Microscopy, Principles and Applications*. New York: Elsevier, 1969.

Sakurai, T., A. Sakai, and H.W. Pickering. *Atom-Probe Field Ion Microscopy and Its Applications*. Boston: Academic, 1985.

Tsong, Tien T. *Atom-Probe Field Ion Microscopy: Field Ion Emisson and Surfaces and Interfaces at Atomic Resolution*. Cambridge: Cambridge University Press, 1990.

Microscope, Optical (Early)

It is not known where, or by whom, the microscope was invented. When it was invented is clearer; almost certainly that occurred in the second decade of the seventeenth century, for Constantijn Huygens reported seeing such an instrument on a visit to London in 1621, and the earliest known representation of a microscope is Isaac Beeckman's drawing of 1631. The instrument was named "microscopium" in 1625 by members of the Accademia dei Lincei in Rome.

To extend the eye's capacity to see minute objects, either a single lens or a combination of two or three lenses may be used. Since the **telescope** was the immediate forerunner of the microscope, the idea of using combinations of lenses to form the compound microscope could be expected to arise. In the seventeenth century, however, there were drawbacks to the use of the compound instrument so serious that better results could be achieved with the single lens of the simple microscope.

The quality of glass available was poor by modern standards, colored and marred by bubbles. The clarity of the image was also affected by two kinds of aberration, chromatic and spherical. The former, caused by the unequal refraction of light rays, produced a colored edge to the image. The latter resulted from the spherical curvature of lenses that caused spread rather than sharp focus, and therefore a blurred image. The history of the development of the microscope is of attempts to banish these defects.

The single-lens microscope was less affected than the compound by these problems, and was therefore of greater scientific importance during the first two centuries of the microscope's history. Chromatic aberration was minimized because with a single lens the eye sees a virtual image, with the colors superimposed, while spherical aberration can be lessened by reducing the aperture and using an intense light source (usually skylight).

The first major optical improvement was initiated by John Dollond, who corrected chromatic aberration in the telescope by using a combination of crown and flint glass for the lenses in 1758. The greater technical problems of achieving the same correction to the much smaller lenses of the compound microscope was solved by the Amsterdam instrument-maker Harmanus van Deijl at the end of the eighteenth century. Spherical aberration had to wait until 1830 for its solution, by Joseph Jackson Lister. What did improve steadily through these two hundred years was the design of the microscope stand, aiming always at greater stability, finer adjustment, and more satisfactory illumination.

The Simple Microscope

The capacity of the simple microscope to achieve high resolution was dependent upon the skill and concentration, as well as excellent natural sight, of the observer. The instrument, because it focused close to the eye, was best suited for looking at transparent objects by transmitted light. A small number of skilled seventeenth-century microscopists achieved remarkable results with the simple microscope.

Antoni van Leeuwenhoek, a cloth merchant of Delft, used a tiny lens contained in a metal plate, with a spike to hold the specimen close to the lens; the instrument was then handheld immediately in front of the eye. Leeuwenhoek made his own lenses from beads or blown bulbs of glass, and with skill and patience he achieved a resolution of about 2 μm. His research, particularly into the reproductive system, was embodied in a series of letters presented to the Royal Society of London. To observe the circulation of the blood in the tail of a fish, Leeuwenhoek devised a different instrument, with a frame holding a glass phial.

Johan van Musschenbroek, an instrument-maker of Leiden, made this type of simple microscope commercially. He also devised what became known as the compass microscope, because the two arms are hinged, as well as a flexible specimen holder for low-power observations, using ball joints that were known as Musschenbroek nuts. His were the instruments used by Jan Swammerdam, the Amsterdam biologist whose observations refuted the concept of metamorphosis in insects. Other notable users of the simple microscope were Marcello Malpighi, who discovered the capillary circulation of the blood, and Nehemiah Grew, who revealed the cellular structure of plants.

As the use of the microscope became increasingly popular, the simple instrument remained in use because it was readily portable, and well adapted for field observation. The compass design continued and was joined by the screw-barrel, again invented by a Dutchman, Nicolaas Hartsoeker, and introduced into England in 1702 by James Wilson. The screw action was used to hold and focus slides containing the specimens, and the simple barrel shape was highly adaptable for use with a handle or a folding foot and could even be converted to a compound instrument. The most famous stand-mounted version was produced by the London instrument-maker Edmund Culpeper.

Natural philosophers of the eighteenth century, and Victorian naturalists, continued to use the simple microscope in many forms. There was the Ellis aquatic microscope, incorporating a watch-glass to observe water creatures; the Withering botanic, contained in a small box and designed to erect itself for use when the box was opened; and the Jones cylindrical naturalist's magnifier.

The Compound Microscope

The compound microscope, close relative of the telescope, achieved instant popularity through the publication of Robert Hooke's *Micrographia* (1665). The earliest compound microscopes were simple barrels, with or without feet, and were held up to the light source when in use. Hooke devised a side-pillar microscope on a solid base that could be used on a table and tilted at the convenience of the user. He described and illustrated the design and showed it with an illuminating arrangement of lamp and bull's eye lens.

The side-pillar was also adaptable for use with transmitted light, a capacity that came into its own in the hands of the London maker John Marshall around 1700. He provided a stage plate attached to the bottom of the pillar that could be replaced with a glass-based trough to hold a fish or frog, so that Harvey's recent discovery of the circulation of blood could be observed. The fish-plate remained a standard microscope accessory for nearly two hundred years.

Henry Baker's *Microscope Made Easy* (1742) provided another new impetus to microscopy. Baker was a skilled microscopist who studied crystal morphology, and he commissioned the instrument-maker John Cuff to make to his design an all-brass microscope, much more convenient in use and with finer focusing. The Cuff-type microscope, a side-pillar on a box foot containing a drawer for accessories, was copied on the Continent and adapted to fold away into the case, being known as the chest microscope.

Later modifications to the side-pillar were made by George Adams, father and son, and by Benjamin Martin, notable London makers and retailers of instruments in the second half of the eighteenth century. Changes produced a much lighter instrument, often with a folding foot and

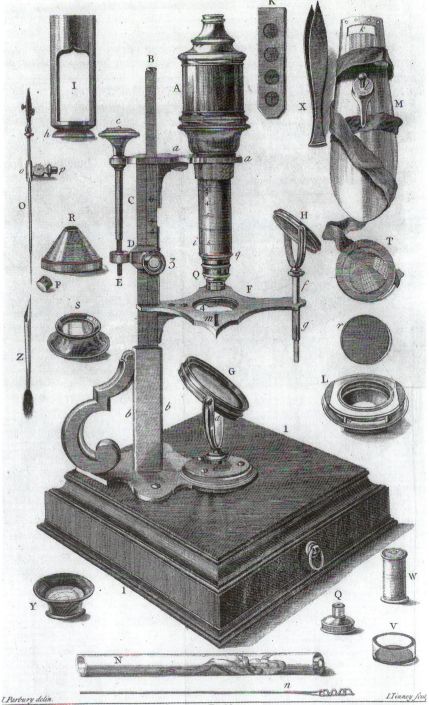

A new constructed *Double Microscope*, as made & sold by the Inventor JOHN CUFF in Fleet street London. Published according to Act of Parliament September 20.th 1744.

Frontispiece to a twelve-page pamphlet showing a compound microscope by John Cuff, dated September 20, 1744. Courtesy of SSPL.

a ball-joint at the top of the pillar to hold the barrel. More and more elaborate accessories were provided in finely fitted cases.

The compound microscope until the 1830s was the popular tool of the naturalist, botanist, and mineralogist, the majority of whom were satisfied to examine the standard specimens and compare notes with other enthusiasts. Some, doing serious research, were pressing for improvements to the optics of the instrument. Chromatic aberration was removed at the end of the eighteenth century. The early years of the nineteenth century were filled with attempts to solve spherical aberration, including the attempt to use jewel lenses in place of glass. The breakthrough came with Lister's discovery of 1830, heralding the great age of the optical microscope.

Gerard L'E. Turner

Bibliography

Bracegirdle, B., ed. *Beads of Glass: Leeuwenhoek and the Early Microscope.* London: Science Museum, 1983.

Fournier, Marian. "Huygens' Design for a Simple Microscope." *Annals of Science* 46 (1989): 575–96.

Turner, G.L'E. *Collecting Microscopes.* London: Studio Vista, 1981.

———. *Essays on the History of the Microscope.* Oxford: Senecio, 1980.

———. *The Great Age of the Microscope: The Collection of the Royal Microscopical Society through 150 Years.* Bristol: Adam Hilger, 1989.

Microscope, Optical (Modern)

The light microscope is today the ubiquitous instrument of science and technology, but it took a long time to become so, even after the seminal work of Joseph Jackson Lister on aplanatic foci, published in 1830. For example, all-brass versions of the Culpeper microscope, with crude optics, were still offered in the 1840s, and achromatic optics did not become the norm until the 1850s. Thereafter, the optics developed steadily in the U.K., Continental Europe, and in the United States. The two main types of stand were the Continental and the English. The Continental was simple in design, relatively inexpensive, and intended for use in the rapidly developing sciences of histology and pathology; they were later used in bacteriology and cytology and, to a lesser extent, materials sciences. The English stand was complex, expensive, and designed for wealthy amateurs eager to look at anything that took their fancy.

Twentieth-century innovations include improved and coated optics, stands finished in black and chrome rather than lacquered brass, and from the 1950s, new techniques of providing contrast. Demand rose, and modern production techniques allowed many more instruments to be made more inexpensively than before.

Optics

With Lister's discovery of aplanatic foci, objectives could be made that were corrected for most of the aberrations otherwise present, and especially noticeable at high magnifications. Achromatic and aplanatic lenses bring to one focus most of the different wavelengths. They also bring to one focus most rays passing through the edges of the lens as well as its center. At the same time coma is corrected—all this was determined experimentally by Lister, a remarkable achievement. He then worked directly with English makers of objectives for some years and achieved quality far better than was then obtainable anywhere else.

The three main English makers during the later nineteenth century were Smith & Beck, Powell & Lealand, and Andrew Ross, and all offered excellent $1/4$-in. objectives. By the late 1850s the norm was the equivalent of a modern $1/6$ in. The leading makers in France were Chevalier and Nachet (from the 1840s); in Germany, Kellner (which became Leitz in 1869), and Carl Zeiss; and C.A. Spencer and R.B. Tolles in the United States.

With an immersion lens, light from the object to the objective passes through a liquid rather than through air. Water immersion objectives were used in the 1840s and had obvious advantages when looking directly at living pond organisms; they are still used. The homogeneous immersion objective was introduced in 1878 by Ernst Abbe of Zeiss, based on an idea by John Ware Stephenson in England. This uses an immersion oil of refractive index and dispersion matching that of glass, giving a system providing 1.5x the resolution of a nonimmersed system. Abbe had published his theory of image formation in 1873. In 1877, he produced his apertometer, to support his concept of Numerical Aperture and to allow it to be measured objectively. In the early 1880s he worked with Friedrich Otto Schott to produce a range of optical glasses, and these were used, with fluorite, to produce apochro-

Powell & Lealand achromatic compound microscope, 1846. SM 1913-291. Courtesy of SSPL.

matic objectives of high optical correction. Apochromatic objectives have even better corrections than achromats. They bring virtually all the wavelengths (colors) to one common focus and correct for spherical aberration almost totally. This gives the highest possible quality images in terms of resolution. A second series followed, and by the end of the century objectives with resolution approaching the theoretical were available from Zeiss and from other firms as well.

From the later 1940s, phase contrast, which had been discovered by Frits Zernike in 1933, was widely applied to study living and other material having low inherent contrast. Coated lenses became the norm in the 1960s.

They reduced glare and allowed the use of many more components than before. In the same decade, differential interference contrast (G.X. Nomarski) was widely applied; this produced color images (to which the eye is very sensitive) emphasizing differences in contrast (to which it is not) while still providing the full resolution of the objective. In the 1970s it became possible to capture microscopical images with a television camera, and then to digitize them. This allowed the image to be manipulated and measured in various ways. Image analysis was further developed in the 1980s.

In the early nineteenth century, each maker had his own threads to attach objectives to his stands. The Microscopical Society of London specified a standard form in 1858; this was quickly taken up by most English makers, and more slowly by those elsewhere.

Stand

The typical Continental stand, which was also available for run-of-the-mill equipment in England and the United States, was relatively simple. It generally had a horseshoe foot with simple stage, a lacquered brass body-tube with coarse focusing by rack and pinion (diagonal teeth were introduced by Swift in England in 1881 and rapidly became popular), and fine focus by screw-operated lever. The substage illuminator was at best a simple Abbe two-lens device with focusing; equally often, just a concave mirror with a substage circle of three apertures. Instruments with machined and interchangeable parts were introduced in the 1870s and became the norm about 1910, reducing the price considerably.

The Zeiss "jug-handle" stand, introduced in 1898 and intended especially for photomicrography, was the recognizable precursor of most stands that followed for about fifty years. The main English contribution to such stands was the "Jackson" limb, introduced in 1851 and used for more than a century; this allows the grooves for the coarse slides and the substage to be machined straight through.

The special market for the English amateur produced expensive and spectacular stands. Most were large, binocular (after 1860, with the Wenham prism), and equipped with an elaborate armory of accessories. The style is typified by the Powell & Lealand No. 1 stand, introduced formally in 1869; this could have fine adjustment to the substage, and in its later years a genuinely apochromatic substage condenser! The design

Zeiss "jug-handle" stand IB, with mechanical stage, 1906. Carl Zeiss. Microscopes and Microscopical Accessories. *33rd edition, Jena, 1906: 47, Figure 20. Courtesy of SSPL.*

was in fact somewhat outmoded when it appeared, being less inherently rigid than the large stands of Ross, for example, and no better made; it is known that a workman put together an entire P & L stand from the raw castings at his bench, and to his death Powell made in person and unaided all the objectives, in conditions of total secrecy. It is amazing that there were enough wealthy enthusiasts to support such a wildly uneconomic trade. Some remarkable stands were made in England and the United States to study the effects of increasing angles of illumination on diatoms especially; this culminated in the Ross "Radial"—a masterpiece of mechanical ingenuity and construction, now known to be based on spurious principles.

As instruments for biological use were being developed, those for what is now called materials science were also coming into use. Two main kinds were used. Both required polarized light, and thus had Nicol prisms to produce it, as well as fittings in the body-tube to allow additional lenses and other parts to be inserted. Relatively small numbers of the petrological instrument for inspecting sections of rocks were and still are supplied. Other microscopes for use with opaque materials, such as metals, required means of sending the illumination down onto the specimen from above, called incident illuminators. These were rarely satisfactory until the 1930s. They required a lot of light and means of directing it actually down through the objective before it bounced back again to form the image.

Toward the end of the century, as scientists around the world began using basic microscopes for routine medical tests and for advanced research, English makers adopted a more pragmatic approach. William Watson, for instance, introduced a machine-made stand of traditional appearance (the "Edinburgh") in 1887; this sold until World War II and could be highly modified at the customer's request. Watson's "Service" stand, introduced in 1919, remained on the market until 1970. Beck, Baker, and Swift also offered increasingly modern designs.

By 1900, Zeiss had produced forty thousand stands, and Leitz over fifty thousand. While production figures for British makers were a close secret, Bausch & Lomb in the United States had made more than sixty thousand stands by 1908. By that time, the production techniques for stands and lenses were similar throughout the world; it was only in design details, to avoid very awkward work where possible, that makers differed.

During the twentieth century, production was increasingly automated in every sphere, and very large numbers of instruments have been sold. Detailed improvements in the fine adjustment and other parts were introduced by many makers, and the binocular instrument became the norm beginning in the 1930s. Large stands were made, especially for photomicrography. In the 1960s and 1970s these were further developed to approach the old concept of a universal stand, with all modes of illumination available at the touch of a button, and with image recording built in. In the 1980s, these stands became automated, with electronics controlling the optical parts, and zoom magnification changers built in.

Flat-field optics were developed from the 1960s, and with the advent of coating of optical surfaces, manufacturers were able to provide highly sophisticated optical systems. With the development of the computer, and its application to optical design (and later, to optical and mechanical production), previously undreamt-of optics were made, including aspheric surfaces.

In the later twentieth century there have developed three distinct markets. One is of basic instruments for student and routine use. These still have vastly improved optics compared with earlier versions. The second is of comprehensive and very expensive instruments for research, as mentioned above. The third is stereo microscopes for use in factories, especially those making electronics products. Quality is uniformly high and so is cost, and the once-proud British makers have virtually all disappeared. The current market has been effectively left to two Japanese and two German companies, where microscopes form only part of their total output.

Illumination

The oil lamp was the usual source of illumination in the nineteenth century, if daylight was not available (see **heliostat**). The incandescent gas mantle, patented by Welsbach in 1885, gave a textured background in the microscope, while the Nernst lamp, introduced in 1899, was a nuisance in use. The carbon arc, from about 1880, needed a lot of attention in use before clockwork-driven models were available by about 1900. Limelight, using jets of oxygen and either hydrogen or town gas playing on a stick of calcium sulphate, was often used for photomicrography, but required more attention than the actual taking of the pictures. The Pointolite lamp, introduced in 1915, was simpler to operate, and gave an intense light, but was costly. Electric filament lamps, of carbon and later of tungsten, were developed by the 1930s to be quite useful for microscopy, in low-voltage forms with compact filaments and quite high outputs. Optical microscopy was revolutionized in the 1960s with the adoption of small, low-voltage tungsten halogen lamps that gave a continuous spectrum bright light. These are now the norm, together with enclosed high-pressure mercury or xenon arcs for special purposes.

Brian Bracegirdle

Bibliography

Bracegirdle, Brian. "Light Microscopy 1865–1985." *Journal of the Quekett Microscopical Club* 36 (1989): 193–209.

Hartley, Walter Gilbert. *The Light Micro-*

scope, Its Use & Development. Oxford: Senecio, 1993.

Turner, Gerard L'E. *The Great Age of the Microscope: The Collection of the Royal Microscopical Society through 150 Years.* Bristol: Adam Hilger, 1989.

Microscope, Scanning Acoustic

The basic idea for an acoustic microscope originated with the Soviet scientist S. Ya Sokolov, who realized that the wavelength of sound waves in liquids approached that of visible light at GHz frequencies. His 1936 patent described a microscope in which the acoustic sensing surface consisted of a two-dimensional array of piezoelectric transducers that converted the acoustic field impinging on it into charge distributions that could easily be detected by a scanned electron beam. The corresponding electronic signal was used to brightness-modulate a scan synchronized CRT display in order to form an image. Since the technology to generate sound waves at GHz frequencies was not yet available, Sokolov built a microscope that operated in the MHz frequency range, where the resolution for acoustic imaging in water is around 1 mm. Although Sokolov's form of ultrasonic microscope is not in use today, various forms of ultrasonic scanners operating at MHz frequencies are routinely used for medical applications, such as fetal monitoring.

Much of the technology to generate and detect GHz frequency acoustic waves emerged in the early 1960s. Hans E. Bommel and Klaus Dransfeld at Bell Laboratories in the United States built devices working at several GHz and measured the ultrasonic absorption and propagation characteristics of various media. Donald K. Winslow et al. at Stanford University developed zinc oxide thin-film transducer technology that was capable of converting electrical energy into sound with better than 50 percent efficiency at GHz frequencies. In 1959, F. Dunn and W.J. Fry introduced an ultrasonic absorption microscope. With this instrument, the sound field at GHz frequencies in water was mapped using a thermocouple that detected the corresponding variations in temperature.

Two groups began working on acoustic microscopy in early 1970—one headed by Calvin Quate at Stanford University and the other by Art Korpel at Zenith Corp.—and two different schemes for achieving high-resolution acoustic micrographs were developed and commercialized. Early efforts were focused on using Bragg diffraction of light off the sound waves to directly visualize the high-frequency sound pattern. James Cunningham and Quate devised an intriguing microscope by dispersing polystyrene spheres in water over the insonified (irradiated with sound) sample surface, which rearranged according to the acoustic pattern over it. The spheres were then photographed using an optical microscope to record the acoustic image at GHz frequencies.

In the Scanning Laser Acoustic Microscope (SLAM) developed by Korpel and L. Kessler, the sample was immersed in a liquid cell and insonified at 150 MHz. The transmitted sound pattern was detected by directing it onto a deformable mirror and monitoring its perturbations using a scanned laser beam—that is, the image records the acoustic transmission of the sample. These systems have essentially remained at 150 MHz or 10-μm resolution and can record real-time acoustic micrographs of samples ranging from semiconductor components to biological specimens.

The Scanning Acoustic Microscope (SAM) developed at Stanford in 1973 by Ross Lemons and Quate was based on a single surface acoustic lens—typically a 100-μm spherical surface ground into a sapphire rod. Because of the large acoustic velocity ratio between sapphire and water, this could focus an incident acoustic beam (generated by a piezoelectric zinc oxide film on the back surface of the sapphire rod) into a diffraction limited spot in the water, roughly a wavelength in diameter. The spot was raster scanned across the sample, and the transmitted or reflected sound amplitude sequentially recorded (using a similar lens in reverse as a receiver) to form the image. In the reflection mode, which is now preferred, acoustic pulse trains are excited and the same lens is used for both transmission and reception by resorting to pulse gating techniques. The resolution of this instrument increased from 10-μm operating at 100 MHz in 1973 to 0.5 μm operating at 3 GHz in 1978—a factor of two increase in resolution each year since 1973.

The attenuation of sound waves in water becomes prohibitive for acoustic microscopy beyond 3 GHz. Further improvements in resolution required media with lower attenuation, lower velocity, or both. Two solutions emerged around 1980. The one at Stanford (Joseph Heiserman et al.) used cryogenic liquids such as

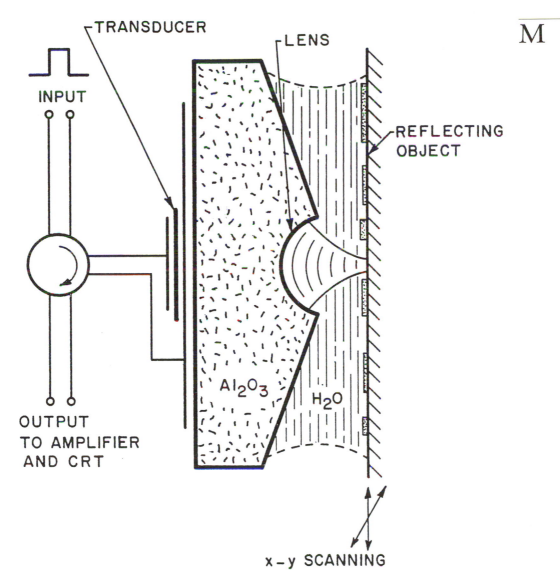

Schematic diagram showing the principle of the scanning acoustic microscope. Courtesy of H. Kumar Wickramasinghe.

argon and helium, in which both the attenuation and velocity are significantly lower. This technology evolved to operating frequencies around 6 GHz and a resolution of 30 nm. The other proposal by Colin Petts and H. Kumar Wickramasinghe used high-pressure gases (argon or xenon), in which the velocities are five times lower and the attenuations become comparable to those of water at several hundred atmospheres pressure. This was shown to work at 150 MHz and 100 atm. with a resolution of 2 μm, a factor of five better than what was achieved in water at the same frequency. Although GHz frequency operation was not pursued in gases, air-coupled

MHz SAMs are currently used for inspection of various components.

Contrast in SAMs derives from the mechanical properties of the sample (elasticity, density, and viscosity). The early work of Ross Lemons showed strong contrast in biological tissue attributable to mechanical properties. The first signs of mechanical contrast in solids was observed by R.G. Wilson and R.D. Weglein in 1977 and put on a firm theoretical basis by A. Atalar and Wickramasinghe at Stanford and Henry Bertoni at Brooklyn Polytechnic in 1978. Contrast was shown to depend on the lens-focusing condition and the coupling into surface acoustic waves within the sample, the so-called v(z) effect. Subsurface contrast and imaging in solids can be achieved by focusing a water-coupled lens below the surface. Eric Ash and colleagues developed aspheric and low numerical aperture lenses coupled with signal processing techniques for subsurface imaging; these are currently used for inspecting diffusion bonds and other subsurface defects such as delaminations.

The acoustic microscope is now a very powerful tool capable of a variety of tasks from imaging through opaque material to studying living processes in cells and organisms.

H. Kumar Wickramasinghe

Bibliography

Kompfner, R., and C.F. Quate. "Acoustic Radiation and Its Use in Microscopy." *Physics in Technology* 8 (1977): 231–37.

Mueller, R.K., and R.L. Rylander. "Seeing Acoustically." *IEEE Spectrum* 19, no. 2 (1982): 28–32.

Quate, C.F. "The Acoustic Microscope." *Scientific American* 241 (October 1979): 62–70.

Wickramasinghe, H.K. "Recent Progress in Scanning Acoustic Microscopy." *Physics in Technology* 12 (1981): 111–13.

Microscope, Scanning Optical

A scanning optical microscope (SOM) produces a magnified image of a specimen by exploring it point by point with a spot of light that scans in a rectangular raster pattern, as in a television system. The image is reconstituted, also point by point, by deriving a signal proportional to the transmitted or reflected light from the specimen and using it to modulate a display scanned in the same rectangular pattern. The magnification is the ratio of the size of the scanned area on the display to that on the specimen.

In 1873, the resolving power of a conventional optical microscope was shown by Ernst Abbe at Zeiss, Jena, to be limited by diffraction to $\lambda/2NA$, where λ is the wavelength of the light, and NA the numerical aperture of the objective lens. With an oil immersion lens, the resolving power can be of the order of 200 nm.

The SOM was proposed in 1928 by Edward H. Synge, a freelance scientist in Dublin. His aim was to overcome the Abbe limitation by what is now called scanning near-field optical microscopy (NSOM)—that is, the production of a very small light probe by collimation through an aperture smaller than the wavelength of the light, the specimen being placed very close to the aperture. In his own words: "We shall suppose . . . that a minute aperture whose diameter is approximately 10^{-6} cm has been constructed in an opaque plate or film and that this is illuminated intensely from below, and is placed immediately beneath the exposed side of the biological section, so that the distance of the minute hole from the section is a fraction of 10^{-6} cm. The light from the hole, after passing through the section, is focussed through a microscope upon a photo-electric cell, whose current measures the light transmitted. The section is moved in its plane with increments of motion of 10^{-6} cm, so as to plot out an area. . . . The different opacities of the various elementary portions of the section, which pass in succession across the hole, produce correspondingly different currents in the cell. These are amplified and determine the intensity of another light source which builds up a picture of the section as in telephotography. . . ."

Synge did not carry out any experiments, and his work was unrecognized until 1989. However, in 1972, Eric A. Ash and G. Nicholls at University College, London, independently demonstrated near-field imaging using 3-cm microwave radiation and achieved $\lambda/60$ resolution. The first NSOM was described in 1984 by Dieter W. Pohl and others at the Zurich Laboratories of IBM; they also were unaware of Synge.

The first SOM was developed in 1951 by John Z. Young and F. Roberts at University College, London. They adapted a conventional optical microscope by placing a cathode-ray tube in front of the eyepiece so that the illuminated spot on the tube screen was projected onto the specimen. The cathode-ray tube was scanned in a rectangular pattern, and the light transmitted through the specimen was detected with a **photomultiplier**. The amplified output modulated the brightness of a cathode-ray tube monitor, the image contrast being controlled by varying the amplifier gain. Young and Roberts used this "flying-spot microscope" to show the magnified image on a large TV screen, but they also pointed out its potential for counting and sizing particles, and for imaging with nonvisible infrared or ultraviolet light.

Modern Instruments

Lasers are now used as the light source in scanning optical microscopes because of their high intensity and coherence. Either the laser beam

Marvin Minsky with his confocal scanning microscope, late 1950s. Courtesy of Marvin Minsky.

can be deflected or the specimen can be scanned mechanically; the latter is simpler but the maximum scan rate is lower.

In 1955, Marvin L. Minsky of the Massachusetts Institute of Technology suggested that the performance of a SOM could be improved by detecting light only from the area of the scanning spot so that scattered light does not affect the image. This is easily arranged if the light spot is fixed and the specimen is scanned mechanically: the detector need only be provided with collector lenses and an aperture. The resolving power of this "confocal" SOM can be higher than that of a simple SOM by a factor of two, and the image contrast is enhanced. Moreover, a slice of a thick transparent specimen can be imaged by focusing the objective and collecting lenses on the same plane; in this way, three-dimensional images can be built up. The technique is particularly advantageous with biological specimens.

A simpler confocal SOM, the tandem SOM, was invented in 1966 by Mojmír Petrán and Milan Hadravsky at Charles University in Pilsen, now in the Czech Republic. Both the light spot and the detector are scanned mechanically by two multiapertured scanning disks revolving at

high speed, and the image is observed directly by eye or by a TV camera. Typically, there are 10^4 holes in each of the disks, which are mounted on the same shaft with the holes aligned to high precision. Alternatively, the optical system can be folded so that a single disk can be used.

Development of the NSOM is continuing in several laboratories. Some of the detailed proposals of Synge are still being applied, including the formation of the aperture at the tip of a quartz taper and the accurate mechanical scanning of the specimen using piezoelectric actuators. Several methods of measuring and controlling the separation between the aperture and the specimen have been developed, and a resolution of the order of 10 nm ($\lambda/50$) can be achieved with an optimum specimen. Biological applications are particularly suitable because the technique is noninvasive, unlike electron microscopy. The study of "near-field optics" has led to other microscopic techniques allied to NSOM.

Dennis McMullan

Bibliography
McMullan, D. "The Prehistory of Scanned
   Image Microscopy. Part 1: Scanned Opti-

cal Microscopes." *Proceedings of the Royal Microscopical Society* 25 (1990): 127–31.

Pohl, D.W. "Scanning Near-field Optical Microscopy." In *Advances in Optical and Electron Microscopy,* edited by T. Mulvey and C.J.R. Shepherd, Vol. 12, 242–312. London: Academic, 1991.

Shepherd, C.J.R. "Scanning Optical Microscopy." In *Advances in Optical and Electron Microscopy,* edited by R. Barer and V.E. Cosslett, Vol. 10, 1–98. London: Academic, 1987.

Synge, E.H. "A Suggested Method for Extending Microscopic Resolution into the Ultra-microscopic Region." *Philosophical Magazine* 6 (1928): 356–62.

Young, J.Z., and F. Roberts. "A Flying-spot Microscope." *Nature* 167 (1951): 231.

Microscope, Scanning Probe

Since 1873, when Ernst Abbe pointed out that the ultimate resolution of a microscope is limited by the wavelength of the radiation used, scientists have been looking for ways to surpass that limit. The family of scanning probe microscopes that are in use today are examples of microscopes that clearly surpass the limit.

The first idea for a super-resolution scanning probe microscope came from the British scientist Edward H. Synge in 1928. He suggested that one could build a tiny aperture at the end of a glass tip and raster scan this over an illuminated sample surface in order to sequentially detect the light transmitted through subwavelength-size regions. A picture could be built up by using the detected signal to brightness modulate a scan-synchronized CRT display. Synge later suggested piezoelectric scanning, electronic magnification control, and contrast enhancement, but he did not perform any experiments. The first demonstration of a near-field, super-resolving scanning probe microscope was performed by Eric A. Ash and G. Nicholls in 1972 using microwave radiation at 3 cm wavelength; they achieved a resolution of $\lambda/60$.

The Scanning Tunneling Microscope (STM) introduced in 1982 by Gerd Binnig and Heini Rohrer is a supreme example of a super-resolution scanning probe microscope; the wavelength of the electrons that scan the sample is on the order of 1 nm, and atomic (0.2-nm) resolution images are routinely obtained using a tip (or "aperture") that is only one atom across. The great success of the STM showed that it is possible to stabilize and scan a fine probe tip with angstrom accuracy in three dimensions using piezoelectric scanners coupled with electronic feedback techniques. In order to achieve such precise control of the tip-sample spacing however, one needs to derive an electronic feedback signal that varies rapidly as the tip-sample distance is varied. In the STM this is achieved by monitoring the (almost exponential) decrease in tunnel current with increasing tip-sample spacing. A predecessor of the STM, the topographiner invented by Russel Young in 1966, had demonstrated piezoelectric scanning and feedback control using field emitted electrons, albeit with somewhat less stability. It is the success of the STM and its capability to resolve surface structure on the atomic scale, however, that encouraged scientists to invent and develop a family of powerful scanned probe microscopes that use the same scanning and feedback principles but rely on a variety of different interactions than the tunnel current between tip and sample to form the image.

In 1984, Dieter W. Pohl et al. at IBM Zurich and Aron Lewis at Cornell University independently introduced the near-field **scanning optical microscope** (NSOM), which bears an uncanny resemblance to the one proposed by Synge in 1928. The technology has improved since 1984, mostly the work of Eric Betzig et al., who introduced drawn and coated optical fibers for efficient light coupling to and from the apertures. The resolution reached with these systems is around 50 nm—that is, $\lambda/10$ in the visible, limited by skin depth of the metal used to form the apertures. Betzig et al. were able to measure the dipole orientation and fluorescence spectrum of a single molecule using these instruments.

In 1985, J.R. Matey and J. Blanc introduced the Scanning Capacitance microscope, which was an adaptation of the sensor used in the RCA video disk. The instrument was capable of measuring capacitance variations at 1 GHz on a 500-nm scale. This was further developed in 1989 by the IBM T.J. Watson Research Center in Yorktown Heights, New York to reach a resolution of 20 nm and applied to dopant profiling in semiconductors.

The inability of the STM to image insulating surfaces led scientists to look for forms of tip-sample interaction that did not rely on tunnel current. In 1985, C.C. Williams and H. Kumar Wickramasinghe developed a Scanning

Commercial scanning tunnelling microscope, by W.A. Technology, 1986. SM 1989-576. Courtesy of SSPL.

Thermal Probe. This was in essence a tiny thermocouple built at the end of a probe tip that was capable of measuring spatial variations of temperature on a 50-nm scale and with millidegree sensitivity. Williams and Wickramasinghe applied it to profile insulating surfaces such as photoresist and probe hot spots in electrical circuits.

The Atomic Force Microscope (AFM) was invented by Binnig in 1986 and developed while he was in Calvin Quate's laboratory at Stanford University. This device resembles a Stylus Profilometer except in that a feedback loop is used to maintain a constant force as the tip scans over a sample. The tip was attached to a very weak cantilever (gold foil) and the repulsive atomic force (typically 0.01 μN) between the atoms on the tip-end and the atoms on the sample was monitored using an STM to measure the canti-lever deflection. In 1987, Yves Martin and Wickramasinghe, motivated by the need for nondestructive measurements of submicron integrated circuits, developed a noncontact (or attractive mode) AFM. This device, an extension of the original AFM, used a resonant cantilever/tip and a laser instead of an STM sensor. Independently, Gary McCleland et al. at IBM Almaden introduced a noncontact AFM based on vibrating the sample instead of the tip. These systems were capable of measuring forces (such as van der Waal's) three orders of magnitude weaker than repulsive-mode AFMs. This extraordinary force sensitivity allowed to be demonstrated the Magnetic Force Microscope (MFM)—using magnetic tips—for recording magnetic images of surfaces such as magnetic disks, and the Electrostatic Force Microscope (EFM)—by applying voltages between tip and sample—for recording charge and potential images.

Meanwhile, the sensitivity of the repulsive-mode AFM was improved an order of magnitude by Paul Hansma et al. by using liquid medium between tip and sample and resorting to laser sensing, a key advance for biological applications. Another key advance was the introduction of all silicon cantilever/tips by Johanne Greschner et al. in 1987 and silicon nitride cantilever/tips by Quate et al. in 1988.

It should be noted in closing that several extensions of STMs and AFMs have also been demonstrated. Notable among these is the Scanning Electrochemical Microscope (introduced by Allen Bard et al. in 1989), which is capable of detecting and measuring electrochemical effects on the nanometer scale; the Inverse Photoemission Microscope (Jim Gimzewski et al. in 1988), which measures light emission from an STM tip; the Ballistic Electron Emission Microscope (William Kaiser et al. in 1988), which measures subsurface information at semiconductor junctions; and the Photovoltage STM (R.J. Hamers et al. in 1990), which locally measures optically induced potential on the nanometer scale. The AFM has been adapted to perform Near-Field Acoustic Microscopy (K. Takata et al. in 1989) at ultrasonic frequencies and Frictional Force Microscopy (Mathew Mate et al. in 1987) on the nanometer scale. All these microscopes belong to the growing family of Scanning Probe Microscopes, which are having increasing impact on biology and materials science.

H. Kumar Wickramasinghe

Bibliography

Binnig, G., and H. Rohrer. "The Scanning Tunneling Microscope." *Scientific American* 253 (August 1985): 40–56.

Quate, C.F. "Vacuum Tunneling: A New Technique for Microscopy." *Physics Today* (August 1986): 26–33.

Rugar, D., and P. Hansma."Atomic Force Microscopy." *Physics Today* (October 1990): 23–30.

Wickramasinghe, H.K. "Scanned Probe Microscopes." *Scientific American* 261 (October 1989): 98–105.

Microscope, Ultra-

The ultramicroscope is used to examine particles of matter at the limit of visible light resolution. It can detect particles as small as 5 nm (5×10^{-6} mm), but its functional range is usually 15–200 nm. The construction of the ultramicroscope is in principle quite simple. Whereas a normal microscope views a sample with light traveling parallel to the viewing angle, an ultramicroscope views the sample with a powerful light shining through a slit at right angles to the viewing angle. By viewing the sample field perpendicularly to the source of illumination and against a dark background, it is possible to identify the presence of particles by the Tyndall effect (the appearance of a light cone when particles suspended in a liquid are strongly illuminated by a narrow beam of light). Individual particles appear as dots of light against the dark background.

Richard Zsigmondy and H. Siedentopf produced their first ultramicroscope in 1903, in response to a growing interest in colloids and a renewed debate about the existence of atoms and molecules. Working with Carl Zeiss of the Zeiss Optical Works at Jena, Germany, Zsigmondy and Siedentopf had access to the most advanced optical materials of the day. Siedentopf was responsible for the construction of the instrument, while Zsigmondy tested the device with standardized samples of gold sols (a solid dispersed in a liquid, typically water or oil) that had been created for him at the J.L. Schrieber glass works at Zombkowice, Russia. Both men also worked on methods for determining particle dimensions, and the ultramicroscope quickly became a standard instrument in many laboratories, particularly those doing research on colloids.

Other researches dealt with the problem of the dark field. In the original slit ultramicroscope, the sample cell was relatively large and the illumination allowed to scatter into the background, thereby illuminating the dark field and decreasing resolution. Focusing was also a problem, requiring a careful hand. Aimé Cotton and Henri Mouton in 1903 suggested an alternative method, the first of the dark field condensers, which used total reflection based on prismatic effects. A much smaller quantity of colloidal material was used, so no appreciable light cone appeared to interfere with observations, and, as long as no light from the illuminating source directly entered the microscope, the illumination could be from any angle. In 1906 Zsigmondy developed a new perpendicular system with a greater aperture for both the illuminating and observing microscopic lenses,

Siedentopf Cardioid Ultramicroscope, by Carl Zeiss, Jena, 1930s. Courtesy of Carl Zeiss, Inc.

increasing the degree of illumination. The immersion ultramicroscope, as it was called, proved to be difficult to use, however, since the lenses had to be in extremely close proximity, limiting the sample cell size. Siedentopf went on to make a paraboloid dark-field condenser in 1907 in an attempt to improve cell size without sacrificing the advantages of the dark-field condenser.

The drawback of these dark-field condensers was that the sample was small, and the walls of the sample cell could influence the behavior of the particles. Siedentopf's cardioid dark-field condenser, developed in 1910, increased the possible cell size without giving up the advantages of the condenser. "One of the most perfect instruments among these dark field condensers is the Zeiss cardioid condenser devised by Siedentopf," wrote The Svedberg in 1923.

The ultramicroscope was developed to experimentally test the limits of microscopic resolvability as determined theoretically by Helmholtz and Abbe, and to explore the kinetic nature of matter. In 1908 Jean Perrin used an ultramicroscope to observe the vertical distribution of colloidal mastic in water and calculated the forces acting on the particles. He independently demonstrated the theoretical conclusions about the physical nature of molecules reached by Einstein in 1905, although his work was not viewed as conclusive. In 1909 Perrin painstakingly traced the motion of individual particles and was then able to calculate the forces moving them. This confirmed the kinetic theory of Brownian motion and supported atomism.

Andrew Ede

Bibliography
Zsigmondy, Richard. *Colloids and the Ultramicroscope.* Translated by Jerome Alexander. New York: Wiley, 1909.

Microtome
A microtome slices material so that light will pass through it and it can be viewed with a **microscope**. The first microtome was constructed for John Hill, to make the specimens described in his book on the structure of timber (1770). This instrument seems to have been automatic, advancing the specimen at each turn of the blade. Custance of Ipswich, who earned his living making the sections of timber that were often sold with microscopes in the late 1700s, did not reveal the design of his microtome. George Adams, however, published the design of his microtome, a small table supporting a well, and he sold some of these instruments in the 1790s.

In the early nineteenth century, Andrew Pritchard had a microtome in which a double-handled blade was pushed across a metal top; the well containing the wood was raised as needed by a screw below. C.R. Topping had a very simple instrument, a T of mahogany with a well attached to one of the top pieces; it was held against the edge of the bench in use, and a blade taken across. He used this to make excellent sections of injected organs. John Thomas Quekett in the 1840s used a microtome like that described by Adams, but most workers preferred to make freehand sections.

By the 1860s, simple section cutters were available in Europe, England, and the United

Cambridge Rocking Microtome, 1885. SM 1885-50. Courtesy of SSPL.

States, but only those similar to the Stirling model of 1861 were widely used. This brass instrument, clamped to the edge of the bench, had a well with a screw to raise the specimen and a top across which to slide the razor.

The specimens to be sectioned were normally soaked in spirit and pushed into the well; only occasionally were they surrounded by pith or carrot to stop them shifting when the blade struck them. The freezing microtome remedied the problem of stability but produced brittle specimens. In the early 1870s, when the original ice/water solution was replaced with a gum solution that stayed slightly soft, the freezing process became widely popular. In 1876 ether was first used to cool the block (by latent heat of evaporation), and section cutting became an all-year activity.

The scientific breakthrough came in 1882, with the introduction of paraffin embedding and infiltration. When a solution of paraffin wax was used to infiltrate the specimen, filling all the cavities, a microtome could cut a ribbon of sections in such a way that their correct order could not be doubted. To exploit this technique, the Cambridge Rocking Microtome was introduced in 1885; suddenly, as many sections

could be cut in an afternoon as in a month previously. The rotating Minot design, introduced in 1887, was more expensive but also popular. Another established design was based on an earlier instrument by Rivet; this was not basically automatic, but it pushed the block up an inclined plane to advance it.

Carbon dioxide was used to cool a new generation of freezing microtomes from about 1900, and it is still universal where quick results are vital. The further evolution of the microtome occurred through specialization of manufacture, slow development of designs, and enclosing microtomes in cold cabinets to provide specimens for use in histochemistry, especially fluorescence work, to allow cell components to be localized in living material. Modern microtomes can cut slices as thin as 2µm.

Finally, it must be recognized that, if sections are to be visible under the microscope, they must be fixed, stained, and mounted. Fixing, which stabilizes the tissue, developed from the 1830s and became universal by the late 1860s. Although natural dyes such as carmine and logwood were used as early as the seventeenth century, the advent of aniline dyes from the 1860s proved of immense use to microscopists. Canada balsam was used for mounting from about 1830; clearing (raising the refractive index to improve visibility) was universal from about 1850.

Brian Bracegirdle

Bibliography

Bracegirdle, Brian. *A History of Microtechnique: The Evolution of the Microtome and the Development of Tissue Preparation.* 2nd ed. Chicago: Science Heritage, 1986.

Mouse

Mus musculus, the house mouse of Europe and North America, is the instrument of biomedical research par excellence. Although experiments have been conducted on mice for hundreds of years, it is only since the late nineteenth century that mice have been increasingly engineered and humanized and used to represent the diseases that affect mankind.

Standards

Living instruments are highly variable entities. This variability has been controlled by genetic standardization and homogeneous husbandry. As stated by the committee for the mouse standard established by the U.S. National Institutes of Health in 1956, pedigreed ancestry means either "genetic uniformity" or "uniform genetic variability." Both are rooted in reproductive control, record-keeping, and naming rules. The former "can only be maintained by continuing brother x sister matings for the entire life of the strain." The latter "can be achieved by a system of rigidly randomized matings." Environmental uniformity is also important, and laboratory protocols and contracts with commercial dealers define normal housing, nutrition, and sanitation. Mice should live in plastic or metal cages between 70°F and 80°F. Beddings should consist of sawdust or shavings. The feed should be of known composition, free of additives, within normal limits of hormone activity, and checked for contaminating microorganisms. All persons entering the breeding rooms shall wash themselves thoroughly and dress in special clothes.

Historical Variants and Usages

Laboratory mice were originally characterized by visible traits or geographical origins. Stocks were labeled white, yellow, spotted, Japanese, British, aggressive, and so on. By 1900, the widespread interest in the fur was reflected in

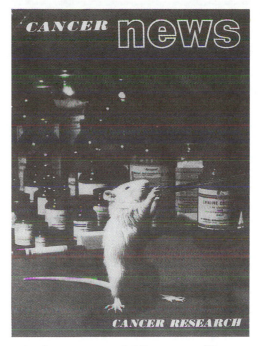

"Mice for cancer research." Front cover of Cancer News *(the journal of the American Cancer Society), May 1948. Reprinted by permission of the American Cancer Society, Inc.*

an increasing number of mendelian coat color factors. The Japanese waltzing mice bred at Abbie Lathrop's New England mouse farm attracted the attention of physiologists and psychologists because they were restless, nervous, excitable, and deaf. In 1908, the biologist Leo Loeb found that spontaneous tumors of the waltzing mice could be grafted with a high degree of success in any waltzer from Lathrop's colony. Loeb and Lathrop then used this strain to investigate host-graft relationships with views on cancer immunity.

In 1908 Clarence C. Little, then a student at Harvard working on the inheritance of coat color in mice, claimed that crossings between closely related kin would provide analogs of plant pure lines. His advisor, William E. Castle, agreed with the majority of breeders and naturalists that inbreeding would diminish variability and weaken the race. Indeed, Little's in-bred mice looked feeble and died of heterogenous diseases. However, after a dozen generations, the offspring of a couple of dilute brown animals exhibited increasing vigor, fertility, and homogeneous color patterns. To the son of an old New England patrician family who was already active in eugenic circles, the purity of the

"Dba" stock was to be prized as both moral and useful. Systematic inbreeding was used in the years after 1910 and the 1920s to generate mice showing genetically controlled high or low incidence of cancer. From the medical side, however, inbred stocks showed stable but artificial characteristics.

Little was an active entrepreneur who served four masters: mammal genetics, cancer research, university management, and eugenics. In 1929 he became managing director of the American Society for the Control of Cancer and established the Jackson Laboratory. The setting was neither a laboratory nor a factory, but a center where scientists would select, preserve, and use inbred lines of mice to "explore man's knowledge of himself, of his development, growth and reproduction." A production system was established to mate and control the genetic quality of inbred lines. Production figures illustrate the growth of the center: 20,000 mice were used by Jackson researchers in 1933, while 100,000 animals were sold in 1939, mainly to large consumers like the Rockefeller Institute or the National Cancer Institute. The original aim of the Jackson system was not to develop mouse genetics but to produce models of human pathologies that embodied methods of work, norms of interpretations and legitimated problems. For instance, a mouse mammary tumor agent transmitted from nursing mothers to offspring was found at Bar Harbor in a few strains showing high cancer incidence. In the 1930s, it circulated with a package including *Jax* cancer mice and the methods used to distinguish various influences of medical interest—that is, genes, hormones, or diet.

In the United States after World War II, cancer research followed the example of antibiotic research. Methods for screening chemicals with promising antitumor properties adopted in the 1950s at the National Cancer Institute consisted in measurements of the effects of inoculated chemicals on the growth of tumors transplanted in inbred mice. Transplanted tumors were cheaper than spontaneous tumors, and easy to transfer with industrylike patterns of work. Uniformization of mice used as graft recipients was an important feature of consensual drug testing. The National Cancer Institute contracted breeding, standardization, and quality control to commercial laboratories that agreed to produce millions of uniform mice to be used as disposable recipients for tumor cells and chemicals.

Geneticists also benefited from increasing investments in mice production. While two dozen genes had been identified during the first forty years of mouse genetics, by the early 1970s textbooks mentioned a few hundred variants. Linkage groups and chromosomal maps were the main products. A few mutants, however, mediated the laboratory and the clinic. *Obese* arose in 1950 as animals of the V stock at the Jackson showed abnormal weight increase. Moderate hyperphagia, marked inactivity, and hyperglycemia in these mice reinforced current views about human obesity. In the late 1950s, *Dystrophia muscularis* boosted the search for biochemical diagnostic assays of human muscular dystrophy. It was also used to play down the possibility of a neurological origin of the human disease. *Nude* emerged in 1962 at the University of Glasgow as a useless variant of *hairless* mice. Originally kept as a marker for linkage studies, *nude* mice were later found to be similar to artificially thymectomized mice and turned into thymus deficient mice. As tolerant hosts of cells and tissues of any background, *nude* have since been wonder tools to immunologists.

Transgenic mice were first produced in the 1980s, as scientists developed techniques for injecting isolated, foreign DNA pieces into fertilized eggs of inbred mice and for implanting these eggs into foster mothers. The first transgenic mice were a pair of giant mice provided with extra copies of gene coding for the synthesis of growth hormone. Other mice have been transformed with human CD4 gene and are susceptible to infection by HIV viruses. According to the Patent Office, which granted the first patent on a strain of transgenic mice in 1988, these constructs are no longer natural biological products but biological entities made by man. Yet, one may wonder whether the laboratory mouse has ever been a natural product.

Jean-Paul Gaudillière

Bibliography

Clark, R. "The Social Uses of Genetic Knowledge: Eugenics and the Career of C.C. Little." M.A. thesis. University of Maine, 1986.

Green, E.L., ed. *Biology of the Laboratory Mouse*. 2nd ed. New York: McGraw Hill, 1966.

Löwy, I., and J.P. Gaudillière. "Disciplining Cancer: Mice and the Practice of Genetic Purity." In *The Invisible Industrialist: Manufactures and the Construction of*

Scientific Knowledge, edited by J.P. Gaudillière, I. Löwy, and D. Pestre. London: Macmillan, forthcoming.

Rader, K.A. "Making Mice: C.C. Little, the Jackson Laboratory and the Standardisation of Mus musculus for research." Ph.D. dissertation. Indiana University, 1995.

Multispectral Scanner

A multispectral scanner collects and records electromagnetic radiation in several spectral bands. It generally uses a reflective optical system with a rotating or oscillating mirror that scans a field of view generally 70° to 120° wide. It is mounted in an aircraft or spacecraft with the scanning motion transverse to its ground track and scans closely spaced lines on the ground to provide complete coverage of the area. The scanner contains a series of discrete detectors, or detector arrays, and uses dichroic beam splitters, prisms, or **diffraction gratings** to disperse the radiation so that each detector receives energy related to a specific band of wavelengths. The detectors are generally semiconductors that generate an electrical signal proportional to the energy received. These signals are digitized and recorded and present images of the terrain covered. Multispectral scanners generally operate in the spectral region from about 0.38 μm to 14 μm, and can measure more than two hundred spectral bands simultaneously.

In the 1950s, multispectral images were created with several cameras using optical filters to limit the spectrum of light that reached the film in each camera. This technique could be used only in the visible and near-infrared spectrum to which films are sensitive and did not produce calibrated data for scientific use.

The multispectral scanner owes its origin to airborne line scanners that were developed after World War II to provide night reconnaissance capabilities for the military. The use of these techniques for scientific or commercial purposes did not occur until elements of the technology were declassified in the early 1960s. The multispectral scanner expanded the spectrum measurements from the ultraviolet to the thermal infrared (generally 0.38 μm to 14.0 μm) and calibrated the process so that the amount of energy reflected or emitted by terrain features could be measured. The space program in the late 1960s provided quantitative measurements of earth surface features from satellites orbiting the earth.

Early studies of the feasibility of multispectral scanners were done at the University of Michigan Willow Run Laboratory and the Purdue University Laboratory for Agricultural Remote Sensing. In 1968, NASA contracted with Bendix Aerospace to develop an ambitious twenty-four spectral channel scanner for earth resource applications. By the early 1970s, many types of multispectral scanners were being developed for both aircraft and satellite use, and advances in optics, detectors, and electronics permitted the simultaneous collection and measurement of energy in many spectral bands with relatively compact instruments.

Modern Instruments

The rapid acceleration of space programs in the late 1970s and 1980s produced a need for more advanced multispectral scanners to measure the properties of the moon and other planets, and to provide more detailed measurements of the earth's atmosphere and oceans. This has led to the development of a vast array of multispectral imagers. Pictured on page 406 is a modern airborne multispectral scanner that is used in many countries to measure environmental conditions in air, land, and water. Many nations have now developed their own earth observing spacecraft, transmitting the data to the earth for analysis. These include the United States, Canada, China, France, India, Japan, and Russia. There are also hundreds of airborne multispectral scanners in use for both research and environmental monitoring programs.

The technology has developed rapidly with significant advances in optics, detectors, electronics, and especially computer image processing and visualization techniques to handle vast quantities of data. Modern instruments may have hundreds of individual spectral bands with widths as narrow as 2 or 3 nm, and they can identify specific minerals or pollutants on the earth's surface and constituents of the atmosphere or ocean waters. The term "hyperspectral" describes those instruments in which the spectral bands are very narrow and the spectra generated are virtually continuous.

Environmental monitoring uses multispectral imaging to establish changes in vegetation and water quality and to identify the causes of such change. Sensors detect and map oil spills and the location and spread of forest fires through dense clouds of smoke. They monitor agricultural crops for early indications of moisture stress or disease and forests for indications

Daedalus enhanced Airborne Thematic Mapper multispectral scanner, 1990s. Courtesy of Daedalus Enterprises, Inc.

of damage caused by acid rain. The whole earth is now routinely mapped by multispectral scanners, with coverage repeated as often as every eighteen days.

Thomas R. Ory

Bibliography

Anon. "Remote Multispectral Sensing in Agriculture." *Research Bulletin*, Vol. 3, 844 (Purdue University Laboratory for Agricultural Remote Sensing), (September 1968): 38, 114.

Lowe, Donald S., John Braithwaite, and Vernon L. Larrowe. "An Investigative Study of a Spectrum-Matching Imaging System." (Contract no. NAS8-21000). Willow Run Laboratory, University of Michigan, October, 1966.

N

Napier's Rods

Napier's rods are a set of rods marked out with the multiplication tables from zero to nine of the numbers zero to nine. They are used for multiplication, division, and the extraction of square and cube roots and are named after the sixteenth-century Scottish laird John Napier of Merchiston, better known to posterity for his invention of logarithms.

These calculating rods were the simplest of three instrumental arithmetical aids described by Napier in *Rabdologia, sue Numerationis per Virgulas,* published posthumously in Edinburgh in 1617. Before the end of that year, a London teacher of mathematics had commended the book, and indicated that the rods "commonly called Napier's Bones are made by Nathaniel Gosse in Hosier lane." Within a decade parts of the text had been translated into German, Italian, and Dutch and reprinted in Latin for European distribution. The earliest English account was published in 1627.

For the novice, the rods provided a readily understood introduction to the apparent mysteries of multiplication. The design is an adaption of the "lattice" method of multiplication. It aroused immediate and widespread interest. Multiplication was reduced to addition, but without the need to memorize multiplication tables. Division and the extraction of square and cube roots could also be undertaken, but the methods lack the simplicity and didactic value of that for multiplication. In 1674, Jonas Moore rightly claimed that "Multiplication by memory is fit for those that have constant practice, but for certainty and ease no invention ever came near that of the Lord Napier by Rods, made either by Wood or Ivory."

A century after Napier's death, arithmetic was becoming integrated into formal education. Teachers now measured competence by the ability to undertake multiplication and division with pen and paper. A once popular aid to beginners slid into redundancy.

Design and Use

On each face of a square sectioned rod are laid out the multiplication tables of a digit; the tens and units separated by a diagonal line. The digits are distributed on the four faces of a rod such that the sum of the digits on parallel faces is nine; in a set of ten rods the various combinations of digits occur once, each digit appearing four times.

In Napier's design, the pair of tables on adjacent faces are inverted with respect to the other pair. In 1648, Seth Patridge suggested that the rods be laid out in the same sense "because it saveth the labour of turning the Rods end to end." After 1648 English texts follow this suggestion, which is implicit in the 1618 German account of the invention. A rod with the squares and cubes of one to nine is used in the extraction of square and cube roots.

Early sets have a loose multiplier rod, bearing the digits 1–9. The first Italian translator suggested the use of a square to align the rods, with the perpendicular numbered as the multiplier and an associated cursor to read off the results of a multiplication. He also suggested a case to store rods, square, and cursor. According to Partridge, sets have "a frame . . . to Tabulate or lay the rods in when you worke with them." The tabulat has a built-in multiplier and a lip.

To undertake a multiplication, rods for the multiplicand are selected and laid out in order

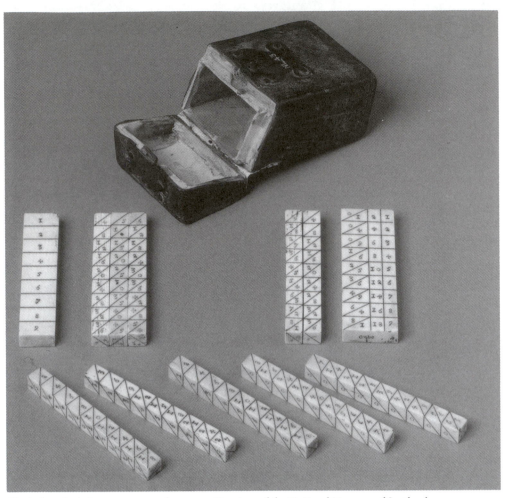

Napier's rods, in ivory, seventeenth century. Courtesy of the National Museum of Scotland.

on the tabulat. Then working from right to left along the line of the multiplier, digits in adjacent triangles are added—the tens of ten times, to the units of one hundred times—with any surplus over nine carried to the left.

Major Design Variations
In 1677, William Leybourn described laminar rods set out on two sides of a slip of wood, arguing that this enables the multiplicand to be selected more speedily. He did not claim to have originated the design. Slip or laminar form design attracted a degree of support from London makers in the decades leading up to and immediately beyond 1700. A 1668 design of the Jesuit encyclopedist Gaspar Schott had the multiplication tables mounted on a series of cylinders set in a box. The surface of each cylinder was divided into ten longitudinal strips carrying the multipli-

cation tables of the digits zero to nine. This allowed the relevant multiplicand to be "dialled," rather than selected from a set of rods. The provision of an addition table in the lid meant that the user did not even have to know how to add!

Seventeenth-century accounts of Napier's rods stressed that they removed the need for written arithmetic. However, this is only the case when multiplying by a single digit. To avoid written intervention, Charles Cotterel (1667) designed an "Instrument for Arithmeticke" that combined slip-form Napier's rods with a bead abacus, the latter used to record and add partial products.

D. J. Bryden

Bibliography
Bryden, D.J. *Napier's Bones: A History and Instruction Manual*. London: Harriet Wynter, 1992.

Napier, John. *Rabdology.* Translated by W.F. Richardson. Cambridge: M.I.T. Press, 1990.

Nephelescope

The nephelescope (or "cloud-examiner") is a vessel in which clouds can be formed and studied. It was developed in the 1830s by the American meteorologist James Pollard Espy in order to support his convective theory of storms and to demonstrate the properties of dry and moist air and other gases as they underwent expansion. Espy had set out to ascertain the expansion of moist air by the evolution of "latent caloric" when a portion of its vapor is condensed into water. For these experiments he used a copper vessel furnished with a stopcock, a bent-tube mercurial **pressure gauge**, and a

thermometer to record the environmental temperature. The copper vessel, containing either dry or moist air, was gradually transferred from one temperature to another. Then the stopcock was opened and closed as soon as possible after the mercury in the two legs of the gauge came to a common level. As the system came to equilibrium, the mercury would again begin to change its level. The difference in final pressures led Espy to conclude that the cooling effect of the expansion of dry air was larger than that of moist air by a factor of about two.

Espy, who developed the theory that storms are driven by the release of latent caloric, reasoned that "there is a great expansion of air containing vapor, when a portion of that vapor is condensed into water." He concluded that air cools about 1.25°F for every one hundred yards it ascends, and also that the base of cumulus clouds at the mo-

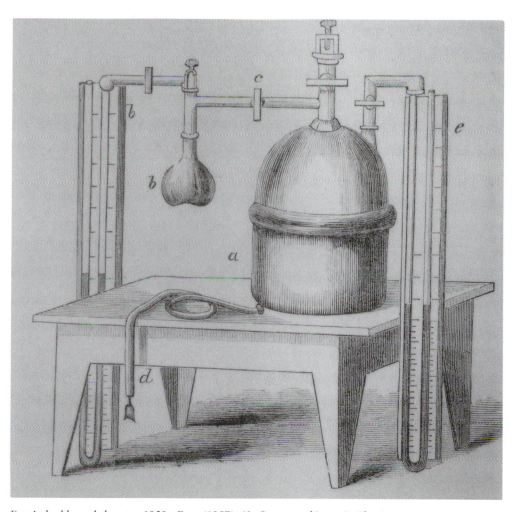

Espy's double nephelescope, 1850s. Espy (1857): 42. Courtesy of James R. Fleming.

ment they form is about one hundred yards high for every degree of difference between the temperature of the air and the dew point.

In 1841 Espy added a condensing pump and employed a glass vessel so that he could view the cloud that formed inside the apparatus that he now called a "nephelescope." Working at higher pressures, he noted that with moist air (but not with dry) the rise of the mercury in the tube was greater when he let the vessel sit for several days before discharging it. From these experiments Espy concluded that stagnant air gradually lost its saturation and, since "aqueous vapor does not penetrate the pores of atmospheric air," it must be carried aloft by the motion of the air itself. In other words, water vapor did not behave as an ideal gas in the free atmosphere and, in the absence of wind currents, its diffusion was extremely slow. This meant that meteorological conditions were more important than Dalton's law of partial pressures in distributing water vapor in the free atmosphere.

In the 1850s, Espy conducted experiments at the Smithsonian Institution, using a double nephelescope to investigate the properties of atmospheric air, oxygen, hydrogen, and carbonic acid. The later experiments, which were related to medical inquiries, were designed "to ascertain whether the quantity of carbonic acid generated by respiration varies with the dew point—as the quantity of [water] vapor generated in the lungs certainly does." In 1859 Espy claimed to have used the double nephelescope to prove that James P. Joule's unit for the mechanical equivalent of heat was equal to his results for the specific caloric of air.

Henry A. Hazen, writing in 1890, observed that Espy's nephelescope experiments had not yet been superseded and formed the basis for his theory of storm formation by the condensation of moisture in expanding air, the release of latent heat, and the generation of uprushing wind currents.

Other scientists, notably John Aitken and C.T.R. Wilson, used nephelescope-like **cloud chambers** to investigate the behavior of microscopic cloud condensation nuclei and the physics of condensation. In 1911 Wilson began to use his cloud chamber as a detector for atomic particles.
James Rodger Fleming

Bibliography

Espy, James P. *The Philosophy of Storms,* vii–viii, 27–37. Boston: Little and Brown, 1841.

———. *Fourth Meteorological Report.* U.S. Senate, Ex. Doc. No. 65, 34th Congress, 3rd Session. Washington, D.C., 1857.

Fleming, James Rodger. *Meteorology in America, 1800–1870,* 98–99. Baltimore: Johns Hopkins University Press, 1990.

Galison, Peter, and Alexi Assmus. "Artificial Clouds, Real Particles." In *The Uses of Experiment: Studies in the Natural Sciences,* edited by D. Gooding, T. Pinch, and S. Schaffer, 225–74. Cambridge: Cambridge University Press, 1989.

Hazen, H.A. "The Tornado: Theories; Objections." *Science* 15 (1890): 351–59.

Neurospora

The fungus *Neurospora crassa* (red bread mold) became in the 1940s a powerful tool for demonstrating that a gene governs the action of a single enzyme (the "one-gene one-enzyme" hypothesis), a key finding in molecular biology. The *Neurospora* is a genus belonging to the *Ascomycetes,* subclass *Pyrenomycetes,* and is the most studied species of all fungi. It thrives in tropical conditions in the wild (and in baking ovens); in the laboratory it grows well on a fully defined medium containing a simple carbon source (sucrose or glycerol), the vitamin biotin, and inorganic salts. It is an excellent tool for genetic research because of its rapid rate of vegetative growth, short generation time, and self-sterility, which permits the making of controlled crosses.

The *Neurospora* was investigated in the 1890s in Java and the Netherlands by the Dutch botanist Friedrich Went. In the 1920s, plant pathologist Bernard O. Dodge at the Brooklyn Botanical Garden domesticated *Neurospora,* worked out its sexual reproduction and life cycle, and foresaw its advantages for genetics. At the time when corn *(Zea mays)* and fruit flies (*Drosophila* melanogaster) were the paradigmatic experimental systems, Dodge tried to persuade the geneticist Thomas H. Morgan at Columbia University to utilize *Neurospora* for genetic research. Dodge's *Neurospora* stocks made their way to the California Institute of Technology when Morgan's group moved there in 1928, and by 1931 Carl C. Lindegren had worked out the cytogenetics of *Neurospora* in his dissertation. Dodge's and Lindegren's works yielded standard procedures for measuring genetic linkage and for determining the occurrence of mutations in same or different alleles. By the mid 1930s *Neurospora* genetics were

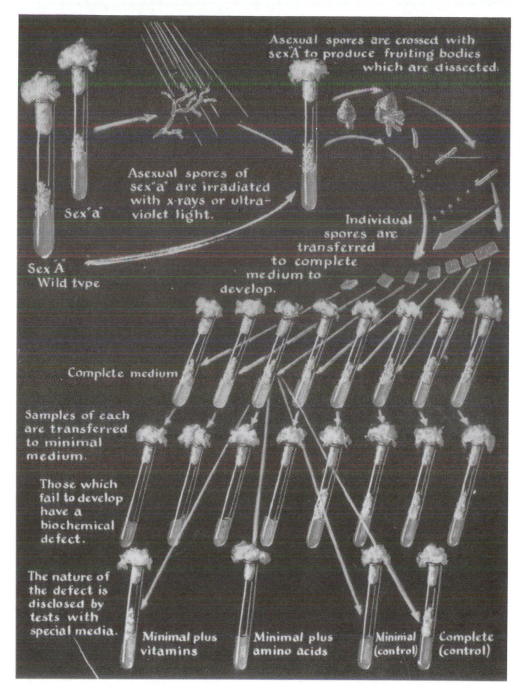

Within the figure (labels):

Asexual spores are crossed with
sex"A" to produce fruiting bodies
which are dissected.

Sex"a"

Asexual spores of
sex"a" are irradiated
with x-rays or ultra-
violet light.

Sex"A"
Wild type

Individual
spores are
transferred
to complete
medium to
develop.

Complete medium

Samples of each
are transferred
to minimal
medium.

Those which
fail to develop
have a
biochemical
defect.

The nature of
the defect is
disclosed by
tests with
special media.

Minimal plus
vitamins

Minimal plus
amino acids

Minimal
(control)

Complete
(control)

Representation of an experiment to determine a single defective gene in Neurospora. *G. W. Beadle. "The Genes of Men and Molds." Scientific American 179 (September 1948): 33. Copyright © 1948 Scientific American, Inc. All rights reserved.*

well documented and its potential as a research tool was appreciated.

George W. Beadle brought the *Neurospora* into center stage of genetics research and, working with biochemist Edward L. Tatum at Stan-ford University in the 1940s, turned it into a remarkably effective experimental system in life science. Having moved from corn genetics at Cornell to *Drosophila* genetics at Caltech, Beadle was interested in the key question of whether genes were enzymes or whether they only made enzymes. Collaborative transplantation experiments in *Drosophila,* performed by Beadle and Boris Ephrussi in the mid 1930s, had already pointed to the probability that genes control the enzyme-catalyzed biochemical reactions involved in the production of eye color (to a correspondence between gene and enzyme), but *Drosophila* was ill suited for such biochemical studies.

Using the *Neurospora,* Beadle reversed his experimental strategy. Instead of starting from a known mutation and working toward the biochemical product, he started from a known biochemical synthesis and worked backward to the gene. If some mutant gene manifested a loss of a particular synthetic step, then that *Neurospora* mutant would be unable to synthesize some essential substance and would thus fail to grow on minimal (or unsupplemented) medium. By finding out which nutrient was needed for survival, a correlation could be established between mutant gene and the specific blockage along a metabolic pathway. The asexual *Neurospora* spores were irradiated with x-rays to produce random mutations, the irradiated spores were then crossed with appropriate mating type, and newly reproduced spores were then isolated and grown in a suitably supplemented medium and tested on unsupplemented medium.

Using this *Neurospora* system, Beadle's group between 1940 and 1945 isolated about eighty thousand spores; of these approximately five hundred had given rise to mutant strains that were unable to carry out essential syntheses, and over one hundred mutant genes controlling vital syntheses had been detected. The majority of mutants were characterized by loss of the ability to synthesize either a vitamin, an amino acid, or nucleic acid component. Mutants for the synthesis of seven B-complex vitamins and twelve amino acids were established, and most of these were shown to be essential for rat, dog, and human metabolism. Without exception, every biochemical pathway leading to the synthesis of a final product—either a vitamin or amino acid—proved to be composed of a series of biochemical reactions. In each case, a specific gene mutation blocked only a single biochemical reaction along the pathway, and by inference correlated with a deficiency of a specific enzyme. This work laid a foundation for biochemical genetics and molecular biology. Using *Neurospora* mutants, Beadle's group also worked out bioassays for cholin, para-ami-

nobenzoic acid, inositol, pyridoxin, and leucin. In fact, in addition to being a genetic tool, the *Neurospora* system also turned out to be a productive tool for food and drug testing and was utilized by several commerical concerns.

In 1958 Beadle and Tatum were awarded the Nobel Prize in physiology (shared with Joshua Lederberg, who worked out important genetic mechanisms in *E. coli*). Ironically, by that time the greater simplicity and shorter life cycle of *E. coli* had partially eclipsed the *Neurospora* as a premier genetic tool.

Lily E. Kay

Bibliography
Fincham, J.R.S., and P.R. Day. *Fungal Genetics.* Oxford: Blackwell Scientific, 1963.
Kay, Lily E. *The Molecular Vision of Life: Caltech, the Rockefeller Foundation, and the Rise of the New Biology.* New York: Oxford University Press, 1993.
———. "Selling Pure Science in Wartime: The Biochemical Genetics of G.W. Beadle." *Journal of the History of Biology* 22 (1989): 73–101.
Kohler, Robert E. "Systems of Production: *Drosophila, Neurospora,* and Biochemical Genetics." *Historical Studies in the Physical and Biological Sciences* 22, part 1 (1991): 87–130.
Perkins, D. "*Neurospora:* The Organism behind the Molecular Revolution." *Genetics* 130 (1992): 163–74.

Nitrogen Determination Apparatus, Kjeldahl

Johann Gustav Christoffer Thorsager Kjeldahl was head of the chemical section of the Carlsberg Laboratory associated with the brewery of that name in Copenhagen. As such, he was well aware of the need for a rapid and routine method for determining the nitrogen content of barley proteins. In Kjeldahl's method, published in 1883, the sample was decomposed by boiling with concentrated sulfuric acid, the nitrogen being converted to ammonium sulphate. After the addition of excess alkali, the liberated ammonia was boiled off and collected in a known volume of standard acid. The quantity of acid left after neutralizing the ammonia (and hence the quantity of ammonia) was measured by titrating with standard alkali, though Kjeldahl at first used a more cumbersome iodometric endpoint.

The process had several antecedents. As early as 1841, Hans Will and Franz Varrentrap had converted organic nitrogen to ammonia by heating the sample with soda-lime. The ammonia was absorbed in acid and determined by weighing the precipitate formed by addition of platinum chloride.

In 1867 James Alfred Wanklyn had determined albuminoid nitrogen in potable waters by boiling with alkaline permanganate. The ammonia was distilled off and measured colorimetrically by adding Nessler's reagent (potassium mercury chloride). With this in mind, Kjeldahl had used permanganate in his early experiments.

Kjeldahl's apparatus was assembled from such ordinary laboratory equipment as flasks, condenser, and connecting tubes. One feature was, however, specially designed by Kjeldahl, the splash bulb that prevented alkaline spray from passing over into the standard acid. The distinctive digestion flask with its pear-shaped bulb and long neck is known as a Kjeldahl flask, but it was not invented by Kjeldahl.

The process of digesting the sample was accelerated by adding potassium sulphate to the sulfuric acid to raise the boiling point. The organic matter charred and the mixture turned black; boiling was continued until the contents of the flask assumed a pale straw color. To assist the decomposition, an oxidant or a catalyst was added. Popular choices were a drop of mercury, a crystal of copper sulphate, or a pinch of manganese dioxide. In 1931, M.F. Lauro proposed the use of selenium, and many analysts found a mixture of selenium with mercury (II) oxide to be almost invincible.

The need for time-consuming back titration of excess acid was obviated in 1913 by Lajos Winkler, who absorbed the ammonia in boric acid solution. Because boric acid does not affect methyl red indicator, the ammonia could be titrated directly with standard hydrochloric acid. Many industrial laboratories continued to use back titration for several decades.

A form of micro-Kjeldahl apparatus was introduced in 1911, but the most popular was that of I.K. Parnas and R. Wagner, which came into use in 1921. In it the ammonia was steam distilled from a vacuum-jacketed flask, the steam entering through the delivery tube that reached to the bottom of the bulb. On cooling, the liquid in the bulb was sucked back into the reservoir and emptied through the tap at the base. The apparatus was then ready for the next analysis. In micro-Kjeldahl determinations, a

Kjeldahl apparatus, 1912. John J. Griffin & Sons Ltd. Griffin's Chemical Handicraft. *London, 1912: 156, Figure 1625. Courtesy of Fisher Scientific UK Ltd.*

few drops of 30-percent hydrogen peroxide were usually added toward the end of the digestion to complete the decomposition.

An interesting extension of Kjeldahl's method to ultramicro-analysis occurred in 1939 (based on an idea of 1933). This was E.J. Conway's diffusion cell, a Petri dish in the center of which was fixed a low-walled circular cell. The digested sample was made alkaline and placed in the central cell and the absorbing acid in the outer portion of the dish. The lid was put on, and after some hours the ammonia diffused into the standard acid, where it was titrated using a horizontal burette.

Kjeldahl's method was excellent for routine laboratory use with biological specimens or with coal and coke, but it did not work with nitro-, nitroso-, or azo-compounds, or with hydrazine derivatives. These could all be converted to a suitable form by preliminary reduction, but this reduced the advantage of speed. Reductions with zinc and acid were not always wholly effective, though the discovery by A. Devarda in 1892 of a reducing alloy of zinc, copper, and aluminum held promise. The best reductant proved to be a mixture of hydriodic acid and red phosphorus, introduced by A. Friedrich in 1933.

A certain amount of ancillary apparatus was sold for use in Kjeldahl determinations, one of the most durable pieces being the digestion stand on which a number of Kjeldahl flasks could be accommodated simultaneously.

W.A. Campbell

Bibliography

Ihde, A. *The Development of Modern Chemistry*, 296. New York: Harper and Row, 1964.

Kjeldahl, J.G.C.T. "Neue Methode zur Bestimmung des Stickstoffs in organischen Korpern." *Zeitschrift für analytische Chemie* 22 (1883): 366–82.

Pregl, Fritz. *Quantitative Organic Microanalysis Based on the Methods of Fritz Pregl*, 78. 4th ed. London: Churchhill, 1945.

Szabadvary, Ferenc. *History of Analytical Chemistry*, 298. Translated by Gyula Svehla. Oxford: Pergamon, 1966.

Thorpe, Jocelyn Field, and Martha Annie Whitely, eds., *Thorpe's Dictionary of Applied Chemistry*, Vol. 2, 619. 4th ed. London: Longmans, 1938.

Nocturnal

A nocturnal is used to find the time of the night from observations of the circumpolar stars. It probably derived from the lore of shepherds and sailors who, knowing the current season of the year, could tell the hour from the position of the "Pointers" of Ursa Major as it appeared to rotate around the pole star.

Although the origin of the nocturnal is unknown, the instrument was popularized by Jacob Köbel of Oppenheim, Germany, who died in 1532. Descriptions and illustrations of nocturnals appeared in several north-German texts from the sixteenth century: Sebastian Munster's *Compositio Horologiorum* (1531); Peter Apian's *Instrument Buch* (1533) and his *Cosmographia* (1584) as expanded by Gemma Frisius; and Johannis Dryander's *Das Nocturnal* (1535), which cites Köbel as its source. The first English ac-count of the construction and use of the nocturnal appears in Thomas Fale's *Horologiographia. The Art of Dialling* (1593), while Edmund Stone's translation and expansion of Nicholas Bion's *Construction . . . of Mathematical Instruments* (1758) describes a device that was already something of a mathematical antique.

Construction

A nocturnal consists of a pair of circular scales and a long-tailed ruler, or alidade, all of which are mounted upon a hollow tubular rivet passing through the center of the circles. The larger circle, usually between 2 and 5 in. in diameter, is attached to a handle so that the instrument can be held upright and at arm's length by the user. This circle is marked with a table of twelve months, commonly divided down to five-day spaces, and a zodiac table. To make the instrument read the correct time, it is necessary that the appropriate date on the month and zodiac scales stand uppermost on the circle when the nocturnal is held vertically. This date position depends upon the stellar epoch for which the nocturnal has been made (which changes with the precession of the equinoxes) and whether it is intended for use with the Julian or Gregorian calendars.

The smaller circle is divided into twenty-four equal-hour divisions, though as the instrument was originally used at night, perhaps without a candle, eighteen of these hour divisions were often cut into pointed teeth so that they could be read by touch. The teeth generally encompassed 4 P.M. to 8 A.M., which are the maximum hours of midwinter darkness.

The hour tooth corresponding to midnight was always made longer and more conspicuous than the rest. Some nocturnals, in addition to providing the time from the "Pointers" of Ursa Major, could also use Ursa Minor. On such instruments the 4-P.M. tooth is also extended to be aligned with the date prior to looking at the sky, to make an empirical solar time conversion from star time.

Use

Before making an observation, the long midnight tooth on the hour scale is turned so that it points to the date of the year on which the observation is to be made, and firmly wedged. When the hour of the night is to be taken, the nocturnal is held vertically with the scales facing the observer, and the pole star sighted through the hole in the central rivet. The observer's arm is then fully extended, with the

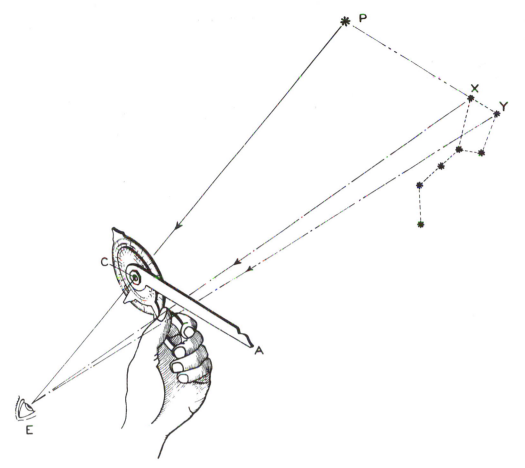

A nocturnal in use. Courtesy of SSPL.

pole star still kept visible through the rivet. The long alidade is then turned until the "Pointers" of Ursa Major sit exactly on its inner edge. In this way, the nocturnal is used to measure the angular proportion between the pole star, the vertical, and the current position of the "Pointers" on their daily rotation around the pole.

Holding the alidade securely in this position, the observer notes which hour on the smaller circular scale is denoted by its inner ruler edge. If working in the dark, the observer runs a finger across the instrument to see which of the teeth before or after midnight corresponds with the ruler.

To work from Ursa Minor, one aligns the large 4-A.M. tooth with the date when setting the instrument. With practice, a nocturnal can be made to read the time to around fifteen minutes, although accuracy depends upon keeping the instrument exactly in the vertical when the stars are being observed.

Subsequent History and Conclusion

The development of accurate mechanical time-keepers rang the death-knell of the nocturnal, though it remained in use at sea well into the eighteenth century, and may have survived even longer in remote rural districts. In World War II, the nocturnal had a limited revival in the form of a celluloid "star clock." Many nocturnals survive in instrument collections around the world; the Museum of the History of Science, Oxford, has a small German instrument in metal dated 1543.

The vernacular origins of the nocturnal suggest that it could have been a widespread homemade instrument in the sixteenth and seventeenth centuries, especially in its wooden form. Thomas Fale provided detailed instructions for making a nocturnal, and other sixteenth-century writers provided engraved paper scales that could be cut out and glued onto wooden parts by an amateur instrument-maker who was perhaps hazy about the astronomy involved. In its day, the nocturnal must have been among the most commonplace of mathematical instruments, bringing together astronomy, printed parts, simple handicraft, and a vernacular scientific tradition.

Allan Chapman

Bibliography

Bion, Nicolas. *The Construction and Principal Uses of Mathematical Instruments*, 252–53. Translated by Edmund Stone. London, 1758.

Dryander, Johannis. *Das Nocturnal Oder Die Nachtuhr*. Frankfurt, 1535.

Fale, Thomas. *Horologiographia. The Art of Dialling*, fols. 53–57. London, 1593.

Fine, Oronce. *De Solaribus Horologiis, et Quadrantibus* [1531], fols. 176, 177. Part 4 of *Protomathesis*. Paris, 1532.

Simcock, A.V. "*Elucidatio fabricae ususque:* Rambling among the Beginnings of the Scientific Bookshelf." In *Learning, Language and Invention*, edited by W.D. Hackmann and A.J. Turner, 273–96. Aldershot and Paris: Variorum, 1994.

Nomogram

A nomogram uses the methods of geometry to perform computation. It can be used by a computational novice, but producing one requires the skills of a mathematician and a draftsman. They are thus used where the long time of preparation is offset by the value of having almost instant results. They have been favored by military engineers and artillery officers, who needed quick results when in action.

Intersection nomograms use the intersections of lines or curves to produce their results. The following diagram is an intersection nomogram for solving a cubic equation of the form $x^3 + px + q = 0$. In this example, the lines $p = 0.2$ and $q = 0.3$ intersect between the lines marked -0.5 and -0.6 and nearer the latter, so we can guess that the solution is about -0.57 (the true solution is -0.5707).

Alignment nomograms align known values on two scales to give the result on a third scale. The simplest form of an alignment nomogram (shown in the illustration above) consists of three parallel scales. The intersecting line aligns the points $x = 5$, $b = 2$ and $a = 3$ and demonstrates that $5 = 2 + 3$. More sophisti-

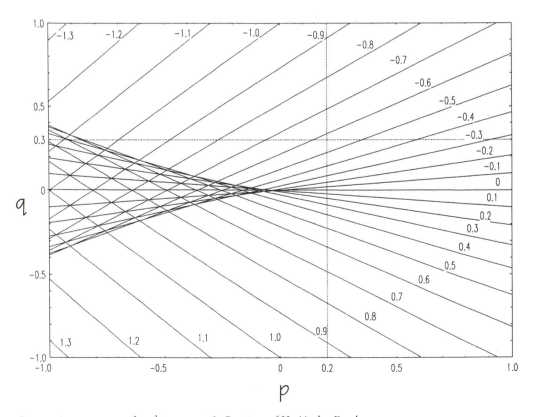

Intersection nomogram for x^3 + px + q = 0. *Courtesy of H. Ainsley Evesham.*

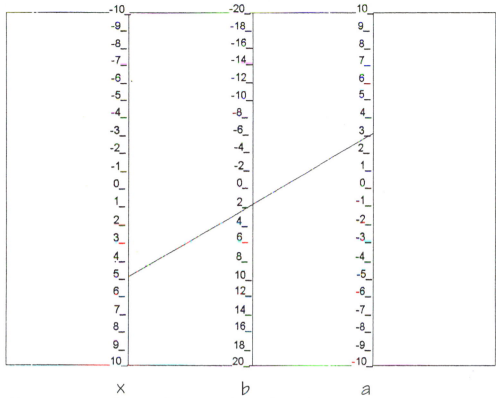

Alignment nomogram for x = a + b. *Courtesy of H. Ainsley Evesham.*

cated alignment nomograms solve more complicated problems.

Geometrical principles have long been used to solve computational problems. Examples include the volvelle diagrams in R. Dudley's "Del l'arcano del Mare" (1661), now in the National Maritime Museum, Greenwich.

Nomography, however, dates from the mid nineteenth century, and the construction of the railway system in France was the impetus for its development. Leon Lalanne, a civil engineer engaged on the project, investigated the subject in a rigorous manner in 1846 and developed a Universal Calculator that performs a variety of computations. Lalanne also concluded that if straight lines could replace curves a more acceptable nomogram would result. The process of replacing curves by straight lines he called anamorphosis. J. Clark, a professor of mathematics at the École Polytechnique in Cairo, later showed that some important and simple nomograms could be produced using curves.

In 1867 Paul de Saint Robert derived a criterion that suggested that some apparently

simple equations could not result in nomograms. J. Massau further developed theoretical aspects of the subject during the construction of the Belgium railways in the 1880s. By this time it had become clear that there was more to nomograms than might at first appear.

The person who did most to develop the theory was Maurice d'Ocagne, an engineer who worked for various French government agencies concerned with roads, bridges, and maps. He coined the term "nomogram"—literally the drawing of laws—in 1891 and introduced the alignment nomogram. He also wrote the authoritative work on the subject in 1899, with a second edition in 1921.

Nomograms have been used in a wide variety of disciplines over many years, in some instances long after they might have been expected to have been replaced by other devices. The petroleum and chemical industries were using them in the 1950s. The Russian journal *Vychiclitelnaya Matematika (Computational Mathematics)* devoted an entire issue to the topic in 1959. In 1973 the British Directorate of Overseas Surveys published nomograms of survey computations, while a set of nomograms for morphometric gravel analysis appeared in 1977, and a nomogram for computing the effective rate of interest in 1980.

H. Ainsley Evesham

Bibliography

Allcock, H.J., J. Reginald Jones, and J.G.L. Michel. *The Nomogram*. London: Pitman, 1963.

Evesham, H.A. "The History and Development of Nomography." Ph.D. dissertation. University of London, 1982.

———. "Origins and Development of Nomography." *Annals of the History of Computing* 8 (1986): 324–33.

Ocagne, Maurice d'. *Traite de nomographie. Theorie des abaques. Applications pratiques*. Paris: Gauthier-Villars, 1899.

Nuclear Magnetic Resonance

See SPECTROMETER, NUCLEAR MAGNETIC RESONANCE

Octant

An octant is an angle comprising an eighth of a circle, or 45°, but the term also refers to an angle-measuring instrument commonly used in navigation and occasionally in surveying. This instrument is known also, perhaps confusingly, as a Hadley quadrant.

The octant employs the principle used in the general class of reflecting instruments, which includes **sextants** and reflecting circles, that if a mirror is rotated through a certain angle, any reflected ray from a stationary object is displaced by twice that angle. Such instruments then rely on rotating a mirror so that the image of one target object is brought into coincidence with that of the other. The angle through which the mirror is rotated to effect this is half the angle between the targets. The ambiguity over the name of the instrument can now be understood: it can measure angles up to 90°, and so is a form of quadrant, but to do so requires a divided arc of only half this angle, and so is an octant. Thus in the octant, a scale 45° in extent is divided into ninety divisions, and each of these divisions represents a degree displacement between the targets.

These design elements were built into instruments designed by Robert Hooke and by Isaac Newton for use at sea, and a group of similar designs appeared in the early eighteenth century from Thomas Godfrey in America, Jean-Paul Grandjean de Fouchy in France, and Caleb Smith and John Hadley in England. Of these, Hadley's proposals, made to the Royal Society of London in 1731 and improved to a standard form in 1734, are the best known.

Two radial arms and an arc bearing the divided scale form a sector, and an index arm is pivoted at the apex (the center of curvature of the arc) and moves across the scale. An index mirror is mounted on the index arm at the pivot; a half-silvered mirror known as the horizon glass is fixed to one stationary arm and a sight on the other. In early examples, though not in Hadley's original design, this was a pinhole sight, but telescopic sights soon became standard accessories. The direct sight is taken across the frame of the instrument, the ray passing through the unsilvered half of the horizon glass, while the second target is seen after two reflections—in the rotatable index mirror and the silvered half of the fixed horizon glass. The zero can be first checked, or adjusted, by viewing the same distant object directly and by reflection; the glasses will be parallel and the scale should read zero, or will indicate a correction to be applied to subsequent measurements. For the observation itself, the frame is held in the plane of the angle required and one target brought into coincidence with the other by moving the index arm and with it the index mirror.

The major navigational problem of the eighteenth century was finding a ship's longitude at sea, and Hadley had hoped that the octant, which offered a significant improvement in accuracy over earlier instruments, would enable lunar distances to be taken at sea as part of a longitude-finding method. However, the angles needed could exceed 90°. For this reason early octants usually have an additional half-silvered glass, set on the same arm as the regular one but fixed at right angles to it, and having its own pinhole sight. Using this glass had the effect of adding 90° to the angle indicated on the scale. However, whereas the index mirror and horizon glass could be adjusted to parallel (index zero), there was no similar adjustment for this extra glass, which over time would

Trade card, depicting an octant in use, by R. Rust, ca. 1783. SM 1934-111. Courtesy of SSPL.

move out of position and was then of little use. In fact the common use of the octant was for finding latitude by measuring the altitude of the pole star, taking another stellar altitude by the technique of equal altitudes, or, most commonly, measuring the meridian altitude of the sun. The instrument was then held vertical, while the direct sight was to the horizon, which explains the term "horizon glass." The additional sight could be used for the far horizon from the sun, if the near one was obscured, and this explains its name of "back horizon glass," but in fact this glass was soon dispensed with.

There was a gradual evolution from mahogany frames with diagonal scales on inlaid boxwood to ivory scales read by verniers, and then ebony frames with brass index arms. By the early nineteenth century, this was the standard form. There were pivoted filters or "shades" for the solar sight, set between the index arm and horizon glass. Unlike the sextant, where there was much experimentation with shapes of frame, the octant retained its characteristic T brace to the arms and limb. The frame might incorporate a hole for a pencil and an inlaid piece of ivory on the back for noting the reading. The octant became the relatively inexpensive, workaday instrument for latitude, while the more expensive and refined sextant was the tool for measuring lunar distances and so finding the longitude.

Jim A. Bennett

Bibliography

Bennett, J.A. *The Divided Circle: A History of Instruments for Astronomy, Navigation and Surveying.* Oxford: Phaidon, 1987.

Cotter, C.H. *A History of the Navigator's Sextant.* Glasgow: Brown, 1983.

Ocular Refraction Instruments

Although the failure of the eyes of some individuals to produce a clear image of distant objects was recognized in antiquity, the complete classification of refractive errors and the development of suitable instruments for their measurement are comparatively recent. In myopia (short sight) the ocular dioptrics are too powerful and hence the defect can be corrected by a diverging lens. In hypermetropia (long sight) the image is focused behind the light-sensitive retina and a converging correction is needed. Lastly, in astigmatism the eye has different powers in different meridians; it is corrected by a cylindrical lens with appropriate power and axis direction. The optics of myopia were understood by Johannes Kepler (1604), but hypermetropia was not clearly differentiated from presbyopia, the progressive failure with age of the dynamic focusing system of the eye, until the work of James Ware (1813) and Frans Donders (1858). Astigmatism was first described by Thomas Young (1801).

There are two basic approaches to the measurement of refractive error. The subjective involves judgments made by the patient, and the objective involves judgments made by the examiner or by a photoelectronic detection system.

Subjective Methods

Although the trial-and-error process to determine which set of lenses gives the patient the sharpest view of a distant object has probably been used since the first convergent spectacle lenses were made in the late thirteenth century, the first effective standard system for classifying the powers of corrective lenses was not adopted until 1875. In this system, lens powers in air are the reciprocal of their focal lengths in meters. Since such powers are additive for thin lenses in contact, any sphero-cylindrical power can be produced by combinations of a relatively modest set of spherical and cylindrical trial lenses.

Most of the common subjective refraction techniques still involve systematically changing lenses in front of each eye to optimize the clarity of a suitable distance target. The lenses may be manually inserted and exchanged in a trial frame. Or they may be fixed around the periphery of several coaxially mounted flat disks that can be separately rotated in front of each eye. Some current instruments are under computer control to speed adjustment and recording of results. Another interesting approach involves lenses whose power can be continuously and smoothly varied.

An alternative method is to directly establish the far point of the uncorrected eye—that is, the position in which an object is clearly in focus. The required correcting lens power is then simply the reciprocal of the distance of the far point in meters, with appropriate allowance for sign. The earliest successful instrument of this type was the optometer developed by William Porterfield in 1759. A vertical line was observed through two slits held close to the eye: in general the line initially appeared doubled but, as it was moved toward the eye, the two images merged when the far point was reached. Thomas Young in 1801 used a single line engraved along the length of the optometer bar. Through the double slit, the line then appeared as an elongated X, with the intersection denoting the far point of the patient. A suitable scale indicated the power of the required correcting lens. By making the instrument reversible and adding a +10D lens at one end, Young solved the problem of measuring hypermetropia and was able to demonstrate his own against-the-rule astigmatism by turning the instrument about its longitudinal axis so that the slits were either horizontal or vertical. Jules Badal suggested further improvements to make the dioptric scale linear in 1876.

Ruka variator, 1932. The two adjustable telescopes acted as variable correcting lenses and were adjusted to achieve maximum clarity for each eye. Courtesy of W.N. Charman.

Other subjective optometers use Galilean and astronomical **telescopes**, and depend on the fact that the separation of the objective and eyepiece affects the divergence of the light leaving the system. Thus, when a distant object is observed, a myope will focus the system so that light leaving the eyepiece is divergent, whereas a hypermetrope will adjust for convergence. With suitable calibration, the spherical ametropia can therefore be deduced from the focus of the telescope. The Ruka Variator of 1934 is based on this principle. It also includes lenses of variable cylindrical power to determine astigmatic corrections. Other subjective refraction methods include utilization of the chromatic aberration of the eye and observation of laser speckle patterns.

Objective Methods

The three basic objective techniques—retinoscopy, retinal image analysis, and coincidence—involve light that is reflected from the retinal surface at the back of the eye.

The retinoscope was introduced by Ferdinand Cuignet in 1873. Here a beam of light is moved across the pupil of the patient's eye, and the examiner deduces the refractive error from the speed and direction of the apparent movements in the pupil plane of the light patch arising from the retinal reflection. An automated retinoscope was introduced around 1970.

Visual optometers or **refractometers** use the same principle as the **ophthalmoscope**. An external target is imaged onto the retina, and diffuse reflection relays this image back through the eye's dioptrics so that it can be observed externally through a suitable optical system. The vergence of the light entering the eye is then changed until the retinal image achieves optimal focus. The first photoelectronic refractometer, patented by Geoffrey Collins in 1936, was the forerunner of many later fully automated devices.

Coincidence optometers go back to the original concept of Christopher Scheiner (1619) that if two small apertures are placed in front of the patient's pupil, the retinal image will appear doubled unless it is precisely in focus: the retinal images are again observed visually or photoelectronically with an ophthalmoscopic arrangement.

Many current microprocessor-controlled instruments (autorefractors) use optoelectronic detection techniques to determine the refractive endpoint: the examiner's role is confined to aligning the instrument with the patient's eye. Use of infrared light allows the measurement beams of the new instruments to be invisible to the patient so that his observation of a simultaneously presented visible target is not disturbed.

The older visual methods of determining ocular refraction are still widely used, as the new automated objective instruments suffer from a variety of limitations, not least their frequent inability to determine the refractive error of patients with small pupils or poorly transmitting ocular media.

W. Neil Charman

Bibliography

Bennett, Arthur G., and Ronald B. Rabbetts. *Clinical Visual Optics.* 2nd ed. London: Butterworths, 1989.

Henson, D.B. *Optometric Instrumentation.* London: Butterworths, 1983.

Levene, John R. *Clinical Refraction and Visual Science.* London: Butterworths, 1977.

Marg, Elwin. *Computer-assisted Eye Examination.* San Francisco: San Francisco Press, 1980.

Odometer

An odometer measures the distance traveled by a wheeled vehicle by counting wheel rotations as the vehicle advances. The distance can then be calculated as the product of the rotation count and the wheel circumference. The counting function is generally accomplished by means of a series of gears driven directly by the rotation of the wheel or, in modern vehicles, by the power transmission proportionally geared to reflect wheel rotations.

The name odometer comes from the Greek word *hodometron,* meaning "way measurer." The instrument is also known in English as viameter, waywiser, milometer, roadometer, sledgmeter, and cyclometer. The **pedometer,** a variant of the wheel odometer, counts the number of steps taken by a person while walking. The distance traversed is then calculated by the relation, step-count times stride length.

Marcus Vitruvius Pollio, the Roman architect and engineer, observed that "the machine for measuring distances when traveling was developed by the ancients and is yet found very useful." Details of these early instruments, however, are lost. Interest in odometers resurfaced with Leonardo da Vinci and increased as Europeans began preparing road maps and establishing boundary lines for civil and military purposes. Many priority claims to the invention of the odometer are found, but these generally apply to specific designs and not to the general concept. People associated with odometers include Christopher Schissler (German instrument-maker), John Newell (English surveyor), M. Meynier (French inventor), Holhfeld (German inventor), Thomas Jefferson (American statesman), Christopher Colles (American engineer and cartographer), and George Everest (English surveyor).

The first British patent for a waywiser was issued to Isaac Fenn in 1765; this described a measuring wheel 31.5 inches in diameter with dial displays that showed distances in poles, furlongs, and miles. A rimless waywiser was patented in London by Richard L. Edgworth in 1767. James Clark received the first American patent for an odometer in 1818; and James Hunter of Scotland received a patent in 1821. By 1995, the United States Patent Office has issued more than five hundred odometer patents.

Odometers have been designed and built in many different ways. One design, popular throughout the nineteenth century, was the pendulum odometer, so called because of its pendulumlike mode of operation. It had a brass plate that could rotate freely within a 2 by 4 in. metal frame. Threads on the central axis of the frame meshed with two geared dials attached to the plate. When in operation, this assembly was inserted into a circular leather or metal case and strapped to the spokes of a wheel. As the wheel rotated, the threads of the central axis drove the two dials, one tooth per wheel rotation. Since the dials contained different numbers of gear teeth (typically 100 and 99), each rotation of the dials produced a one-tooth offset. The instrument could, therefore, count up to ninety-nine hundred rotations of the wheel. Depending on the wheel's

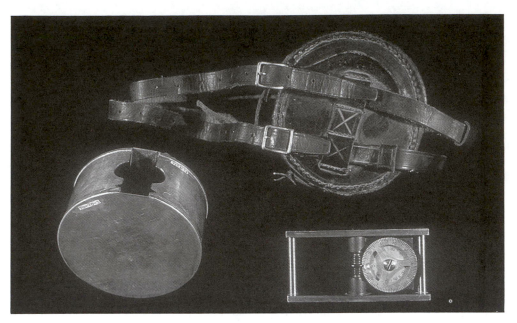

Pendulum odometer, North American, nineteenth century, with case. Courtesy of the Museum of the Rockies.

diameter, this represented a distance of 20 to 30 miles. The origin of the pendulum odometer is unknown, but many of its features are included in a measuring wheel described by John Howell of London in 1678.

With the advent of motor vehicles in the early twentieth century, the role of the odometer was expanded to include important ramifications for the vehicle itself. Vehicle maintenance schedules, terms of warranty, current market value, and decisions to buy and sell were all dictated by odometer mileage data and tampering with an odometer was made a serious crime. The worldwide proliferation of motor vehicles, each with its own "on-board" device, has made the odometer one of the most widely used measuring instruments of all time.

Norman E. Wright

Jane Insley

Bibliography

Beckmann, John. "Odometer." In *A History of Inventions, Discoveries and Origins,* Vol., 1, 5–11. Translated by William Johnston. London: H.G. Bohn, 1846.

Howell, John. "The Description of the Wheel by Which Roads Are Measured." In *A Sure Guide to the Practical Surveyor,* 191. London, 1678.

Pade, Erling. *Milevognen: Og andre oeldre opmalingssystemer.* Copenhagen: Host

and Sons, 1976.

Singer, Charles, ed. *A History of Technology.* Vol. 3, 512–13, 628. New York: Oxford University Press, 1957.

Strandh, Sigvard. *A History of the Machine.* New York: A and W, 1979.

Ophthalmoscope

An ophthalmoscope is a diagnostic instrument used to view the fundus, thereby helping to reveal the eye's anatomical and physiological condition (including the causes of loss of vision) as well as various pathological developments occurring elsewhere in the body.

From the late eighteenth century onwards, several investigators noticed the pupil's occasionally luminous appearance, and in 1818 Bénédict Prevost noted that such luminosity was nothing other than the reflected light that had entered the eye. Some physicians believed that such luminosity was a sign of disease or of an abnormality. Then, in 1846 William Cumming and in 1847 Ernst Brücke independently showed that all healthy human eyes could be made luminous. Yet neither Cumming nor Brücke, nor any other physician or scientist, could account for the eye's luminosity.

That understanding, and the accompanying instrumental advance, came in late 1850, when Hermann von Helmholtz, then a young extraordinary (associate) professor of physiology at the University of Königsberg, invented the ophthalmoscope and soon thereafter reported on its construction, operation, and use while simultaneously explaining the pertinent geometrical and physiological optics of the eye that had guided him in constructing his new instrument. As Helmholtz himself later said, the fundamental idea of the ophthalmoscope was obvious; in principle, it could have been made by any number of individuals. His decided advantage over virtually all others was that he was a physically minded medical doctor and physiologist.

Helmholtz's invention came in response to his desire to demonstrate in a lecture before his medical students Brücke's discovery that reflected light could be emitted from the eye. His central insight was the realization that light rays entering the eye are reflected back along the same path that they had taken in entering it. His invention was an instrument by which the reflected rays could be formed into a distinct image in the observer's eye. In his forty-three-page pamphlet *Beschreibung eines Augen-Spiegels zur Untersuchung der Netzhaut im lebenden Auge* (1851), Helmholtz used the laws of refraction to show that an observer cannot see any light from the observed eye because, in attempting to do so, the observer necessarily cuts off all incident light to the observed eye. To avoid that, Helmholtz used a lamp (or sunlight) to send light to the observed eye indirectly, through reflection from a small, plane glass plate: the observed eye thus saw only the mirror image of the light, thereby allowing the observer simultaneously to view the observed eye.

Helmholtz called his instrument for conducting retinal observations an ophthalmoscope (*Augenspiegel* in German). His first, crude model was made of pasteboard, eye lenses, and a microscopic covering glass. As show in the illustration on page 426, he attached the reflecting plates *hh* at an angle of 56° (to match the optimum angle of incident light) to the circular plate *aa,* thereby forming a triangular prism with the brass piece *gg.* The plate *aa* contained four openings of the form *f,* and rested on the cylinder *bbcc.* It was readily removable from the concave lens *nn* and replaceable by one or more other lenses. The entire prismatic structure was attached to a handle *m.* Seated within a darkened room illuminated by only a single source of directed light, the observer could see the living human retina, and could do so in great detail.

The invention of the ophthalmoscope initiated a revolution in ophthalmology. Ophthalmologists (as these new specialists were soon being called) immediately recognized its diagnostic power, and within two months began making what has become a virtually endless series of improvements on Helmholtz's crude instrument. Fifty years after the instrument's invention, one leading ophthalmologist displayed over 140 examples of different ophthalmoscopes, and by 1971 hundreds of different, new types had been reported and many had been marketed. Although many of these ophthalmoscopes added only minor improvements to their predecessors, there were indeed a number of major improvements or variations on Helmholtz's original ophthalmoscope. These included Epkens's plane silvered mirror ophthalmoscope, which gave increased illumination (1851); Christian Georg Theodor Ruete's development of a lens system that provided an inverted image (the so-called indirect method) and that improved illumination of the retina (1852); Helmholtz's physical explanation of Ruete's developments and of E. Rekoss's development of a disk (containing concave lenses) attached to the ophthalmoscope that made it far easier to change lenses (1852); Wilhelm Frobelius's use of a glass prism for directing light into the eye (1852), with Ernst Adolf Coccius (1853) and Wilhelm von Zehender (1854) providing variations on Frobelius's model; Eduard Jaeger's uniting of the best features of all predecessor ophthalmoscopes (1854); Richard Liebreich's tubular ophthalmoscope, which permitted making photographic images of the retina (1855) and which in its simple form remained a standard-bearer into the twentieth century; and Edward Loring's detachable disks that replaced the Rekoss disk (1869) and which, by 1878, included a set of sixteen lenses. (Loring's instrument long remained one of the most popular.)

The invention of the electric light bulb in 1878–79 opened the possibility of creating self-illuminating ophthalmoscopes. In 1885, W.S. Dennett demonstrated an electric ophthalmoscope, and in the following year Thomas Reid incorporated an electric light source into the ophthalmoscope's handle. It was not, however, until around 1914 that practical electric ophthalmoscopes became available, above all that of Henry L. DeZeng and, especially, that of Charles H. May.

The next major advance in ophthalmoscopic instrumentation did not come until the

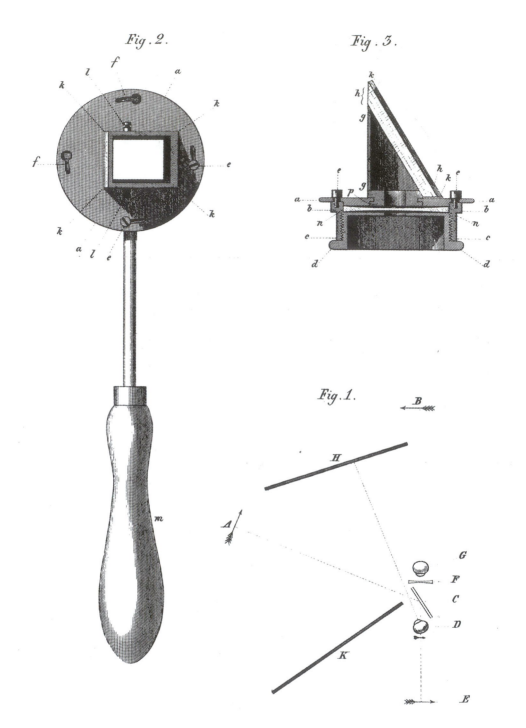

Helmholtz's ophthalmoscope. As shown in Figure 1, the light from the flame A strikes the mirrored glass plate C and is reflected into the observed eye D as if it had originated at the flame B. The reflected light strikes the retina and there produces an inverted image. The light is in turn reflected from the retina back to B, the apparent source (for the observed eye D) of the light. In so doing, part of the light from D is reflected back to A and part is transmitted through the glass plate C, behind which is a concave lens F that makes the convergent rays reflected by the retina divergent and then sends them directly to the nearby observer's eye G, giving an erect image (according to the so-called direct method of ophthalmoscopy). Helmholtz (1851): Volume 2, Plate IV. Courtesy of SSPL.

1940s, when Charles Schepens presented a binocular, self-luminous, indirect ophthalmoscope. Although binocular ophthalmoscopes had appeared in the 1860s, Schepens's instrument did more to advance ophthalmology than any other ophthalmoscope in the post–World War II era. Television ophthalmoscopes and scanning laser ophthalmoscopes, which provide improved images of the retina and its functioning through the use of computerized, televised, and quantitative analyses, represent the latest in current research development of the ophthalmoscope.

Although the use of the ophthalmoscope during the first twenty-odd years of its existence was largely limited to ophthalmologists, from the 1870s onwards general practitioners began using it as part of their routine physical examinations of the eye. The ophthalmoscope made possible the ability to witness, diagnose, and prognosticate about diseases of the eye (such as cataracts and glaucoma) and associated loss of vision, and to help prescribe the necessary corrections for eyeglasses. Moreover, ophthalmologists and other types of medical doctors quickly realized that observation of the state of the fundus could provide them with information on the state of other bodily parts. In time, they have been able to use ophthalmoscopes to help detect such neurological disorders as brain tumors, amaurotic family idiocy, and multiple sclerosis, as well as a host of disorders (for example in the kidneys and heart) belonging to internal medicine.

David Cahan

Bibliography

Friedenwald, Harry. "The History of the Invention and of the Development of the Ophthalmoscope." *Journal of the American Medical Association* 38 (1902): 549–52; appendix, 566–69.

Helmholtz, Hermann von. *Beschreibung eines Augen-Spiegels zur Untersuchung der Netzhaut im lebenden Auge.* Berlin: Förstner, 1851. Reprinted in *Wissenschaftliche Abhandlungen,* Vol. 2, 229–60. Leipzig: Barth, 1882–1895.

Hirschberg, Julius. "Die Reform der Augenheilkunde I." In *Handbuch der Gesamten Augenheilkunde,* edited by A. Graefe, T. Saemisch, C. von Hess, and T. Axenfeld, Vol. 15. 2nd rev. ed. Berlin: Springer, 1918.

Rucker, C. Wilbur. *A History of the Ophthalmoscope.* Rochester, Minn.: Whiting, 1971.

Tuchman, Arleen. "Helmholtz and the German Medical Community." In *Hermann von Helmholtz and the Foundations of Nineteenth-Century Science,* edited by David Cahan, 17–49. Berkeley: University of California Press, 1993.

O

Ophthalmotonometer

An ophthalmotonometer (tonometer for short) measures the intraocular pressure in the eye. This measurement is important because raised pressure can lead to loss of vision. The connection between some forms of visual loss and raised intraocular pressure became clear only in the course of centuries. Hippocrates used the name "glaucoma" for all visual loss resulting from conditions behind the pupil of the eye, especially visual loss that did not respond to treatment. In 1622 Richard Banister pointed out that raised intraocular pressure is an integral symptom of glaucoma. In 1830 the English ophthalmologist William Mackenzie was able to explain most of the symptoms forming the clinical picture of glaucoma by one basic anomaly: the raised intraocular pressure. As the understanding of the condition increased, the meaning of the term "glaucoma" changed.

In 1857 the German ophthalmologist Albrecht von Graefe discovered that acute glaucoma could be treated by iridectomy. In this operation a small piece of the base of the iris is excised, opening the blocked drainage system for the fluid that is produced in the eye and enabling the intraocular pressure to return to normal. The success of this operation led to the development of many instruments for measuring the intraocular pressure. Franciscus Cornelis Donders, the Dutch physiologist/ophthalmologist and director of the first Dutch Eye Hospital, introduced the name ophthalmotonometer in 1863.

There are two main types of tonometers. Impression tonometers measure the relationship between the force applied to the eye by a plunger placed on it and the depth of the indentation produced. Applanation tonometers measure the relationship between the force with which a plate is pressed against the eye and the size of the area that is flattened. Applanation tonometry is now in general use because, with this method, the deformation of the cornea, and thus its rigidity, is an unimportant factor. In older age groups, the increased rigidity of the cornea has a considerable influence on the values found with impression tonometry.

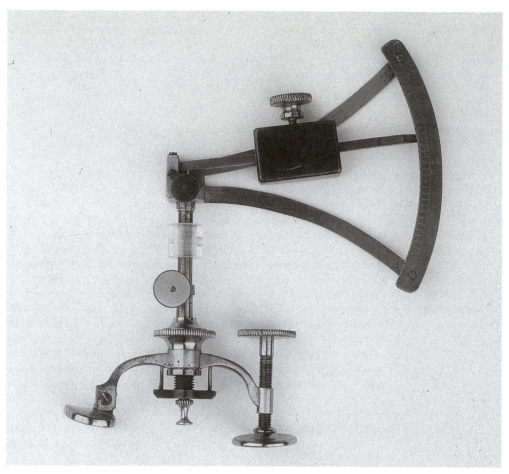

Von Graefe's ophthalmotonometer. Courtesy of the Royal Netherlands Ophthalmic Hospital, Utrecht.

The Utrecht school of ophthalmology, supervised by Donders and Herman Snellen, played a prominent role in the development of tonometry in the nineteenth century. In 1862, von Graefe and Donders, simultaneously but independently, decided to construct impression tonometers.

Von Graefe's ophthalmotonometer had a frame with two supports, a scale, a weighted indicator, and a plunger to which pressure plates of various diameters and curvatures could be screwed. These pressure plates had a very sharp spike at the center and were intended for attachment to the sclerotica. The patient is asked to lie down with the fixed support on the cheekbone and the adjustable support on the eyebrow. When the plunger is freed the weight presses on the sclera. The displacement of the plunger—that is, the depth of the indentation—can be read from the scale. When using the instrument it was found necessary to completely anesthetize the patient with chloroform in order to suppress the eye movements. It appears that measurements were never made with this instrument.

From 1862 to 1904 about twenty impression tonometers were developed, none of which proved to be very successful. The first impression tonometer that came into general use dates from 1905 and was designed by the Norwegian ophthalmologist Hjalmar Schiøtz. For decades it set the trend in large areas of the ophthalmic world, until H. Goldmann designed his universally accepted applanation tonometer (1954).

Bert van Leersum
Isolde den Tonkelaar

Bibliography

Donders, Franciscus Cornelis. *Annual Report of the Netherlands Eye Hospital* 4 (1863): 11.

The original orrery made by John Rowley, 1716. SM 1952-73. Courtesy of SSPL.

————. "Ueber einen Spannungsmesser des Auges (Ophthalmotonometer)(Aus einem schreiben von F.C. Donders am A. von Graefe)." *Archiv für Ophthalmologie 9* (1863): 215–21.

Draeger, Jörg. *Geschichte der Tonometrie.* Basel: Karger, 1961.

Haffmans, J.H.A. "Bijdrage tot de kennis van het glaucoma." *Annual Report of the Netherlands Eye Hospital* 2, Scientific Supplement (1861): 333.

Tonkelaar, Isolde den, Harold Henkes, and Bert van Leersum. "The Utrecht Ophthalmic Hospital and the Development of Tonometry in the 19th Century." *Documenta Ophthalmologica* 68 (1988): 57–63.

Orrery

An orrery is a model of the motions of the earth, moon, and sun that demonstrates such phenomena as day and night, the seasons, eclipses, and lunar phases. Some larger examples also include the other planets and their satellites. Unlike other planetary models (see **planetarium**), orreries demonstrated the sun-centered Copernican cosmology. The London clock- and instrument-maker George Graham, working with Thomas Tompion, created some fine "proto-orreries" at the beginning of the eighteenth century. However, the first "orrery" was made about 1713 by the London instrument-maker John Rowley for Charles Boyle, the fourth Earl of Orrery.

In eighteenth-century England, astronomy was regarded as an appropriate pursuit for members of polite society as it encouraged rational thinking and religious awe. A wide variety of astronomy books aimed at a popular audience, as well as games and souvenirs of astronomical events, were produced and marketed. Orreries, and the books and lectures that accompanied their use, should be considered in this context. Grand orreries were large pieces of furniture, often expensively and richly decorated. Smaller versions could be used by itinerant lecturers. In either case, orreries were often viewed simultaneously by a number of people and incorporated activities designed to be entertaining and inspirational as well as educational. Public displays of orreries were sometimes accompanied by an appeal to the grandeur of the universe; some of the lectures had the flavor of a religious sermon and were accompanied by suitably inspirational and devotional music.

The lecturer Adam Walker devised a large transparent orrery, or Eidourian, in the 1770s. About 20 feet in diameter, the Eidourian was developed further by Walker and his sons and allowed them to provide demonstrations to larger audiences than were possible even with the grand orreries. Interest in orreries was not confined to England. For example, in the United States, David Rittenhouse made orreries for colleges.

Liba Taub

Bibliography

Bedini, Silvio. "In Pursuit of Provenance: The George Graham Proto-Orreries." In *Learning, Language and Invention: Essays Presented to Francis Maddison*, edited by W.D. Hackmann and A.J. Turner, 54–77. Aldershot: Variorum, 1994.

King, Henry C., and John R. Millburn. *Geared to the Stars: The Evolution of Planetariums, Orreries, and Astronomical Clocks.* Toronto:University of Toronto Press, 1978.

Martin, Benjamin. *The Description and Use of Both the Globes, Armillary Sphere, and Orrery.* London, 1762.

Millburn, John R. "Nomenclature of Astronomical Models." *Bulletin of the Scientific Instrument Society* 34 (1992): 7–9.

Walters, Alice Nell. "Tools of Enlightenment: The Material Culture of Science in Eighteenth-Century England." Ph.D. dissertation. University of California at Berkeley, 1992.

Oscilloscope

An oscilloscope displays electrical waveforms. Until the 1890s, the only practical way to determine the waveshape of repetitive alternating voltages (such as mains supplies) was the Joubert "point to point" method, a stroboscopic technique for sampling successive points on the waveform. It used a mechanical rotating contactor that had to be reset for each point on the curve. The readings were then plotted by hand to produce the final trace. Not only was this extremely tedious, but the waveshape might have changed before the measurements were completed. Numerous attempts were made to automate this process, one of the most successful being the "ondographe" invented by Édouard Hospitalier in 1903. Commercial versions of this instrument were produced in France and Britain.

Moving-coil meters were well developed by the turn of the century, but these were useful only for measuring long-term average quantities, such as the root mean square values. The large inertia of the coil made it unable to follow the instantaneous variations of alternating currents of commercial frequencies (that is, 50 or 60 Hz). In 1893, André Eugène Blondel suggested reducing the coil to a rudimentary form consisting of a single loop of wire held under considerable tension, thereby enabling it to follow the waveform throughout the cycle. Movement of the coil was observed by a light beam focused on a small mirror fixed between the limbs of the coil and reflected onto a screen through another rotating mirror. The second mirror moved the spot at right angles to the movement of the small mirror, thereby producing a display showing voltage or current as a function of time.

The idea was taken up by William Du Bois Duddell, who constructed an instrument of this sort, initially for studying alternating electric arcs. His demonstration, given to the Institution of Electrical Engineers in 1899, was a sensation, for his oscillograph promised freedom from the frustrations of the Joubert method. Duddell, in association with the Cambridge Scientific Instrument Co., developed the mechanical oscillograph into a highly successful commercial instrument. Production continued for the next thirty years or so and it appeared in a variety of different versions. It was provided with a rotating or vibrating mirror to display an instantly visible trace, or with photographic accessories to produce a permanent record. It had two special advantages: it was possible to construct multichannel instruments with good insulation between channels; and it was suitable for high-voltage applications where good insulation from ground was required. Indeed, it was used for such applications until well after World War II.

Over the years, various other types of oscillograph were proposed. Blondel favored

Oscilloscope by Allen B. Du Mont Laboratories, ca. 1945. SM 1985-63. Courtesy of SSPL.

moving-iron movements, and he developed these in France. The moving-coil system was also developed in a highly original manner by Henri Abraham, the resulting instrument being known as the rheographe.

The arrival of the cathode ray tube sounded the knell of the mechanical instruments—although they took a long time to die (see **Geissler Tube**). The Frenchman Albert Hess had suggested using a cathode ray tube for waveform display as early as 1894, and Ferdinand Braun, in Germany, provided a practical demonstration of this device in 1897. The cathode rays, magnetically deflected by the applied voltage, were allowed to fall onto a fluorescent target plate. A rotating mirror provided the time axis of the display.

During the first two decades of the twentieth century, there was considerable development of cold cathode tubes with high accelerating voltages, the tubes being demountable and continuously evacuated. Alexandre Dufour was one of the leading experts. Smaller tubes with glass envelopes, both gas-filled and hard vacuum types, were available by the 1930s. It was the tremendous progress in electronics during World War II that made the oscilloscope (as it was by then generally known) the ubiquitous instrument we have today. The cathode ray oscilloscope has the following essential elements:

1. A display tube and associated power supplies.

2. Amplifiers applying the voltages to be examined to the vertical deflection plates. These are often equipped with high-impedance probes so that interference with the circuit under observation is minimized.

3. A time base supplying a sawtooth linear sweep to the horizontal plates. Associated with this is a synchronizing arrangement to ensure that a stationary trace is produced.

In the 1950s, the tubes often had two beams so that two traces could be observed simultaneously. Multitrace display is now more commonly achieved by switching a single beam between signals. Transient signals were more difficult to observe than repetitive waveforms. One way of doing this was to cause one horizontal sweep across the screen at the time of the transient, and to record the trace photographically—the so called "single shot" method. Another technique was to turn off the time base altogether, recording the vertical movements of the spot on a moving film. This was useful for waveforms such as speech signals. In the 1960s, phosphor storage tubes were developed that would hold the trace image on the screen electrostatically for several minutes.

Oscilloscope technology has been revolutionized in the last decade by the introduction of digital storage techniques. These enable the signals, both transient and repetitive, to be captured and held for repeated display on the tube. Connection can also be made to a **digital computer** if required, and a printed copy of the trace is easily provided. There is a tendency now to produce oscilloscopes that not only display the waveforms, but that perform various additional functions as well, such as spectral analysis using Fast Fourier tehniques.

Vivian J. Phillips

Bibliography

Czech, J. *The Cathode Ray Oscilloscope.* Eindhoven, Netherlands: Philips Technical Library, 1957.

Keller, Peter A. *The Cathode Ray Tube: Technology, History and Applications.* New York: Palisades, 1991.

MacGregor-Morris, J.T., and J.A. Henley. *Cathode Ray Oscillography.* London: Chapman and Hall, 1936.

Phillips, V.J. *Waveforms: A History of Early Oscillography.* Bristol: Hilger, 1987.

Osmometers used by Thomas Graham in his experiments on diffusion, ca. 1850. SM 1894-188/5. Courtesy of SSPL.

Osmometer

An osmometer measures the pressure on a membrane separating two regions containing differing quantities of ions. Understanding osmosis is crucial to many investigations in physiology and cellular biology. It is also important in numerous industrial processes, from the isolation of nuclear material to water purification and blood fractioning.

The basic design consists of a chamber separated into two areas by a selectively or semipermeable membrane. Although osmotic pressure can be measured for any fluid mixture that demonstrates the process of osmosis (diffusion through a membrane), it is primarily an issue for ion transport in liquids. Several methods of measuring the pressure have been developed, such as fluid displacement, lifting a column of mercury, or pressure readings made with a manometer. Osmotic pressure can also be measured by establishing an equilibrium point by compressing part of the chamber until the transported material will no longer pass through the membrane.

Osmosis is a key method for the transportation of materials in fluid systems, such as animal and plant cells, and as such has been studied by a wide range of investigators, from physicists to botanists. Abbé Jean-Antoine Nollet, a natural philosopher in Paris, identified osmosis in 1748. The first attempts at quantitative measurement were carried out independently by the French physiologist René Joachim Henri Dutrochet and the German physician Karl Vierordt, who were working between 1826 and 1846 on the passage of salt solutions through a membrane of pig's bladder. The water diffused more quickly than the salt, raising the level on one side of the membrane and creating a hydrostatic pressure. They found that the pressure varied not only with different salts, but also for differing concentrations of salts.

Dutrochet, whose interest in cell behavior was typical of the early investigations of osmosis, was concerned with establishing the mechanical basis of cell behavior. Using simple osmometers with the chambers set perpendicularly, he demonstrated that the pressure was greater than gravity. This important demonstration provided an insight into the movement of materials in cells, and it has become a fundamental part of plant and animal physiology.

The principle of osmosis was also at the heart of the dialyser, invented by the English chemist Thomas Graham in 1850. This device consisted of a pan of parchment paper placed in a water bath that he used to separate crystalloids (substances that would easily form crystals, such as salts) from colloids. Crystalloids would pass through the membrane quickly, while colloids did not pass through, or did so very slowly. Although Graham did not investigate the physical properties of the membrane, the behavior of the osmometer and the dialyser would be examined as part of a larger investigation into the structure and behavior of matter.

Moritz Traube, a German physiological chemist, saw that dialysis was analogous to the behavior of plant cells and reasoned that if there was unidirectional osmosis in a mixture of colloids and crystalloids (which were known to exist in cells), there might also be membranes that acted in the same way to crystalloid mixtures. In 1867, he succeeded in producing several membranes that were selectively permeable to binary solutions of crystalloids. He created these membranes by introducing a drop of nonsetting glue to various solutions, such as tannic acid, lead silicate, and copper silicate. The tannic acid formed a coating on the drop, creating a cell that he found to be selectively permeable. His 1867 paper outlined the various combinations of cell membranes and their permeabilities.

Despite Traube's success at demonstrating selective permeability, his method was not conducive to the study of osmotic pressure, since the cells were extremely delicate. Traube could study osmosis only in dilute solutions and in small quantities. In 1877 the German chemist and botanist Wilhelm Pfeffer introduced a method for forming membranes on the walls of porous earthenware pots, thereby making possible measurements of osmotic pressure amounting to several atmospheres without losing the selectivity of Traube's invention.

In 1885 the Dutch chemist Jacobus Van't Hoff developed a theory of dilute solutions that linked osmotic pressure with the behavior of gases. By showing that the osmotic pressure of a solution is equal to the pressure that the dissolved substance would demonstrate in the gaseous state if it occupied a volume equal to that of the solution, Van't Hoff demonstrated that Avogadro's theorem applied to dilute solutions. This had serious ramifications for both experimental analysis and theoretical ideas about an ideal gas law and the kinetic nature of solutions, since the gas constant (R) would then have the same value as K in the osmotic equation $PV = KT$. The use of osmosis to demonstrate the kinetic nature of ions in solution supported the development of molecular and atomic models of matter.

Another important examination of osmosis was made by the American physical chemists Josiah Willard Gibbs and Frederick Donnan, and led to the Donnan or Gibbs-Donnan equilibrium. Gibbs and Donnan used a simple model of ion flow in mixed solutions (NaCl and albumin, for example) to demonstrate the necessity of an equilibrium of ions on each side of a membrane even in cases where one of the substances passes freely through the barrier and the other does not pass through at all.

Most osmometers have been developed as specific experimental devices to study the behavior and relations of various membranes and solutes, and the instrument never became standardized as did the **microscope** or **barometer**. The exception to this has been the commercial production of membranes, which started with specially washed parchment paper, cellulose, and colloidion around 1900 and has since developed into hundreds of films and membranes with specific kinds of permeability. In industry, osmosis is usually studied with such devices as **flowmeters** and manometers; see also **gauge, pressure**.

Andrew Ede

Bibliography
Graham, Thomas. "On the Diffusion of Liquids." *Philosophical Transactions of the Royal Society of London* 76 (1850): 1–46, 805–36; 77 (1851): 483–94.

Morse, H.N. *The Osmotic Pressure of Aqueous Solutions*. Washington, D.C.: Carnegie Institutions, 1914.

Traube, Moritz. "Experimente zur Theorie der Zellenbildung und Endosmose." *Archiv für Anatomie, Physiologie und Wissenschaftliche Medicin* 87(1867): 87–102.

P

Pantograph

A pantograph is used to copy, reduce, or enlarge maps, plans, and drawings. From the seventeenth century onwards it formed part of the manufacturing repertoire of the mathematical instrument-maker.

The Jesuit astronomer and mathematician Christoph Scheiner published an account of the pantograph in his *Pantographice seu ars delineandi* (Rome, 1631). Scheiner had devised the instrument in 1603 after being intrigued and then frustrated by extravagant reports of a painter's copying instrument whose form and construction were deliberately kept secret. Scheiner's pantograph, based on the geometrical principle of similar triangles, was made of wooden rods joined together in the form of a parallelogram. An attachment fixed the instrument to the copying surface and acted as a fulcrum around which the tracing and drawing points turned. In use, the tracing point was guided around the lines of an image, and, as long as the three points (fixed, tracing, and drawing) were set up in line, the drawing point was constrained to execute the same motions, producing a copy of the original. Besides reproducing drawings to various scales, the pantograph could be set up on a vertically arranged drawing board as a perspective instrument, copying the outline of an object at a distance.

The pantograph was further publicized in print in Italy, but the majority of surviving instruments from the seventeenth century were made in the Netherlands, where Henricus Sneewins and Jacob de Steur, mathematical instrument-makers working in Leiden, produced a redesigned version in brass. Further modifications resulted in the classic form of the instrument, which became standard during the eigh-

teenth century. The basic mechanism consisted of two long and two shorter bars, movable on castor wheels. The positions of the drawing, tracing, and fixed points could be interchanged to configure the instrument for either reducing or enlarging, and the required proportions were set against scales engraved on two of the bars. Instruments of this type, incorporating improvements made by the Parisian maker Claude Langlois, were produced by a succession of French makers such as Canivet and Gourdin in the second half of the eighteenth century. These instruments were typically made of ebony with brass fittings and were sold in their own individually fitted boxes. Pantographs were also available from many mathematical instrument-makers in England, where brass displaced wood as the favored material in the early nineteenth century. To reduce the weight of the instrument (and hence the effects of friction by contact with the paper), the French maker Gavard introduced a tubular construction for the bars in the mid nineteenth century, and this refinement was adopted by other makers such as Stanley in England. In the twentieth century, cheap student versions were made of plastic and other new materials.

Although the pantograph could in principle enlarge or reduce any type of drawing, its performance as an enlarging instrument was suspect because any inaccuracy of line was magnified. Even as a reducing instrument it did not find universal favor. Though it seems to have been used for making reduced copies of maps, artists and architects could not obtain outlines and curves that were sufficiently smooth and reliable. The pantograph's mechanical defects suggested the possibility of improvement, and several new designs were

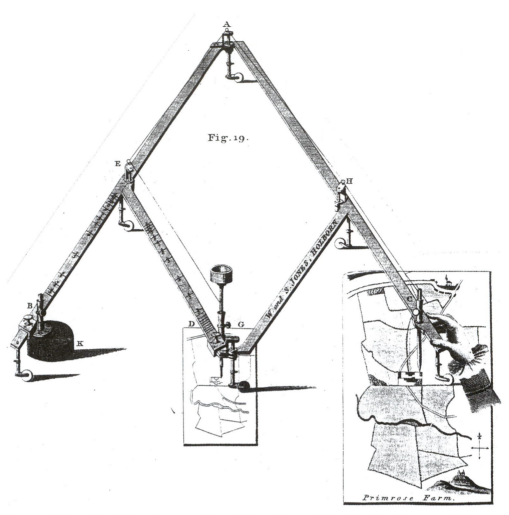

Pantograph in use, late eighteenth century. George Adams. Geometrical and Graphical Essays, *2nd edition. London: William Jones, 1797: Plate XXXI, Figure 19. Courtesy Museum of the History of Science, Oxford.*

forthcoming. There was an especially active period of invention in Scotland in the 1820s when heated controversy surrounded instruments such as Andrew Smith's apograph and his "new" pantograph, as well as John Dunn's pentograph. The most successful and long-lived of these new designs was the eidograph devised by the Edinburgh professor of mathematics William Wallace in 1821. Like the pantograph, the eidograph incorporated tracing, drawing, and fixed points, all three of which remained in a single line during operation. However Wallace's arrangement of these components was novel. The fixed weight was placed centrally and supported a graduated bar at each end of which was a pivoted, adjustable rod, one bearing the tracer and the other the drawing point. A fine chain (later a steel band) was used to link the two rods and ensure that they moved in parallel. Wallace was able to dispense with the pantograph's castors because his instrument was balanced around the central weight.

At the time Wallace was working on the eidograph, Edinburgh was a center for publishing and engraving, and among its characteristic products were multivolume encyclopedias. These were expected to be heavily illustrated with engraved plates whose images would usually be copied from existing publications. Although it was never developed commercially, Wallace devised a special form of eidograph to produce reversed images that were engraved directly onto copper plates for printing.

The simpler form of eidograph was manufactured by the London maker Robert Bate and then, in a reengineered version, by Alexander

Adie. It was further improved by W.F. Stanley in the second half of the nineteenth century and, in parallel with the pantograph, continued to figure in instrument makers' catalogs into the twentieth century.

Stephen Johnston

Bibliography

Hambly, Maya. *Drawing Instruments 1580–1980*. London: Sotheby's Publications, 1988.

Kemp, Martin. *The Science of Art*. New Haven: Yale University Press, 1990.

Simpson, A.D.C., "An Edinburgh Intrigue: Brewster's Society of Arts and the Pantograph Dispute." *Book of the Old Edinburgh Club* 1 (1991): 47–73.

Turner, Anthony. *Early Scientific Instruments: Europe, 1400–1800*. London: Philip Wilson for Sotheby's, 1987.

Wallace, W. "Account of the Invention of the Pantograph, and a Description of the Eidograph, a Copying Instrument Invented by William Wallace." *Transactions of the Royal Society of Edinburgh* 13 (1836): 418–39.

Paper Testing Equipment

Routine paper testing began in the early twentieth century when, realizing the need for quality control and for a common language within the industry, a few American paper and pulp producers formed the Technical Association of Pulp and Paper Industries (TAPPI). The first test methods were published in 1917 and the first edition of TAPPI paper testing methods appeared a few years later. To this day standards such as these are universally accepted and recognized. A number of British Standard Institute (BSI) tests are also in place for the main test routines.

A Mullen paper testing machine, early twentieth century. Cross and Bevan (1916): Plate XV, facing page 376. Courtesy of SSPL.

The most common paper test is for bursting strength, which the BSI defines as "the limiting resistance offered by a test piece of paper or board to a uniformly distributed pressure applied at right angles to its surface, up to a point at which it breaks." The Mullen test, which determines the pressure required to force a rubber diaphragm through the paper when the latter is clamped over the diaphragm, was developed by John Mullen, a paper-maker and superintendent of the Crocker Manufacturing Co. Mullen's first tester, sold to the Parson Pare Co. in 1887, is now in the Henry Ford Museum. By the 1920s there were several other machines on the market giving equivalent results, such as those manufactured by Ashcroft Mfg. Co. (New York) and W.D. Edwards & Sons (London). The Schopper-Dalén tester, introduced in the late 1920s, used compressed air as the pressure device. Many variations of these basic systems are in use today.

Tensile strength is determined by measuring the force required to break a narrow strip of paper when subjected to a longitudinal pull. The Marshall testing machine (by T.J. Marshall and Co. of Stoke Newington [London]) was in common use by the 1920s. Here, narrow strips of uniform width are clamped between the two jaws and the mill-head is turned steadily until fracture takes place. Greater accuracy could be obtained by using the Schopper tester, which was introduced in the late nineteenth century. Here the test strip is held between two screw clamps and forms a connecting link between a screw spindle fitted in a gear box at the lower end of the pillar, and the upper end of a pendulum arm. Any downward movement of the spindle is transmitted via the paper strip and causes the pendulum arm to move over a graduated scale. The force required to raise the pendulum weight is a measure of the tensile strength of the paper. Modern tests (such as using Instron testers) produce stress-strain curves for the paper. Estimates can then be made of the tensile energy absorption (TEA) or "toughness" of the sample and of its creep under tensile loads.

Paper thickness is measured with a vernier or screw **micrometer**. The Schopper Dial Micrometer, accurate to 1/1,000 mm, was common in the early years of the twentieth century. Recent designs, such as those produced by H.E. Messmer (England) in the 1970s, are of the deadweight variety and are fitted with heavy-duty synchronous motors to eliminate the hammering effect on the material being tested and hence increase the overall accuracy.

The color and brightness of paper are determined by comparing the percentage reflectance of the paper surface for the appropriate wavelengths of light, with the reflectance of a white standard using a **spectrophotometer**. The Zeiss Elephro instrument is now standard in the U.K. Opacity is measured by comparing the percentage reflectance of a single sheet of paper backed by a nonreflecting black cavity with that of a pile of sheets of the same material using similar machines used for color and brightness tests.

In the years after 1910, T.J. Marshall was manufacturing the Bibliometer for measuring water absorbency (for blotting paper). Strips of paper are suspended above a trough of distilled water and the rate of rise is noted over finite time intervals. The Kenley tester, designed in the 1960s by the British Paper and Board Industry Research Association and manufactured by Shirley Developments, Ltd., determined stiffness by measuring the force required to produce a standard deflection in a standard size test piece. In the early years of the twentieth century, Schopper introduced a machine to test the folding resistance of paper.

John Griffiths

Bibliography

Cross, Charles Frederick, and Edward John Bevan. *A Text-Book of Paper-Making.* 4th ed. London: Spon, 1916.

Grant, Julius, James H. Young, and Barry G. Watson, eds. *Paper and Board Manufacture: A General Account of Its History, Processes and Applications.* London: British Paper and Board Industry Federation, 1978.

McGill, Robert J. *Measurement and Control in Papermaking.* Bristol: Adam Hilger, 1980.

Mark, Richard E., ed. *Handbook of Physical and Mechanical Testing of Paper and Paperboard.* Vol. 1. New York: Marcel Dekker, 1983.

Rance, H.F., ed. *Handbook of Paper Science.* Vol. 2, *The Structure and Physical Properties of Paper.* Amsterdam: Elsevier Scientific, 1982.

Patch Clamp Amplifier

A patch clamp amplifier measures minute membrane currents, which underlie the electrical excitability of nerve, muscle, and sensory cells. In the classical patch clamp experiment, a tiny pipette is sealed onto a cell surface and current

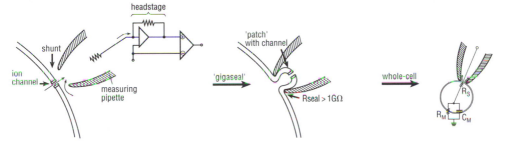

Schematic diagram showing stages of a patch clamp measurement. Courtesy of Erwin Neher.

flowing through the patch of membrane covered by the pipette is measured while the voltage across the patch is clamped to a desired value. Current changes resulting from the opening and closing of single ion channels (porelike macromolecules embedded in the membrane) can be resolved. These currents are very small, typically in the range of picoamperes to nanoamperes.

Early History

Between 1973 and 1980, attempts to measure single channel currents were only partially successful because it was not possible to obtain a tight seal between the measuring pipette and the cell under study. In 1976 single channel currents could be resolved for the first time, but they were obscured by background thermal noise. Consequently, resolution was modest, and it was sufficient to use relatively simple current-to-voltage converters with feedback resistors in the range of 100–1,000 megohms.

Early instruments were usually custom built in the few laboratories in which they were used. Their main part was a small headstage containing a low-noise FET operational amplifier and the feedback resistor, mounted onto a micromanipulator, with the measuring pipette directly attached. The rest of the instrument was not much more than a power supply, an adjustable voltage source for balancing offset potentials, and an additional differential amplifier.

Classical Patch Clamp Amplifiers

In 1980 procedures were found that provide a tight seal between measuring pipette and membrane with resistance values between pipette interior and surrounding bath in the range 1–100 gigaohms. This dramatically reduced the background noise of the signal source. Reduced noise of the signal source called for reduced noise of the amplifier and allowed wider bandwidth (at tolerable noise). To study voltage-

dependent ion channels it was particularly desirable to apply step changes in voltage. This, in turn, required circuitry for compensation of input and pipette capacitance, such that the measured currents would not be contaminated by capacitive charging transients.

The gigaseal also paved the way to whole-cell recording. With this technique the patch of membrane is ruptured, creating a low-resistance current pathway between pipette and cell interior. This can be used to apply voltage commands to the entire cell, and to record the currents that flow in response to such stimuli. This configuration can be represented by a three-component equivalent circuit: a parallel combination of membrane conductance and membrane capacitance, connected to the amplifier input through a series resistance.

Since the main interest in electrophysiology is to study dynamic changes in membrane conductance, it is desirable to compensate the influences of series resistance and membrane capacitance by suitable circuitry. The first low-noise amplifiers incorporating all the compensation circuits were designed by Fred Sigworth. These circuits were quite complex and commercial production and support was indicated. Several brands have been available since the early 1980s, produced by Axon Instruments, Foster City, California; Biologic, Claix, France; Dagan Corporation, Minneapolis, Minnesota; HEKA Electronic, Lambrecht, FRG; List-Elektronik, Darmstadt, FRG; and Nihon-Kohden, Japan.

Properties and Impact of the Patch Clamp Amplifier

A typical patch clamp amplifier can measure pA currents at 30–100 kHz resolution. Its noise spectral density is minimal at 100 Hz–1 kHz, reaching a value of

$$\approx 0.8 \, fA / \sqrt{Hz} \quad .$$

When limited to the dc—3 kHz bandwidth—total noise is typically 0.07 pArms.

In 1995, approximately two thousand to five thousand laboratories worldwide were using patch clamp amplifiers. The impact of patch clamp technology is twofold. On the one hand, it makes it possible to study the opening and closing of individual ion channels. This has been, indeed, the only case in which confirmational changes of single biological macromolecules could be studied in real time. It provided detailed knowledge on the kinetics of protein reactions. It also allowed separation of distinct contributions to membrane current in cases when a given membrane contained multiple channel types.

On the other hand, the whole-cell configuration revolutionized the electrophysiological investigation of cells of mammalian origin, since most cell types of mammalian tissue (in contrast to many cell types from invertebrates) are too small in size for the conventional recording techniques.

Intregrating Headstage
The feedback resistor of the current voltage converter proved to be one of the main noise sources in current amplifier designs, even though the resistance is typically as high as 50 gigaohms. Therefore, one way of improving noise performance is to use capacitance feedback. This means that the input current is integrated, such that subsequent differentiation leads to a signal proportional to input current. In such a configuration any dc current will lead to saturation of the integrating stage—a problem that is handled by intermittent resetting of the integrator.

Computer Controlled Patch Clamp Amplifiers
Detailed biophysical analysis, which is usually performed on current records measured by patch clamp amplifiers, calls for extensive coordination between the amplifier and the data acquisition system. Ideally, the data acquisition system should "know" all the amplifier settings (gain, polarities, compensation settings, and so on) and—even better—control them. The latest generation of the patch clamp amplifier series designed by Fred Sigworth (the EPC-9) has a built-in data acquisition system and computer interface with complete digital control over all amplifier parameters. Many of the hardware functions of conventional amplifiers can then be

implemented by software and some of the compensation features can be automated.

Erwin Neher

Bibliography
Hamill, Owen P., et al. "Improved Patch-Clamp Techniques for High-Resolution Current Recording from Cells and Cell-Free Membrane Patches." *Pflügers Archiv* 391 (1981): 85–100.

Neher, Erwin, Bert Sakmann, and Joe H. Steinbach. "The Extracellular Patch Clamp: A Method for Resolving Currents through Individual Open Channels in Biological Membranes." *Pflügers Archiv* 375 (1978): 219–28.

Sigworth, Frederick J. "Design of the EPC-9, a Computer-Controlled Patch Clamp Amplifier: 1. Hardware." *Journal of Neuroscience Methods* 56 (1995): 195–202.

———. "Electronic Design of the Patch Clamp." In *Single Channel Recording*, edited by B. Sakmann and E. Neher, 95–127. 2nd ed. New York: Plenum, 1995.

———, Hubert Affolter, and Erwin Neher. "Design of the EPC-9, a Computer-Controlled Patch Clamp Amplifier: 2. Software." *Journal of Neuroscience Methods* 56 (1995): 203–15.

Pedometer
A pedometer counts the number of paces walked—and thus, assuming paces of uniform length, the distance traversed. It consists of a pace-counting mechanism and a display. Early pedometers used a dial, or series of dials, to indicate distance. Modern ones use liquid crystal displays and incorporate electronic calculators to give estimates of speed. These are primarily for the recreational market.

Illustrations of pedometers from the sixteenth century survive in the works of Leonardo da Vinci, and also of Melchior Pfintzing, author of *Methodus Geometrica* (Nuremberg, 1598), who showed examples attached both to a man and a horse. John Fischer obtained a British patent for a "geometrical and pedometrical watch" in 1783. This relied on a pusher tied to the wearer's clothes by a piece of string, in turn kept taut by a little instrument containing a watch spring. The motion of the leg turned a wheel of ten teeth one tooth every step, and subsequent gears in the train allowed up to twenty

Sixteenth-century pace counters. Alfred Rohde. Die Geschichte der wissenschaftlichen Instrumente vom Beginn der Renaissance bis zum Ausgang des 18. Jahrhunderts. *Leipzig: Klinkhardt & Biermann, 1923. Courtesy of SSPL.*

thousand paces to be counted. Ralph Gout introduced another version in 1799. This was available in three forms, to suit people, horses (by being fixed to the saddle), and carriages.

An instrument in which the mechanism swings about a lever fixed to the wearer was described in France in the 1720s. In 1831, the Englishman William Payne patented a pedometer with a horizontal pendulum that swings up and down as the wearer moves. This pattern proved popular and long-lived and is still in use today.

Many pedometers were made by watch- and clock-makers trying their hands at another type of gadget. The Science Museum, London, has two eighteenth-century pedometers. One was made by Johann Willebrand, a compass-maker working in Augsburg. The other, bearing the name of George Adams, a prominent instrument-maker of London, was to be worn attached to the belt and with a lever strapped to the leg.

Mechanisms similar to the pedometer appeared in revolution counters for carriage axles (as in the Gout patent), **current meters**, and **odometers**. The idea that the wearer's movements could turn a small mechanism was also used to advantage in the design of self-winding watches.

Jane Insley

Bibliography

Abridgements of Specifications Relating to Optical, Mathematical and Other Philosophical Instruments, A.D. *1636–1866.* London: Her Majesty's Stationery Office, 1875.

Pendulum

In its most basic form, a pendulum is simply a mass suspended at the end of a cord or rod, subject to the force of gravity. When stationary, the device is a plumb bob and acts as a vertical indicator. Plumb bobs have been used since antiquity in astronomy, surveying, and building construction. When the bob swings from side to side, it acts as a pendulum.

For an idealized pendulum consisting of a weightless string and a point mass, the time for one cycle of the swing depends only on the length of the string or rod and the coefficient of gravitational attraction (g). The pendulum can therefore be used to determine either time (from the period of the swing), the length of its own string or rod, or the gravitational coefficient at the location where the pendulum is swinging. If any two of its three variables are held adequately constant, the pendulum can yield the third as a measurement. Pendulums have been used for each of these measurements in a wide variety of scientific and industrial applications.

Time Measurement

Galileo began the scientific study of the pendulum, reputedly after observing a swinging cathedral lamp in 1582. The relation of the pendulum's period to its length was investigated by Marin Mersenne, who experimentally determined the length of a "seconds pendulum" (the length of a pendulum that swings in 1 second) in 1644. Christiaan Huygens implemented the law into a pendulum timekeeping clock in 1656.

In the course of such investigations it was realized that the motion of real pendulums is not adequately described by the theory devised for the idealized version. In 1673 Huygens improved the basic equation to allow for the effect of the distributed mass of the rod and the size of the bob. This improvement in mathematical modeling helped to make pendulum clocks realistic timekeepers. The pendulum clock became standard not just for domestic use but, in increasingly sophisticated forms, also for scientific use.

Length Standards

The eighteenth century saw several initiatives to reform the system of standards. Although the meter was eventually defined in revolutionary France in terms of the meridian arc passing through Paris, an alternative proposal had suggested that a seconds pendulum could provide a natural basis for the ultimate standard of length. This alternative was subsequently pursued in Britain and by act of Parliament the seconds pendulum became the Imperial length standard in 1824. However, problems with reproducibility and an increasing appreciation of the minute factors affecting the precision of this standard led to its official abandonment in 1855.

Gravity Measurement

In the seventeenth century, Huygens, among others, used a pendulum to investigate the value of gravitational attraction at a specific location. This was done by observing the period over many swings and knowing the length. So significant was this means of determining the force of gravity that its unit was expressed in terms of the pendulum length until the nineteenth century, when the unit gal was introduced. Pendulums for the absolute determination of gravity have been used into the twentieth century. Possibly the last gravity pendulum to be developed was a Russian-made apparatus designed by Yu A. Slivin and used in 1972 to link gravity measurements between Moscow and Australia. Five dual pendulums swing four thousand times in five evacuated containers for each determination. Each unit uses different materials and pendulum lengths to statistically reduce errors.

Error Correction and Compensation

Obtaining time or gravity measurements from a pendulum requires highly developed experimental design and practice. Key influencing effects have been gradually brought under control.

Temperature variation was one of the first factors to be tackled. A pendulum rod expands when heated and therefore temperature variation alters the length of the pendulum, causing an error in the period. Using materials with different coefficients of thermal expansion, both George Graham and John Harrison created constant-length pendulums in the 1720s. Graham's mercurial column used a mercury mass fastened to the end of the steel rod. As the steel expanded to lengthen the pendulum rod, the center of the mercury mass moved upwards to compensate by the appropriate amount. Harrison's grid-iron arrangement used brass and iron grids over the full length of the pendulum.

Friction due to air resistance slows the period of swing. In the late nineteenth century, Thomas C. Mendenhall overcame this problem by placing his gravity-measuring pendulum in an evacuated enclosure.

A third error arises in timing precisely when the pendulum passes through the chosen reference position during its cycle. Timing methods were cunningly contrived, such as comparing the rate of the free pendulum with that of the pendulum of a standard clock (late eighteenth century) and using electrical methods (early 1900s) to make a circuit each swing.

Applications

The properties of the pendulum have led to its incorporation as a controlling mechanism in other devices. For example, Giovanni Caselli used pendulums to synchronize telegraph signals in his pantelgraph, a late-nineteenth-century facsimile machine.

A more successful and widespread use for the basic components of the pendulum was as engine governors. When a bob is rotated in a circle at the end of a rod, the degree of its outward swing can be used to control rotational speed. Governors were occasionally used to control windmill speed from around 1740 but did not catch on. Extensive application began with James Watt and Matthew Boulton, who, in 1783, sold a rotary steam engine that incorporated the rotating ball governor. The subsequent surge in interest in the design of the steam engine governor is impressive: from 1836 to 1902 over one thousand patents were granted in the United States alone.

Peter H. Sydenham

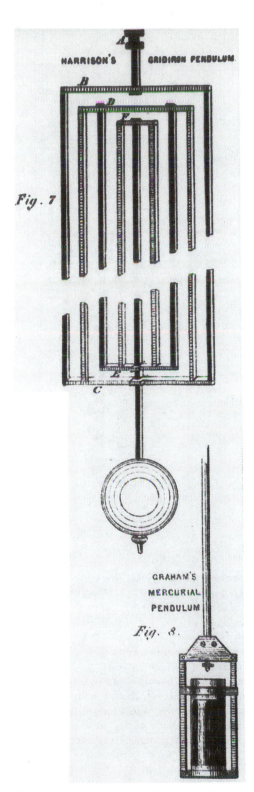

Fig. 7

Fig. 8

GRAHAM'S
MERCURIAL
PENDULUM

Harrison's and Graham's pendulums. Godfray (1880): facing page 41. Courtesy of Peter H. Sydenham.

Bibliography

Godfray, Hugh. *A Treatise on Astronomy.* London: Macmillan, 1880.

Lenzen, Victor F., and Robert P. Multhauf. "Development of Gravity Pendulums in the 19th Century." *Contributions from the Museum of History and Technology.* United States National Museum Bulletin 240, paper 38. Washington, D.C.: Smithsonian Institution Press, 1966.

Privat-Deschanel, A. *Elementary Treatise on Natural Philosophy,* Part 3, translated by J.D. Everett. 12th ed. London: Blackie, 1891.

Simpson, A.D.C. "The Pendulum as the British Length Standard: A Nineteenth-Century Legal Aberration." In *Making Instruments Count,* edited by R.G.W. Anderson, J.A. Bennett, and W.F. Ryan, 174–90. Aldershot: Variorum, 1993.

Sydenham, Peter H. *Measuring Instruments: Tools of Knowledge and Control.* London: Peter Peregrinus for the Science Museum, 1979.

Penetrometer and Penetration Test

Penetrometers cover a large group of instruments that push a probe into a substance; the resistance to penetration gives an indication of the properties. Penetrometers find applications in many fields, but especially in civil engineering, where they are used to investigate the properties of the ground.

Builders have long used simple penetrometers to assess the quality of the ground and to determine the depth at which to set the foundations for a building. The test would consist of hammering a simple iron bar into the ground and noting the resistance to penetration. Soft ground would offer small resistance, while an increased resistance would indicate stronger and thus more suitable ground. A larger-scale test would use a timber pile driven into the ground by a drop weight, working in a guide frame. These early test results for one site were not easily compared with those from another site. Also, since there was no theoretical background, the interpretation of the test results depended entirely on personal experience.

Development of Modern Penetration Tests

The science of geotechnics, or soil mechanics, studies the behavior and properties of the

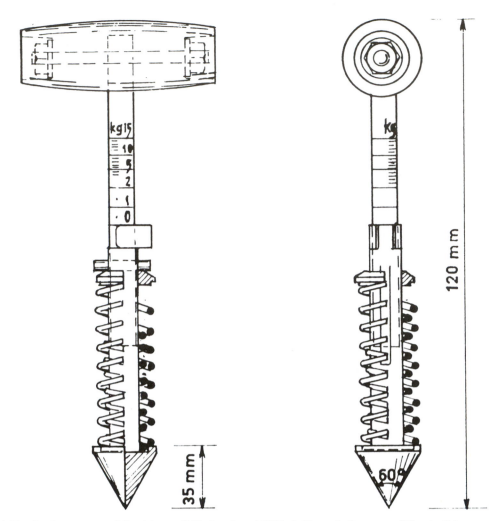

A "Pocket Penetrometer," Danish, ca. 1931. Sanglerat (1972): 3, Figure 2. Courtesy of Elsevier Science Company.

ground as relevant to civil engineering. It also develops theories relating the design of foundations and other structures to the properties of the ground. By the early decades of the twentieth century, geotechnics could be applied to the practical problems of civil engineering design. Extensive research and development led to the establishment of standard penetrometers and test procedures, together with correlations by which the actual properties of the ground could be inferred from the results of penetration tests.

Some of the first standards appeared in Sweden in 1917 and in Denmark in 1927. By the late 1930s there were two main test procedures, both of which have widespread use today: the dynamic penetration test, in which the penetrometer is driven into the ground by repeated blows of a hammer; and the static pen-

etration test, in which the penetrometer is driven into the ground by the continuous thrust of a mechanically or hydraulically operated jack.

Dynamic Penetration Test

The basic procedure is to drive into the ground a string of rods, having a cone point at the lower end, and using a standard dynamic effort. In order to minimize skin friction, the rods are rotated at regular intervals of depth and the applied torque is measured. The number of blows to drive the cone a specified increment of penetration and the torques are recorded against depth. The correlation with the particular ground properties under investigation is determined by laboratory tests on samples taken from boreholes. The correlations are usually site specific and must be done for each new site.

There are various designs for light equipment, operated by hand, that are suitable for shallow depths. Heavier equipment for achieving greater depths is operated by purpose-built rigs that usually can be towed behind a car. Most countries have national standards which, in general, are compatible between countries. For example, the British Standard, BS 1377:1990, covers two tests, both of which use a 90° cone and extension rods. The "Heavy Test" cone has a base diameter of 4.37 cm and requires a driving effort of a 50 kg weight falling 50 cm; the "Super Heavy Test" cone has a base diameter of 5.05 cm and requires a driving effort of a 63.5 kg weight falling 75 cm.

Standard Penetration Test (SPT)

This is a form of dynamic penetration test that is carried out at the bottom of boreholes. It developed in the United States from the practice of taking small soil samples from trial boreholes in order to identify the strata and carry out simple laboratory tests. The sampler consisted of a heavy tube of 2-in. (5.1-cm) outside diameter, with a cutting edge at its lower end that was driven into the ground by a drop weight operating through drill rods. The driving resistance gave a useful indication of the strength of the ground. In the United States in 1947, a standard was proposed by Karl Terzaghi, one of the pioneers of modern soil mechanics, and a national standard for the United States was introduced in 1958. The test now has worldwide use and is covered by compatible national standards. For example, the British Standard, BS 1377:1990 specifies a sample tube of 5.1-cm outside diameter and a drop weight of 63.5-kg (140 lbs.) falling 76 cm (30 in.). The driving effort is comparable to that of the Super Heavy dynamic penetration test. There is a large range of test data covering the use of the SPT in soils and in weak rocks, and many useful correlations have been developed.

Static Cone Penetration Test (CPT)

Driven by a continuous thrust, the penetrometer includes a device enabling the resistance on the cone point to be measured separately from the total resistance. Probably, the CPT was first developed for use in the weak alluvial soils of the delta region of Belgium and the Netherlands. One of the earliest penetrometers was reported in the Netherlands in 1934. The penetrometer and rods were of 3.6 cm outside diameter, and the resistance on the cone point was measured by a string of rods set inside the hollow outer rods. The penetrometer was advanced to the required depth by pushing on the outer rods; the cone resistance was then measured by pushing on the inner rods. Various improvements followed. One, in 1953, was the inclusion of a friction sleeve set just above the cone so as to measure the local skin friction. Penetrometers using electrical transducers to measure the resistances first appeared in 1948, and by the 1960s electrical penetrometers were in general use. National standards generally follow practice in the Netherlands. For example, the British Standard, BS 1377:1990, specifies an electrical penetrometer for measuring cone resistance and local friction. The diameter is 3.57 cm, the cone angle is 60°, the length of the friction sleeve is 13.37 cm, and the standard rate of penetration is 2 cm/second. The CPT gives virtually a direct measurement of the shear strength of the ground, and correlations exist for many other properties.

Penetrometer rigs vary from light 2-ton-thrust rigs to 20-ton-thrust vehicle-mounted rigs with onboard computer equipment for processing and storing the test data.

Later developments of the electrical penetrometer include the piezocone, which also measures the pore water pressure in the ground. Other developments include penetrometers for measuring seismic-wave velocities and for measuring various chemical parameters of the soil and groundwater.

T.R.M. Wakeling

Bibliography

British Standard BS5930:1981. "Code of Practice for Site Investigations." London: British Standards Institution.

British Standard BS1377:1990. "Method of Test for Soils for Civil Engineering Purposes: Part 9. In Situ Methods." London: British Standards Institution.

Clayton, C.R.I. *The Standard Penetration Test (SPT): Methods and Use.* London: Construction Industry Research and Information Association, 1995.

Meigh, A.C. *Cone Penetration Testing, Methods and Interpretation.* London: Butterworths with Construction Industry Research and Information Association, 1987.

Sanglerat, G. *The Penetrometer and Soil Exploration.* London: Elsevier, 1972.

The first peptide synthesizer, built by Merrifield and Stewart in 1965. Courtesy of R.B. Merrifield.

Peptide Synthesizer

A peptide synthesizer carries out the chemical synthesis of peptides or proteins from their component amino acids. Peptides are compounds that occur in every living cell. They play important roles in growth and development, metabolic regulation, immunology, pharmacology and many other areas. To study these functions it is important to have a convenient supply of the natural compounds and suitable analogs.

Ever since Emil Fischer founded the field of peptide chemistry in 1901, the major goals have been to improve the reactions necessary for the synthesis of these compounds and to find ways to simplify and accelerate the process. Initially, the standard procedures of organic synthesis were used, in which reactions were carried out in homogeneous solution, followed by careful purification after each peptide bond was formed, usually by time-consuming crystallization of the product.

R.B. Merrifield introduced the concept of solid phase peptide synthesis in 1963. This technique made it possible to mechanize and automate the synthesis. An α-amino acid was covalently attached to a solid support, such as small cross-linked polystyrene beads, and the subsequent amino acids of the peptide chain were added, one at a time, by a series of chemical reactions. The important feature of this approach was that the support was solvated, but completely insoluble in all solvents, and thus the attached peptide chain was also insoluble. This allowed the rapid separation of the peptide from the soluble reagents, by-products, and solvents by simple filtration and washing steps without transfer of the peptide from a single reaction vessel or the tedious multiple manual manipulations of classical methods of organic chemistry.

The first peptide synthesis instrument was constructed by Merrifield and John M. Stewart in 1965, and described in detail a year later. The apparatus consisted of two units: (1) the liquid-handling system containing the reaction vessel, and the components required to store and select reagents and to transfer them into and out of the vessel; and (2) a programmer that automatically controlled and sequenced the operations of the various components. The reagents were selected by a multiport rotary valve and transferred by a metering pump into a glass reaction vessel (usually 5 to 100 ml) fitted with a sintered glass filter. The reagent and beads with attached peptide were mixed by a gentle rocking motion and after a preset reaction time or after automatic monitoring by a suitable chemical method, the solvent was removed by vacuum filtration. The process was controlled by a stepping drum programmer containing adjustable pins that actuated microswitches that operated the timers and liquid-handling components. After one cycle of one hundred steps of the drum, over a period of 4 hours, one new amino acid was added to the peptide chain. Each remaining amino acid was selected by another rotary valve and added in the same manner by another cycle of the program. Following the assembly of the correct amino acid sequence, the peptide was cleaved from the resin support by a strong anhydrous acid, and the peptide, now soluble, was purified and characterized. The overall time and effort for the synthesis was greatly reduced, especially for large peptides and small proteins. Ribonuclease A, an enzyme containing 124 residues, was soon synthesized on this machine.

Automated peptide synthesis can be conducted in two basic modes: by the original batch process or by a flow process in which the support is packed in a column and reagents are pumped through it. Other variables include the composition of the support (polyacrylamide, polyethylene glycol, carbohydrates, porous glass, and so on), the details of the chemical reactions (protecting groups, coupling reagents), the composition of the monomer units (amino acids or peptides), the programmer (microprocessors, computers) used to control and monitor the process, and the scale of the synthesis, which usually has been in the range of 1 mg to 1 kg of peptide.

All of these variables have been studied in detail and adapted to the construction of instruments in many research laboratories. In addition, several more sophisticated commercial machines have been produced. The first one, made by Schwartz Mann Biochemicals in Orangeburg, New York, was followed by ones from Beckman Instruments in Palo Alto, California, Vega Biotechnologies in Tucson, Arizona, and subsequently by Applied Biosystems in Foster City, California, Millipore Corp. (now PerSpectives Biosystems) in Bedford, Massachusetts, Advanced Chem Tech in Louisville, Kentucky, DuPont in Wilmington, Delaware, Gilson Medical Electronics in Middletown, Wisconsin, and Rainin Instruments in Woburn, Massachusetts. Most of these instruments were designed to synthesize one peptide at a time, but because of the demand for large numbers of peptides for structure-function studies and drug discovery, some can produce many peptides simultaneously by use of multiple reaction vessels and complex valving or robotic arms. The solid phase technique has recently been adapted to combinatorial methods for the simultaneous synthesis of libraries containing millions of peptides, composed of all possible sequences of a selected set of amino acids.

R.B. Merrifield

Bibliography

Merrifield, R.B. "Solid Phase Peptide Synthesis: I. The Synthesis of a Tetrapeptide." *Journal of the American Chemical Society* 85 (1963): 2149–54.
———, John M. Stewart, and Nils Jernberg. "An Instrument for the Automated Synthesis of Peptides." *Analytical Chemistry* 38 (1966): 1905–14.
Schroder, Eberhard, and Klaus Lubke. *The Peptides*. Translated by E. Gross. New York: Academic, 1965–1966.
Veggeberg, S. "Today's Peptide Chemists Face a Dizzying Array of Synthesizer Choices." *Scientist* 9 (1995): 1–7.

Permeameter

Permeability is a measure of the ability of porous media to transmit fluids—the fluid-flow analog of electrical or thermal conductivity. Permeability in a perfectly homogeneous isotropic porous medium is equal in all directions—seldom the case in natural materials. In natural porous media, permeability is tensorial—that is, it varies with direction. Measurement of fluid flow in a given direction is an average of permeability in a single plane.

In the mid nineteenth century, Henry Darcy, a French hydraulic engineer, developed an empirical relationship for the vertical flow of fluid through packed sand for water filtration. Darcy's law states that "the volumetric rate of flow per unit cross-sectional area of permeable media (volumetric flux) is directly proportional (and opposite in direction) to the potential gradient, and inversely proportional to the viscosity of the fluid." One Darcy is defined as that permeability that will permit a fluid of one centipoise viscosity to flow at a rate of 1 cm^3 per second through a cross-sectional area of 1 cm^2 when the pressure gradient is 1 atm/cm. Darcy showed that the apparent velocity of a fluid flowing through a porous medium is proportional to the pressure gradient, and he assumed it would be proportional to the reciprocal of the viscosity.

In natural porous media, permeability values span many orders of magnitude—10^{-6} Darcy or less in tight gas reservoir sands to greater than tens of Darcys in highly permeable

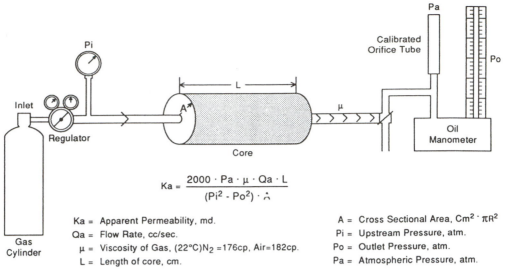

$$Ka = \frac{2000 \cdot Pa \cdot \mu \cdot Qa \cdot L}{(Pi^2 - Po^2) \cdot \overset{\cdot}{A}}$$

Ka = Apparent Permeability, md.
Qa = Flow Rate, cc/sec.
μ = Viscosity of Gas, (22°C)N$_2$ =176cp, Air=182cp.
L = Length of core, cm.

A = Cross Sectional Area, Cm^2 · πR^2
Pi = Upstream Pressure, atm.
Po = Outlet Pressure, atm.
Pa = Atmospheric Pressure, atm.

Single-phase gas permeameter and generalized equation. Courtesy of Robert A. Skopec and Andrew Hurst.

reservoirs. P.Z. Forchheimer, a German hydraulic engineer, showed in 1901 that Darcy's law is limited and restricted to low volumetric fluxes. At higher fluxes, the potential gradient required for a given volumetric flux is greater than that predicted by Darcy's law by an amount proportional to the product of the fluid's density and the square of its volumetric flux. The coefficient of proportionality, designated β, is the inertial resistivity of the porous medium. Inertial energy dissipation is caused by time-rates of change (tortuosity) in the direction and magnitude of velocity.

The permeability of a porous medium to gas (single phase) depends on the mean free path of the flowing gas as well as its absolute pressure. Gas slippage effects first described by the petroleum engineer L.J. Klinkenberg (1941) can cause permeability to be overestimated. Gas slippage is more pronounced in low permeability samples. When permeability is measured at several mean pore pressures, the data can be extrapolated to an equivalent nonreactive fluid permeability. The use of liquids for permeability measurements eliminates problems associated with gas slippage. Liquid flow rates may lead to problems with fluid-rock interaction, fine particle migration, plugging of pores, and microbial damage.

Instruments

Several types of permeameters have been developed for laboratory determinations of permeability from small samples of porous media.

The first permeameters were developed in the nineteenth century for water filtration and groundwater (aquifer) applications. Hydrologists often determine flow potential differences by measuring changes in liquid "heads"—the elevations to which water rises in packed sand columns. In the early twentieth century, petroleum engineers and geologists identified permeability as a critical reservoir parameter because it is the only elementary rock property related directly to fluid flow. The first commercial petroleum core analysis report containing permeability measurements on several subsurface samples was issued by Core Laboratories in 1936 from their Dallas, Texas, facility. There are no standards for the design and fabrication of permeameters, and few instruments are available commercially.

Single-phase permeameters measure single-phase gas or liquid, at steady or unsteady state. Most permeameters used in the petroleum industry measure single-phase gas permeability at steady state, and most are designed for cylindrical samples. Probe permeametry, first described over forty years ago, uses the concept of flowing gas from the end of a tube that is sealed against the surface of a rock sample. The probe permeameter measures several flow parameters, and permeability is calculated from a modified version of Darcy's law; permeability can be measured continuously without the need for cylindrical samples.

Routine permeability measurements require jacketing, booting, or sleeving to ensure reliable data. Sealing the sample radially with a conformable (Hassler) sleeve prevents the measurement fluid from bypassing the sample. Pressure is applied to the conformable sleeve by mechanical, hydraulic, or pneumatic means, and creates a seal between the sample and sleeve. The stress condition under which a measurement is made and the sample orientation may have a significant effect upon permeability. Flow rates during single-phase gas permeability measurements should be sufficiently low to prevent turbulent flow. Permeameter calibration is essential prior to performing measurements. The permeameter must be leak-free to ensure reliable operation.

Most permeability measurements on plug and full diameter samples use single-phase gas (usually air, nitrogen, or helium). In porous media that contain liquids, air permeability should be used on a relative basis and is only an approximation to the more useful and appropriate single-phase liquid permeability. Gas permeability depends upon the particular gas used, conditions of pressure and temperature, and the mean pore pressure. Steady-state gas flow is achieved when the upstream and downstream pressures and the flow rate all become invariant with time.

Single-phase unsteady-state (transient) permeameters use fixed-volume fluid reservoirs upstream (reservoir pressure decline) or downstream (pressure buildup) of the sample. Pulse decay permeameters use a dual (upstream and downstream) sample reservoir approach and are appropriate in low permeability samples where inertial flow resistance may be a problem—for example, in the range 0.1–0.01 x 10^{-7}D. The pressure-falloff method uses a single sample reservoir, a single pressure transient pressure-falloff, and calculation of slippage factors and inertial resistivity.

Unsteady-state methods are superior to steady-state methods when evaluating samples with permeability of $<10^{-3}$D. Unsteady-state tests are performed in a fraction of the time it takes to run steady-state measurements. Some automated data acquisition systems measure Boyle's law porosity and unsteady-state permeability in a single test.

Robert A. Skopec
Andrew Hurst

Bibliography

American Petroleum Institute. "Recommended Practice for Determining Permeability of Porous Media." *American Petroleum Institute* 27 (1956): 27.

Darcy, H. *Les Fontaines publiques de la ville de Dijon.* Paris: V. Dalmont, 1856.

Forchheimer, P. Zeitz. "Wasserbewegung durch Boden." *Zeitschrift Vereines der Deutscher Ingenieure* 45 (1901): 1782–88.

Jones, S.C. "Two-point Determinations of Permeability and PV vs. Net Confining Pressure." *Society of Petroleum Engineering Formation Evaluation Journal* (March 1988): 235–41.

Klinkenbert, L.J. "The Permeability of Porous Media to Liquids and Gases." *Drilling and Production Practice* (1941): 200–13.

PET Scanner

PET is an acronym for positron emission tomography, a technique and a technology for obtaining quantitative images of two-dimensional slices, or tomographs, of biochemical processes in living beings. In contrast to **Computer Tomography Scanning**, which provides structural information (such as bone density) about living beings, PET provides functional, time-dependent images of the rate of flow of specific molecules through a particular area of the body. PET thus provides a solution to the problem of how to obtain useful information about biochemical processes taking place in relatively inaccessible sections of living organisms (for example, the heart and brain). The information that PET presents is both quantitative and visual, demanding careful measurement and complex physiological modeling in order to be interpreted.

PET is currently used in a variety of clinical studies, including heart tissue viability, epilepsy focal localization, bone and breast cancer detection, and head trauma diagnosis. It has also been used in psychophysiological studies—correlating oxygen bloodflow in specific regions of the brain with motor movement, visual attention, and cognitive tasks, as well as more complex cognitive skills. In psychiatry, Seymour Kety, David Ingvar, Monte Buchsbaum, and Jonathan Brodie each led teams that conducted extensive studies of schizophrenia. The brains of people suffering from other mental disorders have also been imaged. These have stimulated speculation on possible biological or molecular explanations of these disorders, but diagnostic ability still eludes investigations.

PET is located at the intersection of a number of disciplines and technical paradigms. Though they are numerous, it is perhaps better to gesture toward the complexity than exclude outright vital participants. One strand fundamental to functional imaging is the biological tracer technique for which Georg von Hevesy was awarded the Nobel Prize in 1944. Hevesy detailed the means whereby a radioactive isotope of a molecule could be used in place of that molecule because it is chemically indistinguishable, yet its radioactivity can be tracked. This technique was used in medical physics and later nuclear medicine, first to follow molecules and later to image their distribution. Unlike x-rays, which are produced externally in tubes and transmitted through organisms in order to reveal their structure, these radioactive tracers emit their rays from within.

Early detection of the pathways of these tracers was with **Geiger-Müller counters** and later with **scintillation counters**. A significant advantage in data gathering was the rectilinear scanner introduced by Bernard Cassen in 1949, which rapidly and precisely took measurements over a bodily area in a zigzag fashion. Around the same time, Harold O. Anger introduced a scintillation camera consisting of multiple scintillation tubes simultaneously collecting data. Both of these devices produced images on film consisting of spots, either darker or lighter relative to the quantity of emission. Improvements on Anger's **gamma camera** were followed by devices using more scintillation counters, arranged and collimated (filtered) to provide better three-dimensional specificity.

Another strand of innovation concerned better and more specific tracers. Chemists, nuclear chemists, and physiologists who were after specific biological processes needed to tag certain molecules (chemicals such as water or pharmaceuticals) with either radioactive isotopes of atoms in them, or with close analogs of those atoms. One class of isotopes is known as positron emitters because they decay radioactively into positrons, which, after traveling a few millimeters, collide with an electron, resulting in mutual annihilation and the production of two 511-KeV gamma-rays traveling almost exactly 180° away from each other. These positron emitters (Carbon[11], Nitrogen[13], Oxygen[15], and Flourine[18]) were explored around 1939 by Martin Kamen and Samuel Ruben, who then discovered Carbon[14] (not a positron emitter) and dropped the others. The positron emitters were difficult to work with for a number of reasons: they have very short half-lives (C^{11} = 20 minutes; O^{15} = 2 minutes; F^{18} = 2 hours) and must be produced with the aid of a cyclotron and bound or tagged onto molecules before being introduced into the organism.

The Atomic Energy Commission's (AEC) postwar policy of promoting the peaceful use of radioactivity was the context for exploring positron emitters within medical research. In 1951, Frank R. Wrenn and colleagues proposed that the two gamma-rays produced could be detected simultaneously to provide very accurate location of the tracer, for instance to localize brain tumors. In 1953, Gordon L. Brownell and William H. Sweet at the Massachusetts General Hospital built a positron scanner to do just that. In the early 1970s, James S. Robertson at Brookhaven National Laboratory built the first positron camera in which the detectors were arranged in a ring, and in the same year David E. Kuhl and Roy Q. Edwards at the University of Pennsylvania developed a tomographic imaging device for single photon (gamma-ray) emission. These set the stage for fully developed PET scanning.

Physiologically, work with positron emitters was carried out by Michel M. Ter-Pogossian and colleagues at Washington University in St. Louis, using O^{15} gas (O_2) for respiratory, brain, and cancer studies. These led to the installation of a cyclotron in the Washington University Medical Center in the mid 1960s with support from both the AEC and the National Institutes of Health (NIH). In the late 1970s, Louis Sokoloff, working at the NIH and building on the work of Seymour Kety, contributed the autoradiographic technique using deoxyglucose as a tracer, which allowed him postmortem to "see" oxygen flow in the brain precisely.

The precipitating event for the PET scanner was the announcement of the CT scanner by the British company EMI, which demonstrated the feasibility of solving the computational problem of how to filter tomographic data using a **computer**. With this inspiration, Michael E. Phelps and Edward J. Hoffman, along with Jerome R. Cox, Donald L. Snyder, and Nizar A. Mullani, developed the first practical PET scanners, the PETT series, under the leadership of Ter-Pogossian. These devices consisted of a hexagon of **scintillation counters** that were electronically linked so that they sent a positive signal only when two opposite ones detected a gamma-ray at the same time. When

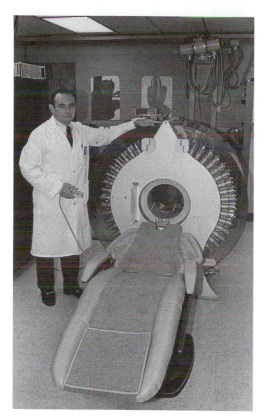

Michel Ter-Pogossian with an early PET scanner. Courtesy of Washington University School of Medicine Archives.

lationship between oxygen concentration in blood, bloodflow in specific areas of the brain, and cognitive processes). This parametric calculation/estimation is known as tracer-kinetics. The resultant image is called functional because it purports to show the rate of flow of a molecule, its concentration through time in a set of regions.

The usefulness of PET depended equally upon radiopharmaceutical constraints as upon technological ones. Much research with PET concentrated on nuclear chemistry ligand work: developing ways to rapidly tag complex molecules such as pharmaceuticals with radioisotopes to show how and where they are used in the body, especially where they are absorbed in the brain. A significant advance came in 1979 when Joanna S. Fowler and Alfred P. Wolf synthesized and used 18-FDG, an analog of glucose, to approximate glucose consumption in the brain. This has remained one of the most-used radiopharmaceuticals. Another significant advance was the demonstration of the ability to image human dopamine receptors carried out by Henry N. Wagner and Michael Kuhar at Johns Hopkins University in 1983.

Following the development of the PETT devices, commercial PET scanners were developed, first by EG&G Ortec (later CTI). In 1979, the NIH funded seven PET centers under a program grant initiating PET as a subfield. In spite of this boost, PET did not enter clinical medicine in the explosive way that CT had. Rather, because PET required tremendous interdisciplinary and financial infrastructure, including an on-site cyclotron, and because its data were not immediately applicable for clinical solutions, the procedure became first a scientific and medical-experimental technique. Nonetheless, by 1983, the number of PET centers in the world exceeded forty. The mid to late 1980s found established medical device providers, Siemens and G.E., taking over the marketing of the PET devices of CTI and Scanditronix, respectively.

PET, along with SPECT (single photon emission computerized tomography), is located in an interdisciplinary space contested by radiology and nuclear medicine. They have also facilitated new disciplinary formations, such as medical imaging and molecular pharmacology—the latter understood as the tracer-imaging counterpart of molecular biology.

In popular culture, PET's ability to provide pictures of the brain in action, as a person per-

this happened, it could be assumed that there was a positron-emitting molecule somewhere along the line between the two detectors. These signals were stored in a computer and then processed mathematically using first an iterative algorithm and later Fourier transforms to reconstruct a two-dimensional (tomographic) slice of the radioactivity. Coincidence detection thus substituted electronic collimation for the physical (and noisier) lead shield collimators used in gamma cameras, and provided significantly more sensitivity and accuracy. Critical improvements in this technology included the practical discovery of bismuth germanate crystals for better detector resolution by Z.H. Cho, and using a stationary ring of detectors rather than a moving hexagon, which provided for easier engineering.

In order to be used medically, however, these data had to be processed in terms of the complex relationships between the molecular circulation in the body, radioactive decay, and the process to be studied (for example, the reforms a cognitive task, and to image different kinds of brains (diseased, disturbed, disabled), have captivated science writers and Hollywood. Courtrooms have recently been faced with the issue of PET's admissibility as scientific evidence in head trauma and insanity cases as well as the vexing question of the possibly prejudicial status of PET images for juries.

In the early 1990s, efforts were underway to make PET a "clinical" technique, which means having insurers, especially the Health Care Finance Administration (which administers Medicare and Medicaid) cover the cost of procedures done with PET. While there was progress in this regard, the issue of coverage depends on cost as well as on clinical efficacy: will enough hospitals be able to afford PET so that everyone has access to approved procedures? The cost of a PET scanner is around two million dollars and the same for a cyclotron. Yearly maintenance and personnel costs (a cyclotron crew, chemistry and PET crew) can cost $300,000 to $700,000. Some of this cost might be reduced with the introduction of regional cyclotrons delivering radioisotopes to groups of nearby hospitals. Additional challenges are being worked out at the regulatory level, with the FDA trying to decide the status of radiolabeled molecules. Finally, there are other techniques of imaging bodily and brain functions, such as SPECT and fastMR, that overlap some of PET's strengths.

Joseph Dumit

Bibliography

Andreasen, Nancy C., ed. *Brain Imaging: Applications in Psychiatry.* Washington, D.C.: American Psychiatric, 1989.

Kereiakes, J.G. "The History and Development of Medical Physics Instrumentation: Nuclear Medicine." *Medical Physics* 14 (1987): 146–55.

Phelps, Michael E. "The Evolution of Positron Emission Tomography." In *The Enchanted Loom: Chapters in the History of Neuroscience,* edited by Pietro Corsi, 347–57. New York: Oxford University Press, 1991.

Reivich, Martin, and Abass Alavi, eds. *Positron Emission Tomography.* New York: A.R. Liss, 1985.

Ter-Pogossian, Michel M. "The Origins of Positron Emission Tomography." *Seminars in Nuclear Medicine* 22 (1992): 140–49.

Petroleum Testing Equipment

This equipment is used in laboratories or refineries to determine key parameters of petroleum products, and to ensure that the product meets specification or regulatory requirements and is of a consistent quality. Specifications and standard methods of test are usually generated by national or international standardization organizations. In the U.K., the Institute of Petroleum (IP) is responsible for standard methods of test, and specifications are covered by the British Standards Institution. In the United States, the American Society for Testing and Materials (ASTM) is responsible for maintaining both specifications and standard methods of test for most products, including those concerned with petroleum.

The requirement for test equipment grew rapidly following discoveries of oil fields and the building of refineries in the nineteenth century. Initially the requirement was based on safety. However, as distillate products became more widely used and as more sophisticated products were developed, the emphasis changed to quality control. Environmental concerns in the 1980s and 1990s led to new instruments and associated test methods.

Each petroleum product has its own requirements for tests, and hence there are many hundreds of test methods and types of instruments. Some of the best known examples are flash point, copper corrosion, lead content, octane/cetane number, oxidation, vapor pressure, and viscosity.

The principles behind many of today's instruments and tests are not new. For example, Isaac Newton's 1713 ideas about the capillary principle of viscosity are still used to determine kinematic viscosity, and liquids are still known as Newtonian or non-Newtonian.

While most standard test methods are written for manual instruments, the 1980s and 1990s saw a rapid expansion of automated instruments. This led to a debate in the United States and U.K. in 1993–1994 on the procedures required to enable such instruments to be specified in test methods without endangering the validity of results.

Flash Point

This is defined as the lowest temperature of the test portion, corrected to a barometric pressure of 101.3 kPa, at which application of a test flame causes the vapor of the test sample to ignite under the specified conditions of test. Na-

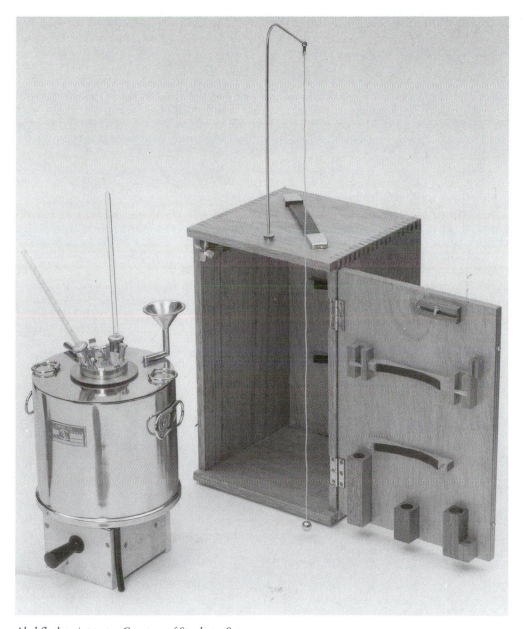

Abel flash point tester. Courtesy of Stanhope-Seta.

tional and international regulations require the flash point testing of fluids for transport and safety reasons.

The growing use of distillates for lighting and heating in place of animal and vegetable oils led to a large number of accidents. These problems were addressed in 1862 by the U.K. Petroleum Act and the adoption, in 1870, of a flash point tester designed by Keates. This act categorized a liquid as being flammable if it had an open cup flash point below 100°F. However,

the test based on Keates's apparatus was difficult to carry out and to reproduce. Sir Frederick Abel was asked to address this problem, and he presented his closed cup design on August 12, 1876. The Abel instrument was subsequently incorporated into the Petroleum Act and the temperature defining flammable reduced to 73°F, that being equivalent to an open cup value of 100°F.

Legislation quickly spread around the world, and many other test instruments were developed. The following list shows when the major surviving instruments were in a form recognizable today and where they were developed:

1876	U.K.	Abel
1880	Germany	Pensky-Martens
1914	U.S.	Tagliabue (Tag)
1915	U.S.	Cleveland
1966	U.K.	Setaflash

There are two basic types of apparatus in common use at present: open cup, which aims to simulate the effects of spillage, and closed cup, which corresponds to the opening of a previously closed vessel. The more controlled conditions used in closed cup tests results in better precision, a lower flash point, and hence a steady move by regulatory bodies to recommend this type of test.

The instruments can be used in various ways. The nonequilibrium test heats the sample at a constant rate, while periodically testing for a flash point. Here the temperature of the vapor lags behind the sample temperature—that is, they are not in equilibrium. These tests take typically 10 to 20 minutes to complete. Equilibrium tests increase the temperature of the sample at a very slow rate such that the sample and vapors are in temperature equilibrium. These tests give more precise results but can take over 60 minutes to complete. The recently developed rapid equilibrium method employs a flash-no flash test, and gives a result in 1 minute.

Requirements for greater manpower efficiency in the 1980s and 1990s led to the development and use of instruments that automated temperature control, the flame dipping mechanisms, and flash detection.

Redwood Viscosity

The Redwood Viscometer is a type of **viscometer** designed by Boverton Redwood in 1885 to measure the viscosity of lubricating oils. Redwood defined the viscosity of an oil in Redwood seconds as the time in which 50 ml of the oil flows through the viscometer jet at the test temperature. Redwood's technique was adopted by the Institute of Petroleum Technologists and the British Admiralty. Although the British Standard Specification for Fuel Oils changed from Redwood seconds to centistokes in the 1960s, boiler engineers and the suppliers of domestic heating oils still refer to fuel oils by their Redwood values, 28- or 35-second oil for kerosene and gas oil.

The viscometer consists of a copper cylinder fitted with an agate jet with a spherical cavity at its upper end. A removable spherical stopper, which fits this cavity, holds the test portion in place. The Redwood Number I has a jet with an internal diameter of 1.620 mm, and the Redwood Number II has a jet with an internal diameter of 3.80 mm.; the flow time for the Number II is 1/10 that of the Number I.

John Phipps
Mike Sherratt

Bibliography

Methods for Analysis and Testing: Part 1 of IP Standards for Petroleum and Its Products, 680–91. London: Institute of Petroleum, 1961.

Redwood, Boverton. *Petroleum: A Treatise on the Geographical Distribution and Geological Occurence of Petroleum and Natural Gas,* Vol. 3, 763–810, 823–26. 4th ed. London: Griffin, 1922.

pH Meter

A pH meter measures the concentration of the hydrogen ion (H^+), or acidity, in an aqueous system. For centuries, certain substances were classified as acids because of a sour taste, or bases because an aqueous solution had a soapy or slippery feeling. The only test for acidity or basicity was the qualitative observation of the change in color the solution imparted to a piece of paper impregnated with a natural dye. This litmus paper was blue in a basic solution, red in an acidic solution. It wasn't until 1887 that Svante Arrhenius proposed his then-controversial theory of ionization of electrolytes, which subsequently was accepted as the rationale for explaining acidity and basicity in terms of the hydrogen ion concentration.

With the acceptance of the Arrhenius concept came the need for a precise evaluation of the hydrogen ion concentration, expressing the measurement with a specific number instead of the crude and nonnumerical litmus test. In 1904 H. Friedenthal and E. Salm developed the first quantitative colorimetric method, using a series of indicators; these were organic acids that underwent a specific color change at a specific hydrogen-ion concentration. This technique was perfected by William Mansfield Clark and others; reasonable numbers could be obtained by comparing the indicator

Beckman's original acidimeter, 1934. Courtesy of the Beckman Heritage Center.

color of an unknown acid concentration with a series of test tubes of known concentrations (and thus colors) until a color match was found.

In 1909 S.P.L. Sørensen suggested that the wide range of numbers associated with aqueous solutions could be compressed on a logarithmic scale, where pH = −log (H+). In pure water, (H+) = 10^{-7}, and thus in a neutral solution the pH = 7. Because of the negative sign in this definition of pH, there is an inverse relationship between the hydrogen ion concentration and the pH. Thus any solution with a pH less than 7 is acidic, and the lower the pH the stronger the acid.

In pure water, the source of the hydrogen ion is the ionization of the water molecule: H_2O = H+ + OH−. Since both ions are formed in equal amounts, a neutral solution will have the hydroxide ion (OH−) concentration also equal to 10^{-7}. Since (H+) x (OH−) always equals 10^{-14} in

aqueous systems, a source of hydroxide ion (a base) added to water causes the hydrogen ion concentration to decrease accordingly. Therefore, a pH greater than 7 means the solution is basic, and the greater the pH above the neutral value of 7, the stronger the base.

At the same time that the colorimetric method was being developed, a more direct electrometric method of measuring the hydrogen ion was being explored. An electrochemical cell consists of two externally connected electrodes that are inserted in a solution to complete a circuit. The chemical reaction that occurs at the electrodes creates an electromotive force measurable according to an equation developed by Walther Nernst in 1889.

By 1915 both Sorensen and Clark had developed systems in which half of the cell was a hydrogen electrode. Although very accurate pH measurements were possible, the use of highly purified hydrogen gas rendered it impractical for routine measurements. M. Cremer had shown in 1906 that an electric potential could develop on a glass surface; and in 1909 Fritz Haber and Z. Klemensiewicz showed that a much simpler glass electrode could replace the hydrogen electrode and that the potential variation was indeed a correct measure of the pH of the solution in which it was inserted. Nevertheless, measurements of the cell emf still required time, patience, and expensive **potientiometers** and **galvanometers**. In 1920 a typical system cost $467.

In 1921, as part of his master's thesis at the University of Chicago, Kenneth H. Goode used the vacuum triode (invented by Lee De Forest in 1909) to measure pH values as they changed continuously during an acid-base titration. Although Goode's discovery simplified pH measurements considerably, because the vacuum tube could be considered a direct-reading, sensitive **voltmeter**, he still used the hydrogen electrode.

The vacuum tube potentiometer was not coupled with the glass electrode until 1928, when two independent groups, H.M. Partridge at New York University and Walter H. Wright and Lucius W. Elder at the University of Illinois, successfully measured solution pH using this combination and considerably reduced the measurement time. But rapid and inexpensive pH measurement would not become a reality until 1934, when Arnold O. Beckman, a young assistant professor of chemistry at the California Institute of Technology, was visited by his University of Illinois classmate, Glen Joseph.

As a chemist at the California Fruit Growers Exchange, Joseph found it difficult to measure the acidity of lemon juice. The glass electrode was not affected by the sulfur dioxide in the lemon juice, but breakage was a constant problem. Moreover, the high resistance of the thin-walled and fragile glass bulb required the use of a highly sensitive galvanometer. Beckman substituted a vacuum tube voltmeter for the galvanometer, and proceeded to assemble a device that used two vacuum tubes and a milliammeter to measure the small current generated by the electrochemical cell and that permitted the use of sturdier glass electrodes.

Within a few months, Joseph was back, asking for another "acidimeter" because his colleagues kept borrowing the first one. Beckman quickly realized that if Joseph "needed two of these instruments in his modest laboratory, perhaps other chemists might also need such an in-

strument." In 1935 he began marketing for $195 a portable and rugged pH meter that initially was met with little enthusiasm by either chemists or scientific equipment dealers. The Arthur H. Thomas Co. of Philadelphia estimated the market at six hundred over a ten-year period.

Low cost and ease of operation quickly made the Beckman pH meter the instrument of choice for pH measurement, and almost six hundred were sold in just two years. Other companies quickly followed Beckman's lead, with constant improvement on the original design. Modern pH meters still require the insertion of two electrodes into the solution to be measured, but they are readily calibrated, can be extremely portable for field use, and have stabilized digital readouts. The new instruments operate on the principle commercialized by Arnold Beckman, but the work can now be done routinely, often automatically, and with minimal operator training.

James J. Bohning

Bibliography

Bates, Roger Gorden. *Electrometric pH Determinations: Theory and Practice.* New York: Wiley, 1954.

Dole, Malcolm. *The Glass Electrode.* New York: Wiley, 1941.

Jaselskis, Bruno, Carl E. Moore, and Alfred von Smolinski. "Development of the pH Meter." In *Electrochemistry, Past and Present,* edited by John T. Stock and Mary Virginia Orna, 254–71. Washington, D.C.: American Chemical Society, 1989.

Mattock, G., and G. Ross Taylor. *pH Measurement and Titration.* New York: Macmillan, 1961.

Stephens, Harrison. *Golden Past, Golden Future: The First Fifty Years of Beckman Instruments, Inc.* Claremont, Calif.: Claremont University Center, 1985.

Photometer

Photometers measure the intensity of light or the brightness of illuminated surfaces. The first extensive photometric investigations were published in 1729 and 1760 by Pierre Bouguer, who concluded that the eye is unreliable for measuring absolute brightness and should be used only to match two light sources. His *lucimètre* consisted of two tubes to be directed at the two light sources, converging to a paper screen viewed by the eye. The light through one tube could be attenuated by masking its aperture or lengthening the tube until the two light spots appeared equal. The ratio of the two intensities was taken as the ratio of the aperture areas or of the squares of the tube lengths (inverse-square law).

The term "photometry" was coined by the German polymath Johann Lambert, who published his mathematically centered researches in 1760. The most careful of eighteenth-century researchers was the American Benjamin Thompson, who in the 1790s employed a simple instrument consisting of a shadow-casting rod and screen. The distance of one light source was adjusted to equate the shadow densities, and the ratio of luminosities determined by applying the inverse-square law. Thompson took precautions to avoid inadvertent bias of the observer and other experimental variables.

There were few applications of photometers in the first half of the nineteenth century, and the techniques were essentially reinvented by each investigator. The principal variant employed visual acuity: brightness would be inferred from the legibility of text of graded sizes or at varying distances from the eye. The more commonly applied comparison principle changed little, although the means of adjusting the reference intensity was refined. In 1834, the English photographic pioneer Henry Fox Talbot proposed using a rotating sector-disk to attenuate the light path. Others employed two polarizers (Malus's law), or a wedge having graded transparency.

The optical head of the photometer also was improved. The grease spot photometer, devised by the German investigator Robert Bunsen in 1843, used a paper screen rendered translucent by a spot of grease or wax at its center; light sources on either side were judged to be matched when the spot disappeared or was of minimum contrast—that is, when the transmitted and reflected intensities were equal. A more precise version based on a cemented prism and viewing eyepiece was developed by Otto Lummer and Eugen Brodhun of the Physikalisch-Technische Reichsanstalt in 1889. Their instrument was widely adopted by the German illuminating gas industry, which had encouraged their work. Its variants remain the state of the art in visual photometers today.

Gas inspectors, particularly after increasing regulation of the industry in the mid nine-

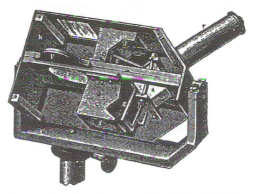

Lummer-Brodhun photometer head. John J. Griffin and Sons Ltd. Scientific Handicraft: An Illustrated and Descriptive Catalogue of Scientific Apparatus, 563, *Figure 2-6016. London, 1914. Courtesy of Fisher Scientific UK Ltd.*

teenth century, were the first significant users of photometers. In accepting an award for his design at the 1893 Chicago Exposition, Lummer chided his academic colleagues for having treated photometry "rather slightingly." He claimed that they had neglected the subject until the needs of the illumination industry and the public had shown them its importance. Reference standards of brightness were motivated by similar concerns. The competition between gas and electric lighting systems from the early 1880s caused an expansion of publications on photometry and interest in photometric practice. The formation of illuminating engineering societies in New York (1905), London (1909), and Germany (1912) served as an impetus for the organization and rationalization of photometric methods.

Astronomers began using photometers to determine stellar magnitudes in the late nineteenth century. Two of the chief proponents were Edward C. Pickering at Harvard, and Johann Zöllner at Potsdam. Pickering's meridian photometer (which used an optical wedge for attenuation, and Polaris as a reference source of light) and Zöllner's version (employing crossed polarizers and a petroleum-burning lamp, respectively) acquired literally millions of observations in the period between 1860 and 1910.

Astronomers also extended photometric techniques by experimenting with photographic recording. In this method, stellar brightness was inferred by examining the diameter or opacity of the photographic image of the star. The measurement of small images necessitated the design of microphotometers, initially based on visual comparison of the photographic plate with a reference light source. Such microphotometers (or **densitometers**) were the impetus for the next transition in instrument technology, namely photoelectric measurement of brightness. Photoelectric vacuum tubes, invented by Johann Elster and Hans Geitel in the 1890s, were applied to the design of densitometers and almost simultaneously to direct photometric measurement through the telescope. Direct photoelectric photometry was problematic until after World War I owing to the exceedingly weak and erratic signal, variable phototube characteristics, and the lack of electrical expertise by the pioneering astronomers.

After the war, the development of reliable photoelectric tubes by companies such as General Electric in Britain and Westinghouse in the United States led to the development and rapid deployment of photoelectric photometers. Phototubes were used initially for nonmeasuring applications such as paper-bale counting and smoke monitoring, but by the early 1930s they had begun to replace visual photometers. The marketing of inexpensive selenium-based photocells in 1932 by the Weston Instrument Co. (and shortly thereafter by competitors such as Everett Edgcumbe & Co.) created a market for new forms of photometer, **colorimeter**, and **spectrophotometer**. By World War II, such instruments were based almost exclusively on photoelectric technology, and had entered the consumer market in the form of photographic **exposure meters** and illumination meters. New photoelectric detectors developed during and after the war further extended the capabilities of such physical, rather than physiological, light-measuring instruments.

Sean F. Johnston

Bibliography

Dibdin, William Joseph. *Practical Photometry: A Guide to the Study of the Measurement of Light.* London: Walter King, 1889.

Harrison, George B. "Instruments and Methods Used for Measuring Spectral Light Intensities by Photography." *Journal of the Optical Society of America* 19 (1929): 267–307.

Huffer, C.M. "The Development of Photo-Electric Photometry." *Vistas in Astronomy* 1 (1955): 491–98.

Johnston, Sean F. "A Notion or a Measure: The Quantification of Light to 1939." Ph.D. dissertation. University of Leeds, 1994.

Walsh, John W.T. *Photometry.* London: Constable, 1926.

Photomultiplier

A photomultiplier converts light energy (photons) into electrical energy (or electric current) and then amplifies that current. The two functions depend on a photocathode, which emits electrons when light falls on its surface, and a series of electrically charged plates, or dynodes, each at a successively higher positive potential, which collect and multiply the electron flux from the cathode and then direct it to an anode and then to a measuring device, such as a **galvanometer** or electronic current amplifier. Photomultipliers are used to detect sources of radiation; the amplified current produced at the anode is a direct measure of the number of photons collected by the photocathode.

Photoelectric Cell

In 1873, Willoughby Smith, an English telegraphy engineer, noticed that when selenium is exposed to light its conductivity increases. After Heinrich Hertz discovered the photoemissive effect in 1887, Johann Elster and Hans Geitel, *Gymnasium* teachers of mathematics and physics in Wolfenbüttel, near Brunswick, Germany, found that electropositive metals such as sodium, potassium, and rubidium are sensitive to light. By the 1890s they had developed an alkali cathode consisting of an amalgam of sodium and mercury that was sensitive to visible and ultraviolet radiation, and they later realized that alkali cathodes can be highly sensitized by passing them through a glow discharge of hydrogen gas. Photoconductive and photoemissive cells came into general use over the next three decades. Photoemissive cells in vacuum tubes allowed for pure electron discharge, whereas those filled with inert gasses amplified the current by collisional ionization.

By 1930, photoelectric cells were widely used in science and industry. They formed the heart of precision photometry (see **photometer**) and spectrophotometry (see **spectrophotometer**) appliances in such diverse areas as biology, atmospheric physics, and astronomy, and appeared as well in recording microphotometers, phototherapy diagnostic devices, and sound film reproduction. Many new photoemissive surface formulations were also developed, such

An early commercial multiplier from RCA, utilizing ten-stage multiplication used for a variety of industrial applications. SM 1936-37. Courtesy of SSPL.

as thin films of cesium on silver for selective emissivity applications in the visual range of the spectrum, or selenium-tellurium and thallium sulfide cells for detecting infrared radiation. Cells were available from such commercial manufacturers as General Electric (which marketed the Osram line), and the British Thomson-Houston Co. (makers of Mazda photoelectric cells).

Photoelectric cells, however, remained far from trouble-free for precision photometry. They often produced systematic errors in performance: high dark current, varying response to different amounts of illumination, variable color sensitivity, nonuniformity of the cathode surface, and leakage or grounding problems in the photoelectric current. There were other problems when the output current had to be amplified, such as in low-light level applications like astronomy. Amplifiers could introduce spurious dark current and noise and distort the all-important proportionality between the photoelectric current and the amount of illumination impinging on the cathode. Amplifiers external to the cells, however—either improved forms of the Lindemann string **electrometer** or dc thermionic devices based upon General Electric's FP-54 Pliotron electrometer tubes—were not as problematic as the distortions within the gas-filled tubes themselves.

Secondary-Emission Multipliers

In the mid 1930s, after H.E. Iams and B. Salzberg showed that secondary emission was a controllable technology, various manufacturers built single-stage multipliers to produce an amplified signal within the tube without the need for a gaseous medium. The first true multipliers using multiple amplifying dynode stages also appeared at this time. RCA's Research Laboratory group headed by Vladimir K. Zworykin developed an electrostatic circular dynode array with nine stages of multiplication capable of amplifying the electron flux from the cathode by a factor of one million. The same structural design was soon available in three cathode formulations to cover different parts of the spectrum.

This new tube (called the RCA 931 and later the 931A) was available commercially by 1940, at a cost of between $12 and $15. It was, however, difficult to obtain one with low-noise (high signal-to-noise ratio) performance, even when the tube was cooled to dry-ice temperatures. The low-noise requirement did not hamper the introduction of the 931A tube into industry, or into scientific areas that did not worry about detecting faint sources of radiation. Typically only one tube in fifty, however, had low enough noise levels to be suitable for astronomical application. This made the use of the tube by astronomers a comparatively expensive affair, and early potential users required intimate knowledge of electron tube technology, or direct access to groups like Zworykin's to obtain good samples and hints on how to make them work properly.

RCA soon developed production-line testing procedures to isolate the factors that gave a few tubes exceptional performance characteristics, and by 1943 Zworykin's group had created the RCA 1P21 tube, which enhanced those factors. Wartime production demands made the 931A and 1P21 plentiful, reliable, and cheap by war's end. RCA photomultipliers and their British counterparts were applied to a wide range of uses during the war, from low light detection to diagnostic analysis, and even as white noise generators for radar jamming. In late 1945, a 1P21 tube cost $47.50, and tubes of that type, along with others with different cathode formulations and dynode chains ranging from nine to fourteen stages, found wide application in color densitometry and spectrophotometry, as well as in signal generators, relay devices and other photoelectric servomechanisms, light and exposure control systems, facsimile transmission technologies, and ultraviolet, x-ray, and scintillation counters.

RCA's early focused dynode designs provided for high collection efficiency and compact design, but the tubes suffered from external magnetic field interference and nonuniform cathode sensitivity. By the 1950s, EMI Electronics in Middlesex, England, brought out an alternative design with dynodes that looked like tiny venetian blinds; but being unfocused, these tubes were initially of lower efficiency, though they were resistive to external fields and were quite reliable. The Allen B. DuMont Laboratories in Passaic, New Jersey, developed a boxlike dynode chain design that combined good collection efficiency with cathode uniformity.

By the 1950s, photomultipliers from a growing list of manufacturers had time constants short enough to allow them to be used with ac amplifiers with synchronous rectification; the earliest samples came from the M.I.T. Radiation Laboratory toward the end of the war. Further refinements included pulse counting circuitry for counting individual photons; improved tubes like the 6094A and 6685 models from EMI had mul-tiplication factors up to 10^9. With increased sensitivity came broader spectral sensitivity, reaching from the ultraviolet to the infrared. The military reconnaissance potential of infrared cells with lead sulfide cathodes sensitive to the 2–4 μm range initially hampered their development for science and industry, but by the 1950s and 1960s such cells, and photomultipliers built upon them, were available from manufacturers such as I.T.T. Laboratories and Farnsworth, even though technical problems caused by increased thermionic emission, which simple cooling could not solve, hampered their use in low-light-level applications.

David DeVorkin

Bibliography

Anderson, John S., ed. *Photo-Electric Cells and Their Applications.* London: The Physical and Optical Societies, 1930.

DeVorkin, David H. "Electronics in Astronomy: Early Applications of the Photoelectric Cell and Photomultiplier for Studies of Point Source Celestial Phenomena." *Proceedings of the IEEE* 73 (July 1985): 1205–20.

Schure, Alexander. *Phototubes.* New York: John F. Rider, 1959.

Whitford, Albert E. "Photoelectric Techniques." In vol. 54 of *Handbuch der Physik,* edited by S. Flügge, 240–88. Berlin: Springer, 1962.

Zworykin, Vladimir K., and E.G. Ramberg. *Photoelectricity and Its Application.* New York: Wiley, 1949.

Photon Counter

According to the semiclassical model of radiation, light propagates with the motion associated with a wave but is emitted and detected as a stream of particles—that is, light possesses a wave-particle duality. In the photoelectric effect, one observes the ejection of individual electrons from the surface of an illuminated material. By analyzing the energy of these electrons, Einstein (1905) postulated that light is quantized into units, called photons, whose energy is related to the frequency of the corresponding classical wave v by the formula $E = hv$, where h is Planck's constant ($\approx 6.63 \times 10^{-34}$ J.s). There is a threshold frequency, v_0, below which there is no emission of electrons. It is now known that the photoelectric effect does not, by itself, provide conclusive evidence for the quantization of the electromagnetic field. There is, however, other strong experimental evidence for this quantization, and the study of photons and their interaction with matter is called quantum optics.

A practical photon counter actually counts the photoelectrons resulting from a light beam's falling on a detector. The counter usually has two properties that enable it to detect individual photons: a primary detection stage of high quantum efficiency, the output of which is an electron in a higher energy state; and an amplification stage that enables the primary event (electron) to be registered unambiguously by a counting circuit.

A **photomultiplier** tube contains a photocathode made of a compound of alkali metals (such as Na_2KSbCs): when a photoelectron is liberated it is accelerated to the first dynode, where it releases a number of electrons, and this cascade process continues along the dynode chain, producing a large pulse at the anode. In an imaging photon counter, a hollow microchannel of approximately 10 μm in diameter performs a function similar to that of the photomultiplier dynode chain. In a solid-state detector, such as an avalanche photodiode, electrons are raised from the valence to the conduction band, hence contributing to the detected current.

Photon counting devices can be divided between those that are spatially integrating and those that are spatially resolved (that is, nonimaging or imaging). Photomultipliers and avalanche photodiodes are single spatially integrat-

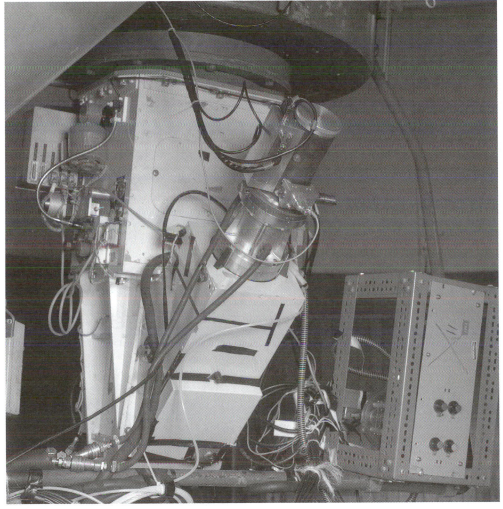

Image Photon Counting System detector (front) in position on a telescope, 1980. Courtesy of the Royal Greenwich Observatory.

ing devices, whose sensitive area varies from a fraction of a square millimeter to several square centimeters. Each detected photon gives a pulse of current whose duration is a few nanoseconds (in a photomultiplier tube), making possible count rates in excess of 10^8 per second. A typical photomultiplier photon counting system consists of a high-voltage power supply, photomultiplier tube (possibly in a cooled housing to reduce dark count), a preamplifier and discriminator, and an electronic counter, linked to a computer.

Spatially resolved photon counters record the position of arrival of a photon as well as the time of arrival. The first widely used device was built in 1972 by Alec Boksenberg, director of the Royal Greenwich Observatory, for use in as-

tronomy: the output phosphor of a four-stage image intensifier was imaged onto a plumbicon television tube, and electronic circuitry was used to identify single photon events. There are several variants of this principle, all using some kind of image intensifier and position-sensitive read-out scheme. Such systems are relatively expensive compared with simple photomultiplier-based instruments. Present-day **charge-coupled devices** have a readout noise associated with each pixel of the order of a few electrons and, therefore, cannot really be said to be photon counters.

The spectral sensitivity of a photon counter is determined by that of the primary radiation-sensitive stage. The photocathode in a photomultiplier may be only blue-green sensitive ("S11"), red sensitive ("S20"), or it may be sensitive in the near-infrared, using gallium ars- enide as the sensitive material. Silicon has a much higher quantum efficiency than photo- cathode materials and is used in avalanche pho- todiode photon counters.

An ideal photon counter would measure the time, position, polarization, and frequency of every arriving photon. Current devices for visible light measure the time to a few nano- seconds and the position to a few μm with a quantum efficiency of approximately 20 percent at best. Future developments in solid state devices may enable the photon energy also to be measured with a high quantum ef- ficiency.

John C. Dainty

Bibliography

Boksenberg, A., and D.E. Burgess. "An Im- age Photon Counting System for Opti- cal Astronomy." *Advances in Electron- ics and Electron Physics* 33B (1972): 835–49.

Csorba, I.P. *Image Tubes*. Indianapolis, Ind.: H.W. Sams, 1985.

Einstein, A. "Über einen die Erzeugung und Verwandlung de Lichtes betreffenden heuistischen Gesichtspunkt." *Annalen der Physik* 17 (1905): 132.

Mandel, L. "The Case for and against Semi- classical Radiation Theory." *Progress in Optics* 13 (1976): 27–68.

Piezometer

Piezometers measure the pressure of fluid within the voids of soils and rocks (the pore pressure). In the 1920s, K. Terzaghi demonstrated that the behavior of soils and rocks is controlled by "ef- fective stress," the difference between normal stress and pore pressure. To apply this concept in practice, one needs to measure pore pressure. The U.S. Bureau of Reclamation (USBR) under- stood the importance of internal seepage pres- sures in embankment dams in 1935 and began making field measurements of pore pressure. After some initial experimentation, they used a hydrostatic pressure indicator. This was a cell containing water in contact with the soil through a carborundum porous filter disk. The water acted on a gold-plated diaphragm that made an electrical contact. The other side of the dia- phragm connected to the measuring point through a small-bore copper tube, and a pressure measurement was made by applying an air pres-

sure until the diaphragm lifted and the contact was broken.

The first modern hydraulic piezometer was introduced in 1939. Here the water in the cell connected directly to a measuring point outside the embankment through two small-bore cop- per tubes. These tubes allowed water to be cir- culated, ensuring that they were filled and that the difference in pressure between the piezom- eter and the measuring point was known. Fif- teen dams were instrumented by 1946. The observations showed that high pore pressures could develop in impermeable fills as they were built, as the increasing load squeezed the pore fluid faster than it could drain out of the soil.

Several embankments in Britain slipped during construction between 1937 and 1941, and this was correctly attributed to incomplete consolidation and high construction pore pres- sures. Muirhead Dam in Scotland failed in 1941. The similar Knockendon Dam was under construction nearby, and construction pore pressures were measured in it, using driven standpipes. The water levels in the standpipes rose to above the level of the fill. The design was modified before construction was completed.

The Building Research Station in Britain began instrumenting dams in 1950, using pi- ezometers similar to those used by USBR, but with plastic tubes. High construction pore pres- sures were observed in the Usk embankment, and again the design was modified before completion. In the 1950s the installation of pi- ezometers in embankment dams became stan- dard practice worldwide. Similar instruments are installed in boreholes below dams to moni- tor foundation behavior, and in many other situations. Hydraulic piezometers do not re- quire calibration and they can be tested to prove that they are operational. Given proper instal- lation, they last well; some of the earliest instal- lations are still operational.

In Continental Europe pore pressure in dams was measured with electrical transducers rather than small-bore water-filled tubes. Here, vibrating wire **strain gauges** measured the de- flection of a diaphragm. These piezometers were manufactured in Germany, Italy, France, and Norway, and installed in dams from about 1950. Such instruments have a good record of longevity and stability, although zero drift has been observed occasionally. They cannot be calibrated in situ. They are expensive but simple to install and may be read using compact por- table equipment. Unlike hydraulic piezometers,

Group of piezometer tips by Soil Instruments Ltd., 1995: (clockwise from top left) Bishop tip, bull-nose tip, cylindrical tip, mini-tip, disc tip, push-in tip. Courtesy of Soil Instruments Ltd.

they are unaffected by the relative levels of the piezometer and the measuring point. They are now used more extensively than twin-tube hydraulic piezometers.

A third type of pressure-sensing system was developed in the United States in the 1960s and adopted widely. Here the pore fluid pressure acted on one side of a neoprene diaphragm, and on the other side the diaphragm closes the ends of two plastic tubes. In practice, an increasing gas pressure is applied to one tube. When this equals the pore pressure, the diaphragm lifts and the gas flows back through the second tube. The reading is unaffected by the relative levels of the tubes. Readings are slow if tubes are long. Pneumatic piezometers have proved less reliable than vibrating wire electric instruments for long-term use.

Piezometers must be installed in boreholes to measure pore pressure in in-situ soil and rock. A. Casagrande's simple borehole piezometer, developed in 1944, monitored the rate of consolidation of soft clay. A borehole was sunk, the casing was withdrawn progressively, and sand and a porous pot on the end of a 0.5-in. plastic tube was placed inside. The bottom of the casing was sealed by alternate layers of bentonite clay balls and sand, and the depth of water in the tube was measured by an electric dip-meter. As only a small flow of water was needed for the water level in the narrow tube to respond to a change in pore pressure, the response was fast enough to monitor consolidation. The Casagrande piezometer has been used extensively ever since, although now the casing is fully withdrawn and the hole back-filled to the top. It is cheap, reliable, and very durable. In clays of low permeability the seal must also be impermeable to prevent errors resulting from seepage along the borehole. Both electrical and pneumatic piezometers can be installed in boreholes, which allows remote readings to be made.

Early hydraulic and electrical piezometers installed in partly saturated fills gave anomalous measurements of pore pressures close to atmospheric pressure. Measurements of the subatmospheric pore pressure in partly saturated shallow agricultural soils had been made by field tensiometers in the 1930s. This pressure controls the availability of soil moisture to plants. Tensiometers were similar to hydraulic piezometers but with a short measuring tube and a filter of fine ceramic. If pressure in partly saturated soil is to be measured directly, the instrument filter must have fine pores so that it can sustain an air/water pressure difference by capillarity greater than that existing in the soil. Otherwise the water in the filter and instrument will be sucked out and replaced by air. The use of ceramic piezometer filters similar to those used in tensiometers began in 1959.

Peter R. Vaughan

Bibliography

British Geotechnical Society. *Proceedings of the Symposium on Field Instrumentation in Geotechnical Engineering.* London: Butterworths, 1973.

British National Society Soil Mechanics and Foundation Engineering. *Proceedings of the Conference on Pore Pressure and Suction in Soils.* London: Butterworths, 1961.

Dunnicliff, John. *Geotechnical Instrumenta-tion for Monitoring Field Performance.* New York: Wiley, 1988.

Kulhawy, Fred H., ed. *Recent Developments in Geotechnical Engineering for Hydro Projects: Embankment Dam Instrumentation Performance, Engineering Geology Aspects, Rock Mechanics Studies.* New York: American Society of Civil Engineers, 1981.

Plane Table

A plane table is a surveying instrument comprising a flat square board, usually of hardwood, mounted on a tripod by some form of leveling arrangement such as a ball-and-socket joint. On top of this board is secured a sheet of paper, often clamped in place by a close-fitting square frame, which may fold up on pivots and hinges. On top of the paper is placed a detached alidade or sighting rule, usually made of brass. The typical plane table alidade has scales engraved on the

Plane table by Benjamin Cole, ca. 1750. SM 1933-7. Courtesy of SSPL.

rule section, which has a beveled edge, and folding plain sights. The sights are often of the double slit and window type; that is, each folding vane has two sighting elements—a thin vertical slit and a slot with a vertical central thread—set one above the other, but with the vertical disposition transposed at either end. This permits sighting in either direction, which is useful for maintaining a line of sight between different stations. Later examples may have a telescopic sight mounted on the rule. Indeed, plane table alidades can be complex and ambitious, with levels, vertical divided circles for altitudes, attached parallel rules, and so forth. The frames can also be marked with scales, both linear and degree. A further and essential accessory is a magnetic **compass**. This can be a detached compass, or it may be incorporated into or attached to one edge of the board. Alternatively, it may form part of the alidade; some alidades have full circular compass cards with a divided scale and so can function as circumferentors.

The plane table makes possible one of the most convenient and direct methods of surveying. A point on the paper is made to represent the first surveying station, with this point and the orientation of the board chosen to take account of the intended progress of the survey. Lines of sight, taken with the alidade, are marked on the paper by drawing along the edge of the rule. The table is moved to the second station, its orientation maintained by the compass and the distance moved transferred to the paper at an appropriate scale. The same targets are sighted and the intersections of the sight lines locate the corresponding positions on the paper. In this manner a plan of the site is drawn as the survey proceeds.

The plane table was introduced into surveying practice in the later sixteenth century, at a time when geometers were trying to reform surveying by introducing angle measurement and triangulation, using an instrument such as a simple **theodolite**. This involved the difficulties of "protraction"—that is, the subsequent construction of a map from measurements taken in the field. The convenience of the plane table, which was favored by the ordinary surveyors, alarmed the geometers, as it threatened to undermine their program of reform. However, the plane table was simply too convenient to be suppressed, and it retained its popularity, particularly for relatively small-scale surveys, into the twentieth century.

Jim A. Bennett

Bibliography

Bennett, J.A. *The Divided Circle: A History of Instruments for Astronomy, Navigation and Surveying.* Oxford: Phaidon, 1987.

Kiely, Edmond Richard. *Surveying Instruments, Their History and Classroom Use.* New York: Bureau of Publications, Teachers College, Columbia University, 1947.

Planetarium

A planetarium demonstrates the relative motions and positions of the sun and planets. In the second half of the twentieth century, the term often describes an optical system used with a projection instrument inside a domed theater, such as those developed by the firm of Carl Zeiss during the first part of the century in Jena, Germany. Recent innovations include the development of other projection systems and the application of **computer** technology. However, the term is also used to describe mechanical models ranging from the room-size planetarium in Franeker, in the Netherlands, completed in 1781 by Eise Eisinga, to the tabletop models found in many museum collections.

There are various references by ancient authors to instruments designed to show planetary motions. While Cicero regarded Archimedes as the founder of the branch of mechanics devoted to the construction of planetaria, some readings of the *Timaeus* suggest that Plato's Academy may have had a planetary model in the fourth century B.C. In the Platonic dialogue, Timaeus claimed that it is impossible to describe the motions of the planets without visible models; the instrument referred to may have corresponded to a type of **armillary sphere**. The school of mathematicians at Cyzicus were interested in building instruments to demonstrate the planetary ideas of Eudoxus. Cicero also credited the philosopher Posidonius with having built a planetary model. In the second century A.D., both the astronomer Ptolemy and the physician Galen referred to models of planetary motion and their makers. While none of these models of planetary motion survive, fragments of a geared *antikythera* mechanism dated to the first century B.C. were salvaged from a wreck in 1901; this device may have been used to demonstrate planetary motions.

During the medieval and early modern periods, planetary motions were demonstrated by two-dimensional moving volvelles and **equatoria**

Luftwaffe training planetarium, by Carl Zeiss, Jena, 1940s. SM 1946-172. Courtesy of SSPL.

and three-dimensional machines. Celebrated examples of the two-dimensional variety appear in the *Astronomica Caesarium* of Peter Apian, published in 1540. Planetary clocks of the period survive, as do written accounts of such clocks. A specialized model showing the spheres used to account for the motions of Mercury within the Ptolemaic system was made by Girolamo Della Volpaia (Hieronymus Vulparius) in the sixteenth century.

In the early modern period, debates concerning the merits of the earth-centered and the sun-centered cosmologies inspired the building of planetary models. Heliocentric models were used to demonstrate the new cosmology and argue against the geocentric worldview. In the seventeenth century, Ole Rømer and Christiaan Huyghens designed mechanical models based on the new conception of the universe. Nevertheless, models of the earth-centered system continued to be used through the early nineteenth century.

The eighteenth and nineteenth centuries saw a proliferation of planetary models marketed by instrument-makers, particularly in London, and used in public lectures. They were available in various sizes and prices, and under different names, such as **orrery** and **cometarium**. (It should be noted that the terminology used to describe astronomical models is complicated, confusing, and inconsistently applied.) The London instrument-maker Benjamin Martin introduced two special types of astronomical models in the 1760s: the tellurian (also known later as tellurium, tellurion, and tellarium), showing the motions of the earth around the sun, and the lunarium, which showed the motions of the moon around the earth.

In the eighteenth century, lecturers, such as John Theophilus Desaguliers, frequently used planetary models as part of their demonstration. Instrument-makers and lecturers, including Benjamin Martin and James Ferguson, published books describing the use of planetary models. In France, planetaria were often incorporated into armillary spheres; elsewhere, the construction of planetaria was rather scattered. The planetarium at Franeker by E. Eisinga was built in his home, in the ceiling of his living room. Other instrument-makers offered smaller versions for home use, including portable models carried by itinerant lecturers. The availability of relatively inexpensive paper versions is indicative of the interest of the public in such instruments.

In general, planetaria provided only approximate representations of astronomical motions. They were not meant to be precise, and did not address such intricacies as the relative distances between planets, or their elliptical orbits. Further, they show mean motions and fixed orbits, without attempting to illustrate perturbations.

Liba Taub

Bibliography

Gingerich, Owen. "The 1582 'Theorica Orbium' of Hieronymus Vulparius." *Journal for the History of Astronomy* 8 (1977): 38–43.

King, H.C., and J.R. Millburn. *Geared to the Stars: The Evolution of Planetariums, Orreries, and Astronomical Clocks.* Toronto: University of Toronto Press, 1978.

Millburn, John R. "Nomenclature of Astronomical Models." *Bulletin of the Scientific Instrument Society* 34 (1992): 7–9.

Price, Derek de Solla. "Gears from the Greeks. The Antikythera Mechanism: A Calendar Computer from ca. 8 B.C." *Transactions of the American Philosophical Society* 64, new series, part 7 (1974): 5–70.

Sedley, David. "Epicurus and the Mathematicians of Cyzicus." *Cronache Ercolanesi* 6 (1976): 23–54.

Planimeter

A planimeter mechanically measures the area bounded by a closed curve. It was one of several devices for carrying out mathematical operations that sold widely in the late nineteenth century. Scientists and engineers increasingly did arithmetic using **slide rules** and newly available commercial adding and **calculating machines** and they used planimeters to perform integration.

At the end of the eighteenth century, surveyors estimated the area of irregularly shaped plots of land or similar closed curves on maps by dividing the area into triangles and trapezoids and taking the sum. This procedure was tedious and not very accurate. Inventors from across Europe suggested improvements. The Bavarian Johannes M. Hermann (1814), the Florentine Tito Gonnella (1825), and the Swiss Johannes Oppikofer (1826) independently proposed planimeters in which the rotation of a disc linked to a tracer and rolling against the side of a cone gave a measure of the area swept out by the tracer. Oppikofer's device was manufactured in Paris by Ernst from about 1836. The Swiss engineer Caspar Wetli and the Austrian instrument-maker Charles Starke patented an important modification of the instrument in Austria in 1849, in which the wheel and cone were replaced by a disc and wheel mechanism. Starke manufactured several of these instruments in the early 1850s. In 1851, the Scottish land surveyor John Sang exhibited a modified wheel-and-cone planimeter at the International Exhibition in London. Sang's "platometer" marks the beginning of Scottish interest in integrating devices. It inspired the physicist James Clerk Maxwell to offer an improved instrument in 1855, and the engineer James Thomson and his physicist brother William to consider more elaborate **harmonic analyzers** in conjunction with research on the winds and tides.

In a footnote to his paper on an improved platometer, Maxwell commented that he had come across an account of a related instrument,

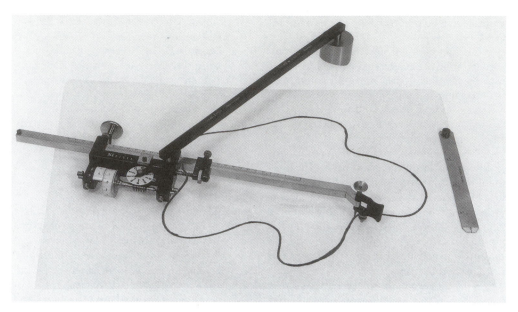

Compensating polar planimeter made by G. Coradi of Zurich, 1914, and sold by the American firm of Keuffel & Esser, showing pole and pole arm (back), adjustable tracer arm (front), and testing rule (right). NMAH Neg 73-1251. Courtesy of NMAH.

the polar planimeter. He believed that "its simplicity, and the beauty of the principle on which it acts, render it worth the attention of engineers and machinists, whether practical or theoretical." Jakob Amsler, inventor of the device, obtained his doctorate in mathematics at Königsberg in 1848 and worked for a year at the Geneva observatory before beginning a teaching career in Zurich. In 1851, he accepted a position at the Gymnasium in the Swiss city of Schaffhausen. Three years later, he turned his attention to precise mathematical instruments, particularly the planimeter. Amsler replaced the complex earlier arrangements of cones or rotating discs with two pivoted metal rods. The end of one rod held a tracer, the end of the other served as a fixed pole. A measuring wheel attached to the tracer arm near the vertex recorded motion parallel to the direction of that arm. Other motions of the arms were angular displacements that made no net contribution to the area swept out by the planimeter when the tracer moved around a closed curve. In fact, the pole arm moved along a circular arc. In some cases, this arc was a complete circle, and the area of this circle was included in the area measured.

Amsler's planimeter was small, sturdy, easy to use, and popular. By 1856, his agents included Lerebours & Secretin in Paris, Amsler & Wirz in Philadelphia, Ertel & Sohn in Munich,

and Elliott in London. From 1857, Amsler devoted full time to precision toolmaking. At his death, the business had produced 50,000 polar planimeters and 700 more complex momentum planimeters. Some sought to improve on Amsler's design. In the early 1880s Gottlieb Coradi of Zurich began selling a "precision disc" planimeter. In this polar planimeter, the recording wheel moves on a smooth disk above the paper on which the curve is drawn, making it possible to measure accurately areas drawn on rough and uneven paper. In 1894 O. Lang noted that the axis of the recording wheel of the planimeter might not be perfectly parallel to the tracer arm. He described a new form of planimeter, built by G. Coradi, in which the curve enclosing the area of interest was traced both clockwise and counterclockwise. This required that the tracer arm be placed on alternate sides of the pole arm. In such "compensating" polar planimeters, the pole arm is higher than the tracer arm and has a steel ball at the vertex that forms a ball joint with the carriage of the tracer arm.

The dimensions of a polar planimeter limit its use. The area to be measured must lie within a circle centered at the pole arm with radius equal to the sum of the lengths of the arms. Hence the instrument is not suited to measuring long, narrow areas. One can divide these regions into smaller parts, measure these areas, and take the sum. From the late 1880s, Coradi sold another instrument for this purpose. One end of the tracer in this rolling planimeter moves in a straight line (in the polar planimeter, the end of the tracer arm near the vertex moves in a circle), while the other traces out the curve. To assure that the instrument moved in a line, it rolled on two heavy wheels with rims slightly roughened to prevent slipping. The wheels were rigidly joined to one another by a heavy axle set in a frame. Such precision came at a price. In 1909, for example, the American firm of Keuffel & Esser offered a polar planimeter on Amsler's pattern for $28.00. It sold the Coradi precision disc planimeter for $85.00 and his rolling planimeter for $82.50 or $95.00, depending on the length of the tracer arm.

As the name suggests, the planimeter was originally envisioned as a way of measuring flat surfaces of land. In the course of the nineteenth century, the steam engine indicator diagram passed from being a closely held trade secret to a standard tool taught in engineering textbooks. Amsler planimeters were sold with modified scales for use by steam engines. In the late nineteenth and early twentieth century, American inventors, such as Edward J. Willis and Alpheus C. Lippincott, designed polar planimeters specifically for reading indicator diagrams. Planimeters intended for the same purpose, but designed with a pole arm that was constrained to move along a straight groove, were sold by the Swiss firm of G. Coradi and designed by the American John Coffin for sale by steam engine gauge manufacturers.

In the twentieth century, planimeters have been widely used not only by surveyors and engineers, but by scientists, medical technicians, and naval architects requiring measurements of areas bounded by closed curves. The firms of Amsler, Ott, and Coradi built other analog instruments intended to find the area under a curve between set limits (integrators), to draw the line representing the integral of a curve (integraphs), and/or to take the integrals to represent a curve by its Fourier expansion (harmonic analyzers). These instruments were the forerunners of the **differential analyzer**. In the second half of the century, they have generally been displaced by electronic digital equipment.

Peggy Aldrich Kidwell

Bibliography

Henrici, O. "Calculating Machines." In *Encyclopaedia Britannica*, Vol. 4, 972–981. 11th ed. Cambridge: Cambridge University Press, 1910.

Horsburgh, E.M., ed. *Handbook of the Napier Tercentenary Celebration; or, Modern Instruments and Methods of Calculation*, Edinburgh: Lothian, 1914.

Lopshits, A.M. *Computation of Areas of Oriented Figures*. Translated by J. Massalski, and Coley Mills, Jr. Boston: D.C. Heath, 1963, pp. 22–32.

Maxwell, J.C. "Description of a New Form of the Platometer." *Transactions of the Royal Scottish Society of Arts* 4 (1856): 429.

Plankton Recorder

Plankton recorders obtain multiple, serial samples of marine plankton and are used to study the spatial distribution of the macroscopic organisms, mostly zooplankton. An early controversy, and a current concern, of biological oceanographers is the extent to which marine plankton are distributed, in patches or uniformly. Alistair Hardy demonstrated horizontal patchiness of near-surface plankton in the Southern Ocean during the "Discovery" expeditions sponsored by Britain's Colonial Office, by towing two cone-shaped plankton nets alternately, each for a few minutes, along many miles of the ships track. He then designed, and in 1925 tested at sea off Antarctica, the first plankton recorder. His design proved so successful that it is still used, almost unchanged, in modern studies.

The Hardy Continuous Plankton Recorder (CPR) is towed like a paravane from the stern of a ship, having fins to stabilize it at 10 meters' depth. Water passes from an orifice in the nose through a tunnel across which a gauze filter of silk bolting cloth (9 in. wide, 60 meshes/in.) is drawn slowly and continuously by the mechanical action of a passive propeller at the back of the towed body. Plankton passing through the tunnel are captured onto the gauze and stored between the filter and another identical gauze strip before passing into a tank of formaldehyde for preservation. Subsequently, the filters are unrolled and cut into segments representing unit towing distance, and the plankton are identified and counted by teams of specialists. The samples obtained in this way record the patchiness of plankton with a resolution of a few miles over distances of several hundred miles.

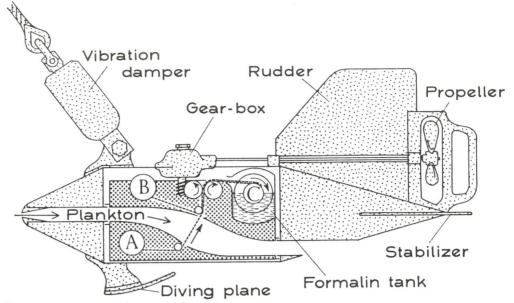

Diagrammatic section of the continuous plankton recorder. R.S. Glover. "The Continuous Plankton Recorder Survey of the North Atlantic." Symposia of the Zoological Society of London 19 (1967): 189–210, Figure 1. Courtesy of the Zoological Society of London.

This system of obtaining data has proved to be well adapted for use from "ships of opportunity," freighters or ferries that frequently ply the same routes; the CPRs are loaded aboard and disembarked by shore staff, and deployed by the ships' crew. Surveys of the North Sea plankton, because of its importance to the herring fisheries, were made in this way during the 1930s by Alistair Hardy from the University of Hull, and progressively expanded after the war by other marine laboratories to cover the entire North Atlantic from Norway to the Gulf of Maine. The data (now approaching a fifty-year series in some regions) have proved critical for a purpose not originally foreseen: they have made possible the analysis of decadal-scale changes in abundance, composition, and distribution of plankton organisms to be monitored across an entire ocean, and in this they are unique. It has been possible to relate the observed biological variability to changes in the circulation of the North Atlantic, and to the industrial eutrophication of the southern North Sea.

Electronic instrumentation of similar recorders is now possible for special studies: the towed bodies can be made to undulate so as to sample a greater depth range, while at small time intervals the instrument records depth, temperature, salinity, light, chlorophyll biomass, and other variables. Some instruments may also count and size (but not identify except by inference) plankton organisms. It is not anticipated that these modern undulating ocean recorders will replace the inexpensive, mechanical CPR for routine surveys.

In the 1960s, the Hardy moving-filter technique was used by a group at Scripps Institution of Oceanography in California in the design of a family of plankton recorders intended to resolve the distribution of plankton on much smaller spatial scales. In these Longhurst-Hardy plankton recorders (LHPR), the instrument is attached to the apex of a conical plankton net that concentrates the plankton before delivering it into the tunnel of the LHPR. The design of the prefiltering net is adjusted to the demands of each sampling operation. The filtering gauze is advanced in steps by an electric motor, and each stepped plankton sample can subsequently be identified with relevant ranges of depth, temperature, salinity, and other variables obtained and recorded electronically. Robert Williams of the Plymouth Marine Laboratory has mounted two LHPRs in tandem, to sample the microplankton and the macroplankton simultaneously. Sampling may be autonomous, or controlled from the research vessel by means of an electrically conducting cable, and it is usually done while the instrument is towed obliquely from 500 or 1,000 meters to the surface.

LHPRs have been especially useful in studying the vertical distribution of plankton in a wide range of oceanic and continental shelf habitats. These studies have led to a wider understanding of the ecological layering of the upper ocean in relation to the physical-chemical gradients (of temperature, density, light, chlorophyll) and especially to the discontinuities in these gradients. The layering of different species, and the aggregation of individuals into depth-discrete layers, revealed by LHPR sampling is now understood to be the most significant inhomogeneity of plankton within the upper kilometer of all oceans. Layering can be resolved by LHPRs to within less than 5 meters under good conditions; other biological profiling techniques (opening-closing nets, and systems with multiple nets) have much lower resolving power, or else enable identification to be made only by inference from an optical or acoustic signal. The LHPR has also become a significant tool in fisheries biology, enabling the fine spatial distribution and ecology of several species of commercial fish to be investigated during the 1980s on the European continental shelf. Such studies with the LHPR return to Alistair Hardy's original objective of understanding the relationship between larval fish, especially herring, and their planktonic food and predators.

Alan Longhurst

Bibliography

Colebrook, J.M. "Environmental Influences on Long-Term Variability in Marine Plankton." *Hydrobiologia* 142 (1986): 309–25.

Hardy, A.C. "Ecological Investigations with the Continuous Plankton Recorder: Object, Plan and Methods." *Hull Bulletins of Marine Ecology* 1 (1939): 1–57.

Herman, A.W. "Emerging Technologies in Biological Sampling." *UNESCO Technical Papers in Marine Science* 66 (1993): 1–48.

Williams, R. "The Double LHPR System, a High Speed Micro- and Macroplankton Sampler." *Deep-Sea Research* 30 (1983): 331–42.

Plethysmograph

A plethysmograph measures blood flow in an organ or limb in a noninvasive manner. When an organ or limb is placed within a sealed chamber, and the flow of blood into and from the organ is not interfered with, short-term alterations in the volume of the structure will reflect alterations in the flow of blood. These changes are detected by the displacement of the air or warm saline in the chamber. Such a device is sensitive enough to record alterations in flow with each heartbeat. The introduction of temporary (5–10 second) repeated blockage or occlusions of the venous drainage permits a measure of the volume of inflowing blood. This development was pivotal in making possible the extension of the technique to human physiological studies.

Although methods of assessing changes in the volume of an isolated muscle or heart had been used since the seventeenth century, the first instrument to record volume graphically, and thus merit the term plethysmograph, was described by a French physician, C. Buison, in 1862. In 1875 Angelus Mosso, a physiologist in Turin, Italy, described a cylindrical chamber plethysmograph used to record blood flow in the human forearm.

T.G. Brodie and A.E. Russell introduced temporary venous occlusion in 1905, in order to measure blood flow in the kidney of an animal. They used a rigid kidney-shaped container with an opening to allow the pedicle containing the blood vessels and ureter to pass to the outside. Their description read: "The plethysmograph as ordinarily applied, gives only qualitative results, which moreover in many cases are difficult to interpret. We have applied a simple modification which enables us to determine the rate of flow quantitatively with considerable accuracy. In principle this consists of blocking the vein of an organ enclosed within the plethysmograph for a short interval of time. The whole of the venous blood is thus retained in the plethysmograph and leads to a rise of the level of the recorder. If the recorder be calibrated the rate at which the level rises enables us to determine the rate of blood flow into the vein. In applying such a method as this it is obviously essential that the blockage of the vein must not be maintained so long as to impede the flow through capillaries. Under all ordinary conditions, the veins are never completely filled, so that it is possible to store up in them a small extra quantity of blood without checking the inflow into them from the capillaries. . . ."

Venous occlusion plethysmography was soon applied to other isolated organs. Instruments used on the kidney, spleen, and so on were called oncometers and distinguished from

Two Roy kidney oncometers, by Cambridge Scientific Instruments, ca. 1899. Cambridge Scientific Instrument Company Ltd. Physiological Instruments. *Cambridge: Cambridge University Press, 1899: 68, Figure 234–5. Courtesy of SSPL.*

plethysmographs used on human limbs. Brodie and Russell realized the potential of their technique for human studies, noting that "the venous outflow can be blocked by a circular ligature applied with so much force as to compress the veins without interfering with the arterial inflow." This technique was first applied to blood flow in human extremities by British physicians A.W. Hewlett and J.G. van Zwaluwenberg (1909), and has since been extended to measure blood flow in the hand (mostly skin), finger (skin), and forearm or calf (mostly skeletal muscle). An arterial occlusion cuff around the upper arm that is rapidly inflated to 50–60 mm Hg for 5–10 seconds occludes venous outflow from the limb while another cuff, inflated to 200 mm Hg at the wrist prior to starting the period of venous occlusion, can be used to separate forearm blood flow from the hand flow.

The seal between the rigid container and the tissues is important. For hand and finger studies, a latex glove (high compliance or very elastic) enclosed within the chamber has been adopted, while forearm and calf plethysmographs have used latex or compliant plastic tubing for a cuff. The chamber is filled with water and the temperature is controlled: the subject is positioned so that the limb to be studied is slightly elevated to induce some collapse of the veins under basal conditions. This ensures that

the venous filling occurs over the linear part of the pressure-volume relationship. In skilled hands the system provides accurate and reliable results, and Henry Barcroft and his co-workers in Belfast, at Queen's University Medical School and at St. Thomas's Hospital Medical School, exploited the technique very effectively.

The introduction of the mercury-in-rubber/ silicone strain gauge technique was a significant development by Robert Whitney (1953). Thin mercury-filled latex or plastic tubing was placed around a limb together with a means of measuring small alterations in resistance. Any transient change in circumference resulting from variations in the blood flow into the limb is sensed by a change in the resistance of the column of mercury. Calculations of volume change were made from several gauges and the high degree of compliance of the tubing ensured high sensitivity. The technique has limited reliability and accuracy but is easy to perform and the subject is not immobilized during measurements.

The mercury-in-silastic strain gauge technique underwent substantial development between 1991 and 1995, and now provides a simple and elegant technique for the noninvasive measurement of blood flow and small-vessel characteristics, including permeability, in the microvasculature of a limb. With the aid of computer software, very small changes in the volume can be measured in real time. Thus, actual levels of blood flow together with rhythmical oscillations can be identified and assessed. The technique clearly has potential for the assessment of peripheral blood flow in critically ill patients as well as in normal physiology.

For measurements of superficial (skin) blood flow, plethysmography is being replaced by laser-Doppler flow techniques that measure blood velocity rather than bulk flow (see **laser diagnostic instruments**). Recent developments in the new imaging techniques enable blood flow to be measured noninvasively in a wide range of human organs and structures.

Plethysmography has also been used to measure respiratory variables involving the chest wall (compliance and resistance). With a whole body plethysmograph, subjects are enclosed in a chamber while breathing from an external circuit.

Cecil Kidd

Bibliography

Barcroft, H., and H.J.C. Swan. *Sympathetic Control of Human Blood Vessels*. London: Edward Arnold, 1953.

Brodie, Thomas G., and A.E. Russell. "On the Determination of the Rate of Blood Flow through an Organ." *Journal of Physiology* 32 (1905): xlvii.

Christ, F., P. Raithel, I.B. Gartside, J. Gamble, K. Peter, and K. Messmer. "Investigating the Origin of Cyclic Changes in Limb Volume Using Mercury-in-Silastic Strain Gauge Plethysmography in Man." *Journal of Physiology* 487 (1995): 259–72.

Mosso, A. "Sopra un nuovo metodo per scrivere i movimenti dei vasi sagruigni nell uomo." *Atti della Reale Accademia delle Scienzi di Torino* 11 (1875–1876): 21–81.

Whitney, R.J. "The Measurement of Volume Changes in Human Limbs." *Journal of Physiology* 121 (1953): 1–10.

Polarimeter, Chemical

Chemical polarimeters evaluate the interaction of a chemical sample with polarized light. They are most frequently used for optically active liquids, which rotate the plane of polarization.

Following the discovery by Dominique François Arago of the effect using quartz crystals, Jean-Baptiste Biot undertook extensive investigations into optical activity. From 1812 to 1838, he published five papers detailing the optical activity of liquids and solids including sugars, essential oils, syrups, and crystalline forms. He found that the rotatory power was proportional to the length of sample, and that it depends on both the wavelength of light used and the sample temperature. Louis Pasteur, from 1848, proposed that the rotation of the plane of polarization in opposite directions by substances of apparently identical composition was caused by dissymmetry, or the existence of mirror-image molecules (optical isomerism). Optical activity figured in theories of stereochemistry in the late nineteenth century and was applied to the analysis of organic and inorganic compounds. Sugar solution, one of the most common optically active materials, was of commercial importance in the food and drink industries. Its analysis spawned the specialized variant of polarimetric saccharimeters. Many of the practical applications centered on the identification or quantitation of components in chemical manufacturing. For this purpose, the optical rotatory power of a wide range of substances, including resins, camphors, oils, and hundreds of carbohydrates were studied.

In the first decades of the twentieth century, considerable effort was devoted to developing the technique of polarimetry by investigators such as Emil Fischer and T.M. Lowry. With the rising popularity of infrared and ultraviolet spectroscopy, the use of polarimetry declined, until innovations in photoelectric and particularly spectropolarimeters revitalized the technique after World War II.

In a typical polarimeter, the light source, frequently monochromatic, illuminates the transparent sample located between the compensator and analyzer polarizers. Polarimetry relies upon measuring the rotation of the plane of polarization by determining an extremum of transmittance through the sample plus instrument. Étienne Malus showed that the intensity of light through two polarizing materials is proportional to the square of the cosine of the angle of polarization. The eye served as the detector of this intensity variation until the introduction of photoelectric detectors from the 1930s.

From 1932, the invention of Polaroid film made available an inexpensive polarizing material employed in nonprecision instruments. An important refinement in sensitivity was provided by the half-shade prism, which made possible the precise location of the angle of minimum transmission. This device introduces an optical phase shift in half the visual field so that small intensity differences can be more easily detected. The

P

Saccharimeter of the form introduced by Leon Laurent in Paris, 1874. This particular instrument was made by Hans Heele in Berlin, late nineteenth century. Courtesy of the Fondazione Scienza e Tecnica, Florence.

angle of rotation generally is measured using some form of divided circle, often with verniers or **micrometer** screw adjustments. When used by a carefully dark-adapted operator, such elaborations permit angular measurements precise to between 0.01° and 0.002°.

Photographic methods have found some application, despite the tedious processes of exposure, processing, and subsequent evaluation of densities using a **microdensitometer**. The available spectral range can be as much as four times wider than in visual work, and the ability to integrate weak intensities makes measurements on highly absorbing samples practicable.

Photoelectric polarimeters have replaced visual instruments, particularly for studies at other than the readily obtainable emission wavelengths of 546 and 589 nm. H. Rudolf devised a photoelectric spectropolarimeter in 1956 that was commercialized shortly thereafter. Recording spectropolarimeters have also been widely applied to problems of stereochemistry. Photoelectric polarimeters have employed a variety of techniques to measure optical activity. In the null method, the transmitted intensity is displayed to locate the minimum, which is then read from a divided circle as in a visual instrument. In the photometric method, the intensity of light is measured and related directly to optical activity by the law of Malus. In the phase-sensitive method, the analyzer is mechanically rotated or the polarization plane is rotated by a Faraday cell to locate the positions of equal transmittance, and hence bracket the minimum.

Polarimetric data are conventionally reported in terms of the wavelength used, sample temperature, and sample solvent. The æoptical rotatory dispersion, Æ, or specific rotation as a function of wavelength, is sometimes measured to identify unknown materials or to infer minor changes in the configuration of a molecule. The corresponding polarimeter is essentially the same as the conventional form, but allowing for the control and measurement of both the temperature of the sample and the wavelength of light incident upon it. This generally incorporates a monochromator to isolate a band of wavelengths that may extend into the ultraviolet. Like **spectrophotometers**, these have been available as both dispersive and Fourier-transform instruments since the 1970s.

Sean F. Johnston

Bibliography

Clark, D., and J.F. Grainger. *Polarized Light and Optical Measurement.* New York: Pergamon, 1971.

Gibb, Thomas R.P., Jr. *Optical Methods of Chemical Analysis.* New York: McGraw-Hill, 1942.

Hyde, W. Lewis, and R.M.A. Azzam, eds. *Polarized Light: Instruments, Devices, and Applications.* Palos Verdes Estates: Society of Photo-Optical Instrumentation Engineers, 1976.

Landolt, H., and J. McRae. *Optical Activity and Chemical Composition.* London: Whittaker, 1899.

Lowry, T.M. *Optical Rotatory Power.* London: Longmans, 1935.

Polarimeter and Polariscope

A polarimeter measures the angle of rotation of a polarized plane of a beam of light when it passes through an optically active substance. The study of polarization began in 1669, when Erasmus Bartholin observed that a transparent crystal of Iceland spar (calcium carbonate) could split a beam of light into two different rays. Christian Huygens studied double refraction a few years later and described some of the effects that we now recognize as polarization of the ordinary and extraordinary rays. But only since the beginning of the nineteenth century has polarization been systematically investigated.

In Paris in 1808, Étienne Malus discovered that light could be polarized by reflection, and he coined the term "polarization." Polarization attracted the immediate interest of such leading physicists as François Arago, Jean Baptiste Biot, and Augustin Fresnel in France, and David Brewster in Scotland. Around 1820, by assuming that light is a transverse wave, Fresnel was able to explain in mathematical terms the phenomena of double refraction and polarization. As the relationship between the optical activity of substances and their molecular structure was recognized, a completely new array of instruments was developed.

Polarimetric techniques were soon found to be useful in chemistry, crystallography, biology, and medicine. Special-purpose polarimeters known as saccharimeters were widely used to measure sugar concentrations in solutions (see **polarimeter, chemical**). Diabetometers measured the sugar content in the urine of diabetics.

The basic polarimeter consists of a polarizer (birefringent crystal, polarizing prism, pile of glass plates, or nonmetallic mirror) and a second device of the same kind called an analyzer, which can rotate in the center of a divided circle. A small telescope attached to the latter allows for observations. The early polarimeters worked on an extinction principle—that is, when the analyzer and the polarizer are positioned at right angles to one another, no light is transmitted. An optically active solution interposed between the crossed polarizer and analyzer rotates the plane of light and, thus, allows some light to be transmitted. The analyzer is then rotated to reestablish the obscurity of the field of vision.

The polarimeter used by Biot and Malus around 1810 used rotating mirrors of black glass for both the analyzer and the polarizer. In a later model, the analyzer was formed by a prism of Iceland spar. In 1828, the Scottish geologist William Nicol described an efficient polarizing prism composed of two pieces of Iceland spar glued in such a way as to allow the extraordinary ray to pass through while deflecting the ordinary ray. Nicol prisms remained in use until the twentieth century. Other polarizing prisms were proposed by William H. Wollaston, Léon Foucault, Adam Prazmowski, Paul Glan, Silvanus Thompson, and others. In 1844, the German chemist Eilhard Mitscherlich introduced a polarimeter equipped with two nicols. Various optical elements such as quartz plates were subsequently introduced in these instruments in order to further increase their accuracy.

Jean François Soleil and his son-in-law and successor, Jules Duboscq, invented and manufactured some of the most successful polarization devices between roughly 1840 and 1880. In

Nörremberg polariscope by Deleuil, late nineteenth century. Courtesy of the Fondazione Scienza e Tecnica, Florence.

Soleil's saccharimeter, the rotation of a polarized beam of white light produced by a sugar solution was compensated for by a double sliding quartz wedge (Soleil's compensator). Other important instrument manufacturers were Franz Schmidt & Haensch, and R. Fuess (both located in Berlin); Hermann & Pfister (in Bern); Steeg & Reuter (in Homburg); and J.G. Hoffmann and Léon Laurent (in Paris).

The polaristrobometer, invented by Heinrich Wildt in 1865, was equipped with a couple of quartz plates that produced interference fringes. A specific rotation of the analyzer eliminated the fringes, thus allowing one to measure the rotation of the polarization plane.

In 1873, Alfred Cornu and Duboscq proposed a half-shadow polarimeter for yellow monochromatic light. In this instrument, the position of polarization plane was determined by comparing and equalizing the luminous intensity of two (or more) sections of the ocular field. In 1874, Laurent described a similar apparatus that attained great popularity in France. In the 1880s, Ferdinand Franz Lippich conceived a half-shadow polarimeter in which the analyzer was composed of a couple of Glan's prisms. This instrument was eventually improved by Hans Heinrich Landolt.

A polariscope enables one to observe the effects of polarization, but not measure their extent. Because polarization phenomena were deemed spectacular, polariscopes were widely used in physics demonstrations. They were often sold with a series of uniaxial and biaxial crystal plates which, in polarized light, exhibit splendid interference patterns and colors. Different types of polariscopes were used in connection with **heliostats** and **magic lanterns**.

In the tourmaline tongs, first described around 1827 by Karl Michael Marx, the specimen to be observed was inserted between two pieces of tourmaline, a birefringent and dichroic crystal that absorbs most of the ordinary ray while allowing the extraordinary ray through. Small presses were also used to produce birefringence in glass plates. Around 1830, the German chemist Christian Nörremberg invented a vertical polariscope in which light was polarized by an inclined glass plate and analyzed by a black mirror or a nicol. This enjoyed popularity for many decades. Around 1850, Duboscq introduced a sophisticated projection polariscope that was eventually copied by several instrument-makers. Many similar devices were proposed, but their working principle remained the same.

Giovan Battista Amici devised a polarizing **microscope** around 1830, and instruments of this sort came into common use for petrographic and crystallographic work in the second half of the century. The cyanopolarimeter enabled one to compare the color of the sky with the colors produced by a polarization system.

Polarizing filters and sheets (Polaroid) were developed during the 1930s by the American inventor Edwin Herbert Land. They are of basically three types: dichroic and orientated microcrystals in a plastic medium; stretched sheet of polyvinylene alcohol with polymeric chain of iodine; or dichroic plastic made of orientated polyvinyl. Polaroids, which superseded most of the old polarizing prisms, are now widely used in industry, in photography, and in many optical instruments.

Paolo Brenni

Bibliography

Khvolson, O.D. *Traité de physique*. Paris: A. Hermann, 1908–1914.

Pellin, Philibert. "Polarimètres et saccharimètres." *Journal de physique théorique et appliqué* 4 (1903): 436–42.

Rosmorduc, Jean. *La polarisation rotatoire naturelle, de la structure de la lumière à celle des molécules*. Paris: A. Blanchard, 1983.

Sidersky, David. *Polarisation et saccharimètrie*. Paris: Gauthier-Villars, G. Masson, 1895.

Polarograph

Polarography is a method of chemical analysis that uses current-potential curves at a dropping mercury electrode to indicate which substances are present and in what quantities. The polarograph was one of the first examples of automatic laboratory equipment. It eliminated tedious point-by-point measurement of current-potential curves and, thereby, started a revolution in analytical methods.

The technique was devised by Jaroslav Heyrovsky at the Charles University in Prague, in 1922, and the first instrument was developed by Heyrovsky, working with a Japanese collaborator, Masuzo Shikata, in 1925. Heyrovsky chose the name in order to emphasize the role of the polarizing electromotive force in the curves obtained by such measurement.

Polarography is particularly suitable for inorganic analysis, since many elements are reduced at the dropping mercury electrode, giving well-defined current-potential curves, called polarograms. Since about thirty metals can be determined at levels down to 1 to 10 ppb, the technique has many applications in metallurgical analysis. It is also widely used in trace analysis, indicating impurities in commercial chemicals, water, sewage, effluents, petroleum, foodstuffs, and biological materials. Many organic compounds, particularly those with a highly polar bond or unsaturation, are also electroactive and yield characteristic polarograms.

Heyrovsky, with colleagues such as D. Ilkovic, Rudolf Brdicka, K. Wiesner, and later Petr Zuman, investigated the fundamental theory of polarography and found applications of the technique in many branches of chemistry. Until 1938, almost all papers on polarography described work either done in Prague or undertaken by chemists trained there. Izaak Kolthoff in the United States and other electrochemists in Germany, Italy, Poland, Russia, and the U.K. started investigations in the late 1930s.

Simple commercial instruments became available during World War II and were tested on analyses either undertaken previously by other methods or for which the older methods had failed. The literature on polarography expanded after the war, and by 1980 the number of papers had passed the twenty thousand mark. In 1959, Heyrovsky received the Nobel Prize for chemistry.

Classical DC Polarography

In 1893, Robert Behrend undertook the first titration in which potential difference rather than color was used to indicate equilibrium. He titrated mercurous nitrate solution with potassium halides and vice versa, using a mercury indicator electrode with a mercury/mercurous nitrate reference electrode. In the early 1920s electromechanical systems were developed, providing the first means of automatic recording of titration curves. This enabled the measurement of the concentration of any ion that could be oxidized or reduced, and not just of acids and bases as in conventional titration.

The polarographic technique developed by Heyrovsky involves the electrolysis of solutions of electroreducible or electro-oxidizable materials in a cell with a polarizable dropping mercury electrode and either a pool of mercury or a reference electrode, usually a saturated calomel electrode. A gradually increasing dc potential is applied to the cell, and the current flowing between the electrodes is plotted against the applied potential. A characteristic steplike current-potential polarogram is obtained for each electroactive species in the solution. The potential at the midpoint of the rising part of each step, the halfwave potential, is a characteristic of the species causing the transition. The height of the step (that is, the diffusion current or wave height) is proportional to the concentration of the species.

The dropping mercury electrode used in classical polarography is a small electrode, in which a steady stream of mercury droplets emerges from a fine-bore (0.05–0.08 mm i.d.) glass capillary at the rate of one drop every 3 to 8 seconds. It was invented in 1903 by Bohumil

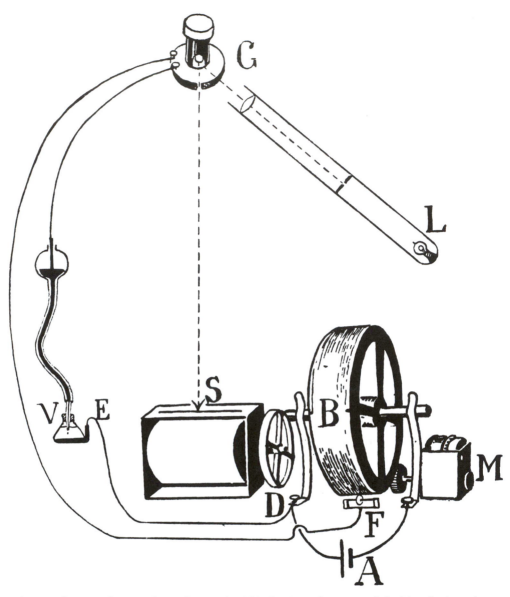

Schematic diagram of Heyrovsky's polarograph, 1925, showing galvanometer light (L); reflecting galvanometer (G), camera slit (S), rotary potentiometer (B), motor (M), and dropping mercury electrode (V). Courtesy of SSPL.

Kucera, who modified the mercury electrode devised in 1873 by Gabriel Lippmann for his capillary electrometer. It is operational over the range +0.3 to −2.8 volts. The dropping mercury electrode has several desirable features. Each drop presents a fresh mercury surface to the solution, and electrolysis products are unable to accumulate. The diffusion current assumes a steady value immediately and is reproducible. These features are offset by the problem that the charging (or capacity) current of the growing drop interferes with the measurement of small wave heights.

The polarograph constructed by Heyrovsky and Shikata in 1925 recorded current-voltage curves photographically. A linearly increasing voltage was applied to the cell by means of a motor-driven **potentiometer,** and a drum carrying photographic paper was rotated by the same motor. Current variations were recorded on the paper by a spot of light reflected from a mirror-**galvanometer.** Voltage increments were marked on the paper automatically, which was then developed.

Commercial photographic polarographs were introduced in the late 1930s, and cost £140 in the U.K. Since the photographic paper had to be processed, it was not possible to observe the polarogram during the recording period. Pen-recording instruments overcame these disadvantages. In the Tinsley instrument, developed in 1944, the current was passed through a mirror-galvanometer and the reflected beam fell on a photocell. The photo current was amplified by a dc amplifier to operate a pen-recording milliammeter. Other pen-recording instruments followed.

Classical dc polarographs can be used to determine electroactive substances in the concentration range, 10^{-2}–10^{-4} M. At lower concentrations, sensitivity is hampered by increasing interference from the charging current. This and other difficulties restricted the use of dc polarography in routine analysis.

Modern Polarography

Attempts to improve sensitivity during the 1950s led to the development of tast, square-wave, and differential pulse instruments that were a thousand times more sensitive than classical dc polarographs. In tast polarography, the current is measured only at its maximum value, before the fall of each drop. This procedure overcomes charging current effects and improves sensitivity. With the arrival of low-cost, fast, stable operational amplifiers in the 1960s, further practical problems were overcome. The great promise of ac, pulse and differential pulse polarography was revealed, thus inducing a major revival of interest.

Modern polarographs are microprocessor controlled, high-performance instruments with facilities for classical dc, tast, square-wave, pulse, and differential pulse polarography. The dropping mercury electrode can be replaced by a glassy carbon or a carbon-paste electrode, thus permitting voltammetric measurements in the anodic region. Differential pulse anodic and cathodic stripping voltammetry make possible measurements of a dozen elements at levels of less than 1 ppb. However, modern chromatographic, fluorimetric, spectrometric, mass spectrographic, and x-ray methods have displaced polarography from its preeminent position (see **chromatograph; spectrometer, mass; spectrophotometer**).

James E. Page

Bibliography

Galus, Zbigniew. *Fundamentals of Electrochemical Analysis*. Translated by R.A. Chalmers, and W.A.J. Bryce. 2nd rev. ed. New York: Ellis Horwood, 1994.

Heyrovsky, Jaroslav, and Jaroslav Küta. *Principles of Polarography*. Prague: Publishing House of the Czechoslovak Academy of Sciences, 1965.

Meites, Louis, *Polarographic Techniques*. 2nd ed. New York: Wiley, 1965.

Milner, G.W.C. *The Principles and Applications of Polarography and Other Electroanalytical Processes*. London: Longmans, 1957.

Vassos, Basil H., and Galen W. Ewing. *Electroanalytical Chemistry*. New York: Wiley, 1983.

Polygraph

Etienne-Jules Marey, a French physiologist, devised the polygraph (from the Greek, meaning "multiple writer") in order to render any physiological movement in graphic form, and to investigate the functional interrelationships between movements occurring simultaneously in an organism. In the twentieth century, the polygraph has been used predominantly for lie detection in forensic, industrial, military, and political contexts. As such, it has been the subject of much epistemological, ethical, and legal controversy.

In the late 1840s, physiologists began to build instruments to translate the motions of respiration, arterial pulse, and the nerve impulse in muscle contraction into a graphic representation along two coordinates. In the 1860s, Marey and his collaborator August Chaveau experimented with a cardiograph that would simultaneously register three separate motions of the heartbeat, using three rubber air-filled tubes to transmit the signal, three separate sphygmograph levers, and a single rotating drum, to produce three curves superimposed upon one another.

Marey extended the principle of transmission at a distance with air tubes to register all sorts of movement. In order to make an instrument capable of adapting to variations in the intensity and duration of different bodily motions, he modified the tambour lever to allow it to better absorb shocks, and he added a long roll of paper (in the manner of the Morse telegraph) to accommodate slowly developing phenomena. Using a bell or a cup to receive the sig-

Keeler polygraph, model 302C, ca. 1950. NMAH 321,642.01. Courtesy of NMAH.

nal, Marey's polygraph could be used to inscribe movements in all parts of the body. The first of these instruments was constructed by Louis Breguet of Paris.

Marey's instrument inspired the production of numerous portable polygraphs for use in clinical diagnosis. One of the most popular of these was the ink polygraph described by James Mackenzie in 1908. This instrument, with its clockwork-driven paper ribbon and one-fifth of a second time marker, was encased in a nickel-plated housing. A projecting arm for registering tambours was connected by means of rubber tubing to the receiving devices, which were simple aluminum cups for the heartbeat and venous pulse, and a pelotte, fixed to the arm by straps, for the arterial pulse. The first Mackenzie polygraphs were built by Krohne and Seseman of London; later models were manufactured by Down Brothers of London, and the Cambridge Scientific Instrument Co.

Forensic Applications

In 1921, James A. Larson, a medical student working for the police department in Berkeley, California, used a polygraph of his own design to simultaneously record the blood pressure, pulse, and respiration of criminal suspects during testimony. Larson's work derived from decades of research on the physiological effect of feelings, emotions, and various kinds of psychological states. The Italian physiologist Angelo Mosso, a close associate of Marey, used graphical methods to measure changes in blood pressure and respiration caused by fear. His countryman Caesare Lombroso, a celebrated criminal anthropologist, attempted to find forensic applications for these studies, on the grounds that fear of being detected is an essential element of deception. Larson's use of the polygraph as a lie-detector was inspired by well-publicized sphygmographic studies of deception at Harvard University conducted by Hugo Muensterberg and William Moulton Marston.

Larson's work gave rise to a veritable industry of polygraph lie-detection in the United States, with two competing schools, each with its own standard instrument and similarly regulated methods of testing. The Keeler polygraph, devised by Larson's assistant Leonarde Keeler, was the preferred instrument of the Scientific Crime Detection Laboratory of Northwestern University. This instrument featured pneumograph tubes circling the chest of the subject and metal tambours producing a pressure curve whose changes were proportional to blood pressure changes in the body. The polygraph designed by John E. Reid of the Reid College of Detection of Deception was a similar instrument, but it was provided with a device to record psychogalvanic skin reflex or electrodermal response. This worked by passing an imperceptible electric current through electrodes attached to the subject's hand and used a **galvanometer** to monitor the variations in the flow of that current.

In the United States, the polygraph has become a potent symbol of the linkage of the authority of scientific instrumentation with the authority of the institutions of the state and private industry. Since its debut in the movie *Northside 777* (in which Keeler himself dramatically administered a lie test to Richard Conte in Joliet Prison, vindicating reporter Jimmy Stewart's suspicion that Conte was innocent), the polygraph has become a staple of the imagery of Hollywood and popular culture. In recent decades, however, scientific criticism of the dependability of the polygraph lie-detector has led to highly restrictive conditions for admissibility in most legal settings. In the wake of Richard Nixon's 1971 remark that "I don't know anything about polygraphs and I don't know how accurate they are, but I know they'll scare the hell out of people," a continuing social outcry against the instrument has arisen, with charges that it serves more as a method of discipline and intimidation than as an assessor of credibility.

Robert Brain

Bibliography

Lykken, David Thoreson. *A Tremor in the Blood: Uses and Abuses of the Lie Detector.* New York: McGraw-Hill, 1981.

Mackenzie, James. "The Ink Polygraph." *British Medical Journal* 1 (1908): 1411.

Marey, Etienne-Jules. *Du Mouvement dans les fonctions de la vie; lecon faites au College de France,* 147–51. Paris: Germer Bailliere, 1868.

Trovillo, Paul V. "A History of Lie Detection." *Journal of the American Institute of Criminal Law and Criminology* 29 (1938–1939): 848–81; 30 (1939–1940): 104–19.

Polymerase Chain Reaction

Polymerase Chain Reaction (PCR) is a method of identifying and rapidly reproducing a gene or a segment of DNA. DNA polymerase is the enzyme catalyst for the reaction; chain reaction refers to the exponential amplification and accumulation of the desired genetic segment. Cloning methods for copying stretches of DNA were introduced in the early 1970s, but it was difficult to get enough DNA with the desired sequence to run the experiments and to separate the desired sequence from the rest of the DNA so that something could be done with it. PCR solved both of those problems.

The process is quite simple. In a test tube, the scientists combine a double strand of DNA containing the gene or segment to be copied (the target sequence) with chemical raw materials used to build new DNA strands (precursors); two short, single strands of DNA (primers) especially constructed so that they will lie on either side of and bracket the segment to be copied; and the DNA polymerase. The mixture is heated, causing the DNA double strands to separate, and then cooled so that each primer can bind to its complementary sequence on a strand. Polymerases start at each primer and copy the sequence of that strand. Within a short time, exact replicas of the target sequence are produced. Every cycle doubles the amount of the target sequence. After twenty cycles there are more than one million copies of the DNA segment.

This procedure was first done by hand, but then special thermal cyclers were developed to automate the process. PCR machines are now almost as common in biomedical laboratories as photocopying machines, and the uses of PCR include detecting pathogens, identifying criminals from DNA fragments, and studying evolution by analyzing the DNA of long extinct creatures.

History of the Concept

The idea for PCR came to Kary B. Mullis in the spring of 1983. Mullis was working for Cetus

A prototype PCR machine, by Cetus Corporation, 1986. SM 1993-339. Courtesy of SSPL.

Corp., a biotechnology company in Emeryville, California, making pieces of DNA (oligonucleotides) for molecular biologists to use in their experiments and thinking about simpler and easier ways to extract and copy the little pieces of DNA that were wanted from a complex piece of DNA. The primers could be used to bracket the fragment one wanted, but then how to copy it without having to repeat the experiment numerous times?

This is where his work with **computers** and writing programs for "loop reiterative processes" came into play. Exponential amplification was an elementary mathematical concept put to powerful uses by computer programmers. Why not apply it to molecular biology and biochemistry? Cyclical heating and cooling, which would cause the DNA to denature and then anneal and the DNA polymerase to extend the annealed primers, would also result in the exponential accumulation of a specific fragment because the primer extension products synthesized in one cycle can serve as a template in the next. Thus the notion of a polymerase chain reaction. A literature search for discussions of this procedure produced nothing. The initial response of his colleagues was negative.

With the help of high school graduate and lab assistant Fred Faloona, Mullis began experiments in the fall of 1983, and he had achieved some convincing results by December. But it was not until the latter half of 1984 that Cetus formed a group to evaluate and apply this technique. Their paper describing the earliest application of PCR, and the first paper to appear on PCR, was published in *Science* in 1985. After a patent and further publications in 1987, PCR was quickly adopted around the world. Mullis won a Nobel Prize for his work in 1993.

History of the Instrument

Since Cetus was not primarily an instrument company, they formed a joint venture with the Perkin-Elmer Corp. of Norwalk, Connecticut. Mr. Cycle, the first instrument built and tested in 1984–1985, consisted of a multi-channel automated liquid handler, called the Pro/Pette™, hooked up to two water baths. The bed of the instrument contained two temperature controlled aluminum blocks. The front block held the samples (in uncapped microcentrifuge tubes) and was connected by a switching valve to two water baths, one at 94°C and the other at 37°C. The back block held solutions of Klenow fragment, the DNA polymerase derived from *E. coli*, also in uncapped microcentrifuge tubes and placed in the same configuration as the samples in the front block. A controller kept track of the incubation times at both high and low temperatures, actuated the switching valve in order to change the front block temperature, and prompted the multichannel head to pick up fresh tips, withdraw aliquots of enzyme solution from the tubes in the back block, and deliver them into the corresponding samples in the front block. This procedure had to be repeated every cycle because the Klenow fragment was thermally unstable and fresh enzyme had to be added after each denaturation step. This made the process tedious and resulted in the rapid accumulation of denatured enzyme in the sample.

Son-of-Cycle, developed in 1985–1986, incorporated two important innovations. One was the use of the Taq DNA Polymerase derived from the bacterium *Thermus aquaticus*. Because Taq was thermostable, it was no longer necessary to add fresh enzyme after each denaturation step. The other was the use of semiconductor elements, called Peltier devices, for heating and cooling the sample holding block.

Several other designs were tried before Perkin-Elmer Cetus introduced a commercial instrument in late 1987. This was called the DNA Thermal Cycler I (TC-1), and it used neither water baths nor Peltier devices. Rather, electrical heaters provided the heating, and a refrigeration unit in the body of the instrument provided the cooling. A microprocessor, with user-programmable files and preprogrammed protocols, regulated the cycling and monitored incubation times and block temperature. The instrument fit on a desk top, weighed 65 lbs., and cost about $8,500.

The DNA Thermal Cycler 480 appeared in 1990, and the DNA Thermal Cycler 9600, with a capacity of ninety-six samples rather than forty-eight, as well as other improved features, was introduced a few years later. Perkin-Elmer Cetus Instruments also began marketing Gene Amp, a DNA amplification reagent kit designed for the patented PCR process.

In 1991, the Swiss pharmaceutical company Hoffmann-La Roche, Inc., bought the rights to PCR and the PCR-related instruments business for $300 million. It established a biomedical laboratory in Alameda, California, now called Roche Molecular Systems, to continue work on new PCR applications. That same year another biotechnology company, Chiron Corp. of Emeryville, California, bought Cetus for nearly $700 million. In this way, one of the first biotechnology companies in the world (founded in 1971) and the birthplace of PCR came to an end. But as a technique and tool and a $1-billion-a-year industry, PCR continues to grow and flourish.

Ramunas Kondratas

Bibliography

Erlich, Henry A., ed. *PCR Technology: Principles and Applications of DNA Amplification.* New York: W.H. Freeman, 1992.

Mullis, Kary B. "The Polymerase Chain Reaction." *Les Prix Nobel* (1993): 102–17.

———, and Fred A. Faloona. "Specific Synthesis of DNA *in vitro* via a Polymerase Catalyzed Chain Reaction." In *Recombinant DNA: Part F,* edited by Ray Wu, 335–50. London: Academic, 1987.

———, F. Ferre, and R.A. Gibbs, eds. *The Polymerase Chain Reaction.* Boston: Birkhauser, 1994.

Yoffe, Emily. "Is Kary Mullis God?" *Esquire* (July 1994): 68–74.

Porometer

A porometer measures the porosity of leaves. This property depends on the stomata (from Greek *stoma* meaning "mouth") situated in the

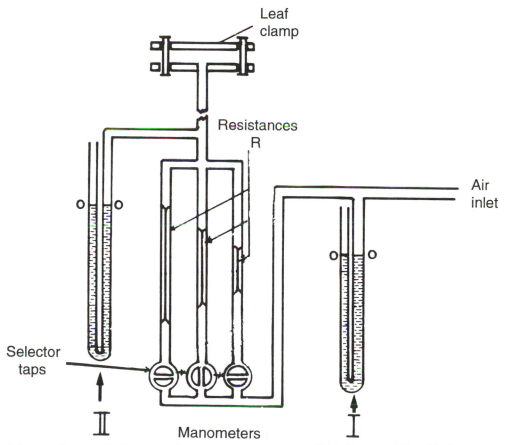

Schematic diagram of a Gregory and Pearse resistance porometer, 1934. Courtesy of Hans Meidner.

epidermis of leaves and the degree of their opening. There is a correlation between this and the intake of carbon dioxide (required for photosynthesis) and the loss of water vapor. These measurements are therefore of practical value, for instance, in agriculture when monitoring crop yields and deciding when to irrigate.

There are two basic kinds of instruments: mass flow porometers, which measure the rate of air flow down a pressure gradient applied across a leaf, and diffusion porometers, which measure the rate of diffusion of gases down their own density gradients. The latter provide the more direct measure of the processes involved because under natural conditions carbon dioxide and water vapor move into and out of leaves by diffusion.

The first mass flow porometer was constructed in the U.K. in 1911 by Darwin and Pertz, who also introduced the term "porometer" for these instruments. The rate of descent of the water column was taken as the measure of leaf porosity (later called leaf resistance or, by its inverse, leaf conductance). The Alvim mass flow porometer, introduced in Brazil, incorporated a **sphygmomanometer** by means of which the rate of decrease in applied pressure gave the measure of leaf resistance.

With the Gregory and Pearse resistance porometer introduced in 1934, the differing readings of manometers I and II were used to calculate leaf resistance in capillary units. With the Heath and Russell **Wheatstone Bridge** porometer of 1951, capillary resistance units could be read off the dial of a calibrated needle valve. The pressure difference porometer, developed in the 1980s, uses a pressure transducer that permits leaf resistance to be calculated by microprocessor and displayed in absolute units (seconds per mm) on LCD. These instruments were introduced in the U.K.

M.J.C. Müller in Germany was making diffusion measurements as early as 1870. His apparatus consisted of a water-filled U tube, one limb of which was of capillary dimensions. Detached epidermal tissue containing stomata was placed across the wide-mouthed limb, and the rate of water vapor diffusion was measured by the rate of decrease in height of the water column in the capillary limb.

Qualitative determinations of diffusion began in 1878 when M. Marget in France used dehydrated palladium chloride to estimate the rate of water vapor diffusion out of leaves. In 1894, Stahl in Germany introduced the use of dry cobalt chloride papers of a standard dark blue color, and measured the time required for the papers to change to a standard light blue. In 1898, Francis Darwin in the U.K. used a horn hygroscope to time the attainment of a certain curvature.

Instruments that measure rates of diffusion of gases such as hydrogen, nitrous oxide, argon, and helium through leaves have been used in France, Australia, and the United States since the 1930s, and have played a significant role in stomatal research.

The construction of instruments that could measure the rate of diffusion of water vapor out of leaves was a major aim of research for many years. In the U.K. in 1951, Meidner and Spanner built a differential transpiration porometer that measured the rate of water vapor diffusion indirectly. Two air streams of different humidities were directed onto two adjacent spots of a leaf, and the resulting differential cooling of the leaf tissue was picked up by a **thermopile** and measured as an electrical output. The lower the leaf resistance, the greater the output.

Decisive progress was made by E.S. Wallihan in the United States with his sensor element porometer of 1964. This measured the rate of change in electrical resistance of a hygroscopic element placed a certain distance above a leaf in a closed space. The faster the diffusion of water vapor out of the leaf, the faster the decrease in electrical resistance of the element. The time taken for a certain decrease in electrical resistance to occur was called the transit time.

Several diffusion porometers costing somewhat less than $10,000 were commercially available in the mid-1990s. For example, the Delta-T measures transit times and draws upon a 1970 design by Stiles, Monteith and Bull; it is made in the United Kingdom. The LI-COR, which is made in the United States, draws upon a 1972 design by Beardsel, Jarvis, and Davidson; this is a null balance instrument that measures the amount of dry air needed to keep the humidity constant in a closed space containing the leaf. Both instruments employ microprocessors with LCD readout of leaf resistance or leaf conductance in absolute units (seconds/mm or mm/seconds).

Hans Meidner

Bibliography

Meidner, Hans, and Terence Mansfield.
   Physiology of Stomata. Maidenhead,
   U.K.: McGraw Hill, 1968.

Weyers, Jonathan, and Hans Meidner. *Methods in Stomatal Research*. Harlow: U.K.: Longman, 1990.

Potentiometer

A potentiometer measures an unknown electromotive force (emf) or potential difference by balancing it by a known emf. The principle was first used by J.C. Poggendorff in 1841 to measure the unknown emf of a **battery** by compensating it for a battery of constant emf. In Poggendorff's compensation method, the emfs of two cells were balanced by means of the resistance wires of different values. One serious problem with this method was that the internal resistance of the constant battery, which was hard to measure, had to be known. Though Du Bois-Reymond significantly improved the Poggendorff method in the 1860s by introducing a graduated slide-scale (a variable resistance) in it, it had the same problem.

Latimer Clark, a telegraph engineer, modified the potentiometer method in such a way that the internal resistance of the source need no longer be known. As shown in the illustration, the wire AB was always maintained at a constant potential difference of V_1 of a standard cell C_1. When there was no deflection in the two **galvanometers**, G_1 and G_2, the following relation was satisfied: $V_2 = V_1 (R_{AC}/R_{AB})$. There was no need to know the internal resistance of C_1. For his potentiometer, Clark devised his own standard cell; the Clark cell used mercury and sulphate of mercury paste with $ZnSO_4$, instead of copper and $CuSO_4$ as in Daniell's cell. With Clark's potentiometer, the wire AB was always maintained at the voltage of a Clark cell, and equilibrium was obtained only when the voltage of a trial cell was smaller than that of a standard Clark cell. Thus, the Clark cell was vulnerable to the inflow of an external current into it.

This limitation was overcome by J.A. Fleming in 1885. His potentiometer used two wires sliding along a scaled wire. It thus no longer mattered whether the voltage of a trial cell was smaller than that of a standard cell. For his potentiometer Fleming used a Daniell's cell of his own design that was not vulnerable to the inflow of the external current into it. In 1887, Fleming first devised a direct-reading potentiometer.

A most important and novel feature of Fleming's potentiometer lay in its purpose. Before Fleming, the potentiometer had been largely used to measure the unknown emf of a battery. Fleming was the first to make the potentiometer read heavy current in amperes. By using a potentiometer and a set of standard resistances, he measured heavy currents up to 500 amperes. Fleming's intention was to use an instrument devoid of a permanent magnet or a moving iron that was used in the direct-reading ampere-meter.

From the late 1880s, precise potentiometers were constructed by K. Feussner in Germany, and J. Swinburne and R.E.B. Crompton in Britain. Crompton's potentiometer in 1893 became a standard model for the power engineering potentiometer. The ac potentiometer was devised by A. Franke in 1891; C.V. Drysdale and A.B. Campbell contributed to the ac potentiometer.

Sungook Hong

Bibliography
Gall, D.C. *Direct and Alternating Current Potentiometer Measurements*. London: Chapman and Hall, 1938.
Rutenberg, D. "The Early History of the Potentiometer System of Electrical Measurement." *Annals of Science* 4 (1939): 212–43.

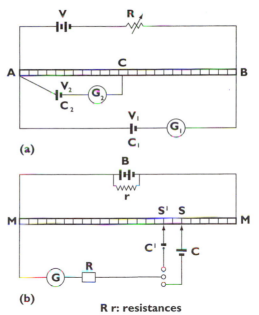

Circuit diagrams of Latimer Clark's potentiometer (top) and J.A. Fleming's improved potentiometer (bottom). Courtesy of SSPL.

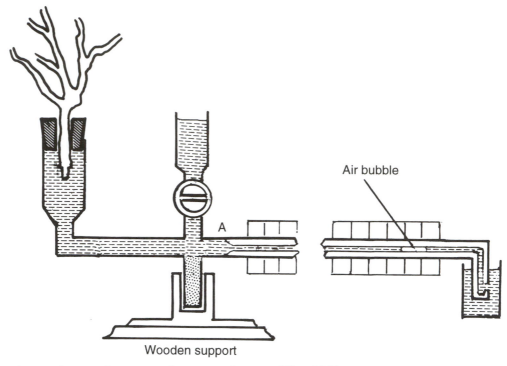

Schematic diagram of a commercial potometer. Courtesy of Hans Meidner.

Potometer

A potometer (from the Greek, *poton,* meaning "drink") measures the rate of water inflow into cut shoots or rooted seedlings under different ambient conditions, such as light, temperature, wind, and humidity. The instrument was invented in the 1870s by the German botanist Julius von Sachs, and modified by Francis Darwin in the U.K. in 1884.

The basic apparatus consists of a water-filled reservoir with an attached capillary tube dipping into a small beaker filled with water. The plant material is sealed into the apparatus and exposed to the desired ambient conditions. A meniscus will form at the inlet to the capillary tube when the beaker is removed for a few seconds; by replacing the beaker once the meniscus has moved 2 or 3 mm, an air bubble can be formed. By timing the movement of the air bubble over a certain distance along the capillary, or simply measuring the time taken by the meniscus to recede, the volume rate of water flowing into the cut shoot or rooted seedling can be calculated. To prevent air from entering the reservoir holding the plant material, the meniscus must be reset when it reaches point A by opening the tap under the settings reservoir. When placed on a balance, a potometer can be used to measure the absorption lag. A micro version can be used with single leaves.

Potometers are available from various educational equipment firms (they cost about $50), but equally satisfactory assemblies can be made from laboratory glassware, fitting a hypodermic syringe (for resetting the air bubble) into the rubber bung holding the plant material; this gives good control.

Hans Meidner

Bibliography

Darwin, Francis. "Absorption of Water by Plants." *Nature* 3 (1884): 180–82.

Pressure Bomb

A pressure bomb measures the water potential (or free energy content of water) of plant material. Fully saturated plant materials have water potentials of zero. If their water content decreases their water potentials decrease and assume a negative numerical value. Botanists use this measurement to plot pressure/volume curves, which provide information on the magnitude of turgor pressures (the forces that keep nonwoody plant tissue in shape, cell walls not providing sufficiently strong support), and also

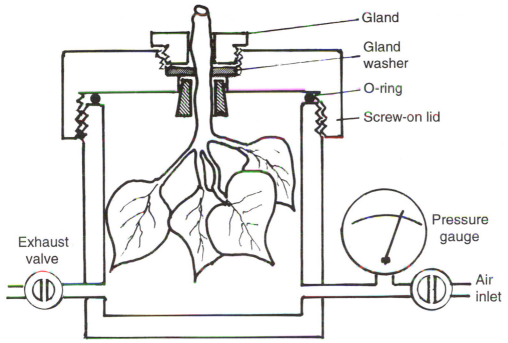

Diagram of Scholander-type pressure bomb in longitudinal section. Courtesy of Hans Meidner.

on the gradients in water potential that determine the water movement within plant tissues.

Extraction of plant sap by mechanical pressure for medicinal purposes was referred to in herbals as early as 600 B.C. The modern pressure bomb, however, dates from 1926, when the English botanist A.C. Chibnall used compressed air to express vacuolar sap separated from cytoplasmic matter. The pressure bomb was subsequently developed for systematic investigations, and by the 1960s the instrument designed by the American botanist P. Scholander had become standard laboratory equipment. In 1997 it was commercially available at a cost of a few thousand dollars.

The bomb is made of strong materials to withstand pressures of up to 5,000,000 pascals (50 bar). The pressure gauge should be sensitive to 20,000 pascals (0.2 bar), and the screw-on lid, as well as the gland around plant stems and petioles must provide airtight seals. In use, a detached twig or leaf is quickly fitted into the bomb, and the pressure is raised gradually. When the first traces of sap appear on the cut surface, the pressure gauge indicates the pressure required to balance the water potential of the material, which will therefore have the same numerical value. If the material has been detached from a fully turgid plant, its water potential will be very close to zero, and the slightest application of pressure will cause sap to appear at the cut end.

For the construction of pressure/volume curves, the material must first be made fully turgid by keeping it with its cut end in water and under a plastic hood. Very small increments of pressure are applied at intervals of 10 to 15 minutes, and the volume of sap expressed is determined after each pressure application. After the highest pressure has been applied, the material within the bomb is cut off and dried to determine its remaining water content. This, plus the cumulative volume of expressed sap, is taken as 100 percent of the water content at full turgor.

Hans Meidner

Bibliography

Meidner, Hans. *Class Experiments in Plant Physiology.* London: Allen and Unwin, 1984.

Scholander, P.F., Edda B. Bradstreet, and A. Hemmingsen. "Sap Pressure in Vascular Plants." *Science* 148 (1965): 339–46.

Tyree, M.T. , and H.T. Hamel. "The Measurement of Turgor Pressure and the Water Relations of Plants by the Pressure Bomb Technique." *Journal of Experimental Botany* 23 (1972): 267–82.

Pressure Gauge

See GAUGE, PRESSURE

Pressuremeter

A pressuremeter measures stiffness and strength of soil or rock in the field in its natural state. It consists of a cylindrical flexible membrane clamped onto a rigid body that supports the membrane over its entire length. Pressuremeters, typically between 40 and 100 mm in diameter and up to 2 meters long, are installed into specially created test pockets in the ground. They can be either prebored (PBP), self-bored (SBP), or pushed in (PIP). All three types can be used in soils; some PBPs and SBPs are designed to operate in rock, though these are often referred to as **dilatometers.**

PBPs are lowered into test pockets drilled using rotary rigs. The diameter of a pocket is nominally 10 percent larger than the diameter of the pressuremeter; therefore the in-situ stresses are reduced by the installation process. SBPs drill their own test pockets, so that the diameter of a pocket is the same as that of the pressuremeter. In that case, the ground is replaced by the pressuremeter and the in-situ stresses are maintained. PIPs are pushed into soil to form a test pocket; that is, the soil is displaced and the in-situ stresses are increased. The installation process affects the ground response curve obtained and therefore the parameters obtained from the interpretation of a test.

Once a pressuremeter is installed in its pocket, a test is carried out by internally pressurizing the membrane using either gas, oil, or water. The membrane expands as the pressure is increased. This expansion is either monitored using displacement transducers mounted at the center of the expanding section or monitored by observing the amount of liquid forced into the membrane, if oil or water is used. A number of test procedures can be followed to allow different ground properties to be determined. All procedures are based on incremental increases in pressure, but the magnitude and number of increments can be altered to produce constant rates of increase of either pressure or expansion.

A graph of applied pressure plotted against membrane expansion is known as the pressuremeter or ground-response curve, and this curve is used to derive either design parameters or in-situ properties of the ground. These properties are used in geotechnical design, for example to predict bearing capacity and settlement of foundations.

History

In 1933, Franz Kögler published a description of a pressuremeter probe and interpretation of a test. Modern pressuremeters have evolved from those developed by Louis Ménard in France and Fukowa in Japan. The Ménard pressuremeter (patented in 1958) and the Japanese Lateral Load Tester (first referenced in 1966) are both PBPs. They are still in use and are the most widely used type of pressuremeters to date.

In 1968 it was recognized by François Jézéquel and others that a test curve more representative of actual ground behavior would be produced if the installation could be improved. The Laboratoire Central des Ponts et Chaussées in France developed the *pressiomètre autoforeuse.* Peter Wroth at the University of Cambridge developed the Cambridge SBP probe, which is sometimes known as the Camkometer, as it was designed to measure K_o, a parameter related to in-situ horizontal stress. The Cambridge probe was introduced into commercial practice in 1978 and has been more widely used than the French probe.

In the late 1960s, following the development of the North Sea oil fields, a push-in pressuremeter was developed from the Cambridge SBP. This reduced the time for installation, since the probe could be pushed in from the base of a borehole without the need to predrill or self-bore a test pocket. This type of probe, now a modified cone **penetrometer**, was introduced to onshore commercial use in the mid 1980s.

Interpretation

A pressuremeter test can be modeled simply as an expanding cavity and interpreted using theories of elasticity and plasticity. In practice, this simple assumption is invalidated by the installation process. Ménard and his co-workers overcame this problem by developing a set of empirical rules that allowed the bearing capacity and settlements of foundations to be predicted directly from the pressuremeter curve. These rules are based on correlations between data obtained from a pressuremeter test and results either from other laboratory and in-situ tests or from foundation performance. They have been the basis of foundation engineering in France and have been incorporated into their design standards. This method of design, a test-

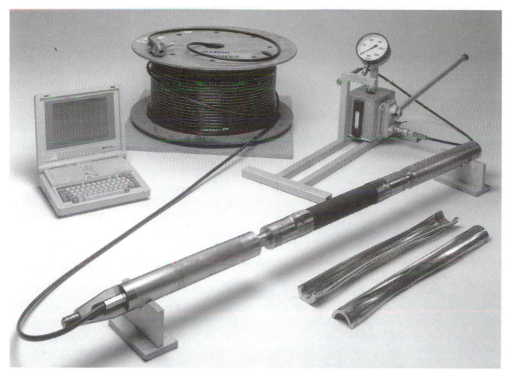

A prebored pressuremeter showing the probe, a protective metal sheath, and testing equipment, 1990. Courtesy of Cambridge Insitu.

specific method, has been used predominantly in French-speaking countries though it is also applied elsewhere.

Improvements in pressuremeter technology and analysis have allowed pressuremeter curves to be interpreted directly, to give properties of the ground that can then be used in design rules and numerical analyses of geotechnical problems. This alternative, indirect design method was first used in the U.K. in the 1960s for the design of coal-fired power stations. This theoretical method uses either a model of the pressuremeter curve that is integrated to produce the ground properties or a model of the ground that is differentiated to produce the pressuremeter curve. The latter model includes linear elastic, perfectly plastic, hyperbolic, parabolic, and other functions.

Summary

PBPs are the most versatile and robust probes, as they can be used in all soils and rocks. The interpretation of PBP test curves is often based on empirical rules because of installation disturbance. SBPs produce test curves that are most representative of the true in-situ ground behavior and, provided a suitable ground model is chosen, the pressuremeter curves can be interpreted to produce shear stress strain curves for the ground. PIPs reduce the installation time and produce repeatable disturbance but, because of this disturbance, a test curve has to be interpreted using semiempirical rules.

Barry Clarke

Bibliography

Baguelin, François, François Jézéquel, and Donald Shields. *The Pressuremeter and Foundation Engineering*. Clausthal: Trans Tech, 1978.

Clarke, Barry. *Pressuremeters in Geotechnical Design*. London: Blackie, 1995.

Mair, Robert, and David Wood. *Pressuremeter Testing: Methods and Interpretation*. London: Butterworth, 1987.

Process Controller

Process controllers form part of a feedback system that controls temperatures, pressures, flow rates, and other variables, in chemical, oil and gas, steel, food, paper, textile, and other process industries. They modify and amplify the error signal (the desired value minus measured value of the controlled variable) to produce an output signal (manipulated variable) that changes a process input such that the controlled variable moves closer to its desired value. Process controllers can be on-off controllers (the manipulated variable takes a minimum or maximum value according to the sign of the error), or modulating controllers giving a continuously variable control signal. Most industrial process controllers use the so-called PI (Proportional + Integral) or PID (PI + Derivative) algorithms. The integral action (reset) compensates for steady-state errors, while the derivative (rate) action provides a faster response to sudden disturbances.

Mechanical Controllers

Liquid level and flow regulators for various purposes are attributed to Ktesibios (ca. 270 B.C.), Philon (ca. 230 B.C.), and Heron (ca. A.D. 50). These direct-acting regulators, using float valves as the measuring and actuating elements, were used in water clocks until the late Middle Ages. They reappeared in England in the eighteenth century to regulate the water level in reservoirs in private houses, steam boilers, and cisterns for water closets.

Temperature regulation began with Cornelis Drebbel, whose system was based on the expansion of a liquid in a closed vessel. The movement, amplified by a lever, adjusted a flue damper that controlled the flow of air to the fire. Similar regulators were described in the eighteenth century by René-Antoine de Réaumur, who credited the inventions to the Prince de Conti (Louis-François de Bourbon); and by William Henry of Lancaster, Pennsylvania (his was called the "Sentinel Register"). Bonnemain, a French engineer of whom we know little, not even his first name, devised temperature regulators suitable for industrial use. Thousands of similar temperature regulators, with mechanical levers to amplify the movement produced by differential expansion of dissimilar metals, were patented during the nineteenth century.

Electromechanical Controllers

Simple industrial on-off temperature controllers based on expansion instruments began to appear in the early 1900s. Electrical contacts placed on either side of the indicating arm operated a relay, and hence controlled an electric motor. The Bristol Co., Cambridge Scientific Instrument Co., and Taylor Instrument Co. were producing controllers of this type around 1906.

During the first decade of the twentieth century, sensors for high temperatures—for example, thermocouples—were introduced. The small change in electromotive force produced by the sensor was detected by a **galvanometer**; potentiometric (H.L. Callendar, 1897, M.E. Leeds, 1911) and direct-acting (W.H. Bristol, 1906) devices were developed to record the galvanometer movement. The Bristol and Leeds recorders used a chopper bar mechanism that periodically clamped the galvanometer arm onto the recording paper. In 1920, Bristol modified the recorder such that when the arm was clamped, relay contacts operated and produced a control output. The Leeds & Northrup Co. (1921), the Wilson-Maeulen Co. (1924), and Taylor Instrument Co. (1926) produced similar controllers, referred to as definite correction controllers.

Pneumatic Controllers

Pneumatic on-off controllers with a pilot valve were introduced by the C.J. Tagliabue Co. (ca. 1900), the Foxboro Co. (1915), and the Taylor Instrument Co. (1915). These controllers had low accuracy because the force to operate the pilot valve affected the measurement. In 1914, Edgar H. Bristol of the Foxboro Co. invented a flapper-nozzle amplifying unit that could be inserted between the bellows and the pilot valve, thus increasing the accuracy of the controller. Flapper-nozzle-based controllers were introduced by Foxboro (1920), Tagliabue (1925), Bristol (1930), and Taylor (1931). The early flapper-nozzle amplifiers had high gain and functioned as on-off controllers. Later controllers (after 1929) provided narrow band proportional action, typically 5 percent of the full-scale movement.

In 1931, Foxboro introduced the Model 10 Stabilog, which incorporated proportional plus reset (PI) action and which provided a significant improvement in control performance. The Stabilog used an invention of Clesson E. Mason that provided negative feedback round the flapper-nozzle amplifier, thus turning it into a high-gain, linear (proportional) amplifier. It also included a pneumatic network with an output proportional to the time integral of the error variable. This device set new standards for controller accuracy and was the first of the modern controllers.

In 1934, Taylor introduced a PI controller, the Fulscope, which provided infinitely variable, field-adjustable settings of the proportional gain. In 1939, a completely redesigned Fulscope controller with "pre-act" (derivative action) was introduced, and Foxboro added "hyper-reset," a form of derivative action to the Stabilog.

Electronic Controllers

During the 1930s, manufacturers began to use electronics in their instruments. The Bailey Co. Galvatron (1934) used both magnetic and electronic amplification; Tagliabue's Celectray (1937) used a photoelectric cell to detect galvanometer movement; and the Wheelco Co. (1938) used a resonant circuit to detect galvanometer movement.

The development of stable dc amplifiers (the operational amplifier) led to replacement of the galvanometer and use of direct amplification of the sensor output. Early examples of such instruments include the Bailey Co. Pyrotron (1940) and Brown Co.'s ElectoniK (1941) range of instruments. Major developments occurred in the mid 1950s with miniaturized panel instruments based transistorized dc operational amplifiers. Examples include Taylor's Transet range (1950) and Foxboro's Consotrol range (1955).

Digital Controllers

Early examples of digital **computers** for process control include two plants that began operating in 1959: the Barton Plant of the Monsanto Co. at Luling, Louisiana, which was controlled by a Ramo-Wooldridge Co. computer; and ICI's soda ash plant at Fleetwood, Lancashire, which was controlled by Ferranti Argus 100 computer. An analog backup was provided for the Barton plant but the ICI plant was totally reliant on the computer system.

Use of digital computers for process control grew following the introduction of the Digital Equipment Co.'s PDP-8 (1965) and PDP-11

Foxboro Stabilog process controller, ca. 1946, showing interior. Courtesy of the Department of Automatic Control and Systems Engineering, University of Sheffield.

(1970). However, these computers were still too expensive for single loop control, and it was only following the introduction of the microprocessor (1974) that the single loop, digital process controller became an economically viable alternative to the analog controller.

Stuart Bennett

Bibliography

Bennett, S. "The Development of Process Control Instruments: The Early Years." *Transactions of the Newcomen Society* 63 (1992): 133–64.

———. *A History of Control Engineering: 1930 to 1955.* Stevenage: Peter Peregrinus, 1994.

Mayr, Otto. *Feedback Mechanisms in the Historical Collections of the National Museum of History and Technology.* Washington, D.C.: Smithsonian Institution Press, 1971.

———. *The Origins of Feedback Control,* Cambridge: M.I.T. Press, 1970. Originally published as *Zur Frühgeschichte der technischen Regelungen.* Munich: Oldenbourg, 1969.

Sydenham, P.H. *Measuring Instruments: Tools of Knowledge and Control.* Stevenage: Peter Peregrinus for the Science Museum, 1979.

Protein Sequencer

Protein sequencers, which sequentially degrade amino acids from peptide chains, have been used to determine the amino acid sequence of many proteins. The construction of the first protein sequencer, announced in 1967, automated the Edman degradation, a popular manual technique for amino acid sequence determination of proteins. Protein sequencers contributed to the rapid growth of protein biochemistry in the 1970s, and could be found in almost all protein chemistry laboratories.

In 1950, Pehr Edman published his degradation technique in which a purified protein was exposed to phenylisothiocyanate, which bound one end of the amino acid chain, activating the protein. When the protein chemical complex was treated with a weak acid, the acid cleaved the amino acid bound to the chemical from the peptide chain. The above steps were repeated until all the amino acids had been cleaved. After the amino acids had been collected, and the order of cleavage carefully noted, the researcher removed the chemical from the amino acid, identified the amino acids by chromatographic means, and deduced the amino acid order in the peptide chain of the protein. In 1967, Edman, and Geoffrey Begg, his colleague at the St. Vincent's Hospital School of Medical Research in Melbourne, Australia, built an instrument that automated the Edman degradation. Called the sequenator, this first protein sequencer reduced the labor and tedium of protein sequencing. For his work on protein sequencing, Edman was awarded the Commonwealth Britannia award and the Berzelius Gold Medal in 1971, and elected to the Royal Society of London in 1974.

The sequenator used a small spinning cup as the reaction vessel. A purified protein was dissolved in a weak acid and placed in the cup. The cup then rotated at a high speed, spreading the protein evenly over the side of the cup. Then a vacuum gently dried the protein. Spreading the protein over the side of the cup provided a large surface, which increased the yield of the chemical reactions. In theory, the sequenator could cleave the first sixty amino acids from a protein, although not all sequencing projects were this efficient. In 1975, more than 150 sequencers based on this design were in use. The majority of these were the Beckman Instruments 890 series, which offered attractive features such as variable speeds for the spinning cup and an apparatus for drying the cleaved amino acids.

The most serious drawback of the sequencer was that it could not sequence the smaller peptides (under thirty amino acids). To solve this problem, Richard Laursen developed a protein sequencer that sequentially degraded proteins bound to an insoluble residue in 1971. Smaller peptides were immobilized on this residue and degraded using the Edman degradation. Sequencers of this type were marketed by LKB and Sequemat. Despite the ability to sequence small protein fragments, these sequencers were not as popular as the spinning cup type. An appropriate type of supporting residue for the peptides could not be found. Supports needed to not react with the reagents, remain permeable, and be stable under the mechanical stresses of the reaction. Also, not all peptides would bind well to each support.

In 1981, Rodney Hewick, Michael Hunkapiller, Leroy Hood, and William Dreyer announced the construction of a protein sequencer that sequentially degraded a wide range of small peptide fragments. This employed gas reagents

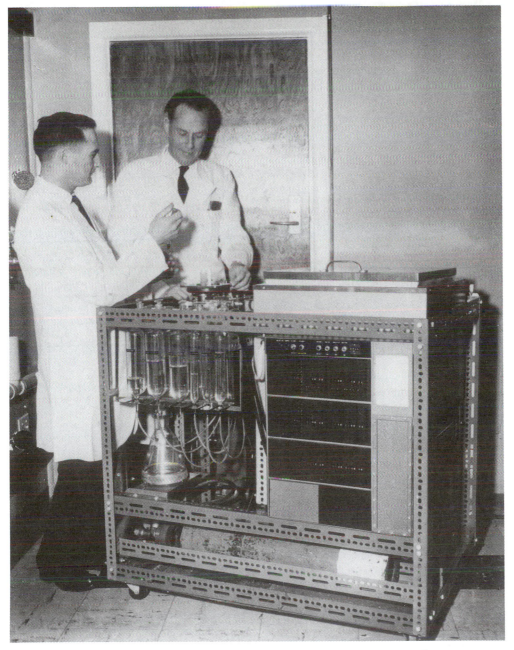

Pehr Edman, with his technical assistant Geoffrey Begg and his prototype sequenator, mid-1960s. Courtesy of St. Vincent's Institute of Medical Research, Melbourne.

at critical moments in the degradation (as opposed to liquid reagents throughout the reactions), and the peptides were immobilized by embedding in a support (as opposed to chemically binding the peptide to a residue). Now researchers not only sequenced shorter peptides to completion, they needed smaller amounts of starting material. Improvements, such as those introduced by Hewick et al., have greatly improved the speed and efficiency of protein sequencers. Now several dozen amino acids from a protein can be degraded overnight from a few micrograms of starting material.

Besides the types of automatic sequencers listed above, other instruments and procedures have been used to determine the amino acid sequence of proteins: **magnetic resonance imaging**, manual degradation of proteins, and the derivation of amino acid sequences from the nucleotide sequences that code for them. Because of its ease and simplicity, DNA sequencing has become the most popular method for determining the amino acid sequence of proteins. Despite contributing to the growth of the field of protein characterization, protein sequencers are now used only when DNA sequencing is not practical.

Phillip Thurtle

Bibliography
Alberts, Bruce, et al. *Molecular Biology of the Cell.* 3rd ed. New York: Garland, 1994.
Croft, L.R. *Introduction to Protein Sequence Analysis: A Compilation of Amino Acid Sequences of Proteins with an Introduction to the Methodology.* Chichester: Wiley, 1980.
Edman, P., and G. Begg. "A Protein Sequenator." *European Journal of Biochemistry* 1 (1967): 80–91.
Hewick, Rodney M., Michael W. Hunkapiller, Leroy E. Hood, and William J. Dreyer. "A Gas-Liquid Solid Phase Peptide and Protein Sequenator." *Journal of Biological Chemistry* 256 (August 1991): 7990–97.
Laursen, Richard A. "Solid-Phase Degradation: An Automatic Peptide Sequencer." *European Journal of Biochemistry* 20 (1971): 89–102.

Psychrometer, Thermocouple

A thermocouple psychrometer (from the Greek *psychros*, meaning "cold") measures the water potential of a sample of soil or plant tissue. It is similar to a standard **hygrometer**, but uses a fine wire thermocouple rather than mercury **thermometers**. It was developed between 1950 and 1970 in the U.K., Australia, and the United States when plant physiologists wanted to estimate the forces residing in the plant that made possible processes like guttation, the ascent of sap, and the maintenance or the reestablishment of turgor—indeed all water movement in plants.

The basic instrument consists of an airtight chamber holding the sample and the thermocouple made from thin chromel/constantan wires. A microvoltmeter calibrated in water potential units must also be available. After allowing for the water vapor pressure in the chamber to equilibrate, an electric current is applied for

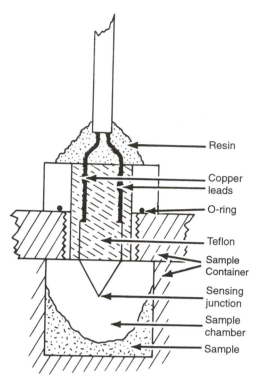

Schematic diagram of a sensing junction holder of thermocouple psychrometer. Courtesy of Hans Meidner/Wescor Inc.

about 15 seconds, cooling the thermocouple to below the dew point, thereby causing a fine film of water to condense on the sensing junction. When the cooling current is switched off, the dew deposit evaporates at a rate that depends on the water vapor pressure in the chamber. The lower the vapor pressure, the faster the rate of evaporation, and the greater the output of the thermocouple as registered on the microvoltmeter.

Since early thermocouple psychrometers had to be kept in a constant-temperature water bath to ensure uniform temperature in the system, they were cumbersome to use. With changes in the electrical circuitry, it is now possible to use the instrument under ordinary conditions and in the field. In 1997 a commercial instrument (the Wescor Dew Point Microvoltmeter) was available at a cost of a few thousand dollars.

Hans Meidner

Bibliography
Brown, Ray W. *Measurement of Water Potential with Thermocouple Psychrometers: Construction and Applications.* USDA Forest Service Research Paper. Intermountain Forest and Range Experi-

ment Station, Ogden, Utah: 1970.

Spanner, D.C. "The Peltier Effect and Its Use in the Measurement of Suction Pressure." *Journal of Experimental Botany* 1 (1951): 145–68.

Pyrheliometer

A pyrheliometer measures the intensity of solar radiation. Its name comes from the Greek *pyr* ("fire"), *helios* ("sun"), and *metron* (measure). The pyrheliometer was devised solely for determining the solar constant (the solar radiation incident on the earth per unit area per unit time). When the value of the solar constant was well established in the mid twentieth century, development of the pyrheliometer waned. The design of the current standard instruments dates from the early 1900s.

As the result of a severe sunburn in 1825, John Herschel became interested in measuring the sun's radiation. He soon developed his **actinometer**, a glass cylinder filled with a dark blue solution of copper sulfate in ammonia. A **thermometer** was soldered to the cylinder to measure the solution's rise in temperature. Placing the cylinder in a box with one transparent side, Herschel alternately shaded and exposed the actinometer to sunlight at 1-minute intervals. He then added the average amount of heating and cooling and calibrated his readings with that of a known energy source. This procedure allowed Herschel to make solar constant measurements. Herschel did not take his research very seriously and was slow to publish his results. Nevertheless, he encouraged James D. Forbes to study atmospheric absorption with an actinometer. Other versions of the actinometer were produced by André P.P. Crova and Jules L.G. Violle. Crova filled the large blackened bulb of a thermometer with alcohol to measure the solar radiation, while Violle placed a thermometer bulb in the center of a double-walled sphere. An icewater bath filled the space between the spheres.

The first instrument that became known as a pyrheliometer was developed by Claude Pouillet around 1837 as a result of his interest in solar radiation. Similar in nature to equipment first used by Benjamin Thompson, Pouillet's device centered on a flat cylindrical disk filled with water. One side of the disk was blackened and the other contained a small opening to allow the bulb of a thermometer to be inserted within. The blackened side was turned toward the sun and its heat would cause the water to increase in temperature. The temperature increase would then be measured by the thermometer. In order to obtain the total effect of the solar radiation, Pouillet also measured the cooling of the pyrheliometer when the sun's rays were blocked. Combining these two measurements, Pouillet could calculate the solar constant.

John Tyndall improved Pouillet's pyrheliometer by substituting mercury for water in the receiving cylinder. This design was further improved by Charles Greeley Abbot at the Smithsonian Astrophysical Observatory in Washington, D.C. Developed during the first decade of the 1900s, Abbot's mercury pyrheliometer immersed the bulb of the thermometer in a thin layer of mercury contained within a small copper receiving disk. The disk was placed within a spherical structure and it received the sunlight through a blackened baffled tube. This instrument underwent several modifications until it reached its final form in 1908 as the silver-disk pyrheliometer, the main development being the replacement of the copper receiving disk with a silver one.

A significant new form of pyrheliometer was developed in 1893 when Knut Ångström built an electric compensation pyrheliometer. The principle behind this instrument is the method wherein two detectors are heated, one by the sun and the other by a known heat source. When the temperatures of the two detectors are determined to be equal, the heat of the solar radiation is considered to be equal to that of the known heat source. Ångström used two blackened platinum detectors, the first exposed to the sun and the second heated by an electric current. A thermocouple was used to determine when their temperatures were the same.

A source of error inherent in the above-mentioned pyrheliometers is caused by that portion of the incident radiation that is convected or radiated outward from the device that measures the temperature. In order to overcome this small but indeterminate error, Abbot set about in 1903 to improve the pyrheliometer. Abbot felt that the key to overcoming the loss of incident radiation would be found in using a black body as a detector. By allowing sunlight to enter a hollow chamber through a small aperture, Abbot would not have to worry about energy loss if he could measure the amount of heat absorbed by the walls of the chamber. Abbot's final version of 1910 had an internal chamber coated with lampblack, which ab-

Silver disk pyrheliometer from the Smithsonian Astrophysical Observatory. NMAH 314,679. Courtesy of NMAH.

sorbed the solar radiation that entered through a collimating tube. The radiation was then absorbed by distilled water (nitrobenzol was initially used) flowing around the chamber. Once the water carried away as much energy as was being absorbed, the amount of solar radiation could be determined by measuring the difference in temperature between the incoming and outgoing water. A double-chamber version of the water-flow pyrheliometer was developed in 1932 and proved to be an extremely stable and accurate instrument.

The most accurate pyrheliometers are the water-flow, silver-disk, and electrical compensation pyrheliometers. They are used to calibrate common operational pyrheliometers so that the latter's readings can be made in terms of absolute energy. The water-flow pyrheliometer, a complicated and difficult instrument, has not been used since the Smithsonian ended its solar constant research around 1960. The silver-disk pyrheliometer is more widely used because the Smithsonian distributed over one hundred of them throughout the world for the purposes of standardizing solar constant readings. The Ångström electrical compensation pyrheliometer remains the primary standard for calibrating all other instruments. The absolute standards are maintained by several Ångström instruments at the World Radiation Center in Davos, Switzerland. Secondary instruments are calibrated against these and are used to transfer the standards to operational instruments.

The modern operational pyrheliometers mainly use **thermopiles** to receive and measure the solar radiation. The most significant of these instruments are the Eppley normal incidence pyrheliometer (made by Eppley Laboratory in the United States), the Linke-Feussner pyrheliometer (made by Kipp and Zonen in Delft, Netherlands), and the Savinov-Yanishevsky pyrheliometer (made in the former Soviet Union). The former Soviet researchers have also used the Michelson bimetallic pyrheliometer, which is actually a bimetallic thermometer.

Ronald S. Brashear

Bibliography

Abbot, Charles Greeley, and Loyal Blaine Aldrich. "The Silver Disk Pyrheliometer." *Smithsonian Miscellaneous Collections,* vol. 56, no. 19. Washington D.C.: Smithsonian Institution, 1911.

———, Frederick E. Fowle, and Loyal Blaine Aldrich. "An Improved Waterflow Pyrheliometer and the Standard Scale of Solar Radiation outside the Atmosphere." *Smithsonian Miscellaneous Collections,* vol. 87, no. 15. Washington D.C.: Smithsonian Institution, 1932.

Ångström, Knut. "The Absolute Determination of the Radiation of Heat with the Electric Compensation Pyrheliometer, with Examples of the Application of This Instrument." *Astrophysical Journal* 9 (1899): 332–46.

Coulson, Kinsell L. *Solar and Terrestrial Radiation.* New York: Academic, 1975.

Kidwell, Peggy Aldrich. "Prelude to Solar Energy: Pouillet, Herschel, Forbes and the Solar Constant." *Annals of Science* 38 (1981): 457–76.

Pyrometer

The original pyrometers measured the expansion or contraction of materials caused by temperature changes and were thus in some sense the converse of **thermometers**, which use the thermal expansion or contraction of materials to measure temperature. Pyrometers were developed in the eighteenth century, and were crucial to solving one of the most pressing technological problems of the time: the making of temperature-invariant oscillators for **chronometers**. In the 1780s, however, the term "pyrometer" came also to refer to high-temperature thermometers. There is no agreed boundary between the ranges dealt with by thermometers and pyrometers, but in practice 500°C is the dividing line. However, electrical thermometers are often used above that temperature.

The Dutch professor of natural philosophy Petrus van Musschenbroek invented a pyrometer in the early 1730s. This was improved by the English watch-maker John Ellicott later in that decade, and substantially changed by the English instrument-makers John Smeaton in the 1750s and Jesse Ramsden in the 1780s.

In principle a pyrometer is a simple instrument: a ruler is placed next to a bar of metal, the temperature is varied, and the change in the length of the metal is measured. In practice considerable ingenuity is needed to make sure that the ruler's own length does not change with varying temperature, which would render it useless. Smeaton's solution to this problem was particularly elegant. He submerged the brass pyrometer in a water bath so that it was at the same temperature as the metal bar being measured. In a separate series of experiments, he established the change in the absolute length of the pyrometer itself over a range of temperatures by placing a steel tipped bar of wood of known length on the pyrometer and measuring its length at 30-second intervals. Since the wooden bar's length expanded by a geometric progression, he could extrapolate back to the time when the bar was first placed into the water of a given temperature, thereby calibrating the pyrometer against the original length of the wooden bar before the heat of the water bath had begun to expand it.

Ramsden adopted a different and, since the bar made no mechanical contact with the ruler, ultimately a more precise solution. His pyrometer held the apparatus containing the ruler at a constant temperature (by surrounding it with an ice bath) and then used **microscopes** that were fixed to the ruler but could be moved by a **micrometer** screw to observe the displacement of the bar as it was heated.

The new meaning of the term originated in 1782 when the British potter Josiah Wedgwood described a "pyrometer" for measuring high temperatures. Wedgwood's instrument was a piece of clay of known size that was placed in the kiln whose temperature was to be measured: on removal, its shrinkage indicated a temperature in degrees Wedgwood.

The measurement of temperature in industry became a significant problem in the second half of the nineteenth century, and a variety of

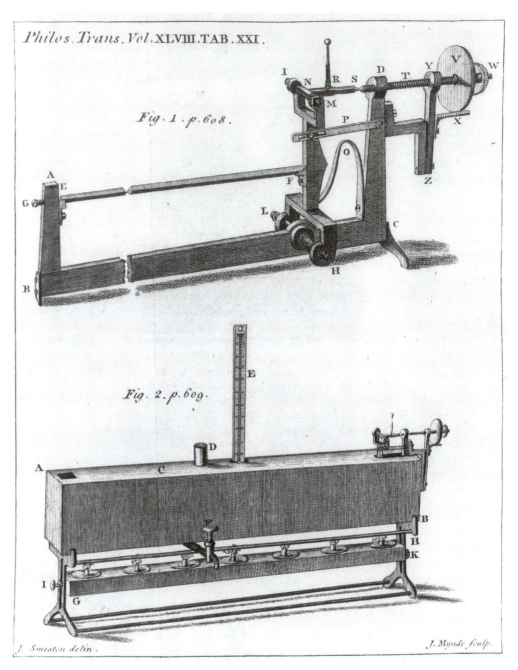

Smeaton's pyrometer and waterbath, 1754. John Smeaton. "Description of a New Pyrometer, with a Table of Experiments Made Therewith." Philosophical Transactions of the Royal Society of London 48, *1754: facing page 608. Courtesy of the Department of Rare Books and Special Collections, Princeton University Libraries.*

instruments of limited accuracy were invented before 1900. The simplest practical solution was the Seger cone, a clay mixture formed into a cone about 10 cm high, that would collapse at a predetermined temperature. Invented by Hermann August Seger of Berlin in 1886 for use in the kiln industries, this was a cheap method that was widely used for a hundred years.

The electrical resistance thermometer was invented by Charles William Siemens in 1871. It was made into an accurate instrument by Hugh Longbourne Callendar, whose work on the platinum resistance thermometer began in 1886. In particular, he demonstrated the need to use highly pure platinum. These instruments were used in the furnace and kiln industries, initially to measure temperatures up to 1,000°C, but later to 1,200° and above with the platinum wire wound on a slip of mica inside a porcelain tube.

Total radiation pyrometers depend on the Stefan-Boltzmann law, which states that the total radiation emitted by a black body is proportional to the fourth power of the absolute temperature, suggested empirically by Joseph Stefan in 1879 and demonstrated theoretically by Ludwig Boltzmann in 1884. The early forms were invented by Charles Féry: the mirror pyrometer (1904), the spiral pyrometer, and the telescope pyrometer.

The first optical pyrometer was made by Henri-Louis Le Chatelier at the end of the nineteenth century. The earliest instrument to find widespread use was the Wanner pyrometer, in which monochromatic light from the hot source was compared with an electric source that could be standardized: comparison was performed with a polarizing system, so it had comparatively complex optical components. Wanner's instrument was successful, but by 1950 the disappearing filament type was in general preferred. This was first made in 1901, independently by Ludwig Holborn and Ferdinand Kurlbaum in Germany and by Harman Northrup Morse in the United States. It operated by varying the current, and thus the temperature and the color, passing through a filament at the focus of a **telescope** pointed at the hot source. The current at which the filament becomes invisible can be empirically converted into a temperature. This instrument is capable of precision measurement and has been used for the verification of other instruments and for laboratory work. It can be used from 600°C to 3000°C.

Optical and total radiation pyrometers can be sited at a distance from the source being measured, and so can be used on hot, moving, or corrosive bodies. By 1920 the limitations of the various types were well understood, and they were increasingly used in processes such as annealing, in which the temperature of an ingot or mass of glass had to be followed and controlled over a period of many hours. Throughout the twentieth century the increasingly large scale of manufacturing, which made waste increasingly costly, and the demand for closer control of quality have led to a larger role for the pyrometer.

Richard J. Sorrenson
John Burnett

Bibliography

Catalogue of the Collections in the Science Museum: Temperature Measurement and Control. London: Her Majesty's Stationery Office, 1976.

DeWitt, D.P., and Gene D. Nutter. *Theory and Practice of Radiation Thermometry.* New York: Wiley, 1988.

Griffiths, Ezer. "Pyrometry, Optical," and "Pyrometry, Total Radiation." In *Dictionary of Applied Physics,* edited by Richard Glazebrook, Vol. 1, 643–77. London: Macmillan, 1922.

Musschenbroek, Petrus van. *Tentamina Experimentorum Naturalium Captorum in Academia del Cimento,* second pagination, 12–57. Leiden, 1731.

"Pyrometer." In *The Cyclopaedia; or, Universal Dictionary of Arts, Sciences, and Literature,* edited by Abraham Rees, Vol. 29. London: Longman, 1819.

Quadrant

A quadrant is a quarter of a circle, and the term refers to several different types of instruments covering an arc of that size.

One of the earliest examples is the large "plinth" described in Ptolemy's *Almagest* and used for measuring the meridian altitude of the sun. Set in the plane of the meridian and adjusted to the vertical, this instrument worked by allowing the shadow of a horizontal peg to fall across a graduated arc of 90°. The Islamic astronomer al-Battani had a mural quadrant, a quadrant fixed to a meridian wall. Nasir al-Din in Maragha had two altazimuth quadrants; these were vertical quadrants that could be rotated to any bearing, so as to measure altitude and azimuth simultaneously.

The astronomical quadrant was adopted by Renaissance astronomers in the West. The most celebrated example was the mural quadrant of 2-meter radius built by Tycho Brahe in 1582. While Islamic instruments incorporated a sighting rule, or alidade, pivoted at the apex and extending to the limb or graduated arc, Tycho tried to reduce moving parts to a minimum by fixing the fore sight into an aperture in a transverse wall and attaching the near sights to a band of brass set in the meridian wall and divided by diagonals. This was the most accurate of the many instruments he devised, and it laid the foundation for his extraordinary success.

The quadrant maintained its role as the principal measuring instrument of astronomy, used in all the leading observatories of the seventeenth and eighteenth centuries. While other forms of mounting were devised, in general the most accurate measurements came from mural quadrants, which kept movement, wear, and flexure to a minimum; this was important for extended observing programs. Observations were restricted to the meridian, but this made for convenient measurement of declination (angular distance from the celestial equator) and avoided the tedious calculations associated with off-meridian work. It was hoped that the introduction of clocks would allow right ascension also to be taken by timing transits through the sights of the mural quadrant, but the instrument was not capable of the fine adjustment required. One very important improvement was the replacement of plain or open sights by telescopic sights. The value of the new sights was the subject of a controversy between Hevelius and Robert Hooke in particular, but by the late seventeenth century **telescopes** had become standard attachments to astronomical quadrants.

In 1725 the London maker George Graham made a particularly successful mural quadrant for Edmond Halley's program of lunar observations at the Royal Observatory, Greenwich. The 8-foot radius arc was braced by a framework of iron bars and the telescopic sight adjusted on the limb by a clamp and tangent **micrometer** screw. John Bird made a similar instrument, with a brass frame, for Greenwich in 1750; a description was published by the Board of Longitude. Further examples were built by London makers such as Sisson, Bird, and Ramsden and exported to observatories across Europe. The success of this and other instrument designs by George Graham established the dominance of London makers in this field into the early nineteenth century. By then, however, quadrants had been replaced by circles as the principal instruments for fundamental measurement in astronomy.

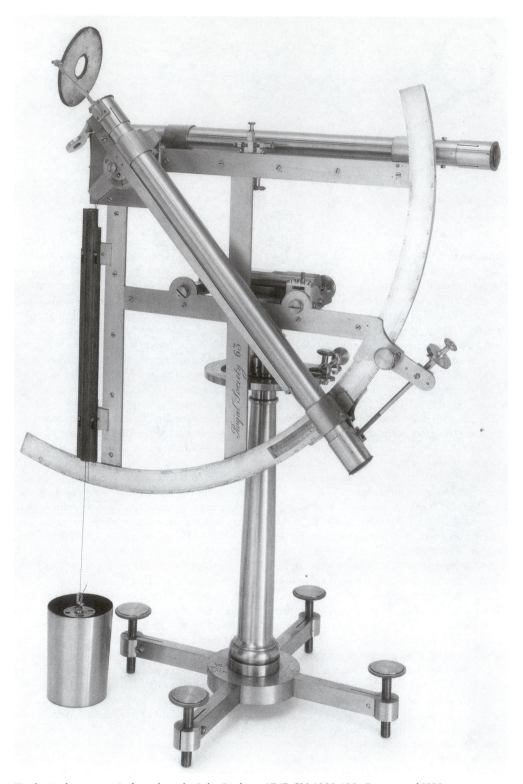

Twelve-inch astronomical quadrant by John Bird, ca. 1767. SM 1900-138. Courtesy of SSPL.

Not all successful quadrant designs were large. In the eighteenth century astronomical instruments on relatively portable stands were made by both French and English makers, such as Langlois, Sisson, and Bird. The French preferred a telescope fixed to a pivoting frame and a vertical, hanging index arm, whereas the English leveled the quadrant frame by a plumbline and arranged the telescope to pivot at the apex of the stationary frame. John Bird supplied portable quadrants of this type for transit of Venus expeditions in the 1760s.

The term "quadrant" has also been attached to rather different instruments, such as the Davis quadrant, otherwise known as the backstaff, or the Hadley quadrant, more commonly called an **octant**. A number of simple surveying and navigation instruments were based on quadrant designs. The most common type of small quadrant was the horary quadrant, a portable instrument generally used to find the time and sometimes to perform astronomical calculations.

The basic measurement taken with an horary quadrant is the altitude of the sun. It can, of course, measure any altitude, and some have features related to the altitudes of certain stars. Generally also there will be a shadow square used for taking altitudes in surveying. A solar sight, however, can be converted into a measure of time in a variety of ways, and from these varieties come the different projections seen on the range of horary quadrants. One of the best known of the early types is the medieval *quadrans vetus* or "old quadrant." This is a universal quadrant—that is to say, it works anywhere on earth. The solar altitude depends on latitude and date as well as on time, so a universal horary quadrant must make allowance for latitude and date before it can offer an instrumental conversion between solar altitude and time. The *quadrans vetus* achieves this by adjusting a bead on a plumb line from the quadrant apex according to a latitude scale and a declination (or date) sliding cursor. When the observation is made, a pair of sights fixed to one edge is aligned with the sun and the plumb line falls across the projection of hour lines. It is where the bead falls in this pattern of lines that indicates the time, in this case in the medieval system of unequal hours—twelve divisions between sunrise and sunset. A later, very popular type of horary quadrant was that designed by Edmund Gunter, which is restricted to a single latitude but offers a number of more advanced astronomical functions.

Jim A. Bennett

Bibliography

Bennett, J.A. *The Divided Circle: A History of Instruments for Astronomy, Navigation and Surveying.* Oxford: Phaidon, 1987.

———. "'The English Quadrant in Europe: Instruments and the Growth of Consensus in Practical Astronomy." *Journal for the History of Astronomy* 23 (1992): 1–14.

Chapman, Allan. *Dividing the Circle: The Development of Critical Angular Measurement in Astronomy 1500–1850.* New York: Horwood, 1990.

Turner, Anthony J. *Early Scientific Instruments: Europe 1400–1800.* London: Philip Wilson for Sotheby's, 1987.

R

Radar

Radar uses electromagnetic (radio) waves to measure the distance (or range) and direction from the observer to a distant reflective object. The acronym RADAR (RAdio Detection And Ranging) was devised by the U.S. Navy in 1940 so that the apparatus could be mentioned openly without fear of security violation. A radar consists of a generator and directional projector of electromagnetic waves, and an antenna and suitable radio to receive the wave echoes from the distant object. The distance to the object is usually determined by noting the time of transit of the waves from transmitter to object to receiver. The direction is determined by noting the direction of the antennas' sensitivity maxima when the echo appears to be strongest. When the transmitter and receiver are colocated, the radar is monostatic; when they are separated, the arrangement is termed bistatic.

The concept of reflecting electromagnetic waves from a metallic object was demonstrated by Heinrich Hertz in his classic 1892 work validating Maxwell's wave equations, but little use was made of the idea by him or by Gugliemo Marconi in his pioneering wireless telegraph development that followed. In 1903, Christian Hülsmeyer devised a wireless transmitter and nearby receiver on the Hohenzollernbrücke over the Rhine in Cologne, Germany, and found that by relocating and adjusting his apparatus he could match the signals received directly from the transmitter against those that were reflected from the river surface below, achieving utter cancellation of these two signals. The passage of a ship under the bridge upset this delicate signal balance and caused a large signal to be received, which rang a bell as part of the receiver's coherer (detector device). Although Hülsmeyer could detect the passage of ships in fog and at night, he failed to sell the idea to the German Navy. Dominik and Scherl resurrected Hülsmeyer's idea during World War I, but they too failed to impress the German Navy.

In 1922, A. Hoyt Taylor and Leo Young, of the U.S. Navy, detected ships on the Potomac River by directing radio transmissions across the river and receiving radio echoes from the ships. They were encouraged to continue their research, and in 1925 they developed a vertically directed radar to detect (and then measure the height of) the earth's ionosphere. By 1934 they were developing radar for Navy ships, and four capital ships were outfitted with aircraft-detecting radars by 1937.

In 1935 in England, Robert Watson-Watt used the radar principle to detect aircraft, using the BBC shortwave transmissions originating at Daventry and receiving equipment set up in a van nearby. His success led to the erection of the Chain Home network of radars used extensively for early warning against German air attack throughout World War II. In the Soviet Union, A.A. Chernyshev experimented with radar techniques aimed at detecting aircraft beyond visual range or at night, from 1934 until 1938 or 1939, but the work apparently received but secondary military priority in the desperate years that followed.

These early efforts were confined to use of signals at relatively low frequencies, from 20 MHz to a few hundred MHz, and the resulting spatial resolution of the reflecting object was necessarily poor, giving only crude images of the object, often reduced to a spatial smear or blob. They all derived from radio communications techniques, using electron tubes as wave generators and receiver amplifiers. In 1939, University

The U.S. Naval Research Laboratory in Washington D.C., 1939, showing four prototype radar antennas. Courtesy of Edwin Lyon III.

of Birmingham scientists (H.A.H. Boot and J.T. Randall, led by Mark Oliphant) discovered that an old electron tube device known as a magnetron could be made into a multicavity magnetron, and produce powerful signals (up to tens of thousands of watts power in each pulse) at frequencies upward of 3,000 MHz with wavelengths in the centimeter range. This led to the rapid development of fine-resolution radars for use in aircraft (to locate other aircraft and to aim guns, for example), aboard all sizes of ships and on the battlefield. The contemporary klystron tube, developed by the Varian brothers in California, could match the magnetron in signal frequency coverage, but could be made small enough to be used in radar receivers, enabling achievement of tremendous sensitivities (typically, a radar of the time could detect and locate an aircraft flying some 150 miles distant). Finally, the development of precision, large-size cathode ray tubes (CRTs) made possible development of maplike radar displays on which radar echoes from targets were electronically plotted, giving the operators a ready understanding of the target situation.

Today, radars operate at signal frequencies from several hundred MHz to a hundred thousand MHz, depending on the mission. Military radars are used for early warning of approaching aircraft, ships, vehicles, personnel, and missiles, as well as for directing weapons offensively. Air traffic control is maintained through the use of radars, located strategically in the areas plied by aircraft and networked to provide integrated overall situation displays and detailed airport traffic listings, displays, and advice. Police use handheld and vehicular radars to record speed limit violators, while weather radars, operating on the echoes from water droplets, provide animated maps showing the development and motion of cyclones and storms. The resolution of modern radars approaches that enjoyed visually, as the radar wavelengths are reduced to millimeters (and less), and as tricks are played on the radar apparatus to simulate larger antenna apertures, for example. Synthetic aperture radar (SAR) obtains an augmented antenna aperture, with its attendant enhancement in spatial resolution of observed reflecting objects, by moving the radar antenna through space (for example, aboard an aircraft), integrating and correlating echo signals as it moves (see **radar, imaging**).

Edwin Lyon III

Bibliography

Fisher, David E. *A Race on the Edge of Time.* New York: McGraw-Hill, 1988.

Page, Robert M. *The Origin of Radar*. Garden City, N.Y.: Anchor, 1962.

Rowe, A.P. *One Story of Radar*. Cambridge: Cambridge University Press, 1948.

Shembel', B.K. *The Origins of Radar in the USSR*. Moscow: Mir, 1977.

Radar, Imaging

Imaging radars use microwave radiation to generate high-resolution images. Single frequency **radar** generates images similar to those produced by black and white photography. Multiple frequency imaging radar generates images similar to those of color photography. The most common imaging radar operates at frequencies ranging from about 400 MHz (a wavelength of 75 cm) to about 15 GHz (a wavelength of 2 cm). Imaging radar sensors use polarized microwave radiation, thus making possible the generation of images with different polarimetric properties. Polarimetric imaging radar provides additional degrees of freedom to map surface properties.

Imaging radars generate their own illuminating signal and measure the reflected signal from the surface. This allows them to operate equally well day or night because they do not depend on the sun's illumination. Also, because they usually use relatively long-wavelength radiation, the signals pass through fog, clouds, and precipitation with little attenuation, making possible surface imaging in all weather conditions and at all times.

These imaging radars can also image objects and features below vegetation canopies and thin covers of dry sand, alluvium, or snow, because those materials have low microwave absorption properties.

Concept and Types

Imaging radars are mounted on moving platforms (usually aircraft or spacecraft). They send a train of microwave pulses to the surface to be examined. Echoes, back-scattered with imprints of the surface morphologic and electric properties, propagate back toward the sensor and are collected by the antenna and detected by the sensor. As the platform moves, an image strip of the surface is formed.

The image resolution is defined by the range resolution across the flight track and by the azimuth resolution along the flight track. The range resolution corresponds to the instantaneous footprint of a transmitted pulse on the surface. Better (that is, smaller) range resolution

can be achieved by transmitting shorter pulses. Resolution of a few meters is easily achievable with modern systems.

For real aperture imaging radar, the azimuth resolution corresponds to the footprint of the antenna on the surface. This footprint is directly proportional to the operating wavelength and the distance between the sensor and the surface, and inversely proportional to the size of the antenna along the flight path. For low-flying airborne sensors, the distance to the surface is short enough that azimuth resolution of a few meters to a few tens of meters is common. However, such fine azimuth resolution cannot be achieved from high-altitude aircraft or from satellites without more sophisticated data handling, which is the case with synthetic aperture imaging radars.

In the case of a synthetic aperture radar, a long virtual azimuth aperture is generated by coherently combining successive echoes as the platform moves. This is fundamentally similar to radio astronomy antenna arrays used to achieve finer radio beams. By combining the successive echoes, virtual apertures of many kilometers' size can be synthesized, allowing us to achieve surface azimuth resolution of a few meters from satellite altitudes.

The different components of echoes emanating from the different surface elements of a pulse footprint have different Doppler shifts depending on the location relative to the plane orthogonal to the flight path. The farther the element is from this plane (or line on the surface), the higher is the Doppler shift. This shift is positive for elements ahead of the line and negative for elements behind it. Thus, by taking successive echoes and tracking segments with different Doppler resolution, very fine resolutions can be achieved.

History and Modern Systems

Airborne imaging radar were developed in the early 1950s (for real aperture) and in the late 1950s (for synthetic aperture). Today sophisticated synthetic aperture radars are commonly used on military and civilian aircraft to obtain reconnaissance images and to map large areas at a very high resolution of 1 to a few meters.

The first spaceborne imaging radar system was flown on the U.S. Seasat satellite in 1978 and was rapidly followed by a series of earth-orbiting missions in the 1980s and 1990s, including the U.S. Shuttle Imaging Radar (SIR) series, the Russian Almaz series, the European ERS-1 and

R

Three-dimensional perspective of the Karakax Valley in Western China, produced from data generated by the Spaceborne Imaging Radar-C/X-band Synthetic Aperture Radar aboard the space shuttle Endeavor, *1994. Courtesy of the Jet Propulsion Laboratory, California Institute of Technology.*

2, the Japanese JERS-1, and the Canadian Radarsat. In 1994 the first multispectral (three frequency) multipolarization spaceborne radar was flown on the shuttle *Endeavor* by a U.S./German/Italian team. This opened the new era of "color" imaging radar.

Imaging radars were also flown to image planetary surfaces, particularly Venus. In 1983–1984 a Russian orbiting imaging radar imaged the continuously cloud-covered Venutian surface at about 1 km resolution. In 1990–1991 a U.S. imaging radar on the *Magellan* mission mapped the total surface of Venus at about 100 meters resolution.

In the mid 1990s a new concept of imaging radar interferometry was demonstrated in which two antennas are used to obtain interferometric surface images that allow the measurement of the surface shape in three dimensions. This allows the generation of topographic information simultaneously with the image, which can then be used to display the images in perspective. By taking images at two separate times, these coherent sensors can measure surface changes at the scale of the wavelength—that is, a few centimeters. This was demonstrated by imaging large areas before and after the occurrence of earthquakes and deriving maps of the resulting surface displacements.

Applications

Imaging radars are commonly used to map large regions for geologic analysis. Surface morphology is easily visible on the images and can be used to infer surface and subsurface structures. Multispectral imaging radars are used to derive quantitative information about the surface cover, particularly the biomass content of forests and the water content of snow. Because of their penetration capability, they are used to map structures and features that are covered by thin layers of sand and alluvium. They are used to map polar ice cover, and to help in navigation of the polar oceans by mapping open leads and transmitting the images to ships at sea. They are used to study ocean surface phenomena by mapping surface waves, eddies, current boundaries, and other phenomena that affect the roughness of the ocean surface. Imaging radar **interferometers** are used to generate digital topographic maps and to map minute surface displacements resulting from earthquakes, glacier flow, and mud slides.

Charles Elachi

Bibliography

Elachi, Charles. "Radar Images of the Earth from Space." *Scientific American* 247 (December 1982): 46–53.

———. *Spaceborne Radar Remote Sensing: Applications and Techniques.* New York: IEEE, 1988.

Harger, R.O. *Synthetic Aperture Radar Systems: Theory and Design.* New York: Academic, 1970.

Stimson, George W. *Introduction to Airborne Radar.* El Segundo, Calif.: Hughes Aircraft Co., 1983.

Ulaby, Fawwaz T., Richard K. Moore, and Adrian K. Fung. *Microwave Remote Sensing: Active and Passive.* Vols. 1, 2, Reading, Mass.: Addison-Wesley, 1981, 1982; Vol. 3, Norwood, Mass.: Artech, 1985.

Radio Telescope

See TELESCOPE, RADIO

Radio Wave Detector

Between 1886 and 1888, Rudolph Heinrich Hertz performed his classic experiments that proved that radio waves, theoretically predicted by James Clerk Maxwell, really did exist. (David Edward Hughes had stumbled upon proof of their existence a decade earlier but, discouraged by the reaction of some members of the Royal Society to whom he had shown his apparatus, he did not continue with his experiments.) In order to show that a burst of radio energy was emitted whenever a spark occurred, Hertz devised a detector that could reveal this to the human senses. For this purpose he used a metal ring, split at one point on its circumference and fitted with a small spark gap at that point. When the transmitter sparked, a small secondary spark was produced at the detector gap.

Others soon realized the need for a more sensitive radio-wave detector and pressed many physical phenomena into service for this purpose. The resulting devices were variously described as "wave revealers," "wave responders," and, for the classically minded, "cymoscopes" (from the Greek *cyma,* "a wave," and *skopein,* "to see"). However, it was the word "detector" that came into general use.

Wireless telegraphy—the use of Hertzian waves to signal by Morse code at a distance without a physical wire connection—required nothing more than a simple device to indicate the presence or absence of a signal in the receiving antenna, and so detection remained an appropriate description of this process. After the introduction of wireless telephony—in which a speech signal was imposed upon the radio wave—the circuits that retrieved the speech signal at the receiver were still referred to as detectors. The name was even applied to frequency changing stages of superheterodyne receivers, although they performed quite a different function.

Early experimenters tried to improve the sensitivity of the secondary spark gap, with limited success. The first breakthrough came in 1891, when Edouard Branly discovered that a loose pile of metal filings normally exhibits a high electrical resistance in poor electrical contacts, but the resistance drops markedly when a small voltage such as that in an antenna is applied. This change can be sensed by external instruments and used to indicate that a signal has been received. The low resistance persists until the filings are shaken back to the sensitive, high resistance condition. Many experimenters used this effect, their detectors commonly consisting of filings contained between metal plugs in a glass tube. Oliver Lodge coined the name "coherer" for these devices. They were often used with an automatic tapping hammer to restore them to the sensitive state. Guglielmo Marconi, in particular, developed the coherer into a commercially reliable receiver. Alexander Popoff independently constructed a similar receiver that he used for the automatic recording of lightning flashes (which are accompanied by emission of radio waves). Upon this receiver the Russians base their claim to have invented radio, although it is generally accepted that Popoff did not construct a transmitter until later.

Another type of detector used around the turn of the century employed changes in the magnetic state of iron when subjected to the effects of a radio-frequency magnetic field. Once again, Marconi produced a commercial version that was used, particularly at sea, up to World War I. Other phenomena used for detection included polarization effects in electrolytic cells (Reginald Aubrey Fessenden in the United States was a notable experimenter with these), capillary effects in liquid films, and vibrating contacts known as "tickers."

Marconi coherer and tapper, ca. 1900. SM 1923-396. Courtesy of SSPL.

It was the rectifying effect (that is, one-way conduction of electric current) found in certain metallic crystal junctions (originally discovered by Ferdinand Braun in the 1870s), and the similar property of the thermionic diode invented by John Ambrose Fleming in 1904, that introduced the concept of detection by rectification. The "cat's whisker" detector, in which the crystal was tickled with a piece of wire to find a sensitive spot, is perhaps the best remembered of these early detectors. Lee De Forest's invention of the triode in 1907 made possible both detection and amplification, a tremendous step forward. The standard vacuum tube detecting circuits, used for many years for receiving amplitude-modulated signals, were the diode "envelope detector" and the so-called "anode bend" and "leaky grid" triode circuits.

By the 1920s, detection had become synonymous with nonlinear circuits, rectification being an extreme form of this. Although the original meaning had been forgotten, the word remained in use until well after World War II, when it was gradually ousted by the more suitable term "demodulation." However, the names "envelope detector" and "ratio detector" persist in our vocabulary even today.

Vivian J. Phillips

Bibliography

Blake, George G. *History of Radio Telegraphy and Telephony*. London: Chapman and Hall, 1928. Reprint. New York: Arno, 1974.

Fleming, J.A. *The Principles of Electric Wave Telegraphy and Telephony*. 1st and 3rd eds. London: Longmans Green, 1906 and 1916.

Phillips, V.J. *Early Radio Wave Detectors*. London: Peter Peregrinus in association with the Science Museum, 1980.

Radiometer, Crookes'

A radiometer is a device that responds to light or other electromagnetic radiation. Crookes' radiometer consists of a glass bulb a few centimeters in diameter, evacuated to a pressure of about 50 mTorr, containing a fly of four vanes pivoted on the tip of a needle. Usually one side of each vane is blackened and the other made white or reflective. When illuminated by visible or infrared radiation, the fly rotates. Although it is more a demonstration device than a measuring instrument, the motion of this hermetically sealed fly with its suggestions of perpetual motion or action at a distance caught the attention and imagination of scientists of the caliber of James Clerk Maxwell and Albert Einstein.

William Crookes invented the radiometer in 1873, and he incorporated one in his arms in 1897 when he was knighted in recognition of his work in chemistry and physics. Crookes' work on the radiometer grew out of studies of discrepancies he observed when weighing hot samples under vacuum. His first device was in the form of a balance with a vane at each end, but he was soon using a "mill" with pith vanes blackened on one side.

Radiometers are easily made, but the theory of their operation has been controversial from the beginning and is now known to be quite complicated. At first Crookes suspected some link between heat and gravity. Later, influenced by Maxwell's electromagnetic theory of radiation (1873), he came to believe that the incident radiation exerted pressure on the absorbing elements. However, since radiation pressure would actually be greater on the reflective surface, the black surfaces should lead in the rotation. In fact, the opposite is observed, consistent with an interaction between the surfaces heated by the radiation and the residual gas. Indeed, experiments by Arthur Schuster and Augusto Righi in 1876 showed that there was a reaction force on the vessel walls in the opposite sense to the vane rotation, proving that a force was being transmitted through the gas.

A simple explanation, advanced by Osborne Reynolds in 1874 and usually given to students today, is that gas molecules rebound from the black surface with high velocities characteristic of its high temperature so that the net recoil force is greater than on the cold side. Such a simple explanation is valid only when the molecular mean free path is so large that collisions between the molecules can be neglected. In fact the actual radiometer force is largest at higher pressures where the mean free path is less than a millimeter. Here the situation is far more complex, and an explanation in terms of Maxwell's "thermal creep," a flow of gas along a surface from cold to hot areas, is more appropriate.

Thermal creep explains the action of several variants of the radiometer that use unpainted metal cups, half cylinders or cones instead of vanes. When illuminated, the fly rotates with the cooler open edges of the cups leading. Molecular flow patterns set up by thermal creep on an absorbing but fixed element (such as a blackened mica disk) can also move a nonabsorbing but mobile element (such as a fly of angled mica vanes) mounted nearby. Crookes called such devices "otheoscopes." Although many details were to be worked out, Osborne Reynolds and Maxwell had explained the basic mechanism by 1879. Crookes, however, was convinced that he could trace "lines of increased molecular pressure" to explain his results. He carried this idea over into his well-known work on gas discharges, where he made a number of important discoveries. Among several "Crookes' tubes" he used were "electrical radiometers" in which the fly acted as an electrode and rotated under the influence of the discharge.

At the turn of the century, most of the major scientific instrument suppliers listed a variety of such tubes named after the authors of papers in which illustrations had appeared. "Zölner radiometers" had angled vanes above a loop of heating wire. "Puluj radiometers" were driven by electrical discharges, and therefore have electrical connections, and often had fluorescent coatings on the vanes. At this time, a basic radiometer cost about $1.50, while variants costs two or three times more.

In spite of its name, the radiometer is not well adapted for quantitative measurement of radiation intensity. However, devices with the same force acting on a vane twisting a torsion fiber through a measurable angle, similar to Crookes' earliest devices, were used in the 1880–1900 period for infrared radiation measurements. A similar geometry was adopted by Pyotr Nicolayevich Lebedev (1899) and by Ernest F. Nichols and G.F. Hull (1901) for measurement of the much smaller true radiation pressure force that remains at extremely low pressures.

Norman R. Heckenberg

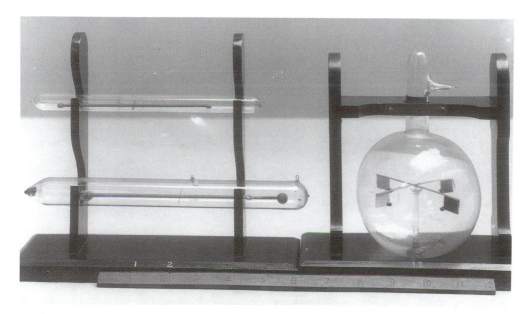

Crookes' original balance (left) and mill-type radiometer tubes, 1873. SM 1888-166. Courtesy of SSPL.

Bibliography

Brock, W.H. "Crookes, William." In *Dictionary of Scientific Biography,* edited by C.C. Gillispie, vol. 3, pp. 474–82. New York: Scribner, 1970.

Brush, S.G., and Everitt, C.W.F. "Maxwell, Osborne Reynolds, and the Radiometer." *Historical Studies in the Physical Sciences* 1 (1991): 105–25.

Crookes, W. "On Attraction and Repulsion Resulting from Radiation Part II." *Proceedings of the Royal Society* 23 (1875): 373–78.

Puluj. J. "Radiant Electrode Matter and the So-called Fourth State." *Memoirs of the Physical Society of London* 1 (1889): 233–331.

Woodruff, A.E. "The Radiometer and How It Does Not Work." *Physics Teacher* (October 1968): 358–63.

Radiometer, Space

A space radiometer operates from the vantage of a space platform, such as a planetary satellite or interplanetary space probe, and measures electromagnetic power radiated by natural objects. Space radiometers producing two- or three-dimensional images are most common. Typical instruments operate at one or more wavelengths in the microwave, infrared, or visible portions of the electromagnetic spectrum. They can measure surface temperature and composition distributions day and night, and three-dimensional temperature, humidity, and aerosol distributions in the atmospheres of earth and other planets. Trace constituents like ozone associated with atmospheric pollution or natural phenomena can also be observed.

The antecedents for this technology lie principally in astronomy, where both radio and optical **telescopes** yield similar radiometric information about the moon, planets, and stars. Early-twentieth-century instruments were little more than sensitive **thermometers** responsive to focused heat rays from the object of interest. These electromagnetic heat rays are the same as those felt while standing before a fire or in bright sunlight, and they extend over the full spectral range. Objects at ordinary temperatures radiate principally at infrared and radio wavelengths longer than 1 µm, which are invisible to the eye.

Radiometers operating at infrared or radio wavelengths can have sensitivities better than 0.01°C, particularly when the observations are averaged for several seconds or more, and when the observed wavelength band is broad. Some space radiometers form images by scanning a single point detector in a raster across the scene, while others view two-dimensional images instantaneously by focusing the incoming radiation upon a focal plane array (FPA) of detectors. Such **infrared detectors** are usually semiconductors with temperature-sensitive resistances that can be measured. In the visible region **charge-coupled devices** (CCDs) are now often used; the intercepted photons excite electrons that can be shifted sequentially from cell to cell and eventually to the edge of the FPA, where they can be measured.

One of the first space radiometers to image the earth was NASA's High-Resolution Infrared Radiometer (HRIR). It measured thermal radiation in the 3.5–4.1 µm (window) region, which is sensitive principally to surface temperature. A spot approximately 8 km in diameter was observed beneath the moving satellite. The HRIR operated for only three and a half weeks after its launch on August 28, 1964. The medium-resolution infrared radiometer (MIRI) was launched on May 16, 1966, on the NASA Nimbus-2 satellite and observed five selected wavelength intervals from 0.2–30 µm. A scanning mirror produced a two-dimensional image beneath the satellite with 55-km resolution yielding information in the 6-µm wavelength water vapor absorption band, a "window" band monitoring surface temperature at 10–12 µm, and the 15-µm carbon dioxide absorption band, which yielded atmospheric temperature profiles. Other channels observed the emitted long-wavelength infrared energy flux for heat budget purposes, and the 0.2–4 µm reflected solar energy. Surface composition and texture can be observed for mineralogical, environmental, and agricultural purposes because each surface type emits differently at different frequencies. A long series of ever-improving space radiometers observing visible and infrared radiation have since been launched by many nations for both peaceful and military purposes.

The first microwave space radiometer observed Venus at close range from the NASA *Mariner-II* space probe in 1961 at 19- and 13.5-mm wavelengths. These verified that the surface of the planet is well over 600K, much too hot to inhabit. The first microwave space radiometer orbiting the earth was on the Soviet satellite *Cosmos-243,* which observed the

Advanced Microwave Sounding Unit (AMSU)—A1, for temperature profiling, 1995. Courtesy of GenCorp Aerojet.

surface temperature, precipitation, snow, and water vapor distributions around the planet. The first microwave space radiometer mapping the atmospheric temperature distribution observed five wavelengths near 5 mm and flew on the *Nimbus-5* satellite in 1972. The first electrically scanned microwave space radiometer also flew on the same spacecraft and imaged surface temperatures, atmospheric humidity, precipitation, and snow and ice distributions at 19 GHz.

Today, infrared space radiometers with more than 2,000 channels are being built for flight on the U.S. Earth Observing System satellites, and microwave imaging systems with more than twenty channels are being built for launch after 1997 on U.S. weather satellites. Such space radiometers play an important role in providing the operational meteorological data necessary to initialize the numerical weather prediction models that have given us increasingly reliable weather forecasts, now approaching a range of one week. Such visible and infrared multiband radiometers also monitor the growth of cities, changing land use patterns, the distribution of biological activity in the top layers of the ocean, and even the spread of agricultural diseases. As the range of uses expands and the quality of the data improves, space radiometers will become increasingly important to our understanding of our planet and our ability to observe, predict, and control change and its impact.

David H. Staelin

Bibliography

Barath, Frank T., et al. "Mariner 2 Micro-
    wave Radiometer Experiments and Re-

sults." *Astronomical Journal* 69 (1964): 49–58.

Basharinov, E., A.S. Gurvich, and S.T. Yegorov. "Determination of Geophysical Parameters According to the Measurement of Thermal Microwave Radiation on the Artificial Satellite 'Cosmos-243.'" *Doklady Akademii nauk SSSR* (1969): 1273.

Chahine, Moustafa T., et al. "Interaction Mechanisms within the Atmosphere." In *Manual of Remote Sensing*, edited by Robert N. Colwell, Vol. 1, 165. 2nd ed. Falls Church, Va.: American Society of Photogrammetry, 1983.

Houghton, John T., F.W. Taylor, and Clive D. Rodgers. *Remote Sounding of Atmospheres*. Cambridge: Cambridge University Press, 1984.

Staelin, David H., et al. "Microwave Spectrometer on the *Nimbus-5* Satellite: Meteorological and Geophysical Data." *Science* 182 (1973): 1339–41.

Radiosonde

The term "radiosonde" refers to any balloon-borne instrument capable of measuring parameters of interest at various altitudes and radioing this information to a receiver-recorder on the ground. Such instruments have been built by researchers to obtain data on various phenomena (such as cosmic rays and ozone concentration). Most commonly, "radiosonde" has a more restricted meaning, referring to the payload of a meteorological data-gathering system consisting of a gas-filled rubber balloon, parachute, and instrument package that radios information on pressure, temperature, and humidity to a receiving station.

The first unmanned balloons carrying self-registering **thermometers** and **barometers** were flown by French scientist Gustave Hermite, beginning in 1892. His constant-volume balloons made of varnished silk were capable of reaching heights of over 9 km before the loss of lift gas caused their slow descent. A notice on the instrument promised the finder a reward for returning it to the central bureau, where the flight record could be read. Soon, other investigators began to use such sounding balloons, or "balloons-sondes," as Hermite had termed them.

In 1896, at the suggestion of the American meteorologist Abbot Rotch, a **hygrometer** was added to the instrument package, marking the advent of the three-sensor system still in use. In 1901, German meteorologist Richard Assmann introduced the use of sealed rubber balloons that could ascend to over 20 km before expanding to their bursting point, allowing the instruments to descend by parachute.

Although useful as a research tool, balloons-sondes were not helpful in weather forecasting because the flight records were not recovered immediately, but only after the lapse of a week or more. The military need for better meteorological information during World War I prompted several scientists to suggest that balloons-sondes equipped with radio transmitters could provide upper atmosphere data on a timely basis for forecasting. This application, however, had to await the development of radio components of suitable size, weight, and cost.

Between 1921 and 1930, work on balloon-borne radio transmitters was carried out in several countries. In 1929, French scientist Robert Bureau flew an instrument in which an aneroid barometer and bimetallic thermometer were linked to a transmitter by an electromechanical transducer that altered the radio signal in a way that could be decoded as values of pressure and temperature. Bureau coined the term "radiosondes" to describe such instruments. In 1930, Russian engineer Pavel Moltchanoff flew an instrument incorporating a complex switching device that caused the output of a barometer, thermometer, and hygrometer to be transmitted in Morse code. Also in 1930, German meteorologist Paul Duckert flew a radiosonde in which sensors, such as a temperature-sensitive capacitor, were components of the transmitter circuit. Changes in the electrical characteristics of such components with variation of the atmospheric parameter being measured altered the frequency of the radio signal in a way that conveyed the data sought.

Features of these three prototype radiosondes appeared in production versions made for the weather bureaus of France, Russia, and Germany, and in the radiosonde developed by America's National Bureau of Standards in 1938, and in Britain's Kew Observatory radiosonde developed in 1940.

Beginning in the 1930s, radiosondes were used in increasing numbers by national weather services. Moreover, as this technology was adapted by investigators interested in measuring nonmeteorological parameters, "radiosonde" acquired a broader meaning. It is impos-

Kew Radiosonde Mark II, 1950s. NMAH 322,313. Courtesy of NMAH.

sible to generalize about the radiosondes developed by individual researchers, but meteorological radiosondes used in many countries are similar. They employ an aneroid barometer to measure pressure, and they rely on temperature and humidity sensors that are either mechanical (bimetallic thermometer, hair hygrometer) or electrical (thermistor, lithium chloride hygrometer). Sensors are coupled to a transmitter operating within a frequency range established by international agreement. Transmission of data is usually based on modulation by a variable audio frequency.

Typical models measure temperature within a degree centigrade, pressure within a millibar, and relative humidity within 3 percent. Cost rather than precision is the chief determinant of their design, since few are recovered in reusable condition. They are purchased in huge quantities by government agencies via open-bid contracts and, as they are built to specifications,

they are not usually considered the product of specific companies.

Special-purpose radiosondes continue to be a valuable tool in high-altitude research. Meteorological radiosondes, launched daily from hundreds of stations worldwide, measure pressure, temperature, and humidity to heights of 30 km, and their flight path, determined by tracking antenna or radar, provides information on the winds aloft. Radiosonde data has long been considered an essential element in weather forecasting.

Charles A. Ziegler

Bibliography

DuBois, John L., Robert P. Multhauf, and Charles A. Ziegler. *The Invention and Development of the Radiosonde.* Washington, D.C.: Smithsonian Institution Press, forthcoming.
Middleton, W.E. Knowles. *Catalog of Meteo-*

rological Instruments in the Museum of History and Technology, 97–122. Washington, D.C.: Smithsonian Institution Press, 1969.

———, and Athelstan F. Spilhaus. *Meteorological Instruments,* 228–65. Toronto: University of Toronto Press, 1953.

Rail Track Recording Device

A rail track recording device assists in the maintenance of rail track to a definite standard for the services to be run. The maintenance of tracks to these standards ensures safety, minimizes cost of the upkeep of both track and the vehicles running on it, and where applicable, maximizes the comfort of passengers.

Background

Before the introduction of recording devices about fifty years ago, there were gangs of men whose sole task was to examine and maintain the track. To test the effectiveness of this system, special vehicles were developed to record the riding conditions of the track. In Great Britain these vehicles were known as Track Testing Cars, and in the United States as Track Geometry Cars. Instruments such as the Hallade Recorder produced graphs, indicating track faults or deficiencies drawn by pendulum-operated pens tracing onto a paper roll driven by a clockwork motor. Defects were marked on the ground by splashes of whitewash released automatically.

In Great Britain, where passenger traffic is most significant, the present-day Track Recording Coaches measure, at high speed, the riding qualities of the coach and indicate where track deficiencies occur; in the United States, where freight traffic is by far the greatest user of the railroads, the Association of American Railroads use their vehicles to evaluate, for example, the effects of substandard track on vehicle springing and thus the cost of maintenance, and the ability of the track to withstand higher wheel loadings and thus higher payloads in the future.

To complement the information of the Track Recording Coaches, British Rail introduced Matiser track recording trolleys, which measured cross-level, alignment and rail flaws. By the addition of a **computer**, these trolleys were upgraded and a fleet of vehicles code named "Neptune" were used from the early 1960s for over twenty years. They operated at slow speeds and could record the track geometry only in an almost static condition under the load imposed by themselves alone. The most recent development in the U.K. has been the High Speed Track Recording coach, which can operate between 15 and 125 mph; in the United States, it has been the Track Loading Vehicle, as part of the Association of American Railroads. In the United States, the Track Train Dynamics Program had as its primary objective the development of improved track maintenance methods and the advancement of vehicle design standards to reduce derailments.

The High Speed Track Recording Coach and Ultrasonic Test Train (British Rail)

The higher axle loadings on British Rail are on the order of 25 tons, and service speeds of 100–125 miles per hour are a regular matter. The High Speed Track Recording Coach has been developed to provide data regarding vehicle behavior and track geometry under that load and at the higher speeds. Neither of these conditions is being met by the Neptune vehicles.

Following its introduction, the high-speed coach was used to examine and record track geometry over 12,500 miles in two months. The examination of 80,000 track miles per annum is the planned use of the vehicle. The coach was developed from a standard British Rail Mark 2f passenger vehicle. It has an instrumentation compartment, a furnished riding compartment, and a two-berth sleeping compartment for the crew. It contains its own diesel generator, and is equipped with both vacuum and air operated brakes. There is a control cable fitted through the coach that allows it to run in a High Speed Train set (with power cars at each end) under the control of the driver in the leading car.

The instrumentation has been developed at the Railway Technical Centre, Derby, and uses noncontacting sensors to measure six basic parameters: vertical profile (both rails), horizontal profile (alignment), cross-levels, curvature, gauge, and variation in gradient. Calculations from this data can produce a number of secondary statistics, such as cross-levels and twist. Vertical movement between the axleboxes and the frame are measured by displacement transducers, and optical scanning devices working from the inside edges of the rails provide data relating to horizontal displacements.

Track loading vehicle used by the Association of American Railroads Transportation Technology Center (commissioned in 1990). Courtesy of the Association of American Railroads Railway Technology Department.

The information collected when working at speed can amount to about five thousand measurements per second. The on-board computer processes this information to standard deviations, and to exceedence counts produced in tabular form. In order that the averaging effect of standard deviations does not cover up bad, isolated defects, threshhold levels are set and recordings above those levels (exceedence) are recorded separately. Gross defects requiring priority attention are charted, and paint is sprayed on the ground to assist in the location of the fault.

The Ultrasonic Test Train uses ultrasonic techniques to examine rails for hidden faults. These are recorded and analyzed automatically thanks to the cooperation of the Nondestructive Testing Centre of the Atomic Energy Authority of the U.K. This vehicle is also equipped with track-marking paint-spraying equipment.

The Track Loading Vehicle (Association of American Railroads)

Flange climbing, gauge widening, and movement of track panels can produce a derailment that is not easily explained. Problems, difficult to define, are associated with side-to-side forces and low vertical forces (when a wheel might lift off the rail) which, in turn, can lead to derailments. The Track Loading Vehicle is designed to simulate controlled derailment conditions and also to determine the dynamic reaction of the track to the loadings applied by the vehicle.

The vehicle is constructed on the underframe of a SD45-X locomotive. The superstructure is fabricated from $1/4$-inch thick steel plate, which provides stiffness and mass, weighing 263,000 lbs. There is in addition to the original locomotive trucks, a fifth wheel set under the center of the vehicle. This is used to apply loads, through hydraulic rams, to the track and also to measure the track reactions both stationary and moving. Specially designed wheel sets incorporate independent wheels and their bearings; the more normal arrangement of two wheels fixed to a common axle can also be fitted if testing conditions require it.

The activation of the load-inducing hydraulic rams is computer controlled and has to accommodate such effects as body displacement on curves automatically adjusting the loading on each wheel. The displacement can amount to 6 in. on commonly found curves and varies continuously while entering or leaving a curve. The vehicle can apply vertical and horizontal loads in excess of 50,000 lbs. The Track Loading Vehicle will examine all the conditions leading to derailment caused by wheel and rail interactions.

Tony Hall-Patch

Bibliography

Coster, Peter J. "Maintaining the Permanent Way 3: Inspection and Day-to-Day Maintenance by Machine." *Modern Railways* 39 (1982): 501–05.

———, "The Railway Civil Engineer 2: Permanent Way Structure and Design." *Railway World* 38 (1977): 58–62.

"Recent Developments in Track Recording and Rail Inspection. *Modern Railways* 34 (1977): 174–75.

Rain Gauge

A rain gauge measures rainfall. It is also called hyetometer (Greek *hyetos-*, "rain" plus *metron-*, "measure"), ombrometer (Greek *ombros-*, "shower of rain"), and pluviometer (Latin *pluvìa*, "rain"). The earliest recorded measurement of rainfall occurs in the Sanskrit work *Science of Politics*, dating from the fourth century B.C., in a passage surveying regional rainfall amounts in India and their effects on agriculture. Presumably a vessel of some standard measure was used to catch the rain. Observers in Palestine during the first two centuries A.D. measured rainfall as a depth of water, again for agricultural purposes. In the fifteenth century, Koreans distributed bronze vases throughout a network of rainfall stations.

These early gauges most likely influenced neither each other nor the first recorded European gauge, a cylindrical glass vessel mentioned by Benedetto Castelli in a letter of 1639 to Galileo. Castelli had used the instrument to estimate the contribution of a rainstorm to the outflow of Lake Trasimeno in Perugia. Around 1663 Christopher Wren devised two different rain gauges for his "weather clock," an automatic recorder of wind, temperature, and rainfall observations. In one design the clock mechanism drew successive square containers under the funnel that collected the rain. As Wren realized, however, water might evaporate from the containers before the observer visited them. The second version used a "tipping bucket," a vessel, known to the Arabs during the Middle Ages, that is so shaped and balanced that its center of gravity shifts as it fills until it tips over, emptying its contents, and subsequently returning to its original vertical position. Wren's colleague Robert Hooke counterpoised the bucket with a cylinder that was gradually drawn out of a liquid bath as the bucket filled, then sank back to its original level when the bucket emptied. In this way the amount of rain was weighed as the bucket filled, and the number of fillings counted by a punch that operated when it emptied.

Regular observations with simple rain gauges were made in the late seventeenth century by Pierre Perrault, who solved an ancient problem when he determined that the amount of rainfall near the headwaters of the Seine was indeed enough to maintain its flow. Edme Mariotte carried out a similar experiment in Dijon, while Philippe de la Hire began regular observations at the Observatoire in Paris. In England, Richard Townley published monthly totals of rainfall.

As occurred with other instruments of natural philosophy, the late eighteenth century brought a concern to eliminate sources of error. One source of error is the loss of raindrops—even those that have fallen into the gauge—that are carried away by eddies and currents generated by the wind's blowing against the instrument's side. James Six found that gauges farther from the ground collected less rain, and it was soon suggested that this was an effect of the wind, which increases with height. One solution was to expose gauges as close to the ground as possible. A second source of error was the splashing of raindrops into or out of the gauge. This effect could be reduced by redesigning the funnel that sat atop the collecting vessel. Luke Howard, author of *The Climate of London* (1818–1820), sank his instrument into the ground so that the mouth of the funnel, furnished with a turned brass rim, was nearly at the level of the turf. Thomas Stevenson, a lighthouse engineer, surrounded his sunken gauge with an annular bristle brush to prevent rain from splashing into it. "Pit gauges" like these, however, did not enjoy great popularity, on account of the expense of placing them, and because too often, as one observer reported, "their chief efficiency was in collecting insects." In 1878 F.E. Nipher of St. Louis invented the shield that carries his name—an inverted cone of wire mesh surrounding the funnel, and whose rim, at the level of the funnel's top, extends outward in a ring like the brim of a hat. The shield prevents splashing almost entirely and breaks up currents and eddies of wind.

Considerable ingenuity has been expended on the invention of recording rain gauges. The simplest type uses a float that rises in the collecting vessel as rain accumulates, and to which a pen is attached; the earliest of these seems to have been constructed in 1827. In other float gauges a rod attached to the float carries a set of inclined planes; the lever operating the pen arm slides along each plane until it drops off the edge to the next, returning the pen to zero. In a third class of float gauges, a siphon empties the chamber once the rain reaches a certain depth; the first of these was described in 1869. W.H. Dines's "tilting-siphon" gauge (1920) uses a trigger device to hold the chamber and siphon off-center on a knife-edge. When the float reaches the proper height, it releases the trigger, and the entire assembly tips, emptying water through the siphon until the float returns to zero.

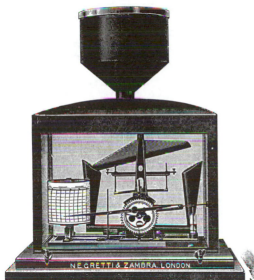

Negretti & Zambra recording tipping bucket rain gauge. Negretti & Zambra. Standard Meteorological Instruments, London, 1931, 54. Courtesy of Meggit plc.

Tipping buckets were also used in recording gauges, as was the case in Wren's and Hooke's gauges. A pair of buckets placed back to back on an arm, and oscillating as first one, then the other, fills and tips, was first used in a rain gauge in 1830. In a version sold at the turn of the twentieth century by the instrument-making firm Negretti and Zambra, the buckets turned a spiral cam as they shifted, raising the pen arm. Dines attached a platinum wire to the bottom of each bucket so that one or the other contacted an insulated pool of mercury. When one of the buckets tipped, both wires made contact, closing a circuit that operated a distant recorder. Electrical gauges of this type remained widespread during the first half of the twentieth century. Though it was long considered useless to attempt to mount rain gauges on ships, due to the rolling of the vessel and the interference of masts and rigging, gauges mounted on gimbals were shown at the end of the nineteenth century to be quite satisfactory and of great importance for the determination of oceanic climate.

Theodore S. Feldman

Bibliography

Abbe, C. "Meteorology: Apparatus and Methods." In *Encyclopaedia Britannica*, Vol. 18, 273–281. 11th ed. Cambridge: Cambridge University Press, 1910.

Middleton, W.E. Knowles. *Invention of the Meteorological Instruments.* Baltimore: Johns Hopkins University Press, 1969.

Rangefinder

A rangefinder, or telemeter, measures distances by triangulation, and was designed primarily for military use. It operates on the principle that a right-angled triangle of known base length can be solved by calculating the size of the second base angle.

The first commercially successful rangefinders, such as the Watkin Mekometer, which was introduced in the U.K. in the 1870s, required two observers to set out a right angled triangle, with the target at the apex. The second observer acquired the range by using an instrument similar to a box **sextant** to measure the second base angle. Such multioperator instruments proved too cumbersome for effective use in action. As artillery and naval guns became more powerful, the need for a rapid and effective means of measuring long ranges became more pressing.

The first practical instrument that could be used by one observer was patented in 1860 by Patrick Adie, a scientific instrument–maker in Edinburgh. It consisted of a metal tube containing a **telescope** at each end, which sent images of the target to a central eyepiece. The observer turned a **micrometer** screw, altering the angle at which one end reflector was set, until the two images of the target were brought into coincidence at the eyepiece. The scale attached to the micrometer translated the angle at which the end reflector was set—the second base angle of the ranging triangle—into a reading of the target's range.

Other inventors, such as Amulf Mallock and Britain's Astronomer Royal, W.H.M. Christie, improved on Adie's design, but were unable to prevent the delicate optical and mechanical parts from becoming damaged or deranged by hard use. These problems were largely overcome in 1888, by Archibald Barr, soon to become the Regius professor of engineering at the University of Glasgow, and William Stroud, professor of physics at the Yorkshire College of Science.

The prototype of the Barr & Stroud rangefinder was rejected by Britain's Royal Artillery, but a modified instrument was adopted by the Royal Navy after trials at sea in 1892. The instrument's

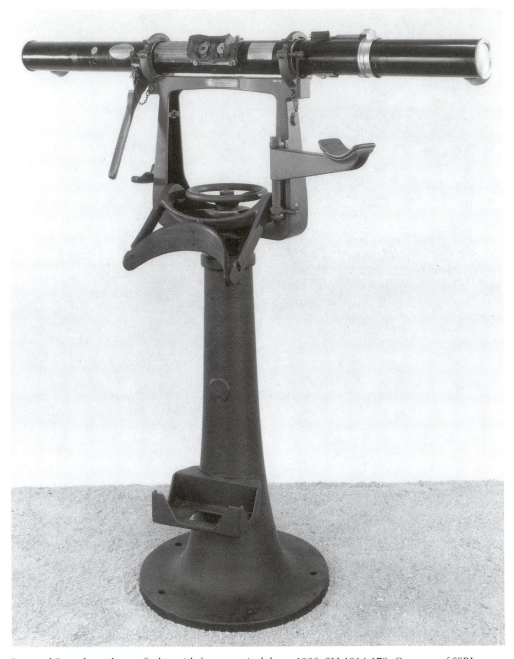

Barr and Stroud naval rangefinder, with forty-two-inch base, 1900. SM 1914-179. Courtesy of SSPL.

main advantage over its predecessor lay in the novel arrangement for measuring the second base angle. Partial images from the fixed end reflectors were transmitted to a central eyepiece, and the observer achieved coincidence by moving an achromatic refracting prism of small angle along the path of the beam of light from one reflector. A scale was calibrated to translate the position of the traveling prism, when coincidence was achieved,

into a reading of the range. As the scale was attached to and moved with the prism, and the reading did not rely on the minute adjustment of delicate optical and mechanical parts, this coincidence rangefinder proved to be far more reliable and sturdy than its predecessors and competitors.

Barr and Stroud formed a company and built a factory in Glasgow to develop and manufacture their invention, and they met with great success in marketing the naval version. By constantly modifying and improving the design of their instruments, and aggressively defending their patents, they succeeded in maintaining a near monopoly of the market for coincidence rangefinders.

The stereoscopic rangefinder was invented by an Alsatian engineer, A. Hector de Grousilliers, and patented in the U.K. in 1893. Zeiss took up the invention, and it went into commercial production in Germany in 1906. The images from the end reflectors of the stereoscopic rangefinder were focused on slides mounted in front of the eyepieces. A series of scale graduations were marked on the slides, and these arrows appeared to stretch back into the stereoscopic field of view. The observer's task was to select the arrow that appeared to lie closest to the target, and read the range.

Zeiss was acknowledged as the world's leading optical engineering firm, and the quality of their lenses and other parts was generally superior to that of the Barr & Stroud instruments. However, many people do not possess true stereoscopic vision, and in others it is impaired by ill health and mental strain. A coincidence rangefinder was easier to use and relied on purely mechanical action by, rather than the physiological attributes of, the observer. It could therefore be used with success by a higher proportion of observers than the stereoscopic instrument.

Coincidence rangefinders were tested in action at the Battle of Tsushima in 1905, when Japanese naval officers praised the performance of their Barr & Stroud instruments during the crushing defeat of Russia's Baltic fleet. By the outbreak of World War I, the single-observer rangefinder had become an integral part of fire control systems on warships throughout the world. However, the greatest naval engagement of the war, the Battle of Jutland in 1916, proved to be an inconclusive test of the comparative merits of the coincidence rangefinder (the Royal Navy was equipped with Barr & Stroud instruments of up to 30 feet in length) and the stereoscopic (German ships were equipped with Zeiss rangefinders of up to 3 meters).

Portable field rangefinders were adopted by most of the world's armies before 1914, particularly for service with artillery, mortar, and machine-gun units. Barr & Stroud and Zeiss were the two greatest suppliers of field rangefinders during the war: during the years between 1913 and 1918, Barr & Stroud supplied over sixteen thousand rangefinders to the British Army and

thirty-three hundred to the French. Such companies as C.P. Goerz of Germany and Bausch & Lomb of the United States achieved some success in marketing their own versions of stereoscopic and coincidence instruments.

After the war, expiration of many of Barr & Stroud's patents, economic turmoil in Germany, and growth of international trade barriers gave other firms of optical engineers the opportunity to develop their own rangefinders. The greatest improvements in design during the interwar years were those that permitted longer base lengths. The biggest rangefinder ever made, with a base length of 100 feet, was manufactured by Barr & Stroud in 1919 and installed at Singapore's harbor defenses in the 1930s. This instrument was accurate to within 17 yards (0.055 percent) at a range of 31,000 yards; the first Barr & Stroud rangefinder, with a base length of 4.5 feet, had been accurate to within 3 percent at 3,000.

During World War II, the naval optical rangefinder was superseded by **radar**. The military version was largely abandoned in the 1950s, and the development of the laser rangefinder in the 1960s apparently sealed its fate (See also **distance measurement, electromagnetic**). However, as a "passive" system of ascertaining ranges, it may yet have a future in low-level guerilla warfare.

Iain Russell

Bibliography

Barr, Archibald, and William Stroud. "On Some New Telemeters or Rangefinders." *Report of the Sixtieth Meeting of the British Association for the Advancement of Science* (1890): 499–512.

Callwell, Charles, and John Headlam. *History of the Royal Artillery, from the Indian Mutiny to the Great War.* London: Royal Artillery Institution, 1931–1940.

Gleichen, Alexander Wilhelm. *The Theory of Modern Optical Instruments.* 2nd ed. London: His Majesty's Stationery Office, 1921.

Moss, Michael S., and Iain Russell. *Range and Vision: The First Hundred Years of Barr & Stroud.* Edinburgh: Mainstream, 1988.

Refractometer

Refractometers measure the refractive index of a sample or compare it to a standard. Samples may be either liquids, solids, or gases, common applications being the measurement of the sugar content of water and the refractive index of transparent solids such as optical glass. Refractometers are commonly used in conjunction with other techniques, such as **polarimeters**, to characterize the fundamental properties of a sample.

Isaac Newton related refraction—that is, the deviation of a ray of light passing into a transparent material—to its mass density. In the nineteenth century, several investigators studied its dependence on temperature and molecular weight. The word "refractometer," and standardized applications, were in use by the 1870s. By the end of the century, a wealth of experimental data had been accumulated, particularly for liquid compounds of organic chemistry. The technique proved most useful for determining the concentration of two-component mixtures such as alcohol and water, or water and milk.

Refractometers have employed a variety of optical principles. The first of these is the angle of refraction of a ray of light passing through a prism-shaped sample. One form of refractometer is thus essentially a spectrometer incorporating a hollow prism into which the sample liquid is poured. The angle of minimum deviation of this prism is determined, and the index of refraction calculated. In a variation of this principle, the Zeiss "dipping" refractometer consists of a viewing **telescope** immersed in the sample liquid to observe the refraction of the rays from a light source located outside the glass wall of the container (see **spectrophotometer**).

A second physical principle employed is that of total internal reflection. In passing from a lower-index to a higher-index medium, light is completely reflected at the interface when the tangent of the angle of incidence is greater than the ratio of refractive indices. In the refractometer of Ernst Abbe, the liquid sample is either sandwiched between two prisms or dropped onto the top of a single prism. A telescope on a graduated circle is used to observe the line of total reflection. Because the index of refraction varies significantly with temperature, the instrument often incorporates a means of measuring and adjusting the sample temperature. The refraction through the prism also disperses the light, causing a colored fringe. This is sometimes removed by interposing a compensating unit consisting of two Amici prisms. Alternatively, the instrument can be used with monochromatic light. The refractometer of Carl Pulfrich also measures the critical angle for total internal reflection, employing a right-angled

prism onto which the sample liquid is placed. Solid samples can be measured by mixing them with an index-matching liquid (which causes the total reflection to disappear) and then measuring the liquid in the refractometer.

The Nichols microrefractometer determines the index of refraction of a liquid by measuring, through a **microscope**, the displacement of a line viewed through two prisms oriented in opposite directions and covered with the sample liquid. The deviation is calibrated with respect to a series of reference liquids of graded refractive index.

Another method relies on the disappearance of a solid transparent object when its refractive index matches that of the liquid. A series of reference solids are employed, which may be powders, single particles, or fibers if a microscope is used for examination. Conversely, unknown solid samples in this form can be measured if reference liquids are available. The microscopic immersion method is in fact the most frequently used technique for solids, for which a smooth refracting surface can be difficult to obtain.

The refractive index may also be measured as the ratio of the real thickness of a transparent material to its apparent thickness, and the apparent thickness can be measured with an **interferometer**. In the Jamin refractometer, the refractive index of a gas is measured by slowly introducing the gas to an evacuated optical cell contained within one arm of an interferometer. By counting the interference fringes, the optical path difference, and hence the refractive index, can be determined.

Manufacturers of refractometers have included many of the major optical instrument companies, such as Hilger & Watts in Britain, Bausch & Lomb in the United States, and Zeiss in Germany. The widely used visual models have been supplemented, particularly for wavelength-dependent studies, by photoelectric recording instruments since World War II.

Sean F. Johnston

Bibliography

Allen, Roy Morris. *Practical Refractometry by Means of the Microscope: With Listings of Index Liquids, and Other Aids for Mineralogists.* New York: R.P. Cargille Laboratories, 1954.

Batsanov, S.S. *Refractometry and Chemical Structure.* Translated by Paul Porter Sutton. New York: Consultants Bureau, 1961.

Pulfrich refractometer, by Hilger, 1921. Arthur H. Thomas Company. Laboratory Apparatus and Reagents. *Philadelphia, 1921: 522, Figure 8660. Courtesy of SSPL.*

Lewin, S.Z. "Refractometry and Dispersometry." In *Treatise on Analytical Chemistry,* edited by I.M. Kolthoff, Philip J. Elving, and Ernest B. Sandell. Vol. 6. New York: Wiley, 1965.

Longhurst, R.S. *Geometrical and Physical Optics.* 3rd ed. London: Longman, 1973.

Regulator Clock

See CLOCK, REGULATOR

S

Scanning Acoustic Microscope
See MICROSCOPE, SCANNING ACOUSTIC

Scanning Optical Microscope
See MICROSCOPE, SCANNING OPTICAL

Scanning Probe Microscope
See MICROSCOPE, SCANNING PROBE

Scintillation Counter

In the traditional scintillation counter, a scintillating crystal—a phosphor—is activated by an incoming nuclear particle, and the resulting flash of light is recorded by the eye. Visual scintillation counters as detectors of nuclear and elementary particles became obsolete in the 1930s, when they were replaced with electronically amplified **Geiger-Müller (GM) counters**. Shortly after the war, the scintillation method was drastically improved into an instrument that physicists soon referred to as the (phototronic) scintillation counter. The trick was to combine the phosphor with a photomultiplier tube—that is, to replace the human eye as a detector of the scintillations with a photomultiplier in which the optical signals are converted into amplified electrical pulses. Such a combined system was pioneered between 1944 and 1947 by American and British physicists. The invention of the modern scintillation counter is sometimes ascribed to the German physicist Hartmut Kallman, who in 1947 developed a technique for detecting beta and gamma rays with a **photomultiplier.**

When the phosphor scintillates, the light (photons) falls upon the tube's photosensitive cathode, which gives off electrons. These are focused on a second plate (dynode) and accelerated toward it by its higher potential. The first dynode emits a shower of "secondary" electrons, which strike a second dynode at a higher potential; they are further multiplied, and so on, until the electron avalanche arrives at a collector plate. By such repeated multiplication of electrons, a tube acts as an enormously efficient amplifier, the net result being an electrical current produced by just a single primary electron. The photomultiplier goes back to about 1936, when a German physicist, Georg Weiss, devised a tube that was built by the Telefunken Co.

As early as 1953, commercially available photomultipliers with fourteen sensitive plates could amplify the number of primary electrons one billion times. The photomultipliers were made by the large manufacturers of vacuum tubes, including RCA in the United States, EMI in England, and Philips in the Netherlands. The first commercial tube used in scintillation counters, RCA's 931A from 1947, had a diameter of 3.3 cm and a length of 9.2 cm. Its nine dynodes yielded an amplification of one million and a maximum current of 1.0 mA.

The success of the new scintillation counters depended not only on developments in tube electronics, but also on advances in the other component of the counter, the phosphors. Whereas almost all visual counters had used zinc sulphide, the photomultiplier technique stimulated the development of a large class of new and still more efficient phosphors. In 1949, the American physicist Robert Hofstadter invented a sodium iodide detector that became a very important instrument in particle physics. The use of organic phosphors started in 1947, when Kallmann discovered that naphthalene

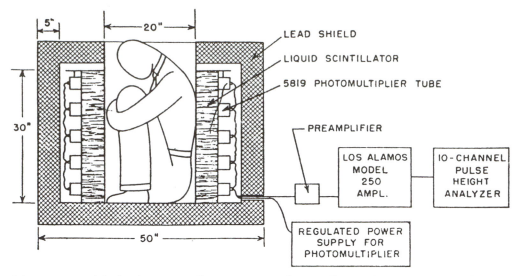

Schematic view of the first human scintillation counter. Carlos G. Bell, Jr., and F. Newton Hayes, eds. Liquid Scintillation Counting. *London: Pergamon Press, 1958: 249, Figure 8. Courtesy of the University of California.*

crystals are efficient phosphors also for beta and gamma radiation. Within a few years a large number of organic crystalline phosphors were developed, of which anthracene proved the most efficient. In addition to the classic use of crystalline phosphors, in the early 1950s organic substances were also used in the form of solutions or mixed with plastics.

The new generation of scintillation counters that emerged about 1950 had great advantages over the traditional GM counter. They had a much better resolution, being able to detect one hundred million scintillations per second, and, since the output is proportional to the intensity of the light, they could also be used to measure the energy of the incident particles. Moreover, they were versatile and relatively simple instruments that could be designed in almost any shape and size, and designed to detect all kinds of particles, including neutrons and gamma rays. By the mid 1950s, scintillation counters had supplanted the GM counter as the premier detector in nuclear and particle physics.

Although commercially manufactured scintillation counters are widely used in industry, biology, and environmental research, it is in high-energy physics that they have made the greatest impact. Various forms of scintillation counters have been essential in virtually all major experiments between 1950 and 1970. Since 1960 the scintillation counter has been developed into a powerful type of detector—a scintillation chamber—in which luminescent tracks of high-energy particles can be directly observed.

Helge Kragh

Bibliography

Birks, John B. *Scintillation Counters*. Oxford: Pergamon, 1953.

———. *The Theory and Practice of Scintillation Counting*. Oxford: Pergamon, 1964.

Brown, Laurie, Max Dresden, and Lillian Hoddeson, eds. *Pions to Quarks: Particle Physics in the 1950s*. Cambridge: Cambridge University Press, 1989.

Collins, George. "Scintillation Counters." *Scientific American* 189 (November 1953): 36–41.

Glasstone, Samuel. *Sourcebook on Atomic Energy*. 2nd ed. Princeton, N.J.: Van Nostrand, 1958.

Sector

A sector solves arithmetical problems by analogical procedures. It is composed of two flat arms hinged together that can be adjusted to form any angle. Each arm is engraved with scales on each of its major faces, and the scales are radial from the center of the hinge. The instrument is equivalent to two radii of a circle and the arc of the circumference that they enclose. The name of the instrument in English derives from the term that Euclid used to designate this area. Problems of proportion may be

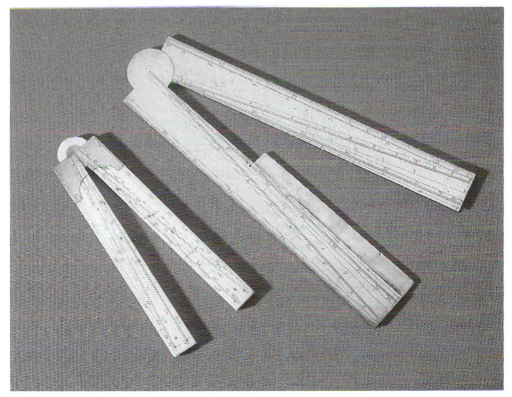

Two sectors: (left) ivory sector by Isaac or Jacob Carver, London, early eighteenth century; (right) brass sector, Gunter's pattern, early seventeenth century. SM 1917-92, 1939-49. Courtesy of SSPL.

resolved without calculation through the use of the scales and a pair of dividers. This use of the instrument is underlined by its name in other European languages—*compas de proportion* in French, *compasso di proporzioni* in Italian, *Proportionalzirkel* in German.

The sector invented by Galileo in 1598/1599 could solve all the problems of practical mathematics of his day. It originated in the context of the search, general to early modern Europe, for ways to carry out mathematical operations without calculation. Other instruments developed for this purpose, and that have a relation with the sector, include the reduction compass; the proportional compass in the various forms produced by Frederico Commandini and Simone Baroccio (1568), Jost Burgi, Latino Orsini (1582), and Milles Denorroy and Philippe Danfrie (1587/1588); the *pantomètre* of Michel Coignet, developed between 1580 and 1620; the sector of Thomas Hood (1598); and the geometrical and military compass of Galileo (1595–1597). The distinguishing feature of Galileo's sector was the incorporation of a scale known as the line of equal parts. This scale was

so important that Edmund Gunter was to name it the "line of lines" in his *de Sectore et Radio* (1623) in which he fixed the form that the general calculating sector would take in England for the next two centuries.

The line of equal parts had appeared on Thomas Hood's sector of 1598, an instrument intended primarily as an aid to land-surveying. Hood had introduced this line to help with the transfer of observed values to paper in the production of survey maps. Galileo, who had no knowledge of Hood's work, included some scales with specific purposes, such as a scale for fitting regular polygons into a circle (useful in the laying out of polygonal fortresses). However, his instrument was specifically adapted to calculation in general, and it is this universality of use that is the distinguishing mark of the sector as it came to be standardized during the late seventeenth and eighteenth centuries.

Galileo claimed to have had made and distributed some three hundred of his sectors, and he published a description of this instrument in his *Le Operazione del compasso geometrico e militare* in 1606. Because the instrument responded to a clear need it spread rapidly, and by 1620 forms of the universal sector and literature about it were available throughout Europe. The unauthorized Latin version of Galileo's work, prepared by Mathias Bernegger in 1613, was a clear and accurate version that included valuable explanations and commentaries by Bernegger himself.

During the early and middle decades of the seventeenth century there continued to be a good deal of variety both in the size of sectors made and in the scales that were marked on them. English instruments were often heavily charged with scales, with lines for operations such as the laying out of **sun-dials** being particularly popular. French sectors, on the contrary, were frequently restricted to the minimum of four scales, those of the line of lines, planes, chords, and solid figures.

Manufactured in silver, brass, ivory, or boxwood, sectors, especially the larger models, were often supplied with a cross-strut so that they could be fixed to a 45° or 90° opening. The instrument could also be mounted on a stand and fitted with sighting pinnules and, thus, made useful for surveying, navigation, and military uses. By the closing decades of the seventeenth century, small sectors were routinely included in cases of mathematical instruments. They prevailed as a kind of established ornament well into the nineteenth century, by which time the instrument had lost all practical usefulness.

Anthony Turner

Bibliography

Galilei, Galileo. *Galileo Galilei, Operations of the Geometric and Military Compass* [1606]. Edited and translated by Stillman Drake. Washington, D.C.: Smithsonian Institution Press, 1978.

Garvan, Anthony N.B. "Slide Rule and Sector, a Study in Science, Technology and Society." *Actes du Xe congrès internationale d'histoire des sciences*, August 26, 1962–September 2, 1962, pp. 397–400. Paris: Hermann, 1964.

Heather, J.F. *Mathematical Instruments, Their Construction, Adjustment and Use*, 42–52. Enl. ed. London: Crosby, Lockwood, 1880.

Rasquin, Victor A. "Les règles à calcul anciennes et leur utilisation en navigation, les compas de proportion, les règles de Gunter." *Académie Royale de Marine de Belgique, A.S.B.I. Communications* 28 (1986–1988): 53–87.

Schneider, Ivo. *Der Proportionalzirkel, ein universelles Analogrecheninstrument der Vergangenheit*. Munich: R. Oldenberg, 1970.

Seismograph

A seismograph records the displacement of the ground, its velocity or its acceleration, at a particular point on the earth's surface. It consists of a sensor, usually a mass hanging from a spring, and a recorder, which can be either direct or remote. The sensor breaks the seismic signal up into three orthogonal components, two horizontal and one vertical. Modern seismic instruments can amplify the ground motion some million times, and **computers** are used as active elements between the sensor and recorder.

Instruments with short oscillation periods can detect earthquakes located within some hundred kilometers of the instrument, while long-period instruments are more suitable for recording earthquakes located up to some thousand kilometers away. The latest instruments have broadband sensors that are sensitive to a wide range of seismic frequencies and amplitudes and that are suitable for a wide range of applications at the global and regional level.

In China in A.D. 132, Chang Hêng invented a seismic instrument that indicated the direction but not the magnitude of seismic movements. Over a thousand years later, seismic instruments were used in Maraghah (Iran). Jean De Haute-Feuille's mercury seismoscope of 1703 was a vessel with broad edges below which eight deep cavities were connected by means of channels to a central container full of mercury. When an earthquake occurred, the mercury passed into one of the lower containers in greater or lesser quantities depending on the intensity and duration of the shock, while the direction of the movement was shown by the position of the container in which the mercury was found. This design was revised by Niccolò Cacciatore, and his models of 1818 and 1827 still survive.

Several seismic instruments were designed and used in Italy in the eighteenth century. Following the strong earthquake of March 20, 1731, for instance, the Neapolitan naturalist Nicola Cirillo observed, with two pendular instruments writing on sand, the effects of the aftershocks at different distances from the major effects area. Further instrument develop-

Gray-Milne seismograph, by J. White, Glasgow, 1885. SM 1885-115. Courtesy of SSPL.

ment followed in Europe, and particularly in Italy, in the nineteenth century. Much of this, however, was fairly independent of the theoretical models of earthquakes.

The construction of the first true seismograph and the birth of seismology as a discipline were nearly contemporaneous. Luigi Palmieri made his first electromagnetic seismograph in 1856, and after the earthquake of December 16, 1857, the Irish engineer Robert Mallet outlined the first theoretical framework of the science of earthquakes, which he named seismology.

Palmieri's instrument, designed to examine Vesuvius's seismic activity, was a particularly sensitive synthesis of previous devices, including James D. Forbes's reverse pendulum of 1844. The oscillation of mercury inside pipes or the pouring of it from containers, and the oscillation of springs or **pendulums**, were recorded on a telegraph paper ribbon through an electromagnetic system. Owing to its complexity and high manufacturing cost, only four models were made; three remained in Naples, and one was ordered by the Japanese government in 1874.

Most early seismic instruments were actually seismoscopes—that is, instruments that showed the effects of earthquakes but at best were capable of recording them on sand or blackened glass. The first instrument that left a graphic representation of the earth's movement dates from 1875. It was designed by Filippo Cecchi of the Ximeniano Observatory of Florence. This was the electric seismograph with moving smoked paper. In the 1880s, seismographs were constructed in Italy, Japan, and Germany, and the instrumental approach to the study of earthquakes began in earnest. Seismologists began to pay attention not only to the characteristics of their instruments, but also to their territorial spread and to their organization into survey networks. An international network of standard instruments was introduced at the turn of the century.

The free period of a simple pendulum must be longer than the principal periods of the seismic signal if it is to reproduce ground motion accurately. This condition is more easily achieved in a horizontal-component seismometer than in a vertical one. In 1880 Ewing made the first horizontal pendulum that could detect earthquakes, and also a three-component seismograph. At the turn of the twentieth century, John Milne promoted the creation of the first worldwide network made up of his standard seismograph.

Experimentation with detecting equipment led to an appreciation of the importance of the sensor's proper oscillation period and the damping in characterizing its function. In the early twentieth century, Emil Wiechert in Göttingen and Boris B. Galitzin in Pulkovo introduced a viscous damping system in the instruments they designed, as well as astatization. Wiechert first used an air damping system, then he used an oil one, while Galitzin preferred electromagnetic damping. While astatization guaranteed natural periods long enough to detect ground motions,

the damping provided a more reliable recording of them. Increasingly sensitive instruments were made, with an amplification that had been unimaginable until that time (1,000 to 2,000 times), using large masses (up to 22 tons) in the mechanical recording systems or galvanometric recording systems on photographic paper.

Finally, the meeting of two cultures—the European culture of the fugitives from Nazi Germany and the Californian culture of the twenties—led to the development of two important seismographs: the Wood-Anderson horizontal instrument and the Benioff vertical one.

Seismographs having different characteristics are used for the localization of seismic events, from imperceptible to destructive earthquakes, for the study of seismic sources (seismogenesis), for civil defense (seismic hazard, earthquake prediction), and for geophysics studies (seismic tomography). In 1935 Hugo Benioff introduced the strainmeter, to record variations in the distance between two points of the earth's surface. Tiltmeters measure the slow angular displacement of the ground extending over considerable periods of time. The last twenty years have seen the development of ocean bottom seismometers (OBS). The **accelerometer** is used by engineers to measure the seismic acceleration of the ground during destructive earthquakes; this yields useful information for aseismic building design.

Graziano Ferrari

Bibliography

Bullen, K.E., and Bruce A. Bolt. *An Introduction to the Theory of Seismology.* 4th ed. Cambridge: Cambridge University Press, 1985.

Dewey, James W., and Perry Byerly. "The Early History of Seismometry (to 1900)." *Bulletin of the Seismological Society of America* 59 (1969): 183–277.

Ferrari, Graziano. "Seismic Instruments." In *Sciences of the Earth: An Encyclopedia of Events, People and Phenomena,* edited by Gregory A. Good. New York: Garland, 1977.

———. *Two Hundred Years of Seismic Instruments in Italy, 1731–1940.* ING-SGA Bologna: Storia Geofisica Ambiente, 1992.

Sextant

Since the term "sextant" refers to an arc of 60°, several large astronomical instruments used by

Sextant by Troughton, with double-frame design, ca. 1790. Courtesy of the Whipple Museum of the History of Science, Cambridge.

Tycho Brahe, Joahnnes Hevelius, and John Flamsteed were known as sextants. However, the more common reference is to a portable instrument that measures angles between distant objects working on the reflecting principle used in the **octant** and reflecting circle. These sextants were designed for navigation, but were also used for astronomy, surveying, and hydrography. They have an arc of 60°, measuring to 120°, and,

like octants, an index mirror and a half-silvered horizon glass. They almost always have a telescopic sight, and their frame is almost always made of metal.

While a sextant resembles an octant, it actually evolved from a reflecting circle. Tobias Mayer's design of this instrument was submitted to the British Board of Longitude and tested in the late 1750s by Captain John Campbell, using an instrument made by John Bird. Campbell was attracted by the idea, but found the full circle unnecessarily cumbersome. He therefore arranged for Bird to apply the design to a 60° arc, which he judged would be adequate for the lunar distance measurements required for finding longitude.

The first sextants were large and heavy, requiring a pole supported in a belt to keep them in place while in use, but the development of **dividing engines** for setting out the scales mechanically made the same level of accuracy possible on a much smaller instrument. A clamp and tangent screw became standard for the final adjustment of the vernier index.

There was much experimentation in the late eighteenth and early nineteenth centuries to design a frame that would be rigid but light. Ramsden used a lattice structure of brass struts between the arms and limb; another of his designs was the bridge type, in which an open brass framework on the upper half of the sextant served both to improve its rigidity and to protect the optics. Edward Troughton adopted the double-frame design, in which two thin T-braced frames in brass plate were connected by a series of turned brass pillars. This design survived through the nineteenth century as one of the more expensive models.

A variety of lattice designs appeared in the nineteenth century; in one popular type, the central area was filled by three circles of brass. By this time, oxidized rather than lacquered brass was used for the frame, while an inlaid silver scale was usually set in the limb. The scale would typically be divided to 10 minutes of arc and could be read by the vernier to 10 seconds. Both the index and the horizon glasses would be provided with sets of shades, mounted on pivots on the frame, and there would be a variety of alternative telescopic sights, with their own screw-fit filters. Often a dark tube, with no optics, was also supplied. There were attempts to introduce lighter alloys, as well as aluminum, in the twentieth century, when the vernier scale was replaced by the graduated drumhead of a **micrometer** screw.

Sextants were also used for astronomical measurements, mostly in temporary observatories or on expeditions, and altitude measurements on land would need an accompanying **artificial horizon**. The artifical horizon would be a flat reflecting surface—a trough of mercury or a leveled mirror—and the observer would measure the angle between the body and its reflection, half of which would be the required altitude.

Surveying sextants, used for taking bearings, had no shades, as there is no intention of sighting the sun. A special instance of the surveying sextant is the sounding sextant, used to locate the position of a boat when the sea depth is being measured in an offshore hydrographic survey. In this case the telescope will have a larger field of view, to help identify landmarks on the shore, and again there is no need of shades.

Jim A. Bennett

Bibliography

Bennett, J.A. *The Divided Circle: A History of Instruments for Astronomy, Navigation and Surveying.* Oxford: Phaidon, 1987.

Cotter, C.H. *A History of the Navigator's Sextant.* Glasgow: Brown, 1983.

Sextant, Aircraft

Two features distinguish the sextants used for aircraft navigation from those used on board ship. First, the critical measurement to find position, whether at sea or in the air, is the angle between the true horizontal and the line of sight to a celestial body. From the deck of a ship, a small correction accounts for the fact that the natural horizon appears slightly below the true horizonal. From a high-flying aircraft, the angle from the true horizontal to the natural horizon can be very large, and when the aircraft is flying above the clouds, the horizon can not be seen at all. The solution was to fix sextants with an **artificial horizon** to establish a true horizontal line of reference. Balloonists of the late nineteenth century used marine sextants fitted with a spirit level to indicate when the sextant line of sight was horizontal.

Artificial horizons based on **pendulums** and **gyroscopes**, which were popular for seagoing navigation, were tried repeatedly for aircraft sextants in the early twentieth century, but never succeeded because their orientation changed with accelerations of the aircraft. The U.S. Army Air Corps's first designated sextant, A-1, was a gyrosextant developed in 1922; a Sperry Gyroscope Co. candidate appeared in 1933; an electrically driven gyro octant by Pioneer Instrument Co. was tried in 1939. The fact that **gyroscopes** respond to accelerations made them the heart of the **inertial guidance** systems developed in the 1950s that quickly made sextants obsolete for aircraft navigation.

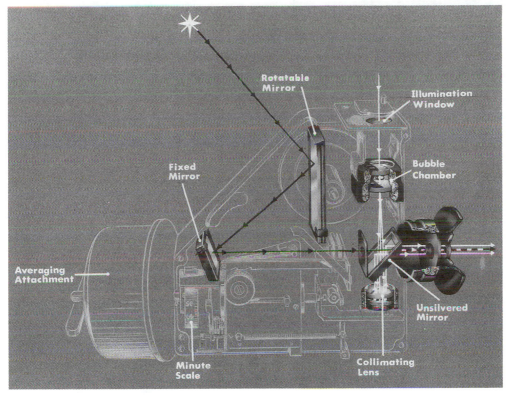

Schematic diagram of a bubble sextant. Courtesy of SSPL.

The second feature unique to aircraft sextants arises from the fact that it is difficult to make an accurate observation in the cramped quarters of a fast-moving aircraft. The solution here was to average several observations taken over a short period of time. The early aircraft navigators did this manually, but virtually all aircraft sextants after the mid 1930s had mechanical means of averaging several shots without having to take the sextant down to record each sight.

Early averagers required the navigator to hold the sextant steady on the celestial body for two minutes. An improvement permitted the observer to record the sight whenever it was properly aligned. The most sophisticated system, first used on the Plath SOLD sextants, continuously integrated the sights over a preselected period of 40, 120, or 200 seconds.

Early aircraft navigators took their sights from an open cockpit, and spoke of the wind rushing by and almost tearing the sextant from their hands. To address this problem, Thomas Yeomans Baker of the Royal Navy invented a periscope sextant in 1919. This had a prism for an index mirror and two special horizon mirrors—one for observing the horizon directly below the celestial body and one for simultaneously observing the horizon behind the observer.

Richard Evelyn Byrd of the U.S. Navy designed the sextant used by the navigators of the historic transatlantic flights of the Navy's NC seaplanes in May 1919. The Byrd sextant was held in the left hand, leaving the right hand free to record the observation without having to put the sextant down. And it provided a spirit level artificial horizon; this was basically a mirror placed beyond the horizon mirror reflecting the image of the bubble into the line of sight.

In 1919, Admiral Gago Coutinho of the Portuguese Navy described a spirit level artificial horizon built into the frame of a conventional sextant, and he called his instrument a precision astrolabe. He later added a second spirit level to indicate when the sextant was held vertically. Coutinho did not patent his ideas and the design was picked up and produced for many years by Hughes of London and C. Plath of Hamburg.

A major advancement in aircraft sextant design was the invention of a new form of bubble artificial horizon in 1919 by Lionel Burton

Booth and William Sidney Smith, superintendent of the Royal Aeronautical Establishment at Farnborough. Here a bubble floats in a liquid contained in a chamber with a domed top. When the chamber is held vertically, the bubble floats to the center of the dome and forms a vertical line of reference. The bubble was originally placed in the line of sight, but the fluid in the chamber tended to obscure the sight of faint stars. A better design, patented in 1925 by Robert Wheeler Willson of Harvard University, placed the bubble chamber outside the line of sight and used mirrors to project the image into the line of sight.

A bubble artificial horizon appeared on the R.A.E. Mark I sextant of 1919. The MK II of 1920 featured a device for adjusting the size of the bubble. Other modifications appeared in the MK V of 1925 and the MK VI of 1926. By this time the frame of the sextant had been completely redesigned to accommodate the bubble chamber and a simple averaging device. A small electric light to illuminate the bubble for night observations soon became standard.

The German Plath SOLD bubble sextant, used extensively by the Luftwaffe in World War II, was similar to the British MK VIII of 1935. The Royal Air Force MK IX, designed by P.F. Everest, was widely used by the Allied air forces from the early years of World War II to as late as the 1960s. These could average sixty sights over a 1- or 2-minute interval.

In the United States, early aircraft instrument development was largely in the hands of the National Bureau of Standards. Their first success was the BUSTD MODA, designed in 1925 by I. Beige and manufactured by Bausch & Lomb. Modifications quickly followed. The BUSTD series of instruments used the same reflecting index glass plate optical system found in the British Hughes series of sextants.

Hughes provided most of the sextants for the British and Canadian air forces. Plath supplied Germany, Tamaya produced for Japan, and a host of suppliers in the United States joined the war effort: Pioneer (whose Victor E. Carbonara had patented a compact bubble sextant with prism optics in 1931), Bausch & Lomb, Link Aviation, Fairchild, and Agfa-Ansco.

When aircraft cabins became pressurized, navigators could no longer lean out of the cockpit to take a star sight. Sighting through the window was awkward, and visibility of the stars was sharply limited. Clear hemispherical astrodomes 18 to 24 in. in diameter soon were added on the top of the aircraft, providing an unobstructed 360° view of the heavens. As aircraft flew faster, astrodomes caused unacceptable aerodynamic drag; periscope sextants that protruded only 4 or 5 in. through the aircraft skin were developed to solve this problem.

Just as the advent of inertial guidance systems marked the demise of handheld sextants for aircraft navigation, so the use of the **Global Positioning System** (GPS) will replace inertial systems.

Peter Ifland
Jeremy P. Collins

Bibliography
Beij, Karl Hilding. *Astronomical Methods in Air Navigation.* Washington, D.C.: Government Printing Office, 1925.
Booth, Lionel Barton. "The Aerial Sextants Designed by the Royal Aircraft Establishment." In *Proceedings of the Optical Convention 1926*, Vol. 2, 720–28. London: Optical Convention, 1926.
Hughes, Arthur J. *History of Navigation.* London: Allen and Unwin, 1946.
Rogers, Francis M. *Precision Astrolabe.* Lisbon: Academia Internacional da Cultura Portuguesesa, 1971.
Weems, P.V.H. *Air Navigation.* New York: McGraw-Hill, 1931.

Skid Resistance Testing Instruments

Skid resistance is the frictional force between a vehicle tire and the pavement surface available to oppose skidding. The measurement of the skid-resisting properties of the pavement surfaces of highways, airport runways, and the materials used in their construction is required in the specification of new works, and in the maintenance of quality of existing facilities.

The slipperiness of highway surfaces, which had traditionally been considered only in relation to the foothold available to horses, became a problem with the introduction of automobiles. In the U.K., Parliament set up a select committee to investigate the causes and control of skidding in 1906. Scientific investigation began in 1911 when the National Physical Laboratory established that skid resistance depended on the vehicle speed and weather conditions. Highway conditions were found to be most dangerous immediately after a dry surface had been made wet; conditions improved slightly after prolonged rain. A program for

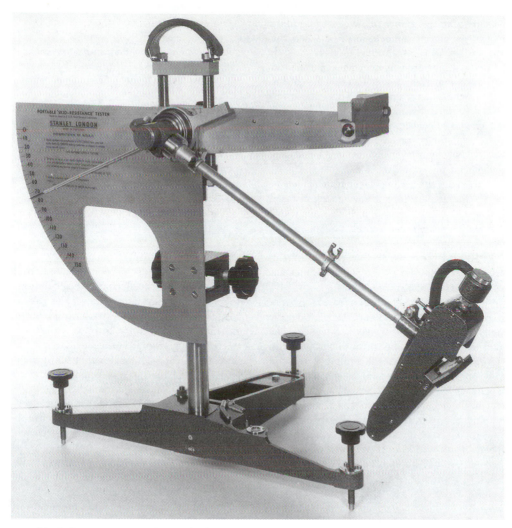

Portable skid resistance tester, by Stanley, 1970s. Courtesy of the Transport Research Laboratory.

systematic standardized testing was undertaken on surfaces that had been artificially watered by sprinklers. The distinct concepts of braking force coefficient (BFC) and sideway force coefficient (SFC) were introduced in 1927.

BFC is a measure of the resistance of a wheel to forward sliding on the pavement surface—in other words, to the condition when brakes are applied to a wheel having forward motion only. The BFC is expressed as the ratio of the horizontal force in the plane of the wheel to the load on the wheel when it is on the point of skidding. This is usually undertaken by an instrumented trailer that can be towed at speeds as high as 160 km/h on airport runways and 130 km/h on highways. A typical BFC test sequence results in the trailer wheel(s) being locked for about 2 seconds

and the associated brake torque being measured. The instruments became less expensive and more consistent with the introduction of load-cells in the 1950s. Recording systems also developed from the direct reading and noting of gauges to punched paper tape, light sensitive traces, and latterly magnetic tape. Early BFC trailers were of light construction, sometimes with only a single wheel, towed by an automobile on the pre-sprayed test surface. In the 1980s a larger two-wheeled trailer was developed with one braking wheel (the other wheel continues to rotate), load-cells in its axle, and its own spray-head to wet the path immediately in advance of the test wheel. The heavier trailer is towed by a powerful pickup truck that carries a water tank to serve the spray-head.

The sideway force coefficient (SFC) is a measure of the resistance of a wheel to skidding on the pavement surface, applied when the wheel is free to rotate but has sideways as well as forward motion. It is expressed as the ratio of the force at right angles to the plane of the wheel to the load on the wheel. This test evolved from a 1930s test with a motorcycle and a sidecar. The latter's wheel was able to be set at 20° to the direction of travel. This was developed in the 1950s as a fifth wheel mounted centrally beneath a front-wheel drive car.

To avoid the need for a separate vehicle to wet the highway surface before a medium speed SFC test, a truck carrying a 3,000-liter water tank with a test wheel assembly and measuring and recording equipment was specified by the U.K. Road Research Laboratory and built in Bristol in 1968. It is called a SCRIM (Sideway-force Coefficient Routine Investigation Machine) vehicle. The vehicle can travel at speeds up to 80 km/h on trafficked roads and water the highway surface immediately in advance of its own test wheel for a continuous 50-km run before the water tank needs refilling. To extend this range, larger water tanks are now often specified.

In the 1930s decelerometers were used to investigate tire tread patterns in tests in which all four tires of an automobile traveling at speeds of up to 50 km/h were locked for a 1-second period. Although unsuitable for use on bends or trafficked roads, this test continued to be used in the 1950s for skid-resistance experiments.

A simple surrogate is the portable skid-resistance tester, developed in 1960 by the U.K. Road Research Laboratory from a U.S. National Bureau of Standards test for the slipperiness of flooring. A pad of tire-tread natural rubber is mounted on the end of a pendulum arm. The arm is allowed to swing from a standard height over a standard length of highway surface. The skid resistance is assessed by the loss in energy of the pendulum arm. This has proved to be useful for investigations of low-speed skidding, particularly after traffic accidents.

Robert C. McWilliam

Bibliography
Bransford, T.L., ed. *Highway Skid Resistance.* Philadelphia: American Society for Testing and Materials, 1969.
Croney, David. *The Design and Performance of Road Pavements.* London: Her Majesty's Stationery Office, 1977.
Giles, C.G., Barbara E. Sabey, and K.H.F. Cardew. *Development and Performance of the Portable Skid-Resistance Tester.* London: Her Majesty's Stationery Office, 1964.
Hosking, Roger. *Road Aggregates and Skidding.* London: Her Majesty's Stationery Office, 1992.
Salt, George Frederic. *Research on Skid-Resistance at the Transport and Road Research Laboratory (1927–1977).* Washington, D.C.: Transportation Research Board, National Research Council, 1977.

Slide Rule

A slide rule permits the speedy instrumental performance of relatively complex calculations with minimal written intervention and to a reasonable degree of accuracy. Computation is performed by the manipulation of calibrated scales following standard procedures that could be learned by rote. The scales are usually logarithmic, and calculation was usually performed by sliding one scale across another. The slide rule was invented in England in the early seventeenth century. It became an indispensable tool for a wide range of practitioners in science, engineering, and commerce, and was forced into obsolescence only by the widespread availability of the pocket electronic calculator in the 1970s (see **calculating machine**).

John Napier published his invention of logarithms in 1614, and by 1623 Edmund Gunter had suggested that logarithms, in the form reformulated by Henry Briggs, be applied to practical computations in navigation by laying them out on the limbs of a **sector**, or on the transom of a **cross-staff**, with instrumental solutions achieved through the manipulation of a pair of dividers. The mathematician and Anglican divine William Oughtred was the effective inventor of the slide rule. However, his insistence that comprehension of theoretical principles precede practical application, and in particular that instrumental solutions taught to the uninitiated would produce not scholars but "only doers of tricks, and as it were Juglers," made him reticent to publish his inventions. Oughtred's former pupil Richard Delamain had no such inhibitions and was happy to provide an artifact whereby the mathematically unskilled could attain solutions to otherwise intractible problems.

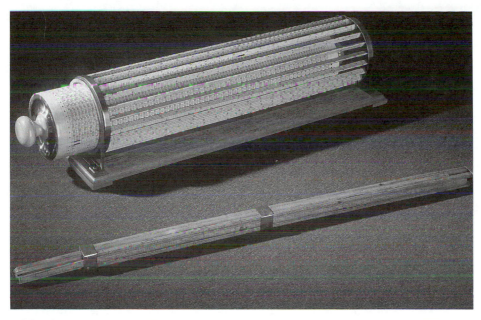

Two slide rules: (rear) Thacher's cylindrical slide rule, by Keuffel & Esser, New York, 1884; (front) linear rule by Robert Bissaker, London, 1654. SM 1898-30, 1914-579. Courtesy of SSPL.

Delamain's 1631 account of the circular slide rule stung Oughtred into publishing an account of circular and linear slide rules. It is symptomatic of Oughtred's disdain of the practical that he was content for the definitive form, the "Circles of Proportion," to be left to the London mathematical instrument-maker Elias Allen. In this instrument, logarithmic scales of numbers, sines, and tangents were laid out in a series of circles. The sliding function was performed by a pair of stiffly-hinged radial arms. Oughtred also designed linear rules with scales selected for computation in navigation and in ullaging—that is, computing the partial contents of a cask of alcoholic liquor (see, **gauge, level**). Thomas Brown expanded the scale of numbers by setting it out on a spiral line.

Oughtred's linear slide rule was two rulers with similar logarithmic scales set out on adjacent faces. This design remained in use into the early eighteenth century for particular trade purposes, notably as the glazier's rule. The conventional slide rule with scales set out on a central stock, and others on runners set in groves in the stock, appeared in the mid seventeenth century. Seth Partridge's 1662 publication gives the earliest account but does not claim to have originated the design. The features described by Partridge, with other scales, appear on a London-made rule dated 1654, preserved in the Science Museum, London.

Most seventeenth- and eighteenth-century English slide rules were designed for specific trades and professions, those for the carpenter, gauger, glazier, and navigator being the most numerous. John Robertson's sliding rule for navigators (1778) had a brass cursor and a slow-motion screw to improve the read-out accuracy. About this time the engineer James Watt developed a simple instrument with single, double, and triple radius logarithmic scales of numbers that would provide rapid solutions to engineering problems. With the "Soho" rule, mathematically competent employees of Boulton & Watt could undertake computations with squares, square roots, cubes, and cube roots. By contrast, earlier claims for universal slide rules achieved the desiderata through the inclusion of a multiplicity of scales. By the late nineteenth century there were designs for uses as particular as stock control for publicans, carcass weights for butchers, directing fire for gunners, developing time for photographic printing, or scaling grades for schoolteachers.

Other than for specific trade use, the slide rule is little mentioned in eighteenth century literature. Outside Britain, the instrument does not seem to have been widely used even in trade. In the nineteenth century the situation changed; while specific rules continued to be designed for particular needs, general rules were designed and used for speedy and approximate mathematical calculation. In 1815, P.M. Roget, who compiled the first English-language thesaurus, or dictionary of synonyms, published an account of a "logometric" scale—that is, of logarithms of logarithms. Roget suggested that this scale would be useful in computations associated with population growth and chance. The general usefulness of the log log scale was appreciated later in the century for computations in, for example, thermodynamics. The basic design and layout of the linear slide rule, familiar for over a century to generations of practitioners in science and engineering, followed that published in 1851 and 1853 by the French military engineer Amédée Mannheim. Made by Gravet-Lenoir in Paris, the Mannheim rule soon became the norm; in the last decades of the nineteenth century, German and American manufacturers pioneered the production of easily read scales on white celluloid.

While small size and ease of use for the nonmathematician were seen as advantages in the specific rule, the fact that solutions were only approximate was a weakness for some arithmeticians. A few early-nineteenth-century makers, notably Lenoir in Paris, were known for the accuracy with which they made logarithmic slide rules, but many designers sought increased precision by expanding the scale. The grid slide rules of Joseph Everett (1866), and John C. Hannyngton (1884), the spiral rule laid out on a cylinder by George Fuller (1878), and the linear scales set longitudinally on a cylinder by Edwin Thacher (1881) claimed an accuracy of the same order as four- or five-figure tables of logarithms.

D. J. Bryden

Bibliography

Bryden, D.J. "A Patchery and Confusion of Disjointed Stuffe: Richard Delamain's *Grammelogia* of 1631/3." *Transactions of the Cambridge Bibliographical Society* 6 (1974): 158–66.

Cajori, Florian. *A History of the Logarithmic Slide Rule and Allied Instruments.* New York: Engineering News, 1909.

———. "On the History of the Gunter's Scale and the Slide Rule during the 17th Century." *University of California Publications in Mathematics* 1 (1912–1920): 187–209.

Delehar, P. "Notes on Slide Rules." *Bulletin of the Scientific Instrument Society* 3 (1984): 3–10.

Williams, W.D. "Some Early Chemical Slide Rules." *Bulletin of the History of Chemistry* 12 (1992): 24–29.

Solar-Neutrino Detector

A solar-neutrino detector measures the fluxes of neutrinos that come from the sun and that form an ideal probe of the solar interior. All other forms of solar radiation provide evidence only of processes that occurred millions of years earlier in the center of the sun. Solar neutrinos, on the other hand, arrive at earth 8 minutes after they are produced in the core of the sun. Because neutrinos interact so little with matter, they travel straight through the sun. For this reason, however, solar neutrinos are enormously difficult to detect.

The detectors are massive, often comprising several hundred tons of target material, and they must be located either in deep mines or under mountains to provide rock shielding from cosmic rays. Such detectors are very expensive. The first detector, built by Raymond Davis at the Brookhaven National Laboratory in 1964, cost $600,000. Later (gallium) experiments funded in the 1980s cost many millions of dollars and required large international collaborations. Solar neutrino science today is very much "big science."

The predominant chain of nuclear reactions in the sun—the pp-chain—produces neutrinos of different energies. The highest energy neutrinos are produced from the decay of B^8 and these are the easiest to detect. Neutrinos are also produced from the fundamental $p + p$ reaction, from the $p + e^- + p$ reaction, and the decay of Be^7. The pioneering radio-chemical detection experiments of Davis searched primarily for B^8 neutrinos. Davis's experiment consisted of a large tank of perchloroethylene, C_2Cl_4, placed in a deep mine in South Dakota. The reaction Davis looks for is the neutrino capture of Cl^{37} to form the radioactive isotope, Ar^{37}. By adding an argon carrier and sweeping the tank every month with helium, Davis is able to extract the accumulated Ar^{37}, which can then be detected from its characteristic radioactive decay. The technical difficulties are enormous. Davis is literally looking for a few atoms of Ar^{37} in a tank containing billions upon billions of atoms.

Davis's results, first reported in 1967, have caused puzzlement because he has persistently detected fewer neutrinos (about one-third) than

Raymond Davis's solar-neutrino detector in Homestake Gold Mine, South Dakota. Courtesy of Brookhaven National Laboratory.

expected from the standard solar model. The "solar-neutrino puzzle" was born from this clash between experimental results and standard solar theory. Many, many solutions have been proposed to the discrepancy, including radical ideas that neutrinos have a nonzero mass. Davis's experimental procedures have come under close examination, and he has carried out a variety of calibration tests. Over the years he has in general satisfied his critics, and most scientists do not think the puzzle arises from a fault in his experimental methods.

The first replication of Davis's result came in 1988 from a group of Japanese physicists operating the Kamiokande II Detector in the Kamioka metal mine in Japan. It is a Čerenkov detector, which uses 2,140 tons of water. By measuring the energy and track direction of the recoil electrons, it is possible to obtain information on the neutrino arrival time, direction, and energy spectrum. The Japanese group was able to confirm Davis's low result and also show that the origin of the B^8 neutrinos is solar.

Because the B^8 neutrinos are very sensitive to temperature variations and hence the details of the solar model, a more direct confirmation of nuclear processes in the sun would come from the detection of the low-energy neutrinos produced by the fundamental $p + p$ reaction. Two radiochemical detectors have been built that are sensitive to these neutrinos. Both use the reaction $Ga^{71} + v = Ge^{71} + e^-$.

The GALLEX project is an international collaboration based at the Max-Planck-Institut in Heidelberg. The detector (Gran Sasso Underground Laboratory, Italy) consists of 30 tons of gallium in the form of a concentrated aqueous chloride solution. The Ge^{71} is extracted by nitrogen purging and detected in proportional counters.

The SAGE project is a Russian-American collaboration that uses a 60-ton target of pure molten gallium (underground in the Northern Caucasus). A germanium carrier is added and the accumulated Ge^{71} extracted by chemical means. The amount of Ge^{71} present can again be determined by its characteristic radioactive decay.

The results of both gallium experiments are lower than expected and not entirely consistent. One favored interpretation is that these results show the presence of the "must see" pp flux and a low B^8 flux and the absence of the Be^7 flux. Since the B^8 flux is directly dependent upon the earlier formation of Be^7 in the sun, it is today argued that the solar-neutrino puzzle has become even more serious. Nonzero rest mass neutrinos could solve the dilemma, and a variety of new forms of detector have been proposed to investigate this possibility.

Trevor Pinch

Bibliography

Bahcall, John. *Neutrino Astrophysics*. Cambridge: Cambridge University Press, 1989.
Pinch, Trevor. *Confronting Nature: The Sociology of Solar Neutrino Detection*. Dordrecht: Kluwer, 1986.
Raghavan, Roger. "Solar Neutrinos—From Puzzle to Paradox." *Science* 267 (1995): 45–51.

Solid-State Gas Sensors

The technology for detecting gases has developed in parallel with the progressive industrialization of society during the twentieth century. The need for gas detection and monitoring has emerged as organic fuels and other chemicals have become an essential part of domestic and industrial life, and as the awareness of the need to protect the environment has grown.

There are three types of gas sensors. Oxygen sensors are used in connection with the protection of breathable atmospheres and to control combustion processes (boilers and internal-combustion engines). Oxygen concentrations must be monitored in the region of 20 percent and 0–5 percent respectively in the two applications. Flammable gas sensors are used to protect against the unwanted occurrence of fire or explosion. In this case concentrations to be measured are in the range up to the lower explosive limit, which, for most gases, is up to a few percent in air. Toxic gas sensors monitor concentrations around the exposure limit, which in most cases is a few parts per million in air.

Most of the well-established sensors are solid-state devices that combine rugged construction with sufficiently low purchase cost to make possible widespread deployment. There are three major types.

Solid Electrolyte Sensors

The use of electrical measurements of solids to provide information about atmospheric composition began with the pioneering work of W. Nernst on solid electrolytes around the turn of the century. His discovery that defect structure oxides such as stabilized zirconium exhibit a significant ionic conductivity at temperatures below 1,000°C while remaining electronically insulating paved the way for the production of an electrochemical cell that forms the basis of the oxygen sensors that are used in today's automobile exhaust systems. The potential difference between electrodes on opposite sides of a stabilized zirconia ceramic membrane, often in the form of a closed end tube, provides a measure of the ratio of the respective oxygen partial pressures.

Catalytic Sensors

Potentially explosive mixtures of a flammable gas such as methane can be monitored by means of a catalytically active solid-state sensor developed in 1959 by A. Baker at the Health and Safety Executive laboratories in Sheffield (U.K. patent no. 892,530). The device, often referred to as the "pellistor," is essentially a catalytic microcalorimeter. It consists of a catalytic surface constructed around a temperature sensor, and a heater that maintains the catalyst at a sufficiently high temperature to ensure rapid combustion of any flammable gas molecules present. The heating and temperature measurement functions are usually combined: a platinum coil is embedded in a refractory bead of aluminum that is maintained at 500°C by a current through the wire. The sensor detects gas concentrations by monitoring changes in the resistance of the wire resulting from temperature increases produced by combustion.

The response of the catalytic sensor is not selective but depends on the product of the concentration of a flammable gas and its heat of combustion. The sensor thus offers a different response to different gases at a single concentration, expressed on a volume percent basis, but gives a universal measure of all flammable gases expressed as a percentage of the lower explosive limit. This measure of the "explosiveness" of an atmosphere is often more important than the identification of the individual components of the atmosphere.

Semiconducting Oxide Gas Sensors

This is a gas-sensitive resistor in which a sensing element, usually a semiconducting oxide presenting a high surface to bulk ratio, is deployed on a heated insulating substrate between two metallic electrodes. Reactions involving gas molecules can take place at the oxide surface to change the density of charge carriers available in the oxide. Hence the conductance of the device changes progressively with changing atmospheric composition. Semiconductor gas sensors were first commercialized in Japan (see N. Taguchi's 1970 U.K. patent no. 1,280,809) but, using tin oxide as the sole sensitive component, were limited in application by a characteristic lack of specificity between gases. A range of more specifically reacting materials is now being used, and oxygen, flammable gases, and toxic gases can be monitored. This is the fastest-growing type of gas sensor at the present time.

Patrick T. Moseley

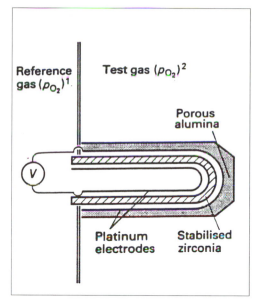

An oxygen probe based on the Nernst principle. Courtesy of Patrick T. Moseley.

Bibliography

Moseley, P.T., and B.C. Tofield, eds. *Solid-State Gas Sensors*. Bristol: Adam Hilger, 1987.

Moseley, P.T., J.O.W. Norris, and D.E. Williams, eds. *Techniques and Mechanisms in Gas Sensing*. Bristol: Adam Hilger, 1991.

Sonar

Sonar (SOund Navigation And Ranging) is an ultrasonic technique for detecting and determining the position of underwater objects. It was begun in World War I as a desperate attempt to contain the U-boat menace. Unlike **radar**, sonar has never caught the public's imagination.

The Royal Navy had paid scant attention to submarines, and when war broke out, radical organizational and technical methods were needed to detect and destroy this new threat. No avenues were left unexplored, including such novel methods as using sea lions as underwater ears and training seagulls to recognize periscopes, but to no avail. The most promising approach turned out to be detection by underwater sound, since electromagnetic waves attenuate too rapidly in the sea. By the end of the war, hydrophones, or underwater microphones, based on contemporary telephone technology, were being used extensively but had been responsible for only four "kills."

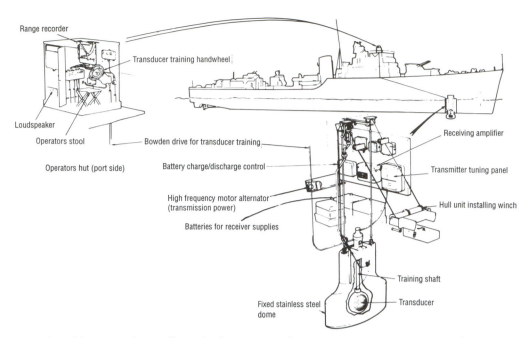

Range recorder

Transducer training handwheel

Loudspeaker

Operators stool

Bowden drive for transducer training

Operators hut (port side)

Battery charge/discharge control

High frequency motor alternator
(transmission power)

Batteries for receiver supplies

Receiving amplifier

Transmitter tuning panel

Hull unit installing winch

Training shaft

Fixed stainless steel
dome

Transducer

Typical World War II asdic installation for destroyers. Hackmann (1984): xxviii, Figure 1. British Crown Copyright © 1984. Reproduced with the permission of the Controller of Her Majesty's Stationery Office.

Of greater importance for future submarine warfare was the work begun in France by Paul Langevin and the Russian electrical engineer Constantin Chilowsky in 1915 on ultrasonic echo-ranging, in which high-frequency sound waves were reflected off submarines. Similar work was undertaken by civilian scientists in the Royal Navy led by the Canadian physicist R.W. Boyle. If World War I had continued for a few more months, this device would have become operational. In late 1918, prototype equipment detected submarines at ranges of over 400 yards. During World War II, the average range was only 1,300 yards.

In England, this system became known as "asdics." The term appeared in July 1918 and was made famous by the fiercely fought Battle of the Atlantic in World War II. According to the *Oxford English Dictionary,* it is the acronym for the Allied Submarine DetectIon Committee, but as no such committee has been recorded at that time, it is more likely that it stood for the Admiralty department that supervised this research and coordinated the navy's response to the U-boat: Anti-Submarine Division-ICS. The modern acronym "sonar" was coined by F.V. Hunt, director of the wartime Harvard Underwater Sound Laboratory, as the phonetic analog of "radar." Hunt withdrew his first sug-

gestion "sodar" (Sound Detection and Ranging), the acoustic equivalent of "radar," because it sounded unpleasant. The term "sonar" replaced "asdics" in the Royal Navy in the early 1950s, to the chagrin of some of the older naval officers who felt that now the key British contribution to the developments of this system would be forgotten.

The backbone of echo-detection is the electroacoustic transducer, which converts an electrical signal into an acoustic signal and vice versa, and thus can be used for both transmission and reception. In the sonar transducer, the energy conversion is based on either magnetostriction (1846) or piezoelectricity (1880). The first successful transducer was the low-frequency electrodynamic oscillator that R.A. Fessenden patented in 1913. The first ultrasonic transducer was the quartz-steel sandwich of Langevin and Chilowski, which the Royal Navy adopted at the end of World War I, and which formed the basis of their asdic transducer used to such good effect in World War II. Only in the 1950s was it superseded by much more powerful sonars based on magnetostriction. Shortly after World War I, the Americans replaced quartz with synthetic Rochelle salt crystal transducers (soluble in water), and in the mid twenties with high-powered, rugged magnetostrictive transducers.

During the interwar years, influenced by the Admiralty's preoccupation with what naval strategists called defending sea-lines of communication against submarines, the Royal Navy developed an integrated sonar system for the U.K. This was basically an active sonar "searchlight" system in which a mechanically rotated transducer beamed out high-frequency sound waves and received the returning echoes. Navy scientists developed the three components of this system: the quartz transducer, the streamlined dome or casing around the transducer that allowed the antisubmarine vessel to keep up with the fleet, and the chemical range recorder that made it possible to plot and predict the submarine's course during an attack. The range recorder was based on the "fultograph" for the transmission of newspaper pictures (1929). This technology was passed on to the U.S. Navy in Reverse Lend-Lease. The German Navy, which was forbidden to rearm with submarines until 1935, developed sophisticated passive listening arrays to give their capital ships long-range warning of torpedo attacks by submarines, in order to take evasive action.

In most respects the battle against the U-boat in World War II was a repeat of the previous war's, except that the submarines and countermeasures were technologically more sophisticated. The postwar search for ever faster submarines, culminating in the first atomic submarine, the USS *Nautilus* (1954), made contemporary sonar technology virtually obsolete overnight. The departure point of the next generation of sonars was the wartime German passive hydrophone arrays, and the electronic scanning techniques developed for radar and used in the massive postwar magentostriction attack sonars. Modern sonars incorporating advanced signal-processing techniques are still an important element in the armory to contain the nuclear strategic submarine.

The military sonar technology found many civilian applications, including the ultrasonic cleaning and scanning used in medicine. Oceanography, which has always been dominated by military considerations, became especially important from the 1920s, as scientists recognized that sea conditions (temperature, salinity, hydrostatic pressure, air pressure, and especially temperature gradients or "thermoclines") affect the behavior of the underwater sound beam (its refraction, reflection, scattering, spreading, and absorption).

The echo sounder used to map the sea bed had strong affinities with the Royal Navy's chemical range recorder developed for attack sonars. Large-scale use of echo sounders for detecting fish began after World War II, and its impact on the fish industry and fish stock has been dramatic. High-resolution narrow-beam sonars, designed to detect mines on the sea bed, were used for other purposes. The first test of this new generation of sonars was to locate HM Submarine *Affray,* tragically lost with all hands in the English Channel in 1951. Another development was the high-resolution side scan sonars for large-scale exploration of the sea floor. "GLORIA" (Geological LOng-Range Inclined Asdic), built by the National Institute of Oceanography in the late 1960s, can make an acoustic shadow-graph of the topography of the sea bed to a distance of 12 miles (22 km) athwart the observing ship, to a depth of 18,000 feet (5.5 km). It is impossible to determine to what extent naval involvement in oceanography may have distorted research priorities, but, on the other hand, it is undeniable that naval involvement has been of great benefit.

Willem D. Hackmann

Bibliography

Hackmann, Willem D. *Seek and Strike: Sonar, Anti-Submarine Warfare and the Royal Navy 1915–54.* London: Her Majesty's Stationery Office, 1984.

———. "Underwater Acoustics and the Royal Navy, 1893–1930." *Annals of Science* 36 (1979): 255–78.

Sonometer

A sonometer is a simple mechanical device for investigating the behavior of vibrating strings. It consists of a resonant box and one or more strings, each of which is stretched between two pegs and free to vibrate. The box maximizes the volume of sound the device can create. A sonometer with one string is also known as a monochord. Experimenters can stop a sonometer string at any point along its length to affect the pitch of the note it produces. On some sonometers, string tension can also be altered by suspending weights from one free end.

The sonometer is one of the earliest instruments to have been used in the scientific study of sound. An account of the Pythagorean brotherhood in Greece in the sixth century B.C., written by Philolaus of Crotona about fifty years after Pythagoras' death, mentions the brotherhood's profound interest in rationalizing certain

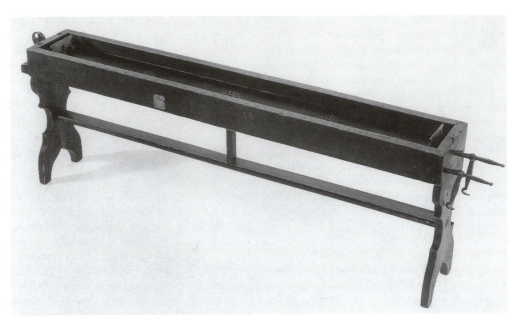

Sonometer from the collection of Stephen Demainbray, probably early eighteenth century. SM 1927-1244. Courtesy of SSPL.

acoustic phenomena and suggests that they developed the sonometer for scientific experimentation. But, as secrecy was a tenet of this sect for much of its existence, there are no primary sources that confirm this account.

The brotherhood was also deeply interested in mathematics and metaphysics based on mathematical principles, and they believed numbers to be the fundamental constituents of the world. Philolaus, who was a follower of Pythagoras, stated that "everything that can be known has a number; for it is impossible to grasp anything with the mind or to recognize it without this."

The musical consonance of the perfect fourth, fifth, and octave had been noted long before the time of Pythagoras. However, the Pythagoreans experimented with sonometers or similar devices to identify the length ratios of strings that produced them. Their work on musical consonance, often referred to as "cannonics" or "harmonics," showed that consonant intervals were produced by strings of lengths in whole-number ratios. They could extract from these ratios the numbers one, two, three, and four—the sacred tetractys that combined to produce the perfect number ten. These findings firmly established musical consonance as a fundamental element of Pythagorean cosmogony. The world, which

could be rationalized using numbers, was in harmony.

Musical thought became so central to the study of numbers that, in the fourth century B.C., Archytas of Tarentum, a pupil of Philolaus, described mathematics as a discipline composed of four related studies: astronomy, geometry, arithmetic, and music. These four related studies evolved into the quadrivium, the scientific curriculum of the medieval scholar.

In the thirteen century, the Arab musical theorist Safi al-Din experimented with vibrating strings to relate their thickness, length, and tension to pitch. His contemporary Al-Jurjani described the considerable problems Safi al-Din would have encountered with these investigations: "To date we have no means to measure the thickness or thinness of a string, nor to measure its tension or relaxation." Three centuries later, Galileo experimented with these relationships. He outlined his findings in his *Discoursi* (1638), and suggested that the pitch of a vibrating string is directly related to its frequency of vibration.

As developments in transport enabled musicians to travel more widely, the need increased for an absolute measure of frequency. Musical pitches varied widely in Europe until the end of the nineteenth century. Church organs in operation between the thirteenth and nineteenth centuries had A tuned to any pitch from 275 to 500 Hz.

In 1636, the Franciscan Marin Mersenne made an admirable attempt to find the absolute frequency of musical notes. He built extremely long sonometers, 100 to 120 feet in length, which could produce vibrations of a very low frequency. These vibrations would have been inaudible but slow enough for Mersenne to count. Mersenne applied the inverse relationship between string length and frequency to estimate the frequency of musical notes. Although well conceived, Mersenne's experiments were flawed by extremely inaccurate measurements.

At the beginning of the eighteenth century, J. Sauveur of Paris successfully devised a means of standardizing musical pitch. Through experiments with the sonometer, he also identified the complex harmonic nature of vibrating strings. In 1877, Lord Rayleigh published *The Theory of Sound,* in which the ideas of Sauveur were successfully combined with Fourier's complex mathematical theorem of periodic motion. Fourier analysis and synthesis is still used by many modern acoustic instruments to process waveforms.

As electroacoustic devices developed in the twentieth century, the sonometer became a less important component of the science laboratory. The sonometer was incorporated into some frequency-detecting devices, but these were soon superseded by electronic bandpass filters. Today, sonometers are most often found in school or college laboratories, and are chiefly used as didactic tools. Developing scientists can use it to experience the key acoustic phenomena that Mersenne, Galileo, Safi al-Din, and the Pythagoreans first tried to understand.

Sarah Angliss

Bibliography

Hunt, Fredrick V. *Origins in Acoustics: The Science of Sound from Antiquity to the Age of Newton.* New Haven: Yale University Press, 1978.

Lippman, Edward A. *Musical Thought in Ancient Greece.* Columbia: Columbia University Press, 1964.

Miller, Dayton Clarence. *Anecdotal History of the Science of Sound to the Beginning of the 20th Century.* New York: Macmillan, 1935.

Rayleigh, John William Strutt, Baron. *The Theory of Sound.* London: Macmillan, 1877.

Sound Level Meter

A sound level meter is an electroacoustic device that measures the amplitude of sound in air. Modern sound level meters combine a microphone and amplifier, digital or analog level indicator, and power supply in a single handheld device. They are an indispensable instrument for acousticians and noise control engineers who need to take real-time measurements of an acoustic environment. They are invariably designed to measure sound pressure level (SPL). This is a decibel rating of sound energy, relative to the minimum sound energy the ear can detect.

Sound level meters are always used in ensemble with a pistonphone and **barometer**. A pistonphone is a calibrating device that fits snugly over the microphone of a sound level meter and produces a pure tone of constant amplitude. A barometer enables acousticians to determine how to adjust sound level readings when local air pressure varies.

The basic sound level meter is a highly accessible tool, easily used by any prospective acoustician with a basic grasp of calibration methods and the decibel scale. More sophisticated models have built-in or add-on networks that can store readings, weigh measurements, detect impulses, integrate sound over time, filter sounds into octaves or part octaves, and perform many other complex functions. These make the sound level meter a highly adaptable tool capable of the most sophisticated acoustic analyses.

The scientific study of sound originated with the Pythagorean brotherhood in Greece in the sixth century B.C. However, until the late nineteenth century, work on the quantification of the amplitude of sound was notable by its absence. Theorists focused on phenomenological and qualitative acoustics and experimented with the subjectively measured relative pitches of vibrating devices. Early-seventeenth-century pioneers, such as the Franciscan Marin Mersenne, experimented, with varying degrees of success, to determine the absolute pitch of vibrating strings and the velocity of sound in air. Later that century, Robert Boyle, suggesting the general relationship between loudness and pressure variations, discussed "touching the spring of air." However, it was not until 1870 that L. Boltzman and A. Toepler made the first recorded attempt to measure the pressure variations that create sound.

As sound is created by minute changes in air pressure—as small as 2×10^{-5} Pa in amplitude—it is not surprising that there were technical obstacles to the development of sound-measuring devices. Sound pressure levels could be reliably measured only after transducers had been developed that could convert these pressure fluctuations into other, directly measurable phenomena such as changes in electric current. Furthermore, complex physical theories had to be fully developed before sound pressure could be related to other measurements.

As early as 1375, the Arab scholar Al-Jurjani had identified the technical problems of quantitative acoustics. On the subject of sound, he commented: "One cannot measure quantitatively with the same ease the value of these causes."

Until the twentieth century, there was little incentive to measure the level of sound. Acousticians were concerned mainly with the rationalization of musical consonance and tuning, and their science had been used primarily to develop the timbre and increase the chromatic flexibility of musical instruments. However, as the world became more industrialized in the twentieth century, the measurement of sound—and particularly unwanted noise—increased in importance.

Following the work of L. Boltzmann and A. Toepler, Lord Rayleigh (John William Strutt) in 1877 developed a spinning disk to measure the absolute intensity of sound. This was followed in 1893 by the oscillograph (see **oscilloscope**), devised by A. Blondel of Paris, which detected sound with a telephone receiver and recorded it photographically. The oscillograph remained an indispensable piece of laboratory equipment until the late 1930s, when the first integrated sound level meters were built.

These early sound level meters had large microphones, typically 1 in. in diameter. As a microphone of this size had a significant effect on the sound field it was placed in, even at fairly low frequencies, this severely restricted the useful range of the device. From the mid 1950s onwards, sound level meters were used with much smaller microphones—sometimes only 0.25 in. in diameter—to increase the useful upper-frequency limit of the devices.

Any instrument used to indicate human exposure to noise must be designed to account for the nonlinear frequency response of the human ear. In 1933, H. Fletcher and W.A. Munson of the Bell Telephone Laboratories made a detailed survey of human hearing at

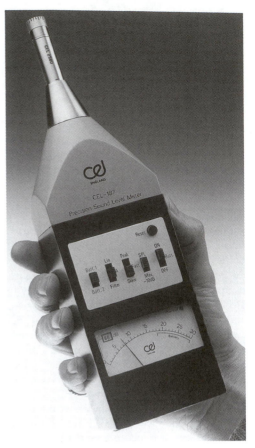

Sound level meter CEL-187, by CEL Ltd., 1995. Courtesy of CEL Ltd.

different frequencies and amplitudes. The results of their work were later used to design a series of standard weighting networks that converted sound level measurements into measures of perceived sound. Different weighting networks were used to mimic the human response to sound at different amplitudes.

Twentieth-century concern about unwanted noise was reflected in the U.K. Health and Safety at Work Act of 1974. The act precisely specified an upper limit of noise exposure for individuals throughout a working day. Sound level meter manufacturers responded by adding networks that could measure noise dosage in accordance with the act's guidelines. As other noise sources, such as air traffic noise, became causes for concern, new networks were designed to enable sound level meters to quantify them.

Major manufactures of early sound level meters were the General Radio Co., Dawes, and the Danish company Brüel and Kjaer. Dawes, which is now a part of Lucas CEL, and Brüel and Kjaer still manufacture acoustic instruments today.

Almost all modern sound level meters use digital technology. As models have increased in functionality, acousticians have required fewer additional acoustic instruments to complete most analyses. Priced in the mid 1990s at about $11,000, the sound level meter had developed into an accessible and highly adaptable handheld device.

Sarah Angliss

Bibliography

Fletcher, Harvey. *Speech and Hearing in Communication.* 2nd ed. New York: Van Nostrand, 1953.

Hunt, Fredrick Vinton. *Origins in Acoustics: The Science of Sound from Antiquity to the Age of Newton.* New Haven: Yale University Press, 1978.

Miller, Dayton Clarence. *Anecdotal History of the Science of Sound to the Beginning of the 20th Century.* New York: Macmillan, 1935.

National Physical Laboratory, Teddington. *Noise Measurement Techniques.* London: Her Majesty's Stationery Office, 1963.

Rayleigh, John William Strutt, Baron. *The Theory of Sound.* London: Macmillan, 1877.

Space Radiometer
See RADIOMETER, SPACE

Spectrofluorimeter

A spectrofluorimeter measures the intensity of the radiation emitted by a sample when it is irradiated by light. Molecules absorb radiation at certain characteristic wavelengths. In some situations this stimulates an excited state. When the molecule loses that excitation energy, some of it can appear as radiation, usually of longer wavelength, thus less energy, than the exciting radiation.

Both atoms and molecules can display fluorescence. Atoms must be in the vapor state and free of all molecular bonding. Molecules will fluoresce in liquid solutions and, in some cases, as solids. Physicists have used the fluorescence of gaseous atoms for many scientific purposes since the middle of the nineteenth century. The American physicist Robert W. Wood was particularly successful in the early twentieth century.

Most molecular absorption bands are broad, and, in complex mixtures of different molecular compounds, these absorption bands overlap to such an extent that quantitative analysis by absorption spectrometry becomes difficult or impossible. Since spectrofluorescence involves both a specific absorption band and an equally specific emission band, the likelihood of molecular overlap is greatly reduced. In addition, the fluorescence measurement of small signals is often more sensitive than the absorption measurement of small differences between large signals, thus making fluorescence a more sensitive detector of trace molecular compounds.

Several aspects of the fluorescence process are measured to increase the specificity of the method even further. When the molecule is excited, there is some time delay before the relaxation occurs with the consequent emission. This relaxation time provides important information concerning the molecule. If the relaxation time is very long, the process is called phosphorescence, another important aspect of fluorimetry.

In the 1950s simple fluorimeters were made commercially to take advantage of the sensitivity of the technique. A bright lamp emitting ultraviolet radiation, usually a mercury arc lamp, irradiated the sample and the fluorescent signal was isolated with filters. Such simple instruments provided very sensitive measurements of large biological molecules and were important in biochemistry, which was beginning to blossom in that period. Simple fluorimetry was also the method of choice for assaying uranium ores in that period when nuclear energy was beginning to become important.

David Hercules from the Massachusetts Institute of Technology pioneered the successful implementation of sophisticated fluorescence methods to analytical chemistry in the late 1950s and into the 1960s. The first commercial spectrofluorimeters, in which monochromators replaced the filters in both the excitation and emission beams, appeared at that time. This period also saw the development of the xenon arc, an intense source of ultraviolet radiation, and the **photomultiplier,** a very sensitive detector of ultraviolet and visible radiation. Spectrofluorimeters provided the opportunity of identifying complex molecules by their emission and excitation spectra, each scanned in sequence. Several Nobel Prize winners have credited the availability of spectrofluorimeters for the explosive progress of biochemistry in the 1960s and

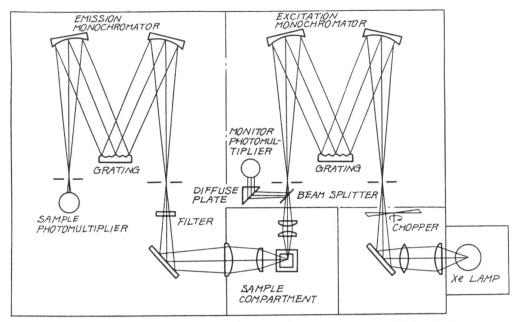

Schematic diagram showing the optical system of a spectrofluorimeter. Courtesy of Walter Slavin.

1970s. Much of this work was stimulated by the collaboration of Robert Bowman and Sidney Udenfriend at the National Institutes of Health in Bethesda, Maryland. They also stimulated the commercial development of instrumentation.

In some situations it is important to know the emission and excitation spectra on a physical basis, free of instrumental artifacts like the wavelength-dependent brightness of the light source, the sensitivity of the detector, and so forth. This has been done by adding a thermocouple detector to sample a fraction of the light from the excitation monochromator. The thermocouple responds linearly to the energy of the signal, independent of wavelength. Such an instrument is called an energy-recording spectrofluorimeter and is used, for example, to characterize the phosphor coatings of fluorescent lamps.

In recent years, spectrofluorimeters have been frequently used as a detector for liquid and gas **chromatographs** because of their sensitivity and specificity. They remain an important tool in the arsenal of instrumentation for both qualitative and quantitative analytical chemistry.

Walter Slavin

Bibliography

Hercules, David. *Fluorescence and Phosphorescence Analysis.* New York: Wiley-Interscience, 1966.

Rendell, David. *Fluorescence and Phosphorescence.* Chichester: Wiley, 1987.

Slavin, Walter. "Energy-recording Spectrofluorimeter." *Journal of the Optical Society of America* 51 (1961): 93–97.

Udenfriend, Sidney. *Fluorescence Assay in Biology and Medicine,* Vol. 2. New York: Academic, 1969.

Winefordner, James D., S.G. Schulman, and Thomas C. O'Haver. *Luminescence Spectrometry in Analytical Chemistry.* New York: Wiley-Interscience, 1972.

Spectrometer, Atomic Absorption

An atomic absorption spectrometer measures the intensity of the radiation absorbed by an atomic vapor that has been irradiated by light of just the wavelength characteristic of that particular element. An atomic absorption spectrometer differs from other spectrometers (see **spectrophotometer**) designed for the ultraviolet and visible spectral regions in the following ways: it has interchangeable light sources, one for each element to be determined, a sample compartment that accommodates a flame or an electrical furnace, and electronic circuits that handle quite different signals. That is done by making a light source of the desired element and isolating the specific wavelength with a spec-

Perkin-Elmer Model 303 atomic absorption spectrophotometer, ca. 1967. Courtesy of Perkin-Elmer Ltd.

trometer. The ratio of the intensity of the radiation before the sample is vaporized to that when the atomic vapor is present (in other words, the fraction of the radiation absorbed) is proportional to the amount of element in the sample.

In the mid-nineteenth century, G. Kirchhoff and R. Bunsen made absorption measurements for astronomical and analytical purposes but, after their pioneering work, analytical spectroscopy used only emission methods. In 1955, simultaneously and independently, Alan Walsh in Australia and C.T.J. Alkemade in the Netherlands rediscovered atomic absorption spectroscopy (AAS).

Walsh and his colleagues used a flame to convert the sample to an atomic vapor. By using acetylene-air mixtures and later acetylene–nitrous oxide mixtures, they developed combustion mixtures that were much hotter than Bunsen's. They also developed an electrical discharge lamp using the element of interest as the cathode. These hollow cathode lamps were fitted to spectrophotometers very similar to those being used commercially at that time for molecular spectrophotometry. By this time the dispersing device was a grating and the detector was a **photomultiplier** tube.

In the late 1950s, most elemental analysis was being done by emission spectroscopy using an electric arc or spark, by colorimetry using compounds that bound the element of interest, or by electrochemistry. The first completely successful commercial atomic absorption spectrometer was introduced in 1963, eight years after Walsh's publication. Within the next ten years, this technique had largely replaced other methods for the determination of metallic elements. Thousands of instruments are sold every year.

Walsh's first publication was read by Boris L'vov, a Russian graduate student looking for a project on which to base his Ph.D. dissertation.

Despite the objections of his advisor and hundreds of obstacles, L'vov developed an electrical **furnace** to vaporize the sample. He showed that this improvement provided several orders of magnitude greater sensitivity than flame AAS and that it required only micrograms of sample. This improvement was introduced commercially in 1970. In fact, though, the instrumental requirements of furnace AAS are quite different from those for flame AAS, and it was not until the 1980s that properly designed furnace AAS instruments became available.

The instrumentation for furnace AAS is more complex and expensive than that for flame. As we conclude the twentieth century, simple and relatively inexpensive flame AAS instruments are sold for the purposes for which it is adequate, and furnace instruments are sold for the more exacting requirements.

Walter Slavin

Bibliography

L'vov, Boris V. "A Personal View of the Evolution of Graphite Furnace Atomic Absorption Spectrometry." *Analytical Chemistry* 63 (1991): 924A–931A.

Mavrodineanu, Radu, and Henri Boiteux. *Flame Spectroscopy.* New York: Wiley, 1965.

Slavin, Walter. *Atomic Absorption Spectroscopy.* New York: Interscience, 1968.

———. "Atomic Absorption Spectroscopy: Why Has It Become Successful?" *Analytical Chemistry* 63 (1991): 1033A–1038A.

Welz, Bernhard. *Atomic Absorption Spectrometry.* Weinheim: VCH, 1985.

Spectrometer, Gamma Ray

A gamma ray spectrometer measures the energies of gamma rays. Penetrating gamma radiation was observed and named by the French physicist Paul Villard in 1900. Early energy-measurement devices could determine if radiation was penetrating, but could not distinguish between energies. One of the more sophisticated instruments was a focusing curved-crystal spectrometer that diffracted x-rays or low-energy gamma rays at angles depending on their energy. Sequential measurements at different angles under carefully controlled geometric conditions distinguished gamma rays with different energies and determined their abundances. In another method, gamma rays were directed onto a thin foil (called a radiator) that would eject electrons whose energies were equal to the gamma ray energy minus the binding energies of the atoms in the foil. The energies of the electrons could then be measured with a magnetic spectrometer. In still other methods, gas-filled proportional counters measured the energies of x-rays and low-energy gamma rays. None of these methods, however, were efficient for higher energy gamma rays.

In 1948 it was found that gamma rays interacting with a crystal of thallium-activated sodium iodide (NaI) would produce flashes of light that could be detected. The intensities of the flashes were found to be proportional to the gamma ray energy, and they could be transformed to an electronic pulse with a photomultiplier tube, and then amplified and fed into pulse height analyzers to determine the gamma ray energies and abundances. These detectors, which measured many gamma rays simultaneously and efficiently, were a boon for scientific studies of nuclear structure and permitted a much clearer understanding of the energies and decay patterns of nuclear states.

The new detectors also led to the rapid growth of the field of activation analysis—that is, the determination of element abundances in a target by measurement of nuclear radiations arising from irradiation with neutrons, charged particles, x-rays, or gamma rays. The irradiations induce either radioactivity or fluorescence, and these latter radiations can simultaneously distinguish many of the elements in the target and indicate their abundances. Because of the general availability of nuclear reactors with large fluxes (10^{13}–10^{14} neutrons/second/cm^2) since World War II, neutron activation analysis has been the preferred technique of activation analysis. This technique is particularly useful where accurate data are needed for abundances ranging from percentages down to parts-per-million and below. It has been used in industry to test for impurities in high-purity materials; in archaeology to determine the place of origin of artifacts of pottery, obsidian, stone, and metal; in geology to determine the origin of rocks; and in crime detection and medical research.

In the 1960s scientists discovered that solid-state detectors made from germanium crystals with lithium drifted into the surface and, kept at liquid nitrogen temperatures and in a vacuum, could measure gamma ray energies with much better resolution (smaller peak widths) than possible with NaI. Many studies of gamma ray emissions from radioactive isotopes previously made with NaI detectors were profitably redone with germanium (Ge).

Using NaI and then Ge detectors, physicists could more easily measure gamma rays emitted one after the other from an atomic nucleus—that is, in coincidence. This procedure had a tremendous impact on nuclear science and caused a significant improvement in activation analysis.

One of the most recent developments in the latter field is the Luis W. Alvarez Iridium Coincidence Spectrometer, conceived by the Nobel Laureate in physics. This device measures minute abundances of the element iridium (Ir) by counting coincidences between two gamma rays of Ir^{192} formed in the neutron irradiation of geochemical samples. Spurious Ir coincidences due to Compton scattering of high-energy gamma rays are monitored by two mineral oil shields that together nearly completely surround the Ge detectors. The mineral oil is doped with a scintillator, and **photomultiplier** tubes and their associated electronics veto coincidences registered by the Ge system whenever radiation is detected by the mineral oil. The spectrometer was built with a minimum budget ($200,000) and used mineral oil as a shield rather than the more efficient NaI or bismuth germanate because of the lower cost.

The measurement of Ir has received much interest in recent years because it was fundamental in demonstrating that a mass extinction of species sixty-five million years ago, which possibly included those of the dinosaurs, was likely due to the impact of a 10-km-diameter asteroid or comet on the earth. Between 1987 and 1989, over half of all measurements of Ir abundances in this field were made with the spectrometer discussed above.

The Gammasphere gamma ray spectrometer array at the Lawrence Berkeley National Laboratory, 1995. Courtesy of the Lawrence Berkeley National Laboratory.

A number of Ge spectrometer arrays, used predominantly with targets excited by the beams from charged-particle **accelerators** and capable of measuring a multitude of gamma rays (with groups of two or three in coincidence), have been built for nuclear science studies. These led to the discovery of superdeformation: very deformed, highly excited, high-spin nuclear states that decayed by cascades of gamma ray emission to lower energy states. The work resulted in a renaissance in nuclear structure physics.

By the beginning of 1995 three instruments stood out in their ability to measure multiple coincidences between gamma rays efficiently. These were the first phase of the Gammasphere at the Lawrence Berkeley National Laboratory (University of California) in Berkeley, California, the Gasp Array in the Laboratori Nazionali di Legnaro in Padova, Italy, and the Eurogram Array, initially in the Daresbury Laboratory in the U.K., and later in the Centre de Recherches Nucléaires Strasbourg in France. Like earlier array spectrometers, these suppressed background radiation connected to Compton scattering by surrounding each Ge detector with arrays of bismuth germanate (BGO) detectors and vetoing pulses from the former that occurred simultaneously with those in the latter.

Two more powerful gamma ray spectrometers were subsequently constructed. One of these, the moveable full Gammasphere, had 100 of its planned 110 detectors functioning by the end of April 1997. The other, Euroball III, built by Denmark, France, Germany, Italy, Sweden, and the U.K. is expected to be operational in 1997. Euroball III will be used first at the Laboratori Nazionali di Legnaro and later at the Centre de Recherches Nucléaires Strasbourg. These instruments are complex and expensive (the Gammasphere will cost about $20,000,000), and the cooperative efforts of more than one laboratory and sometimes more than one country are necessary for their construction and operation.

Frank Asaro

Bibliography

Alvarez, L.W., W. Alvarez, F. Asaro, and H.V. Michel. "Extraterrestrial Cause for the Cretaceous-Tertiary Extinction: Experimental Results and Theoretical Interpretation." *Science* 208 (1980): 1095–1108.

Hofstadter, Robert. "Alkali Halide Scintillation Counter Studies." *Physical Revue* 74 (1948): 100–101.

Lee, I-Yang. "Gammasphere." In *Exotic Nuclear Spectroscopy,* edited by William C. McHarris, 245–58. New York: Plenum, 1990.

Lieder, Ranier M. "New Generation of Gamma-Detector Arrays." In *Experimental Techniques in Nuclear Physics,* edited by D.N. Poenaru and W. Greiner, 1–56. Berlin: Walter de Gruyster, 1995.

Michel, H.V., F. Asaro, W. Alvarez, and L.W. Alvarez. "Geochemical Studies of the Cretaceous-Tertiary Boundary in ODP Holes 689B and 690C." *Proceedings of the Ocean Drilling Program, Scientific Results* 113 (1990): 159–68.

Spectrometer, Mass

Mass spectrometers constitute a large, very diverse, and widely employed and produced class or family of instruments. It is likely that no other type of complex instrument has been as important for so many fields of science in the twentieth century. The defining characteristics of this vast range of devices are operational (or functional) and hypothetical in nature, more than material or structural. As Cooks, Busch, and Glish stated in 1983: "Instruments that go by the name of mass spectrometer are appearing in ever-increasing variety with an astonishing range of applications." A mass spectrometer is whatever operates by processes that could be used to produce a mass spectrum, no matter how different its design and processes may be from those of any other mass spectrometer. The mass spectrum of any substance or mixture is a record of the distribution of materials of different masses that can be found when a sample is ionized. The instruments were first created as experiments early in the twentieth century, attained great scientific and technological importance by mid century, and proliferated most dramatically both in terms of new types developed and number of machines in use during the last third of the century.

The heart of any mass spectrometer is its analyzer. This is a region of high vacuum through which ions extracted from sample substances are made to move by some kind or kinds of static or oscillating electromagnetic field. Ions of different mass, velocity, and charge are moved differently by the field(s). Taking account of velocity and charge effects, ions of specific masses can be separately collected if the field is carefully controlled, and their numbers and masses precisely determined. Mass spectrometers accordingly must have vacuum systems and arrangements to produce, control, and vary the analyzing field(s), as well as ways to introduce samples, to create ions from the sample and get them into the analyzer, to collect analyzed ions, and to display or record the results. Within these shared requirements, different types, arrangements, and uses of analyzers, different sources of samples, and different modes of ionization have resulted in a remarkably extensive set of different types of mass spectrometers, each of which could warrant its own entry.

"Mass spectrometry" (MS) refers to these machines, to information about them, and to development of techniques of employing them in the several branches of natural science and industry; it labels as well a range of research areas in various fields of chemistry that have been intensively developed with these devices. Some significant instruments earlier in the century that used photographic plates to collect ions were called mass "spectrographs," as distinct from "spectrometers," while "mass spectroscope" and "mass spectroscopy" served as inclusive labels, but that distinction and terminology have become uncommon except in reference works.

The origin of all mass spectrometers was the turn-of-the-century research on *kanalstrahlen,* the streams of positive ions formed from residual gases in cathode ray tubes, initially found coming through channels cut in the cathode plate. Local magnetic and electrostatic fields differentially deflected these positive rays depending on their mass; they made diverging traces on a photographic plate. J.J. Thomson was the crucial experimenter, and the first evidence for the existence of stable (nonradioactive) isotopes was the most dramatic result.

Since World War I, a rough cycle of five recurrent, overlapping processes, phases, or stages of development of mass spectrometers is discernible. These can conveniently be called demonstration, familiarization, routinization, radiation, and diversification. In the first, a mass spectrometer *was* the experiment; instead of an integrated unit, an instrument used to do work defined in other terms, it was the arrangement of equipment composing essentially the whole experiment. Successful experiments provided particular results, but also demonstrated that apparatus of this design could be made to work. An experimental arrangement that was successfully copied for use in further research (and named) made more scientists familiar with its potentials. When a design was standardized and treated as a reliable entity by more people in more contexts, it became a routine instrument. The instruments were spread in wider areas of application where their basic viability was not at issue. Inevitable limitations spurred trials of alternative components and designs, generating diverse types of equipment that in turn needed demonstration of viability, founding new lines of instrument development.

The clear demonstration of mass spectrometry came at the end of World War I by Francis W. Aston (who had helped design Thomson's equipment and make it work) and Arthur J. Dempster, in Cambridge and Chicago, respectively. Dempster used a magnetic analyzer that focused ions into an electrical collector, while Aston used both electrostatic and magnetic fields to focus ions on a photographic plate. Their continued work, along with that of Joseph H.E. Mattauch, R.F.K. Herzog, Kenneth T. Bainbridge, and Alfred O.C. Nier, among others, produced major results in atomic and nuclear physics, including discovery of the existence, and measurement of the abundances and masses, of numerous isotopes and the determination of their nuclear stabilities and energies. Such work led to Aston's Nobel Prize (in chemistry) and created some familiarity with such equipment in the 1930s.

Stabilizing the esoteric and "touchy" experimental apparatus into routine instruments and applying them to new kinds of tasks, required extensive effort. Most influential in the first cycle were the papers, devices, and students of Alfred Nier (often cooperating with various others) from the end of the 1930s to the early 1950s. Nier incorporated recent developments in vacuum technologies and electronics for power supplies, ion detection, and so on, while providing the foundation for determining the age of the earth. His work significantly improved magnetic focusing instruments, establishing that good results could be obtained with ions being sent merely through a comparatively modest wedge-shaped sector magnetic field rather than having as their entire path a semicircle within an analyzer completely confined between the poles of a massive magnet (prior standard practice). A more practical electron-bombardment ion source, along with several other crucial aspects of construction and technique, also brought improvements in performance, convenience, and costs. Double-focusing machines, attaining greater precision by adding an electrostatic analyzer, were also greatly refined. During these years machines and expertise spread outward from a few physics laboratories, founding precise geochronology and cosmochronology, facilitating isotopic tracer studies, providing the analytic and vacuum controls that made the Manhattan Project's uranium enrichment facilities workable, and making the instruments common in the petroleum industry. Commercial production of mass spectrometers began in the 1940s.

By 1953, convenient handbooks of design and practice had appeared in the United States, the U.K., Germany, and Russia, and annual conferences of mass spectrometrists began. Instrument designs created for isotopic analysis soon were applied to analysis of complex organic molecules. Meanwhile, the demonstration of quite different instrument types was well underway. Analyzers based on the different times of flight over a set path for different accelerated ions, and others using various types and combinations of fields had some success. In 1953 Wolfgang Paul and his colleagues initiated development of what became the most common type of those mass spectrometers having no magnetic field, the quadrupole mass analyzer (and ion trap), using crossed radio-frequency and electrostatic fields. This eventuated in Paul's Nobel Prize (in physics). The middle and later 1950s saw the first wave of effort to concatenate mass spectrometers with other significant types of instruments, in this case creating various types of gas **chromatograph** mass spectrometers, which have become the most widely sold of all mass spectrometer instrumentation.

Despite the growing familiarity of these and other types, the great majority of mass spectrometers in service well into the 1960s were magnetic sector or double-focusing machines, mostly producing ions by electron bombardment. A score of companies marketed the standard models, costing thousands and tens of thousands of dollars. The spread of mass spectrometers from physics into geology, chemistry, physiology, and other industries continued. They performed gas analyses in venues as disparate as hospital operating rooms and rockets in the upper atmosphere. From the perspec-

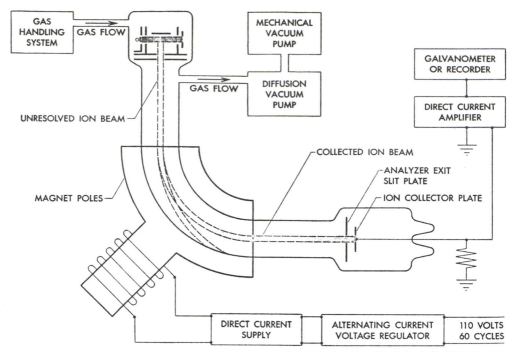

Schematic diagram of a single-focus magnetic sector mass spectrometer. Alfred O. Nier. "The Mass Spectrometer." Scientific American 188 (March 1953): 68.

tive of earlier decades, their numbers and impact seemed to be growing quite rapidly, but by comparison with later decades, the expansion of numbers, uses, and types had hardly started.

Since then a host of workers have transformed mass spectrometers, and founded an array of new families of machines of vastly enhanced scope and precision, based particularly on different approaches to ion production but also on other modes of analysis. Cooks, Busch, and Glish rightly noted that "latitude in methodology, and characteristics of the hardware which demand interaction with the equipment, have made mass spectroscopists likely to modify instrumentation or to develop entirely new instruments." Each new type has grown (despite the substantial cost of the machines), being commercialized in turn and approaching or surpassing the total growth of the 1950s; three score companies were in the market early in the 1990s.

In the 1960s, chemical ionization mass spectrometry (or CIMS) and field desorption MS (FDMS) emerged, and several mass spectrometry journals began publication. In the 1970s, secondary ionization MS, Fourier transform MS, plasma desorption MS, electrohydro-

dynamic MS, laser desorption MS, thermal desorption MS, spark source MS, and glow discharge MS were invented or developed significantly, and additional journals were started. At the same time, the scale of the machines went to opposite extremes, with the quest for high performance and the development of tandem MS (in which machines are combined, one serving as a source for the next) leading to large "grand scale" instruments, with particle accelerators being used as new forms of mass spectrometer, with instruments being shrunk for portable medical uses, and others miniaturized for missions to Mars, Venus, Halley's comet, and beyond.

Clearly identifiable developments of the 1980s, beyond still more new journals, included laser resonance ionization MS, matrix-assisted laser desorption MS, fast atom bombardment MS and its continuous flow transformation, the astonishingly sudden development of ion trap MS, a dramatic advance in electrospray MS, as well as a considerable development of liquid chromatography MS. These lists are hardly complete, nor do they include combinations. One review found over ten new types of machine per year appearing in the literature at the start of the 1990s. Yet earlier designs have not been dropped; what are called "Nier-machines" and quadrupoles remain very numerous and productive. And in a crucial sense all these diversified instruments still compose a single class, sharing their fundamental functional characteristic: they all sort ions by mass. Although the inferences drawn from their data vary enormously, there are many different ways of producing the same basic kind of information.

Originally designed to work with atomic isotopes or comparatively light gases, mass spectrometers now deal with a range of substances that is almost unlimited. By the early 1960s the ever-increasing precision in measurement of isotopic masses and abundances drove physicists and chemists to new international standards for atomic mass and weight. Capable of precision to a part in a billion in dealing with the mass of an atom, the instruments also provide extremely precise measurements when dealing with ever larger molecules, along with a flood of structural information, all on the basis of minuscule samples. In the early 1980s, it seemed amazing that mass spectrometers could handle ions even with a molecular weight of over 10,000, yet by the 1990s the proven range extended to several hundred thousand, and no material seemed so involatile or unstable as to be beyond the capabilities of all the techniques.

Several applications of mass spectrometers have been mentioned above. To be comprehensive about the uses to which these instruments have been put and the results achieved, at even the most superficial level, requires little less than a survey of the full range of natural scientific endeavor in the twentieth century and some account as well of a wide range of medical, industrial, and governmental concerns. A partial list is all that is suitable here.

Analyses by mass spectrometers are crucial for astronomical studies of the components of our solar system, for all geochronology (including the histories of climates and of life's evolution), for isotope archaeology, and for much else in geophysics and geochemistry as well. No less than the geological fields, chemistry is "awash" in mass spectrometers, for their use constitutes both one of the most precise modes of experimentation and most powerful methods of chemical analysis. The same can be said increasingly of their biological, biochemical, and medical uses. Mass spectrometry is employed in the identification of complex natural products

and of metabolic pathways. The capabilities of detecting and identifying mere trace presences in tiny samples have led to use of mass spectrometers in toxicology, drug abuse diagnosis, environmental pollution monitoring, and elsewhere. These instruments have long played a significant role in materials analysis and process monitoring in the petroleum, chemical, and pharmaceutical industries, and they are being used in food processing and electronics industries. Mass spectrometers are the key to noninvasive (thus politically viable) international monitoring of nuclear facilities. They are even returning to some prominence in physics, where they had become less central since determining the masses of stable and unstable nuclides. They are becoming important tools in studies of surface phenomena, and of the solid state several atoms deep, which may well lead to further industrial applications. Finally, mass spectrometers are the key to coping with next to nothing at all, for they are essential to vacuum technology, as leak detectors and as the most sensitive gauges for the most extreme vacua we can produce.

Despite this importance, mass spectrometers have received hardly any attention from historians of science and technology, and remain almost totally unknown among the generally educated public. A notable chronicle literature exists, but the history remains largely unexplored. Even in as laudatory a work as Claude Allègre's survey *From Stone to Star,* in which almost all the growth of our understanding of how the solar system, the earth, the atmosphere, and the biosphere all developed is ascribed to accurate mass spectrometry, the instruments themselves are left highly praised yet essentially undiscussed and invisible.

Keith A. Nier

Bibliography

Cooks, R. Graham, Kenneth L. Busch, and G.L. Glish. "Mass Spectrometry: Analytical Capabilities and Potentials." *Science* 222 (1983): 273–91.

Cornides, I. "Mass Spectrometric Analysis of Inorganic Solids—The Historical Background." In *Inorganic Mass Spectrometry,* edited by F. Adams, R. Gijbels, and R. Van Grieken, 1–15. New York: Wiley, 1988.

Falconer, Isobel. "J.J. Thomson's Work on Positive Rays, 1906–1914." *Historical Studies in the Physical and Biological*

Sciences 18 (1988): 265–310.

Remane, Horst. "Zur Entwicklung der Massenspektroskopie von den Anfängen bis zur Strukturaufklärung organischer Verbindungen." *NTM—Schriftenreihe Geschichte der Naturwissenschaft, Technik, und Medizin* 24 (1987): 93–106.

Svec, Harry J. "Mass Spectroscopy—Ways and Means: A Historical Prospectus." *International Journal of Mass Spectrometry and Ion Processes* 66 (1985): 3–29.

Spectrometer, Nuclear Magnetic Resonance

Nuclear Magnetic Resonance (NMR) is the most widely used of several radio-frequency spectroscopy methods that appeared immediately after World War II and that are based on electronics technology developed from war-related projects. NMR spectra arise from the selective, or resonance, absorption of electromagnetic radiation by spinning atomic nuclei when the resulting magnetic dipole moments are oriented in a high magnetic field. The energy levels responsible for NMR are a result of the nuclear Zeeman effect. The frequency of radiation absorbed by the nuclei is influenced by the chemical environment of the nucleus, giving rise to the NMR chemical shift. Other nearby magnetic nuclei may also alter the frequency of the NMR signal, as well as introduce additional frequencies, through the phenomenon of nuclear spin-spin coupling.

All NMR spectrometers contain the following components: (a) a magnet capable of producing a high and very uniform magnetic field within a volume of a few cubic cm; (b) a stable, low-noise radio-frequency transmitter and receiver and a suitable antenna, coil, or cavity, contained in a probe, that couples the radiation to the sample; and (c) a data system to process and display the radio-frequency power absorbed by the sample at various frequencies. The earliest NMR spectrometers employed magnetic fields of around 1 tesla (10,000 gauss), corresponding to a resonance frequency of 40 MHz for protons. Modern spectrometers may use fields in excess of 10 tesla and observing frequencies of up to 750 MHz. Although low-frequency spectrometers have used permanent magnets or conventional electromagnets, most modern instruments employ superconducting magnets. Over the years, data recording on strip chart recorders has been replaced by comprehensive data accumulation, processing, display, and storage using **computers**. Until the early 1970s, virtually all commercial NMR spectrometers generated the NMR spectrum by varying the magnetic field while fixing the frequency. Modern spectrometers fix both the magnetic field and the transmitter frequency, and detect the spectrum of frequencies broadcast by nuclei after stimulation by brief and intense radio-frequency pulses. The NMR spectrum is generated from the transient response by numerical Fourier transformation.

The existence of nuclear spins and magnetic moments was inferred from observations of hyperfine lines in atomic and molecular spectra during the early 1930s. At about the same time, resonant transitions between nuclear Zeeman states were detected using atomic beams. It was not until 1946, however, that direct observation of nuclear magnetic resonance in condensed matter was reported by Edward Purcell at Harvard University and Felix Bloch at Stanford University. The development of commercial NMR spectrometers was pioneered by Varian Associates in Palo Alto, California, which had accumulated early expertise in the area of microwave generators for **radar**. Although other companies, most notably Bruker Instruments of Karlsruhe, Germany, have contributed to spectrometer development, most of the refinements in design that made modern high-resolution NMR commercially feasible originated at Varian. In 1966, Weston Anderson and Richard Ernst, who was at that time at Varian, perfected the technique of Fourier Transform NMR. This method, which was incorporated in commercial spectrometers within a decade, improved the sensitivity of NMR by nearly a hundredfold for the types of samples of most interest to chemists. Further advances in NMR instrumentation have kept pace with increases in the magnitude of fields available from superconducting magnets and the evolution of computational, data storage and graphics display capabilities of computers.

All of the naturally occurring nonradioactive chemical elements, except argon and cerium, have at least one isotope suitable, in principle, for study by NMR. The minimum number of nuclei detectable by NMR decreases with increasing magnetic field strength and increasing magnitude of the nuclear magnetic moment. Even using the highest achievable magnetic fields, however, and working with nuclei, such as protons, which possess large magnetic

Early NMR apparatus, built by Rex Richards at the Physical Chemistry Laboratory, Oxford, 1950s. Courtesy of the Photographic Department, Physical and Theoretical Chemistry Laboratory, University of Oxford.

moments and constitute nearly 100 percent of the naturally occurring isotope of the element, it is rarely possible to detect fewer than 10^{17} nuclei, corresponding to 1 cm^3 of sample containing a solute at a concentration of 10^{-4} molar. Although NMR signals have been detected from gases, the low intrinsic sensitivity of the technique has largely confined it to the study of condensed matter. Liquid samples exhibit more highly resolved spectra than do solids, unless special line-narrowing methods are employed

for the latter. Furthermore, spin $^1/_2$ nuclei, such as H^1, C^{13}, N^{15}, F^{19}, and P^{31}, usually exhibit much narrower absorption lines than those with spin $> {}^1/_2$, such as O^{17} and N^{14}, which possess electric quadrupole moments.

NMR has now become a standard technique for the chemical analysis of moderately concentrated solutions of nearly any substance that contains spin $^1/_2$ nuclei. Since the mid 1950s, NMR has played an increasingly important role in organic chemistry. The sensitivity of the chemical shift and spin-spin coupling to subtle variations in molecular structure has made it possible for chemists to monitor the progress of reactions designed to prepare complex chemical substances that have medicinal or other properties of value to society. Furthermore, pulsed techniques developed since the early 1980s have made NMR one of the principal methods used to study the geometries of proteins, nucleic acids, and other biological macromolecules in solution. The technique of **magnetic resonance imaging**, which has revolutionized medical imaging, is a direct descendant of applications of NMR to chemical analysis.

In 1997, commercially available NMR spectrometers ranged in price from $50,000 to more than $1 million. The low-end instruments operate at low frequencies, with small magnets, and are used primarily in education or for specialized applications, such as moisture analysis, where high resolution and sensitivity are not required. The most expensive instruments incorporate state-of-the-art magnet and computer technology. On a logarithmic price scale, NMR instruments occupy a place midway between low-cost equipment, available in nearly any scientific laboratory, and national or international facilities such as particle accelerators, space satellites, and large telescopes. Although the average price of an NMR instrument is still within the range affordable by a single institution, it is too high for most individual scientists. The most expensive NMR instruments are now being shared by institutions and managed in much the same way as other multiuser facilities.

Ronald G. Lawler

Bibliography

Freeman, Ray. *A Handbook of Nuclear Magnetic Resonance.* New York: Wiley, 1988.

Jonas, Jiri, and Herbert S. Gutowsky. "NMR in Chemistry—An Evergreen." *Annual Review of Physical Chemistry* 31 (1980): 1–27.

Wehrli, Felix W. "The Origins and Future of Nuclear Magnetic Resonance Imaging." *Physics Today* 45 (June 1992): 34–42.

Spectrophotometer

A spectrophotometer, a combination of **spectroscope** and **photometer**, measures the intensity of light of a particular color (actually, of a very narrow band of wavelengths). It is usually used to determine the change in the intensity of this light after it has been reflected by or transmitted through a sample.

Spectroscopes are used to observe light in the visible region. By contrast, spectrophotometers, which use some form of photoelectric detection, and spectrographs, which use photographic film, can detect infrared and ultraviolet as well as visible radiation. Usually the spectrum is split into ultraviolet and visible light in one type of instrument, and infrared in another.

Ultraviolet Spectrophotometry

Walter Noel Hartley built an ultraviolet spectrograph in 1877–1878, while working on bacteriology at King's College, London. Hartley's apparatus used a spark spectrum of an alloy of tin, lead, cadmium, and bismuth as the light source, a quartz prism placed at the angle of minimum deviation, and a quartz focusing lens. His major innovation was the use of gelatin photographic plates to record the spectrum after it had been focused using a fluorescent screen.

Hartley was interested in ultraviolet spectroscopy as an analytical tool, especially for metallurgical assaying. Nevertheless, he also studied the ultraviolet spectra of organic compounds, including the relationship between colorless aromatic substances (such as benzene and naphthalene) and synthetic dyes. With James Dobbie, he used ultraviolet spectroscopy in 1898–1899 to study the vexed issue of tautomerism, and he was able to show that isatin has a keto (lactam) rather than an enol (lactim) structure.

Hartley worked closely with Frank Twyman of Adam Hilger of London, who introduced the first fixed adjustment quartz spectrograph in 1906, and the sector photometer to measure the absorption in 1910. Hilger remained the leader in the production of ultraviolet spectrographs for many years, replacing the photographic sector photometer with the photoelectric Spekker photometer in 1931 (see **absorptiometer, Hilger-Spekker**).

Another important commercial spectrophotometer was the Koenig-Martens, manufactured by Franz Schmidt & Haensch in Berlin. When he went to work for this Optisch-Mechanische Werkstätten in 1896, Friedrich Franz Martens had just received a Ph.D. in physics from the University of Berlin. His spectrophotometer, a modification of an instrument designed by Arthur Koenig in the previous de-

GE-Hardy recording spectrophotometer, designed by A.C. Hardy and used at the Catholic University of America. NMAH 329,779. Courtesy of NMAH.

cade, remained in use until well into the second quarter of the twentieth century.

In the Koenig-Martens spectrophotometer, the two light beams are dispersed by a prism and are then polarized at right angles to each other by passing through a Wollaston prism. One beam passes through (or is reflected from) a standard of some sort, while the other beam has a similar interaction with the material to be tested, and the two are then reunited by the nicol prism. If the two paths are optically identical, the two beams will have the same amplitude when they come together. If, however, the paths are different, the amplitudes of the two beams can be balanced (or one could be extinguished) by the proper rotation of the nicol.

By the methods then in use, a reasonably precise spectrum consisted of thirty points, and each point required five readings laboriously obtained by fallible and tiring visual comparisons. By the 1920s, photoelectric devices had progressed enough for scientists to dream that they might equal or even better the eye as a comparative intensity detector.

One person who believed this was the physicist Arthur C. Hardy. Soon after arriving at M.I.T. in 1922, Hardy obtained two new state-of-the-art cesium photocells and began designing a spectrophotometer that would detect intensities by electronic and photoelectric means. He ultimately produced an instrument that set the paradigm for automated spectrophotometric devices.

In 1928, after an early promising prototype for a spectrophotometer that moved through the visible wavelengths without human guidance and produced a paper and ink graph of intensity versus wavelength (a spectrum), Hardy struck an agreement with General Electric to produce a commercial version of his new automated apparatus. In an unrealistic excess of zeal, G.E. gave Hardy "only 10 days to redesign the optics, with the understanding that the instrument must be no larger than a console radio." Cooperation with G.E. gave Hardy access to unparalelled facilities in both metal fabrication and electronics. By 1931 he was designing a new optical system based on rotating polarizers and a detector related to the flicker photometer. The basic design was set by early 1932, construction of a prototype began in the spring, tests were made in the fall, and the machine was placed into operation in January of 1933. It was an immediate and lasting success. The first production instrument went to the research laboratories of the International Printing Ink Corp. in late 1933. The later production instruments differed markedly from the prototype apparatus.

Investigators at the National Bureau of Standards quickly realized that this new machine could produce transmission and reflectance curves several times faster than the several Koenig-Martens and other machines in their laboratories. This was particularly important for the group working on color standards. Thus

G.E.-Hardy was installed at NBS in 1936. For more than a quarter of a century, it tested pigment and dyes for many manufacturers, and set all the textile and paint color standards in the United States. It also set the standards for all signal lights in all areas of ground, sea, and air transportation. In the 1950s, as demand for these standards continued to grow, the Bureau acquired a second G.E.-Hardy machine.

The machine was well received by the few who could afford it. In 1943 the G.E.-Hardy spectrophotometer cost $6,400; in 1947 it cost almost $8,000. The 1943 spec sheet for the "Recording Photoelectric Spectrophotometer" gave a (partial) list of users that read like a *Who's Who* of major commercial firms, large universities, and government agencies: Illinois and Purdue universities, American Cyanamid, Bausch & Lomb, Dow, DuPont, Kodak, Mohawk Carpet, Monsanto, Technicolor in Hollywood, the Bureau of Engraving, the Food and Drug Administration, the Frankford Arsenal, Wright Field, and the National Bureau of Standards. Although G.E.-Hardy machines were made until well into the 1970s and their price eventually came down, they were never as popular as some other machines.

If the G.E.-Hardy was the Rolls-Royce of commercial spectrophotometers, the DU designed by Arnold Beckman and Howard Carey was the Volkswagen. Several thousand were made from 1941 through 1976, and most scientists in chemical, biological, and industrial laboratories got their first taste of sophisticated instrumentation from the DU and the equally ubiquitous Beckman Model G **pH meter**. Although not automatic, its manual method could produce spectral points rapidly and accurately. It covered not only the visible region but the ultraviolet and near infrared as well, and it was affordable. An automated version, the DR, was built in 1947, but it was not until the DK-1 came out in 1954 that an instrument with a level of automation comparable to the GE-Hardy became generally available.

Infrared Spectroscopy

Leopoldi Nobili and Macedoni Melloni laid the foundations of infrared spectroscopy between 1829 and 1833 with the development of the thermopile detector and the rock-salt prism. Fifty years later, William de Wiveleslie Abney and Edward Robert Festing related the bands in the absorption spectra of organic compounds to their chemical bonds. Their work was extended by the American physicist William Weber Coblentz, who compiled an atlas of the spectra of 112 organic compounds between 1900 and 1905.

Hilger marketed the model D83 infrared (IR) spectrophotometer in 1922. This had a Nernst filament, a rock salt prism, and a Raschen-type mirror **galvanometer**. The first major breakthrough in the development of the modern IR spectrophotometer was the introduction of the prism-grating arrangement, which greatly improved the precision of measurements, by Harrison Randall of the University of Michigan in 1939.

Commercial infrared spectrophotometers became commonplace in the wake of the growing use of infrared spectroscopy to identify petroleum hydrocarbons just before and during World War II. R. Bowling Barnes at American Cyanamid collaborated with the neighboring firm of Perkin-Elmer to develop the model 12. For the crash program to make synthetic rubber, the U.S. government commissioned Arnold Beckman to develop the IR-1, which appeared in 1942. In Britain, infrared spectrophotometers were introduced by Adam Hilger (a double-beam instrument based on Hardy's system), Grubb Parsons, and Unicam of Cambridge. Baird Associates' double-beam optical spectrophotometer (1947) presented the spectrum in terms of percent transmission wavelength. The Perkin-Elmer 21 followed two years later. Grubb Parsons developed the first double-beam grating instrument, the GS-2, in 1956, and within two years Beckman had produced the similar IR-7. The introduction of the inexpensive Perkin-Elmer 137 in 1957 brought infrared spectrophotometry within the reach of the ordinary chemistry laboratory and, in time, even the undergraduate teaching laboratory. When such machines became widely available they changed far more than the appearance of the laboratory; they changed the way chemists spent their day.

Peter Fellgett of the University of Cambridge recorded the first Fourier transform infrared (FTIR) spectrum in 1949, and Grubb Parson and Research Industrial Instruments Company brought out far-infrared instruments developed by Alistair Gebbie of the National Physical Laboratory in the early 1960s. The first commercial mid-IR FTIR instrument was marketed by Block Engineering (later Digilab, now Bio-Rad) in 1963. However, the full development of this technique required the introduction of powerful microcomputers in the late 1960s and the application of the Cooley-Tukey fast Fourier transform to interferometry in 1966. The falling cost of computers enabled the production of moderately priced FTIR instruments in the early 1980s that have gradually displaced classical infrared spectrometers.

Raman spectroscopy, a technique discovered by the Indian physicist Venkata Raman in 1928, observes light scattered (rather than absorbed) by molecules. Raman spectroscopy can provide important clues about the symmetry or even detailed geometry of molecues. Since water does not cause interference, Raman spectra can be obtained in aqucous solutions. And, Raman spectra can be recorded directly on a photographic plate, while early IR spectroscopy required manual plotting.

A commercial Raman instrument was successfully marketed by Lane-Wells Co. of Pasadena, California, in the early 1940s. With the growing availability of automatically recording IR spectrophotometers after 1945, the importance of Raman spectroscopy declined, especially in organic chemistry. It remained useful, however, in inorganic chemistry and for organic molecules that absorb weakly in the IR region. The Cary 81 model was introduced in 1953. In 1962, S.P.S. Porto and D.L. Wood developed a Raman spectrometer that used a laser instead of the original mercury arc or mercury-silica arc light. This advance was soon commercialized and forms the basis of modern Raman spectroscopy. FT-Raman has also been commercialized.

Jon Eklund
Peter Morris

Bibliography

Banwell, Colin N., and Elaine M. McCash. *Fundamentals of Molecular Spectroscopy.* 4th ed. London: McGraw-Hill, 1994.

Beckman, Arnold O., et al. "History of Spectrophotometry at Beckman Instruments, Inc." *Analytical Chemistry* 49 (1977): 280A-300A.

Boltz, David F., et al. "Analytical Spectroscopy." In *A History of Analytical Chemistry,* edited by Herbert A. Laitinen and Galen W. Ewing. Washington, D.C.: American Chemical Society, 1977.

Denney, Ronald C., and Roy Sinclair. *Visible and Ultraviolet Spectroscopy.* Chichester: Wiley on behalf of ACOL, 1987.

George, Bill, and Peter McIntyre. *Infrared Spectroscopy.* Chichester: Wiley, 1987.

Jones, Ronald Norman. "Analytical Applications of Vibrational Spectroscopy: A Historical Review." *European Spectroscopy News* 70 (1987): 10–20; 72 (1987): 10–20; 74 (1987): 20–34. Originally published in *Chemical, Biological and Industrial Applications of Infrared Spectroscopy,* edited by James R. Durig, 1–50. Chichester: Wiley, 1985.

Rabkin, Yakov M. "Technological Innovation in Science. The Adoption of Infrared Spectroscopy by Chemists." *Isis* 78 (1987): 31–54.

Spectrophotometer, Dobson

A Dobson spectrophotometer measures ozone concentration in the earth's atmosphere by measuring ultraviolet absorption (ozone absorbs ultraviolet radiation at 0.22 to 0.33 μm.). Estimates of the total amount of ozone in a vertical column can be made by comparing the intensity of two wavelengths of sunlight, one corresponding to the absorption band of ozone and the other to a reference band. The vertical distribution of ozone is found by measuring upwards at different angles when the sun is low. This process is called the umkehr effect.

A Dobson spectrophotometer contains prisms that spilt incoming sunlight into two selected wavelengths that are isolated by a double monchromator. A rotating shutter causes the two wavelengths to fall alternately onto a **photomultiplier**. Optical wedge filters equalize the intensity of the two signals, and the positions of the optical wedges provide, after calibration, the relative intensities of the two beams.

The Dobson spectrophotometer was developed by Gordon Miller Bourne Dobson, who spent much of his career at the University of Oxford, studying atmospheric ozone. In the late nineteenth century, W.N. Hartley and A. Cornu had observed a concentration of ozone in the upper atmosphere and noted a blocking of ultraviolet light that they correctly attributed to ozone. In 1910 Fabry and Buisson measured atmospheric ozone for short periods by observing its absorption at certain radiation wavelengths. Their equipment, however, was not convenient for routine use out of doors. Dobson adopted their technique, and built his own spectrophotometer in 1924, using a prism and an optical wedge to isolate the wavelengths. Unwanted visible light was filtered out by a

Photoelectric Dobson ozone spectrophotometer, ca. 1980. British Crown Copyright © 1996. Reproduced with the permission of the Controller of Her Majesty's Stationery Office.

bromine-chlorine filter. The relative intensities of the spectral lines were recorded photographically. Dobson's first instrument is now in the Science Museum, London.

Measurements in 1925 established the main features of seasonal variation of ozone over Oxford. To further study the relationship between ozone distribution and meteorological patterns, Dobson obtained a Royal Society grant to buy five fer prisms for new spectrophotometers. These new instruments were sent to various locations around Europe, including Ireland, Switzerland, and Germany. Other instruments were sent to California, Egypt, India, and New Zealand in 1928. By the end of 1929, the main features of ozone variation with latitude and season had been established.

The recording mechanism of these first Dobson spectrophotometers was onto photographic plates that were sent back to Oxford for processing. Later models used a photoelectric cell as the recording mechanism.

Dobson spectrophotometers have since been built by R. & J. Beck (now Ealing Electro Optics), U.K., and the network of meteorological observation stations using them has increased steadily. In 1956 there were forty-four Dobson spectrophotometers distributed around the world. The International Geophysical Year (IGY) in 1957 increased the demand for new instruments with most of the sixty stations involved with ozone observations during IGY using Dobson spectrophotometers for measurements. By 1968, R. & J. Beck had completed instrument number one hundred. In May 1977 the World Meteorological Organization produced a list of the locations of all 120 Dobson spectrophotometers. By 1992 the manufacturers had completed number 130 for Taiwan. A few Dobson spectrophotometers were made in Japan and the USSR.

The basic design of the Dobson spectrophotometer has not changed radically since the 1920s. Operation of the instrument has been improved by changes to the electric power supply, and a move to fused silica optics instead of natural quartz. Otherwise the diagrams of the spectrophotometers in the IGY handbook and current trade literature are almost identical.

Ozone Depletion

In the mid 1980s, data from a Dobson spectrophotometer enabled a group of scientists from the British Antarctic Survey to identify ozone loss over the Antarctic. In fact Dobson spectrophotometers had been used since 1956 to measure ozone over Halley Bay, Antarctica, but ozone depletion was not established until one of the Dobsons was sent back to check that it was not giving faulty readings. Satellite data had not indicated the loss because the computer analyzing the data had been programmed to reject low values as being impossible. However, as a result of the Dobson spectrophotometer measurements, the satellite data was reinterpreted and confirmed a reduction of ozone. The significance of Dobson to ozone measurement is indicated by the fact that stratospheric ozone is measured in Dobson units.

Anna Bunney

Bibliography

Dobson, Gordon Miller Bourne. "The Development of Instruments for Measuring Atmospheric Ozone during the Last Fifty Years." *Journal of Physics. E: Scientific Instruments* 6 (1973): 938–39.

———. "Forty Years Research on Atmospheric Ozone at Oxford." *Applied Optics* 7 (1968): 387–405.

———, and C.W. Normand. "Observers' Handbook for Ozone Spectrophotometer." *Annals of the International Geophysical Year* 5 (1957): 90–114.

Farman, J.C., B.G. Gardiner, and J.D. Shanklin. "Large Losses of Total Ozone in Antarctica Reveal Seasonal CLOx/NOx Interaction." *Nature* 315 (1985): 207–10.

Houghton, J.T., and C. Desmond Walshaw. "Gordon Miller Bourne Dobson." *Biographical Memoirs of the Fellows of the Royal Society* 23 (1977).

Spectroscope (Early)

A spectroscope disperses light into a spectrum, enabling it to be observed and analyzed. The first spectroscopes were made by Robert Bunsen and Gustav Kirchhoff in Germany in 1859. Before that, spectroscopic observations were made with a simple prism or **diffraction grating**, mounted so the spectrum could be observed.

In 1666 Isaac Newton was one of the first to use a glass prism to analyze light, though his work was not published until 1672. He split white light into seven colors and showed that these colors could not be further decomposed. In the 1810s, while working to improve optical glass, the Bavarian glass-maker Joseph [von] Fraunhofer found that flame spectra are characterized by discrete bright lines. He also found a number of dark lines crossing the continuous spectrum of the sun, and noted that their positions were invariable. These dark lines were subsequently named after Fraunhofer, and the letters that he allocated to the most prominent lines are still used today.

While spectral lines facilitated the calibration of optical instruments, their meaning eluded satisfactory explanation for many years. Indeed, the physical interpretation of the lines played a major role in the debate over the nature of light (wave versus particle) that raged during the 1820s and 1830s. William Henry Fox Talbot suggested in 1826 that spectral lines might be used for chemical analysis. This idea, however, was not pursued, largely because the generally poor quality of glass prisms made it difficult to achieve replicable results, as did the impurities present in chemical substances.

From his work on photochemistry in the 1850s, the professor of chemistry at the University of Heidelberg, Robert Wilhelm Eberhard Bunsen, became convinced that the light emitted from flames is uniquely characteristic of the chemical elements present in those flames. In 1860–1861, using what was then known as spectrochemical analysis, Bunsen discovered two hitherto unknown chemical elements, which he named cesium and rubidium, that occurred in trace quantities in mineral waters. In 1861, William Crookes discovered the chemical element thallium using spectrochemical methods.

During the same period, Bunsen collaborated with the professor of physics, Gustav Robert Kirchhoff, and the two men were able to show experimentally that the bright yellow lines characteristic of sodium correspond with Fraunhofer's dark D lines in the solar spectrum. This extension of chemical analysis to the sun and stars (which the French philosopher Auguste Comte had given in 1835 as an example of something that it was impossible ever to know) led to the new science of astrophysics. In the ensuing decades, spectroscopical observations allowed astronomers to develop theories of the evolutionary sequence of stars. Somewhat later, using the measurements and analyses of the distribution of

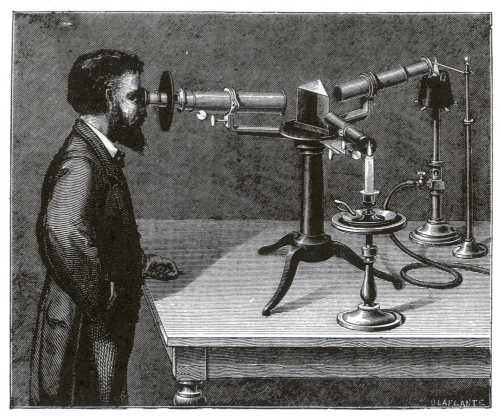

Spectroscope with reflected scale, 1870s. J. Norman Lockyer. The Spectroscope and Its Applications. *London, 1873: 29, Figure 16. Courtesy of SSPL.*

lines emitted by particular elements, physicists began to investigate the internal composition of matter, ultimately leading to the development of quantum mechanics.

The spectroscope's obvious benefits to a wide range of scientific activities led to commercial manufacture by such instrument-makers such as Steinheil in Munich, Elliott Brothers and John Browning in London, and Duboscq and Hoffmann in Paris. Although the instrument was developed and refined over the next few decades, its basic principles did not undergo any major change until the invention of the mass spectrometer (see **spectrometer, mass**) in 1919. From Kirchhoff's work onwards, most spectroscopes were provided with scales by which the position of a spectral line could be measured; the term "spectrometer" and "spectroscope" did not denote any significant difference in the principle of the instrument (see **spectrophotometer**). Refinements that were made to spectroscopes included using **diffraction gratings,** or hollow prisms filled with carbon bisulphide, instead of a glass prism.

The prisms of some spectroscopes were arranged such that the spectroscope could be apparently used in the same way as a telescope—"direct vision spectroscopes." But despite these modifications, the spectroscopes used in school chemical laboratories today would be instantly recognizable to Bunsen and Kirchhoff.

Frank A.J.L. James

Bibliography

Bennett, James A. *The Celebrated Phaenomena of Colours.* Cambridge: Whipple Museum of the History of Science, 1984.

James, Frank A.J.L. "The Discovery of Line Spectra." *Ambix* 32 (1985): 53–70.

———. "The Establishment of Spectro-Chemical Analysis as a Practical Method of Qualitative Analysis 1854–1861." *Ambix* 30 (1983): 30–53.

———. "The Practical Problems of 'New' Experimental Science: Spectro-Chemistry and the Search for Hitherto Unknown Chemical Elements in Britain 1860–

1869." *British Journal for the History of Science* 21 (1988): 181–94.

McGucken, William. *Nineteenth-Century Spectroscopy: Development of the Understanding of Spectra, 1802–1897*. Baltimore: Johns Hopkins University Press, 1969.

Spectroscope, Astronomical

In 1814, Joseph [von] Fraunhofer discovered more than five hundred dark lines crossing the continuous bright spectrum of the sun. In 1859, the work of Gustav Kirchhoff and Robert Bunsen provided the method of spectral analysis for determining the chemical composition of the sun and the stars. Efforts to photograph the solar spectrum began in the 1840s. The first photograph of the spectrum of a star (Vega) was accomplished by Henry Draper in 1872.

Early investigators worked with direct vision **spectroscopes** (made by Merz of Munich) or with a train of prisms for faint stars (such as those made by John Browning of London). High-dispersion spectrographs designed specifically for photographing the spectrum were introduced in the 1870s. In 1888, using the 28-cm refractor at the Potsdam Astrophysical Observatory with a spectrograph made by Otto Toepfer in Potsdam, Hermann Carl Vogel obtained the first reliable measures of line shifts caused by the Doppler effect. The comparison spectrum was obtained by a **Geissler tube** or by a spark spectrum.

At the turn of the century, large spectrographs were built by John A. Brashear of Pittsburgh, Howard Grubb of Dublin, Carl Zeiss of Jena, and Askania of Berlin. Using the Coudé focus, very large spectrographs can be placed in a separate room. The registration of the spectrum can be made in the laboratory with micro**photometers**. The line profiles contain information about temperature and pressure of the stellar atmosphere.

In order to observe or photograph many stellar spectra at the same time, especially for classification purposes, an objective prism is mounted in front of the objective lens of the telescope (an idea of Fraunhofer's). Because incident starlight is already parallel, the collimator and the slit can be omitted. The prism angle is normally small (about 7°), otherwise the long focal length of the telescopes would produce too large a dispersion. By observing visually with a Merz objective prism, Angelo Sec-

chi sorted the stars into three spectral types in 1866. Harvard astronomers began a spectrographic survey in 1885, eventually producing the Henry Draper Catalogue in which Annie J. Cannon classified the stars into seven spectral types. For survey work, objective prisms are still used today (dispersion only about 100–1,000 Å/mm). In the 1940s, R.W. Wood used objective transmission gratings of great light efficiency by concentrating most of the spectral light into one first-order spectrum (see **diffraction grating**).

Ultraviolet Spectroscopy

In 1875, William Huggins designed an ultraviolet spectrograph with a quartz collimating lens, an Iceland spar prism made by Adam Hilger of London, and a sensitive dry plate. To obtain spectra of very faint sources such as nebulae, slitless quartz spectrographs were used, for example, at Lick Observatory around the turn of the century.

In the 1930s, Karl-Otto Kiepenheuer measured the ultraviolet radiation (UV) of the sun with a quartz spectrograph in a balloon in the stratosphere. This UV double monochromator was made by Carl Leiss of Berlin-Steglitz. In 1942, Kiepenheuer developed the idea of using a rocket to photograph the ultraviolet spectrum. In 1946, under the auspices of the U.S. Naval Research Laboratory, an ultraviolet spectrograph was transported into space by an A4 (V2) rocket. In 1974, the *Skylab* space station provided information on solar spectra in the extreme ultraviolet.

Solar Spectroscopy

Solar prominences were discovered during a solar eclipse in 1842 and were visible only during solar eclipses until 1868, when J. Norman Lockyer and Pierre J. Janssen found that by widely opening the slit of their spectroscope, they could study prominences at any time. Charles A. Young photographed prominences in this way in 1870. The small prism spectroscopes attached to the eye end of a refracting telescope eventually developed into solar spectrographs, which can be as large as the telescope with which they are used. Diffraction gratings that produced high-dispersion normal spectra (that is, in which the positions of the spectral lines are proportional to their wavelength) were introduced in the 1880s. The American physicist Henry A. Rowland began ruling diffraction gratings on concave surfaces. Using a mounting in which the entrance slit, the concave grating, and the photographic

Seven-prism astronomical spectroscope for observing solar prominences, ca. 1868. J. Norman Lockyer,
Contributions to Solar Physics. *London: Macmillan, 1874, Figure 84. Courtesy of SSPL.*

plate lie on a circle, Rowland produced a photographic atlas that showed twenty thousand lines of the solar spectrum. The American astronomer and engineer F.L.O. Wadsworth designed a compact and achromatic mounting for a concave grating that enabled astronomers to record and identify spectra of small solar structures.

Plane gratings were easier to produce than concave gratings of similar perfection, and they give a better definition over the usable spectral range. A Littrow or autocollimating spectroscope (the collimator lens is also the camera lens) is used at the Mount Wilson Solar Observatory. The Czerny spectroscope at McMath-Hulbert Observatory in Michigan produces coma-free images.

In 1908, using a spectrograph fed by a coelostat (see **heliostat**) mounted on a tower, George Ellery Hale at Mount Wilson was able to observe and to measure the line doubling caused by the Zeeman effect, and thus to determine magnetic fields in sunspots.

Since the 1970s, astronomers have used gratings with a few grooves per millimeter (called échelles)—an idea of Robert McMath's in the 1950s. By an appropriate form of grooves, because of a certain reflection angle (blaze angle), the main intensity of a given order could be concentrated in one direction. With the échelles, large dispersions can be obtained: for stars several Å/mm and for the sun 0.1 Å/mm.

The spectroheliograph was invented independently in 1890 by George Ellery Hale in Chicago and Henri Deslandres in Paris-Meudon, in order to investigate the chromosphere, the reddish-colored envelope surrounding the sun. This instrument produces a monochromatic photograph by selecting with a filter a narrow band of light—usually the red hydrogen line Hα 6,563 Å or the violet calcium line 3,933 Å (but the infrared line of helium can also be used)—and by photographing only one slice of the sun at a time. With the Rumford spectroheliograph at Yerkes Observatory, Hale took the first photographs in the Hα lines and discovered the dark hydrogen or calcium flocculi in 1903. In 1926, Hale invented the spectrohelioscope, an instrument for visual observation of short-timescale chromospheric phenomena. With this instrument it is possible to observe the movements of prominences and especially the solar flares (eruptions of high energy).

Gudrun Wolfschmidt

Bibliography

Birney, S.D. *Observatorial Astronomy.* Cambridge: Cambridge University Press, 1991.

Hearnshaw, J.B. *The Analysis of Starlight: One Hundred and Fifty Years of Astronomical Spectroscopy.* Cambridge: Cambridge University Press, 1986.

Kitchin, C.R. *Astrophysical Techniques.* 2nd ed. Bristol: Adam Hilger, 1991.

Ulrich, M.H., ed. *High Resolution Spectroscopy with the VLT. Proceedings No. 40 of the ESO Workshop 1992.* Garching, Bavaria: European Southern Observatory, 1993.

Voigt, H.H., ed. *Landolt-Bornstein: Numerical Data and Functional Relationships in Science and Technology.* Group 6, vol. 3, *Astronomy and Astrophysics. A: Instruments, Methods, Solar System.* Berlin: Springer, 1993.

Wall, J.V., and A. Boksenberg. *Modern Technology and Its Influence on Astronomy.* Cambridge: Cambridge University Press, 1990.

Speedometer

A speedometer indicates the speed of a moving motor vehicle. In the early days of motoring, with relatively few vehicles on the road, a speed indicator was not an important requirement of safe travel, an **odometer** being a more useful accessory to indicate distance traveled. Many steam-driven delivery vehicles were traveling average annual distances of 12,000 miles by the early 1900s. On October 1, 1937, it became a legal requirement for all motor vehicles in the U.K., registered for the first time on or after that date, to be fitted with a speedometer, exceptions being invalid carriages or vehicles restricted at all times to twelve miles per hour.

In England one of the earliest speedometers was produced by Smiths in 1904 for a Daimler owned by King Edward VII. Samuel Smith, a watch- and clock-maker, founded his business in London around 1851. With the rapid popularization of motor vehicles the business expanded, and S. Smith and Sons (Motor Accessories) was formed in 1914. Some fifty thousand speedometers were then in use. Allan Gordon Smith, Samuel's fifth child, invented the mileometer, a simple device usually fitted to the hub of the wheel to record distance traveled.

Further development, and the king's wish to know the speed of his vehicle, led to the production of a speedometer, often combined with the odometer as an instrument to be fitted to the bulkhead or windscreen pillar of the vehicle.

There were many early designs, including an electric speedometer that relied on the road wheel's turning a small magnetic dynamo connected to a hot wire **voltmeter** giving a proportionate reading of speed to current. This rather fragile device had largely disappeared by 1911, replaced by robust instruments needed to survive the rigorous road conditions.

The principle speedometer manufacturers in England were Smiths, Watford, and Elliott. The early manufacturers in Europe included O.S. and Jaeger; the A.T. (or Auto-Tempometer) was introduced in Germany and later bought by Smiths. American firms included Jones, A.C., North East, Stewart, and Waltham.

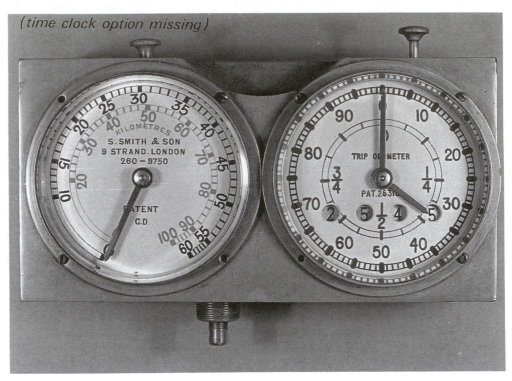

An early Smith's speedometer and odometer. Courtesy of Vintage Restorations.

The Jones speedometer was first used on the New York to Buffalo endurance run in 1901, and rapidly became popular, production quickly increasing to at one time a thousand a day. The Warner speedometer was patented in 1903. The company was sold to John K. Stewart in 1912, and the Stewart Warner Speedometer Co. was founded.

Developed at about the same time, the Governor speedometer was based on a device invented to control steam engines. It had a shaft with spring-loaded weights that opened under centrifugal force, pulling a slide connected to a mechanism operating the pointer, speed being indicated on the dial in proportion to the amount of movement made by the slide. A worm gear cut on the revolving shaft connected to the odometer mechanism wheels. This type of instrument required a fast rotating cable to give the necessary impetus to the governor, usually in the region of 3,000 revolutions per mile. Because of this high speed, the governor shaft was mounted on ball bearings.

The air mechanism of the American Waltham speedometer relied on a cable driving two cups fixed close together, over which was poised a similar double aluminum cup with an air gap of about 0.01 in. between the pairs. The air friction between the cups was sufficient to revolve the driven cup, which was restrained by a hair spring. The edge of the outer cup was printed with the speed, indicated through a slot in the dial.

Later the Magnetic speedometer used a magnet rotated by a flexible cable at a speed proportional to the speed of the vehicle. Concentric with the magnet, an aluminum cup or disk was mounted on a spindle that carried the pointer above the dial and a hair spring below. The magnet when turned produces a rotating magnetic field that causes eddy currents in the aluminum disk that is then carried in the direction of rotation of the magnet. The amount of movement is controlled by the hair spring of a given strength. On early examples, the speed scale was printed on the edge of the aluminum cup and viewed through a slot in a cover dial. Beneath the magnet a worm gear was fitted to operate the odometer mechanism. These instruments were of simpler construction, not requiring such high cable revolutions or ball bearing mountings to the spindle. Because of economics of production, the same magnetic principle of operating the speed pointer and odometer mechanism remain to the present day, in spite of the development of electromechanical and solid-state display instruments.

The Chronometric mechanism consists of a geared drive and a balance wheel escapement similar to that of a watch or clock. The escapement controls the speed of rotation of a camshaft, which causes the recording mechanism to be engaged with the drive at regular intervals. During these intervals, the turns of the mechanism are counted and indicated on the dial by the pointer, which, moving from one position to the next, gives a very accurate, steady reading. The complex nature of this mechanism required intricate parts to be manufactured to fine limits, and that meant high costs of production. The magnetic instrument, less complicated and simpler to manufacture, became more favored.

Other indicators of speed have been developed for aircraft and for boats and ships.

John E. Marks

Bibliography

Kennedy, Rankin. *The Book of the Motor Car: A Comprehensive and Authoritative Guide on the Care, Management, Maintenance, and Construction of the Motor Car and Motor Cycle.* London: Caxton, 1913.

————. *The Encyclopaedia of Motoring: Containing Full Definitions of Every Term Used in Motoring, with Special Articles on Roadside Troubles, Electric Ignition and Similar Important Subjects,* edited by R.J. Mecredy. 3rd ed. Dublin: Mecredy, Percy, 1909.

Spherometer

An instrument for measuring the curvature of surfaces or the thickness of a thin plate. John Herschel termed it an "elegant invention" which, "by substituting the sense of touch for that of sight in the measurement of minute objects, permits the determination of their dimensions with a degree of precision which is fully adequate to the nicest purposes of scientific enquiry." Although there is some indication that the spherometer was invented by the French optician Laroue, the first spherometer of which we have positive knowledge was that devised and named around 1810 by the French optician Robert-Aglaé Cauchoix and made by the French mechanician Nicolas Fortin. Cauchoix's design—a three-legged base supporting a central **micrometer screw**—was quickly adopted as the basic standard, and remains in use to this day. The Conservatoire National des Arts et Métiers in Paris has a spherometer made by Fortin; another, made by Cauchoix and used by Biot, that reads to 1/1,000 millimeter; and another, made by the French mechanician Perreaux that reads to 1/4,000 millimeter.

German instrument-makers were producing spherometers by the 1820s, if not earlier. Particularly notable was the instrument made by Georg Reichenbach, probably for the use of Joseph [von] Fraunhofer, with a contact lever that significantly increased the precision of the instrument. The first English spherometer-maker seems to have been Andrew Ross, who received a silver medal from the Royal Society of Arts for this work in 1841.

Spherometers are small, often no more than 5 in. high, with a graduated circle of less than 4 in. diameter. Precise instruments were relatively expensive. In 1874, for instance, J.W. Queen & Co. of Philadelphia offered one for $50. By the turn of the century, however, many

Spherometer by Perreaux, 1866. Courtesy of Musée National des Techniques, CNAM–Paris.

dealers were offering serviceable instruments for under $5.

While originally designed for the use of opticians, spherometers were probably most often to be found in physics laboratories. They were eagerly adopted by physicists such as J.B. Biot (1811), J. Herschel (1820), and E. Mitscherlich (1824), who found them essential for their investigations of the colors produced by thin plates of translucent material. Later in the century, when physics professors stressed the importance of precision measurement, spherometers became standard pieces of pedagogical equipment. They were made by most precision instrument-makers and were available from most scientific instrument dealers.

Deborah Jean Warner

Bibliography

Biot, Jean Baptiste. *Traité de Physique,* Vol. 4, 343–45. Paris: Deterville, 1816.

Conservatoire National des Arts et Métiers. *Catalogue des Collections,* 397–98. Paris: Dunod, 1882.

Herschel, John Frederick. *Preliminary Discourse on the Study of Natural Philosophy,* 355. London: Longman, 1830.

Ross, Andrew. "Spherometer." *Transactions, Royal Society of Arts* 53 (1839–1841): 74–78.

Sphygmomanometer

A sphygmomanometer measures arterial blood pressure. The term is derived from the Greek word *sphygmos* (pulse) and the French word *manometre* (**pressure gauge**). The standard unit is millimeters of mercury.

Since antiquity, healers have been fascinated with the pulse, feeling that its rate and quality provide clues to a person's state of health. Most ancient cultures established elaborate systems of pulse diagnosis and recognized that a bounding pulse often signified diseased states.

In 1733, Stephen Hales reported his experience with measuring blood pressure in horses. Approximately fifteen years earlier, he had inserted a brass pipe in a horse's artery, connected it to a glass pipe, and made the first determination of arterial blood pressure. Over one hundred years elapsed before a German physiologist, Carl Ludwig, developed the **kymograph** in 1847 and opened the door to graphical exploration of human physiology. Using the kymograph, Ludwig and his colleagues inserted cath-

eters into the arteries of experimental animals and obtained numerical and graphical measurements of blood pressure. The technique of cannulating arteries was invasive and risky, however, and could not be practically applied to clinical medicine.

Many physiologists experimented with devices for measuring arterial blood pressure without opening an artery. In 1855, German physiologist Karl Vierordt developed a sphygmograph to measure the pressure needed to obliterate the arterial pulse. In 1860, French physiologist Etienne-Jules Marey developed an improved, more clinically useful sphygmograph. While these machines accurately depicted the rate and regularity of the pulse, they could not reliably determine blood pressure.

In 1881, Samuel Siegfried Karl Ritter von Basch invented his sphygmomanometer, a simple device that used a water-filled bag connected to a manometer to measure the pressure needed to obliterate the radial pulse. His determinations of blood pressure were confirmed by direct arterial catheterization, proof that an indirect measure could be reliable. Von Basch's instrument was not widely adopted clinically, in part because doctors were wary of any technology that replaced time-honored methods of diagnosis, and in part because the practitioner had yet to be convinced that the information gleaned from the instrument had practical applications. Although a number of physiologist-physicians adapted von Basch's design—some using plethysmographic principles, others using a spring manometer—these instruments did not gain widespread use. Critics called attention to their bulkiness, frequent need for calibration, propensity to break, and inaccuracy in acutely ill patients.

In 1896, Scipione Riva-Rocci, an Italian physician, announced his invention of the prototype of the modern sphygmomanometer. His device circumferentially squeezed the arm with an inflatable rubber tube, and thus occluded the brachial artery. As the pressure was released, a mercury manometer measured the point at which the pulse returned, the systolic pressure. Riva-Rocci's technique required the physician to palpate the radial pulse during the procedure. The American neurosurgeon Harvey Cushing discovered Riva-Rocci's device while traveling in Italy in 1901 and brought it to Johns Hopkins University, making minor alterations to make it easier to use in the hospital. Cushing

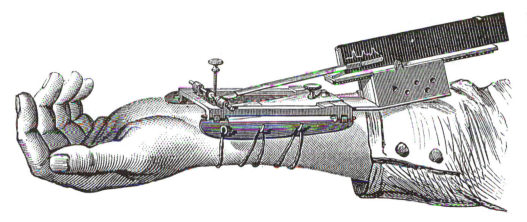

Marey direct-recording sphygmograph. Étienne Jules Marey. La Méthode Graphique. *Paris: Libraire de l'Académie de Médecine, 1878: 281, Figure 142. Courtesy of SSPL.*

and George Washington Crile, a Cleveland surgeon interested in shock, became the foremost American proponents of sphygmomanometry, advocating its use in the operating room and as a diagnostic, therapeutic, and prognostic instrument.

In 1905, Nikolai S. Korotkoff, a Russian surgeon, discovered that both the systolic and diastolic pressures could be determined if the physician auscultated the pulse with a **stethoscope**, instead of palpating it. With the acceptance of his auscultory method, physicians symbolically "let go" of pulse palpation in the determination of blood pressure. Korotkoff's technique provided more accurate and reliable information about the underlying pathophysiology and is the method most widely used today.

Significance

The sphygmomanometer symbolized the transformation occurring in late-nineteenth- and early-twentieth-century medicine in which disease and health became entities that could be measured and quantified. Sphygmomanometers, and many other physiological instruments adapted for clinical use, provided new access to bodily processes and allowed them to be presented in numerical and often graphical terms. Quantitative data was touted as superior to the qualitative descriptions that had dominated medicine until the late nineteenth century. Armed with the power of the "graphic method," leading doctors stressed thinking about disease as a process that could be measured. These new methods of presenting information fundamentally changed the way in which doctors communicated with each other, replacing largely descriptive phrases with more precise terms. Accordingly, medical education was transformed, with a heightened emphasis on knowledge that is measurable and reproducible. By the 1920s, the sphygmomanometer was a standard tool in the doctor's armamentarium.

Before the sphygmomanometer's information could be useful, researchers had to establish normal and abnormal values. Theodore Janeway, a passionate advocate of sphygmomanometry, examined blood pressure measurements of hundreds of patients over time and discovered "essential hypertension," or an elevated blood pressure that signaled future disease. The sphygmomanometer not only quantified a bodily function that had heretofore been merely described, it also enabled doctors to discover a pathological state that was largely asymptomatic.

The impact of the sphygmomanometer on the doctor patient relationship has been profound. Instruments such as this one contributed to a rising feeling that the human body is a machine and the doctor a mechanic. Critics have argued that these instruments of precision distanced the patient from the doctor; advocates have stressed that with information gathered using the instruments, the doctor actually knew the patient more intimately.

Hughes Evans

Bibliography

Booth, Jeremy. "A Short History of Blood Pressure Measurement." *Proceedings of the Royal Society of Medicine* 70 (1977): 793–99.

Davis, Audrey B. *Medicine and Its Technol-*

ogy: *An Introduction to the History of Medical Instrumentation.* Westport, Conn.: Greenwood, 1981.

Evans, Hughes. "Losing Touch: The Controversy over the Introduction of Blood Pressure Instruments into Medicine." *Technology and Culture* 34 (1993): 784–807.

Janeway, Theodore. *The Clinical Study of the Blood-Pressure: A Guide to the Use of the Sphygmomanometer in Medical, Surgical, and Obstetrical Practice, with a Summary of the Experimental and Clinical Facts Relating to the Blood-Pressure in Health and Disease.* New York: Appleton, 1904.

Reiser, Stanley Joel. *Medicine and the Reign of Technology.* Cambridge: Cambridge University Press, 1978.

Spinthariscope by Adam Hilger Ltd., 1924, used by James Chadwick. SM 1982-1708. Courtesy of SSPL/University of Liverpool.

Spinthariscope

The spinthariscope is a simple instrument that visually shows individual alpha particles by means of the scintillations they produce when hitting a screen of a suitable phosphorescent material. Whereas the spinthariscope itself was of little scientific value, it was soon developed into methods of quantitative determinations of radiations from radioactive substances by means of such scintillations. In the present context, "spinthariscopes" include simple **scintillation counters** insofar as the counting was done visually.

In a lecture before the Royal Society on March 19, 1903, William Crookes reported that if a screen coated with phosphorescent zinc sulphide is exposed to the radiation from an alpha-active substance—he used radium nitrate—a brilliant luminosity appeared; by means of a magnifying glass he showed that it consisted of a large number of scintillating points that he identified as effects of collisions of the alpha particles with the crystals. Eighteen days later the German physicists Julius Elster and Hans Geitel announced that they had known the phenomenon "for some time" and described experiments similar to Crookes's.

Crookes devised an instrument that he called a spinthariscope, a word derived from the Greek *spintharis,* meaning "scintillation" or "spark." It consisted of a trace of a radium salt placed 1 millimeter away from a small zinc sulphide screen fixed at one end of a short brass tube; at the other end of the tube there was a convex lens through which the scintillations on the screen could be observed in a dark room. Crookes's spinthariscope quickly became popular. In the summer of 1903 it was manufactured by several instrument-makers who designed it as a waistcoat-pocket instrument. In 1904 F.H. Glew, a London instrument-maker, invented the "scintilloscope," a version with a replaceable double glass plate, one of the plates being coated with a radioactive salt and the other with a phosphor. The public's fascination with radioactivity for a period made spinthariscopes and scintilloscopes popular among people who wanted to demonstrate their interest in science.

The pocket-spinthariscope functioned as a demonstration instrument and a toy. Some years later, improved instruments, in which the number of flashes could be counted, became important in radioactive research. In 1908, Erich Regener of Berlin University devised a method of counting scintillations by observing them with a **microscope.** He concluded that almost each alpha particle hitting the screen produces a scintillation, from which he was able to infer the charge of the alpha particle. Regener also found that beta particles produce scintillations in barium platinocyanide, but these were too feeble to be used for quantitative purposes. During the following two decades, fine crystals of zinc sulphide with traces of copper were mostly used as phosphor (pure zinc sulphide does not scintillate). It was by means of counting scintillations that Ernest Rutherford and Hans Geiger clarified the nature of the alpha particle, and it was also this method they used in measuring the scattering of alpha particles that in 1911 led to the discovery of the atomic nucleus.

Visual counting of scintillations was used extensively until the early 1930s and proved invaluable in the study of radioactivity and nuclear physics. It was only in the late 1920s that the method was investigated systematically, especially by physicists in the Cavendish Laboratory. It was shown that the duration of each scintillation was about 10^{-4} second, and that about one-quarter of the energy of the alpha particle was converted into visible light, a surprisingly high ratio. However, the mechanism of the production of the scintillations remained obscure.

One of the last successes of the visual scintillation method was its use in the famous experiment of John Cockcroft and Ernest Walton in 1932 on the disintegration of lithium nuclei by artificially accelerated protons. Cockcroft and Walton used a scintillation counting method with zinc sulphide screens and microscopes that had not changed much over twenty years. At that time visual scintillation counting was becoming obsolete, and electronically improved **Geiger-Müller counters** began to dominate particle detection. Unable to make use of the new electronics, the scintillation method seemed on its way to being relegated to museums. However, after World War II, the method experienced a spectacular revival with the emergence of the electronic scintillation counter.

Helge Kragh

Bibliography

Chariton, J., and C.A. Lea. "Some Experiments Concerning the Counting of Scintillations Produced by Alpha Particles." *Proceedings of the Royal Society* A122 (1929): 304–52.

Crookes, William. "The Emanations of Radium." *Proceedings of the Royal Society* 71 (1903): 405–8.

Regener, Erich. "Über Zählung der α-Teilchen durch Szintillation und die Grösse des elektrischen Elementarquantums." *Verhandlungen der Deutschen Physikalishcen Gesellschaft* 10 (1908): 78–83.

Rutherford, Ernest, James Chadwick, and Charles Ellis. *Radiations from Radioactive Substances*. Cambridge: Cambridge University Press, 1930.

Spirometer

A spirometer measures quantities of air expired from the lungs. Most types are variants of the simple gasometer. Although sometimes presented as a key example of the nineteenth-century interest in the numerical measure of physiological function, there is little evidence that spirometers were in common usage until comparatively recently.

A succession of eighteenth-century experimenters, including Alphonso Borelli, Daniel Bernouilli, and Stephen Hales, measured inspiration or expiration. Their investigations were more often the fruits of natural philosophical investigation or natural historical recording than of strictly medical interests. In 1800, following a visit to James Beddoes' Pneumatic Institution, William Clayfield produced a "mercurial air holder," which allowed volumes of expired air to be measured.

John Hutchinson, who is generally credited as the inventor of medical spirometry, introduced his device in 1846. This consisted of a counterweighted sealed cylinder inverted inside another, with a reservoir of water providing an airtight seal. The person being tested blew through a pipe into the base of the inner cylinder, causing it to rise to an extent that could be read off on a calibrated scale. Hutchinson developed a classification of different volumes of air in respiration: breathing, complemental, reserve, and residual air. The combination of the first two (the greatest voluntary expiration following the deepest inspiration) he named "vital capacity" and made it his standard measure. Hutchinson, perhaps reflecting developments in medical statistics, derived a measure of normal vital capacity by testing more than four thousand individuals, ranging from dwarfs to giants and pugilists to gentlemen. He established that this vital capacity was linearly related to height, but not to weight.

Variations

Most subsequent spirometers took a similar approach. Dry spirometers either have a mechanical seal in place of the water, or have taken the form of concertinalike bellows incorporating a central sticklike calibrated gauge. An exception is Robert Lowne's portable spirometer, patented in 1870. In this the quantity of breath was measured by means of an enclosed paddle wheel connected via gears to a watchlike gauge.

Most spirometers gave a simple numerical measure of Hutchinson's "vital capacity." During the twentieth century it has become common to investigate the rate as well as the volume of expiration. Sometimes timers have been conof respiratory function. Two instruments have been developed to measure this. The Wright peak flow meter is a cylindrical box containing a vane pivoted so that it moves in a circle when air is blown in via an orifice at the side. A dial connected to the pivot gives the reading. The peak flow gauge, shaped like a pistol, is simpler yet, consisting of a piston running in a cylinder.

The other main postwar development has been the electronic spirometer, in which electronic circuitry translates signals from sensors into standard measures. Various sensor techniques have been used, including channeling exhaled breath over a heated wire whose resistance is proportional to the air flow rate. Another approach is to place in the air path a small propellerlike sail wheel whose rate of rotation is read by means of an optical device.

Contexts of Use

Since the time of Hutchinson, champions of spirometry have proclaimed its promise as a routine diagnostic technique, although the frequency with which inventors write piously of the wish that it should become more common belies this supposed potential. Only since the introduction of the Wright peak flow meter and gauge has spirometry gained a foothold in routine clinical use. In the hospital, the rise of the technique of artificial ventilation from the late 1930s has established a niche for spirometry as a monitoring technique. Spirometric modules using electronic sensors are now standard items of life-support equipment.

In public health, spirometry has been used more widely. The measure of "vital capacity" was beguiling to medical practitioners in the insurance industry, especially as spirometry could be used to diagnose tuberculosis, a disease whose high prevalence caused considerable concern to the calculators of premiums. But it is in the physiological laboratory that spirometry has probably seen greatest use, and especially with the rise of the study of lung diseases in occupational health since the 1930s. In this context many techniques have been developed, including double spirometers to record the ventilatory capacity of each lung separately (in this case it is necessary to pass a special catheter down the trachea to gain the two readings). Another example is calculating the residual volume of the lungs (the air that cannot voluntarily be expelled) using a spirometer in conjunction with a katharometer to measure the quantity of an

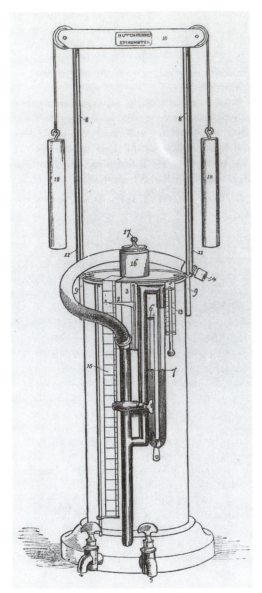

Hutchinson's spirometer. John Hutchinson. "On the capacity of the lungs. . . ." Medico-Chirurgical Transactions 29 (1846): 234. Courtesy of SSPL.

nected to spirometers. But most often recordings have been made by connecting a **ky-mograph** to the counterweight thread of the instrument. In the Vitalograph a pen writing on a triggered fast-moving chart is connected on an arm to the top of the wedge-shaped bellows, which receive the expired air. Recording spirometers are occasionally called spirographs.

One of the most notable postwar developments has been the establishment of forced expiratory volume (FEV_1) as the main measure

unreactive gas, usually helium, mixed with the air breathed by the subject.

Timothy M. Boon

Bibliography

Bass, B.H. *Lung Function Tests: An Introduction.* 4th ed. London: H.K. Lewis, 1974.

Davis, Audrey B. *Medicine and Its Technology: An Introduction to the History of Medical Instrumentation.* Westport, Conn.: Greenwood, 1981.

Reiser, Stanely Joel. *Medicine and the Reign of Technology.* Cambridge: Cambridge University Press, 1978.

Spriggs, E.A. "The History of Spirometry." *British Journal of Diseases of the Chest* 22 (1978): 165–80.

Wright, B.M., and C.B. McKerrow. "Maximum Forced Expiratory Flow Rate as a Measure of Vital Capacity." *British Medical Journal* 2 (1959): 1041–47.

SQUID

A SQUID (Superconducting Quantum Interference Device) essentially measures magnetic flux changes but has been developed to permit exquisitely sensitive measurements of a wide range of physical properties including voltage, displacement, biomagnetic signals, and magnetic microscopy. Its operational principle is based on a combination of two pivotal aspects of superconductivity, both discovered in the 1960s— namely, magnetic flux quantization and the Josephson effects.

History

Superconductivity was a little-understood phenomenon that included loss of electrical resistance and exclusion of magnetic field (the Meissner effect) exhibited by certain metallic samples when they were cooled below a transition temperature characteristic of each material. The phenomena were explained in terms of quin in the mid 1950s. An important conceptual leap involved realizing that a piece of superconductor could be treated as a single macroscopic quantum system, a little like a single giant atom. The implications of this explained the observed magnetic field exclusion but also implied that the magnetic flux linking any hole through a piece of superconductor should be quantized, existing only as an integer multiple of the flux quantum $\Phi_o = h/2e$ (where h is Planck's constant and e is the charge of an elec-

tron). The second major event that led to the discovery of the SQUID involved British physicist Brian Josephson's enunciation in 1962 of the effects that occur when two pieces of superconductor are coupled weakly together, so that a small supercurrent of electron pairs (<1 mA, typically) can flow by quantum mechanical tunneling or classical transport means between them. These effects, with their counter-intuitive existence of direct voltage drops driving an alternating supercurrent, can also be best understood in terms of the macroscopic quantum nature of superconductivity.

The first SQUID was made some four years after Josephson's prediction of the effects that bear his name and consisted of two tunneling junctions in a thin film structure. It demonstrated all the effects expected but did not have a practically useful magnetic field sensitivity because of its extremely small cross-sectional area. Within two years a single junction or radio-frequency SQUID, constructed from a bulk piece of niobium and with a cross-sectional area of a few square millimeters, was perfected. This two-hole SQUID could be coupled to the outside world by means of a superconducting flux transformer (a magnetic flux linking circuit based on the persistent supercurrent flowing in a superconducting coil whose ends were welded together). The magnetic sensitivity shown by this early device established SQUIDs as the most sensitive magnetometry devices available, exceeding by two orders of magnitude the sensitivity achieved with the much bulkier magnetic resonance **magnetometers**.

Fundamental Physics

Initial use of SQUIDs was mainly confined to physics laboratories, where their unique properties contributed to a number of basic measurements. An early demonstration of the magnetic vector potential using the Aharonov-Bohm effect was followed in later years by their use in searches for quarks, magnetic monopoles, gravity waves, and a very sensitive test of the equivalence principle of general relativity.

Applications

SQUIDs began to move into the wider world when the reproducibility and reliability of the devices were improved. This process began with development of the Nb-Insulator-Nb trilayer thin film process, arising out of Josephson junction computer projects that were carried out in a number of countries during the 1970s and

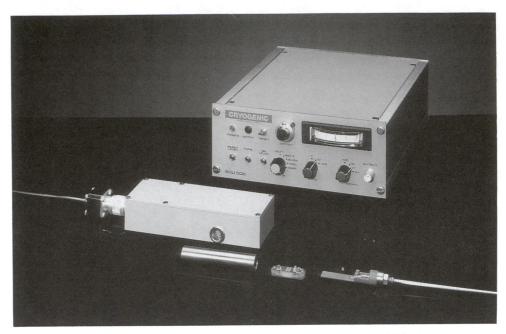

SQS6/SCU500 SQUID system, by Cryogenic Consultants Ltd., ca. 1991. Provided by Cryogenic Consultants Ltd.

1980s. As a result thousands of circuits with properties matched to within a few percent could be made reproducibly. New thin film coupling coils and strucures with improved efficiency also resulted, allowing SQUIDs to be coupled to a variety of physical parameters. Since the end of the Cold War it has been revealed that military applications for the remote detection of the magnetic signature of submerged submarines was probably the earliest developed application. The use of as many as 256 SQUIDs to remotely image the magnetic fields arising from electrical activity in the human brain (typically only tens of fem-totesla in amplitude) is probably the most impressive demonstration of SQUID technology at the time of this writing.

High-Temperature Superconductors

The remarkable increase in the transition temperature of superconductors, which arose from Bednorz's and Muller's 1986 discovery of superconductivity in two-dimensional copper oxide perovskite structured compounds, led to a rapid development of SQUIDs that could be used at temperatures as high as 110°K, well above the boiling point of liquid nitrogen (77°K). Within six years, high temperature SQUID systems were on sale and many of the applications originally envisaged using liquid helium–cooled SQUIDs had been demonstrated, at least in pro-

totype form, with high-temperature versions. The Josephson junction technologies are not yet as developed as for low-temperature SQUIDs. True tunnel junctions have not yet been demonstrated, but reasonably reproducible grain boundary junctions are used where the grain boundary may be engineered at any required point in an otherwise epitaxial thin superconducting film. The resulting devices are as sensitive as the best liquid helium–cooled SQUIDs of the 1970s and, since cooling should be much less difficult, may be expected to be used much more in extra-laboratory applications.

John Gallop

Bibliography

Clarke, J. "SQUIDs." *Scientific American* 271 (February 1994): 46–53.

Gallop, J.C. *SQUIDs, the Josephson Effects and Superconducting Electronics*. Bristol: Adam Hilger, 1991.

Station Pointer

A station pointer is used to plot positions that have been fixed by measuring the horizontal angles between three objects of known position. Its principal application is in marine surveying, for the insertion of soundings onto a chart. Fixes by measurements of the horizontal angles are known as resection fixes. The theory of re-section fixes was described by John Collins in 1674 and Edmond Halley in 1701, both of whom realized their potential value for marine surveyors. But the process of calculating the point of observation mathematically was time consuming and impractical.

The instrumental solution of the problem was suggested in 1774 by the surveyor Murdoch Mackenzie, Sr. In his words: "Provide a graduated semicircle of brass, about 6 inches in diameter, having three radii with chamfered edges, each about 20 inches long . . . one of which radii to be a continuation of the diameter that passes through the beginning of the degrees on the semicircle, but immoveably fixed to it, the other two moveable round the center, so as to be set and screwed fast to the semicircle at any angle. In the center let there be a small socket, or hole, to admit a pin for marking the central point on the draught."

The observed angles were to be set between the movable arms and the fixed arm and the instrument then laid on the chart and its position adjusted until the index of one of the three arms passed through each of the three points used. The observer's position was then at the center of the instrument and could be pricked onto the chart. Mackenzie concluded that "such an instrument as this may be called a station-pointer; and would be found convenient for finding the point of station readily and accurately."

Mackenzie had already retired from active surveying when he wrote this, but the idea was taken up by his nephew and successor as Admiralty surveyor Lt. Murdoch Mackenzie and his assistant, Graeme Spence, who suddenly were able to increase the number of soundings included in their work. They may already have had a prototype station pointer; or they may have used a piece of tracing paper with the angles drawn on it, another solution suggested by the elder Mackenzie. A later report credits Spence with developing a new station pointer in about 1784, and certainly by 1788 the Navy Board owned two station pointers that they issued to Spence for surveying.

Station pointers came into general use over the next thirty years, enabling British hydrographers charting large areas of the world to insert numerous soundings accurately. A surveyor with a good sextant and three well-fixed points to observe could take fixes quickly and independently of the errors of compass bearings. Use of

Station pointer by Joseph Huddart. Nichelson (1804): Plate 1, facing page 80. Courtesy of SSPL.

station pointers has declined with the introduction of electronic fixing methods.

The first illustration of a station pointer, published in 1804, shows a design that has altered little since. The only significant difference from the instrument envisaged by Mackenzie is that the scale is a full circle. Verniers, usually reading to 1 minute, were added to the movable arms at an early stage. Scales, graduated to 20 or 30 minutes, could be brass, favored for boat work as easier to read, or silver, which can be divided more accurately, for work on board ship. Extension pieces for lengthening the arms, a magnifier for reading the scale, and a pin for pricking the chart were supplied with instruments. Instrument size has ranged from 2.5-in. diameter scales with 10-in. arms, to 12-in. scales with arms up to 6 feet long when fitted with their extension pieces. The firm of Troughton was particularly associated with the earliest instruments, but since coming into common use they have been supplied by most major instrument-makers.

Susanna Fisher

Bibliography
Fisher, Susanna. "The Origins of the Station Pointer." *International Hydrographic Review* 68, no. 2 (1991): 119–26.
Mackenzie, Murdoch. *A Treatise of Maritim* [sic] *Surveying.* London, 1774.
Nichelson, William. "Description and Use of the Station Pointer." *Journal of Natural Philosophy* 7 (1804): 1–5.

Stereoscope

A stereoscope produces the illusion of a single three-dimensional image from two slightly different flat images. It works only when the flat images are of identical subjects drawn or photographed from viewpoints approximately equal in separation to the distance between the human eyes, and when the stereoscope is constructed so that each eye sees only the appropriate image—that is, the left eye sees the left viewpoint and the right eye the right viewpoint.

Binocular vision, the means by which the slightly different images seen by the two eyes separately are fused in the brain into one solid image, has interested scientists for centuries. The differences in the image seen by the two eyes were described by Euclid about 280 B.C., but there is no evidence to suggest that he understood the principles of stereoscopy. Similar observations were also made by the physician Galen in the second century A.D. In the sixteenth century binocular vision was studied by several European philosophers, including Leonardo da Vinci and Giambattista della Porta.

The principle of stereoscopic vision was established by the English physicist Charles Wheatstone, who had two types of stereoscope constructed by the London opticians Murray and Heath toward the end of 1832. The earliest published mention of Wheatstone's work on stereoscopic vision appeared in the third edition of Herbert Mayo's *Outlines of Human Physiology* (1833). In 1838 Wheatstone published his own account of his work in a long paper to the Royal Society that includes details of a reflecting stereoscope. In this instrument two images were fixed at opposite ends of a horizontal bar so that they faced a pair of central mirrors sited midway between them at right angles to each other. An observer facing the mirrors would see the two reflected images simultaneously as one solid image.

The reflecting stereoscope proved suitable only for showing diagrams of simple geometric figures and as such was no more than an interesting aid to the study of the physiology of vision and an intriguing optical toy. It was the introduction of the first practicable photographic processes in 1839, making possible a series of similarly detailed pictures to be produced with great accuracy, that led to Wheatstone's instrument's assuming greater significance. The inventor of negative-positive photography, W.H.F. Talbot, and his associate, Henry Collen, were soon persuaded to make suitable calotype images. Wheatstone also attempted to use photographs made by the rival daguerreotype process, but these proved unsuitable.

Wheatstone showed only limited interest in exploiting the reflecting stereoscope commercially, but a development of another of his earlier instruments, a refracting stereoscope, was described by David Brewster in 1849. Brewster's stereoscope, a more compact instrument, used prisms or lenses in a binocular eyepiece to view two small photographs side by side. An adaptation of Brewster's instrument made by the Parisian optician Jules Duboscq was shown at London's Great Exhibition of 1851 and particularly aroused the admiration of Queen Victoria. The queen's interest stimulated a craze for stereoscopic photography. A mass market for stereoscopic photographs was soon established, and the stereoscope, often in ornate forms, became a common feature in nineteenth-century homes. The binocular stereoscope eventually became one of the most popular scientific toys of the age.

Brewster's refracting stereoscope underwent many improvements and refinements, but the basic binocular pattern has remained constant up to the present day. Its popularity as a device for viewing photographs diminished after World War I, but a small core of enthusiasts have continued to practice stereoscopic photography and use binocular stereoscopes to view the results of their endeavors. Throughout the twentieth century various forms of the binocular stereoscope have been produced as optical novelties and children's toys and, until the widespread use of film and video, it found favor with salesmen and commercial travelers as a sales aid.

Modern science has found several uses for the stereoscope. Stereocomparators, introduced in the early years of the twentieth century, re-

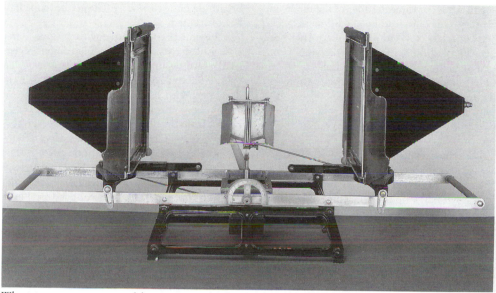

Wheatstone stereoscope, used for viewing medical radiographs, ca. 1920. SM 1973-395. Courtesy of SSPL.

vealed small discrepancies between one astronomical photograph and another, and led to the discovery of numerous faint, moving celestial objects (see **camera, aerial** and **comparator, astronomical**). Using sophisticated techniques largely developed during World War II, the instrument has been widely used for the analysis of aerial camera photographs and for aerial survey work. Stereomicrography allows microscopic objects to be viewed in relief through a binocular viewer. Stereoradiography records a three dimensional image of an internal structure using x-rays. These radiographs can be viewed with either a binocular viewer or a Wheatstone mirror stereoscope. The latter type is favored for large plates or where stereoscopic distance measurements in space are required.

John Ward

Bibliography

Bowers, Brian. *Sir Charles Wheatstone, FRS, 1802–1875*. London: Her Majesty's Stationery Office, 1975.

Coe, Brian. *Cameras: From Daguerreotypes to Instant Pictures*. London: Marshall Cavendish, 1978.

The Focal Encyclopedia of Photography. Rev. ed. London: Focal, 1965.

Gernsheim, Helmut, and Alison Gernsheim. *The History of Photography from the Camera Obscura to the Beginning of the Modern Era*. Rev. and enl. ed. London: Thames and Hudson, 1969.

Stethoscope

A stethoscope couples the ear of a medical examiner to the surface of a patient's body for the purpose of listening to sounds generated within the body. Although it was invented in 1816 by the French physician René Laennec, its origins lie within a clinical research enterprise that stretches back at least to the middle of the eighteenth century. Leopold Auenbrugger, a Viennese physician, sought to reveal the presence of pathological alterations within the thorax by tapping firmly upon the patient's chest. Auenbrugger published an account of his new technique in 1761, but thoracic percussion, as it was called, did not gain any degree of popularity until the early decades of the nineteenth century. Even in the eighteenth century, however, Auenbrugger was not alone in attempting to discern and locate pathological changes in the internal structures of the living body. Giovanni Morgagni, in Padua, for example, palpated the abdomen and thorax of his patients to detect abnormalities. Morgagni's use of physical examination was guided by the principle of correlating the symptoms observable in the living patient with the findings of post mortem dissection. He sought to detect the same swellings and lesions that the dissecting knife would enable him to see after death.

The systematic correlation between clinical signs and symptoms, on the one hand, and pathological anatomy, on the other, was very characteristic of the "anatomico-clinical" method of the members of the Paris School in the first two or three decades of the nineteenth century. One of its leading practitioners, Nicholas Corvisart, revived and refined Auenbrugger's innovation of thoracic percussion. Corvisart also encouraged his colleagues to use the older diagnostic method of auscultation—listening to the sounds within the body cavities, especially the thorax—which had been known to the ancient Greek physicians but had fallen out of use.

Laennec, who had been a student of Corvisart's, took a special interest in diseases of the chest. On one occasion, he was consulted by a young woman with the symptoms of heart disease. The patient was rather plump and Laennec was unable to get her chest to resonate upon percussion. Still a fairly young doctor, Laennec felt inhibited from pressing his head firmly against the bosom of his female patient. So, remembering a game played by French children in the street, he picked up a sheet of paper, rolled it up into a tube, and placed one end against his patient's chest. He was amazed to be able to hear the sounds of her heart and her

breathing quite distinctly. The stethoscope had been invented.

Leannec experimented with various materials and shapes for his new instrument, eventually settling upon a simple hollow wooden cylinder about 25 cm long and about 3.5 cm in diameter. With this tool, Laennec undertook a comprehensive investigation of the sounds emanating from the heart and lungs, wherever possible correlating his findings in detail with pathological alterations observed upon autopsy. His results were published in *On Mediate Auscultation* (1819). Many of the technical terms describing thoracic sounds introduced by Laennec are still in use, and his treatise is the basis of modern understanding of the pathology of the lung.

While there was a certain amount of opposition to the use of the stethoscope by the more conservative members of the profession, who were either unable to perceive the value of the technique or felt the use of an instrumental aid would compromise their professional dignity, Laennec's innovation came into general use quite

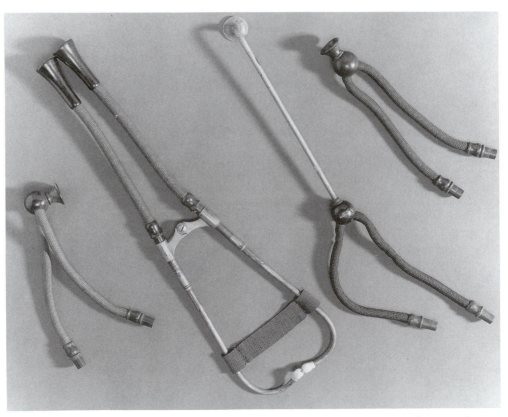

Differential binaural stethoscope (third from left) with interchangeable attachments, early twentieth century. SM A625089. Courtesy of SSPL.

quickly. The ground had been prepared by advances in pathological anatomy. The expansion of clinical teaching in the hospitals provided students wishing to learn stethoscopy with the necessary supply of patients upon whom they could educate their ears. By the 1850s, the stethoscope had become a virtually indispensable badge of office of the medical practitioner. Its widespread adoption gave a considerable stimulus to the development and application of other methods of physical diagnosis, and accustomed patients to being examined by the doctor.

It should be noted, however, that despite Laennec's claims to the contrary, the stethoscope possessed few technical advantages over applying one's ear directly to the patient's chest. In most cases, the instrument did not make the thoracic sounds any louder or clearer than they would be to the naked ear. What was so attractive about Laennec's invention was that it enabled the physician to examine the patient's chest more conveniently and more hygienically, while preserving his personal and professional dignity and respecting the sensibilities of his patients. In other words, the real improvement that the stethoscope brought to medical practice was a social one.

Such considerations of professional convenience were partly to shape further developments of stethoscope design. In 1828, N.P. Comins, an Edinburgh physician, designed an instrument with a hinge between its two tubes that he claimed would enable the examiner to "explore any part of the chest, in any position, and in any stage of disease, without pressure or inconvenience to the patient or to himself." A longer tube could be screwed on if the patient was particularly dirty or modest. Numerous other design modifications were tried, to improve the acoustics or the ease of use of the instrument. Amplification of the heart and lung sounds was experimented with. The now familiar binaural stethoscope, with flexible rubber tubes, came into common use in the 1890s. At the chestpiece, it has either an open bell or a closed diaphragm, or sometimes both. While to a large extent now displaced from its position of supreme authority in the diagnosis of lung disorders by the introduction of radiographic imaging, the stethoscope is still indispensable to cardiologists and general physicians. Numerous applications have been found for it outside of the thoracic region, such as in the monitoring of pregnancy and of bowel function, the measurement of blood pressure, and the detection of the bubbles within tissue that are diagnostic of gas gangrene.

Malcolm Nicolson

Bibliography
Davis, Audrey B. *Medicine and Its Technology: An Introduction to the History of Medical Instrumentation.* Arlington: Printer's Devil, 1981.
Nicolson, Malcolm. "The Art of Diagnosis: Medicine and the Five Senses." In *The Companion Encyclopaedia of the History of Medicine,* edited by W.F. Bynum and R. Porter, Vol. 2, 801–25. London: Routledge, 1993.
————. "The Introduction of Percussion and Stethoscopy to Early Nineteenth-Century Edinburgh." In *Medicine and the Five Senses,* edited by W.F. Bynum and R. Porter, 134–53. Cambridge: Cambridge University Press, 1992.
Reiser, Stanley Joel. *Medicine and the Reign of Technology.* New York: Cambridge University Press, 1978.
————. "The Science of Diagnosis: Diagnostic Technology." In *The Companion Encyclopaedia of the History of Medicine,* edited by W.F. Bynum, and R. Porter, Vol. 2, 826–51. London: Routledge, 1993.

Strain Gauge (Electrical Resistance)

The bonded electrical resistance strain gauge, the most important type of strain gauge in the late twentieth century, consists of a thin wire or foil of conducting material that can be bonded to the surface of a component or testpiece. When the object to be tested is loaded, the strain causes a small change in the gauge resistance; this change can be readily quantified in terms of the out-of-balance reading in a suitable **Wheatstone bridge** circuit. There is a direct proportional relationship between the change in electrical resistance and mechanical strain (first elucidated by William Thomson in 1856); consequently the bridge reading provides a measure of the specimen strain. The importance of such measurements in a very wide range of engineering applications cannot be overstated. Stresses in critically loaded components can be inferred from strain measurements. Force transducers (devices in which an applied force can be determined or monitored from the output of a strain gauge incorporated in the device) are used in numerous applica-

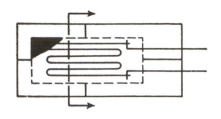

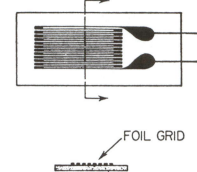

PAPER — FELT COVER — WIRE FILAMENTS — CEMENT

FOIL GRID — BACKING

Schematic diagram showing the construction of wire (left) and foil (right) strain gauges. Charles C. Perry, and Herbert Lissner. The Strain Gage Primer. *New York: McGraw-Hill, 1955: 21, Figure 2-1. Courtesy of McGraw-Hill Inc.*

tions, from large-scale testing to commercial weighing machines.

Stein, whose work has been essential to this article, notes that Charles Wheatstone "had the strain gauge in his hand" in 1843 when he recorded, in his introductory presentation on the bridge circuit that now bears his name, that "slight differences . . . in the tensions of the wires" could disturb the bridge balance. Almost a century was to pass, however, before the appearance of the first bonded wire strain gauge. One of the first important developments that preceded this was the unbonded wire gauge intended for use on dams and large concrete structures; this was patented by Roy Carlson in 1934 and produced commercially. Also notable was the bonded carbon gauge developed in 1936 by Charles M. Kearns, who simply filed a flat side on a cylindrical carbon resistor that he then bonded to an aluminum specimen. The bonded carbon gauge was instrumental in practically eliminating in-flight propeller failures at Kearns's company in the late 1930s. It was also used successfully in Europe.

The bonded electrical wire strain gauge also emerged at this time. The relevant patents are in the names of Edward E. Simmons (the "basic" patent) and Arthur C. Ruge (the "development and improvement" patents). Working at the California Institute of Technology in 1936, Simmons proposed a bonded wire strain gauge transducer for dynamic force measurements; the transducer was made by Gottfried Dätwyler and consisted of a length of constantan wire bonded to the faces of a prismatic steel bar. It proved successful in this work. In 1938, working quite independently, Ruge, a professor

of civil engineering at M.I.T., produced a successful bonded gauge consisting of a 12.25-cm length of Elinvar (an Fe-Ni-Cr alloy) wire bonded to a celluloid bar. This was quickly developed for strain measurements on a water tank model. Alfred V. De Forest, working in the Mechanical Engineering Department of M.I.T., had already introduced an important development of Kearns's bonded carbon gauge. (His company, Magnaflux Corp., produced the brittle coating material, Stresscoat, the basis of a very useful technique that can be applied as a preliminary to a strain gauge study.) He recognized the importance of Ruge's work and redirected his own efforts into the development of the bonded wire gauge. Ruge and de Forest eventually joined forces, and the commercial exploitation of the gauge by the Baldwin-Southwark organization quickly followed.

The first mention of the resistance strain gauge in England appears to have been in a 1939 note to the Engineering Department of the Royal Aircraft Establishment by F. Postlethwaite. Within a year or two, gauges were being made by Tom Baldwin's group in the LMS Railway Co. and at the National Physical Laboratory under F. Aughtie; the Aero Engine Division of Rolls-Royce and the Royal Aircraft Establishment were also active over this period. Commercial production in the U.K. began in 1942. D.C. Gall of H. Tinsley & Co. patented a technique for gauge production in 1944. In 1946, papers on "practically every aspect of strain gauges" were presented at an Institute of Physics conference in Manchester, and gauge production was demonstrated at the Physical Society Exhibition at Imperial College. A notable development in the early 1950s was the introduction of the foil strain gauge by Peter Jackson of Saunders Roe in 1952; most gauges in use today are of this type. Semiconductor gauges first appeared in 1960.

The resistance strain gauge is conceptually simple, but in its present form it is the product of a great deal of research and development work in many organizations throughout the world. Gauges are now available with a strain resolution of 0.1×10^{-6}. They range in active gauge length from 0.2 mm to 150 mm and can be used over the temperature range $-270°C$ to $350°C$, and higher in special applications. The most widely used gauge material remains the Cu-Ni alloy constantan; Ni-Cr alloys are also used, and Pt-W gauges are available for high-temperature applications. The role of the bond between the gauge and the strained body is crucial. Many of the available adhesives are highly specific, and surface preparation is invariably important. Weldable gauges are available. Reliable gauge protection techniques have been developed that are particularly relevant for long-term monitoring or submerged applications. Major advances have been made in the associated circuitry and signal processing. Digital displays are now commonplace, and many systems provide data analysis and storage facilities.

Peter Stanley

Bibliography

Gall, M.W. "Early Days of the Resistance Strain Gauge." *Strain* 25 (1989): 83–88.

The Measurement of Stress and Strain in Solids. London: Institute of Physics, 1948.

Stein, Peter K. "A Brief History from Conception to Commercialization of Bonded Resistance Strain Gages and Brittle Coatings." In *Fifty Years of Bonded Resistance Strain Gages—History and Future*, 25–38. Tokyo: Society for Instrument and Control Engineers of Japan, 1989.

Window, A.L., ed. *Strain Gauge Technology.* London: Applied Science, 1992.

Strain Gauge (General)

A strain gauge is a sensitive instrument for measuring small deformations in machines or structures. While early extensometers worked on mechanical or optical principles, modern gauges are usually based on either electrical or acoustic principles.

Extensometers

The need to detect small distortions in large structures was particularly apparent to those maintaining Gothic buildings. One solution was to cement a thin piece of glass across a crack in a structure that was settling. The subsequent cracking of the glass indicated that the structural crack was continuing to grow. Such telltales are still used for monitoring cracks in small masonry arches.

Direct linear measurement using verniers and **micrometers** was refined during the nineteenth century. Levers were also used, and optical techniques such as photogrammetry (see **aerial camera**) were used to examine structures and machines. And metrological instruments such as the **comparator** found their way into measuring the extension of structural components under load.

Notable early extensometers include E. Hodgkinson's 1856 wedge gauge; screw extensometers incorporating micrometers, electrical contacts, and telescopic sighting; and W.C. Unwin's 1883 touch micrometer. Successful use of this latter instrument depended on the skill of a mechanic "accustomed to take dimensions with callipers with very great accuracy." C. Cowper's extensometer was used in testing the long bars for Kiev Bridge in 1850; W. H. Paine's lever extensometer was used in tests at the East River Bridge; and H. Flad's extensometer was used to test materials for the St. Louis Bridge. By the turn of the century, a number of highly accurate, but delicate, instruments had evolved for laboratory purposes. Notable examples include the differential **cathetometers** made by both H. Streinitz (1877) and A.B.W. Kennedy; the level extensometer (1879) also by Kennedy; J. Bauschinger's roller and mirror extensometer; Unwin's mirror extensometer; and O. Strohmeyer's roller extensometer. Several extensometers using the principles derived last century are still in use, including mechanical systems, such as the extensometers of J.A. Ewing and of Lindley; the mechanical opening of electrical contacts in Hounsfield's extensometer; and the optical Marten's mirror extensometer.

Dial indicators (also known as dial gauges) began to be manufactured around 1890. In a dial indicator a plunger is geared to a pointer that shows, by its rotation on a dial, the displacement of the plunger. Although dial indicators are usually associated with production engineering, they continue to be used as parts of structural deflectometers, usually for beams under load. Here a tightly strung invar wire connects the dial gauge to the loaded structure. Dial indicators were also incorporated in self-contained instruments such as the fulcrum-plate strain gauge introduced by H.L. Whittemore in 1928, which in turn led to H.C. Berry's strain gauge. The latter used an invar tube and was initially developed for the U.S. National Bureau of Standards to investigate the large arch dams being built in the 1930s.

By 1930 the Swedish inventor Carl Edvard Johansson had successfully developed and was widely marketing a novel strain gauge: the Mikrokator. In this instrument, linear displacement is converted directly into the rotational movement of a pointer at the midpoint of a twisted metal strip of rectangular cross-section. Also around 1930, pneumatic flow was first used experimentally for the measurement of strain. Dynamic strain measurement remained difficult to measure with mechanical equipment, the most widely used surrogate being the scratch recording strain gauge developed by Professor Alfred De Forest at M.I.T. It has no provision for the magnification of the motions measured, and the record had to be viewed with a **microscope**.

In addition to optical instruments using lenses and mirrors, experiments were made with optical systems that relied on phenomena such as interference fringes and the properties of polarized light. The latter concept using photoelastic coating was initiated by the French researcher A. Mesnager in 1930, but it was not developed successfully until 1955. Three-dimensional models, utilizing the diphase properties of synthetic resins, which helped identify the stress concentrations likely in different shapes of components, enjoyed a short period of intense interest in the late 1950s and early 1960s.

Early Electrical Gauges

In spite of their size and cost, mechanical and optical extensometers continue to be used for accurate measurement in research laboratories. In the field, however, or in research on complicated structures, their accurate use is seldom possible.

In the 1930s and early 1940s there was much experimentation with **electrical strain gauges**. Other devices also relied on electrical inductance or on electrical capacitance. An electrical inductance gauge is a device in which the displacement being measured produces a change in the magnetic field, and, hence, in the impedance of a current-carrying coil. The impedance of a coil depends on its inductance and on its effective resistance, and either or both of these quantities can be made sensitive to the mechanical quantity being measured. The inductance that is changed can be either the self-inductance of the coil or its mutual inductance with respect to another coil.

Four basic forms of electrical inductance gauge had been developed by the mid 1940s: variable airgap, moving-core solenoid, eddy current, and magnetostriction. Flux leakage

Johansson Mikrokator twisted strip strain gauge (right) and calibration stand, ca. 1947. NMAH 81.0423.30.01-02. Courtesy of NMAH.

resulted in the nonlinear response of the simple single gap gauges offered by C.M. Hathaway in 1937, while the Westinghouse Co. offered a more complicated double-gap gauge until it developed systems to obtain a linear response from single-gap gauges in 1944. The variable-coupling moving-core solenoid gauge, known as a "linear variable differential transformer" (LVDT), developed by H. Schaevitz in 1947 remains widely used as a transducer in a variety of applications, including as an "electrical extensometer." Eddy current gauges had by 1947 been found to be most effective at measuring the thickness of nonmetallic coatings. Electrical inductance gauges were also found by 1944 to be well suited to measure strains in rotating components by incorporating a device relying on magnetostriction such as the General Electric Co.'s "Electomagnetic Torque-meter."

Electrical capacitance gauges were developed in the 1940s to obtain more precise results than could be achieved by either resistance gauges or inductive elements. Their main value was in cases in which the temperature was beyond the limit for resistance gauges, and this resulted in extensive trials in aircraft engines at the U.K. Royal Aircraft Establishment in the 1940s. All early inductance and capacitance gauges were also known collectively as electric strain gauges; it was not until the early 1950s that the term began to be confined to those gauges that rely on electrical resistance and **Wheatstone bridge** circuits.

Later Electrical Gauges

The foil strain gauge, which is now the most widely used type of strain gauge throughout the world, was invented by Peter Jackson, working at the Saunders Roe Co. on the Isle of Wight, in 1952. At that time, printed circuit techniques were appearing, and he decided to make a strain gauge by etching the grid from a thin foil of the appropriate resistance material. Jackson hoped that foil gauges would cost only a few pennies each.

The early foil gauges were large and could be made only with a resistance of about 50 ohms, but they could dissipate heat readily and, it was argued, could carry far more current than a wire gauge. In theory, they could be just as effective as a wire gauge, although the use of multichannel circuits would require considerably more power. It was, however, some time before foil gauges were made with sufficient precision to

cause any serious competition to wire gauges. This was mainly because imperfect etching resulted in a jagged edge to the foil, resulting in poor fatigue characteristics. The Saunders Roe patent deterred other British manufacturers from making the necessary improvements.

Meanwhile the art of producing foil gauges was perfected in the United States, and foil gauges were made in very large quantities. They remained expensive, however, because the equipment needed to make and heat-treat the foil, to do the photography and the artwork, and to carry out the chemical etching and polishing involved considerable capital expenditure. Wire gauges, on the other hand, were made with simple tools and from readily available materials. Latterly, much effort has been directed toward improved control and understanding of gauge materials, characteristics, and design. New production techniques included die cutting rather than etching and vacuum deposition. Related work pertained to brittle lacquers, photoelasticity using polarized light, and photoelastic coatings. All these techniques played their part in the great advances made in stress analysis work in the 1950s and 1960s.

Semiconductor strain gauges employing the piezoresistive effect were introduced in 1960. These gauges often use a crystal of germanium or silicon, treated with an impurity to make its resistance sensitive to strain. They are about a hundred times as sensitive as ordinary strain gauges and can be made small enough to measure strain virtually at a point. However, they are more expensive and less stable than resistance strain gauges.

The principle of capacitance is also used to measure strains at very high temperatures. The Hughes Aircraft Company's, first capacitance gauges were made in 1966, using mica as the dielectric material. Boeing's gauge used an air gap system, as did the device designed specifically for monitoring turbo-generating machinery in power stations by the Central Electricity Generating Board in the U.K.

Acoustic Gauges

A vibrating wire strain gauge consists of a thin steel wire held in tension between two anchorages. The wire is set into transverse vibration by exciting it with a short burst of current passed through the coil of an electromagnet positioned near the midpoint of the wire. The same coil is then used to detect the frequency of the vibrating wire. When the distance between the anchorages changes, the tension of the wire and its natural frequency also change. This form of gauge has been shown to be stable over periods longer than twenty years, and it has the advantage that its frequency is not changed by the resistance or length of the leads.

The first report of a vibrating wire strain gauge was made by the Russian engineer N. Davidenkoff in 1928. Although Davidenkoff mentioned a design suitable for embedment in concrete, most early experimental gauges were for measuring surface strains. Concrete is not a homogeneous material, and an embedded gauge is required to measure the changes in strain within a large slab subjected to three-dimensional loading. By the mid 1960s, embedded vibrating wire gauges were developed for comparing the predicted and actual behavior of prestressed concrete pressure vessels as nuclear containments, for monitoring concrete mine shafts and pit bottom roadway linings, and for measuring the contraction of prestressed concrete beams resulting from creep and shrinkage.

Robert C. McWilliam

Bibliography

Browne, R.D., and L.H. McCurrich. "Measurement of Strain in Concrete Pressure Vessels." In *Conference on Prestressed Concrete Pressure Vessels,* edited by Marilyn S. Udall, 615–25. London: Institution of Civil Engineers, 1968.

Hetényi, M., ed. *Handbook of Experimental Stress Analysis.* New York: Wiley, 1950.

Neubert, Hermann K.P. *Strain Gauges: Kinds and Uses.* London: Macmillan, 1967.

Unwin, William Cawthorne. *The Testing of Materials of Construction.* 2nd ed. London: Longmans, 1899.

Window, A.L., and G.S. Holister, eds. *Strain Gauge Technology.* London: Applied Science, 1982.

Strength of Materials–Testing Instruments

Knowledge of the properties of timber, stone, and metal has traditionally been in the hands and eyes of such craftsmen as carpenters, stonemasons, smiths, and ironfounders, and it was transmitted through apprenticeship. An intellectual interest in the mechanical behavior of materials emerged in the seventeenth century, based on the assumption of perfect elastic response to load.

The materials testing machine proper appeared early in the nineteenth century, and was designed to test materials in tension only. A notable example was the machine installed in Woolwich Naval Dockyard, which Peter Barlow used for his pioneering experiments, the results of which were published in 1817.

The first generation of tensile testing machines tended to hold the specimen horizontally, but the preferred method in recent times is vertical alignment. By gripping the specimen at one end with a shackle attached to a screw thread and using a wheel nut to apply the load, one can apply a gradually increasing load in ever-decreasing increments as critical stages are reached. Hydraulic pressure acting on a ram in a cylinder also delivers a steady, controllable load to the specimen. Water was first used as the hydraulic medium, although oil is now preferred.

The oldest method is dead weight application, measuring with weights on a scale, and multiplying by the leverage ratio if levers were used. When using hydraulic pressure, the load on the specimen was measured with the pressure gauge, multiplied by the cross-sectional area of the ram. This technique was discredited, as it ignored the friction loss between the leather seal and the hydraulic ram. The favored method was, and in many cases still is, to use a system of hardened, eccentric, steel knife-edges, a lever system, and a steelyard to determine the load applied.

Many of the large testing machines produced from the middle of the nineteenth century were designed to be multipurpose devices. In the twentieth century, smaller testing machines were designed to carry out single types of tests, thus eliminating the shut-down time as a universal machine was rerigged to carry out another type of test.

David Kirkaldy's universal testing machine was built by Greenwood and Batley, of Leeds, and installed in London in 1866. Kirkaldy then practiced as an independent materials tester, as did his son and grandson until 1974. The machine remains, in working condition, as the centerpiece of the Kirkaldy Testing Museum at 99 Southwark Street, London. It has a horizontal cast iron bed 47 feet long and was designed to apply a maximum load of 446 tons by means of a hydraulic ram and measured by a steelyard. It was originally adapted to test tension, compression, bending, torsion, shear, punching, and bulging.

The Emery testing machine installed at Watertown Arsenal, 1879. Report of the United States Board Appointed to Test Iron, Steel, and Other Metals, *Vol. 2. Washington, D.C.: Government Printing Office, 1881. Courtesy of NMAH.*

In 1872 a committee of American engineers urged the U.S. government to sponsor a series of tests on American iron and steel. The sum of $75,000 was made available, and in 1875 A.H. Emery was commissioned to design a machine capable of applying a load of 400 tons and of testing specimens in tension up to 28 feet long and 30 in. wide and in compression columns up to 30 feet long. The machine, installed at the Watertown Arsenal in 1879, was then probably the largest testing machine in the world. Smaller versions of this machine were subsequently built by the Yale & Towne Manufacturing Co. of Stamford, Connecticut.

Testing machines have been used in government and independent testing laboratories, engineering works, universities (for research and teaching), and large construction sites. Since the late nineteenth century, a wide range of designers and manufacturers have produced a great variety of machines and measuring instruments. The principal names are Fairbanks (New York), Yale & Towne (Stamford), Tinius Olsen (Philadelphia), and Riehle Brothers (Philadelphia) in the United States; J. Buckton & Co. (Leeds), W. & T. Avery (Birmingham), Greenwood & Batley (Leeds), Tangye Brothers (Birmingham), S. Denison & Sons (Leeds), Edward G. Herbert (Manchester), and Daniel Adamson (Manchester) in the U.K.; and Alfred J. Amsler (Schaffouse, Switzerland), Grafenstaden (Mulhouse, France), and Ludwig Werder (Germany).

With the enormous growth of equipment and techniques, some form of international standardization was seen to be necessary if testers hoped to compare their results. The German portland cement manufacturers and the railway administrations made tentative efforts in this direction in the 1870s. In 1884, J. Bauschinger of Munich called a convention for the "Purpose of Adopting Uniform Methods for Testing Constructional Materials," and this eventually led to the foundation of the International Society for Testing Materials.

Denis Smith

Bibliography

Kirkaldy, William G. *Illustrations of David Kirkaldy's System of Mechanical Testing.* London: Sampson Low, 1891.

Popplewell, William Charles. *Experimental Engineering.* Vol. 2. Manchester: Scientific, 1901.

Unwin, William Cawthorne. *The Testing of the Materials of Construction.* 2nd ed. London: Longmans, 1899.

String Galvanometer

See GALVANOMETER, STRING

Sun-dial

A sun-dial indicates time by the position of the shadow of a marker cast by the sun on a grid of hour or month lines. It may indicate the time in the year, if a scale showing the sun's position in the zodiac or among the months is drawn, or in the day if hour lines are drawn, or even at night if the dial is fitted with a scale for converting from sidereal to solar time. Sun-dials should be distinguished from simple gnomons (shadow markers used with a set of tables showing the length of shadow cast by a vertical stick of standard height as a function of solar declination throughout the year), and from meridians (sun-dials that simply mark the moment of noon).

The earliest evidence of sun-dials are two Egyptian fragments, datable respectively to ca. 1500 B.C. and to ca. 1000 B.C., and an inscription with illustration in the Cenotaph of Seti I (1318–1304 B.C.). None of these show any compensation for the change in solar declination throughout the year, although in Assyria at least this may have been known by 1000 B.C. as tables about it are to be found among the *Mu'l Apin* texts. These tables, however, relate to vertical gnomons, not to true sun-dials, and there is no evidence to show where the development of dials with attached hour-scales incorporating a compensation for the change of solar declination first occurred. In Egypt and Greece, the development seems to have taken place by the late fourth century B.C. although the earliest datable dial surviving from Greek regions (Delos) derives from the third century B.C.

In Greece, sun-dial designs multiplied from the late fourth century B.C. onwards. In the brief passage in *de Architectura,* which is our major source of evidence for ancient dialing, Vitruvius mentions fifteen different kinds of dial of which four are portable models. At least half of the dials mentioned by Vitruvius can be identified among surviving Graeco-Roman dials. Nearly three hundred dials of all classes from the Roman empire have also survived.

Most dials surviving from antiquity and the Middle Ages are fixed dials, while all portable dials from before the fourteenth century are altitude dials, measuring time by the sun's altitude rather than its angular displacement along the local horizon. In the Roman empire dials were usually large, decoratively sculpted pieces, set up in public places for utility and adornment. Sun-dials found a new application, as markers of the time of prayer, in Christian monasteries from the fifth and sixth centuries onwards, and later in Islamic mosques.

For the purposes of organized Christian life, a simple form of direct south facing vertical dial with its gnomon set at right-angles to the dial face was used. Among the twelve hour lines on such dials, those (the third, sixth, and ninth) that were of particular importance to Christians were often distinguished by a cross, and on some dials the intervening lines were suppressed as being of no utility. Particularly abundant in Britain and north west Europe, such dials gradually degenerated into the "mass" or "scratch" dial, examples of which are plentiful on the walls of churches up to the sixteenth century.

In the Islamic regions of the Near East, where it may be assumed Graeco-Roman dials survived relatively plentifully *in situ,* the revival of Greek mathematics led to the development of several ingenious and sophisticated designs for dials. Because regular prayers were incumbent upon Muslims, and because the periods when the prayers were to be performed were astronomically determined, special lines to indicate them were added to both fixed and portable dials. From the Islamic regions knowledge of certain kinds of dials—in particular the portable pillar or cylinder dial—was transmitted from the tenth and eleventh centuries onwards to Christian Europe, while the revival of cities, commerce, and travel favored the reappearance of dials, especially the portable varieties.

The most important development in this area in the Middle Ages, however, was linked with the magnetic compass in the late thirteenth century. The compass made possible the development of portable direction dials that must be accurately oriented along the meridian. A second crucial innovation resulted from the appearance of the weight-driven clock, which caused the old system of unequal hours (one-twelfth part of the day or night period, the length of which varies in the course of the seasons), to be replaced by a system of equal hours (one twenty-fourth part of the whole day and night period, which is invariable) in the fourteenth century. This led to the introduction of the polar gnomon—that is, a gnomon inclined on the dial plate by an angle equal to the co-latitude of the place where it was to be used so that the gnomon lies parallel to the north-south polar axis of the earth.

In Renaissance Europe, dialing reached the apogee of its popularity and sophistication. Many new types of dial were invented, a large literature was published in Latin and the main vernacular tongues, and a flourishing trade developed. Large and elaborate multifaceted, polyhedral dials cut in stone were designed by architects in the Vitruvian tradition and by mathematicians and mathematically inclined gentlemen and executed by local masons or other craftsmen. Portable dials made in silver, brass, ivory, or precious woods were manufactured by highly skilled mathematical instrument-makers, and assimilated to the luxury trades.

Dials of the mid fifteenth to mid seventeenth centuries display exuberant decoration, complex designs, and many different indications (hours, minutes, place of sun in the zodiac, scales for different hour systems and convertors for them, time of sunrise and sunset, length of day and night, calendrical information). From the late seventeenth century onwards, however, dials became increasingly functional, and subsidiary indications were abandoned in the interests of producing a dial on which accurate time could be easily read. This period also saw the increasing popularity of large public meridians that accurately marked the instant of noon, and against which clocks and watches could be checked and tested. The increasing accuracy of clocks and watches stimulated increasingly accurate dials, and even the introduction of dials with geared minute hands.

Faced with redundancy caused by telegraphic and radio time signals and the development of standard time zones in the late nineteenth century, dialists responded by developing instruments that indicated standard time as well as local solar and mean time. Such dials could again claim a place as useful public timepieces and this, combined with their decorative qualities, has led to a minor renaissance in dialing during the last decade of the twentieth century.

Anthony Turner

Bibliography

Gotteland, Andrée, and Georges Camus. *Cadrans solaire de Paris*. Paris: CNRS, 1993.

Gouk, Penelope. *The Ivory Sundials of Nuremberg 1500–1700*. Cambridge:

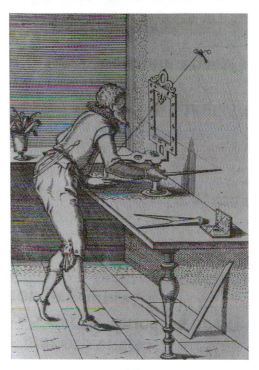

A sixteenth-century sun-dial maker at work. B. L(eeman). Instrumentum Instrumentorum: Horologiorum Sciotericorum. *Zurich, 1604. Courtesy of the Houghton Library, Harvard University.*

Whipple Museum of the History of Science, 1988.

Higgins, Kathleen. "The Classification of Sundials." *Annals of Science* 9 (1953): 341–58.

King, D.A. "Mizwala." In *Encyclopaedia of Islam,* vol. 7, 210–11. Leiden: Brill, 1991.

Turner, A.J. "Sun-dials, History and Classification." *History of Science* 27 (1989): 303–18.

Waugh, Albert E. *Sundials: Their Theory and Construction*. New York: Dover, 1973.

Surface Analytical Instruments

Surface analytical instruments are used predominantly to measure the chemical composition of the outermost atomic layers of a solid specimen. The most common types are Auger-electron spectroscopy (AES), x-ray photoelectron spectroscopy (XPS), and secondary-ion mass spectrometry (SIMS) (see **spectrometer, mass**). The surface sensitivity attained in practice depends on the specimen material, the analytical technique, and the operational parameters, and can typically range from one to about twenty atomic layers. Information on variation of composition with depth ("depth profiles"), particularly in the vicinity of interfaces, is frequently obtained by removal of specimen material by ion sputtering and concurrent measurement of the composition of the newly exposed surface. Sustained work on the development of XPS at Uppsala University from the 1950s led to the selection of Kai Siegbahn as a Nobel physics laureate in 1981.

Surface and interface properties are crucial for the fabrication and performance of a wide range of advanced materials (such as ceramics, composites, alloys, polymers, superconductors, diamond thin films, and biomaterials), semiconductor devices, optoelectronics, high-density magnetic-storage media, sensors, thin films, and coatings. Surface analysis is commonly used for the characterization of surfaces and interfaces so that correlations can be made with specific properties or processes such as catalysis, corrosion (or degradation), adhesion, lubrication, wear, segregation, and diffusion.

Principles

The figure on page 591 shows a schematic outline of a surface analysis instrument. The specimen is irradiated with electrons (AES), x-rays (XPS and AES), or ions (SIMS), and measurements are made of the energy spectrum of electrons leaving the surface (AES and XPS) or of the mass spectrum of ions leaving the surface (SIMS). AES and XPS instruments may be equipped with an auxiliary source of ions (often 0.5–5 keV argon ions) so that the specimen surface can be eroded by sputtering.

In AES, the incident electron beam energy is generally between 5 and 25 keV, and the beam can be focused to a diameter of between 20 nm and 10 μm. Measurements are made of Auger-electron features that occur at characteristic kinetic energies for particular elements in the secondary-electron energy distribution in the range of 20 to 2,500 eV.

With XPS, the specimen is irradiated by x-rays, often generated in tubes with Al or Mg anodes; an x-ray monochromator may also be employed with characteristic Al x-rays in order to increase the overall energy resolution and to eliminate complications caused by the presence of other x-ray lines or *bremsstrahlung* from conventional x-ray tubes. Measurements are made of characteristic photoelectron peaks resulting from the photoionization of core electrons in the specimen material; these peaks (and often also Auger-electron peaks) occur in the energy spectrum of the emitted electrons in the range 250–1,500 eV. The spatial resolution is typically between 5 μm and about 1 mm depending on the sophistication of the x-ray optics or the electron optics.

Small variations in the positions of the Auger-electron and photoelectron peaks and variations in the shapes of these peaks give information on the chemical state of the particular element. All elements can be detected by AES and XPS with the exception of hydrogen and helium. A major advantage of AES is that it can be used to obtain surface-compositional information with higher spatial resolution than the other methods; major advantages of XPS are that surface analyses can be made on specimens that might be modified by electron bombardment in AES and that chemical-state information is more readily obtained for many materials.

With SIMS, the specimen is bombarded by ions (often Ar^+, O_2^+, O^-, Cs^+, or Ga^+) of energy between 2 and 30 keV. The mass spectrum of secondary ions leaving the specimen is measured by a quadrupole, magnetic-sector, or time-of-flight mass spectrometer. Surface analyses by SIMS are usually performed in either the static or the dynamic modes. In the static mode, a mass spectrum is obtained with a relatively low incident-ion current density from a relatively large specimen area such that much less than a surface atomic or molecular layer is removed by ion sputtering. The dynamic mode is usually employed for depth-profiling applications; here the incident-ion current densities are much higher than for static SIMS and the erosion rate can be as high as 10 nm/s. The principal advantage of SIMS is that its sensitivity for the detection of trace elements can be several orders of magnitude larger than the corresponding values found in AES or XPS; a major complication, however, is that the sensitivities can vary substantially with matrix and with the excitation conditions.

Historical Development

In a series of papers beginning in 1923, P. Auger at the Sorbonne observed and interpreted the effect that now bears his name. While there were many investigations of the photoelectric effect at around the turn of the century, the first XPS experiments were performed by H.R.

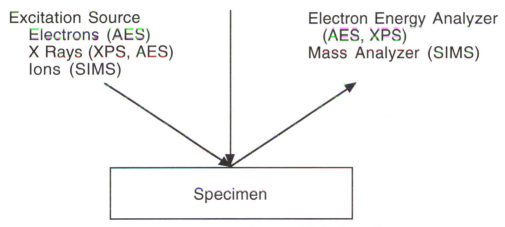

Schematic outline of a surface analysis instrument. Courtesy of Cedric J. Powell.

Robinson and W.F. Rawlinson at the University of Manchester in 1914. The first observation of secondary ions resulting from ion impact on surfaces was reported by J.J. Thomson at the University of Cambridge in 1910.

Subsequent development was slow, largely because of the considerable difficulty in producing ultrahigh vacua. Unless the pressure in the analysis chamber was in the vicinity of 10^{-8} Pa, the surface composition of many materials would change during typical measurement times because of reactions with or adsorption of residual gas. Ultrahigh vacuum chambers were generally constructed from glass prior to 1960; it was then a major undertaking to develop functioning equipment and to introduce and process specimen materials. Nevertheless, surface phenomena such as photoelectron and secondary-electron emission and surface reactions were successfully investigated in the 1920s and 1930s; electron diffraction, discovered in 1927, was a useful monitor of surface conditions in some experiments. It was not until the development of a new generation of stainless steel chambers, demountable flanges, vacuum pumps, and pressure gauges in the 1960s that commercial instruments for AES, XPS, and SIMS became available.

The past three decades have seen many improvements in instrumental capabilities. The development of brighter electron (field-emission) and ion (liquid-metal) sources has led to higher spatial resolution in images that depict the variations of composition on a surface in AES and SIMS, respectively. More intense x-ray sources have also been developed, together with improved x-ray monochromators for XPS. Different types of electrostatic and magnetic electron-optical systems have been developed for AES and XPS that make possible collection of larger fractions of the emitted Auger electrons and photoelectrons for a selected energy resolution; other systems have been designed to produce electron or ion images ("microscope" mode) when the specimen was irradiated by relatively broad electron, x-ray, or ion beams. Extremely efficient time-of-flight mass analyzers have been developed for SIMS. Parallel detectors have been introduced to increase the rate of data collection. Extensive **computer** software has been developed for each technique so that the analyst is assisted with instrument setup, data acquisition, and data reduction. There are now many thousands of these instruments in operation throughout the world. In 1997, the cost of a complete instrument was between $200,000 and $1,000,000, depending on the features selected and the sophistication of the design.

Other methods used for the determination of surface and near-surface composition include sputtered-neutral mass spectrometry, Rutherford backscattering spectroscopy, and ion-scattering spectroscopy. Low-energy electron diffraction and reflection high-energy electron diffraction are often employed for the determination of surface atomic structure, while photoelectron spectroscopy and inverse photoelectron spectroscopy are commonly used for the measurement of surface electronic structure.

The topography of surfaces is measured by scanning electron microscopy, (see **microscope, electron**), scanning probe microscopy (see **microscope, scanning probe**), reflectance of scattered light, and mechanical profiling methods (see **surface texture, measurement of**).

Cedric J. Powell

Bibliography

Benninghoven, A., F.G. Rudenauer, and H.W. Werner. *Secondary Ion Mass Spectrometry: Basic Concepts, Instrumental Aspects, Applications and Trends.* New York: Wiley, 1987.

Palmberg, Paul W. "Ultrahigh Vacuum and Surface Science." *Journal of Vacuum Science and Technology* A12 (1994): 946–52.

Powell, C.J. "Compositional Analyses of Surfaces and Thin Films by Electron and Ion Spectroscopies." *Critical Reviews in Surface Chemistry* 2 (1993): 17–35.

———. "Inelastic Interactions of Electrons with Surfaces: Application to Auger-Electron Spectroscopy and X-Ray Photoelectron Spectroscopy." *Surface Science* 299/300 (1994): 34–48.

Riviere, J. C. *Surface Analytical Techniques.* Oxford: Clarendon, 1990.

Surface Texture, Measurement of

The assessment of the roughness of a surface is important to its suitability for engineering applications. Until the 1930s this was done almost entirely by touch, visual inspection, and subjective judgment, which might be aided by comparison with a set of graded reference samples. With more stringent demands on engineering components, especially in aircraft engines, it became important to obtain an objective, quantified measure of surface texture.

In 1929, Gustav Schmaltz in Germany devised an instrument to make a photographic trace of the deflection of a light ray by a mirror attached to a stylus drawn across the surface. A magnification of up to four thousand times could be obtained, but a magnification ten times that was needed to make the result useful. The first to achieve that sort of magnification was Ernest James Abbott, of the Physics Research Co. in the United States in 1936.

In the Abbott profileometer the vibration of the stylus, drawn over the surface by hand or motor, was amplified electronically. The instrument was dynamic, working rather like a phonograph pickup, the result depending on how fast the stylus was moved, which limited the objectivity of the reading.

Richard Reason, of Taylor, Taylor & Hobson, devised the Talysurf in 1937. In this instrument also the movement of a stylus is amplified electronically, but it is its displacement and not its rate of movement that is represented by the paper trace, which is therefore a record of the surface profile itself. A diamond stylus of about 0.0025 mm radius is used. The geometry of the stylus, of the skid that is usually drawn across the surface with it as a vertical datum, and of their relation to one another, do affect the accuracy of the record somewhat.

The Talysurf quickly became very widely used, despite prejudice in mechanical engineering against the use of electronic amplification and the very real problems of the use of thermionic tubes, and instruments of the same type are in current use. Modern versions employ solid-state electronics.

Reason went on in 1949 to develop the Talysurf to make a record of the roundness of circular components, the sensing and amplifying system being made to record a trace on a circular chart turning with the component under test. At first this facility was available only through consultancy, but Rank Taylor Hobson marketed the instrument as the Talyrond in 1954.

Interferometry (see **interferometer**) affords another means of examining surface quality, but only when the surface has a sufficiently high finish to yield an adequate reflection, and the upper limit to surface roughness that can be examined in this way is a full range from valley to crest of about 0.0003 mm. Commercial instruments using interferometry have been developed by Hilger & Watts, Baker, and Zeiss.

On a yet smaller scale, a range of techniques is now used experimentally to explore surface structure at an atomic or molecular level. The principles employed include spectroscopy, electron diffraction and microscopy, x-ray diffraction, and molecular beam and ion scattering. A significant impetus behind this work is the relevance of surface detail to the behavior of catalysts.

Michael Wright

Bibliography

Hume, Kenneth J. *A History of Engineering Metrology.* London: Mechanical

Talysurf surface meter, by Taylor Hobson Ltd., 1937. Courtesy of Rank Taylor Hobson Ltd.

Engineering, 1980.

Moore, Wayne R. *Foundations of Mechanical Accuracy.* Bridgeport, Conn.: Moore Special Tool, 1970.

Somorjai, G.A. "Modern Concepts in Surface Science and Heterogeneous Catalysis." *Journal of Physical Chemistry* 94 (1990): 1013–23.

T

Tachistoscope

A tachistoscope provides short visual exposures and is used primarily to study reading and visual attention. The name, sometimes abbreviated to T-scope, comes from the Greek *tachistos,* "very rapid," and *skopein,* "to see." The instrument furnishes a field upon which subjects may fix their attention, supplanting this for a brief instant by another containing the test material. There are thus a preexposure field (containing a fixation mark), an exposure field, and a postexposure field, the contents of the exposure or stimulus field depending on the object of the experiment. The early instruments used various mechanical devices for brief presentation, while current forms employ electronic means.

In the experimental psychology that emerged in the latter half of the nineteenth century, apparatus and techniques were often transferred from the preceding physiological laboratories; the first work defining the new discipline was Wilhelm Wundt's *Principles of Physiological Psychology* (1873), which announced "an alliance between two sciences." While psychologists have made most use of the tachistoscope, the first exposure apparatus was probably a gravity form devised by Alfred W. Volkmann (1850), in which a falling screen opens a viewing aperture for an instant; it was reported on by Hermann von Helmholtz in his *Treatise on Physiological Optics* (published in German in 1896). Helmholtz recommended use of an electric spark produced by an **induction coil** for illumination, because its short duration would reduce the possibility of eye movement; the subject looked through eyeholes in a hollow box painted black inside. A variety of early devices were described by G.M. Whipple (1910). Most early psychologists preferred the fall or gravity form, in which a guillotine effect is achieved by a

screen perforated with a horizontal slit dropping down before a card bearing the exposure field; Wundt developed a large demonstration model of this version, as well as a **pendulum** exposure apparatus. Other variants of the gravity form were achieved by a rubberband and shutter or a photographic shutter. Wundt's pendulum model was featured in the catalogue of the instrument-makers Zimmermann of Leipzig in 1897.

Wundt in 1899 laid down ten criteria for a good tachistoscope. Technical controversies relating to the effectiveness of the apparatus and consequent interpretation of results secured by it in its first half-century of use, as outlined by Whipple, are (a) how essential is absolute simultaneity of exposure over the entire field? (b) how carefully are convergence and accommodation controlled by the fixation point? (c) how long is and should be the actual duration of the retinal excitation set up by the exposure? and (d) what are the optimal conditions of general and local adaptation?

Today's versions allow presentation of a stimulus pattern, usually on a card, for a period of time controlled electronically and with a controlled level of illumination of the viewing field. Most are fitted with a hood to restrict the subject's field of view, and the stimulus field is viewed by reflection in a mirror silvered on the front surface to minimize multiple reflections. The usual means of illumination is a miniature fluorescent tube driven from a dc supply to prevent flicker. It is possible to construct multifield tachistoscopes using mirrors, with means for switching between fields, or to use conventional slide projectors with electromechanical shutters, directed at the same screen, for groups of subjects. With a single field it is important to match features such as light intensity and spectral char-

Front (left) and side (right) views of Wundt's demonstration version of the gravity tachistoscope. Courtesy of the Psychology Museum, University of Sydney.

acteristics across the adaptation (or fixation) and the stimulus (or exposure) fields; as more stimulus fields are added the issue of matching background characteristics across these becomes critical.

Initially the tachistoscope was used in the reaction experiment much favored by the first psychologists, in which the material has either to be reacted to, as in the simple discriminative reaction setup, or identified as well; this is described in Edward Bradford Titchener's classic *Experimental Psychology: A Manual of Laboratory Practice* (1905). Early on it became fashionable among pedagogical psychologists for the experimental investigation of reading, in which the exposure contained such materials as printed texts, words, nonsense syllables, or single letters. It was also used to determine range of attention for visual apprehension of groups of lines, drawings, objects, colors, and the like. As well, it has been used to measure the capacity to apprehend

a number of disparate objects by visual examination during a short period; here the stimulus is more complex and the exposure period longer than in the former situation. Some models have been adapted for the study of memory, in investigations in which control of duration of observation is considered important; the so-called memory drum, a clockwork **kymograph** used in conjunction with a screen with an exposure slit, is an example. Its potential in the construction of tests of individual ability or cognitive type or in the plotting of lifespan changes in reading style was recognized by early-twentieth-century psychologists, but current use is primarily in the fields of fundamental human cognitive and perceptual processes.

Alison M. Turtle

Bibliography

Cleary, Alan. *Instrumentation for Psychology.* Chichester: Wiley, 1977.

Schulze, R. *Experimental Psychology and Pedagogy for Teachers*. Translated by Rudolf Pintner. New York: Macmillan, 1912.

Titchener, Edward Bradford. *Experimental Psychology: A Manual of Laboratory Practice*. New York: Macmillan, 1901–1905.

Whipple, Guy Montrose. *Manual of Mental and Physical Tests*. Baltimore: Warwick and York, 1910.

Wundt, Wilhelm. "Zur Kritik tachistosckopischer Versuche." *Philosophische Studien* 15 (1899): 287–317.

Tachometer

A tachometer measures the velocity of shafts and rotating bodies and is calibrated in revolutions per minute (rpm). The name derived from the Greek *tacho*, "speed," plus meter. Tachometers differ from simple revolution counters in that they give a direct reading of velocity as a function of time. Some are mechanical and some electrical. Contact tachometers are directly connected by belt, chain, gears, or friction to the item being timed, while noncontact instruments have no physical link with the equipment they analyze.

In 1810, Bryan Donkin, an inventor, mechanic, and civil engineer of Bermondsey, England, described a device he invented to measure the speed of machinery and which he termed a "tachometer." Before this time, the only means for determining the speed of a rotating body was to observe the number of revolutions it made while simultaneously recording the time it took. Donkin's use of centrifugal force proved so practical that nearly all subsequent mechanical tachometers operated on the same principle.

The need to measure rpm came about only with the rise of industrialization and the development of manufacturing machinery. Precise information about the speed of steam engines and machines enabled operators to make immediate, accurate adjustments and to optimize certain operations. Without a tachometer, an operator could only sense the need for change. They were particularly useful in the manufacture of textiles and paper, where consistent speeds were critical to a uniform product. In the early twentieth century, aircraft and automobiles were added to the growing list of users of tachometers. Although it became a standard instrument on aircraft, it was not so universally applied to the automobile.

In 1874, Edward Brown, an instrument-maker of Philadelphia, patented one of the first tachometers to be mass produced for use on steam engines. An upright mercury column was positioned at the center of a pair of rotating reservoir tubes. As the reservoirs revolved, centrifugal force caused mercury to gather in them and pass from the column. The volume in the reservoirs was directly proportional to their speed. Looking much like a thermometer, the column was calibrated in revolutions per minute and the height of the mercury indicated the speed.

The construction of most centrifugal tachometers was nearly identical to that of the flyball-type governor used to control the speed of steam engines. Movable weights revolving about an axis provided the impetus for their operation. As the weights rotated, they sought to move outward in a straight line, but because of the linkage used to suspend them, they pivoted in an arc as they were thrown out. This movement was used to impart other action, and in the case of the tachometer it moved a pointer that indicated speed. Mechanical refinements in these instruments included worm gear drive and ball-bearing-mounted shafts.

Curtis H. Veeder, a mechanical engineer in Hartford, Connecticut, invented a noncentrifugal, liquid-type tachometer in 1903. It consisted of two columns partially filled with fluid and joined together by a small pump. When it was in operation, fluid was pumped from the reservoir tube into the calibrated indicator tube. Although Veeder believed the instrument would be particularly useful on automobiles, it did not win wide acceptance. Adjustments required to maintain it and the need to replenish evaporated liquid may have been enough to discourage motorists.

The vibrating-reed tachometer has no revolving parts, and its operation relies on vibrations inherent in operating machinery. It consists of a series of reeds or carefully tempered spring steel strips, each tuned to vibrate at a specific frequency. The instrument is attached to a piece of equipment, and movement within the machine sets up a sympathetic vibration in the reeds. Those reeds with a resonance most closely corresponding to the machine's vibration move the greatest amount, and they indicate the speed when read against a calibrated scale.

Tachometer by the Veeder Manufacturing Co., 1920s. NMAH 330,328. Courtesy of NMAH.

The first electric tachometer was developed in the early decades of the twentieth century. Here a small generator attached to a rotating shaft produced an electric current, and the voltage produced by the generator was directly proportional to the speed of the machine.

A hybrid of the electric- and centrifugal-type tachometers appeared in the 1920s. This was based in part on the rotating mercury column, but added to it were an electrical inductance coil and movable armature. Resting on the surface of the mercury was a float that supported an armature; around the armature, but not connected to it, was an inductance coil. As centrifugal force moved mercury from the column to the rotating reservoirs, the position of the armature relative to the electrical field of the coil changed. Both elements were connected by wires to an identical movable armature and coil. Changes in the position of the tachometer armature caused a like change in the indicator or recorder. A pointer attached to that armature gave the speed on a calibrated scale. As there was literally no friction involved in the movement of the mercury and armatures, the slightest change in speed was registered almost instantaneously.

The photoelectric tachometer is a mid-twentieth-century development that requires no direct contact with the operating machine. A beam of light is aimed at a spot of reflective material placed on the rotating part. As the spot passes in front of the light, the beam is reflected back onto a photoelectric cell. The cell in turn gives off an electrical impulse. Each impulse represents one revolution of the moving part, and, taken altogether, the series of impulses when computed represents the speed of the object. With the introduction of a laser light source, the device is useful in all lighting conditions and increases the number and type of reflective surfaces that can be used.

A more recent tachometer employs a small permanent magnet attached to the rotating element with a stationary electronic sensor placed close by. Each time the magnet passes the pickup point, electrical impulses are transmitted to a unit that computes the rpms.

William E. Worthington, Jr.

Bibliography

Donkin, Bryan. "An Instrument to Ascertain the Velocities of Machines, Called by Him a Tachometer." *Transactions of the Society of Arts, Manufactures, and Commerce* 28 (1811): 185–91.

Drysdale, C.V., and A.C. Jolley. *Electrical Measuring Instruments*. London: Chapman and Hall, 1952.

Moyer, James Ambrose. *Power Plant Testing*. New York: McGraw Hill, 1926.

Pullen, W.W.F. *The Testing of Engines, Boilers, and Auxiliary Machinery*. 2nd ed. Manchester: Scientific Publishing, 1911.

Telescope (Early)

There are two fundamentally different designs of telescope used with the human eye: the refractor, in which the objective is a lens, and the reflector, in which the objective is a mirror.

Although Galileo is popularly supposed to have invented the refracting telescope, and he was certainly one of its early users, the invention was that of Sacharias Jansen, a spectacle-maker of Middelburg in the province of Zeeland in the Netherlands. The invention was made during 1608, and the question of a patent was debated by the States General on October 2, 1608. There is no evidence from the writings of the key scientists in Europe interested in optics that they knew of a telescope before that year. During 1609 the news spread to Thomas Harriot in England and to Galileo in Italy. Harriot made the earliest record of the use of a telescope in July 1609, and in the same month Galileo ordered a telescope to be made to the Dutch pattern.

In a refracting telescope, all the optical parts are lenses, and the name derives from the fact that light is refracted when it enters glass. This earliest type of telescope developed in three different forms. The first is the astronomical telescope, which has two lenses, both of which converge the light and are known as positive lenses: the image is inverted, which presents no problems for observing the heavens. The second form is that for terrestrial use, having a three-lens erecting eyepiece system in addition to the objective lens. All the lenses are positive and the image is upright. The third type consists of an objective that is a converging, positive lens with a diverging, or negative, eye lens. These telescopes are known as Galilean type, because Galileo popularized this arrangement from 1610. The advantage is cheapness, because only two lenses need to be figured and the image is upright. The disadvantage is that magnification is not great. This arrangement was to become restricted to opera and field glasses (see **binocular**).

The refractor was the only type of telescope in general use during the seventeenth century and until about 1750. In addition to measuring stellar position, astronomers also wished to penetrate space, to examine planets and nebulae. For this purpose wide objective lenses were made with very long focal lengths, even up to 50 meters. A reason for this was the inherent defects in the image brought about through the nature of light and the colors produced by refraction and dispersion within a glass lens (chromatic aberration), and the spherical shape of the ground and polished surface of the lens (spherical aberration).

Chromatic aberration is caused by the unequal refraction of light rays of different color, which means that the blue and red ends of the spectrum come to a focus at different points, resulting in a colored edge to the image. Spherical aberration arises as follows. In a lens ground and polished to a spherical surface (nonspherical lens have been produced only in the mid

A group of early refracting telescopes set up for use. Johannes Hevelius. Machinae Coelestis. *Gedani, 1673: facing page 382. Courtesy of SSPL.*

twentieth century), the focal point of those rays that pass through the lens near its edge come to a focus closer to the lens than do the central rays. As rays from all parts of the object pass through all parts of the lens, the whole of the image is unsharp. The reflecting telescope has no chromatic aberration because all colors reflect equally from a mirror surface, the incident and reflected rays always being in the same medium—that is, air. The early refracting telescopes suffered from the poor quality of glass used for their lenses, and from aberrations in the image. The extremely long tube required to provide for the focal length made them unwieldy and impractical.

The first really important improvement to refracting instruments, first the telescope and after some years the microscope, was the work of John Dollond. The son of a Huguenot refugee living in London, his hobby was geometry, and in middle life he joined his son Peter in his instrument-making business. John Dollond achieved the remarkable feat of correcting chromatic aberration in the refracting telescope by using a combination of crown glass and flint glass for the components of the objective lens. The dense flint glass has greater dispersion than crown glass, so that a positive crown with a negative flint, pressed together, will give in combination a positive lens with virtually no chromatic aberration. Objectives of this type were marketed from 1758 by the Dollonds. The invention was to earn John Dollond a Gold Medal and Fellowship of the Royal Society.

The common reflecting telescope produces an erect image, and this type was the eighteenth century's most popular telescope, because it did not suffer from chromatic aberration. Also, it was considerably shorter in length, not more than 3 meters, and could be made with an objective mirror of considerable width, up to 45 cm, which made possible much greater light gathering and hence penetration into space. The concave mirror is known from classical time, and was used for focusing the sun's rays for burning. Its incorporation into a telescope was not made until the middle of the seventeenth century. James Gregory, a Scottish mathematician, published his design in 1663, but its fabrication proved too difficult for the technology of that time. This fact persuaded Isaac Newton to make a small reflector entirely himself. He achieved a telescope 6 in. in length in 1669. Newton reported that this, the first reflecting telescope ever to be made, could magnify forty times in diameter, "more than any 6 foot Tube can do I believe with distinctness."

There are three types of reflecting telescope. The Gregorian reflector has a concave objective mirror and a concave secondary mirror, which reflects light from the objective through a small hole in the middle of the objective mirror into the eyepiece (which is composed of two glass lenses). A similar-looking reflector is known as the Cassegrainian type, in which the secondary mirror is convex, and the image is inverted. It is named after a scarcely known Frenchman. In both these forms, the telescope is put to the eye and pointed straight at the object to be viewed. With the third type, the Newtonian reflector, the observer stands at right angles to the direction in which the telescope is pointing. This is because the objective mirror collects light and reflects it onto a small plain mirror set at 45° to the axis of the telescope. The eyepiece is, therefore, at right angles to the tube, and at the top end of the telescope. The most famous Newtonian telescopes were those produced at the end of the eighteenth century by William Herschel for astronomical space penetration. The smallest Herschel reflector has a metal mirror 15.5 cm in diameter and a 2.1-meter focal length.

In the eighteenth century, the London instrument-making trade included many fine makers of reflecting telescopes, of whom the most notable was the Scotsman James Short. His skill at founding the copper-tin alloy, and polishing by hand the pairs of metal mirrors that provided the optics for his Gregorian-type telescopes, was such that they were bought by most of the observatories in Europe and the New World. Short's achievement was built upon and extended by William Herschel at the end of the eighteenth century. Large reflecting telescopes were in use in observatories throughout the nineteenth century, and with even larger mirrors, are still employed today.

Gerard L'E. Turner

Bibliography
King, Henry C. *The History of the Telescope.* London: Charles Griffin, 1955.
Simpson, A.D.C. "James Gregory and the Reflecting Telescope." *Journal for the History of Astronomy* 23 (1992): 77–92.
Turner, Gerard L'E. "James Short, FRS, and His Contribution to the Construction of Reflecting Telescopes." *Notes and Records of the Royal Society of London* 24 (1969): 91–108.
———. "Three Late-Seventeenth Century Italian Telescopes, Two Signed by Paolo Belletti of Bologna." *Annali dell'Istituto di Storia della Scienza di Firenze* 9 (1984): 41–64, xxi plates.
Van Helden, Albert. "The Invention of the Telescope." *Transactions of the American Philosophical Society* 67 (1977): part 4.

Telescope (Modern)
Refractor

Although the achromatic refractor was invented in the 1750s, its development followed the remarkable improvement in optical glass-making in the German workshop in Benediktbeuern in the early nineteenth century. There Joseph [von] Fraunhofer was able to produce crown and flint glass of high quality and of previously calculated dispersion, combined these to correct the chromatic aberration, and calculated appropriate curvatures for the four lens surfaces. Fraunhofer was able to offer much larger achromatic lenses than the Dollonds; his refractors for the observatories in Dorpat (1824) and Berlin (1835) had an aperture of 9 Paris in. (24.4 cm). Fraunhofer also improved the stability and functionality of telescopes by developing the equatorial mount. With this "German mounting," a telescope could be pointed to any part of the sky above the horizon, with otherwise inaccessible regions being reached by reversing the telescope about its polar axis. Fraunhofer's work was continued by Merz & Mahler, who produced 14-Paris-in. (38-cm) refractors for Pulkovo Observatory in St. Petersburg (1839), and the Harvard College Observatory in Cambridge, Massachusetts (1847).

Other important large refractors include the 27-in. for the Vienna Observatory (1880) made by Howard Grubb; the 30-in. for the Pulkovo Observatory (1884), with optics by Alvan Clark & Sons of Cambridgeport, Massachusetts, and mounting by Repsold of Hamburg; the 80-cm for the Potsdam Astrophysical Observatory (1899), with optics by C.A. Steinheil & Sons of Munich and mounting by Repsold of Hamburg; the 83-cm for the Meudon Observatory (1893), with optics by Paul Pierre Henry and his brother Prosper Mathieu Henry and mounting by P. Gautier of Paris; the 36-in. for the Lick Observatory (1888); and the 40-in. (1897) for the Yerkes Observatory, both with optics by Alvan Clark & Sons and mounting by Warner & Swasey of Cleveland, Ohio.

Most achromatic refractors were corrected for visual observations. The increasing importance of photography in the latter decades of the nineteenth century led to the development of refracting telescopes that produced sharp images at blue wavelengths. These astrographs had a wide field, short focal length, and thus an aperture ratio (ratio between objective diameter and focal length) of 1:4 to 1:10 instead of the usual 1:15 to 1:20. Many of them (up to 40 cm in. diameter) were made by Zeiss of Jena.

The era of the great refractors came to an end at the end of the nineteenth century, as objective lenses reached their practical limit; flexing of the heavy disks of glass tended to cause distortion and absorb much of the transmitted light, especially in the blue spectral region, which is important for photography. Mirrors, on the other hand, are inherently free from chromatic aberration; they can be supported from the back as well as from the sides, thus lessening distortion; and they absorb only a slight amount of incident light.

Silvered Glass Reflector

Several large reflectors with speculum metal mirrors were built in the late eighteenth and early nineteenth centuries, but the reflexivity was not very high, and even the best polish degraded quickly in the earth's atmosphere. Thus the new method of covering a glass surface with silver introduced by Justus von Liebig in 1835 (published in 1856) was readily adopted for astronomical purposes. Carl August Steinheil in Munich and Jean Bernard Léon Foucault in Paris (independently of each other) were soon building good telescopes with silvered glass mirrors of 32 to 80 cm aperture. Foucault also developed an accurate testing technique. By the 1870s, opticians such as George Calver, John Browning, and A. Ainslie Common in England, and Henry Draper and John A. Brashear in the United States, had constructed reflecting telescopes up to 1 meter. Although they are very useful, especially for astronomical spectroscopy, photometry, and photography, professional astronomers did not rely on reflectors until the early twentieth century (see **camera, photographic; photometer;** and **spectroscope, astronomical**). The only notable early example was the 36-in. Crossley reflector made by Common (1879); this was transferred to the Lick Observatory in 1895 and used by James E. Keeler to investigate nebulae. In 1904, Carl Zeiss began producing reflecting telescopes in cooperation with the improved glass of the Schott works in Jena. In the United States, the 24-in. reflecting telescope at the Yerkes Observatory (1901) led to the 60-in. and 100-in. telescopes at the Mount Wilson Observatory (1908 and 1917). These three instruments were promoted by George Ellery Hale, and all three mirrors were figured by George Willis Ritchey. From photographs of the spectrum taken with the 100-in. telescope, Edwin Hubble made his famous discovery of the velocity-distance relation of galaxies (1929).

The Yerkes forty-inch refracting telescope on display at the World's Columbian Exposition, Chicago, 1893. Worcester R. Warner and Ambrose Swasey, A Few Astronomical Instruments. *Cleveland: Warner & Swasey, 1900: Plate XXXVI. Courtesy of SSPL.*

The largest reflectors are the 200-in. (5-meter) Hale telescope on Mount Palomar (planned since 1928 and opened in 1948), and the 6-meter Soviet reflector in Selencukskaja in the Caucasus Mountains (1976). Most of the astronomically useful reflectors, however, have mirrors in the 4-meter range, and with these one can observe in the prime focus (aperture ratio 1:3 to 1:5), or the Newtonian focus for photography, or in the Cassegrain focus (1:10 to 1:20), or the Coudé focus (1:30 to 1:40) for spectroscopy.

New materials with small coefficients of thermal expansion have further increased the efficiency of reflecting telescopes. Pyrex was first used in the 1930s and became widespread in the 1950s. Glass ceramics with extremely small coefficients of thermal expansion (such as, ZERODUR by Schott Glassworks of Mainz) were introduced in the 1970s. Modern concave mirrors have very high quality surfaces: the deviation of the 3.5-meter mirror of the Calar Alto telescope in southern Spain (1981/1982) from the ideal surface shape is little less than $1/_{10,000}$ of a millimeter.

Schmidt Telescope

A reflector with a parabolic mirror produces a distortion-free image only if the incident rays of light are parallel to the optical axis. Rays incident at an angle to the optical axis produce asymmetric, cometlike images (coma). Therefore, the parabolic mirror has only a small usable field of view (about 15 minutes), thus thirty-two photographic plates are required to cover only 1 square degree. The entire sky contains of 41,253 square degrees! This new problem—needing a good quality not only for one star in the center but over a wide field—came up with the rise of photography. The first step toward larger fields of view was the Ritchey-Chrétien reflector. Henri J. Chrétien suggested the design in 1922, and Ritchey produced the difficult aspheric surface. This system avoided coma, but still had astigmatism and field curvature. Karl Schwarzschild suggested a special two-mirror telescope that retained only the image defect of astigmatism.

A wide field of view (up to 15°) and distortion-free-image quality were achieved by Bernhard Schmidt, an Estonian-born optician working for the Hamburg Observatory. In 1930, Schmidt used a simple spherical mirror in order to avoid coma, and placed a thin aspherical correction plate in the center of curvature of this mirror to remove spherical aberration. In addition, he had the brilliant idea of producing this correction plate using vacuum technique.

Schmidt's first telescope of this sort had a spherical mirror of 44-cm diameter, and correction plate of 36-cm diameter (aperture ratio 1:1.75 and focal length 62.5 cm); since 1962 this has been used at the Boyden Observatory in Bloemfontein, South Africa. His second telescope had a spherical mirror of 60 cm. Shortly after Schmidt's death in 1935, the director of the observatory published details on the invention and production of the Schmidt telescope. Although a few Schmidt telescopes were made in the United States in the late 1930s, this form did not become widely used until after World War II. Independently, Yrjö Väisälä had developed the principle of the Schmidt telescope in Turku, Finland.

The Schmidt telescope, one of the most important inventions of twentieth-century astronomy, does have some small disadvantages—most notably, the film must be curved, and the overall length of the telescope is very large (the tube length is twice the focal length). Efforts have been made to overcome these problems. F.B. Wright proposed modifications like a Schmidt-Newtonian. In 1940, James G. Baker introduced a Schmidt-Cassegrain system that has a shorter tube length (one-third of the focal length) and a flat field. In 1944, Dimitri D. Maksutov in Leningrad (now St. Petersburg) introduced a system that uses a thick spherical meniscus lens to correct the spherical aberration of the primary spherical mirror. This had a very short tube length but curved photographic fields. For survey cameras, the Schmidt and Maksutov systems were combined to produce a telescope with extreme aperture ratio of 1:0.7 and a wide field of 50°. The largest Schmidt telescopes are the 1.3-meter in Tautenburg near Jena, Germany (1960), the 1.2-meter on Mt. Palomar, California (1948), and an instrument of similar size in Australia (1973).

Gudrun Wolfschmidt

Bibliography

King, Henry C. *The History of the Telescope.* London: Griffin, 1955.

Marx, Siegfried, and Werner Pfau. *Himmelsfotografie mit Schmidt-Teleskopen.* Leipzig: Urania, 1990.

Osterbrock, Donald E. *Pauper and Prince: Ritchey, Hale, and Big American Telescopes.* Tucson: University of Arizona Press, 1993.

Riekher, Rolf. *Fernrohre und ihre Meister: Eine Entwicklungsgeschichte der Fernrohrtechnik.* Berlin: Technik, 1957.

Wilson, Raymond Neil. *Reflecting Telescope Optics.* Berlin: Springer, 1995.

Telescope, New Technology

Since the 1970s, several steps have been taken to develop ever larger and more powerful telescopes and to avoid the perturbations caused by the atmosphere of the earth (if it is not possible to observe in orbit as it is done by the Hubble Space Telescope). These include multiple mirror telescopes, active optics, adaptive optics, speckle imaging, and the Very Large Telescope.

Multiple Mirror Telescopes

The performance of a telescope depends on the size of its objective—the larger the objective, the fainter objects it can "see." Although mirrors can be made much larger than the largest objective lenses, even these are limited by weight and finishing techniques. This limitation has led to the development of large reflecting telescopes with objectives consisting of several individual mirrors. The Multiple Mirror Telescope, opened in 1979 on Mount Hopkins in Arizona (a joint venture of the Smithsonian Astrophysical Observatory and the University of Arizona), has six 72-in. diameter mirrors mounted together on a tracking structure; the collecting area corresponds to a telescope of 176-in. diameter. The 10-meter Keck Telescope SMT (Segmented Mirror Telescope) erected on Mauna Kea in Hawaii in 1992 has thirty-six segmented 1-meter mirrors (honeycomb pattern). Segmented mirror telescopes of even 25-meters are under discussion. Such segmented mirrors cost less because many similar segments can be produced at the same time; and it is possible to build such telescopes in space step by step.

Active Optics

In 1976, using ideas from the 1960s, Raymond Neil Wilson developed the concept of active optics using thin flexible mirrors. The first active telescope mirror arrangement was tested in a laboratory at the European Southern Observatory (ESO) at Garching near Munich in 1986, and the 3.6-meter New Technology Telescope (NTT) became operational at ESO in La Silla, Chile, in 1989. This has the possibility of intercontinental remote control from Garching via a satellite link.

This new type of telescope mirror is so thin that it can be slightly deformed. Deviations from the ideal shape can arise from imperfect finishing, and deformations can also arise from gravitational, thermal, and mechanical changes during operation caused by temperature variations, weather, and wind. The thin active telescope mirrors can be continuously controlled, and deviations can be immediately corrected by computer-activated supports ("actuators"). This ensures that the NTT will have the best possible image quality in every position. Active mirrors are lighter and therefore less expensive than conventional mirrors: the active 3.6-meter mirror for the NTT is 24 cm thick and weighs only 6 tons, while the conventional 3.5-meter mirror at Calar Alto (Spain) is 55 cm thick and weighs 13 tons!

Adaptive Optics

Stars appear to twinkle because light is distorted by turbulence in the earth's atmosphere. Thus, observing is effectively determined by the state of the atmosphere during the exposure, which is referred to as astronomical "seeing" (normally 1 or 2 arc seconds, related only to the observation site, but independent of telescope size). The parallel wave fronts of the stars are more or less distorted by the atmosphere, so that we can not reach the theoretically possible limit of image quality, the "diffraction limited imaging." (The theoretical resolution of a 1-meter telescope in visible light, for example, is 0.1 arc second.) Adaptive optics compensate for atmospheric aberration and, thus, increase the image sharpness. The first ideas go back to 1953, but the technology was first developed in the late 1970s for military purposes. The first astronomical image with adaptive optics was taken in 1989 by a team of ESO and French astronomers. Adaptive optics works by measuring the distortion of incoming light with a wavefront sensor, and rapidly (within a few milliseconds) correcting this distortion with a small computer-controlled deformable mirror. Precondition for the correction is the existence of a comparison light source—for example, either a star or an artificial light source. These atmospheric corrections are additional to those of active optics.

Adaptive optics, such as the COME-ON system used at the ESO 3.6-meter telescope, have been especially successful in the infrared spectral region. Astronomers hope that, with

Active 3.6m NTT mirror, with 78 computer-controlled active supports, at the European Southern Observatory, 1990. Courtesy of the European Southern Observatory.

this new technology, ground-based telescopes will produce images almost as sharp as if the telescope were situated in space.

Speckle Imaging

Another method of reaching the theoretical resolution of a telescope is to improve the photographic image (after the exposure) through speckle interferometry, a technique developed in 1970 by Antoine Labeyrie. Here one uses hundreds of photographs of extremely short exposure times, an interference filter with a narrow pass width, recording film or video cameras with very sensitive image amplifiers and large telescopes. In the 1980s speckle cameras were developed with photon counters—for example, PAPA (Photo Analog Precision Address) used at Harvard Smithsonian, or with digital **charge-coupled devices** (CCD) data recorded on optical disks (see also **photon counter**).

Each snapshot of a binary system taken through the earth's atmosphere shows a blurred spot consisting of many small speckles, representing frozen air turbulences—a changing pattern with each exposure. It thus provides information about the rapidly varying distortion structure of the atmosphere and also time-constant information about the object itself. In "speckle-masking interferometry" the artificial comparison star is simulated with the aid of a special mask. The key is not to add the speckle images themselves—that would be comparable to a long exposure image—but to make appropriate correlations that contain the information about the object in an encoded form. Speckle interferometry uses a computer to reconstruct by Fourier analysis the true (diffraction limited) image from a great many individual, flawed images. It is hoped that speckle interferometry, in combination with the Very Large Telescope, will produce images with more than 0.01 arc second resolution in visible light.

Very Large Telescope—Optical Interferometers

The production of images and spectra with fascinating resolution is the great advantage of optical **interferometers**. The idea for the interferometry technique comes from radio astronomy.

The Very Large Telescope (VLT) of the European Southern Observatory at Paranal in Chile will be the largest optical interferometer yet built. The project was started in 1986, and the first telescope mirror was completed in 1995; expected completion of the entire structure is around the turn of the century. The Very Large Telescope will be formed of four 8.2-meter reflecting telescopes with active and adaptive optics, and the same capacity as a telescope with a diameter of 16.4-meters. The large mirrors are made of ZERODUR by the Schott glassworks in Mainz, and were polished in 1993 by REOSC (Recherches et Études d'Optique et de Sciences Connexes) near Paris. Each mirror will be supported by 150 hydraulic actuators, and the light received by each mirror can be combined in a common focal point. The VLT will make possible optical and infrared observations of the faintest, most remote, and oldest objects known in the universe.

Gudrun Wolfschmidt

Bibliography

Alloin, D.M., and J.M. Mariotti, eds. "Diffraction-Limited Imaging with Very Large Telescopes." *Proceedings of the NATO Advanced Study Institute on Diffraction-Limited Imaging with Very Large Telescopes, Cargese, September 13–23, 1988.* Dordrecht: Kluwer, 1989.

Beckers, J.M., and Fritz Merkle, eds. *High Resolution Imaging by Interferometry II.* Proceedings no. 39 of the European Southern Observatory (ESO) Conference, 1991. Garching: European Southern Observatory, 1992.

Crowe, Devon G., ed. *Selected Papers on Adaptive Optics and Speckle Imaging.* SPIE Milestone Series vol. MS 93. Bellingham, Wash.: SPIE Optical Engineering, 1994.

Merkle, Fritz, ed. *Active and Adaptive Optics.* Proceedings no. 48 of the European Southern Observatory (ESO) Conference, 1992. Garching: European Southern Observatory, 1993.

———, ed. *NOAO-ESO Conference on High-Resolution Imaging by Interferometry: Ground-Based Interferometry at Visible and Infrared Wavelengths, 15–18 March 1988.* Garching: European Southern Observatory, 1988.

Tyson, Robert K. *Principles of Adaptive Optics.* London: Academic, 1991.

Ulrich, M.H., ed. *Progress in Telescope and Instrumentation Technologies.* Garching: European Southern Observatory, 1993.

Telescope, Radio

A radio telescope collects and records radio waves from extraterrestrial objects. It consists of an aerial, or array of aerials, that collect the electromagnetic radiation, and a receiver that amplifies the signal and produces an inscription, often in the form of a pen-recording. The largest instruments were very expensive, and their operation involved teams of astronomers, engineers, and support staff. Radio astronomy grew rapidly in the years after World War II. This new scientific specialty articulated a universe radically different from that described by optical astronomers: a violent universe including radio stars, pulsars, and quasars.

For Karl Jansky, a Bell Telephone Laboratories radio engineer, cosmic radio noise was one component of the static produced in the development of sensitive radio communication receivers. Grote Reber, another American radio engineer working in the 1930s, built an instru-

The Mark I Radio telescope at Jodrell Bank, Cheshire, England. Courtesy of Nuffield Radio Astronomy Laboratories/University of Manchester.

ment to measure cosmic radio noise collected by a parabolic dish reflector of 9.5-meter diameter. However, it was skills learned by academic and military scientists through the wartime development of radar and the investigation of interfering signals that crucially shaped the new postwar specialty. Important radio astronomy groups were set up in Britain, Australia, Holland, the United States, France, Canada, and Russia.

The configuration and design of the aerial constrains the capabilities of a radio telescope. Radio waves are longer than light waves, and for comparable resolution, or beamwidth, a radio telescope aerial or array must be proportionately larger, or work with higher frequencies. Much early work used aerials made from ex-army Würzburg radar dishes or arrays of dipoles. Through the 1950s and 1960s engineers and astronomers designed a series of large single filled aperture steerable dishes, notably the 250-foot Mark I radio telescope at Jodrell Bank in Britain, the Green Bank 140-foot telescope of the National Radio Astronomy Observatory (NRAO) in the United States, and the 210-foot Parkes telescope of the

Commonwealth Scientific and Industrial Research Organization (CSIRO) of Australia. The construction of these expensive and spectacular instruments, fueled by national competition, reached a working culmination with the 100-meter steerable radio telescope at Effelsburg in Germany. However other schemes, such as the 1,000-foot Mark IV at Jodrell Bank and the American 600-foot Sugar Grove telescope, foundered as the alliances of government, military, and scientific bodies that had secured the resources for the earlier dishes loosened. The only completed single filled dish on this scale, the 300-meter-diameter Arecibo radio telescope operated by Cornell University, sacrificed steerability and was built in the 1960s in a natural hollow.

With small dishes and arrays, the design and construction was done by the astronomer. As the scale, complexity, and time-scale of these projects grew, a new relationship between astronomer and engineer had to be managed. The design of a large and heavy dish required the skills of a mechanical engineer; its subtle and accurate guidance meant the innovation of special servomechanisms and computer control. The establishment of on-site engineers mirrored on a smaller scale the changes in social organization found contemporaneously in nuclear physics facilities such as particle **accelerators**.

A large single dish was not the only route to higher resolution. Arrays of smaller aerials, such as the Mills Cross in Australia, could also produce the pencil-beam sensitivity of a filled parabolic reflector. An alternative method was to combine several aerials together through the technique of interferometry to achieve the resolving power of a larger telescope. In an **interferometer** the output varies as signals received through carefully spaced aerials combine in and out of phase. The shape of the output can provide information about the size and intensity of the radio source.

Groups at the University of Cambridge and the CSIRO at Sydney independently began constructing radio interferometers soon after 1945. Both groups used their interferometers to produce catalogues of radio sources, but disparities between the two caused controversy in the 1950s. The Cambridge group under Martin Ryle developed an important interferometry technique called aperture synthesis that was incorporated in their two major instruments: the 1-mile and 5-km radio telescopes. Aperture synthesis is also the basis of the NRAO's Very Large Array (VLA) built in the 1970s in New Mexico out of twenty-seven steerable radio telescopes along three arms, each 21 km long. Even greater resolving power was achieved by increasing the baseline still further, such as through Long Baseline Interferometry (LBI), in which a radio link between aerials is used, or Very Long Baseline Interferometry (VLBI), in which the signals are carefully recorded on-site and combined at a later date. The technique of interferometry allowed radio astronomers to observe structures in astronomical objects of arc-second dimensions, and thereby compete with optical astronomers.

There were also important changes in receiver technology. The introduction of liquid-helium-cooled maser and parametric amplifiers in the late 1950s and 1960s cut internally generated noise and improved sensitivity. Computers were integrated into the radio telescope system both to control the aerials, and to reduce and analyze data, which, particularly in the case of interferometers, was a formidable task.

The design of radio telescopes depended partly on intended use. Instruments for special purposes, such as the Culgoora radio heliograph built in 1967 to map the sun, had specialized designs. The design of aerials could also have broader significance: there was considerable overlap between the manufacture of radio telescopes, and the aerials used for early-warning systems, and commercial or military satellite communication. For example, a major dish for British Telecom's Goonhilly transatlantic station was a reproduction of Jodrell Bank's Mark II telescope.

Radio telescopes possessed a social component: the astronomers who judged and valued the output and who worked with engineers to design and construct the instruments. In some instances, the technical choice of radio astronomy groups (and hence the development of techniques within the groups) depended as much on the group's social structure as on the scientific program pursued. Public, government, or military bodies can also be important in accounting for the design and interpretation of radio telescopes.

Jon Agar

Bibliography

Agar, Jon. "Making a Meal of the Big Dish: The Construction of the Jodrell Bank Mark I Radio Telescope as a Stable Edifice, 1946–57." *British Journal for the History of Science* 27 (1994): 3–21.

Edge, David O., and Michael J. Mulkay. *Astronomy Transformed: The Emergence of Radio Astronomy in Britain*. New York: Wiley, 1976.

Needell, Allan. "Lloyd Berkner, Merle Tuve, and the Federal Role in Radio Astronomy." *Osiris* 3 (1987): 261–88.

Robertson, Peter. *Beyond Southern Skies: Radio Astronomy and the Parkes Telescope*. Cambridge: Cambridge University Press, 1992.

Sullivan, Woody T., III, ed. *The Early Years of Radio Astronomy*. Cambridge: Cambridge University Press, 1984.

Telescope, X-ray

An x-ray telescope detects high-energy x-radiation, having wavelengths around 1 Å, emitted by the sun and other celestial bodies. The category includes ionization chambers that collect x-ray photons and metallic tubes having polished inner surfaces that direct x-radiation to spectrometers and imaging devices (see **spectrophotometer**). These instruments have made x-ray astronomy, an important part of celestial studies through the discovery and understanding of high-energy phenomena such as black holes and pulsing neutron stars.

Special Nature of X-ray Astronomy

X-ray astronomy, the study of celestial objects in the high-energy portion of the electromagnetic spectrum (from about 0.01Å [1,000 keV] to about 120Å [0.1 keV]), is heavily dependent on space technology and special instrumentation. Because x-rays are absorbed high in the earth's atmosphere—at about 100 km—observation of the high-energy radiation from the earth's surface is impossible. When rockets became available for scientific research after World War II, scientists employed ionization chambers to take their initial glimpses of a universe previously invisible to them. Normal optical telescopes are useless when studying x-rays because the high-energy radiation has properties more akin to those of a photon than an electromagnetic wave. Partly as a result, advances in x-ray astronomy instrumentation came from people trained as physicists, accustomed to high-energy particle experimentation, rather than from those trained in classical astronomy.

T

Ionization Chambers

During the early days of the science, experimentalists used such ionization chambers as **Geiger** and proportional counters, which work on the same principle to detect x-rays: when an x-ray photon interacts with inert gas inside the instrument, it generates a cascade of electrons that is electronically amplified and recorded. Using a variety of thin plastic or metal windows through which the radiation passes, scientists can limit the energy levels of the incident radiation and determine a crude spectrum. The sensitivity of the counter depends on the materials used for the window and the gas inside. But most important, the size of the window determines how many X-ray photons can be collected, with a large aperture being the most useful.

Interest in celestial x-rays arose from practical military concerns. In the 1930s, Edward O. Hulburt, a scientist working for the Naval Research Laboratory (NRL) in Washington, D.C., hypothesized that the sun emits x-rays that cause ionization of the E-region of the earth's atmosphere (90–160 km high). The ionization appeared to affect radio communications around the globe—a subject of vital interest to the navy. In 1949, Herbert Friedman, another NRL scientist, took advantage of a modified German V-2 rocket to launch a Geiger counter to a height of 150 km, verifying Hulburt's theory while obtaining the first data concerning the nature of solar x-rays. Throughout the 1950s, Friedman and colleagues at the NRL refined their instruments and rocket techniques to obtain almost all the empirical information about the sun's x-radiation.

The Origin of Nonsolar X-ray Astronomy and Development of New Instruments

An explosion of activity in x-ray astronomy followed the Russian launch of Sputnik in 1957 and the creation of the National Aeronautics and Space Administration (NASA) in the following year. Though only a small element in the larger space program, funding for x-ray astronomy—primarily for advances in instrumentation and spacecraft—enabled the science to expand dramatically. Aside from work performed by NRL scientists, research was begun by cosmic ray physicists Bruno Rossi, an M.I.T. professor, and Riccardo Giacconi, who worked at the privately owned American Science and Engineering Co. (AS&E) Motivated by the American government's interest in space science, the two scientists hypothesized that other

celestial objects besides the sun might emit x-radiation. This was a remarkable suggestion, since the sun, if placed at the distance of the nearest star outside our solar system, would produce a minuscule flux of x-rays. But Rossi and Giacconi suggested that x-rays could be produced not only by high-temperature thermal radiation, the source of solar x-radiation, but also from magnetic *bremsstrahlung,* or "synchrotron" radiation, in which magnetic fields capture and deflect high-energy electrons.

The low flux of x-rays from nonsolar sources suggested the need for extremely sensitive detectors. While Rossi and Giacconi obtained funding, starting in 1960, to produce conventional ionization chamber detectors to look for x-ray sources, they also began work on a true x-ray telescope that focused the radiation. Giacconi fortuitously discovered that a German scientist, Hans Wolter, had offered a theory for making x-ray microscopes in the late 1940s and 1950s. Using parabolic and hyperbolic mirrors in conjunction, x-rays could be reflected at very shallow angles ("grazing angles") of incidence and focused onto a detector. Practical difficulties in making small instruments like these for microscopy meant that no successful x-ray microscopes were constructed. But Giacconi realized that the construction constraints would not exist when making large mirrors for telescopes. Meanwhile, Rossi offered the useful suggestion of nesting several mirror surfaces concentrically within one telescope, which increased the instrument's power. Though called a "telescope," the instrument acted more like a funnel to direct x-rays to other detectors.

Work on the mirror telescope proceeded slowly, even after the discovery in 1962 of unexpectedly intense x-ray sources in the sky. Using rocket-borne ionization chambers, AS&E and NRL scientists spent the decade of the 1960s identifying about thirty nonsolar x-ray emitters, which included some supernova remnants. The use of a large-area ionization chamber on *Uhuru,* the first x-ray astronomy satellite launched in 1970, resulted in acquisition of unprecedented amounts of data that allowed scientists to understand the nature of many x-ray sources: they consisted of neutron stars and possibly black holes accreting matter from a binary partner and heating that matter to temperatures on the order of 1,000,000°.

The x-ray mirror telescope found its first use not to observe any of these exotic celestial objects, but to look at the sun in 1973. Oper-

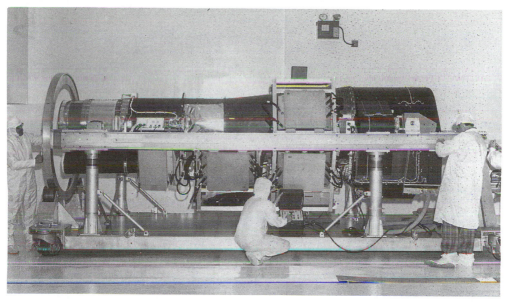

The x-ray telescope from HEAO-B being checked out at NASA-Marshall Space Flight Center, 1977. Courtesy of NASA.

ated by astronauts on the *Skylab* space station, the telescope obtained dramatic pictures of x-ray emission from the solar corona. With the success of this instrument, Giacconi and colleagues worked confidently on design and construction of a 0.6-meter-diameter x-ray mirror telescope to be carried into space by the second High Energy Astronomy Observatory (HEAO). Nicknamed "Einstein" because it made its initial observations in 1979, the one-hundredth anniversary of Albert Einstein's birth, the telescope took x-ray pictures of explosive extragalactic objects and supernova remnants as well as calmer phenomena such as coronal x-ray emission from sunlike stars. It also observed weak x-radiation emitted from the magnetic fields of Jupiter and Saturn.

Since the early 1980s, x-ray astronomy research has continued with satellite-borne experiments, many of them designed and launched by European and Japanese space organizations. Both large ionization chambers and x-ray mirror telescopes have been used for studying x-radiation that can offer clues about the "Big Bang" and star formation. In February 1993, the Japanese launched the *Asuka* satellite, which contained four American-built x-ray mirror telescopes used for examining x-ray emissions at the edge of the universe. Another x-ray mirror telescope is planned to be used in the American Advanced X-Ray Astrophysics Facility, but congressional funding cutbacks have delayed launch

of that instrument until the year 2000 at the earliest. The delay illustrates how advances in x-ray astronomy, though spectacular and occurring in a relatively short time, depend on rapid technological innovation and government support.

Richard F. Hirsh

Bibliography

Friedman, Herbert. "Discovering the Invisible Universe." *Mercury* 20 (January/February 1991): 42–49.

Hirsh, Richard F. *Glimpsing an Invisible Universe: The Emergence of X-Ray Astronomy.* Cambridge: Cambridge University Press, 1983.

Mecham, Michael. "Launch of X-Ray Satellite Will Aid Big Bang Studies." *Aviation Week and Space Technology* 138 (March 1, 1993): 9.

Tucker, Wallace, and Riccardo Giacconi. *The X-Ray Universe.* Cambridge: Harvard University Press, 1985.

Theodolite

A theodolite is an altazimuth surveying instrument designed for taking angles in two coordinates. It is provided with both a vertical and a horizontal arc or circle and a telescopic sight, so that altitudes and azimuths can be taken from a single sighting. Designs for such instruments were proposed in the sixteenth century,

Ramsden's three-foot geodetic theodolite, used for the Principal Triangulation of Great Britain and Ireland, 1792. SM 1876-1203. Courtesy of SSPL.

but at that time the customary understanding of the word "theodolite" was an instrument with only a horizontal circle, used for taking azimuths or bearings. Historians who have not been careful over the terms used in the primary literature have been able to trace spurious lines of development from the early designs to the present day. After the modern meaning of "theodolite" had come into use, W.F. Stanley chose to refer to the azimuth instrument as a "simple theodolite" and that terminology should be adopted to avoid further misunderstanding.

The simple theodolite was a tool of a new method of surveying introduced in the sixteenth century to replace much of the primitive linear measurement taken with ropes and poles by location using angular measurement. When the technique of triangulation was first explained by Gemma Frisius in 1533, the angles required at either end of a baseline were to be taken with the alidade and degree scale on the back of an **astrolabe**, to which would be added a small magnetic **compass** for orientation. There was no need, however, for the complexity of the main astrolabic scales and projections, and so a simplified instrument with only the components required for surveying soon emerged. One such design was the "theodelitus" of Leonard Digges, first described in print in 1571. Digges also explained the much more complicated altazimuth instrument, which he called the "topographicall instrument." Although some of these were made, they did not find a role in everyday surveying.

Several attempts were made to introduce the altazimuth theodolite to the surveyors of the eighteenth century. Jonathan Sisson and his son Jeremiah produced a variety of arrangements for adding a vertical arc to the simple theodolite. Other English makers, such as Thomas Heath and Benjamin Cole, made ambiguous instruments, in which a detachable vertical arc with a telescopic sight was mounted on the plain alidade of the simple theodolite, so that the surveyor was not tied to either alternative. Sophisticated designs were also introduced by Jesse Ramsden in England and by Georg F. Brander in Germany. Nevertheless, the simple theodolite was still referred to as "the common theodolite" by George Adams in his *Geometrical and Graphical Essays* of 1791.

The altazimuth theodolite came to be accepted as the standard design in the nineteenth century, and while there were many variants, three general types are worth noting. The earliest to gain acceptance was the plain theodolite, in an arrangement that was sometimes attributed to Ramsden. Here two A-supports on the horizontal plate carried a horizontal axis for a vertical semicircle and telescopic sight. The semicircle was positioned between the two supports and it carried the **telescope** above. F.W. Simms cited this model as the exemplary theodolite in 1834. Simms also described the Everest theodolite, in which the telescope was positioned at the center of the horizontal axis, after the manner of the astronomer's transit instrument; the axis itself was carried by a fork mount, and two short arcs toward either end of the telescope were read at both extremities of a horizontal index arm.

In the transit theodolite, the supports for the horizontal axis were sufficiently tall to allow the telescope to transit, and thus point in either direction. It was fitted with a full vertical circle, which was typically read at either end of a horizontal index arm. The transit theodolite in effect combined the best features of the plain and Everest designs, and it remained the standard design into the twentieth century. The scales were increasingly enclosed for protection, to be read through apertures by the use of micrometer microscopes. The optics of scale reading became increasingly sophisticated, and both vertical and horizontal measurements were not only taken from a single sighting on the target, but were also presented to the surveyor together in the same field of view.

Jim A. Bennett

Bibliography

Bennett, J.A. *The Divided Circle: A History of Instruments for Astronomy, Navigation and Surveying.* Oxford: Phaidon, 1987.

Thermobalance

A thermobalance measures weight changes of samples subjected to a controlled temperature regime in a preselected atmosphere. The technique is thermogravimetry (TG) or thermogravimetric analysis (TGA). A thermobalance is usually a microbalance controlled by a servo mechanism providing a record via an X-Y recorder or by a computer work station. The record is that of weight (w) plotted against temperature (T), or time (t) if the variation of temperature with time is indicated. An example of decomposition that is often quoted in TG is the dissociation of calcium carbonate to calcium oxide and carbon dioxide. From the record of weight against temperature, the decomposition can be followed. In corrosion from a metal, the plot shows an increase in weight. Such information is often plotted in alternative ways such as the percentage weight change, the fractional weight change, or fractional extent of reaction (α) against temperature. The record of weight against temperature is called the thermogravimetric curve. Derivative thermogravimetry (DTG) involves plotting dw/dt against temperature.

TGA requires a **balance** and a **furnace**. The art of weighing was known in Egypt around 2800 B.C., but perhaps the earliest example of weighing to follow a reaction was in the Ptolemaic Period (332–30 B.C.) when gold was re-

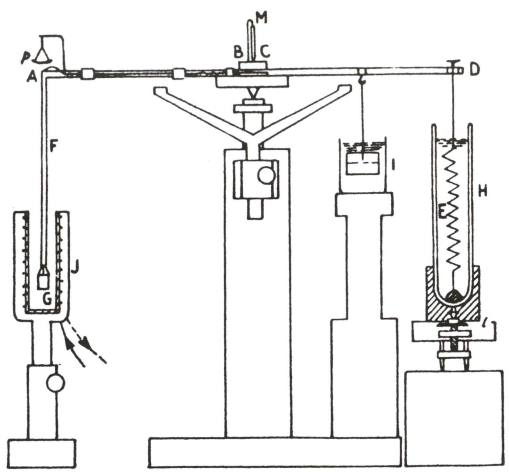

Schematic diagram of the Honda thermobalance, 1915. The furnace is shown at (J). Clément Duval. Inorganic Thermogravimetric Analysis. *Translated by R.E. Oesper. Amsterdam: Duval (1963): 5, Figure 1.*

fined by amalgamation with mercury. In his *Experiments and Observation . . . on Calcareous Cements* (1780), Bryan Higgins described how he heated limestone at different temperatures and followed the decomposition to calcium oxide; he used a balance to measure weight changes caused by heating, but could not effectively measure the temperature. With the improvement of **thermometers** in the nineteenth century, the development of a thermobalance became possible.

Early Development

Emil G. Warburg and T. Ihmori introduced the microbalance in Germany in 1886. In 1903 Walther Nernst and Ernest H. Riesenfeld, from Germany, reported using a microbalance to follow weight changes of Iceland spar, opal, and zirconia on heating. In thermal analysis, a restoration type microbalance is favored as the

sample resides in the same region of the furnace throughout.

Otto Brill described the effect of heat on calcium carbonate in 1905. He heated the sample in a platinum tube furnace, removed it at regular intervals, and recorded the weight on a Nernst microbalance. In 1912, the French chemist Georges Urbain constructed an apparatus incorporating a conventional balance modified for null point electromagnet compensation, as introduced by K. Angström in 1895. This was a true thermobalance, as the sample could be weighed in the furnace and both temperature and weight measured. Its potential however was never realized, probably because it was unreliable.

In 1915, Kataro Honda in Japan published "On a Thermobalance," in which reliable equipment is described and the word "thermobalance" used for the first time. The design was influenced by Honda's use of a similar unit for studies on magnetochemistry. Honda's thermobalance was modified by his students, and the thermal analysis of many hundreds of precipitates were reported by the Japanese school. Another early form of the thermobalance was described by a French scientist, Marcel Guichard, in 1923, and he and his co-workers carried out a comprehensive series of thermal analysis investigations. Pierre Dubois and later Pierre Vallet employed photographic recording of the thermogravimetric curves.

Modern Instruments

Reliable commercial thermogravimetric equipment began with the introduction of the Pierre Chevenard thermobalance in France in 1943. Mainly as a result of criticism by his colleague Clement Duval, a more reliable modification was produced in 1947. Since the early 1950s there has been great progress in the development of the thermobalance, with the use of many weighing systems and a great improvement in furnace design and temperature programming. The scope of thermogravimetry now extends beyond simply confirming gravimetric techniques and includes studies in the fields of kinetics, thermodynamics, metallurgy, corrosion, and polymers.

The most important trend in the design of thermobalances has been the miniaturization of both the microbalance and the furnace. There is some criticism of this in that small samples may not be representative in industries such as coal, cement, glass, and ceramics. Some balances are capable of taking heavy loads, but still provide great accuracy in noting small weight changes. In other developments, the equipment may operate in the presence of corrosive gases. The advent of the computer work station has facilitated new ways of presenting the data and provided easy access to further calculations dealing, for example, with kinetics and the DTG plot. An increasing facility being offered is the simultaneous measurement of Differential Scanning Calorimetry (DSC), Differential Thermal Analysis (DTA), or Evolved Gas Analysis (EGA) with TGA.

David Dollimore

Bibliography

Duval, C. *Inorganic Thermogravimetric Analysis*. 2nd ed. Translated by R.E. Oesper. Amsterdam: Elsevier Science, 1963.

El-Badry, H.M., and C.L. Wilson. "Report of a Symposium on Microbalances." *Lectures, Monographs, and Reports of the Royal Institute of Chemistry* 4 (1950): 23–48.

Honda, K. "On a Thermobalance." *Science Reports of Tohoku University* 497 (1915): 97–103.

Keattch, C.J. "The History and Development of Thermogravimetry." Ph.D. dissertation. University of Salford. U.K., 1977.

Thermocouple Psychrometer

See PSYCHROMETER, THERMOCOUPLE

Thermometer

Any instrument that measures temperature is a thermometer. The most common are alcohol and mercury-in-glass thermometers, and other expansion thermometers that used metals and gases. The electrical properties of materials and the electrical effects at the junctions of different metals also make possible the measurement of temperature. High-temperature thermometers are usually known as **pyrometers**.

Early History

The air thermometer was in use by 1612, when Santorio Santorio published investigations into the heat of the human body made with one. It is probable that either he or Galileo was the inventor; Robert Fludde and Cornelis Drebbel have less forceful claims. Giuseppe Bianconi used the word "thermoscopium" in 1617, and Jean Leuréchon used the word "thermomètre" in 1626. The word reached English seven years later in William Oughtred's translation of Leuréchon.

The first liquid-in-glass thermometers were those designed by the Grand Duke Ferdinando de' Medici in 1654 at the latest, and made by Antonio Alamanni for the Accademia del Cimento. They were filled with spirit of wine and probably had one fixed point, conceivably two, and were very highly regarded by natural philosophers. They apparently gave mutually consistent measurements, but how they were standardized is not clear. There are a large number of these instruments in the Museo di Storia della Scienza, Florence. Florentine instruments were distributed all over

Europe and were copied with various degrees of competence. Robert Hooke in London made them with "a great certainty and tendernesse."

The Eighteenth Century

The Danish astronomer Ole Rømer was the first to calibrate thermometers with two fixed points, the melting point of ice and the boiling point of water, in 1702. Daniel Gabriel Fahrenheit, who learned from Rømer how to calibrate thermometers, added careful craftsmanship and a determination to remove error. He settled in Amsterdam and by 1717 had adopted mercury as the thermometric fluid for his best thermometers and was selling them commercially. He later used the blood heat of the human body, which he set at 96°, as the upper fixed point, but after his death the boiling point of water was used by other makers, particularly John Bird of London. Some of Bird's instruments were said to have "Bird's Fahrenheit" scale. Fahrenheit's instruments, and copies using the same scale, were widely used in the Netherlands, Britain, and Germany, and two survive in the Museum Boerhaave, Leiden.

Few instruments have a history as contorted as that of the thermometer of René de Réaumur. His original conception was based on a single fixed point—the freezing point of water—and a knowledge of the expansion of spirit of wine. Réaumur's status as a savant brought it into widespread use in France, and its shortcomings induced reform. By the end of the century, following detailed research by Jean-André DeLuc and Antione-Laurent Lavoisier and widespread discussion, the Réaumur scale was generally defined by the same fixed points as the Fahrenheit thermometer. The hundred-degree scale that now bears the name of Anders Celsius was probably first used, in an inverted form, by his compatriot Carl Linné about 1740, though there are several contenders for this honor in Sweden, Switzerland, and the Netherlands.

In the first half of the eighteenth century, the thermometers produced by various savants were not regarded as having different scales but as being distinct instruments, for it was widely known that they were made on different principles. George Martine's *Essays Medical and Philosophical* (1740) presented a table of comparisons that made it possible to convert readings from one thermometer to another. This was done definitively by Jan Hendrik van Swinden

in his *Dissertation sur la Comparison des Thermomètres* (1778). At the same time, leading savants such as de Luc, Lavoisier, and Henry Cavendish were working on the improvement of the accuracy of the thermometer. By the 1770s some instruments were being divided to $1/10°$F, but it is likely that these very sensitive instruments were made to measure small changes and did not always give accurate values for the gross temperature. The first metallic thermometers were devised in London in the 1730s, and high-quality ones were made by Hans Loeser near Wittemberg in 1746–1747. James Six and John Rutherford devised successful maximum and minimum thermometers at the end of the eighteenth century.

By the middle of the eighteenth century, the thermometer was being used in many sciences. It was essential to the creation of the concepts of specific heat and latent heat by Joseph Black and Johan Carl Wilcke. It was also used in medicine, meteorology, oceanography, chemistry, and natural philosophy. Some London brewers gave it an industrial application in the 1750s.

The Nineteenth and Twentieth Centuries

As science and its applications grew, thermometers were made for more specific purposes in more distinctive forms. Their size, sensitivity, range, and shape were all specific to the measurements they were required for: laboratory thermometers were very different from instruments used in jam-making or for taking the temperature of a baby's bath. Perhaps the most sensitive thermometer made in quantity was the adjustable-range instrument invented by Ernst Beckmann in 1888. It had a tube with an extremely narrow bore and a reservoir above the bulb into which mercury could be transferred from the bulb. Consequently the range could be set by the user, usually covering about 5° with intervals of 0.01°C. It was used in chemical laboratories.

Thermometers were used for physiological purposes in the seventeenth and eighteenth centuries, and were introduced into medical practice in Paris around 1840. Karl August Wunderlich made an exhaustive argument for the medical use of thermometers in *Das Verhalten der Eigenwarme in Krankheiten* (1868), and within twenty years they were commonplace. In the twentieth century, the clinical thermometer has been the type made in the largest numbers. A large manufacturer said, "We are kept in business by clumsiness at the bedside." Each instrument had to be

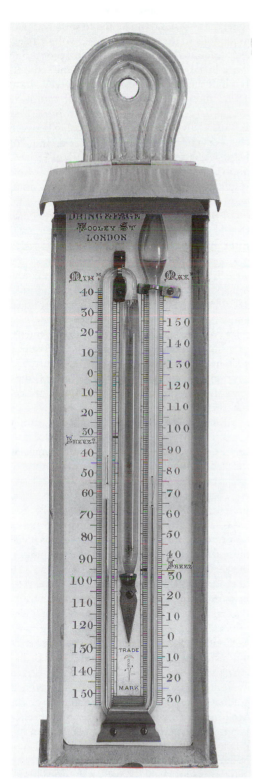

Six's maximum and minimum thermometer, by Dring & Fage, 1876. SM 1876-856. Courtesy of SSPL.

made individually until constant-bore tubing became available about 1970.

National characteristics were established in the nineteenth century. Stems with etched scales were most common in Britain, but enclosed scales were more usual on the Continent. These instruments had a thin-walled capillary with a "milk" or "opal"—that is, white—glass scale enclosed in an outer glass tube. While this arrangement was more robust, there was a possibility that the scale might move in relation to the tube. Of great importance was the discovery in the 1840s of the "aging" of thermometer bulbs—that is, their contraction over a period of some two years, which resulted in the instruments' reading several degrees higher than their calibration. New glasses that did not show aging effects were developed from the 1880s onwards, initially by Friedrich Otto Schott, whose work on optical glass is famous. His soda-lime glass containing zinc oxide numbered Jena 16^{III} became designated "normal thermometer glass."

The electrical measurement of temperature became increasingly important in the late nineteenth century. Thermocouples, which measure the current in a closed loop of two dissimilar metals when their junctions are at different temperatures, are based on Thomas Johann Seebeck's discovery of thermoelectricity in 1822 (see **thermopile**). Thermocouples using two wolfram-rhenium alloys can be used up to 3,000°C. Perhaps the most important use of a material new to thermometry was the platinum resistance thermometer, which was suggested by Carl Werner Siemens in 1871. The first fully practicable instrument was made by Hugh Longbourne Callendar in 1887, and platinum resistance thermometers are now widely used for temperatures between −260° and 1,000°C.

The modern history of the standardization of thermometers began with the work that Pierre Chappuis carried out in the 1880s for the Bureau International des Poids et Mesures, comparing excellent mercury thermometers made by Tonnelot of Paris with constant-volume gas thermometers. In 1887 the Comité International des Poids et Mesures adopted a constant-volume hydrogen scale from the ice to the steam point as standard. It was replaced in 1927 by the International Scale, which used a platinum resistance thermometer from −193° to 650°C and then a thermocouple to up to 1,100°. This scale was revised in 1948 and again in 1968. It was replaced in 1990 by ITS-90, which consists of four overlapping scales starting from 0.65K, following a platinum resistance thermometer in the range from 13.8033K to 961.78°C.

In the twentieth century, mercury and alcohol have been by far the most common thermometric fluids, and the latter is used down to −80°C. Toluene has been used to −100°C, and pentane to −200°C.

John Burnett

Bibliography

Chaldecott, J.A. *Catalogue of the Collections in the Science Museum: Temperature Measurement and Control.* Part 2. London: Her Majesty's Stationery Office, 1976.

Higgins, William F. "Thermometry." In *A Dictionary of Applied Physics,* edited by Sir Richard Glazebrook, Vol. 1, 988–1022. London: Macmillan, 1922.

Michalski, L., K. Eckersdorf, and J. McGhee. *Temperature Measurement.* Chichester: Wiley, 1991.

Middleton, W.E. Knowles. *A History of the Thermometer and Its Use in Meteorology.* Baltimore: Johns Hopkins Press, 1966.

Thermopile

A thermopile illustrates the thermoelectric effect and can be used either to record changes in temperature or to generate electric currents. Thomas Johann Seebeck discovered the thermoelectric effect in 1822 while studying the influence of heat on galvanic arrangements. To test his hypothesis that heat might create magnetism, Seebeck joined a semicircular piece of bismuth with a similar piece of copper into a circle. When he applied heat to either of the bismuth-copper junctions, a magnetic needle placed nearby behaved as if the circle were a closed, current-carrying circuit. After many experiments with different pairs of metals and other conductors, Seebeck was able to order them in a thermoelectric series with bismuth at the extreme negative and tellurium at the extreme positive end. In all, he ranked twenty-eight materials and observed that their order was not the same as for the voltaic series. Although Seebeck persisted in describing this effect as thermomagnetic, Hans Christian Oersted identified it with thermoelectricity. With the help of J.B.J. Fourier, Oersted soldered several pairs together in series to make the first thermopile, analogous to the electrochemical voltaic pile.

James Cumming, noted for his pioneering work in galvanometry, discovered the same effect independently, published his experiments in 1823, and managed to drive a small motor by means of thermoelectricity. Antoine César Becquerel investigated the relationship between chemical effects and thermoelectricity and, not being well acquainted with the work of Seebeck and Cumming, was surprised by some of his results. Becquerel was keen to use this phenomenon to extend temperature measurements beyond the usual limits. With a couple made of two platinum samples, he measured temperatures in the flame of his alcohol lamp in 1826.

Leopoldo Nobili in Florence, Italy, began working with thermopiles in 1829 and was joined by Macedonio Melloni from 1831 until 1839, when Melloni moved to Paris in political exile. Nobili made a large number of thermopiles, ranging from six to two hundred elements of bismuth and antimony, using them to supply current for his galvanometric experiments, and calling them thermomultipliers. Indeed, they were the only practical constant source of electric current before reference voltages could be supplied by the standard cells of J. Latimer Clark (1873) and E. Weston (1893) (see **battery**). Georg Simon Ohm used a thermopile as the electric source when formulating his law of electrical resistance (Ohm's Law, 1827).

On September 5, 1831, Nobili and Melloni presented a thermopile to the Académie des Sciences in Paris for investigating the properties of heat (radiant energy). This thermopile was much more sensitive than the differential **thermometer,** in that it could detect the heat of a hand at a distance of a meter. It was immediately copied by instrument-makers and became commonly known as the Nobili-Melloni thermopile. It was primarily used for radiant heat experiments with Melloni's bench. This consisted of a number of units such as screens with apertures and diaphragms, a Leslie cube, a hollow brass prism, **goniometer,** and a heat source, all clamped to a graduated brass bar secured to a mahogany base. Melloni used five sources of heat: Locatelli's lamp with reflector, Argand lamp, platinum spiral in the flame of a spirit lamp, blackened copper plate kept at a temperature of about 400°C, and a copper tube, blackened on the outside and filled with water at boiling point.

The very low currents produced by the thermocouple made observations of some of the

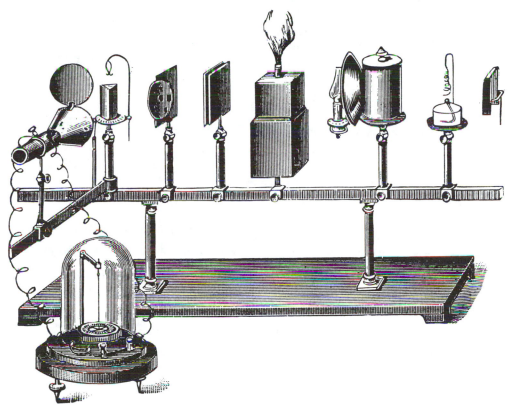

Commercial version of Melloni's thermo-electric apparatus, ca. 1912. John J. Griffin & Sons Ltd. Scientific Handicraft: An Illustrated and Descriptive Catalogue of Scientific Apparatus. *London, 1914: 487, Figure 2-2355. Courtesy of Fisher Scientific U.K. Ltd.*

ordinary phenomena associated with electricity impossible. This allowed Seebeck, who died in 1831, to maintain that he had discovered a magnetic effect. Thermoelectric sparks, thermoelectric resistance heating, and thermoelectric decomposition of water were all demonstrated in the late 1830s, and in 1837 Francis Watkins announced that he had raised 94 lbs. with a thermoelectromagnet.

In 1834, Jean Charles Athanase Peltier discovered that heating or cooling occurs at the junction of a thermocouple when an electric current is driven through. In 1838, Emil Khristianovich Lenz succeeded in freezing water with a Peltier junction. Attempts to explain this phenomenon became an important aspect of thermodynamics, which eventually resulted in the formulation of the Second Law of Thermodynamics by William Thomson and R.J.E. Clausius. It has been argued that in the history of thermoelectricity, sensitivity of instrumentation was of less importance than the ingenuity of the experimenter.

Thermocouples were also used to measure the temperature difference between two points (the thermoelectric **pyrometer**). In many applications the temperature of one junction is maintained at a known temperature, often by means of a bath of melting ice, and the other junction acts as a sensitive thermometer probe. For accurate temperature measurements up to 1,700°C, junctions of platinum against a platinum-rhodium alloy are used as a standard thermometer; for temperatures up to 1,300°C, the junctions are made of the alloys chromel and alumel; and for lower temperatures up to a few hundred degrees C, junctions of copper and the alloy constantin are widely used.

Willem D. Hackmann

Bibliography

Darling, Charles C. *Pyrometry: A Practical Treatise on the Measurement of High Temperature.* London: Spon, 1911.

Finn, Bernard S. "Thermoelectricity." *Advances in Electronics and Electron Phys-*

Improved Newman tide gauge, by Negretti & Zambra, 1886. Negretti & Zambra. Encyclopaedic Illustrated and Descriptive Catalogue. *London, ca. 1880: 98, Figure 100. Courtesy of SSPL.*

ics 50 (1980): 176–240.

Hackmann, Willem D. *Catalogue of Pneumatic, Magnetic, Electrostatic, and Electromagnetic Instruments in the Museo di Storia della Scienza.* Florence: Giunti, 1995.

Tide Gauge

Coastal measurements of sea level have a long history, not least because of the importance of tides for navigation, marine industries based in shallow waters, and the construction of docks and harbors. Vertically mounted poles have been used for thousands of years, and many harbors have marked scales set in the walls. In calm conditions, observation of the reading causes no difficulty, but in stormy weather or at night this is more problematic.

Although the basic idea was described in 1666 by Robert Moray, first president of the Royal Society of London, the first self-recording gauge appears to be the one designed by Henry Palmer in the 1830s, installed at Sheerness in the Thames estuary, and described by John Lubbock to the Royal Society of London. Palmer's gauge consisted of a float set vertically in a well connecting with the sea; this was connected to a pen and a chart recorder with a time indicator. A later version incorporated a separate cylinder that was engaged for only the 30 minutes around high tide and time marks in the form of punctures every minute.

Another device, constructed by T.G. Bunt on the River Avon at Bristol in 1837, was described by William Whewell. Both Lubbock and Whewell were, with George Airy, the Astronomer Royal, concerned with the theory of tides, and they presented papers on the subject to the British Association for the Advancement of Science through the 1830s and 1840s. By the 1850s, recording float gauges had been set up at major ports in Britain and elsewhere; in the 1980s the British network consisted of some thirty gauges, and the U.S. National Ocean Service had over 150.

Although gauges were robust and relatively simple to operate, their expense, limited accuracy in measuring level and time, and the physical behavior of the wells themselves encouraged the development of tide measurement by other principles. In 1908, a British patent was granted to A.M. Field and H.E. Purley-Cust, hydrographer and assistant hydrographer to the Admiralty, for an "Improved Method and Apparatus for Indicating and Recording the Rise and Fall of the Tide." This used the principle that if a closed vessel containing air under pressure is connected by a pipe to an open nozzle immersed under the surface of the water, air escapes through the nozzle until the pressure in the air system is equal to the pressure due to the vertical height of the surface of the water above the nozzle. The variation of water level was then measured using a **pressure gauge**. Pneumatic bubbler systems such as this have been used extensively through the twentieth century. They employ cheap and expendable components, and make it possible to place the underwater pressure point some hundreds of meters away from the recorder. This type of system can be used at virtually all coastal sites, provided the tubing is protected as it passes through the zone of breaking waves.

The acoustic gauge uses the time taken by sound to travel from the source to a reflecting surface and back as a measure of distance. These are gradually replacing the float type in the U.S. National Ocean Service network.

The 1980s saw the development of pressure instruments, expensive to make, deploy, and retrieve, but justified for hydrographic survey, navigation of ships or oil rigs through narrow channels, and the scientific study of ocean and shelf sea hydrodynamics. Satellite altimetry is also in use, but it requires greater datum stability than presently available for measuring long-term trends in sea level.

Jane Insley

Bibliography

Darwin, George Howard. *The Tides and Kindred Phenomena in the Solar System.* Boston: Houghton, 1898.

Deacon, Margaret. *Scientists and the Sea, 1650–1900: A Study of Marine Science.* London: Academic, 1971.

Pugh, David T. *Tides, Surges and Mean Sea Level.* Chichester: Wiley, 1987.

Tide Predictor

The study of tides has been of interest from the time that people first started to fish, but it became of great commercial interest when large ships began to sail. In 1867 the British Association for the Advancement of Science formed a commission to consider methods of predicting tides. Their report, written by William Thomson and published in 1868, proposed

William Thomson's first tide predicting machine, by Légé, 1872. SM 1876-1129. Courtesy of SSPL.

that the complex wave form produced by a record of tide measurements could be approximated by the sum of a series of periodic functions such as cosines, a fact that had been known for some time. It then suggested that this procedure be used to solve the tide prediction problem by obtaining careful measurements of the tides at a given location, finding the sum of a series of cosines that would approximate this data, and evaluating this series to predict the tidal variations into the future.

The main impediment to this plan was that simulating the complex nature of tides required many cosine terms. The amount of arithmetic involved in determining the coefficients for each term in this series, and in evaluating the series to give even modest predictions, prohibited the calculation of tides for any except the most important locations. The process of finding the coefficients of the cosines in the series is known as harmonic analysis, and, although Thomson suggested mechanical devices that would help with this task (see **harmonic analyzer**), practical instruments to perform this aspect of the calculation were not to be available for many years.

The process of creating an instrument to evaluate the cosine series, once the harmonic analysis had been done, was much simpler. Several machines were invented for this purpose, but the most famous, and certainly one of the simplest, is that devised by Thomson himself. It relies on the fact that a simple oscillating motion, generated by a rod attached to a gear, can be used to trace a periodic function such as a cosine. The amplitude of the function is controlled by the length of the rod and the period of the function by the speed of the rotation of the gear (usually controlled by the number of teeth and size of the gear). If a number of these mechanisms are connected in series so that their combined outputs produce the final trace, then, after ensuring the periods and amplitudes are correct, the trace will approximate the tides for a given area. Machines to this design were put to use almost immediately to calculate tidal variations around the coasts of Britain and India.

The major problem with this device was that the cord or wire connecting the components together would stretch while the machine was in use and thus introduce inaccuracies into the final trace. Various attempts were made to correct this problem. One of them led to a different principle for creating a tide predictor, and formed the basis of an instrument that could be used to actually calculate the coefficients of the cosines.

The Coast and Geodetic Survey was responsible for these matters in the United States and, in 1882, one of their employees, William Ferrel, designed a similar machine using seventeen mechanisms in series, which would give only the times of high and low tides with no intermediate information. In 1905, Rollin A. Harris, a mathematician with the Coast and Geodetic Survey, together with Ernest G. Fisher, their chief instrument-maker, began the design of a much more ambitious machine that would use thirty-seven terms of the periodic equation, give continuous plots of the tides, and make estimates of the tidal currents to be expected. The development of this "Great Brass Brain" took five years, but by 1910 it was in use to predict tides around the American coastline for 1911. This machine was impressive—it was about 11 feet long and 7 feet high, and weighed some 2,500 pounds—and it produced graphs that showed the height of the tide to the nearest tenth of a foot for each minute of the year. It remained in use until the late 1960s, when an IBM 7090 computer took over the job. Even when **digital computers** finally took over from analog instruments, the amount of arithmetic needed to properly evaluate the cosine series was so vast that, once again, the output had to be limited to simply times of high and low tide for any particular area. This was overcome only when, during the 1970s, digital computers became powerful enough to provide essentially unlimited amounts of computational power to be applied to the problem.

Michael Williams

Bibliography

Collins, A. "The Great Brass Brain." *Datamation* (November 15, 1979): 32–36.

Horsburgh, E.F., ed. " Instruments of Calculation." In *Handbook of the Napier Tercentenary Celebration; or, Modern Instruments and Methods of Calculation*, Section G, 181–277. Edinburgh: Royal Society of Edinburgh, 1914.

Torquetum

The torquetum, or turquet, was used to measure the position of celestial bodies and to demonstrate the principles of Ptolemaic astronomy. It should not be confused with the triquetrum—a simple set of jointed rods for determining zenith distances.

Although details of its origins remain unclear, the torquetum is believed to date from the latter half of the thirteenth century. The Hispano-Muslim astronomer and mathematician Abū Muḥammad Jābir ibn Aflaḥ al-Ishbīlī (known in the West by the Latinized name Geber) has frequently been named as its inventor, but he was responsible only for an instrument similar in function. Likewise, Muḥammad ibn Muḥammad ibn al-Ḥasan al-Ṭūsī (Naṣir al-Dīn), director of the Marāgha observatory, has also been put forward as a candidate, but evidence has yet to be found that the torquetum originated in the Islamic East. On the basis of the extant manuscript sources, it appears that the torquetum was an invention of Christian Europe, the two earliest known accounts of it being provided by Bernard of Verdun (Bernardus de Virduno, a Franciscan) and Franco of Poland (Franco de Polonia).

Unfortunately, it is impossible to ascribe priority to either man. Bernard's account (which formed part of his *Tractatus super totam astrologiam*) is of unknown date. The earliest manuscripts based on Franco's account can be dated accurately to 1284; their far greater frequency and wider dispersal, compared with manuscripts based on Bernard's tract, means that Franco can be credited with responsibility for the dissemination of knowledge about the torquetum across Europe, if not unequivocally with its invention. It was Franco's account that served as the model, particularly in regard to its precise terminology, for other descriptions of the torquetum until the late fifteenth and early sixteenth centuries, when it was superseded by a number of new accounts, most notably those provided by Johannes Regiomontanus, Petrus Apianus, and Johannes Schöner.

The etymologies of the various terms by which the instrument has been known are fascinating and at the same time perplexing. Manuscripts based on Franco's tract use the term "turquetus" or "turketus," which, despite what has already been said, must have meant the "Muslim instrument," *turkus* being a medieval Latin word covering a more general area than Turkey or Turkmenistan alone. It is this original meaning that is reflected in the English "turquet" and German *Türkengerät*. Bernard of Verdun also used "turchetus" and in one instance "truquetus," which, like the old French *troche,* seems to suggest simply some sort of "assemblage," perhaps in reference to the instrument's strange silhouette. Regiomontanus called the instrument the "torquetum"—from the Latin *torqueo,* "to twist." This, it appears, was taken up by Robert Recorde and others as "torquete."

The torquetum is complex, but essentially unvarying in structure, despite differences between individual instruments in the shapes and relative sizes of their constituent parts. A table, termed by Franco the *tabula orizontis,* forms the base of the instrument and represents the plane of the horizon. A second table, the *tabula equinoctialis,* is hinged to the first and, being supported by a prop (the *stilus*) at an angle equal to the complement of the observer's latitude, represents the equatorial plane. This table is inscribed with a circle, usually graduated with hours. A third table, the *tabula orbis signorum,* lies above the second, being held at an angle equal to the obliquity of the ecliptic by a rotating structure, the *basilica,* which has a pointer, the *almuri,* at its base. The *tabula orbis signorum* represents the plane of the ecliptic and

is inscribed with degrees and a zodiacal calendar. These three tables support the head and shoulders, as it were, of the device, namely a divided circle, the *crista,* which is oriented in a plane perpendicular to that of the ecliptic by means of a second rotating stand, the base of which forms an alidade, the *turnus.* An additional alidade, the *alidada circuli magni,* moves over the *crista.* To this alidade is fixed a semicircular plate, the *semis,* marked with degrees and lines of unequal hours; a plumb line, the *perpendiculum,* hangs from its midpoint.

In operation the torquetum, true to its name, rotates about its various axes to allow the position of celestial bodies sighted through the *alidada circuli magni* to be measured in each of the three different coordinate systems. In normal use the divisions on the *crista* indicate celestial latitude, the position of the *perpendiculum* over the *semis* altitude, the position of the *turnus* in the ecliptic circle celestial longitude, and the position of the *almuri* in the circle of hours on the equatorial plane right ascension. With the ecliptic table folded, the *crista* also measures declination; with all the tables folded, it simply indicates azimuth and altitude.

Early instances of the torquetum having been used to take such measurements can certainly be found: Jean de Murs, astronomer and writer on arithmetic and music at Paris, used a torquetum to observe the entry of the sun into Aries on March 12, 1318, and Peter of Limoges, Canon of Evreux and fellow of the Collège de Sorbonne, found that the initial position of the comet of 1299 "as determined by a *turquetum*" was "in the 18th degree of Taurus on a circle passing through the poles of the zodiac." The question remains, however, whether the torquetum was used primarily as an observing instrument or whether it found greater utility as a means of demonstrating the principles of Ptolemaic astronomy and for accomplishing, without the need for calculation, the otherwise difficult task of converting between coordinate systems. Certainly by the sixteenth century, with the advent of other large, specialized instruments, it must have had little useful observational role. That it continued to be made, in various highly decorative incarnations, testifies to its value as an aid to explanation, not to mention the desire of its owners to demonstrate their familiarity with astronomical science.

Torqueta are now very rare. Only two medieval examples survive: the instrument owned by Cardinal Nicolas of Cusa, dated to 1444 and

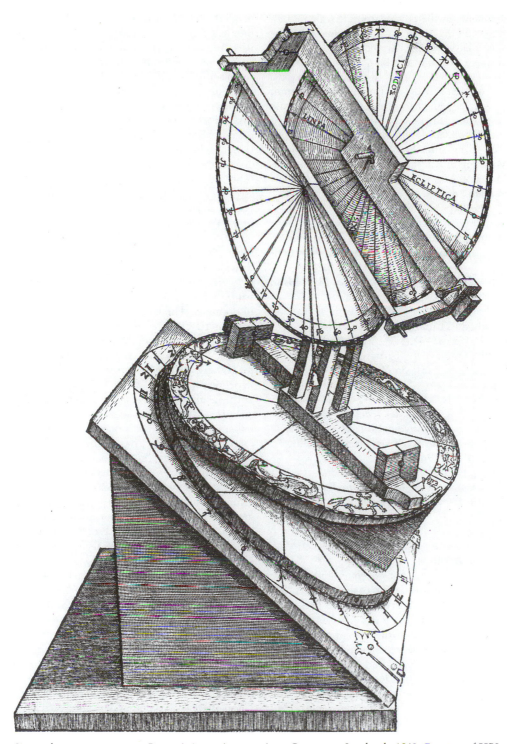

Sixteenth-century torquetum. Petrus Apianus. Astronomicum Caesareum. Ingolstadt, 1540. Courtesy of SSPL.

housed in the Hospice des Viellards de Cues on the Mosel, and that constructed by Hans Dorn of Vienna, ca. 1487, for Martin Bylica of Olkusz, conserved at the University of Cracow. At least eight examples from the sixteenth century are known, including unsigned instruments in the Observatoire Royale de Belgique and the Mathematisch-physikalischer Salons at Dresden; an instrument marked with the initials L.M.N. in the Bamberger Heimatmuseum; a signed example by Johann Praetorius, dated 1586, in the Germanisches Museum, Nuremberg; an instrument of copper and brass in the University Library, Königsberg, associated with Jakob Cuno; and three instruments attributed to Erasmus Habermel, in the Hamburg Museum für Kunst und Gewerbe, the Deutsches Museum, Munich, and the Hessisches Landesmuseum, Kassel.

Perhaps the most famous depiction of a torquetum is found in the background of Hans Holbein the Younger's painting *The Ambassadors,* which hangs in the National Gallery, London.

Giles M. Hudson

Bibliography

Gunther, R.T. *Early Science in Oxford,* Vol. 2, 35–37, 370–75. Oxford: 1923.

Poulle, Emmanuel. "Bernard de Verdun et le turquet." *ISIS* 55 (1964): 200–208.

Thorndike, Lynn. "Franco de Polonia and the Turquet." *ISIS* 36 (1945–1946): 6–7.

Virduno, Bernardus de. *Tractatus super totam astrologiam.* Edited by Polykarp Hartmann. Werl/Westfalen: Dietrich-Coelde, 1961.

Zinner, Ernst. *Deutsche und neiderländische astronomische Instrumente des 11. bis 18. Jahrhunderts.* 2nd ed. Munich: Beck, 1967.

Torsion Balance

The torsion balance has been used to observe electric and magnetic forces ever since 1784, when Charles-Augustin Coulomb presented his instrument to the Paris Academy of Sciences and proposed the law of torsion for metallic wires. A year later, in the first of seven memoirs on electricity and magnetism, Coulomb investigated the force-distance relation in the case of electric repulsion, and formulated the main elements of the now classic inverse-square law of electrostatics. Coulomb's training as an engineer gave him an excellent knowledge of mechanics and mathematics and enabled him to establish electricity on the model of mechanics; his torsion balance served as a device for checking these assumptions. His engineering background also provided the skills needed to devise the apparatus. His torsion balance came out of a series of instruments used to measure the friction and rigidity of ropes, and it served initially to determine fluid resistance.

For studies of magnetism, a needle suspended by a silk wire twisted in response to the slightest changes in magnetic force. The angle of the twisted thread was taken to be proportional to the elastic force with which it strained against the magnetic force to unwind itself. This represents a generalization of Hooke's law: stress (external force, in this case magnetic) bears a constant ratio to strain (elastic deformation). The torsion balance could also be used to measure electrical forces. In Coulomb's instrument, the wire was a thin, 76-cm-long, metal thread, and the magnetic needle was replaced by a silk thread or straw (soaked in Spanish wax) that on one end carried a pith ball 0.5 cm in diameter. The balance had a height of approximately 1 meter and was completely covered by a glass cylinder (to protect the needle against wind currents) with a torsion **micrometer** at the upper end; a strip of paper marked off in degrees was pasted around the glass cylinder at the height of the needle for reading its exact position. At the beginning of the experiment the ball and a second (fixed) one were put in contact; they were then charged by a conductor, leading to the repelling of the movable ball. After the equilibrium position was read, the torsion of the wire was increased with the micrometer in order to draw the balls closer together, and the position of the movable ball was read again; the electrostatic repulsion between the two balls was canceled by the torsion of the silver wire. The balance's most fragile part was the extremely thin metal wire, which tended to break very easily. In the 1820s, the price of the electrical balance was approximately 500 francs (roughly the standard monthly salary of a professor).

Coulomb's torsion balance engendered very different reactions: immediate acceptance and praise in France; indifference in Italy; doubt, even refutation (with another law) in Germany. These responses depended on a large number of factors, including the circulation of Coulomb's papers, changing criteria of evaluation, and cultural and institutional frameworks. In Paris the torsion balance fit into a vision, common to members of the Academy of Sciences, centering on the possibility of capturing physical phenomena through simple and univer-

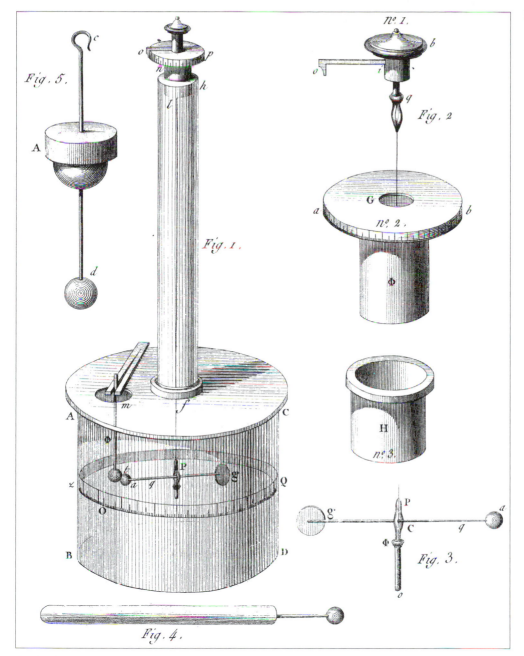

Coulomb's torsion balance. Charles-Augustin Coulomb. "Premier mémoire sur l'électricité et le magné-tisme." Mémoires de l'Académie Royale des Sciences *(1785): Plate XIII. Courtesy of NMAH.*

sal mathematical laws. Italian physicists, on the other hand, regarded Coulomb's experiment as a composite phenomenon that could not be captured by a simple law. Alessandro Volta, who regarded electricity as a chemical phenomenon, aimed at defining new electrical magnitudes of both a qualitative and quantitative character; he introduced his own balance of a

different design. German physicists objected that Coulomb did not provide enough numerical values and did not perform his experiments in public. Unlike Coulomb, who did not teach, the German physicists tried to replicate experiments for their students. They considered the balance to be inappropriate for this function, and they put Coulomb's law and balance in doubt with the help of alternative instruments until 1825.

Physicists had difficulties using the torsion balance for precise electrical measurements, finding it to be too sensitive and to depend too strongly on the competence of a single observer. These disadvantages also hampered its commercialization. Nevertheless, balances were found in the physical cabinets of most nineteenth-century French teaching institutions, often exhibited but rarely manipulated. The lecturer would describe Coulomb's experiment and quote the three numerical values Coulomb had given in his 1785 memoir. Fixed in this form and fetishized, Coulomb's balance became the symbol of the foundation of electrostatics. The situation was different, however, for magnetic observations. The French astronomer Jean-Dominique Cassini had used a torsion balance for this purpose in the late eighteenth century, and in the 1820s the French instrument-maker Henri-Prudence Gambey provided a large variety of different types of torsion balances *(boussoles)* that were widely used in first attempts of simultaneous measurements of the earth's magnetic field.

The principle of the torsion balance—the measurement of electrical or magnetic forces by the angle of the rotation of a thread—lay at the heart of its two technological progeny: the **galvanometer** for measuring electric forces, and the **magnetometer** for measuring magnetic forces. The international campaign to measure the earth's magnetic field, launched by Wilhelm Weber and Carl Friedrich Gauss in 1834, led to the first successful standardized use of the balance on a worldwide scale. Weber and Gauss introduced absolute measurements, abandoning comparative methods in favor of precisely measurable mechanical units like space, time, and weight. Their magnetometer differed from the torsion balance in size and in the manner of reading the measurements. Gauss and Weber also replaced the monofilar suspension by a bifilar suspension, which had the advantage of avoiding the method of oscillation and obtaining the data instantly. Weber then used the intimate knowledge of devices acquired during this project in the conception of the galvanometer and other electrical measuring instruments in the 1840s. This line of electromechanical instruments was superseded in accuracy during the second half of the twentieth century by microelectronic devices such as the digital **voltmeter**.

Matthias Dörries

Bibliography

Blondel, Christine, and Matthias Dörries, eds. *Restaging Coulomb, usages, controverses et réplications autour de la balance de torsion.* Firenze: Olschki, 1994.

Dörries, Matthias. "Prior History and Aftereffects: *Nachwirkung* and Hysteresis in 19th-Century Physics." *Historical Studies in the Physical Sciences* 22 (1991): 25–55.

Gillmor, C. Stewart. *Coulomb and the Evolution of Physics and Engineering in Eighteenth-Century France.* Princeton: Princeton University Press, 1971.

Heilbron, J.L. *Electricity in the 17th and 18th Century: A Study of Early Modern Physics.* Berkeley: University of California Press, 1979.

Transit Circle

A transit circle integrates the function of a **transit instrument** and a mural **quadrant** or circle in a single instrument, and so enables astronomers to simultaneously measure the right ascension and declination of a star (the celestial equivalent of longitude and latitude used on the earth). It is used in conjunction with an accurate clock to time the meridian passage of stars and to measure their angular distance from the zenith.

In his *Basis Astronomiae* (1735), Peter Horrebow described the "Rota Meridiana" that the Danish astronomer Ole Rømer had designed for his new observatory at Copenhagen in 1704. Rømer's meridian circle consisted of a transit instrument supported on stout wooden piers with a graduated circle 1.5 meters in diameter. The instrument along with most of Rømer's observations were lost in the 1728 fire that destroyed most of Copenhagen.

For most of the eighteenth century the transit circle was neglected, astronomers choosing instead to measure star positions using the quadrant and the transit instrument. The first successful transit circle in England was built by Edward Troughton in 1806 for Stephen Groombridge, a talented amateur astronomer. The instrument consisted of two graduated circles four feet in diameter enclosing a **telescope** of $3^1/2$ inches in aperture and with a focal length of 5 feet. The conical shafts bearing the transit circle pivoted on two stone piers. Leveling of the instrument was achieved in a manner similar to that of a transit instrument. The divided circles were read using four **micrometer** microscopes

Four-foot transit circle made by Edward Troughton for Stephen Groombridge, 1806. Abraham Rees. The Cyclopedia; or, Universal Dictionary of Arts, Sciences, and Literature, *Vol. 1. London: Longman, 1820: Plate X. Courtesy of SSPL.*

that could be zeroed using either a plum bob or a vertical collimator. The latter tool consisted of a small telescope mounted vertically to an annulus that floated in a bath of mercury. The transit circle was checked by pointing its tele-scope at the nadir. A coincidence of the reflected image of the cross-hairs in both telescopes confirmed the vertical. Groombridge used this instrument to produce a valuable catalogue of four thousand circumpolar stars. The ease with which the instrument could be used is given in an account by Thomas Firminger, an assistant at the Royal Observatory, Greenwich, from 1799 to 1807. He recalls that Groombridge's observatory was attached to the house and that often he would leave family and friends at dinner to make an observation. He would then return with his measurements, recorded on slates, that he reduced later at his leisure.

During the first half of the nineteenth century, German companies such as Pistor, Reichenbach, Martins, and Repsold installed transit circles at most of the major Continental observatories. Later in the century, French makers such as Secretan and Gambey became significant builders of transit circle instruments. The large divided circles were often attached at the pivot end of the instrument, a form that later became standard. Thomas Jones installed a transit circle at the Radcliffe Observatory, Oxford, in 1836. The instrument was a compromise and had many of the features of a mural circle, being supported on two unequal stone pillars.

The first large transit circle installed in Britain dates from 1850. This instrument was designed by the Astronomer Royal George Biddell Airy and replaced two mural circles and a transit instrument at the Royal Observatory, Greenwich. The heavy engineering for the transit circle was provided by Ransomes and May of Ipswich, with the optics, divided circle, and other instrumentation being produced by Troughton and Simms. The telescope for the transit circle was of 8.1 in. aperture and 11 feet 7 in. focal length. The transit circle had a single circular scale 6 feet in diameter mounted on the west side of the instrument. The divided circle was read using six micrometer microscopes, each of which could be read to a fraction of an arc second. A later innovative feature was the use of a **chronograph** linked to the micrometer wires of the observer's eyepiece. Electrical contacts on the traveling metal wires of the eyepiece micrometer provided a paper strip record of the timing of transit observations. It replaced the long-used ear and eye method of transit observation using an adjacent regulator clock. The new transit circle defined the Greenwich meridian and hence Greenwich Mean Time. In 1884, an international conference held in Washington agreed to the adoption of the Greenwich meridian as the prime meridian of the world—namely, zero degrees longitude. The world's system of longitude and timekeeping had thus become dependent on a unique transit circle, now known as Airy's Transit.

Changes in the design of the transit circle during the twentieth century have been concerned mainly with improvements in accuracy and automation. Later instruments have used glass-etched circular scales and diamond-tipped bearings, and have antifreeze in their hollow iron pillars to counteract thermal movement. The eyepiece micrometers used for transit observation were automated to remove any personal component to the measurements. Likewise, the reading of the circular scales by eye was replaced by photography. In fully automated transit circles, the human observer has been replaced by **computers** and electronic detectors. A good example is the Danish Carlsberg Telescope installed at the La Palma Observatory in the Canary Isles. This instrument is capable of making hundreds of measurements each night at a speed far beyond that of any human observer. Further improvements in the accuracy of star measurement are being achieved by the use of spacecraft, such as *Hipparchus,* built by the European Space Agency. The need for increased precision is driven by the desire to obtain accurate distances to more remote stars using parallax, a yardstick to the scale of our universe.

Kevin L. Johnson

Bibliography
"Astronomical Instruments." In *The Cyclopedia; or, Universal Dictionary of Arts, Sciences, and Literature,* edited by Abraham Rees, Vol. 1. London: Longman, 1820.
Bennett, J.A. *The Divided Circle: A History of Instruments for Astronomy, Navigation and Surveying,* 174–77. Oxford: Phaidon, 1987.
Howse, Derek. *Greenwich Observatory: The Buildings and Instruments,* Vol. 3, 43–48. London: Taylor and Francis, 1975.
King, Henry C. *The History of the Telescope,* 103–4, 172, 234–35, 393–94. New York: Dover, 1979.

Transit Instrument

A transit instrument consists of a refracting **telescope** mounted on a pair of trunnions set at right angles to its optical axis, in the manner of a cannon, and capable of describing a meridian circle. The meridian itself is defined by the vertical wire in the telescope's field of view, and the passages of astronomical bodies across it are timed against an accurate clock. In this way, it

Transit instrument used in observations of the transit of Venus, 1874. J. Norman Lockyer. Stargazing Past and Present. *London: Macmillan, 1878: 236, Figure 113. Courtesy of SSPL.*

can be used to define the point of solar noon for the calculation of mean time, and to measure the right ascension, or hour angles, of the stars and planets. The transit instrument carried no divided scales and measured its east-west positions as timed fractions of the 360° of the sky in the horizontal plane.

Around 1580, Tycho Brahe demonstrated the ease and accuracy of taking the positions of astronomical bodies in the meridian. But the planes of large-radius quadrants, such as the one used by Tycho, are difficult to maintain, as supporting walls can be susceptible to movement. The application of the telescope to regular astronomical measurement by 1670, moreover, had brought about a dramatic increase in accuracy over the naked-eye observations of Tycho, while at the same time, astronomical instruments became more specialized in their operations. The transit epitomized these tendencies in technological development, being an instrument that was fixed in the meridian plane with no facilities for sideways movement, and using its telescope to perform a single task with critical accuracy.

Early History

The first transit telescope was devised and set up in Ole Rømer's observatory in Copenhagen, Denmark, in 1675. It was positioned across the casement of a south-facing window, where it could be used in conjunction with a pendulum clock. In 1721 the English craftsman George Graham built a transit with a 5-foot-focus telescope as part of the new set of instruments intended to re-equip the Royal Observatory, Greenwich, following the accession of Edmond Halley to the office of Astronomer Royal. It is difficult to ascertain the extent to which Graham and Halley were influenced by any accounts of Rømer's prototype of nearly fifty years before, though no significant transits are known to have been made in the intervening years, apart from a small one, also by Graham, for the private observatory of Halley's associate James Pound in the years after 1710. It was the Greenwich model, however, that became influential for the observatories of Europe and America in the eighteenth century. The Greenwich transit was described in detail in Robert Smith's *Compleat System of Opticks* (1738) and Diderot's *Encyclopédie* (1765), while numerous other writers provided accounts of transits in their published works.

The Rømer and Graham transits did not set their meridian-defining telescopes in the centers of their trunnion-carrying axes, and so they could not be checked by reversing them in their pivots. In 1750, John Bird built a new transit for James Bradley, who was Halley's successor at

Greenwich. Bird's design produced the transit in its definitive form. The 8-foot-long telescope tube was placed in the middle of the trunnion axis. To prevent flexure, this axis was fabricated from a pair of large brass cones that were joined to the telescope tube at their bases, while their apexes culminated in the machined trunnion bearings upon which the instrument was balanced. By 1760, transit instruments had become standard in all observatories that used European instruments as the best way of defining the meridian and precise moment of noon. In the days before standard mean time signals, clockmakers used small transits to regulate their clocks; David Rittenhouse was using one in Philadelphia in the 1770s.

The transit could also be used to provide a check upon the perfect verticality of the 90-degree scale of large mural quadrants. Bradley and other astronomers, working in conjunction with an assistant, observed simultaneous meridian passages of the same star with the transit and the adjacent mural quadrant so that any eastward or westward distortion of the quadrant's plane could be noted and tabulated.

Adjustment

The axial trunnions that supported the telescope were set in a pair of self-centering V-bearings that were fixed to a pair of stone or iron piers, due east and due west of the telescope. These Vs could be moved slightly using set screws to achieve a critical adjustment of the instrument. A special spirit **level,** when hung from these trunnions, was used to set the exact east-west alignment, while the equal, east and west arcs of the circumpolar stars were used to define the meridian itself. In 1742, James Bradley used the bright circumpolar star Capella to realign the Graham-Halley transit at Greenwich. Using an accurate pendulum clock, he adjusted the V-bearings until the star took exactly one-half of a sidereal day to pass through its eastern and western semicircles about the pole.

When the transit was aligned to the horizontal and described a meridian arc, its telescope was brought down to view the horizon so that distant meridian marks could be set up to the north and south to keep the adjustment in check thereafter. Once the instrument had been modified by placing the telescope in the exact center of the trunnion-axis, around 1750, it became easy to lift the instrument out of its V-bearings and reverse it, left to right and in rotation. If the telescope's cross-wires fell upon the distance meridian markers in both the normal and in the reverse position, then its accuracy was reliable.

Using the Transit Instrument

Before the transit could be successfully developed, it needed the accuracy of the new pendulum clock, which also became available in the 1670s. In addition to regulating the clocks, and checking the plane of the quadrant, the transit was used to measure the right ascension of stars. It did this by noting which stars were on the meridian for every timed fraction of the sidereal day, as measured by the clock. These differences in hours, minutes, and seconds of time, as the objects moved west, corresponded to the degrees, minutes, and seconds of arc to provide the hour angles of all bodies in their longitudinal relationships to each other.

The transit instrument declined in research significance in the nineteenth century, when Troughton, Reichenbach, Ertel, Simms, and other designers combined its reversing, meridian-defining principle with that of the graduated circle, to produce the **transit circle.** It remained popular in minor and in amateur observatories, however, where it was still used to set clocks. Portable transits were used on geodetic surveying expeditions until superseded by electronic and satellite-based techniques of position-finding in the late twentieth century. Numerous transits survive in museums around the world.

Allan Chapman

Bibliography

Bradley, James. *Miscellaneous Works and Correspondence of the Rev. James Bradley.* Edited by S.P. Rigaud. Oxford: Oxford University Press, 1832.

Chapman, Allan. *Dividing the Circle: The Development of Critical Angular Measurement in Astronomy 1500–1850,* 2nd ed. New York: Horwood, 1995.

Howse, Derek. *Greenwich Observatory,* Vol. 3, *The Buildings and Instruments.* London: Taylor and Francis, 1975.

Pearson, William. *An Introduction to Practical Astronomy.* Vol. 2. London: Privately printed, 1829.

Smith, Robert. *A Compleat System of Opticks in Four Books.* Cambridge, 1738.

Traverse Board

A traverse board is a recording device, used with a **compass** and **log,** for keeping track of the

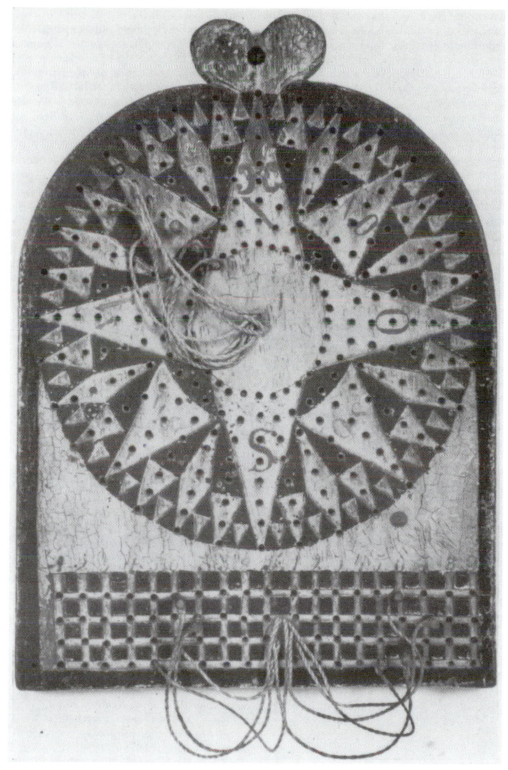

Traverse board, sixteenth century. David Waters, The Art of Navigation in England in Elizabethan and Early Stuart Times. *London: Hollis, 1958: Plate X. Courtesy of the National Maritime Museum.*

course traversed by a ship during a watch. It consisted of a wooden board with thirty-two radiating lines representing the points of the compass, and eight equidistant holes in each line for each half hour of the watch. Eight small pegs were attached to the center of the board by lengths of twine, and after each half hour the quartermaster placed a peg into a hole on the compass point on which the ship had run during that period, the nearest hole to the center representing the first half-hour, the next outward the second half-hour, and so forth. The varying appearance of preserved specimens indicates that traverse boards were made by local craftsmen or carpenters aboard ship.

Traverse boards originated before the seventeenth century, but there is no evidence of the time or region of their first use. In the seventeenth century when log-lines came into use, traverse boards were provided with four horizontal lines with equidistant holes, their numbers varying from twelve up to more than twenty. These were used to record the speed of the ship in knots and fathoms. At the end of the watch the navigator could write down the course and make calculations from the positions of the pegs with regard to leeway and compass variation. In the later years of the seventeenth century a "rough log" as a rough record was also kept on a log board, where space was given for recording the speeds, courses sailed, and winds experienced during those intervals. Also private journals with several columns for these data have been called "traverse-books."

Traverse boards are devices typical for the navigation of the sailing ship era and were still used in some countries at the end of the nineteenth century.

Jobst Broelmann

Bibliography

Hewson, J.B. *A History of the Practice of Navigation*. Glasgow: Brown, 1963.

Robertson, J. *The Elements of Navigation*. 3rd ed. London: Nourse, 1772.

Taylor, E.G.R. *The Haven-Finding Art: A History of Navigation from Odysseus to Captain Cook*. London: Hollis and Carter, 1956.

Tromometer

A tromometer detects the small and natural movements of the ground. It was invented in 1870s by Timoteo Bertelli in Florence, Italy; the name comes from the Greek word *tromòs*, "tremor." It was a simple and inexpensive descendant of the pendular instruments designed and used in Italy since 1731 (see **seismograph**).

After the presentation of his first results, Bertelli received positive comments and suggestions from many scholars, including Michele Stefano de Rossi and Giovanni Cavalleri, but also sharp criticism from Pietro Monte, a professor of physics at Livorno. In order to answer Monte's criticism and dispel the doubts of others, Bertelli and de Rossi, separately but in constant exchange of letters, undertook a long series of experiments with pendulums of different lengths in different environmental conditions.

In its ultimate form (1875), the tromometer consists of a cylindrical mass of 100 g hanging by a thin thread of annealed copper having a diameter sufficient to hold up its weight. A thin metal rod is soldered coaxial to the mass; it ends with a disk on which a small cross is carved. A small **telescope** containing a slide graduated into decimillimeters allows one to observe the deflections of the pendulum by measuring the shifts of the cross reflected by a prism. The telescope rotates on its axis so that it is possible to observe the cross on orthogonal planes and to measure quantity and direction of the shift of the **pendulum**. The thread of the pendulum is fixed to a stirrup bricked up into a pillar separated from the building where the observer stands, and it is shielded by a sheet-metal-tube. The lower part of the tromometer, including the mass and the measuring cross, is shielded by a small cubical glass box. The instrument can detect deflections of some μrad. Tromometers equipped with electric contacts could work as seismic warning devices.

Most tromometers were built by local craftsmen, or by the Florentine instrument-maker Giuseppe Poggiali. Around 1877, the Officina Galileo in Florence began making an industrial variant of the standard tromometer, as well as of Bertelli's orthoseismometer.

French authorities were interested in using tromometers in coal mines as signalers of microseisms connected with firedamp discharges. John Milne, William E. Ayrton, and John Perry in England also had some interest in these instruments. Most of the interest, however, was in Italy, where, from about 1875 to 1885, tromometers were the seismic instruments par excellence. By 1880, thirty-one tromometers had been installed in as many private, ecclesiastic, and public observatories (this number was later raised to over

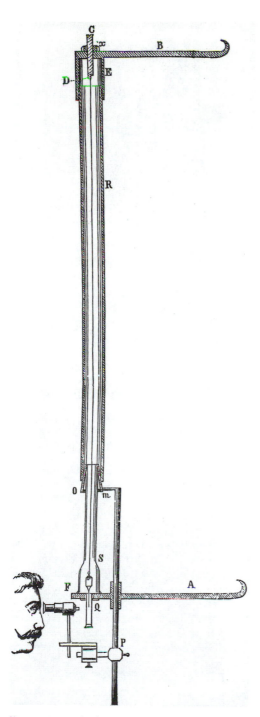

Economic standard trommometer, 1874. Courtesy of Graziano Ferrari.

nological catalogue of seismic events. A new reading of the data, with the present theoretical models and modern processing techniques, indicates that trommometers were able to detect the slow aseismic slip of near faults or the coseismic deformation step.

Graziano Ferrari

Bibliography

Ferrari, Graziano. "The Origin and Development of a Method of Measurement in Early Seismology." In *Proceedings of the Eleventh International Scientific Instruments Symposium: Held at Bologna University, Italy, 9–14 September 1991*, edited by Giorgio Dragoni, Anita McConnell, and Gerard L'E. Turner, 179–89. Bologna: Grafis, 1994.

———. "Seismic Instruments." In *Sciences of the Earth: An Encyclopedia of Events, People, and Phenomena*, edited by Gregory A. Good. New York: Garland, 1990.

———, ed. *Tromometri Avvisatori Sismografi: Osservazioni e Teorie dal 1850 al 1880 (Tromometers, Seismoscopes, Seismographs: Observations and Theories between 1850 and 1880)*. Bologna: Storia Geofisica Ambiente, 1991.

———, ed. *Two Hundred Years of Seismic Instruments in Italy, 1731–1940*. Bologna: Storia Geofisica Ambiente, 1992.

Tuning Fork

The tuning fork is a simple vibrating pitch carrier composed of a U-shaped steel bar. When the prongs oscillate, they produce a nearly pure and permanent tone. Its invention for musical purposes in 1711 has been generally attributed to the English trumpeter and lutenist John Shore. But it was only after 1850 that many efforts were made to standardize the frequencies of tuning forks used in music, which varied from different countries between around 455 and 435 Hz. In 1939 the standard was establish at a' = 440 Hz but, as happened in the past, this pitch tended to creep upward.

Despite the fact that Pieter Van Musschenbroek and Jacob Willem 'sGravesande illustrated tuning forks (just a folded bar with no stem) in their treatises on natural philosophy, these devices were quite rare in eighteenth-century physics collections. Tuning forks became an invaluable scientific instrument and a reference standard of frequency only in the nineteenth

fifty). Observations were made three times a day at regular intervals, and detected microseisms as well as strong earthquakes.

In the nineteenth century, trommometer observations were used simply to compile a chro-

century, when experimental acoustics aroused very large interest. Laboratory forks were often fixed vertically on a rectangular wooden box with one of the faces removed and with specific dimensions. This resonator box amplifies the fundamental tone of the fork, while dampening the inharmonic, high partial ones. In the last century the unity of acoustic frequency was the "simple vibration" (2 VS = 1 Hz).

The first tonometer, devised by Johann Heinrich Scheibler in 1834, consisted of an array of fifty-six tuning forks (between 220 and 440 Hz at intervals of 4 Hz). This was used to accurately determine the frequency of a musical note by counting the beats produced by the note and one of the forks. Jules Antoine Lissajous proposed a standard fork and, in 1855, described an optical method for comparing the frequencies of two tuning forks. He studied the curves produced by a spot of light reflected in turn by a small mirror set on one prong of each of two forks that vibrate in orthogonal planes. The curves (called Lissajous's figures) depend on the frequencies, amplitudes, and phases of the two oscillations. The analysis of the figures produced by a standard fork with a vibrating system allowed one to determine its frequency. Lissajous also invented the vibration **microscope** whose objective was fixed on one of the prongs of a tuning-fork. With this instrument it was possible to study Lissajous's figures produced by vibrations of small amplitude.

The tuning fork became a precision device in the second half of the nineteenth century, due to the research of the acoustic instrument-maker Rudolph Koenig of Paris. At the 1876 Centennial Exhibition in Philadelphia, Koenig presented an astounding tonometer comprising more than 650 tuning forks (which is now in the National Museum of American History). Furthermore, he was able to determine absolute frequencies with great accuracy through his legendary chronographic fork. Within this instrument, a mechanical clock is regulated by a precision tuning fork (64 Hz) whose vibrations are maintained by the clock itself. An ocular and an objective mounted on one of the prongs form a vibration microscope with which it is possible to determine the frequency of an oscillating system by means of the Lissajous's figures. The fork-clock is matched to an unknown frequency, which can be determined by observing the loss or gain of time between a standard clock and the one with the fork.

Koenig's clock with tuning fork control. Koenig (1889). Courtesy of SSPL.

Koenig's catalogue of 1889 described several sets of forks whose cost varied from a few tens of francs (for the simplest ones) to 3,000 francs (for a 67-fork, high-accuracy tuning fork tonometer). Most of Koenig's acoustic instruments were copied by many instrument-makers.

After 1850, electrically maintained forks appeared. The vibrations of one of the prongs, which formed a kind of hammer breaker, periodically excited an electromagnet fixed between the prongs themselves.

For his fundamental acoustical researches published in 1862, Hermann von Helmoltz devised an ingenious synthesizer that was composed of several electromagnetic tuning forks, each positioned in front of a resonator. One fork acts as a breaker for the electromagnet, which drives the other forks. With a keyboard it is possible to control the opening and closing of the resonators. Helmholtz used this instrument to demonstrate his theory of vowel frequencies.

Lord Rayleigh (John William Strutt) and Paul La Cour independently invented the first phonic wheels, which were electric motors driven by an electromagnetic fork. Since the late nineteenth century, phonic wheels of various types have been used for **chronographs,** stroboscopic devices, and also to determine frequencies and to control the speed of more powerful motors.

Around 1920 electronic vacuum tube–excited tuning forks could produce standard supersonic and radio-frequencies. Experiments were also made with electromagnetic forks and phonic wheels in the first experiments of electromechanical television.

Tuning forks have now been superseded by sophisticated electronic pitch carriers and oscillators.

Paolo Brenni

Bibliography

Brenni, Paolo. *Gli Strumenti del Gabinetto di Fisica dell'Istituto Tecnico Toscano, I. Acustica.* Firenze: Provincia di Firenze, 1986.

Koenig, Rudolph. *Catalogue des Appareils d'Acoustique.* Paris: Koenig, 1889.

Tyndall, John. *Sound: A Course of Eight Lectures Delivered at the Royal Institution of Great Britain,* 140–50. 2nd ed. London: Longmans, 1869.

Wood, Albert Beaumont. *A Textbook of Sound; Being an Account of the Physics of Vibrations with Special Reference to Recent Theoretical and Technical Developments,* 117–33. London: G. Bell, 1930.

T

U

Ultracentrifuge

See CENTRIFUGE, ULTRA-

Ultramicroscope

See MICROSCOPE, ULTRA-

Ultrasound, Diagnostic

Ultrasound is sound waves at frequencies above 18,000–20,000 Hz, undetectable by the human ear. It is produced by piezoelectric materials that translate electrical excitation into mechanical wave motion and vice versa. The echoes of ultrasonic pulses can be displayed as an image on an **oscilloscope** in a number of ways: as a plot of amplitude of echoes over time (A-mode), as a two-dimensional image (B-mode), or as Doppler shifting of sonic echoes to track motion.

The development of diagnostic ultrasound was preceded by a long period of research on the physical properties of high-frequency sound for underwater detection. Even though the French physicist Paul Langevin noted biological effects of ultrasound during his work on echo ranging, it was several Americans, R.W. Wood and A.L. Loomis in 1927 and E. Newton Harvey in 1930, who first conducted a systematic study of the effect of ultrasound on living materials. Their work marked the beginning of the use of ultrasound in the preparation of pharmaceuticals and in physical therapy, which hit a zenith in the 1940s.

Simultaneously in the late 1930s, a number of investigators began to look at ultrasound as a source of information, rather than as simply a source of energy. André Denier of France devised an ultrasonic instrument to locate foreign objects in cattle brains, but when he pub-licized his work after World War II, A. Dognon and L. Gougerot, leading authorities on the biological properties of ultrasound, harshly rejected his results and squelched any further work. In 1937 two Austrian brothers, Karl and Friedrich Dussik, used ultrasound transmitted through the brain to produce a two-dimensional image. The clinical utility of their images was later disputed by Theodor Hueter and H. Ballantine, Jr., at the Massachusetts Institute of Technology, and by a team led by W. Guttner in Germany, who independently showed that the skull overshadowed any useful patterns from ultrasound transmitted through the brain.

Diagnostic Imaging

Between 1948 and 1954, a large number of clinicians, physicists, and bioengineers began working on the clinical applications of ultrasound as the electronics expertise accumulated from work on **sonar** and **radar** during the war, and as surplus ultrasonic flaw-detecting equipment and trained personnel were made available for civilian applications. Clinicians literally wheeled flaw-detectors borrowed from local industries or military bases into the hospital or clinic and applied them directly to humans, making modifications to the equipment as necessary to adapt them to different diagnostic needs.

Diagnostic ultrasound was simultaneously developed in a number of centers for a variety of very different clinical uses. R.P. McLoughlin and G.N. Guastavino developed an instrument for two-dimensional imaging in 1949, while working for an Argentinian laboratory of RCA charged with finding commercial applications for RCA's electronics expertise. Douglass Howry, a radiologist at the University of Colorado, began using 2-MHz ultrasound in 1949

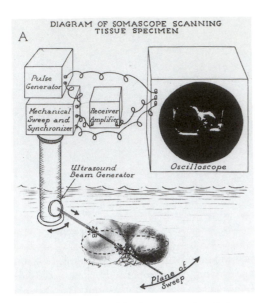

DIAGRAM OF SOMASCOPE SCANNING
TISSUE SPECIMEN

A

Pulse Generator

Mechanical Sweep and Synchronizer

Receiver Amplifier

Ultrasound Beam Generator

Oscilloscope

Plane of Sweep

Schematic diagram of the first in a series of ultrasonic mapping instruments devised by Douglass Howry and colleagues between 1949 and 1957. Courtesy of American Institute of Ultrasound in Medicine Archives, Laurel, Md.

to image soft tissues that x-rays depict poorly. John Wild, an Englishman on a surgical fellowship at the University of Minnesota, used 15-MHz ultrasound to characterize tissue as malignant or benign.

Ian Donald, a professor of midwifery at the University of Glasgow, met John Wild in 1954 and soon after began his own program in Glasgow. He was more successful than Howry and Wild in gaining clinical credibility, industry collaboration, and funding support for ultrasonic diagnosis in 1955, when he applied a Kelvin & Hughes flaw detector modified by Tom Brown to the abdomens of his female patients. This led eventually to the first commercial two-dimensional scanner, one that allowed the transducer to be placed directly on the patient.

Ultrasound quickly found a home in many medical specialties. In addition to radiology, surgery, obstetrics, and gynecology, ultrasound was applied to cardiology, neurology, ophthalmology, and oncology. Inge Edler and Helmuth Hertz modified Kelvin & Hughes and Siemens equipment in Sweden for use in cardiac diagnosis; L. Leksell in Sweden and R.C. Turner in London investigated the use of Kelvin Hughes flaw detectors in diagnosis of brain lesions; and Yoshimitsu Kikuchi, Rokuro Uchida, Kenji Tanaka, and Toshio Wagai applied it to cancer diagnosis.

Despite the extensive clinical research, ultrasound was not widely available commercially, or accepted in clinical practice, until the late 1970s, after investigators in the United States, England, and Russia had established dosimetry standards that allowed control of exposures and the meaningful comparison of results from different clinical centers. The work done by George Kossoff in Australia on gray scale scanning in 1969 also did much to improve the clinical acceptance of ultrasonic diagnosis, since gray scale scans conveyed far more information than earlier scans. As the image quality of ultrasonic scans continued to be improved, especially with the use of **computers,** insurance companies and national health programs began to pay for ultrasonic examinations, giving a large boost to the clinical acceptance of the technique.

Because of its development within a large number of medical specialties, ultrasound continues to be controlled by many different types of medical specialists and produced by many different equipment manufacturers. Ironically, a diagnostic instrument that was first developed for identifying abnormalities is now used most often in demonstrating normality—in obstetrics, where the vast majority of pregnant women now take home pictures of a fetus that is developing normally, listen to their babies' heartbeats through a Doppler ultrasound device, and have the progress of their labor tracked by an ultrasonic fetal monitor. It is just such routine and widespread application of a medical technology that has prompted the greatest criticism.

Ellen B. Koch

Bibliography

Blume, Stuart. *Insight and Industry: The Dynamics of Technological Change in Medicine.* Cambridge: M.I.T. Press, 1992.

Goldberg, Barry, and Barbara Kimmelman. *Medical Diagnostic Ultrasound: A Retrospective on Its 40th Anniversary.* Philadelphia: Jefferson University Hospital, 1988.

Hill, C.R. "Medical Ultrasonics: An Historical Review." *British Journal of Radiology* 46 (1973): 899–905.

Kelly, Elizabeth, ed. *Ultrasound in Biology and Medicine.* Washington, D.C.: American Institute of Biological Sciences, 1957.

Koch, Ellen. *In the Image of Science? American Research on Medical Ultrasound.* Cambridge: MIT Press, forthcoming.

Vacuum Gauge
See GAUGE, VACUUM

Vacuum Pump
See AIR PUMP

Van Slyke Gasometric Apparatus

Donald Dexter Van Slyke and his colleagues at the Hospital of the Rockefeller Institute devised a gasometric apparatus in 1917, in order to measure the carbon dioxide in blood. It was soon used also for the determination of oxygen, carbon monoxide, total nitrogen, amino acids, lactic acid, sugars, calcium, and so on.

In the original apparatus, gases are liberated from the solution into an evacuated chamber, brought to atmospheric pressure, and their volume measured. In the more precise version developed in 1924 by Van Slyke and James M. Neill, the released gas is brought to a specific volume and the amount of gas present is determined from the pressure measured by an attached manometer.

"The apparatus consists of a 50-cc. pipette with a cock sealed at each end, the lower end being attached to a heavy walled rubber tube connecting with a mercury leveling bulb, the upper end serving for reception of blood samples and reagents. The analysis is carried out by filling the apparatus with mercury, then measuring in the blood sample, either preceded or followed by the reagents to free the gases. The latter are extracted from solution by lowering the mercury until a vacuum is obtained in the pipette, which is then shaken for one to three minutes. The liquid is then drawn off into a small bulb sealed at the bottom, and mercury is readmitted until the pressure is restored to atmospheric. The volume of gas is read in the graduated stem of the pipette" (Peters and Van Slyke 1932, 230).

Prehistory

Early chemical methods of gas analysis were systematized by Robert Bunsen in *Gasometrische Methoden* (1857). Toward the end of the century, physiologists used various gasometric methods and apparatus in their research on, among others, plant and animal respiration and blood gases. Detailed descriptions of such instruments can be found in Abderhalden's *Handbuch* (1910).

For use in physiology, gases often had to be extracted from solutions such as blood. Complete extraction of gases was difficult, and recourse had to be taken to heating under diminished pressure in a blood pump. The analysis was time consuming and the foaming of blood made accurate measurements problematic.

In 1901, Joseph Barcroft and John Scott Haldane described a method of measuring blood gases by releasing oxygen (by adding ferricyanide) or carbon dioxide (by adding tartaric acid) from a sample of blood in a closed chamber filled with air at atmospheric pressure, and then measuring increases in gas volume by changes in pressure (see **blood gas analyzer**). The Van Slyke apparatus incorporates elements of this method and of the blood pump: gases are extracted with chemical reagents, but in a vacuum rather than in air at atmospheric pressure. Moreover, the liquid is drawn off before the volume of gas is measured, preventing reabsorption of the gases.

Prototypes and Development

Van Slyke's original apparatus existed in two versions: a large one used for determining the

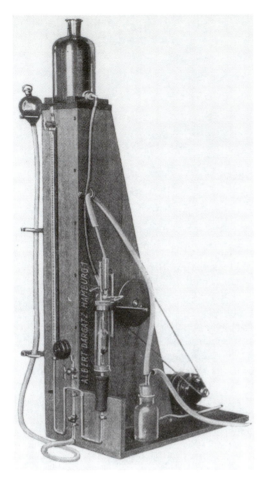

surrounded by a water jacket and equipped with a motor to run the shaker.

Use

The appropriateness of the Van Slyke apparatus for routine clinical laboratory use was ensured by the fact that it was simpler to use than the previous methods, that determinations could be made repeatedly without recalibrating or cleaning the apparatus, and that they could be made quickly (a series of determinations could be made at a rate of one every 3 to 4 minutes). Nevertheless, the use required considerable technical skill and relatively complex calculations.

Van Slyke had designed his apparatus to detect diabetic acidosis, which manifests itself in the depletion of blood bicarbonate. Given that the state of alkali reserve, and more generally of the acid-base equilibrium in the blood, provides significant information on a number of other pathological conditions (nephritis, respiratory and cardiac disorders, for example) and that the apparatus could be used to measure other gases and substances, it was widely used in clinical diagnostic laboratories and in physiological and biochemical research. Van Slyke's own studies of blood as the physico-chemical system relied heavily on determinations made with the gasometric apparatus.

Later Developments

Although the Van Slyke apparatus was gradually replaced by electrodes for measuring blood gases, it remained the standard for the measurement of the oxygen content of blood as late as the 1970s and continued to be listed in instrument supply catalogues well into the 1980s.

Olga Amsterdamska
Anne Löhnberg

Van Slyke manometric apparatus. Handbuch der biologischen Arbeitsmethoden: Methoden der allgemeinen vergleichenden Physiologie, *Vol. 3, edited by Emil Abderhalden, Berlin, 1938: 141. Courtesy Urban and Schwarzenberg.*

gases in approximately 1 cc of blood or blood plasma, and a microapparatus for small amounts of solution (0.2 cc). In 1921, William C. Stadie added a mechanical shaker, and the bore of the graduated stem of the pipette was made smaller to allow for more precise measurements. The manometric version, introduced in 1924, increased the accuracy of measurement for research purposes.

The apparatus was originally manufactured by Emil Greiner in New York, but since it was relatively simple, it could be assembled in most laboratories and manufactured by a number of firms. In the early 1920s, various versions of the volumetric apparatus were sold, for example, by Eimer & Amend of New York, at prices ranging from $10 for basic glassware to $60 for an instrument mounted on a stand,

Bibliography

Amsterdamska, Olga. "Chemistry in the Clinic: The Research Career of Donald Dexter Van Slyke." In *Molecularizing Biology and Medicine: New Practices and Alliances 1930s–1970s,* edited by Soraya de Chader-evian and Harke Kamminga. Reading, England: Harwood Academic, 1997.

Büttner, Johannes, ed. *History of Clinical Chemistry.* Berlin: Van de Gruyter, 1983.

Peters, John P., and Donald D. Van Slyke. *Quantitative Clinical Chemistry,* Vol. 2, *Methods.* Baltimore: Williams and Wilkins, 1932.

Van Slyke, Donald D. "Studies of Acidosis. II. A Method for the Determination of Carbon Dioxide and Carbonates in Solution." *Journal of Biological Chemistry* 30 (1917): 347–68.

———, and James M. Neill. "The Determination of Gases in Blood and Other Solutions by Vacuum Extraction and Manometric Measurement. I." *Journal of Biological Chemistry* 61 (1924): 523–73.

Vapor Density, Boiling Point, and Freezing Point Apparatus

In 1882 Francois Marie Raoult, working on the alcohol content of wines in Grenoble, enunciated the law known by his name: the vapor pressure of a solution is lower than that of the pure solvent, and the extent of lowering depends on the number of molecules of solute in the solution.

This law has three consequences. A solution freezes at a lower temperature than the pure solvent (a fact noticed by Richard Watson in 1771 and stated quantitatively by Charles Blagden in 1788); a solution boils at a higher temperature than the pure solvent; and a solution separated from a pure solvent by a membrane through which solvent, but not solute, molecules can pass develops an osmotic pressure. Elevation of boiling point, depression of freezing point, and osmotic pressure were termed "colligative properties" by Wilhelm Ostwald, since they depend only on the number of solute molecules in a certain weight of solvent, and not on their chemical identity. If the weights of solute and solvent, and the value of one of the colligative properties, are known, then the relative molecular mass or molecular weight can be calculated.

The temperature changes are small, so special **thermometers** are needed for their measurement. The most successful, invented by Ernst Otto Beckmann in 1889, had a scale of only five or six degrees graduated in $1/100$ths of a degree. A reservoir of mercury at the top of the tube allowed the mercury level to be adjusted to the boiling point of the chosen solvent. Adjusting the Beckmann was a skilled operation involving repeated heating, tapping, and shaking; all too often the expensive thermometer was broken in the process.

Ordinary procedures for determining boiling points were inadequate for molecular weight work, and special equipment was designed. Two popular forms were those of Beckmann and W. Landsberger; both were modified by James Walker.

In the Beckmann apparatus, the solution was contained in an inner tube surrounded by vapor from a solvent boiling in an outer vessel. Both solution and solvent were heated by bunsen burners; an essential part of the apparatus was the asbestos heating box that distributed heat to both inner and outer vessels, though a later modification made use of direct electric heating. The inner tube contained glass beads or platinum tetrahedra to ensure even heating, and a short piece of platinum wire was sealed into its base. Both vessels were fitted with reflux condensers.

In the Landsberger-Walker apparatus, the solution was heated by passing into it the vapor of boiling solvent; as long as the temperature of the solution was below its boiling point, vapor would condense and release its latent heat. The bulbed inner tube was graduated in $1/10$ths of a cc. It was closed by a cork through which passed a thermometer and a delivery tube; near the top, a small hole allowed vapor to escape into the outer vessel from which it passed to a condenser. Solvent was boiled in a separate flask and led to the delivery tube.

Beckmann also devised an apparatus for the depression of freezing point, or cryoscopic, route to molecular weights. It consisted of a stout tube with an angled side arm; a Beckmann thermometer and a wire stirrer passed through the cork by which the tube was closed. The lower portion of the tube was encased in a wider tube, and the whole was immersed in a beaker containing a freezing mixture and provided with a stirrer. The temperature of the freezing bath was about $5°$ lower than the freezing point of the solution.

A useful adaptation of the cryoscopic method was made by Karl Rast in 1922. Camphor has a very high freezing point depression constant, and if one part of solute and ten parts of camphor are melted together and thoroughly mixed, the freezing point can be observed in an ordinary melting point tube.

Molecular weights found by ebulloscopic or cryoscopic means are accurate only to 5 or 10 percent. If, however, an empirical formula for the solute has been established by chemical analysis, the approximate molecular weight would suffice to decide the factor by which the empirical formula should be multiplied to ob-

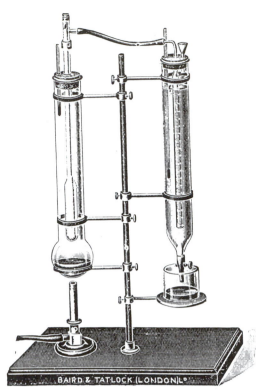

Victor Meyer vapor density apparatus. Baird & Tatlock Ltd. Price List of Apparatus for Experiments in Practical Physics. *London, 1912: 334. Courtesy of SSPL.*

placed. On reaching the heated zone, the sample boiled, blew out the stopper, and pushed an equal volume of air out through the side arm that led to a measuring tube. A good deal of skill was needed to obtain useful results.

The instruments described in this article continued in use until the late 1950s when **mass spectrometry** began to provide a new route to accurate molecular weights.

W.A. Campbell

Bibliography
Beckmann, Ernst O. "Bestimmung des molekulargewichts aus Siedpunktserhöhungen" *Zeitschrift für physikalische Chemie* 3 (1889): 603–4.
Landsberger, W. "Ein neues Verfahren der Molekelgewichtsbestimmung nach der Siedemethode," *Berichte der deutschen chemischen Gesellschaft* 31 (1898): 458–73.
Demuth, Robert and Victor Meyer. "Verfahren zur Bestimmung der Dampfdichte von Körpern unterhalb ihre Siedetemperatur," *Berichte der deutschen chemischen Gesellschaft* 23 (1890): 311–16.
Walker, James. *Introduction to Physical Chemistry*, 197–217. London: Macmillan, 1919.

tain the molecular formula from which the accurate molecular weight could be calculated.

Jean Baptiste André Dumas invented a method for determining molecular weights from vapor density in 1826. This apparatus consisted of a thin-walled glass bulb of about 200 cc capacity with its neck drawn out to a capillary. A small quantity of a volatile liquid was placed in the weighed bulb, which was then immersed in a bath of boiling water. When all the liquid had boiled off and the bulb was filled with vapor, the tip of the neck was sealed in a flame and the bulb weighed again. The volume of vapor was calculated from the weight of water that rushed in to fill the bulb when the sealed tip was broken off under water.

Victor Meyer's vapor density apparatus of 1889 consisted of a long narrow corked tube blown into a cylindrical bulb at its lower end and fitted with a short side arm about 5 cm from the top. This tube was supported in an outer jacket of glass or copper in which water was boiled. The sample was introduced in a small weighing tube, and the cork quickly re-

Variation Compass
See COMPASS, VARIATION

Visceroctome
A visceroctome, which allows rapid sampling of cadaver liver tissue, is composed of a tube with a sliding top and a stainless steel blade. Visceroctomes were used to ascertain if deaths in a given geographic area were the consequence of suspected yellow fever, and the device played an important role in epidemiological studies of this disease. In addition, however, the instrument and the related technique (visceroctomy) cannot be dissociated from legal prescriptions that made visceroctomy obligatory, from the network of visceroctome stations that made possible the execution of these legal prescriptions, and from the institutionalized supervision of visceroctome posts. The visceroctome is thus a key element in a complex network of social relations.

In 1912 the Brazilian physician Rocha Lima noticed characteristic degenerative changes ("pepper and salt necrosis") in the livers of pa-

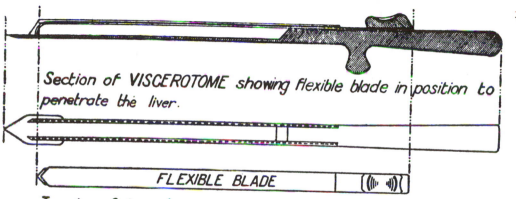

Section of VISCEROTOME showing flexible blade in position to penetrate the liver.

FLEXIBLE BLADE

Top view of viscerotome with flexible blade withdrawn

Cutting end of viscerotome with flexible blade in position to penetrate the abdominal wall of the body

The same end of the viscerotome with the flexible blade in position to enter the liver

Viscerotomes, showing different positions of the blade. Rickard (1937): Figure 2. Courtesy of the American Journal of Tropical Medicine and Hygiene.

tients who had died from yellow fever. This observation was confirmed in the 1920s by C.M. Torres, W.H. Hoffman, and O. Klotz, and applied to epidemiological studies of yellow fever in 1930. In the 1920s experts from the International Health Division of the Rockefeller Foundation hoped to eliminate yellow fever from northern Brazil through the eradication of its vector, the mosquito *Aedes aegypti,* from endemic urban areas. They successfully eliminated the mosquito but not the disease, a failure that led them to the conclusion that hidden foci of yellow fever must exist in Brazil's interior. Routine autopsies of all the persons deceased from suspicious "fever" could, they and their Brazilian colleagues believed, uncover these hidden foci and guide mosquito eradication campaigns. The systematic carrying out of autopsies in that vast and underdeveloped country was not, however,

an easy task. Thus the visceroctome was devised to sample cadaveric tissue in rural areas in the absence of a medical infrastructure.

The first visceroctome (originally called a liver punch) was developed in the summer of 1930 by two physicians, Elmer Rickard of the Rockefeller Foundation and Decio Pareiras of Brazil's National Department of Public Health. Fred Soper, head of the Rockefeller Foundation office in Brazil, decided to patent Rickard's instrument, in order to prevent counter-patenting for profit by Pareiras. Wilbur Sawyer, director of the International Health Division, opposed patenting a medical instrument. A compromise was finally found: a patenting process was started to block competitors, but then was left open. Visceroctomes were mass produced in Brazil and used in that country, then in the entire Latin American continent.

The diffusion of the visceroctome in Brazil was closely related to the implementation of visceroctome posts and to the introduction of regulations concerning burial of suspicious "fever" cases. The first regulations were issued by local sanitary authorities, but the authoritarian regime of Getulio Vargas (in power in Brazil since 1930), which strongly supported Rockefeller Foundation experts, made visceroctomy obligatory throughout the country. A decree of May 24, 1932, prohibited burials without the visa of the visceroctomy service, and fixed punishments for transgression of these regulations. This legislation, coupled with the organizational efficiency of the Rockefeller specialists, led to a rapid extension of the network of visceroctome posts in Brazil. The practice of visceroctomy demonstrated the existence of silent foci of yellow fever in rural areas and led to the description of a new epidemiological form of this disease, jungle yellow fever. It also guided Aedes aegypti eradication and oriented anti–yellow fever vaccination campaigns.

Visceroctomy was occasionally seen as offensive by the families of deceased persons. Several employees of the visceroctomy service were killed in fights over tissue sampling. These incidents, and even more the fear of a negative image of the Rockefeller Foundation activities, prompted Sawyer in 1937 to propose a drastic reduction of the number of visceroctome posts. Soper disagreed, insisting that visceroctomy was an indispensable tool for epidemiological surveys. Rockefeller Foundation experts enrolled the support of local politicians and clergymen in favor of visceroctomy. They fought against burial without a visceroctomy visa, "clandestine cemeteries," bribing of visceroctomy officials to allow burial without tissue sampling, and also against numerous attempts to increase the number of liver samples sent to the central laboratory in order to get the premium paid for each sample. A complicated system of control over persons and inscriptions was installed to ensure the reliability of the visceroctomy service. This service was gradually phased out in the 1940s and 1950s with the reduction of the number of cases of yellow fever in Latin America.

Ilana Löwy

Bibliography

Ribeiro, Leonido. *Brazilian Medical Contributions,* 106–7. Rio de Janeiro: J. Olympio, 1939.

Rickard, Elmer R. "The Organization of Visceroctome Service of the Brazilian Cooperative Yellow Fever Service." *American Journal of Tropical Medicine* 17 (1937): 163–90.

Soper, Fred L. "Present Day Methods for the Study and Control of Yellow Fever." *American Journal of Tropical Medicine* 17 (1937): 655–76.

———, E.R. Rickards, and P.J. Crawford. "The Routine Post-Mortem Removal of Liver Tissue from Rapidly Fatal Cases for the Discovery of Silent Yellow Fever Foci." *American Journal of Hygiene* 19 (1934): 549–66.

Viscometer

Viscometers measure viscosity—the resistance of a fluid to flow, which Isaac Newton in 1687 defined as a ratio of shear stress to shear rate. Viscosity is a function of temperature, its common unit being centipoise (cP), the SI unit being Pascal second, where 1mPa s = 1 cP. Kinematic viscosity expressed in centistrokes (cSt) is dynamic viscosity divided by density. Water at 20°C has a viscosity of 1.009 cP. There are three basic types of viscometers: capillary/orifice, rotational, and moving body.

Capillary Viscometers

These are widely used for Newtonian liquids, in which viscosity is independent of shear rate. The principle is based on the Hagen-Poiseiulle law (1840), which correlates dynamic viscosity with flow rate, pressure drop, and tube dimensions, for steady state, isothermal, laminar capillary flow. The basic instrument designed by W. Ostwald in 1920 consists of a glass U-tube with reservoir bulbs separated by a capillary. The time required for a fixed volume of liquid to flow from the upper reservoir under a hydrostatic head is a measure of viscosity. The instrument is calibrated with a reference fluid at a constant temperature, and measures kinetic viscosity by multiplying efflux time with the calibration constant.

The original Ostwald viscometer has undergone considerable improvements to achieve better accuracy. Instruments sold commercially have capillary diameters from 0.3 to 4.0 mm and cover viscosity ranges from 0.6 to 30,000 cSt. Examples are Cannon-Fenske for transparent (1939) and opaque (1941) liquids, Ubbelhode suspended level (1938), Fitz-Simon (1935), Zeitfuchs cross-arm (1946), and SIL (1941). The

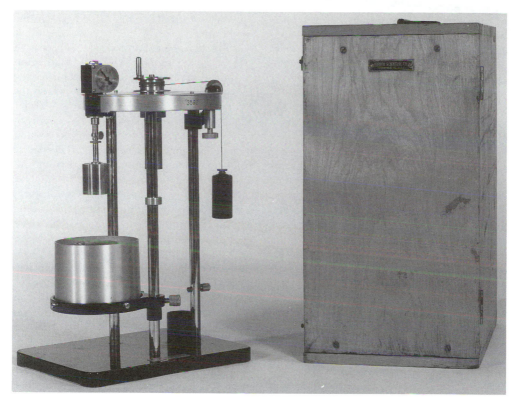

Stormer viscometer, ca. 1909. NMAH 336,370. Courtesy of NMAH.

ASTM-D-445 gives detailed dimensions and methods of use of glass capillary viscometers.

Orifice Viscometers

The time taken for a fixed volume of liquid to flow out of a cup with a hole at the bottom is a measure of viscosity. This idea, used in 1540 B.C. in Amenemhet's waterclock, is the principle of the orifice viscometer, first constructed by Engler in 1885. Orifice viscometers used include the Ford, Zahn, and Shell cups for paint and inks, and the Saybolt Universal, Redwood, and Furol instruments common in the petroleum industry. The efflux times give comparable viscosity covering ranges up to 5,000 cSt.

Rotational Viscometers

The first concentric cylinder rotational viscometer devised by M.M. Couette in 1890 consisted of a rotating cup with an inner cylinder supported by a torsion wire and resting on the cup bottom. Measuring the torque, radius, and height of the inner cylinder, cup radius, and the relative angular velocity gives the dynamic viscosity of the fluid sheared in the narrow annulus between two surfaces, through Margules's equation (1880).

G.F.C. Searle designed a viscometer with a rotating inner cylinder in 1912, while E. Hatscheck improved the Couette apparatus with better guard rings in 1913. The year 1915 saw the first commercial Couette-type viscometer (MacMichael), preceded by one by E.J. Stormer (1909). Here a constant torque is applied to an inner cylinder or paddle and its rate of rotation becomes a measure of viscosity.

Rotational viscometers are versatile and measure viscosity as a function of shear rate and time of non-Newtonian materials. Important commercial types include the Rotovisco, Rheomat, Brookfield Syncho-Lectric, and Mooney Disk. These have low to high shear rate capabilities and cover viscosity ranges from 2 to 10^9 cP. In the cone-and-plate type of rotational viscometer, a low-angle cone rotates at a constant shear rate against a flat plate with the test fluid between them. Commercially available types are Ferranti-Shirley and ICI-Cone-Plate.

Moving Body or Falling Ball Viscometers

These are based on Stokes's law (1845) relating the viscosity of a Newtonian fluid to the velocity of a ball falling down a cylindrical tube filled with the fluid. The most common is the Hoepper falling/rolling sphere viscometer (1933) having a water-jacketed precision bore glass tube mounted 10° from the vertical. The instrument is calibrated with standard oils. Series of balls of different diameters allow wide range of viscosity measurements.

Modern Trends

Viscometers measuring the stress-strain-time relationship of materials exhibiting both viscous and plastic properties are called rheometers. Examples are the pressure-driven piston-cylinder capillary viscometer for polymer melts and the Weissenberg Rheogoniometer for measuring normal stresses and dynamic rheological properties. Modern instruments are typically microcomputer controlled with automated data acquisition. Rheometers are widely used for continuous in-plant quality and process control and also for new product development. Extensive applications of rheological instruments are found for food products, biological fluids, lubricants, paints, printing inks, rubbers, soaps, plastics, and pharmaceuticals.

Asitesh Bhattacharya

Bibliography

Kirk-Othmer. *Encyclopedia of Chemical Technology,* Vol. 20, 259–319. New York: Wiley, 1982.

Merrington, A.C. *Viscometry*. London: Edward Arnold and Co., 1949.

Meskat, W. "Viskometrie." In *Messen und Regeln in der Chemischen Technik,* edited by J. Hengstenberg, B. Sturm, and O. Winkler, 856–994. Berlin: Springer, 1964.

Sherman, Philip. *Industrial Rheology*. London: Academic, 1970.

van Wazer, J.R., et al. *Viscosity and Flow Measurement*. New York: Interscience, 1963.

Vocational Aptitude Tests (Psychotechnics)

Vocational aptitude tests are designed to predict achievement in an occupation and are typically administered before selection for training. The term "psychotechnics" originally denoted applied psychology, but it was never generally accepted in the English-speaking world and has lost its acceptance on the European Continent; it is now used by historians to denote the heavy apparatus aptitude testing used between the world wars.

Psychotechnical tests were first used on a large scale during World War I. Hugo Münsterberg described an arrangement for testing Boston streetcar drivers in 1912, but it was the apparatus developed in 1915 by Walther Moede and Curt Piorkowski to test applicant automobile drivers in the German Army that became the significant prototype. This device combined a simulation of the real driving situation with a setup for research on reaction time and attention from the psychological laboratory, consisting of stimulus producing, reaction recording, and time registering components. The applicant was seated in a driver's seat with steering wheel, pedals, gear shift, and other devices, all connected to registration instruments. On the opposing wall various lights and signals appeared that simulated diverse traffic situations. Various instruments controlled and recorded stimuli and reactions.

Comparable installations were introduced to select military aviation applicants and such military specialists as wireless telegraphers, hydrophone operators, observers, and sound ranging parties. These instruments tested specific sensory aptitudes, and typically simulated the real instruments, but altered stimulus input and recording technique.

A modified version of the Moede-Piorkowski apparatus was used to test applicant engineers for the Saxonian Railroads in 1917, and another for drivers of the Berlin Streetcar Co. in 1918. This opened the way for civilian applications to spread to many countries after the war. Such installations were expensive, not producible in series, and affordable only to companies with a sizable number of drivers' jobs and serious financial risks in the case of accidents.

As psychotechnical aptitude testing caught on, more tests for civilian occupations were introduced. Important domains were the testing of train, streetcar, bus, and automobile drivers, industrial apprentices and employees, railroad workers, telephone operators, office clerks, and stenotypists. Some instruments tested specific sensorimotor abilities, such as the weight discrimination test, the joint test, the touch test, the falling rod test, or the tremometer. The dexterity or motor ability tests were less specific; these included various tapping tests, tracing tests, dotting tests, finger or rod mazes, peg tests, aim-

Moede's two-hand coordinator, simulating a lathe-bearer carriage, 1919. Courtesy of the Institute for the History of Modern Psychology, Passau University, Germany.

ing apparatus, mirror drawing apparatus, and pursuit apparatus. Notable are hand-foot co-ordination tests and Moede's two-hand coor-dinator, which simulated a lathe bearer car-riage. The cognitive-motor tests included mechanical aptitude tests such as Moede's hammer mill or Walther Schulz's pump, which resemble mechanical toys to be assembled by the applicant. Others tested specific cognitive skills: memory tests, attention tests, or unspe-cific cognitive abilities such as Fritz Heider's mechanical puzzles or Richard Couvé's classi-fication tests. Another group gauged emo-tional features such as emotional stability, or personality traits such as recklessness; both were used by Adolph Judah Snow for testing car drivers.

In several instances, large companies insti-tutionalized their own psychological laborato-ries and services and developed special instru-ments simulating their specific jobs. Notable here were the railroads, the post and telegraph services, the police, and the military.

Although psychotechnics started with indi-vidual performance tests using complex appa-ratus, there was a marked tendency toward less complex instruments, group tests, and nonper-formance (paper-and-pencil) tests. The motive was obviously economic, not scientific.

Many of these tests did not simulate any real situation or activity, and often simple stan-dard ability assessment was used to infer apti-tude. Most of the later and simpler instruments would be combined into test batteries for dif-fering diagnostic purposes. They were trans-portable, inexpensive, and produced in series. Comparability over different users was a prob-lem with the usually custom-made, heavy appa-ratus performance type of instruments, whereas the less expensive serial models were more eas-ily standardized.

In the 1920s, there was a psychotechnics craze in Europe, with many inventors patenting constructions of uncertain merit, believing that money could be made with the right instrument. Manufacturers like Zimmermann in Leipzig, Organisations-Institut in Berlin, Verdin-Boulitte in Paris, or Stoelting in Chicago offered a ple-thora of models, many of which have not sur-vived. Large corporations, however, usually had exclusive instruments produced in their own workshops.

Psychotechnical apparatus of the performance type was introduced in the 1920s in Europe and the Soviet Union. Americans put more emphasis on paper-and-pencil procedures. Today, laboratorylike performance testing is still prevalent where selection and evaluation for intricate tasks with expensive or dangerous machinery is at stake: space navigation, aviation, maritime navigation, railroads, road traffic, and, combining all these, the military.

The worth of psychotechnical instruments must be judged according to psychological testing theory, especially the criteria of objectivity, reliability, and validity, even though the early period of psychological testing had vague notions about test quality criteria. In psychotechnical equipment, objectivity can, as a rule, be estimated as high, as there is usually an uncomplicated reading of scales or counting of instants. Reliability is more difficult to assess than is validity. Simulations of the future job rely heavily on content validity. The less an instrument simulates the actual task, the less can be said about its validity; research into criterion validity (concurrent or predictive) was minimal in the early days of psychotechnics and construct validity had not yet been formulated.

Horst U.K. Gundlach

Bibliography

Sokal, Michael M., ed. *Psychological Testing and American Society 1890–1930.* New Brunswick: Rutgers University Press, 1987.

Walsh, W. Bruce, and Samuel Osipow, eds. *Handbook of Vocational Psychology: Theory, Research, and Practice.* Hillsdale, N.J.: Lawrence Erlbaum, 1983.

Voltameter

A voltameter measures quantities of electricity. It was invented by the British electrochemist Michael Faraday and introduced in 1834 as the volta-electrometer. This term and its shortened form, voltameter, are now effectively obsolete. The modern term, "coulometer," was introduced by Theodore William Richards in 1902.

According to Faraday's laws, a definite quantity of electricity will bring about 1 gram-equivalent of electrochemical action, such as the decomposition of water, deposition or dissolution of a metal, or oxidation or reduction of a species in solution. This quantity, now termed the Faraday, is 96486.18 ±0.13 coulombs per gram equivalent.

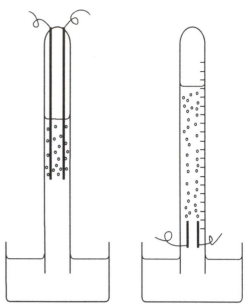

Original (left) and revised versions of the water voltameter. Courtesy of John Stock.

Faraday used the principle of the electrolytic decomposition of acidulated water at platinum electrodes, followed by measurement of the resulting volume of hydrogen, oxygen, or their mixture. He initially tried the device diagrammed at left in the illustration above, but noted that the gas mixture began to disappear when the electrolysis was stopped. He was experiencing the platinum-catalyzed interaction of the gases to form water. With totally submerged electrodes, as diagrammed at right, the gas volume was stable. Faraday described various forms of the water voltameter. Development by many others continued into the present century. A disadvantage of any form of gas voltameter is the need to correct for temperature and pressure and to convert the result into a corresponding mass.

In 1835, the Italian scientist Carlo Matteucci briefly described the silver deposition voltameter; change in mass is the measured variable. Johann Christian Poggendorf developed a form that was used by many investigators. Here, the platinum bowl cathode contains silver nitrate solution, into which dips a silver anode. The dried bowl is weighed before and after the electrolysis, thus giving the mass of the deposit.

Further refinements, especially in the early years of the present century, led to results so precise that the ampere, the unit of current strength, could be defined internationally in terms of the rate of the electrolytic deposition of silver. This definition endured until 1948. A technique based on the measured electrolytic dissolution of silver has been used for the high-precision determination of the Faraday.

A voltameter with hydrazine sulphate as electrolyte, yielding a hydrogen-nitrogen gas mixture, has been used for measuring small amounts of electricity. The electrolysis of a bromide-containing solution between a silver anode and a platinum cathode produces hydroxyl ions. This can be titrated with standard acid solution. A voltameter that involves the titration of iodine liberated from potassium iodide solution is capable of very high precision.

Electrical and Electronic Devices

The manipulations associated with any form of chemical voltameter also permit a direct readout in coulombs or in any arbitrary units. Such devices are based on the relationship

$$Q = \int_0^t I.dt,$$

where Q is the number of coulombs, I the current in amperes, and t the time in seconds. If, as in coulometric titrimetry, the current is known and constant, Q is directly proportional to the total time of current flow. Integration is needed if the current is variable.

One form of integrator is a counter that is driven by a motor with linear speed-to-current characteristics. It and its associated timer are started and stopped simultaneously. Alternatively, a constant-speed motor may drive the counter through a variable gear, the ratio of which is controlled by the prevailing current strength. The most important integrator, however, is that based on an electronic current-to-frequency converter, the pulsating output of which can drive a counter.

Applications

Important in fundamental studies, the voltameter has also proved valuable in other directions. For example, in preparative chemistry, the oxidative or reductive intensity can be nicely adjusted by controlled-potential electrolysis, during which the current decreases as the reactants are used up.

When Thomas Alva Edison developed his direct-current supply system around 1880, the customer had a dissolution voltameter through which a known fraction of the supply current was passed. At intervals, the customer was billed according to the decrease in mass of the zinc anode. Later, two voltameters were coupled so as to bring about the period tilting of a beam. This operated a counter, so that weighing was not needed. Various other chemical-mechanical supply meters, including prepayment (coin in the slot) devices, were patented before the progressive changeover to purely electrically operated meters and to ac supplies, which began in the early 1900s (see **electricity supply meter**).

John T. Stock

Bibliography

Lingane, James J. *Electroanalytical Chemistry,* chap. 19. 2nd ed. New York: Interscience, 1958.

Stock, John T. "A Century and a Half of Silver-based Coulometry." *Journal of Chemical Education* 69 (1992): 949–52.

———. "Coulombs for Customers." *Journal of Chemical Education* 66 (1989): 417–19.

———. "From the Volt-electrometer to the Electronic Coulometer." *Journal of Chemical Education* 70 (1993): 576–79.

Voltmeter

A voltmeter measures the difference in electric potential, or voltage, between two points in an electrical circuit. It is distinct from the **voltameter**, an electrochemical device invented by Michael Faraday for measuring the total charge that has flowed through a circuit. All voltmeters are built to work accurately only within a specified range, often around an order of magnitude (such as 10-100 volts), although this range can usually be scaled up or down by the addition of resistive shunts. There are a range of different operating mechanisms for voltmeters: electromagnetic (moving-iron, moving-coil, **dynamometer**), electrothermal (hot-wire, thermocouple), and electrostatic. These are used in different applications for appropriate levels of versatility, robustness, and accuracy.

Two features are common to the design and use of all voltmeters. Since the role of the voltmeter is to gauge the voltage drop between the terminals of a circuit element, this element is always connected in parallel with it. Voltmeters are thus designed with a resistance (impedance, for ac work) much larger than that of the

Early direct-reading moving coil voltmeter, by Weston Electrical Instrument Co., 1888. SM 1935-322. Courtesy of SSPL.

circuit element across which the voltage is to be measured. This feature ensures that the effective resistance of the circuit element is not significantly lowered by the connection of the voltmeter, and hence that the potential differ-

ence is not distorted by the act of measurement itself.

Up to the late 1870s, the industries of telegraphy and electroplating usually cited potential differences simply as the number of Grove or

Clark cells used to generate the current required. If a more specific measurement was required, Ohm's law was employed to get a value of potential difference by multiplying together the readings of a resistance **potentiometer** and a **galvanometer**. The need for a specialized instrument to measure voltage arose with the rise of electric lighting in the 1880s. The brightness of the new Edison-Swan incandescent lamps was sensitively dependent on the potential difference across their filaments, hence electrical engineers sought more direct and immediate ways of monitoring the potential difference generated by the dynamos used to power the lighting circuits.

The early history of the voltmeter is closely tied to that of the **ammeter**. Prototypes of both were developed in 1881–1884 to monitor the stability and efficiency of power-lighting networks, as well as in fault-diagnosis after breakdowns in electrical circuits. These sibling instruments were at first given a common basic moving-iron design by their inventors, William Ayrton and John Perry. So close was the initial similarity that an early (nondirect reading) ammeter could be converted into a voltmeter simply by rewinding its coils with high-resistance wire. From 1884/1885, however, voltmeters like ammeters were increasingly manufactured as direct-reading devices calibrated with scales in the recently standardized unit of potential difference, the volt.

In the 1880s and 1890s, the market for such devices in the U.S. and U.K. was highly competitive. Consequently, diverse innovative designs were introduced to meet the needs of the fast-developing lighting and power industry. One design that maintained the generic similarity between ammeters and voltmeters was William Siemens's dynamometer, which operated by the magnetic attraction of two current-carrying wires: by appropriate connections and winding, this could be used to measure either voltage or current. The hot-wire technique initiated by Philip Cardew proved, however, to be rather more effective for voltmeters than ammeters. His method harnessed the heating expansion generated by a flowing current to elongate a taut silver-platinum wire, yielding a dial-reading in proportion to the current or voltage being measured. While the heat losses were relatively negligible in the high-resistance voltmeter version of this instrument, they were not so in the low-resistance ammeter version. Hence only the hot-wire voltmeter was found to be accurate enough for mass production.

The hot-wire voltmeter is now used in cars and other applications that derive most benefit from its inexpensive and robust if not highly sensitive characteristics. In other contexts it has the distinct advantage of being able to measure voltages in both dc and ac systems—useful in as much as large ac systems have existed alongside small localized dc installations since the 1890s. This dual-use is common to most other major patterns of voltmeter design: the dynamometer, electrostatic, and moving-iron forms. However, it is not a feature of (unmodified) moving-coil voltmeters. At all but the lowest frequencies of alternating current, these instruments do not register a reading. This is because over the course of the voltage cycle, the electromagnetic forces involved undergo reversal too rapidly to overcome the inertia of the moving parts (coil and indicator needle). Moving coil voltmeters can be used to measure alternating potentials only if the current is rectified to one direction only.

For special purposes the technologies of rapid signal sampling and digitization have been deployed in recent decades to make high-precision digital voltmeters. In nonspecial applications requiring flexibility and portability, the design of the voltmeter and ammeter have reconverged in the operation of the analog and digital multimeter. State-of-the-art digital multimeters can log readings of current, voltage, and resistance directly onto computers.

Graeme J.N. Gooday

Bibliography

Aspinall-Parr, George D. *Electrical Engineering Measuring Instruments for Commercial and Laboratory Purposes.* London: Blackie, 1903.

Bolton, William. *Electrical and Electronic Measurement and Testing.* Harlow, U.K.: Longman, 1992.

Warburg Manometer

An adaptation of the Haldane-Barcroft instrument for blood gas analysis, the Warburg manometer became the dominant apparatus used during the 1920s and the following decades for measuring respiration and other processes connected to the absorption or release of gases in animal or plant tissues (see **blood gas analyzer; porometer;** and **Van Slyke gasometric apparatus**).

A manometer has been defined since the eighteenth century as an instrument for measuring the rarity or density of the air, or, after the discovery of the general gaseous state, as the pressure of a gas or vapor. Simple manometers have often consisted of a U-tube partially filled with a liquid, with one end connected to the gas whose pressure is to be determined, the other open to the atmosphere. The pressure is measured, respective to the reference pressure of the atmosphere, by the difference in height of the liquid in the two arms of the tube. Through the relation between pressure and volume established by Boyle's law, changes in pressure can be used to calculate changes in the volume of the enclosed gas.

In 1902 two British physiologists, John Scott Haldane and Joseph Barcroft, devised a "method of estimating the oxygen and carbonic acid in small quantities of blood." Their apparatus, a simple but ingenious modification of an ordinary manometer, consisted of two tubes connected at the bottom by a piece of rubber tubing with a screw clamp that enabled them to change the volume. The closed end of the tube was connected to a vessel in which they placed a blood sample. They displaced first the oxygen from the blood with ferricyanide. The increased volume of gas caused the liquid to descend in the closed tube and rise in the open tube. By adjusting the clamp, they returned the level in the closed tube to its original mark. The difference between the two levels then became a measure of the change in pressure, from which the volume of the gas released could be calculated. The carbon dioxide was then displaced by means of tartaric acid and similarly determined. To correct for changes in atmospheric pressure and temperature, a second instrument containing a control vessel was mounted beside the experimental apparatus.

Barcroft used this apparatus particularly to study the changes in the content of the blood gases perfused through isolated organs. In this situation a comparison between two blood samples to ascertain the changes incurred was more relevant than a determination of the absolute quantities of the blood gases. For this purpose he developed a differential manometer, in which the two vessels were attached to the two arms of a single instrument.

In 1910 the German biochemist Otto Warburg adopted the original Haldane-Barcroft method to measure the consumption of oxygen in sea urchin eggs. Because he needed only to determine the change in the quantity of oxygen, Warburg was able to dispense with the ferricyanide and compute the absorption directly from the decrease in the pressure in the manometer. During the 1920s Warburg simplified the design of the manometer and applied it to an expanding range of problems associated with tissue respiration. A central advantage of his method was that it allowed one to read changes in the level of the manometric fluid at short intervals, so that one could easily follow changes in the rate of a respiratory process.

One could directly measure only the overall change in the gaseous volume, so that in res-

Sir Hans Krebs with manometers. Courtesy of SSPL.

piratory exchanges one could measure the oxygen absorbed only if the carbon dioxide was absorbed in potash, or the carbon dioxide produced anaerobically could be measured. Warburg, however, devised a method that enabled him to measure both gases in a single experiment by using duplicate runs with different volumes of fluid in the vessel. The difference in the solubilities of the two gases provided the basis for the calculation. In 1923 Warburg devised the method of studying the respiratory exchanges in very thin slices of mammalian tissues placed in a fluid medium in which cellular activity survived for several hours.

The combination of tissue slices and manometric measurements proved, during the 1930s, to be a powerful tool for the study of intermediary metabolism. It was applied, not only to measure respiratory gaseous exchanges, but also to many other intermediary reactions that could be linked to a reaction producing or absorbing a gas. Both the Warburg manometer and the Barcroft differential manometer were used for this purpose, but the simplicity and versatility of the Warburg eventually made it the standard instrument in metabolic biochemistry. In the postwar years various refinements increased its sensitivity, and it has continued to play a major role in biochemical experimentation, although gradually replaced by more recent methods.

Frederic L. Holmes

Bibliography

Barcroft, Joseph. "Differential Method of Blood-Gas Analysis." *Journal of Physiology* 37 (1908): 12–24.

——— and J.S. Haldane. "A Method of Estimating the Oxygen and Carbonic Acid in Small Quantities of Blood." *Journal of Physiology* 28 (1902): 232–40.

Dixon, Malcolm. *Manometric Methods as Applied to the Measurement of Cell Respiration and Other Processes.* 2nd. ed. Cambridge: Cambridge University Press, 1943.

Warburg, Otto. *The Metabolism of Tumors.* Translated by Frank Dickens. London: Constable, 1930.

Water Sample Bottle

Taking a sample of seawater involves getting the container down to the required depth, opening and closing it on demand, and bringing it back to the surface without mixing the contents with water from higher levels. A multitude of bottle forms have been devised as scientists and instrument-makers grappled with the problems of investigating the temperature, chemical composition, and salinity of a largely unknown environment.

In the late seventeenth century, Robert Hooke described a weighted wooden bucket with valved top and bottom that would be open on lowering and held closed on being hauled to the surface. Hooke's device was satisfactory in

shallow water, but at greater depths the wood became waterlogged and the sample contaminated. Alexander Marcet, a chemist interested in the composition of seawater, compared the performance of a number of water bottles in 1818 and devised several forms of his own. As it was impossible to keep a steady pull on the line, and as valved lids could open on return to the ship, Marcet provided a spring mechanism to hold the bottle open until it hit the bottom and closed on the way up; he later developed a more robust design that could be closed at any depth. One indication of the popularity of this instrument is in the *Edinburgh Philosophical Journal,* which cited a dozen scientists using bottles with hinged lids and bottoms in 1825. Some years later, George Aimé, working off the coast of Algeria, developed "messengers"— weights clipped to and slid down the line to trigger releases and catches for instrument control. Some of his instruments are preserved in the Monaco Oceanographical Museum.

The early measurement of temperature at depth was accomplished by hauling up the **thermometer** and water sample together. In 1821, Captain R. Wauchope used a thermometer inside no fewer than five tin cases and an outermost wooden one, with tops and bottoms hinged to be open on the way down, and closed on the way up. A weighted rope carried this contraption to about 1,000 fathoms, and the friction of the seawater on the rope was so great it took one hundred men an hour and 20 minutes to get the thermometer back on board. By the time of the *Challenger* expedition of 1872–1876, steam-driven winches were available to take some of the effort out of deep-sea investigations.

The best form of thermometer to take was also discussed. William Rutherford's design for a minimum thermometer was preferred in the 1820s, but it had to be held still and read directly. The scientist François Walferdin described his ideas for a new form of thermometer in 1836.

The reversing bottle introduced by Jean-Baptiste Biot attracted much attention in the 1830s. This was a hollow glass cylinder, open at one end, and closed at the other by a solid plate of metal. When the cylinder reached the required depth, the investigator pulled a cord attached to its lower extremity, causing the cylinder to turn upside down. The weight of the bottle was thus taken by the piston, which, in rising, filled the bottle. A small valve kept the container gas- and watertight during the haul to the surface. The Biot bottle also provided for the escape of any compressed air, which could burst the apparatus on return to the surface, into a gas bladder; the gas too could then be analyzed back on board. The action of reversing the bottle could be used as part of the procedure for ensuring that the bottle closed, trapping the water sample securely inside. It could also be the mechanism whereby the thermometer, frequently mounted alongside the water bottle, would be made to indicate the temperature at depth.

In 1890, Vagn Walfrid Ekman and Otto Petersson organized a series of cruises for hydrographic research in the Baltic and the North Sea. Petersson devised a water bottle that was insulated, and tripped shut by a propeller mechanism when the bottle started upward to the surface. As the walls of the bottle were made up of spaced concentric cylinders of brass or celluloid, with top and bottom plates made of rubber, the bottle was insulated by the seawater itself. Fridtjof Nansen modified this design—most notably, by including the thermometer in the bottle—and his pattern became the international standard for many years.

Ekman was also responsible for several bottle designs. The longest-lived was a cylindrical tube having top and bottom plates fitted with rubber gaskets. The moving parts were suspended in a frame, and when the whole was lowered, water could pass freely through the cylinder. When the catch was released by a messenger, the cylinder rotated by 180 degrees, pressing the end plates firmly against the cylinder and securing the sample. The Ekman bottle also carried a reversing thermometer. By 1910, messengers had almost completely replaced the propeller mechanism. Nansen experimented with attaching water bottles and thermometers to a reversing frame from 1900 onwards; he described this combination as a "reversing water bottle."

For temperature measurement at depth, the reversing thermometer was superseded from 1938 onward by the **bathythermograph**, which could produce temperature depth profiles continuously. The pressure for its development was antisubmarine warfare.

In 1942, Harald Sverdrup, Martin Johnson, and Richard Fleming recorded in their textbook the basic requirements for any water sampler. It should be constructed of noncorrosive metals that will reduce contamination to a minimum; it should have a draincock and air vent for removing the sample; and it should be painted white for visibility on hauling in. The

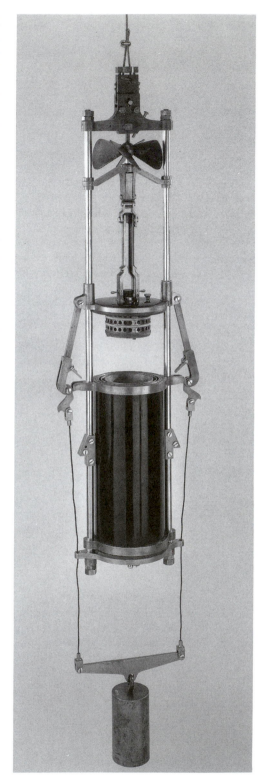

Nansen-Petersson water sampling bottle, ca. 1905. SM 1975-26. Courtesy of SSPL.

procedure for paying out the line began with a 50 to 100 lb. weight, to keep the wire taut and to reduce the angle of the wire. More wire was paid out to avoid the weight's hitting the ship while the lowest bottle was attached or detached. The bottle was adjusted to its set position on the wire, the thermometers were checked, and the meter wheel set to zero. The wire was then lowered a chosen amount, the next bottle and a messenger were attached, and so on until the complete configuration was achieved. At the required depth, the bottles were held for 10 minutes to allow the thermometers to register, then a messenger was clipped to the wire and released. At depths of less than 500 meters it was possible to feel the jerks when the messengers struck the bottles by keeping a finger on the wire. At greater depths, more time was allowed for the messenger to reach and trigger the final bottle, as when the angle is greater the messenger travels more slowly.

An alternative process uses electronic triggers from the ship, if communicating cable can be suspended alongside the wire. The choice of bottle and thermometer determines whether the bottle rotates, or a frame holding the thermometer rotates. A rosette sampler is a device that carries twelve to twenty bottles, controlled by electrical command from the deck, and is used with a conductivity-temperature depth sensor. The CTD readings are compared, and the bottles are used at will to obtain samples to confirm interesting features in the water property profiles.

Jane Insley

Bibliography

Carpine, C. *Catalogue des appareils d'océanographie en collection au Musée Océanographique de Monaco. 4: Bouteilles de prélevement d'eau.* Monaco: Musée Océanographique, 1994.

Deacon, Margaret. *Scientists and the Sea 1650–1900.* London: Academic, 1971.

Lenz, W., and M. Deacon, eds. *Ocean Sciences, Their History and Relation to Man.* Hamburg: Bundesant für Seeschiffart und Hydrographie, 1990.

McConnell, Anita. "The Development of Apparatus for Physical Oceanography, 1800–1914." Ph.D. dissertation. University of Leicester, 1978.

Ponko, Vincent. *Ships, Seas and Scientists: U.S. Naval Exploration and Discovery in the 19th Century.* Annapolis: Naval Institute, 1974.

Wattmeter

A wattmeter measures the power dissipated in an electrical circuit. The need to measure power arose with the growth of electricity supply systems for electric lighting from the early 1880s. Previously, the main application of electricity had been in telegraphy, where power levels were low. Wattmeters are particularly important in ac systems where, unlike dc systems, power cannot be calculated from current and voltage measurements.

Most wattmeters use an electrodynamometer movement with two sets of coils. One set is fixed and connected in series with the circuit, and the other is movable and connected across its ends. The magnetic fields of the coils interact to produce a torque that is a function of the power dissipation.

William Edward Ayrton and John Perry designed what may have been the first wattmeter in 1882. They called it an "arc horse-power measurer" and it was a direct reading instrument. Charles William Siemens advocated the use of an electrodynamometer wattmeter in 1883, in a form adapted from the Siemens **ammeter** introduced a few years earlier. In this instrument, a torsion head was turned to restore the moving coil to the undeflected position. Torsion wattmeters were also designed by Charles Vickery Drysdale in 1901, and by William Du Bois Duddell and Thomas Mather in about 1903. The Drysdale instrument was manufactured until at least the 1960s. It was also available as a double wattmeter, for measuring power in three-phase circuits.

Torsion instruments were suitable for the laboratory or test room, but instruments with a pointer and scale were needed for use in the field or on a switchboard. William Thomson patented an engine room wattmeter in 1893. Like many others, it was designed to be astatic and therefore unaffected by external magnetic fields. John Thomas Irwin patented an astatic wattmeter in 1912, and this was made for many years. The major manufacturers of industrial electrical instruments produced ranges of wattmeters, both single and double, to meet a variety of needs. Most wattmeters contained no magnetic iron, but some used laminated iron cores to obtain a greater magnetic field, careful design being necessary to minimize problems introduced by the iron.

Electrostatic instruments can also function as wattmeters. G.L. Addenbrooke used an electrostatic wattmeter as early as 1884–1885. At the National Physical Laboratory, near London, in

Heap and Smith pattern wattmeter, by Elliott Brothers, 1901. SM 1931–682. Courtesy of SSPL.

1913, C.C. Paterson, E.H. Rayner, and A. Kinnes designed a precision electrostatic wattmeter that was used extensively for calibrating other meters.

As with other electrical measurements, by the 1980s electronic wattmeters were taking over from the traditional instruments.

C.N. Brown

Bibliography

Drysdale, Charles Vickery, and Alfred Charles Jolley. *Electrical Measuring Instruments, Part 1.* London: E. Benn, 1924.

Paterson, C.C., E.H. Rayner, and A. Kinnes. "The Use of the Electrostatic Method for the Measurement of Power." *Journal of the Institution of Electrical Engineers* 51 (1913): 294–354.

Perry, John. "The Future Development of Electrical Appliances." *Journal of the Society of Arts* 29 (1880–1881): 457–70.

Wave Recorder

A wave recorder measures the parameters of sea waves, usually height and period. From this information, such parameters as wavelength and speed can be determined if water depth and current speed are known.

In Algiers Roads in 1843, George Aimé tried to determine to what depth horizontal water oscillations were detectable. He used a small float equipped with prongs and attached by a short cord to a weighted board. The apparatus was lowered to the seabed and left until a storm had passed; the horizontal water oscillations moved the float and impaled the prongs on the board. The number of holes in the board indicated the water movements at that depth.

Thomas Stevenson's wave dynamometer, also devised in 1843, resembled a railway buffer inside a box. It was fixed to a rock, and each crashing wave pushed the buffer back against a spring, which displaced a leather washer. This displacement enabled Stevenson to calculate the pressure of the most powerful wave.

The first instrument that recorded the waves themselves, rather than their effects, was designed by two French naval officers, Admiral Pâris and his son, in 1867. This consisted of a buoyant pole weighted at its base and protruding 10 meters above the water surface. A toroidal float was placed around the pole and attached by elastic to its top. An indicator was clamped to the elastic one-tenth of the way below its top. As the float rose and fell, the indicator inscribed a one-tenth scale wave trace on a clockwork-driven chart.

From 1908 to 1929, the British Tyneside Port Authority used a **theodolite** to measure the vertical motion of two buoys located 100 meters off the piers at the mouth of the River Tyne. This motion was taken to be the wave height.

Attempts to use stereophotography to determine the contours of the sea surface were made, for example by Schumacher in 1936, but because a large amount of work was needed to extract any data, use of this method has been spasmodic.

In the 1930s, pressure recorders were developed by the German Testing Establishment for Aeronautics, and by the British Admiralty working in conjunction with the Cambridge Scientific Instrument Co.

Modern Developments

Practical systems include surface-piercing techniques, pressure recorders, inverted echo-sounders, **accelerometer** buoys, shipborne wave recorders, fixed radar sensing, and satellite-based instruments.

Wave recorder built by Admiral François-Edmond Pâris and his son, 1860s. Pâris (1867). Courtesy of SSPL.

One of the earliest surface-piercing techniques was the step gauge, used extensively in the United States. A series of equally spaced electrodes with a resistance wired between each pair was held vertically through the sea surface. When the water immersed each pair, its resistance was shorted out and the resistance between the two ends of the gauge was (inversely) related to the wave height. Modern step gauges use individual electronic circuits to detect when each electrode is under water, with the number immersed being recorded digitally.

Many offshore oil platforms use the Baylor wave gauge. This consists of two steel ropes stretched vertically through the sea surface, forming an electrical transmission line terminated by the sea surface. The impedance of this line, which is directly related to its length above the water surface, is measured at 0.65 MHz. These devices are vulnerable to collision and have largely been replaced by radar gauges.

The early pressure recorders, flexible bag devices, were superseded by pressure-sensing cells such as piezoelectric crystals, or capacitance sensors detecting the bending of a stiff metal membrane. Commercial pressure gauges can now measure the pressures under waves, trading small deficiencies in absolute accuracy and zero stability for ruggedness and reliability. They are usually frequency-modulated devices with the frequency being averaged over 0.5 second. It is difficult to correct for the attenuation of the pressure fluctuations with depth, and there is some doubt as to whether the classic formulae apply accurately over a possibly porous or nonrigid seabed. But, for obtaining on-site data, it can be a practical and reliable method.

An echo-sounding wave recorder is mounted on the sea bed facing upwards in relatively shallow water. It detects the distance of the surface, but tends to lose the echo when the surface is aerated. It works fairly well when the waves are predominantly swell, but not in local storms.

Accelerometer buoys are the most widely used and generally give the most reliable results. The U.K.'s Cloverleaf Buoy measured pitch, roll, and heave of each of three floats placed at the corners of an equilateral triangle, plus alignment of the buoy. It was a successful research tool for relatively early wave studies, but as it required the attendance of a research vessel it could not be used for routine measurements. The most successful sensor was developed by Wemelsfelder in the Netherlands, originally for the Waverider. It consists of a sphere filled with a fluid, with a vertical accelerometer mounted on a horizontal platform that uses the inertia of the water sphere to form a pendulum with a very long period; this stabilizes the platform against the motion due to waves. The output is integrated twice and gives the vertical displacement of the buoy. For directional recording, a buoy that follows the surface slope is usually used, with the tilt of the buoy relative to the stabilized platform being measured on two perpendicular axes. The Wavec, a directional buoy developed from the Waverider, measures the E-W and N-S components of acceleration of the buoy, which is assumed to follow the wave particle motions. The signals from these buoys are normally radioed ashore.

M.J. Tucker of the British National Institute of Oceanography conceived the Shipborne Wave Recorder in the early 1950s. This used two vertical-seeking accelerometers placed symmetrically, one on each side of the ship. Pressure recorders were placed next to each accelerometer and connected to the seawater by a small hole through the hull; these measured the height of those waves that were short compared with the length of the ship. The two signals were added, yielding a total wave record. The combination of the four sensors eliminated most of the effect of an almost stationary ship's motion. Later, modifications were made to analytical methods to compensate for second-order effects due to the ship's reaction to the waves. This device made the largest instrumental contribution to the embryonic study of sea waves by providing reliable data on waves unaffected by shallow water.

With fixed **radar** sensing, a narrow-beam distance-measuring radar is mounted vertically on, for example, an oil platform to measure the rise and fall of the sea surface-yielding wave height and period. The EMI infrared radar, although expensive, is the most accurate and reliable of these devices. The most serious problem is that the amplitude of the echo from the sea surface varies over a wide range, necessitating a receiver with a high dynamic range. Ordinary horizontal PPI microwave radars can be used to look at the backscatter from the sea-surface roughness. This is a complicated process using a simple radar, and only the predominant direction of travel of the waves can be obtained. However, if a succession of radar images is recorded, a more sophisticated analysis yields an estimate of the shape of the directional spectrum: its amplitude must be calibrated by the use of, for example, a Waverider. Other microwave radars (such as the Miros radar developed in Norway) measure the particle velocities in the waves using the Doppler effect and, by turning the radar, can measure the directional spectrum.

Satellites carrying precision altimeters now measure waves accurately from a location over a hundred kilometers above the earth's surface. They use microwave radars pointing downwards with a very sharp leading edge to the pulse. When backscattered from a sea surface covered in waves, the time difference between reflections from the crests and troughs smears the leading edge of the returning pulse; the amount of this smearing can be interpreted to give the significant waveheight with a specified accuracy of the worse of either ±0.5 meter or ±10 percent. But, by calibration against surface buoys, this accuracy can be improved by a factor of two. The device produces one reading per second, each covering a small footprint, and over a period of years it is capable of giving a global wave climate. Some satellites, notably *Seasat* and *ERS1,* have carried Synthetic-Aperture Radars that image wave patterns on the sea surface (see **radar, imaging**). However, Doppler shifts in the radar echoes due to the wave particle velocities confuse the aperture synthesis process, which degrades the resolution and so complicates the interpretation.

Laurence Draper

Bibliography

Pabst, von Wilhelm. "Uber ein Gerat zur Messung und Aufzeichnung des Seeganges." *Zeitschrift für Flugtechnik und Motorluftschiffahrt* 21 (1933): 598–619.

Pâris, François Edmond. "Note sur un trace-roulis et sur un trace-vague inventés par MM PARIS Pere et Fils." *Comptes Rendus de l'Academie des Sciences* 63 (867): 731–38.

Schumacher, A. "Untersuchung des Seegangs mit Hilfe der Stereophotogrammetrie." In *Jahrbuch 1936 der Lilienthal-Gesellschaft für Luftfahrtforschung,* 239–47. Berlin: Oldenbourg, 1936.

Stevenson, Thomas. *The Design and Construction of Harbours: A Treatise on Maritime Engineering.* 2nd ed. Edinburgh: Black, 1875.

Tucker, Malcom J. *Waves in Ocean Engineering: Measurement, Analysis, Interpretation.* Chichester: Ellis Horwood, 1991.

Wheatstone Bridge

The Wheatstone bridge is an electrical circuit for comparing resistances, but the term is also used for instruments embodying that circuit. It was described by Charles Wheatstone, professor of experimental philosophy at King's College, London, in *Philosophical Transactions of the Royal Society* in 1843. The same principle had been described by Samuel Hunter Christie in the same journal in 1833. Wheatstone acknowledged Christie's priority in a footnote to his paper, but there is evidence that this was added at a very late stage. Christie's paper had attracted little attention: his analysis was difficult to follow, in part because (like many of his contemporaries) he did not appreciate Ohm's law. The term "Wheatstone bridge" seems to have originated on the continent of Europe. Wheatstone called the circuit a "differential resistance measurer." What is believed to be one of Wheatstone's original bridge circuits survived at King's College and is now in the Science Museum, London.

The circuit consists of four resistances connected in a loop, with a battery connected between two opposite junctions and a **galvanometer** connected between the other two. One or more of the resistances are adjusted until no current flows through the galvanometer. When the bridge is balanced in this way, the ratio of the resistances A/B is equal to the ratio X/Y, and if three resistances are known the fourth can be calculated. Because the bridge is a null instrument—that is, measurements are made when no current flows through the galvanometer—the results are not dependent on the calibration of the galvanometer or the steadiness of the **battery,** and high precision is achieved more easily.

To avoid using a large number of standard resistances, two of the resistances can be replaced by a length of uniform resistance wire with a sliding contact that can be moved along the wire until a balance is obtained. Slide-wire bridges suitable for use in electrical laboratories

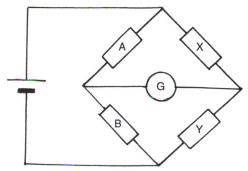

Circuit diagram of a Wheatstone bridge. Courtesy of SSPL.

Post Office pattern Wheatstone bridge, *by Latimer Clark, Muirhead and Co., ca. 1885. SM 1989-965. Courtesy of SSPL.*

were marketed in the latter part of the nineteenth century, but their most widespread use was in school laboratories, where they survived (in Britain) until at least the 1970s.

For general use the plug bridge was preferred, a box containing a set of resistances arranged to form three known resistances of a Wheatstone bridge circuit. The values were adjusted by removing (or inserting, according to type) metal plugs. A common form was the Post Office pattern, so called because of its use in the Telegraph Department of the British Post Office, but there were other forms designed for greater precision. Plug bridges were available commercially by the 1880s. Later, when suitable switch mechanisms were developed, the plug arrangement was replaced by rotary switches. High-quality instruments were always used with a separate galvanometer and battery, but portable versions had a built-in galvanometer; in later years, some included a dry battery. For special purposes there were variants of the Wheatstone bridge, such as the Carey Foster bridge for comparing nearly equal resistances, the Kelvin double bridge for measuring low resistances, and the Callendar

and Griffiths bridge for use with resistance thermometers.

The Wheatstone bridge will operate with alternating currents if the ordinary galvanometer is replaced by a suitable detector, such as earphones, a vibration galvanometer, or an ac galvanometer (when such instruments became available). The arms of the bridge may contain resistors, capacitors, or inductors, and the bridge is balanced when the ratios of two pairs of impedances are the same. Bridges for measuring inductance or capacitance were not so common as resistance bridges and were not available until later, but they were marketed by the makers of high quality instruments. For more general purposes, the "universal" bridge came into use in the second half of the twentieth century, capable of measurements on electrical components of all types.

Though largely superseded for routine use by electronic instruments, the old forms of Wheatstone bridge have not totally disappeared in the early 1990s, and highly sophisticated forms of bridge are still indispensable in standards laboratories.

C.N. Brown

Bibliography

Ekelöf, Stig. "The Genesis of the Wheatstone Bridge." Papers presented at the fifth IEE weekend meeting on the history of electrical engineering. London, April 1–6, 1977.

Fleming, John Ambrose. *Handbook for the Electrical Laboratory and Testing Room*, Vol. 1. London: The Electrician, 1901.

Wheatstone, Charles. "An Account of Several New Instruments for Determining the Constants of a Voltaic Circuit." *Philosophical Transactions of the Royal Society* 133 (1843): 303–28.

X-ray Diffraction

Crystals are distinguished from other solid materials in their tendency to display symmetrically arranged external forms, derived from the underlying regularity of the internal arrangement of their constituent atoms or molecules. The unit cell of a crystal represents the basic building block of the structure, which, theoretically, is repeated ad infinitum in three dimensions (a typical crystal of 1 mm^3 may contain something like 10^{20} unit cells). A consequence of this repetition is the existence in the structure of many rows and planes of atoms or molecules, like the rows of trees in a well-planned orchard. Crystal structure analysis exploits this property by measuring the intensity I(hkl) with which an x-ray beam is scattered from each crystal plane, characterized by three integers, h, k, l, which define the intercepts made by the plane on the unit cell axes.

X-ray diffraction provides the most accurate representation possible of atomic and molecular structures in crystals, over a very wide range of molecular weights in organic molecules (such as penicillin), inorganic substances (such as rock salt), and complex biological molecules—including the discovery of structure and activity relationships in hemoglobin, insulin, and other molecules of fundamental importance in biology and medicine. Although the accuracy that can be achieved depends on the three-dimensional ordering of the molecular arrangement in the crystal, outstandingly important achievements have been made on less ordered structures, most notably with the genetic material of DNA, as well as hair, collagen, and muscle. The determination of crystal structures by x-ray diffraction techniques requires instrumentation to record and quantify x-radiation

weakly scattered from the many thousands of hkl planes associated with the crystal lattice. X-rays used for this purpose, whether from conventional laboratory generators or from a more powerful synchrotron source, will be in the wavelength range of 0.5–2.5 Å (1 Å = 10^{-8}cm). With the exception of the Laue method, measurement of I(hkl) values may be assumed to employ a monochromatic x-ray beam. Many instruments have been devised for this purpose since the discovery of x-ray diffraction, in 1912, in the laboratory of Max Theodor Felix von Laue, an assistant lecturer in Munich who was undertaking experiments to examine the nature of x-rays.

There are two principal methods for detecting x-rays. In the photographic method, the position of diffraction spots—defining hkl—and their blackening—defining intensity I(hkl)—are measured using optical techniques. This method is currently used to establish the quality of diffraction and to provide unit cell and symmetry information from crystalline specimens. Electronic diffractometers and area detectors rely on the ability of x-rays either to ionize gases or solids, or to produce fluorescence in a crystal. These instruments are used for accurate measurement of crystal geometry parameters and I(hkl) values.

Single Crystal X-ray Diffraction Geometry
In 1912, William Lawrence Bragg, a physicist working at the University of Cambridge, provided a simple but effective model relating the position of a diffraction spot on an x-ray film to the glancing angle θ, that the x-ray beam makes with an hkl plane, and the interplanar spacing d(hkl) for a given wavelength λ. Paul Peter Ewald showed in 1921 that the hkl dif-

Bragg's x-ray spectrometer. SM 1926-1021. Courtesy of SSPL.

fraction spots lie on a (conceptual) lattice, reciprocal to the crystal lattice, and thus provided a geometrical analog which, together with Bragg's equation, forms the basis for interpreting x-ray diffraction photographs.

X-ray Cameras

The Laue camera is the easiest method for recording x-ray diffraction, as the crystal is fixed behind the film in a heterogeneous x-ray beam. (The fortuitous alignment of an hkl plane in the presence of a wavelength suitable for satisfying Bragg's condition will produce one of the many diffraction spots occurring on the film.) Al-

though it was the original method for recording x-ray diffraction, and for many years it was used simply to determine crystal symmetry, the Laue method has recently come into its own as a powerful and rapid means of obtaining intensity data from even weakly diffracting samples such as protein crystals, by using a high-intensity synchrotron source. The most obvious disadvantage of the Laue method is that each spot requires assignment of the appropriate x-ray wavelength, selected by the hkl plane from the mixture of wavelengths in the incident beam of x-rays. All the other devices discussed below require the use of monochromatic x-rays of known wavelength.

The oscillation camera produces x-ray diffraction spots as the crystal is rotated through a small angular range, thus moving the hkl planes through the Bragg position. Versions of this camera were produced in the 1920s, and the theory for interpretation of the photographs was largely developed by the pioneering x-ray crystallographer John Desmond Bernal around 1926, working at the Royal Institution in London. The film was held in a cylindrical cassette whose axis was concentric with the crystal rotation or oscillation axis. Bernal, Dorothy Crowfoot (later Dorothy Hodgkin), and Max Perutz, all pioneers in structural and molecular biology, used this method for studying protein crystals, which have large unit cells, with most useful results. An improved version, designed by molecular biologists Ulrich Wolfgang Arndt and Alan John Wonnacott, working at the MRC Laboratory in Cambridge, England, and produced by Enraf-Nonius in the mid 1970s, provided a means for automatically moving through a series of exposures with different oscillation ranges. This method was specifically designed for the collection of intensity data from crystals of large biological molecules such as proteins.

The most popular x-ray camera, especially for teaching purposes, is that developed by Karl Weissenberg around 1924. Here the film cassette is translated parallel to the oscillation axis and screened to record a distorted map of part of the reciprocal lattice. This design was adopted by Charles Harold Carlisle, a crystallographer at Birkbeck College, London, for recording protein data, and it is also used in a contemporary image plate diffractometer.

In 1938 Wieger Fokke de Jong and Johannes Bouman showed that it was conceptually possible to record geometrically undistorted layers of the reciprocal lattice if both crystal and film were made to undergo the same (or parallel) motions. These ideas enabled the prolific American crystallographer Martin James Beurger of M.I.T. to develop the precession camera in the mid 1940s. This is an ideal tool for studying lattice and symmetry properties of crystals. The pictures are very easy to interpret, although they generally require more skill to produce than either oscillation or Weissenberg photographs.

Although x-ray cameras have largely been replaced by diffractometers and image plate devices, some scientists advocate their use in teaching and some basic aspects of research. Companies producing Weissenberg and precession cameras include Stoe et Cie (Darmstadt) and Enraf-Nonius (Delft).

X

Diffractometers

Perhaps the most obvious advantage of using a counting device (**Geiger counter**, proportional counter, **scintillation counter**, semiconductor detector) to collect diffracted x-rays lies in the ease of quantification of the signal received. The concept arises from the x-ray **spectrometer** of William Henry Bragg, father of W.L. Bragg, a physicist of Leeds University, England (ca. 1915). It used an ionization chamber/electroscope detector. X-ray reflections are recorded individually as the crystal rotates through a preset Bragg position. The process of collecting a complete data set for a given crystal (often many one thousands of hkl's) using a modern diffractometer is slow but highly accurate, particularly in the case of stable specimens.

One of the first commercial models was the linear diffractometer designed by U.W. Arndt and David Chilton Phillips, a structural molecular biologist working at the Royal Institution, London (ca. 1960) and marketed by Hilger & Watts Ltd. (London). This was a **computer**-controlled reciprocal lattice analog device for rapid measurement of intensity data from protein crystals. A triple counter was later introduced to speed up data collection, and digitized output was produced on paper tape. Around the same time, the Charles Supper Co. (New York) produced a semiautomatic diffractometer, essentially based on Weissenberg geometry with intensity data output on punched cards. Several versions of the four-circle diffractometer appeared between 1965 and 1975. These have three crystal-orienting axes and a fourth that carries the counter. Under computer control, a crystal can be characterized and oriented prior to automatic measurement of a set of intensity data for structure analysis. The measurements are typically undertaken at the rate of 1 hkl about every 30-60 seconds. This is too slow to enable a complete set of data to be measured from proteins and other crystals that deteriorate under x-radiation. Examples of these machines include the Philips (Eindhoven) PW1100, Siemens-Hoppe (Karlsruhe, Germany) AED, Stoe (Darmstadt, Germany) STAD14, and Hilger & Watts Y290/A328.

The Enraf-Nonius CAD4 diffractometer, one of the most popular four-circle instruments currently available for single crystal work, is characterized by its kappa-**goniometer**. The crystal is mounted on the kappa-block and is oriented by rotation about theta, kappa, and omega. The counter is mounted on the horizontal two-theta block. When recording I(hkl) the hkl planes are thus oriented vertically.

Area Detectors

The need for rapid data collection, in the case of unstable biological materials, for example, prompted the design in the 1980s of instruments with the recording capability of photographic film combined with the electronic measuring capability of the diffractometer. Such devices use the concept of the area detector or electronic film. Several such instruments are currently available.

The Enraf-Nonius FAST Area Detector, based on a design by Arndt, employs the basic goniometer of the CAD4 diffractometer. By rotating the crystal through a small angle, many x-ray reflections are produced. These are received on a Gd_2O_2S:Tb phosphor layer, deposited on a flat fiber-optics faceplate and connected via an image intensifier to a camera tube. After digitization, the image is ready to be processed by special software. The process is then repeated until a complete data set has been obtained (usually 24-48 hours). Although originally conceived for large molecule work, a modified version of this instrument employed in the SERC service from around 1993 run by Michael Brian Hursthouse (Cardiff) is suitable for a wide range of materials.

The mar Image plate IP, developed from a design by Joules Hendrix and Arnold Lentfer, has a reusable photosensitive $BaFBr$:Eu^{2+} film. X-ray photons produce a latent image on the plate that can be liberated, by scanning with 6,330-Å He-Ne laser light, in the form of 3,900 Å luminescence that is measured by a photomultiplier in a reader head and converted to a digitized output for processing. The plate is restored for further exposure to x-rays by means of an erasing lamp. Complete data sets can usually be recorded within 24–48 hours using a high-intensity rotating anode x-ray source, or in a fraction of this time with synchrotron x-rays. Such procedures ensure optimal production of intensity data from valuable crystal specimens that have a limited lifetime in the x-ray beam. Some image plate diffractometers are also able to record Laue diffraction patterns.

Rex A. Palmer

Bibliography

Ewald, Paul Philip, ed. *Fifty Years of X-Ray Diffraction*. Utrecht: Oosthoek, 1962.

Helliwell, John Richard. *Macromolecular Crystallography with Synchrotron Radiation*. Cambridge: Cambridge University Press, 1992.

Ladd, Marcus Frederick Charles, and Rex Alfred Palmer. *Structure Determination by X-Ray Crystallography*. 3rd ed. New York: Plenum, 1993.

Lonsdale, Kathleen. *Crystals and X-Rays*. London: G. Bell, 1948.

X-ray Machine

When W.C. Röntgen first described x-rays (1895), his earliest findings had been made with a collection of common laboratory devices: an **induction coil**, gas discharge tube, and fluorescent screen. The x-ray tube was the gas discharge tube—a partially evacuated glass bulb with electric terminals fused into the glass to allow current to be passed across it. Such devices were well known to late-nineteenth-century scientists experimenting on electrical discharge phenomena. High voltage across the tube caused ionization of the gas atoms within, with positive ions being driven toward the cathode. This bombardment of the cathode caused cathode rays (electrons) to be emitted from it. On striking a target (in Röntgen's case, the glass wall of the tube), cathode rays cause the emission of x-rays.

Modifications were quickly made to these gas tubes. Making the cathode cup-shaped (as in the Jackson focus tube) served to focus the electron beam on the target, giving the small x-ray source essential for sharp radiographs. Metal targets for x-ray production (instead of the glass wall) were to become standard, with tungsten eventually the preferred choice. Heat dissipation from the target was a major problem, as was controlling the degree of vacuum within the tube. Early workers used laboratory clamps to hold tube and x-ray plate at the requisite distances from the object or body part under examination. The penetrating power of the x-rays produced was temperamental and hard to control with these setups. It was affected, for example, by the degree of vacuum in the tube. Patients had often to remain motionless for several minutes to get an image. Pictures of many body parts, some showing fractures or foreign bodies, were obtained in the early years.

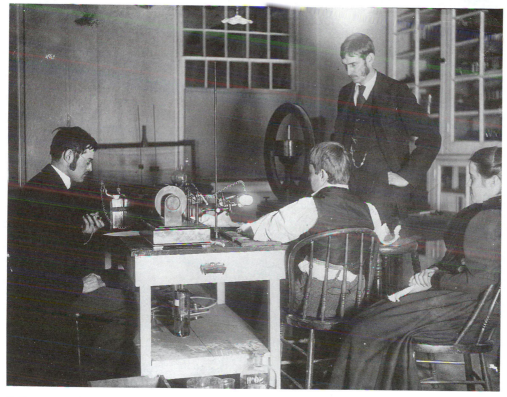

Early x-ray machine and patient at Dartmouth College, ca. 1900. Courtesy of NMAH.

However much medical work remained experimental until World War I.

Subsequent x-ray "machines" enclosed the basic components in durable housings, could work from the mains, had movable patient tables, often incorporating film cassette holders, and accurate means of lining up and adjusting source-patient-film distances. As well as permanent installations for consulting rooms, portable x-ray sets were produced for home visiting or for military use. Experience in the field during World War I probably familiarized many doctors with x-ray machines for the first time.

In the interwar years, x-ray machines were increasingly installed in dedicated hospital departments and their operation restricted to trained personnel. Interpretation of radiographs became the province of doctors rather than technical staff. The paramedical role of the radiographer was defined. Growing technical sophistication of x-ray apparatus went hand in hand with greater automation. Technical changes included use of the more controllable thermionic or Coolidge tube, which gradually replaced gas tubes. Here the vacuum was near perfect and electron production depended on the heating of a tungsten filament in the cathode to incandescence. Transformers replaced induction coils, allowing easier control of penetrating power and x-ray dosage. In the 1920s Metalix tubes, comprising a metal chamber sealed to glass end pieces, protected the user from stray radiation. In general, however, minimizing exposure for operator or patient was not yet a paramount concern. "Screening"—x-ray examination substituting a fluorescent (barium platinocyanide) screen for the x-ray plate—was still common, especially for the chest. It produced transient, real-time moving images on the screen, but entailed high radiation doses. Subsequently x-ray tubes were enclosed in metal housings to protect the user from electric shock and incorporated a lead coating for radiation protection.

From 1924 the Potter-Bucky diaphragm minimized blurring of radiographs resulting from scattering of radiation by the part under examination. A fine grid of lead strips ensured that only rays directly from the source reached the plate. By this time, the original glass x-ray plates had been replaced by film. Although lighter and less fragile, the early cellulose nitrate film was a fire hazard. It was replaced by cellulose acetate safety film in the 1920s. Subsequent developments in film and film handling included improved emulsions and sandwiching of film between fluorescent intensifying screens. There was also increasing standardization, and some automation, of dark room techniques.

Two major developments in diagnostic radiology involved the application of technology from other spheres. Drawing on wartime experience, G.N. Hounsfield used computers to devise **computer tomography** in 1967. In this innovative technique, multiple x-ray images taken around an axis were electronically combined to produce pictures of thin "sections" of the head or body.

The technology of television and image intensification has also had an integral part to play in diagnostic radiology. X-ray workers had long sought a means to permanently record moving x-ray images. Russell Reynolds had limited success with his cineradiography outfit in the 1920s and 1930s but produced an apparatus too cumbersome for widespread use. The essential technical problem remained production of an image bright enough for recording purposes. In image intensifiers, after passing through the patient, x-rays excite a screen of cesium iodide. The emitted light is converted to photoelectrons, which are focused and energized by an electric field before being converted back to light with a higher intensity. The resultant smaller, brighter image can be recorded with a TV or cinecamera.

Use of image intensifiers became routine for examinations such as barium swallows, in which real-time passage of barium (a contrast medium opaque to x-rays) could be observed. They were also integral to the increasing number of invasive procedures now carried out by radiologists. Such techniques allow the placement of radiopaque catheters, for example, in the heart or other organs, to be carried out under direct vision.

Digitization of the image has facilitated other forms of electronic image enhancement now central to diagnostic radiology. The presence of contrast media in small blood vessels may be masked by larger anatomical structures. Electronic subtraction of the precontrast image can reveal these. Dosages of contrast media have been substantially reduced and some hazardous techniques largely superseded because of this.

Much research is being carried out into filmless x-ray systems. Using a digital x-ray transducer, image capture is digitized, and film—and its storage requirements—largely eliminated. Hard-copy reproduction (conversion of digital images to film) can be performed, as in computerized tomography, but is not generally cost effective. Images would normally be consulted via appropriate VDU systems (usually line scan TV monitors), and stored on, for example, optical disk. Electronic processing of images, both during raw data capture and subsequently, holds much potential for improved diagnosis with x-rays.

X-ray machines have been used for radiotherapy, largely, but not exclusively, against cancer, from the early days. High-voltage (up to 1,000-kV) machines were produced for this purpose in the interwar period. After World War II came the development of supervoltage apparatus: Van de Graaff generators, cyclotrons, and linear **accelerators**.

Ghislaine M. Lawrence

Bibliography

Brecher, R., and E. Brecher. *The Rays: A History of Radiology in the United States and Canada.* Baltimore: Williams and Wilkins, 1969.

Glasser, Otto. *Wilhelm Conrad Röntgen und die Geschicte der Röntgenstrahlen.* Berlin: Springer, 1931/1958.

Mould, R.F. *A History of X-rays and Radium with a Chapter on Radiation Units: 1895–1937.* Sutton: I.P.C. Building and Contract Journals, 1980.

Pallardy, Guy, Marie-Jose Pallardy, and Auguste Wackenheim. *Histoire Illustrée de la Radiologie.* Paris: R. Dacosta, 1989.

Pasveer, Bernike. "Knowledge of Shadows: The Introduction of X-Rays into Medicine." *Sociology of Health and Illness* 11 (1989): 360–81.

X-ray Telescope
See TELESCOPE, X-RAY

Index

The main entry for each topic is listed in **boldface**

Conservatoire National des Arts et Métiers, France, 186, 569
Conte, R., 481
Conway, E.J., 413
Cooper, J.T., 57
Cooper, S., 219
Copernicus, N., 30
Coradi, G., 304, 468
Core Laboratories, 448
Cormack, A.M., 144
Cornell University, 60, 151, 398, 411, 608
Cornu, A., 476, 561
corona, instruments for observing the, 147–49
coronagraph, 147
Corvisart, N., 580
cosmic ray detector, 149–51
Cosmos-243 (satellite), 512
Cosmotron, 11, 98
Cosslett, V.E., 216
Cotterel, C., 408
Cotton, A., 400
Couette, M.M., 647
Coulier, J.P., 100
Coulomb, C.-A., 177, 209, 257, 296, 369, 626
coulometer, 650
Coulter, J.R., 154
Coulter, W., 153, 243
counter, colony, 151–53
counter, Coulter, 153–55
counting rods, 155–56
counting-table, 5
Cour, P. La, 637
Courant, E.O., 11
Coutinho, G., 533
Couvé, R., 649
Cowper, C., 583
Cox, J.R., 450
Cox, O., 336
Cramer, J.A., 68
craniometer, 157–59, 336
Crawford, A., 78
Creed, R.S., 219
Cremer, E., 107
Cremer, M., 66
Crile, G.W., 571
Crocker Manufacturing Co., 438
Crompton, R.E.B., 485
Cronstedt, A.F., 68
Crookes, W., 280, 510, 563, 572
Crookes' radiometer. *See* radiometer, Crookes'
Crookes' tube, 279
Crooks, L., 368
Crosland-Taylor, P.J., 243
Cross, J., 312
cross-staff, 159–60
Crova, A.P.P., 51, 70, 495
Crowfoot, D., 669
CSIRO, Australia, 608
CTI, 451
Cuff, J., 388
Cuignet, F., 422

Cullen, W., 514
Culpeper, E., 388
Cumming, A., 51
Cumming, J., 123, 221, 257, 259, 618
Cumming, W., 424
Cummins, H.Z., 247, 349
Cunaeus, A., 353
Cunningham, J., 394
Cuno, J., 626
Curie, J., 327
Curie, P., 327
current meter, 160–62, 441
Cushing, H., 570
Custance, 401
Cuthbertson, J., 223
Cyblusky, N., 207
cyclometer, 423
Cyclone (computer project), 141
Cyclotron, 11, 451, 672
cystoscope, 225
cytometer. *See* flow cytometer

D

Daft, L., 199
Dagan Corp., 439
Daguerre, L.J.M., 87, 90
daguerreotype, 87
Dalton, J., 7, 262
Dalton, J.L., 77
Dalton Adding Machine Co., 77
Damadian, R., 368
Damköhler, G., 107
Dancer, J.B., 365, 371
Daneel, H., 66
Dantzig Natural Philosophy Society, 353
D'Arcy, H., 247
Darcy, H., 447
d'Arcy, P. Le C., 220
Daresbury Laboratory, 551
Darwin, F., 484, 486
Dätwyler, G., 582
Davidenkoff, N., 586
Davis, J., 159
Davis, R., 538
Dawes, 546
De Forest, A.V., 582, 584
De Forest, L., 456, 510
De Luca, C.J. 211
Deacon, G.F., 245
Dean, L., 39
decelerometer, 13, 536
declinometer, 370
Decoudin, J., 237
Defries, N., 264
Dehmelt, H., 119
Deijl, H. van, 387
Delage, Y., 161
Delamain, R., 536
Dellmann, J.F.G., 210
Delpy, D., 65

E

Ealing Electro Optics, 562
ear oximeter, 63
Earnshaw, T., 114, 123
earth conductivity measurements, 199–201
Earth Observing System (satellite), 513
earth strain meter, 201–03, 530
East India Co., Netherlands, 36, 160
Eastern Telegraph Co., 91
Eastman, G., 124
Ebbinghaus, E., 263
echo sounder, 543, 639, 661. *See also* depth
    sounder
Eck and Krebs, 278
Eckert, P., 139
Eckhold, C.A., 180
École des Ponts et Chaussées, France, 357
École Polytechnique, Cairo, 417
Eddy and Co., 98
Edelmann, M., 260
Eden, E.M., 351
Edgcumbe, E., & Co., 336, 458
Edgworth, R.L., 423
Edinburgh University, 45
Edison, T.A., 40, 70, 203, 651
Edlén, B., 148
Edler, I., 640
Edman, P., 492
EDSAC (computer), 140
Edward VII, King of England, 567
Edwards, R.Q., 450
Edwards, W.D., & Sons Ltd., 438
Egli, H.W., 77
Ehrlich, G., 387
eidograph, 436
eidourian, 430
Eimer & Amend, 642
Einstein, A., 134, 339, 345, 401, 460, 510
Einthoven, W., 205, 207, 210, 259
Eisinga, E., 465
Ekman, V.W.-F., 161, 658
Ekström, D., 186
Elder, L.W., 456
Electric Heat Control Apparatus Co., 253
electricity supply meter, 203–04, 651
electrocardiograph, 204–07, 259
electroencephalograph, 207–08
electromagnet, thermo-, 619
electromagnetic torquemeter, 585
electrometer, 205, 208–11
electromyograph, 211–13
electron capture detector, 213–14
electron probe microanalyzer, 214–16
Electronic Associates, Inc., 142
electrophoretic apparatus, 216–18
electroretinograph, 218–19
electroscope, 219–21, 257
electrostatic machine, 221–24
Elliott, J., 121, 220, 497
Elliott Brothers Ltd., 133, 142, 468, 564
ellipsograph, 193

ellipsometer, 224–25
Ellis, R., 157
Elsner, H., 225
Elster, J., 458, 572
Elton, J., 31
Emery, A.H., 357, 587
EMI (co.)
    computer tomography scanner, 144
    electronic analog computer, 142
    MRI, 368
    PET scanner, 450
    photomultiplier, 460
    scintillation counter, 525
    wave recorder, 662
endoscope, 225–27
English Electric Co. Ltd., 142
ENIAC (computer), 139
Enraf-Nonius, Netherlands, 669
Eötvös, R. von, 296
Ephrussi, B, 412
equatorium, 227–29, 465
Erlanger, J., 212
Ernst, R., 59, 556
ERS-1 (satellite), 507, 663
Ertel und Sohn, 468, 632
Escherich, T., 230
Escherichia coli, 230–32, 412
Esmarch, E. von, 151
Espy, J.P., 409
Euclid, 578
Eudiometer, 232–34
Eudoxus, 465
Euler, L., 298
Euroball III, 551
Eurogram Array, 550
European Center for Nuclear Research. *See* CERN
European Molecular Biology Laboratory, 283
European Space Agency, 630
Evans, D.J., 174
Everad, T., 270
Everest, G., 423
Everest, P.F., 534
Everett, J., 538
Evershed and Vignoles Ltd., 335
Evershed, S., 335
Ewald, J.R., 116
Ewald, P.P., 116, 667
Ewing, J.A., 245, 583
Ewing, W.M., 56
explosives, instruments to test the ballistic force of,
    234–36
exposure meter, 236–38, 458
extensometer, 583, 584
extinction meter, 237

F

Fabrikant, V.A., 345
Fabry, C., 340, 346, 377
FACS. *See* fluorescence-activated cell sorter
facsimile machine, 104, 442

Dobson spectrophotometer, 562
early optical microscope, 388
early telescope, 601
electrostatic machine, 221
hydrometer, 312
octant, 419
protein sequencer, 492
radio wave detector, 509
spinthariscope, 572
stereoscope, 578
tide gauge, 621
Wheatstone bridge, 663
Ruben, S., 450
Rubens, H., 71
Rubner, M., 80
Rudberg, F., 169
Ruddock, J.C., 226
Rudolf, H., 474
Rueprecht, A., 47
Ruete, C.G.T., 425
Ruge, A.C. 581
Ruhmkorff, H.D., 258, 330
rule (drawing instrument), 38, 193, 297, 464, 501, 536
ruling engine, diffraction grating and, 171–73, 186, 291, 405, 563, 565
Rumsey-Loomis Co., 62
Runge, F.F., 107
Runge, V., 368
Ruska, E., 216, 382
Russell, A.E., 471
Russell, F.A., 141
Rutherford, E., 10, 100, 277, 572
Rutherford, J., 616
Rutherford, W., 657
Rutherfurd, L.M., 171
Ryle, M., 608

S

saccharimeter, 473, 475, 476
saccharometer, 312
Sachs, J. von, 42, 486
Sahli, H., 310
Sakurai, T., 386
Salcher, P., 88
Salleron, J., 375
Salm, E., 454
Salzberg, B., 459
al-Samh, I. , 228
Samzee, L., 263
Sanders, J.H., 346
Sanford, E.C., 115
Sanford, J.C., 60
Sang, J., 467
Sanger, F., 281
Sanguet, J.L., 180
Santorio, S., 615
Santoni, E., 84
Santorre, S., 25
Sartorius, F., 47

satellite
aerial camera, 84
atomic clock, 120
cosmic ray detector, 150
current meter, 162
Dobson spectrophotometer, 563
global positioning system, 284
imaging radar, 507
inertial guidance, 333
multispectral scanner, 405
new technology telescope, 605
radio telescope, 609
space radiometer, 512
tide gauge, 621
transit instrument, 632
wave recorder, 661
x-ray telescope, 611
See also individual satellite names
al-Sarraj, I., 34
Saunders-Roe, Ltd., 142, 582, 585
Saussure, H.B. de, 15, 314
Sauty, C.V. de, 91
Sauveur, J., 545
Savart, F., 106, 257
Savery, S., 381
Sawyer, W., 645
Schaevitz, H., 585
Schaffer, E., 274
Schaffner, K. , 15
Scheibler, J.H., 636
Scheimpflug, T., 84
Scheiner, C., 422, 435
Schepens, C., 427
Schering, H., 92
schety, 6
Scheutz, E., 77, 138
Scheutz, G., 77, 138
Schickard, W., 75
Schilt, V., 76
Schindler, R., 226
Schiøtz, H., 428
Schissler, C., 423
Schlumberger, C., 189, 199
Schlumberger, M., 199
Schluze, E.A., 374
Schmaltz, G., 592
Schmidt, A., 177, 370
Schmidt, B., 604
Schmidt, F.&H., 476, 558
Schmidt, H.D., 379
Schöner, J., 229, 624
Scholander, P., 487
Schopper-Dalén tester, 438
Schott, F.O., 59, 87, 390, 617
Schott, G., 90, 408
Schott Glassworks, 602, 607
Schreiber, P., 51, 375
Schreyer, H., 139
Schrieber, J.L., Glassworks, 400
Schütz, W., 59
Schuler, M., 133